ISBN 978-0-266-92575-0
PIBN 10910804

DEO,

PATRIÆ,

TIBI.

Procemium.

OVR Author, a gentleman of an antient and faire descended Familie *de Littleton*, tooke his name of a Towne so called, as that famous chiefe Iustice Sir *Iohn de Markham*, and diuers of our profession and others haue done. The name and degree of our Author.

Thomas de Littleton Lord of Frankley, had issue *Elizabeth* his only childe, and did beare the Armes of his Ancestours, *viz.* Argent, a Cheuron betweene three Escalop shelles Sable. The bearing hereof is verie antient and honourable, for the Senators of Rome did weare bracelets of Escalop shelles about their armes, and the knights of the honourable Order of Saint *Michaell* in France doe were a coller of gold in the forme of Escalop shelles at this day. Hereof much more might be said, but it belongs vnto others. His Armes. Instituted by *Lewis* the eleuenth, King of France, 9. *E.* 4. 1469.

With this *Elizabeth* married *Thomas Westcote* Esquire, the Kings seruant in Court, a Gentleman antiently descended, who bare Argent, a Bend betweene two Cotisses Sable, a Bordure engrayled Gules, Bezantie. *Thomas Westcote.*

But she beeing faire and of a noble spirit, and hauing large possessions and inheritance from her Ancestors *de Littleton*, and from her Mother the daughter & heire of *Richard de Quatermains*, and other her ancestors (ready meanes in time to worke her owne desire) resolued to continue the honor of her name (as did the daughter and heire of *Charleton* with one of the sons of *Knightley*, and diuers others) And therfore prudently, whilest it was in her owne power, prouided by *Westcotes* assent before marriage, that her issue inheritable should be called by the name of *de*

Littleton. These two had issue foure sonnes, *Thomas, Nicholas, Edmund,* and *Guy*, and foure daughters.

Our Author bare his Mothers surname.

Thomas the eldest was our Auhor, who bare his fathers Christian name *Thomas*, and his mothers surname, *de Littleton*, and the armes *de Littleton* also; and so doth his posteritie beare both name and armes to this day.

Camden.

Camden in his Britania saith thus, *Thomas Littleton* alias *Westcote* the famous Lawyer, to whose treatise of Tenures the Students of the Common Law are no lesse beholding, than the Ciuilians to *Iustinians* Institutes.

*Psalm.*92.13. The iust shall flourish like the Palme tree, and spread abroad like the Cedars in Libanus.
* The best kind of quartering of Armes.

The dignitie of this faire descended Familie *de Littleton*, hath grown vp together, and spred it selfe abroad by matches with many other antient and honourable Families, to many worthy and fruitfull branches, whose posteritie flourish at this day, and quartereth many faire Coates, * and enioyeth fruitfull and opulent inheritances thereby.

Of the Inner Temple.
His Reading.
Seriant.
Kings Seriant *Rot.Pat.*33.*H.*6. *Parte* 1.*M.*16.
*Mich.*34.*H.*6 *fo.*3.*a.*
Iudge of the Common Pleas, *Rot.Pat.*6.*E.*4. *Parte* 1.*M.*15.
* Knight of the Bath 15.*E.*4.

He was of the Inner Temple, and read learnedly vpon the Statute of *W.* 2. *De donis conditionalibus*, which we haue. He was afterward called *Ad statum & gradum Seruientis ad legem*, and was Steward of the Court of the Marshalsey of the Kings houshold, and for his worthinesse was made by King *H.*6. his Seriant, and rode Iustice of Assise the Northerne Circuit, which places he held vnder King *E.*4. vntil he in the sixt yeare of his raigne constituted him one of the Iudges of the Court of Common Pleas, and then he rode Northamtonshire Circuit, The same King in the 15. yeare of his raigne, with the Prince, & other Nobles and Gent. of antient blood, honored him with Knighthood of the Bath.

When he wrote this Booke.
14.*E.*4.*tit.Garranty.*5.
*Lit.Sect.*692, 729. & 730.

He compiled this Booke when hee was Iudge, after the fourteenth yeare of the raigne of King *E.*4. but the certaine time we cannot yet attaine vnto, but (as we conceiue) it was not long before his death, because it wanted his last hand, for that Tenant by Elegit, Statute Merchant, and Staple, were in the table of the first printed Booke, and yet hee neuer wrote of them.

The deceases of his Contemporanes.
(a) He died 27.*H.*6.
(b) He died 39.*H.*6.
(c) Died 11.*E.*4.
(d) Died 16.*H.*7.
(e) Died 7.*E.*4.
(f) Ouerliued our Author.
(g) Suruiued him also.
(h) Died. 23.*H.*6.
(i) Suruiued our Author.
(k) Died 33.*H.*6.
(l) Died 18.*H.*6.
(m) Died 10. *H.*6.
(n) Remoued 1.*E.*4.
(o) Remoued 8.*E.*4.
(p) Died 28.*E.*4.

Our Author in composing this worke had great furtherance, in that hee flourished in the time of many famous and expert Sages of the Law. (a) Sir *Richard Newton*, (b) Sir *Iohn Prisot*, (c) Sir *Robert Danby*, (d) Sir *Thomas Brian*, (e) Sir *Pierce Arderne*, (f) Sir *Richard Choke*, (g) *Walter Moyle*, (h) *William Paston*, (i) *Robert Danuers*, (k) *William Ascough*, and other Iustices of the Court of Common pleas. And of the Kings Bench, (l) Sir *Iohn Iune*, (m) Sir *Iohn Hody*, (n) Sir *Iohn Fortescue*, (o) Sir *Iohn Markham*, (p) Sir *Thomas Billing*: and other excellent men flourished in his time.

And of worldly blessings I account it not the least, that in the beginning of my study of the Lawes of this Realme, the Courts of Iustice, both of Equitie and of Law, were furnished with men of excellent Iudgement, Grauitie, and Wisedome; As in the Chancerie Sir *Nicholas*

Bacon,

Bacon, and after him Sir *Thomas Bromley*. In the Exchequer Chamber the Lord *Burghley*, Lord high Treaſurer of England, and Sir *Walter Mildemay* Chancellour of the Exchequer. In the Kings Bench, Sir *Chriſtopher Wray*, and after him Sir *Iohn Popham*. In the Common Pleas Sir *Iames Dyer*, and after him Sir *Edmund Anderſon*. In the Court of Exchequer, Sir *Edward Saunders*, after him Sir *Iohn Ieffrey*, and after him Sir *Roger Manwoode*, men famous (amongſt many others) in their ſeuerall places, and flouriſhed, and were all honoured and preferred by that thrice noble and vertuous Queene *Elizabeth* of euer bleſſed memorie. Of theſe reuerend Iudges, and others their aſſociates, I muſt ingeniouſly confeſſe, that in her raigne I learned many things, which in theſe Inſtitutes I haue publiſhed; And of this Queene I may ſay, that as the Roſe is the queene of flowers, and ſmelleth more ſweetely when it is pluckt from the branch: ſo I may ſay and iuſtifie, that ſhee by iuſt deſert was the Queene of Queens, and of Kings alſo, for Religion, Pietie, Magnanimitie, and Iuſtice; who now by rememberance thereof, ſince Almightie God gathered her to himſelfe, is of greater honour and renowne, than when ſhee was liuing in this World. You cannot queſtion what Roſe I meane: For take the Red or the White, ſhee was not onely by royall deſcent, and inherent Birthright, but by Roſial Beautie alſo, heire to both. Queene *Elizabeth*.

And though we wiſh by our labours (which are but *Cunabula Legis*, the cradles of the Law) Delight and Profit to all the Students of the Law, in their beginning of their ſtudie (to whome the firſt part of the Inſtitutes is intended) yet principally to my louing friends, the Students of the honourable and worthie Societies of the Inner Temple, and Cliffords Inne, and of Lyons Inne alſo, where I was ſometime Reader. And yet of them more particularly to ſuch as haue bin of that famous Vniuerſitie of Cambridge, *alma mea matre*. And to my much honoured and beloued Allies and Friends of the Counties of Norffolke, my deare and natiue Countrie; and of Suffolke, where I paſſed my middle age; and of Buckinghamſhire, where in my old age I liue. In which Counties, we out of former Collections compiled theſe Inſtitutes. But now returne we againe to our Author. Inner Temple, Cliffords Inne, Lyons Inne.

He married with *Iohan* one of the daughters and coheires of *William Burley* of Broomeſcroft Caſtle in the County of Salop, a Gentleman of antient deſcent, and bare the Armes of his Family, Argent, a Feſſe Checkie Or and Azure, vpon a Lyon Rampant Sable, armed Gules. And by her had three ſonnes, Sir *William*, *Richard* the Lawyer, and *Thomas*. His marriage. His Iſſue.

In his life time, he, as a louing Father & a wiſe man, prouided matches for theſe three ſonnes, in vertuous and antient Families (that is to ſay) for his ſonne Sir *William*, *Ellen* Daughter and Coheire of *Thomas Welſh* Eſquire, who by her had iſſue *Iohan* his onely childe, married to Sir The eſtabliſhment of his poſteritie, by the matches of his three ſonnes, with Vertue, and good Blood.

Iohn

Iohn Aston of Tixall Knight: And for the ſecond wife of Sir ***William***, ***Mary*** the Daughter of ***William Whittington*** Eſquire, whoſe poſteritie in Worceſterſhire flouriſh to this day. For ***Richard Littleton*** his ſecond ſonne(to whome he gaue good poſſeſſions of inheritance) ***Alice*** daughter & heire of ***William Winsbury*** of Pilleton-hall in the County of Stafford, Eſquire, whoſe poſterity proſper in Staffordſhire to this day. And for ***Thomas*** his third ſonne(to whom he gaue good poſſeſſions of inheritance) ***Anne*** daughter and heire of ***Iohn Botreaux*** Eſquire, whoſe poſteritie in Shropſhire continue proſperouſly to this day. Thus aduanced he his poſteritie, and his poſteritie by imitation of his Vertues haue honoured him.

He gaue poſſeſſions of inheritance to his yonger ſonnes for their better aduancement.

His laſt Will.

His Executors.

His Superuiſor.

Hee made his laſt Will and Teſtament the two and twentieth day of Auguſt in the one and twentieth yeare of the raigne of King ***Edward*** the fourth, whereof he made his three Sonnes, a Parſon, a Viccar, and a Seruant of his executors, & conſtituted ſuperuiſor thereof, his true and faithfull friend ***Iohn Alcocke*** Doctor of Law, of the famous Vniuerſitie of Cambridge, then Biſhop of Worceſter (a man of ſingular Pietie, Deuotion, Chaſtitie, Temperance, and holineſſe of life) who amongſt other of his pious and charitable workes, founded Ieſus Colledge in Cambridge, a fit and faſt friend to our honourable and Vertuous Iudge.

His Age.
His Departure.

He left this life in his great and good age, on the three and twentieth day of the month of Auguſt, in the ſayd one & twentieth yere of the raigne of King ***Edward*** the fourth; For it is obſerued for a ſpeciall bleſſing of Almightie God, that few or none of that profeſſion dye ***Inteſtatus & improles***, Without Will and without Childe; which laſt Will was proued the Eight of Nouember following in the Prerogatiue Court of Canturburie, for that he had ***Bona notabilia*** in diuers Dioceſſes. But yet our Author liueth ſtill in ***ore omnium iuris prudentium.***

1.H.7.fol.27.
21.H.7.fol.32.b.

Littleton is named in 1.*H*.7. and in 21.*H*.7. Some doe hold, that it is no error either in the Reporter or Printer; but that it was ***Richard*** the ſonne of our Author, who in thoſe daies profeſſed the Law, & had read vpon the Statute of *W*.2. ***quia multi per malitiam***, and * vnto whom his Father dedicated his Booke; And this ***Richard*** died at Pilleton-hall in Staffordſhire, in 9.*H*.8.

W.2.2.cap.12.
* See *Littleton Sect.749.*

His Sepulchre.

The bodie of our Author is honourably interred in the Cathedrall Church of Worceſter, vnder a faire Tombe of Marble, with his ſtatue or portrature vpon it, together with his owne match, and the matches of ſome of his Anceſtors, and with a memoriall of his principall Titles; and out of the mouth of his ſtatue proceedeth this prayer, ***Fili Dei miſerere mei***, which he himſelfe cauſed to be made and finiſhed in his life time, and remaineth to this day. His wife ***Iohan*** Lady ***Littleton*** ſuruiued him, and left a great inheritance of her Father, and ***Ellen*** her Mother(Daughter and heire of ***Iohn Grendon*** Eſquire) and other her

Anceſtors to Sir *William Littleton* her ſonne.

This worke was not publiſhed in Print, either by our Author himſelfe, or *Richard* his ſonne, or any other, vntill after the deceaſes both of our Author, and of *Richard* his ſonne. For I find it not cited in any Booke or Report, before Sir *Anthony Fitzherbert* cited him in his *Natura breuium*; who publiſhed that Booke of his *Natura Breuium* in 26.*H*.8. Which worke of our Author in reſpect of the excellencie thereof (by all probabilitie) ſhould haue bin cited in the Reports of the raignes of *E*.5.*R*.3.*H*.7.or *H*.8.or by S. *Iermyn* in his booke of the Doctor and Studient (which he publiſhed in the three & twentieth yere of *H*.8.) if in thoſe dayes our Authors Booke had bin printed. And yet you ſhall obſerue, that time doth euer giue greater authoritie to Workes and Writings, that are of great and profound learning, than at the firſt they had. The firſt impreſſion that I find of our Authors Booke was at Roane in France, by *William le Tailier* (for that it was written in French) *Ad inſtantiam Richardi Pinſon*, at the inſtance of *Richard Pinſon* the Printer of King *H*. 8. before the ſaid Booke of *Natura Breuium* was publiſhed; & therefore vpon theſe and other things, that we haue ſeen, we are of opinion, that it was firſt printed about the foure and twentieth yeare of the raigne of King *H*.8. ſince which time he hath beene commonly cited, and (as he deſerues) more and more highly eſteemed.

When this Worke was publiſhed.

F.N.B. 212.c.

Nota.

When this Worke was firſt imprinted.

Hee that is deſirous to ſee his picture, may in the Churches of Frankley & Hales Owen ſee the graue and reuerend countenance of our Author, the outward man, but hee hath left this Booke, as a figure of that higher and nobler part (that is) of the excellent and rare endowments of his minde, eſpecially in the profound knowledge of the fundamentall Laws of this Realm. He that diligently reads this his excellent Worke, ſhall behold the child & figure of his mind, which the more often he beholds in the viſiall line, and well obſerues him, the more ſhall he iuſtly admire the iudgement of our Author, and increaſe his owne. This only is deſired, that he had written of other parts of the Law, and ſpecially of the rules of good pleading (the heart-ſtring of the Common Law) wherein he excelled, for of him might the ſaying of our Engliſh Poet be verified:

His Picture.

The figure of his Mind.

Chaucer.

There to he could indite and maken a thing,
There was no Wight could pinch at his writing.

So farre from exception, as none could pinch at it. This skill of good

Good Pleading.

good pleading he highly in this Worke commended to his ſonne, and vnder his name to all other Studients ſons of his Law. He was learned alſo in that Art, which is ſo neceſſary to a compleat Lawyer (I mean) Logicke, as you ſhal perceiue by reading of theſe Inſtitutes, wherein are obſerued his Sillogiſmes, Inductions, and other arguments; & his Definitions, Deſcriptions, Diuiſions, Etymologies, Deriuations, Significations, & the like. Certain it is that when a great learned man (who is long in making) dyeth, much learning dyeth with him.

Logicke.

Seneca.

That which we haue formerly written, that this Booke is the ornament of the Common Law, and the moſt perfect and abſolute Worke that euer was written in any humane Science: and in another place, that which I affirmed and tooke vpon mee to maintaine againſt all oppoſites whatſoeuer, that it is a Worke of as abſolute perfection in his kind, and as free from errour, as any Booke that I haue knowne to be written of any humane learning, ſhall to the diligent and obſeruing Reader of theſe Inſtitutes, be made manifeſt, and we by them (which is but a Commentary vpon him) bee deemed to haue fully ſatisfied that, which wee in former times haue ſo confidently affirmed and aſſumed. His greateſt commendation, becauſe it is of greateſt profit to vs, is, that by this excellent Worke, which hee had ſtudiouſly learned of others, he faithfully taught all the profeſſors of the Law in ſucceeding ages. The Victory is not great to ouerthrow his oppoſites, for there was neuer any learned man in the Law, that vnderſtood our Author, but concurred with me in his commendation. ***Habet enim iuſtam venerationem quicquid excellit***, For whatſoeuer excelleth hath iuſt honour due to it. Such, as in words haue endeauoured to offer him diſgrace, neuer vnderſtood him, and therfore wee leaue them in their ignorance, and wiſh that by theſe our Labours, they may know the truth and be conuerted. But herein wee will proceede no further. For ***Stultum eſt abſurdas opiniones accuratius refellere***, It is meere folly to confute abſurd opinions with too much curioſitie.

The commendation of his Worke.
Lib.1.fo.67.
Epiſt.10.li.10.

Cicero.

Ariſtotle.

And albeit, our Author in his three Bookes cites not many Authorities, yet he holdeth no opinion in any of them, but is proued and approoued by theſe two faithfull witneſſes in matter of Law, Authority, and Reaſon. Certaine it is, when he raiſeth any queſtion, and ſheweth the reaſon on both ſides, the latter opinion is his owne, and is conſonant to Law. Wee haue knowne many of

his

his cases drawne in question, but neuer could find any iudgement giuen against any of them, which wee cannot affirme of any other Booke or Edition of our law. In the raigne of our late Soueraign Lord King *Iames* of famous and euer blessed memory, It came in questiō vpon a demurrer in Law, whether the releas to one tres-passer should be auaileable or no, to his companion. Sir *Henrie Hobart* that honourable Iudge, and great Sage of the Law, and those reuerend and learned Iudges *Warburton*, *Wynch*, and *Nichols* his companions, gaue iudgement according to the opinion of our Author, and openly sayd, That they owed so great reuerence to *Littleton*, as they would not haue his Case disputed or questio-ned, and the like you shall find in this part of the Institutes. Thus much (though not so much as is due) haue we spoken of him, both to set out his life, because he is our Author, and for the imitation of him by others of our profession.

Nota.

Mich. 13. Iac. in Communi Banc. inter Cock & Hoours.

We haue in these Institutes endeauoured to open the true sence of euery of his particular cases, & the extent of euery of the same either in expresse words, or by implication, and where any of them are altered by any latter Act of Parliament, to obserue the same, and wherein the alteration consisteth: Certaine it is that there is neuer a period nor (for the most part) a word, nor an (&c.) but affordeth excellent matter of learning. But the module of a Preface cannot expresse the obseruations, that are made in this worke, of the deepe Iudgement and notable Inuention of our Author. Wee haue by comparison of the late and moderne impressions with the originall print, vindicated our Author from two iniuries; first from diuers corruptions in the late and moderne prints, and restored our Author to his owne. Secondly, From all additions, and incroachments vpon him, that nothing might appeare in his worke but his owne.

What is indeauoured by these Institutes.

Our hope is, that the yong Studient, who heretofore meeting at the first, and wrastling with as difficult termes and matter, as in many yeares after, was at the first discouraged (as many haue bin) may by reading these Institutes, haue the difficultie and darke-nesse both of the Matter and of the Termes and Words of Art in the beginnings of his Studie facilitated, and explained vnto him, to the end hee may proceed in his Studie cheerefully, and with delight; and therefore I haue tearmed them Institutes, because my desire is, they should institute, and instruct the studious, and guid him in a readie way to the knowledge of the nationall Lawes of England.

The benefit of these Institutes.

Wherefore called Institutes.

Wherefore published in English.

This part wee haue (and not without president) published in English, for that they are an introduction to the knowledge of the nationall Lawes of the Realme; a worke necessarie, and yet heeretofore not vndertaken by any, albeit in all other professions there are the like. We haue left our Author to speake his owne language, and haue translated him into English, to the end that any of the Nobilitie, or Centrie of this Realme, or of any other estate, or profession whatsoeuer, that will be pleased to read him and these Institutes, may vnderstand the language wherein they are written.

I cannot coniecture that the generall communicating of these Lawes in the English tongue can worke any inconuenience, but introduce great profit, seeing that *Ignorantia iuris non excusat*, Ignorance of the Law excuseth not.

Regula.

36.E.3.cap.15.

And heerein I am iustified by the Wisedome of a Parliament the words whereof be, *That the Lawes and Customes of this Realme the rather should bee reasonably perceiued and knowne, and better vnderstood by the tongue vsed in this Realme, and by so much euery man might the better gouerne himselfe without offending of the Law, and the better keepe, saue, and defend his heritage and possessions. And in diuers Regions and Countries where the King, the Nobles, and other of the sayd Realme haue beene, good gouernance and full right is done to euerie man, because that the Lawes and Customes bee learned and vsed in the Tongue of the Countrey*: as more at large by the said Act, and the puruiew thereof may appeare, *Et neminem oportet esse sapientiorem Legibus*, No man ought to bee wiser than the Law.

Regula.

Our Authours kind of French.

And true it is that our Bookes of Reports and statutes in auntient times were written in such French, as in those times was commonly spoken and written by the French themselues. But this kind of French that our Author haue vsed is most commonly written and read, and very rarely spoken, and therefore cannot be either pure, or well pronounced. Yet the change thereof (hauing beene so long accustomed) should bee without any profit, but not without great danger and difficultie: For so many antient Termes and Words drawne from that legall French, are growne to bee *Vocabula artis*, Vocables of Art, so apt and significant to expresse the true sence of the Laws, and are so wouen into the Laws themselues, as it is in a manner impossible to change them, neither ought legall Termes to be changed.

36.E.3. vbi supra.

In Schoole Diuinitie, and amongst the Glossographers and

Inter-

Interpreters of the Ciuile and Cannon Lawes, in Logicke and in other liberall Sciences, you shall meet with a whole Armie of words, which cannot defend themselues *in Bello Grammaticali*, in the Grammaticall Warre, and yet are more significant, compendious, and effectuall to expresse the true sence of the matter, than if they were expressed in pure Latine.

This Worke we haue called The first part of the Institutes, for two causes: First, For that our Author is the first Booke that our Studient taketh in hand. Secondly, For that there are some other parts of Institutes not yet published, (*viz.*) The second part being a Commentary vpon the Stat. of *Magna Carta*, *Westm.* 1. and other old Statutes. The third part treateth of Criminall causes and Pleas of the Crowne: which three parts we haue by the goodnesse of Almightie God alreadie finished. The fourth part we haue purposed to be of the Iurisdiction of Courts; but hereof wee haue onely collected some materialls towards the raising of so great and honourable a Building. Wee haue by the goodnesse and assistance of Almightie God brought this twelfth Worke to an end: In the eleuen Bookes of our *Reports* we haue related the opinions and iudgements of others; but herein wee haue set downe our owne. Wherefore called the first part.

Before I entred into any of these parts of our Institutes, I acknowledging myne owne weakenesse and want of iudgement to vndertake so great Workes, directed my humble Suite and Prayer to the Authour of all Goodnesse and Wisedome, out of the Booke of *Wisedome*; *Pater & Deus Misericordia, Da mihi sedium tuarum assistricem sapientiam, mitte eam de Coelis sanctis tuis & a sede magnitudinis tua, vt mecum sit, & mecum laboret, vt sciam quid acceptum sit apud te*; Oh Father and God of Mercie, giue mee Wisedome, the Assistant of thy Seates; Oh, send her out of thy holy Heauens, and from the Seate of thy Greatnesse, that shee may bee present with mee, and labour with mee, that I may know what is pleasing vnto thee, *Amen*. Li. Sap. ca. 9. vers. 4. 10.

Our Authour hath diuided his whole Worke into three Bookes: In his first hee hath diuided Estates in Lands and Tenements, in this manner; For, *Res per diuisionem melius aperiuntur*. Bracton.

A Figure of the diuision *of Possessions.*

- *Estates*
  - *By the common Law*
    - *Into the state of Freehold*
      - *Inheritance*
        - *Fee simple.*
        - *Fee taile*
          - *Generall*
          - *Speciall*
      - *For term of life*
        - *For terme of life of the Tenant*
          - *Tenant in taile after possibilitie of Issue extinct*
          - *Tenant by the Curtesie*
          - *Tenãt in Dower*
            - 1 *By the Common Law.*
            - 2 *By the Custome.*
            - 3 Ad ostium Ecclesiæ.
            - 4 Ex assensu Patris.
            - 5 De la pluis Beale.
        - *For terme of life of another*
    - *Vnder the state of Freehold.*
      - *Tenant for yeares, or halfe a yeare, &c.*
      - *Tenant at will*
        - *Expressed*
        - *Implied*
  - *By Custome, these may be so diuided, as Estates haue bin by the Common Law.*

Our Authour dealt onely with the Estates and termes aboue sayd; Somewhat Wee shall speake of Estates by force of certaine Statutes, as of Statute Merchant, Statute Staple, and *Elegit*, (whereof our Authour intended to haue written) and likewise to Executours to whome lands are deuised for payment of Debts, and the like.

And

And when the Reader ſhall in any part of this Worke finde no perfect ſence, or the Caſe apparantly againſt Law, or miſquotations, or incongrue Latyne, or falſe Orthographie, or the like; I ſhall deſire of him three things:

Firſt, Before hee enter (vpon the firſt apprehenſion thereof) into any euill conceit, That hee would aduiſedly peruſe ouer the *Errata* in the end of this Booke, & correct his booke accordingly, and then I am perſuaded he ſhall in many things receiue ſatisfaction.

Secondly, That he will impute no more or greater faults to the Printer, than he deſerues, in reſpect I was in the Countrey during all the time of the impreſſion hereof, and for that hee might eaſily miſtake my hand writing, beeing in many places not eaſie to be read but by him that was well acquainted therewith: and the rather, becauſe the *Errata* be not ſuch, (ſauing a verie few) but that the iudicious Reader vpon the Context and other parts of this Worke, will eaſily vnderſtand my meaning.

Thirdly, That the learned Reader will not conceiue any opinion againſt any part of this painefull and large Volume, vntill he ſhal haue aduiſedly read ouer the whole, and diligently ſearched out and well conſidered of the ſeuerall Authorities, Proofes, and Reaſons which wee haue cited and ſet downe for warrant and confirmation of our opinions throughout this whole Worke.

Regula. *Inciuile eſt parte vna perſpecta, tota re non cognita, de ea iudicare.*

Myne aduice to the Studient is, That before hee read any part of our Commentaries vpon any Section, that firſt hee read againe and againe our Authour himſelfe in that Section, and doe his beſt endeauours, firſt of himſelfe, and then by conference with others, (which is the life of Studie) to vnderſtand it, and then to read our Commentarie thereupon, and no more at any one time, than hee is able with delight to beare away, and after to meditate thereon, which is the life of reading. But of this Argument we haue for the better direction of our Studient in his Studie, ſpoken in our Epiſtle to our firſt Booke of *Reports*.

And albeit the Reader ſhall not at any one day (doe what he can) reach to the meaning of our Author, or of our Commentaries,

taries, yet let him no way diſcourage himſelfe, but proceed; for on ſome other day, in ſome other place, that doubt will bee cleared. Our Laboures herein are drawne out to this great Volume, for that our Author is twice repeated, once in French, and againe in Engliſh.

**
*

ciarios ad placita forestarum quas idem Frater noster habet ex dono domini Regis Henrici patris nostri secundum assis'. forestæ tenend, &c. In this case the grantee and his heires had a personall inheritance in making of a request to haue Letters patents of Commission to haue Justices assigned to him to heare and determine, of the pleas of the forests, and concerneth neither lands or tenements. And so it is if an Annuity be granted to a man and his heires, It is a fee simple personall, & sic de similibus. And lastly hereditaments mixt both of the realty and personalty. As the Abbot of Whitbye in the County of Yorke hauing a forrest of the gift of William of Percye founder of that Abby, and by the Charters of king Iohn and of other his progenitors, king Henry the third did graunt Abbati & conuentui de Whitbye quod ipsi & eorum successores imperpetuū habeant viridarios suos proprios de libertate sua de Whitbye eligend de cetero in pleno com Eborum prout moris est ad responsiones & presentationes, faciend de transgressionibus quas amodo fieri continget de venatione infra metas forestæ suæ de Whitbye quam habent ex donatione Willi. de Percey & Alani de Percey, filij eius & redditione & concessione domini Iohanis quondam regis Angliæ patris nostri, & confirmatione nostra coram Iusticiarijs nostris itinerantibus ad placita forestæ in partibus illis & non alibi sicut viridarij forestæ nostræ huiusmodi responsiones & presentationes facere debent & consueverunt. Et si contingat aliquos forinsicos qui non sunt de libertate predictorum Abbatis & conuentus transgressionem facere de venatione infra metas forestæ predictæ quos predicti viridarij attachiare non possunt. Volumus & cōcedimus pro nobis & heredibus nostris quod huiusmodi transgressores, per Iusticiarios forestæ nostræ vltra Trentam attachientur ad presentationem viridariorū predict ad respondendū inde coram Iusticiarijs nostris itinerantibus ad placita forestæ nostræ in partibus illis cum ibid. ad placitandum venerint prout secundum assisam & consuetudinem forestæ nostræ fuer faciend. Which Charter was pleaded vpon the Clayme made by the Abbot of Whitbye before Willoughby, Hungerford, and Hanbury, Justices in Eire in the forrest of Pickering, which Eire began Anno 8. E. 3. And these before them were allowed. And when the King createth an Earle of such a County or other place, To hold that Dignity to him and his heires, This Dignity is personall, and also concerneth lands and tenements. But of this matter more shalbe said in the next Chapter, Sect. 14. & 15.

Ro. Pat. an. 47. H. 3. Itin. Pickering. 8. E. 3. Ro. 42.

¶ *Et est appel en Latine feodum simplex quia feodū idem est, quod hereditas.* Here Littleton himselfe teacheth the signification of feodum, according to that which hath beene said, which only is to be applied to fee simple pure and absolute And this and all his other interpretations of words and Etymologies throughout all his three bookes (wherein the studious reader will obserue many) are perspicuous, and euer per notiora & nunquam ignotum per ignotius, and are most necessary, for ignoratis terminis ignoratur & ars.

Bract lib. 4. cap. 9. fo. 263. Britt. ca. 32. & 79.
For interpretation of words and Etimologies.
Vid. Sect. 9. 18. 95. 116. 119. 135. 154. 164. 174. 184. 186. 194. 204. 234 267. 258. 332. 337. 424. 520. 592. 645. 689. 73.

¶ *Simplex idem est quod legittimum vel purū*, hereof he treateth only in this place. And Litt: saith well, that Simplex idem est quod purum. Simplex enim dicitur quia sine plicis & purū dicitur, quod est merū & solum sine additione Simplex donatio & pura est vbi nulla addita est conditio sive modus, simplex enim datur quod nullo additamento datur.

Bract. lib. 2. ca. 39. fo. 92. 62. b. lib. 4. ca. 28. Fleta lib. 3. ca. 8. Bract. lib. 2. ca. 5. & 6. Britt. ca. 34.

¶ *Hereditas legitima vel hereditas pura.* And therefore it is wel said, quod donationū alia simplex & pura, quæ nullo iure civili vel naturali cogente, nullo precedente metu vel interveniente ex mera gratiutaque libertate donantis procedit, & vbi nullo casu velit donator ad se reuerti quod dedit, alia sub modo conditione vel ob causam, in quibus casibus non proprie sit, donatio, cum donator id ad se reuerti velit, sed quedam potius feodalis dimissio, alia absoluta & larga, alia stricta, & coarctata, sicut certis heredibus quibusdam a successoribus exclusis, &c. And therefore seeing Fee simple is hereditas legittima vel pura, it plainly confirmeth, that the diuision of Fee is by his Authority rather to be diuided as is aforesaid then fee simple. And he saith wel in the disiunctiue legittima vel pura, for euery fee simple is not legittimum. For a disseisor, abator, intruder, vsurper, &c. haue a fee simple, but it is not a lawfull fee. So as euery man that hath a fee simple, hath it either by right or by wrong. If by right, then he hath it either by purchase, or discent. If by wrong, then either by disseisin, intrusion, abatement, vsurpation, &c. In this Chapter he treateth only of a lawfull fee simple, and deuideth the same as is aforesaid.

Fleta. lib. 3. ca. 2.

¶ *Car si home purchase.* Persons capable of purchase are of two sorts, persons naturall created of God, as I. S. I. N. &c. and persons incorporate or politique created by the policie of man (and therefore they are called bodies politique) and these be of two sorts, viz. either sole, or aggregate of many: againe aggregate of many, either of all persons capable, or of one person capable, and the rest incapable or dead in law, as in the chapter of Discontinuance, Sect. 57. shall be shewed. Some men haue capacitie to purchase but not ability to hold. Some capacitie to purchase and abilitie to hold or not to hold, at the election of them or others. Some capacitie to take and to hold. Some neither capacitie to take nor to hold. And some specially disabled to take some particular thing.

Vid. Sect. 57.
Who haue abilitie to grant.
Persons capable of purchase.

If an alien Christian or infidell purchase houses, Lands, tenements, or hereditaments to him and

11. Eliz. Dier. 283. 11. H. 4. 20. & 26. 7. E. 4. 29.

32.H.6.23. Pl.Com.483.
5.Mar.Br.tit.Deniz.en 22.
Pasch.29.Eliz.in Sir Iames Crofts case.
49.Ass.pl.2.49.E.3.11.

and his heires, albeit he can haue no heires, yet he is of capacitie to take a fee simple but not to hold. For vpon an office found, the King shall haue it by his prerogatiue of whom soeuer the land is holden. And so it is if the alien doth purchase land and die, the law doth cast the freehold and inheritance vpon the King. If an alien purchase any estate of freehold in houses, lands, tenements, or hereditaments, the King vpon office found shall haue them. If an alien be made Denizen and purchase lands, and die without issue, the lord of the fee shall haue the escheat, and not the King. But as to a lease for yeares, there is a diuersitie betweene a lease for yeares of a house for the habitation of a merchant stranger being an alien, whose King is in league with ours, and a lease for yeares of lands, meadowes, pastures, woods, and the like. For if he take a lease for yeares of lands, meadowes, &c. vpon office found, the King shall haue it. But of a house for habitation he may take a lease for yeares as incident to Commercery, for without habitation he cannot merchandize or trade. But if he depart or relinquish the realme, the King shall haue the lease. So it is if he die possessed thereof, neither his Executors or Administrators shall haue it but the King, for he had it only for habitation as necessary to his trade or traffique, and not for the benefit of his Executor or administrator. But if the alien be no merchant, then the King shall haue the lease for yeares, albeit it were for his habitation, and so it is if he be an alien enemie. And all this was so resolued by the Iudges assembled together for that purpose in the case of Sir Iames Croft, Pasch 29, of the raigne of Queene Elizabeth. Also if a man commit felonye, and after purchase lands, and after is attainted, he had capacity to purchase, but not to hold it, for in that case the Lord of the fee shall haue the Escheat. And if a man be attainted of felony, yet he hath capacitie to purchase to him and to his heires, albeit he can haue no heire, but he cannot hold it, for in that case the King shall haue it by his prerogatiue, and not the Lord of the fee, for a man attainted hath no capacitie to purchase (being a man civiliter mortuus) but only for the benefit of the King, no more then the alien nee hath.

Magna Carta ca.36.
7.E.1.de religiosis.
W.2.13.E.1.ca.33.
15.R.2.ca.5.23.H.8.ca.10.
39.Eliz.ca.5.
23.H.3.Ass.436.
29.Ass.p 17.Brit.f.32.
Fleta.lib.3.cap.4.& 5.
19.E.2.tit.Vil.34.
29.E 3.Ibid.13.21.E.3.5.
4.H 6.9 19 H.6.63.65.
3.E 4 14 1 E … Mortm.8
34.H.6.37 9.… 3 19.H.6.63.
7.E.4.14.
Pl.Com.193.en Wrottesleyes case.

If any sole Corporation or aggregate of many, either Ecclesiasticall or temporall (for the words of the statute be Si quis religiosus vel alius) purchase Lands or Tenements in fee, they haue capacity to take but not to retayne, (vnlesse they haue a sufficient Licence in that behalfe) for within the yeare after the alienation, the next Lord of the fee may enter, and if he doe not, then the next immediate lord from time to time to haue halfe a yeare, and for default of all the mesne Lords, then the King to haue the land so aliened for euer, which is to be vnderstood of such inheritance as may be holden. But of such inheritances as are not holden as Villeins, rents-charges, commons, and the like, the King shall haue them presently by a fauourable interpretation of the statute. An Annuity graunted to them is not mortmaine, because it chargeth the person only. Some haue said that it is called mortmaine Manus mortua, quia possessio eorum est immortalis, manus pro possessione, & mortua pro immortali, and the rather for that by the lawes and statutes of the realme, all Ecclesiasticall persons are restrained to alien. Others say it is called manus mortua per Antiphrasin, because bodies politique and corporate neuer die. Others say that it is called Mortmaine by resemblance to the holding of a mans hand that is ready to die, for that he then holdeth he letteth not goe till he be dead. These and such others are framed out of wit and inuention, but the true cause of the name, and the meaning thereof, was taken from the effects, as it is expressed in the statute it selfe, per quod quæ servitia ex huiusmodi feodis debentur, & quæ ad defensionem regni ab initio provisa fuerunt indebite subtrahuntur & capitales domini eschaetas suas amittunt; so as the lands were said to come to dead hands as to the Lords, for that by alienation in Mortmaine, they lost wholly their escheats, and in effect their knights seruices for the defence of the Realme, wards, Marriages, Reliefes, and the like, and therefore was called a dead hand, for that a dead hand yeeldeth no seruice.

Le statut.de Religiosis.7.E.1.

I passe ouer Villeins or Bondmen, who haue power to purchase lands, but not to reteyne them against their Lords, because you shall reade at large of them in their proper place in the Chapter of Villenage.

An infant or minor (whom we call any that is vnder the age of 21. yeares) haue without consent of any other, capacitie to purchase, for it is intended for his benefit, and at his full age, he may either agree thereunto, and perfect it, or without any cause to be alleaged, waiue or disagree to the purchase, and so may his heires after him, if he agreed not thereunto after his full age.

A man of non sane memory may without the consent of any other purchase lands, but hee himselfe cannot waiue it, but if he die in his madnesse, or after his memorie recouered without agreement thereunto, his heire may waiue and disagree to the state, without any cause shewed, and so of an Ideot. But if the man of non sane memory recouer his memory, and agree vnto it, it is vnauoydable.

43.Ass.p.23.
Bract.lib.2.fo.12.& 32.

If an Abbot purchase lands to him and his successors without the consent of his Couent, he himselfe cannot waiue it, but his successor may vpon iust cause shewed, as if a greater rent were reserued thereupon then the value of the land, or the like, but he cannot waiue it vnlesse it be vpon iust cause, & sic de similibus prælatus Ecclesiæ suæ cōditionē meliorare potest, deteriorare nequit. And in another place he saith, Est enim Ecclesia eiusdem conditionis, quæ fungitur vice minoris.

Yet

But no simile holds in every thing, according to the antient saying, Nullum simile quatuor pedibus currit. An Hermophrodite may purchase according to that Sexe which preuaileth. A feme Couert cannot take any thing of the gift of her husband, but is of capacitie to purchase of others without the consent of her husband. And of this opinion was Littleton in our books, and in this booke Sect.677. but her husband may disagree thereunto, and deuest the whole estate, but if he neither agree nor disagree, the Purchase is good, but after his death, albeit her husband agreed thereunto, yet she may without any cause to be alleaged waiue the same, and so may her heires also, if after the decease of her husband she her selfe agreed not thereunto.

1.H.7.16.7.H.4.17. 18.H.6.8.39.E.3.30. 15.E.4.fol.1.b.27.H.8.24

A name of purchase.

A wife, (Vxor) is a good name of Purchase without a Christian name, and so it is, if a Christian name be added and mistaken, as Em for Emelyn, &c for vtile per inutile non vitiatur. But the Queene, the consort of the King of England, is an exempt person from the king by the Common law, and is of ability, and capacitie to Purchase and grant without the King. Of which see more at large, Sect.206.

2.H.4.25. 1.H.5.8. 46.E.3.22. 12.Ass.16. 30.E.3.18.1.Ass.11. 11.H.4.33.9.E.4.49. 13.E.3. Estoppel.231. F.N.B.97.a.

The Parishioners or Inhabitants, or probi homines of Dale, or the Churchwardens, are not capable to Purchase lands, but goods they are, vnlesse it were in ancient time when such grants were allowed.

12.H.7.28.37.H.6.30. 10.H.4.3.b.

An ancient grant by the Lord to the Commoners in such a waste, that a way leading to their common should not be streightened, was good, but otherwise it is of such a grant at this day. And so in ancient time a grant made to a Lord, & hominibus suis tam liberis quam natiuis or the like was good, but they are not of capacitie to Purchase by such a name at this day. But yet at this day if the King grant to a man to haue the goods and chattels de hominibus suis, or de tenentibus suis, or de residentibus infra feodum, &c it is good, for there they are not named as purchasers or takers, but for another mans benefit, who hath capacitie to purchase or take. And regularly it is requisite that the Purchaser be named by the name of Baptisme and his surname, and that speciall heed be taken to the name of Baptisme, for that a man cannot haue two names of Baptisme as he may haue diuers surnames. And it is not safe in writs, pleadings, grants, &c. to translate surnames into Latine. As if the surname of one be Fitzwilliam, or Williamson, if he translate him to filius Willi. if in truth his father had any other Christian name then William, the writ, &c. shall abate, for Fitzwilliam or Williamson is his surname whatsoeuer Christian name his father had, therefore the Lawyer neuer translates surnames. And yet in some cases, though the name of Baptisme be mistaken, (as in the case before put of the wife) the grant is good.

32.E.3.lare 261. 33.E.3.grant 83. 18.E.3.50.12.Ass.35. 14.H.6.12.34.Ass.p.11. 40.Ass.p.21. Bract.lib.4.tract.1.ca.20. Britton fol.12.122. 3.E.3.78.25.E.3.43. 26.Ass.61.30.Ass.16. 46.E.3.22.39.E.3.17. 3.H.6.25.19.H.6.2. 30.H.6.1.34.H.6.19. 11.H.4.27.9.E.4.29. 5.E.4.46.65. 14.H.7.11. 20.Eliz.D er.259. 8.E.3.436.29.E.3.25. 1.H.4. 3.H.6.26. 19.H.6.2.

So it is if Lands be giuen to Robert Earle of Pembroke where his name is Henry, to George Bishop of Norwich, where his name is Iohn, and so of an Abbot, &c. for in these and the like cases there can be but one of that Dignity or name, And therefore such a grant is good, albeit the name of Baptisme be mistaken. If by Licence lands be giuen to the Deane and Chapter of the holy and indiuided Trinitie of Norwich, this is good, although the Deane be not named by his proper name, if there were a Deane at the time of the grant, but in pleading he must shew his proper name. And so on the other side, If the Deane and Chapter make a Lease without naming the Deane by his proper name the Lease is good, if there were a Deane at the time of the Lease, but in pleading, the proper name of the Deane must be shewed, and so is the Booke of 18.E.4. to be intended, for the same Judges in 13.E.4 held the grant good to a Maior, Aldermen, and Commonaltie, albeit the Maior was not named by his proper name, but in pleading it must be shewed, as it is there also holden. If a man bee baptized by the name of Thomas, and after at his Confirmation by the Bishop he is named Iohn, hee may purchase by the name of his Confirmation. And this was the case of Sir Francis Gawdye, late chiefe Justice of the Court of Common-pleas, whose name of baptisme was Thomas, and his name of Confirmation Francis, and that name of Francis by the aduice of all the Judges in Anno 36.H 8. he did beare, and after vsed in all his purchases and grants. And this doth agree with our antient bookes, where it is holden that a man may haue diuers names at diuers times, but not diuers Christian names. And the Court said, that it may be that a woman was baptized by the name of Anable, and 40. yeares after shee was Confirmed by the name of Douce, and then her name was changed, and after she was to be named Douce, and that all purchases, &c. made by her by the name of Baptisme before her Confirmation remaine good, a matter not much in vse, nor requisite to be put in vre, but yet necessary to be knowne. But Purchases are good in many cases by a knowne name, or by a certaine description of the person without either Surname, or name of Baptisme, as Vxori I.S as hath beene said, or primogenito filio, or secundo genito filio, &c, or filio natu minimo I. S, or seniori puero, or omnibus filijs or filiabus I S. or omnibus liberis seu exitibus of I.S. or to the right heires of I.S.

34.H.6.19.5.E.4.55. 27.H.8.11.1.H.5.5. 18.E.3.32.27.E.3.85. 8 E. 3.427. 7.H.6.29. 9.H.5.9. 40.E.3.22.Fitzwilliam. 24.E.3.60. Fitz Iohn. 39.E.3.34. Fitz robert. 27.E.3.85.tit.grant 67. 18.E.3.23,24. 18.E.4.8.b. 14.H.7.31.32. 13 E.4.8. 5.E.2.Voucher.179. 17.E.3.35. where the proper name is mistaken.

21.R.2.brief.936. 12.R.2.feffments 58. 9.E.3.14.46,E.3.22. 3.H.6.26.34.H.6.19. 1.H.7.29.5.E.2.brief.741. 14.H.7.11. 17.E.3.29.18.E.3.59. 30.E.3.18.11.H.4.84. Pl.Com.525.21.R.2.deuise. 41.E.3.19.15.E.3.Counterplea de vouch.43.35.Ass.13. 37.H.6.30.11.E.4.2. 7.H.4.5.40.E.3.9. 37.H.8.Nosme 40.Br.

But if a man doe infranchise a Villeine, cum tota sequela sua, that is not sufficient to infranchise his children borne before, for the incertaintie of the word sequela. But regulerly in writs, the demandant or tenant is to be named by his Christian Name and Sirname, vnlesse it bee in cases of some Corporations or bodies politique.

15.H.7.14. 8.E.3.437.29.E.3.44. 19.E.4.11.21.E.4.19. 9.H.6.29.

39.E.3.11.24.17.E.3.42. 35.Ass.13.41.E.3.19.

A Bastard hauing gotten a name by reputation may purchase by his reputed or knowne name to him and his heires, although he can haue no heire. A man make a Lease to B for life, remainder to the eldest issue male of B. and the heires males of his body. B. hath issue a bastard sonne, he shall not take the remainder, because in law he is not his issue, for qui ex damnato coitu nascuntur inter liberos non computentur. And as Littleton saith, A bastard is quasi nullius filius and can haue no name of reputation as soone as he is borne. So it is if a man make a Lease for life to B the remainder to the eldest issue male of B to be begotten of the body of Iane S. whether the same issue be legitimate, or illegitimate. B hath issue a bastard on the body of Iane S. this sonne or issue shall not take the remainder, for (as it hath beene said) by the name of issue, if there had beene no other words he could not take, and (as it hath beene also said) a Bastard cannot take, but after he hath gained a name by reputation, that he is the sonne of B. &c. And therefore he can take no remainder limitted before he be borne, but after he be borne, and that he hath gained by time a reputation to be knowne by the name of a sonne, then a remainder limitted to him by the name of the sonne of his reputed father is good. But if he cannot take the remainder by the name of issue at the time when he is borne he shall neuer take it. And so it seemeth, and for the same cause, if after the birth of the issue B had married Iane S so as he became Bastard eigne, and had a possibilitie to inherit, yet he shall not take the remainder.

Vid. Sect 188.

So it was resolued. M.38.& 39 Eliz. in Bre. de errore for land in Partington in com. Salop.

39.E.3.11.24.35.Ass.13. 41.E.3.19.17.E.3.42.

Persons deformed hauing humane shape, ideots, mad men, leapers, bastards, deafe, dumbe, and blinde, minors, and all other reasonable creatures haue power to purchase and reteyne Lands or Tenements. But the Common law doth disable some men to take any estate in some particular things. As if an office either of the grant of the King or Subiect which concerne the administration, proceeding, or execution of Iustice, or the Kings Reuenue, or the Commonwealth, or the interest, benefit, or safetie of the subiect, or the like; if these, or any of them bee granted to a man that is unexpert, and hath no skill and science to exercise or execute the same, the grant is meerely voyde, and the partie disabled by law, and incapable to take the same, pro commodo regis & populi; for only men of skill, knowledge, and abilitie to exercise the same are capable of the same to serue the King and his people. An infant or minor is not capable of an office of Stewardship of the Court of a Mannor either in possession or reuersion. No man though neuer so skilfull and expert, is capable of a iudiciall office in reuersion, but must expect untill it fall in possession. And see Sect 378. where bargaining or giuing of mony or any manner of reward, &c. for offices there mentioned, shall make such a purchaser incapable thereof, which is worthy to be knowne, but more worthy to be put in due execution.

5.E.4.tit. offic.& officer. B.48.Vintors case. 5.Mar.Dier.fo.150. Seroggs case.

M.40.& 41.Eliz. in the Kings bench betweene Scamler and Walters. Lib.11.fo.2. in Auditor Curles case. Vid.Sect.378.

Some are capable of certaine things for some speciall purpose, but not to use or exercise such things themselues. As the King is capable of an office, not to use but to grant, &c.

A monster borne within lawfull matrimonie, that hath not humane shape cannot purchase, much lesse reteine any thing. The same law is de professis & mortuis seculo, for they are civiliter mortui, whereof you shall reade at large in his proper place, Sect 200.

1.H.7.31. Bract.lib.5.fo.421. 415.B itt.ca.22.39. Flet.lib.[illegible].ca.41. 1.E.3.9.44.E.3.4. 3.H 6.24.21.R.2.iudgement 263.7.H.4 2.14.H.8.16. Doct.& Stu.141.

¶ *Purchase.* In Latin perquisitum of the verbe perquirere, Littleton discribeth it in the end of this chapter in this manner, Item, purchase est appel le possession de tres ou tenements que home ad per son fait, ou per son agreement, a quel possession il ne avient per title de discent de nul de ses ancesters, ou de ses cosens per son fait demesne. So as I take it, a purchase is to be taken, when one commeth to lands by conuevance or title, and that disseisons, abatements, intrusions, usurpations, and such like estates gained by wrong, are not said, in law purchases, but oppressions and iniuries.

Pl.com.fo.47. Brit.ca.33.

Note that purchasers of lands, tenements, leases, and hereditaments for good and valuable consideration, shall auoide all former fraudulent and couinous conueyances, estates, grants charges and limitations of uses, of or out of the same, by a Statute made since Litt: wrote, whereof you may plainely and plentifully reade in my reports, to which I will adde this case, I C. had a Lease of certaine lands for 60. yeares if he liued so long, and forged a lease for 90. yeares absolutely, and he by Indenture reciting the forged Lease for valuable consideration bargained, and sold the forged Lease: and all his interest in the Land to R G. It seemed to me that R.G. was no purchaser within the statute of 27 Eliz for he contracted not for the true and lawfull interest, for that was not knowne to him, for then perhaps he would not haue dealt for it, and the visible and knowne tearme was forged, and although by generall words the true interest passed, notwithstanding he gaue no valuable consideration nor contracted for it. And of this opinion were all the Iudges in Seriants Inne in Fleetstreete.

27.Eliz.ca 4. 13.Eliz.c.5. Lib.3 fo 80 82.83 Twines. Case Lib.5 f.60.Gooches case. lib.6.fo.72.Burrels case. lib.11.fo.74. Pasch.12.Ia.Inter.Iones.p'. and Sir Rich.Grobham def. in eiectione firme in euidence al Iu re.

In Ancient time when a man made a fraudulent feoffement it was said, quod posuit terram illam in brugam, where brugam doth signifie wrangle, contencion, or intricacy, for fraud is the mother of them all. And on the other side, purchases, estates, and contracts may bee avoyded since Littleton wrote by certaine Acts of Parliament against Usurie aboue ten in the hundred, in such manner and forme as by those Acts it is prouided. Which statutes are well expounded in my bookes of reports which may be read there. To them that lend money my cautat is, that

Hil. 18.E.3.coram Rege in thesaw. 37.H.8.cap.6. 13.Eliz.ca.8.lib 5. fo.69.Burtons case. eodem. lib.fo.7.Claytons case.

neither

neither directly nor indirectly, by art, or cunning invention, they take aboue Ten in the hundred, for they that seeke by sleight to creepe out of these Statutes, will deceiue themselues, and repent in the end.

¶ *Purchase terres.* Littlet. here and in many other places putteth Lands but for an example, for his rule extendeth to Segniories, rents, aduowsons, commons, estouers, and other hereditaments of what kind or nature soeuer.

Lands and other things to be purchased.

¶ *Terre.* Terra, Land, in the legall signification comprehendeth any ground, soile or earth whatsoeuer, as meadowes, pastures, woods, moores, waters, marishes, furses and heath, terra est nomen generalissimũ, & comprehendit omnes species terre, but properly terra dicitur a terendo, quia vomere teritur, & anciently it was written with a single r, and in that sense it includeth whatsoeuer may be plowed, and is all one with arvũ ab arando. It legally includeth also all castles, houses, & other buildings: for castles, houses, &c. consist vpon two things, viz. land or ground, as the foundation and structure thereupon, so as passing the land or ground, the structure or building therupon passeth therewith. Land is anciently called Fleth, but land builded is more worthy then other land, because it is for the habitation of man, and in that respect hath the precedencie to be demanded in the first place in a præcipe, as hereafter shall be said. And therefore this element of the earth is preferred before the other elements; first and principally, because it is for the habitation and resting place of man, for man cannot rest in any of the other elements, neither in the water, ayre or fire. For as the heauens are the habitation of Almightie God, so the earth hath he appointed as the subburbs of heauen to be the habitation of man; Cœlum cœli domino, terram autem dedit filijs hominum. All the whole heauens are the Lords, the earth hath he giuen to the children of men. Besides, euery thing as it serueth more immediatly or more meerely for the food and vse of man (as shall be said hereafter) hath the precedent dignitie before any other. And this doth the earth, for out of the earth commeth mans foode, and bread that strengthens mans heart, Confirmat cor hominis, and wine that gladdeth the heart of man, and oyle that makes him a cheerefull countenance. And therefore terra olim ops mater dicta est quia omnia hac opus habeant ad viuendum. And the Diuine agreeth herewith, for he saith, Patriam tibi & nutricem, & matrem, & mensam, & domum posuit terram deus, sed & sepulchrum tibi hanc eandem dedit. Also the waters that yeeld fish for the foode and sustenance of man are not by that name demaundable in a Precipe, but the land whereupon the water floweth or standeth is demandable (as for example) viginti acr̃ tre aqua coopert̃, and besides the earth doth furnish man with many other necessaries for his vse, as it is replenished with hidden treasures, namely, with gold, siluer, brasse, Iron, tynne, leade, and other mettals, and also with great varietie of pretious stones, and many other things for profit, ornament and pleasure. And lastly, the earth hath in law a great extent vpwards, not only of water as hath beene said, but of ayre and all other things euen vp to heauen, for cuius est solum eius est vsque ad cœlum, as it is holden, 14 H. 8. fo. 12. 22. H. 6. 59. 10. E. 4. 14. Registr. originall, and in other bookes.

Pl. Com. 168. b. & 170. a. & 151.
Lib. 4. 87. b. Lutterels case.
4 E. 3. 161. & 6 E. 3. 283.
8. E. 3. 377.
Temps. E. 1. Bre. 811.
28. H. 8. Dier 47.
Tr. 7. E. 3. coram Rege Northampt. in the saur.
Psal. 115. 16.
Psal. 104. 15.
Chrysost. hom 30.

And albeit land whereof our Author here speaketh, bee the most firme and fixed inheritance, and therefore is called solum, quia est solidum, and fee simple the most highest and absolute estate that a man can haue, yet may the same at seuerall times be moueable, sometime in one person, and alternis vicibus in another, nay sometime in one place, and sometime in another. As for example, if there be 80. acres of meadow which haue beene vsed time out of minde of man, to be deuided betweene certaine persons, and that a certaine number of acres appertaine to euery of these persons, as for example, to A. 13. acres to be yeercly assigned and lotted out, so as sometime the 13. acres lie in one place, and sometime in another, and so of the rest. A. hath a moueable fee simple in 13. acres, and may be parcell of his mannor, albeit they haue no certaine place, but yearely set out in seuerall places, so as the number only is certaine, and the particular acres or place wherein they lie after the yeare incertaine. And so was it adiudged in the Kings Bench vpon an especiall verdict.

Vid. Sect. 59. where in this case liuery shall be made.
Vid Sect. 648.
How these 13. acres may be charged.
Hill: 34. Eliz. rot. 489. in tini. inter Welden & Bridgewater in banco Regis.

If a partition be made betweene two coparceners of one and the selfe-same land, that the one shall haue the land from Easter vntill Lammas and to her heires, and the other shall haue it from Lammas till Easter to her and her heires, or the one shall haue it the first yeare, and the other the second yeare alternis vicibus, &c. there it is one selfe-same land wherein two persons haue seuerall inheritances at seuerall times. So it is if two coparceners haue two seuerall mannors by discent and they make particion, that the one shall haue the one mannor for a yeare, and the other the other mannor for the same yeare, and after that yeare, then she that had the one mannor shall haue the other, & sic alternis vicibus for euer, and albeit the mannors be seuerall, yet are they certaine, and therefore stronger then Bridgewaters case, so as this doth make a diuision of states of inheritances of lands, viz. Certaine or vnmoueable whereof Littleton here speaketh, and incertaine and moueable, whereof these three cases for examples haue beene put. Wherein it is to be noted, that the possession is not only seuerall, but the inheritance also.

Temps. E. 1. tit. partition 21. F. N. B. 62. I.
F. N. B. 62. K.
Vid. Sect. 184. where aduowsons, &c. may be appendant and in gros.

It

By what names &c. lands &c. shall passe.
Vid. Sect. 279.
14.H.8 6.4.H 7.3.
10.H.7.24.11.H.7.21.
14 H.7.4.6. 21.H.7 36.37.
9.H.6.52 37.H 6.35.
22.E.4. barre.116.
11.H.4.90.18.E.3.execution 56.4.E.3.48. 8.E.3.13.
9.Ass.p.12.38.E.3.24.
Bract. fo.222.
17.E.3.75.39.H.6.38.
11.Eliz Dier.285.
Pasch. 12.Ia. Inter Dockwray & Tomes in evidence al Jury in Banke le Roy.
Vid. Sect 279.
Bract fo.208.
40.E.3.45.Pl.com.154.
10.H.7.24.28.7.H.7.13.
18.H.6 29.34.H.6.43.
20.H 6.4.18 E.4.4.
4.E.3.48.1.E.3.4.32.E.3. Scir.fac.100.
22.E.4 barre.116.
12.H.3.Ass.427.34.Ass 11
13.E.3.tit.entrie.57.
20.E.3.Bre.685.W.2.ca.24
Tr.11.R.2 in tres.neent imprimee ne abridge 11.H.7.4.
9.E.3.342 3.Ass 9.10.
7.Ass.9.
45.E.3.tit.feoffments & faits.90.14.H.8.6.
Pl.com.541.b.F.N.b.fo 8.
12.E.3.D.wer 90.
9.Ass.p.12.9.E.3.443.466.
Domesday.
7.R.1.inter fines in Thesaur.
Int.inquisit.apud Launcest. anno.6.E.1.in thesaur.
Mich.1.H.5 coram Rege rott.3.in thesaur.
Tr.7.Eliz.in banco regis lib.5 fol.11.Iues case.
14.H 8.1.46 E.3.22.
28.H.8 Dier.19.
32.H.8.Br.reseruat.39.
7.E.6 Dier.79.
** Glanuil.lib.8.cap.3.*
Domesday Regist.F.N.B.2.
8.E.2 Wast.111.
7.Ass 18.11..Ass.p.13.
41.E.3.Wast.82.
** Hill.14.E.3.coram Rege Lanc.in thesaur.*
** Inter inquisit.apud Lanc. in com. cornubie coram Iustic. Ind.anno 6.E.1.in thesaur. the B.of Excesters case.*
Domesday.
Camden.462.151.
Pasch.44.E.3.coram Rege in Thesaur.
Hill.13.E.2.Lanc.coram Rege in Thesaur.
Camden Brit.247.
rot.parl.18.E.1.8.
Euesque de Carliles case.
Pl.com.169.a.
4.E.2.Bre.792.793.
3.E.3.86.4.E.4.1.
27.H.8.12.
20.Ass.pl.9.
Pl.com.169.a.13.E.3.
Bre.241.33.E.3. Entrie 80.
Domesday.F.N.B.2.Regist.

It is also necessary to be seene by what names lands shal passe. If a man hath 20. acres of land, and by deede granteth to another and his heires *vesturam terræ*, & maketh livery of seisin *secundum formam cartæ*, the land it selfe shall not passe, because he hath a particular right in the land, for thereby he shall not have the houses, timber trees, mines, and other reall things parcell of the inheritance, but he shall have the vesture of the land, (that is) the corne, grasse, underwood, swepage, and the like, and he shall have an action of trespasse, *quare clausum fregit*. The same Law, if a man grant *herbagium terræ*, he hath a like particular right in the land, and shall have an action *quarum clausum fregit*, but by grant thereof and livery made, the soile shall not passe as is aforesaid. If a man lett to B. the herbage of his woods, and after grant all his lands in the tenure, possession, or occupation of B. the woods shall passe, for B. hath a particular possession and occupation, which is sufficient in this case, and so it was resolved. So if a man bee seised of a River, and by deed doe grant *seperalem piscariam* in the same, and maketh livery of seisin *secundum formam cartæ*, the soile doth not passe nor the water, for the grantor may take water there, and if the river become drie, he may take the benefit of the soile, for there passed to the grantee but a particular right, and the livery being made *secundum formam cartæ*, cannot enlarge the grant. For the same reason, if a man grant *aquam suam*, the soile shall not passe, but the pischarie within the water passeth therewith. And land couered with water shall be demaunded by the name of so many acres *aqua coopert*, whereby it appeareth that they are distinct things. So if a man grant, to another to dig turues in his land, and to carry them at his will and pleasure, the land shall not passe, because but part of the profit is given, for trees, mines, &c. shall not passe. But if a man seised of lands in fee by his deed granteth to another the profits of those lands, to have and to hold to him and his heires, and maketh livery *secundum formam cartæ*, the whole land it selfe doth passe, for what is the land, but the profits thereof, for thereby Vesture, herbage, trees, mines, and all whatsoever parcell of that land doth passe.

By the grant of the Bolloury of Salt, it is said that the soile shall passe, for it is the whole profit of the soile. And this is called *Saliua* of the French word *salure* for a salt pit, and you may reade *de Saliua* in *Domesday*, and *Selda*, signifieth the same thing: and where you shall reade in Records *de lacerta in profunditate aque salie*, there *lacerta* signifieth a fathom. A man seised of divers acres of wood, grants to another *omnes boscos suos*, all his woods, not only the woods growing upon the land passe, but the land it selfe, and by the same name shalbe recovered in a *præcipe*, for *boscus* doth not only include the trees, but the land also whereupon they grow.

The same law if a man in that case grant *omnes boscos suos crescentes*, &c. yet the land it selfe shall passe, as it hath beene adiudged * *frassetum* signifieth a wood, or ground that is woodie. If a man hath a wood of Elder trees contayning 20. acres, and granteth to another 20. *acras Alneti* (with an N not a V) the wood of Elders, and the soile thereof shall passe, but no other kinde of woods shall passe by that name. *Alnetum est vbi alni arbores crescunt*, * And *sullings* are taken for elders. *Salicetū* doth signifie a wood of willows, *vbi salices crescunt*, these trees in our books are called *Sawces*. *Selda*, is a wood of sallowes, willowes or withies. A brakie ground is called *filecetum, vbi filices crescunt*. A wood of Ashes is called *fraxinetū, vbi fraxini crescunt*, and passeth by that name, and *lupulicetum* where hoppes growe, and *Arundinetum* where reeds growe. Some say that *Dene* or *Denne*, whereof *Dena* commeth, is properly a valley or dale. *Dena siluæ*, and the like, as *drofden*, or *drufden*, or *druden*, signifieth a thicket of wood in a valley, for *druf*, or *dru*, signifieth a thicket of wood, and is often mentioned in *Domesday*. And sometime *Dena* or *Denna* signifieth, as *villa* and *denne*, a towne.

Cope signifieth a hill, and so doth *Lawe*, as *Stanlawe* is *saxeus collis*. *Howe* also signifieth a hill. And *hope combe*, and *Stow* are valleyes, and so doth *clough*. And *Dunum* or *Duna*, signifieth a hill or higher ground, and therefore commonly the townes that end in *Dun*, have hills of higher grounds in them, which we call Downs. It commeth of the old French word *Dun*.

In our Latin a wood is called *boscus*, *Graua* signifieth a little wood, in old deeds, and *Hirst* or *Hurst* a wood, and so doth *Holt* and *Shawe*. *Twaite* signifieth a wood grubbed up, and turned to errable. *Stethe* or *Stede*, betokeneth properly a banke of a river, and many times a place, as *Stowe* doth, and *Wic*, a place upon the Sea shore, or upon a River. *Lea* or *Ley* signifieth pasture.

If a man doth grant all his pastures, *pasturas*, the land it selfe imployed to the feeding of beasts doth passe, and also such pastures or feedings, as he hath in another mans soile. *Leswes* or *Lesues* is a Saxon word, and signifieth pastures. Betweene *pastura* and *pascuum*, the legall difference is that *pastura* in one signification containeth, the ground it selfe called pasture, and by that name is to be demanded. *Pascuū* feeding, is wheresoever cattell are fed, of what nature soever the ground is, and cannot be demanded in a *præcipe* by that name.

If a man grant *omnia prata sua*, all his meadowes, the land it selfe of that kinde passe, *& dicitur pratum quasi paratum*, because it groweth *sponte* without manurance. A man grant *omnes brueras suas*, the soyle where heath doth grow passeth, and may be demanded by that name

in

in a præcipe, it is derived from bruyer a French word for heath, and it is called Ros in the Brittish tongue.

Roncaria or Runcaria, signifieth land full of brambles and briers, and is derived of Roucier the French word, which signifieth the same, and as much as senticetum. By the grant of omnes Iuncarias or Ioncarias, the soile where rushes doe grow, doth passe for Ionc in French is a Rush, whereof Ioncaria commeth. A man grant omnes Ruscarias suas, the soile where rusci. i. knee-holme, or butchers pricks or broome doe grow, shall passe, and so in the verse in the Register it is called, but in F.N.B. fol. 2 in the verse Pischaria, is put in stead of Ruscaria. And Iampna commeth (of Ionc, and nower) a waterish place, and is all one in effect with Ioncaria, He that granteth omnes mariscos suos, all his fennes or marish grounds doe passe. Mariscus is derived of the French word mares or marets; the Latyn word for it, is palus or locus paludosus. Mora is derived of the English word Moore, and signifieth a more barren and unprofitable ground then marshes, dangerous for any cattell to goe there, in respect of myrie and moorish soile, neyther serves it for getting of turves there: you shall reade in Record, that such a man perquisivit trescent. acr. maretti, &c. this word marettum is derived of mare the sea, and tego, and properly signifieth a moorish and gravelly ground, which the sea doth cover and overflow at a full sea, and lyeth betweene the high water marke and the lowe water marke, infra fluxum & refluxum maris. By grant of these particular kindes, the lands of these particular kindes only doe passe, but as hath beene said by the grant of land generall, all these particular kindes and some others doe passe. Non mihi si centũ linguæ sint oraq; centum, omnia terrarum percurrere nomina possem. And therefore let us turne our eye to generall words, which doe include lands of severall sort and qualities. By the name of an honor, which a subiect may have, divers mannors, and lands may passe. So by the name of an Isle insula, many mannors, lands and tenements may passe.

Holme, or Hulmus signifieth an Isle or fenny ground. * A Commote is a great Segniorie, and may include one or divers mannors; By the name of a castle, one or more mannors may be conveyed, & è converso. by the name of a mannor, &c. a castle may passe. In Domesday I reade, Comes Alanus habet in suo castellatu 200. maneria, &c. præter castellariam habet 43. maneria, and in that booke a castle is called castellum, and castrum, and domus defensibilis, and mansus muralis. But note by the way, that no subiect can build a castle or house of strength imbattelled, &c. or other fortresse defensible, called in Law by the names aforesaid, and sometimes domus kernellatæ, or Carnellatæ, imbattellatæ, tenellatæ, machecollatæ, mese carnelet, &c. without the licence of the King for the danger which might ensue, if every man at his pleasure might doe it. And they be called imbattlements, because they are defences against battels in assaults. Tenellare or tanellare, is to make holes or loopes in walls to shoote out against the Assailants. Machecollare or machecoulare, is to make a warlike device over a gate or other passage like to a grate, through which scalding water, or ponderous, or offensive things may bee cast upon the assaylants. But to returne to the matter from whence upon this occasion we are fallen.

By the name of a towne Villa, a mannor may passe. In Domesday, Alodium (in a large sence) signifieth a free mannor, and Alodiarij or Alodarij, lords of the same, and Lannemanni there signifie lords of a mannor, having socam & sacam de tenentibus & hominibus suis. And by the name of a Mannor, divers townes may passe, quod olim dicebatur fundus nunc manerium dicitur, by the name of a ferme or fearme firma, houses, lands and tenements may passe, and firma is derived of the Saxon word feormian, to feede or releeve, for in ancient time they reserved upon their Leases, cattell and other victuall and provision for their sustenance. Note a fearme in the North parts is called a Tacke, in Lancashire a Fermeholt, in Essex a wike. But the word fearme, is the generall word, and anciently fundus signified a fearme and sometime land. Lands making a Knights fee, shall passe by the grant of a Knights fee de uno feodo militis.

Unum solinum, or solinus terræ in Domesday booke conteyneth two plow lands and somewhat lesse then an halfe, for there it is said, Septem Solini, or Solinæ terræ sunt 17. carucat'. Una Hida seu carucata terræ, which is all one as a plow-land, viz. asmuch as a plough can till, Sullerye also signifieth a plow-land. Una virgata terræ, a yard land, the Saxons called it Zirdland, and now the G. is turned to a Y. as in some Countries 10 in some 20. in some 24. in some 30. &c. Una bouata terræ, an oxgange, or an oxgate of land, is as much as an oxe can till. But carucata terræ, and bovata terræ, are words compound, and may conteyne meadow, pasture, and wood, necessary for such tillage. Iugum terræ in Domesday, conteyneth halfe a plow-land. And by all these names in the raigne of R. 1. lands were usually demanded and long after.

By the name of a Grange, grangia a house or edifice, not only where corne is stored up like as in barnes, but necessary places for husbandry also, as stables for hay and horses, and stables and styes for other cattell, and a curtilage, and the close wherein it standeth shall passe, and it is a French word, and signifieth the same, as we take it.

Stagnum, in English a poole doth consist of water and land, and therefore by the name of

Regist. 1. E. 3. 4. F.N.B. 7. 16. Ass. p. 9. Register.
Iampna.
Pasch. 41. E. 3. coram Rege Lincoln. rot. 28.
Mag. Carta. ca. 31. Walingford. Nott. Bolon, Lanc. &c.
Trin. 33. E. 1. coram Rege in Thes. honor de Huntingdon.
Mich. 9. E. 2. coram Rege in Thes. 18. E. 2. Ass. 377.
26. Ass. p. 60.
6. E. 3. 56. 47. E. 3. 21. honor de peverel. 49. E. 3. 24. honor de Egles. 9. H. 6. 27. 36. H. 8. Dier. 58. honor de Glouc. F.N.B. 265 honor Abbath. de Merle. 5. E. 4. 129. 7. H. 6. 39. 1. E. 3. 4. &c.
13. E. 3. iurisdict. 23. Lib. 4. fo. 88. Lutterels case. 5. H. 7. 9. 14. H. 4. in recordo longo.
8. H. 4. pl. Com. 168.
8. H. 7. 1. 4. E. 4. 16.
* 13. E. 3. iurisdict. 23.
26. Ass. 54. 29. E. 3. 15.
29. H. 6. travers. 4.
Bract. fo. 434. 1. E. 3. 4.
5. H. 7. 9. 3. E. 2. Avowry 188
37. H. 6. 24. 18. H. 6. 11. [illegible] fol. 18. [illegible], carta
Cap. escheatrie, fo. 162.
Britten. c. 20.
Rot. Parliam. 45. E. 3. nu. 34. 6. H. 4. nu. 19. 1. E. 4. 1.
Rot. Parliament. 1. E. 3. 2. pars. Alano [illegible] barton.
22. E. 3. 2. pars. Thoma Barkley &c.
Lamb. exposit. verb. fermo.
Pl. Com. 195.
Pl. Com. 169. Regist. 227. b. eiect. firma.
17. E. 3. fo. 8. 5. E. 3. 213.
16. E. 3. bre. 165. 12. E. 2. bre. 814.
4. E. 3. 161. 6. E. 3. 283.
2. E. 3. 5. 35. H. 6. 29.
Pl. Com. 168. 7. Ass. 8.
11. Ass. 17.
Lamb. expos. verb. Hyde & virgat. terræ.
Glanuil. lib. ca. Domesday.
Bract. lib. 2. ca. 26. 27. & lib. 5. fo. 434. Reg. fo. 72.
45. E. 3. fine 49. 13. E. 3. fine. 67. 39. H. 6. 8.
4. E. 3. 159. 8. E. 3. 377.
Bract. fol. 180. 269. 431.
5. H. 3. Droit. 66. Pl. Com. 168.
13. E. 3. bre. 241. 2. E. 3. 57. temps. E. 1. bre. 811. pl. com. 168.
Pl. com. 169. Linwood.
44. E. 3. 21. 4. E. 3. 32.
4. E. 3. tit. feffmentz & faits 79. 14. E. 3. Formdon. 34.
34. Ass. pl. 11.

11.E.3.4.4.E.3.143. 8.E.1.38..10.E.3.482. 11.E.3.entry 57. F.N.B.191.h. Domesday.

Stagnum or a poole, the water and land shall passe also. In the same manner Gurges, a deepe pit of water, a gors or gulfe consisteth of water and land, and therefore by the grant thereof by that name, the soile doth passe, and a præcipe doth lye thereof, and shall lay his esplees in taking of fishes, as Breames and Roches. In Domesday it is called guort, gort & gors plurally, as for example, de 3.gorz mille anguills.

Temps.E.1.bre.861. 4.E.3.5.10.H.7.30. 44.E.3.12.43.E.3.24. 35.H.6.55.3.H.6.2. Domesday.Bracton. lib.4.fo.235.

So it is of a Forest, Parke, Chase vivarye, and warren in a mans owne ground, by the grant of any of them, not only the priviledge, but the land it selfe passe, for they are compound. In the booke of Domesday, that is called leuuad and leuga, and leuued, and leuue, which in Latyn is called leuca.

Int.adiudicat.coram Rege. p.39.E.3.lib.2.f.95.in Thesaur. 40..Ass.38.4.H.6.14. 35.E.1.ca.6. Anno 10.R.1.inter fines in Thesaur.Ferlingus terra conti. 32.acras. Domesday. Frustrum.16.E.3.tit. common 9. Mich 8 H.3.in cipien.9. Coram Rege.Warr.Ro.6. Virg.eglog.1.4. Bract.211.233.22.E.4.trns. 140.pl.com.168.171.

Stadium, or ferlingus sive ferlingum, or quarentena terræ, is a furlong of land, and is as much as to say, a furrow long, which in ancient time was the eight part of a mile, and land will passe by that name. And some hold, that by that name land may be demanded. And de ferlingis & quarentenis, you shall reade divers times in the booke of Domesday, and there you shall reade, In insula Rex habet vnũ frustrũ terræ vnde exeunt sex vomeres. Nota Frustrũ, signifieth a parcell. Warectum or wareccum, or varrectum, doth signifie fallow; Terra jacet ad Warectũ, the land lyeth fallow: but in truth the word is vervactum, quasi verè novo victũ seu subactum, terra novalis seu requieta quia alternis annis requiescat, Tam culta novalia. By the grant of a messuage, or house mesuagium, the orchard, garden, and curtilage doe passe, and so an acre or more may passe by the name of a house. It is derived of the French word mese. In Domesday, a house in a Citie or Burrough, is called haga; other houses are called there mansiones, mansuræ & domus, and in an ancient plea concerning Feuersham in Kent, hawes are interpreted to signifie mansiones. In Normans French it is called mesiul or mesuil: Bye signifieth a dwelling, bye an habitation, and byan to dwell.

23.H.8.Br.feffments 53. 9.Ass.p.21.35.H.6..44. pl.com.169. Domesday. Pasch.30.E.1.coram Rege Kanc.in Thesaur. Statut.de extent.manerii Domesday. Domesday.

It is to be noted, that in Domesday there be often named bordarij seu borduanni, cosces, cosset, cotucami cotarij, are all in effect bores or husbandmen, or cotagers, saving that bordarij, which commeth of the French word borde for a cottage signifieth, there bores holding a little house with some land of husbandry bigger then a cottage, and coterelli are meere cottagers, qui cotagia & curtilagia tenent.

Villani in Domesday (often named) are not taken there for bondmen, but had their name de villis, because they had fermes, and there did worke of husbandrie for the lord, and they were ever named before bordarij, &c. and such as are bondmen are called there servi.

Int.placita coram domino Rege Mich.10.E.3.Rot.26.

Coleberti often also named in Domesday, signifieth Tenants in free socage by free rent, and so it is expounded of record Radmans and Radchemistres, (Rad, or rede, signifieth firme and stable) there also often named, these are liberi tenentes qui arabant & herciebant ad curiam domini, seu falcabant, aut metiebant, because their estates are firme and stable, and they are many times called Sochemans and sokemanni, because of their plough service.

Lamb.exposit.verb.Thanus.

Dreuchs signifieth free tenants of a Mannor there also named. Taini or thaini mediocres were freeholders, and sometime called milites regis, and their land called Tainland, and there it is said, hæc terra T R E. fuit Tainland, sed postea conversa in Reueland. But thainus regis is taken for a Baron, for it is said in an ancient Author, Thainus regis proximus comiti est, & ibidem mediocris thainus, & alibi Baro sive thainus.

Lib Rub.cap.15. & cap.41. & 76.W.2.c.46. 7.H.4.38. Lib.dentries tit.Ass. corps.pol.2. Domesday. 7.H.4.38. Fleta lib.2.ca.35.

Berqualia or Bercaria, commeth of Bere, an old Saxon word, used at this day for barkes or rindes of trees, and signifieth a Tanhouse, or a heath house, where barkes or rindes of trees are laid to tanne withall, and Berquarij are mentioned in Domesday.

By Vaccaria in law, is signified a Dairy house, derived of vacca the cow. In Latyn it is, Lactar um or Lactitium, and vaccarius is mentioned in Domesday. And Fleta maketh also mention of porcaria a swinestye.

Domesday. 10.R.1.Inter fines.

The content of an Acre is knowne, the name is common to the English, German, and French. In legall Latyn it is called, Acra, which the Latinists call iugerum. In Domesday it is called Arpeu prati, silvæ, &c 10.R.1. inter fines acra, in Cornewall, continet 40. perticatas in longitudine & 4. in latitudine & quelibet perticata de 16. pedibus in longitudine.

9.E.3.39.Temps.E.1. br.866.Mich.30.E.1. coram Rege Glouc.in Thesaur.

By the grant of a Selion of land, Selio terræ, a ridge of land, which containeth no certainty, for some be greater and some be lesser, and by the grant de vna porca, a ridge doth passe: Selio is derived of the French word Sellon for a ridge.

Bract.fo.377.431.43.E.3.27 Regist.fo.1.94.248.249. F.N.B.fo.87.F.I. Regula.

By the grant de centum libratis terræ, or 50. libratis terræ, or centum solidatis terræ, &c land of that value passeth, and so of more or lesse, and in ancient time by that name it might have beene demanded. And many things may passe by a name, that by the same name cannot bee demanded by a præcipe (for that doth require more prescript forme) but whatsoever may be demanded by a precipe, may passe by the same name by way of grant.

7.R.1.inter fines Sussex.

Frythe is a plaine betweene woods, and so is lawnd or lound, Combe, hope, dene, glyn, hawgh, howgh signifieth a Vally. Howe hoo, knol law peu, and cope a hill. Ey, lug and worth signifieth a watry place or water. Falesia is a banke or hill by the sea side, it commeth of falaize, which signifieth the same: of all these you shall reade in ancient bookes, charters, deedes,

and

and records, and to the end that our student should not be discouraged for want of knowledge when he meetes with them (nescit enim generosa mens ignorantiam pati) we haue armed him with the signification of them, to the end he may proceed in his reading with alacritie, and set vpon, and know how to worke into, with delight, these rough mines of hidden treasure.

(m) By the name of Minera or fodina plumbi, &c. the land it selfe shall passe in a grant if livery be made, and also be recouered in an assise, & sic de similibus.

(m) 17. E.3.7. 43. E.3.33.b. Regist. 165. 10. H.7.31. Pl. Com. 191. 195. Bract. 211. 325.

By the grant of a fouldcourse or the like lands and tenements may passe. (n) Tenementū, Tenement is a large word to passe, not only lands, and other inheritances which are holden, but also offices, rents, commons, profits apprender out of lands and the like, wherein a man hath any frankteneme̅t, and whereof he is seised, vt de libero tenemento. But hereditamentum, hereditament, is the largest word of all in that kinde, for whatsoeuer may be inherited is an hereditament, be it corporeall or incorporeall, reall or personall or mixt.

(n) 45. E.3. Voucher 72. 33. E.3. grant. 102. 11. H.6.22.27. 14. E.4.4. 20. Ass. p.9. 3. E.4.19. 1. H.7.25.

(o) A man seised of lands in fee hath diuers Charters, deeds, and euidences, and maketh a feoffment in fee, either without warranty, or with warranty only against him & his heires, the purchaser shal haue all the Charters, deeds and euidences, as incident to the lands, and ratione terræ, to the end he may the better defend the land himselfe, hauing no warranty to recouer in value, for the euidences are as it were the sinewes of the land, and the feoffor being not bound to warrantie, hath no vse of them. But if the feoffor be bound to warranty, so that he is bound to render in value, then is the defence of the title at his perill, and therefore the feoffee in that case shall haue no deeds that comprehend warranty, whereof the feoffor may take aduantage. Also hee shall haue such Charters as may serue him to deraigne the warrantie paramount; Also hee shall haue all deeds and euidences, which are materiall for the maintenance of the title of the land, but other euidences which concerne the possession, and not the title of the land, the feoffee shall haue them.

(o) Lib.1. fo.1. & 2. in Seignior Buckhursts case. 44. E.3.11.b. 39. E.3.17.a. 19. H.6.65.b. 34. H.6.1.a. 10. E.4.9.b. 18. E.4.14.15. 6. H.7.3.b. H.7.33.a.

¶ *A auer & tener.* These two words doe in this place proue a double signification, viz. a auer to haue an estate of inheritance of lands discendible to his heires; and tener to hold the same of some superior lord.

There haue beene eight formall or orderly parts of a deede of feoffment; viz. 1. the premisses of the deed implied by Littleton, 2. the habendum where Littl. here speaketh, 3. the tenendum mentioned by Litt. 4. the Reddendum. 5. the clause of warrantie. 6. the In cuius rei testimonium, comprehending the sealing. 7. The date of the deede contayning the day, the moneth, the yeare, and stile of the King, or of the yeare of our Lord. (a) Lastly, the clause of hijs testibus; and yet all these parts were contained in very few and significant words, (b) Hæc fuit candida illius ætatis fides & simplicitas, quæ pauculis lineis omnia fidei firmamenta posuerunt.

Vid. Sect. 40. & 370. 371. many things de cartis & factis. Fleta lib.3. cap.14. Britton. 100. 101. Bracton lib.5. fo.396.a. 399. 38. H.6.31.36. Pl. com. Wrotesl.ys case, fo.96. (a) Vid. Throgmortons case, pl. com. (b) Lib.6. fo.43. in Sir Anthony Mildemayes case.

The office of the premisses of the deede is twofold: First rightly to name the feoffor and the feoffee. And secondly to comprehend the certainty of the lands or tenements to be conueyed by the feoffment, either by expresse words, or which may by reference be reduced to a certainty; for, id certum est quod certum reddi potest. The habendum hath also two parts, viz. first, to name againe the feoffee, and secondly to limit the certaintie of the estate. The Tenendum at this day where the fee simple passe, must be of the chiefe lords of the fee. And of the Reddendum more shalbe said in his proper place in the chapter of Rents. Of the clause of warrantie more shall be said in the chapter of warranties. In Cuius rei testimonium sigillum meum apposiui was added, for the Seale is of the essentiall part of the deed. The date of the deede many times Antiquitie omitted, and the reason thereof was for that the limitation of prescription or time of memory did often in processe of time change, and the law was then holden that a deede, bearing date, before the limitted time of prescription was not pleadable, and therefore they made their deedes without date, to the end they might alleage them within the time of prescription. And the date of the deedes was commonly added in the raigne of E.2. and E.3. and so euer since.

Vid. Sect. 278. Britt. fol. 101. (p) Lamb. exposit. verb. terra ex scripto. Vid. Fortescue. cap. 32. see the second part of the Institut. cap. 38.

And sometimes antiquitie added a place, as Datum apud D. which was in disaduantage of the feoffee, for being in generall, he may alleage the deede to be made where he will. And lastly, Antiquitie did adde, hijs testibus in the continent of the deede after the In cuius rei testimonium, written with the same hand that the deede was, which witnesses were called, the Deede read, and then their names entred. (p) And this is called charter land, and accordingly the Saxons called it Bockland, as it were booke land which clause of hijs testibus in subiects deeds continued vntill and in the raigne of H.8. but now is wholly omitted. And it appeareth by the antient Authors and Authorities of the Law; that before the Statute of 12. E.2. ca.2. Processe should be awarded against the witnesses named in the deede, testes in carta nominatos, (a) and that the same Statute was but an affirmance of the Common law, which not being well vnderstood, hath caused varietie of opinions in our bookes. But the delay therein was so great, and sometimes (though rarely) by exceptions against those witnesses, which being found true, they were not to be sworne at all, neither to be ioyned to the Jury, nor as witnesses; (b) as if the witnesse were infamous, for example, if he be attainted of a false verdict, or of a conspiracie at the suite

12. E.2. c.2. see the second part of the Institutes, Marlbr. cap.6. & cap 14. (a) Britton fo.65.101. 11. E.3. Proces.170. 6. H.3. proces.229. 8. H.3. proces.210. 4. E.2. gard 119. (b) Mirror cap.4. § de infamies & periurie. Glanuil. lib.2 cap.15. Bract. lib.5 fo.288.292. Britt. fo.134.135.101. Fleta lib.5. ca.22. 8. E.2. Ass.356. 2. E.3.22. 24. E.3.34.

43.E.3. Conspir.12. 27.Ass.59. 33.H.6.55.21.H.6.30. (c) Fortescu.cap.26. Pas.55.H.3.m.3. Stanf.Pl.Cor.174.a.

suite of the King, or conuicted of periury, or of a Premunire, or of forgerie vpon the Statute of 5. Eliz. cap 14. and not vpon the Statute of 1. H.5. cap. 3. or conuict of felony, or by iudgement lost his eares, or stood vpon the pillory, or tumbrell, or beene stigmaticus branded, or the like, whereby they become infamous for some offences, quæ sunt minoris culpæ sunt maioris infamiæ. (c) If a champion in a writ of right become recreant or coward, hee thereby looseth liberam legem and thereby becomes infamous, and cannot be a witnesse, for regularly hee that looseth liberam legem, becommeth infamous and can be no witnesse. Or if the witnesse be an infidell, or if non sane memory, or not of discretion, or a partie interessed or the like.

(d) Fortescue.ca.25.

(d) But often times a man may be challenged to be of a Jury, that cannot be challenged to be a witnesse; and therefore though the witnesse be of the neerest alliance, or kindred, or of councell, or tenant, or seruant to either partie, (or any other exception that maketh him not infamous, or to want vnderstanding, or discretion, or a partie in interest) though it be proued true, shall not exclude the witnesse to bee sworne

(e) 22.Ass.12.& 41. 23.Ass.11. 19.E.2.tit.Ass.409.

(e) but hee shall bee sworne, and his credit vpon the exceptions taken against him left to those of the Jury, who are tryers of the fact, insomuch as some bookes haue said that though the witnesse named in the Deede be named a Disseisor in the writ, yet he shalbe sworne as a witnesse to the deede,

(f) 34.E.1.Proces.208.

(f) A witnesse amongst others named in a Deed was outlawed, & no Proces was awarded against him by the Statute, because he was extra legem, and an outlawed person cannot be an Auditor. And the Court in some books haue said, that they haue not seene witnesses challenged, which is regularly to be vnderstood, with the limitations aboue said, but such as are returned to be of a Jury, are to bee challenged for the causes aforesaid for outlawrie, and diuers other causes (for the which a witnesse cannot be challenged) and such proces against witnesses vanished. But seeing the witnesses named in a Deede shall be ioyned to the Inquest, and shall in some sort ioyne also in the verdict (in which case if Jury and witnesses finde the Deede that is denied to bee the Deede of the partie, the aduers partie is barred of his attaint, because there is more then 12. that affirme the verdict.) It is reason that in that case of ioyning, such exception shall bee taken against the witnesse as against one of the Jury, because he is in the nature of a Juror.

(a) 34.E.1.tit.proces.208. 11.Ass.p.19.20.12.Ass.p.1. 13.41.18.Ass.p.11. 22.Ass.15.23.Ass.15. 40.Ass.23.48.Ass.p.5. 21.H.6.30.

(a) And therefore to put one example if hee be outlawed in a personall action hee cannot bee ioyned to the Jurie, but yet that is no exception against him to exclude him to be sworne as a witnesse to the Jury. And the reason of all this is, for that if he with others should ioyne in verdict with the Jury in affirmance of the Deede, the partie should be barred of his Attaint. But note there must be more then one witnesse, that shall be ioyned to the Inquest. And albeit they ioyne with the Jury, and finde it not his Deede, notwithstanding this ioyning, the partie shall haue his attaint, for it is a maxime in Law,

(b) 48.E.3.30.12.H.6.fo 6.a 50.E.3.16.43.E.3.32. 12.H.4.9.19.E.2.Ass.408. Pasch.14.E.3.coram Rege Deum.in Thesaur. Fleta.lib.6.cap.6. Fitz.N.B.106.H.& 97.e. (c) Mirror.ca.3. Pl.Com.fo.10. Bract.lib.5.fo.400.

(b) That witnesses cannot testifie a negatiue, but an affirmatiue. And if one of the witnesses named in the Deede be one of the panell, he shalbe put out of the panell, and all these secrets of law, doe notably appeare in our bookes.

To shut vp this point, it is to be knowne, (c) that when a tryall is by witnesses, regularly the affirmatiue ought to be proued by two or three witnesses, as to proue a summons of the tenant, or the challenge of a Juror, and the like. But when the tryall is by verdict of 12. men, there the iudgement is not giuen vpon witnesses, or other kinde of euidence, but vpon the verdict and vpon such euidence as is giuen to the Jury they giue their verdict. And Bracton saith, there is probatio duplex, viz. viua, as by witnesses viua voce, and mortua, as by deedes, writings, and instruments. And many times Juries, together with other matter, are much induced by presumptions, whereof there be three sorts, viz violent, probable, and light or temerarie. Violenta presumptio is many times plena probatio, as if one be runne thorow the body with a sword in a house, whereof he instantly dieth, and a man is seene to come out of that house with a bloody sword, and no other man was at that time in the house, presumptio probabilis moueth little, but, Presumptio levis seu temeraria, moueth not at all.

Fleta lib.6.ca.33. 8.E.3.390.37.E.3.21.b. Glanvil.lib.10.ca.12. Fleta lib.6.ca.33.

So it is in the case of a Charter of feoffment, if all the witnesses to the Deede be dead (as no man can keepe his witnesses aliue, and time weareth out all men) then violent presumption which stands for a proofe is continuall and quiet possession, for ex diuturnitate temporis omnia presumuntur solenniter esse acta, also the deed may receiue credit, per collationem sigillorum, scripturæ, &c. & super fidem cartarum mortuis testibus erit, ad patriam de necessitate recurrendum.

Pasch.10.Ia.in Com.banco vpon the Stat. of Bankrouts.

Note, it hath beene resolued by the Justices, that a wife cannot be produced either against or for her husband, quia sunt duæ animæ in carne vna, and it might be a cause of implacable discord and dissention betweene the husband and the wife, and a meane of great inconuenience, but

(d) Fleta lib 2 ca.44. 13.E.1.tit.Vill.36 37. 19.E.2 Ibid 32. (e) Tr.8 Ia in Com banco. Smiths Case. in euidence vpon an information vpon the statute of Vsury.

(d) in some cases women are by law wholly excluded to beare testimony, as to proue a man to be a Villeine, mulieres ad probationem status hominis admitti non debent. It was also agreed by the whole Court (e) that in an Information vpon the statute of Vsurie, the partie to the vsurious contract shall not be admitted to be a witnesse against the Vsurer, for in effect hee should be testis in propria causa, and should auoide his owne bonds and assurances, and discharge himselfe of the money borrowed, and, though he commonly raise vp an Informer to exhibite the Information, yet in rei veritate he is the partie. And herewith in effect agreeth Britton.

Brit.fo.134.

ton, that he that challengeth a right in the thing, in demand cannot be a witnesse, for that he is a partie in interest. But now let us returne to that from the which by way of digression (upon this occasion) we are fallen.

And the ancient Charters of the King which passed away any franchise or revenue of any estate of inheritance had ever this clause of hijs testibus, of the greatest men of the kingdome, as the Charters of creation of Nobility, yet have at this day: when hijs testibus was omitted, and when teste me ipso came in into the Kings grants, you shall reade in the second part of the Institutes magna charta, ca.38. I have tearmed the said parts of the Deed, formall or orderly parts, for that they be not of the essence of a Deede of feffment, for if such a Deede be without premisses, habendum, tenendum, reddendum clause of warrantie, the Clause of In cujus rei testimonium, the Date. and the clause of his testibus, yet the Deede is good. (f) For if a man by Deede give lands to another, and to his heires without more saying, this is good, if he put his Seale to the Deede, deliver it, and make livery accordingly. (g) So it is if A. give lands, to have and to hold, to B. and his heires, this is good, albeit the feoffee is not named in the premisses. And yet no well advised man will trust to such Deedes, which law by construction maketh good ut res magis valeat, but when forme and substance concurre, then is the Deede faire and absolutely good. The sealing of Charters, and Deeds is much more ancient then some, out of error, have imagined, for the Charter of the King Edwyn, brother of King Edgar, bearing date Anno Domini, 956. made of the land called Iecklea in the Isle of Ely, was not only sealed with his owne Seale (which appeareth by these words, Ego Edwinus gratia dei totius britannicæ telluris rex meum donum proprio sigillo confirmavi) but also the Bishop of Winchester put to his Seale, Ego Ælswinus Wintoñ Ecclesiæ divinus speculator propriũ sigillũ impressi. And the Charter of King Offa, whereby he gave the Peter-pence, doth yet remaine under Seale. But no King of England, before, or since the Conquest, sealed with any seale of Armes, before King R.1. but the Seale was the King sitting in a chaire on the one side of the Seale, and on horsebacke on the other side in divers formes. And King R.1. sealed with a Seale of two Lyons, for the Conqueror for England bare two Lyons, and King Iohn in the right of Normandy (the Duke whereof bare one Lyon) was the first that bare three Lyons, and made his Seale accordingly, and all the Kings since have followed him. And King E.3. in anno 13. of his raigne, did quarter the Armes of France with his three Lyons, and tooke upon him the title of King of France, and all his successors have followed him therein.

(f) *Mirror ca* 1.§.6. & *ca* 5 § 1. *Glanvil. lib* 10 *ca.*12. *Bract lib.*5.*fo* 396. *Fleta lib* 6.*ca.*32.*Brit fo* 66.

(g) *Vid tearmes of the law, verb faits.* *Vid Glanvil lib.*10 *cap.*12. *Mirror, cap.*1.§.3. & *cap.*3.

The antiquity of sealing.

In ancient Charters of feoffment there was never mention made of the delivery of the Deed or any livery of seisin indorsed, for certainly the witnesses named in the Deede, were witnesses of both: and witnesses either of delivery of the Deede, or of livery of seisin by expresse tearmes was but of latter times, and the reason was in respect of the notorietie of the feoffment. And I have knowne some ancient Deedes of feoffment having livery of seisin indorsed suspected, and after detected of forgerie. As if a Deede in the stile of the King name him Defensor fidei before 13.H.8. or supreame head before 20.H.8. at what time hee was first acknowledged supreame head by the Cleargie, albeit the King used not the stile of supreame head in his Charters, &c. till 22.H.8. or King of Ireland, before 33.H.8. at which time he assumed the title of the King of Ireland, being before that called Lord of Ireland, it is certainly forged, & sic de similibus.

21.H 8.ca.16.

And some have observed, that Grace was attributed to King H.4. Excellent grace to King H.6. Maiestie to King H.8. and before the King was called, Soveraigne Lord, Liege Lord, Highnesse, and Kingly Highnesse, which in Latyn in legall proceedings is called regia celsitudo, as the beginning of the Petition of right to the King is, humilimè supplicavit vestræ celsitudini regiæ, &c. and the like. And upon this occasion it shall not be impertinent, seeing it is part of the formall Deede, to set downe the severall stiles of the Kings of England since the Conquest.

Vid 2.*H.*4 *ca.*15. *where Roy* all Maiesty *is attributed to the King, and* Crimen lese Maiestatis *is farre more ancient.*

William the Conqueror commonly styled himselfe Willielmus rex, and sometimes Willielm. rex Anglorum. And the like did William Rufus, and sometimes Willielmus dei gratia rex Anglorum.

Henry the first, Henricus rex Anglorum. and sometimes Henricus dei gratia rex Anglorum.

Mawde the sole daughter and heire of H.1. wrote Matildis imperatrix Henrici regis filia & Anglorum domina. Divers of whose creations and grants I have seene.

King Stephen used the stile that King H.1. did.

Henry the 2. Fitz emprice omitted dei gracia, and used this stile, Henricus rex Angliæ, dux Normanniæ, & Aquitaniæ, & comes Andegaviæ, hee having the Dutchie of Aquitaine, and Earledome of Poitiers in the right of Elianor his wife heire to both: And the Earledome of Aniowe Tournie and Maine, as sonne and heire to Ieffery Plantagenet by the said Mawde his wife, daughter and sole heire of King H.1. She was first married to Henry the Emperour, and after his death to the said Ieffery Plantagenet. Which Dutchie of Aquitaine doth include, Gascoigne and Guian.

King R.1. used the stile that H.2. his father did, yet was he King of Cyprus, and after of Ierusalem, but never used either of them.

King Iohn used that stile, but with this addition Dominus Hiberniæ, and yet all that he had in Ireland was conquered by his father King H. 2. which tytle of Dominus Hiberniæ, hee assumed, as annexed to the Crowne, albeit his father, in the 23. yeare of his raigne, had created him King of Ireland in his life time.

King H. 3. stiled himselfe as his father King Iohn did, untill the 44. yeare of his raigne, and then he left out of his stile Dux Normanniæ, & comes Audegauiæ, and wrote only Rex Angliæ dominus Hiberniæ, & dux Aquitaniæ.

King E. 1. stiled himselfe in like manner as King H. 3. his father did, Rex Angliæ dominus Hiberniæ, & dux Aquitaniæ. And so did King E. 2. during all his raigne. And King E. 3. used the selfesame stile untill the 13. yeare of his raigne, and then he stiled himselfe in this forme Edwardus dei gratia Rex Angliæ & Franciæ, & dominus Hiberniæ, leauing out of his stile dux Aquitaniæ. He was King of France, as sonne and heire of Isabell wife of King E. 2. daughter and heire of Philip la beau King of France, he first quartered the French armoryes with the English in his great Seale, Anno domini 1338. & regni sui 14.

King R. 2. and King H. 4. used the same stile that King E. 3. did. And King H. 5. untill the 8. yeare of his raigne continued the same stile, and then wrote himselfe, Rex Angliæ hæres & regens Franciæ, & dominus Hiberniæ, and so continued during his life.

Vid. Rot. Parliam. anno 1. H. 6. nu. 15. he was stiled Rex Franciæ & Angliæ & dominus Hiberniæ.

King H. 6. wrote, Henricus dei gratia Rex Angliæ & Franciæ, & dominus Hiberniæ; this King being crowned in Paris King of France used the said style 39. yeares, till he was dispossessed of the Crowne by King E. 4. who after he had raigned also about tenne yeares, King H. 6. was restored to the Crowne againe, and then wrote, Henricus dei gratia rex Angliæ & Franciæ, & dominus Hiberniæ ab inchoatione regni sui 49. & recaptionis regiæ potestatis primo.

King E. 4. R. 3. and H. 7. stiled themselues, Rex Angliæ & Franciæ, & dominus Hiberniæ.

King H. 8. used the same stile till the tenth yeare of his raigne, and then hee added this word (Octavus) as Henricus octavus dei gratia, &c. In the 13. yeare of his raigne he added to his stile fidei Defensor. In the 22. yeare of his raigne, in the end of his stile hee added supremum caput Ecclesiæ Anglicanæ. And in the 33. yeare of his raigne he stiled himselfe thus Henricus octavus dei gratia Angliæ, Franciæ & Hiberniæ rex fidei defensor, &c. & in terra Ecclesiæ Anglicanæ & Hiberniæ supremum caput.

King E. 6. used the same stile, and so did Queene Mary in the beginning of her raigne, and by that name summoned her first Parliament, but soone after omitted supremum caput. And after her marriage with King Philip, the stile notwithstanding that omission was the longest that euer was, viz. Philip and Mary by the grace of God King and Queene of England and France, Naples, Ierusalem and Ireland Defendors of the Faith, Princes of Spaine and Cicilie, Archdukes of Austria, Dukes of Millaine, Burgundie, and Brabant, Countees of Hasburgh, Flanders and Tyroll. And this stile continued till the fourth and fift yeare of King Philip and Queene Mary, and then Naples was put out, and in place thereof both the Cicilis put in, and so it continued all the life of Queene Mary.

I need not mention the stile of Queene Elizabeth, King Iames, nor of our Soueraigne Lord King Charles, because they are so well knowne, and I feare I haue beene too long concerning this point, which certainely is not unnecessary to be knowne for many respects. But to shew the causes and reasons of these alterations would aske a treatise of it selfe, and doth not sort to the end, that I haue aymed at. And now let us returne to the learning of Charters and deeds of Feoffments and Grants.

Livery of seisin incident to a feoffment. Vid. Sect. 59.

Very necessary it is, that witnesses should be underwritten or indorsed, for the better strengthening of Deedes, and their names (if they can write) written with their owne hands. For Livery of seisin. See hereafter Sect. 59. and for Deedes, Sect. 66. and of conditionall Deedes. See our Author in his Chapter of conditions. And now let us proceede to the other words of our Author.

Mirr. ca. 2. §. 15. Bract. lib. 2. fo. 62. b. Flet. lib. 6. ca. 1. & 54. & lib. 1. ca. 13. Glanvill lib. 7. ca. 1. & ca. 12. & 13.

¶ *A luy & a ses heires.* Hæres, in the legall understanding of the Common Law, implyeth that he is ex iustis nuptijs procreatus, for Hæres legittimus est quem nuptiæ demonstrant, and is he to whom lands, tenements, or hereditaments by the act of God, and right of blood doe discend of some estate of inheritance, for solus Deus hæredem facere potest non homo: dicuntur autem hæreditas & hæres ab hærendo, quod est arctè insidendo, nam qui hæres est hæret, vel dicitur ab hærendo quia hæreditas sibi hæret, licet nonnulli hæredem dictum velint quod hæres fuit, hoc est dominus terrarum, &c. quæ ad eum perueniunt.

(a) Bract. lib. 5. fo. 437. 438. Britt. ca. 66. fo. 167. & ca. 83. Fleta lib. 1. ca. 5.

A monster which hath not the shape of man kinde, cannot be heire or inherit any land, albeit it be brought forth within marriage, (a) but although he hath deformitie in any part of his bodie, yet if he hath humane shape he may be heire. Hij qui contra formam humani generis conuerso more procreantur, vt si mulier monstrosum, vel prodigiosum enixa, inter liberos non computentur partus tamen, cui natura aliquantulum ampliauerit vel diminuerit, non tamen superabundantur (vt si sex digitos vel nisi quatuor habuerit) bene debet inter liberos connumerari.

Si

Si inutilia natura reddidit, ut si membra, tortuosa habuerit, non tamen is partus monstrosus. Another saith, ampliatio seu diminutio membrorum non nocet. (b) A Bastard cannot bee heire, for (as hath beene said before) qui ex damnato coitu nascuntur inter liberos non computentur. Every heire is either a male, or female, or an Hermophradite, that is both male and female. And an Hermophradite (which is also called Androgynus) shall bee heire, either as male, or female, according to that kinde of the sexe which doth prevaile. Hermophradita, tam masculo, quam feminæ comparatur, secundum prævalescentiam sexus incalescentis. And accordingly it ought to be baptized. See more of this matter, Sect 35.

(b) Vid. Sect. 188. 399. Bract. lib. 2. fo. 9. Britton, fo. Fleta lib. 1. ca. 5. & lib. 6. ca 8 Felta. vbi sup. 4. 3. R. 2. entr. cong. 38.

(c) A man seised of lands in fee hath issue an Alien that is borne out of the Kings ligeance, he cannot be heire, propter defectum subiectionis, albeit he be born within lawfull mariage. If made Denizen by the Kings Letters patents, yet cannot he inherite to his father or any other. But otherwise is it, if he be naturalized by act of Parliament, for then hee is not accounted in law alienigena, but indigena. But after one bee made Denizen, the issue that hee hath afterwards shalbe heire to him, but no issue that he had before. If an Alien commeth into England and hath issue two sonnes, these two sonnes are indigenæ subiects borne, because they are borne within the realme. And yet if one of them purchase lands in fee, and dieth without issue, his brother shall not be his heire, for there was never any inheritable blood betweene the father and them, and where the sonnes by no possibility can be heire to the father, the one of them shall not be heire to the other. See more at large of this matter, Sect. 198. This is not law. v. Sid: 1198.

(c) Mirror ca. 1. Ca. 3. §. ca. 5 §. Bract. lib. 5 fo. 415 427. Britt fo. 29. Fleta lib. 6. c. 47. 13. E. 3. br. 677. 25. E 3. de natis ultra mare. 31. E. 3. Cosinage 5. 42. E. 3. 2. 11. H. 4. 26. 14. H. 4. 19 20. 3. H. 6. 55. 22. H. 6. 38. 9 E 4 7. lib. 7 fo. 1. in Caluyns case.

If a man be attainted of treason, or felony, although hee be borne within wedlocke, hee can be heire to no man, nor any man heire to him propter delictum, for that by his attaindor his blood is corrupted. And this corruption of blood is so high, as it cannot absolutely bee salued, and restored but by Act of Parliament, for albeit the person attainted obtaine his Charter of pardon, yet that doth not make any to be heire whose blood was corrupted at the time of the attainder, either downward or upward. (d) As if a man hath issue a sonne before his attainder and obtaineth his pardon, and after the pardon hath issue another sonne, at the time of the attainder the blood of the eldest was corrupted and therefore he cannot be heire. But if hee die liuing his father the younger sonne shall bee heire, for he was not in esse at the time of the attainder, and the pardon restored the blood as to all issues begotten afterwards. But in that case if the eldest sonne had suruiued the father, the younger sonne cannot be heire, because he hath an elder brother which by possibilitie might haue inherited, but if the elder brother had beene an Alien the younger sonne should bee heire, for that the alien never had any inheritable blood in him. See more plentifully of this matter, Sect. 646, 647.

1. E. 3. 4. 6. E. 3 55. 27 E. 3. 77. 3. E. 2 discent. Br. 64. 31. E. 1. discent 17. 46. E. 3. Petition 20. 26. Ass p. 2. 49. Ass pl 4. 29. Ass p 11. 9. H. 5. 9. (d) Stanf. pl. cor. 195. 196. Bract. lib 3. fo. 132. 133. 276 & lib. 5 fo. 374. Britt fo. 215. b. Fleta lib. 1. ca. 28.

If a man hath issue two sonnes, and after is attainted of treason, or felony, and one of the sonnes purchase lands and dieth without issue, the other brother shall be his heire, for the attainder of the father corrupteth the lineall blood only, and not the collaterall blood betweene the brethren, which was vested in them before the attainder, and each of them by possibilitie might haue beene heire to the father, and so hath it beene adiudged, (*) but otherwise in the case of the alien nee, as hath beene said. (e) But some haue holden that if a man after he be attainted of treason or felony haue issue two sonnes that the one of them cannot bee heire to the other because they could not be heire to the father, for that they never had any inheritable blood in them.

* In the Exchequer, Mich 40. & 41. Eliz. in le Case de Holby. (e) Bracton lib. 3. fol 130. Britton fol. 15. Fleta. lib 1. cap 58.

(f) One that is borne deafe and dumbe may be heire to another, albeit it was otherwise holden in ancient time, And so if borne deafe, dumbe and blinde, for in hoc casu, vitio parcitur naturali, but contract they cannot. Ideots, leapers, madmen, outlawes in debt, trespasses, or the like; persons excommunicated, men attainted in a præmunire, or conuicted of heresie, may be heires.

(f) Bract. lib. 5 fo. 421. 430. 434. lib. 2. fo. 12. Fleta lib. 6. ca. 39. 47. 14. H. 3. bre. 877. 32 E. 3. Age. 8. 10. E. 3. 535. 18. E. 3. 53. 13. E. 3. Ley 49.

(g) If a man hath a wife, and dieth, and within a very short time after the wife marrieth againe, and within 9. moneths hath a childe, so as it may be the childe of the one or of the other. Some haue said, That in this case the childe may choose his father, quia in hoc casu filiatio non potest probari, and so is the booke to be intended, for auoyding of which question and other inconueniences, this was the Law before the Conquest; Sit omnis vidua sine marito duodecim mensibus, & si maritauerit perdat dotem.

(g) 21. E. 3. 39. Tanarollus noua reperta 485. &c. Opus eximium 48 b. Lambard de priscis Anglorum legibus 120. 72. arc.

(h) A man by the Common Law cannot be heire to goods or chattels, for hæres dicitur ab hæreditate. (i) If a man hath diuers fishes, as Carps, Breames, Tenches, &c, and put them in his Pond and dieth, in this case the heire shall haue them and not the Executors, but they shall goe with the inheritance, because they were at libertie and could not bee gotten without industrie as by nets, and other ingines, otherwise it is if they were in a trunke or the like. Likewise Deere in a Parke, conies in a warren, and Doues in a doue-house young and old shall goe to the heire. (k) But of ancient time the heire was permitted to haue an action of debt upon a bond made to his Auncestor and his heires, but the Law is not so holden at this day. Vid. Sect. 12.

(h) Bracton lib. 4. ca. 9. fo. 265 lib. 2. fo. 62. b. Fleta. lib. 6. ca. 1. Lib. 8. fo. 54. Symes case. (i) Mich. 36. & 37. Eli. Rot. 25. Inter. Gray and Tanles in the Kings bench. Stanford 25. b. 18. E. 4 8. 22. Ass. 25. 18. H. 8. 2. (k) 13. E. 3. dett. 135. 139. 140. 47 E. 3. 23. 25. E. 3. fo. 48. 26. E. 3. fo. V. d. for an heireloome hereditarum et principalius, Sect. 12

(l) It is to be noted that one cannot be heire till after the death of his auncestor, he is called hæres apparens, heire apparant.

(l) Mirror. ca. 1. §. 3.

In

In our olde bookes and records there is mention made of another heire, viz. hæres astrarius, so called of Astre that is an harth of a house, because the auncester by conveyance hath set his heire apparant, and his family in a house and living in his life time, of whom Bracton saith thus, (a) Item esto quod hæres sit astrarius, vel quod aliquis antecessor restituat hæredi in vita sua hæreditatem, & se dimiserit, videtur quod nullo tempore iacebit hæreditas, & ideo quod nec relevari possit, nec debet nec relevium dari. (b) For the benefit, and safetie of right heires contra partus suppositos, the Law hath provided remedy by the writ de ventre inspiciendo, whereof the rule in the Register is this, Nota si quis habens hæreditatem duxerit aliquam in vxorem & postea moriatur ille sine hærede de corpore suo exeunte, per quod hæreditas illa fratri ipsius defuncti descendere debeat, & vxor dicit se esse pregnantem de ipso defuncto cum non sit, habeat frater & hæres breve de ventre inspiciendo. It seemeth by Bracton and Fleta which followed him, that this writ doth lye, Vbi vxor alicuius in vita viri sui se pregnantem fecit cum non sit, vel post mortem viri sui se pregnantem fecit cum non sit ad exherædationem veri hæredis, &c ad quærelam veri hæredis per præceptum domini regis, &c. Which is to be understood according to the rule of the Register: when a man having lands in fee simple dieth, and his wife soone after marrieth againe, and faine her selfe with childe by her former husband, in this case though shee be married, the writ de ventre inspiciendo doth lye for the heire. But if a man seised of lands in fee (for example) hath issue a daughter, who is heire apparant, she in the life of her father cannot have this writ for divers causes; first because she is not heire, but heire apparant, for as hath beene said nemo est hæres viventis, and this writ is given to the heire to whom the land is discended. And both Bracton and Fleta saith, that this writ lieth ad quærelam veri hæredis, which cannot be in the life of his ancester, and herewith agreeth Britton and the Register. Secondly, the taking of a husband in the case aforesaid being her owne act, cannot barre the heire of his lawfull action once vested in him. Thirdly, the Law doth not give the heire apparant any writ, for it is not certaine whither he shall be heire, solus deus facit hæredes. Fourthly, the inconvenience were too great if heires apparant in the life of their ancester should have such a writ to examine and trie a mans lawfull wife in such sort as the writ de ventre inspiciendo doth appoint, and if she should be found to be with childe, or suspect, then shee must be removed to a Castle and there safely kept untill her delivery, and so any mans wife might bee taken from him against the lawes of God and man.

(a) Bract. lib. 2. fo. 85. Heref. p. 8. E. 1. Ro. 80. de Banco. Mirror. cap. 2. §. 18. Britton 151. b.
(b) Registr. fo. 227. Bracton. lib. 2. fo. 69. Britton. fo. 165. Fleta lib. 1. ca. 14.
Britton. fo. 165. b. Regist. vbi supra.
Vid. Bracton Britton. & Fleta vbi supra. Registr. vbi supra. Bracton and Fleta vbi supra have (ad exheredationem.)

The words of the writ de ventre inspiciendo make this evident, Rex vic: salutem, monstravit nobis A. quod cum R. *quæ fuit vxor Clementis* B. pregnans non sit, ipsa falsò dicit se esse pregnantem de eodem Clemente, *ad exhæredationem* ipsius A. desicut terra quæ fuit eiusdem C. *ad ipsum A. iure hæreditario descendere debeat* tanquam *ad fratrem & hæredem* ipsius C. si prædict R. prolem de eo non habuerit, &c. but this rather belongs to the treatise of originall writs, and therefore thus much herein shall suffice.

And it is to be observed that every word of Littl: is worthy of observation, first (Heires) in the plurall number, for if a man give land to a man and to his heire in the singular number, hee hath but an estate for life, for his heire cannot take a fee simple by discent, because he is but one, and therefore in that case his heire shall take nothing. Also observable is this coniunctive (Et), For if a man giveth lands to one, To have & to hold to him or his heires, he hath but an estate for life for the uncertaintie. (Ses, suis) If a man give land unto two, To have and to hold to them two & hæredibus (c) omitting suis, they have but an estate for life for the uncertainty, whereof more hereafter in this Section. But it is said if land be given to one man & hæredibus, omitting suis, that notwithstanding a fee simple passeth, but it is safe to follow Littleton.

¶ (d) *Et ses assignes*. Assignee, commeth of the verbe assigno. And note there be assignes in Deede, and assignes in Law, whereof see more in the chapter of Warrantie, Sect. 733.

¶ *Ceux parolx (ses heires) tant solement font lestate denheritance en touts feoffments & grants.* (e) Si autem facta esset donatio, vt si dicam, do tibi talem terram, ista donatio non extendit ad hæredes sed ad vitam donatoris, &c. (f) Here Littleton treateth of purchases by naturall persons, and not of bodies politique or corporate; (g) for if lands bee given to a sole body politique or corporate, (as to a Bishop, Parson, Vicar, master of an Hospitall, &c.) there to give him an estate of inheritance in his politique or corporate capacitie, he must have these words, To have and to hold to him and his successors, for without these words Successors in those cases there passeth no inheritance, for as the heire doth inherite to the ancestor, so the successor doth succeed to the predecessor and the executor to the testator. (h) But it appeareth here by Littleton that if a man at this day give lands to I. S and his successors, this createth no fee simple in him, for Littleton speaking of naturall persons saith that these words (his heires) make an estate of inheritance in all Feoffments and Grants whereby he excludeth these words (his successors) (i) And yet if it be in an ancient grant it must bee expounded as the Law was taken at the time of the grant. (k) A Chantry priest incorporate tooke a Lease to him

(d) Lib. 5. fo. 96. 97. Brit. fo. 28. H. 8. Dier. Pl. Com. 287. 288.
(e) Bract. lib. 2. cap. 39 fo. 92. b. Brit. ca. 39. fo 99. b. Fleta. lib. 6. ca. 1. 2. & lib. 3. cap 2. 20. H. 6 35. 36. 19. H. 6. 17. 22. 74. 22. E. 4. 16. b. 4 E. 6. pl com 26.
(f) Vid. Sect 413.
(g) 7. E. 3. 25. Vid. Sect. 686. 25. E. 3. 35. Bract. lib. 2. fo. 62. b. Vid. Sect. 413.
(h) Pl. Com 242. Seguior Berkleys case.
(i) Vid. Brit. fo. 86 121. & 130. 17. E 3. 25. b. 33. H 6. 22. 10. H. 7. 13. 14. 9. H. 7. 11. 16. H. 7. 9. 15. E. 4 13 14. H 6. 12. 35. H. 6. 54. 24. Ass. 14. 40. Ass. 21. Tr. 5. E. 3. Ro. 4. in Scaccario. 3. E. 3. 32 7 E 3. 40. 11. H 4. 84. 12. H. 4. 12. 18. E. 3. Counsans 39. b. 5. E. 4. 121. 38. E 3. 4. Lib. 9. fo. 28. in Case. de Abb. de Strata Marcella.
(c) 10 H. 6. 7. 22. H. 6. 15. Pl. Com. 28. b. 22. E. 4. 16. 2. H. 4. 13. 20. E. 3. br. 377.

him and his successors for a hundred yeares, and after tooke a release from the Leasor to him and his successors, and it was adiudged that by the release he had but an estate for life, for he had the Lease in his naturall capacitie for it could not goe in succession, and (his successors) gave him no estate of inheritance for want of these words (his heires.) (l) If the King by his Letters patents giueth lands Decano & Capitulo, habendem sibi & hæredibus & successoribus suis, In this case albeit they be persons in their naturall capacitie to them and their heires, yet because the Grant is made to them in their politique capacitie, it shall enure to them and their successors. And so if the King doe grant lands to I S. Habendum sibi & successoribus siue hæredibus suis, this grant shall enure to him and his heires.

(l) 18.H.6.11.b & c. adiudge.

(m) B. hauing diuers sonnes and daughters A. giueth lands to B. & Liberis suis & a lour heires, the father and all his children doe take a fee simple ioyntly by force of these words (their heires) but if he had no childe at the time of the feoffment the childe borne afterward shall not take.

(m) 15.E.3.tit. Counterplea de Voucher. 43. 37.H.6.30.11 E.4 2.

These words (his heires) doe not only extend to his immediate heires, but to his heires remote, and most remote borne and to be borne, (n) Sub quibus vocabulis (hæredibus suis) omnes hæredes propinqui comprehenduntur, & remoti, nati, & nascituri, And hæredum a ppellatione veniunt hæredes hæredum in infinitum. And the reason, wherefore the Law is so precise to prescribe certaine words to create an estate of inheritance, is for auoyding of uncertainty, the mother of contention and confusion.

(n) Fleta lib.3 ca.8.
Pl Com.163.

There be many words so appropriated, as that they cannot be legally expressed by any other word, or by any periphrasis, or circumlocution: Some to estates of Lands, &c. as here and in (a) other places of our Author. In this place these words tantsolement, not solement alone; but tantsolement all only; .i. solummodo, or duntaxat, are to be obserued; (b) Some to tenures; (c) Some to persons, (d) Some to offences; (e) Some to formes of originall writs eyther for recouery of right, or remouing, or redresse of wrong; (f) Some to warrantie of Land. These haue I touched for examples, I leaue others to the studious reader to obserue, and adde holding this for an undoubted verity, that there is no knowledge, case, or point in Law, seeme it of neuer so little account, but will stand our studient in stead at one time or other, and therefore, in reading, nothing to be pretermitted.

(a) Sect. 17.62.133.
(b) Sect. 156.161.
(c) Sect. 184.
(d) Sect. 190.194.746.
(e) Sect 9 67.194.204 234. 236.241.405 485.478. 651.655.646.620.614.637 674.692.
(f) Sect. 733.

¶ *Font lestate.* Status dicitur a stando, because it is fixed, and permanent. The Isle of Man, which is no part of the kingdome, but a distinct territorie of it selfe, hath beene granted by the great Seale to diuers subiects and their heires. (g) It was resolued by the Lord Chancellor, the two chiefe Iustices and chiefe Baron, that the same is an estate discendible according to the course of the Common law, for whatsoeuer state of inheritance passe under the Great Seale of England, it shall be discendible according to the rules, and course of the Common Law of England.

(g) Tr. 40. Eliz. in le Countee de Derbys case, by the Lo: Chancellor, les 2. chiefe Iustices & chiefe Baron.

¶ *En touts feoffments & grants.* Here hee giueth the feoffment the first place, as the ancient and the most necessary conueyance, both for that it is solemne and publique, and therefore best remembred and proued, (g) and also for that it cleareth all disseisins, abatements, intrusions, and other wrongfull or defeasible estates, where the entry of the feoffor is lawfull, which neither fine, recouery, nor bargaine and sale by Deede indented and inrolled doth. And here is implyed a diuision of fee, or inheritance, viz, (h) into corporeall (as Lands and tenements which lye in livery) comprehended in this word feoffment, and may passe by livery by Deed, or without Deed, which of some is called hæreditas corporata, and incorporeall, (which lye in grant, and cannot passe by livery, but by deede, (as Aduowsons, Commons, &c. and of some is called hæreditas incorporata) and, by the delivery of the Deed, the freehold, and inheritance of such inheritance, as doe lye in grant, doth passe) comprehended in this word Grant. And the Deede of incorporeate inheritances doth equall the livery of corporeat. And therefore Littleton saith, in all Feoffments and Grants. Hæreditas, alia corporalis, alia incorporalis: Corporalis est, quæ tangi potest & videri, incorporalis quæ tangi non potest, nec videri.

(g) Vid S & 59. & 66.
(h) Mirror. ca 2.§.15 & ca. 5.§.1. Bract. lib 2 fo. 53. 366. 368. Fleta lib. 3 ca. 1.2 15 Brit. 84. 87.a. & fo 63.101 102 141.142. agreeth herewith Pl. Com. 171. Hill & Grange
Mirror ca. 5 §.1. Brit. ca 34.

Feoffment is deriued of the word of art feodum, quia est donatio feodi, for the ancient writers of the Law called a feoffment donatio, of the verbe do or dedi, which is the aptest word of feoffment. And that word Ephron used, * when he enfeoffed Abraham, saying, I giue thee the field of Machpelah ouer against Mamre, and the Caue therein I giue thee, and all the trees in the field and the borders round about, all which were made sure unto Abraham for a possession, in the presence of many witnesses.

For the Antiquitie of Feoffments. See the second part of the Institutes Merlebridge ca. 9 8.E 3.24.18 H.6.24. 39.H.6.39.
** Genesis 23.*

By a Feoffment the corporeate fee is conueyed, & it properly betokeneth a conueyance in fee, as our Author himselfe hereafter saith, * in his chapter of Tenant for life. And yet sometime improperly it is called a feoffment when an estate of freehold only doth passe, Done est nosme generall plus que nest feoffment, car done est generall a touts choses moebles & nient moebles, feoffment est riens forsque del soyle. And note there is a difference inter cartam & factũ, for carta is

** Vid. Sect. 57.*
Brit. ca. 34.
44.E.3.42.
See more of feoffment Sect. 60.
See of Factum, Sect. 259.

entended a Charter which doth touch inheritance, and so is not factum vnlesse it hath some other addition.

Lib.3 fo.63. in Lincolne Colledge case.

Grant, Concessio, is properly of things incorporeall which (as hath beene said) cannot passe without Deede. And here it is to be obserued (that I may speake once for all) that euery Period of our Author in all his three bookes containe matter of excellent learning, necessarily to be collected by implication, or consequence, for example hee saith here, that these words (his heires) make an estate of inheritance in all feoffments and grants, he expressing feoffments and grants, necessarily implyeth, that this rule extendeth not, first to Last wills and testaments, for thereby, (i) as he himselfe after saith, an estate of inheritance may passe without these words (his heires) (k) As if a man deuise 20. acres to another, and that he shall pay to his executors for the same tenne pound, hereby the deuisee hath a fee simple by the intent of the deuisor, albeit it be not to the value of the land. (l) So it is if a man deuise lands to a man imperpetuum, or to giue, and to sell, or in feodo simplici, or to him and to his assignes for euer, In these cases a fee simple doth passe by the intent of the Deuisor, but if the deuise bee to a man and his Assignes without saying (for euer) the Deuisee hath but an estate for life. (m) If a man deuise land to one & sanguini suo that is a fee simple, but if it be semini suo, it is an estate taile

(i) Litt. lib.3. ca. de Attorn. Sect 5.8.6.
4.E 6 Estates Br.78.
29 H 8. Testaments 18.
22. Eliz Dier 371.
Temps H.8 tit. Conscience Br 25.
(k) 21.E.3.16.24.H.6.7.
19 H.8.9. lib.3. fo.21. in Bonastons case lib.6. fo.16.17. lib.10. fo 67.
(l) Vid. Sect 585.
(m) Mich.40 & 41. Eliz. in Error Int. Downhall & Catesby adiudge. Brooke tit. taile 21

(n) Secondly, that it extendeth not to a fine sur conusans de droit come ceo que il ad de son done, by which a fee also may passe without this word (heires) in respect of the height of that fine, and that thereby is implyed that there was a precedent gift in fee.

(n) Lib.1. fo.100 Shellyes case. 42.E.3.7.
19.H 6.17.b 22 b.
Pl. Com.248.

Thirdly, Nor to certein Releases, and that three manner of wayes, (o) first when an estate of inheritance passeth and continueth, as if there be three coparceners or ioyntenants, & one of them release to the other two, or to one of them generally without this word (heires) by Litt. owne opinion they haue a fee simple as appeareth hereafter. Secondly, by release (p) when an estate of inheritance passeth & continueth not, but is extinguished, as where the Lord releases to the tenant or the grantee of a rent, &c release to the tenant of the land generally all his right, &c. hereby the Seigniorie, rent, &c. are extinguished for euer, without these words (heires) Thirdly (q) when a bare right is released, as when the disseisee release to the disseisor all his right, he neednot saith our Author in another place speake of his heires But of all these, and the like cases, more shall be treated in their proper places, Fourthly, nor to a Recouery, A. seised of land suffereth B. to recouer the land against him by a common recouery where the iudgement is quòd prædictus B. recuparet versus præd'. A tenementa prædicta cum pertin. yet B. recouereth a fee simple without these words (heires) for regularly euery recouerer recouereth a fee simple. Fiftly, nor to a creation of Nobilitie by writ, for when a man is called to the vpper house of Parliament by writ, hee is a Baron and hath inheritance therein without the word (heires) yet may the King limit the generall state of inheritance created by the Law and custome of the Realme to the heires males, or generall, of his body by the writ, as he did to Bromflete who in 27. H.6. was called to Parliament by the name of the Lo: Vescie, &c. with the limitation in writ to him and the heires males of his body, but if he be created by patent, he must of necessitie haue these words (his heires) or the heires males of his body, or the heires of his body, &c. otherwise he hath no inheritance. The first creation of a Baron by patent that I finde was of Iohn Beauchampe of Holte created Baron by patent in 11.R 2. for Barons before that time were called by writ. And it is to be obserued, that of ancient times Earles, &c. were created by girding them with a sword, and nominating him Earle, &c. of such a County or place and this with a calling of him to Parliament by writ, by that name was a sufficient creation of inheritance.

(o) Litt. lib.2 ca. tenant in Common. Sect.304 305. cap. Attorn. Sect.374.
Dier 9. Eliz. 263.
(p) Litt lib.3. ca. Releases, Sect.479.480
20.H.6.17.19.H.6.17.22.
(q) Litt. ca. Releases Sect.467.
27.H.6. Lo. Vescies case.

But out of this rule of our Author the Law doth make diuers exceptions (& exceptio probat regulam) for sometime by a feoffment a fee simple shall passe without these words (his heires.) For example, first, (r) if the father infeoffe the sonne, To haue and to hold to him and to his heires, and the sonne infeoffeth the father as fully as the father enfeoffed him, by this the father hath a fee simple, quia verba relata hoc maximè operantur per referentiam vt in esse videntur. (s) Secondly, in respect of the consideration, a fee simple had passed at the Common Law without this word (heires) and at this day an estate of inheritance in tayle, as if a man had giuen land to a man with his Daughter in Francke marriage generally, a Fee simple had passed without this word (heires) for there is no consideration so much respected in Law, as the consideration of marriage, in respect of Alliance, and posterity. (t) Thirdly, if a feoffment or Grant be made by Deed to a Mayor and communalty or any other Corporation aggregate of many persons capable, they haue a fee simple without the word (Successors) because in iudgement of the Law they neuer die. (u) Fourthly, in case of a sole corporation a fee simple shall sometime passe without this word (successors) as if a feoffment in fee be made of land to a Bishop, To haue and to hold to him in libera eleemosina, a fee simple doth passe without this word (Successors) (w) And so if a man giue lands to the King by Deede inrolled, a fee simple doth passe without these words (successors or heires) because in iudgement of Law the King neuer dieth. Fiftly, in Grants sometimes an Inheritance shall passe without this word (heires)

(r) 39. Ass.12.41.E.3. tit. Feoffments & faits 254.
14.H.4.13.34.E.3. Auowry.258.
(s) Vid. Sect.17.
12.H.4.19. in Formdon.
(t) 8.E.3.27.11.H.7.12.
22.E.4. 11.H.4.84.
2.H.4.13.
(u) 19.H.6.74.20.H.6.36.
(w) Pl. com. Lo. Berkleyes Case.

(heires)(x) as if partition be made betweene copercenèrs of Lands in fee simple, and for owelty (x) 29. Ass. 23. 15. H. 7. 14.
of partition the one grant a rent to the other generally, the grantee shal haue a fee simple without 2 H. 7. 5. 11. H. 4. 3.
this word (heires) because the grantor hath a fee simple in consideration whereof he granted the 21. E. 3. 1. 21. Ass.
rent, ipsæ etenim leges cupiunt vt jure regantur. Sixtly, by the Forrest law if an assart be granted by the King at a Justice seat (which may be done without Charter) to another Habendum
& tenendũ sibi imperpetuũ, he hath a fee simple without this word (heires) (y) for there is a speciall Law of the Forrest, as there is a law Marshall for wars, and a Marine law for the seas. (y) 40. H. 7. 7.
(z) And this rule of our Author extendeth to the passing of estates of inheritances in exchanges, (z) 22. E. 3. 3. 45. E. 3. 20.
releases, or confirmations that enure by way of enlargement of estates, warranties, bargaine 9. E. 4. 21.
and sales by Deed indented & inrolled, & the like in which this word (heires) is also necessary Lib. 4. fo. 121. Bustardi case. Vid. Sect. 465. 469 610.
for they doe tant amount to a feoffment or grant or stand vpon the same reason that a feoffment 19. H. 6. 17. 22.
or grant doth, for like reason doth make like law, vbi eadem ratio, ibi idem jus. And this is to be 17. E. 2. garr. 85.
obserued throughout all these three books, that where other cases fall within the same reason, our
Author doth put his case but for example, for so our Author himselfe in another place * expla- * Sect. 301.
neth it, saying, Et memorandũ q̃ en touts auters cases coment que ne sont icy expressement moves
& specifies si sont en semblable reason sont en semblable ley. And here our Author is to bee vnderstood to speake of heires when they are inheritable by discent, for they are capable of land also
by purchase, and then the course of discent is sometime altered, as if lands of the nature of Gaul-
kinde be giuen to B. and his heires hauing issue diuers sonnes, all his sonnes after his decease
shall inherite, but if a lease for life be made, the remainder to the right heires of B. and B. dieth,
his eldest sonne only shall inherite, for he only to take by purchase is right heire by the Common
law. So note a diuersitie betweene a purchase and a discent, but where the remainder was limitted to the right heires of B. it need not to be said and to their heires, for being plurally limitted it includeth a fee simple, and yet it resteth but in one by purchase.

Out of that which hath beene said it is to be obserued, that a man may purchase lands to him
and his heires by Ten manner of conueyances, (for I speake not here of estoppells.) First by
Feoffment, secondly by Grant (of which two our Author here speaketh.) Thirdly by Fine
which is a feoffment of record. Fourthly by common Recouery which is a common conueyance
and is in nature of a feoffment of record. Fiftly by Exchange which is in nature of a grant.
Sixtly, by Release to a particular tenant. Seuenthly by Confirmation to a particular tenant
both which are in nature of Grants. Eighthly, by grant of a reuersion or remainder with at- 27. H. 8. ca. 16.
tornment of the particular tenant, of all which our Author speaketh hereafter. Ninthly, by bar- 32 H. 8 ca. 2.
gaine and sale by Deede indented and inrolled ordained by statute since Littleton wrote. Tenth- 34. H. 8. ca. 5.
ly, by deuise by custome of some particular place, as he sheweth hereafter, and since he wrote, by
will in writing generally by authority of Parliament.

What words are apt words for a feoffment or grant Vid. §. 531. Our Author speaketh of feoff- Sect 531.
ments and grants, wherby is implyed lawfull conueyances, & therfore this rule extendeth not to 37. Ass. p. 8. 38. Ass. p. 9.
disseisins, abatements or intrusions into lands or tenements or to vsurpations to aduousons, &c. 12. E. 4. 9. &c.
in which cases estates in fee simple are gained by the act and wrong of the disseisors, abators,
intruders and vsurpers, and if a disseisin abatement or intrusion be made to the vse of another if
cẽy que vse agreeth thereunto in pays by this bare agreement he gaineth a fee simple without
any liuery of seisin or other ceremony.

Section 2.

¶ ET si home pchase tres en fee simple & deuy sans issue chescun q̃ est son prochine cosin collateral del entire sanke, de quel pluis long degree q̃ il soit, poet inheriter & auer m̃ la tre come heire a luy.

AND if a man purchase land in fee simple and die without issue hee which is his next cosen collaterall of the whole blood, how farre so euer hee bee from him in degree, may inherit & haue the land as heire to him.

¶ Littleton sheweth here who shalbe heire to lands in fee simple, for hee entendeth not this case of an estate taile, for that he speaketh of an heire of the whole blood for that extendeth not to estates in taile as shall bee said hereafter in this chapter, Section 6.

¶ *Prochein cosin collaterall.* Neyther excludeth he brethren or sisters, because he hath a speciall case concerning them in this chapter, Sect. 5. and in his chapter of parceners, but this is intended where a man purchase lands and dieth without issue, and having neither brother nor sister, then his next cousin collaterall shall inherite. So as here is implyed a division of heires, viz. lineall (who ever shall first inherit,) and collaterall, (who are to inherite for default of lineall) For in discents it is a maxime in law quod linea recta semper prefertur transuersali. Lineall discent is conveyed downward in a right line, as from the grandfather to the father, from the father to the sonne, &c. Collaterall discent is derived from the side of the lineall, as grandfathers brother, fathers brother, &c. Prochein cousin collaterall enheritera doth give a certaine direction to the next cosin to the sonne, and therefore the fathers brother and his posterity shall inherite before the grandfathers brother and his posterity. Et sic de ceteris, for propinquior excludit propinquum & propinquus remotum, & remotus remotiorem.

Glanvil lib. 7 ca. 3. 4. Bract. lib. 2. ca. 30 fo. 65. Britt. ca 119. Fleta lib. 6. cap. 1. & 2.

Bract lib 2. ca. 30 f. 64. Fleta lib. 5 ca 5 & lib 6 ca 1. & 2. Britt. ca 119. Mirror 11. ca. 1. §. 3. 30. Ass. p. 47.

Upon this word (Prochein) I put this case. One hath issue two sonnes A and B. and dieth, B. hath two sonnes C and D. and dieth. C. the eldest sonne hath issue and dieth: A. purchaseth lands in fee simple and dieth without issue, D. is his next cousin, and yet shall not inherite, but the issue of C. for he that is inheritable is accounted in law next of blood. And therefore here is understood a division of next, viz. next, iure repræsentationis, and next, iure propinquitatis, that is, by right of representation and by right of propinquitie. And Littleton meaneth of the right of representation, for legally in course of discents he is next of blood inheritable. And the issue of C. doth represent the person of C. and if C. had lived he had beene legally next of blood. And whensoever the father if he had lived, should have inherited, his lineall heire by right of representation shall inherite before any other, though another be iure propinquitatis neerer of blood. And therefore Littleton intendeth his case of next cosin of blood immediately inheritable. So as this produceth another division of next of blood, viz. immediatly inheritable, as the issue of C and mediatly inheritable as D. if the issue of C. die without issue, for the issue of C. and all that line be they never so remote shall inherite before D. or his line, and therefore Littleton saith well de quel pluis long degree que il soit. And here ariseth a diversity in law betweene next of blood inheritable by discent, and next of blood capable by purchase. And therefore in the case before mentioned if a Lease for life were made to A. the remainder to his next of blood in fee. In this case as hath beene said D. shall take the remainder, because he is next of blood and capable by purchase, though he be not legally next to take as heire by discent.

19. R. 2. tit. gar. 170.

30. Ass. p. 47.

Section 3.

¶ Mes si soit pier & fits, & le pier ad un frere que est uncle a le fits, & le fits purchase tre en fee simpl & mort sans issue vivant son pier, luncle avera la terre come heire al fits & nemy le pier, uncore le pier est pluis prochein de sank; pur ceo que est un maxime en le ley, Que enheritance poet linealment discender, mes ney ascender. Uncore si le fits en tiel case mort sans issue, & son uncle entra en la tre come heire a le

But if there bee father & son, & the father hath a brother that is uncle to the son, & the son purchase land in fee simple, and die without issue, living his father, the uncle shal have the land as heire to the son, & not the father, yet the father is neerer of blood; because it is a maxime in law, That inheritance may lineally discend, but not ascend. Yet if the son in this case die without issue, and his uncle enter into the land as heire to the

¶ Uncore le pier est pluis prochein de sanke. And therefore some doe hold upon these words of Littleton that if a Lease for life were made to the sonne the remainder to his next of blood that the father should take the remainder by purchase, and not the uncle, for that Littleton saith the father is next of blood, and yet the uncle is heire. As if a man hath issue two sonnes, and the eldest sonne hath issue a sonne and die, a remainder is limited to the next of his blood, the younger sonne shall take it, yet the other is his heire

5. E. 6. tit. Administr. Br. 47. Ratcliffes case ubi supra. See after in the chapter of Socage.

¶ (p) Est un Maxime en le Ley que enheritance poet linealment discender mes nemy ascender.

(p) Pl. Com. 293. b. Oiborns case.

Maxime, i. A sure foundation or ground of art, and a

fits (si come il deuoit p la ley) & apres lun-cle deuia sans issue, viuant le pier, donqs le pier auera la terre cõe heire al vncle, & nēy cõe heire a son fits, pur ceo que il veigne al terre p collaterall discent & nēy p lineall ascention.

sonne (as by law hee ought) and after the vncle dieth without issue, liuing the father, the father shall haue the land as heire to the vncle, & not as heire to his son, for that hee commeth to the land by collateral discent & not by lineall ascent.

conclusion of reason so called (q) quia maxima est eius dignitas & certissima authoritas, atque quod maximè omnibus probetur, so sure and vncontrolable as that they ought not to be questioned. (r) And that which our Author here and in other places calleth a Maxime, hereafter he calleth a Principle, and it is all one with a Rule, a common ground, Postulatum or an Axiome, and it were too much curiositie to make nice distinctions betweene them. And it is well said in our bookes, (s) nest my a disputer lancient principles del ley. I neuer read any opinion in any booke old or new against this Maxime but only in lib. rub. where it is said, (t) si quis sine liberis discesserit pater aut mater eius in hæreditatem succedat, vel frater & soror si pater & mater desint, si nec hos habeat, soror patris vel matris & deinceps qui propinquiores in parentela fuerint hæreditario succedant, & dum virilis sexus extiterit, & hæreditas abinde sit, fæmina non hæreditat'. But all our ancient Authors and the constant opinion euer since doe affirme the maxime.

(q) *Pl. Com. 27. b.*
(r) *Sect. 90. 648.*
(s) *12. H. 4.*
Glanuill lib. 7. ca. 1.
Bract. lib. 2. cap. 29.
(t) *Lib. Rub. cap. 70.*

By this maxime and the conclusion of his case, only lineall ascention in the right line is prohibited, and not in the collaterall, (u) Quælibet hæreditas naturaliter quidem ad hæredes hæreditabiliter discendit, nunquam quidem naturaliter ascendit, discendit itaque jus quasi ponderosum quod cadens deorsum recta linea vel transuersali, & nunquam reascendit ea via qua discendit post mortem antecessorum, à latere tamen ascendit alicui propter defectum hæredum inferius prouenientium; so as the lineall ascent is prohibited by law, and not the collaterall. And in prohibiting the lineall ascent, the Common Law is assisted with the Law of the 12. tables.

Brit. ca. 119.
Fleta lib. 6. cap. 1.
Num. b. ca. 27.
Ratcliffs case vbi supra.

Here our Author for the confirmation of his opinion draweth a reason and a proofe (as you haue perceiued) from one of the maximes of the Common law: Now that I may here obserue it once for all, his proofes and arguments, in these his three bookes, may bee generally deuided into two parts, viz. from the Common law and from Statutes, of both which, and of their seuerall branches I shall giue the studious reader some few examples and leaue the rest to his diligent obseruation.

From the Common Law his proofes and arguments are drawne from 20. seuerall fountaines or places.

(a) First from the Maximes, Principles, Rules, Intendment, and Reason of the Common Law, which indeede is the Rule of the Law as here, and in other places our Author doth vse.

(b) Secondly, from the bookes, records, and other authorities of Law cited by him, Ab authoritate, & pronunciatis.

(c) Thirdly, from originall Writs in the Register, à rescriptis valet argumentum.

(d) Fourthly, from the forme of good pleading.

(e) Fiftly, from the right entry of iudgements.

(f) Sixtly, à præcedentibus approbatis & vsu, from approued Precedents and Vse.

(g) Seuenthly, a non vsu, from not vse.

(h) Eightly, ab artificialibus argumentis, consequentibus & conclusionibus, artificiall arguments consequents and conclusions.

Ninthly, (i) a communi opinione jurisprudentum, from the common opinion of the sages of the Law.

Tenthly, (k) ab inconuenienti, from that which is inconuenient.

Eleuenthly, (c) a diuisione from a diuision vel ab enumeratione partium from the enumeration of the parts.

Twelfthly, (m) a maiore ad minus, from the greater to the lesser, or (n) from the lesser to the greater, (o) a simili, (p) a pari.

13. (p) ab impossibili from that which is impossible.

14. (q) A fine from the end.

15. (*) Ab vtili vel inutili from that which is profitable or vnprofitable.

16. (r) Ex absurdo for that thereupon should follow an absurdity quasi à surdo prolatum, because it is repugnant to vnderstanding and reason.

17. (s) A natura et ordine naturæ, from nature or the course of nature.

(a) *Sect. 5. 8. 90. 96 52. 93. 57. 59. 65 99. 139. 146 156. 169. 178. 231. 293. 302. 352. 360. 376. 377. 396. 410. 440. 441. 346. 347. 462. 43.*
(b) *Sect. 20. where a number other are quoted.*
(c) *Sect. 67. 132. 170. 234. 241. 263. 613 614.*
(d) *Sect. 58 170. 183. 369.*
(e) *Sect. 248. 249.*
(f) *Sect. 88. 74. 76. 145. 332. 371. 372. 445.*
(g) *108. 733.*
(h) *Sect. 170. 264. 283. 302. 429. 464. 629. 633. 686. 340. 418. 613. 686 739.*
(i) *Sect. 697. 59. 104. 288. 332. 478*
(k *Sect. 87. where many others are quoted.*
(l) *Sect. 13. where many more are quoted but see chiefly, Sect. 381.*
(m) *Sect. 438. 439. 441.*
(n) *Sect. 18. (o) 301. &c.*
(p) *291. 298. 409. &c.*
(p.) *129. 440.*
(q) *Sect. 46. 194.*
* *Sect. 360.*
(r) *Sect. 722.*
(s) *Sect. 114. 223. 129. 211. 107. 108.*

18 (t) Ab ordine religionis, from the order of Religion.
19. (u) A communi præsumptione from a common presumption.
20. (w) A lectionibus iurisprudentium, from the readings of learned men of Law.

From Statutes his arguments and proofes are drawne.

1. (x) From the rehearsall or preamble of the Statute.
2. By the bodie of the Law diuersly interpreted.

Sometime by other parts of the same Statute, which is benedicta expositio, & ex visceribus causæ.

(y) Sometime by the reason of the Common Law. But euer the generall words are to be intended of a lawfull Act, (z) and such interpretation must euer be made of all Statutes, that the innocent or he in whom there is no default may not be damnified.

¶ *En la ley.* There bee diuers Lawes within the Realme of England. As first, (a) Lex Coronæ, the Law of the Crowne.

2. (b) Lex & consuetudo parliamenti. Ista lex est ab omnibus quærenda, à multis ignorata, à paucis cognita.

3. (c) Lex naturæ, the Law of nature.

4. (d) Communis lex Angliæ, the Common Law of England sometime called Lex terræ, intended by our Author in this and the like places.

5. (e) Statute Law, Lawes established by authoritie of Parliament.

6. (f) Consuetudines. Customes reasonable.

7. (g) Ius belli. The Law of Armes, warre, and Chiualrie, in republica maximè conseruanda sunt iura belli.

8. (h) Ecclesiasticall or Canon Law in Courts in certaine Cases.

9. (i) Ciuill Law in certaine cases not only in Courts Ecclesiasticall, but in the Courts of the Constable and Marshall, and of the Admiraltie, in which Court of the Admiraltie is obserued la ley Olyron, anno 5. of Richard the first, so called, because it was published in the Isle of Olyron.

10. (k) Lex forestæ, Forest Law.

11. (l) The law of Marque or reprisall.

12. (m) Lex mercatoria, Merchant, &c.

13. (n) The Lawes and Customes of the Isles of Iersey, Gernesey and Man.

14. (o) The Law and priuiledge of the Stanneries.

15. (p) The Lawes of the East West, and middle Marches which are now abrogated.

But hereof this little taste for our Studient, that he may bee capable of that which hee shall reade concerning these and others in Records, and in our Bookes, and orderly obserue them, shall suffice.

¶ *Et son vncle enter en la terre.* For if the vncle in this case doth not enter into the land, then cannot the father inherite the land, for there is another maxime in law herein implyed. (q) That a man that claymeth as heire in fee simple to any man by discent, must make himselfe heire to him that was last seised of the actuall freehold and inheritance. And if the Uncle in this case doth not enter, then had he but a freehold in Law, and no actuall freehold, but the last that was seised of the actuall freehold was the sonne to whom the father cannot make himselfe heire, And therefore Littleton saith, Et son vncle enter en la terre (sicome deuoit per la ley) to make the father to inherit, as heire to the vncle. (r) Note that true it is that the vncle in this case is heire, but not absolutely heire, for if after the discent to him the father hath issue a sonne or daughter, that issue shall enter vpon the vncle. (s) And so it is if a man hath issue a sonne and a daughter, the sonne purchaseth Land in fee and dieth without issue, the daughter shall inherit the land, but if the father hath afterward issue a sonne, this sonne shall enter into the Land as heire to his brother, and if he hath issue a daughter and no sonne, she shalbe coperconer with her sister.

¶ *Sicome il deuoit per la ley.* These words as a key doe open the secrets of the Law, for hereupon it is concluded, that where the vncle cannot get an actuall possession by entrie or otherwise, there the father in this case cannot inherit. And therefore if an Aduowson be granted to the sonne and his heires, and the sonne die, and this discend to the vncle, and he die before he doth or can present to the Church, the father shall not inherit, because he should make himselfe heire to the sonne which he cannot doe. And so of a Rent and the like. But if the vncle had presented to the Church, or had seisin of the rent there the father should haue inherited. For Littleton putteth his case of an entrie into Land, but for an example, If the sonne make a Lease for life, and die without issue, and the reuersion discend to the vncle, and he die, the reuersion shall not discend to the father, because in that case hee must make himselfe heire to the sonne. A, infeoffe the sonne with warrantie to him and his heires, the sonne dies, the vncle enters into the Land and dies, the father if he bee impleaded shall not take aduantage of this warrantie,

(t) *Sect. 202.*
(u) *Sect. 440.*
(w) *Sect. 81.*
(x) *Sect. 134. &c. Sect. 731. 692. 635. 633. 441. 103. 193. 154. 140. 2.*
(y) *Sect. 464.*
(z) *Sect. 737. 685.*
(a) *17. E. 3. Rot parl. nu. 19. 25. E. 3. cap. 1. Regist. inter Iura regia 61 &c.*
(b) *Commonly spoken of in Parliament Rolls.*
(c) *13. E. 4. 9. Lib. 7. Culwyns case. Pl. com. Sharingtons case.*
(d) *This Law appeareth in our bookes and in iudiciall records.*
(e) *These are of record in Rolls of Parliament.*
(f) *Whereof you shall reade in our author, and in our bookes.*
(g) *Rot. parlim. 2 R 2. nu 3. 13. R 2 ca. 2.*
(h) *Lib. 7. Caudries case ar-icul. super cartas. &c.*
(i) *37. H. 6 21. Fortesc ca. 32. 13. H 4. 4. 28. H 8. ca 15.*
(k) *Carta de foresta &c. the eires of the Forest.*
(l) *27. E. 3. ca. 17. Wi. ca 23. 4. H. 5. ca. 7.*
(m) *Mirror des Iustic. ca. 1. Bract. 334. 444. Fleta. lib. 2 ca. 51. 52. &c. 5. E 3. 11. 38. E. 3. 7. 27. E. 3. cap 8 Fortesc. 32. F. N. B. 119 13. E. 4. 9. Rot. parl. 6. H. 4. nu. 43. 10. H. 7. 16. 47. E. 3. 22. 30. E. 1. Accompt 127. Carta mercatoria 31. E. 1. rot. patent.*
(n) *Mich. 41. E. 3. coram rege in thesaur. 1. E. 3. fol. 7. 12. H. 8 fol. 5. Rot parl. an. 20. E. 1. Lib. 7. Calwyns case fol. 21. Regist. fol. 22.*
(o) *50. E. 3. Rot. parl. 50. E. 3. Rot. patent. &c.*
(p) *31. H. 6 ca. 3. 4. Ia. ca. 1.*
(q) *11. H. 4. 11. 10. ass. 27. 34 ass. p. 20. 19. E. 2. quar. imped. 177. 45. E. 3. 13. 40. ass. p. 6.*
(r) *11. ass p. 6. Doct. & Stud. 12. b. 32. H. 6. 35.*
(s) *19. H. 6. 61.*

rantie, for then hee must vouch A. as heire to his sonne, which hee cannot doe, for albeit the warrantie discended to the vncle, yet the vncle leaueth it, as hee found it, and then the father by Littletons (deuoit) cannot take aduantage of it. For Littleton Sectione 603. saith that warranties, shall discend to him that is heire by the Common Law, and Sect.718 he saith that euery warrantie which discends, doth discend to him that is heire to him which made the warrantie by the Common Law, which proueth that the father shall not be bound by the warrantie made by the sonne, for that the father cannot bee heire to the sonne, that made the warrantie. And a warrantie shall not goe with tenements, whereunto it is annexed to any especiall heire, but alwayes to the heire at the Common Law. And therefore if the vncle be seised of certaine lands, and is disseised, the sonne release to the disseisor with warrantie, and die without issue, this shall bind the vncle, but if the vncle die without issue, the father may enter, for the warrantie cannot discend vpon him. So if the sonne concludeth himselfe by pleading concerning the tenure and seruices of certaine lands, this shall bind the vncle, but if the vncle die wit out issue, this shall not bind the father, because he cannot be heire to the sonne, and consequently not to the estoppell in that case; but if it be such an estoppell as runneth with the land, then it is otherwise.

*Vid.Sect.*603.718.

Vid.Sect. 735.736.737.

35.*H*.6.33.*Iohn Crookes case.*

Section 4.

¶ En tiel case, lou le fits purchase terre en fee simple, & deuie sauns issue, ceux de son sanke de part son pier enheriteront cõe heires a luy, deuant ascun de sanke de pt sa mere: mes s'il nad ascun heire de part son pier, donques la tre discendera a les heires de part la mere. Mes si home p̃rent enheritrix des tres en fee simple, qux ont issue fits, & deuiont, & le fits enter en les tenements, cõe fits & heire a sa mere. & puis deuie sans issue, les heires de part la mere doient enheriter les tenemts & iammes les heires de part le pier. Et s'il ny ad ascun heire de part la mere, donque le seignior, de que la terre est tenus, auera la

AND in case, where the sonne purchaseth land in fee simple, and dies without issue, they of his bloud on the fathers side shall inherit as heires to him, before any of the bloud, on the mothers side. But if he hath no heire on the part of his father, then the land shall discend to the heires on the part of the mother. But if a man marrieth an inheritrix of lands in fee simple, who haue issue a son, and die, and the sonne enter into the tenements, as sonne and heire to his mother, and after dies without issue, the heires of the part of his mother ought to inherit, and not the heires of the part of the father. And if hee hath no heire on the part of the mother, then the Lord

¶ By this it appeareth, that our author deuideth heires into heires of the part of the father, and into heires of the part of the mother. (a) And note, it is an olde, and true Maxime in Law, That none shall inherit any lands as heire, but only the bloud of the first purchaser. for * refert à quo fiat perquisitum. As for example, Robert Coke taketh the daughter of Knightley to wife and purchaseth lands to him and to his heires, and by Knightley hath issue Edward, none of the blond of the Knightleys though they be of the bloud of Edward shall inherit, albeit hee had no kindred but them, because they were not of the bloud of the first purchaser, viz. of Robert Coke.

¶ (b) *Ceux del sank de part son pier.* Here it is to bee vnderstood, that the father hath two immediate bloods in him, viz. the bloud of his father, and the bloud of his mother, both these bloods are of the part of the father. (c) And this made ancient Authors say, that if a man be seised of lands in the right of his wife, and is attainted of felonie, and after hath issue, this issue should not inherit his mother, for that he could deriue no bloud inheritable from the father. And both these bloods of the part of the father must bee spent before

*Vid.Sect.*354.*an excellent point.*

(a) *Pl.com.Sir Edward Cleres case.* 447.

(*) *Fleta.lib.*6.*ca.*1.2.*&c. Bracton lib.*2.*fol.*65.67.68. 69.*&c.Britton.ca.*119. 24.*E*.3.50.39.*E*.3.29.30.38 49.*E*.3.12. 49.*ass.p.*4.12.*E*.4.14. *pl.com.*445.*&* 450. 7.*E*.6 *Dier* 6. 24.*E*.3.24.37 *ass.*4. 40.*E*.3.9.42.*E*.3.10. 45.*E*.3.*Releases* 28. 7.*H*.5.3.4.8.*ass.*6. 35.*ass.*2.5.*E*.4.7. 3.*H*.5.21.*H*.7.33. 40 *ass.*6. *Ratcliffs case lib.*3.*fol.*41.

(b) *Bracton. vbi supra. Fleta. vbi supra. Britton.ca.*118.119. *pl.com.*445.*Cleres case. Tr.*19.*E*.1. *in banco Rot.*25. *Lincoln.Will.Seels case.*

(c) *Britton.fol.*15. *Fleta.lib.*1.*ca.*18. *pl.com.*445.446.*&c. Cleres case.*

terre per Escheat. En mesme le manner est, si tenemẽts discendont a le fits de part le pier, & il enter & puis morust sans issue, cel terre discendra as heires de part le pier, & nẽy as heires de part la mere. Et sil ny ad ascun heire de part le pier, donques le seignior, de que la terre est tenus, auera la terre per Escheat. Et sic vide diuersitatem, lou le fits purchase terres ou tenements, en fee simple, & lou il vient eins a tiels terres ou tenements per discent de part sa mere ou de part son pier.

of whom the land is holden, shall haue the land by Escheate. In the same manner it is, if lands discend to the sonne, of the part of the father, and hee entreth, and afterwards dies without issue, this land shall discend to the heires on the part of the father, and not to the heires on the part of the mother, And if there bee no heire of the part of the father, the Lord of whom the Land is holden shall haue the land by Escheate. And so wee see the diuersitie, where the sonne purchase lands or tenements in fee simple, and where hee commeth to them by discent on the part of his mother, or on the part of his father.

before the heire of the bloud of the part of the mother shall inherit, wherein euer the line of the male of the part of the father, (that is) the posteritie of such male, bee they male or female (who euer in discents are preferred) must faile before the line of the mother shall inherit, (d) and the reason of all this is for that the bloud of the part of the father is more worthy and more neere in iudgement of law, than the bloud of the part of the mother.

(d) 19 R.2. garr 100.

Britton ca.118 119. Fleta.lib 6.ca.2.

¶ *Deuant ascun del sanke del part del mere.* And it is to be obserued, that the mother hath also two immediate bloods in her (viz.) her fathers bloud, and her mothers bloud. Now to illustrate all this by example. Robert Fairefield sonne of Iohn Fairefield and Iane Sandie, take to wife Anne Boyes daughter of Iohn Boyes and Iane Bewpree and hath issue William Fairefield who purchaseth lands in fee. Here William Fairefield hath foure immediate blouds in him, two of the part of his father, viz the bloud of the Fairefields, and the bloud of the Sandyes, and two of the part of his mother, viz. the bloud of the Boyses, and the bloud of the Bewprees, and so in both cases vpward in infinitum. Now admit that William Fairefield die without issue, first the bloud of the part of his father, viz of the Fairefields, and for want thereof the bloud of the Sandyes (for both these are of the part of the father) if both these faile, then the heires of the part of the mother of William Fairefield shall inherit, viz. first the bloud of the Boyses, and for default thereof the bloud of the Bewprees.

It is necessary to be knowne in what cases the heire of the part of the mother shall inherite, and where not. If a man be seised of lands as heire of the part of his mother and maketh a feoffment in fee, and taketh backe an estate to him and to his heires, this is a new purchase, and if he dieth without issue, the heires of the part of the father shall first inherite. If a man so seised maketh a feoffment in fee vpon condition, and die, the heire of the part of the father which is the heire at the Common law shall enter for the condition broken, but the heire of part of the mother shall enter vpon him, and enioy the land. (m) A man so seised maketh a feoffment in fee reseruing a rent to him, and to his heires, this rent shall goe to the heires of the part of the father; but, (n) if he had made a gift in taile, or a lease for life reseruing a rent, the heire of the part of the mother shall haue the reuersion, and the rent also, as incident thereunto, shall passe with it, but the heire of the part of the mother shall not take aduantage of a condition annexed to the same, because it is not incident to the reuersion nor can passe therewith. (o) If a man had beene seised of a mannor as heire on the part of his mother, and before the statute of Quia emptores terrarum had made a feoffment in fee of parcell to hold of him by rent and seruice, albeit they be newly created, yet for that they are parcell of the Mannor, they shall with the rest of the mannor discend to the heire of the part of the mother, quia multa transeunt cum vniuersitate quæ per se non transeunt. If a man hath a rent secke of the part of his mother, and the tenant of the land

9.H.7.24.

(m) 7.H.6.4. Lib.1. fol.100. Shellyes case.

(n) 5.E.2.111. auowry.207.

(o) 5.E.2. auowry 207.

granteth a distresse to him and his heires, and the grantee dieth the distresse shall goe with the rent to the heire of the part of the mother as insident or appurtenant to the rent, for now is the rent secke become a Rent charge.

(p) A man so seised as heire on the part of his mother maketh a Feoffment in Fee to the use of him and his heires, the use being a thing in trust and confidence shall insue the nature of the land, and shall discend to the heire on the part of the mother. (q) A man hath a seignory as heire of the part of his mother, and the tenancy doth escheate, it shall goe to the heire of the part of the mother. If the heire of the part of the mother of land whereunto a warranty is annexed is impleaded and Vouche; and iudgement is giuen against him, and for him to recouer in value, and dieth before execution (r) the heire of the part of the mother shall sue execution to haue in value against the Vouchee; for the effect ought to pursue the cause, and the recompence shall ensue the losse.

(p) 5 E.4.4.lib.1.fol.100. Shellyes case. 27.H.8. Dier Buckenhams case.32.H.8 gard. Brooke.93. 13.H.7 6.

(q) 16.E.3.age.46.

Pl Com 292.& 515.See more of this in the Chap' er of Warranties.

If a man giueth lands to a man, to haue and to hold to him and his heires on the part of his mother, yet the heires of the part of the father shall inherit, for no man can institute a new kind of inheritance not allowed by the Law, and the words (of the part of his mother) are voide, as in the Case that Littleton putteth in this Chapter, If a man giueth lands to a man to him and his heires males, the Law reiecteth this word males, because there is no such kind of inheritance, whereof you shall reade more in his proper place.

A man hath issue a sonne, and dieth, and the wife dieth also, Lands are letten for life, the remainder to the heires of the wife, the sonne dieth without issue, the heires of the part of the father shall inherit, and not the heires of the part of the mother, because it vested in the sonne as a Purchaser. And the rule of Littleton holdeth aswell in other kind of Inheritances, as in Lands and Tenements. (s) And therefore if there be Lord, fem mesne, and tenant, and the Mesne bind her selfe and her heires by her deed to the acquitall of the tenant, the Mesne take husband, the Tenant by his Deed granteth to the husband and his heires, that hee or his heires shall not be bound to acquitall, the husband and wife haue issue, and die, this issue, being bound as heire to his mother, shall not take benefit of the said grant of discharge, for that extends to the heires of the part of the father, & not to the heires of the part of the mother, and therefore the heire of the part of the mother was bound to the Acquitall. And thus much for the better understanding of Littletons Cases concerning the heire of the part of the mother shall suffice.

(s) 38.E.3.12.

¶ *Mes si home prist feme inheritrix &c.* **Heere there is another** maxime, (t) That whensoeuer Lands doe discend from the part of the mother, the heires of the part of the father shall neuer inherit. And likewise when Lands discend from the part of the father, the heires of the part of the mother shall neuer inherit. Et sic paterna paternis, & è conuerso, materna maternis For more manifestation hereof, and of that which hereafter shall be said touching Discents, see a Table in the end of this Chapter.

(t) 39.E.3.27. 49.E.3.12.

¶ *Auera la terre per Escheat.* (u) *Escheat*, Eschaeta **is a word of** art, and deriued from the French word Eschear (id est) cadere, excidere or accidere, and signifieth properly when by accident the Lands fall to the Lord of whom they are holden, in which Case we say the fee is escheated. And therefore, of some, Escheats are called excadentiæ or terræ excadentiales (w) Dominus vero capitalis loco hæredis habetur quoties per defectũ vel delictum extinguitur sanguis sui tenentis, loco hæredis & haberi poterit nisi per modum donationis fit reuersio cuiuscuque tenementi. And Ockam (who wrote in the raigne of Henry the second) treating of tenures of the King, saith, Porro eschaetæ vulgo dicuntur, quæ decedentibus hijs quæ de Rege tenent &c. cum non existit ratione sanguinis hæres ad fiscum relabuntur. (x) So as an Escheat doe happen two manner of wayes, aut per defectum sanguinis .i. for default of heire, aut per delictum tenentis .i. for felonie, and that is by iudgement three manner of waies aut quia suspensus per collum, aut quia abiurauit regnum, aut quia vtlegatus est, And therefore, they which are hanged by martiall Law, in furore belli forfeit no Lands: and so in like Cases Escheats by the Ciuilians are called Caduca.

(u) Vid Sect.130. Glanvil.lib.7.cap 17. Bract l.b.3 fol.118. Fleta l.b.5.cap.5.& lib 3. cap.10. Britton.ca.37.& cap.119. F.N.B 100. Tr.19.et in banco Rot.25.

(w) Fleta lib.6.cap.1. Ockam.cap. quod non absoluatur. &c.

(x) Pl.Com. Dame Hales case.

(y) The father is seised of Lands in fee holden of I.S. the sonne is attainted of high treason, the father dieth the Land shall escheat to I.S. propter defectum sanguinis, for that the father dieth without heire, And the King cannot haue the Land because the sonne neuer had any thing to forfeit. But the King shall haue the escheate of all the Lands whereof the person attainted of high treason was seised, of whomsoeuer they were holden.

(y) Pl.Com. in Nichols case.

(z) In an Appeale of Death or other Felonie, &c. processe is awarded against the defendant, and hanging the processe the defendant conueyeth away the Land, and after is outlawed, the Conueyance is good and shall defeat the Lord of his escheate, but if a man be indited of Felonie, and hanging the processe against him, hee conueyeth away the Land, and after is outlawed, the Conueyance shall not in that case preuent the Lord of his escheate. And the reason of this diuersitie is manifest: For in the case of the Appeale, the writ containeth no time when

(z) 38.E.3.fo.37.30.H 6.5. Bract l.2.title de Forf. Stanf. Pl.Cor.192. and according to this diuersitie was it resolued in 5.E.6. as it appeareth by my Lord Diers Manuscript.

the Felonie was done, and therefore the escheate can relate but to the outlawrie pronounced. But the inditement containeth the time when the felonie was committed, and therefore the escheate vpon the outlawrie shall relate to that time. Which Cases I haue added, to the end the student may conceiue, that the obseruation of Writs, Inditements, Processe, Judgements, and other Entries, doth conduce much to the vnderstanding of the right reason of the Law.

(a) Mirror.ca.1.§.5. 51.H.3.statutum de Scac. Britt.n.fo.33.34. Fleta.lib.1.cap.36. & lib 2.ca 34.35. Regist.301.his Oath 18.E.1. Ro.Parl. Tol.21.E 1. Rot 1.29.E.1.stat. de Eschaetoribus,14.E.3.ca.8. 28.E.1. ca.18.F.N.B.100.e. Stanf. Prar.81.1.H.8.ca.8. 3.H.8.ca 2. Capitula Eschaetria in Vet. magna carta.fo.160.161.&c.

Of this word (eschaeta) here vsed by our Author, commeth (a) Eschaetor, an ancient Officer so called, because his office is properly to looke to Escheats, Wardships, and other Casualties belonging to the Crowne. In ancient time there were but two Escheators in England, the one on this side of Trent, and the other beyond Trent, at which time they had Subeschaetors. But in the raigne of Edward the second, the Offices were diuided, and seuerall Escheators made in euerie Countie for life, &c. and so continued vntill the raigne of Edward 3. And afterwards by the statute of 14.E.3. it is enacted by Authoritie of Parliament, that there should bee as many Escheators assigned, as when King Edward 3. came to the Crowne, and that was one in euerie Countie, & that no Escheator should tarry in his office aboue a yeere, and by another Statute to be in office but once in three yeers, the Lord Treasurer nameth him. And hereof also commeth eschaetria, which signifieth the Escheatership or the office of the Escheater. But now let vs heare what our Authour will further say vnto vs.

* Sect.147.149 248. 287.417.667.&c.

¶ Et sic vide, &c. This kind of speech is often vsed by our Author, and doth euer import matter of excellent obseruation, which you may find in the Sections noted in the margent *.

(b) 7.E.4.12.13. Fitz N.B.33.9.E.3.26. 17.E.2.statut. de templariis.

And it is to be well obserued, that our Author saith, Sil nad ascun heire, &c. la terre eschaetera. In which words is implied a diuersitie (as to the Escheate) betweene fee simple absolute, which a naturall bodie hath, and fee simple absolute with a bodie politique, or incorporate hath. (b) For if land holden of I. S. be giuen to an Abbot and his successors: In this case if the Abbot and all the Couent die so that the bodie politique is dissolued, the Donor shall haue againe this land, & not the Lord by escheat. And so if land be giuen in fee simple to a Deane and Chapter, or to a Maior and Cominaltie, and to their successors, and after such bodie politique or incorporate is dissolued, the Donor shall haue againe the land, and not the Lord by Escheate. And the reason, and cause of this diuersitie is for that in the case of a body politique or incorporate the fee simple is vested in their politique or incorporate capacitie created by the policie of man, and therefore the Law doth annex a condition in Law to euery such gift and grant That if such body politique or incorporate be dissolued, that the Donor or grantor shall re-enter, for that the cause of the gift or grant faile, but no such condition is annexed to the estate in fee simple vested in any man in his naturall capacitie, but in case where the Donor or Feoffor reserue to him a tenure, and then the Law doth imply a Condition in Law by way of escheate. Also (as hath beene said) no writ of escheate lyeth but in the three cases aforesaid, and not where a body politique or incorporate is dissolued.

Section 5.

¶ Item si soint trois freres, & le mulnes frere purchase terres en fee simple & deuie saunz issue leigne frere auera la terre per discent & nemy le puisne, &c. Et auxi si soint trois freres & le puisne purchase terres en fee simple & deuie sans issue, leigne frere auera la terre per discent &

ALso if there bee three brethren, and the middle brother purchaseth lands in fee simple, and die without issue, the elder brother shall haue the land by discent, and not the younger, &c. And also if there be three brethren, and the youngest purchase lands in fee simple, and die without issue, the eldest brother shall

¶ Now commeth our Author to the discent betweene brethren, which hee purposely omitted before. ¶ Discent discensus commeth of the Latyn word discendo, and, in the legall sence, it signifieth when lands doe by right of blood fall vnto any after the death of his Ancestors: or a discent is a meanes whereby one doth deriue him title to certaine lands, as heire to some of his Ancestors. And of this, and of that which hath beene spoken doth arise another diuision of estates in fee simple, viz. euery man that hath a lawfull estate in fee simple, hath it either by discent, or by purchase.

nemy le mulnes, pur ceo que leigne & pluis digne de sanke.

haue the land by discent & not the middle, for that the eldest is most worthy of blood.

¶ *Leigne est pluis digne de sanke.* It is a maxime in Law, that the next of the worthiest blood shall euer inherite, as the male and all discendant from him before the female, and the female of the part of the father before the male or female of the part of the mother, &c. because the female of the part of the father is of the worthiest blood. (c) And therefore among the males the eldest brother and his posterity shall inherite lands in fee simple as heire before any younger brother, or any discending from him, because as Littleton saith he is pluis digne de sanke. Quod prius est dignius est, and qui prior est tempore potior est iure. Si quis plures filios habuerit jus proprietatis primo discendit ad primogenitum, eo quòd inuentus est primo in rerum natura; In King Alfreds time Knights fees descended to the eldest sonne, for that by diuision of them betweene males the defence of the Realme might be weakened, but in those dayes Soccage fee was deuided betweene the heires males, and therewith agreeth Glanuill * Cum quis hæreditatem habens moriatur, &c; si plures reliquerit filios, tunc distinguitur vtrum ille fuerit miles, sive per feodum militare tenens, aut liber Sockmannus quia si miles fuerit aut per militiam tenens tunc secundum jus regni Angliæ primogenitus filius patri succedit in toto, &c. si verò fuerit liber Sockmanus, tunc quidem diuidetur hæreditas inter omnes filios, &c. But hereof more shall be said hereafter in his proper place.

(c) *Britton cap.* 119. *Bract. lib.* 2. *cap.* 30. 277. 279. 3. *E.* 3. 26. 3. *Eliz. Dier* 138. *Stanford prar.* 52. 58. 3. *E.* 1. *tit. au.wry.* 235. 32. *E.* 3. *discent.* 80. *Bract. lib.* 4. 211. *Fleta. lib.* 6. *ca.* 2. *Glanuill. lib.* 7. *ca.* 1. *Mirror cap.* 1. §. 3. * *Glanuill. lib.* 7. *ca.* 3. & *ca.* 1. *Vid. Pl. com.* 229. *b.*

Section 6.

Item est ascauoir, que nul auera terre de fee simple per discent come heire a ascun home, si non que il soit son heire dentire sanke. Car si home ad issue deux fits per diuers venters & leigne purchase terres en fee simple & morust sans issue, le puisne frere nauera la terre, mes luncle leigne frere, ou auter son procheine cosin ceo auera, pur ceo que le puisne frere est de demy sanke al eigne frere.

Also it is to bee vnderstood, that none shall haue land of fee simple by discent as heire to any man, vnlesse he be his heire of the whole blood, for if a man hath issue two sonnes by diuers venters, and the elder purchase lands in fee simple, and die without issue, the younger brother shall not haue the land but the Vncle of the elder brother, or some other his next cosin shall haue the same, because the younger brother is but of halfe blood to the elder.

¶ No man can bee heire to a fee simple by the Common Law, (d) but he that hath sanguinem duplicatum the whole blood; that is both of the father and of the mother, so as the halfe blood is no blood inheritable by discent because that he that is but of the halfe blood cannot be a compleat heire, for that hee hath not the whole and compleate blood, and the Law in discents in fee simple doth respect that which is compleat and perfect. And this maxime doth not only hold where lands (whereof Littleton here speaketh) are claymed or demanded as heire (e) but also in case of appeale of death; for, if one brother bee slaine, the other brother of the halfe blood shall neuer haue an appeale (albeit hee shall recouer nothing therein either in the realty or personalty) because in the eye of the Law hee is not heire to him. Also this rule extends to a warrantie as our Author himselfe elsewhere holdeth.

(d) *Bract. lib* 4. 279. *b. idem lib.* 2. *fo.* 65. *Britton. ca.* 119. *Fleta. lib.* 6. *ca.* 1. 1. *E.* 3. 19. *Iohn Giffords case.* 31. *E.* 3. *Counterpl. de Voucher* 88. 40. *Ass.* 6. 4. *E.* 2 *Formed.* 49. *Vid. Ratcliffs case lib* 3. *fo.* 40. 41.

(e) 7. *E.* 4. 15.

Sect. 737.

Section 7.

¶ Et si home ad issue fits & file

And if a man hath issue a sonne and a

¶ This is put for an example to illustrate that which hath beene

Britton. ca. 119.

beene (said needeth no explanation. And herewith agreeth Britton.

per vn venter, & fits p auter venter, & le fits del primer venter purchase terres en fee, & mor sans issue, la soer auera la terre p discent, come heire a sa frere & nemy le puisne frere, pur ceo que la soer est de le entire sanke a son eigne frere.

daughter by one venter, & a son by another vēter, & the son of the first venter purchase lands in fee and die without issue, the sister shall haue the land by discent as heire to her brother, and not the younger brother, for that the sister is the whole blood of her elder brother.

Sect. 8.

(f) 24. E. 3. 24. 30. 38 E. 3. Count de Vouch. 88. 32 E. 3. tit. Voucher. 37. Ass. p. 4. 40. E. 3. 9. 42. E. 3. 10. 39 E. 3. 7. H. 5. 3.

(g) 5. E. 4. fo. 7. Pl. Com. fo. 58. in Wimbishes case.

(h) 10 Ass. 27. 34. Ass. 10. 31. E. 3. Count de Voucher. 88. 32. E. 3. tit. Vouch.

¶ *Seisie de terres en fee simple.* These words exclude a seisin in fee taile, albeit he hath a fee simple expectant. (f) And therefore if lands bee giuen to a man and his wife, and to the heires of their two bodies, the remainder to the heires of the husband, and they haue issue a sonne, and the wife dieth, and hee taketh another wife, and hath issue a sonne, the father dieth, the eldest sonne entreth, and dieth without issue, the second brother of the halfe blood shall inherite because the eldest sonne by his entrie was not actually seised of the fee simple being expectant but only of the estate taile. And the rule is that possessio fratris de feodo simplici facit sororem esse hæredem, and here the eldest sonne is not possessed of the fee simple but of the estate taile. And where Littleton speaketh only of lands, (g) yet there shall be possessio fratris of an vse, of a Seigniory, a rent, an aduowson and of other hereditaments.

¶ *Et leigne fits enter.* (h) These words are materially added when the father die seised of lands in fee simple, for if the eldest sonne doth not in that case enter, then without question the youngest

¶ Et auxi ou hōe est seisie de terres en fee simple, & ad issue fits & file per vn venter, & fits per auter venter, & mor, & leigne fits enter, & mor sans issue, la file auera les tenements, & nemy le puisne fits, vncore le puisne fits est heire a le pere, mes nemy a son frere, mes si leigne fits ne entra en la tre apres la mort son pere, mes mor deuant ascun entrie fait per luy, donqs le puisne frere poit enter, & auera le terre come heire a son pere. Mes lou leigne fits en le case auandit entra apres la mort son pere, & ad ent possession, donqs la soer auera la terre

AND also where a man is seised of lands in fee simple, and hath issue a sonne, and daughter by one venter, and a son by another venter, and die, and the eldest son enter, and die without issue, the daughter shall haue the land, and not the younger sonne, yet the yonger son is heire to the father but not to his brother, but if the elder son doth not enter into the land after the death of his father but die before any entrie made by him, then the younger brother may enter, & shal haue the land as heire to his father but where the elder son in the case aforesaid enters after the death of his father, and hath possession,

Quia possessio fratris de feodo simplici facit sororem esse hæredem. **Mes si sont deux freres per diuers venters, & leigne est seisie de terre en fee, & mort sans issue, & son vncle entra come prochein heire a luy quel auxi mort sans issue, ore le puisne frere puit auer la terre come heire al vncle, pur ceo que il est de lentier sanke a luy, coment que il soit de demy sanke a son eigne frere.**

there the sister shall haue the land, Because *Possessio fratris de feodo simplici facit sororem esse hærede.* But if there bee two brothers by diuers venters, & the elder is seised of land in fee, and die without issue, and his vncle enter as next heire to him, who also die without issue, now the younger brother may haue the land as heire to the vncle, for that he is of the whole blood to him, albeit he be but of the halfe blood to his elder brother.

sonne shall be heire, because as it hath beene said before regularly he must make himselfe heire to him that was last actually seised (as to the purchasor) and that was to the father where the eldest sonne did not enter. And therefore Littleton addeth that the sonne is heire to the father. (i) But when the eldest sonne in this case doth enter, then cannot the youngest sonne being of the halfe blood bee heire to the eldest, but the land shall discend to the sister of the whole blood. Yet in many cases albeit the sonne doth not enter into lands discended in fee simple the sister of the whole blood shall inherite, and in some cases where the eldest sonne doth enter, yet the younger brother of the halfe blood shall bee heire.

(i) 11.H.4.11. 40.E 3.30. 45 E.3.13. 40.Ass. p.6. Ratcliffes case.lib.3.fo.41.

(k) If the father maketh a Lease for yeares, and the Lessee entreth & dieth, the eldest sonne dieth during the tearme before entrie or receipt of rent, the younger sonne of the halfe blood shall not inherite but the sister, because the possession of the lessee for yeares is the possession of the eldest sonne, so as hee is actually seised of the fee simple, and consequently the sister of the whole blood is to be heire. The same Law it is, if the lands be holden by Knights seruice, and the eldest sonne is within age, and the Gardian entreth into the lands. And so it is if the gardian in Socage enter.

(k) 5.E 4.7.b. 3.H 7.5. 8.Ass.p 6. 45.E.3 tit Release.28.

But in the case aforesaid, if the father make a Lease for life or a gift in taile, and dieth, and the eldest sonne dieth in the life of tenant for life or tenant in taile, the younger brother of the halfe blood shall inherite because the tenant for life or tenant in taile is seised of the freehold, and the eldest sonne had nothing but a reuersion expectant vpon that freehold or estate taile, and therefore the youngest sonne shall inherite the land as heire to his father, who was last seised of the actuall freehold. And albeit a rent had beene reserued vpon the Lease for life, and the eldest sonne had receiued the rent and died, yet it is holden by some * that the younger brother shall inherite because the seisin of the rent is no actuall seisin of the freehold of the land. But 35.Ass. pl.2. seemeth to the contrary, because the rent issueth out of the land and is in lieu thereof, wherein the only question is, whither such a seasin of the rent, be such an actuall seasin of the land in the eldest sonne as the sister may in a writ of right make her selfe heire of this land to her brother. But it is cleere that (l) if there be bastard eigne, and mulier puisne, and the father maketh a Lease for life or a gift in tayle be reseruing a rent and die, and the bastard receiue the rent and die, this shall barre the mulier, for the reason of that standeth vpon another maxime as shall manifestly appeare in his apt place, Sect.399.

* 7.H.5 3 4. per Hulls & Lodington. 35.Ass.p 2. (l) 14.E.2 Bastardy. 26. Vid.Sect. 399.

¶ *Seisie des terres.* (m) **But in this case if the eldest sonne doth** enter and get an actuall possession of the fee simple, yet if the wife of the father be indowed of the third part and the eldest sonne dieth the younger brother shall haue the reuersion of this third part notwithstanding the elder brothers entrie, because that his actuall seisin which hee got thereby was by the endowment defeated. But if the eldest sonne had made a Lease for life, and the Lessee had endowed the wife of the father, and tenant in dower had died, the daughter should haue had the reuersion, because the reuersion was changed and altered by the Lease for life, and the reuersion is now expectant on a new estate for life.

(m) 7.H.5.2.3.4.

¶ *Enter.* **Hereupon the question groweth whither if the father** be seised of diuers seuerall parcels of lands in one Countie, and after the death of the father the sonne entreth into one parcell generally, and before any actuall entry into the other dieth, this generall entry into part shall vest in him an actuall seisin in the whole, so as the sister shall inherite the whole. And this is a quære in 21.H.7.33.a.

21.H.7.33.a.

And some doe take a diuersitie when an entrie shall vest, or deuest an estate, that there must be seuerall entries into the seuerall parcels, but where the possession is in no man, but the free-hold in law is in the heire that entreth, there the generall entrie into one part reduceth all into his actuall possession. And therefore if the Lord entreth into a parcell generally for a Mortmain, or the Feoffor for a condition broken, or the Disseisee into parcell generally, the entrie shall not vest nor deuest in these or like cases, but for that parcell. But when a man dies seised of diuers parcels in possession, and the freehold in law is by law cast vpon the heire, and the possession in no man, there the entrie into parcel generally seemeth to vest the actual possession in him in the whole. But if his entrie in that case be speciall, viz. that he enter only into that parcell and into no more, there it reduceth that parcell only into actuall possession.

(g) 19. E. 2. quare impedit. 177. 3. H. 7. 5.

(h) 7. E. 3. 66. iii. barre. 293. 3. H. 7. 5.

¶ *Home seisie des terres.* **What then is the Law of a Rent,** Aduowson, or such things that lie in grant? (g) If a Rent, or an Aduowson doe discend to the eldest sonne, and hee dieth before hee hath seison of the Rent, or present to the Church, the Rent or Aduowson shall discend to the youngest sonne, for that he must make himselfe heire to his father, as hath beene oftentimes said before. The like Law is of Offices, Courts, Liberties, Franchises, Commons of inheritance, and such like. (h) And this case differeth from the case of the tenant by the courtesie, for there if the wife dieth before the rent day, or that the Church become void, because there was no laches or default in him, nor possibilitie to get seison, the law in respect of the issue begotten by him will giue him an estate by the courtesie of England. But the case of the discent to the youngest sonne standeth vpon another reason, viz. to make himselfe heire to him that was last actually seised as hath beene said.

(i) 8. E. 3. 11. 49. E. 3. 12. Ratcliffes case lib. 3. fol. 41.

¶ *En fee simple.* (i) **For halfe bloud is not respected in estates** in taile, because that the issues doe claime in by discent, per formam Doni, and the issue in taile is euer of the whole bloud to the Donee.

(k) Bracton. lib. 2. fol. 65. & lib. 4. f. l. 279. Britton. cap. 119. Fleta. lib. 6. ca. 1. 24. E. 3. 30.

(l) Ratcliffes case lib. 3. fo. 43.
(m) Britton. ca. 119.

¶ (k) *Possessio fratris de feodo simplici facit sororem esse haeredem.* Hereupon foure things are to be obserued, euery word almost being operatiue, and materiall. First, That the brother must bee in actuall possession. For possessio est quasi pedis positio. Secondly, De feodo simplici, exclude estates in taile. Thirdly, Facit sororem esse hæredem. So as (l) Soror est hæres facta, and therefore some act must bee done to make her heire, and the younger sonne is hæres natus (m) if no act be done to the contrarie. And albeit the words be facit sororem esse hæredem, yet this doth extend to the issue of the sister, &c. who shall inherit before the younger brother. Fourthly, Of Dignities whereof no other possession can be had but such as discend (as to bee a Duke, Marquesse, Earle, Vicont, or Baron) to a man and his heires, there can be no possession of the brother to make the sister to inherit, but the younger brother being heire as Litleton saith to the father, shall inherit the Dignitie inherent to the bloud, as heire to him that was first created noble.

6. H. 4. 1.

(n) 34. H. 6. fo. 34. Pl. Com. fo. 245. 23. E. 3. ca. de natu vltra mare.

And you shall vnderstand that concerning Discents, there is a law, parcell of the lawes of England, called Ius coronæ, and differeth, in many things, from the generall law concerning the subiect. As for example, The King in any suite for any thing that pertaine to the Crowne shall not shew in certaine his cosinage as a subiect shall do, or as he himselfe shall do, for things touching his Duchie. (n) And in the case of the King, if he hath issue a sonne and a daughter by one venter, and a sonne by another venter, and purchaseth lands and dieth, and the eldest son enter and dieth without issue, the daughter shall not inherit these lands, nor any other fee simple lands of the Crowne, but the yonger brother shall haue them. Wherein note that neither possessio fratris doth hold of lands of the possessions of the Crowne, nor halfe bloud is no impediment to the discent of the lands of the Crowne, as it fell out in experience after the decease of King Edward the sixt to the Queene Marie, and from Queene Marie, to Queene Elizabeth, both which were of the halfe bloud, and yet inherited not only the lands which King Edward or Queene Marie purchased, but the ancient lands parcell of the Crowne also.

Pl. Com. vbi supra.

A man that is King by discent of the part of his mother, purchase lands to him and his heires and die without issue, this land shall discend to the heire of the part of the mother, but in the case of a subiect, the heire of the part of the father shall haue them.

Pl. Com. fol. 247.

So King Henrie the eight purchased lands to him and his heires, and died hauing issue two daughters, the Ladie Marie, and the Ladie Elizabeth after the deceale of King Edward, the eldest daughter Queene Marie did inherit only, all his lands in fee simple. For the eldest daughter, or sister of a King shall inherit all his fee simple lands. So it is if the King purchaseth lands of the custome of Gauelkind, and die hauing issue diuers sonnes, the eldest sonne shall only inherit these lands. And the reason of all these cases is, for that the qualitie of the person doth in these and many other like cases alter the discent, so as all the lands, and possessions whereof the King is seised in iure Coronæ, shall secundum ius Coronæ, attend vpon and follow the Crowne, and therefore to whomsoeuer the Crowne discend, those lands and possessions discend also for the Crowne and the lands, whereof the King is seised in iure Coronæ, are concomitantia. If the right heire of the Crowne be attainted of Treason, yet shall the Crowne discend to him, and eo instante (without any other reuersall) the attainder is vtterly auoided, as it fell out in the case of Henrie the seuenth. (o) And if the King purchase lands to him and his heires, he is seised thereof in iure Coronæ, à fortiori, when he purchases land to him his heires and successors.

Pl.Com. 238. 1.*H.*7.*fol.*4.

(o) 43.E.3.*fol* 20.

But hereof this little taste shall suffice.

Section 9.

CEt est ascauoir que c parol (enheritãce) nest pas tãtsolement entendue, lou home ad tres ou tenements per discent denheritage, mes auxi chescun fee simple, ou taile que home ad p son purchase puit estre dit enheritance, pur ceo que ses heyres luy purront enheriter. Car en briefe de Droit que home portera de terre que fuit de son purchase demesne, le bre dirra: Quam clamat esse ius & hæreditatem suam. Et issint serra dit en diuers auters briefs, qux hõe ou fẽe porta d s purchase ðmesn, cõe apiert p l Regist.

AND it is to wit, that this word (*inheritance*) is not only intended where a man hath Lands or Tenements by discent of inheritage, but also euery fee simple or taile which a man hath by his purchase may bee said an inheritance, because his heires may inherit him. For in a Writ of right which a man bringeth of land that was of his owne purchase, the Writ shall say, *Quam clamat esse ius & hæreditatem suam*. And so shall it be said in diuers other Writs which a man or woman bringeth of his owne purchase, as appeares by the Register.

C*Et est ascauoire.* This kinde of speech is vsed twice in this Chapter, and oftentimes by our Authour in all his three Bookes, and euer teacheth vs some rule of Law, or generall or sure leading point, as you shall perceiue by reading, and obseruing of the same, which for the ease of the studious Reader I haue obserued.

*Sect.*45.46.57.59.80.100. 146.164.170.184.229.243. 259.274 280.293.300.305. 419.420.421.489.632.697. 749.

Quam clamat esse ius & hæreditatem suam. (a) Here our Author declareth the right signification of this word (inheritance). And true it is that in the writ of right Patent, &c. quando dominus remittit Curiam suam. The words of the writ be, Quam clamat esse ius & hæreditatem suam. And in the Præcipe in capite, in a cui in vita, (b) when the Demandant claimeth by purchase, the writ is quam clamat esse ius & hæreditatem suam. And with Littleton agreeth the Register, fol.4. & 232. and the Booke in 49.E.3. 22. against sodaine opinions 7 H.4.5. 10.H.6.0. 39.H 6.38. Pl.com. Wimbishes case 47. And yet in 7.H.4.5. which is the Booke of the greatest weight Sir William Thirning Chiefe Justice of the Common Bench (as it seemeth doubting of it) went into the Chancery to enquire of the Chancerie men the forme of the writ in that case, and they said that the forme was both the one way and the other, so as thereby the opinion of Littleton is confirmed. and the Booke in 6.E.3.fol.30. is notable, for there in an action of waste the Plantife supposed, that the Defendant did hold de hæreditate sua, and it is ruled, that albeit the Plantife purchased the reuersion, yet the writ should serue. And there it is said, It hath beene seene, that in a Cui in vita, the writ was, which the Demandant claymed as her right and inheritance, when it was her purchase. And so this point wherein there might seeme some contrarietie in Bookes is manifestly cleered. But in the Statute of W.2.ca.5. de hæreditate vxorum by construction of the whole Statute is taken only for the wiues inheritance by discent, and not by purchase, as appeareth in 1.E.2. tit. Quare imped. 43.35.H.6.54. F.N.B.34.b.

(a) *Sect* 732. *Bract.lib.*2.*fol.*62.*b.* *Fleta lib.*6.*ca.*1.

(b) *Regist.fol.*1.2.

*Regist fol.*4.232.49.*E.*3.22. 7.*H.*4.5.10.*H.*6.9. 39.*H.*6.38.6.*E.*3.30. *Pl.com. Wimbeshes case* 47. & 58.*b.*

6.*E.*3.30.

*W.*2.*ca.*5. 1.*E.*2.*tit.quare imped.*43. 35.*H.*6.54. *F.N.B.*34.*b.*

There be some that haue an inheritance (c) and haue it neither by discent nor properly by purchase but by Creation, as when the King doth create any man a Duke, a Marquesse, Earle Viscount, or Baron to him and his heires, or to the heires males of his bodie, &c. hee hath an inheritance therein by Creation. A man may haue an inheritance in title of Nobilitie and Dignitie three manner of wayes, that is to say, by Creation, by Discent, and by

(c) *Lib.*6. *fol.*52.53. *Countee de Rutlands case.lib.*8.*fol.*16. 17. *the Trenest case.*

Prescription. By Creation two manner of ordinarie wayes (for I will not speake of a Creation by Parliament) by Writ and by Letters Patents. Creation by Writ is the ancienter way, and here it is to be obserued, that a man shall gaine an inheritance by Writ. King Richard the second created Iohn Beauchampe de Holte Baron of Kedermister by his Letters Patents, bearing date the 10. of October, anno regni sui, 11 before whom there was neuer any Baron created by Letters Patents, but by Writ. And it is to be obserued, that if hee be generally called by Writ to the Parliament, he hath a fee simple in the Baronie without any words of inheritance. But if he be created by Letters Patents, the state of inheritance must be limited by apt words, or else the grant is void. If a man bee called by Writ to the Parliament, and the Writ is deliuered vnto him, and he dieth before he commeth and sits in Parliament, whether hee was a Baron or no? And it is to bee answered that hee was no Baron, for the direction and diliuerie of the Writ to him maketh not him Noble; for the better vnderstanding whereof it is to be knowne that the words of the Writ in that case are, Rex, &c. E.B. de D. Chiualier salutem. Quia de aduisamento & assensu concilij nostri pro quibusdam arduis & vrgentibus negotijs statum & defensionem regni nostri Angliæ, &c. concernen̄ quoddam Parliamentum nostrum apud Ciuitatem Westm. à 21. Octob. proxim. futuro teneri ordinauimus, & ibid. vobiscum & cum Prælatis, Magnatibus & Proceribus dicti regni nostri colloquium habere & tractatum; vobis in fide & ligeancia quibus nobis tenemini firmiter iniungendo mandamus, quod consideratis dictorum negotiorum arduitate, & periculis imminentibus cessante excusatione quacunque, dictis die & loco personaliter intersitis nobiscum & cum Prælatis, Magnatibus, & Proceribus supradictis, super dictis negotijs tractaturis vestrumque concilium impensuris, &c. And this Writ hath no operation or effect vntill he sit in Parliament, and thereby his bloud is ennobled to him and his heires lineall, and thereupon a Baron is called a Peere of Parliament. (d) And if issue be ioyned in any action, whether hee bee a Baron, &c. or no, it shall not be tried by Jurie, but by the Record of Parliament, which could not appeare vnlesse he were of the Parliament. Therefore a Duke, Earle, &c. of another Kingdome, are not to be sued by those names here, for that they are not Peeres of our Parliament. And albeit the Creation by Writ is the ancienter, yet the Creation by Letters Patents is the surer, for he may be sufficiently created by Letters Patents, and made Noble, albeit he neuer sit in Parliament.

Lib. 6. fol. 52. 53. Countesse of Rutlands case. 8. H. 6. 10. 48. E. 3. 30. 35. H. 6. 46. Pl. Com. 223. (d) 35. H. 6. 46. 48. E. 3. 30. b. 48. Ass. p. 6. 22. Ass. p. 24. Regist. 287. 11. E. 3. breue. 472. 20 E. 4. 6.

(e) And it is to be obserued that Nobilitie may be granted for tearme of life, by act in law without any actuall Creation; as if a Duke take a wife by the intermarriage she is a Duches in Law, and so of a Marquesse, an Earle, and the rest, and in some other case. And there is a diuersitie betweene a woman that is Noble by Discent, and a woman that is Noble by marriage. (f) For if a woman that is Noble by Discent, marrie one that is vnder the degree of Nobilitie, yet she remayneth Noble still; but if shee gaine it by marriage, shee looseth it, if she marrie vnder the degree of Nobilitie, and so is the rule to be vnderstood, Si mulier nobilis nupserit ignobili desinit esse nobilis. (g) But if a Duchesse by marriage marrieth a Baron of the Realme she remayneth a Duchesse and looseth not her name because her husband is Noble, & sic de cæteris.

(e) Lib. 6. fol. 52. 53. Countes de Rutlands case. 2. H. 6. 11. 22. Ass. 24. 12. E. 3. breue 254. 8. H. 4. 19. 11. H. 4. 15. V. Fleta lib. 6. ca. 10. (f) Lib. 4. fo. 118. Actons case Tempore Mariæ Reginæ. Brooke nosme de dignitie 69. 14. H. 6. 18. 2. H. 6. 11. (g) 22 H. 6. 52.

And as an estate for life may be gained by marriage, so may the King create either man or woman Noble for life (h) but not for yeeres, because then it might goe to Executors or Administrators. The true diuision of persons is, that euery man is either of Nobilitie that is, a Lord of Parliament of the vpper House, or the degree of Nobilitie, amongst the Commons, as Knights, Esquires, Citizens and Burgesses of the lower House of Parliament, commonly called the House of Commons, and hee that is not of the Nobilitie is by intendement of Law among the Commons.

(h) Lib. 9. fol. 97. 98. Sir George Reynells case.

¶ *Come appiert per le Register.* **Which booke in the Statute of** W. 2. cap. 24 is called Registrum de Cancellaria, because it containeth the formes of Writs at the Common Law that issue out of the Chancerie, tanquam ex officina Iustitiæ. There is a Register of originall Writs, and a Register of Judiciall Writs, but when it is spoken generally of the Register it is meant of the Register originall. For the antiquitie and excellencie of this Booke. See in my preface to the eight part of my Commentaries. This excellent Booke our Author voucheth diuers times in these Bookes, and so doth hee diuers other Authorities in law of seuerall kinds, but with this obseruation, that he citeth no Authoritie, but when the Case is rare or may seeme doubtfull, which appeareth in this, that hee putteth no Case in all his three Bookes but hath warrant of good Authoritie in Law. For hee knew well the rule that perspicua vera non sunt probanda. And the like obseruation is made of Justice Fitzherbert in his Booke of Natura Breuium, that he neuer citeth Authoritie, but when the Case is rare or was doubtfull to him. The Authorities which our Author hath cited in his three Bookes I haue collected.

Vide Sect. 88. 94. 96. 101. 157. 234. 318. 383. 412. 420. 433. 514. 643. 644. 657. 660. 692. 702. 729.

Section 10.

¶ Et de tielx choses de quex home poit auer vn manuel occupation possessiō ou resceit, sicōe des terres, tenemēts, rents, & huiusmodi, la home dirr en coūt countant, & en plee pledant, que vn tiel fuit seisie en son demesne come de fee. Mes de tiels choses que ne gisont en tiel Manuel occupation, &c. sicome de aduowson desglise, & huiusmodi, la il dira que il fuit seisie come de fee, & nemy en son demesne come de fee, & en Latin il est en lun cas, quod talis seisitus fuit, &c. in dominico suo vt de feodo, & en lauter case, quod talis seisiius fuit, &c. vt de feodo.

And of such things whereof a man may haue a Manuell occupation, possession, or receipt, as of Lands, Tenements, Rents, and such like, there a man shall say in his Count Countant and Plea Pleadant that such a one was seised in his demesne as of fee, but of such things which doe not lie in such Manuell Occupation, &c. as of an Aduowson of a Church and such like, there he shall say, that hee was seized as of fee, and not in his Demesne as of fee. And in Latine it is in one Case, *Quod talis, seisitus fuit in dominico suo vt de feodo*, and in the other Case, *Quod talis seisitus fuit, &c. vt de feodo.*

¶ In Count Countant. Coūt .i. narratio cōmeth of the French word Conte which in Latine is Narratio, & is vulgarly called a Declaration. The originall Writ is according to his name Breue, briefe and short, but the Count which the Plaintifè or Demandant make is more narratiue and spacious and certaine both in matter and in circumstance of time & place, to the end the Defendant may bee compelled to make a more direct answere; so as the Writ may be compared to Logique, and the Count to Rhetorique, and it is that, which the Ciuilians call a Libell. And in that ancient Booke of the Mirror of Justices, lib. 2. ca. des Loiers, Contors are Seriants skilfull in law so named of the Count as of the principall part, and in W. 2. ca. 29. he is called Seriant counter. *Mirror. des Iustices.* *W. 2. cap. 29.*

¶ *En plea pleadant.* Placitum. Here Littleton teacheth good pleading in this point, of which in his third Booke and Chapter of Confirmations, Sect. 534. he thus saith, *Et saches mon fits que est vn des pluis honorables, laudables, & profitable choses en nostre ley, de auer le sciente de bien pleader en actions reals & personels, & pur ceo, ieo toy counsaile especialment de mettera ton courage, & cure de ceo apprender.* And for this cause this word Placitum is deriued a placendo, quia bene placitare super omnia placet, and is not, as some haue said, so called per Antiphrasin, quia non placet.

¶ *Seisie; Seitus*, commeth of the French word *seisin* .i. possessio, sauing that in the Common Law seised, or seisin is properly applied to freehold, and possessed or possession properly to goods and chattels; although sometime the one is vsed in stead of the other. *Bract. lib. 4. fol. 263.* *Idem lib. 5. fol. 372.* *Britton. fol. 205 206.* *Fleta lib. 5. ca. 5.* *Stanf. prær. 8.* *Pl. Com. fol. 191.* *Wretesleys case.*

¶ *En son demesne come de fee*, in Dominico suo vt in feodo. Dominicum is not only that inheritance, wherein a man hath proper dominion or owner-ship, as it is distinguished from the lands which another doth hold of him in seruice, but that which is manually occupied, manured, and possessed, for the necessarie sustentation, maintenance and supportation of the Lord and his houshold, and sauoureth de domo, of the house, either ad mensam, for his or their bord and sustentation, or manually receiued (as Rents) for bearing and defraying of necessarie charges publike or priuate. Of these (saith our Author) he should plead, that he is seised in dominico suo vt de feodo. i. de feodo dominicali, seu terra Dominicali, seu redditu Dominicali, which is as much to say as Demeyne or Demaine, of the hand, .i. manured by the hand, or receiued by the hand, and therefore he calleth it manuall occupation, possession, or receipt. And in Domesday demeane land is called Inland, as for example, 4. bouatas terræ de Inland, & 10. bouatas in seruitio. *Domesday.*

¶ *En tiel manuel occupation, &c.* There is nothing in our Author but is worthy of obseruation. Here is the first (&c.) and there is no (&c) in all his three Bookes (there being as you shall perceiue very many) but it is for two purposes First, it doth imply some other necessary matter. Secondly, that the studient may together with that which our Author hath said inquire what authorities there be in Law that treate of that matter, which will worke three notable effects; First, it will make him vnderstand our Author the better; Secondly, it will exceedingly adde to the readers inuention. And lastly, it will fasten the matter the more surely in his memory, for which purpose I haue for his ease in the beginning set downe in these Institutes the effect of some of the principall Authorities in Law as I conceiue them concerning the same. In this place the (&c.) implyeth possession or receipt, and such other matter as appeareth by my notes in this Section As for the Authorities of Law, you shall finde the effect of them in this Section, and the like of the rest of the (&c.) which you shal finde in the Sections hereafter mentioned, omitting those (for auoyding of tediousnesse) that either are apparant, or which are explaned in some other places, viz. Sect. 20. 48. 102. 108. 120. 125. 136. 137. 146, 149, 154. 164. 166. 167. 168. 177. 179. 183. 184. 194. 200. 202. 210. 211. 217. 220. 226. 233. 240. 242. 244. 245. 248 262. 264. 269, 270. 271. 279 320. 322. 323. 325. 326. 327. 329, 330. 335. 336. 341. 347. 348. 349 350. 352. 355. 356. 359. 364. 365. 374. 375. 377. 381. 384. 389. 393. 395, 397. 399. 401. 402. 410 417. 428. 433 447. 449. 464. 470. 471. 477. 483. 489. 500. 501. 522. 532. 552. 553. 556. 558. 562. 578. 591. 592. 593. 594. 603. 613. 624 625. 630. 632. 634. 637. 638, 648. 659. 660. 661. 669. 687. 693. 700. 718. 745. 748. 749. All which I haue obserued and quoted here once for all for the ease of the studious reader

Britton 205. 206. *optime.*
Fleta lib. 6. *ca.* 5.
Idem lib. 3. *ca.* 15.

¶ *Vt de feodo.* Where (vt) is not by way of similitude, but to bee vnderstood positiuely that he is seised in fee. And so it is where one plead a discent to one vt filio & hæredi that is to so S. that is sonne and heire, & sic de ceteris where (vt) denotat ipsam veritatem.

(i) 7. E. 3. 63. 24. E. 3. 74. 34. H. 6. 34. 19. E. 3. *quar. imp.* 154. *Mirror. cap.* 2. § 17.

(k) *Lib.* 6. *fo.* 51. *Boswels case.*

(l) 8. E. 2. *Presentment al Eglise.* 10. 7. E. 3. 39. 27 E. 3. 89. 29. E. 3. 5. 31. E. 3. *Estopel* 240. (m) 7. E. 3. 63. *Bracton.* 263. 372. *Fleta lib.* 5. *ca.* 5.

¶ *Sicome de advowson.* Of an Aduowson (i) wherein a man hath as absolute ownership and propertie as he hath in lands or rents, yet he shall not pleade, that he is seised in Dominico suo vt feodo, because that inheritance, sauouring not de domo, cannot either serue for the sustentation of him and his houshold, nor any thing can bee receiued for the same for defraying of charges. And therefore he cannot say, that he is seised thereof in dominico suo de feodo, whereby it appeareth how the Common law doth detest Simony and all corrupt bargaines for presentations to any benefice, but that (k) idonea persona for the discharge of the cure should be presented freely without expectation of any thing; nay so cautious is the Common law in this point that the pl. in a quare impedit should recouer no damages for the losse of his presentation vntill the statute of W 2. cap 5. And that is the reason that Gardian in Socage (l) shall not present to an Aduowson, because he can take nothing for it, and by consequent he cannot account for it. And by the law he can meddle with nothing that he cannot account for. (m) And in a writ of right of Aduowson, the patron shall not alledge the exploes or taking of the profits in himselfe but in his incumbent. And hereby the old bookes shall bee the better vnderstood, viz. Bracton, lib. 4. tract. 1. cap nu. 5. Est autem dominicum quod quis habet ad mensam, & proprie sicut sunt Bordlands Anglice. And Fleta lib. 5. ca 5. Est autem dominicum proprie terra ad mensam assignata. Dominicum etiam dicitur ad differentiam eius quod tenetur in seruitio. But of an Aduowson and such like he shall plead, that he is seised de aduocatione vt de feodo & jure.

7. E. 3. 4. 45. E. 3. 5.

¶ *Aduowson.* Aduocatio, signifying an aduowing or taking into protection, is as much as ius patronatus. Sir William Herle in 7. E. 3. fo 4. saith, that it is not long past, that a man did know what an Aduowson was, but when a man would grant an aduowson he granted Ecclesiam, the Church, and thereby the aduowson passed. Vid. 45. E. 3. 5. But surely the word is of greater antiquity, for in the Register there is an originall writ de recto Aduocationis, and in the originall writ of Assise de darreine presentment the patron is called Aduocatus. (n) Vid. W. 2. ca 5. And so doth (o) Bracton call him. Aduocatus autem dici poterit ille ad quem pertinet jus aduocationis alicujus, vt ad Ecclesiam præsentet nomine proprio & non alieno. And (p) Fleta lib. 5 ca. 14. agreeth herewith almost totidem verbis: Aduocatus est ad quem pertinet jus aduocationis alterius Ecclesiæ, vt ad Ecclesiam nomine proprio non alieno possit præsentare; And (q) Britton cap. 92. The Patron is called Auow, And the patrons are called aduocati for that they be either Founders or mainteyners or benefactors of the Church either by building, dotation or increasing of it, in which respect they were also called Patroni, and the Aduowson jus patronatus.

(n) *W.* 2 *ca.* 5.
(o) *Bract. lib.* 4. *fo.* 240.
(p) *Fleta lib.* 5 *ca.* 14.
(q) *Britton. ca.* 92.
(r) 33. *H.* 6. 11. *b per Prisot* 14. *H.* 6. 15. *per Newton.* 31. *E.* 1. *droit.* 68. 69. *F. N. B.* 31. *b. Lib.* 10. 135. 136. *R. Smythes case.* 45. *E.* 3. *Fines* 41. 45. *E.* 3. 12. 19. *E.* 3. 78. 17. *E.* 2. *Dower* 163.

And it is to be vnderstood that there is a great (r) diuersity inter aduocationem medietatis Ecclesiæ, &c. & medietatem aduocationis Ecclesiæ, and of their seuerall remedies for the same. For the Aduowson of the moity is when there be seuerall Patrons, and two seuerall incumbents in one Church, the one of the one moity thereof, and the other of the other moity, and one

part

part aswell of the Church as of the towne allotted to the one, and the other part thereof to the other, and in that case each Patron if he be disturbed shall haue a quare impedit, quod permittat ipsum præsentare idoneam personam ad medietatem Ecclesiæ.

But if there be two Coperceners, and they doe agree to present by turne each of them in truth hath but a moity of the Church, but for that there is but one incumbent, if either of them be disturbed she shall haue a Quare impedit, &c. præsentare idoneam personam ad Ecclesiam; for that there is but one Church and one incumbent, and so of the like. But in (s) the said case of two Coperceners one of them shall haue a Writ of right of Aduowson de meditate aduocationis for in truth she hath but a right to a moity, but in the other case where there be two Patrons and two incumbents in one Church each of them shall haue a Writ of right of Aduowson de aduocatione medietatis.

(s) *Britton.fo.*235. 31.*E.*1.*droit* 68.69. *F.N B.*31.*b.c.*33.*a.* 5.*H.*7.8. 17.*E* 3.38.75.76. 7.*E.*3 327. 8.*E.*3.425. 32.*Ass.p.*33. 14.*H.*4 10. 33.*E.*3.*quar.imp.*196.

And as there may (as hath beene said) be two seuerall Parsons in one Church, so there may be two that may make but one Parson in a Church. (t) Britton saith, Si ascun Eglise soit done a diuers persons per vn sole avowe nul ne se pura pleadre per assise de iuris vtrum ne nul estre implede sauns lautre, &c. And therewith agreeth Fleta. (u) Item licet aliqua Ecclesia diuisa fuerit inter duos, sive bona sua habeant comunia siue seperata, dum tamen vnicum habeant advocatum nullus eorum sine alio agere poterit vel implacitari. And Fitzh. saith, that two Prebendaries may be one Parson of a Church, who shall ioyne in a Iuris vtrum, so as one Rectory may be annexed to two seuerall Prebends, and both of them make but one Parson. But where one is Parson of the one moity of a Church and another of the other moity as hath beene said, there one of them shall haue a juris vtrum against the other, and in the Writ shall name him persona medietatis Ecclesiæ, &c. But for auoyding of suspition of curiositie if wee should proceed any further herein, we will attend what Littleton will further teach vs.

(t) *Britton.fo* 235.
(u) *Fleta lib.*5.*ca* 19.
*F.N.B.*49. o.
*F.N.B.*49.*p.*

Section 11.

¶ Et nota que home ne poit auer pluis ample ou pluis greinder estate denheritance, que fee simple.

And note that a man cannot haue a more large or greater estate of inheritance than Fee simple.

This doth extend aswell to fee simples conditional and qualified, as to fee simples pure and absolute. For our Author speaketh here of the amplenesse, and greatnesse of the estate, and not of the perdurablenesse of the same. And he that hath a fee simple conditionall or qualified hath as ample and great an estate as hee that hath a fee simple absolute, so as the diuersitie appeareth betweene the quantitie and qualitie of the estate.

From this state in fee simple, estates in taile, and all other particular estates are deriued, and therefore worthily our Author beginneth his first booke with Tenant in Fee simple for a principalioribus seu dignioribus est inchoandum.

¶ *Ne poet auer pluis ample ou greinder estate, &c.* For this cause two (a) fee simples absolute cannot be of one, and the selfe-same land. If the King make a gift in taile and the Donee is attainted of treason, in this case the King hath not two simples in him, viz the ancient reuersion in fee, and a fee simple determinable vpon the dying without issue of Tenant in taile, but both of them are consolidated and conioyned together; and so it is if such a Tenant in taile doth conuey the land to the King his heires and Successors, the King hath but one estate in fee simple vnited in him, and the Kings grant of one estate is good, and so was it adiudged in the Court of Common pleas. And yet in seuerall Parsons by act in Law a reuersion may be in fee simple in one, and a fee simple determinable in another by matter Ex post facto; as if a gift in taile be made to a Villeine, and the Lord enter, the Lord hath a fee simple qualified, and the Donor a reuersion in fee, but if the Lord infeoffe the Donor, now both Fee simples are vnited, and he hath but one fee simple in him; but one fee simple cannot depend vpon another by the grant of the partie, as if lands be giuen to A. so long as B. hath heires of his body the remainder ouer in fee, the remainder is voide.

(a) *Pl.Com* 349. & 248. 19.*H.*8.*Dier* 4. 29.*H.*8. *Dier* 33. 16.*Eliz.* *Dier.* 330. 2.*Mariæ Dier.*107. *Austens case.* *Pa.*38.*Eliz.rot.* 108. *In quar.imp. betweene the Queene Pl. and the Bishop of Lincolne, Hussey and others deff.* 15.*E.*4.6.8.

Sect. 12.

Item purchase est appel la possession de terres ou

Also purchase is called the possession of lands or

¶ Purchase in Latyn is either acquisitum of the verbe acquiro, for so I finde it in the originall Register 243. In terris vel tenementis

mentis quas viri & mulieres coniunctim acquisierunt, &c. Bracton calleth it perquisitum;

Bracton.lib.2.fo 65.
(b) Glanuil.lib.7 ca.1.
Britton ca 33.fo 84. & 121.

and by (b) Glanuil it is called questus or perquisitum.

A purchase is alwayes intended by title, and most properly by some kinde of conueyance either for money or some other consideration, or freely of gift: for that is in Law also a purchase. But a discent, because it commeth meerely by act of Law, is not said to be a purchase; and accordingly the makers of the act of Parliament in 1.H.5.ca.5. speaketh of them that haue lands or tenements by purchase or discent of inheritance. And so it is of an escheate or the like because the inheritance is cast vpon, or a title vested in the Lord by act in Law and not by his owne deede or agreement as our Author here saith. Like Law of the state of Tenant by the courtesie tenant in dower or the like. But such as attaine to lands by meere iniury and wrong, as by disseisin, intrusion, abatement, vsurpation, &c. cannot be said to come in by purchase no more then Robberie, Burglary, Pyracy or the like can iustly be tearmed purchase.

Pl. Com, Wimbishes case, 47.b.
1.H.5.ca.5.

If a Noble man, Knight, Esquire, &c. be buried in a Church, and haue his coat armour and Pennions with his armes, and such other ensignes of honour as belong to his degree or order set vp in the Church, or if a grauestone or tombe bee laid or made, &c. for a monument of him. (c) In this case albeit the freehold of the Church be in the parson, and that these be annexed to the freehold, yet cannot the Parson or any take them or deface them, but he is subiect to an action to the heire, and his heires in the honor and memory of whose Auncestor they were set vp. And so it was holden, Mich.10.Ia. and herewith agreeth the Lawes (d) in other Countries. Note this kinde of inheritance: and some hold that the wife or Executors that first set them vp may haue an action in that case against those that deface them in their time. And note that in some places chattels as heire-loomes, (as the best bed, table, pot, pan, cart, and other dead chattels moueable) may goe to the heire, and the heire in that case may haue an action for them at the Common-law, and shall not sue for them in the Ecclesiasticall Court, but the heireloome is due by custome and not by the Common law. And the (e) ancient iewels of the Crowne are heire loomes, and shall discend to the next successor, and are not deuisable by testament.

(c) 9.E.4.14.
Mich.10.I..Obiter in Com. banco. in Tyms case.
(d) B. Cassanans fo.13. Concl.29.
30.E.3.2.& 3.
39.E.3.6.9.10.
1.H.5.tit. Executors.108.
tit. Discent. Br.43.
9.E.4.15. Madam Wiches case.
(e) Vid.28.H.8.24.

An heire loome is called principalium or hereditarium.

Consuetudo hundredi de Stretford in Com' Oxoñ est quod hæredes teñtorum infra hundredum prædictum existeñ post mortem antecessorum suorum habebunt, &c. principalium Anglice an heire Lombe, viz. De quodam genere catallor, vtensilium, &c. optimum plaustrum Optimam carucam, optimum ciphum, &c.

Pat. adiudicata coram Rege. Tr.41.E.3.lib.2.fo.104. in Thesaur.

Our Author hath not spoken of parceners in this Chapter for that he hath particular chapters of the same.

Sect.241.242.&c.

tenements que home ad p son fait, ou per agreement, a quel possession il ne auient per title de discent de nul de ses auncesters, ou de ses cousins mes per son fait demesne.

tenements that a man hath by his deed or agreement, vnto which possession hee commeth not by title of descent from any of his ancestors, or of his Cousins but by his owne deed.

CHAP. 2. *Sect.* 13.

¶ T*Enant en Fee Taile.* Tallium, or Feodum talliatum, is deriued of the French word tailler, scindere, for so Littleton himselfe in his Chapter Sect.18. saith.

Mirror.ca.2.§.15. & cap.1.§.5.

¶ *Le Statute de W.*2. This Statute was made in 13.E.1. and is called West.2. because the Parliament was holden at Westminster, and

TEnant in Fee tail est p force de le statute de West.2. ca.1. Car deuant le dit statute, touts Enheritãces fuer fee simpl; car touts les dones q sõt specifies deins

TEnant in Fee Taile is by force of the Statute of *W.2.cap.*1. for before the said Statute, al Inheritances were Fee simple; for al the gifts which bee specified in yt stat. were fee simple

hath

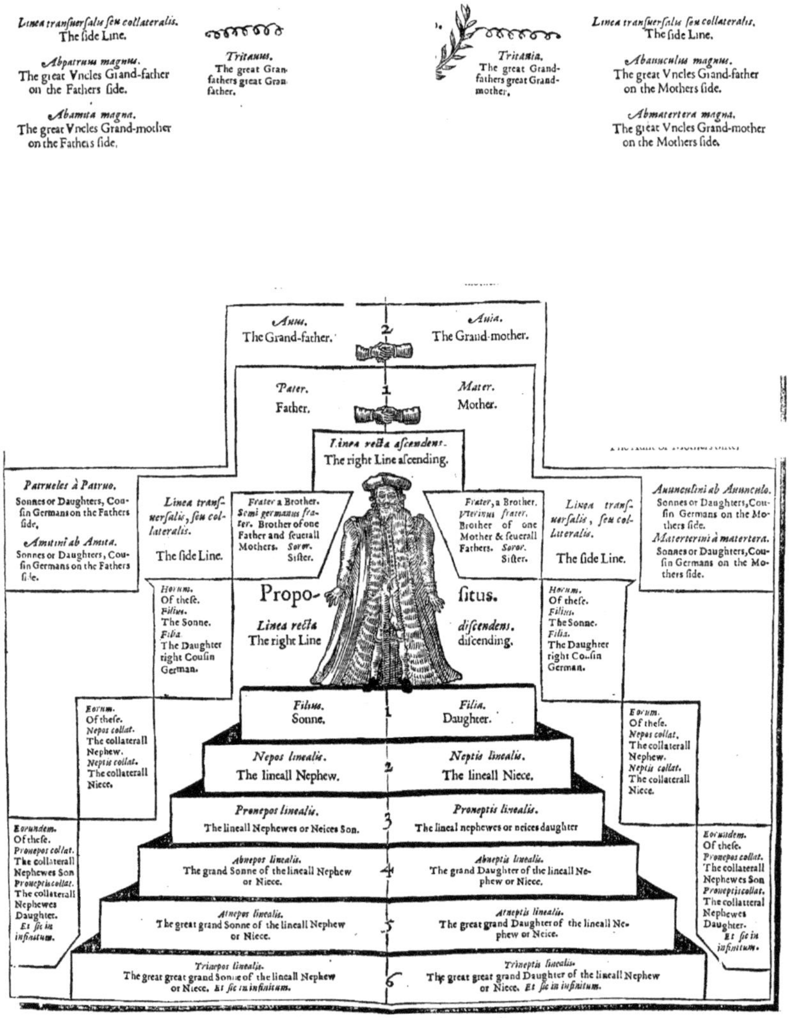

Place this next before Folio 19.

Bracte
(b) G
Britt.

Pl. C
1. H.

(c) 9.

Mich.
banco.
(d) E
Covel.
30. E.
39. E.
1. H. 5
nit. D
9. E. 4.
Wiche
(e) V

Pat. anh
Tr. 41.
in Thes

Sect. 2

Mirro.
& cap.

This Statute was made in 13. E. 1. and is called West. 2. because the Parliament was holden at Westminster, and

taces fuer fee simple; car touts les dones q sont specifies deins

simple; for al the gifts which bee specified in yt stat. were fee simple

hath

m l'estat, fuet fee simple côditional al comon ley, côe appiert p' rehersal d' m l'statute. Et ore p cel stat tenât en l' taile est en deux manñs, cestascawoire, tenant en taile generall, & tenant en taile special.

cōditional at the common law, as appeareth by the rehearsall of the same Statute. And now by this Statute, Tenant in Taile is in two manners, that is to say, Tenant in taile generall, and Tenant in taile speciall.

hath the name of the second, because another Parliament was formerly holden at Westminster in the third yere of the same Kings raigne, which was called Westminster the first. And albeit manie Parliaments were after holden at Westminster besides these, yet were they two onely, propter excellentiam, called the Statutes of Westminster. And the Act intended by Littleton, is W.2.c.1. Upon which Statute, our Authour in the Inner Temple did learnedly read, whose reading I haue. Of King Ed.1. and of this Statute, Sir William Herle chiefe Justice of the Court of Common Pleas, in 5.E.3.14. saith, That King E.1. was the wisest King that euer was: 5.E.3.14.
and the cause of the making of this Statute, was to preserue the Inheritance in the bloud of them to whom the gift was made. And in 9 E.3.22. he saith, That they were sage men that 9.E.3.22.
made this Statute. See more of this in the Chapter of Warranties, Sect.746.

Of this estate Taile it is said, (a) Modus legem dat donationi, & tenend' est etiam conuentio, quia Modus & Conuentio vincunt legem: Vt si alicui cum vxore fiat donatio, habendum & tenendum sibi & hæredibus quos inter eos legitime procreabunt, ecce quod donator vult tales hæredes in hæreditate paterna & materna succedant, alijs hæredibus eorum remotioribus penitus exclusis: Et quod voluntas donatoris obseruari debet manifeste apparet per hæc Statuta, quia autem dudum Regi durum videbatur, &c. (a) *Fle'a lib.3.cap.9 Bract.lib.2.ca.5.&c. Brit.cap.24.& 36.*

¶ *Deuant le dit Statute* (b) *touts Inheritances fueront Fee simple.* Here Fee simple is taken in his large sence, including as well conditionall or qualified, as absolute, to distinguish them from estates in Taile since the said Statute. Before which Statute of Donis conditionalibus, If Land had beene giuen to a man, and to the heires males of his bodie, the hauing of an Issue female had beene no performance of the Condition; but if he had issue male, and died, and the issue male had inherited, yet hee had not had a fee simple absolute, (c) for if he had died without issue male, the Donor should haue entred as in his reuerter. By hauing of issue the Condition was performed for three purposes; First, to Alien: Secondly, to Forfeit: Thirdly, to charge with Rent, Common, or the like. But the course of discent was not altred by hauing issue; for if the Donee had issue and died, and the land had descended to his issue, (d) yet if that issue had died (without any alienation made) without issue, his colaterall heire should not haue inherited, because hee was not within the forme of the gift, viz. heire of the bodie of the donee. (f) Lands were giuen before the Statute in frankmarriage, and the donees had issue and died, and after, the issue died without issue, it was adjudged, that his colaterall issue shall not inherite, but the donor should re-enter. So note, that the heire in Taile had no fee simple absolute at the Common Law, though there were diuers discents.

(b) *Vid.Sect.18. Brit.ca.35.fol.93. Pl.Com 235.562.Shelleys Case.lib.1.fol.103.*
(c) *44.E.3.3. 30.E.1. Formedon 66. 7.E.3.6.7. 7.H.4.31. 12.H.4.1.*
(d) *18.E.3.46.18.Ass.p.5. 12.E.4.3.*
(f) *4.H.3.Formedon 34. 18.Ass.5. 12.E.4.3. Pl.Com.247.b. 18. E.2. tit. Formedon 58.59.*

If Lands had beene giuen to a man and to his heires males of his bodie, and hee had issue two Sonnes, and the eldest had issue a Daughter, the Daughter was not inheritable to the Fee simple, but the yonger sonne per formam Doni. And so if Land had beene giuen at the Common Law to a man and the heires Females of his bodie, and he had issue a Sonne and a Daughter, and died the Daughter should haue inherited this Fee simple at the Common Law, for the Statute of Donis Conditionalibus, createth no estate taile, but of such an estate as was fee simple at the Common Law & is discendible in such forme as it was at the Common Law. If the Donee in taile had issue before the Statute, & the issue had died without issue, the alienation of the Donee, at the Common Law, hauing no issue at that time had not barred the Donor.

(g) If Donee in taile at the Common Law had aliened before any issue had, and after had issue, this alienation had barred the issue, because he claimed a Fee simple, yet if that issue died without issue, the Donor might reenter for that he aliened before any issue, at what time he had no power to alien to barre the possibilitie of the Donor. (h) But if Feme tenant in taile had taken husband, and had issue, and the husband and wife had aliened in Fee by Deed before the Statute, yet the issue might haue had a Formdon in discender for the alienation was not lawfull: but otherwise it is, if it had beene by fine. And these things though they seeme ancient are necessarie, notwithstanding to be knowne, aswell for the knowledge of the Common Law, as for Annuities and such like Inheritances as cannot be intailed, within the said Statute, and therefore remayne at the Common Law. (i) If the King before the Statute of Donis 6.E.3 56.Ie. of Elthams case.

(g) *30.E.1.formdon 65. Tempt E.1.ibidem.62. 19.E.2.formdon 61. Pl.Com.246.*
(h) *4.E.2.formdon 59.*

conditionalibus had made a gift to a man, and to the heires of his bodie begotten, the Donee Post prolem suscitatam might haue aliened aswell as in the case of a common person. (k) But if the Donee had no issue, and before the Statute had aliened with warrantie, and died, and the warrantie had discended upon the King, this should not haue bound the King of his Reuersion without assets: but otherwise it was in the case of a common person. (l) Of the other side, if Lands had beene giuen to the King and to the heires of his bodie, hee could not before issue haue aliened in Fee, but only to haue barred his issue as a common person might haue done, but not to haue barred the reuersion, for that should haue beene a wrong in the case of a subiect, and the Kings Prerogatiue cannot alter his case, nor make it greater, then the Donor gaue unto him: And it is a maxime in Law, That the King can doe no wrong. When all Estates were Fee simple, then were Purchasers sure of their Purchases, Farmors of their Leases, Creditors of their Debts, the King and Lords had their Escheates, Forfeitures, wardships, and other profits of their Seigniories; and for these and other like cases, by the wisdome of the Common Law all estates of inheritance were Fee simple; and what contentions and mischiefes haue crept into the quiet of the Law by these fettered inheritances, daily experience teacheth us. But see more of this matter in the aforesaid Chapter of warrantie, Sect. 746.

(k) 45. *Ass. p.* 6.

(l) *T. l. Com.* 246. *b.*

Lib. 10. *fol.* 38. *in Tort. cast.*

¶ *Common ley.* See for explication hereof, Sect. 170.

¶ *Come appeirt per le rehersall de mesme lestatute.* Here, by the authoritie of our Author, The rehearsall or preamble of a Statute is to be taken for truth; for it cannot be thought that a Statute that is made by authoritie of the whole Realme, aswell of the King as of the Lords Spirituall and Temporall, and of all the Commons will recite a thing against the truth.

Doct. & Stud. lib. 2. *cap.* 55.

¶ *Et ore per cel statute tenant en taile est en* 2. *Manners, .S. tenant en tayle generall, & tenant en tayle especiall.*

This diuision of an estate taile is perfect and sound, For the membra diuidentia, viz. generall and speciall are conuerted properly with the thing defined, and they are proued by many Authorities of Law, and approued of all learned men; and so are all the diuisions through all his three Bookes which the studious and diligent Reader will obserue. And how excellent and difficult a thing it is to diuide rightly and properly, especially in the Law the learned doe know.

By this Statute the land is as it were appropriated to the Tenant in taile, and to the heires of his bodie, and therefore (r) if an estate be made, either before or since the Statute of 27. H. 8. cap. 10. to a man and the heires of his bodie, either to the use of another and his heires, or to the use of himselfe and his heires, this limitation of use is utterly void. For before the said Statute of 27. H. 8. he could not haue executed the estate to the use, and so was it adiudged (s) in an Eiectione firmæ betweene Iohn Cowper Plantife, and Thomas Franklin &c. Defendant.

(r) 24. *H.* 8. *tit. feoffments al uses* 4. 27. *H.* 8 *fo.*

(s) *Pasch.* 14 *Ia. in the Kings Bench.*

Section 14. 15.

¶ *Terres*, Terra, in his generall and legall signification (as hath beene said before) includeth not only all kind of grounds, as medow, pasture, wood, &c. but houses and all edifices whatsoeuer. In a more restrained sence it is taken for arrable ground.

Vid. Sect. 1.

¶ *Tenements*, tenementa This is the only word which the said Statute of W. 2. that created Estates taile useth, and it includeth not only all Corporate Inheritances, which are or may be holden, but also all Inheritances issuing out of any of

¶ Tenãt en taile generall, est lou tres ou tenemẽts sont dones a un hõe & a ses heires de son corps engendres: En ceo case est dit generall taile, pur ceo q̃ quelcunq; feme q̃ tiel tenant espousa (sil auoit plusors femes, & per chescun d' eux il ad issue) uncore chescun de les issues

Tenant in taile generall, is where Lands or Tenements are giuen to a man, and to his heires of his bodie begotten. In this case it is said generall taile, because whatsoeuer woman that such tenant taketh to wife (if he hath many wiues and by euery of them hath issue) yet euerie one of these issues by pos-

per possibilitie poit enheriter les tenements per force del done, pur ceo que chescun tiel issue est de son corps engendre.

posſibilitie may inherit the Tenements by force of the gift; becauſe that euerie ſuch iſſue is of his bodie ingendred.

¶ En mesme le maner est lou terres ou tenements sont dones a un feme, & a ses heires de sa corps issuants, coment que el auoit diuers barons, uncore lissue que el poit auer per chescun baron, poit enheriter come issue en le taile per force de tiel done, & pur ceo tielx dones sont appelles generall tailes.

IN the ſame manner it is, where lands and Tenements are giuen to a woman, and to the heires of ~~their~~ her bodie, albeit that ſhe hath diuers husbands, yet the iſſue which ſhee may haue by euery Huſband may inherit as iſſue in taile by force of this gift. And therefore ſuch gifts are called generall tailes.

those Inheritances, or concerning, or annexed to, or exercisable within the same, though they lie not in tenure, therefore all these without question may be intailed. As (t) Rents, Estouers, Commons, or other profits whatsoeuer granted out of Land; Or Uses, Offices, Dignities which concerne Lands or certaine places may be entailed within the said Statute; because all these sauour of the Realtie. But if the grant be of an Inheritance mere personall, or to be exercised about Chattels, and is not issuing out of land, nor concerning any land or some certaine place, such Inheritances cannot be intailed, because they sauour nothing of the realtie. But examples will illustrate and make this learning cleere.

(t) 7.E.3.363.18.E.3.27. 7.H.6.8. 32.H.28. 5.E.4.3. 1.H.7.28.4.H.7.9.1.H.5.1 H.8.fol.3. Neuils case.lib. fol.33.34. Pl.Com.in Manxels case fol.2. & 3.

The writ of Assise (u) was De libero tenemento, & made his pleint of the Office of the fourth part of the Seriant of the Common Place, and the writ adiudged good, and seeing that a man hath a freehold, Liberum tenementum in it, by consequent it may bee intailed.

(u) 7.Ass.p.12. 7.E.6.1.

The Office of the keeping of the Church of our Ladie of Lincolne, was intailed, and a Formedon there brought vpon that gift of the Office by the issue in taile. The (x) Office of the Marshall of England intailed. The (y) Office of one of the Chamberlaines of the Exchequer intailed. 1.H.7.28. The Office of a Fostership intailed. 4.H.7.10 9.E.4.56.b. Charters intailed. 19.H.8.3 Use intailed. (z) Nomination to a Benefice intailed.

18.E.3.27. (x) 5.E.4.3. 10.E.4.14. (y) 11.E.4.1. 1.H.7.28. 4.H.7.10. 9.E.4.526. 19.H.8.3. 1.H.5.1.

Also a name of dignitie may be intailed within the Statute, (a) as Dukes, Marquesses, Earles, Uiscounts, and Barons, because they be named of some Countie, Mannor, Towne, or Place. If the issue in taile (b) in a Formedon in the discender be barred by a false verdit, his release is no barre to his issue, albeit the action is at the Common Law.

(a) Lib.7.fol.33.34. Neuils case. 28.H.6. Lord Veseyes case. (b) 14.Ass.2. 3.Eliz. Dier.188.

The like Law is of a writ of Errour 3.Eliz. Dier 188. If a gift in taile bee made with warrantie, the Donee releases the warrantie, this shall not bind the issue in taile; for to all these cases and the like the said Statute doth extend. But if I grant to a man, and to the heires of his bodie to be Keeper of my Hounds, or Master of my Horse, or to be my Faulconer, or such like with a fee therefore, yet these cannot bee intailed within the said Statute, for that they be not issuing out of Tenements nor annexed to, or exercisable within, or concerning Lands or Tenements of Freehold or Inheritance, but concerning Chattels, and sauour nothing of the realtie. And so it is if I by my deed for me and my heires grant an annuitie to a man, and the heires of his bodie, for that this only chargeth my person and concerneth no land nor sauoureth of the realtie.

Pl.Com. in Manxels case

In all these cases he hath a fee conditionall, as they were before the Statute, and the grantee by his grant or release may barre his heire, as hee might haue done at the Common Law, for that in these cases he is not restrained by the said Statute.

¶ *Et a ses heires de son corps engendres.* In gifts in taile these words (heires) are as necessary, as in Feoffments and Grants; for seeing every estate taile, was a fee simple at the Common Law, and at the Common Law no Fee simple could bee in Feoffements and Grants without these words (heires) and that an estate in Fee taile is but a cut or restrained Fee, It followeth that in gifts in a mans life time, no Estate can bee created without these words (heires) vnlesse it bee in case of Frank-marriage as hereafter shall bee shewed. And where Littleton saith (heires) yet (heire) in the singular number in a speciall

case

39.Ass.p.20. 20.H.6.35. 5.H.4.7.b. 14.H.4.15.

case may create an Estate taile, as it appeareth by 39.Ass. P.20. hereafter mentioned. And yet if a man giue lands to A. & hæredibus de corpore suo, the remainder to B. in forma prædicta, this is a good Estate taile to B. for that in forma prædicta do include the other. If a man letteth lands to A. for life the remainder to B. in taile, the remainder to C. in forma prædict. this remainder is void for the incertaintie. But if the remainder had beene, the remainder to C. in eadem forma, this had beene a good Estate taile, for idem semper proximo antecedenti refertur. If a man giue Lands or Tenements to a man & semini suo, or exitibus vel prolibus de corpore suo, to a man and to his Seed, or to the Issues or Children of his bodie, he hath but an estate for life, for albeit, that the Statute prouideth that Voluntas donatoris secundum formam in charta doni sui manifestè expressam de cætero obseruetur. Yet that will and intent must agree with the rules of Law. And of this opinion was our Authour himselfe, as it appeareth in his learned reading aforementioned vpon this Statute: where he holdeth if a man giueth land to a man. Et exitibus de corpore suo legitime procreatis, or semini suo, hee hath but an estate for life, for that there wanteth words of Inheritance.

Vid. Shelleyes case lib.1.fol.

¶ *De son corps.* These words are not so strictly required but that they may be expressed by words that amount to as much; For the example that the statute of W.2. putteth hath not these words (de corpore) but these words (hæredibus) viz. Cum aliquis dat terram suam alicui viro & ejus vxori & hæredibus de ipsis viro & muliere procreatis. If lands be giuen (c) to B. & hæredibus quos idem B de prima vxore sua legittimè procrearet. This is a good estate in especiall taile (albeit he hath no wife at that time without these words (de corpore.) So it is (d) if lands be giuen to a man, and to his heires which he shall beget of his wife: (e) or to a man & hæredibus de carne suâ, or to a (f) man & hæredibus de se. In all these cases these be good estates in taile, and yet these words de corpore are omitted. It is holden (g) by some opinion, that if there be grandfather, father and sonne, and lands are giuen to the grandfather, and to his heires begotten by the father, the father dieth, the grandfather dieth, the sonne is in as heire to the grandfather begotten vpon the body of his father, and the wife of the grandfather in that case shall be indowed. But certaine it is, that in some cases one shall haue the land per formam doni that is not issue of the body of the Donee which see Section 30.

(c) 3.E.3.tit.breue 743. 3.E.3.tit. Estates.
(d) 12.H.4.2.
(e) 37.H.6.15.
(f) 5.H.5.6.
(g) 12.H.4.2. per Herton.

¶ *Engendres.* This word may in many cases be omitted or expressed by the like, and yet the state in taile is good, as, Hæredibus de carne, hæredibus de se, hæred quos sibi contigerit, &c. as is aforesaid, and where the word of Littleton is, ingendred, or begotten, procreatis, yet if the word be procreandis, or quos procreauerit, the estate in taile is good: and as procreatis shall extend to the issues begotten afterwards, so procreandis shall extend to the issues begotten before.

18.E.2.tit.Bre.836. 24.E.3.28.

Section 16.

TEnant en Taile speciall est lou terres ou Tenements sont dones a vn home & a sa feme, & a les heires de lour deux corps engendres; en tiel case nul poet inherit per force de le dit done, forsque ceux que sont ingendres perenter eux deux. Et est appel le speciall Taile, pur ceo que si la fee deuy, & il prent auter fee, & ad issue, lissue del se-

TEnant in taile speciall is where Lands or Tenements are giuen to a man and to his wife, and to the heires of their two bodies begotten; In this case none shall inherit by force of this gift, but those that bee engendred between them two. And it is called especiall taile, because if the wife die, and hee taketh another wife, and haue issue, the is-

¶ A *Vn home & sa feme.* (a) Then put the case that lands bee giuen to a man and a woman vnmarried, and the heires of their two bodies: for the apparant possibilitie to marry, they haue an estate taile in them presently. (b) So it is where lands bee giuen to the husband of A. and to the wife of B. and to the heires of their bodies, they haue presently an estate in taile, in respect of the possibilitie. If a feme sole doe infeoffe a married man causa matrimonij prælocuti, it is good for the possibilitie. But put the case that the premisses and the habendum bee in other manner than Littleton hath put, and let vs see

(a) 5.H.7.10.11.E.3 Formdon 30. Tl.Com.35.

(b) Lib.1.fol.120 Chudleys case, 40.Ass.pl.13.34.Ass. pl.1. Fleta lib.5.ca.34.

what

cond feme ne serra jammes inheritable p force d tiel done, ne auxy lissue del second baron, si le prim Baron deuie.

sue of the second wife shall not inherit by force of this gift, nor also the issue of the second husband, if the first husband die.

what the Law is in these cases. (c) As if a man in the premisses giue lands to another and the heires of his bodie, habendum to him and his heires for euer; in this case he hath an estate taile, and a fee simple expectant: And so (it is said) via versa, if lands be giuen to a man and to his heires in the premisses, habendum to him and to the heires of his bodie, that he hath an estate taile, and a fee simple expectant. (d) If lands be giuen to B. and his heires, to haue and to hold to B. and his heires, if B. haue heyres of his bodie, and if he die without heires of his bodie that it shall reuert to the donor, this is adiudged an estate taile, and the reuersion in the donor. (e) For, Voluntas donatoris in charta doni sui manifestè expressa obseruetur; and therefore in the case next precedent, if these or the like words be added, (and if he die without heires of his bodie, that the lands shall reuert to the donor) that then the habendum shall by authoritie of diuers Bookes bee construed vpon the whole deed, to be a limitation or a declaration, what heires are meant in the premisses, to inherit, and that in that case the reuersion is in the donor.

(c) 21.H.6.7.

(d) 30 *Ass.p.*47. 35.*Ass.p.*14.37.*Ass.*15. 5.*H.*5.6.

(e) *W.*2.*ca.*21.

(f) If a man make a Charter of feoffement of an acre of land to A. and his heires, and another deed of the same acre to A. and the heires of his bodie, and deliuer seisin according to the forme and effect of both deeds: In this case he cannot take a fee simple onely, as some hold, for that liuerie was made according to the deed in taile, as well as to the Charter in fee, neither can the liuerie enure onely to the deed of estate taile with a fee simple expectant, for that liuerie was made as well vpon the deed in fee simple, as the deed in taile. Therefore others hold, That in that case it shall enure by moities, that is, to haue an estate taile in the one moitie, with the Fee simple expectant, and a fee simple in the other moitie: And so the liuerie shall worke immediately vpon both deeds.

(f) 2.*H.*6.25.45.*E.*3.20.

Section 17.

¶ EN mesme le maner est lou tenements sont dones p vn home a vn auter oue vn feme, que est la file ou cousin al donour en frankmariage, l quel doñ ad vn enheritance per ceux parolx (frankmariage) a ceo annexe, coment que ne soit expressement dit, ou reherce en le done, cestascauoir, que les donees auerõt les tenemẽts a eux & a lour heires penter eux deux engendres. Et ceo est dit especial taile, pur ceo que lissue del se-

¶ IN the same maner it is, where tenements are giuen by one man to another, with a wife (which is the daughter or cousin to the giuer) in frankmariage, the which gift hath an enheritance by these words (frankmariage) annexed vnto it, although it bee not expresly said or rehearsed in the gift (that is to say) that the donees shall haue the tenements to them and to their heires betweene them two begotten. And this is called especiall taile, because

¶ A *Vn home oue vn feme.* Albeit the gift is made of the land to the man with his daughter, &c. yet is the gift good to them both in speciall taile, and therefore that of Stephan de la More in (g) 5.E.3. is very remarkeable, where the case was, that Robert gaue the reuersion of lands which Agnes his wife did hold for her life to Stephen de la More, Habendum post mortem dictæ Agnetis in liberum maritagium cum Iohanna filia eiusdem Roberti, and it is adiudged that it is a good estate taile: wherein three things are to be obserued; First that Ioane the daughter tooke with her husband an estate in especiall taile, albeit she were named but vnder a cum, viz. cum Iohanna, &c. 2. That that cum doth come after the habendum, for that it is but all one sentence, 3. That these words, in liberum maritagiũ, doe create an estate of inheritance in speciall taile as Littleton

*Vid.Sect.*19.20.

5.*E.*3.17.
(g) *This case is vouched in Pl. Com.*158. *to bee in* 4.*E.*3. *which being not found in that yeare it is there so left without any further reference, but you shall finde it as aboue said in* 5.*E.*3.17.

tleton saith, Le donee ad vn inheritance per reason de ceux parolz (frankmariage) a ceo

cond feme ne poit inheriter, &c.

the issue of the 2. wife may not inherite.

W.2.ca.1.
19.E.3.tit.taile.1.

annexe, coment que ne soit expressement dit, &c. But this had neede of some interpretation, for if lands be giuen by these words (in frankmariage) according to the rules of Law, then doe these words create an estate of inheritance in speciall taile; for the consideration of mariage is in that case more fauoured in Law than any other consideration: But though the gift bee in these words, yet if it be not consonant to the rules of Law in other things requisite thereunto, there they create but an estate for life. And therefore to speake once for all; Foure things bee incident to a frankmariage. First, that it bee giuen for consideration of mariage either to a man with a woman or, as some haue held, to a woman with a man: For in (h) 6 E.3.33. in Peirs de Saltmarsh his case, a man gaue land to his sonne in Frankmariage, and Fitz N.B 172. taketh the Law so also. And 7.E.4.12. per Moyle against a new opinion in temps H 8.Br.tit. Frankmariage the former bookes being not remembred. Secondly, that the woman or man, that is the cause of the gift (i) be of the blood of the Donor, but it may bee made aswell after mariage as before, and it may be made with a widow, &c. Thirdly, if the gift be made of such a thing as lyeth in tenure, that the Donees hold of the Donor at the time of the estate in Frankmariage made. A rent seruice (k) may be giuen in Frankmariage because it may bee holden. And so may a Rent charge or Rent secke as Fitz N.B. holdeth; and it appeareth in our bookes that a Common was granted in Frankmariage. Fourthly, that the Donees shall hold freely of the Donor till the fourth degree be past. And therefore if land be giuen to a woman, with a sonne of the Donor in Frankmariage, there passeth an inheritance, but if the Donee that is the cause of the gift be not the blood of the Donor, then there passeth but an estate for life if Liuery be made. Also if (l) lands be giuen to a man with a woman of the blood of the Donor in liberum maritagium, the remainder in fee either to a stranger or to the Donees they haue no estate taile, because there is no tenure of the Donor, but if (m) in that case, the remainder had beene limitted to another in taile reseruing the reuersion in fee to the Donor there the said words (in liberum maritagium) create an inheritance because the Donees hold of the Donor. And this is the cause that it is holden, That a man cannot deuise land in Frankmariage because the Donee cannot hold of the Donor. And Cesty que vse before the statute of 27.H.8. could not haue made a gift in Frankmariage because the reuersion was in the Feoffees. (n) And if the Donor doth giue lands in liberum maritagium reseruing a rent, this reseruation shall take no effect till the fourth degree be past, but the Frankmariage is good, for if the reseruation should be good, then could not the Donees haue an Estate taile for want of words of the heires of their bodyes.

(h) 6.E.3.33.
Fitz.N.B.172.
7.E.4.12.
15.E.2. Cui in vita.
Sect.24.
(i) 4.E.3.8.
31.E.1.taile.30.
Bracton.lib.2.cap.7.
(k) 22.R.2.tit.discont.50.
Fitz.N.B.212.
9.H.6.35.b.
W.2.ca.1.acc.
(l) Temps H.8.Br frankm.11
13.E.1. formdon 63.
Vid.32.E.1.tail.25.
2.E.2.Feoffment & faitz.9.
17.E.3.5.a.45.E.3.20.
(m) 20.E.2.aid 174.
31.E.3.Gard 216.
(n) Bracton.lib.2.cap.7.
32.E.1.taile.31.
13.H.4.74.4.H.6.17.
26.Ass.66.31.E.3.garr.29.

¶ *En Frankmariage.* Liberum maritagium, **Free mariage**; Maritagium is taken for Fee taile, and deuideth maritagium into liberum & seruitio obligatum: and herewith agreeth Bracton (o) lib.2.cap.34.& 39. Maritagium est aut liberum aut seruitio obligatum. & lib 2.ca.7.nu. 3 & 4. liberum maritagium dicitur, vbi donator vult quod terra. sic data quieta sit & libera ab omni seculari servitio. And so, before Bracton, said Glanuill. lib.7. ca.18. Maritagium autem aliud nominatur liberum aliud seruitio obnoxium; liberum dicitur maritagium quando aliquis liber homo aliquam partem terræ suæ dat cum aliqua muliere in maritagium, ita quod ab omni servitio terra illa sit quieta, &c. And after both of them Fleta that followed them both, lib.3.cap.1 saith, Est autem quoddam maritagium liberum ab omni servitio solutum donatori vel ejus hæredi, &c. Et est similiter maritagium servitio obligatum & oneratum, &c. And these words (in liberum maritagium) are such words of art, and so necessarily required, as they cannot be expressed by words equipollent, or amounting to as much. As if a man giue lands to a man with his daughter in connubio soluto ab omni servitio, &c. Yet there passeth in this case but an estate for life, for seeing that these words (in liberum maritagium) create an estate of inheritance against the generall rule of Law, the Law requireth that they should be legally pursued. But then it may be demanded if a man had giuen lands at the Common law in libero maritagio, whether had the Donees a fee simple without these words (heires) for that it appeareth by that which hath beene said before that all gifts in taile were fee simple at the Common Law, and that the statute of W.2. did not create any estate in Fee taile but out of an estate in Fee simple. To this it is answered that these words (in liberum maritagium) did create an estate in fee simple at the Common law; and it is holden in 31.E.3. gard.116. Per ceux parolx in frankmariage les donees aueront les terres a eux & a lour heires parenter eux engendres, & ceo est dit especial taile. But yet betweene Donees in Frankmariage and other Donees in speciall taile there be many notable diuersities. If the King giue land to a man and a woman, and the heires of their two bodies, and the woman die without issue, yet shall the man be tenant in taile apres possibilitie? But if the King giue land to a man with a woman of his kindred in a frankmariage and the woman dieth without issue the man in the Kings case shall not hold it for his life because the woman was the cause of the gift, but otherwise

26.Ass p.66 per Wilbye.
(o) Bract lib.2 ca.34. & 39. & lib.2.ca.7.nu.3.& 4.
Glanuill, lib.7.ca.1.& ca.18.
Fleta.lib.3.ca.1.
30.E.1.tit.Formdon.66. adiudg.acc.
31.E.3.tit.Gard.116.
Mirror.cap.2.§.15.acc.
9.H.3.Dower 202.

wife it is in the case of a common parson. If lands be giuen to a man and a woman in especiall taile and they are diuorced causa præcontractus both shall hold the lands for their liues, But in (p) case of frankmariage if they be so diuorced, the woman shall enioy the whole land, because she was the cause of the gift. If lands holden in Socage (q) be giuen in especiall taile and the Donees die the issue being within the age of 14. yeares, (r) the next of kinne of the part of the father or of the part of the mother which can hap the custody shall haue it, but in case of frankmariage the heire of the part of the mother shall haue it, because as it hath beene said, shee was the cause of the gift.

7.H.4.16.

(p) *13.E.3.tit.Ass. 19.E.3.Ass.83. 12.Ass.12. 19. Ass.2. 8.E. Ass.45.*

(q) *Pl.Com.Carrils case.*

(r) *17.H.3.111 Gard.146. 27.E.3 79.*

Section 18.

¶ ET nota, quod hoc verbum (Tallaire) idem est quod ad quandã certitudinem ponere, vel ad quoddam certum hæreditamentum limitare. Et pur ceo q̃ est limit & mis en certaine, quel issue inheritera per force de tiels dones, & come longement lenheritance endurera, il est appell' en Latin, feodũ talliatum, .i. hæreditas in quandam certitudinem limitata. Car si tenant in general taile moruist sans issue, l' donor ou ses heires poiẽt enter cõe en lour reuersion.

AND note that this word (*Talliare*) is the same as, to set to some certaintie, or to limit to some certaine inheritance. And for that it is limitted and put in certaine, what issue shall inherite by force of such gifts, and how long the enheritance shall indure, it is called in Latine, *feodum talliatum, .i. hæreditas in quandam certitudinem limitata.* For if tenant in generall tayle dieth without issue, the Donor or his heires may enter as in their reuersion.

¶ E*T nota.* This, in our Author throughout his three bookes, betokeneth some notable point of instruction worthy of more speciall obseruation which is often (s) vsed by him as you may perceiue by the Sections noted in the margent.

(s) *Sect.* 18.37.42.43.47. 52.64.72.89 90 104 108. 114.116.147.158.161. 168.170.183.254. 279. 346.387.452.467.618. 619.637.642.670.982. 684.711.717.729.738.

¶ *Feodum talliatum .i. hæreditas in quandam certitudinem limitata.* Here our Author doth interpret what feodum talliatum is. Of all the estates tayle most coarcted or restrained that I finde in our bookes, is the estate taile in 39. Ass. Pl 20 where lands were giuen to a man and to his wife and to one heire of their bodies lawfully begotten and to one heire of the body of that heire only. This case being adiudged in the point is an exception (some say) out of the generall rule put before by Littleton. Sect 13, that all estates tailes were fee simple at the Common Law, for (say they) by this limitation (hæredi) in the singular number the Donees had not had a fee simple at the Common law. Vide registrum iudiciale, fo.6. a gift made to a man & hæredi masculo de corpore suo.

West.2.cap.1. Pl.Com.251.a.

39. Ass. pl 20.

Sect.13. Vid.pl.com. fo 29.b.

Regist iudic fo.5

Section 19.

¶ EN mesm le maner est del tenant en special taile, &c. Car en chescun done en le taile sauns pluis ouster dire, le reuersion del fee simple est en le donor. Et les donees &

IN the same manner it is of the tenant in especiall taile, &c. For in euery gift in taile without more saying, the reuersion of the fee simple is in the donor. And the donees and

¶ E*N chescun done en taile sans pluis ouster dire, le reuersion del fee simple est en le donor.* This is wrought by the construction of the statute of W.2. cap.1. which hath turned the fee simple of the Donee into a particular estate of inheritance, and the possibility of the Donor to a reuersion in him expectant vpon the estate taile, so

lour issues ferront al Donor & a ses heires autielx seruices, cōe le donor fait a son Seignior ꝑchein a luy Paramont, forsprise les donees in frankmarriage, les queux tiendront quietment de chescun maner de seruice, sinon que soit per fealtie tanque le quart degree soit passe, & apres ceo q̄ le quart degree soit pass, lissue en le cinqz degree, & issint oustř lauťs des issues apres luy, tiendrōt del donō ou ses heires cōe ils teignōt ouster, cōe il est auāť dit.

their iſſue ſhall doe to the Donor, and to his heires the like ſeruices, as the Donor doth to his Lord next Paramont, except the Donees in Frankmarriage who ſhall hold quietly from all manner of ſeruice (vnleſſe it bee for fealtie) vntill the fourth degree is paſt, and after the fourth degree is paſt, the iſſue in the fift degree, and ſo forth the other iſſues after him, ſhall hold of the Donor or of his heires as they hold ouer, as before is ſaid.

(c) 12.E.4.23. 5.H.7.14. *West.* 2.ca.13. *Pl. Com.* 247. 248.251.562.2.E.2.*tit. resceit.* 147. 33.H.6.27.39.E.3.18.45. E.3.20.

so as there be two inheritances of one land, yet this was doubted in our Bookes (c) & there resolued according to Littleton. But I see no cause wherefore that point should be drawne in question, for at the same Session of Parliament (in which the Statute de donis conditionalibus was made) viz. ca.3. it is expressely said, vel per donum in quo reseruatur reuersio, so as by the iudgement of the same Parliament a reuersion was setled in the Donor.

¶ *Le reuersion del fee simple est en le donor.* A reuersion is where the residue of the estate alwayes doth continue in him that made the particular estate, or where the particular estate is deriued out of his estate, as here in the case of Litt. Tenant in Fee simple, maketh a gift in taile, so it is of a Lease for life, or for yeares. If a man extend Lands by force of a statute Merchant, staple, recognizance or Elegit, he leaueth a reuersion in the Conusor. But since Littleton wrote, the description must be more large vpon the Statute of (a) 27, H.8. for at this day, if a man seised of lands in fee make a Feoffment in fee, (and depart with his whole estate) and limit the vse to his daughter for life, and after her decease, to the vse of his sonne, in taile, and after to the vse of the right heires of the Feoffor. In this case, albeit he departed with the whole fee simple by the feoffment, and limitted no vse to himselfe, yet hath he a reuersion (b) for whensoeuer the Ancestor takes an estate for life, and after a limitation is made to his right heires, the right heires shall not be purchasors. And here in this case when the limitation is to his right heires, and right heire hee cannot haue during his life (for non est heres viuentis) the Law doth create an vse in him during his life, vntill the future vse commeth in esse, and consequently the right heires cannot bee purchasors, and no diuersitie when the Law creates the estate for life, and when the partie. And all this was adiudged betweene (c) Fenwick and Mitford in the Kings Bench; and if the limitation had beene to the vse of himselfe for life, and after to the vse of another in taile, and after to the vse of his owne right heires, the reuersion of the fee had beene in him, because the vse of the fee continued euer in him; and the Statute doth execute the possession to the vse in the same plight, quality and degree as the vse was limited.

(a) 27.H.8.ca.10.

(b) 38.E.3.26.27.E.3.age 118.24.E.3.36. 40.E.3.

(c) Tr. 31. Eliz. inter Fenwicke & Mitford. 32.H.8. gard. 93. 28.H.8. Dier. 8.9.10. &c. Buckenhams case. 5. Marie. Dier 163.

(d) 1.H.5.8.4.H.6.20. 9. Eliz. Dier. Bromleys case.

(d) If a man make a gift in taile or a lease for life, the remainder to his own right heires, this remainder is void, & he hath the reuersion in him, for the Ancestor during his life, beareth in his bodie (in iudgement of law) all his heires, and therefore it is truly said that Hæres est pars antecessoris. And this appeareth in a common case, that if land be giuen to a man and his heires, all his heires are so totally in him; as he may giue the lands to whom he will.

(e) Dier. 5. Marie 156. Grefwolds case adiudge. Bendlowes Seriant in his report agreeth.

(e) So it is if a man be seised of lands in Fee and by indenture make a Lease for life, the remainder to the heires male of his owne bodie, this is a void remainder, for the Donor cannot make his owne right heire a purchaser of an Estate taile without departing of the whole Fee simple out of him: as if a man make a Feoffment in fee to the vse of himselfe for life, and then to the vse of the heires males of his bodie, this is a good Estate taile executed in himselfe, and the limitation is good by way of vse, because it is raised out of the state of the Feffees, which the Feffor departed with, and that is apparant; for a limitation of vse to himselfe had without question beene good.

(f) 20. Eliz. Dier.

(f) If a man make a Feoffment in fee to the vse of himselfe in taile, and after to the vse of the Feoffee in fee, the Feffee hath no reuersion, but in nature of a remainder, albeit the Feoffor haue the Estate taile executed in him by the Statute, and the Feoffee is in by the Common Law, which is worthy of obseruation.

To conclude this point (g) whosoeuer is seised of land, hath not only the Estate of the land in him, but the right to take profits, which is in nature of the vse, and therefore when he makes a Feoffment in Fee without valuable consideration to diuers particular vses, so much of the vse, as he disposeth not, is in him, as his ancient vse in point of reuerter. As if a man be seised of two Acres, the one holden by Knights seruice, by prioritie, and the other by Knights seruice holden by posterioritie, and maketh a feoffment in fee of both Acres to the vse of himselfe and his heires, the old vse continued in him, and the prioritie and posterioritie remayne. So it is of lands of part of the mother, the vse shall goe to the heire of the part of the mother, which could not be, if it were not the old vse, but a thing newly created: the like law of lands, of the custome of Boroughenglish Gauelkind, &c.

(g) 13.*H*.7.6. 28.*H*.8.*Dier*.12.

5.*E*.4.7. *Lib*.1.76.84.85.100.&c. *Chudley*. *Lib*.2.56.57.58.77.78. *Lib*.4.22. *Lib*.6.34.43.

¶ *Les dones & lour issues serront al donor & a ses heires autiels seruices come le donor fait a son seignior procheine a luy paramount.* The reason of this is, that when by construction of the said Statute, there was a reuersion setled in the Donor for that the Donee had an Estate of inheritance, the Iudges resolued that hee should hold of his Donor, as his Donor held ouer: as if the Tenant had made a Feoffment in Fee at the Common Law, the Feoffee should haue holden of the Feoffor as he held ouer; and before the Statute of W.2. the Donee had holden of the Donor as of his person, and now of him as of his reuersion: but if a man make a Lease for life, or yeares, and reserue nothing, hee shall haue fealtie only and no rent, though the Lessor hold ouer by rent, &c. And this that Littleton saith, is regularly true, if the Donor maketh no speciall reseruation, for then the speciall reseruation excludes the tenure which the Law would create. As if Tenant by Knights seruice maketh a gift in taile reseruing Fealtie and Rent, the Donee shall hold in Socage, by Fealtie, and Rent, and not by Knights seruice. But if a man hold land of the King in grand Seriantie, and maketh a guift in taile generally, in this case the Donee shall not hold of the Donor by graund Seriantie, because no man can hold by graund Seriantie, but of the King only, as hereafter shall be said, and therefore seeing graund Seriantie doth include Knights Seruice, he shall in that case hold of the Donor by Knights Seruice. If a man seised of land in the right of his wife holden by Knights Seruice giueth the same lands in taile generally, the Donee shall not hold of him by Knights Seruice, because his wife held the land, and he had nothing but in her right. And in that case the Baron hath gained a new reuersion by wrong, and therefore such a Donee shall doe Fealtie only.

A. seised of two acres of land, holdeth the one of B. by Knights Seruice, and twelue pence Rent, and the other of C. in Socage and one pennie Rent, and makes a gift in taile of both Acres without any expresse reseruation of any tenure, In this case the Donor hath but one reuersion. And yet he shall make seuerall auowries, because there be seuerall tenures created by Law, in respect of the seuerall tenures ouer: and the auowrie is made in respect of the tenures.

Lord, Mesne and Tenant, the Tenant holdeth by foure pence, and the Mesne by twelue pence, the Tenant makes a gift in taile without reseruing any thing, by reason whereof he holdeth by foure pence, in respect of the tenure ouer. Afterwards the reuersion escheate, now shall the Donee hold by twelue pence, for the Mesnaltie which was foure pence is extinct, and the law reserued the tenure vpon the gift in taile, in respect of the Mesnaltie, and when the Mesnaltie is extinct, the former Rent betweene the Donor and Donee is extinct also, and then by the same reason that the Donee shall take aduantage, if the Donor by release or confirmation had holden by lesser Seruices, by the same reason he shall be preiudiced, when he holdeth by greater seruices.

49.*E*.3.10.

¶ *Forsprise les donees en Frankmarriage.* It is to bee vnderstood, that although the Land be giuen in liberum maritagium, in free marriage generally, yet first the Law doth make a limitation of this word (free) viz. till the fourth degree bee past, for the reason that our Author here yeeldeth. And 2. albeit it bee free marriage, yet the Donees and their issues vntill the fourth degree be past shall doe fealtie, for that is incident to euerie tenure (except Frankealmoigne) and cannot be separated from it, and therefore the Donees and their issues shall hold it as freely till the fourth degree be past, as the Donor can make it. See more of this in the Chapter of Frankalmoigne.

Bracton.*lib*.2.*fol*.21. *Britton*.*cap*.119. *Fleta lib*.3.*cap*.11.& *lib*.6.*cap*.2. *Vide Sect*.17.20.

Sect. 20.

¶ ET les degrees en frankmarriage serrót accópts en tiel maner, s. de

AND the degrées in frankmariage shal bee accounted in this manner, *viz*. from

¶ WHere Littleton saith (a) that the Donees in frankmariage shall hold by fealtie only vntill the fourth degree

(a) *Vide Sect*.17.19.138. 268.269.271.733.

degree be past & then the issue in the fift degree shall hold of the Donor as the Donor holdeth ouer, (b) Vide Bracton vbi supra, Ita quod ille cui terra sic data fuit, nullum inde faciat seruitium vsque ad tertium hæredem & vsque quartum gradum, ita quod tertius hæres sit inclusus. And herewith also agreeth, Fleta vbi supra. And the (c) learning of degrees set out in the Ciuill and Canon Law (wherein I finde some difference) is worth the knowledge, to the end that Littleton and the law in this case may the better bee vnderstood, which I will deuide into certain rules, whereof the first is; That a person added to a person in the line of Consanguinitie maketh a degree. And it is to bee vnderstood that a line is threefold, viz. the line ascending, discending, and collaterall. And first for example, of the ascending line, take the Sonne and adde the Father, and it is one degree ascending, adde the Grandfather to the Father, and it is a second degree ascending.

(b) *Glanuil. lib. 7. cap* 18. *Bract. lib* 2 *fol.* 21. *Britton. cap.* 119. *Fleta lib.* 3. *cap.* 11. & *lib.* 6. *cap.* 2.

(c) *Vide* 10. *E.* 3. *tit. mortwry.* 157. 31. *E.* 3. *cessauit.* 22. 31. *E.* 3. *gard.* 116. 21. *H.* 7. 30.

1. *Rule.*

So as how many persons there be, take away one, and you haue the number of degrees. If there be foure persons it is the third degree, if fiue the fourth, for one must exceed, and then you haue the degree. Likewise by the discending, take the Father, and adde the sonne, and it is one degree, then take the Sonne and adde the Grandchild, and it is the second degree, and so likewise further, wherein obserue that the Father, Sonne and Grandchild, albeit there are three persons, yet they make but two degrees, because (as it hath beene said) one must exceed for making a degree.

It is to bee noted, that in euery line the person must be reckoned from whom the computation is made. And there is no difference betweene the Canon and Ciuill Law in the ascending and discending line, for those whom the Ciuilians doe reckon in the second degree, the Canonists doe reckon in the first, and those whom they place in the fourth, these place

le Donor a les donees en frankmarriage, le primer degree, pur ceo que la feme que est vn des donees couient estre file, soer, ou aut cousin a le donor. Et de les donees tanque a lour issue il serra accompt le second degree, & de lour issue tanque a son issue, le tierce degree, & issint ouster &c. Et la cause est, pur ceo que apres chescun tiel done les issues queux veignont de le donor, & les issues queux veignont de les donees apres le quart degree passe de ambideux parties en tiel forme destre accompt, poyent enter eux per la ley de saint Esglise entermarie. Et que le donee en frankmarriage serra dit le prime degree de les quart degrees home poit veier en vn plee sur vn briefe de Droit de Garde P. 21. E. 3. Lou le Pl. counta, que son tresaiel fuit seisie de cert terre, &c. & ceo tenust dun autre per seruice de chiualer, &c. quel dona la terre a vn Rafe Holland ouesque sa soer en frankmariage, &c.

the Donor to the Donees in frankmarriage the first degree, because the wife, that is one of the donees ought to be daughter, sister, or other cosen to the Donor, & from the donees vnto their issue shall be accounted the second degree, and from their issue vnto their issue the third degree, and so forth. And the reason is, because that after euery such gift, the issues of the Donor, & the issue of the Donees after the fourth degree past of both parties in such forme to bee accounted may by the Law of the holy Church entermarrie. And that the Donee in frankmarriage shall be said to bee the first degree of the foure degrees, a man may see in a plea vpon a Writ of Right of Ward, P. 21. *E.* 3. where the Pl. pleadeth that his great Grandfather was seised of certaine Lands, &c. and held the same of another by Knight Seruice, &c. who gaue the Land to one *Raphe Holland* with his sister in Frankmarriage, &c.

in the second. Therefore if wee will know in what degree two of kindred doe stand according to the Ciuile Law, wee must begin our reckoning from one, by ascending to the person from whom both are branched, and then by discending to the other to whom wee doe count, and it will appeare in what degree they are. For example, In brothers & sisters sonnes, take one of them and ascend to his father, there is one degree from the father to the grandfather, that is the second degree, then descend from the grandfather to his sonne, that is the third degree, then from his sonne to his sonne, that is the fourth. But by the Canon Law there is another computation, for the Canonists doe euer begin from the stocke, namely from the person of whome they doe discend, of whose distance the question is. For example, if the question be, In what degree the sonnes of two brothers stand by the Canon Law: wee must begin from the grandfather, and discend to one sonne, that is one degree; then discend to his sonne, that is another degree, then descend againe from the grandfather to his other sonne, that is one degree; then discend to his sonne, that is a second degree, so in what degree either of them are distant from the common stocke, in the same degree they are distant betweene themselues: And if they bee not equally distant, then wee must obserue another rule. In what degree the most remote is distant from the common stock, in the same degree they are distant betweene themselues, and so the most remote maketh the degree. And albeit the donee be a Cosine in the third or fourth degree from the donor, yet in this computation it maketh the first degree: Gradus dicitur a gradiendo, quia gradiendo ascenditur & discenditur. And thus much of the Ciuile and Cannon Law is necessarie to the knowledge of the Common law in this point: And herewith agreeth our Author in the words following:

¶ *Les issues queux veignont de le donor, & les issues queux veignont de les donees apres le 4. degree passe dambideux parties in tiel forme deste accout poient enter eux per le Ley de Saint Esglise entermarrier.* (De Saint Esglise) (d) So as hereby it appeareth, That the computation of the degrees in this case, must bee according to the Cannon Law. But it is necessarie to bee knowne concerning marriages betweene persons of kindred one to another, that it is enacted (e) by the Statute of 32. H. 8. that no reseruation or prohibition (Gods Law except) shall trouble or impeach any marriage without the Leuiticall degrees.

(d) Brit ca. 119. Accord. Flet. lib. 3. ca. 11. & li. 6. c. 2.

(e) 32. H. 8. ca. 38.

The case vouched by Littleton in 31. E. 3. you shall find abridged by Fitzh tit. gard 116. And albeit this yeare of 31. E. 3. was neuer in print till Fitzhebert did abridge it and publish it in print anno 11 H. 8. and goeth vnder the name of broken yeares, yet heere it appeareth by our Author, that the same is of authoritie in Law, as hereafter also in other places shall bee obserued.

Sect. 21.

¶ ET touts ceux tailes auãtdits, sont specifies en l' dit estatute de W. 2. Auxy sont diuers auts estates en le taile, coment q̄ ne sont specifies per expresse parols in le dit estatut, mes ils sont prises per le equitie de l' dit Statute. Sicome Terres sont dones a vn home & a ses heires males de son corps engendres, en

AND all these Entailes aforesaid be specified in the sayde Statute of *W.* 2. Also there bee diuers other estates in taile, though they bee not by expresse words specified in the said Statute, but they are taken by the equitie of the same statute. As if lands be giuen to a man, and to his heires males of his bodie begotten, in this case his issue male shal

¶ *ET touts ceux Tailes auaunt-dits sont specifies en le dit Statute de Westminster* 2. And so it appeareth by the sayd Statute, Auxy sont diuers auters estates en le taile, &c. And herewith agreeth Carbonels Case, 33. Edw. 3. titulo Taile 5.

That the cases of the statute are set downe but for examples of estates taile, generall and speciall, and to exclude other estates taile. 3. E. 3. 32. 18. Ass. p. 5. 18. E. 3. 46. 1. Mar. Dyer 46. Pl. Com. Seignior Barkleys case, fo. 251. For, Exempla illustrant non restringunt legem.

3. E. 3. 32. 18. E. 3. 46. 18. *Ass. p.* 5. 1. *Mar. Dy.* 46. *Pl. Com.* 251.

¶ *Equitie* is a construction made by the Iudges, that cases out of the letter of a Stat. yet being within the same mischiefe, or cause of the making of the same, shall bee within the same remedie that the Statute prouideth: And the reason hereof is, for that the Law maker could not possibly set downe all cases in expresse termes, Equitas est conuenientia rerum quæ cuncta coæquiparat, & quæ in paribus rationibus paria iura & iudicia desiderat. And againe, Equitas est perfecta quædam ratio quæ ius scriptum interpretatur & emendat, nulla scriptura comprehensa, sed solum in vera ratione consistens. Equitas est quasi equalitas. Bonus judex secundum equum & bonum iudicat, & equitatem stricto iuri præfert. Et ius respicit æquitatem.

tiel case s̃ issue male inherita, & le issue female ñ vnq; enherita pas, vncor in l's auts tailes auantdits auterment est.

inherit, and the Iſſue female ſhall neuer inherit, and yet in the other entailes aforeſaid, it is otherwiſe.

Bract. lib. 4. fol. 186. (b) 18. Aſſ p. 5. 18. E. 3. 46. 33. E. 3. tit. Taile 5. 3. E. 3. 32. Pl. Com. Seignieur Barkleys caſe, 1. Mar. Dy. 46. V. Sect. 24.

¶ *Sicome terres sont done a vn home & a les* (b) *heires males de son corps engendres, en tiel case son issue male inheritera, & lissue female ne vnques inheritera, &c.* This shall be explained afterward, Sect. 24.

Sect. 22. & 23.

¶ These two Sections, or any thing therein, do neede no explanation, in respect they shall be also explaned hereafter in the next Section, sauing onely these words (queux doient inheriter) are verie obseruable, for they implie a diuersity betweene a discent and a purchase. For when a man giueth lands to a man and the heires females of his body, and dyeth hauing issue a son and a daughter, the daughter shall inherit, for the will of the donor (the Statute working with it) shall bee obserued. But in case (g) of a purchase it is otherwise: For if A. haue issue a sonne and a daughter, and a lease for life be made, the remainder to the heires females of the bodie of A. A. dieth, the heire female can take nothing, because she is not heire; for shee must bee both heire and heire female, which she is not, because the brother is heire, and therefore the will of the giuer cannot be obserued, because heere is no gift, and therefore the statute cannot worke thereupon. And so it is if a man hath a a sonne and a daughter, and dieth, and lands bee giuen to the daughter, and the heires females of the bodie of her father, the daughter shall take

(g) 9. H. 6. 24. 11. H. 6. 13. 14 37. H. 8. Br. tit. Done 42. Tit. meſme 1. & 40. Dyer 23. El. 374. Shelleys caſe lib. 1. fo.

¶ In m̃ l' manner lest, si tres ou tenemẽts soint dones a vn hõe & a les h'res females de son corps engendres; en tiel case son issue female luy inherita p force & form de l' dit done, & nemy issue male, pur ceo que en tiels cases de dones faits en le taile, queux doient enheriter, & quex nemi, la volunt dl donor sert obserue.

IN the ſame manner it is, if Lands or Tenements bee giuen to a man, and to his heires females of his bodie begotten; In this caſe his iſſue female ſhall inherit by force and forme of the ſaid gift, and not his iſſue male. For in ſuch caſes of gifts in taile, the wil of the Donor ought to bee obſerued, who ought to inherit, and who not.

¶ Et en le case q̃ terres ou tenements sont dones a vn hõe, & a ses heires males d' s̃ corps issuants, & il ad issue deux fits, & deuy, & leign fitz entra come h' male, & ad issue file & deuy, s̃ frer aũa la t'r, & nemi la file, pur

ANd in caſe where lands or tenemẽts be giuen to a man, and to the heires of his bodie, and hee hath iſſue two ſonnes, and dieth, and the eldeſt ſon enter as heire male, and hath iſſue a daughter, and dieth; his brother ſhall haue the land, &

nothing

ceo que le frere est heire male. Mes autermt sra en auters tailes qux sont specifies en le dit Statute.

not the daughter, for that the brother is heire male. But otherwise it is in the other entailes, which are specified in the sayd Statute.

nothing but an estate for life, because there is no such person, she being not heire. But where a gift is made to a man, and to the heires female of his bodie, there the Donee being the first taker, is capable by purchase, and the heire female by discent, secundum formam doni: And therefore Littleton purposely added these words, Queux doient inheriter.

*Sect.*24.

¶ Auxy si tẽs soient donẽs a vn hõe, & a ses hẽs males de son corps ingendres, & il ad issue file, q̃l ad issue fits & duy, & puis apres le donee deuie, en cest case le fits de la file ne inheritera passe p force de le taile, pur cẽ que quecunque que serra inherit per force dun done en le taile fait as hẽs males, couient conueier son discent tout per les Heyres Males. Mes en tiel case le donor poet ent p cẽ q̃ le donee est mort sans issue male en la Ley, entaunt que lissue del file ne poet conueyer a luy mesme le discent per Heyre male.

Also if lands be giuen to a man and to the heires males of his bodie, and he hath issue a daughter, who hath issue a sonne, and dieth, and after the donee die; In this case, the son of the daughter shall not inherit by force of the entaile, because whosoeuer shall inherit by force of a gift in taile made to the heires males, ought to conuey his discent wholly by the heires males. Also in this case the donor may enter, for that the donee is dead without issue male in the law, insomuch as the issue of the daughter cannot conuey to himself the discent by an heire male.

¶ *Quecunque serra enheriter per force dun done en Taile, &c.* Vide Tr. (h) 28. H.6. Tit. Deuise 18. (Which is not in the booke at large, but written verbatim out of Stathã) If a man deuise lands to a man, and to the heires males of his bodie, and hath issue a daughter, which hath issue a sonne, this sonne shall be inheritable, and notwithstanding in a gift in taile the Law is otherwise, and that by the opinion of all the Judges, in the Exchequer Chamber. But I hold this case to be ill reported, vnlesse you will refer the opinion of the Judges to the gift in taile last mentioned. For first, albeit a Deuise may create an Inheritance by other words than a gift can, yet cannot a Deuise direct an inheritance to discend against the rule of Law. Secondly, there is no intent of the deuisor appearing, that the sonne of the daughter should, against the rule of Law, inherit, and the Statute prouideth, that voluntas Donatoris, &c. obseruetur. And I haue heard this case often denied to bee Law, both in the Kings bench, and in the Common pleas, Vide Pl. Coment. 414. b. And so it is (i) mutatis mutandis, when a gift in taile is made to a man, and to his heires females of his bodie, and he hath issue a sonne, who hath issue a daughter, this daughter shall neuer inherit, because she must conuey by discent from females. And for the reason hereof, see a notable Case in 15. E. 2. tit. Corone 385. Where it is adiudged (as before it had beene) That the sonne of a female should haue an appeale of the death of a cosine; and yet the daughter her selfe should neuer haue had it. But there it is agreed, that the sonne of a female (k) in a Libertate probanda, should be no witnesse or proofe against the issue of the male. And the reason of this diuersitie is verie obseruable: For by the Common Law the female might

Vide Sect.719.
(h) 1. H.6.24 11. H.6.13.14 28. H.6. tit. Deuise 18. Statham tit. Deuise. Pl. Com. in in Scholast. case, 414. b. 20. H.6.43. 37. H.8. Br. tit. Done & Rem. 61. tit. nosme 1. & 40.

(i) 11. H.6.13.

15. E.2. Tit. Cor. 386.

(k) *Mirror c.2. §.7. Vi. Glanuile lib 14. cap. 3.*

Vid. Seignior de la Warre case. lib. 11. fo. 1.

might haue had an appeale as heire to any of her Ancestors, as well as the male. But by the Statute of magna carta, cap. 34. Nullus capietur aut imprisonetur propter appellam feminæ de morte alterius quam viri sui, which restraineth not the sonne of the female. And there Scrope saith Per tout le Serjant d' Angliterre, that is, by all the Judges of the Coife in England, it was awarded, that the issue of the female should haue an appeale for the death of his cousin. But in a libertate probanda, the issue of the blood female shall not be receiued to proue Villenage in the issue of the blood male, for the mother was disabled by the Common law, & the mother might be a neife De en & trene, that is of the water and whip of three corde, (meaning such a bondwoman as is used to seruile workes and correction) and enfranchised by her husband.

17. E. 4. 1.
30. H. 6. 43.

All which appeareth in the said booke. And it is holden in 17. E. 4. 1. that if a man bee slaine which hath no heire of the part of his father, that his uncle of the part of his mother shall haue the appeale, and yet he must of necessity make his conueyance by a woman. Vid. 20. H. 6. fo. 33. the question suddenly demanded and debated, and no consideration or mention had of the said former judgements and authorities; there it is compared to a gift in taile to a man and to his heires males of his body, that the heire male of the daughter shall not inherit which hath no affinitie to it, and yet the authoritie of the bookes is great, for it is by the assent of all the Justices of the one bench and the other in the Exchequer chamber, and therefore I leaue the learned and judicious reader to his owne judgement.

(l) Stanford, 58. b. 15. E. 2. tit. Coron. 384.

(l) Vid. Stanford. 58. b 15. E. 2. 384. If a man giue lands to a man and to the heires males of his body begotten, remainder to him and to his heires females on his body begotten, the Donee hath issue a sonne who hath issue a daughter, who hath issue a sonne, this sonne is not inheritable to either of both these estates taile, because as Littleton saith, The Male must make his conueyance only by males and so must the Females by Females. But in this case the land shall reuert to the Donor, And therefore the safest way when a man will entaile his lands to the heires males and females of his body, is to limit the first estate to him and the heires males of his body, the remainder to him and to the heires of his body, and then all his issues whatsoeuer are inheritable. But if A. hath issue a sonne and a daughter and dieth, and the sonne hath issue a daughter and dieth, and a Lease for life is made, the remainder to the heires females of the body of A. In this case the daughter of A. shall not take causa qua supra. But albeit the daughter of the sonne maketh her conueyance by a male she shall take an estate taile by purchase, for she is heire and a female, but if lands be deuised to one for life, the remainder to the next heire male of B in taile, and B. hath issue two daughters and each of them hath issue a sonne and the father and daughters die, some say this remainder is voide for the uncertaintie, some say that the eldest shall take it because he is worthiest, and others say that both of them shal take for that they both make but one heire.

11. H. 6. 13.
9. H. 6. 25.

If lands be giuen to a man and to his heires males or females of his body hee hath an estate in generall taile in him.

Section 25.

EN mesme le maner est, lou tenements sont done a un hōe, & a sa feme, & a les heires males de lour deux corps engendres, &c.

IN the same manner it is, where lands are giuen to a man and his wife, and to the heires males of their two bodyes begotten, &c.

21. E. 3. Formdon. 25.

¶ A *Vn home, & a sa feme.* But what if tenements be giuen to a man, and to a woman being not his wife, and to the heires males of their two bodies, they haue also an estate taile, albeit they bee not married at that time. And so it is if lands bee giuen to a man which hath a wife, and to a woman which hath a husband, and the heires of their two bodies, they haue presently an estate taile (m) for the possibility that they may marry.

(m) 15 H. 7. 10. Lib. 1. Dilon & frems case. 40. Ass. p. 13.
(n) 24. E. 3. 29. a.

But if lands be giuen to two husbands and their wiues, and to the heires of their bodies begotten (n) they shall take a joynt estate for life and seuerall inheritances, viz. the one husband and his wife the one moitie, and the other husband and wife the other moitie, and no crosse remainder or other possibility shall be allowed by law, where it is once settled and take effect.

(o) 7. H. 4. 16. 16. E. 3. 78. Littleton fo. 66. 15. Eliz. Dier. 326.

But if lands bee giuen to a man and two women and the heires of their bodies begotten, (o) In this case they haue a joynt estate for life and euery of them seuerall inheritance, because they cannot haue one issue of their bodies, neither shall there be by any construction a possibility upon a possibilitie, viz. that he shall marry the one first and then the other.

(p) 44. E. 3. tit. taile. 13.

And the same Law it is (p) when land is giuen to two men and one woman, and to the heires of their bodies begotten.

Section 26.27.

26.27. These two Sections need no explanation at all.

¶ Item si tenēts soient dones a vn home & a sa feme, & a les heires del corps del home engendres, en c̄ case le barō ad estate en le taile generall, et la feme forsque estate pur terme de vie.

Also if tenements be giuen to a man and to his wife, and to the heires of the body of the man; In this case the husband hath an estate in generall taile, and the wife but an estate for terme of life.

¶ Item si tres soient dones a le baron & sa feme, & a les heires le baron, quux il engendra de corps sa feme, en ceo case le baron, ad estate en le taile special, & la feme forsque pur terme de vie.

Also if lands bee giuen to the husband and wife, and to the heires of the husband which hee shall beget on the body of his wife, In this case the husband hath an estate in especiall taile and the wife but an estate for life.

Sect. 28.

¶ Et si le done soit fait al baron & a sa feme, & a les heires la feme de sa corps per le baron engendres, donques la feme ad estate en special taile, & le baron forsque pur terme de vie: Mes si terres sont dones a le baron & a la feme, & a les heires que le baron engendra de corps la feme, en ceo case ambideux ont estate en la taile, pur ceo que cest parol (heires) nest limit a lun pluis que a lauter.

And if the gift be made to the husband and to his wife, and to the heires of the body of the wife by the husband begotten, there the wife hath an estate in speciall taile, & the husband but for terme of life: but if lands be giuen to the husband & the wife, and to the heires which the husband shall beget on the body of the wife, in this case both of them haue an estate taile, because this word (heirs) is not limitted to the one more then to the other.

¶ *Heires.* This word (heires) is nomen operatiuum, to which of the Donees it is limitted, it createth the estate taile; but if it incline no more to the one than to the other, then both doe take as here Littleton putteth the case. And therewith accordeth the case of (q) 3.E.3. where it appeareth; Quod Robertus de S. dedit Iohanni de Riperijs & Matildæ vxori eius, & hæredibus quos idem Iohannes de corpore ipsius Matildæ procrearet, &c. and this adiudged to be an estate in especial taile in them both, because the state is equally tailed to the heires of the baron as to the heires of the wife. If lands be giuen to the husband and the wife, and to the heires of the body of the suruiuour, the gift is good, and the suruiuour shall haue an estate in taile generall, but the estate taille vesteth not till there be a suruiuour. And hereby it appeareth (r) that a gift made to a man and to the heires of his body, is as good as to his heires of his body.

19.H.6.75.a. Regist. 239. 17.E.2.tit. Taile 23. 3.E.3.32. 4.E.3.43. 5.E.3.29.b.& 34.a. 21.E.3.43. 12.H.4.1.

(q) 3.E.3.32. 21.E.3.43. 19.H.6.95. per Hody.

Regist. 239.

(r) 20.E.3. Bre. 377.

Section 29.

Item si terre soit done a un home & a ses heires que il engendra de corps sa feme, en ceo case le baron ad estate en especial taile, & la feme nad riens.

Also if land bee giuen to a man and to his heires which he shall beget on the body of his wife, In this case the husband hath an estate in especiall taile, and the wife hath nothing.

20.H.6.36.
(f) Lib.1.fo.140.b. Chaulrights case adiudge.

¶ This is euident by that which hath been said and needeth no explanation. But it hath beene said, (f) that if a man giue land to another and to his heires of the body of such a woman lawfully begotten, that this is no estate taile for the uncertainty by whom the heires shall bee begotten, for that the brother of the Donee or other cousin may haue issue by the woman which may be heire to the Donee, and estates in taile must be certaine. Therefore our Author to make it plaine in all his cases added to these words (his heires) which hee shall ingender. But that opinion is since our Author wrote ouer-ruled, and that estate adiudged to be an estate taile, and begotten shall be necessarily intended begotten by the Donee.

Section 30.

Item si home ad issue fits, & deuie, & terre est done al fits, & a les heires de corps son pier engendres, ceo est bone taile, & uncore le pier fuit mort al temps de la done. Et mults auters estates en taile y sont per le equitie del dit estatute que icy ne sont specifies.

Also if a man hath issue a sonne and dieth, and land is giuen to the sonne, and to the heires of the body of his father begotten, this is a good entaile, and yet the father was dead at the time of the gift. And there bee many other estates in the taile by the equity of the said statute, which bee not here specified.

17.E.2.Taile 23. 2.E.3.1. tit.Taile 7.4.& 5.Ph.& Mar.Dier 156. 12.H.4.1. 15.H.7.10.

¶ *Si home ad issue fits & deuie, &c.* John de Mandevile by his wife, Roberge had issue Robert and Mawde, Michael de Morevill gaue certaine lands to Roberge and to the heires of Iohn Mandeuile her late husband on her body begotten, and it was adiudged that Roberge had an estate but for life, and the fee taile vested in Robert (heires of the body of his father being a good name of purchase) and that when he died without issue, Mawde the daughter was tenant in taile as heir of the body of her father per formam doni, and the Formedon which shee brought supposed, Quod post mortem prefatæ Robergiæ & Roberti filij & hæredis ipsius Iohannis Mandauile & hæred' ipsius Iohannis de prefata Robergia per præfatum Iohannem procreat, prefat' Manlda filiæ predict' Iohannis de prefatâ Robergia per præfatum Iohannem procreata sorori & hæredi predicti Roberti discendere debet per formam donationis predict'. And yet in truth the land did not discend unto her from Robert but because she could haue no other writ, it was adiudged to be good. In which case it is to be obserued that albeit Robert being heire tooke an estate taile by purchase, and the daughter was no heire of his body at the time of the gift, yet she recouered the land per formam doni, by the name of heire of the body of her father, which, notwithstanding her brother was and he was capable at the time of the gift; and therefore when the gift was made she tooke nothing, but in expectancie, when she became heire per formam doni. But where a man by deede gaue lands to Emme late wife of John Master, habendum & tenendum predict' Emme & hæredibus Iohannis Master de corpore eiusdem Emme procreat'. In that case the sonne and heire of John Master begotten on the body of Emme tooke no estate with Emme in the lands because he was named after the Habendum.

5.H.4.3.a.

If a man hath issue two daughters, and dieth seised of two acres of land in Fee simple, and the one Coparcener giueth her part to her sister, and to the heires of the body of her father, In this case the Donee hath an estate taile in the moity of the Donors part, for the Donee is not entire heire but the Donor is heire with the Donee, and shee cannot giue to the heires of her owne body, and the Donee hath the other moity of her sisters part for life. If a man hath issue a sonne and a daughter, and dieth, and land is giuen to the daughter and to the heires females

of

of the body of the father, she taketh but an estate for life because she is not heire female to take by purchase as before hath beene said.

¶ *Et a les heires de corps le pier.* **These words** (les heires) **are observable**, for if they were (ses heires) it clearely altereth the case. And therefore if lands be giuen to the sonne and to his heires of the body of his father, the sonne cannot take as heire of the body of his father, because the grant is to him and to his heires, &c. and consequently he hath a Fee simple. But if there be Grandfather, Father and Sonne, and the father dieth, and lands bee giuen to the Sonne, and to the heires of the body of the Grandfather, this is a good estate taile in the Sonne, so as Litleton did put his case of the Father but for an example.

¶ *Et mults auters estates en le tayle y sont, &c.* **This needeth no explanation.**

Section 31.

¶ Mes si home done terres ou tenements a vn auter, a auer & tener a luy & a ses heires males, ou a ses heires females, il a que tiel done est fait ad fee simple, pur ceo que nest my limit per le done de quel corps lissue male ou female issera, & issint ne poit en ascun maner estre prise per lequitie del dit estatute & pur ceo il ad fee simple.

BVt if a man giue Lands or Tenements to another, To haue and to hold to him and to his heires males, or to his heires females, he to whom such a gift is made, hath a Fee simple, because it is not limited by the gift, of what bodie the issue male or female shall be, and so it cannot in any wise bee taken by the equitie of the said Statute, and therefore he hath a Fee simple.

¶ *Terres ou Tenements.* **This** rule extendeth but to Lands or Tenements, and not to the Inheritance that Noblemen and Gentlemen haue in their Armories or Armes. For where the Nobleman or Gentleman hath a Fee simple in his Armories or Armes, yet is the same discendible to the heires males lineall or collaterall. For albeit a Female be heire at the Common Law, yet the Shield, Armories and Armes discend vnto them that are able to beare them (farre exceeding the nature of Gauelkind, but with seuerall differences.) And all the females of that Family in respect that they be of the same bloud, may in a losenge or vnder a Curtaine manifest of what Family they bee by expressing the Armories and Armes beelonging to that Family, and the husband of them may impale them or quarter them with their owne as the case shall require. And for distinction and better explanation hereof. If the King by his Letters Patents giueth lands or Tenements to a man, and to his heires males; the grant is void, for that the King is deceiued in his grant, in asmuch as there can be no such inheritance of Lands or Tenements as the King intended to grant. But if the King for reward of seruice granteth Armories or Armes to a man, and to his heires males without saying (of the bodie) this is good, and as hath beene said they shall discend accordingly. 18.H.8.tit.Patents. Br.104.

If a man by his last will deuise Lands or Tenements to a man and to his heires males, this by construction of Law is an Estate taile, the Law supplying these words (of his bodie.) Vide the Princes (t) Case where it appeareth that an Act of Parliament may limit an Inheritance of Lands or Tenements, otherwise then Common Law would doe, and create a new Estate of Inheritance, and many Authorities in Law there cited worthy of note and obseruation. Rot. Parliam. anno 1.E.4.nu.26. The (u) Duchie of Lancaster is intailed to King Edward the fourth and his heires Kings of England. And King Henrie the sixt did by his Letters Patents grant Iohanni filio Iohannis Talbot quod ipse & hæredes sui Domini manerij de Kingston Lisle in comitatu Berk. exnunc. Domini & Barones de Lisle Nobiles & Proceres regni habeantur, teneantur, & reputentur, &c. by this he had a Fee simple qualified in the Dignitie.

27.H.8.27.

(t) *Lib.8.fol.1. The Princes case.*

21.E.3.4. 22.E.3.3. 24.E.3.53. 9.H.6.25. 9.E.4.15. 1.Marie. Dier.94.

(u) *Per literas patentes authoritate Parliamenti.*

2.H.5.fol.1. A grant was made to a man, and to his heires Tenants of the Mannor of Dale. A man seised of Lands in Gauelkind, giue or deuise the same to a man and to his eldest heires, he cannot hereby alter the customarie Inheritance, but as in the case of our Author,

Mich. 26. & 27. Eliz. in Com. Banco. Lenard Louelace case.

thor, Vt res magis valeat, the Law rejecteth (Males) so in this case the Law rejecteth this Adjectiue (eldest.) And so it is if Lands be giuen to a man, and to the eldest heires females of his bodie, yet all his Daughters shall inherit as it hath beene resolued.

¶ *Et issint ne poet estre prise per lequitie del dit statute, &c.* For it is a certaine rule in law that in euery estate in taile within the said statute, it must be limited either by expresse words or by words equipollent of what bodie the heire inheritable shall issue. And it was (x) adiudged in Parliament, that where lands were giuen to a man, and to his heires males, that this was a Fee simple, and that as well the heires females as heires males should inherit, for the grant of a subiect shall be taken most strongly against himselfe.

(x) 18. Ass. p. 5. 18. E. 3. 46. 6. 9. H. 6. 23. 25. lib. 8. fol. 1. The Princes case. Ancient tenure f. l. 3.

¶ *Et pur ceo il ad Fee simple.* Littletons reason being shortly collected is this. Whosoeuer hath an Estate of inheritance, hath either a Fee simple or a Fee taile, but where lands be giuen to a man and his heires males, he hath no Estate taile, and therefore he hath a Fee simple.

What actions tenant in taile may haue and cannot haue, vide Sect. 595. What great alterations haue beene made since Littleton wrote concerning not only Leases to bee made by tenant in taile, but barres also of the Estate taile it selfe by force of certaine Acts of Parliament made since Littletons time, you shall read Sect. 56. and 708.

Chap. 3. Sect. 32.

Tenant in taile apres possibilitie dissue extinct.

¶ Littleton hauing spoken of Estates of Inheritance, viz. Fee simple and Fee taile, now he treateth of tenants of freehold tantum, that is, for terme of life, and therein first of Tenant in taile after possibilitie of issue extinct, and hee giueth vnto him the first place because this Tenant hath eight qualities and Priuiledges which tenant in taile himselfe hath, and which Lessee for life hath not. (a) As first he is dispunishable for waste. Secondly, Hee shall not be compelled to atturne. Thirdly, He shall not haue aide of him in the reuersion. Fourthly, Upon his alienation, no writ of entrie in consimili casu, lieth. Fiftly, After his death no writ of intrusion doth lie. Sixtly, Hee may ioyne the mise in a writ of right, in a speciall manner. Seuenthly, In a Præcipe, brought by him hee shall not name himselfe tenant for life. Eightly, In a Præcipe brought against him hee shall not bee named barely tenant for life. And yet hee hath foure other qualities which are not agreeable to an

(a) Temps E. 1. wast. 125. 39. E. 3. 16. 31. E. 3. aid 35. 42. E. 3. 22. 43. E. 3. 1. 45. E. 3. 22. 28. E. 3. 96. 46. E. 3. 13. 27. 2. H. 4. 17. 7. H. 4. 10. 11. H. 4. 15. 21. H. 6. 56. 10. H. 6. 1. 26. H. 6. aid 77. 3. E. 4. 11. 13. E. 2. Entre Conge. 56. Fitz. N. B. 203. Lewes Bowles case lib. 11. fo. 8.

¶ Tenant en fee taile aps possibilitie dissue extinct est, lou tenemts sont dones a vn home & a sa feme en especiall taile, si lun de eux deuy sans issue, celuy q̃ surueſquist est tenant en taile apres possibilitie dissue extinct. Et sils auoyent issue, & lun deuie, coment q̃ durant la vie, lissue celuy q̃ surueisquist ne serra dit tenant en taile aps possibilitie dissue extinct, vncore si lissue deuy sans issue, issint que ne soit ascun issue en vie que poit enheriter p̃ force de le taile, donque celuy que surueſquist

Tenant in Fee Taile after possibilitie, of issue extinct is, where Tenements are giuen to a man, and to his wife in especiall taile, if one of them die without issue, the suruiuor is tenant in taile after possibilitie of issue extinct, and if they haue issue, and the one die, albeit that during the life of the issue, the suruiuour shall not bee said tenant in taile after possibilitie of issue extinct, yet if the issue die without issue, so as there bee not any issue aliue which may inherit by force of the taile, then the suruiuing partie of the Donees

de les donees est tenant en le taile apres possibilitie dissue extinct.

nees is tenant in taile, after possibilitie of issue extinct.

Estate in taile, but to a bare Lessee for life. (b) First, if he maketh a feoffment in fee, this is a forfeiture of his Estate. Secondly, If an Estate in fee, or in fee taile in reuersion, or remainder discend or come to this tenant, his Estate is drowned, and the fee or fee taile executed. Thirdly, He in the reuersion or remainder shall be receiued vpon his default, as wel as vpon bare tenant for life. Fourthly, an exchange betweene a bare tenant for life and him is good, for their estates in respect of their quantitie are equall, so as the difference standeth in the qualitie, and not in the quantitie of the Estate. And as an Estate taile was originally carued out of a fee simple, so is the estate of this tenant out of an estate in especiall taile. And he is called tenant in taile after possibilitie of issue extinct, because by no possibilitie hee can haue any issue inheritable to the same Estate taile. But if a man giueth land to a man and his wife, and to the heires of their two bodies, and they liue till each of them be C. yeere old, and haue no issue, yet doe they continue tenant in taile for that the law seeth no impossibilitie of hauing children. But when a man and his wife bee tenant in especiall taile, and the wife dieth without issue, there the Law seeth an apparant impossibilitie, that any issue that the husband can haue by any other wife should inherit this estate. And let this tenant keepe his estate for he hath these priuiledges in respect of the priuity of his estate, and of the inheritance that was once in him. (c) For in the Case of Euens, Mich. 28. & 29. Eliz. it was adiudged that where tenant in taile after possibilitie of issue extinct granted ouer his estate to another, that his grantee was compelled to attorne in a quid Iuris clamat, as a bare tenant for life, and so be named in the writ, for by the assignement the priuitie of the Estate being altered, the priuiledge was gone, and this iudgement was affirmed in a writ of Error, and herewith agreeth 27. H. 6. tit. aid. Statham 29. E. 3. 1. b.

(b) 13. E. Entre Cong. 56. 45. E. 3. 22. 28. E. 3. 96. 27. Ass. p. 60. F. N. B. 159. 32. E. 3. tit. ag. 55. 55. E. 3. 4. 9. E. 4. 17. 2. R. 2. resceit. 147. 41. E. 3. 12. 20. E. 3. resceit. 38. E. 3. 33. Lewes Bowles case vbi supra.

(c) Lib. 11. fol. 83. Lewes Bowles case. 27. H. 6. tit. aid. Statham. 29. E. 3. 1. b.

27. H. 6. tit. aid. 29. E. 3. 1. b.

Section 33.

Item si tenements sont dones a vn home & a ses heires que il engendra de corps sa feme, en cest cas la feme nad ryen en les tenements, & le baron est seisie come donee en special taile. Et en ceo cas, si la feme deuy sans issue de son corps engendres per son baron, donques le baron est tenant en taile apres possibilitie dissue extinct.

Also if Tenements be giuen to a man and to his heires which hee shall beget on the bodie of his wife. In this case the wife hath nothing in the Tenements, & the husband is seised as Donee in especiall taile. And in this Case if the wife die without issue of her bodie begotten by her husband, then the husband is Tenant in Taile after possibilitie of issue extinct.

Si la feme deuie sans issue. So as the estate of this tenancie must bee altered by the act of God, and that by dying without issue, for if a feoffment in fee be made to the vse of a man and his wife for tearme of their liues and after to the vse of their next issue male to bee begotten in taile, and after to the vse of the husband and wife, and of the heires of their two bodies begotten they hauing no issue male at that time; In this Case the husband and wife are tenants in especiall taile executed, and after they haue issue a sonne in this case, they are become tenants for life, the remainder to the sonne in taile, the remainder to them in speciall taile, for albeit their Estate taile is turned to an Estate for life, yet they haue but a bare Estate for life, but if the issue die, and the husband die hauing no other issue, and then the sonne die without issue, the wife shall haue the priuiledges belonging to a tenant in taile after possibilitie of issue extinct, as it appeareth in Lewes Bowles Case vbi supra. Where it is said, that the state of this tenant must be created by the act of God, and not by limitation of the partie, ex dispositione Legis, and not ex prouisione hominis. (d) If land be giuen to a man and to his wife, and to the heires of their two bodies, and after they are diuorced causa Praecontractus or Consanguinitatis, or Affinitatis, their estate of inheritance is turned to a ioint Estate for life, and albeit they had once an inheritance in them, yet for that the Estate is altered by their owne act, and not by the act of God, viz. by

Lewes Bowles case lib. 11. fo. 80

(d) 7. H. 4. 16. 8. E. 1. Ass. 415. 12. Ass. 22. 19. Ass. p. 2. 13. E. 3. Ass. 92. in fine.

the

the death of either partie without issue, they are not tenants in taile after possibilitie of issue extinct. Lands are giuen to the husband and wife, and to the heires of the bodie of the husband, the remainder to the husband and wife, and to the heires of their two bodies begotten, the husband die without issue, the wife shall not be tenant in taile after possibilitie, for the remainder in speciall taile was vtterly void, for that it could neuer take effect, for so long as the husband should haue issue, it should inherit by force of the generall taile, and if the husband die without issue, then the speciall Estate taile cannot take effect, in as much as the issue which should inherit the especiall, must be begotten by the husband, and so the generall which is larger and greater, hath frustrated the especiall which is lesser. And the wife in that Case shall be punished for waste.

Section 34.

¶ If lands be giuen to a man with a woman in Frankmarriage, albeit the woman (which was the cause of the gift) dieth without issue, yet the Husband shall bee tenant in taile, apres possibilitie, &c. for that hee and his wife were Donees in especial taile, and so within the words of Littleton, the residue of this Section is euident.

¶ Et nota q̃ nul poit estre tenñt en le taile ap̃s possibility dissue extinct, forsq; vn des donees, ou le donee en le special taile. Car l' donee en generall taile ne poit estr̃ vnq; dit tenñt en taile ap̃s possibility dissue extinct, pur ceo q̃ tout tẽps durant sa vie, il poit per possibility auer issue que poit inheriter per force de mesme le taile. Et issint en m̃ le mañ, lissue q̃ est heire a les donees en vn especial taile, ne poit estre dit tenñt ẽ taile ap̃s possibilitie dissue extinct, causa quà supra.

AND note that none can be tenant in taile after possibility of issue extinct, but one of the Donees, or Donee in especiall taile. For the Donee in generall taile cannot be said to bee tenant in taile after possibilitie of issue extinct, because alwayes during his life, he may by possibilitie haue issue which may inherit by force of the same entaile. And so in the same manner the issue which is heire to the Donees in especiall taile, cannot be tenant in taile after possibilitie of issue extinct, for the reason abouesaid.

* This and that which follow, is not in the first Edition (which I haue.) And therefore (that I may speake it once for all) it was wrong to the Authour to adde any thing, (especially in one Context) to his worke.

* Et nota que tenant en taile apres possibility dissue extinct ne serra vnq; puny de wast, pur lenheritance que fuit vn foits en luy, 10. *Hen.* 6. 1. * Mes cestuy en le reuersion poit enter sil alien en fee, 45. E. 3. 22.

And note that tenant in taile after possibilitie of issue extinct shall not be punished of waste, for the inheritance that once was in him. 10. *H.* 6. 1. But he in the reuersion may enter if hee alien in fee, 45. *E.* 3. 22.

Chap. 4. *Sect.*35.

Curtesie Dengleterre.

Tenant p la Curtesie Denglectre est, lou home prent feme seisie en fee simpl, ou en fee tail general, ou seisie come heire de le taile special, & ad issue per mesme la feme, male ou femal, oyes ou vife, soit lissue apres mort ou en vie, si la feme deuie, le baron tiendra la terre durant sa vie, per la ley Dangleterre. Et est appel tenant per le Curtesie Dengleterre, pur ceo que ceo est vse en nul auter realme, forsque tantsolement en Engleterre.

Et ascuns ont dit, queil ne serra tenant p le curtesie, sinon que lenfant quil ad p sa feme soit oye crie, car p le crie est prove que le enfant fuit nee vife: Ideo quære.

Tenant by the curtesie of England is where a man taketh a wife seised in fee simple, or in fee taile generall or seised as heire in taile especiall and hath issue by the same wife, male or female borne aliue, albeit the issue after dieth or liueth, yet if the wife dies, the husband shall hold the land during his life by the law of England. And he is called Tenant by the curtesie of England, because this is vsed in no other realme but in England only.

And some haue said, that he shall not be tenant by the curtesie, vnlesse the childe which he hath by his wife be heard crie; for by the cry it is proued that the childe was borne aliue. Therfore Quere.

Prist feme seisie. And first of what season a man shall be tenant by the curtesie. (e) There is in Law a two fold seisin, viz. a seisin in Deed, and a seisin in Law, whereof more shalbe said, Sect. 468. & 681. And here Littleton intendeth a seisin in Deed if it may be attained vnto. (f) As if a man dieth seised of lands in Fee simple or fee taile generall, and these lands discend to his daughter, and she taketh a husband and hath issue, and dyeth before any entry, the husband shall not be tenant by the curtesie and yet in this case shee had a seisin in Law, but if she or her husband had during her life entred, he should haue beene tenant by the Curtesie. (g) A man seised of an Aduowson or rent in fee hath issue a Daughter, who is married, and hath issue, and dieth seised, the wife before the rent became due, or the Church became voide, dieth, shee had but a seisin in Law, and yet hee shall bee tenant by the Curtesie, because hee could by no industrie attaine to any other seisin, *Et impotentia excusat legem.* But a man shall not be tenant by the Curtesie of a bare right, title, vse, or of a reuersion or remainder expectant vpon any estate of free hold, vnlesse the particular estate be determined or ended during the couerture.

(e) *F.N.B.* 194.

(f) 1. *Mar. Dyer.* 95.

(g) 7. *E.* 3. 66. 3. *H.* 7. 5.

At the Coronation of King R. 2. saith the Record, (h) Iohannes Rex Castiliæ & leg onis Dux Lancastriæ, coram dicto domino rege & consilio suo comparens clamauit vt comes Leicestriæ officium Seneschalciæ Angliæ, & vt dux Lancastriæ ad gerendum principalem gladium domini Regis vocat' Curtana die coronationis eiusdem regis, & vt comes Lincoln ad scindendum & secandum coram ipso domino Rege sedente ad mensam dicto die coronationis, & quia fact' diligenti examinatione coram peritis de consilio regis de premissis satis constabat eidem consilio, quod ad ipsum ducem tanquam tenentem per legem Angliæ post mortem Blanchiæ quondam vxoris suæ pertinuit officia predict' prout superius clamabat exercere, consideratum fuit per ipsum regem & consilium suum predictum, quod idem Dux officia predicta per se & sufficientes deputatos suos faceret & exerceret, & feoda debita in hac parte obtineret. Qui quidem

(h) *Process. fact. ad Coronationem R.* 2. *Anno Regni sui primo rot. claus. m.* 45.

dux officium Seneschalciæ predict' personaliter adimpleuit, &c. And every man that claymed to hold by graund Seriantie to doe any seruice to the King at his Coronation exhibited his petition to the said Duke as Steward of England, who vpon hearing the proofes either allowed or disalowed the same.

Rot. Patent. Anno 20. H. 6.

In Letters patents made by King H. 6. to Richard Earle of Salisbury you shall finde this clause, Quodque charissimus consanguinius noster Richardus nunc comes Sarum qui Aliciam filiam & hæredem Thomæ nuper comitis Sarum adhuc superstitem duxit in vxorem, & cum eadem Alicia prolem tempore mortis predictæ Thomæ habuit & habet superstitem de presenti, eoque pretextu idem Richardus nunc comes Sarum nomen, statum & honorem comitis Sarum, &c. habet, & pro tempore, vitæ suæ de iure pretextu premissorum habere debet. The name of the issue which the said Richard Earle of Salisbury had by the said Alice was Richard, who married with Anne the sister and heire of Henry Beauchamp Earle of Warwicke, who was Earle of Warwicke to him and to his heires, and Duke of Warwicke to him and to the heires males of his body. And Richard the sonne hauing then no issue by his wife, King H. 6. in 27. yeare of his raigne granted to him that he should be Earle of Warwicke Licet ipse & predicta Anna exitum inter eos ad præsens non habent. These and many more I haue read concerning this matter, and only say to the reader, Vtere tuo iudicio, nihil enim impedio.

Rot. Patent. de anno 27. H. 6. m.

(i) Vid. 1. E. 3. 6. 5. E 3. 26.

(i) If an estate of freehold in Seigniories, Rents, Commons, or such like be suspended, a man shall not be tenant by the curtesie, but if the suspension be but for yeares, he shall bee tenant by the curtesie. As if a tenant make a Lease for life of the tenancie to the Seignioresse, who taketh a husband, and hath issue, the wife dieth, he shall not be tenant by the curtesie, but if the Lease had beene made but for yeares he shall be tenant by the curtesie.

¶ *En Fee simple ou en Fee taile generall, ou seisie come heire de la taile speciall & ad issue per la feme male ou female.* **Secondly of what estate.**

W 2. ca. 1. Litt. cap Dower fo. 10. Sect. 52. Paines case lib. 8. fo. 34.

If lands be giuen to a woman and to the heirs males of her body she taketh a husband and hath issue a daughter and dieth, he shal not be tenant by the curtesie, because the daughter by no possibilitie could inherite the mothers estate in the land, and therefore where Littleton saith, issue by his wife male or female, it is to be vnderstood, which by possibility may inherite as heire to her mother of such estate. Littleton himselfe explaneth this by expresse words Cap. Dower. fo. 10. Sect. 52. And therefore if a woman tenant in taile generall maketh a Feoffment in fee, and taketh backe an estate in fee, and take a husband and hath issue, and the wife dieth, the issue may in a Formedon recouer the land against his father, because he is to recouer by force of the estate taile as heire to his mother and is not inheritable to his father.

¶ *Et ad issue.* 3. **The time of hauing the issue.** 4. **What kinde of issue.** If a man seised of Lands in fee hath issue a daughter, who taketh husband and hath issue, the father dieth, the husband enter, hee (a) shalbe tenant by the curtesie, albeit the issue was had before the wife was seised. And so it is albeit the issue had died in the life time of her father before any discent of the land, yet shall he be tenant by the curtesie. If a woman (b) seised of lands in fee taketh husband, and by him is bigge with childe, and in her trauell dieth, and the childe is ripped out of her body aliue yet shall he not be tenant by the curtesie, because the childe was not borne during the marriage nor in the life-time of the wife, but in the meane time the land discended, and in pleading he must alledge, That he had issue during the marriage.

(a) Old tenures 21. H. 3. tit. Dower 198.

(b) Vid. Paines case. vbi supra.

(c) Bract. lib. 5. 437. 438. Britt. ca. 66. & ca. 83. Fleta lib. 1. ca. 5. & lib 6. ca. 54.

If the wife be (c) deliuered of a Monster which hath not the shape of mankinde, this is no issue in the Law, but although the issue hath some deformity in any part of his body, yet if he hath humane shape this sufficeth. Hij qui contra formam humani generis conuerso more procreantur (vt si mulier monstruosum vel prodigiosum fuerit enixa) inter liberos non computentur, partus tamen cui natura aliquantulum ampliaverit vel diminuerit non tamen superhabundantur, vt si sex digitos vel nisi quatuor habuerit benè debet inter liberos commemorari. Si inutilia natura reddidit membra, vt si curvus fuerit aut gibbosus vel membra tortuosa habuerit non tamen est partus monstruosus Item puerorum alij sunt masculi alij feminæ alij hermophraditæ, hermophradita tam masculo quam feminæ comparatur secundum prævalescentiam sexus incalescentis.

If the issue be borne deafe or dumbe or both, or be borne an Ideot, yet is it a lawfull issue to make the husband Tenant by the curtesie and to inherite the land.

(d) 28. H. 8. 25. Dier. Paines case vbi supra.

¶ *Oyes ou vine.* **If it be borne aliue** (d) **it is sufficient though it** be not heard crye; for peraduenture it may be borne dumbe. And this is resolued clearely in Paines case Vbi supra. For the pleading (as hath beene said) is, That during the marriage he had issue by his wife, and vpon that point the triall is to be had, and vpon the euidence it must be proued, that the issue was aliue, for moruus exitus, non est exitus, so as the crying is but a proofe that the childe was borne aliue, and so is motion stirring and the like. And it is said by an ancient Author (e) that it was ordeyned in the raigne of King H. 1. Que touts que surrequissent

(e) Mirror cap. 1. §. 3.

sent lour femes dount ils vssent conceiue tenuissent les heritages lour fems pur lour vies.

By the custome of Gauelkinde (f) a man may be Tenant by the curtesie without hauing of any issue.

(f) 9.E.3.38. 16.E.3. aid.129. *Stat. de Consuetudinibus Kancie.*

¶ *Soit leissue apres mort ou en vie.* **And therefore** (g) **if a woman** Tenant in taile generall taketh a husband and hath issue, which issue dieth and the wife dieth without any other issue, yet the husband shall be tenant by the curtesie albeit the estate in taile be determined, because he was intitled to be tenant Per legem Angliæ before the estate in taile was spent and for that the land remaineth. But if a woman maketh a gift in taile and reserue a Rent to her and to her heires, and the Donor taketh husband and hath issue, and the Donee dieth without issue, the wife dieth, the husband shall not be tenant by the curtesie of the Rent for that the rent newly reserued is by the act of God determined and no state thereof remaineth. But (h) if a man be seised of a Rent and maketh a gift in taile generall to a woman, she taketh husband and hath issue, the issue dieth, the wife dieth without issue, he shall be Tenant by the curtesie of the Rent, because the rent remaineth. The diuersitie appeareth.

(g) 21.H.3. tit. Dower 198. *Paynes case, Vbi supra.*

(h) *Brooke, tit. per le Curtesie* 86. 10.E.3.27.

¶ *Si la feme deuie le baron tiendra la terre, &c.* **Foure things doe belong** to an estate of Tenancy by the curtesie, viz. Marriage; Seisin of the wife; Issue, and death of the wife. But it is not requisite, that these should concurre all together at one time: And therefore if a man taketh a woman seised of Lands in fee and is disseised, and then haue issue, and the wife die, he shall enter and hold by the curtesie. So if he hath issue which dieth before the discent as is aforesaid.

And albeit the state be not consummate untill the death of the wife, yet the state hath such a beginning after issue had in the life of the wife as is respected in law for diuers purposes.

First, after issue had, he shall doe homage alone, and is become tenant to the Lord, and the atnowr: shall be made only vpon the husband in the life of the wife, as shall bee said hereafter when we come to the apt place. Secondly, if after issue (i) the husband maketh a Feoffment in fee, and the wife dieth, the Feoffee shall hold it during the life of the husband, and the heire of the wife shall not during his life recouer it in Sur cui in vita; for it could not be a forfeiture, for that the estate, at the time of the feoffment, was an estate of Tenancie by the curtesie inniitiate and not consummate. And it is adiudged in 29.E.3 that the tenant by the Curtesie cannot clayme by a Deuise, and waiue the state of his tenancie by the Curtesie, because saith the booke, the freehold commenced in him before the Deuise for terme of his life.

(i) 34.E.2. *Cui in vita* 13. 2.E.2. *Cui in vita* 26. 10.E.3.12. *Dier.*21.*Eliz.*363.

29.E.3.

¶ *Et est appel tenant per le curtesie dengliterre pur ceo que nest vse en auter realme forsque tantsolement en Engliterre.*

¶ *Per le Curtesie.* **In Latyn** Per legem Angliæ.

¶ *Tantsolement en Engleterre.* **It is also vsed within the realme of** Scotland, and there it is called Curialitas Scotiæ. And so it is in the Realme of Ireland.

¶ *Et ascuns ount dit qui il ne serra tenant per le curtesie sinon que lenfant que il ad per sa feme soit oye crie, car per le crie est proue que le enfant fuit nee vife.* **Our Author hauing deliuered his owne opinion before,** viz. Oyes ou vife, now he sheweth the opinions of others: for so it is said in the (k) Statute De tenentibus per legem Angliæ: and of that opinion is Glanuile (l) lib.7.cap.8. Bracton lib.5. tract.5.cap.30. Britton cap.50.fo.132. Fleta lib.6.ca.50.&c. But the reason is against their opinion; For by the crye it is proued, &c. so as it is but an euidence to proue the life of the enfant.

(k) *Vet.mag.cart.part* 1. *fol.*90.

(l) *Glanuil.lib.*7.*cap.*8. *Bract.lib.*5.*tract* 5.*ca.*30. *Brit.ca.*50.*fo.*132. *Fleta.lib.*6.*cap.*54.

¶ *Ascuns ont dit.* **But these and the like speeches our Author in**tendeth that the point had beene controuerted, but thereby except it be in this Section where formerly he deliuered his opinion as hath beene said, hee tacitely insinuateth his owne iudgement which in all the rest holdeth for good Law and warranted by good Authority throughout his three bookes, which kinde of speach and the like I haue collected together as it appeareth by the Sections in (l) the margent.

(l) *Sect.*40.319.132.136. 137.138.141.145.148.156. 170.179.192.202.227.234. 269.336.339.357.400.435. 436.440.443.460.462.478. 501.503 506.522.523.524. 534.576.601.633.634.640. 642.643.644.646.658.675. 689.721.723.726.730.731. 733.734.

¶ *Ideo quære.* **This** Quære **is not in the originall edition of** Littleton, and therefore to be reiected.

And some haue said that in diuers cases a man shall by hauing of issue be tenant by the Curtesie where a woman shall not be endowed. And therefore they say if lands bee giuen to two women and to the heires of their two bodyes begotten, and one of them take husband and haue issue and die, the inheritances being seuerall the husband shall be tenant by the Curtesie as it is adiudged 7.E.3. and in other bookes (m) this iudgement is cited and allowed. But certaine it is, That if land be giuen to two men and to the heires of their two bodyes begotten, and the one taketh wife and dieth, she shall not be endowed for no estate in the land is altered by that marriage. But I leaue the reader to his owne opinion or rather to suspend it untill he come

7.E.3.6.

(m) 17.E.3.51.

to the proper place in the next Chapter. If lands holden of the King by Knights service in capite discend to a woman, and after office found she intrude and taketh husband and hath issue. In this case the husband shall be tenant by the Curtesie; And yet if the heire Male after office in the like case intrudeth and taketh wife, his wife shall not be endowed, for so it is provided by the statute of Prerogatiua reg. cap. 13. that in that case there accrue to the heire no freehold nor Dower to the wife, which by interpretation is as much to say that the heire shall haue no freehold as to this respect to giue any dower to his wife. If a man marrie the niefe of the King by licence and hath issue by her, and after lands discend to the niefe and the husband enter, the neife dieth, he shall be tenant by the curtesie of this land, and the King vpon any office found shall not euict it from him, because by the marriage, the niefe was infranchised during the couerture. But if a free woman marrie the Villaine of the King by licence, and lands discend to the Villaine, the Villaine dieth, the wife shall not be endowed, but vpon an office found the King shall haue the land, for the Villaine remained still a Villaine to the King. A woman (n) taketh husband, and hath issue, lands discen: to the wife, the husband enters, and after the wife is found an Ideot by office, the lands shall be seised by the King, for the title of the tenancie by the curtesie, and of the King begin at one instant, and the title of the King shall be preferred. A man shall be tenant by t e curtesie of a Castle (o) which serueth for the publike defence of the Realme, but a woman shall not be endowed thereof, as shall be said more at large hereafter.

Prerog. Regis ca. 13.

33. E. 3. ti. Trauers 36.

(n) Pl. Com. Dame Hales Case. 263.

(o) Magna Carta. 30. E. 1. Dower 81. b. 17. H. 3. Dower. Bract. lib. 2. fol. 46. & 314.

(p) 4 H. 3. Dower 180. Bract. fol. 93. Fleta lib. 5. ca. 23. 2. E. 2. Dower 123. 3. E. 3. Dower. B. 102. 9. H. 7. 1. 30. E. 3.

A man shall be tenant by the curtesie of a common sauns nomber, but a woman shall not be endowed thereof, because it cannot be deuided. A man shall be tenant by the curtesie (p) of a house that is Caput Baroniæ, or Comitatus: But it appeareth by 4. H. 3 Dower 180. that a woman shall not be endowed of it. For the Law respecteth Honour and Order. A man is entitle ; to be tenant by the curtesie, and maketh a feoffment in fee vpon condition, and entreth for the condition broken, and then his wife dieth, he shall not be tenant by the curtesie, because albeit the state giuen by the feoffement, be conditionall, yet his title to be tenant by the curtesie was inclusiuely absolutely extinct by the feoffment, for the condition was not annexed to it. As if the Lord disseise the Tenant, and maketh a Feoffment in fee of the land vpon condition, and entreth for the condition broken, yet the Seignorie is extinct for that was inclusiuely extinct by the feoffment. See more of Tenant by curtesie. Section 52.

Chap. 5. Sect. 36.

Dower.

Tenant en dower. Tenens in dote. Dos Dower in the Common Law (q) is taken for that Portion of Lands or Tenements which the wife hath for terme of her life of the Lands or Tenements of her husbands after his decease for the sustenance of her selfe, and the nurture and education of her children. Propter onus matrimonij & ad sustentationem vxoris & educationem liberorum cum fuerint procreati si vir præmoriatur: & hoc proprie dicitur Dos mulieris secundum consuetudinem Anglicanam. And Dos is deriued ex donatione, & est

(q) Lib. rub. ca. 70. Glanuil. lib. 6. cap. 1. Bract lib. 2 fol. 92. Britton. cap. 101. Fleta lib. 5. cap. 22.

Tenāt en Dower est lou hōe est seisie de certaine terres ou Tenements en fee simple, taile generall, ou come heire de le taile speciall, & prent feme, & deuie, la feme apres le decesse de la baron serra endow de la tierce part de tiels terres & tenements que fueront a sa Baron en ascun temps du-

Tenant in Dower is where a man is seised of certaine Lands or Tenements in fee simple, fee taile generall, or as heire in speciall taile, and taketh a wife, and dieth, the wife after the decease of her husband shall bee endowed of the third part of such Lands and tenements as were her husbands at any time during the couerture.

rant

rant le couerture, a auer & tener a mesme la feme en seueraltie per metes & bounds pur terme de sa vie, le quel el auoit issue per sa baron ou nemy. & de quel age que la feme soit, issint que el passe lage de neuf ans al temps de le mort sa baron, car il couient que el soit passe lage de neuf ans al temps del mort sa baron, ou auterment el ne serra my endow.

To haue and to hold to the same wife in seueraltie by metes and bounds for terme of her life, whether shee hath issue by her husband or no, and of what age soeuer the wife be, so as shee bee past the age of nine yeeres at the time of the death of her husband, for she must bee aboue nine yeeres old, at the time of the decease of her husband otherwise shee shall not be endowed.

quasi donarium, because either the Law it selfe doth (without any gift) or the husband himselfe giueth it to her as shal be said hereafter. And at this day Dos or Dower is not taken by the professors of the Common Law, either for the land which the wife bringeth with her in marriage to her husband, for then it is either called in Frankmarriage or in marriage as hath beene said, nor for the portion of money or other goods or chattels, which she bringeth with her in marriage, for that is called her marriage Portion. And yet of ancient time (r) Dos mulieris, the Dower or Dowrie of the woman was also applyed to them. But it is commonly taken for her third part which she hath of her husbands lands or tenements.

(r) *Britton.ca.*101. *Bracton.lib.*2.*fol.*92. *Glanvil.lib* 6.*ca.*1.*lib.*7.*ca.*1. *Lib.*2.*fol.*93.*Binghams case.* 4.*H.*3.*Dower* 179.

In Domesday, Dos is called Maritagium.

To the consummation of this Dower three things are necessarie. Viz. marriage, seisen and the death of her husband.

Dos (s) the very name doth import a freedome, for the Law doth giue her therewith many freedomes: Secundum consuetudinem regni mulieres viduæ &c. debent esse quietæ de tallegijs &c. And tenant in Dower shall not bee distreyned for the debt due to the King by the husband in his life time in the lands which she held in Dower. And other priuiledges she hath; Of all which Ockam yeelds the reason, Doti eius parcatur quia præmium pudoris est.

(s) *Claus.*11.*H.*3 *nu.*17. *Regist.*142.143. *F.N.B.*150 *Ockham. fol.*40.

¶ *Lou home.* If the husband be an alien (t) the wife shall not be indowed. So if the husband be the Kings Villaine, the wife shall not bee endowed (as hath beene said) but if the husband be a Villaine to a common person, the wife shall bee indowed if she be intitled to Dower before the entrie of the Lord. And so if a free man take a neife to wife and dieth she shall be indowed. The wife of an Ideot, non Compos mentis, outlawed or attainted of Felonie or trespasse, attainted of heresie, præmunire or the like) shall bee indowed. But if the husband be attainted of treason, albeit it bee treason done after the title of Dower she shall not be indowed as shall be said hereafter.

(t) *Bract.fol.*298.19.*E.*2. *Dower* 171. *Dame Hales case;* 13.*E.*3.*Dower. Starham.* 13.*E.*1.*tit.Dower.*

The wife of one attainted of Felony shall not be Endowed vid: Sect: 747. –

¶ *Seisie.* Here this word (seised) extendeth it selfe aswell to a seison in law, or a ciuill seison, as to a seison in deed, which is a naturall seison: but seised hee must be either the one way or the other during the couerture. For a woman shall bee indowed of a seison in law. As where lands or tenements discend to the husband, before entrie, he hath but a seison in Law, and yet the wife shall be endowed, albeit it bee not reduced to an actuall possession, for it lieth not in the power of the wife to bring it to be an actuall seison, as the husband may doe of his wiues land, when he is to be tenant by curtesie, which is worthy the obseruation. And yet of euery seison in Law, or actuall seison of lands or Tenements, a woman shall not be indowed. For example, If there be grandfather, father, and sonne, and the grandfather is seised of three Acres of land in fee, and taketh wife and dieth, this land discendeth to the father, who dieth either before or after entrie, now is the wife of the father dowable. The father dieth and the wife of the grandfather is indowed of one acre and dieth, the wife of the father shall be endowed only of the two Acres residue, for the Dower of the grandmother is paramount, the title of the wife of the father, and the season of the father which discended to him (be it in law or actuall) is defeated, and now vpon the matter the father had but a reuersion expectant vpon a freehold, and in that case, Dos de dote peti non debet; although the wife of the grandfather dieth liuing the fathers wife. And here note a diuersitie (w) betweene a Discent and a Purchase. For in the case aforesaid, if the grandfather had infeoffed the father, or made a gift in taile vnto him, there in the case abouesaid, the wife of the father, after the decease of the grandfathers wife should haue beene endowed of that part assigned to the grandmother

True, not at Common Law; but by Statute 1 Ed. 6 cap. 12 &c. She may; See Sect. 41. & also Cokes Comment on Sect. 747 & above quoted

(u) 43.*E.*3.32. 45.*E.*3.13. 9.*E.*3.4. *F.N.B* 149. 8.*E.*3.*tit.Ass.*393. 19.*E.*2.*Dower* 170. 23.*E.*3. *Dower* 30.

(w) 5.*E.*3.*tit.Voucher.* 249. *Parkes case.* 9.*E.*3.4.

mother, and the reason of this diuersitie is, for that the reason that discended after the decease of the grandfather to the father is auoided by the indowment of the grandmother whose title was consummate by the death of the grandfather. But in the case of the purchase or guift that tooke effect in the life of the grandfather (before the title of Dower of the grandmother was consummate) is not defeated but only quoad the grandmother, and in that case there shall be Dos de dote. And yet there is another diuersitie (x) where the wife of the Father, is first indowed, and where the wife of the grandfather, for in the same case after the decease of the grandfather and father the sonne entreth and indoweth his mother of a third part, against whom the grandmother recouereth a third part and dieth, the mother shall enter againe into the land recouered by the grandmother, because she had in it an estate for terme of her life, and the estate for the life of the grandmother is lesser in the eye of Law, as to her then her owne life. Also the husband (y) may be seised in his Demesne, as of the fee absolutely, yet the woman shall not be indowed, as she shall not be indowed both of the land giuen in exchange, and of the land taken in exchange, and yet the husband was seised of both, but shee may haue her election to be endowed of which she will.

(x) 8.E.3.tit.Ass.303. 13.R.2.Dower.55. 22.E.3.5 8.E.3.3.7.H.6.4.

(y) 6.E.3.50. F.N.B.149.

Also of a seison for an instant a woman shall not be indowed. As if Cesty que vse (z) after the Statute of 1.R.3. and before the Statute of 27.H.8. had made a feoffment in fee, his wife should not be indowed.

(z) 27.H.8.23.F.N.B. 17.H.3.Dower 192.

Likewise if two ioynt tenants be in fee, and the one maketh a feoffement in fee, his wife shall not bee indowed. And so if the Conusee of a fine doth grant and render the land to the Conusor, the wife of the Conusee shall not be indowed, for it is not possible that the husband could haue indowed his wife of such an estate as the vsuall pleading is, Lib intrat 225. Quia dicit quod W. quondam vir suus nunquam fuit seisitus de tenementis prædictis de tali statu ita quod eandem A. inde dotasse potuit.

Vid.Sect.242.

¶ *Des terres ou tenements.* **Of a Castle that is maintained for** the necessarie defence of the Realme, a woman shall not be endowed, because it ought not to be diuided, and the publique shall be preferred before the priuate. But of a Castle that is only maintained for the priuate vse and habitation of the owner, a woman shall bee endowed. And so it was adiudged in the Court of (a) Common Pleas, where in a writ of Dower, the demand was, De tertia parte Castri de Hilderker in Comitatu Northampt: And the Statute of Magna Charta cap.7. whereby it is prouided, nisi domus illa sit Castrum, is to be vnderstood, a Castle maintained for the necessarie and publique defence of the Realme. And this agreeth with antient Records, (b) (albeit in the argument of the said case they were not vouched) the effect whereof be, Non debent mulieribus assignari in dotem castra quæ fuerunt virorum, suorum & quæ de guerra existunt vel etiam homagia & seruicia aliquorum de guerra existent. Wherein it is to be obserued, That the Law is not satisfied with the names of things, or nominatiues, but with things reall and substantiall. But of the principall Mansion, or capitall Messuage, the wife shall be endowed, (c) si non sit caput Comitatus, siue Baroniæ, for the honour of the Realme, or (as hath beene said) a Castle for the publique defence of the Realme. And so are the old bookes to be intended, as it was resolued Tr. 17.Eliz. in the Court of Common pleas, which I heard and obserued. And of an estate taile in lands determined, a woman shall bee endowed in the like manner and forme as a man shall bee Tenant by the Curtesie Mutatis mutandis.

(a) Pasc.23.Eliz.in Com. Banco. Bract.fol.96. Brit.ca.103. Flet.li.5.c.23. 30.E.1.tit.Dower 81.b. 30.E.1.Vouch.298. 17.H.3.192.8.Hen.3.Dower 196.8.H.3.ib.194. (b) Pat.1.E.1.part.1.m.17. Esch.4.E.1.nu.88.

(c) Bract.l.2.f.93.Brit.c.103. Fleta lib.5 ca.22. Trin.17.El.in Com.Banco.

¶ *En fee simple, fee taile general, &c.* **If a man be Tenant in fee** taile generall, (d) and make a feoffement in fee, and taketh backe an estate to him and to his wife, and to the heires of their two bodies, and they haue issue, and the wife dieth, the husband taketh another wife, and dieth, the wife shall not be endowed, for during the couerture, hee was seised of an estate taile generall, and yet the issue which the second wife may haue, by possibilitie may inherit.

(d) 41.E.3.30. 44.E.3.26. 30.H.8.Dyer 41.

The same Law it is, if in this case he had taken backe an estate in fee simple, and after had taken wife and had issue by her; yet she shall not bee endowed, for that the fee simple is vanished by the remitter, and her issue hath the land by force of the entaile. But in that case the Tenant cannot plead, that the husband was neuer seised of such an estate whereof the demandant might be endowed, but he must plead the speciall matter.

30.H.8.Dyer 41.

¶ *Et prent feme.* **If a man so seised as is aforesaid, taketh an** Alien to wife, and dieth, she shall not be endowed: but if the King take an alien borne, & dieth, she shall be endowed by the law of the Crowne. And Edmond the brother of King Edward the first, married the Queene of Nauarre, and died, and it was resolued (e) by all the Judges, that she should be endowed of the third part of all the lands whereof her husband was seised in fee.

(e) Rot.Parl.26.E.1.rot.1.

If a Jew borne in England taketh to wife a Jew borne also in England; the husband is conuerted to the Christian Faith, purchaseth lands, and infeoffeth another, and dieth, the wife

brought

brought a writ of Dower, and was barred of her dower, and the reason yeelded in the record (f) is this, Quia verò contra justiciam est, quod ipsa dotem petat vel habeat de Tenemento quod fuit viri sui ex quo in conuersione sua noluit cum eo adherere & cum eo conuerſ.

(f) D. 15. claus. 18. H. 3. m. 1.

¶ *Del tierce part de tiels Terres & Tenements per seueraltie per metes & bonds.* **Albeit of many Inheritances that bee entire, whereof no** diuision can be made by metes and bonds, a woman cannot be endowed of the thing it selfe, yet a woman (g) shall be endowed thereof in a speciall and certaine manner. As of a Mill a woman shall not be endowed by Mets and Bounds, nor in common with the heire; but either she may be endowed of the third tolle dish, or de integro molendino per quemlibet 3. mensem. And so of a Villeine, (h) either the third dayes worke, or euerie third weeke or moneth. A woman shall be endowed of the third part of the profit of Stallage, of the third part of the profits of a faire, of the third part of the profits of the office of the Marshalsie, of the (i) third part of the profites of the keeping of a Parke. Of the third part of the profit of a Doue house; and likewise of the third part of a Piscarie, (k) viz. tertium piscem, vel iactum retis tertium. Of the third presentation to an aduowson. A writ of Dower lieth de 3. parte exituum prouenientium de custodia gaolæ Abathiæ Westm. And herewith agreeth reuerend antiquitie, De (l) nullo quod est sua natura indiuisibile, & secationem, siue diuisionem non patitur nullam partem habebit, sed satisfaciat ei ad valentiam. Of the third part of profits of Courts, (m) fines, heriots, &c. Also a woman shall be endowed of tithes. And the surest endowment of tithes, is of the third sheafe, for what land shall be sowne is vncertaine.

(g) Bract. lib. 2. fol. 97. b. 23. H. 3. tit. ass. 415 F. N. B. 149. 45. E. 3. Dower 50.

(h) 2. H. 6. 11. Bract. lib. 2. fol. 97. Brit. 247. 11. E. 3. tit. Dower 85. 15. E. 1. ibid. 81. 2. E. 3. 57 F. N. B. 8.

(i) 4. E. 2. T. 233. 26. E. 3. 58 45. E. 3. Dower 50.

(k) Bract. 98. 208. Brit. 247. Flet. lib. 5. cap. 23. 17. Ed. 2. Dower 104. 163. 19. Edw. 3. Quar. Imp. 154. 7. E. 3. 7.

(l) Bract. 97. Brit. 146. 147.

(m) Lib. Intr. Indemne. 18. fo. 230. Lib. 11. fo. 25. 26. Harpers case.

But in some cases of lands and tenements which are diuisible, and which the heire of the husband shall inherit, yet the wife shall not be indowed. As if the husband (n) maketh a lease for life of certaine lands, reseruing a rent to him and his heires, and he taketh wife and dieth; the wife shall not be endowed, neither of the reuersion (albeit it is within these words Tenements) because there was no seisin in deed or in law, of the freehold, nor of the rent, because the husband had but a particular state therein, and no fee simple. But if the husband maketh a lease for yeares, reseruing a rent, and taketh wife, the husband dieth, the wife shall bee endowed of the third part of the reuersion by metes and bonds, together with the third part of the rent, and execution shall not cease during the yeares. And herewith agreeth the common experience at this day. But if the husband maketh a gift in taile, reseruing a rent to him and to his heires, and after the donor taketh wife and dieth, the wife shall be indowed of this rent, because it is a rent in fee, and by possibilitie may continue for euer.

(n) 28. Ass. 3. 8 R. 2. Dower 184. 1. E. 6. Dow. B. 89 acc.

Vid. 1. E. 6. B. 89.

Of a Common certaine a woman shall be indowed, but of a Common sauns nomber en grosse she shall not be endowed, as hath beene said before. And so of a rent seruice, rent charge, and rent secke, she shall be endowed: but of an annuitie that chargeth onely the person, and issueth not out of any lands or tenements, she shall not be endowed. But if the freehold of the rents common, &c. were suspended before the couerture, and so continue during the couerture, she shall not be endowed of them. If after the couerture the husband doth extinguish them by release or otherwise, yet she shall be endowed of them; for as to her dower they in the eye of the Law haue continuance.

Lib. 7. fo. 38. Hillin-stons case. Lib. 6. fo. 78. Seig. Abergauenies case.

If the wife be entituled to haue dower of three acres of marsh, euerie one of the value of twelue pence, the heire by his industrie and charge maketh it good Meadow, euerie acre of the value of ten shillings, the wife shall haue her dower according to the improoued value, and not according to the value as it was in her husbands time: for her title is to the quantitie of the land, viz. one iust third part.

And the like law it is, if the heire improoue the value of the land by building: And on the other side, if the value be impaired in the time of the heire, she shall be indowed according to the value at the time of the assignement, and not according to the value as it was in the time of her husband.

V. 30. E. 1. Vouch. 298.

¶ *Ascuns temps durant le couerture.* **For the better vnderstanding** whereof it is to be knowne, that (as hath beene said) to dower three things bee belong, viz. marriage, seisin, and the death of the husband. Concerning the seisin, it is not necessarie that the same should continue during the couerture, for albeit the husband alieneth the lands or tenements, or extinguisheth the rents or commons, &c. yet the woman shall be endowed. But it is necessarie that the marriage doe continue during the couerture, for if that be dissolued, the dower ceaseth, vbi nullum matrimonium, ibi nulla dos. But this is to bee vnderstood when the husband and wife are diuorced à vinculo matrimonii, as in case of precontract consanguinitie, affinitie, &c. and not à mensa & thoro onely, as for adulterie. And yet it is said, that if the assignement of dower ad hostium eccl' bee specified, viz. That notwithstanding any diuorce shall happen, yet that she shall hold it for her life, that this is good.

Bract. 92. Brit. cap. 101. Brit cap. eodem.

If the wife elope (o) from her husband; that is, if the wife leaue her husband, and goeth away and tarrieth with her adulterer, she shal lose her dower vntill her husband willingly with-

(o) W. 2 ca. 34. Lib. Intr. 234. Fleta lib. 5. c. 22. Brit. c. 10p. Mirror. cap. 5. §. 5.

one

out coertion ecclesiasticall be reconciled unto her, and permit her to cohabit with him; all which is comprehended shortly in two Hexameters, Sponte virum mulier fugiens, & adultera facta, dote sua carear, nisi sponsi sponte retracta. And (p) if she goeth willingly with or to the avowtrer, this is a departure and a tarrying; albeit she remaineth not continually with the avowtrer, or if she tarrieth with him against her will, or if he turne her away, or if she cohabit with her husband, by the censures of the Church, in all these cases she loseth her dowrie. But see notable matter hereof, in the exposition upon the Statute of W.2.cap.34.

(p) 3.E.3.2.6.E.3.29. 9.E.3.20.19.E.3.Dower. 94.41.E.3.19. Vid. Fitz.N.B.150.h. 8.E.2.Dower 153.

¶ *En seueraltie per metes & bonds.* And yet in some cases where the husband was sole seised, the wife shal not be endowed in severaltie by metes and bonds. As for example, (q) If a man seised of lands in fee, take a wife and infeoffed eight persons, a writ of Dower was brought against these eight persons, and two confesse the Action, and the other sixe plead in barre, and discend to issue, the demandant shall have judgement to recover the third part of two parts of the land, in eight parts to be divided, and after the issue being found for the demandant against the sixe, the demandant shal have judgement to recover against them the third part of sixe parts of the same lands, in eight parts to be divided, which is worthie the observation. But of this more shall be afterwards said in this chapter.

(q) M.2.& 3.Eliz. Dier 187.b. 10.Ass.p.2. 27.E.3.4. Tr 10.H.5.Rot.447.

But regularly Littletons words are to be intended, where the husband was sole seised, for where he was seised in Common, there she cannot be endowed by metes and bonds, as it appeareth in this chapter, Sect.44. Nota, the endowment by metes and bonds, according to the common right, is more beneficiall to the wife, than to be endowed against common right, for there she shall hold the land charged, in respect of a charge made after her title of dower.

36.E.3.Dower 133. 10.E.3.31. 17.E.2.Dower 164. 19.E.3 qua.imp.154. 12.E,4.2. 18.H.6.27. per Paston.

¶ *Le quel el auoit issue per sa baron ou nemy.* Herein the tenant in Dower, as in many other, is preferred before the tenant by the Curtesie; But yet this great disadvantage the wife hath, that she cannot enter into her Dower by the Common Law, but is driven to her writ of Dower to recover the same, wherein sometimes great delayes are used, and therefore the well advised friends of the wife will provide for a joynture to be made to her as shalbe said hereafter; For by the statute of (r) Magna carta cap.7. shee shall tarrie in the chiefe house of her husband but by the space of 40.dayes after the death of her husband, within which time dower shall be assigned unto her, unlesse it were formerly assigned, &c. but of little effect was that act, for that no penaltie was thereby provided if it were not done: which terme of 40.dayes is in law called Quarentena. But if she marry within the 40 dayes she loseth her Quarenten. But some have said that by the ancient Lawe of England the woman should continue a whole yeare in her husbands house within which time if Dower were not assigned, she might recover it: and this certainly was the Law of England before the Conquest (s) Mulieres viduæ bis senos menses viduas exigunto, atque tum demum cui velint nubant, sin quæ ante annum nupserit dote mulctata fortunis omnibus à priore marito relictis priuatur. But for the reliefe of the widow it was provided by the Statute of Merton made in Anno 20.H.3.cap.1. (which by (t) Bracton is called Noua constitutio) that the wife shall recover damages in her writ of Dower from the time of the death of her husband. But herein divers things are observable. First in what kinde of writ of Dower she shall recover her damages. In a writ for a Dower ad ostium Ecclesiæ, or ex assensu patris she shall recover no damages because she may enter, and the words of the Statute be Et dotes suas habere non possunt sine placito. Also I have read in an ancient and learned reading upon this Statute, that it extendeth only to a writ of Dower, Vnde nihil habet, and not to a writ of right of Dower, for in no writ of right damages are to be recovered. 2. She shal recover damages only when her husband die seised, (that is) seised of the freehold & inheritance, (u) for albeit the husband before the title of Dower had made a Lease for yeares reserving a Rent the wife shall recover the third part of the reversion with a third part of the rent and damages, for the words of the Statute be, De quibus viri sui obierunt seisiti. 3. Some say that the Demandant in a writ of Dower, that delayeth her selfe shall not recover damages, therefore let the Demandant take heed thereof. 4. It is necessary for the wife after the decease of her husband as soone as shee can to demand her Dower before good testimony, for otherwise she may by her owne default lose the value after the decease of her husband and her damages for deteyning of her Dower. For if she bring a writ of Dower against the heire, and the heire commeth into the Court upon the summons the first day, and pleade that he hath beene alwayes ready and yet is to render Dower, &c. If the wife have not requested her Dower, shee shall lose the meane values and her damages, but if she hath requested her Dower shee may pleade it and issue may be thereupon taken.

(r) Magna carta cap.6. Fleta lib 5 cap.21. Bracton lib.2.fol.96. Britton ca.103. 19.H.6.24. 6.E.6. Dyer 76. F.N.B. 161. Regist.orig.175. 1.Marie Dower 101.

(s) Lamb.sect.120.71. & divers ancient Manuscripts, See the 2.part of the institutes cap.7.

(t) Bract.lib.4.312. & lib.2.96. Britton cap.103. Fleta lib.5.cap.23.

(u) Regist.judic.4. Origin.173. Dier 11.El.284. Rast.pl.fo.226.&c. 16.E.2. tit.Damages.83. 8.E.2.ibid.11.

But it is holden in some bookes (w) that a request in Pays is not sufficient, and that it is the folly of the wife, that she brought not her writ of Dower sooner. But the Law and many (x) bookes be against it, and the words of the plea (that he hath beene alwayes ready, &c.) prove the same, and the words of the Statute also prove this, Et dotes suas habere non possunt sine placito.

(w) 5.E.3.2.41.E.2. Dower 46. and not in the booke at large.
(x) 6.E.3.Dower 57. 2.H.4.7.9.H.4.4. tit. issue 133.11.H.4.40. 13.E.4.7.14.H.8.25.b.

And the reason why tout temps prist is a good plea in a writ of Dower brought against the heire to barre her of the meane values and damages is, because the heire holdeth by title, and doth no wrong till a demand be made. But in a writ of Aiell, Cosinage, &c. where the land and damages are to be recovered, there such a plea is not good, for there the tenant of the land hath no title, but holdeth the land by wrong. And the Feoffee of the heire cannot at the first day plead Tout temps prist, because he had not the land all the time, since the death of the Ancestor. 5. It is to be observed that the meane values and damages are to be recovered against the tenant in a writ of Dower, as it appeareth in a notable Record (y) betweene Belfield and Rowse, the Tenant as to parcell pleaded Non-tenure, and for the residue, Deteyniment of Charters, upon which pleas they were at issue, and both issues found by the Jury against the Tenant, and found further that the husband died seised such a day and yeare, and had issue a sonne; and that the Demandant and the sonne by 6. yeares after the decease of the husband together tooke the profits of the land, and after the sonne such a day and yeare died without issue, after whose decease the land discended to the Tenaunt as uncle and heire to him, by force whereof hee entred and tooke the profits untill the purchasing of the originall Writ, and found the value of the land by the yeare, and assessed damages for the deteyning of the Dower, and costs, and upon this verdict, after often debating the demandant had iudgement to recover her damages for all the time frō the death of her husband without any defalcation. In which case many things apparāt therein are observable. Let the Tenant therefore take heede how he plead false pleas. 6. That this Statute of Merton doth extend to Coppiholds (z) where the custome is that women be dowable. 7. That if the wife hath Dower assigned to her in Chauncery she shall have no damages (a) for the words of the statute be Et viduæ per placitum recuperaverint, &c. So it is if the heire or his feoffee assigne Dower, and the wife accepteth it she loseth her damages.

(y) *Mich.8.&9.E.2. rot.904. in Communi banco*

(z) *Tr.37.Eliz.lib.4. fo 30.b. Shawes case.*

(a) *43.Ass.pl.32.*

A man seised of lands in fee taketh a wife and granteth a rent charge and after maketh a Feoffment in fee, and taketh backe an estate tayle and dieth, the wife recovereth Dower against the issue in tayle by reddition, the wife maketh a surmise that her husband died seised, and prayeth a writ to enquire of the damages, and that is granted to her. In this case she hold the land charged with the rent charge, for by her prayer she accepteth her selfe dowable of the 2. estate, for of the first estate whereof shee was dowable her husband died not seised, and so shee hath concluded her selfe, wherefore if the rent charge be more to her detriment then the damages beneficiall to her, it is good for her in that case to make no such prayer.

14.H.8.28.

¶ *De quel age que la fēe soit, issint que el passe lage de neufe ans al tēps del mort son barō.* Fēe, **wife, here** Lit. **speaketh of a wife generally, & generally** it is to be understood aswel of a wife de facto as de jure. Therfore if the wife bee past the age of 9. yeres (b) at the time of the death of her husbād she shalbe endowed, of what age soever her husband be, albeit he were but 4 yeres old, Quia juñ non potest dotē præmerī neq; victū sustiñ; nec obstabit mulieri petenti minor ætas, viz wherein it is to be observed, that albeit Consensus non concubitus facit matrimonium, and that a woman cannot consent before twelve, nor a man before fourteene, yet this inchoate and imperfect mariage (from the which either of the parties at the age of Consent may disagree) after the death of the husband shall give Dower to the wife, and therefore it is accounted in law after the death of the husband legittimum matrimonium, a lawfull mariage, quoad dotem. If a man taketh a wife of the age of seven yeares, and after alien his land, and after the alienation the wife atteyneth to the age of 9. yeares, and after the husband dieth, the wife shall be indowed, for albeit she was not absolutely dowable at the time of the marriage yet she was conditionally dowable, viz. if she attained to the age of 9. yeares before the death of the husband, for so Litleton here saith, so that she passe the age of 9. yeares at the death of her husband, for by his death the possibilitie of Dower is consummate.

(b) *13.E.1.Dower. Itin.North. 8.E.2.Dower.122. 7.E.2.Dower.147. 12.E.2.ibid.159. 21.E.3.28. 15.E.3.Dower.67. 12.R.2.Dower.54. 12.H.4.3. 35.H.6.40. 7.H.6.11 12. 12.H.4. Doct.& Stud. Fitz.N.B.149.b. 22.Eliz.Dower 369. Bract.f.l.92. Fleta lib.5.ca.22. Lib.Intrat.fo.123.*

And so it is if the husband alien his land and then the wife is attainted of felony now is she disabled, but if she be pardoned before the death of the husband she shal be indowed. If the sonne indow his wife at her age of seven yeares ex assensu patris if she before the death of her husband attaine to the age of 9. yeares the Dower is good. But otherwise it is of an originall absolute disabilitie, as if a man take an Alien to wife, and after the husband alien the land, and after she is made Denizen, the husband dieth she shall not be indowed because her capacitie and possibility to be indowed came by the denization, otherwise it is if shee were naturalized by act of Parliament whereof see more in the chapter of Villinage.

And the Bishop upon an issue ioyned in a Writ of Dower, Quod nunquam fuerunt copulati legitimo matrimonio, ought to certifie that they were coupled in lawfull marriage, albeit the man were under fourteene, or the wife above nine, and under twelve. So it is if a marriage de facto, be voidable by Divorce, in respect of Consanguinitie, Affinitie, Precontract, or such like, whereby the marriage might have beene dissolved, and the parties freed à vinculo matrimonij, yet if the husband die before any divorce, then for that it cannot now be avoyded, this wife de facto shall bee endowed (c) for this is legitimum matrimonium (as in the other case

(c) *10.E.3.35. Fleta.lib.5.ca.22. Britt.cap.107.*

when the wife is infra annos nubiles) quoad dotē. And so in a Writ of dower the Bishop ought to certifie, that they were legitimo matrimonio copulati, according to the words of the writ. And herewith agreeth 10.E.3.35. And (d) Bracton: quamdiu durauit matrimonium, durauit dotis exactio, ea deficiente deficit dotis petitio, &c. poterit tamen replicare contra exceptionem illam, quod si aliquando fuit matrimonium propter Consanguinitatem, &c. inter eos accusatum nūquam tamen fuit in vita viri sui solutum nec diuortium celebratum. But if they were diuorced à vinculo matrimonij in the life of her husband she loseth her Dower: Otherwise it is if they were diuorced (e) Causa adulterij, which is but à mensa & thoro, and not à vinculo matrimonij, as it was adiudged. But some doe hold that a wife de facto shall not haue an appeale of the death of her husband, but only she that is a wife, De iure in fauorem vitæ. Vide 50. E.3. fol. 15. 28. E.3.92.27 Ass. Stanford Pl. Cor 59. and that there vnques accouple in loyall matrimonie shall be taken de iure strictly. And so in some case a wife shall haue Dower where shee cannot haue an appeale, (f) and in other Cases she shall haue an appeale, where she cannot haue a writ of Dower, as if she elope &c. she is barred of her Dower, but not of her appeale: and the reason is for that the Statute (g) barreth her of her Dower, but not of her appeale. So if the husband be attainted of treason, &c. his wife shall not bee endowed, and yet if any doe kill him, the wife shall haue an appeale, the reason of the diuersitie shall appeare hereafter in this Chapter.

(d) *Bract. lib. 4. fol. 304. Britton. ibidem. Fleta lib. 5. cap. 23. 32. E. 1. Dier 156.*

(e) *Tr. 2. Ia. Rot. 1815. in Communi Banco. Inter Stowell & Wikes in Dower.*

(f) *50. E. 15. b.*

(g) *W. 2. cap. 34.*

¶ *Apres le mort le Baron.* (h) mortuo viro hinc confirmatur Dos. This is intended of a naturall, not of a ciuill death. For if the husband entred in religion, (i) the wife shall not be endowed vntill he be naturally dead.

And in this Chapter Littleton deuideth Dower into fiue parts, viz. Dower by the Common Law. Secondly, Dower by the Custome. Thirdly, Dower ad ostium Ecclesiæ. Fourthly, Dower ex assensu patris. And fiftly, Dower De la pluis beale. And all these Dowers were instituted for a competent liuelihood for the wife during her life. (k) Propter onus matrimonij & ad sustentationem vxoris & educationem liberorum cum fuerint procreati si vir præmoriatur.

(h) *Britton. cap. 106. Bracton. lib. 4. fol. 301.*

(i) *31. E. 3. tit. collusion 29.*

(k) *Bract. lib. 2. cap. 39. fol. 92. &c. Fleta. lib. 5. cap. 22. Britton cap. 101.*

Section 37.

¶ ET nota, que per le common ley la feme nauera pur sa Dower forque la tierce part des tenements que fueront a sa Baron durant le Espousels, mes per custome dascun pais el auera le moitie, & per le custome en ascun Ville & Burgh, el auera lentiertie. Et en touts tiels cases, el serra dit tenāt en Dower.

AND note, that by the common law, the wife shall haue for her Dower, but the third part of the Tenements which were her husbands during the Espousals, but by the custome of some countie shee shall haue the halfe, and by the custome in some Towne or Borough, shee shall haue the whole. And in all these Cases shee shall be called Tenant in Dower.

¶ *Nota per le common ley la feme nauera pur sa dower forsque* (l) *la teirce part, &c.* This third part is called rationabilis dos, or Dos legitima, because it is the Dower that the Common Law giueth rationabilis autem Dos est cuiuslibet mulieris de quocunque tenemento tertia pars omnium terrarum; & tenemētorum quæ vir suus tenuit in dominico suo vt de feodo, &c.

(l) *Glanuil. lib. 6. cap. 1. Bracton. vbi supra. Britton. vbi supra. Fleta vbi supra. Mirror. cap. 1. §. 3. Magna Carta cap. 7.*

¶ *Mes per Custome dascun pais el auera le moitie, & per le custome en ascun Ville & Burgh el auera lentiertie.* Such a (m) custome may extend to a County, City, or an ancient Burgh without question, and so this custome as here it appeareth by Littleton, may extend to vpland Townes, which are neither, Counties, Cities, nor Boroughs. But the surer pleading in this and the like Cases, is to lay the custome within a Mannor or Seigniorie if the truth of the case will so beare it. By the custome of Gauelkind (n) the wife shall be indowed of the moitie, so long as she keepe herselfe sole, and without child, which she cannot waiue and take her thirds for her life. For in that case, Consuetudo tollit communem legem.

And as custome may enlarge, so may custome abridge Dower, and restraine it to a fourth part, &c.

Fitz. N. B. 150. o.

(m) *21. E. 4. 53. 54. 7. H. 6. 26. 22. H. 6. 14. 21. H. 7. 17. 40. Ass. 27. 41. 16. E. 2. prescription 53. 43. E. 3. 32. 45. Ass. 8. Dier. 363. 39. E. 3. 2. 10. 14. E. 3. Barre 277. 13. E. 3. tit. Dower. 65.*

(n) *Vide le statute de consuetud. Kancia, &c. Trin. 17. E. 3. coram Rege Kan. in Thesaur. in which record Senecia signifieth Widdowhood.*

Section 38.

This shall be explained by that which shall be said in the two Sections next ensuing.

¶ Aulx sont deux auters manners de dower, cestascauoir, dower que est appelle dowment ad ostium Ecclesiæ, & dower appelle dowment ex assensu patris.

Also there bee two other kinds of Dower, *viz.* Dower which is called Dowment at the Church doore, and Dower called Dowment by the fathers assent.

Section 39.

¶ Dowment ad ostium Ecclesiæ, est lou home de pleine age seisi en fee simple que serra espouse a un feme, quant il vient al huis del monastery ou del esglise destre espouse, & la apres affiance enter eux fait, il endowe la feme de sa entier terre, ou de la moitie, ou dautre meindre parcel & la ouertment declare le quantitie & la certainty de la terre que el auera pur sa dower, in ceo case la feme, apres le mort le baron, poit enter en le dit quantitie de terre dont le baron luy endowa, sans auter assignement de nulluy.

Dowment at the Church doore, is where a man of full age seised in Fee simple, who shall be married to a woman, and when he commeth to the Church doore to be married, there, after affiance & troth plight betweene them, he endoweth the woman of his whole land or of the halfe or other lesser part thereof, and there openly doth declare the quantitie and the certaintie of the land which shee shall haue for her Dower. In this case the wife after the death of the husband, may enter into the said quantitie of land of which her husband endowed her, without other assignement of any.

¶ If this dower bee made ad ostium castri siue messuagij it is not good, but ought to be made, ad ostium Ecclesiæ siue Monasterij. 10. H. 3. Dower. 200.

Et sciendum est (o) quod hæc constitutio fieri debet in facie Ecclesiæ, & ad ostium Ecclesiæ, non enim valet facta in lecto mortali, vel in camera, vel alibi vbi clandestina fuere coniugia. For the law require that this and like matters bee done publickly and solemnely.

(o) Bracton. lib. 2. cap. 38. Mirror. cap. 1. §. 3. & cap 5. 10. H. 3. Dower 201. F. N. B. 150. m. n. Fleta. lib. 5. cap. 22. &c. Britton. cap. 101. 108. &c.

¶ *Ou home de pleine age.* That is of one and twentie yeares. Anno 9. H 3. Dower 197. A man of the age of eighteene yeeres tooke a wife, and by assent of his garden endowed her, ad ostium Ecclesiæ, and it was adiudged a good endowment, albeit, the husband died before the age of one and twentie yeeres; but I hold Littletons opinion to be good Law. 9. H. 3. Dower. 197.

¶ *La apres affiance enter eux.* Affidare est fidem dare. Affiance or sponsalitie, and is derived of this word spondeo, because they contract themselues together, & ideo sponsalia dicuntur (p) futurarum nuptiarum conuentio, & repromissio. But this Dower is euer after marriage solemnized, and therefore this Dower is good without deed, because he cannot make a Deed to his wife. For no assignement of dower ad ostium Ecclesiæ, can be made before marriage, for that before marriage the woman is not intitled to haue dower.

(p) Glanuill lib. 6. cap. 1. 40. E. 3. 43. Vide Vrmoni case lib. 4. fo. 1. 2

¶ *De sa entier terre ou de le moitie.* In ancient time (q) as it

(q) Glanuill. lib. 6. cap. 1. Bract. lib. 2. cap. 38. 39. & lib. 4. tract. 6. cap. 1. & 6. Britton cap. 101. &c. Fleta lib. 5. cap. 22. &c.

(r) F.N.B. 150.
(s) 20.E.3. Barre 132.
45.E.3.6. Fleta. lib. 5.23.

appeareth by Glanuill, lib. 6. cap. 1. It was taken that a man could not haue endowed his wife *ad ostium Ecclesiæ*, of a more then a third part, but of lesse he might. But at this day (r) the Law is taken as Littleton here holdeth. An assignement of dower (s) where the husband was sole seised, cannot bee made of the third or fourth part in common, but ought to bee in seueraltie.

(t) Britton. cap. 101.
Bracton. lib. 2. cap. 18.

¶ *Et la ouertment* (t) *declare le quantitie & certeintie del terre.* Here be two things that the Law doth delight in, viz. first, to haue this and the like openly and solemnely done. Secondly, to haue certaintie, which is the mother of quiet and repose. And this word (moitie) abouesaid is to be entended of the halfe in certaintie, and not of the moitie in Common, which cleerely (u) appeareth in that here Littleton saith, the quantitie and certaintie of the land.

(u) Vide 14.H.3. Dower 189
9.H.3. Dower 190.
8.H.3. Dower 195.
F.N.B. 150.
40.E.3.43.

¶ *En ceo case la feme poet enter en le dit quantitie del terre.* And afterwards Sectione 43. he saith, Nota, que en touts cases lou le certaintie appeirt queux terres ou tenements feme auera pur sa dower la fem poet enter apres la mort son Baron. It was instituted in fauour and reliefe of wiues, that a man after marriage might assigne to his wife certaintie of Dower, to the end that the widow should not bee driuen to a long and chargeable suit wherein delay might be vsed, and in the meane time her life spent, together with her money also. For albeit the (w) law hath prouided, *Quod vidua post mortem mariti sui non det aliquid pro dote sua & maneat in capitali mesuagio mariti sui per quadraginta dies post obitum mariti sui infra quos dies assignetur ei dos sua, nisi prius ei assignata fuerit, &c & habeat rationabile estouerium suum interim in Communi*, yet because there was no penaltie or punishment inflicted, the tenant of the land may driue her to sue for her Dower. And this continuance of the widow in the capitall Messuage is in Law called a Quarentine, *Quarentina*, for that it is by the space of fortie dayes, as is aforesaid. And if the heire or other tenant of the land put her out, she may haue her writ, *De quarentina habenda.* If the wife marrie within the fortie dayes she loseth her Quarentine for her habitation in the house is personall to her, and only giuen to her in iudgement of Law during her widowhood, albeit the words of the Law bee generall. And therefore to the end that widowes might haue certaintie of estate, and that they might enter and not be driuen to suit, the Law hath prouided Dower *ad ostiam Ecclesiæ*, and as it shall appeare hereafter, Dower *ex assensu patris*, And lastly, by making of a ioynture, of which (being no Dower but made in satisfaction of Dower either before or after Marriage) it is necessarie that some thing should be said hereafter in his apt place, for that this now falleth out to be the surest way.

(w) Magna Carta cap. 7.
See the second part of the Institutes, cap. 7.
Fleta lib. 5. cap. 23.
Britton. cap. 103.
Bract. lib. 2. cap. 40.
Regist. 175.
Vide Dier 6.E.6.76.b. & 161.a. F.N.B. 161.
1. Marie. Br. 101.

Nota. surest way.

¶ *En touts cases quant le certeintie appeirt &c. la feme poet enter apres le mort del Baron.* This is to be intended where the certaintie appeareth vpon an assignement of dower, *ad ostium Ecclesiæ*, or *ex assensu patris* For if a woman bring a writ of dower of six pound rent charge, & she hath iudgement to recouer the third part, albeit it be certain that she shal haue fortie shillings, yet she cannot (x) distreine for 40. shillings before the Sherife doe deliuer the same vnto her: for wheresoeuer the writ demand land, rent, or other things in certaine, the demandant after iudgement may enter or distreine before any season deliuered to him by the Sherife vpon a writ of *habere facias seisinam.* But in Dower where the writ demandeth nothing in certaine, there the demandant after the iudgement cannot enter or distreine vntill execution sued, by which execution the Sherife is by the Kings writ to deliuer the third part in certaintie to the demandant. And so it is when the wife of one tenant in common demand a third part of a moitie, yet after iudgement she cannot enter vntill the Sherife deliuer to her the third part, albeit the deliuerie of the Sherife shall reduce it to no more certaintie then it was.

(x) 45.E.3.26.
48.E.3.36. 22. Ass. 87.
39.E.3.12. 37.H.6.38.
39.H.6.25.
1.8. 5.8. Breu. 199.
30.E.3.30. 21.E.4.3.
Vide lib. 1. Shelleys case.
40.E.3.22.

¶ *Sans auter assignement de nulluy.* For as concerning Dower at the Common law, there must be assignement either by the Sherife (as hath beene said) by the Kings writ, or else by the heire or other tenant of the land by consent and agreement betweene them To a perfect assignement of Dower eight things are to be obserued: (a) First regularly the assignement must be certaine, as our Author here saith.

(a) 8.E.2. Gar. 75. 40.E.3.21
45.E.3.5.6.
(b) 1. Mar. Dier 91.
1.E.2. Dower 146. 28.H.6.2.
Dier 9. El. 263. 26. Ass. 41.
31.E.3. Scir. fa. 99. 33.H.6.2
Vernons case, li. 4. f. 1.
5.E.4.22.

Secondly, It (b) must be either of some part of the land whereof she is dowable, or of a rent or some other profit issuing out of the same, either before iudgement or after, which Rent may be assigned to her by parol. But an assignement of other land whereof she is not dowable, or of a rent issuing out of the same, is no barre of her dower.

Thirdly, The assignement must be absolute, and not conditionall, or subiect to any limitation.

Fourthly, It must be made by him that is Tenant of the land, but herein certaine diuersities are to be obserued.

(c) 7.H.6.34. 10.E.2. Dower 169. 10.E.3.38.

If two or more be Ioyntenants of lands, (c) the one of them may assigne Dower to the

wife,

wife of a third part in Certaintie, and this shall binde his companions, because they were compellable to doe the same by Law. But if one of them assigne a rent out of the land to the wife, this shall not binde his companion, because hee was not compellable by the Law thereunto. If the husband make severall Feoffments of severall parcels, and dieth and the one Feoffee assigne Dower to the wife of parcell of land in satisfaction of all the Dower which shee ought to have in the land of the other feoffees, the other feoffees shall take no benefit of this assignement, because they are strangers thereunto, and cannot pleade the same. But in that case if the husband dieth seised of other lands in fee simple and the same discend to his heire, and the heire indoweth the wife of certaine of those lands in full satisfaction of all the Dower that shee ought to have aswell in the lands of the feoffees as in his owne lands, this assignement is good, and the severall feoffees shall take advantage of it. And therefore if the wife bring a writ of Dower against any of them, they may vouch the heire, and hee may pleade the assignement which he himself hath made in safetie of himselfe, least they should recover in value against him, (d) so as there is a privitie in this respect betweene the heire and the feoffees, and by this meanes the same may be pleaded by the heire that made it. And so it is adiudged in our books, which is a notable case for many purposes.

(d) 33.E.3.*Tit* *Iudgm*.254. 8.E.3.69. 17.E.3.58.b. 3.E.3.*tit.Dower* 76. 3.E.3.*Vouch*.196. *See the second part of the Instit W.*1. *cap*.49.

Fiftly, If assignement be made (e) by any disseisor, abator, intruder, or any wrong doer, of lands or tenements, if they came to that estate by collusion and covin betweene the widdow and them, albeit the widdow hath iust cause of action and the assignement bee indifferently made after iudgement by the Sherife of an equall third part, yet shall the Disseisee, &c. avoyd it, for covin in this case shall suffocate the right that appertained to her, & so the wrongfull manner shal avoyd the matter that is lawfull.

(e) 25.*Ass*.p.1. 44.*Ass* 27. 44.E.3.46. 27.*Ass* 74. 11.H.4.60. 15.E.4.4. 19.H.8.12. *Lit*.83.151.

Sixtly, An assignement by (f) a disseisor, abator, intrudor, &c. if there be no covin, is good, unlesse it be preiudiciall to the disseisee, &c. As if the husband (g) infeoffeth the younger sonne with warrantie, the eldest sonne disseise the youngest sonne, and endow the widdow, in this case the younger sonne shall avoyd this assignement, for otherwise he shall lose his warrantie: but a disseisor, abator, intrudor, &c. cannot assigne a rent out of the land to her for her dower, to bind the disseisee, &c.

(f) 12.*Ass*.p.20.21.E.3.12. (g) 3.E.3.*tit.Dower* 77. 18.E.2.*tit.Dower Statham.*

Seventhly, No assignement can be made, but by such as have a freehold, (as hath bin said) or against whom a writ of Dower doth lie, and therefore (h) an assignement by a gardein in socage is void, but a gardein in chivalrie may assigne dower, as shall be said hereafter, because a writ of dower lieth against him, and not against a gardein in socage.

(h) 31.E.1.*Dower* 151. 29.*Ass* 68. 15.E.3.*Dower* 67.

Eightly, And before the gardein in chivalrie enter, the heire within age (i) may assigne dower, for the gardein may waive the wardship. And so briefely have you heard, of what, by whom, and to whom the assignement must be made. But there needeth neither liverie of seisin, nor writing, to any assignement of Dower, because it is due of common right.

(i) 7.R.2. *admesurement* 4. F.N.B.148.f.

Section 40.

DOwment ex assensu Patris est lou le pier est seisie de Tenements en fee, & son fits & heire apparent, quant il est espouse, endowe sa feme al huys del Monasterie ou del Esglise, de parcel de Terres ou Tenements son pier, de assent son pier, & assigne la quantitie & les parcels. En ceo case apres le mort le fits,

DOwment by assent of the father is, where the father is seised of Tenements in fee, and his sonne and heire apparent when he is married, endoweth his wife at the Monasterie or Church doore, of parcel of his fathers lands or Tenements with the assent of his Father, and assignes the quantity and parcels; In this case after the death of the

¶ *Lou le piere est seisie de Tenements en fee.* Tenant for life of a Carue of Land, the reversion to the father in fee, the sonne and heire apparent of the father endoweth his wife of this Carue, by the assent of the father, the Tenant for life dieth, the husband dieth, the reversion was a Tenement in the father, and yet this is no good endowment ex assensu patris, because the Father at the time of the assent had but a reversion expectant upon a freehold, whereof hee could not have endowed his owne wife; and albeit the tenant for life died, living the husband, yet, quod initio non valet tractu temporis non convalescet.

Brit c.109. *Flet.li*.5 c.22.23 *Bract.li*.5.305. 6.E.3.34. F.N.B.150.

ualescet. And for the most part, Dower ad ostium Ecclesiæ, and ex assensu patris, ensue the nature of a Dower at the Common Law. And for these the wife may haue a writ of Dower, albeit they be certaine, as for the third part at the Common Law.

¶ *Et son fits & heire apparent.* It must be such a sonne and heire apparent, as must continue an heire apparent, and therefore the youngest sonne and heire apparent cannot endow his

la feme entera en mesme le parcell sauns auter assignement de nulluy. Mes il ad este dit en cest case, que il couient a la feme dauer vn fait de le Pier prouant son assent & consent de cel endowment, M.44.E.3. fol.45.

sonne, the wife shal enter into the same parcell without the assignement of any. But it hath beene said in this case, That it behoueth the wife to haue a Deed of the father, to prooue his assent and consent to this endowment. *M.* 44.*E.*3.*f.*45.

wife ex assensu patris, of lands whereof the father is seised in fee of the nature of Borough English, because the father may haue another sonne, and then the husband is not heire apparent: and it is in respect of the constant and perpetuall apparance, that the sonne and heire apparant may endow his wife of his fathers land. And so it is of lands in Gauelkind: (k) and this is the reason that Dower ex assensu fratris, or consanguinei, is not good, for that albeit he is heire apparant at that time, yet for the common possibilitie that hee may haue issue, and euery issue that the brother or cosine should haue afterwards, shall exclude him, hee is no such heire apparent as the Law intendeth. (l) But an endowment ex assensu matris, is as good as ex assensu patris, because there is an apparance of a constant and perpetuall heire. And some haue said, that if the father after his assent be attainted of treason or felonie, that the wife in that case loseth her dower, because her husband doth not continue heire.

(k) 8.*H.*3.*Dower* 193. 9.*H.*3.*Dow.*19.11.*H.*3. *Dower.F.N.B.*150.*l.* 29.*E.*3.*Dower* 134.

(l) *F.N.B.*150.*e Flet.lib.*5. *cap.*22. *Bract.lib.*4.305. *Ambr.Gorges case.li.*6 *fo.*22.

¶ *Quant il est espouse, endow sa feme.* (m) **In this case, albeit the** Freehold and Inheritance is in the father, yet in respect (as hath been said) of the constant and perpetuall appearance of the heire, the heire apparent doth endow, and the father doth but assent. And therefore where the father did endow the wife of his sonne and heire apparent, that endowment was holden void, because the husband in that case must endow, and the father assent.

(m) 2.*H.*3.*Dower* 199. 6.*E.*3.34. 8.*E.*2.*Dow* 154.

And it is holden in 2.H.3.Dower 199. That if the heire apparent be within age, yet the endowment ex assensu patris is good. Note, Littleton in the case of Dower ad ostium Ecclesiæ, doth put the husband of full age, but here of the dower ex assensu patris, he speaketh generally.

2.*H.*3.*Dower* 199.

¶ *Et assigne le quantitie & les parcels.* **So as both in Dower** ad (n) ostium Ecclesiæ, & ex assensu patris, the certaintie must be expressed. And therefore where Bookes speake of a moitie, it is intended, (as hath beene said) of an halfe in certaine.

(n) 9 *H.*3.*Dower* 190. *F.N.B.*150.*m.*

¶ *Apres la mort le fitz sa feme entera:* **In this case after the death** of the husband the wife shall enter, or haue a writ of Dower albeit the father be aliue.

8.*E.*2.*Dower* 154.

¶ *Que il conient al feme dauer vn fait prouant sont assent a cel endowment.*

¶ *Vn fait*, **a Deed** factum, **this word (Deed) in the vnderstanding** of the Common Law is an Instrument written in parchment or paper, (o) whereunto ten things are necessarily incident: Viz First, writing. Secondly, in Parchment or Paper. Thirdly, a person able to contract. Fourthly, by a sufficient name. Fiftly, a person able to be contracted with. Sixtly, by a sufficient name. Seuenthly, a thing to be contracted for. Eightly, apt words required by Law. Ninthly, Sealing. And tenthly, Deliuerie. A Deed cannot be written vpon wood, leather, cloath, or the like, but onely vpon parchment or paper, for the writing vpon them can be least vittated, altred, or corrupted.

(o) *Bract.li.*2.*fol.*33.*&c.* & *li.*5.*fol.*396.*Brit.fol* 34. 65.66.101. *Flet.li.*3.*ca.*14. & *li.*6.*c.*32.& *li.*3 *c.*3,4,5.6

If a deed (p) be alledged in Count or Plea, regularly it must be shewed to the Court, to the end the Court may iudge whither there be apt words to make it a good contract according to the rule of Law, whereof more shall be said in the chapter of conditions. But if non est factum be pleaded, because thereby the sealing, deliuerie, or other matter of fact is denied, it shal be tried by the Countrie. Of Deeds some be indented, and some be Deeds poll. Of indented, some be bipartite, some tripartite, some quadripartite, &c. whereof more shall be said in the Chapter of Conditions. Also of Deeds, some be inrolled, and some (q) be not inrolled; if it bee inrolled according to the Statute of 27.Hen.8.cap.10. it must be inrolled in parchment for the strength and continuance thereof, and not in paper, and so was it resolued in Parliament by the Iudges

(p) 4.*E.*2.*Fines* 116.14.*E.*2 *Ley* 79.4.*E.*2.*Ley* 78. 27.*H.*6. 0.27.*H.*8.22. *F.N.B.*122.*I.*

(q) *Brit.fo.*101.*Bract.li.*2. *fol.*33. *Fleta lib.*3.*ca.*14.

ges in anno 23.Eliz. Now for the rest of the parts of a Deed, you shall read thereof plentifully in our Bookes, and in my Reports; which by this short instruction you shall easily understand.

¶ *Vn fait de feoffement*. It is properly called Charta feoffamenti, and yet if such a deed be denied, the plea is non est factum. So as of deeds, some concerne the realtie, as here a deed of feoffement; some the personaltie, as a Deed of gift of goods, Obligations, Bills, &c. And some mixt, whereof more shall bee said in the Chapter of Releases.

If a man deliuer a writing sealed, to the partie to whom it is made, as an escrow to be his Deed vpon certaine conditions, &c. this is an absolute deliuerie of the Deed, being made to the partie himselfe, for the deliuerie is sufficient without speaking of any words, (otherwise a man that is mute could not deliuer a Deed) and Tradition is onely requisite, and then when the words are contrarie to the act which is the deliuerie, the words are of none effect, non quod dictum, sed quod factum est inspicitur. And hereof though there hath beene (r) varietie of opinions yet is the Law now settled agreeable to iudgements in former times, and so was it resolued by the whole Court of Common-pleas. But it may be deliuered to a stranger, as an escrowe, &c. because the bare act of deliuery to him without words worketh nothing. And this is the ancient diuersitie (s) in our bookes the record whereof I haue seene agreeable with the reason of our old bookes. And as a Deed may be deliuered to the partie without words, so may a Deed be deliuered by words without any act of deliuery, as if the writing sealed lyeth vpon the table, and the feoffor or obligor saith to the feoffee or obligee, Goe and take vp the said writing, it is sufficient for you; or it will serue the turne, or take it as my Deede, or the like words, it is a sufficient deliuery.

35.Ass.Pl.11. Tr.27.H.8. Dier 95.
(r) Tr.43.Eliz. inter Hankesby & Lacher in the Kings bench. Hill.12.Ia.R. in the Common place.
(s) 13.H.8. 19 H.8.8. 4.E.3.18.13.H.4.8.

Of Deeds and their destinctions you shall reade excellent matter in Antiquitie. (t) Cartarum, alia regia, alia priuatorum, & regiarum, alia priuata, alia communis, & alia vniuersitatis. Priuatarum, alia de puro feoffamento & simplici, alia de feoffamento conditionali siue conuentionali, alia de recognitione pura, vel conditionali, alia de quiete clamantia, alia de confirmatione, &c. Verba intentioni non é contra debent inseruire.

(t) Brott. lib.2.fo.33.b. Fleta lib.3.ca.14.

Carta non est (u) nisi vestimentum donationis. Carta non est nisi vestimentum orationis. Nemo tenetur armare aduersarium suum contra se. Scriptum est instrumentum ad instruendum quod mens vult. Carta est legatus mentis. (w) Benignæ sunt faciendæ interpretationes cartarum propter simplicitatem laicorum vt res magis valeat quam pereat. Nihil tam (x) conueniens est naturali equitati quam voluntatem domini volentis rem suam in alium transferre ratam habere.

(u) Fleta lib.6.ca.28. Bratton. Bratton lib.2 fo 34.
(w) Bratton lib 2.fo.94.95.
(x) Idem lib.2 fo 18.

Re, verbis, scripto, consensu, traditione
Iunctura vestes sumere pacta solent.

(y) Pl.Com. in Throgmortons case fo.161.b.

Verba cartarum fortius accipiuntur contra proferentem. Generale dictum generaliter est intelligendum. Verba debent intelligi secundum subiectam materiam. Carta de non ente non valet.

Note, the father may (a) make a Deede to the wife of his sonne, and so is the Law holden for that the fathers land by his assent is charged with a future freehold whereunto a Deede is requisite, but to a Dower Ad ostium Ecclesiæ no Deede is requisite. And here it is not well done (of him that made the addition to our Author) to vouche 44.E.3.fo.45. because the Author himselfe vouched it not, for if he (b) meant to haue vouched authorities, hee would haue vouched more then one in this case, and those that (c) hee vouched hee would haue cited truly, but this case is mistaken both in the yeare and in the Leafe, for where it is cited in 44.E.3. it is in 40.E.3. and where he saith it is fo.45. it is fo.43.

(a) 3.E.2.Dower 126. 8.E.2.Dower 154. 6.E.3.34. 40.E.3.43.
(b) 11.H.3.Dower 186. 14.H.3.Dower.
(c) 2.E.2.Dower 125. Vid. Statut. Walliæ anno. 12.E.1.fo.18. in veteri magna carta. 47.H 3.Dower 174.

An assignment of Dower (d) either ad ostium Ecclesiæ or ex assensu patris may be made of more than a third part. But the ancient Law was that no greater assignement could bee made in those cases but of a third part, but lesse he might, as it appeareth in Glanuill.

(d) F.N.B.150.p. Glanuil. lib.6.ca.1.2.3.

Section 41.

CET cel apres le mort le baron el enter & agree a ascun tiel dower de les dits dowers ad ostium ecclesiæ, &c. Donque

AND if after the death of her husband she entreth, and agree to any such dower of the said dowers at the Church dore, &c. then

CEL *est conclude a claimer ascun anter dower per la common ley*. Wherein a diuersitie is be obserued betweene a Dower ad ostium Ecclesiæ, or ex assensu patris, and a ioyncture

el est conclude de claimer ascun auter dower per le common ley, dascuns terres ou tenements quex fuerent a sa dit baron. Mes si el voit, el poit refuser tiel dower ad ostium ecclesiæ,&c. & donqz el poit estre endow solonqz le cours del common ley.

she is concluded to claime any other dower by the Common law of any the lands or tenements which were her husbands, but if shee will, shee may refuse such dower at the Church dore,&c. and then she may bee endowed after the Course of the Common law.

Vernons case lib.4.fo.1. 1.Marie.Dier 91. 31.E.3. Scire fac.99. 20.E.4.3.

joynture or estate made to the wife in satisfaction of her Dower, for one of those Dowers being assented unto is a barre of the Dower at the Common Law, but a joynture was no barre of her Dower at the Common law. For a right or title that one hath to a freehold cannot bee barred by acceptance of collaterall satisfaction. But a woman cannot haue a double dower, viz. ad ostium Ecclesiæ,&c. and at the Common law, for the wife of one husband can haue but one dower. But since Littleton wrote by the Statute of 27.H.8. if a joynture be made to (a) the wife according to the purview of that statute it is a barre of her dower so as the woman shall not haue both joynture and dower, and to the making of a perfect joynture within that statute sixe things are to be obserued. First, her joynture by the first limitation is to take effect for her life in possession, or profit presently after the decease of her husband, Secondly, that it be for the tearme of her owne life, or greater estate. Thirdly, it must be made to her selfe, and to no other for her. Fourthly, it must be made in satisfaction of her whole dower, and not of part of her dower. Fiftly, it must either be expressed, or auerred to be in satisfaction of her dower. And sixtly, it may be made either before or after mariage.

27.H.8. cap.10. (a) 12.E.2. Dower.158. 27.H.8.ca.10. versus finem.

Concerning the first, if a man make a Feoffment in fee of Lands or Tenements either before or after mariage to the use of the husband for life, and after to the use of A. for life, and then to the use of the wife for life in satisfaction of her dower, this is no joynture within the statute, because by the first limitation it was not to take effect in possession or profit presently after the death of her husband, And albeit in that case A. should dye liuing the husband, and after the death of the husband the wife entreth, yet this is no barre of her dower, but she shall haue her dower also because it is not within the said statute, and (as it hath beene said) by the Common law it was no bar of her dower. 2. It must be either in fee taile, or for term of her own life, for an estate for life or liues of one or many other, [redacted] or to her for a C. or 1000. yeares,&c. if she liue so long, or without such limitation is no barre of her dower, albeit they be expressely made in satisfaction of her dower, causa qua supra. 3. If an estate bee made to others in fee simple, or for her life upon trust so as the estate remaine in them, albeit, it be for her benefit, and by her assent, and by expresse words to be in full satisfation of her dower, yet is this no barre of her dower. The fourth is so plaine as it needeth not any example. 5. A deuise by will cannot be auerred to be in satisfaction of her dower, unlesse it bee so expressed in the will. 6. If the joynture be made before marriage, the wife cannot waiue it and clayme her dower at the Common law, but if it be made after mariage, she may waiue the same and claime her dower. I haue touched these points the more summarily, because they are resolued at large with the reasons thereof in Vernons case vbi supra. So as to comprehend all in few words, a joynture (which in common understanding extendeth as well to a sole estate as to a joynt estate with her husband) is a competent liuelihood of freehold for the wife of Lands or Tenements,&c. to take effect presently in possession or profit after the decease of the husband for the life of the wife at the least if she her selfe be not the cause of determination or forfeiture of it. Which see more at large in Vernons case vbi supra. If a joynture bee made to a wife of lands before the Couerture, and after the husband and wife Alien by fine those lands so conueyed for her joynture, she shall not be endowed of any of the other lands of her husband. But if the joynture had beene made after mariage notwithstanding the alienation by the husband and wife thereof by fine, yet seeing her estate was originally waiuable, and the time of her election came not till after the decease of her husband she may claime her dower in the residue of her lands. But in the other case, the joynture of the wife made before mariage was not waiueable at all, now as the dower ad ostium Ecclesiæ and ex assensu patris is better for the wife, because in respect of the certainty, she may enter, then the dower at the Common Law, where shee is driuen to her reall action, and therefore Britton calleth Dower ad ostium Ecclesiæ and ex assensu patris establishment of dower by the husband and assignement of Dower after his decease (for nothing that is uncertaine is established.) So a joynture that hath the force of a barre of Dower by the said act of 27.H.8.) is as hath beene said more sure and safe for the wife then either Dower

Leake & Rardals case, lib.4.fol.4.

Vid. Vernons case vbi supra, fo.2.b.

Dier, 19.Eliz.358.

Britt, cap.102.103.

ad

ad ostium Ecclesiæ or ex assensu patris, for besides it is as certaine as those others, and shee may enter into it, after the death of her husband and not be driuen to her action. She shall not be barred of her ioynture albeit her husband cõmit treason or felonie, as she shalbe both of her Dower ad ostium Ecclesiæ and ex assensu patris by the Common Law. But now at this day by the statutes of 1.E.6.cap.2. and 5.E.6.cap.11. a wife shall not lose any title of Dower which to her was accrued by the attainder of her husband for any manner of murder or other felony whatsoeuer. But (a) if the husband be attainted of high treason or petie treason she shalbe (b) barred of her dower at this day, so long as that attaindre standeth in force.

Bract.311.lib.4. Britton.ca.15.

1.E.6.ca 6. 5.E.6.ca.11.

(a) Stanford.195.b

(b) Vid. in the chapter of Garranty. Sect.

¶ *Conclude*, commeth of the (c) verbe concludo which is deriued of con and claudo to determine, to finish, to shut vp, to estoppe, or barre a man to pleade or clayme any other thing, Vid. Estoppell.

(c) T. Com.276.b. per Walsh. Vid. Sect.693.695. 667.679.

Section 42.

ET nota que nul feme serra endow ex assensu patris en le forme auantdit, mes lou sa baron est fits & heire apparant a son pier. Quære de ceux deux cases de dowment ad ostium Ecclesiæ, &c. si la feme al temps del mort sa baron, ne passe lage de ix. ans, si el auera dower ou non.

And note that no wife shall bee endowed *ex assensu patris* in forme aforesaid, but where her husband is sonne and heire apparant to his father. *Quære* of these two cases of dowment *ad ostium ecclesiæ, &c.* if the wife at the time of the death of her husband bee not past the age of 9. yeares, whither shee shal haue dower or no.

Vl feme serra endowed, &c. Of this sufficient hath beene said before.

¶ *Quære de ceux deux cases de dowment ad ostium Ecclesiæ, &c.* And it seemeth that these Dowers being made by assent, &c. that the same are good albeit the wife bee within the age of Nine yeares, for Consensus tollit errorem. But without question, a ioynture made to her vnder or aboue the age of Nine yeares, is good.

Section 43.

ET nota que en touts cases lou le certainty appiert queux tres ou tenements feme auer pur sa dower, la le feme poit entrer aps la mort sa baron, sans assignement de nuluy. Mes lou le certaintie ne appiert, si come : destre endow de la tierce part dauer en seueraltie, ou del moitie solonque le custome de tener

And note that in all cases, where the certaintie appeareth what lands or tenements the wife shall haue for her dower, there the wife may enter after the death of her husband without assignement of any. But where the certaintie appeares not, as to be endowed of the 3. part to haue in seueralty, or the moity according to the custom

ET nota que en touts cases, &c. In all cases where the demaund of the Dower is certaine as in case of Dower ad ostium Ecclesiæ or ex assensu patris, there the wife after the death of the husband may enter. But where the demaund is vncertaine as in writs of Dower at the Common Law, there albeit the thing it selfe be certaine, yet shall she not take it without assignement, As if a woman bring a writ of dower of three shillings rent, albeit shee ought to bee endowed of one shilling, yet cannot shee after iudgement distreine for twelue pence before assignement, because the demaund was vncertaine

40.E.3.22.43. 45.E.3.4. 20.E.3.barre.132. 8.E.2.Entry 75.

taine. And so it is if two tenants in common bee, and the wife of one of them bring a writ of dower to be endowed of a third part of a moitie, and haue iudgement to recouer, yet cannot shee enter without assignement, albeit the assignement cannot giue her any certaintie because her husbands state was incertaine. See more of this before Section 39.

en seueraltie, en tielx cases il couient que sa dower soit a luy assigne aps le mort del baron, pur ceo que non constat deuant assignemēt quel part des terres ou tenements el auera pur sa dower.

to hold in seueraltie. In such cases it behoooueth that her Dower bee assigned vnto her after the death of her husband, because it doth not appeare before assignement what part of the lands or tenements she shall haue for her dower.

Sect. 44.

Of this sufficient hath beene said before, and that in this case, the wife cannot enter without assignement.

¶ MEs si soient deux iointenants de certaine terre en fee, & lun alien ceo que a luy affiert a vn auter en fee, que prent feme & puis deuie; en ceo cas la feme pur sa dower auera le tierce part de la moitie que sa baron ad purchase, a tener en common (come sa part amountera) ouesque lheire sa baron, & ouesque lauter iointenant que ne aliena pas, pur ceo que en tiel cas sa dower ne poit estre assigne per metes & bounds.

BVt if there be two ioyntenants of certaine land in fee, and the one alieneth that which belongeth to him, to another in fee, who taketh a wife, and after dieth. In this case the wife for her dower shal haue the third part of the moitie which her husband purchased, to hold in common (as her part amounteth) with the heire of her husband, and with the other ioyntenant, which did not alien. For that in this case, her dower cannot be assigned by metes and bounds.

Sect. 45.

¶ THe reason of this diuersitie is for that the iointenāt which suruiueth, claymeth the land by the feoffment, and by suruiuorship, which is aboue the Title of Dower, and may plead the feoffment, made to himselfe without naming of his compagnion that died, as shall bee said hereafter in his proper place, but Tenants in common haue seuerall Freeholds and Inheritances, and their moities shall discend to their seueral heires, & therefore their wiues shall be indowed.

¶ Est ascauoir, q̄ la feme ne serrā my endow de terres ou tenements q̄ sa baron tient iointment ouesque vn auter al temps de son morant: mes lou il tient en common auterment est, come en le case prochein auantdit.

ANd it is to be vnderstood that the wife shall not bee endowed of lands or tenemēts which her husband holdeth iointly with another at the time of his death: but where hee holdeth in common, otherwise it is as in the case next abouesaid.

Sect. 46.

¶ Et est ascauoir que si tenant en le taile endowa sa feme ad ostium Ecclesiæ, come est auantdit, ceo seruera pur petit ou rien al feme, pur ceo que apres la mort sa baron, lissue en le taile puit entrer sur le possession la feme: Et issint puit celuy en le reuers. si ne soit issue en le taile en vie &c.

And it is to bee vnderstood, that if tenant in taile endoweth his Wife at the Church doore, as is aforesaid, this shall little or nothing at all auaile the wife, for that, that after the decease of her husband, the issue in taile may enter vpon her possession, and so may he in the reuersion, if there bee no issue in taile then aliue.

¶ The Reason of this is, for that tenant in taile is restrained by the said statute of 13. E. 1. De donis conditionalibus. And so did our Authour take the law in his Learned reading. Here our Authors reason is à fine, and therefore such an Endowment is not to bee made because it is to ends.

Vide Sect. 194.

Sect. 47.

¶ Auxy si home seisi en fee simple esteant deins age endowa sa feme al huis del monasterie ou deglise, & deuie, & sa feme enter, en ceo cas lheire la baron luy puit ouster. Mes auterment est (come il semble) lou le pier est seisie en fee, & le fits deins age endow sa feme ex assensu patris, le pier donque esteant de plein age.

Also if a man seised in Fee Simple beeing within age endoweth his wife at the Monasterie or Church doore, and dieth, and his wife enter, in this case the heire of the husband may out her. But otherwise it is, (as it seemeth) where the father is seised in fee, and the sonne within age endoweth his wife *ex assensu patris*, the Father being then of full age.

¶ The reasō of this diuersitie is for that in the first case the husbād within age is seised and therefore hee beeing within age cannot by a voluntarie act bind himselfe: otherwise it is where he doth an act whereunto hee is compellable by law, but in the latter case the Father which giueth the assent, is seised of the freehold and Inheritance, and the Sonne therein hath nothing, and therefore his Heire shall not auoide it in respect of his Infancie.

Vid. 9. *H.* 3. *tit. dower* 197.

Section 48.

¶ Auxy il y ad vn auter endowment, que est appel dowment de la pluis beal. Et ceo est come en tiel case, que home seisie de xl. acres de terre, & il tient vint

Also there is another dower which is called dowment *de la pluis beale*. And this is in case where a man is seised of fortie acres of land, and hee holdeth twentie acres of

¶ *Et le Seignior de que le terre est tenus en Chiualrie enter en les vint acres tenus de luy.* For hee is not possessed as a Garden against whom a Writ of Dower lieth, vntill hee doth enter: of the wardship of the bodie hee is possessed before seisure, because it

Vid. le statut. de bigamis cap. 3.

(a) 44 E.3.13. 4.H.6 11. *Sta f. pier.* 13. 6.E.3.15. 16.E.3.*breue* 657. *Temps* E.1.*breue* 863. 11.E.3. *breue* 473. 45.E.3.5. 17.E.3.70. 3.H.7.17. 4.H.7.1. 4.H.7. *aid le Roy* 33. 38.E.3 13. 9.H.6.6.b. 39.E.3.8. 8.E.2. *Dower* 169. 8 E.2. *breue* 809. 22.E.4. *Dower* 16.

8.E.3.52.

2.E.3.15. & 31. 38.E.3.37. 47 E.3.9.b.

it is transitorie, but hee is not possessed of the land untill hee enter because it is permanent. And therefore if hee doth not enter, the heire within age may assigne Dower as hath beene said, and as it appeareth afterwards.

¶ *Si en tiel case el port breue de dower enuers le Garden en Chiualrie.* Albeit (a) the Garden in Chiualrie or the Grantee of the King of a Wardship hath but a chattle during the minoritie of the heire, and the woman shall recouer a freehold in her writ of Dower, yet after the Garden as is aforesaid, hath entred into the land, that writ lieth against him, and not against the heire who is tenant of the freehold, because the law hath trusted the Garden to plead for the heire within age, and that is in his custodie, and also for his owne particular interest, and by this diuersitie all the Bookes bee reconciled. So likewise if the Garden dieth, the wife shall haue a writ of Dower against his Executors, and if there bee two Executors, and one of them alone take the profits, the writ of Dower shall bee maintained against him only. If a man bee possessed of the Wardship of certaine land, either joyntly with his wife or in the right of his wife, yet the writ of Dower lieth against the husband only. Garden in Socage shall not endow herselfe de la pluis beale without judgement, as shall be said hereafter.

¶ *Le Garden en Chiualrie poit pleader.* The authoritie of Littleton is direct that the Garden may plead this plea. But hereof ariseth two questions. First, whither if the heire bee vouched by the tenant in the writ of Dower in the gard of the Garden, whither he comming in as Vouchee may plead that plea. The second is, whither if the Garden in socage haue

acres de les dits xl. acres de terre dun per seruice de chiualrie, & les autres vint acres de terre dun auter en socage, & prist feme, & ount issue fits, & morust, son fits esteant deins lage de xiiij. ans, & le Seigniour de que la terre est tenus en chiualrie, entre en les xx. acres tenus de luy, & eux ad come gardein en Chiualrie durant le nonage lenfant, & la mere de lenfant enter en le remnant, & ceo occupie come gardein en socage: si en tiel case le feme port briefe de dower enuers le gardein en chiualrie, de estre endow de les tenements tenus per seruice de chiualer en le Court le Roy, ou en auter Court, le gardein en chiualrie puit plede en tiel case tout cest matter & monstre coment la feme est gardein en socage, coment deuant est dit; & prie que serra adiudge per la Court que le feme luy mesme endowera de le pluis beale de les tenements que el ad come gardein en socage solonque le value de le tierce part

the said fortie acres of one by Knights Seruice, and the other twentie acres of another in Socage, and taketh wife, and hath issue a sonne, and dieth, his sonne being within the age of fourteene yeeres, and the Lord of whom the Land is holden by Knights Seruice entreth into the twentie acres holden of him, and holdeth them as Garden in Chiualrie, during the nonage of the infant, and the mother of the infant, entreth into the residue, and occupieth it as Garden in Socage. If in this case the Wife bringeth a Writ of dower against the garden in Chiualrie to be endowed of the tenements holden by Knights Seruice, in the Kings Court or other Court, the Garden in Chiualrie may pleade in such case all this matter, and shew how the wife is Garden in Socage, as aforesaid, and pray that it may bee adiudged by the Court, that the wife may endow her selfe *de le pluis beale* .i. of the most faire, of the tenements which shee hath as Garden in So-

que

que el claime dauer de les tenements tenus en chiualrie per sa briefe de Dower. Et si la feme ceo ne puit dedire, donq̃ le iudgement serra fait, que le gardeine en chiualrie tiendra les terres tenus de luy durant le nonage lenfant, quit de la feme, &c.

cage, after the value of the third part which shee claimes by her writ of dower, to haue the tenements holden by Knights Seruice. And if the wife cannot gainsay this, then the iudgement shall be giuen, that the Garden in Chiualry shall hold the Lands holden of him during the nonage of the infant, quite from the woman, &c.

not sufficient, as if the Land holden by seruice of Chiualrie be thirtie Acres, and the lands holden in Socage but fiue Acres, whether she shall be endowed by parcels, viz. to recouer fiue Acres against the Garden in Chiualrie, and to retaine fiue Acres. And as to the first the Garden shall aswell plead it, when he come in as Vouchee, as when he is tenant. And as to the second some say that the demandant in the writ of Dower must haue Assets in her hands to the value of her Dower, so as she shal not be partly endowed against the Garden, and partly retaine in her owne hands. And they say, that the iudgement should be in part, that is, as to the land in Socage in seueraltie, and as to the land in Chiualrie to recouer the third part, and compare it to the Case in 8.E.4.3. that damages shall not be recouered, partly against the defendant in an appeale, and partly against the Abettors, but entirely either against the one or the other. And Littleton here putteth his Case that the Garden in Socage hath Assets in value, and seeing it is a Dower against common right, they hold that she must be intirely endowed either by her selfe against common right, or against the Garden according to common right. But (a) yet by the Booke in 25.E.3 52.b and others it appeareth that she may in this very case retaine for part, and recouer against the Garden for part.

5.E.3.60. 2.E.3 31. Lib.intrat. Dow.fol.225.a. 18.E.3.4.b.

14.H 7.26. Keble.

(a) 25.E.3.52.b. 4.E.2. tit.diss in 10. Regist.iudic.26. Lib.Intrat.22. 16.E.3.breue 657.20.E.3.iudgement 175.

(Gardein in Chiualrie (b) shall plead in barre of her dower, detainment, or eloigning of the bodie of the ward, because his marriage doth appertaine vnto him: And if the heire come in (c) as vouchee, hee shall plead the same plea. But he shall not plead detainment of the Charters, (d) because the Charters concerning the inheritance of the heire, belong not to the gardein. The gardein in Chiualric (e) may assigne dower of the lands and tenements he hath in ward, or if he assigne a rent out of those lands in allowannce of her dower, it is good. If the Gardein in Chiualrie assigne too much for her dower, the heire shal haue a writ of Admesuremt by the Common Law. And so (f) if the heire within age assigne before the gardeine enter, to the wife too much in the dower, the Gardein shall haue a writ of Admesurement, by the statute of West.2.cap.7. And if the heire within age, before the gardein enter into the land, assigne too much in dower, he himselfe shall haue a writ of Admesurement at full age: and some haue said, that in that case he may haue it within age. (g) But if the heire (before the gardein enter) endow the wife of more than she ought, and the gardeine assigne ouer his estate, his assignee shall haue no writ of Admesurement, because it was a thing in action. Also the heire shall haue an (h) Admesurement for the assignement in the life of his ancestor, by the Common Law, (i) and a writ of Admesurement lieth vpon an assignement in Chancerie.

(b) 7.E.3.57.8.E.3.71.
(c) 17.E.3.58.
(d) 10.E.3.50.6.El.Dy.230
(e) 3.E.3.Dow.75. 8.Ed.2. Dower 155. W.2.cap.7.
(f) Bract.li.4.314.Reg. origin.171.Flet.li.5.ca.22. 7.E.2.tit.Admes.13. F.N.B.149.
(g) 7.R.2.Admes.4 F.N.B.148.1.
(h) 7.R.2 vbi sup.F.N B.149.a
(i) 7.R.2.vbi sup.12.H.6. Admes.9.F.N.B.149. 25.E.3.51.

¶ *Donques le judgement serra fait que le gardein en Chiualrie tiendra les Terres tenus de luy durant le nonage lenfant, quite de la feme, &c.*

¶ *Iudgement.* Iudicium quasi iuris dictum, the verie voyce of Law and right, and therefore, iudicium semper pro veritate accipitur. The antient words of Iudgment are verie significant, Consideratum est, &c. because that Iudgement is euer giuen by the Court vpon due consideration had of the Record before them: and in euerie Iudgement there ought to be three persons, Actor, Reus, and Iudex. Of Iudgements, some be finall, and some not finall, whereof you shall read more hereafter. And now to returne to our Author, it is materiall that these words (& cætera) be explaned at large, viz. Et quod prædicta A. (the Demandant) capiat de terris hæred̃ prædicti in custodia sua existeñ ad valentiam p̃d. 3. partis cum pertineñ teneñ nomine dotis suæ pro præd̃ 3. parte superius per eam petit̃. Now some are of opinion, that vpon this iudgement the demandant may not in any sort endow her selfe of the land, because she cannot doe an act to her selfe, but he shall recoupe the third part of the profits vpon her account, and be endowed against the heire at his full age. But obserue what Littleton saith in the next Section: but before you come to that, obserue what priuiledge the common Law giueth to the land holden by Knights seruice, viz that it shall not be dismembred, but the

22.E.4.Dow.16.16.E.3. Wast.120.45.E.3.6.

whole dower taken of the lands holden in Socage, and the reason is, for that Knights service is for the defence of the Realme, which is pro bono publico, and therefore to be fauoured.

Section 49.

ET nota, que apres tiel judgement done, la feme puit prender ses Vicines, & en lour presenc endower luy mesme p metes & Bonds, de la pluis beale part de les tenemts que el ad cōe gardein en Socage, dau͂ et tener a luy pur terme de sa vie, & tiel Dower est appel Dower de la pluis beale.

AND note, That after such a Iudgement giuen, the wife may take her Neighbours, and in their presence endow her selfe by Metes and Bonds, of the fairest part of the Tenements which shee hath as Gardein in Socage, to haue and to hold to her for terme of her life: & this Dower is called *Dower de la plus beale*.

And the iudgement, viz. Tenend' noīe dotis, proueth, that she may haue it for terme of her life, for euerie dower is for terme of life.

Section 50.

15.E.3.Dow.69.
16.E.3.tit.Wast.100.

¶ *LOu le iudgement est fait, &c.* For without such a iudgement, as appeareth before, Gardeine in Socage cannot endow her selfe, as likewise hath bin said before.

Bract.li.5.329.F.N.B.7,8.

¶ *Ou en auter court.* That is by writ of Right of Dower in the Court of the heire, if he haue any, or of the Lord of whome the Land is holden.

¶ *Et ceo est pur saluation del estate del gardein en Chiualrie, durant le nonage de lenfant.* For the heire (before the entre of the Gardein) cannot plead the said plea, that the demandant should endow her selfe de la pluis beale. And the reason of this dower de la pluis beale to be all of the Socage land, was for aduancement of Chiualrie for the defence of the Realme.

ET nota, q̄ tiel Dowment, ne puit estre, mes lou le iudgement est fait en le court le Roy, ou en auter court, &c. et ceo est pur saluation del estate del Gardeine in Chiualrie durant le nonage le Enfant.

And note, that such dowment cannot be, but where a iudgement is giuen in the Kings Court, or in some other Court, &c. And this is for the preseruation of the estate of the gardein in Chiualrie, during the nonage of the Infant.

Sect. 51.

This is manifest of it selfe, and therefore needeth no explanation.

ET issint poyes veier cinque manners de dower, s̄, Dower per le common Ley, Dower per le custome, Dower ad ostium Ecclesiæ, Dower ex assensu patris, & Dower de la pluis beale.

AND so you may see fiue kinds of Dower, *viz.* Dower by the Common Law, Dower by the custome, Dower *ad ostium Ecclesia*, Dower *ex assensu Patris*, and Dower *de la pluis beale*.

Sect.52.

Sect.52.

EEt memorandū que en cheſcun caſe lou home prent feme ſeiſie de tiel eſtate de tenemēts, &c. iſſint que liſſue que il ad per ſon feme poit p poſſiblitie enheriter meſmes les tenements de tiel eſtate que la feme ad come heire al feme, en tiel caſe apres le mort la feme il auera meſmes les Tenements per le curteſie de Angleterre, & autrement nemy.

ANd *memorañ*, that in euerie caſe where a man taketh a wife ſeiſed of ſuch an eſtate of Tenements, &c. as the iſſue which he hath by his wife may by poſſibilitie inherit the ſame Tenements of ſuch an eſtate as the wife hath, as heire to the wife; In this caſe after the deceaſe of the wife, he ſhall haue the ſame tenements by the curteſie of England, but otherwiſe not.

M*Emorandū*, This word doth euer betoken ſome excellēt point of learning, which our author hath vſed in other places, as appeareth in the margent. *Sect*.234.301.335.

The matter hereof hath bin partly explaned in the Chapter of Tenant by the curteſie. If a man (a) taketh a wife ſeiſed of lands or tenements in fee, and hath iſſue, and after the wife is attainted of felonie, ſo as the iſſue cannot inherit to her, yet he ſhall be tenant by the Curteſie, in reſpect of the iſſue which he had before the felonie, and which by poſſibilitie might then haue inherited. But if the wife had beene attainted of felonie before the iſſue, albeit hee hath iſſue afterward, he ſhal not bee tenant by the Curteſie. (a)21.*E*.3.9. 11.*H*.7. 3.*H*.7.17.*Stamf*.195. 27.*E*.3.77.46.*E*.3.*Pet*.20. 26.*Aſſ.p*.2.13.*H*.4.8.

¶ *Come heire al fee.* This doth implie (b) a ſecret of Law, for except the wife be actually ſeiſed, the heire ſhall not (as hath been ſaid) make himſelfe heire to the wife: and this is the reaſon that a man ſhall not be Tenant by the Curteſie, of a ſeiſin in Law. (b) *Li*.8.*fo*.34.*in Paines caſe*.

Section 53.

EEt auxy en cheſcun caſe lou le feme prent baron ſeiſie d tiel eſtate des tenements, &c. Iſſint q ſi p poſſibilitie il puiſſoit happer q ſi le feme auoit aſcun iſſue p ſa barō, & que m liſſue puiſſoit per poſſibilitie enheriter meſmes les Tenements de tiel eſtate que l baron ad, come heire a l baron, de tiels Tenemēts el auer ſa dower, & autrement nemy. Car

ANd alſo in euerie caſe where a woman taketh a husband ſeiſed of ſuch an eſtate in tenements, &c. ſo as by poſſibilitie it may happen that the wife may haue iſſue by her husband, and that the ſame iſſue may by poſſibilitie inherite the ſame Tenements of ſuch an eſtate as the husband hath, as heire to the husband. Of ſuch tenements ſhee ſhal haue her dower, & otherwiſe not. For

¶ I*Sſint que ſi per poſſibilitie il puit happer que le feme auoit aſcun iſſue per ſon baron.* Albeit the wife bee a hundred yeares old, or that the husband at his death was but foure or ſeuen yeares old, ſo as ſhee had no poſſibilitie to haue iſſue by him, yet ſeeing the Law ſaith, That if the wife be aboue the age of nine yeares at the death of her husband, ſhe ſhall be endowed, and that women in antient times haue had children at that age, whereunto no woman doth now attaine, the Law cannot iudge that impoſſible, which by nature was poſſible. And in my time, a woman aboue threeſcore yeares old hath had a child, and ideo non definitur in 12.*H*.4.2.7.*H*.6.11,12.

in iure, And for the husbands being of such tender yeres, he hath habitum, though hee hath not potentiam at that time, and therefore his wife shal be endowed.

¶ *Et que mesme lissue puissoit per possibilitie inheriter mesmes les tenements, &c.* A man seised of land in generall taile, taketh wife, & after is attainted of felonie, before the said Statute of 1. E. 6 the Issue should haue inherited, and yet the wife should not haue been endowed: For the Statute of W. 2. ca. 1. relieueth the issue in taile, but not the wife in that case. But at this day, if the husband be attainted of felonie, the wife shall be endowed, and yet the issue shall not inherit the Lands which the father had in fee simple. If the wife elope from her husband, &c. shee shall bee barred of her dower, as hath beene said, and yet the Issue shall inherit.

si tenemẽts sont donẽs a vn hõe & a les heires que il engendra de corps sa feme, en tiel case la feme nad riẽs en les tenements, & le baron ad estate forsque come donee en especiall taile; uncore si le baron deuy sans issue, mesme la feme serra endow de mesmẽs les tenemẽts, pur ceo que lissue que el per possibilitie puissoit auer per mesme le baron, puissoit enheriter mesmes les tenements. Mes si la feme deuiast, viuant sa baron, & puis le baron prist auter feme, & morust, sa second feme ne serra my endow en cest case, causa qua supra.

if tenements be giuen to a man, and to the heires which hee shall beget of the bodie of his wife, in this case the wife hath nothing in the tenements, and the husband hath an estate but as donee in speciall taile; yet if the husband die without issue, the same wife shall bee endowed of the same tenements, because the issue which shee by possibilitie might haue had by the same husband, might haue inherited the same tenements. But if the wife dieth, liuing her husband, & after the husbãd takes another wife & dieth, his 2. wife shall not be indowed in this case for the reasõ aforesaid

Section 54.

5. *E.* 3. *Voucher* 249.
8. *E.* 3. *Ass.* 393.
4. *H.* 6. 24. F. N. B. 149.

¶ You may easily perceiue by the context that this shaft came neuer out of Littletons quiuer of choice arrowes, And therefore I will leaue it. Only for Students sake I will referre them to 5. E. 3. Voucher 249. 8. E. 3. Ass. 393. 4. H. 6. 24. F. N. B. 149.

¶ NOta si vn home soit seisie de certaine terres & prist vn feme, et puis aliena mesme la terre oue garrantie, & puis le feoffor, & le feoffee deuiont, & le feme de le feoffor port vn action de dower enuers le issue le feoffee, & il vouch lheire le feoffor, & pendant le voucher & nient termine, la feme le feoffee port son action de dower enuers le heire le feoffee, & demaunda la tierce part de ceo

NOte if a man be seised of certaine lands, and taketh wife; and after alieneth the same land with warrantie, and after the feoffor and feoffee dye, and the wife of the feoffor bring an action of dower against the issue of the feoffee, and he vouch the heire of the feoffor, and hanging the voucher and vndetermined, the wife of the feoffee brings her action of dower against the heire of the feoffee,

de que sa baron fuit seisie, & ne voile demaunder le tierce part del eux deux parts de que sa baron fuit seisie, fuit adiudge, que el nauera iudgement tanque lauter plee fuit determine.

feoffee, & demand the third part of that whereof her husband was seised, and will not demand the third part of these two parts of which her husband was seised, It was adiudged, that she should haue no iudgement vntill such time as the other plea were determined.

Section 55.

CET nota que Vauisour dit, Que si vn home soit seisie de terre et fait felonie, & puis alien, & puis est attaint, la feme auera bone action de Dower enuers le feoffee: Mes si soit eschete al Roy, ou al seignior, el nauera bre de dower. Et sic vide diuersitatem, & quære inde legem.

AND note *Vauisor* saith that if a man be seised of land and cōmitteth felony, and after alieneth, and after is attaint the wife shall haue a good action of dower against the feoffee: but if it be escheated to the King, or to the Lord, she shal not haue a writ of dower. And so see the difference, and inquire what the law is herein.

¶ This is also of the new addition, & explosa est hæc opinio, for it is cleere in Law that the wife at the Common law should not haue beene endowed against the feoffee. For to deterre and retaine men from committing of treason or felony, the Law hath inflicted fiue punishments vpon him that is attainted of treason or felony. 1. Hee shall lose his life and that by an infamous death of hanging betweene heauen and the earth as vnworthy in respect of his offence of either. 2. His wife that is a part of himselfe (Et erunt animæ duæ in carne vna) shall lose her Dower. 3. His blood is corrupted, and his children cannot be heires to him, and if he be noble or gentle before, he and all his posteritie are by this attainder made ignoble. 4. He shall forfeit all his lands and tenements, And fiftly all his goods and chattels, and all this is included by the Law in the iudgement Quod suspendatur per collum. But this is not intended of all felonies but of felony by stealing of goods aboue the value of xii. pence, and not of petit larceny vnder the value. So as the woman shall lose her dower aswell against the feoffee as against the Lord by escheate. And so it was resolued in a writ of Dower brought by Mary Gates late wife of John Gates, who after the couerture had infeoffed Wisman in fee, and after committed high treason, and was thereof attainted, that the wife should not be endowed against the feoffee, and in that case it was resolued, that so it was at the Common Law in case of felony. And it is to be vnderstood, that the wife shall not only lose her reasonable Dower at the Common Law for the felony of her husband, but also her dower ad ostium Ecclesiæ and ex assensu patris for felony done after the Dower assigned, and dower by custome also. And the reason of all this is yeelded by Littleton himselfe in the chapter of warranties, Section 746. to the end that men should be affraid to commit felony. But at this day the wife of a man attainted of felony (as often hath beene said) shalbe endowed by force of the Statutes in that case prouided.

And it appeareth by Britton Que fem de homicide ne teigne nul dower de tenants que lour fuit assigne per lour barons, so as the wife of a felon attainted by the Common Law was disabled to recouer dower ad ostium Ecclesiæ and ex assensu patris, as well as her reasonable dower which the Common Law gaue her. See in Bracton many barres of dower as the Law was then held.

Vid. Sect. 746.
Vid. Britton, cap. 109. *lib.* 1.
Bracton title euident, lib. 4. *fol.* 307. 30. 311.
Stanf. pl. cor. 194. 195.
Britton fol. 15. *cap.* 5.
Vid. Sect. 746.
M. 3. & 4. *Ph. & Mar. Ro.* 760. *in com. banco.*
8. *E.* 3. 20. 12. *H.* 4. 30.
Bracton lib. 4. *fo.* 311.
Vid. Sect. 746.
Britton cap. de homicide, fol. 15.
Bracton, lib. 4. *fol.* 308. & *Fleta vbi supra* & *Britton vbi supra.*

Chap. 6. *Sect.* 56.

Tenant a Terme de vie.

Tenāt pur terme de vie est, lou home lessa terres ou tenements a vn auter pur terme de vie le lessee, ou pur terme de vie dun auter home, en tiel case le lessee est tenant a terme de vie. Mes per cōmon parlance celuy que tient pur terme de sa vie demesne, est appel tenant pur terme de sa vie, & cestuy que tient pur terme dauter vie, est appel tenant pur term dauter vie.

Tenant for terme of life is, where a man letteth Lands or tenements to another for terme of the life of the Lessee, or for terme of the life of another man. In this case the Lessee is tenant for terme of life. But by common speech hee which holdeth for terme of his owne life, is called tenant for terme of his life, and he which holdeth for terme of anothers life, is called tenant for terme of another mans life.

Cuy pur terme de vie dun auter home. Now it is to be vnderstood that if the lessee in that case dieth liuing cesty que vie, (that is he for whose life the Lease was made) hee that first entreth shall hold the land during that other mans life, and hee that so entreth is within Littletons words, viz. tenant pur auter vie, and shalbe (a) punished for waste as tenant pur auter vie, and subiect to the payment of the rent reserued, and is in law called an occupant (occupans) because his title is by his first occupation. And so if tenant for his owne life grant ouer his estate to another, if the grantee dieth there shall bee an occupant. In like manner it is of an estate created by Law, for if tenant by the curtesie or tenant in dower grant ouer his or her estate, and the grantee dieth there shalbe an occupans. But against the King there shalbe no occupant, because nullum tempus occurrit regi. And therefore no man shall gaine the Kings land by prioritie of entrie. There can be no occupant of any thing that lyeth in grant, and that cannot passe without Deede, because euery occupant must claime by a que estate and auerre the life of Ce' que vie. It were (c) good to preuent the incertaintie of the estate of the occupant to adde these words, (to haue and to hold to him and his heires during the life of Ce' que vie) and this shall preuent the occupant, and yet the Lessee may assigne it to whom he will, or if he hath already an estate for another mans life without these words, then it were good for him to assigne his estate to diuers men and their heires during the life of Ce' que vie.

Bract. lib. 2. *ca.* 5. *& cap.* 9. *fol.* 26. *Fleta lib.* 3. *ca.* 12. *Britton fol.* 83. *Bracton* 4. *fol.* 170. *Vid. Sect.* 381.

(a) *Vid. le Deane de Worcest. case, lib.* 6. *fo.* 37. 27. *Ass.* 31. 39. *E.* 3. 1. 27. *H.* 6. *Recognizance Statham pl. vltimo.* 38. *H.* 6. 27. *Bracton lib.* 2. *fol.* 9. *Britton fol.* 84. 85.

(b) 27. *Ass. p* 31. *& Pl. com fol.* 28 *b. in Coltherst case tit. Barre* 303.

(c) *Littleton* 167. 11. *H.* 4. 42. 17. *E.* 3. 48. 39. *E.* 3. 25. 7. *H.* 4. 46. 8. *H.* 4. 15. *Dier.* 8. *Eliz.* 253.

Note that (d) to euery tenant for life, the Law as incident to his estate without prouision of the partie giueth him three kinde of estouers, (that is) housbote which is twofold, viz. estouerium edificandi & ardendi, Ploughbote, that is estouerium arandi. And lastly Hayebote, and that is estouerium claudendi and these estouers must bee reasonoble estoveria rationabilia. And these the Lessee may take vpon the land demised without any assignement, vnlesse hee be restrained by speciall couenant for modus et conuentio vincunt legem. Bote in the Saxon tongue and estouers in the French in this case are of all one signification, that is to haue compensation or satisfaction for these purposes. Estouiers commeth of the French word estouer. And the same estouers that tenant for life may haue, tenant for yeares shall haue.

(d) *Bract. lib.* 4. *fo.* 222. 231. 232. *& vid. fo.* 136. 137. *Fleta lib.* 4. *ca.* 19. 25. 26. 27. 8. *E.* 3. 54. 55. 21. *E.* 3. 41. 48. *E.* 3. 31. 7. *E.* 4. 28. 21. *H.* 6. 46. 10. *E.* 4. 3. *F. N. B.* 180. *lib.* 4. 86. 87. *in Luttrels case.*

You haue perceiued, That our Author diuides Tenant for life into two branches, viz. into Tenant for terme of his owne life, and into Tenant for terme of another mans life: to this may be added a third, viz. into an estate both for terme of his owne life, and for terme of another mans life.

Vid. Sect. 381.

As if a Lease be made to A. to haue to him for terme of his owne life, and the liues of B. and C. for the Lessee in this case hath but one Freehold, which hath this limitation, During his owne life, and during the liues of two others. And herein is a diuersitie to bee obserued betweene seuerall estates in seuerall degrees, and one estate with seuerall limitations. For in the first, an estate for a mans owne life is higher than for another mans life, but in the second it is not. As if A. be tenant for life, the remainder or reuersion to B. for life, A. may surrender to B.

Rosses case lib. 5. *fo.* 13.

for

for the estate of B. for terme of his owne life is higher than an estate for another mans life: And therefore if Tenant for life infeoffe him in the remainder for life, this is a surrender, and no forfeiture. And albeit an estate for terme of a mans own life be but one freehold, yet may severall freeholds in certaine cases be derived out of the same, whereof our books are verie plentifull, and wherewith you may disport your selves for a time. As if tenant for life maketh a Lease by Deed, or without Deed, to him in the remainder of reversion, in taile or in fee, for the term of the life of him in the rem. or reversion, and after he in the remainder taketh wife and dieth, his wife shall not be endowed, for tenant for life shal enjoy the land again, for forfeiture it cannot be, for he in the rem' was partie, and surrender it cannot bee, for that his whole estate was not given.

24.E.3.32.& 68.30.ass.p.47
19.E.3.Sur.8.
13.R.2.Dow 95.7.H.6.3. per Cur.18.E.3.48.

The heire maketh a lease for life, reserving a rent, against whom the wife recovereth her dower, and dieth, the Lessee shall have the land againe for his life, and the rent is revived.

7.H.5.4.

So it is, if Tenant for life take husband, and by Deed indented they make a Lease to him in the reversion for the life of the husband, reserving a rent, this is neither forfeiture, nor absolute surrender, for the cause aforesaid, and the reservation is good.

29.Ass.p.64.

B. seised of lands in fee, taketh to wife I.S. and infeoffe C. in fee, who take Alice to wife: C. dieth, Alice is endowed, B dieth, I.S. recovereth dower against Alice, and dieth, Alice shall enjoy the Land againe during her life.

8.E.2.ass 393.45.E.3.13.

A. and (a) B. Joyntenants, A. for life, and B. in fee, joyne in a lease for life, A. hath a reversion, and shall joyne in an Action of Wast.

(a) 2.H.5.7.13.H.7.15. 18.E.2.Br.835. F.N.B.59.f

Tenant for (b) life, and he in the reversion joyne in a lease for life, it is said, that they shall joyne in an Action of Wast, and that the Lessee for life shall recover the place wasted, and he in reversion, dammages.

(b) 37.H.8.13.13 H.7.15. 22.H.6.24.17.E.3.9.b.

If a man grant (c) an estate to a woman dum sola fuit, or durante viduitate, or quam diu se bene gesserit, or to a man and a woman during the coverture, or as long as the grantee dwell in such a house, or so long as he pay x.l. &c. or untill the grantee bee promoted to a Benefice, or for any like incertaine time, which time, as Bracton saith, is tempus indeterminatum: In all these cases, if it be of lands or tenements, the lessee hath in judgement of law an estate for life determinable, if liverie be made; and if it be of rents advowsons, or any other thing that lie in grant, he hath a like estate for life by the deliverie of the Deed, and in count or pleading he shall alledge the lease, and conclude, that by force thereof hee was seised generally for terme of his life.

(c) 37.H 6.27.26.E.3.69. 14.E.2.Grant 92.3.E.3.15. 14.H.8.13.
Bract li.4.f.207 Fl.l.3.c.12

If a man make a lease of a Mannor, that at the time of the lease made is worth xx.l. per annum, to another untill C.l. be paid, in this case because the annual profits of the manor are incertain, he hath an estate for life, if livery be made determinable upon the levying of the C.l. But if a man grant a rent of xx.l. p an untill C.l. be payd, there he hath an estate for five yeares, for there it is certaine, and depend upon no incertaintie. And yet in some cases a man shal have an incertaine interest in lands or tenements, and yet neither an estate for life, for yeares, or at will. As if a man by his will in writing, devise his lands to his Executors for payment of debts, and untill his debts be paid; in this case the Executors have but a Chattell, and an incertaine interest in the land untill his debts be paid; for if they should have it for their lives, then by their death their estate should cease, and the debts unpaid: but being a Chattell, it shall goe to the Executors of Executors for the payment of his debts; and so note a diversitie betweene a devise and a conveyance at the Common Law, in his life time. And tenant by Statute merchant, by Statute staple, and by Elegit, have incertaine interests in lands or tenements, and yet they have but Chattels, and no freehold, whose estates are created by divers Acts of Parliament, whereof more shall be said hereafter. And so have Gardeins in Chivalry which hold over for single or double value incertaine interests, and yet but Chattels.

33 Ass p.2.
Li.8.fo.9. Mannings case. 3.H.7 13.27.H.8.5. 14.H.8.13.21.Ass p.8.

If one grant lands or tenements, reversions, remainder, rents, advowsons, commons, or the like, and expresse or limit no estate, the lessee or grantee (due ceremonies requisite by Law being performed) hath an estate for life. The same law is of a declaration of a use. A man may have an estate for terme of life determinable at will; As if the King doth grant an office to one at will, and grant a rent to him for the exercise of his office for terme of his life, this is determinable upon the determination of the office.

V.Sect.381.7.Ass pl.1. 13.El.Dyer 300.
7.E.4.23.

A. tenant in fee simple make a lease of lands to B. to have and to hold to B. for terme of life, without mentioning for whose life it shall be, it shall be deemed for terme of the life of the lessee, for it shall be taken most strongly against the lessor, and as hath beene said, an estate for a mans owne life is higher then for the life of another. But if tenant in taile make such a lease without expressing for whose life, this shall be taken but for the life of the lessor, for two Reasons.

V.Sect.381.

First, when the construction of any act is left to the Law, the Law which abhorreth injurie and wrong will never so construe it, as it shall worke a wrong: and in this case, if by construction it should be for the life of the lessee, then should the estate taile be discontinued, and a new reversion gained by wrong: but if it be construed for the life of the tenant in taile, then no wrong is wrought. And it is a generall rule, that whensoever the words of a Deed, or of the parties without Deed may have a double entendement, and the one standeth with law and

4.E.2.Wast.11. 17.E.3.7.

right, and the other is wrongfull and against Law, the intendement that standeth with Law, shall be taken.

Secondly, The Law more respecteth a lesser estate by right, then a larger estate by wrong, as if tenant for life in remainder disseise tenant for life, now he hath a fee simple, but if Tenant for life die, now is his wrongfull estate in fee by iudgement in law changed to a rightfull estate for life.

19.H.6.7.H.4.32. 6.E.3 17.7.E.3.66. 18.E.3.60.23.E.3.ca.1.&c. 11.H.4.44. 38.E.3.23.24.

If a man retaine a seruant generally without expressing any time, the Law shall construe it to be for one yeare, for that retainer is according to Law. Vide 23.E.3.cap.1.&c. To shut vp this point it hath beene adiudged, that where Tenant in taile made a lease to another for terme of life generally, and after released to the lessee and his heires, albeit betweene the Tenant in taile, and him a fee simple passed, yet after the death of the lessee, the entrie of the issue in taile was lawfull; which could not bee, if it had been a lease for the life of the lessee, for then by the release it had bene a discontinuance executed. But let vs now returne to Littleton.

Section 57.

¶ This and the rest that follow in this chapter concerning the description of Feoffor and feoffee, Donor and Donee, and Lessor and Lessee are euident.

¶ *Et est ascauoir que il y ad le Feoffor, & le Feoffee, &c. Vide Sect.* 2. where a light touch is giuen who may purchase, now somewhat is to be said, who haue abilitie to enfeoffe, &c. and may be a Feoffor, Donor, Lessor, &c. whosoeuer is disabled by the Common Law to take, is disabled to infeoffe, &c. But many that haue capacitie to take, haue no abilitie to infeoffe, &c. As men attainted of Treason, Felonie, or of a Premunire, Aliens borne, the Kings Villaines, Traitors, Felons, &c. he that hath offended against the Statutes of Premunire, after the offences committed if Attainders ensue, Ideots, Madmen, a man deafe, dumbe, and blind from his Natiuitie, a Fem, Couert, an Infant, a man by dures: for the feoffements, &c. of these may bee auoided. But an Hereticke, though he be conuicted of heresie, a Leper remoued by the Kings Writ from the societie of men, Bastards, a man Deafe, Dumbe, or blinde, so that hee hath vnderstanding and sound memorie, albeit he expresse his intention by signes, Villaine of a common

Bracton.lib.5.fol 415. Britton.fol 88. Fleta lib.3. cap.3. & lib.6.cap.39.40.

2.H.5.cap.7. which is repealed Doct.& Stud.lib.2.cap.29.

¶ ET ē ascauoire que il y ad le Feoffor & le Feoffee, Donor & le Donee, & Lessor & l Lessee. Le feoffor est propermt lou home enfeoffa vn auter en ascuns terres ou tenements en fee simple, celuy que fist le feoffement est appel feoffour, & celuy a que le feoffmēt est fait, est appel feoffee. Et le donour est propermeni lou vn home done certaine terres ou tenements a vn auter en le taile, celuy que fist le done est appel le donor, & celuy a que le done est fait, est appel le Donee. Et le Lessor est propermeni lou vn home lessa a vn auter certaine terres ou tenements pur terme de vie, ou pur terme des ans, ou a tener a volunt celuy que fist le leas est appell les-

AND it is to be vnderstood, that there is Feffor and Feffee, Donor and Donee, Lessor and Lessee, Feoffor is properly where a man enfeoffes another, in any Lands or Tenements in Fee simple, hee which maketh the feoffment is called the Feoffor, and he to whom the feoffment is made, is called the Feoffee. And the Donor is properly where a man giueth certaine lands or tenements to another in taile, he which maketh the gift, is called the Donor, & he to whom the gift is made, is called the Donee. And the Lessor is properly where a man letteth to another lands or tenements for terme of life or for terme of yeares, or to hold at will: Hee which maketh the Lease is called Lessor,

for

ſoꝛ ⁊ celuy a que le leas eſt fait, eſt appel Leſſee. Et cheſcun que ad eſtate en aſcun terres ou tenements pur terme de ſa vie ou pur terme dauter vie, eſt appell tenant de franktenement, ⁊ null auter de meindꝛe eſtat poit auer franktenement, mes ceux de greinder eſtate ont franktenement car ceſtuy en fee ſimple ad franktenement, ⁊ celuy en le taile ad franktenement, ⁊c.

and hee to whom the Leaſe is made, is called Leſſee. And euery one which hath an eſtate in any Land or Tenements for terme of his owne or another mans life, is called tenant of freehold, and none other of a Leſſer eſtate can haue a Freehold, but they of a greater Eſtate haue a Freehold; For hee in Fee ſimple hath a Freehold, and Tenant in taile, hath a Freehold, &c.

perſon befoꝛe entrie, oꝛ the like may infeoffe, ⁊c.

(a) All feoffments, gifts, grants, and Leaſes by Biſhops, albeit they bee confirmed by the Deane and Chapter, by any of the Colledges oꝛ Halls in either of the Uniuerſities, oꝛ elſewhere, Deans and Chapters, Maſter oꝛ Gardein of any Hoſpital, parſon, Uicar, oꝛ any other hauing Spirituall oꝛ Eccleſiaſticall liuing, are alſo to bee auoyded, (b) and all the ſayd bodies politique oꝛ coꝛpoꝛate, are by the Statutes of the Realme diſabled to make any conueyances to the King, oꝛ to any other, as it hath bin adiudged: which ſtatutes haue been made ſince Litlet. wrote.

(a) 32.H.8.cap.28.1.El. not printed. 13.El.ca.10.14.El. ca.11.18.El.ca 20. Ia.ca.

(b) Lib.4.fo.76.120.libr.5. fo.6.14. Li.5.fo.37. li.11. fo 67. Magdalen Colledge caſe. Vide Leſt.de W.2.ca.41.

It is prouided (c) by the Statute of Magna Charta, quod nullus liber homo det de cætero amplius alicui de terra ſua quam vt de reſiduo terræ ſuæ poſſet ſufficienter fieri domino feodi ſeruitium ei debitum quod pertinet ad feodum illud. Upon which act I haue heard great queſtion (d) made, whether the feoffment made againſt that Statute were voidable oꝛ no, and ſome haue ſaid, that the Statute intended not to auoid the feoffment, but implicite to direct the tenure, viz that the tenant ſhould not infeoffe another of parcell to hold of the chiefe Loꝛd (that is of the next Loꝛd) but to hold of himſelfe, and then the Loꝛd may diſtraine in euery part foꝛ his whole ſeruice without any pꝛeiudice vnto him. But this opinion is againſt (e) the authoꝛitie of our Bookes, and againſt the ſaid Statute of Magna Charta. Foꝛ firſt it is agreed in 10.H 7. that aſwel befoꝛe the Statute as after a tenant which held two Acres might haue aliened one of the Acres to hold of him, and notwithſtanding the Loꝛd might haue diſtrained in which of the Acres he would foꝛ his whole ſeruices: and reaſon teacheth that befoꝛe that Statute a tenant could not haue aliened parcell to hold of the chiefe Loꝛd; Foꝛ the Seigniory of the Loꝛd was intire, foꝛ the which the Loꝛd might diſtraine in the whole oꝛ in any part, and which the Tenant by his owne Act cannot diuide to the pꝛeiudice of the Loꝛd to barre him to diſtraine in any part foꝛ his Seruices, as hee ſhould doe, if hee ſhould enfeoffe another of parcell to hold of the chiefe Loꝛd. But the Tenant might haue made a Feoffment of the whole to hold of the chiefe Loꝛd, foꝛ there no pꝛeiudice inſued to the Loꝛd. Others haue ſaid, and they ſaid truly, that the intention of the Statute was that the Tenant could not alien parcell (which might turne to the pꝛeiudice of the Loꝛd) without his aſſent, and this appeareth cleerely by the Miroꝛ. And by this Statute the King tooke benefit to haue a fine foꝛ his licence, befoꝛe which Statute no fine foꝛ alienation was due to the King. Foꝛ it is (f) adiudged that foꝛ an alienation in time of Henry the ſecond, no fine was due, and it appeareth in our Bookes, that if an alienation had beene made befoꝛe 20.H.3. no fine was due to the King foꝛ alienation: Now it is to be obſerued; that oftentimes foꝛ the better vnderſtanding of our Bookes, the aduiſed Reader muſt take light from Hiſtoꝛie and Chꝛonicles eſpecially foꝛ diſtinction of times. And therefoꝛe Matthew Paris (who in his Chꝛonicle reciteth Magna Charta) teſtifieth that King Henry the third by euill counſell (and eſpecially as the truth was of Hubert de Burgo then chiefe Juſtice) ſought to auoide the great Charter firſt granted by his Father King Iohn, and afterward granted and confirmed by himſelfe in the ninth of Henry the third, foꝛ that as he ſaid King Iohn did grant it by Dures, and that he himſelfe was within age when he granted and confirmed it. But foꝛaſmuch as afterwards the ſaid King Henry the third, in the twentieth yeare of his Raigne, at what time hee was nine and twentie yeare old, did grant and confirme the ſaid great Charter, foꝛ that cauſe to put out all ſcruples is the twentieth yeare of Henry the third named, albeit in law the Kings Charter granted in the ninth yeere of Henry the third, was of foꝛce and validitie notwithſtanding his nonage, foꝛ that, in iudgement of Law the King, as King, cannot be ſaid to be a Minor

(c) Magna Charta cap.32. Mirror.cap.5.§.2. Glanuil.lib.7.cap.1. Bract.lib.1. britton.88.&c. Fleta lib.3 cap.3.

(d) Vide an excellent declaration hereof inter adiudicat coram Rege. Trin.E.1.fol.2.in Theſa. Nott.& Derb.

(e) Bract lib.1. 10.H.7.fol.10.b. 33.E.3.auowry 255. Stanf.prer.fol.29. 8.E.4 12.

Mirror.cap.5 §.2. Fleta lib 3.cap.3.

(f) 26.Aſſ.p.37. 20.Aſſ.p.17 20.E.3.auowrie 126. 34.E.3.cap.15. Vide Stanf. 29.30. Matt. Paris. Walſingham 37.39.

Vide 5.H.3. Mordanc. 53. Magna Charta there vouched, which was the Charter of King Iohn, for it was eited before. 9.H.3.

nor, for when the Royall Bodie Politique of the King doth meete with the naturall capacitie in one person, the whole Bodie shall haue the qualitie of the Royall Politique, which is the greater and more worthy, and wherein is no Minoritie. For Omne maius trahit ad se quod est minus. And it is to bee obserued, that no Record can bee found, that either a licence of alienation was sued or pardon for alienation was obtained for an alienation without licence at any time before the twentieth yeare of Henrie the third, and it is holden in the twentieth of Edward the third, that a licence for alienation grew by this Statute.

40. Ass. pl. 17. by Skipwith.

Now in the case of a common person it was the common opinion, that if the tenant had aliened any parcell contrary to the said act, that he himselfe was bound by his owne act, but that his heire might haue auoyded it, and in the Kings Case many held the same opinion. For Britton saith, Ne Countes, ne Barons, ne Chiualer, ne Seriants, que teignont en chiefe de nous: ne purr' my dismember nous fees sanus licence: que nous ne puissent per droit engettre les purchasors, &c. And herewith agreeth Fleta, and our Bookes. But now by the Statute 1. E. 3. cap. 12. & 34. E. 3. cap. 15. although the Kings tenant in chiefe, or by grand seriantie doe alien all or any part without licence, yet is there not any forfeiture of the same, but a reasonable fine therefore to be paid. And note, it appeareth by the preamble in 1. E. 3. that complaint was made that land holden of the King in Capite, being aliened without licence was seised as forfeited. And in the case of a common person, the Statute of 18. E. 1. De quia emptores terrarum hath made it cleere, for this hath in effect as to the common persons taken away the said Statute of Magna Charta cap. 32. for thereby it is prouided, Quod liceat vnicuique libero homini terras suas seu tenementa sua, seu partem inde ad voluntatem suam vendere, ita quod feoffatus teneat, &c. de Capitali Domino. And herein are diuers notable points to bee obserued. First, that this word liceat proueth that the tenant could not, or at least wayes was in danger to alien parcell of his tenancie, &c. vpon the said Act of Magna Charta. Secondly, that vpon the feoffment of the whole, the tenant shall hold of the chiefe Lord. Thirdly, that the tenant might infeoffe one of part to hold pro perticula of the chiefe Lord. But this Act (the King being not named) doth not take away the Kings fine due to him by the Statute of Magna Charta.

Britton. fol. 28. 88. 186. 187. 245. 247. Prer. Regis cap. 7. Fleta lib. 6. cap. 29. acc. 20. E. 3. Ass. 122. 29. Ass. pl. 19. 14. E. 3. quare imped. 45. 14. H. 4. 2. 3. 9. E. 3. fol. 26. 1 E. 3. cap. 12. 34. E. 3. ca. 15. lib. 2. fol. 81. 82. in Seignior Cromwels case.

Regist. int les breues de onerand pro rata portione.

¶ *Franktenemẽt.* Here it appeareth that tenant in fee, tenant in taile, and tenant for life are said to haue a franktenement, a freehold, so called because it doth distinguish it from tearmes of yeares, Chattels vpon incertaine interests, lands in Villenage or Customary, or Coppihold lands. Liberum autem tenementum dicitur ad differentiam Villenagij, & villanorum qui tenent Villenagium quia non habent actionem nec assisam, &c. item quod sit suum & non alienum, hoc est si teneat nomine alieno vt firmarius & ad terminum vel sicut creditor ad vadium. And note that tenant by statute Merchant, statute staple or elegit are said to hold land Vt liberum tenementum vntill their debt be paid, and yet in troth they (as hath beene said) haue no freehold, but a Chattle, which shall goe to the Executors, and the Executors also if they be ousted shall haue an Assise. But (vt) is similitudinarie, because they shall by the statutes haue an Assise as tenant of the freehold shall haue, and to that respect hath a similitude of a freehold, but Nullum simile est idem.

Bracton. lib. 4. fol. 224. Britton. cap. 32. & 47. Bracton. lib. 4. fol. 22. Regist. indic. 68. 73.

28. Ass. p. 7. W. 2. cap. 18. Statut. de mercatoribus anno 13. E. 1. 27. E. 3. cap. 9. 23. H. 8. cap. 6. F. N. B. 178. 7.

Chap. 7. *Sect.* 58.

Tenant for tearme of yeares.

¶ Lou home *lessa terres &c. lessa* and Lease is (a) deriued of the Saxon word leapum, or leasum, for that the Lessee commeth in by lawfull meanes (b) and dimittere is in French laysser to depart with or forgoe.

When Littleton wrote many persons might make Leases for yeares, or for life or

(a) Mirror. cap. 2. §. 17. Bracton. lib. 2. cap. 26. & lib. 4 fol. 220. Fleta. lib. 3. cap. 12. & lib. 5. cap. 34.
(b) For the word (dimitto) See Sect. 531.

¶ Tenãt pur terme dans ẽ lou hõe lessa terres ou tenements a vn auter pur terme de certaine ans solonque le number des ans que est accord perenter le les-

¶ Tenant for tearme of yeares is, where a man letteth Lands or Tenements to another for tearme of certaine yeares after the number of yeares that is accorded between the

for

for & le lessee. Et quant le lessee enter per force del leas, donque il est tenant pur terme des ans. Et si le lessor en tiel case reserue a luy un annuall rent sur tiel leas il poit eslier a distrainer pur le rent en les tenements lesses, ou il poit auer un action de debt pur les arrerages enuers le lessee. Mes en tiel case il couient que le lessour soit seisie de mesmes le tenemēts al temps del leas, car il est bone plee pur le lessee a dire, que le lessor nauoit riens en les tenemēts al tēps de le leas sinon que le leas soit fait per fait endent, en quel case tiel plee donque ne gist en le bouch le lessee a pleader.

Lessor and the Lessee, and when the Lessee entreth by force of the Lease, then is hee tenant for tearme of yeares, and if the Lessor in such case reserue to him a yearely Rent vpon such Lease, hee may chuse for to distraine for the Rent in the Tenements letten, or else he may haue an Action of debt for the Arrerages against the Lessee. But in such case it behooueth that the Lessor be seised in the same Tenements at the time of his lease, for it is a good plee for the Lessee to say, that the Lessor had nothing in the tenements at the time of the lease, except the lease bee made by deed, indented, in which case such plee lieth not for the Lessee to plead.

liues at their will and pleasure, which now cannot make them firme in Law. And some persons may now make leases for yeares, or for life or liues (obseruing due incidents) firme and good in law who of themselues could not so doe when Littleton wrote, and this by force of diuers Acts of Parliament (c) as namely 32. H 8. 1. Eliz. 13. Eliz 18. Eliz. and 3. Iac. Regis of which statutes one is inabling, and the rest are disabling. When Littleton wrote, Bishoppes with the confirmation of the Deane and Chapter, Master & Fellowes of any Colledge, Deanes and Chapters, Master or Gardian of any Hospitall, and his Brethren, Parson or Vicar, with the consent of the Patrone and Ordinary, Archdeacon, Prebend, or any other bodie Politique Spirituall and Ecclesiasticall (Concurrentibus hijs quæ in iure requiruntur) might haue made Leases for liues or yeares without limitation or stint. And so might they haue made gifts in tailes or states in fee at their will and pleasure, whereupon not only great decay of Diuine Seruice, but Dilapidations and other inconueniences ensued, and therefore they were disabled and restrained by the said Acts of 1. Eliz. 13. Eliz. and 3. Iac. Regis to make any estate or Conueyance to the King at all or to the subiect, but there is excepted out of the restraint or disabilitie, leases for three liues, or one and twentie yeares; with such reseruation of Rent, and with such other prouisions and limitations as hereafter shall appeare. Also they may make grants of ancient Offices of necessitie with ancient fees Concurrentibus hijs quæ in iure requiruntur, for those grants are not within the statute of 32. H 8. but by construction, they are not restrained by the statutes of 1. Eliz. or 13. Eliz. because these ancient Offices be of necessitie, and with the ancient fees, and so no diminution of reuenue.

(c) 32. H. 8. ca. 28. 1. Eliz. not printed but in the abridgement. 13. Eliz. cap. 10. 18. Eliz. cap. 6. 3. Iac. cap. 3.

Lib. 5. fol. 14. case de Ecclesiasticall persons. Lib. 11. fol 66 Magdalen Colledge case. Leuesque de Sarums case l b. 10 fol. 60. 61.

There be three kinds of persons, that at this day may make leases for three liues, &c. in such sort as hereafter is expressed which could not so doe when Littleton wrote. Viz. First, Any person seised of an estate taile in his owne right. Secondly, Any person seised of an estate in fee simple in the right of his Church. Thirdly, Any husband and wife seised of any estate of inheritance in fee simple, or fee taile in the right of his wife, or ioyntly with his wife before the couerture or after, viz. the tenant in taile, by deed to bind his issues in taile, but not the reuersion or remainder, the Bishop, &c. by deed without the Deane and Chapter to bind his successors, the husband and wife by deed to bind the wife and her and their heires, and these are made good by the statute of 32. H. 8. which inableth them thereunto. But to the making good of such leases by the said statute there are nine things necessarily to bee obserued belonging to them all, and some other to some of them in particular.

First, The lease must be made by Deed indented, and not by Deed, Poll, or by Paroll.

Lib. 5. fol. 6. Seig. Mountioyes case.

Secondly, It must be made to begin from the day of the making thereof, or from the making thereof.

Thirdly,

Thirdly, If there be an old lease in being, it must be surrendred or expired, or ended within a yeare of the making of the lease, and the surrender must be absolute and not conditionall.

Lib.5 fol.2. Elmers case.

Fourthly, There must not bee a double Lease in beeing at one time, as if a Lease for yeares bee made according to the statute, hee in the reversion cannot expulse the Lessee, and make a Lease for life or lives according to the statute, nor è converso, for the words of the statute be to make a lease for three lives, or one and twentie yeares, so as one or the other may be made, and not both.

Fiftly, It must not exceed three lives, or one and twentie yeares, from the making of it, but it may be for a lesser terme or fewer lives.

Sixtly, It must bee of Lands, Tenements, or Hereditaments, Manurable or Corporeall, which are necessary to be letten, and whereout a rent by law may be reserued, and not (d) of things that lie in grant, as Aduowsons, Faires, Markets, Franchises, and the like whereout a rent cannot be reserued.

(d) Lib.5.fol.2. Iewels case. 17.E.3.75.9. Ass.24.14.E.3. Scire facias 22. 10.H.6.2. 3.H.6.21.

Seuenthly, It must be of Lands or tenements which haue most commonly beene letten to farme, or occupied by the Farmers thereof by the space of 20 yeares next before the lease made, so as if it be letten for 11. yeares at one or seuerall times within those 20. yeares it is sufficient. A grant (e) by copie of Court roll in fee for life or yeares is a sufficient letting to farme within this statute, for he is but tenant at will according to the custome, & so it is of a lease at will by the Common Law, but those lettings to farme must be made by some seised of an estate of Inheritance, & not by a Gardein in Chiualrie, tenant by the curtesie, tenant in dower or the like.

(e) Lib 6.fol.37. Deane and Chapter of Worcester case.

Lib.5.fol.6. Seignior Mountioyes Case.

Eightly, That vpon euery such lease there be reserued yearely during the same lease due and payable to the Lessors their heires and Successors, &c. so much yearely farme or rent, or more, as hath beene most accustomably yeelded or paid for the lands, &c. within twentie yeares next before such lease made. Hereby first it appeareth (as hath beene said) that nothing can be demised by Authoritie of this act, but that whereout a rent may be lawfully reserued. Secondly, That where not only a yearely rent was formerly reserued, but things not annuall, as heriots; or any fine or other profit at or vpon the death of the farmor, yet if the yearely rent be reserued vpon a lease made by force of this statute, it sufficeth by the expresse words of the Act. Thirdly, If he reserue more then the accustomable rent it is good also by the expresse letter of the Act; but if twentie Acres of land haue beene accustomably letten, and a lease is made of those twentie, and of owne Acre which was not accustomably letten, reseruing the accustomable yearely Rent, and so much more as exceed the value of the other Acre, this lease is not warranted by the Act, for that the accustomable Rent is not reserued, seeing part was not accustomeably letten, and the Rent issueth out of the whole. Fourthly, If tenant in taile let part of the land accustomably letten, and reserue a Rent pro rata, or more, this is good for that is in substance the accustomable Rent. Fiftly, If two Coperceners be tenant in taile of twentie Acres euery one of equall value, and accustomably letten, and they make partition, so as each haue ten Acres, they may make leases of their seuerall parts each of them, reseruing the halfe of the accustomeable rent. Sixtly, If the accustomeable Rent had beene payable at foure dayes or Feasts of the Yeare, yet if it be reserued yearely payable at one Feast, it is sufficient, for the words of the statute be, reserued yearely.

Lib.6.fol.37.38. Deane and Chapt. of Worcester Case.

Lib.5.fol 5. Seignior Mountioyes Case, lib.6.fol.37.

Lord Mountioyes Case vbi supra.

Ninthly, Nor to any lease to be made without impeachment of waste, therefore if a Lease be made for life, the remainder for life, &c. this is not warranted by the statute, because it is dispunishable of waste. But if a lease bee made to one during three liues this is good, for the occupant if any happen; shall be punished for waste. The words of the statute be (seised in the right of his Church) yet a Bishop that is seised iure Episcopatus, a Deane of his sole possessions in iure Decanatus, an Archdeacon in iure Archidiaconatus, a Prebendarie and the like are within the statute, for euery of them generally is seised in iure Ecclesiæ

Deane and Chapter of Worc. Case. Vbi supra.

Deane and Chapter of Worc. Case. Vbi supra.

But a Parson and Vicar are excepted out of the statute of 32.H.8. and therefore if either of them make a lease for three liues, &c. of lands accustomeably letten, reseruing the accustomed Rent, it must be also confirmed by the Patrone and Ordinarie, because it is excepted out of 32.H.8. and not restrained by the statutes of primo or 13.Eliz. And what hath beene said concerning a lease for three liues, doth hold for a lease for one and twentie yeares.

3.E.6 1.Mar.tit.leases Bre.62.

Thus much shall suffice to haue spoken of the inabling statute of 32.H.8. the better to inable the Reader to vnderstand both this and that which follow. Now to speake somewhat of the disabling Statutes of 1. Eliz. and 13. Eliz. the words of the exception out of the restraint and disabilitie of 1. Eliz. are, Other than for the terme of twentie one yeares, or three liues, from such time as any such grant or assurance shall bee giuen, whereupon the old and accustomed yearely rent, or more, shall be reserued: And to that effect is the exception in the Statute of 13. Eliz. First, It is to be vnderstood, that neither of these disabling Acts, nor any other, doe in any sort alter or change the inabling Statute of 32 H.8. but leaueth it for a patterne in many things for leases to be made by others. Secondly, It is to be knowne, that no Lease made according to the exception of 1. Eliz. or 13. Eliz. and not warranted by the Statute of 32.H.8. if it bee made by a Bishop, or any sole Corporation, but it must be confirmed by the Deanes and Chapters, or others that haue interest, as hath beene said in the case of the Parson and Vicar, but examples doe illustrate. If a Bishop make a lease for 21. yeares, and all those yeares being spent sauing three or more; yet may the Bishop make a new lease to another for twentie one yeares, to begin from the making, according to the exception of the Statute, but not a Lease for life or liues, as hath beene said, and this concurrent Lease hath beene resolued to be good, as well vpon the exception of 1. Eliz. in the case of Bishops, as vpon 13. Eliz. which extend to spirituall and ecclesiasticall Corporations, aggregate of many, as Deanes and Chapters, &c. which 32. H. 8. did not: but in the case of the concurrent lease, in the case of the Bishop it must be confirmed. Also the exception of 1. Eliz. and 13. Eliz. doth differ from the statute of 32. H. 8. for the leases for yeares to bee made according to the exceptions of the statutes of 1. and 13. Eliz. must beginne from the making, and not from the day of the making, but by force of 32. H. 8. from the day of the making. And although the statutes of the first or thirteenth of Eliz. doe not appoint the lease to be made by writing, yet must it therein and in the other eight properties or qualities before mentioned and required by 32. H. 8. follow the paterne thereof (the concurrent lease only excepte). Although the exception in 1. and 13. Eliz. concerning the accustomed rent is more generall then that of 32. H. 8. and there is not any prouision for leases made dispunishable of waste, &c. yet must the paterne of 32. H. 8. be followed: for leases without impeachment of waste made by such Spirituall and Ecclesiasticall persons are vnreasonable and causes of dilapidations. Thus much haue I thought good to lead the studious Reader by the hand, and to conduct him in the right way. And to put all these things together vpon consideration had of all the statutes, which otherwise might haue *prima facie* seemed to him a diffuse and darke laborinth. And albeit it be prouided by the said Acts of 1. and 13. Eliz. that all grants, &c. leases, &c. made, &c. (other then leases for three liues, or one and twentie yeares according to those Acts) should be vtterly void and of none effect, to all intents constructions and purposes, yet grants, or leases, &c. not warranted by those acts are not void, but good against the Lessor, if it be a sole Corporation, or so long as the Deane or other head of the Corporation remaine, if it be a Corporation aggregate of many, for the statute was made in benefit of the successor. But let vs now returne to our Author.

Lib. 3. fo. 59. 60. Lincolne Colledge case. T. 39. Eliz. Inter Hunt. & Singleton. ibidem.

¶ *Home lessa.* Here Littleton putteth this case where one letteth, &c. It is therefore necessary to be seene what the Law is where diuers ioyne in a Lease. If the tenant of the Land, and a stranger which hath nothing in the Land ioyne in a lease for yeares by Deed indented of one and the selfe-same land, this is the Lease of the tenant only, and the confirmation of the stranger and yet the Lease as to the stranger workes by conclusion.

Vide Sect. 346. 11. H. 4. 1. 5. E. 4. 4. a. 27. H. 8. 16.

If two seuerall tenants of seuerall lands, ioyne in a lease for yeares by Deede indented, these be seuerall Leases and seuerall Confirmations of each of them, from whom no interest passeth, and worke not by way of conclusion in any sort; because seuerall interests passe from them. E. tenant for life of C. and he in the remainder or reuersion in fee, hauing seuerall estates in the one and the same Land ioyne in a lease for yeares by Deede indented, this demise shall worke in this sort, during the life of C. it is the Lease of B. and Confirmation of him in the reuersion or remainder, and after the decease of C. it is the Lease of him in the reuersion or remainder, and the Confirmation of B. for seeing the Leasors haue seuerall estates, the Law shall construe the Lease to moue out of both their estates respectiuely, and euery one to let that which he lawfully may let, and not to be the lease only of tenant for life, and the Confirmation of him in the remainder or reuersion, neither is there any conclusion in this case, as shall be said hereafter. Tenant for life and he in the remainder in fee, made a lease for yeares by Deed indented, the Lessee was eiected, and brought an *Eiectione firme*, and declared vpon a demise made by tenant for life and him in remainder, and vpon not guilty pleaded this speciall matter was found and that tenant for life was liuing and it was adiudged (a) against the pl', for during the life of the tenant (as hath beene said) it is the Lease of the tenant for life, and therefore during his life he ought to haue declared of a Lease made by him, and after his decease he ought to declare of a Lease made by him in remainder. (b) And the Deed indented could be no Estoppell in this case, because there passed an interest from them both. And whensoeuer any interest passeth from the partie there can be no Estoppell against him, and (c) so it was adiudged. Hereby you shall vnderstand your bookes the better which treate of these matters; and accordingly it was adiudged that where tenant in taile and he in the remainder in fee ioyned in a grant of a rent charge by Deed in fee, and after tenant in taile died without issue, the grantee distreyned and auowed by force of a graunt from him in the remainder and vpon *non concessit*, the Jury found the speciall matter, and it was adiudged for the auowant; for euery one granted according to his estate and interest.

(a) 27. H. 8. fo. 13. a. 13. H. 7. 14. 2. H. 5. 7. Lib. 1. fol. 76. Bredons Case.

(b) Mich. 36. & 37. Eliz. in the Kings Bench. Vide Mich. 6. & 7. Eliz. Dier 234. 235.

(c) Hill. 44. Eliz. Rot. 1459. in Communi Banco inter Ellice & Cowne.

Leases for liues or yeares are of three natures, some be good in Law; some be voydable by entrie, and some voide without entrie. Of such as be good in Law, some be good at the Common Law as made by tenant in fee whereof Littleton here putteth his case, some by Act of Parliament, as tenant in taile, a Bishop seised in fee in the right of his Church alone without his chapter, A man seised in fee simple or fee taile in the right of his wife together with his wife (as hath beene said) may by deede indented make Leases for 21. yeares or three lives in such manner and forme as hath beene said and by the Statute (d) is limitted; all which were voydable by the Common Law when Littleton wrote, and now are made good by Parliament.

(d) 32.H.8.cap.28.

An infant seised of Land holden in Socage, may by custome make a lease at his age of 15. yeares, and shall binde him, which Lease was voydable by the Common Law; Voydable, some by the Common Law, after the death of the lessor as of tenant in taile a Bishop, &c. Or after the death of the husband (intended of Leases not warranted by the said statute of 32.H.8.) Some voydable by Act of Parliament, as by a Bishop though it be confirmed by Deane and Chapter, if it be not warranted by the Statute of 32.H.8. and so of a Deane and Chapter after the Death of the Deane; Some voydable at times by the lessor himselfe or his heires, as by an infant and the like. Some voyde in futuro, and some voide in presenti. In futuro as if a tenant in taile make a Lease for yeares and die without issue, it is voide, as to them in reversion or remainder, though it be made (e) according to the said Statute. If a Prebend, Parson or Vicar make a Lease for yeares, it is voyde by death, if it be not according to the Statutes. Otherwise it is of a Lease for life for that is voydable, & sic de similibus.

(e) 33.H.8.Dier. lib.3.fo.59.60.in Lincolne Colledge case. Hunts case vouched.

Some voide in presenti as if one make a Lease for so many yeares as he shall live, this is voide in presenti for the incertaintie. Et sic in similibus whereof Littleton himselfe will teach you next and immediately and I know you would now gladly heare him.

¶ *Par terme*. Pro termino, Terminus **in the understanding of the** Law doth not only signifie the limits and limitation of time, but also the estate and interest that passeth for that time. As if a man make a Lease for 21. yeares, and after make a lease to begin A fine & expiratione prædicti termini 21. annorum dimiss. and after the first Lease is surrendred, the second Lease shall begin presently, but if it had beene to begin Post finem & expirationem predict' 21. annorum, in that case although the first tearme had beene surrendred, yet the second lease should not begin, till after the 21. yeares be ended by effluxion of time, and so note the diversitie betweene the terme for 21. yeares, and 21. yeares; and (f) herewith agreeth the Lord Pagets Case.

Pl.com.Wrotesl.198. 35.H.8.tit.exposition des parols 44. lib.1.fo.145.in Daveuports case.

(f) Lib.1.fo.154.in the Rector of Chedingtons case.

(g) Words to make a lease be, demise, grant, to fearme let, betake, and whatsoever word amounteth to a grant may serve to make a lease. In the Kings case (h) this word Committo doth amount sometime to a grant, as when he saith Commisimus W.de B officium seneschalciæ, &c. quamdiu nobis placuerit, and by that word also he may make a lease: and (i) therefore a fortiori a common person by that word may doe the same.

(g) Vid.Sect.531.
(h) Register.F.N.B.270.e.

(i) 8.H.6.34.

¶ *De certaine ans*. **For regularly in every Lease for yeares the** terme must have a certaine beginning, and a certaine end, and herewith (k) agreeth Bracton, terminus annorum certus debet esse & determinatus. And Littleton is here to bee understood, first, that the yeares must be certaine when the Lease is to take effect in interest or possession. For before it takes effect in possession or interest, it may depend upon an incertaintie, viz. upon a possible contingent before it begin in possession, or interest, or upon a limitation or condition subsequent. Secondly albeit there appeare no certainty of yeares in the lease, yet if by reference to a certaintie it may be made certaine it sufficeth, Quia id certum est quod certum reddi potest. For example of the first. If A. seised of lands in fee grant to B. that when B. payes to A. xx. shillings, that from thence forth he shall have and occupie the land for 21. yeares, and after B. payes the xx. shillings, this is a good lease for 21. yeares from thenceforth. For the second if A. leaseth his land to B. for so many yeares as B hath in the Mannor of Dale, and B. hath then a terme in the mannor of Dale for 10. yeares, this is a good lease by A. to B. of the land of A. for 10 yeares. If the parson of D. make a lease of his gleabe for so many yeares as hee shall bee parson there, this cannot be made certaine by any meanes, for nothing is more uncertaine then the time of death. Terminus vitæ est incertus, & licet nihil certius sit morte, nihil tamen incertius est hora mortis. But if he make a lease for three yeares, and so from three yeares to three yeares, so long as he shall be parson, this is a good lease for 6. yeares, if he continue parson so long, first for three yeares, and after that for three yeares; and for the residue uncertaine.

(k) 14.H.8.14.3.Mar.leases Br.67. 2.Mar. ibid.67. Say & Fullers case, Pl.com. 273. & Weldens case ibid. 4.H.6.12. 21.H.7.38. Vid. le case del evesque de Bathe.lib.6.fo.34.35. Bract.lib.2.ca.9. Vid.lib.1.fo.155.156. Rector de Chedingtons case.

Bracton lib.2.ca.9. So resolved Hill.26. Eliz. rot.935. in com. banco.

If a man maketh a lease to I.S. for so many yeares as I.N. shall name, this at the beginning is incertaine, but when I.N. hath named the yeares, then it is a good lease for so many yeares.

A man maketh a lease for 21. yeares if I.S. live so long, this is a good lease for yeares, and yet is certaine in incertaintie, for the life of I.S. is incertaine. See many excellent cases concerning this matter put in the said case of the Bishop of Bathe and Wells. By the ancient Law of England for many respects a man could not have made a lease above 40. yeares at the most, for then

Pl.com.Say & Fullers case. Mirror cap.2.§.17. & cap.5.§.1.

then was it said that by long leases many were preiudiced, and many times men disherited, but that ancient Law is antiquated.

In the eye of the Law any estate for life being as Littleton hath said an estate for Freehold, against whom à precipe quod reddat doth lye, is an higher and greater estate then a lease for yeares though it be for a Thousand or more which neuer are without suspition of fraude, and they were the lesse valuable, for that at the Common Law they were subiect unto, and under the power of the tenant of the Freehold, the learning whereof standeth thus and is worthy to bee knowne. When Littleton wrote if a man had made a lease for yeares by writing, and he that had the Freehold had suffered himselfe to be impleaded in a reall action by collusion to barre the Lessee of his terme, and made default, &c. The Statute of Glouc' gaue the Lessee for yeares some remedy by way of receipt, and a triall whether the Demandant did moue the plea by good right or collusion, and if it were found by collusion then the termor should inioy his tearme, and the execution of the iudgement should stay untill after the tearme ended. But this Statute extended not to 5. Cases. 1. If the lease were without writing for the words of this act are, (so that the termor may haue recouery by writ of Couenant.) 2 It extended not but to a recouery by default. 3. The termor could not be relieued by this statute, unlesse he knew of the recouery and were receiued, &c. 4. By the better opinion of bookes, it extended not to tenants by Statute merchant, statute staple or elegit. 5. Not to gardein. (l) But now the statute of 21 H. 8. doth giue remedy in all the said cases sauing the case of the gardian, and giueth them power to falsifie all manner of recoueries had against the tenants of the freehold upon fained and untrue titles, &c. Now the (m) statute saith that it was a doubt before that statute whither a Termor for yeares might falsifie or no, but yet it seemeth by the better opinion of bookes in so great varietie, that he hauing but a chattel, was not able by the Common Law to falsifie a couenous recouery of the freehold, because he could not haue the thing that was recouered. (a) And Thrning and Hankford doe hold that a gardian is not within the statute of Glouc.

Lib. 11. fo. 33.

(l) 21. H. 8. ca. 15.

(m) That a termor might falsifie at the Common Law. Vid. 19. E. 3. Ass. 82. 21. E. 3. 1. 7. H. 7. 11. b. 1. H. 7. 9. b. Pl. com. 83. 10. E. 3. 46. 19. E. 3. resceit 212.
That he could not. 30. H. 6. Fauxes recouery 9. 43. Ass. 41. 26. H. 8. 2. 9. E. 4. 38. F. N. B. 198. E. 14. H. 8. 4. lib. 9. fo. 135. Asseonghes case.
(a) 7. H. 4. 12. 33. H. 8. Dier 52.

If two Copercener be, and one of them let her part to another for yeares and after upon a writ of partition brought against the Lessor too little is alotted to the Lessor, it is holden by some that the Lessee cannot auoide it for that it is made by the oath of men, and iudgement is thereupon giuen that the partition shall remaine firme and stable. But if there be two Coperceners of three acres of land euery one of equall value, and the one Copercener letteth her part, and after make partition, and one acre is alotted only to the Lessor, the Lessee is not bound hereby, but he may enter and take the profits of another halfe acre, for that of right belong unto him. Thus much haue I thought good to set downe for it sufficeth not to know what the Law is in these cases, unlesse he understand the reason and cause thereof.

And albeit (as hath beene said) a lease for yeares must haue a certaine beginning, and a certaine end, yet the continuance thereof may be incertaine, for the same may cease and reuiue againe in diuers cases. As if tenant in taile make a lease for yeares reseruing xx. shillings, and after take a wife and die without issue, now as to him in the reuersion the lease is meerely voide, but if hee indow the wife of tenant in taile of the land, (as she may be though the estate taile be determined) now is the lease as to the tenant in dower (who is in of the state of her husband) (a) reuiued againe as against her, for as to her the estate taile continueth; for she shal be attendant for the third part of the rent seruices, and yet they were extinct by act in Law. So it is if tenant in taile make a lease for yeares vt supra, and dieth without issue, his wife enseint with a sonne, he in the reuersion enter, against him the lease is voide, but after the sonne be borne the lease is good, if it be made according to the (b) statute, and otherwise is voydable.

(a) 16. E. 3. 26. 34. Ass. 15. 23. E. 3. Dower 130.

(b) 32. H. 8. ca. 28.

The King made a gift in taile of the Mannor of Eastfarleigh, in Kent to W. to hold by Knights seruice; W. made a lease to A. for thirtie sixe yeares, reseruing thirteene pound rent, W. dyed, his sonne and heire of full age, all this was found by office: as to the King this lease is not of force, for he shall haue his primer seisin as of lands in possession, but after liuerie, the lessee may enter; and if the issue in taile accept the rent, the lease shall bind him, for the Kings primer seisin shall not take away the election of the issue in taile, for it may be that the rent was better than the land: (c) and so it was adiudged in Awstens case, as I had it of the report of Master Edmond Plowden, a graue and learned Apprentice of Law.

(c) Pasch. 2. & 3. ph. & Mar. in an information of Intrusion in the Exchequer against Austen.
Vid. Dier Pasch. 2. & 3. Ph. & Mar. 115. 13. Eliz. ca. 10.

If tenant in fee take wife, and make a lease for yeares and dieth, the wife is endowed, shee shall auoyd the lease, but after her decease the lease shall bee in force againe. But if the Patron grant the next auoydance, and after Parson, Patron, and Ordinarie, before the Statute, (d) had made a lease of the glebe for yeares, and after the Parson dieth, and the grantee of the next auoydance had presented a Clerke to the Church, who is admitted, instituted, and inducted, and dieth within the terme, the Patron presents a new Clerke, and he is admitted, instituted, and inducted, albeit he commeth in under the Patron that was partie to the lease, yet because the last incumbent, who had the whole state in him, auoyded the lease, it shall not reuiue againe, no more than if a feme couert leuie a fine alone, if the husband enter and auoyd the fine, and die, the whole estate is so auoyded as it shall not bind the wife after his death.

(d) 6. E. 6. Dier. 72. 17. E. 3. 52. 17. Ass. p. 17. 2. R. 3. 20. 9. H. 6. 33.

2.E.3.8.per Scroope. If a woman be endowed of an aduowson which is appropriated, and she present, and her incumbent is admitted, instituted, and inducted, albeit the incumbent die, yet is the appropriation wholly dissolued, because the incumbent which came in by presentation, had the whole state in him, and so was it adiudged, as the case is to be intended.

Pl.Com.437.a. Tenant in taile make a lease for fortie yeares, reseruing a rent, to commence ten yeares after, tenant in taile die, the issue enter and infeoffe A. ten yeares expire, the lessee enter, if A. accept the rent, the lease is good, for he shall haue the same election that the issue in taile had, either to make it good, or to auoyd it, so as it could not be precisely affirmed, whither by the entrie of the issue this executorie lease was auoyded, but it dependeth incertainly upon the will of the feoffee. But now I know you are desirous to heare Littleton, who is speaking to you.

¶ *Et quant le lessee enter per force del lease, donques il est tenant pur terme des ans.* **And true it is, that to many purposes he is not Tenaunt** for yeares untill he enter: as a release made to him is not good to him to increase his estate, before entrie; but he may release the rent reserued before entrie, in respect of the priuitie. Neither can the Lessor grant away the reuersion by the name of the reuersion, before entrie, vide Sect. 567. But the lessee before entrie hath an interest, interesse termini grantable to another, vide Sect. 319. And albeit the lessor die before the lessee enters, yet the lessee may enter into the lands, as our Author himselfe holdeth in this chapter. And so if the lessee dyeth before he entred, yet his executors or administrators may enter, because hee presently by the lease hath an interest in him: And if it be made to two, and one die before entrie, his interest shall suruiue. Vid Sect. 281.

V.Sect.454.455.

V.Sect.665. more fully of this matter. He that hath a lease for yeares, hath it either in his owne right, whereof Littleton hath heere spoken, or in anothers right, and that in diuers manners, as a man may haue a terme for yeares in the right of his wife, whereof the husband hath power to dispose at any time during his life, and if he suruiueth his wife, the law doth giue the lease to him. But if he make no disposition thereof, and his wife suruiue him, it remaineth with the wife: but of this in another place more fully.

If a man be possessed of a terme of fortie yeares in the right of his wife, and maketh a Lease for twentie yeares, reseruing a rent, and die, the wife shall haue the residue of the terme, but the executors of the husband shal haue the rent, for it was not incident to the reuersion, for that the wife was not partie to the lease. So note, a disposition of part of the terme is no disposition of the whole. But if the husband grant the whole terme, upon condition that the grantee shall pay a summe of money to his executors, &c. the husband die, the condition is broken, the Executors enter, this is a disposition of the terme, and the wife is barred thereof, for the whole interest was passed away.

Hil.17.El.in the kings Bench. If a lease be made to a baron and feme for terme of their liues, the remainder to the Executors of the suruiuor of them, the husband grant away this terme and dieth, this shall not barre the wife, for that the wife had but a possibilitie, and no interest.

37.Ass.p.11.Pl.Com.418.b If the husband and wife be eiected of a terme in the right of his wife, and the husband bring an eiectione firmæ in his owne name, and haue iudgement to recouer, this is an alteration of the terme, and uesteth it in the husband.

If a lease for yeares be made to a Bishop and his successors, yet his executors or administrators shall haue it in auter droit, for regularly no Chattell can goe in succession in a case of a sole Corporation, no more than if a lease be made to a man and his heires, it can goe to his heyres. But let us returne to Littleton.

Li.5.fo.1.Claytons case 12. Eliz. Dyer 286.

14.El.Dy.307.5.El.Dy.218 Touching the time of the beginning of a lease for yeares, it is to be obserued, that if a lease be made by Indenture, bearing date 26. Maii, &c to haue and to hold for twentie one yeares, from the date, or from the day of the date, it shall begin on the twentie seuenth day of May. If the lease beare date the twentie first day of May, &c. to haue and to hold from the making hereof, or from henceforth, it shall begin on the day in which it is deliuered, for the words of the Indenture are not of any effect till the deliuerie, and thereby from the making, or from henceforth take their first effect. But if it be à die confectionis, then it shall begin on the next day after the deliuerie. If the habendum be for the terme of twentie one yeares, without mentioning when it shall begin, it shall begin from the deliuerie, for there the words take effect, as is aforesaid. If an Indenture of lease beare date, which is voyd or impossible, as the thirtieth day of Februarie, or the fortieth of March, if in this case the terme be limitted to begin from the date, it shall begin from the deliuerie, as if there had beene no date at all. (a) And so it is, if a man by his Indenture of lease, either recite a lease which is not, or is voyd, or misrecite a lease in point materiall which is in esse, To haue and to hold from the ending of the former lease, this lease shall begin in course of time from the deliuerie thereof.

Li.2 fo.5.Goddards case.

(a) Pl.Com.148.3.E.6.tit. Leases Br.62.3.El.W.195. 1.Mar.Dyer 116.

¶ *Et si le lessor en tiel case reserue a luy un annual rent sur tiel case, il poet eslier a distreyner pur le rent, ou il poet auer action de debt pur les arerages.*

¶ *Reserne a luy vn annual rent,&c.* **First it appeareth (b) here by** Littleton that a rent must be reserued out of Lands or Tenements, whereunto the Lessor may haue resort or recourse to distreine, as Littleton here also saith, and therefore a rent cannot be reserued by a common person out of any incorporeall inheritance, as Aduowsons, Commons, Offices, Corodie, multure of a Mill, Tythes, Faires, Markets, Liberties, Priuiledges, Franchises and the like. (c) But if the lease be made of them by Deede for yeares, it may be good by way of Contract to haue an action of debt, but distreine the Lessor cannot. Neither shall it passe with the graunt of the reuersion for that it is no rent incident to the reuersion. But if any rent be reserued in such case vpon a lease for life, it is vtterly voide, for that in that case no action of debt doe lye. But if a man demiseth the vesture or herbage of his land he may reserue a rent, for that the thing is maynorable, and the Lessor may distreine the chattel vpon the Land: And so a reuersion, or a remainder of lands or tenements may be granted reseruing a rent, for the apparant possibility that it may come in possession, and they are tenements within the words of Littleton.

(b) *Li.7.fo.23.Butt case. Li.10.fo.39.60.*
(c) 30.*Ass.p.*5.12.*Ass.*20. 20.E.4.10. 1.*H.*4.1,2,3.11.*H.*4.82. 19.*E.*2.*Fines* 126.44.*E.*3.45 9.*Ass.*24.26.*ass.*60.14.*E.*3. *Ser.fac.*122.5.*E.*3.68. 17.*E.*3.75.11.*H.*4.40. 3.*H.*6.21.45.10.*H.*6.12. 21.*H.*6.11.5.*H.*7.30. 21.*H.*7.19.17.*E.*2.*Ex.*112. 23.*El. Dyer* 377.

(a) It appeareth by Littleton that reservando is an apt word of reseruing a rent, and so is reddendo, solvendo, faciendo, inveniendo, dummodo, and the like.

(b) And note a diuersitie betweene an exception (which is euer of part of the thing granted and of a thing in esse) for which exceptis, saluo, praeter, and the like be apt words; and a reseruation which is alwayes of a thing not in esse, but newly created or reserued out of the land or tenement demised. (c) Poterit enim quis rem dare & partem rei retinere, vel partem de pertinentiis, & illa pars quam retinet semper cum eo est & semper fuit. (d) But out of a generall a part may be excepted, as out of a Mannor, an Acre, Ex verbo generali aliquid excipitur, and not a part of a certaintie, as out of twentie Acres, one.

It is further to bee obserued that the Lessor cannot reserue to any other but to himselfe, for Litt. sayth reserue a luy, reserue to himselfe. (e) If two ioyntenants be, & they make a lease for yeares by paroll, or deed poll reseruing a rent to one of them, this shall enure to them both, but if it bee so reserued by deed indented, it shall enure to him alone by way of conclusion.

(f) Littleton here is putting of a case, and not making a lease, for then he would not reserue the rent to him, but to him, and his heires, for otherwise the rent shall determine by his death if he die within the terme. (g) But if he reserue a rent generally without shewing to whom it shall goe, it shall goe to his heires. If he reserue a rent to him and his Assignes, yet the rent shall determine by his death, because the reseruation is good but during his life. So it is if he reserue a rent to him and his Executors it shall end by his death, because the heire hath the reuersion, and the rent was incident to the reuersion. So if a man warrant land to B. and his assignes, the assignee must vouche during the life of B. for the warrantie continue but only during the life of B. for the warrantie is but for life, for want of words of inheritance. But if the warrantie be to B. his heires and assignes, so as he hath an inheritance therein, then his assignee shall vouche after his decease. So if the rent be reserued to the Lessor his heires and assignes, so as it be incident to the inheritance, then shall all the assignees of the reuersion enioy the same.

(a) 40.E.3.47.8.E.3.67. 21.E.4.62.3.*H.*6.45. 31.*ass.p.*30.3.*ass.*9.26 *ass.*66. 32.*E.*3.*Br.*291.8.*E.*4.8. 10.*El.Dy.*276.*Pl.Com.en Browning & Beestons case fo.*131.132.&c.
(b) 50.E.3.12.13.*Ass.*9. 38.*E.*3.10.21.*E.*3.4.34.*ass.*11.29 E.3.14. 3.*H.*6.45. 10.*H.*6.8.41.33.*H.*6.1. 35.*H.*6.34.17.*ass.*14.*H.*8.1. 44.*E.*3.43.*Pl.Com.*361.
(c) *Bract li.*2.*f.*32.*b.&f.*249
(d) 9.*El.Dy.*264.38 *H.*6 38 14.*H.*8.1.22.*E.*3.8. 2.*E.*3.56.5.*E.*3 66. 34.*Ass.*11.
(e) 5.*E.*4.4. 14.*E.*3. *bro.*282 *lib.*8.*fo.*70.71.
(f) *Vid.Sect.*314.215.216. &c. 10.*E.*4.18. 11.*E.*3. *Ass* 86. 27.*H.*8.19. 21.*H.*7.25.30.*H.*8.*Dy.*45.
(g) *Mich.*5.*Ia.in repl inter Wootton & Edwin bank le roy. Hil.*33.*El.Rot.*1431.*in ba ke le roy enter Rickmond & Butcher.*

¶ *Annual rent.* **So it is if the rent be reserued euery two or three** or more yeares. Of Rents Littleton doth excellently treate hereafter in his Chapter of rents, and therefore in this place thus much shall suffice.

¶ *A distreiner pur le rent.* **Here it is necessarie to be seene of what** things a distresse may be taken for a rent, and how the distresse ought to be demeaned. (h) First it must be of a thing, whereof a valuable propertie is in some body, and therfore Dogs, Bucks, Doas, Conies and the like that are fere naturæ cannot be distreyned. Secondly, although it be of valuable propertie as a horse, &c. yet when a man or woman is riding on him, or an axe in a mans hand cutting of wood and the like, they are for that time priuiledged and cannot bee distreyned. (i) 2. Valuable things shall not be distreined for rent for benefit and maintenance of trades, which by consequent are for the Common-wealth, and are there by Authority of Law, as a horse in a Smithes shop shall not be distreyned for the rent issuing out of the shop, nor the horse, &c. in the Hostry, nor the materials in the weauers shop for making of cloth, nor cloth or garments in a Taylors shop, nor sacks of corne or meale, in a Mill nor in a Market; nor any thing distrayned for damage fesaunt, for it is in custody of Law, and the like.

*Vi. for this word Distreine, Sect.*136.
(h) 14.*H.*8.25.2.*E.*2.*tit. Distresse* 6.*R.*2. *Rescous* 11. 7.*E.*3.*Auowr.*199.15.*E.*2. *Auowry* 2.
(i) 22.*E.*4.49.*b.*7.*H.*7.1.*b.* 22.*E.*4.36.4 *E.*6.*tit.Dist. Br.*74.

(k) 4. Nothing shall be distreyned for rent, that cannot be rendered againe in as good plight as it was at the time of the distresse taken, as sheaues or shocks of corne or the like cannot be distreyned for rent, but for damage fesant they may be distreyned. But charrets or carts with corne may be distreyned for rent for they may be safely restored.

(l) 5 Beasts belonging to the plow, aueria carucæ shall not be distreined (which is the ancient Common Law of England for no man shall be distreyned by the vtensills or instruments of his trade or profession, as the axe of the Carpenter, or the bookes of a scholler) while goods

(k) 18.*E.*3.4.*a.*11.*H.*7. 14.*a.*21.*H.*7.39.*b.*22.*E.*4. 50.*b.*2.*H.*4.15.
(l) *Okeham* 38.39. *Bra.li.*4.*f.*217.*F.N.B.*90.*a Reg.*97. *Flet.li.*2.*ca.*41. *Mirr.cap.*2.§.15.16. 4.*E.*3.1.29.*E.*3.17.

(m) 21.*H*.7.26. 3.*E*.3.*Ass*.46.9.
(n) 7.*H*.7.1.*b*.10.*H*.7.21. 11.*H*.7.4.*a*. 15.*H*.7 17. 18.*E*.2.*avowrie* 219. 6.*E*.4. 22.*E*.4.49. 4.*E*.3.*distres*.18.27.*E*.3.80. 2.*H*.4.16.
(o) *Marlebr.cap*.4. *W*.1.*cap*.16. 2.& 3.*Ph.& mar.cap*.13. *Fleta lib*.2.*cap*.20. 6.*H*.3 *avowrie* 242. 30.*Ass*.38. 1.*H*.6.9. 22.*E*.4.11.*F.N.B*.89. *Doctor & Student. lib*.2.*cap*.27. 5.*H*.7.*fol*.9.
(p) 33.*H*.8.*tit.distres*.*Br*.65

or other beasts which Bracton cals animalia (or catalla) otiosa may be distrained (m). 6. Furnesses, Caudrons or the like fixed to the freehold, or the doores or windowes of a house, or the like cannot be distrained. (n) Lastly, beasts that escape may be distrained for rent, though they have not beene leuant and couchant. (o) Note that he that distraines any thing that hath life must impound them, in a lawfull pound within three miles in the same Countie, and that is either Ouert or Open, in a Pinfold made for such purposes, or in his owne Close, or in the Close of another by his consent. And it is therefore called Open, because the Owner may give his Cattle meate and drinke without trespasse to any other, and then the Cattle must be sustained at the perill of the Owner. (p) Or it is a Pound Couert or Close as to impound the Cattle in some part of his house, and then the Cattle are to bee sustained with meate and drinke at the perill of him that distraineth, and he shall not have any satisfaction therefore. But if the distresse be of Utensils of houshold or such like dead goods which may take harme by wet or weather, or be stolne away, there he must impound them in a house or other Pownd couert within three miles within the same Countie, for if he impound them in a Pownd ouert hee must answer for them.

(q) 4.*E*.6.*tit.distres*.74. *F.N.B*.100.*E*.

(q) If the distresse be taken of goods without cause the Owner may make Rescous, but if they distrained without cause, and impounded, the Owner cannot breake the Pownd and take them out, because they are then in the custodie of the Law.

(r) 3.*E*.3.*tit.trans*.11.
(s) 34.*H*.6.18.

(r) But if a man distraine Cattle for damage feasant, and put them in the pownd, and the Owner that had common there make fresh suite, and find the doore unlocked, he may iustifie the taking away of the Cattle in a parco fracto. (s) If the Owner breake the Pownd, and take away his goods, the partie distraining may have his Action de parco fracto, and hee may also take his goods that were distrained wheresoever he find them, and impownd them againe.

(t) *Regist. F.N.B*.100.101.

It is called a Writ de parco fracto of these words in the writ (t) Parcum illum vi & armis fregit. And the forme thereof appeare in the Register and F.N.B.

But it is to be obserued that for the rent due the last day of the Tearme, the Lessor cannot distraine because the Terme is ended, and therefore some use to reserve the last halfe yeares rent, at the Feast of the Natiuitie of Saint Iohn Baptist before the end of the Terme, so as if the rent be not then paid, he may distraine betweene that and Michaelmasse following.

(u) 7.*H* 6.13.*lib*.4.*fol*.49. *Lib*.3.*fol*.16. 34.*E*.1.*tit. avowrie* 233. 32.*H*.8.*Br. reliefe* 11.*F.N.B*.82.83. *Glanvil.lib*.9.*cap*.35. *Fleta lib*.2.*cap*.40.& *lib*.3.*cap*.14. *Bracton.lib*.2.*fol*.36. *W*.1.*cap*.35. 25.*E*.3 *cap*.11. *Britton.fol*.57.& 70.

¶ *Action de debt.* *Note* a diversitie betweene a rent reserved upon a lease for yeares, reserving a yearely rent; the Lessor may have severall Actions of debt for every yeares rent. But upon a bond or contract for payment of severall summes, no Action of debt lieth till the last day be past. But otherwise it is of a Recognizance, which see at large and the reason thereof cap. Releases Sect 512.513. (u) Note that the Lord shall not have an action of Debt for releife or for escuage due unto him, because hee hath other remedie, but his Executors or Administrators shall have an Action therefore, because it is now become as a flower falne from the stocke, and they have no other remedie. Neither shall the Lord have an Action of debt for aide, pur file marier or faire fitz Chiualer for the cause aforesaid.

¶ *Mes en tiel case il covient que le lessor soit seisie de mesmes les tenements al temps del lease, car est bone plea pur le lessee a dire que le lessor navoit riens en les tenements al temps del lease.* And the reason of this is, for that in every contract there must be quid pro quo, for contractus est quasi actus contra actum, and therefore if the Lessor hath nothing in the land, the Lessee hath not quid pro quo nor any thing for which he should pay any rent. And in that case he may also plead, that the Lessor non dimisit, and give in evidence the other matter.

(x) 45.*E*.3.9.20.*E*.4.10. 34.*H* 6.48. 35.*H*.6.34. 1.*H*.6.35.11.*H*.4.22.
(y) 2.*E*.2.*Estop*.253. 39.*E*.3.13. *Pl.Com*.434. 18.*E*.3.16. 15.*E*.3.*Estop*.236. 14.*H*.4.32.
(z) 14.*H*.6.23. 8.*H*.4.7.
(a) *Resolue.Pasch*. 2.*Eliz. in Communi Banco.*
(b) *Mich*.31.& 32.*Eliz. in Communi Banco adiudge in Londons case.*
(c) 38.*H*.6.24. 30.*E*.3.21.

¶ *Si* (x) *non que le lease soit per fait indent, &c.* If the lease be made by deed indented then are both parties concluded; (y) but if it be by deed poll the Lessee is not estopped to say that the lessor had nothing at the time of the Lease made. A. lessee for the life of B. makes a lease for yeares by deed indented, and after purchase the reversion in fee, B dieth, A. shall avoid his owne Lease, for he may confesse & avoid the lease which took effect in point of interest, and determined by the death of B. But if A. had nothing in the land, and made a Lease for yeares by deed indented, and after purchase the land, the Lessor is aswell concluded, as the Lessee to say that the Lessor had nothing in the land, and here it worketh only upon the conclusion, and the Lessor cannot confesse and avoid as hee might in the other case. (z) If a man take a Lease of his owne Land by deed indented reserving a Rent the Lessee is concluded. (a) But if a man take a Lease of the herbage of his owne Land by Deed indented, this is no conclusion, to say that the Lessor had nothing in the Land, because it was not made of the land it selfe: (b) but if a man take a Lease for yeares of his owne Land by deed indented, the estopell doth not continue after the terme ended. For by the making of the lease the estoppell doth grow and consequently by the end of the lease, the estopell determines (c) and that

part

part of the indenture which belonged to the lessee, doth after the terme ended, belong to the lessor, which should not be if the estoppell continued.

Section 59.

CEt est ascauoire, Que en lease pur terme de ans per fait ou sans fait, il ne besoigne ascun liuerie de Seisin deste fait al Lessee, mes il poet enter quant il voet p force de mesme de Lease. Mes des Feoffmts faits en pais, ou dones en l' Taile, ou lease pur term de vie, en tiels cases ou franktenement passera, si ceo soit per fait ou sauns fait, il couiēt auer vn liuery de seisin.

AND it is to be vnderstood, That in a lease for yeares by deed or without deed, there needs no Liuery of seisin to be made to the Lessee, but he may enter when he will by force of the same lease. But of Feoffements made in the Countrie, or gifts in Taile, or Lease for terme of life, in such cases where a Freehold shall passe, if it be by Deed, or without Deed, it behoooueth to haue Liuerie of Seisin.

¶ *Liuerie de seisin.* Traditio, or deliberatio seisinæ is a solemnitie that the Law requireth, for the passing of a Freeholde of Lands or Tenements by deliuerie of Seisin thereof. (b) Interuenire debet solennitas in mutatione liberi tenementi ne contingat donationem deficere pro defectu probationis.

18.*E*.3.*fo*.16.41.*E*.3.17. 40.*Ass*.10.2.*Ass*.1.2 *E*.3.4 43.*E*.3.*Feoff*.51 *Pl.Com*. 25.*a*.& 303.*b.V.Sect*.66.

(b) *Bract.li*.2.*ca*.15.

And there be two kinds of liuerie of seisin, viz. a liuerie in (c) Deed, and a liuerie in Law. A liuerie in Deed, is when the Feoffor taketh the ring of the doore, or turfe or twigge of the land, and deliuereth the same vpon the land to the Feoffee in name of seisin of the land, &c. per hostium & per haspam & anulum vel per fustem vel baculum, &c.

(c) *Bract.li*.2.*ca*.15.& 18. *Brit.ca*.33.*in fine fo*.87. *Flet.li*.3.*ca*.15.

A seised of an house in fee, and being in the house, (d) saith to B. I deuise to you this house for terme of my life; this is a good beginning to limit the state, but here wanteth liuerie. A liuerie in Deed may be done two manner of wayes by a solemne act and words, as by deliuerie of the ring or haspe of the doore, or by a branch or twig of a tree, or by a turfe of the land, and with (e) these or the like words, the feoffor and feoffee both holding the Deede of feoffement, and the ring of the doore, haspe, branch, twigge, or turfe: and the feoffor saying, Here I deliuer you seisin and possession of this house, in the name of all the Lands and Tenements contained in this [illegible] according to the forme and effect of this Deed. Or by words without any Ceremonie [illegible], as the feoffor being at the house doore, or within the house, Here I deliuer you seisin [illegible] possession of this house, in the name of seisin and possession of all the lands and tenements contained in this Deed, Et sic de similibus, or enter you into this house or land, and haue and enioy it according to the Deed; or, Enter into the house or land, and God giue you ioy, or I am content you shall enioy this land according to the Deed, or the like. For if words may amount to a liuerie within the view, much more it shall vpon the land. But if a man deliuer the Deed of feoffement vpon the land, this amounts to no liuerie of the land, for it hath another operation to take effect as a Deed: but if he deliuer the Deed vpon the land in name of seisin of all the lands contained in the Deed, this is a good liuerie: and so are other books entended that treat hereof, that the Deed was deliuered in name of seisin of that land. Hereby it appeareth, That the deliuerie of any thing vpon the land in name of seisin of that land, though it be nothing concerning the land, as a ring of gold, is good, and so hath it beene resolued by all the Judges, and so of the like.

(d) *Li*.6.*fo*.26.*Sharps case*.

(e) *See of this more, Sect*.60.

41.*E*.3.17.*b*.41.*Ass.p* 10. 38.*Ass.p*.2.38.*E*.3.11. 39.*Ass.p*.12.26.*Ass*.39. 27 *Ass.p*.61.18.*E*.3.16. *Li*.6 *fo*.26. *Sharps case*.

43.*E*.3.*tit.Feoffm*.51. 35.*H*.8.*Feoffm.Br*.

50.*E*.3.*Rot.Parl.nu*.30.

If diuers parcells of land be conteyned in a Deed, and the Feoffor deliuers seisin of one parcell according to the Deed, all the parcels doe passe albeit he saith not (in name of all, &c) because the Deed conteyneth all. And so if there be diuers Feoffees, and hee make liuery to one according to the Deed, the land passeth to all the Feoffees, and yet the playner way is to say (in the name of the whole, or of all the Feoffees.)

13.*E*.3.*Estop*.177.

If a man make a Charter in fee, and deliuer seisin for life secundum formam cartæ, the whole fee simple shall passe, for it shall be taken most strongly against the Feoffor. Note that these words (Secundum formam cartæ) are vnderstood according to the quantitie and qualitie of the effectuall estate conteyned in the Deed. If a man make a lease for yeares by Deed, and deliuer

Ibidem.

7.*E*.4.25.29.*Ass*.40. 10.*Ass*.19.43.*Ass*.20.

Mich.33.& 34.Eliz. in the Kingsbench Inter Hegge & Crosse for lands in London. Vid. Pl.com.395.

* *See more of this Sect.66. 11.H.4.71. 19.Ass.9. 19.H.8.9.b.*

liuer seisin according to the forme and effect of the Deede, yet he hath but an estate for yeares, and the liuery is voide as Littleton saith. So if A. by Deed giue land to B. to haue and to hold after the death of A. to B. and his heires, this is a voide Deed, because he cannot reserue to himselfe a particular estate, and construction must be made vpon the whole Deed, and if liuery be made according to the forme and effect of the Deed, the liuery also is voide because the liuery referreth to a Deed that hath no effect in Law, and therefore it cannot worke secundum formam & effectum cartæ. And so it was adiudged, & sic de similibus. * And it is to be obserued that neither the Feoffor being absent, can make liuery, nor the Feoffee being absent can take liuery; but by warrant of Attorney, by Deed and not by parol, because it concerneth matter of freehold.

Bridgewaters Case.

Vid. Sect.1.

Vide Sect.1. in Bridgewaters Case, where a man hath a moueable estate of inheritance, for example there put, in 13. acres: the question is where liuery shall be made. First, if they be parcell of a Mannor, they may passe by the name of the Mannor; but if they be in grosse then the Charter of Feoffment must be of 13. acres, lying and being in the meadow of 80. acres, generally without bounding or discribing of the same in certaintie, and liuery of the seisin of any 13. acres allotted to the feoffee for a yeare secundum formam cartæ is a good liuery to passe the content of 13. acres wheresoeuer the same lie in that meadow. In the second case where one entire Mannor is seperate and deuided, as is aforesaid, there is no question but the liuery must be made of that Mannor, but in the other case where two Mannors are separate, and deuided alternis vicibus, there the Charter of feoffment must be made of both, and liuery in that Mannor which he is seised of in any one yeare secundum formam cartæ, and the next yeare in the other secundum formam cartæ: for there are two distinct Mannors, and seuerall estates in them.

38.E.3.11. 38.Ass.p.2. 43.Ass.p.20. Temps H.8. Tit. Feoffments Br.70. 18.E.3.16 b. 28.H.8.F.18. 9.E.4.39. per Moyle. Bract.lib.2.cap.18.& lib.4.fo.225.a.

(a) 9.E.4.39. 38.E.3.11.
(b) 9.E.4.28.40. 5.H.7.9. 3.H.6.tit.Pleint.1. 11.H.4.32. 11.E.3.Ass.86.
(c) 38.Ass.p.23.

A liuery in Law is when the Feoffor saith to the Feoffee being in the view of the house or land, (I giue you yonder land to you and your heires and goe enter into the same, and take possession thereof accordingly,) and the Feoffee doth accordingly in the life of the Feoffor enter this is a good feoffment for signatio pro traditione habetur. And herewith agreeth Bracton, Item dici poterit, & assignari quando res vendita vel donata sit in conspectu quam venditor & donator dicit se tradere: And in another place he saith, in seisina per affectum & per aspectum. But if either Feoffor or the Feoffee die before entry the liuery is voyde. And liuery within the view is good where there is no Deed of feoffment. (a) And such a liuery is good albeit the land lie in another country. (b) A man may haue an inheritance in an vpper chamber, though the lower buildings and soyle be in another, and seeing it is an inheritance corporeall it shall passe by liuery. (c) A man maketh a Charter of feoffment and deliuers seisin within the view, the Feoffee dares not enter for feare of death, but claimes the same, this shall vest the freehold and inheritance in him, albeit by the liuery no estate passed to him, neither in Deed, nor in Law, so as such a claime shall serue, aswell to vest a new estate and right in the Feoffee, as in the cōmon case to reuest an ancient estate and right in the disseisee, &c. as shalbe said hereafter more at large in the chapter of continuall claime. And so note a liuery in Law shalbe perfected and executed by an entry in Law. (d) If a man be disseised, and make a Deed of feoffment, and a letter of Attorney to enter and take possession, and after to make liuery secundum formam cartæ, this is a good feoffment albeit he was out of possession at the time of the Charter made for the Authority giuen by the letter of Attorney is executorie, and nothing passed by the deliuery of the Deed till liuery of seisin was made. And in ancient letters of Attorney power is giuen to others to take possession for the Feoffor. But if a man be disseised, and make writing of Lease for yeares and deliuer the Deed, and after deliuer it vpon the ground, the second deliuery is voide, for the first deliuery made it a Deed, and for that the lease for yeares must take effect by the deliuery of the Deed, therefore the Deed deliuered when he was out of possession was voide. But so it is not of a Charter of feoffment, for that takes effect by the liuery and seisin. But if the Lessor had deliuered it as an escrowe, to be deliuered as his Deed vpon the ground, this had beene good.

(d) Hill:37.Eliz.rot.620. in com.banco, inter Browne & Tirrey adiudged. Dier 16.Eliz.234. 3.Eliz. Dier 131.

Lib.3.fol.35. inter Iennings & Bragge.

A man makes a lease for yeares and after makes a Deed of feoffment and deliuers seisin, the Lessee being in possession and not assenting to the feoffment, this liuery is voyde, for albeit the Feoffor hath the freehold and inheritance in him, yet that is not sufficient, for a liuery must bee giuen of the possession also: but if the lessee be absent, and hath neither wife nor seruants (though he hath cattell) vpon the ground the liuery of seisin shall be good.

Lib.2.fo.31.32. Bettisworths case.

If a man be seised of an house, & of diuers seuerall closes in one Countie in fee, and makes a lease thereof for yeares, and afterward maketh a feoffement in fee of the same, and makes liuerie of seisin in the Closes, (the Lessee or his wife or seruants then being in the house) the liuery is voyd for the whole: for the lessee cannot be vpon euery parcell of the land to him demised, for the preseruation and continuance of his possession therein. And therefore his being in the house, or vpon any part of the land to him demised, is sufficient to preserue and continue his possession in the whole, from being ousted or dispossessed.

Note

Note a great diuersitie, when a man hath two wayes to passe lands, and both of the wayes be by the Common Law, and he entendeth to passe them by one of the wayes, yet vt res magis valeat it shall passe by the other. But where a man may passe Lands either by the Common Law, or by raising of an vse, and setling it by the statute, there in many cases it is otherwise. For example, If a man be seised of two acres in fee, and letteth one of them for yeares, and intending to passe them both by feoffement, maketh a Charter of feoffement, and maketh liuerie in the acre in possession, in name of both, onely the acre in possession passeth by the liuerie. Yet if the lessee attorne, the reuersion of that acre shall passe by the deed and attornement, for he is in by the Common Law, and in the per in both, and so in the like. But otherwise it is, if the father make a Charter of feoffement to his sonne, and a letter of Attorney to make liuerie, and no liuerie is made, yet no vse shall rise to the son, because he should be in by the statute in another degree, viz in the post, and the intention of the parties worke much both in the raising and direction of vses. So if Cesty que vse and his feoffees had ioyned in a feoffement after the statute of 1.R.3.&c. it had beene the feoffement of the feoffees, and the confirmation of Cesty que vse, for the state at the Common Law shall be preferred. So to conclude in this point, Of Freehold and Inheritances, some be corporeall, as houses, &c. lands, &c. these are to passe by liuerie of seisin, by Deed or without Deed; some be incorporeall, as Aduowsons, Rents, Commons, Estouers, &c. these cannot passe without Deed, but without any liuerie. And the law hath prouided the Deed in place or stead of a liuerie. And so it is if a man make a lease, and by Deed grant the reuersion in fee, here the freehold with attornement of the lessee by the Deede doth passe, which is in lieu of the liuerie. See Bract. lib. 2. cap. 18. Et est traditio de re corporali de persona in personam de manu, &c. gratuita translatio, & nihil aliud est traditio in vno sensu, nisi in possessionem inductio, de re corporali; & ideo dicitur, Quod res incorporales non patiuntur traditionem sicut ipsum ius quod rei siue corpori inhæret, & quia non possunt, res incorporales possideri sed quasi, ideo traditionem non patiuntur, &c.

7.E.4.20.a. per touts les Iust. 11.H.4.71. Pl.Com.152. 10.E.4.3.

Li.2. fo.35.36. Sir R. Heywards case.

1.R.3.ca.1. 21.H.7.

This antient manner of conueyance by feoffement and liuery of seisin, doth for many respects exceed all other conueyances. For (as hath beene said) if the feoffor be out of possession, neither fine, recouerie, Indenture of bargaine and sale inrolled, nor other conueyance, doth auoyd an estate by wrong, and reduce cleerely the estate of the feoffee, and make a perfect Tenant of the Freehold, but onely liuerie of seisin vpon the land: the other conueyances being made off from the ground, doe sometimes more hurt than good, when the feoffor is out of possession. And yet in some cases a freehold shall passe by the Common Law without liuerie of seisin: As if a house or land belong to an office, by the grant of the office by Deed, the house or land passeth as belonging thereunto. So if a house or chamber belong to a Corodie, by the grant of a Corodie, the house or chamber passeth. A Freehold may by custome be surrendred without liuerie, as hereafter shall be said: and so of assignement of Dower ad ostium Ecclesiæ, or otherwise, and by exchange a Freehold may passe without liuerie, as hereafter shall be said in this Chapter.

Lib.2. fo.55 Bucklers case.

1.H.7.28. 8.H.7.4.

31.H.6.16. 8.H.7.4. M.31.E.1 coram Rege. Ranu ph Huntingfels case. 3.E.3. Coron.310. 11.H.4.83 V. Sect.74.

Section 60.

MEs si home lessa terres ou Tenements per fait, ou sans fait, a terme des ans, le remainder ouster a vn auter pur terme de vie, ou en taile, ou en fee donque en tiel case il couient que le lessor fait vn liuerie de seisin a le lessee per terme de ans, ou autrement riens passa a eux en le remaind coment q le lessee ent en

BVt if a man letteth lands or tenements by Deed or without Deed for terme of yeares, the remainder ouer to another for life, or in taile, or in fee; in this case it behooueth, that the lessor maketh liuery of seisin to the lessee for yeres, otherwise nothing passeth to them in the remainder, although that the lessee enter into the

¶ *Per fait, ou sauns fait.* For seeing that the remainders take effect by liuerie, there needs no deed.

22.H.6.1. 10.E.4.1. 18.E.4.13.

¶ *Le remainder* is a residue of an estate in land depending vpon a particular estate, and created together with the same, and in Law-Lattin it is called Remanere.

¶ *Fait vn liuery de seisin al Lessee.* This Liuery is not necessarie in this case for the lessee himselfe, because he hath but a Terme for yeares, but it is for the benefit of them in the rem', so as the liuery the lessee shal enure for the benefit of them in the rem': for the liuerie of the possession could not be made to the next in remainder, because the

les tenements. Et si le termor en tiel cas entra deuant ascun liuerie de seisin fait a luy, donque est le franktenemēt & auxy le reuersion en le lessor: Mes si il fait liuerie de seisin a le lessee, donque est le franktenement oue le fee a eux en le remainder, solonque le forme del grant & le volunt del lessor.

tenements. And if the Termour in this case entreth before any liuery of seisin made to him, then is the Freehold and also the reuersion in the Lessor. But if he maketh liuerie of seisin to the Lessee, then is the Freehold together with the fee to them in the remainder acording to the forme of the grant, & the wil of the lessor.

the possession belonged to the lessee for yeares, and for that the particular terme, and all the remainder make in Law but one estate, and take effect at one time therefore the liuerie is to bee made to the lessee. But if a lease for yeares without deed bee made to A. and B. the remainder to C. in fee, and liuerie is made to A. in the absence of B. in the name of both; it seemeth the liuerie is good to vest the remainder; and there is a diuersitie, betweene two ioynt Attornies to receiue liuerie for another, and liuery and seisin is made to one of them, in the name of both, this is cleerely void, because they had but a mere and bare authoritie, and they both doe, in Law make but one Attorney, vnlesse the warrant bee ioyntly and seuerally, but the lessee for yeares hath an interest in the land. Againe, if A. is to make a feoffment to B. and C and their heires without deed, and A. makes liuerie to B. in the absence of C. in the name of both, and to their heires; this liuerie is void to C. because a man being absent cannot take a freehold by a liuery, but by his Attorney being lawfully authorised to receiue liuerie by deed, vnlesse the feoffment be made by deed, and then the liuerie to one in the name of both is good.

10.E.4.1.12.E.4.16. 15.E.4.18.22.E.4.35. 40.E.3.10.41. Temps H.8. Feffments 72. 6.H.4.2.b. Litt.153. 3.H.7.13.

Note there is a diuersitie betweene liuerie of seisin of land, and the deliuerie of a Deed; for if a man deliuer a Deed without saying of any thing, it is a good deliuerie; but to a liuery of seisin of land, words are necessarie; as taking in his hand the Deed, and the Ring of the doore (if it be of an house) or a turffe or twigge (if it be of land) and the feoffee laying his hand on it, the feoffor say to the feoffee, Here I deliuer to you seisin of this house, or of this land, in the name of all the land, contained in this Deed, according to the forme and effect of the Deed, (as hath beene said) and if it be without Deed, then the words may be, Here I deliuer you seisin of this house or land, &c. to haue and to hold to you for life, or to you and the heires of your bodie, or to you and your heires for euer as the case shall require.

Ruth.cap.4. verse 7.8. Deut.25.9.10. Genesis 23. verse 11.

When the Kinsman of Elimelech gaue vnto Boas the parcell of land that was Elimelechs, he tooke off his shooe, and gaue it vnto Boas in the name of seisin of the land (after the manner in Israel) in the presence, and with the testimonie of many witnesses. And when Ephron infeoffed Abraham of the field of Machepela, hee said to him, Agrum trado tibi, &c. I deliuer this field to thee.

A man makes a lease for yeares to A. the remainder to B. in fee, and makes liuery to A. within the view; this liuerie is void, for no man can take by force of a liuerie within the view, but he that taketh the freehold himselfe.

¶ *Et si le termor en tiel case enter deuant ascun liuery fait, &c.* By the entrie of the lessee he is in actuall possession, and then the liuery cannot be made to him that is in possession, for Quod semel meum est, amplius meum esse non potest. But if the lessor and lessee come vpon the ground, of purpose for the lessor to make, and for the lessee to take liuery, there his entrie vest no actuall possession in him vntill liuerie be made; for as (a) Affectio tua nomen imponit operi tuo, And therefore if it be agreed betweene the disseisor and disseisee, that the disseisee shall release all his right to the disseisor vpon the land, and accordingly the disseisee entreth into the land, and deliuereth the release to the disseisor vpon the land, this is a good release, and the entrie of the disseisee, being for this purpose did not auoid the disseisin, for his intent in this case did guide his entrie to a speciall purpose. And so was it resolued (b) by Sir Iames Dier, and the whole Court of Common Pleas, Pasch. 18. Eliz. vpon euidence which I my selfe heard and obserued. But if the disseisor infeoffe the disseisee and others, there albeit the disseisee came to take liuerie, yet when liuerie is made, the disseisee is remitted, to the whole in iudgement of law, as shall be said more at large in the Chapter of Remitter in his proper place.

(a) Bracton, lib. 1.

(b) T.19.Eliz. in Communi Banco. Tl.Com.in Ass.de fresh-force. 91. 29.Ass.26. 43.Ass.p.3. 3.H.6.19. in formdon.

Section 61.

ET si home voile faire feoff. per fait ou sans fait, de tres ou tenements que il ad en plusors villes en un Countie, le liuerie de seisin fait en un parcel de les tenements en un ville en le nosme de touts suffist pur touts les autres terres & tenements comprehendes deins m l'feoffement, en toutz les autres villes deins m le countie. Mes si home fait un fait de feoffement des terres ou tenements en diuers Counties, la il couient en chescun Countie auer un liuerie de seisin.

And if a man wil make a feoffement by deed or without deed, of lands or Tenements, which hee hath in diuers Townes in one Countie, the liuerie of seisin made in one parcell of the Tenements in one Towne in the name of all the rest is sufficient for all other the Lands and Tenements cōprehended within the same feoffment in all other the Townes in the same Countie, but if a man maketh a Deed of Feoffement of Lands or Tenements in diuers Counties, there it behoueth in euery Countie to haue a liuerie of seisin.

EN *un Countie.* A Countie is fetched frō the French, and Shire from the Saxon. For Styran in the Saxon tongue signifieth partiri, because euerie Countie or Shire is deuided and parted by certaine metes and bounds from another, and in Latine is called Comitatus à comitando, for accompanying together. And for as much as the men of one Countie doe not accompanie together with men of another Countie at Countie Courts, Turnes, Leets and other Courts, therefore in iudgement of Law they shall take no notice of a liuerie in another Countie to passe any lands in their owne Countie. But of this more shall be said hereafter. 45. E. 3. 21.

Section 62.

ET en ascun cas home auera per le grant dun auter fee simple, fee taile, ou frankten. sans liuerie de seisin. Sicome deux homes sont, & chescun deux est seisie dun quantitie de terre deins un countie, & lun granta sa terre a lauter en eschange pur la terre que lauter ad, & en mesme le manner lauter granta sa ter-

And in some case a man shall haue by the grant of another a fee simple, fee taile, or freehold without liuery of seisin. As if there bee two men and each of them is seised of one quantitie of Land in one Countie, and the one granteth his Land to the other in exchange for the Land which the other hath, and in like maner the other gran-

HEre Littleton putteth a case where Freehold, &c. shall passe without liuerie of seisin, and thereupon putteth the case of an exchange of lands in one Countie that is good by deed or without deed, without any liuerie, but if it bee in seuerall Counties there must bee a deed. 45. E. 3. 21. 3. E. 4. 10. 9. E. 4. 21. 7 H. 4 1. 8. H. 7. 4. Also of things that lie in grant as Aduowsons, Rents, Commons, &c. an exchange of them albeit they bee in one Countie, is not good, vnlesse it be by deed, and therefore Littleton putteth his case warily of land. And in case of a fine, which is a feoffment of Record; of a deuise by a last will, of a surrender, of a release or confirmation to a lessee for yeares, or at will, In all 28. H. 6. 2.

Vide Sect. 1.
all these and some other cases a freehold, &c. (as hath beene said) may passe without liuerie. But this word (exchange) which our Authour here vseth, is so appropriated by Law, to this case as it cannot bee expressed by any Pariphrasis or circumlocution.

¶ *En ceo case chescun poet enter, &c.* For by the exchange the parties, albeit the lands bee all in one Countie, haue no freehold in Deed or Law in them before they execute the same by entrie; and therefore if one of them dieth, before the exchange be executed by entrie, the exchange is void; for the heire cannot enter and take it as a Purchasor, because he was named only to take by way of limitation of estate in course of discent.

9. E. 4. 38. 39. 45. E. 3. 20. 21. 45. E. 3. exchange 10.

re a le primer grantor en eschange pur la terre que le primer grantor ad, en ceo cas chescun poit enter en lauter terre issint mise en eschange sans ascun liuerie de seisin, & tiel eschange fait per parolx de tenemts deins mesme le Countie sans escript, est Assets bone.

teth his Land to the first Grantor in exchange for the Land which the first Grantor hath. In this Case each may enter into the others land, so put in exchange without any liuerie of seisin. And such exchange made by paroll of tenements within the same Countie without writing, is good enough.

Section 63.

¶ This is euident enough. But of what things an exchange may be made (which was a conueiance frequent in former times) is to be seene, and herein many things are to bee obserued.

(a) 30. E. 1. Esch. 15. 3. E. 4. 10. 9. E. 4. 21. 14. H. 8. 20.
First, That the things exchanged (a) need not to be in esse at the time of the exchange made. (As if I grant a rent newly created out of my lands in exchange, for the mannor of Dale, this is a good exchange.

(b) 6. E. 56. 30. E. 1. Esch. 16. 16. E. 3. Esch. 2. 7. H. 4. 34. 3. E. 4. 11.
(b) Secondly, There needeth no transmutation of possession, and therefore a release of a Rent, or Estouers, or right to land in eschange for land is good.

(c) 9. E. 4. 21. 9. E. 3. 56. 21. E. 3. 6.
The things (c) exchanged need not be of one nature, so they concerne lands or Tenements whereof Lutleton here speaketh. As land for rent or common, or any other inheritance which concerne lands or tenements, or spirituall things, as Tythes, &c. for temporall, and tenure by a diuine Seruice for a temporall Seigniorie, &c. But Annuities or such like which charge the person only, and doe not concerne lands or tenements, cannot be exchanged for lands or tenements.

¶ Et si les terres ou tenements, soient en diuers counties, cestascauoire ceo que lun ad est vn Countie & ceo que lauter ad est en auter Countie la il couient de auer vn fait indent destre fait enter eux de tiel eschange.

AND if the lands or tenements bee in diuers counties, *viz.* that which the one hath in one countie, and that which the other hath in another countie, there it behoueth to haue a deed indented, made betweene them of this exchange.

Section 64. 65.

Estates. Vide Sect. 65.
¶ *En eschange, il couient que les estates soient egales, &c.* Equalitie in lands is threefold, viz. First equalitie in value;

¶ Et nota que en exchange il couient que les estates soient egales, que

AND note that in exchanges it behooueth that the estates which both par-

ambideux tielx parties aueront en les tres issint eschanges, car si lun voit & grant que lauter aueroit la terre en fee taile, pur le terre que il aueroit del grant de le auter en fee simple, coment que lauter soit agree a cel, cest eschange est voide, pur ceo q̃ les estates ne sont my egales.

ties haue in the lands so exchanged, be equall, for if the one willeth and granteth that the other shall haue his land in fee taile for the land which he hath of the grant of the other in fee simple, although that the other agree this, yet this exchange is voide, because the estates be not equall.

CE En mesme le manner est, lou il est grant & agree enter eux, que lun auera en lun terre fee taile, & lauter en lauter terre forsque a terme de vie, ou si lun auera en lun terre fee taile generall, & lauter en lauter terre fee taile especial, &c. Issint touts foits il couient que en eschange les estates dambideux parties soiẽt egales cestascauoire, si lun ad fee simple en lun terre, que lauter auera tiel estate en lauter terre, & si lun ad fee taile en lun terre il couient que lauter aũa semblable estate en lauter terre, &c. & sic de alijs statibus, mes nest my riens a charger del egal value des terres, car

IN the same manner it is, where it is granted and agreed betweene them, that the one shall haue in the one land fee taile, and the other in the other land but for terme of life, or if the one shall haue in the one land fee taile generall, and the other in the other land fee taile especiall, &c. So alwayes it behoueth that in exchãge the estates of both parties bee equall, *viz.* if the one hath a fee simple in the one land that the other shall haue like estate in the other land, and if the one hath Fee taile in the one land the other ought to haue the like estate in the other land &c. and so of other estates, but it is nothing to charge of the equal

Secondly, equalitie in quantitie of estate giuen and taken. Thirdly, equality in qualitie or manner of the estate giuen and taken. But as Littleton after saith, Equalitie in value of lands in an exchange is not requisite; Neither equalitie in the qualitie or manner of the estate. And therefore if two ioyntenants giue lands ioyntly to two men, and their heires, and the other in exchange of other lands to them and their heires in common, this is a good exchange, and yet the manner of their estates is not equall, for the estate of one partie is ioynt, and the other in common. And so it is if two men giue lands in exchange to A. and his heires for lands from A. to them two and their heires, though the one partie haue a ioynt estate, and the other a sole estate, yet the exchange is good. The like is if the one land be of a defeasible title, and the other of an undefeasible title, yet the exchange is good till it be auoyded.

(a) An exchange with the King is good and yet the King is seised in his politique capacitie, and the subiect in his naturall capacitie. But equalitie of the quantitie of the estate is requisite, as it appeareth cleerely in the cases put by Littleton. (b) But therein it is to be obserued that it is not necessarie that the parties to the exchange be seised of an equall estate at the time of the exchange made: for if Tenant in taile, or a husband, seised in the right of his wife, exchange lands, and both by the exchange, giue a fee simple, this is good untill it be auoyded by the issue in taile, or by the wife after the death of the husband, (d) so as Littleton saith that in exchanges it behoueth that the estates which both parties haue in the land so exchanged be equall is as much to say as that the state reciprocally giuen in exchange ought to bee equall. (c) But in a partition the estates allotted to either partie need not to bee equall

(a) *Bracton lib. 5. fo. 389. 17. E. 3. 12. b. 4. H. 4. 2.*

(b) *14. H. 6. 6. E. 2. Exch. 12. 8. E. 2. Cui in vita 28. 10. E. 2. Exch. 13. 16. E. 3. Exch. 2. 3. E. 3. 19. 12. H. 4. 12. 21. H. 6. 25. 13. E. 4. 3.*

(d) *44. E. 3. 20. 38. E. 3. 15. 39. E. 3. 1. 9. E. 4. 21. 7. H. 4. 17. 30. E. 1. tit. bre. 884. 30. E. 1. tit. exchange, 15.*

(c) *F. N. B. 62. m.*

quall, as shall be obserued in his proper place.

To shut vp this point, There be fiue things necessary to the perfection of an exchange. 1. That the estates giuen be equall. 2. That this word (excambium exchange) be vsed (f) which is so indiuidually requisite, as it cannot be supplied by any other word or described by any circumlocution; and herewith agreeth Littleton afterwards in this chapter Sect. In the booke of Domesday I finde hanc terram cambiauit Hugo Briccuino quod modo tenet comes Meriton, & ipsum scambium valet duplum.
Hugo de Belcamp pro escambio de warres,

(f) 9.E.4.21. 25.H.6 56. 19.H.6.27. 44.E.3.24. 50.Ass. Dorset. Walen. Bedf. Sandeia.
(h) 9.E.4.39.15.E.4.3. 45.E.3.30.

coment que la terre lun vault mult pluis que la terre de lauter ceo nest riens a purpose: issint que les estates per leschange fait, soient egales. Et issint ẽ leschange sont deux grants car chescun partie grant son tre a lauter en eschange, &c. & en chescun de lour grants mention serra fait de leschange.

value of the lands, for albeit that the land of the one be of a farre greater value than the land of the other, this is nothing to the purpose, so as the estates made by the eschange be equall. And so in an eschange there be two grants, for each partie granteth his land to the other in eschange, &c. and in each of their grants mention shalbe made of the eschange.

3. That there be an execution by entrie or claime in the life of the parties, as hath bin said. (g) 4. That if it be of things that lye in grant, it must be by Deede. (h) 5. If the lands be in seuerall Counties there ought to be a Deede indented, or if the thing lye in grant albeit they be in one Countie.

(i) If an infant exchange lands and after his full age occupie the lands taken in exchange, the exchange is become perfect, for the exchange at the first was not voyde (because it amounted to a liuery, and also in respect of the recompence) but voidable.

¶ *Coment que lauter agree a cel cest eschange est voide.* The agreement of the parties cannot make that good which the Law maketh voide.

45.E.3.eschange 1.
(g) 28.H.6.2.
(h) 45 E.3.20. 7.H.4.11.
(i) 4.E.2.tit.exch.10. 12.H.4.12.

Section 66.

¶ *SI home lessa terre a un auter pur terme dans, Coment que le lessor morust deuant, &c.* The reason is because the interest of the tearme (as hath beene said) doth passe and vest in the Lessee before entrie, and therefore the death of the Lessor cannot deuest that which was vested before.

¶ *Attorney.* Is an ancient English word and signifieth one that is set in the turne, stead or place of another, and of these some be priuate (whereof our Author here speaketh) & some bee publike, as Attorneys at Law; whose warrant from his master is ponit loco suo talem Attornatum suum which setteth in his turne or place such a man to be his Attorney.

¶ ITem si home lessa terre a vn auter pur term dans, coment que le lessor morust deuant que le lessee enter en les tenements, uncore il poit enter en mesmes les tenements apres le mort le lessour, pur ceo que le lessee per force de le lease ad droit maintenãt dauer les tenements solonqz le forme de le lease. Mes si home fait vn fait de feoffement a vn auter, & vn letter dattorney a vn

ALso if a man letteth land to another for terme of yeares, albeit the lessor dieth before the lessee entreth into the tenements, yet he may enter into the same tenements after the death of the lessor, because the lessee by force of the lease, hath right presently to haue the tenements according to the forme of the lease, but if a man maketh a deed of Feoffment to another, & a letter of Attorney to

home a deliuerer a luy seisin per force de mesme le fait, uncore si liuerie de seisin ne soit fait en la vie celuy que fesoit le fait, ceo ne vault riens, pur ceo que lauter nad pas ascun droit dauer les tenẽts solonqz le purport de le dit fait, deuant le liuerie de seisin. Et si nul liuerie de seisin soit fait, donqz apres le mort celuy que fist le fait, le droit de tiels tenements est maintenant en son heire, ou en ascun auter.

one to deliuer to him seisin by force of the same deed, yet if liuery of seisin be not executed in the life of him which made the deed, this auaileth nothing, for that the other had nought to haue the tenements according to the purport of the said Deede before liuery of seisin made, & if there be no liuery of seisin, then after the decease of him who made the Deed, the right of these tenemẽts is forthwith in his heire, or in some other.

¶ *Et vn letter dattorney a vn home a deliuer a luy seisin per force de mesme le fait.* *Vid.Sect.*196.

Here first it appeareth that the Authority to deliuer seisin (as hath beene said) must be by Deede; For Letter dattorney is as much as a warrant of Attorney by Deede for Littere doe signifie sometime a Deed as litteræ acquietanciæ doe signifie a Deede of Acquittance, and herewith (a) agreeth Britton. (a) 24.*E*.3.27.11.*H*.7.13. *Britt*.101.*b*.

2. Littleton here speakes generally a vn home, and few persons are (b) disabled to be priuate Attorneys to deliuer seisin; for Monks, infants, fem couerts, persons attainted, outlawed, excommunicated, villeins, aliens, &c. may bee Attorneys. A fem may be an Attorney to deliuer seisin to her husband, and the husband to the wife, and he in the remainder to the lessee for life. 21.*E*.4.18. *Br.feoffments*.50 21.*H*.6.30. 13.*E*.3.*Attorney* 73.

3. It appeareth here that the Attorney must (c) pursue his warrant, otherwise he doth not deliuer seisin by force of the Deed, as Littleton speaketh. Now his Authoritie is twofold, expressed in his warrant, and implied in Law, both which he must pursue and first of his expresse authority. A man seised of blacke acre and white acre makes a Deede of feoffment of both, and a letter of Attorney to enter into both acres, and to deliuer seisin of both of them according to the forme and effect of the Deede, and he entreth into blacke acre and deliuers seisin secundum formam cartæ, this liuery and seisin is good, albeit he did not enter into both, nor into one in the name of both; for when he deliuereth seisin of one secundum formam cartæ, this is tantamount and implieth a liuery of both. So when the feoffment is made to two or more, and the Attorney is to make liuery of seisin to both, and the Attorney make liuery of seisin to one of the Feoffees secundum formam & effectum cartæ, this is good to both, and yet in that case he that is absent may waiue the liuery. If Lessee for life make a Deede of Feoffment and a letter of Attorney to the Lessor to make liuery and the Lessor maketh liuery accordingly, notwithstanding he shall enter for the forfeiture, but if Lessee for yeares make a feoffment in fee and a letter of Attorney to the Lessor to make liuery and he make liuery accordingly, this liuery shall binde the Lessor, and shall not be auoided by him; for the Lessor cannot make liuery as Attorney to the Lessee, because he had no freehold, whereof to make liuery; but the freehold was in the Lessor. If the Lessor make a deed of Feoffment, and a letter of Attorney to the Lessee for yeares to make liuery, and he doth it accordingly, this shall not drowne or extinguish his tearme, because he did it as a minister to another and in another right, and is accounted in iudgement of Law the act of the other and the Feoffee claimeth nothing by him.

(c) 12.*Ass.pl*.24.26.*Ass*.39. 11.*H*.4.3. 10.*H*.7. 11.*H*.7.13. 40.*Ass*.38.

27.*Ass*.61. 41.*Ass*.10. 41.*E*.3.17.

Tr.7.Eliz.in com.banco.

If one as Procurator or Attorney to another present to his owne benefice, he putteth himselfe out of possession, because he commeth in by the induction and institution of the Ordinary. If the tenant deuise that the Lord shall sell the land, and dieth, and the Lord selleth it, the Seigniory remaine. But if the Lord or a grantee of a Rent charge had beene also Cc' que vse of the land and after the statute of R.3. and before the statute of 27.H.8. Cc' que vse had made a feoffment in fee of the land, albeit the land passeth from the Feoffees, and his feoffment is warranted by the power giuen to him by the statute, yet the Seignory or rent charge is extinct by his feoffment, for that he hath not a bare Authority as the Attorney hath. 17.*E*.3.61.

If a man be disseised of blacke acre and white acre, and a warrant of Attorney is made to enter into both and to make liuery, there if the Attorney enter into blacke acre only and makes liuery secundum formam cartæ there the liuery of seisin is voide; because he doth lesse then his warrant for the estate of the disseisor in white acre cannot bee deuested without an entry.

But

But there is a diuersitie betweene an authoritie coupled with an interest, and a bare authoritie. For example, A custome within a mannor time out of mind of man used, was to grant certain lands parcell of the said mannor in fee simple, and neuer any grant was made to any, and the heires of his bodie, for life or for yeares, and the Lord of the said mannor did grant to one by Copie for life, the remainder ouer to another, and the heires of his bodie: And it was (k) adiudged, that the grant and remainder ouer was good; for the Lord hauing authoritie by custome, and an interest withall, might grant any lesser estate: for in this case, the custome that enableth him to the greater, enableth him to the lesser, Omne maius in se, continet minus. But hee that hath but a bare authoritie, as he that hath a warrant of Atturney, must pursue his authority, (as hath been said) and if he doe lesse, it is voyd.

(k) Hil. 36 El. Rot. 492. Inter Stanton & Barnes, in Eiectione firma, in the Kings bench.

A man make a lease for life, and after make a Charter of feoffement, with a Letter of Attorney to deliuer seisin, the Atturney enters upon the Lessee, this is sufficient to conuey away the reuersion; for (that it may be said once for all) liuerie of seisins being to perfect the common assurance of lands, is alwayes expounded fauourably, vt res magis valeat quam pereat. And all this was adiudged and (l) resolued by the Court of Common Pleas, and after affirmed by all the Judges of the Kings Bench, in a Writ of Error.

2. & 3. Ph. & M. Dyer 131. 17. El. Dyer 40.

(l) Pasc. 31. El Rot. 514. in Com. Banc. inter Carter pl. & Claypole & al. def. In Eiectione firma, & in Briefe de Error. Hil 32. El. Rot. 791.

And it is to be knowne, that a deed of feoffement beginning Omnibus Christi fidelibus, &c. or Sciant præsentes & futuri, &c. or the like, a Letter of Atturney may bee contained in such a Deed; for one continent may containe diuers Deeds to seuerall persons, but if it be by Indenture betweene the Feoffor on the one part, and the Feoffee on the other part, there a Letter of Atturney in such a Deed is not good, unlesse the Atturney bee made a partie in the Deed indented.

Now the authoritie of an Atturney implyed in the Law, is, though the warrant bee generall, to deliuer seisin: yet the Atturney cannot deliuer seisin within the view, for his warrant is intendable in Law of an actuall and expresse liuerie, and not of a liuerie in law, and so hath it beene resolued. See more hereof here next following.

Pas. 3. El. in Com. Banc. in Tathams case.

¶ *Vncore si liuerie & seisin ne soit fait en la vie celuy que fesoit le fait.* Here albeit the warrant of Atturnie be indefinite, without limitation of any time, yet the Law prescribeth a time, as Littleton here saith, in the life of him that made the Deed: but the death not onely of the Feoffor, of whom Littleton speaketh, but of the feoffee also, is a countermand in Law, of the Letter of Atturney, and the Deed it selfe is become of none effect, because in this case nothing doth passe before Liuerie of Seisin, For if the Feoffor dieth, the Land descends to his heire, and if the Feoffee dyeth, liuerie cannot be made to his heire, because then hee should take by purchase, where heires were named by way of limitation. And herewith agreeth Bracton, Item oportet, quod donationem sequatur rei traditio, etiam in vita donatoris & donatorij. Therefore a Letter of Attorney to deliuer Liuerie of Seisin after the decease of the Feoffor, is voyd.

22. H. 6. 6.

Bract. li. 2. fo. 16. 40. ass. pl. 38. 29. H. 6. 7. a. 14. b. 4. 2. 18. E. 3. 16. b.

Fourthly, In all cases the Atturney must pursue the warrant in substance and effect, that he hath to deliuer Seisin.

11. H. 7. 13. &c.

Fiftly, All this is to be understood of sole persons, or of a Corporation or bodie consisting of one sole person, or a Bishop person, &c. But it holdeth not in a Corporation aggregate of manie persons capable. And therefore if a Maior and Commonaltie make a Charter of feoffement, and a Letter of Attorney to deliuer Seisin, the Liuerie of Seisin is good after the decease of the Maior, because the Corporation neuer dieth. The like of a Deane and Chapter, Et sic de similibus.

18. H. 8. 3. 11. H. 7. 19.

Lastly, If the Lessor by his Deed licence the Lessee for life or yeares, (which is restrained by condition not to alien without Licence) to alien, and the Lessor dieth before the Lessee doth alien, yet is his death no countermand of the licence, but that he may alien, for the licence exempteth the Lessee out of the penaltie of the Condition, and it was executed on the part of the Lessor as much as might be. And so was it resolued, Michael 3. Iacob. in Communi Banco. As if the King doth Licence to alien in Mortmaine, and dieth, the Licence may bee executed after.

Mich. 3. Ia. in Com. Banco. F. N. B. 223. 2. E. 3. Offic. de Court. 29. Stamf. Prar. 30.

Sect. 67.

¶ *SI le Lessee fait wast. Wast*, Vastum dicitur à vastãdo, of wasting and depopulating: and for that wast is often alled-

¶ ITem si Tenements soiẽt lesses a un home p̃ term de demy an, ou pur le

ALso if tenements be let to a man for terme of halfe a yeare, or for a quarter of a

ges

quarter de vn an, &c. En tiel case, si l'lessee fait wast, l'lessor auera enuers luy briefe de Wast, & le Briefe dirra, Quod tenet ad terminum annorum: Mes il auera vn speciall Declaration sur le veritie de son matter, & le Count nabatera le Briefe, pur ceo que il puit auer nul auter briefe sur le matter.

yeare, &c. In this case if the Lessee commit wast, the Lessor shall haue a Writ of Waste against him; and the Writ shall say, *Quod tenet ad terminum annorum*: but he shall haue an especiall declaration vpon the truth of his matter, and the Count shall not abate the Writ, because he cannot haue any other writ vpon the matter.

ged to be in timber, which we call in Latin Maremium, or maresnium, or maresmium, it is good to fetch both of them from the originall. First, Timber is a Saxon word. Secondly, Maremium is derived of the French word Marreun, or Marrein, which properly signifieth timber.

An Action of wast doth lie against tenant by the Curtesie, tenant in Dower, tenant for life, for yeares, or halfe a yeare, or gardein in Chiualry, by him that hath the immediate estate of inheritance, for wast or destruction in houses, gardens, woods, trees, or in lands, meadowes, &c. or in exile of men to the disherison of him in the reuersion or remainder.

V. Merib ca. 23. 2. part of this Instit.

There be two kinds of wasts, viz. Uolantarie or actuall, and permissiue. (a) Wast may be done in houses, by pulling or prostrating them downe, or by suffering the same to be vncouered, whereby the sparres or rafters, plaunchers, or other timber of the house are rotten. (b) But if the house be vncouered when the Tenant commeth in, it is no wast in the Tenant, to suffer the same to fall downe. But though the house be ruinous at the tenants comming in, yet if hee pull it downe, it is wast vnlesse he re-edifie it againe. (c) Also if glasse windowes (though glased by the tenant himselfe) be broken downe, or carried away, it is wast, for the glasse is part of his house. And so it is of wainscote, benches, doores, windowes, furnaces, and the like, annexed or fixed to the house, either by him in the reuersion, or the tenant.

(a) 34. E. 3. Wast. 145.

(b) 40. ass p. 22. 2. Mar. Dyer 117. 23. H. 6. 24. 10. H. 7. 2. 44. E. 3. 4. 29. E. 3. 33. li. 4. fo. 63. Herlakendens case.

(c) 22. H. 6. 18. 12. H. 8. 1. 13. H. 7. 21. 21. E. 4. 18. 21. E. 4. 39. 10. H. 7. 2. Reg. Judic. 76.

(d) Though there bee no timber growing vpon the ground, yet the Tenant at his perill must keepe the houses from wasting. If the Tenant doe or suffer wast to be done in houses, yet if he repaire them before any Action brought, there lieth no action of wast against him, but he cannot plead, Quod non fecit vastum, but the speciall matter.

(d) 41. E. 3. 21. 38. ass. 1. 4. E. 3. Wast. 22. 10. El. Dyer 276. li. 5. fo. 119. in Whelpdales case. 19. E. 3. Wast. 30. 44. E. 3. 44.

A wall vncouered when the tenant commeth in, is no wast if it be suffred to decay (e) If the tenant cut downe or destroy any fruit trees growing in the garden or orchard, it is wast, but if such trees grow vpon any of the ground which the Tenant holdeth out of the garden or Orchard, it is no wast.

(e) 7. H. 6. 38. 44. E. 3. 44.

(f) If the Tenant build a new house, it is wast, and if he suffer it to be wasted, it is a new wast. (g) If the house fall downe by tempest, or be burnt by lightning, or prostrated by enemies, or the like, without a default of the Tenant, or was ruinous at his comming in, and fall downe, the Tenant may build the same againe with such materialls as remaines, and with other timber which he may take growing on the ground for his habitation, but hee must not make the house larger than it was. If the house be discouered by tempest, the tenant must in conuenient time repaire it.

(f) 42. E. 3. 21. 49. E. 3. 2. 9. H. 6. 52. 17. E. 2. Wast 118.

(g) Li. 4. fo. 63. Herlakendens case. 43. E. 3. 6. 26. E. 3. 76. 11. H. 4. 32. 12. H. 4. 5. 22. H. 6. 18. 19. E. 3. wast. 30.

(h) If the Tenant of a Doue house, warren, Parke, Uiuarie, Estangues, or the like, doe take so many, as such sufficient store be not left as he found when he came in, this is wast, and to suffer the pale to decay, whereby the Dere are dispersed, is wast.

(h) Temps E. 1. Wast. 128. Brit. fo. 34. 3. R. 2. Wast. 97. 12. H. 8. 1. Pl. com. 322. 7. H. 3. Wast. 141.

And it is to be obserued, That there is wast, destruction, and exile. Wast properly is in houses, gardens, (as is aforesaid) in timber trees, (viz. Oke, Ashe, and Elme, and these be Timber trees in all places) either by cutting of them downe, or topping of them, or doing any Act whereby the timber may decay. Also in Countries where timber is scant, and Beeches or the like are conuerted to building for the habitation of man, or the like, they are also accounted timber. (i) If the Tenant cut downe timber trees, or such as are accounted timber, as is aforesaid, this is wast, and if he suffer the young germyns to be destroyed, this is destruction. (k) So it is, if the Tenant cut downe vnderwood, (as he may by law) yet if he suffer the young germins to be destroyed, or if he stubbe vp the same, this is destruction.

(i) 22. H. 6. 11. a. 9. H. 6. 66. 11. H. 6. 1. F. N. B. 59. m.

(k) 10. E. 3. Wast. 32. 10. H. 7. 2. 42. E. 3. 6. b. 5. E. 4. 100. 41. E. 3. Wast. 82. 20. Edw. 3. Wast. 32. 12. E. 4. 1.

(l) Cutting downe of willoughes, beech, birch, aspe, maple, or the like, standing in the defence and safeguard of the house, is destruction. (m) If there be a quickeset Fence of white thorne, if the tenant stubbe it vp, or suffer it to be destroyed, this is destruction, and for all these and the like destructions, an action of wast lieth. (n) The cutting of dead wood, that is, vbi arbores sunt aridæ, mortuæ, cauæ, non existent maeremium, nec portantes fructus, nec folia in æstate, is

(l) 40. E. 3. 15. b. & 35. 12. E. 4. 1. 12. H. 8. 1. b. 10. H. 7. 2. 8. E. 2. Wast. 111. 4. E. 6. Wast. Br. 136.

(m) 46. E. 3. 17. 9. H. 6. 10. 12. H. 8. 1.

(n) 16. El. Dy. 332. 20. E. 3. Wast. 32. F. N. B. 59. m.

no wast; but turning of trees to coles for fewel, when there is sufficient dead wood, is wast. (o) If the Tenant suffer the houses to be wasted, and then fell down timber to repaire the same, this is a double wast. (p) Digging for gravell, lime, clay, bricke, earth, stone, or the like, or for mines of mettall, cole, or the like, hidden in the earth, and were not open when the tenant came in, is wast; but the Tenant may dig for gravell or clay for the reparation of the house, aswel as he may take convenient timber trees.

(o) 44.E.3.44. 30.E.3. Wast.32. F.N.B.59.b. 19.E.3 Wast.30.
(p) 22.H.6.18.b. 9.E.4.35. 41 E.3. Wast.82. 17.E.3.7. 9.H 6 66. 2.H.7.14. F N.B.59.a & 149.e. 20.Ed.3. Wast.32.

(q) It is wast to suffer a wall of the sea to be in decay, so as by the flowing & reflowing of the sea, the meadow or marsh is surrounded, whereby the same becomes unprofitable: but if it bee surrounded suddenly by the rage and violence of the sea, occasioned by wind, tempest, or the like, without any default in the tenant, (r) this is no wast punishable. So it is, if the Tenant repaire not the bankes or walls against rivers, or other waters whereby the meadowes or marshes be surrounded, and become rushie and unprofitable.

(q) Anno 6. El. Of the Report of Iustice Dalison in Griffins case. 17 E.3.65. Br. u. fo.168.b.
(r) 20.H.6.1. F.N.B.59.n. 6.El. ubi supra.

(s) If the Tenant convert erable land into wood, or è converso, or meadow into erable, it is waste; for it changeth not only the course of his husbandry but the proofe of his evidence.

(s) 28.H.8. Dyer 37. 22.H.6.24. 10.H 7.5.a. 44.E.3.44.

(t) The tenant may take sufficient wood to repaire the walls, pales, fences, hedges and ditches, as he found them, but he can make no newe: and he may take also sufficient plowbote, firebote, and other housbote.

(t) 16.El. Dy.332. 21.H.6.47. L.5.E.4.100. 12.E.3. Wast.28.48.E.3.25. Temps E.1.123. 20 E.3 Wast.32. 19.E.3. Wast.30.

The tenant cutteth downe trees for reparations and selleth them, and after buyeth them againe, and imploy them about necessary reparations, yet it is waste by the vendition: hee cannot fell trees and with the money cover the house, burning of the house by negligence or mischance is waste.

(u) If a man make a Lease for life and by Deed grant that if any waste or destruction bee done, that it shall be redressed by neighbours, and not by sute or plea, notwithstanding an action of waste shall lye, for the place wasted cannot be recovered without a plea.

(u) 3.E.3 Wast.5. Bracton lib.4 fo.315.

(w) Bracton, Fleta and Britton, doe use the same division as is aforesaid, viz. Vastum, destructio, & exilium, in their proper signification.

(w) Bracton fo.168. Fleta.lib.1.cap.11. 16.H.3. wast.135. 3.E.2. tit. Wast.2. 17.E.2. Wast.118. 10.H.7. 2.H.6.11. 9.H.6.52. 11.E.2. W.st.113. F.N.B. 56.H. & 55.e. Regist. indic.25.

Now somewhat is to be spoken of Exile or destruction of men; Exile or destruction of Villeines, or Tenants at will, or making them poore where they were rich when the Tenant came in, wherby they depart from their tenures, is waste. (a) And yet the statute of Glouc' speaketh not of exile, but it is comprehended under the generall word of waste. The statute of W.1. hath destructionem, the statute of Magna Carta hath Vastum & destructionem, the statute of Merlebridge hath vastum, venditionem & exilium in domibus, boscis, vel hominibus, &c.

(a) Glouc. cap.5. W.1. ca.21. Magna Carta. cap.4. Merleb. ca.23.

But waste and destruction in their larger sence are words convertible. (b) Item de hoc quod dicit vastum & exilium, sciendum est quod non sunt referenda ad eundem intellectum, sed vastum & destructio fere idem sunt, vastum idem est quod destructio, & é converso, & se habent ad omnem destructionem generaliter.

(b) Bract. lib.4. fo.316. & 317.

(c) Vastum autem & destructio fere equipollent & convertibiliter se habent in domibus, boscis, & gardinis, sed exilium dici poterit, cum servi manumittantur & à tenementis suis iniuriose eijciantur, fortuna autem & ignis vel huiusmodi eventus inopinati omnes tenentes excusant.

(c) Fleta lib.1. ca.11.

(d) No person shall have an action of waste, unlesse he hath the immediate state of inheritance, but sometime another shall ioyne with him for conformity. As if a reversion be granted to two and to the heires of one; they two shall ioyne in an action of waste: and in like sort the surviving Coparcener, and the tenant by the Curtesie shall ioyne in an action of waste: and if two ioyntenants be, and to the heires of one of them, and they make a Lease for life, they shall ioyne in an action of waste. (e) If the estate taile determine, hanging the action of waste, and the plt. become tenant in taile after possibilitie, the action of waste is gone. (f) If the Tenant doth waste, and he in the reversion dieth, the heire shall not have an action of waste for the waste done in the life of the Ancestor; nor a Bishop, master of an Hospitall, Parson, or the like in the time of the Predecessor. (g) And so if Lessee for yeares doth waste, and dieth; an action of waste lyeth not against the Executor or Administrator, for waste done before their time. But if two Coparceners be of a reversion, and waste is committed, and the one of them die, the Aunt and the Neece shall ioyne in an action of waste.

(d) 7.E.3.54.b. 2.H.5.7. 22.H.6.24. 13.H.7. 27.H.8.13. F.N.b.59.f. 8.R.2. Wast.147.
(e) 2.H.4.22.
(f) 2.H.4.2.
(g) 10.E.4.1. 49.E.3 25. 2;.H.8. tit. Wast. Br. 38.E.3.17. 44.E.3.8. 45.E.3.3. 46.E.3.31. 11.E.2. Wast.115. 2 Mar. wast.117. 8.E.2. wast.110.

(h) If lands be given to two and the heires of one of them, he that hath the Fee shall not have an action of waste upon the statute of Glouc: for that they are ioyntenants, but his heire shall have an action of waste against tenant for life.

(h) 24.E.3.27. 50.E.3.3. 8.H.6.13.

Note after waste done there is a speciall regard to be had to the continuance of the reversion in the same state that it was at the time of the waste done, for if after the waste he granteth it over, though he taketh backe the whole estate againe, yet is the waste dispunishable. So if he grante the reversion to the use of himselfe and his wife, and of his heires, yet the waste is dispunishable, and so of the like, because the estate of the reversion continueth not, but is altered, and consequently the action of waste for waste done before (which consist in privity) is gone.

(i) A Prohibition of waste did lye against Tenant by the curtesie, Tenant in dower, and a gardian in Chivalry by the Common Law, but not against tenant for life, or yeares, because

(i) Bract. lib.4 f.315.316.317 Fleta lib.1. ca.11. Britt. fo.168. Doct. & Stud. lib.2. cap.1. 12.H.4.3. 10.H.3. Wast.142 20 H.6.1. 4 H.3. Wast 140. 9.H.3. ibid.136.

they

they came in by their owne act, and he might haue prouided that no waste should be done. (i) A tenant by the curtesie or in dower can hold of none but of the heire, and his heires by discent, and therefore if they grant ouer their whole estate, and the grantee doth waste, yet the heire shall haue an Action of waste against them, and recouer the land against the assignee: but if the heire either before the assignement had granted, or after the assignement doth grant the reuersion ouer, the stranger shall haue an Action of waste against the assignee, because in both Cases the priuitie is destroyed: in all other Cases the Action of wast shall be brought against him that did the waste (for it is in nature of a trespasse) vnlesse it be in the case of a ward (k) for there if the Gardian doth wast and assigne ouer, the action lieth against the assignee (l). A Gardian shall not be punished for waste done by a stranger, it is so penall vnto him, for he shall lose the wardship both of the bodie and of the land, though the waste be but to the value of twentie shillings, and if that sufficeth not to satisfie for the wast, then he shall recouer damages of the waste, ouer and aboue the losse of the ward. But tenant by the curtesie, tenant in dower, tenant for life, yeares, &c. shall answere for the waste done by a stranger, and shall take their remedie ouer. (m) But if there be two ioyntenants of a ward, and one of them doe waste both shall answer for it.

(n) If the Gardian doth waste and the heire within age bring an action of waste, the Gardian shall lose the wardship as is aforesaid, but if the heire bring an action of waste at his full age, then he shall recouer treble damages, for then he cannot lose the wardship.

(o) An infant and Baron and Fem shall be punished for waste done by a stranger, and so shal the wife that hath the state by suruiuour, for wast done by the husband in his life time, if she agree to the Estate, though there hath beene varietie of opinions in our Bookes.

(p) But if Fem tenant for life take husband, and the husband doth waste, and the wife dieth, no Action of waste lieth against the husband in the tenuit, for he was seised but in iure vxoris and his wife was tenant of the freehold, but if a Feme bee possessed of a terme for yeares, and take husband, and the husband doth waste, and the wife dieth, the husband shall be charged in an Action of waste, for the Law giueth the terme to him.

(q) If tenant for life grant ouer his Estate vpon condition, and the grantee doth waste, and the Grantor re-entreth for the condition broken, the Action of waste shall bee brought against the grantee, and the place wasted recouered.

(r) If a lease for life be made to a Villaine, and waste is done, the Lord entreth, he shall not be punished for the waste done before, but for waste done after he shall.

(s) An occupant shall be punished for waste, and so if an Estate bee made to A. and his heires during the life of B. A. dieth, the heire of A. shall be punished in an Action of waste.

(t) If a lease be made to A. for life, the remainder to B. for life, the remainder to C. in fee in this case where it is said in the Register, and in F.N.B. that an Action of waste doth lie, it is to be vnderstood after the death or surrender of B. in the meane remainder for during his life, no Action of waste doth lie.

But if a lease for life be made, the remainder for yeares, the remainder in fee, an Action doth lie presently during the terme in remainder for the meane terme for yeares is no impediment.

But if a man make a lease for life or yeares, and after granteth the reuersion for yeares, the Lessor shall haue no Action of waste during the yeares, for he himselfe hath granted away the reuersion, in respect whereof he is to maintaine his Action. (*) Otherwise it is, if hee had made a lease in reuersion which had beene but a future interest, for there an action of waste lieth during the terme, and so is the Booke to be vnderstood, and terme shall be saued in that case.

(u) No action of waste lieth against a garden in socage, but an account or trespasse, nor against tenant by statute, staple, &c. or elegit.

(w) If tenant for life or yeares or their assigne make a grant ouer, and notwithstanding take the profits, an action of waste lieth against him, by him in the reuersion or remainder by the statute, Nota.

(x) If waste be done sparsim here and there in woods, the whole woods shall be recouered, or so much wherein the waste sparsim is done. And so in houses so many roomeths shall be recouered wherein there is waste done, but if wast be done sparsim throughout, all shall bee recouered. It hath bin said that if the hall be wasted, the whole house shall be recouered, because the whole house is denominated of the hall: but later Authoritie is to the contrarie.

(y) There is waste of a small value, as Bracton saith, Nisi vastum ita modicum sit propter quod non sit inquisitio facienda. Yet trees to the value of three shillings and foure pence, hath bin adiudged waste, and many things together may make waste to a value. But let vs now returne to our Authour.

¶ *Brief de waste.* **See in the Register fiue seuerall Writs of** waste; Two At the Common Law for waste done by Tenant in Dower, or the Garden, and Three by speciall or statute law, for waste done by tenant for life, for yeares and tenant by the curtesie.

(i) F.N.B.56.e.et f. Temps E.1.wast.122.18.E.3.3.30.E.3.16.38.E.3.23.11.H.4.18.4.E.3.25.Regist.72.lib.3.fol.23.Walters case.lib.9.fol.142.Beaumonts case.

(k) 27.E.3.81.26 E 3.Waste.10.

(l) 12.H.4.3.Bract.lib.4.315.317.Fleta.lib.1.cap.11.Britt.168.34.E.3.Wast 146.44.E.3.27.F.N.B.59.a.& 60.g.& T.

(m) 33.E.3.Wast.6.

(n) 44.E.3.27.48.E.3.10.F.N.B.60.t.12.H.4.3.19.E.2.Wast.117.41.E.3.Wast.81.3.E.2.Wast.3.7.E.3.12.

(o) 15.H.3.Wast.16.Temps E.1.Wast.128.2.H.4.3 a.3.E.3.13.76.11.Ass.11.21.H.6.24.b.33.H.6.31.a.42 E.3.22.19.E.3.breue 246 46.E.3.25.7H.6.2.b.3.E.3.46.10.E.3.17.18.9.E.3.42.9.E.3.breue 246.17.E.4.7.9.H.6.52.F.N.B.36.b.Doct.& Stud.lib.2.cap.1.23.H.8.Wast.138.lib.8.fol.44.Willinghams case.

(p) Lib.5.fol.75.(l)ftons case 46.E.3.25.46.E.3.Wast.Statham.10.H.6.11.12.

(q) 30.E.3.16.

(r) 48.E 3.19.

(s) Lib.6.fol.37.le Deane and Chapter of Worcest.case.lib.10.fol.9.b.

(t) 4.E.3.18.Coles case.3.E.3.18 F.N.B.58.c.& 59 h.50.E.3.3.33.E.3.Wast.144 11.E.3.resceit.118.10.E.4.9 Regist.74.lib.2.fol.92.inter Paget & Carie in Binghams case.lib.5 fol.76.Pagets case.lib.10.fol.44.Iennings case.F.N.B.59.h.4.E.3.18.

(*) 4.E.3.18.F.tit.Wast.18.

(u) Merlbridge cap.17.21.E.3.30.16.E.3.tit.wast.100.14.E.3.wast.107.2.E.2.Wast.1.28.H.6.wast.9.32.H.6.7.F.N.B.59.E.

(w) 11.H.6.cap.5.Lib.5.fol.77.Boothes case.

(x) 8.E.2.wast.112.4.E.6.wast.136.4.E.3.32.15.H.7.11.15.E.3.Wast.134.Temps E.1.wast.134.18.H 8 1.

(y) Bract.lib.4.fol.316.38.E.3.7 b.34.E.3.wast 146 14.H.4.11.b.F.N.B.60 c.Temps E.1.wast.124.19.H.6.8.

(z) Vi. Brast. lib. 5. fo. 413. b. Fleta lib. 2. cap. 12. See the second part of the Institutes. W. 2. cap. 24.

De vasto. Brast. lib. 4. fol. 315. 316. 317. Fleta. lib. 1. cap. 11. & lib. 5. cap. 33. Britt. fol 162. & 168. 46. E. 3. 31. F. N. B. 60. e. 4. E. 4. 13. 37. H. 6. 26. b. 7. H 7. 2. 14. H. 8. 12. 18. E. 3. 27.

Vide Marle'ridge cap. 23. 2. part of the institutes.

¶ *Brief dirra.* The Writs originall of the Register (z) (as Bracton saith) formed, and of course had their first authoritie by Act of Parliament, and therefore without an Act of Parliament they cannot be altered, or changed, which is proued by the statute of W 2 cap. 24. whereby remedie is prouided in many cases. But heare what Bracton saith. Sunt quædam breuia formata in suis casibus, & quædam de cursu, quæ concilio totius regni sunt approbata, quæ quidem mutari non possunt, absque eorundem contraria voluntate. Magistralia autem sæpe variantur secundum varietatem casuum, &c. And this is the reason that in this case of halfe a yeare the words of the writ shall be without change, Quod tenet ad terminum annorum, and the pl' must make a speciall declaration according to his case, for otherwise hee should bee without remedie. In this particular case the statute of Glouc. cap. 5. which giueth the Action of waste against the Lessee for life or yeares (which lay not against them at the Common Law) speaketh of one that holdeth for tearme of yeares in the plurall number, and yet here it appeareth by the authoritie of Littleton. That although it be a penall Law, whereby treble damages and the place wasted shall be recouered, yet a tenant for halfe a yeare being within the same mischiefe, shall be within the same remedie, though it bee out of the letter of the Law, for Qui hæret in littera, hæret in cortice, which is an excellent example, whereupon in many like cases a man may settle a certaine iudgement. You may obserue in the said ancient Authors, what remedie was giuen for waste at the Common Law, and against whom, and what was adiudged waste, destruction, and exile.

(a) 12. H. 8. 1.

F. N. B. fol. 127.

In many cases a tenant for life or yeares may fell downe timber to make reparations, albeit hee be not compellable thereunto, and shall not bee punished for the same in any action of waste. As (a) if a house be ruinous at the time of the lease made, if the lessee suffer the house to fall downe he is not punishable, for he is not bound by law to repaire the house in that case. And yet if he cut downe timber vpon the ground so letten, and repaire it, he may well iustifie it, and the reason is, for that the law doth fauour the supportation and maintenance of houses of habitation for mankind. And therefore if two or more ioyntenants or tenants in common be of a house of habitation, and the one will not repaire the house, the other shall haue by the law a writ De reparatione facienda, and the writ saith, Ad sustentationem eiusdem domus teneantur. So it is if the Lessor by his Couenant vndertaketh to repaire the houses, yet the lessee (if the Lessor doth it not) may with the timber growing vpon the ground repaire it though hee be not compellable thereunto. In the same manner, if a man make a lease of a house and land without impeachment of waste for the house, yet may the lessee with the timber vpon the ground repaire the house, though he may vtterly waste it if he will, and so in many other cases. A man hath land in which there is a Mine of Coales, or of the like, and maketh (b) a lease of the land (without mentioning any Mines) for life or for yeares, the lessee for such Mines as were open at the time of the lease made, may digge and take the profit thereof. (c) But he cannot digge for any new Mine, that was not open at the time of the lease made, for that should be adiudged waste. And if there be open Mines, and the Owner make a lease of the land, with the Mines therein this shall extend to the open Mines only, and not to any hidden Mine, but if there be no open Mine, and the lease is made of the land together with all Mines therein, there the lessee may digge for Mines, and enioy the benefit thereof, otherwise those words should be void. I haue beene the more spacious, concerning this learning of waste, for that it is most necessarie to be knowne of all men.

(b) 17. E. 3. 7. 9. H. 6. 56. 22. H. 6. 18. 9. E. 4. 35. 12. E. 4. 8. F. N. B. 149. e. & 59. n.

(c) Lib. 5. fol. 12. Sanders case.

Now hath Littleton spoken of an estate for life, and an estate for yeares in seuerall persons. Now let vs see how they stand simul and semel in one person.

If a man letteth lands to another for life, the remainder to him for 21. yeares, hee hath both estates in him so distinctly, as he may grant away either of them; for a greater estate may vphold a lesser, but not è conuerso, and therefore if a man make a lease to one for 21. yeares, the remainder to him for terme of his life, the lease for yeares is drowned.

(d) 19. E. 2. couenant. 25. 19. E. 3. couenant. 24. 32. E. 3. Quid iuris cl. 5. 17. E. 3. 29. 46. E. 3. 31. 40. E. 3. 5. 11. H. 4. 34. 14. Eliz. Dier. 309. M. 40. & 41 Eliz. in Communi Banco. Rot. 2215. in tresp. inter Sparke & Sparke. Hill. 42. Eliz. Sir Iohn Sauages case in Curia Wardorum.

(d) If a man make a lease for life to one, the remainder to his Executors for 21. yeares, the terme for yeares shall vest in him, for euen as Ancestor and Heire are corelatiua, as to Inheritance (as if an estate for life bee made to A. the remainder to B. in taile, the remainder to the right heires of A, the fee vesteth in A, as it had beene limitted to him and his heires) euen so are the Testators and the Executors corelatiua as to any Chattell. And therefore if a lease for life be made to the testator, the remainder to his Executors for yeares, the Chattle shall vest in the lessee himselfe, as well as if it had beene limited to him and his Executors.

Chap. 8. *Sect.* 68.

Of Tenant at will.

¶ Tenant a volũt eſt, ou terres ou tenements ſont leſſes per vn home a vn auter, a auer & tener a luy a la volunt le leſſor, p force de quel leaſe le leſſee eſt en poſſeſſion, en tiel cas le leſſee eſt appel tenant a volunt, pur ceo que il nad aſcun certaine ne ſure eſtate, car le leſſor luy poit ouſter a quel temps que il luy plerroit: vncore ſi l' leſſee emblea l' terre & le leſſor apres lembleer, & deuant q̃ les blees ſont matures luy ouſta, vncore le l'ſſee auera l's blees, & aũra, frãk entr̃, egres & regres a ſcier & de carier les blees, pur c̃ q̃ il ne ſcauoit a quel temps le leſſor voloit entre ſur luy. Autermẽt eſt ſi tenãt pur terme dans q̃ conuſt le fine de ſon terme emblea ſa terre, & le terme eſt finy deuant que les blees ſont matures en ceo cas le leſſor, ou celuy en la reuerſion

Tenant at will is, where lands or tenements are let by one man to another, to haue and to hold to him at the wil of the leſſor, by force of which leaſe, the leſſee is in poſſeſſion, In this caſe the leſſee is called tenant at will, becauſe hee hath no certain nor ſure eſtate, for the leſſor may put him out at what time it pleaſeth him. Yet if the leſſee ſoweth the land, and the leſſor after it is ſowne, and before the corne is ripe put him out, yet the leſſee ſhall haue the corne, and ſhall haue free entrie, egreſſe and regreſſe to cut and carrie away the Corne, becauſe hee knew not at what time the leſſor would enter vpon him. Otherwiſe it is if Tenant for yeares, which knoweth the end of his terme, doth ſow the land, and his terme endeth before the corn is ripe; In this caſe the leſſor, or he in

¶ *Tenant a volunt eſt, ou terres ou tenements, ſont leſſes per vn home a vn auter, a auer & tener a luy a la volunt le leſſor, &c.* It is regularly true that euery leaſe at will muſt in law bee at the will of both parties, and therefore when the leaſe is made, To haue and to hold at the will of the Leſſor, the law implyeth it to be at the will of the leſſee alſo; for it cannot bee only at the will of the Leſſor, but it muſt be at the will of the leſſee alſo. And ſo it is when the leaſe is made To haue and to hold at the will of the Leſſee, this muſt be alſo at the will of the Leſſor; and ſo are all the Bookes, that ſeeme prima facie to differ, cleerely reconciled.

¶ *Pur ceo que il nad aſcun certaine ou ſure eſtate, &c.* Alia poſſeſſio eſt præcaria & alia pro prece conceſſa, vt ſi quis ſine ſcripto conceſſerit alicui habitationem vel vſumfructum in re ſua tenenda ad voluntatem ſuam hæc quidem poſſeſſio præcaria eſt & nuda eo quod tempeſtiue & intempeſtiue pro voluntate Domini poterit reuocari.

¶ *Vncore ſi le leſſee emblea la terre, & le leſſor apres le embleer, &c.* The reaſon of this is, for that the Eſtate of the Leſſee is vncertaine, and therefore leaſt the ground ſhould be vnmanured, which ſhould bee hurtfull to the Common-wealth, hee ſhall

Fleta lib. 3. *cap.* 15.

18. *H.* 6. 1. 38. *H.* 6. 21. 9. *E.* 4. 1. *b.* 10. *E.* 4. 18. *b.* 21. *H.* 7. 38. 13. *H.* 8. 16. 14. *H.* 8. 11. 14.

Fleta lib. 3. *cap.* 15.

auera les blees, pur ceo que le termor conuſt le certaintie de ſ͞ terme quant ſ͞ tme ſerroit ſiny.

the reuerſion ſhal haue the corne becauſe the Leſſee knew the certaintie of his tearme, & when it ſhould end.

ſhall reape the Crop which hee ſowed in peace, albeit the Leſſor doth determine his will before it be ripe. And ſo it is if he ſet roots, or ſow Hempe or Flax, or any other annuall profit if after the ſame bee planted, the Leſſor ouſt the Leſſee, or if the Leſſee dieth yet he or his Executors ſhall haue that yeares crop. But if he plant young fruit trees, or young Okes, Aſhes, Elmes, &c. or ſowe the ground with Acornes, &c. there the Leſſor may put him out notwithſtanding, becauſe they will yeald no preſent annuall profit. And this is not only proper to a Leſſee at will, that when the Leſſor determine his will that the Leſſee ſhall haue the Corne ſowne, &c. but to euery particular Tenant that hath an eſtate incertaine, for that is the reaſon which Littleton expreſſeth in theſe words (Pur ceo que il nad aſcun certeine ou ſure eſtate.) And therefore if Tenant for life ſoweth the ground, and dieth his Executors ſhall haue the Corne, for that his eſtate was vncertaine, and determined by the act of God. And the ſame law is of the Leſſee for yeares of Tenant for life. So if a man be ſeiſed of land in the right of his wife, and ſoweth the ground, and he dieth, his Executors ſhall haue the corne, and if his wife die before him he ſhall haue the Corne. But if huſband and wife be ioyntenants of the land, and the huſband ſoweth the ground and the land ſuruiueth to the wife, it is ſaid (a) that ſhe ſhall haue the Corne. If Tenant pur terme dauter vie ſoweth the ground, and Ceſty que vie dieth, the Leſſee ſhall haue the Corne. If a man ſeiſed of lands in fee and hath iſſue a daughter and dieth his wife being enſeint with a ſonne, the daughter ſoweth the ground the ſonne is borne, yet the daughter ſhall (b) haue the Corne becauſe her eſtate was lawfull, and defeated by the act of God, and it is good for the Common wealth that the ground be ſowen. (c) But if the Leſſee at will ſowe the ground with Corne, &c. and after he himſelfe determine his will and refuſeth to occupie the ground, in that caſe the Leſſor ſhall haue the Corne becauſe he loſeth his Rent. And if a woman that holdeth land Durante viduitate ſua ſoweth the ground and taketh huſband, (d) the Leſſor ſhall haue the embleaments becauſe that the determination of her owne eſtate grew by her owne act. But where the eſtate of the Leſſee being incertaine is defeaſible by a right paramount, or if the Leaſe determine by the act of the Leſſee as by forfeiture, condition, &c. (e) There he that hath the right paramount, or that entreth for any forfeiture, &c. ſhall haue the Corne.

18.*E.*4.18.

*Tempi E.*1.*br.*25.
10.*Aſſ.pl.*6.
10.*E.*3.29.
46.*E.*3.1.
7. *H.*4.17.
7.*Aſſ.*19.
*Lib.*5.126. *Olands caſe.*

(a) 8.*Aſſ.*21.
8.*E.*3.54.
Dier 316.

(b) 18.*H.*6.6.
(c) *Lib.*5 *fo.*106.
Olands caſe.
(d) *Olands caſ. vbi ſupra.*

(e) 33.*E.*3.*treſp.F.*254.
42.*E.*3.25.
Olands caſe.
Vbi ſupra.

If a Diſſeiſor ſowe the ground and ſeuer the corne, and the Diſſeiſee re-enter (f) hee ſhall haue the corne becauſe he entreth by a former title, and ſeuerance or remouing of the corne altereth not the caſe, for the regres is a recontinuation of the freehold in him in iudgement of Law from the beginning.

(f) 27.*H.*6.1. 37.*H.*6.6.
12.*E.*4.45. 14.*E.*4.6.
15.*E.*4.31. 2.*H.*7.1.
5.*H.*7.17. 12.*H.*7.25.
10.*H.*4.1. 28.*H.*8.32.
Dier.

(g) If tenant by ſtatute Merchant ſoweth the ground, and then a ſodaine and caſuall profit falleth by which he is ſatisfied, he ſhall haue the emblements.

(g) 44.*E.*3.15.
*Fleta lib.*3. *cap.*15.

¶ *Le leſſor luy puit ouſter.* **There is an expreſſe** ouſter, **and implied** ouſter, an expreſſe, as when the Leſſor commeth vpon the land, and expreſly forewarneth the Leſſee to occupie the ground no longer; an implied, as if the Leſſor without the conſent of the Leſſee enter into the land and cut downe a tree, this is a determination of the will, for that it ſhould otherwiſe be a wrong in him, vnleſſe the trees were excepted, and then it is no determination of the will, for then the act is lawfull albeit the will doth continue. If a man leaſeth a Mannor at will whereunto a Common is appendant, if the Leſſor put in his beaſts to vſe the Common this is a determination of the will. The Leſſor may by actuall entrie into the ground determine his will in the abſence of the Leſſee, but by words ſpoken from the ground the will is not determined vntill the Leſſee hath notice. No more then the diſcharge of a Factor, Attorney, or ſuch like in their abſence is ſufficient in Law vntill they haue notice thereof.

(h) 35.*H.*6.24. 21.*H.*6.9.
1.*E.*4.3. 21.*E.*4.5.
Pl.com. perſon de Heuylands caſe.

14.*E.*4.6.
8.*E.*4.11.&c.

(a) If a woman make a Leaſe at will reſeruing a Rent and ſhe taketh huſband, this is no countermand of the Leaſe at will, but the huſband and wife ſhall haue an action of debt for the Rent, and ſo it is if a Leaſe be made to a woman at will reſeruing a Rent and the Leſſee taketh huſband this is no countermand of the Leaſe but the Leſſor may haue an action of debt or diſtreine them for the Rent: ſo if the huſband and wife make a Leaſe at will of the wifes land reſeruing a Rent and the huſband die, yet the Leaſe continueth. In like manner if a Leaſe be made by two to two others at will and the one of the Leſſors or of the Leſſees die the Leaſe at will is not determined in neither of thoſe caſes; which are neceſſarie points to be knowne.

(a) *Lib.*5.*fol.*10.
Henſteads caſe.
10.*Eliz.Dier.*269.*b.*

¶ *Apres lembleer, & deuant que les blees ſont matures.* **Then put the** caſe that the corne is ripe and ready cut downe, and the Leſſor before the Leſſee reapeth it, enter, and put out the Leſſee, whither ſhall the Leſſee haue the corne? and it is without all queſtion that the Leſſee ſhall haue it, for by the ſame reaſon that he ſhall haue it when he is put out before

it

it be ripe, he shall haue it when he is put out when it is ripe, *Et vbi eadem est ratio, ibi idem jus.*

¶ *Et auxi franke entrie, egres & regres.* (b) For when the Law doth giue any thing to one, it giueth impliedly whatsoeuer is necessary, for the taking and enioying of the same *Quando lex aliquid alicui concedit, concedere videtur, & id sine quo res ipsa esse non potest*, and the Law in this case driueth him not to an action for the corne, but giueth him a speedy remedy to enter into the land, and to take and carry it away, and compelleth not him to take it at one time, or to carry it before it be ready to be carried; and therefore the law giueth all that which is conuenient, viz. free entrie egresse and regresse as much as is necessary.

(b) *Temps E. 1. tit. grant 4. 9. E. 4. 35. 5. E. 3. tresp. 13. 21 H. 7. 14 b. 8. H. 6. 18. b. 2. R. 2. barre 237. 14. H. 8. 2. 27. H. 8. 18. b.* Holt 524, 1 Salk. 19.

If the Lessee be disturbed of this way which the law doth giue vnto him, he shall haue his action vpon his case, and recouer his damages, and this action the law doth giue vnto him; for whensoeuer the law giueth any thing, it giueth also a remedy for the same. But here is to be obserued a diuersity, betweene a Priuate way, whereof *Littleton* here speaketh, and a common way. For if the way be a common way, if any man be disturbed to goe that way, or if a ditch be made ouerthwart the way so as he cannot goe, yet shall he not haue an action vpon his case, and this the law prouided for auoyding of multiplicity of suites, for if any one man might haue an action, all men might haue the like. But the law for this common nusance hath prouided an apt remedy, and that is by presentment in the Leete or in the Torne, vnlesse any man hath a particular damage as if he and his horse fall into the ditch whereby he receiued hurt and losse, there for this speciall damage which is not common to others, he shall haue an action vpon his case, and all this (c) was resolued by the Court in the Kings bench: And in that case it was said that it had beene adiudged in that Court betweene *Westbury* and *Powell* that where the Inhabitants of Southwarke had by custome a watering place for their cattell which was stopped vp by *Powell* that in that case any Inhabitant of Southwarke might haue an action, for otherwise they should be without remedy because such a nusance is not presentable in the Leete or Torne: Note the diuersitie.

(c) 27. H. 8. 27. 2. E. 4. 9. 5. E. 4. 2. *Tr. 41. Eliz. betweene Finenx and Houenden. Vid. lib. 5. fo. 72. Williams case.*

There be three kinde of wayes, whereof you shall (d) reade in our ancient bookes. First a foote way, which is called *Iter, quod est jus eundi vel ambulandi hominis*, and this was the first way.

(d) *Fleta lib. 4. ca 27. Bracton. lib. 4. fo. 232.*

The second is a foote way and horse way, which is called *actus ab agendo*, and this vulgarly is called packe and prime way, because it is both a foot way, which was the first or prime way, and a packe or drift way also.

The third is *via* or *aditus* which conteyne the other two, and also a cart way, &c. for this is *jus eundi, vehendi, & vehiculum & iumentum ducendi*; and this is twofold, viz. *Regia via* the Kings high way for all men, & *comunis strata* belonging to a Citie or Towne, or betweene neighbours and neighbours. This is called in our bookes *chimin* being a French word for a way, whereof commeth *chiminage chiminagium*, or *chimmagium*, which signifieth a Toll due by custome, for hauing a way through a Forrest; and in ancient Records it is sometime also called *Pedagium*.

32. E. 3. barre 261. 27. E. 3. 78. 6. E. 3. 23. Carta de foresta cap. 14.

If the Lessee at will by good husbandrie and industry, either by ouerflowing or trenching, or compassing of the meadowes, or digging vp of bushes or such like make the grasse to growe in more abundance, yet if the Lessor put him out, the Lessee shall not haue the grasse, because that the grasse is the naturall profit of the earth. And the same law is if he doth sowe hay seed, and thereby encreaseth the grasse.

¶ *Auterment est de tener a terme dans que conust le fine de son terme, &c.* Well said *Littleton* (which knoweth the end of his terme) that is, where the end of the terme is certaine, but where the Lease for yeares depends vpon an incertainty, as vpon the death of tenant for life being made by him, or of a husband seised in the right of his wife or the like, there it is otherwise.

Section 69.

¶ Item si vn mese soit lessee a vn home a tener a volunt, par force de quel le lessee enter en le mese, deins quel mese

Also if a house bee letten to one to hold at will, by force whereof the lessee entreth into the house, & brings his houshold-

¶ *Si vn mese soit lesse a vn home a tener a volunt, &c.* The reason of this is euident vpon that which hath beene said before.

¶ *Mese*, or mai-son,

son, called in legall Latine Messuagium, containeth (as hath beene said) the Buildings, Curtelage, Orchard, and Garden.

Cottage, Cotagium is a little house without land to it. (a) See 31. Eliz. cap. 1. and Cottagers, in Domesday booke are called Cotterelli: And in antient Records haga significth a house. If a man hath a house neere to my house, and he suffereth his house to be so ruinous, as it is like to fall vpon my house, (b) I may haue a Writ de domo reparando, and compell him to repaire his house. But a Præcipe lieth not de domo, but de messuagio.

(a) 31. El. ca. 1. in Domesday.

(b) Reg. 153. F.N.B. 127. 4.E. 2. Vouch. 244. Six acres of land may be parcel of a house.

¶ *Per reasonable temps.* (c) This reasonable time shall be adiudged by the discretion of the Iustices, before whome the cause dependeth; and so it is of reasonable fines, customes, and seruices, vpon the true state of the case depending before them: for reasonablenesse in these cases belongeth to the knowledge of the Law, and therefore to be decided by the Iustices. (d) Quam longum esse debet non definitur in iure, sed pendet ex discretione Iusticiariorum: And this being said of time, the like may be said of things incertaine, which ought to be reasonable; for nothing that is contrarie to reason, is consonant to Law.

(c) 22. E. 4. 27. 34. H. 6. 40.

(d) Bract. li. 2. ca. 52. b.

¶ (e) *Sicome home seisi dun mese en fee simple, ou fee taile, &c.* This is so euident, as it needeth no explanation.

(e) 2. H. 6. 15. 21 H. 6. 30.

il porta ses vtensils de meason, & puis le Lessor luy ousta, vncore il auera franke entre egresse & regresse en mesme le mese per reasonable temps, de carrier ses biens & vtensils. Sicome home seisie dun mese en fee simple, fee taille, ou pur terme de vie, le quel ad certaine biens deins mesme le mese, & fait ses executors, & dey, quecunque apres sa mort ad l' mese, vncore les executors avont frank entry egresse & regres d' carier hors de mesme le mese les biens lour testator per reasonable temps.

stuffe into the same, and after the Lessour puts him out, yet he shall haue free entrie, egresse and regresse into the said house, by reasonable time to take away his goods and vtinsels. As if a man seised of a mese in fee simple, fee taile, or for life, hath certaine goods within the sayd house, and makes his Executors, and dieth, whosoeuer after his decease hath the house, his Executours shall haue free entrie egresse and regresse to carrie out of the same house the goods of their testatour by reasonable time.

Section 70.

¶ Here it appeareth, That if the Feoffee doth enter, he is tenant at will, because hee entreth by the consent of the Feoffor.

¶ *Et deliuer a luy le fait.* Albeit the Deed be deliuered vppon the Ground, yet doth it not amount to a liuerie of seisin of the Land; For it hath his naturall effect to make it a Deed. (f) Donationum alia perfecta, alia incepta & non perfecta: Vt

(f) Flet. li. 3 ca. 3. & ca. 15. 43. E. 3. Tit Feof. & faits 51. 35. H. 8. Feof. Br. 27. Ass. 61. 38. Ass. 2. 39. Ass. 12. 41. E. 3. 17. li. 6. fo. 26. Sharps case.

Item si vn home fait vn fait de Feoffement a vn auter de certaine terre, & deliuer a luy le fait, mes nemy liuerie de Seisin, en ceo case, celuy a que le fait est fait, poit enter en le Terre, & tener & occupier a la volunt celuy que fist le

Also if a man make a Deed of Feoffement to another, of certaine lands, and deliuereth to him the Deed, but not liuerie of seisin; in this case he to whom the Deed is made, may enter into the Land, and hold and occupie it at the will of him which

le fait, put ceo que il est proue per les parols del fait, que il est la volunt que le auter auera la terre, mes celuy que fist le fayt luy poet ouste quaunt luy pleist.

made the Deed, because it is prooued by the words of the Deed, that it is his will that the other should haue the land; but hee which made the Deed may put him out when it pleaseth him.

si donatio lecta fuerit & concessa ac traditio nondum fuerit subsecuta. But if the Deede be deliuered in name of seisin of the Land, or if the Feoffor saith to the Feoffee, Take and enioy this Land according to the Deed, or enter into this Land, and God giue you ioy, these words doe amount to a liuery of seisin.

Section 71.

Item si vn mese soit lesse a tener a volunt, le lessee nest pas tenus a susteiner ou repairer le Meason, sicome Tenant a terme dans est tenus. Mes si le Lessee a volunt fait voluntarie wast, sicome en abatement des measons, ou en couper des arbres, il est dit que le Lessor auera de ceo enũs luy action de Trespasse. Sicome ieo bayle a vn hōe mes barbits a cōpester sā t̃r, ou mes boefes a arer la terr, & il occist mes auers, ieo puissoy bn̄ aũ vn acc̃ d̃ tr̃s enũs luy nient obstant l'bailement.

Also if a house be leased to hold at will, the Lessee is not bound to sustain or repaire the house, as Tenant for terme of yeres is tied. But if Tenant at will commit voluntarie wast, as in pulling downe of houses, or in felling of trees, it is said that the Lessor shall haue an action of Trespasse for this, against the Lessee. As if I lend to one my Sheepe, to tathe his land; or my Oxen to plow the land, and he killeth my Cattle, I may well haue an action of Trespas against him, notwithstanding the lending.

¶ *Si vn mese soit lesse a tener a volunt le lessee nest passe tenus, &c.* For the statute of Gloucester aboue mentioned extends not to a Tenant at will, and therefore for permissiue wast, the lessor hath no remedie at all.

¶ *Mes si Lessee a volunt fait voluntary wast, &c.* (g) And true it is, That if Tenant at will cutteth downe timber Trees, or voluntarily pul downe and prostrate houses, the Lessour shall haue an action of Trespasse against him, quare vi & armis, for the taking vpon him power to cut timber, or prostrate houses, concerneth so much the freehold and inheritance as it doth amount in Law to a determination of his will, (h) and so hath it beene adiudged.

(g) 21. H. 6. 38. 28. E. 3. 25. 12. H. 4. 3. 22. E. 4. 50.

(h) Mich. 28. & 29. E. 1?. Rot. 318. in Com. Banc. enter Walgraue & Somerset. V. le Counte de Shrewsburies case, li. 5. fo. 13.

(i) If Tenant at will granteth ouer his estate to another, and the Grantee entreth, he is a Disseisor, and the lessor may haue an Action of Trespasse against the grantee, for albeit the grant was void, yet it amounteth to a determination of his will.

(i) 27. H. 6. 3. 22. E. 4. 5.

¶ *Sicome ieo baile a vn home mes barbits a compester son terre, &c.* And the reason is, (k) that when the Bailife hauing but a bare vse of them, taketh vpon him as an owner, to kill them, he loseth the benefit of the vse of them. Or in these cases hee may haue an action of Trespasse sur le case, for this conuersion, at his election.

(k) V. 11. H. 4. 24. 1. E. 4. 9. 12. E. 4. 8. 21. E. 4. 19. & 76. 22. E. 4. 5. 3. H. 7. 4. 21. H. 7. 14.

¶ *Trespasse.* Transgressio deriuatur a transgrediendo, because it passeth that which is right: Transgressio autem est cum modus non seruatur, nec mensura: debet enim quilibet in suo facto modum habere, & mensuram: Nota, In the lowest and the highest offences there are no accessaries, but all are principals, as in ryots, routs, forcible entries, and

Flet. li. 2. ca. 1.

other transgressions vi & armis, which are the lowest offences; and so in the highest offence which is crimen lesæ majestatis, there be no accessaries: but in felonies there be accessaries both before and after.

Sect. 72.

21.H.7.39.b. 2.E.4.6.b. 7.E.4.27.a. 6.R.2. Auowrie 86.

Nota si le lessor sur tiel lease a volunt reserue a luy vn annual rent, il poit distrainer pur le rent arere, ou auer de ceo vn action de debt a son election.

Note if the lessor vpon a lease at will, reserue to him a yearely rent, he may distreine for the rent behinde, or haue for this an action of debt at his owne election.

Il poet distreyner pur le rent arere ou auer de ceo vn action de debt, &c. But if he impound the distresse vpon the ground letten at will, the will is determined. Note he may distreine for the Rent, and yet it is no Rent seruice, for no fealty belongeth thereunto, but a Rent distreinable of common right.

(l) Bracton lib. 4. fol. 318. 4.E.3.39. 7.E.3.13. 24.E.3.24. 38.E.3.28. 7.R.2. fauour deff. 30. 8.E.4.25. 4.H.6.30. 22.E.4.38. 18.E.4.25. F.N.B. 201. D. 203. 8.E.2. entre 87. Tempe H.8.b.15. tit. tenant a volunt. Pl. com. 138. 4.H.7.3. (m) 13.H.7.10.a. 21.H.6.54. 5.E.4.3. 22.R.2. tit. Discent. 48.E.3.23. pl. com. 435. 19.E.3. bre. 468. 15.E.4. Discont. 30. 6.E.3.56.57. 21.E.4.5. 21.H.7.38. 10.E.4.18. Per Choke & Litt. (n) Statu' de Merlbridge cap. 26. Abb. Ass. 120.b. F.N.B. 196. 11.E.4.10. & 11. Bract. lib. 4. fo. 252. 253.

There is a great diuersity betweene a tenant at will, and a Tenant at sufferance; for Tenant at will is alwayes by right, and Tenant at sufferance entreth by a lawfull Lease, and holdeth ouer by wrong. A Tenant at sufferance is he that at the first came in by lawfull demise, and after his estate ended continueth the possession and wrongfully holdeth ouer. (l) As Tenant pur terme dauter vie, continueth in possession after the decease of Ce' que vie, or tenant for yeares holdeth ouer his tearme, the Lessor cannot haue an action of trespasse before entrie. Now that a writ of entrie ad terminum qui preterijt lyeth against such a Tenant as holdeth ouer, is rather by admission of the demandant, then for any estate of Freehold that is in him, for in iudgement of Law he hath but a bare possession, but against the King there is no tenant at sufferance, but he that holdeth ouer in the cases aboue said is an intruder vpon the King, because there is no laches imputed to the King for not entring. (m) If Tenant in taile of a Rent grant the same in fee and dieth, yet the issue in taile may bring a Formedon and admit himselfe out of possession. The like Law is it if a man maketh a Lease at will and dieth, now is the will determined, and if the Lessee continueth in possession he is Tenant at sufferance, and yet the heire by admission may haue an assize of Mordanc' against him. (n) But there is a diuersity betweene particular estates made by the terretenaunt, as aboue is said, and particular estates created by act in Law: as if a gardian after the full age of the heire, continueth in possession, he is no Tenant at sufferance, but an Abator, against whom an Assize of Mordancester doth lye, Et sic de similibus.

Chap. 9. Section 73.

Tenant by Coppie.

Tenant p copie de court rolest, deins quel manor il y ad vn custome que ad este vse de temps dont memorie ne court, que certaine tenants deins mesme le manor, ont vse dauer terres & tenements, a tener a

Tenant by copy of Court Roll is, as if a man be seised of a mannor, within which manor there is a custome, which hane beene vsed time out of minde of man, that certaine tenants within the same manor haue vsed to haue lands and te-

Tenant per copie, &c. Tenens per copiam rot. Cur'. Copie we call in Latyn copiam, though copia in his proper signification signifieth plenty, but we haue made a Latyn word of the French word copie and this is ancient for in the Register fo. 51. there is a writ de copia libelli deliberanda, which is grounded vpon the statute of 2.H.4.ca. There is no tenant in the Law, that holdeth

eux & a lour heires en fee simple, ou en fee taile, ou a terme de vie, &c. a volunt le Seignior solonque le custome de mesme le manor.

nements to hold to them and their heires in fee simple, ou fee taile or for terme of life, &c. at the will of the Lord according to the custome of the same manor.

by copie but only this kinde of customary tenant, for no man holdeth by copie of a Charter, or by copie of a fine, or such like, but this tenant holdeth by copie of Court roll.

(a) Bracton calleth Copiholders Villanos Sockmãnos, not because they were bond, but because they held by base tenure by doing of Villein seruices.

(a) *Bracton lib. 2. ca. 8. fo. 26. & lib. 4 fo. 209. Britton. 165. Fleta lib. 1. cap. 8. & lib. 2. cap. 6. Item de custuma. iii. Octaro Cap. quod mardrum. F.N.B. fo. 12. c.*

And Britton saith that some that be free of blood doe hold land in Villenage, and Littleton himselfe in the next chapter calleth them tenants by base tenure: and in F.N.B. fo. 12. C. Et cest terme que est ore a cest jour appel copitenaunts ou copiholders, ou tenaunts per copie, est forsque vn novel nosme trove, car dancient temps ils fuer' appelles tenants in Villenage, ou de base tenure, &c (b) And yet in 1. H. 5. 11. they be called Coppiholders in 14. H. 4. 34. tenant per le verge in 42. E 3 25. Tenant per Roll solonque le volunt le seignior; and in the statute of 4. E. 1. called extenta manerij they are called Custumarij tenentes, and so doth Fleta call them; And before him Ockam (who wrote in the raigne of H. 2.) speake of them and how and vpon what occasion they had their beginning.

(b) *1. H. 5. 11. 14. H. 4. 34. 42. E. 3. 25. Vid. lib. 4. fo. 2. Brownes case.*

(c) Terra ex scripto Saxonice Bockland, fundũ veteres aut ex scripto qui Bockland. i. booklãd, aut sine scripto qui Folkland dicebatur, possidebant, que fuit ex scripto possessio commodiore erat possessione libera, atque immunis, fundus sine scripto censum pensitabant annuũ, atque officiorum seruitute quadam est obligatus, priorem viri plerunque nobiles, atque ingenui, posteriorem rustici fere & pagani possidebant.

(c) *Lamb. verb. terra ex scripto.*

¶ *Court.* Curia, Court is a place where Justice is iudicially ministred and is deriued a cura quia in curijs publicis curas gerebant. (d) The Court baron must be holden on some part of that which is within the Mannor, for if it be holden out of the Mannor it is voide, vnlesse a Lord being seised of two or three Mannors hath vsually time out of minde kept at one of his Mannors Courts for all the said Mannors, then by custome such Courts are sufficient in Law, albeit they be not holden within the seuerall Mannors. And it is to be vnderstood that this Court is of two natures, the first is by the Common Law, and is called a Court baron, as some haue said for that it is the freeholders or freemans Court, (for barons in one sence signifie freemen) and of that Court the freeholders being suitors be iudges, and this may be kept from three weekes to three weekes; The second is a customary Court, and that doth concerne Coppiholders, and therein the Lord or his Steward is the iudge. Now as there can be no Court baron without freeholders, so there cannot be this kinde of customary Court without Coppiholders or Customary holders. And as there may be a Court baron of Freeholders only without Coppiholders, and then is the steward the Register, so there may be a customary Court of Coppiholders only without Freeholders, and then is the Lord or his steward the iudge. And when the Court baron is of this double nature, the Court Roll conteineth aswell matters appertaining to the customary Court as to the Court baron.

(d) *Vid. 4 fo. 24. inter Murrell & Smith eodem lib fo. 27. inter Clifton & Molineux.*

Lib. 4. fo. 26. Melwitches case. Britton fol 274.

And forasmuch as the title, or estate of the Copiholder is entred into the Roll whereof the steward deliuereth him a copie, thereof he is called Copiholder. (e) It is called a Court baron because amongst the lawes of King Edw: the Confessor it is said: Barones vero qui suam habent curiam de suis hominibus, &c. taking his name of the Baron who was Lord of the Mannor, or for that properly in the eye of Law it hath relation to the Freeholders, (f) who are Judges of the Court. And in Ancient Charters and Records the Barons of London, and Barons of the Cinque ports doe signifie the free men of London and of the Cinque ports.

(e) *Lamb fo. 128 & 136. Cambden Brit. fo. 121. b. Britton fo 274.*

(f) *Mirror cap. 1. §. 3.*

¶ *Seisie dun mannor.* Manerium dicitur a manendo secundum excellentiam sedes magna fixa & stabilis. Lageman .i. habens socam & sacam super homines suos, &c. (g) Et sciendum est quod manerium poterit esse per se ex pluribus edificijs coadiuuatum siue villis & hamletis adjacentibus. Poterit etiam esse manerium & per se & cum pluribus villis & cum pluribus, Hamletris adjacentibus, quorum nullum dici poterit manerium per se sed villæ suæ hamlettæ, poterit etiam esse per se manerium capitale, & plura continere sub se maneria non capitalia, & plures villas & plures Hamlettas quasi sub vno capite aut dominio vno. And afterwards, Manerium autem fieri poterit ex pluribus villis vel vna, plures enim villæ poterunt esse in corpore manerij sicut & vna, And in these (h) ancient Authors you shall see the difference, inter mansionem, villam, & manerium. Concerning the institution of this Court by the Lawes and Ordinances of ancient Kings and especially of King Alfred, it appeareth

Domesday.

(g) *Bracton lib. 4 fol. 212. Fleta lib. 4. cap. 15. & lib. 6. cap. 49. Britton fol. 124.*

(h) *Bract lib. 5 fo. 434. Fleta vbi supra. Mirror. cap. 1. §. 3.*

that the first Kings of this Realme had all the Lands of England in Demeane, and les grand Manors & Royalties they reserued to themselues, and of the remnant they, for the defence of the Realme, enfeoffed the Barons of the Realme with such iurisdiction as the Court Baron now hath, and instituted the Freeholders to be Judges of the Court Baron. And herewith agreed the aforesaid Law of Saint Edward. And it is to be obserued, that in those ancient Lawes vnder the name of Barons were comprised all the Nobilitie.

There may be a customarie Manor granted by Copie of Court Roll, so although the word be (seisie) which properly betokeneth a Freehold, yet Tenant for yeares, Tenant by statute, Merchant, Staple, Elegit, and Tenant at will, Garden in Chiualrie, &c. who are not properly seised but possessed are Domini pro tempore, not only to make admittance, but to grant voluntarie Copies of ancient Copyhold lands which come into their hands. And therefore there is a diuersitie betweene Disseisors, Abators, Intrudors, and others that haue defeasible Titles, for their voluntary grants of ancient Copihold lands, shall not binde the Disseisors or others that right haue. And voluntarie grants by Copie, made by such particular Tenants as is aforesaid, shall bind him that hath the Freehold and Inheritance, because all these be lawfull Lords for the time being, but so is not a Tenant at sufferance, because he is in by wrong as hath beene said, and so (i) was it adiudged P. 29. Eliz. inter Rowse & Arteis lib. 4. fol. 24. But admittances made by Disseisors, Abators, Intruders, Tenant at sufferance or others that haue defeasible Titles, stand good against them that right haue because it was a lawfull act, and they were compellable to doe them.

(i) Lib. 4. fol. 24. p. 29. Eliz. inter Rous & Arteis.

(k) And yet in some speciall case an Estate may be granted by Copie, by one that is not Dominus pro tempore, nor that hath any thing in the manor. As if the Lord of a manor by his will in writing, deuiseth that his Executor shall grant the customary Tenements of the Manor according to the custome of the Manor for the payment of his debts, and dieth, the Executor hauing nothing in the Manor may make grants according to the custome of the Manor.

(k) Dier. Mich. 7. & 8. Eliz. Manuscript.

¶ *Deins quel mannor il y ad vn Custome que ad este vse de temps dont memory ne court, &c.* **Of this custome here spoken of there bee** three supporters. The first is time, and that must be out of memory of man, which is included within this word (custome) so as Copihold cannot begin at this day. (l) The second supporter is that the Tenements be parcell of the Mannor or within the Mannor, which appeare by these words of Littleton, que certeine tenants deins mesme le mannor, &c. The third supporter is that it hath beene dimised and dimisible by copie of Court Roll, for it neede not to be dimised time out of mind by copie of Court; but if it be dimisible it is sufficient. For example: If a Copihold tenement escheat to the Lord, and the Lord keepeth it in his hands by many yeares, during this time it is not demised but demisible, for the Lord hath power to dimise it againe.

(l) Vide lib. 4. fol. 24. inter Murrel & Smith.

¶ *A volunt le seigniour solonque le custome.* **So as he is not a bare** tenant at will, but a tenant at will according to the custome of the mannor, as shalbe spoken more hereafter in this chapter.

¶ *Certaine tenements.* **What things may be granted by copie, is** necessarie to be knowne: First, a Manor may be granted by copie. Secondly, vnderwoods without the soile may be granted by copie to one and to his heires, and so may the herbage or vesture of land. Thirdly, generally all lands and tenements within the Manor and whatsoeuer concerneth lands or tenements may be granted by copie: as a faire appendant to a Manner may be granted by copy, &c.

Lib. 11. 17. Sir H. Neuils case.

Lib. 4. fol. 30. 31. inter Hoe & Tayler.

¶ *Consuetudines.* **This word** Consuetudo **being deriued** a Consueto, properly signifieth a Custome, as here Littleton taketh it: But in legall vnderstanding it signifieth also Tolles, Murage, Pontage, Pauage, and such like newly granted by the King; and therefore when the King grantes such things, the words be Concessimus &c. in auxillium villæ prædict' pauiand' &c. consuetudines subscriptas, viz. de quolibet summagio, &c. And it was an Article of the Justices in Eire to inquire, De nouis consuetudinibus leuatis in regno siue in terra, siue in aqua, & quis eas leuauit & vbi. Where consuetudo is taken for Tolles, and such like Taxes or Charges vpon the subiect.

Regist. F. N. B. 270. d. Vet. mag. Carta in cap. Itin. fol. 151. Bract. lib. 3. 117. Fleta. lib. 1. cap. 20.

Section 74.

¶ *ET tiel tenant ne puit aliener sa terre, &c.* And this is

¶ ET tiel tenant ne puit alien sa terre per fait, car

AND such a tenant may not alien his land by deed, for then

don=

donques le Seignior poit entre come en chose forfeit a luy, mes s'il voit alien sa terre a vn auter, il couient solonque ascun custome de surrender les tenemẽts en ascun Court &c. en le maine le Seignior, al vse celuy que auera le state, en tiel forñ, ou a tiel effect.

the Lord may enter as into a thing forfeited vnto him. But if hee will alien his land to another, it behoueth him after the custome to surrender the tenements in Court, &c. into the hands of the Lord to the vse of him that shall haue the Estate in this forme or to this effect.

Ad hanc Curiam venit *A.* de *B.* & sursum reddidit in eadem Curia, vnum mesuagium, &c. in manus Domini, ad vsum *C.* de *D.* & hæredum suorum, vel hæredum de corpore suo exeuntiũ, vel pro termino vitæ suæ, &c. Et super hoc venit prædictus *C.* de *D.* & cœpit de Domino in eadem Curia, mesuagium prædictũ, &c. Habendum & tenendum sibi & hæredibus suis, vel sibi & hæredibus de corpore suo exeuntibus, vel sibi ad terminum vitæ, &c. ad voluntatem domini, secundum consuetudinem manerij, faciendo & reddendo inde redditus, seruitia, & consuetudines inde, prius debita & consueta, &c. Et dat Domino pro fine, &c. Et fecit Domino fidelitatem, &c.

A. of *B.* commeth vnto this Court, and surrẽdreth in the same Court a Mease, &c. into the hands of the Lord, to the vse of *C.* of *D.* and his heires, or the heires issuing of his bodie, or for terme of life, &c. And vpon that, commeth the aforesaid *C.* of *D.* and taketh of the Lord in the same Court, the foresaid Mease &c. To haue and to hold to him and to his heires, or to him and to his heires issuing of his bodie, or to him for terme of life, at the Lords will, after the custome of the Manor to do and yeeld therefore the Rents, Seruices, and Customes thereof before due & accustomed, &c. and giueth the Lord for a fine, &c. and maketh vnto the Lord his fealtie, &c.

true in Case of alienation, but when a man hath but a right to a Copihold, he may release it by deed or by Copie, to one that is admitted Tenant de facto.

Lib. intrat. 131. *Lib* 4. *fol.* 25.*b. inter Kite & Queinton.*

¶ *Alien per fait.* Here it appeareth by Littleton that there must be an alienation: for the making of the Deed alone, vnlesse somewhat passe thereby is no forfeiture: as if he make a Charter of feoffement, or a Deed of demise for life, and make no liuery, this is no forfeiture, because nothing passeth, and therefore no alienation, but otherwise it is of a lease for yeares.

¶ *Forfeit a luy.* This Adiectiue in Latine is forisfactus, the Verbe is forisfacere, and the Nowne forisfactura, they are all deriued of foris, (that is) extra and facere, quasi diceret extra legem seu consuetudinem facere to do a thing against or without Law or Custome, and that legally is called a forfeiture. Littleton vseth this word but once in all his book. What shall be said (k) forfeitures of Copiholds you may read at large in my Reports.

(k) *Lib.* 4. *inter les Copihold cases* 21. 23. 25. 27. 28. *Lib.* 8. 92. 99. 100. *Lib.* 9. 75. 107. *Lib.* 10. 131.

¶ *En ascun Court.* (l) This is the generall custome of the Realme that euerie Copiholder may surrender in Court and need not to alleadge any custome therefore. So if out of Court hee surrender to the Lord himselfe, he need not alleadge in pleading any custome, but if he surrender out of Court into the hands of the Lord by the hands of two or three, &c. Copiholders, or by the hands of the bayliffe or Reeue, &c. or out of Court by the hand of any other, these customes are particular, and therefore he must plead them.

(l) *Bract. lib.* 2 *cap.* 8. & *lib.* 4 49. 15. *H.* 4. 34. 1. *H.* 5. 11.

(m) Bracton lib. 4. fol 209. speaking of these kind of customary Tenants, saith, Dare autem non possunt tenemẽta sua, nec ex causa donationis ad alios transferre non magis quam villani puri, & vnde si transferre debeant restituunt

(m) *Bract. lib.* 4. *fol.* 209. & *lib.* 2. *cap.* 8. &c. 14. *H.* 4. 34.

ea Domino vel Baliuo & ipsi ea tradant alijs in villenagium tenenda, but although it be incident to the estate of a Copyhold, to passe as our Author saith by surrenders, (b) yet so forcible is custome that by it a Freehold and Inheritance, may also passe by surrender (without the leave of the Lord) in his Court and delivered over by the Baily to the feoffee according to the forme of the Deed, to be inrolled in the Court or the like.

(b) *Coram rege Mich.31.E.3 Ranulph Huntingfelds case. 3.E.3.Corona 310. 11.H.4.83. per Thirning.*

(c) *Vide lib.4. inter les cases de Cop.holds.*

¶ *Ad hanc Curiam venit* A. *de* B. *& sursum reddidit, &c.* Here Littleton putteth an example of a surrender in Court, and in this example three (c) things are to be observed.

First, That the surrender to the Lord be generall without expressing of any Estate, for that he is but an instrument to admit Celty a que use, for no more passeth to the Lord, but to serve the limitation of the use, and Ce' que use, when hee is admitted, shall bee in by him that made the surrender, and not by the Lord.

Secondly, if the limitation of the use be generall, then Ce' que use taketh but an estate for life, And therefore here Littleton expresseth upon the declaration of the use the limitation of the Estate, viz. in fee simple, fee taille, &c.

(d) *Mich.2.& 3.Ph.& M. in Com.Banco, by the whole Court in Constables case of Pickenham in Norfolk.*

Thirdly, The Lord cannot grant a larger Estate then is expressed in the limitation of the use. Littleton here putteth his case of one. If two joyntenants be of Copyhold lands in fee, and the one out of Court according to the custome surrender his part to the Lords hands, to the use of his last will, and by his will deviseth his part to a stranger in fee, and dieth, and at the next Court the surrender is presented; by the surrender and presentment the joynture was severed, and the devisee ought to be admitted to the moitie of the lands, for now by relation, the state of the land was bound by the surrender.

(e) *Fleta.lib.2.ca.65.& 71.*

¶ *In manus Domini. Dominus manerij.* The Lord of a Manor is described (e) by Fleta as he ought to be in these words. In omnibus autē & supra omnia decet quēlibet Dominū verbis esse veracem, & in operibus fidelem, Deū & Iustitiam amantem, fraudem & peccatum odientem, voluntariosque, maleuolos, & iniuriosos contemnentem, & apud proximos pietatem vultumque motibilem & plenum, ipsius enim interest potius consilio quam viribus uti, proprioue arbitrio: non cuiuslibet voluntarij iuuenis menestralli, vel adulatoris sed iurisperitorum virorum fidelium & honestorum, & in pluribus expertorum consilio debet fauere. Qui bene sibi vult disponere & familiæ suæ, scire veram executionem terrarum suarum necessarium erit, vt perinde sciat quantitatem suarum facultatum & finem annuarum expensarum. And the residue is fit for every Lord of a Manor to know and follow which were too long here to be recited, only his conclusion having spoken of the Lords revenue and expenses I will adde, Quæ omnia distincte scribantur in membranis, vt perinde sagacius vitam suam disponat & facilius conuincat mendacia compostariorum.

(f) *See more of this lib.4. the cases of Copiholds. Trin.1.Ja.Rot.854. inter Shapland & Ridler in repl. in Com.Banco, the case of the Garden in Socage adiudged.*

(f) If the Lord of the Manor for the time being be Lessee for life or for yeares, garden, or any that hath any particular interest, or tenant at will of a Manor (all which are accounted in law Domini pro tempore) doe take a surrender into his hands, and before admittance the Lessee for life dieth, or the yeares interest or custodie doe end or determine, or the will is determined, though the Lord commeth in above the Lease for life or for yeares, the custodie or other particular interest or tenancie at will, yet shall he be compelled to make admittance according to the surrender, and so was it holden in 17.Eliz. in the Earle of Arundels Case, which I my selfe heard.

¶ *Et dat Domino de fine.* For the signification of this word (finis) vide Sect. 174.183.194.441.

Of fines due to the Lord by the Copiholder, some be by the change or alteration of the Lord, and some by the change or alteration of the tenant, the change of the Lord ought to be by Act of God, otherwise no fine can be due, but by the change of the tenant either by the Act of God, or by the act of the partie a fine may be due: for if the Lord doe alledge a custome within his Manor to have a fine of every of his Copiholders of the said Manor at the alteration or change of the Lord of the Manor, be it by alienation, demise, death, or otherwise; This is a custome against the Law, as to the alteration or change of the Lord by the act of the partie, for by that meanes the Copiholders may be oppressed by multitude of fines, by the act of the Lord. But when the change groweth by the act of God, there the custome is good as by the death of the Lord. And this, upon a Case in the Chancerie (g) referred to Sir Iohn Popham Chiefe Justice, and upon conference with Anderson, Periam, Walmesley, and all the Judges of Serjants Inne in Fleetstreet, was resolved, and so certified into the Chancerie. But upon the change or alteration of the Tenant, a fine is due unto the Lord.

(g) *T.39.Eliz. betweene the Coppiholders of the Manor of Gaultons, in the Countie of Northumberland and Armestrong, Lord of the Manor in Chancerie.*

Of fines taken of Copiholders some be certaine by custome, and some bee incertaine but that fine though it be incertus, yet must it bee rationabilis. And that reasonablenesse shall bee discussed by the Justices upon the true circumstances of the Case appearing unto them, and if the Court where the cause dependeth, adiudgeth the fine exacted unreasonable, then is not the

Copi-

Copiholder compellable to pay it. And so was it adiudged (h) for all excessiuenesse is abhorred in Law. See more concerning fines of Copiholders in my Reports (i) which are so plainly there set downe, as they need not be rehersed here.

(h) Pasch. 1. Iac. in com. banco rot. 1845. inter Stallon & Brady.

(i) Lib. 4. the cases of Copiholds.

Sect. 75.

CEt tiels tenants sont appelles Tenants per copie de court Rolle, pur ceo que ils nont auter euidence concernãt lour tenemẽts, forsque les Copies des Rolles d' Court.

AND these tenants are called tenants by copie of court Rolle, because they haue no other euidence concerning their tenements but only the Copies of Court Rolles.

¶ *Ils nont auter euidence.* This is to be vnderstood of euidences of alienation, for a release of a right by Deed a Copiholder (that commeth in by way of admittance) may haue, and that is sufficient to extinguish the right of the Copihold which he that maketh the release had.

Section 76.

CEt tiels tenãts ne empledérõt, ne serront empledes de lour tenements p briefe le Roy. Mes sils voilent empleder auters pur lour tenements, ils aueront vn plaint fait en le Court le Seignior en tiel forme, ou a tiel effect: A. de B. queritur versus C. de D. de placito terræ, videlicet, de vno mesuagio, quadraginta acris terr', quatuor acris prati, &c. cum pertin. & facit protestationem sequi querelam istam in natura breuis domini Regis assisæ mortis antecessoris ad communẽ legẽ, vel breuis domini regis assisæ Nouæ disseisinæ ad cõmunem legem, aut in natura breuis de for-

AND such tenants shall neither impleade nor be impleaded for their tenements by the Kings writ, but if they will implead others for their tenements, they shall haue a plaint entred in the Lords Court in this forme, or to this effect. A. of B. complaines against C. of D. of a plea of land, viz. of one messuage, forty acres of land, foure acres of meadow, &c. with the appurtenances, and makes protestation to follow this complaint in the nature of the Kings writ of assise of Mordancester at the Common Law, or of an assise of nouel disseisin, or formedon in the discender at the

¶ *Tiels tenants ne empledéront, ne serront empledes, &c.* This is euident and needes no explanation.

4. H. 4. 34. adiudge in Parliament.

¶ *Mes sils violent empleder auters, ils aueront, &c.* Put the case that the Demandant in a pleint in nature of a reall action recouereth the land erroniously, what remedy for the partie grieued? For he cannot haue the Kings writ of false iudgement in respect of the basenesse of the estate and tenure, being in the eye of the law but a Tenant at will and the freehold being in another, he shall haue a petition to the Lord in the nature of a writ of false iudgement, and therein assigne errors and haue remedie according to Law.

14. H. 4. 34. 1. H. 5. 11. Vet. N. B. 18. 13. R. 2. tit. Faux iudgement. 7. E. 4. 19 21. E. 4. 80.

¶ *De forma donationis in discender ad communem legem.* By the opinion of Littleton as there may be an estate taile by custome with the co-operation of the Statute of W. 2. cap. 1. so may he haue a Formedon in discender, but as the Statute without a custome extendeth not to Copiholds, so a custome

L. 6. 3 fo. 8. 9. in Heydons case. Lib. 4. fo. 22. 23. 15. H. 8. Br. tit. taile.

stome without the statute cannot create an Estate taile. Now it is not a sufficient proofe that lands haue beene granted in taile, for albeit lands haue anciently and vsually beene granted by Copie to many men and to the heires of their bodies, that may be a Fee simple conditionall as it was at the Common Law. But if a remainder haue been limited ouer such Estates and enioyed, or if the issues in taile haue auoyded the alienation of the ancestor, or if they haue recouered the same in Writs of Formedon in the discender, these and such like be proofes of an Estate taile. (y) But if by custome, Copihold may bee intailed, the same by like custome, by surrender may be cut off, and so hath it beene adiudged, (z) some haue holden that there was a Formedon, in the discender at the Common Law.

ma donationis in discendere ad communem legem, ou en nature dascun auter briefe, &c. Plegij de prosequendo, F.G.&c

Common Lawe, or in the nature of any other Writte, &c. Pledges to prosecute F.G.&c.

(y) T.29.Eliz. inter Hill & Vpcheir. Custome deins le manor de Onerhall in Essex. 21.Eliz. Dier 356. 23 Eliz. Dier 373.

(z) 10.E.2.formdon.55. 21.E.3.47.Pl.Com.240. 4.E.2.formdon 50.

Sect. 77.

¶ CAr (il est dit) que si le Seignior, &c. And here Littleton saith truly that it is said so, for so it is said in 13.E.3.13.R.2. 32.H.6,& 7.E.4.19.

13.E.3.tit.prascript.20. 13.R.2.feiux iudgement 7. 32.H.6.tit.Subpena 2. 7.E.4.19.

But hee setteth not downe his own opinion, but rather to the contrarie, as hereafter in this chapter appeareth. But now magistra rerum Experientia, hath made this cleere and without question, that the Lord cannot at his pleasure put out the lawfull Copyholder without some cause of forfeiture, and if he do the Coppiholder, may haue an action of trespasse against him, for albeit hee is tenens ad voluntatem Domini, yet it is secundum consuetudinem Manerij.

Vide Sect.81.82.84.132.

(b) And Britton speaking of these kinde of Tenants saith thus, & ceux sont priuiledges en tiel maner que nul de les doit ouster de

(b) Vid.42.E.3.25. Britt.fol.165.

¶ ET coment que ascun tiels tenants ont inheritāce solonque le custome del Manor, vncore ils nont estate forsque a volunt le Seignior solonque le course del common ley. Car il est dit, si le Seignior eux ousta, sils nont auter remedy forsque de suer a lour Seigniors per petition, car sils aueront auter remedie, ils ne seront dits tenants a volunt le seignior solonque le custome del Manor, mes le Seignior ne voile enfreinder le custom que est reasonable en tiels cases.

¶ Mes Brian Chiefe Justice dit, que son opinion ad touts foits este, & vnquez sera, si tiel tenant per le custome payant ses seruices soit eiect per le Seignior, que il auera action de trns vers luy, H.21, Ed.4. Et issint fuit lopinion de Danby chiefe Justice, M. 7.Ed. 4.

AND although that some such Tenants haue an Inheritance according to the custome of the Manor, yet they haue but an Estate but at the will of the Lord according to the course of the cōmon law. For it is said, that if the Lord doe oust them, they haue no other remedy, but to sue to their lords by petitiō, for if they shold haue any other remedy, they should not be said to be tenāts at wil of the lord accor ding to the custome of the Manor. But the Lord cānot breake the custome which is reasonable in these cases.

¶ But *Brian* Chiefe Iustice said, that his opinion hath alwayes been and euer shall be, that if such tenant by custome paying his seruices be eiected by the Lord, hee shall haue an Action of trespasse against him. *H.21.Ed.4.* And so was the opinion of *Danby*, Chiefe Iustice in 7.*Ed.4.*

Car

Car il dit que le teñ per le custome est ciblen enheriter de auer son terre solonq; le custome, come celuy que ad frankteñement al common ley.

For hee saith that tenant by the custome is as well inheritour to haue his land according to the custome as he which hath a freehold at the Common Law.

tiels tenements, tantcome ilz font les seruices que a lour tenements appendent, ne nul ne poet lour seruices acrestre ne change a faire autres seruices ou pluis. And herewith agreeth Sir Robert Danby chiefe Justice of the Court of Common pleas M. 7. E. 4. 19. and Sir Thomas Brian his successor M. 21. E. 4. 80. viz. that the Copiholder doing his customes and seruices, if hee be put out by his Lord, hee shall haue an action of trespasse against him.

CHAP. 10. *Sect.* 78.

Tenant per le Verge.

¶ TEnāts p le Verge, sont en tiel nature come Tenants per le copy de Court Roll. Mes la cause purque ils sont appelles tenāts per la Verge, est p ceo que quant ils voilēt surrender lour teneměts en le maine lour seignior al vse dun auter, ils aueront vn petite verge (per le custome) en lour maine, le quel ils baillera al Seneschall, ou al bailife solonque le custome & vse del manor, & celuy q̄ auera la terre, prendra m̄ la terre en le court, & son prisel serra enter en le roll, & le Seneschal, ou le bailife, solonq; le custome deliuera a ce-

TEnants by the Verge are in the same nature as tenants by Copy of Court roll. But the reason why they bee called tenants by the Verge is, for that when they will surrender their tenements into the hands of their Lord to the vse of another, they shall haue a little rod (by the custome) in their hand, the which they shall deliuer to the steward, or to the bailife according to the custome of the manor and hee which shall haue the land shal take vp the same land in Court, and his taking shalbe entred vpon the roll, and the steward or bailiffe, according to the custom

¶ *Tenants per le Verge.* This Tenant per le Verge is a meere Copiholder, and taketh his name of the Ceremony of the Verge. 14. H. 4. 33. Tenure in Villenage or by base tenure is thus described by Britton, (a) Villenage est, teñ de demeynes de chescun Seignior baille a tener a son volunt p Villeines seruices de enprover al opes le Seignior, & liuere per verge & nient per title de estrit, ne per succession de heritage dont gards de mariages ne auters seruices reals come homage & reliefes ne ponent des amnones de demeynes ne de villenage ests demand. (a) *Britton fol. 165. a. F. N. B. fol. 12. Liberatio per Virgam.*

¶ *A le seneschall.* (which wee call a steward) Seneschallus is deriued of sein a house or place, and Schalc an officer or gouernour, some say that sen is an ancient word for Justice, so as Seneschall should signifie officiarius Iustitiæ, and some say that steward is deriued of Stewe (that is) a place, and Ward, that signifieth a Keeper, warden or Gouernour; And others that it is deriued of Stede, that signifieth a place also and Ward as it were the keeper or gouernour of that place; but it is a word of

Vid. Sect. 93. & 379. Fleta lib. 2 cap. 66. Vid. Statut. de extent. maner. 14. E. 1.

of many significations. In this place it signifieth an officer of Justice viz. a keeper of Courts, &c. Fleta describeth the office and duty of this officer at large most excellently; Prouideat sibi dominus de seneschallo circumspecto & fideli, viro prouido & discreto & gratioso, humili, pudico, pacifico & modesto, qui in legibus consuetudinibusque prouinciæ & officio seneschalciæ se cognoscat & jura domini sui in omnibus teneri affectet, quique subballivos domini in suis erroribus & ambiguis sciat instruere & docere, quique egenis parcere, & qui nec prece vel pretio velit à tramite justiciæ deviare, & peruerse judicare, cuius officium est curias tenere maneriorum & de subtractionibus consuetudinum, seruiciorum, reddituum, sectarum ad cur', mercata, molendina domini & ad visus francpledg: aliarumque libertatum domino pertinentium inquirat, &c. The residue pertaining to his office is worth your reading at large. Euery steward of Courts is either by Deed or without Deed, for a man may be retayned a steward to keepe his Court baron and Leete also belonging to the Mannor without Deed, and that reteyner shall continue untill hee be discharged. The Lord of a Mannor may make admittances out of Court and out of the Mannor also, as at large appeareth in my reports.

Vid. lib. 4. Cases de Copiholds, fo. 26. 27. 30.

luy que prist la terre, mesme l'verge, ou un auter verge en nosme del seisin, & pur cel cause ils sont appeles tenants per le verge, mes ils nont auter euidence, sinon pur copy de Court roll.

shall deliuer to him that taketh the land the same rod, or another rod in the name of seisin, and for this cause they are called tenants by the verge but they haue no other euidence but by copy of Court roll.

Section 79.

Vid. Lamb. exposition of Saxon words.

¶ A *Le bailie.* This word bailie as some say commeth of the French word Baylife, in Latyn balivus but in truth Bailie is an old Saxon word and signifieth a safe keeper or protector, and baile or ballium is safe keeping or protection, And thereupon we say when a man upon suretie is deliuered out of prison traditur in ballium he is deliuered into baile, that is, into their safe keeping or protection from prison; and the sherife that hath Custodiam comitatus, is called balivus and the Countie baliva sua.

¶ *Reue* is deriued of the Saxon word geresa or gereve, and by contraction or rather corruption Gereue or Reue and is in Latyn præfectus or præpositus. It signifies as much as appruator a disposor or director, as woodreeue, sheepe reeue, shire reeue, &c. whereof more shalbe said hereafter. Vide Fleta lib. 2. cap. 67. where hee treateth of the office of the Baillife, and cap. 69. de officio præpositi of

Fleta lib. 2. ca. 67.

¶ Et auxy en diuers seigniories & manors, il y ad tiel custome, si tiel tenant que tient per custome voloit aliener ses terres ou tenements, il poit surrender ses tenements a le Baily, ou a le Reeue, ou a deux probes homes del seigniory, al vse cestuy que auera le terre, dauer en fee simple, fee taile, ou pur terme de vie, &c. Et tout ceo ils presenteront al procheine Court, & donques celuy que auera la terre per Copy de Court Rol, auera mesme la terre solonque lentent del surrender.

And also in diuers Lordships and mannors there is this custome, viz. if such a tenant which holdeth by custome will alien his lands or tenements hee may surrender his tenements to the Bailife or to the Reeue or to two honest men of the same Lordship to the vse of him which shall haue the land to haue in fee simple, fee taile, or for terme of life, &c. and they shall present all this at the next court, & then he which shall haue the land by copy of Court Roll, shall haue the same according to the intent of the surrender.

the office of the reeue, and what belongeth of dutie and right to either of them, which words are too long here to be inserted, only this I will take out of him, balivus autem cuiuscunque manerij esse debet in verbo verax, & in opere diligens & fidelis ac pro discreto appruatore plegiatus & electus qui de moribus & legibus pro tanto officio sufficient' se cognscat, & quod sit ita justus quod ob vindictam seu cupiditatem non quærat versus tenentes domini nec alios, &c. Præpositus autem tanquam appruator & cultor optimus, &c. domino vel eius seneschallo palam debet presentari cui injungatur officium illud indilate, non ergo sit puer aut somnolentus sed efficaciter & continue comodum domini adipisci nitatur & exarare, &c. The residue concerning both the Offices being worth your reading.

¶ *A le bailie ou a le Reeue.* Littleton intendeth into the hands of the Lord by the hands of the Bailiffe or the Reeue.

¶ *Ou al deux probes homes del seigniorie.* The custome doth guide these surrenders out of Court, and the custome must be pursued.

¶ *Et tont ceo ils presenteront al procheine court, &c.* By the surrender out of Court the Copihold estate passeth to the Lord vnder a secret condition that it be presented at the next Court according to the custome of the mannor. And therefore if after such a surrender, and before the next Court he that made the surrender dieth, yet the surrender standeth good, and if it be presented at the next Court Ce'a que vse shalbe admitted thereunto; but if it be not presented at the next Court according to the custome, then the surrender becommeth voide, and so was it clearely holden Pasch. 14 Eliz. in the court of Common pleas which I my selfe heard. *Vid. lib. 4. fol. 25. Kt. & Quaintons case.*

Sect. 80.

¶ Et issint est asçauoire, que en diuers seigniories, & diuers manors, sont plusors & diuers customes en tielx cases, quant a prender tenements, & quant a pleder, & quant as auters choses & customes a faire, & tout ceo que nest pas encounter reason, poit bien estre admitte & allow.

And so it is to bee vnderstood, that in diuers Lordships, and in diuers manners, there be many and diuers customes, in such cases as to take tenements, and as to plead, and as to other things and customes to bee done, and whatsoeuer is not against reason, may well bee admitted and allowed.

¶ *Sont plusors & diuers customes.* This was cautiously set downe, for in respect of the varietie of the customes in most Mannors, it is not possible to set downe any certaintie, only this incident inseparable euery custome must haue, viz. that it be consonant to reason, for how long soeuer it hath continued, if it be against reason, it is of no force in Law.

¶ *Encounter reason.* This is not to be vnderstood of euery vnlearned mans reason, but of artificiall and legall reason warranted by authority of Law: Lex est summa ratio.

Section 81.

¶ *Ils sont appelles tenants per base tenure.* Of this sufficient hath beene spoken before.

¶ Et tiels tenants q̃ teignont solonq̃ le custome dun seigniorie, ou dun manor, coment que ils ont estate denheritance solonq̃ le custome del Seigniory ou mañ, vnc̃ pur ceo q̃ ils nõt assez

And these tenants which hold according to the custome of a Lordship or Mannor, albeit they haue an estate of inheritance according to the custome of the Lordship or Mannor, yet because

franktenement per le cours del common ley, ils sont appelles Tenants p base tenure.

they haue no freehold by the course of the common law, they are called tenants by base tenure.

Sect. 82.

¶ ET diuers diuersities y sont perenter tenant a volunt, que est eins per lease son lessor per le course del common ley, & tenant solonq; le custome del manor en le forme auantdit. Car t a volūt solonq; le custom puit auer estate denheritance (cõe est auantdit.) al volūt le seignior solōq le custome & vsage del manor. Mes si home ad terres ou Tenements, queux ne sont deins tiel manor ou Seigniorie, ou tiel custome ad este vse en le forme auantdit, & voile lesser tiels terres ou tenemēts a vn auter, a auer & tener a luy & a ses heires a le volunt le lessor, ceux parolx (a les heires de le lessee) sont voids, Car en cest case si le lessee deuie & son heire enter le lessor auera bon action de trespas enuers luy, mes nemy issint enuers lheire le terre per le custome en ascun cas, &c. pur ceo que le custome de le manor en ascun cas luy puit aide de barrer son seignior en action de trespasse, &c.

AND there are diuers diuersities betweene tenant at wil which is in by lease of his lessor by the course of the Common Law, and tenant according to the custome of the Manor in forme aforesaid. For tenant at will according to the custome may haue an estate of inheritance (as is aforesaid) at the will of the Lord, according to the custome and vsage of the Manor. But if a man hath lands or tenements which bee not within such a Manor or Lordship, where such a custome hath beene vsed in forme aforesaid, and will let such lands or tenements to another, to haue and to hold to him and to his heires at the wil of the lessor, these words (to the heires of the Lessee) are void. For in this case if the lessee dieth, and his heire enter, the Lessor shal haue a good Action of trespasse against him, but not so against the heire of tenant by the custome in any case, &c. for that the custome of the Manor in some case may aide him to barre his Lord in an action of Trespasse, &c.

¶ *Tenant a volunt solonque le custome puit auer estate denheritance, &c.* Here note that Littleton alloweth that by the custome of the Manor, the Copiholder hath an Inheritance, and consequently the Lord cannot put him out without cause.

¶ *Mes si home, &c. voile Lesser Terres ou tenements a vn auter a auer & tener a luy & ses heires a volunt le lessor, ceux parols (a les heires de le lessee) sont voides, car en cest case si le lessee deuie, & son heire enter le lessor auera action de trespasse enuers luy, &c.* By which it is proued that by the death of the lessee, the Lease is absolutely determined, which is proued by this that if the heire enter the Lessor shall haue an action of trespasse, quare vi & armis, before any entrie made by the Lessor.

10.*E*.4.18. 21.*E*.4.13. 2.*R*.2.*barre* 237. 11.*H*.7.22. 21.*H*.7.12.

¶ *Pur ceo que le custome de le Manor en ascun case luy puit aider de barrer son seignior en action de trespasse, &c.* Hereby it appeareth that by the opinion of Littleton, the Lord against the custome of the Manor cannot oust the Copiholder.

Section 83.

¶ ITem lun tenãt per le custome ẽ ascuns lieux doit repairer & susteiner ses measons, & lauter tenant a volunt nemy.

ALso the one tenant by the custome in some places ought to repaire and vphold his houses, and the other Tenant at will ought not.

¶ PEr le Custome. For what a Copiholder may or ought to doe, or not doe, the custome of the Manor (a) must direct it, for Consuetudo Manerij est obseruanda. (b) But if there be no custome to the contrary, wast either permissiue or voluntarie of a Copiholder, is a forfeiture of his Copihold.

(a) Bracton. lib. 2. fol. 76.

(b) Vide lib. 4. fol. 21. 22. &c. in cases de Copiholds.

Sect. 84.

¶ ITem lun tenant per le custome ferra fealtie, & lauter nemy. Et plusors auters diuersities y sont perenter eux.

ALso the one tenãt by the custome shall do fealtie and the other not, and many other diuersities there be betweene them.

¶ L *Vn tenant per le custome ferra fealtie, & lauter nemy.* And the doing of fealtie by a Copiholder, proueth that a Copiholder so long as he obserues the custome of the Manor & payeth his seruices hath a fixed Estate. For Tenant at will that may bee put out at pleasure shall not doe fealtie. For to what end should a man sweare to bee faithfull and true to his Lord, and should beare faith to him which he claymeth to hold of him, and that lawfully hee shall doe his customes and seruices, &c. when hee hath no certaine estate, but may bee put out at the pleasure of the Lessor, or hee himselfe may determine it at his pleasure, of these kind of customarie Tenants, and of many things concerning them, you may read more in the fourth Booke of my Reports, fol. 21. 22. 23. &c. Thus much as I haue here set downe, may suffice for the vnderstanding of such Cases and Opinions as Littleton hath expressed.

Vide Sect. 132.

Lib. 4. fol. 21. 22. 23. &c.

Finis Libri primi.

THE SECOND BOOKE of the firſt part of the Inſtitutes of the LAWES of ENGLAND.

CHAP. I. *Homage.* *Sect.* 85.

¶ Homage eſt le pluis honorable ſeruice, & pluis humble ſeruice de reuerence, q̃ frank tenant puit faire a ſon Seignior. Car quãt le tenant ferra homage a ſon Seignior, il ſerra diſcinct & ſon teſt diſcouer, & ſon Seignior ſeera, & le tenant genulera deuaunt luy ſur ambideux genues, & tiendra ſes maines extendes, & ioyntes enſemble euter les maines le Seignior, & iſſint dirra: Jeo

Homage is the moſt honorable ſeruice & moſt humble ſeruice of reuerence that a Frank-tenant may doe to his Lord: For when the Tenant ſhall make Homage to his Lord, hee ſhall be vngirt, and his head vncouered, and his Lord ſhall ſit, and the Tenant ſhal kneele before him on both his knees, and hold his hands ioyntly together betweene the hands of his Lord, and ſhall ſay thus: I become your man

¶ Our Author hauing taught vs in his former booke the ſeuerall diſtinct eſtates of lands and tenements as moſt neceſſary to be knowne, for the vnderſtanding of theſe two other bookes doth in this ſecond booke treat of the tenures and ſeruices, whereby the ſaid lands and tenements beene holden, which he deuideth into twelue parts, viz. Homage, Fealtie, Eſcuage, Knight ſeruice, Socage, Frankalmoigne, homage auncestrel, grand Serieantie, petit Seriantie, tenure in Burgage, in Villenage, and into Rents, wherein his method is moſt excellent, for hee beginneth with homage, becauſe it is the moſt humble ſeruice of reuerence expreſſing the dutie of the tenant to his Lord, and the affectionate loue and protection of the Lord towards his tenant as hereafter ſhall appeare. Secondly, Fealty a ſacred

deveigne vostre home de cestiour en avant, de vie, & de member, & de terrest honor, & a vous serra foiall & loiall, & foy a vous porta des tenements que ieo claime de tener de vous, salue la foy que ieo doy a nostre Signior le Roy, & donques le Signior issint seyant, luy basera.

from this day forward of life and limme, and of earthly worship, & vnto you shall be true and faithful, and beare you faith for the Tenements that I claime to hold of you, (sauing the Faith that I owe vnto our Soueraigne Lord the King.) And then the Lord so sitting shall kisse him.

sacred seruice, expressing by oath his fidelitie to his Lord.

Thirdly, Escuage, which is Seruitium scuti, the seruice of the Shield.

Fourthly, Knights Seruice, for the defence of the Realme against outward hostilitie and inuasions, which the better might be effected, if such dutie, fidelitie, & loue were betweene Lords and tenants, as ought to be, and as the law expecteth.

Fiftly, Socage, the seruice of the Plough, aptly placed next Knights seruice, for that the Ploughman maketh the best souldier, as shall appeare in his proper place.

Sixtly, Frankalmoigne, Seruice due to Almightie God, placed towards the middest for two causes; First, for that the middest is the most worthie and most honourable place; And secondly, because the first fiue preceding Tenures and Seruices, and the other sixe subsequent, must all become prosperous and vsefull, by reason of Gods true Religion and seruice, for Nunquam prospere succedunt res humanæ, vbi negliguntur diuinæ: Wherein I would haue our Student follow the aduice giuen in these antient Verses, for the good spending of the day.

Sex horas somno, totidem des Legibus æquis.
Quatuor orabis, des Epulisque duas.
Quod superest vltro sacris largire camænis.

Seuenthly, Homage auncestrel, Antient Families enioying with their bloud the antient inheritance of their forefathers, as a great blessing of the Almightie.

8, & 9. Serjeantie grand & petit, due to the King onely, to whom the highest and most eminent honour, ligeance, and reuerence of all kind is due; which hath two notable effects: First, Imperij Maiestas est tutelæ salus, according to the old rule. And secondly, it is an assured meanes of long continuance of houses and families in prosperous estate, whereof our Authour speaketh in the Chapter before.

10 Then followeth the Tenure of Burgage, of antient Burghes and Cities, &c. which are to be supported for the honour of the King, and for the maintenance of trade and trafique, the life of all Commonwealths, especially of Islands.

11 Villenage, for the performance of seruice, yet necessarie seruice for the clensing of Cities, Boroughs, Mannors, &c. and for the better manuring of arrable grounds, and increase of Husbandrie.

12 And lastly, Tenure by Rents, which are called Viui redditus, because the Lords and owners thereof doe liue by them, which they shall enioy the better, if trade and traffique be maintained, and our natiue commodities, which are rich and necessarie, holden vp and saleable at a reasonable value. And now vnderstanding his method, let vs peruse our Authors words.

And as our Author began his first Booke with Fee simple, which is the most principall and worthiest estate, so he beginneth his second Booke with Homage, which is the most honourable and humble seruice.

(a) Glanu. li. 9. ca. 1. Bract. fo. 78. 80. Brit. fo. 170. 172, 173. Flet. li. 3. c. 16. Mir. c. 3. de Homage, & li. 5. §. 1.

Homage is derived of (a) Homo, and it is called Homage, because when he doth this seruice, he saith, Ieo deveigne vostre home: And in English Homage is called Manhood, so as the manhood of his Tenant, and the homage of his Tenant is al one. Mutua quidem debet esse Dominij & Homagij fidelitatis connexio, ita quod quantum homo debet domino ex homagio, tantum illi debet Dominus ex Dominio præter solam reuerentiam.

(b) Lib. Rub. ca. 55.

¶ *Feial & Loyal.* These words are of great extent, for they extend to the obseruation of the Lords Councell in whatsoeuer is honest and profitable, (b) Omnis homo debet fidem Domino suo de vita & membris suis, & terreno honore, & obseruatione concilij sui per honestum & vtile (comprehended in these words Foyall & Loyall) salua Fide Deo & terræ Principi.

¶ *Seruice.* (c) Seruitium in Lege Angliæ regulariter accipitur pro seruitio quod per tenentes Dominis suis debetur ratione feodi sui: But seruitium est duplex, Spirituale, whereof more shall be said in the Chapter of Frankalmoigne; & Temporale, whereof our Author here treateth: And he beginneth with Homage, first, because it is most honourable, for, Honor plus est in honorante, quam in honorato. 2 It is Pluis humble de reuerence, and both of these for fiue causes on the part of the Tenant. First, The Tenant when he doth his homage is discinctus, disarmed or ungarded. Secondly, Nudo capite, bare headed. Thirdly, Ad pedes Domini super genua proiectus. Fourthly, Ambas manus iunctas inter manus Domini porrigit. Fiftly, Per verba omni supplici veneratione plena, he saith, Ieo deueigne vostre hõe, &c. And for three causes on the part of the Lord: First, The Lord doth sit. Secondly, Hee incloseth his Tenants hands betweene his owne. Thirdly, The Lord sitting kisseth the Tenant. Prudent antiquitie did for the more solemnitie and better memorie and obseruation of that which is to be done, expresse substances under ceremonies.

(c) 2.H.4.6.

Glanuil & Mir. vbi supra.

Nil sine prudenti fecit ratione vetustas.

¶ *Ieo deueigne vostre home de vie & de member.* And therefore he is discinctus, for that he must neuer be armed against, or opposite to his Lord, but both life and member must be readie for the lawfull defence of his Lord.

¶ 2 *De Terrene honor,* Expressed by kneeling at the feet of his Lord.

Bract fo.80. Brit. f.173.b &c. Flet. li.3.ca.16.

3 Debet quidem tenens manus suas vtrasque ponere inter manus vtrasque domini sui per quod significatur ex parte Domini protectio, defensio, & warrantia, & ex parte tenentis reuerentia & subiectio. So as the holding up of the Tenants hands betokeneth reuerence and subiection, and the Lords inclosing of his Tenants hands betweene his owne, betokeneth protection and defence.

¶ 4 *Et a vous serra foyal & loyal, & foy a vous portera, &c.* This faith, Fides, or Fœdus perpetuum, this perpetuall league betweene the Lord and the Tenant, is expressed by the Lords kissing of the Tenant: And some say, That Fœdus dicitur à fide, quia fides interponitur: And so firme and strong was this league betweene them, that by the antient Law of England, Nihil facere potest tenens propter obligationem homagij, quod vertatur Domino ad exhæredationem, vel aliam atrocem iniuriam. Nec Dominus tenenti è conuerso, quod si fecerint dissoluitur & extinguitur homagium omnino & homagij connexio & obligatio & erit inde iustum iudicium cum venerit contra homagium & fidelitatis Sacramentum quod in eo in quo delinquunt puniantur, s. in persona Domini, quod amittat dominium, & in persona tenentis, quod amittat tenementum.

Bract. vb sup Brit. fo.174.

¶ *Des tenements queux ieo claime a tener de vous.* Britton saith, That (a) in doing of homage he must name the Lands or Tenements for which he doth homage in certaintie, and the reason is, Ne in captione homagij contingat Dominum per negligentiam decipi vel per errorem.

(a) Brit vbi sup. Bract. vb sup. Glanuil. li 9. ca.1. Mir. Ca.3. de Homage.

For the better understanding of that which shall be said hereafter, it is to be knowne, That first, there is no land in England in the hands of any Subiect, (as it hath beene said) but it is holden of some Lord by some kind of seruice, as partly hath beene touched before.

Secondly, All the Lands (b) within this realme were originally deriued from the Crowne, and therefore the King is soueraigne Lord, or Lord paramont, either mediate or immediate of all and euery parcell of land within the Realme.

(b) 18.E.3.35. 44.E.3.5. 48.E.3.9. 8.H.7.12.

Thirdly, That in antient time Lords upon the creation of their Tenures did not onely reserue rents, seruices, and profit, &c. for which they might destreyne and haue other remedie, but also tooke an humble submission of his Tenant by promise and oath, (for to homage fealtie is incident) to be true and faithfull to him for the Tenements holden of him, which submission is called homage and fealtie, according to the tenure reserued.

¶ *Salue le foy que ieo doy a nostre Seignior le Roy.* Both because there is Homagium ligeum which is due to the King onely, and also because he is soueraigne Lord ouer all.

Glanuil li.9. ca.1. Mir. cap.3. de Fealtie. Bract. Vbi sup. Brit. vbi sup.

I haue seene an antient Record in Anno 6. Edw.1. in these words, Michael de North qui sequitur pro Rege quæritur quod cum Dominus Rex ratione regiæ dignitatis & Coronæ suæ tale habeat priuilegium quod nullus in regno suo de aliquo qui sit in regno Angliæ alicui homagium facere debeat, vel aliquis huiusmodi homagium ab aliquo recipere debeat nisi facta mentione de homagio Domino Regi debit eidem Domino Regi fideliter obseruand Walterus Exoñ Epus, in

Inter Inquis. apud Lanceston, anno 6.E.1. Cornub. in Thes.

in contemptu domini regis & ad manifestam quoad priuilegium predictum ipsius domini regis exhæredationem, & ad damnum & dedecus ipsius domini regis ad Valenciam decem Mill' librarum de Henrico de Pomeray Thoma de Kanc' Iohanne de bello prato Laurencio filio Ric. Iohanne le Soer, Willielmo de Alex', Eudone de Tranael Rogero le gros, Iohanne le Lunge, Rad'o de Beuill, Guidone Nouant, Willielmo de Rouskerrek, & Hen: Cannel accepit seruitia contra priuilegium predict', nulla facta mentione de homagio & fidelitate domino regi debitis. And iudgement in the end was giuen against the said Bishop.

(d) *Mirror ca.* 1. §. 2. & *ca.* 2 §. 1. & 2. *Bracton fo.* 5. 107. 368. 369. 340. *Fleta. lib.* 1. *cap.* 5. *Fortescu: cap.* 8. & 37. *Stanf. pl. cor.* 58. 99. & *Trer.* 65.
(e) *Glanuill lib.* 9. *ca.* 1. *Bracton fo.* 78. *b.* *Britton. ca.* 68. *fo.* 170. 171. *Fleta lib.* 3. *ca.* 16.
(g) *Glanu l, lib.* 9. *cap.* 1. *Bracton. lib.* 2. 78. *Fleta lib.* 3. *cap* 16. *acc.* 21. *E.* 3. 40. 26. *E.* 3. 63. 64. 32. *E.* 3 *age.* 80. & *tit. per que seruitia.* 9. 13. *H.* 4. 5. 33. *H.* 6. 16. 20. *E.* 3. *per que seruic.* 24.
(h) *Britton fo.* 171.
(i) *Glanuil. lib.* 9. *ca.* 1. *F.N.B.* 157. *Regist.* 296. *Britton ibi supra* *Mirror ca.* 1. §. 3.

¶ *Roy.* Our Ancestors the Saxons termed him Coning or Cyning a name signifying power and skill, which by way of contraction we now call King. This name the Saxons with a small alteration had from the Brittaines who called him Koningh or Konincke; in French he is called Roy, in Italian Re, in Spanish Rey all deriued from the Latyn (Rex) of the true signification whereof you shall reade (d) plentifull matter in our old books.

So as homage is deuided first In homagium ligeum, & non ligeum.

2. In homagium antecessoriū, & non antecessoriū. It is here necessary to be knowne, what tenant, that holdeth by homage shall do homage. (e) Item videndū quis potest homagium facere. Sciendū est quod quilibet liber homo tam masculus quam femina, clericus & laicus, maior & minor, dum tamen electi in episcopos, post consecrationem homagium non faciant, quicquid fecerint ante, sed tantum fidelitatem. Conuentus autem Homagium non faciet de iure sicut nec Abbas, nec Prior eo quod tenent nomine alieno scilicet nomine Ecclesiarum.

(g) One within the age of 21. yeares may doe homage, but Bracton saith hee cannot doe fealty, because in doing of fealty he ought to be sworne which an infant cannot be. But some opinions be in our bookes to the contrary, viz. that an infant shall doe fealtie, but I take it to be meant of homage; and herewith (h) agreeth Britton who saith, Et tout soit que enfant deins age fait homage, pur ceo ne volons nous my que il face serement de fealtie, iesque a taunt que il soit de pleine age; & tout soit ceo comon dit del people que fait de enfant fait deins age ne soit fait my a tener estable: volons nequedent que chescun home & chescun feme de quel age que ils soient, facent homage a lour seigniour solonque lestatut de la grand charter.

Glanvill saith. (i) women shall not doe homage, but Littleton saith that a woman shall doe homage, but she shall not say, Ieo deveigne vostre feme, but Ieo face a vous homage, and so is Glanuill to be understood, that she shall not doe compleate homage.

Sect. 86.

¶ Mes si vn Abbe, ou vn Pryor, ou auter hōe de religion ferra homage a son seignior, il ne dirra: Ieo deueigne vostre home, &c. pur ceo q̄ il ad luy professe pur estre tant solement le home de Dieu: mes il dirra issint, Ieo vous face homage & a vous serra foial & loial, & foy a vous portera des tenements que ieo teigne de vous, salue la foy que ieo doy a nostre Seignior le Roy.

BVt if an Abbot or a Pryor or other man of religion shall doe homage to his Lord, he shall not say, I become your man, &c. for that hee hath professed himselfe to be only the man of God. But hee shall say thus. I doe homage vnto you, and to you I shall bee true and faithfull, and faith to you beare for the tenements which I hold of you (sauing the faith which I doe owe vnto our Lord the King.

(k) *Glanuill lib.* 1. *cap.* 9. *in fine.* *Britton lib.* 2. 78. *Bracton cap.* 68. *Fleta lib.* 3. *cap.* 16.
(l) *Vid. Sect.* 96. & 133.

¶ No man of Religion when (k) hee doth homage shall say, Ieo deueigne vostre home, because hee hath professed himselfe the man of God, yet shall he doe homage, and shall say, (l) Ieo face a vous homage, & à vous serra foyall & loyall, &c. and note that here religion is taken largely, for it extends not only to regular persons as Abbots and the like, but also to all Ecclesiasticall persons, as Bishops, Deanes or any other sole Ecclesiasticall body politique, and so it is in vse at this day which also appeareth in our old bookes.

And it is to bee obserued that in old bookes and records, the homage which a Bishop, Abbot or other man of religion doth is called Fealtie, for that it wanteth these words (Ieo deveigne vostre home.) But yet in iudgement of law it is homage, because he saith (I doe to you homage, &c. and so of a woman.

Sect. 87.

Pur ceo que neſt conuenient, &c. **By this it appeareth** (m) **that** argumentum ab inconuenienti plurimum valet in lege, **as often ſhall bee obſerued hereafter.** Non ſolum quod licet, ſed quid eſt conueniens eſt conſiderandum, nihil quod eſt inconueniens eſt licitum.

(m) *For like reaſons ab inconuenienti. Vid. Sect.* 138. 139. 231. 269. 440. 478. 665. 722. 730. 21.*H*.7.13. *F.N.B.*230.*d.* 16.*H*.7.9.

Item ſi feme ſole ferra homage a ſon ſeignior, el ne dirra: Jeo deueigne voſtre feme, pur ceo que neſt conuenient que feme dirra q̃l el deuiendra feme a aſcun home forſque a ſa baron quant el eſt eſpouſe, mes el dirra: Jeo face a vous homage, & a vous ſerra foial & loial, & foy a vous portera des tenements que ieo teigne de vous, ſalue la foy que ieo doy a noſtre ſeignior le Roy.

ALſo if a woman ſole ſhall [illegible] doe homage, ſhee ſhall not ſay I become your woman, for it is not fitting that a woman ſhould ſay that ſhe will become a woman to any man but to her husband when ſhee is married, but ſhe ſhall ſay, I doe to you homage, and to you ſhall bee faithfull and true and faith to you ſhall beare for the tenements I hold of you. Sauing the faith I owe to our Soueraigne Lord the King.

Sect. 88.

Item home puit veier en vn bone note M.15.E.3. Lou vn home & ſa feme fiſt homage & fealty en le common banke, q̃l eſt eſcrie en tiel form̃. Nota que J. Leukner & Elizabeth ſa feme, fiſt homage a W. Thorpe en ceſt maner, lun & lauſt tiendront iointm̃t lour mains enter les mains W. T. & le baron dit en ceſt forme: Nous vous ferromus homage, & foy a vous porterons, pur les tenements q̃ nous teignomus de A. vr̃e conuſor, q̃ a vous ad graunt noſtre ſeruices en B. & C. et auters villes, &c.

ALſo a man may ſee a good note in M. 15.E.3. where a man and his wife did homage and fealtie in the Common place which is written in this forme. Note that *I. Lewknor* & *Eliz.* his wife did homage to *W. Thorpe* in this manner. The one and the other held their hands ioyntly betweene the hands of *W.T.* and the husband ſaith in this forme. Wee doe to you homage, and faith to you ſhall beare for the tenements which wee hold of *A.* your Conuſor, who hath granted to you our ſeruices in *B.* and *C.* and other townes, &c. againſt all nations,

In this (n) **record three things are to bee obſerued.**

1. How neceſſary, and profitable records and obſeruations are; albeit they were not publiſhed in print, for at the time when Litleton **wrote, this record was not printed.**

2. That the husband and wife doing homage, the husband ſhall ſpeake the words for them both, viz. **(Wee doe you homage, &c.**

3. That the homage which the husband and wife doe, is the very homage which the wife ſhould doe alone but this ioynt homage done by the husband and wife is intended to bee before iſſue had betweene them whereof more ſhall bee ſaid hereafter. (o) **And it is to bee obſerued that very**

(n) *Mich.*15.*E.*3. *tit.* [illegible] 109.

(o) *Vid. Hill.* 17.*E.*2. *Rot. Perlia. &c.*

very few cases ruled or resolued in the raigne of Edward the Third, but the same or the like had been ruled or resolued in the Raignes of Edward the Second, Edward the First, or before, as for example for warrant hereof.

encounter touts gents: salue la foy que nous deuons a nostre Seignior le Roy, & a ses heires, & a nostre auters seigniors: & lun & lauter luy baserôt, En puis ils fect fealtie, et lun et lauter tyendrôt lour mains sur vn liure, & le barõ dit les polx, et ambidẽ baseront le liu.

sauing the faith which we owe to our Lord the King and to his heires, and to our other Lords, and both the one and the other kissed him. And after they did fealtie, and both of them hold their hands vpon the Booke, and the husband said the words, and both kissed the Book.

Sect. 89.

¶ *Et a mes auters Seigniours.* This sauing for other Lords is good for explanation, albeit the homage is referred only to the Tenements which he holdeth of him to whom he doth the homage.

¶ NOta si vn home ad seueral tenancies queux il tient de seuerals Seigniors, s. chescun tenancy per homage, donque quant il fait homage a vn des Seigniors, il dirra en le fine de son homage fait, salue la foy que ieo doy a nostre Seignior le Roy, & a mes auters Seigniors.

NOte if a man hath seuerall Tenancies which he holdeth of seuerall Lords, that is to say, euery tenancie by homage, then when hee doth homage to one of his Lords, hee shall say in the end of his homage done, sauing the faith which I owe to our Lord the King, and to my other Lords.

Sect. 90.

¶ EN *droit dun auter.* As the Husband and wife in the right of his wife; the Bishop in right of his Bishoprike, &c. the Abbot or Prior in right of his Monasterie, &c. But no Corporation aggregate of many persons capable, bee the same Ecclesiasticall or Temporall can doe homage, as a Deane and Chapter, Maior, and Comminaltie; and such like, albeit they bee seised in fee of lands holden by homage yet shall not they doe homage. And the reason is because that homage must be done in person, and a Corporation aggregate of many cannot ap-

(p) 33. H. 8. tit. fealtie Br. 13. Lib. 4. fol. 11. Lib. 7. fol. 10. Lib. 10. fol. 31.

¶ NOta que nul ferra homage, mes tiel que ad estate en fee simple, ou en fee taile, en son droit demesne, ou en droit dun auter. Car il est vn Maxime en ley que il q̃ ad estate forsq; pur terme de vie, ne ferra homage, ne prendra homage. Car si feme ad terres ou tenements en fee simple, ou ẽ fee taile,

NOte, none shall do homage but such, as haue an estate in fee simple, or fee taile in his owne right, or in the right of another. For it is a maxime in law, that hee which hath an estate but for terme of life, shall neither doe homage or take homage. For if a woman hath lands or tenements in fee simple or in fee taile

queux

queux el tient de son Seignior per homage, & prent baron, & ont issue, donque le baron en la vie la feme ferra homage, pur ceo que il ad title davoir les tenements per le curtesie Dengleterre sil survesquist la feme, & auxy il tient en droit de sa feme. Mes si la feme deux devant homage fait per le baron en la vie sa feme, & le baron soy tient eins come tenant per le curtesie, donques il ne ferra homage a son seignior, pur ceo que il adonque nad estate forsque pur terme de vie.

which shee holdeth of her Lord by homage and taketh husband, & haue issue, then the husband in the life of the wife shall doe homage, because he hath title to haue the tenements by the curtesie of Eng. if he suruiueth his wife, and also hee holdeth in right of his wife, but if the wife dies before homage done by the husband in the life of his wife, and the husband holdeth himselfe in as tenant by the curtesie, then hee shall not doe homage to his Lord, because hee then hath an estate but for terme of life.

¶ Plus serra dit de homage en le tenure per homage auncestrel.

¶ More shall bee said of homage in the tenure of homage ancestrell.

peare in person, for albeit the bodies naturall whereupon the bodie Politique consists may bee seene, yet the bodie Politique or Corporate it selfe cannot bee seene, nor doe any act but by Atturney, and homage, must euer be done in person, &c. And albeit an Abbot and Couent is a Corporation aggregate of many, yet because the Couent are all dead persons in law, the Abbot alone in nature of a sole Corporation shall doe homage.

¶ *Vn maxime en Ley.* A maxime is a proposition, to bee of all men confessed & granted without proofe, argument, or discourse Contra negantem principia non est disputandum. But of this somewhat hath beene said before.

¶ *Il que ad estate forsque pur terme de vie.* (q) A Parson or Vicar of a Church that hath a qualified fee, (r) and yet to many intents upon the matter but an estate for life can neither receiue homage nor doe homage as a Bishop an Abbot, or any such like that hath a fee absolute may. (s) So if a man and his wife be seised in fee of a Seigniorie in the right of his wife, the husband shall not receiue homage alone but he and his wife together. (t) But if the husband in that case hath issue by his wife, then he shall receiue homage alone during the life of his wife, and the reason is because he by hauing of issue is intitled to an estate for terme of his owne life, in his owne right, and yet is seised in fee in the right of his wife, so as he is not a bare tenant for life. But if his wife die, then he hath only but an estate for life, and then he cannot receiue homage. Yet tenant for life or yeares of a Seigniorie, (u) shall haue ward, Marriage and Reliefe, and shall suppose that the Tenant died in the fealtie of the Pl. (w) Fieri possunt homagia libero homini tam masculo quàm feminæ tam Maiori quàm minori tam clerico quam laico.

(q) Glanuil. lib. 9. cap. 2. Britton. fol. 170. Temps E. 1. tit. Iuris vtrum 13. (r) 8 E. 4. 28. 39. E. 3. 15. 3. E. 3. auowrie 175.

(s) 2. E. 2. auowrie 183. F. N. B. 257. 13. E. 3. gard. 39.

(t) 27. Ass. p. 51. F. N. B. 257. 13. H. 6. auowrie 21. 43. E. 3. 13. 44. E. 3. 41. 3. E. 3. auowrie 175. 13. E. 3. 2. gard. 39. 22. E. 3. fol. 19. gard. 44. (u) 6. E. 2. gard. 122. 13. E. 3. gard 39. 22. E. 3. gard. 44. (w) Glanuil lib. 9. cap. 3. 18. E. 3. 7. 43. E. 3. 13. 44. E. 3. 41. 13. H. 6. auowrie. 21. 8. H. 6. 13. 7. E. 4. 27. F. N. B. 257.

¶ *Et ount issue, donque le baron en la vie la feme ferra homage.* The reason hereof is rendred before, & also that after the death of his wife he being but a bare tenant for life shall doe no homage; for regularly it is true that hee that cannot receiue homage in respect of the weaknesse of his estate in the Seigniorie, shall not do homage if he hath a like estate in the tenancie.

If a man hold of the King and hath issue diuers daughters and dieth, the King shall haue homage of euery one of these Daughters And this (a) appeareth by the Statute de Hibernia anno 14. H. 3. to be the Common Law, for that Act saith. In regno nostro Angliæ talis est lex & consuetudo quod si quis tenuerit de nobis in capite, & habuerit filias herædes ipso patre defuncto antecessores nostri habuerunt & semper nos habuimus & cepimus homagium de omnibus huiusmodi filiabus, & singulæ earum tenerent de nobis in capite in hoc casu. And therefore where by the (b) Statute De prærogatiua Regis, it is prouided, Si vna hæreditas, &c. that is but an affirmance of the Common Law. (c) But this is to bee understood where the coheires be of full age, for if they within age and in ward to the King, Primogenita tantum faciet homa-

(a) 14. H. 3. tit. prærog. 5.

(b) Prærog. Regis cap. 5.
(c) Statut. de homagio capiendo Temps E. 1.

homagium pro se & sororibus suis, & aliæ sorores cum ad ætatem peruenerint faciet seruitia Dominis fœdorum per manum primogenitæ. (d) And therefore if a man holds of a common person by the seruice of homage, and hath issue diuers daughters and dieth, the eldest daughter only shall doe homage for her and all her sisters. And this appeareth also by the Statute of Hibernia. Primogenita tantum faciet homagium Domino pro se & omnibus sororibus suis. And the reason is there rendred afterward, Quia omnes sorores sunt quasi vnus hæres de vna hæreditate. (e) But if the Coparceners in that case make partition, then euery one shall doe homage, because now it is not Vna sed diuersa hæreditas (f) And so it is if, one make a feoffment in fee (which is a partition in law for that part) that feoffee shall doe homage, for euery Tenant in common shall doe seuerall seruices. And it hath beene adiudged (g) in our Bookes that if the eldest Coparcener doe homage to the Lord, and afterwards the younger sister maketh a feoffment in fee of her part, the Lord shall haue homage for the part of the younger sister, for that which was vna hæreditas, one Inheritance by law, by the alienation which is her act is (as hath beene said) diuided and become in grosse and the Coparcenarie defeated.

(d) Glanuill. lib. 7. cap. 3. & lib. 9. cap. 2. Bract. lib. 1. de homag. cap. end. & lib. 2. fol. 78. 82. Britton. fol. 168. b. 171. 172. Fleta lib. 3. cap. 16. & lib. 2. cap. 60. & lib. 5. ca. 9. F.N.B. 161. 159. 259. Staunf. prær. 23. 24.
(e) F.N.B. 162. Vide 11. E. 3. auowrie. 101.
(f) 45. E. 3. 23. 24. E. 3. 73. Marlbridge cap. 9. F.N.B. 162.
(g) 2. E. 2. auowrie. 179.

But if Tenant enfeoffe diuers men in fee iointly, (h) all these iointenants shall iointly doe their homage, and their fealtie also. (i) If homage bee due by the Tenant, and hee maketh a feoffment in fee, the Feoffor shall not doe homage, because albeit he is supposed to be Tenant in some Cases quant al auowrie, yet the Feoffee is very Tenant, and homage shall euer bee done by the verie Tenant, but that very Tenant needeth not to be very Tenant of the Land, and therefore the Mesne because he is very Tenant to the Lord Paramont (though he be not Tenant of the land) shall doe homage. And so it is of the Disseisee, and of Tenant in taile, after a feoffment in fee, for in that case the Donee is very Tenant to the Donor.

(h) 7. E. 4. 27. 28. 14. H. 4. 38. 1. H. 5. grant. 43. 31. E. 3. gard. 116.
(i) 48. E. 3. 8. 15. E. 4. 13. 5. E. 4. 3.

If a Tenant that holdeth by homage maketh a feoffment in fee of part (k) that Feoffee shall doe homage, and so shall euery Feoffee of what part soeuer.

(k) 22. E. 4. 22.

If there be two Coparceners or Iointenants of a Seigniorie, if the Tenant doth homage and fealtie to one of them (l) he shall be excused against the other.

If homage be parcell of a tenure, it is a presumption that the tenure is by Knights seruice, vnles the contrarie be proued, but of it selfe it maketh not Knights seruice. And yet by custome the heire of him that holds by homage only may be in ward.

More shall be said of homage in the title of homage ancestrell.

(l) 3. E. 2. auowrie 187. 13. H. 4. 5. 13. R. 2. tit. auowrie 89. 8. H. 3. tit. prescription 38. Hill. 22. E. 1. coram Rege Rot. 43.

Chap. 2. Section 91.

Fealtie.

¶ Fealtie, idem est quod fidelitas en Latin, Et quant franktenant ferra fealtie a son Seignior, il tiendra sa maine dexter sur vn Lieur et dirra issint; Ceo oyes vous mon Seignior, que ieo a vous serra foial et loial, et foy a vous portera des tenements que ieo claim a tener de vous, et que loialment a vous ferra les customes et seruices que faire a vous doy as termes assignes, sicome moy aide Dieu et ses

Fealtie is the same that *fidelitas* is in Latine. And when a freeholder doth fealtie to his Lord, he shall hold his right hand vpon a Booke, and shall say thus. Know ye this my Lord, that I shall bee faithfull and true vnto you, and faith to you shall beare for the Lands which I claime to hold of you, and that I shall lawfully do to you the customes and seruices which I ought to doe at the termes assigned, so helpe me God and his Saints, &c.

¶ *Fealtie* in French is feaulty, and is (a) deriued of the Latine word fides, or fidelitas.

(a) Bract. lib. 2. fol. 80. Britton. Regist. origin. 302. Mirror. cap. 3. de serement, & de fealt. Statut. de 17. E. 2. tit. homage.

¶ *Et quant franktenant.* Euery Freeholder except Tenant in Frankalmoigne shall doe Fealtie. (b) And yet some that are not tenants of any Freehold shall doe fealtie, as a tenant for yeares shall doe fealtie. Bracton saith, De nullo tenemento quod tenetur ad terminum, fit homagij sit tamen inde fidelitatis Sacramentum.

(b) Bracton. lib. 2. fol. 80. a. Britton. fol. 173. Fleta lib. 3. cap. 16. Littleton. fol. 29. nu. 132. 40. E. 3. 34. 9. H. 6. 43. 10. H. 6. 13. 5. H. 5. 12. 9. E. 4. 1. 21. E. 4. 29. 5. H. 7. 11.

¶ *Que a vous serra foial & loial, &c. & foy a vous portera des tenements que ieo claime a tener de vous, & que loialment a vous ferra les customes & seruices, &c.*

(c) Fealtie is a part of homage, for all the words of Fealtie are comprehended within homage, and therefore fealtie is incident to Homage.

(c) *Mirror, cap.3. de serend. & de Fealtie.*

¶ *Sicome moy aide Dieu.* As homage is the more honourable service, so Fealtie is a seruice more sacred because he is sworne thereunto. And the reason wherefore the Tenant is not sworne in doing his homage to his Lord is, for that no subiect is sworne to another subiect to become his man of life and member but to the King only, and that is called the oath of Allegiance or homagium ligeum. And those words for that purpose are omitted out of Fealtie, which is to be done vpon oath. And Littleton said well (when a Freeholder doth Fealtie) (d) for the Fealtie of him that holdeth in Villenage differeth from the fealtie of the Freeholder. For the Villeine holding his right hand vpon the booke shall say thus to his Lord, Heare you my Lord A. that I A B. from this day forward shall be to you true and faithfull, and shall owe you Fealtie for the land that I hold of you in Villenage and shalbe iustified by you in body and goods so helpe me God, &c. as by the act appeareth.

(d) *Stat. de 17. E. 2. tit. Homage, in le abridgement.*

Section 92.

¶ Et graund diuersitie y ad perenter feasans de fealtie et de homage, car homage ne poit estre fait forsque al Seigniour: Mes le Seneschal de court le Seignior, ou Bailife, puit prender fealtie pur le Seignior.

And there is great diuersitie beetweene the doing of fealty, and of homage; for homage cannot be done to any but to the Lord himselfe, but the steward of the Lords Court, or Bailife may take fealtie for the Lord.

¶ Bracton lib. 2. fo. 80. saith thus; Sciendum est quod non per procuratores nec per litteras fieri poterit homagium sed in propria persona tam domini quam tenentis, capi debet & fieri.

Bracton. lib. 2. fo. 8. 21. E. 4. 17. acc. 2. E. 3. 10. 32. H. 6. 23. lib. 9. fo. 76.

¶ *Mes le seneschal &c. ou Bailife poet prender fealtie.* This is so euident as it needeth no explanation.

(e) *Vid For the signification of Seneschal and Bailife Sect. 78. 79. 248. & 379.*

Sect. 93.

¶ Item tenant a terme de vie ferra fealtie, et uncore il ne ferra homage. Et diuers auters diuersities y sont perenter homage et fealtie.

Also tenant for terme of life shall doe fealtie, and yet hee shall not doe Homage. And diuers other diuersities there be between Homage and fealtie.

¶ The Tenant must do fealtie in person because hee must bee sworne vnto it, and no man can sweare by the Common Law by Attorney or Procter.

Lib. 9. fo. 76.

Section 94.

¶ Item home poit veier 15. E. 3. coment home et sa feme fieront homage et fealtie en common banke, quel est escript deuant en Tenure de homage.

Also a man may see in 15. *E.* 3. how a man and his wife shall doe homage and fealty in the Common place, which is written before in the tenure of Homage.

¶ This is euident and appeareth before, and if Lords knew what benefit they may reape by receiuing of Homage and Fealtie they would not neglect them, (e) for by the receiuing of either of them, it is a sufficient seisin of all manner of seruices as by the words (f) of either of them appeareth. Now if it be demanded, what

(e) *Lib. 4. fo. 8. & 9. Bevills case. 13. E. 4. 5.*

(f) *Vid. Sect. 113. 130. 131. 138.*

What difference is betweene the oath of Fealtie, when it is done to the King in respect of a Tenure, and the oath which euerie Subiect ought to take in respect of his allegeance, Littleton here setteth downe the oath of Fealtie. Now the (g) Oath of Allegeance is thus, You shall sweare, &c.

Plus serra dit de Fealtie en le tenure en Socage, & en l'tenure en Frankealmoigne, & en le tenure per homage Auncestrel.

More shall bee sayd of Fealtie in the Tenure in Socage, and in Frankealmoigne, and in the Tenure by homage Auncestrell.

Then it may be demanded, where and when is this oath to be taken, and it is answered, That whosoeuer is aboue the age of twelue yeares, is to be sworne in the Tourne, vnlesse hee bee within some Leet, and then in the Leet: And I read amongst the lawes of Saint Edward, Quod hanc Legem inuenit Arthurus, qui quondam fuit inclitissimus Rex Britanorum, & ita consolidauit & confederauit Regnum Britanniæ vniuersum semper in vnum. Huius legis authoritate expulit Arthurus prædictus Saracenos & inimicos a regno. Lex enim ista diu sopita fuit & sepulta donec Eadgarus Rex Anglorum excitarit, & erexit in lucem, & illam per totum Regnum obseruari pręcepit. Which law in some maner is obserued at this day. But to returne to Littleton.

(g) Brit ca. 29. Caluins case, li. 7. fo. 6. b. 12. H. 7. 18.

Lambert 135.

¶ Escuage. (a) In Latine Scutagium, (id est) Seruitium scuti, Seruice of the Shield, hereby it appeareth, that right interpretations and etymologies are necessarie: For, ad recte docendum oportet primum inquirere nomina, quia rerum cognitio a nominibus rerum dependet.

Nomina si nescis, perit cognitio rerum.

And herewith agreeth that which is said, Primo excutienda est verbi vis ne sermonis vitio obstruetur oratio, siue lex siue argumentis.

Scutum in French is Escue, and thereof commeth the Escuer, (i.) Scutifer, which wee vsually call Armiger. (b) Of this Bracton saith, Item scutagium dicitur quòd talis præstatio ptinet ad scutum quòd assumitur & seruitium militare. And Fleta saith, Sunt quædam seruitia forinseca, & dici possunt regalia quæ ad scutum præstantur, & inde habemus scutagium, & ratione scuti pro feodo militari reputatur. And Ockam saith, Hæc itaq; summa quia nomine scutorum soluitur, scutagium nuncupatur.

(a) Mir. ca. 1. §. 3. Brit fo. 162. &c. Ockam cap. Quid sit scutagium.

(b) Bract. li. 2. fo. 35. a. Flet. li. 3. ca. 14. Ockam vbi supr. 27. Ass. 52. 31. Ass. 38.

CEscuage est appel en Latine Scutagium, cestascauoire, Seruitium Scuti. Et tiel tenant que tient sa terre per Escuage, tient p seruice de Chiualer. Et auxy il est communement dit, que ascun tient per vn fee d seruice de Chiualer, Et ascun per le moity dun fee d Seruice d chiualer, &c. Et il est dit, que quant le Roy face voyage royall en Escoce pur subduer les Scotes, donqs il que tient per vn fee de Seruice de chiualer, couient estē oue le Roy per 40. iours, bien et cōuenablement array pur le Guerre. Et celuy que tient sa Terre per le

Escuage is called in Latine, *Scutagium*, that is, Seruice of the Shield; and that Tenant which holdeth his Land by Escuage, holdeth by Knights seruice. And also it is commonly said, That some hold by the seruice of one Knights fee, and some by the halfe of a Knights Fee. And it is said, That when the King makes a voyage royall into Scotland to subdue the Scots, then he which holdeth by the seruice of one Knights Fee, ought to be with the King fortie dayes, well and conueniently arrayed for the War: and hee which holdeth his land by the moity of a Knights

moitie dun Fee de chiualer couient estre oue le Roy per 20. iours. Et il que tient son Terre per le quart part dun Fee de chiualer couient estre oue le Roy per 10. iours, et issint que pluis, pluis, et que meins, meins.

fee, ought to bee with the King twentie dayes: and hee which holdeth his land by the fourth part of a Knights fee, ought to be with the King ten dayes, and so he that hath more, more, and he that hath lesse, lesse.

¶ (c) *Et tiel tenaunt que tient son terre per Escuage tient per seruice de Chiualer.* (d) For as Fealty is incident to homage, so homage and Knight Seruice be incident to Escuage, and by the grant of Seruices, Escuage passeth with the rest. Euerie Tenure by Escuage is a tenure by Knights Seruice: but euerie Tenant that holdeth by Knights seruice, holdeth not by Escuage, as shall be said hereafter. But note here the wisedome of Antiquitie, (e) mavult enim Princeps domesticos quam stipendiarios bellicis apponere casibus, that is, to be serued in his warres by his owne subiects, rather than by stipendarie Foreners.

(c) *Mir. ca. 1. §. 3.*

(d) 2. E. 3. 8. b. 19. E. 3. *Auowrie* 294. 26. *H.* 8. 1. a. 20 *E.* 3. *Per qua Seruic.* 11. 43. *E.* 3. 22. *F. N. B.* 83. 84.

(e) *Lib. rub.*

¶ *Vn fee de seruice de Chiualer.* (f) There is great diuersitie of opinions concerning the Contents of a Knights Fee, that is, how much land goeth to the liuelyhood of a Knight; for some say that a Knights fee consisteth of eight hides, and euery hide conteyneth an hundred acres, and so a Knights fee should containe 800. acres; others say that a Knights fee containeth 680. acres; others say that an organge of lands containeth 15. acres, and eight organgs make a plowland; by which account a plowland containes 120. acres, and that virgata terre, or a yard land containeth 20. acres. But I hold that a Knights fee, an hide or plowland a yardland or Organge of land doe not containe any certaine number of acres. But a knights fee is properly to be esteemed according to the qualitie and not according to the quantitie of the land, that is to say, by the value and not by the content. And therefore it is very true which Master Camden in his Brittannia pa. 136. saith, viz. Subsequenti ætate ex censu vt colligitur facti fuerunt equites, &c. And Antiquitie thought that twenty pound land was sufficient to maintaine the degree of a Knight, as appeareth in the ancient treatise de modo tenendi Parliamentum tempore regis Edw: filij regis Etheldredi. Where it appeareth that comitatus (to wit) an Earledome constat ex viginti feodis vnius militis, quolibet feodo computato ad viginti libratas: Baronia constat ex 13. feodis, & 3. parte vnius feodi militis secundum computationem predictam; Vnum feodum militis constat ex terris ad valentiam 20. l. Which Antiquitie I cite for that it concurreth with the act of Parliament, anno 1. E. 2. de militibus, by which act Census militaris the state of a Knight is measured by the value of xx. pound per annum, and not by any certaine content of acres; and with this agreeth the statute of W. 1. cap. 35. and F. N. B. fol. 82. where twenty pound of land in Socage is put in Equipage of a Knights fee, and this is the most reasonable estimate, for one acre may be better then many others, so as he which hath 680. or 800. acres of some barren land had not according to the ancient account a sufficient reuenue to maintaine the degree of a Knight, and he which had a lesse number of acres of some land of the value of xx. pound per annum had a sufficient liuelyhood in those dayes for the maintainance of a Knight. So Antiquity thought that 400. markes of land per Annum was a competent liuelihood for a Baron and 400. pound per annum, Ad sustinendum nomen & onus of an Earle, and of late time 800. markes per Annum of a Marquesse, and 800. pound per Annum of a Duke, so that their yearely reuenue was estimated by the value and not by the content. And one plowland, carucata terræ, or a hide of land, hida terræ (which is all one) is not of any certaine content, but as much as a plow can by course of husbandry plow in a yeare. And therewith agreeth Lambard verbo Hide. And a plow land may containe a messuage wood meadow and pasture, because that by them the plowmen and the cattell belonging to the plow are maintained. Vide Temps E. 1. tit. Briefe 860. 4. E. 3. 47. Pl. com. in Hill and Granges case, fo. 168. Vid. 6. E. 3. fo. 42. and 39. H. 6. 8. 2. And venerable Beda calleth a Plowland familiam a family, because it containeth necessary things for the maintenance of a family. And Prisot well saith in 35. H. 6. fo. 29 that a plow may till more land in a yeare in one Country then in another, and therefore it stands with reason, that a plowland should be lesse in one place than in another. 41. E. 3. tit. fine 40. and 11. E. 3. fine 67. A fine shall not be receiued De vna virgata terræ for the vncertaintie vid. 39. H. 6, 8. But an acre of land is certaine by the statute De terris mensurandis. Note also (Reader) that euery plowland of ancient time was of the yearely value of fiue nobles per Annum, and these was the liuing of a plowman or Yeoman, and Ex duodecim carucatis constabat vnum feodum militis which amount to 20. pound per Annum. And this you may see Termino pasch. anno 3. E. 1. Coram Rogero de Seyton & socijs suis Iusticiarijs apud

(f) *Lib. 9. fo. 123. in Lowes case.*

Vid. lib. 7. fol. 33. 34. Neuils case.

Westm. Ebor. Ro. 10. Radulphus de Normanville petens in brevi de medio queritur contra Luciam de Kyme quod cum ipsa teneat de ipso duas carectatas terræ in Coningston per homagium & servitium militare, unde duodecim carucatæ terræ faciunt unum feodum militis pro omni servitio, ipsa distrinxit ipsum ad faciendũ sectam ad curiam suam de Thorneton in Craven, &c.

And it is to be observed that the reliefe of a Knight and all above him which be noble, is the fourth part of their yearely Revenue, as of a Knight five pound which is the fourth part of 20. pound. So Una baronia constat ex 13 feodis militum & de 3. parte unius feodi militis, which amount to 400. Markes, and therefore his reliefe is the fourth part of this, viz. 100, markes; and an Earledome consists of twenty Knights fees which amount to 400. pound (as before it appeareth by the said ancient Record De modo tenendi Parliamentum, &c.) and therefore his reliefe is 100. pound. And this also appeareth by the statute of Magna Carta, cap. 2. and by the equitie of this statute, insomuch as a Marquisdome which consists of the revenue of two Baronies which amount to 800. markes, shall pay according to that just proportion for his releife 200, markes, and because a Dukedome consist of the revenues of two Earledomes, viz. 800. pound per Annum, a Duke shall pay 200. for a relife, which is also the fourth part of his revenue, and with this agree the Records of the Exchequer.

Note (Reader) At the time of the making of the statute of Magna Carta, 5.9. H 3. there was not any Duke, Marquesse or Vicount in England (and therefore the statute could not make mention of them) and Edward the eldest sonne of King E. 3. called the blacke Prince was the first Duke in England after the Conquest, and Robert Earle of Oxford in the raigne of R. 2. was the first Marquesse. Sic enim inter ordines Angliæ in sua Brittannia testatur Camden ubi supra. Et titulus Marchionis serius ad nos devenit, nec ante R. 2. tempore cuiquam delatus ille enim Robertum Vere Oxoniæ comitem delicias suas primum marchionem Dubliniæ designavit, merumque erat honoris nomen, Hæc, ille. And before the raigne of H. 6 there was not any Viscount. Sic enim idem Author ubi supra asserit. Post comites vicecomites ordine sequuntur Vicounts nos vocamus; hæc vetus officij sed nova dignitatis appellatio, & H. 6. tempore ad nos primum audita, Hæc ille, Et dominus de Bello monte was the first Viscount Created by King H. 6. Vide Cassianeum in gloria mundi parte 4. considef 55. that this Dignity of a Viscount is of great antiquitie in other Realmes.

7 H.4.9. 31. Ass. 30. 26. Ass. 66. 27. Ass. 52. 8. E.3. 154.

Bracton lib. 2. 36. Item sunt quædam servitia quæ dicuntur forinseca, quamvis sunt in carta de feoffamentis expressa & nominata, & quæ ideo dici possunt forinseca, quia pertinent ad dominum regem, & non ad dominum capitalem, nisi cum in propria persona profectus fuerit in servitio, vel nisi cum pro servitio suo satisfecerit domino regi, &c.

7. E.3.29. 21. H.4.7. F.N.B. 28.b. & 83.g. 3. H.4.16. 28. H.6.1.b. 39. H.6.38. 6. R.2. protection. 46. 19. R.2. gard. 165. 27. H.6. Protection 56. 7. E.4.27. 11. H.4.7. 3. H.4.16.

¶ *Voyage royall.* **A voyage royall is not only when the King** himselfe goeth to warre, as Littleton here saith, but also when his Lieftenant or Deputy of his Lieftenant goeth. And what shall be said a Voyage royall shall be adiudged in this case by the Judges of the Common Law as an incident to Escuage and not by the Constable and Marshall or any other, & sic de similibus.

There is also another kinde of Voyage Royall, viz. when one goeth with the Kings daughter beyond sea to be married, &c. for such a voyage is for the good of the whole Realme, (for more proffit for the Realme cannot be then to make alliance with another Nation, but of this Voyage Royall Littleton speaketh not here, but only of the Voyage Royall to warre; so as there is a Voyage Royall of warre, and a Voyage Royall of peace and amitie. And it is to be observed that he that holdeth by Castle gard or cornage holdeth by Knights service, and yet hee shall pay no Escuage because he holdeth not to goe with the King to warre.

Lib. Rub in Scacc. 47.48. 19. R.2. gard. 95. 6. R 2. Protection 46. 6. H.3. Avowrie 242. Vid. Rot. Clauss. 8. H.3. & Finium 8. H.3. & patent. 9. H.3. multi solverunt scutagium pro exercit. in Walliam. memb. 30. & ante. Clauss. 6. H.3. memb. 3.

¶ *En Escoce.* In Scotiam, **this is put but for an example, for if the** tenure be to go in Walliam Hiberniã Vasconiã, Pictaviã, &c. it is all one. See an ancient record Rott. De finibus Termino, Mich. 11. E. 2 Sir Rich: Rockesley Knight did hold lands at Seaton by Serjanty to be Vantrarius Regis, that is to be the Kings fore-footman when the King went into Gascoigne, donec per usus fuit pari solutarum precij 4. d. that is untill he had worne out a paire of shoes of the price of foure pence. And this service being admitted to be performed when the King went to Gascoigne to make warre, is Knight service.

¶ *Il que tient per un fee de seruice de chivalier covient este ove le Roy per 40. iours.* **But this is to be understood of a Tenant that holdeth of** the King immediately, for every man is bound by his tenure to defend his Lord, and both hee and his Lord the King and his Countrie, and therefore if the Lord goeth not his tenant is excused. But yet if the tenant peravaile goeth with the King, it excuseth all the meanes

Magna Carta cap. 37. Fleta lib. cap. 60.

And it is to be observed that for every pound of the ancient value of a Knights fee accounting twenty pound land, the Tenant must goe with the King two dayes, which commeth just to 40. dayes for a whole Knights fee by the Statute of Magna Carta it is provided that scutagium de ceter' capiatur sicut capi consueuit tempore Henr. regis avi nostri.

Section 96.

MEs il appiert p les plees & arguments faits en vn bon plee sur briefe de Detinue de vn escript obligatorie port per vn H: Gray T.7.E.3. que ne besoigne a celuy q̃ tient per Escuage de aler oue le Roy luy mesm, sil voile trouer vn auter person able pur luy conuenablement array pur le guerre, de aler oue le Roy. Et ceo semble estre bon reason, car poit estre q̃ celuy que tient per tiels seruices est languishant, issint q̃ il ne poit aler ne chiuaucher. Et auxy vn Abbe, ou auter home de Religion, ou feme sole q̃ tient per tiels seruices, ne doit en tiel cas aler en proper person. Et Sir W. Herle adonque chiefe Justice d̃ common bank, disoit en tiel plee, que escuage ne serra graunt, mes lou le Roy alast luy mesme en son proper person. Et fuit demurre en iudgement en mesme le plee, le quel les xl. iours serront accompts de le primer iour del mu-

BVut it appeareth by the pleas and arguments made in a plea vpon a Writte of detinue of a writing obligatorie brought by one *H.Gray 7.E.3.* that it is not needfull for him which holdeth by Escuage to goe himselfe with the King if hee will finde another able person for him conueniently arrayed for the warre to goe with the King. And this seemeth to be good reason. For it may be that he which holdeth by such seruices is languishing, so as he can neither goe nor ride. And also an Abbot or other man of Religion, or a feme sole, which hold by such seruices ought not in such case to goe in proper person. And Sir *William Herle* then chiefe Iustice of the Common place said in this plea, that escuage shall not bee granted but where the King goes himselfe in his proper person. And it was demured in iudgement in the same plea, whither the 40. dayes should bee accounted from the first day of

TR.7.E.3.&c. This is the first book at large that our Author hath cited & it is to be obserued that this point is not debated in the said booke, but only it is there admitted, & yet is good authority in law, for our Author saith that it appeareth by this book, now both by Littleton himselfe, and by the booke of 7.E.3. it is apparant that albeit the tenure is that he which holdeth by a whole Knights fee ought to be with the King, &c. to doe a corporall seruice, yet he may finde another able man to doe it for him. T.7.E.3.*fol.*39.

By the statute of Magna Carta, cap.20. it is prouided, that no Knight that holdeth by Castle-gard shall bee distreyned to giue money for the keeping of the Castle, Si ipse eam facere voluerit in propria persona sua vel per alium probum hominem faciet si ipse eam facere non possit propter rationabilem causam.

Some haue thought that he that holds by escuage is taken by the equitie of this statute that speaketh only of Castle gard, but it is holden that this statute is but an affirmance of the Common law. For where that Act saith, (propter rationabilem causam) that reasonable cause is referred to the Tenants owne discretion and choyce, and the cause is not materiall or issuable no more then in the case that Littleton here putteth as hereafter appeareth. And I would aduise our student, that when hee shall be enabled and armed to set vpon the yeare bookes, or reports of Law, that hee bee furnished with all the whole course of the Lawe that when hee heareth a case vouched and applied either in Westminster Hall, (where it is necessary for him to bee a diligent hearer, and obseruer of cases of Law) or at readings or other exercises of learning, hee may finde out and reade the case so vouched, for that will both fasten it in his memory, and bee to him as good as an exposition of that case, but that must not hinder his timely and orderly reading which (all excuses set apart) he must bind himselfe unto, for there be two things to be avoyded by him, as enemies to learning, Præpostera lectio, and præpropera praxis. But let us now heare what our Author will say.

ster de host le Roy, fait per les Commons, & per commandement le Roy, ou de la iour que le Roy primes entra en Escoce: Ideo Quære de hoc.

the muster of the kings host made by the commons, & by the commandement of the King or from the day, that the King first entred into *Scotland*. Therefore inquire of this.

Et ceo semble bone reason, &c. Here Littleton sheweth three reasons wherefore the Tenant should not be constrained to doe his seruice in person.

First. It may be the Tenant is sicke, so as he is neither able to goe nor rule. And euer such construction must be made in matters concerning the defence of the Realme or common good, as the same may be effected and performed. To the former disabilitie may be added where a Corporation aggregate of many, as Deane and Chapter, Maior and Comminaltie, &c. or an Infant beeing a Purchaser, for these also must finde an able man. But it may bee obiected that in these particular Cases the Tenant might find a man, but not when he himselfe is able without all excuse or impediment. To this it is answered, that Sapiens incipit à fine. And the end of this seruice is for defence of the Realme, and so it be done by an able and sufficient man, the end is effected.

Secondly, Seeing there are so many iust excuses of the Tenant it were dangerous, and tending to the hindrance of the seruice, if these excuses should bee issuable, Multa in iure communi contra rationem disputandi pro communi vtilitate introducta sunt.

Lastly, both Littleton and the Books in the seuenth of Edward the Third, giueth the Tenant power, without any cause to be shewed to find an able and sufficient man, and oftentimes Iura publica ex priuato promiscue decidi non debent.

Vn Abbe ou auter home de religion. Note that if the King had giuen Lands to an Abbot and his Successors to hold by Knights seruice, this had been good, and the Abbot should doe homage & find a man, &c. or pay Escuage, but there was no wardship or reliefe or other incident belonging thereunto. And though the Law saith that this was a Mortmayne, that is, that they held fast their Inheritances, yet if the Abbot with the assent of his Couent, had conueyed the land to a naturall man and his heires, now Wardship and Reliefe and other incidents belonged of common right to the tenure. And so it is, if the King giue Lands to a Maior and Comminaltie, and their Successors to be holden by Knights Seruice. In this case the Patentees (as hath beene said) shall doe no homage, neither shall there be any wardship or Reliefe, only they also shall find a man, &c. or pay Escuage. But if they conuey ouer the lands to any naturall man and his heires, now Homage, ward, Mariage, and Reliefe, and other incidents belong hereunto. And yet this possibilitie was remota potentia, but the reason hereof is, Cessante ratione legis cessat ipsa lex, the reason of the immunitie was in respect of the Bodie Politique, which by the conueyance ouer ceaseth, which is worthy of obseruation.

And it is to bee obserued, that euery Bishop in England hath a Baronie, and that Baronie is holden of the King in Capite, and yet the King can neither haue wardship or Reliefe.

If two ioyntenants bee of Land holden by Knights Seruice, if one goeth with the King, it sufficeth for both, and both of them cannot be compelled to goe, for by their tenure one man is only to goe.

6. H. 3. Auowry 242. F. N. B. 83. 84. If the Tenant perauaile goeth, it dischargeth the Mesne, for one Tenancie shall pay but one Escuage.

Ou auter home de Religion. Here this word (Religion) is taken largely, viz. not only for regular, or dead persons, as Abbots, Monkes, or the like. But for Secular persons also, as Bishops, Parsons, Vicars, and the like, for neither of them are bound to goe in proper person. For nemo militans Deo implicet secularibus negotiis.

Languishant. So it may be said of an Ideot, a mad Man, a Leaper, a man maymed, Blind, Deafe, of decrepit age, or the like.

Ou fem sole. Seeing that a fem sole, that cannot performe Knights Seruice may serue by deputie, it may bee demanded wherefore an heire male being within age of 21. yeares may not serue also by Deputie, beeing not able to serue himselfe.

To this it is answered, that in cases of Minoritie, all is one to both sexes, *viz.* if the heire male be at the death of the Ancestor vnder the age of one and twentie, or the heire female vnder the age of fourteene, they can make no Deputie but the Lord shall haue wardship as an incident to the tenure: therefore Littleton is here to be vnderstood of a fem sole of full age, and seised of Land holden by Knights Seruice either by purchase or discent.

¶ *Couenablement arraie pur le guerre.* **So as here are foure things** to be obserued.

First (as hath beene said) that he may find another.

Secondly, That he that is found must be an able person.

Thirdly, He must be armed at the costs and charge of the Tenant; and herein is to be noted, Quod non definitur in iure, with what manner of Armor the Souldier shall be arrayed with for time, place, and occasion doe alter the manner and kind of the Armour.

Fourthly, He must haue such Armour, as shall be necessarie, and so appointed in readinesse.

Ferdwit is a Saxon word & significat quietanciam murdri in exercitu. Worscott is an old English word and signifieth, Liberum esse de oneribus armorum. *Fleta.lib.1.cap.42.*

It is truly said, Quod miles hæc tria curare deber, corpus vt validissimum & pernicissimum, habeat arma apta ad subita imperia, cætera Deo, & Imperatori Curæ esse. *Liuius.*

Sapiens non semper it vno gradu, sed vna via, non se mutat sed aptat. Qui secundos optat euentus, diuinet arte, non casu. In omni conflictu non tam prodest multitudo quam virtus. *Vegetius.*

Est optimi ducis scire & vincere, & cedere prudenter tempori. Multum potest in rebus humanis occasio, plurimum in bellicis. *Polibius.*

Quid tam necessarium est quam tenere semper arma quibus tectus esse possis. But I will take my leaue of these excellent Authors of Art Militarie, and referre them to those that professe the same, and will returne to Littleton. *Vegetius.*

¶ *Muster.* **I find this word in the Statute of 18.H.6.cap.19.** and the ancient Militarie Order is worthy of obseruation, for before and long after that statute, when the King was to be serued with Souldiers for his warre. A Knight or Esquire of the Countrie, that had Reuenues, Farmors and Tenants would couenant with the King by Indenture inrolled in the Exchequer to serue the King for such a terme with so many men (specially named in a List) in his warre, &c. an excellent institution that they should serue vnder him, whom they knew and honored, and with whom they must liue at their returne, these men being mustered before the Kings Commissioners, and receiuing any part of their wages, and their names so recorded, if they after departed from their Captaine within the Terme, contrarie to the forme of that Statute it was felonie. But now that Statute is of no force, because that ancient and excellent forme of militarie course is altogether antiquated: but later Statutes haue prouided for that mischiefe. *Lib.6.fol.27. the Souldiers Case.*

To muster is to make a shew of Souldiers well armed and trained before the Kings Commissioners in some open field. Vbi se ostendentes præludunt prælio. In Latine it is Censere, seu lustrare exercitum.

By the Law before the conquest that musters and shewing of Armour should be Vno eodem die per vniuersum regnum ne aliqui possint arma familiaribus & notis accommodare, nec ipsi illa mutuo accipere, ac iustitiam Domini Regis defraudare, & Dominum Regem & Regnum offendere. *Lamb. fol.135.b.*

Concerning the point in Law, demurred in iudgement, in the seuenth of Edward the third, here mentioned by our Author, The Law accounteth the beginning of the fortie dayes after the King entreth into the forreine Nation, for then the warre beginneth, and till he come there, he and his hoste are said to goe towards the warre, and no Militarie seruice is to be done, till the King and his hoste come thither.

¶ *Sir William Herle.* **A famous Lawyer constituted chiefe Justice** of the Common Pleas by Letters Patents dated, 2.die Martij anno 5.E.3. It appeareth by Littleton, and by the Record that he was a Knight against the conceit of those, that thinke, that the Chiefe Justices of the Court of Common Pleas were not Knighted till long after.

Our Student shall obserue that the knowledge of the Law is like a deepe well, out of which each man draweth according to the strength of his vnderstanding. He that reacheth deepest, he seeth the amiable, and admirable secrets of the Law, wherein, I assure you, the Sages of the Law in former times, (whereof Sir William Herle was a principall one) haue had the deepest reach. And as the Bucket in the depth is easily drawne to the vppermost part of the water, (for Nullum elementum in suo proprio loco est graue) but take it from the water, it cannot bee drawne vp but with great difficultie. So albeit beginnings of this studie seeme difficult, yet when the Professor of the Law can diue into the depth it is delightfull, easie, and without any heauie burthen, so long as he keepe himselfe in his owne proper element.

Glanuile lib.2.cap.6.&c.

¶ *Iustice.* In Glanuill he is called Iustitia in ipso abstracto, as it were Iustice it selfe, which appellation remaines still in English and French, to put them in mind of their duties and functions. But now in legall Latine they are called Iusticiarij tanquam iusti in Concreto: and they are called Iusticiarij de Banco, &c. and neuer Iudices de Banco, &c.

¶ *De Comon Banke.* *Banke* is a Saxon word, and signifieth a Bench or high seate, or a tribunall, and is properly applyed to the Iustices of the Court of Common Pleas, because the Iustices of that Court set there as in a certaine place: for all Writs returnable into that Court are Coram Iusticiarijs nostris apud Westmon. or any other certaine place where the Court set, and Legall Records tearme them Iusticiarij de Banco. But Writs returnable into the Court called the Kings Bench, are Coram nobis (.i. Rege) vbicunque fuerimus in Anglia. And all iudiciall Records there are stiled coram Rege. But for distinction sake it is called the Kings Bench, both because the Records of that Court are stiled (as hath beene said) Coram Rege, and because Kings in former times haue often personally set there. For the antiquitie of the Court of Common Pleas they erre, that hold that before the Statute of Magna Charta there was no Court of Common Pleas, but had his Creation by, or after that Charter: for the learned know, that in the sixe and twentieth yeare of Edward the Third. The Abbot of B. in a Writ of Assize brought before the Iustices in Eire claymed Conusance and to haue Writs of Assize, and other originall Writs out of the Kings Court by prescription, time out of mind of man, in the raignes of Saint Edmond, and Saint Edward the Confessor before the Conquest. And on the behalfe of the Abbot were shewed diuers allowances thereof in former times in the Kings Courts, and that King Henrie the first confirmed their vsages, and that they should haue Conusance of Pleas, so that the Iustices of the one Bench, or the other should not intermeddle. And the Statute of Magna Charta, erecteth no Court, but giueth direction for the proper iurisdiction thereof in these words. Communia Placita non sequantur Curiam nostram, sed teneantur in aliquo certo loco. And properly the Statute saith, non sequantur, for that the Kings Bench did in those dayes follow the King vbicunque fuerit in Anglia, and therefore enacteth that Common Pleas should be holden in a Court resident in a certaine place. In the next Chapter of Magna Charta (made at one and the same time) it is prouided. Et ea quæ per eosdem (s. Iusticiarios itinerantes) propter difficultatem aliquorum articulorum terminari non possunt, referantur ad Iusticiarios nostros de Banco, & ibi terminentur. And in the next to that (Assisæ de vltima præsentatione semper capiantur coram Iusticiarijs de Banco, & ibi terminentur. Therefore it manifestly appeareth that at the making of the Statute of Magna Charta, there were Iusticiarij de Banco, which all men confesse to be the Court of Common Pleas. And therefore that Court was not erected by or after that Statute. For the Authoritie of this Court, it is euident by that which hath beene said, that it hath iurisdiction of all Common Pleas. But let vs returne to Littleton.

26.Ass.p.24. 4.E.3.fol.19. Bracton.lib.3.fol.105.b. Brit.fol.1.& 2. Fleta lib.2.cap.2. Mirror.cap.5.§.1. Fortescue cap.51. See in the Preface to the third part of my Reports.

Mirror.cap.5.§.2. Fleta.lib.2.cap.54.

¶ *Demurre en iudgement.* A Demurrer commeth of the Latine word demorari to abide, and therefore he which demurreth in Law, is said, he that abideth in Law, Moratur, or demoratur in lege. Whensoeuer the Councell learned of the partie is of opinion, that the Count or Plea, of the aduerse partie is insufficient in Law, then he demurreth or abideth in Law, and referreth the same to the iudgement of the Court, and therefore well saith Littleton, here demurre en iudgement, the words of a Demurrer being Quia narratio, &c. materiaque in eadem contenta minus sufficiens in lege existit, &c. and so of a Plea, Quia Placitum, &c. materiaque in eodem content minus sufficiens in lege existit, &c. vnde pro defectu, sufficientis narrationis siue placiti &c. petit iudicium, &c. But if the Plea be sufficient in Law, but the matter of fact is false, then the aduerse partie taketh issue thereupon, and that is tried by a Iury, for matters in Law are decided by the Iudges, and matters in fact by Iuries, as elsewhere is said more at large.

Now as there is no issue vpon the fact, but when it is ioyned betweene the parties, so there is no Demurrer in Law, but when it is ioyned, and therfore when a Demurrer is offered by the one partie as is aforesaid, the aduerse partie ioyneth with him, (for example) saith, Quod Placitum prædictum &c. materiaque in eodem contenta bonum & sufficiens in lege existunt, &c. & petit iudicium, and thereupon the Demurrer is said to be ioyned, and then the Case is argued by Councell learned of both sides, and if the points bee difficult, then it is argued openly by the Iudges of that Court, and if they or the greater part concurre in opinion, accordingly iudgement is giuen, and if the Court bee equally deuided, or conceiue great doubt of the case, then may they adiorne it into the Exchequer Chamber, where the case shall be argued by all the Iudges of England, where if the Iudges shall bee equally diuided, then (if none of them change their opinion) it shall bee decided at the next Parliament by a Prelate, two Earles, and two Barons which shall haue power and Commission of the King in that behalfe, and by aduice of themselues, the Chancellor, Treasurer, the Iustices of the

Vid. Bract. lib.5.fol.352.b.

14.E.3.cap.5. Statut.1.

the one Bench and the other, and other of the Kings Councell, as many and such as shall seeme conuenient, shall make a good iudgement, &c. And if the difficultie be so great as they cannot determine it, then it shall be determined by the Lords in the vpper house of Parliament. See the statute, for it extends not only to the case aforesaid, but also where iudgements are delayed in the Chancery, Kings bench, Common bench, and the Exchequor, the Iustices assigned, and other Iustices of Oyer and Terminer, sometime by difficultie, sometime by diuers opinions of Iustices, and sometime for other causes. (a) Before which Statute, if iudgements were not giuen by reason of difficultie, the doubt was decided at the next Parliament (which then was to be holden once euery yeare at the least) (b) Si autem talia nunquam prius euenerint, & obscurum & difficile sit eorum iudicium, tunc ponatur iudicium in respectum vsque ad magnam curiam vt ibi per concilium curiæ terminentur. But hereof thus much shall suffice. (r) He that demurreth in Law confesseth all such matters of fact as are well and sufficiently pleaded. If there be a demurrer for part and an issue for part, the more orderly course is to giue iudgement vpon the demurrer first, but yet it is in the discretion of the Court to trie the issue first if they will. After demurrer ioyned in any Court of record, the iudges shall giue iudgement according as the very right of the cause and matter in Law shall appeare, without regarding any want of forme in any Writ, Returne, Pleint, Declaration, or other pleading, Proces, or course of proceeding, except those only which the partie demurring shall specially and particularly set downe and expresse in his demurrer. (a) Now what is substance and what is forme you shall reade in my Reports.

Rot. Parliam. 14. E. 3. nu. 31. a proceeding in Sir Iohn Stantons Case vpon difficultie in the Court of Common Pleas. Vid. Britton, fo. 41. 21. E. 3. 37. 38. 39. E. 3. fo. 1. 21. 35. 40. E. 3. 34. 13. H. 4. 3. 4.
(a) 4. E. 3. ca. 14.
(b) Bracton lib. 1. cap. 2. nu. 7. Britt. fo. 41. 1. E. 3. 7. 8. 2. E. 3. 6. 7.
(r) 17. E. 3. 50. b. 47. E. 3. 13. 14. 5. H. 7. 1. 13. E. 4. 7. b. Pl. Com. 85. 411. 172. 48. E. 3. 15. 2. R. 2. inquest. 2. 38. E. 3. 25. 11. H. 4. 5. 75. 3. E. 4. 2.
(a) Lib. 3. fo. 57. Linc. Coll. case. Lib. 5. fo. 74. Wymeks case. Lib. 10. fo. 88. vsque 98. Doctor Leyfields case.

And in some cases a man shall alledge speciall matter, and conclude with a Demurrer, (b) as in an action of trespasse brought by I. S. for the taking of his horse, the defendant pleades that he himselfe was possessed of the horse vntill he was by one I. S. dispossessed, who gaue him to the plaintife, &c. the plaintife saith that I. S. named in the barre, and I. S. the plaintife were all one person & not diuers; and to the plea pleaded by the defendant in the manner, he demurred in Law, and the Court did hold the plea and demurrer good, for without the matter alledged hee could not demurre. Now as there may be a demurrer vpon counts and pleas, so there may be of Aide prior, Voucher, Receite, waging of Law, and the like. (c) By that which hath beene said it appeareth, that there is a generall demurrer that is shewing no cause, and a speciall demurrer which sheweth the cause of his demurrer. Also by that which hath beene said, there is a demurrer vpon pleading, &c. and there is also a demurrer vpon euidence. (d) As if the plaintife in euidence shew any matter of Record, or Deeds or writings, or any sentence in the Ecclesiasticall Court, or other matter of euidence by testimony of witnesses, or otherwise whereupon doubt in Law ariseth, and the defendant offer to demurre in Law thereupon, the plaintife cannot refuse to ioyne in demurrer, no more then in a demurrer vpon a Count, replication, &c and so E conuerso may the plaintife demurre in Law vpon the euidence of the defendant.

(b) 13. E. 4. 7. 31. E. 3. estoppel. 244. 33. H. 6. 9. 10. 22. E. 4. 50. 1. H. 7. 21.
(c) 14. H. 4. 31. 37. H. 6. 6.
(d) Lib. 5. fo. 104. a. Bakers case.

But if euidence for the King in an Information or any other suite be giuen, and the Defendant offer to demurre in Law vpon the Euidence, the Kings counsell shall not be enforced to ioyne in Demurrer: but in that case, the Court may direct the Jury to finde the speciall matter.

(e) 38. H. 8. Dyer 53.

¶ *En iudgement.* For the signification of this word, Vid. Sect. 366

Sect. 97.

¶ ET apres tiel voyage royal en Escoce, il est communement dit, que per authoritie de Parliament lescuage serra assesse & mis en certaine, s. certeine summe dargent, quant chescun que tient per entier fee de seruice de chiualer, quel ne fuit

AND after such a voyage royall into Scotland, it is commonly said, that by authority of Parliament, the escuage shall be assessed and put in certeine, s. a certaine summe of money, how much euery one which holdeth by a whole Knights fee,

¶ *APres voiage royal, &c. il est communement dit que per Authority de Parliament escuage serra assesse.* Nota here is a secret of Law included, that albeit escuage incertaine bee due by tenure, yet because the assessment thereof concerned so many and so great a number of the subiects of the realme, it could not bee assessed by the King or any other but by Parliament: (a) and

(a) 13. H. 4. 5.

(b) 8. H. 3. Rot. Claus. & Rot. finium memb 30. & ante.

Staff. p 14. E. 1. de Banco.

F. N. B. 84.

Bract. lib. 2. 36. a.

F. N. B. 84.

Rot. Parl. 9. R. 2. nu 40.

(a) and this was by the common Law.

(b) No Escuage was assessed by Parliament since the raigne of Edward the second, and in the eighth yeare of his raigne Escuage was assessed.

If the Tenant goeth with the King, and dieth in exercitu, in the host or armie, hee is excused by Law, and no Escuage shall be demanded.

And it is to obserued, that if he that hold of the King by Escuage, goeth, or findeth another to goe for him with the King, &c. then hee shall haue escuage of his Tenants that hold of him by such seruice, which must be assessed by parliament.

But if the Kings Tenant goeth not with the King, then he shal pay for his default Escuage, and shall haue no escuage of his Tenants. Richard the second making a voyage Royall into Scotland, at the petition of his Commons pardoned the payment of Escuage.

per luy mesme, ne per vn auter pur luy, oue le Roy paiera a son Seignior de que il tient la Terre per escuage. Sicome mittomus, que il fuit ordaine per authoritie de la Parliament, que chescun que tient per entire fee de Seruice de chiualer, que ne fuit oue le Roy, payera a son Seignior 40. s. donque celuy que tient per moitie dun fee de chiualer ne payera a son seignior forsque xx. s. & celuy que tient per la quart part de fee de chiualer ne payera forsque x. s. & sic que pluis, pluis, & que meins, meins.

who was neither by himselfe nor by any other, with the King, shall pay to his Lord of whom he holds his land by Escuage. As put the case that it was ordained by the authoritie of the Parliament, That euery one which holdeth by a whole Knights fee, who was not with the King, shall pay to his Lord fortie shillings; then he which holdeth by the moitie of a Knights fee, shall pay to his Lord but twentie shillings, and hee which holdeth by the fourth part of a knights Fee, shall pay but x. s. & he which hath more, more, and which lesse, lesse.

Sect. 98.

Vide Sect. 120.

25. E. 3. Tit. Avow. 215. 26. Ass. 65. 30. E. 3. 23. b. Lib 4. fo. 88. in Luttrels case.

¶ *Ascuns teignont per custome, &c.* Nota, that Escuage is directed by custome.

¶ *Mes auterment est de Escuage certain.* Here it appeareth, that Escuage is two fold, viz. Escuage incertaine, whereof Litleton here speaketh; and escuage certaine, Quemadmodum incertitudo scutagij facit seruitium militare, ita certitudo scu-

ET ascuns teignont per la custome que si lescuage courge per authoritie de Parliament, a ascun summe de money, que ils ne paieront forsque la moitie de ceo, & ascuns teignont que ils ne payeront forsque le quart part de ceo. Mes pur ceo que lescuage que ils paieront est non certain pur ceo que nest certaine coment le Parliament

AND some hold by the custome, That if Escuage bee assessed by authoritie of Parliament, at any summe of mony, that they shal pay but the moitie of that summe, and some but the fourth part of that summe. But because the Escuage that they should pay, is vncertaine, for that it is not certaine how the Parliament will assesse the escuage they hold by Knights ser-

asseffera lescuage eux teignont per Seruice de Chiualer. Mes auterment est de lescuage certaine, de que serra parle en le tenure de Socage.

uice. But otherwise it is of Escuage certaine, of which shall be spoken in the tenure of Socage.

tagij facit Socagium. But more of this in the Chapter of Socage Sect.120.

¶ *Per Parliament.*

Of the Antiquitie and Authoritie of this Court see Sect.164.

Sect. 99.

ET si home parle generalment descuage, il serra entendue per l'common parlance descuage noncertaine, que est Seruice de chiualer, & tiel escuage trait a luy homage, & homage trait a luy Fealtie, car fealtie est incident a chescun manner de seruice forsque a le Tenure en Frankalmoigne, come serra dit apres en le Tenure de Frankalmoigne. Et issint il que tient per Escuage, tient p homage fealtie & Escuage.

AND if one speake generally of Escuage, it shall be intended by the common speech of Escuage incertaine, which is Knights seruice: And such Escuage draweth to it Homage, and Homage draweth to it fealtie; for Fealtie is incident to euerie manner of seruice, vnlesse it be to the Tenure in Frankalmoigne, as shall bee said afterward in the Tenure of Frankealmoigne. And so he which holdeth by Escuage, holds by Homage, Fealtie and Escuage.

¶ *ET si home parle generalment descuage il serra intend per le common parlance descuage non certain.*

Entendments en Ley Sect.100. 110.367.377,393.406.462. 463.

5.E.2.Ref.165.20.H.6.23. 21.H.6.8.37.H. 29. 13.H.4.4.6.El.Dyer 236. 10.E.4.11.32.E.3. Gard.31

Verba æquiuoca & in dubio posita intelliguntur in digniori & potentiori sensu. Tenure in Capite ex vi termini is a Tenure in Grosse, and it may be holden of a Subiect, but being spoken generally, it is secundum excellentiam, intended of the King, for he is Caput Reipublicæ.

But fo 163.

¶ *Et tiel escuage trait a luy homage, & homage trait a luy Fealtie, car Fealtie est incident a chescun manner de seruice forsque a tenure en Frankealmoigne.*

40.E.3.22.8.H.7.4.

Sect.100.

This is gathered by the effects of their Tenure, for essences are found out by properties, fountains by Riuers, and causes by effects: for amongst others, the Lords shal haue Escuage. Of their Tenants, &c. as it followeth.

ET est ascauoire, Que quant escuage est tielment assesse per authority de Parliament chescun Seignior de que la terre est tenus per Escuage, auera lescuage issint assesse per Parliament pur ceo que il est in-

AND it is to be vnderstood, that when Escuage is so assessed by authoritie of Parliament, euerie Lord of whom the land is holden by Escuage, shall haue the Escuage so assessed by Parliament, because it is intended by the Law, That at

tendus p la ley, q al comencement tiels tenemts fuer dones p les Snrs a lez tenats de tener per tielx seruices a defender lour Snrs, auxy bien come le Roy, & mitter en quiet lour Snrs & le Roy, de les Scotes auandits.

the beginning such tenements were by the Lords to the tenants to hold by such seruices to defend their Lords aswell as the King, and to put in quiet their Lords and the King from the Scots aforesaid.

Sect. 101.

¶ Et pur ceo que tiels tenemts deuiendront primes des seigniors, il est reason q ils aueront lescuage de lour tenants. Et les Seigniors e tiel case purront distrein pur lescuage issint assesse, ou ils en ascuns cases purront au bre le roy, direct as Vicots de m les Counties, &c. de leuier tiel escuage pur eux, sicome appiert p le Register. Mes d tiels tenants queux teignont per escuage de Roy, queux ne fueront oue le roy en Escoce, le Roy mesme auera lescuage.

And because such tenements came first from the Lords, it is reason that they should haue the Escuage of their tenants. And the Lords in such case may distreine for the escuage so assessed, or they in some cases may haue the kings Writts directed to the Sheriffs of the same Counties, &c. to leuie such escuage for them, as it appeareth by the Register. But of such tenants as hold of the King by escuage which were not with the King in Scotland, the King himselfe shall haue the escuage.

F.N.B. 84. Register. 88. de Scutagio habendo.

¶ *Les seigniours aueront lescuage, &c.* This is euident.

¶ *Breife le roy.* This commeth of the Latyne word Breue.

Fitz. in his Preface to his N.B. saith of them, that they be those foundations whereupon the whole Law doth depend.

(a) Bracton lib. 5. fol. 413. Fleta lib. 2. cap. 13. Britton, fol. 122, 227.

(a) Bracton describeth a writ thus, Breve quidem cum sit formatum ad similitudinem regulæ juris quia breuiter & paucis verbis intentionem proferentis exponit & explanat sicut regula iuris rem que est breviter enarrat, non tamen ita breve esse debeat quin rationem & vim intentionis contineat.

Of writs some be originall, brevia originalia, and some be iudiciall, brevia judicialia.

Also of Originals, quædam sunt formata sub suis casibus & de cursu, & de communi consilio totius regni concessa & approbata, que quidem nullatenus mutari poterint absque concensu & voluntate eorum; & quædam sunt Magistralia, & sæpe variantur secundum varietatem casuum factorum & querelarum, as for example actions vpon the case which varie according to the varietie of euery mans case and the like, and these being not of course, the masters being learned men did make: Item breuium originalium alia sunt realia, alia personalia, alia mixta. Item breuium originalium, alia sunt patentia siue aperta, & alia clausa. Certaine it is that the originall writs are so artificially and briefely compiled, as there is nothing redundant or wanting in them, of which an honourable Secretary of state once said, that it was not possible to comprehend so much matter, so perspicuously in fewer words: of all these kinde of writs you shall reade plentifully in the Register whereof Littleton maketh mention in this place, and also in Fitz N.B.

¶ *Sicome appiert per le Register.* Register, is the name of a most ancient booke and of great authority in Law, containing all the originall writts of the Common Law, of which book see more in the Preface to the ninth part of my Reports, & containeth also Breuia iudicialia quæ sepius variantur secundu varietate placitoru proponentis & respondentis.

Bracton vbi supra. Britton vbi supra. Regist. 88. F.N.B. 84.

Also it appeareth by the Register that the King shall haue escuage of his tenants which hold of him as of a Mannor which he hath in ward, or by reason of a vacation of a Bishopricke.

F.N.B. 84.

And so shall a common person, if he hath an estate for life or for yeares of a Seigniory.

Section 102.

¶ ITem en tiel caſe auandit, lou le Roy face vn voyage royall en Eſcoce, & leſcuage eſt aſſeſſe per Parliament, ſi le ſñr diſtreine ſon tenant que tient de luy per ſeruice dentier fee de chiualer pur leſcuage iſſint aſſeſſe, &c. & le tenãt plede, & voit auerrer que il fuit oue le Roy en Eſcoce &c. per xl. iours, & le Seignior voit auerrer le contrarie, il eſt dit, que il ſerra trie per le certificat del Marſhal del hoſt le Roy en eſcript ſouth ſ͂ ſeale q̃ ſerra mis a les Juſtices.

ITem, in ſuch caſe aforeſaid, where the King maketh a voyage royall into Scotland, and the Eſcuage is aſſeſſed by Parliament, if the Lord diſtraine his tenant that holdeth of him by ſeruice of a whole Knights fee, for the Eſcuage ſo aſſeſſed, &c. and the tenant pleadeth and will auer that he was with the King in Scotland, &c. by 40. daies, and the Lord will auerre the contrary, it is ſaid that it ſhall bee tried by the certificat of the Marſhall of the kings hoſt in writing vnder his ſeale, which ſhall be ſent to the Iuſtices.

¶ *ET voet averre, que il fuit ove le roy en Eſcoce per 40. iours, &c.* (a) *il eſt dit que il ſerra trie per le certificat del Marſhall.* This is a triall appointed by the Law, Ne curia regis deficeret in Iuſticia exhibenda. (b) Herewith agreeth the Regiſter, where the Marſhall is is called Conſtabularius exercitus noſtri.

(a) 2.E.4.11. 4.E.4.10. 21.E.4.10. F.N.B.85. 11.H.7.5. L.b.9.fo.32. Caſe de Strat. Marc:

(b) Regiſt.88. F.N.B.84. 2.E.4.1.4.E.4.10. 9.H.4.3. 11.H.7.5. 21.H.6.50. 33.H.6.1.45.

¶ *Marſhall de hoſte le roy.* Mareſchallus exercitus, in Saxon Mariſchalk. i. equitum magiſter. This word Marſhall is either deriued of Mars or of Marc an horſe and ſchalc which ſignifieth in the Saxon tongue, a Maſter or Gouernour. (c) In the Lawes before the Conqueſt it is ſaid. Mareſchalli exercitus, ſeu ductores exercitus Heretoches per Anglos vocabantur, illi ordinabant acies denſiſſimas in prælijs & alas conſtituebant prout decuit, & prout ei melius viſum fuerit ad honorem coronæ & ad vtilitatem regni. (d) And here it is to be obſerued, that his Certificate in this caſe is a triall in Law. I read of ſixe kindes of Certificates allowed for trialls by the Common Law; the Firſt whereof Littleton here ſpeaketh of, in time of warre out of the Realme, 2. In time of peace out of the Realme: (e) As if it be alledged in auoydance of an Outlawrie, that the defendant was in priſon at Burdeaux in the ſeruice of the Maior of Burdeaux, it ſhall bee tried by the Certificate of the Major of Burdeaux. 3. For matters within the Realme, (f) the Cuſtome of London ſhall be certified by the Maior & Aldermen by the mouth of the Recorder. 4. By certificate of the Sherife vpon a writ to him directed (g) in caſe of priuiledge if one be a Citizen or a Forreiner. 5. Triall of Records by certificate of the Judges in whoſe cuſtody they are by Law. All theſe be in temporall cauſes. 6 In cauſes Eccleſiaſticall, as loyaltie of marriage, generall baſtardie, excommengement, profeſſion. Theſe and the like are regularly to be tried by the Certificate of the ordinarie.

(c) Lamb.fo.136.

(d) 2.E.4.1.6.4 E.4.10. 23.E.4.47. F.N.B.85.

(e) 4.E.4 10.

(f) 5.E.4.30. 21.E.4.18.

(g) 10.H.6.10.

And there be diuers other trialls allowed by the Common Law, then by a Jury of 12, men which you may reade at large in the ninth booke of my Reports, fo.30.31. &c. in the caſe of the Abbot of Strata Marcella, which are as plainely ſet downe there, as they can be here: and in this caſe, if the triall ſhould not be by Certificate, it ſhould want triall which ſhould be inconuenient; Only in this place I will adde ſomething of a forreine triall which I finde not in any of the Treatiſes lately publiſhed againſt ſingle combats, becauſe it may deterre men from that vngodly and vnlawfull kinde of reuenge, whereupon many murders haue enſued, and preuent all hope of impunitie for default of triall in that caſe

If a ſubiect of the King be killed by another of his ſubiects out of England in any forreine Countrey, the wife or he that is heire of the dead may haue an appeale for this murder or homicide before the Conſtable and the Marſhall, whoſe ſentence is vpon teſtimony of witneſſes or combate. And accordingly where a ſubiect of the King was ſlaine in Scotland by others of the

Stat. de 1.H.4.cap.14. 13.H.4.fo.5. Vid. Rot. Parliam. 8.H.6. nu.38. Stanf.pl. Cor.fo.65.

(*) Anno 25. Eliz.

the Kings subiects, the wife of the dead had her appeale therefore before the Constable and the Marshall. And so it was (*) resolued in the Raigne of Queene Elizabeth in the case of Sir Francis Drake who strooke off the head of Dowtie, in partibus transmarinis, that his brother and heire might haue an Appeale, Sed Regina noluit constituere Constabularium Angliæ, &c. & ideo dormiuit appellum.

If a man be mortally wounded in France, and dieth thereof in England, it is said that an Appeale doth lie vpon the said Statute, for it is not punishable by the Common Law, and the proceeding there (as hath beene said) is vpon witnesses or combate, and not by Jurie, and the mortall wound was giuen out of the Realme.

CHAP. 4. Sect. 103.

Knights Seruice.

¶ Tenure per homage, fealtie, & escuage, est a tener per seruice de chiualer, & trait a luy garde, mariage, & reliefe. Car quant tiel tenant morust, & son heire male est deins lage de 21. ans, le seignior auera la terre tenus de luy tanque al age del heire de 21. ans, le quel est appell pleine age, pur ceo que tiel home per entendement del ley nest pas able de faire tiel seruice de chiualer, deuant lage de 21. ans: Et auxy si tiel heire ne soit marie al temps de mort de tiel auncester, donque le seignior auera le garde & le mariage de luy. Mes si tiel tenant deuie, son heire female esteant dage de 14. ans, ou de plus, donque le Seignior na-

Tenure by homage, fealtie and escuage is to hold by Knights Seruice, and it draweth to it Ward, Mariage, and reliefe. For when such tenant dieth, and his heire male bee within the age of 21. yeares, the Lord shall haue the land holden of him vntill the age of the heire of 21. yeares, the which is called full age, because such heire by intendement of the Law is not able to doe such Knights Seruice before his age of 21. yeares. And also if such heire be not maried at the time of the death of his Ancestor, then the Lord shall haue the Wardship & mariage of him, but if such Tenant dieth, his heire female being of the age of 14. yeares, or more, then the Lord shall not haue the

(a) Glanuil. lib. 7. cap. 10.
(b) Regist. 2. 30. E. 3. 24.
(c) Glanuil. lib. 7. cap. 14.
(d) Glanuil. lib. 7. cap. 9. & 1. Fleta. lib. 1. cap. 8. Bract. lib. 2. fol. 85. Britton. fol. 162. & fol. 28. & 95. Ockam in diuersis locis. Mirror cap. 1. §. 3. Sudey Diton.

¶ Seruice de Chiualer. Nota, it appeareth by (a) the Register, that it is (b) said vnum fœdum militis, and not fœdum vnius militis, as it was said (c) by some of old, and so duo fœda militis, &c. and sometime these fees are called fœda militaria. Our Authour hauing before treated of Homage, Fealtie and Escuage, now commeth, to Knight Seruice it selfe. In Domesday, it is thus recorded Episcopus Baiecensis ille qui tenet de Modardo reddit ei 50. s. & seruitium vnius militis.

(e) Bracton. lib. 2. fol. 36. 37. Britton. fol. 164. 165. Fleta lib. 3. cap. 14. 19. E 2. auowrie 224. 26. Ass. 65. 31. Ass 30. 30. E. ..23. 8. E. 3. 67. 7 H. 4. 19.

¶ Chiualer .i. eques, Knight is a Saxon word, and by them written, Cnite. Chiualer taketh his name from the horse, because they alwayes serued in warres on horsebacke. The Latines called them Equites, the Spaniards, Caualleroes, the Frenchmen, Chiualiers, the Italians Cauallieri, and the Germanes Reiters, all from the horse. It is necessary to bee seene by what names this seruice of a Knight is called. It is called (e) Seruitium forinsecum quia pertinet ad Dominum Regem & non ad capitalem Dominum nisi cum in propria persona profectus fuerit in seruitio, & nisi cum pro seruitio suo, satisfecerit Domino Regi, &c. ideo forinsecum dici potest, quia fit & capitur foris siue extra seruitium quod fit

nauera my le garde del terre ne de corps pur ceo que feme de tiel age poit auer baron able de faire seruice de chiualer. Mes si tiel heire female soit deins lage de 14. ans, & nient marie al temps de la mort son auncester, donque le Seignior auera le garde de la terre tenus de luy, tanque al age de tiel heire female de 16. ans, pur ceo que il est done per le Statute de Westm̃. 1. cap. 22. Que per 2. ans procheine ensuant les dits 14. ans, le seignior poit tender couenable mariage sãs disparagement a tiel heire female. Et si le Seignior deins les dits 2. ans ne luy tend̃ tiel mariage, &c. donque el al fine des dits 2. ans, poit enter & ouste son Seignior. Mes si tiel hẽre female soy marie deins lage de 14. ans en la vie sõ ancester, & son auncester deuy el esteant deins lage de 14. ans, le Seignior nauera forsq; la garde de la terre, iesques a fine de 14. ans, dage de tiel heire female, & donq;

Wardship of the land, nor of the bodie, because that a woman of such age may haue a husband able to doe Knights Seruice, but if such heire female bee within the age of 14. yeares, and vnmaried at the time of the death of her ancestors, the Lord shal haue the Wardship of the Land holden of him vntill the age of such heire female of 16. yeares. For it is giuen by the Statute of W. 1. cap. 22. that by the space of two yeares next ensuing the said 14. yeares, the Lord may tẽder conuenable mariage without disparagement to such heire female. And if the Lord within the said two yeares do not tender such mariage, &c. then shee at the end of the said two yeres may enter, and put out her Lord; but if such heire female bee maried within the age of 14. yeres in the life of her Ancester, & her Ancester dieth, shee beeing within the age of 14. yeares, the Lord shall haue only the Wardship of the Land vntill the end of the 14. yeares of age of such

Domino capitali. And it is called Scutagium, as it appeareth (f) by Littleton and many authorities before recited. Sometime droit de espee. Also it is called (g) Regale seruitium, quia specialiter pertinet ad Dominum Regem. Vt si dicatur in Carta, faciendo inde fornisecum seruitium, vel Regale seruitium, vel seruitium Domini Regis quod idem est, &c. And another saith. Et sunt quædam seruitia forniseca quæ dici poterunt Regalia quæ ad scutum præstantur, & inde habemus Scutagium, & ratione scuti pro fœdo militari reputatur, &c. So as in respect of him that doth it, it is called seruitium militis, but in respect of him for & to whom it is done, viz. to the King, & for the Realme it is called seruitium Regale, or seruitium Domini Regis, &c. (h) In ancient time they which held by Knights Seruice were called Milites, qui per loricas, &c. defendunt & deseruiunt, &c. and sometime this seruice is called seruitium hauberticum. And in ancient time such as held by Knights seruice for the defence of the Realme had many Priuiledges granted to them by Law: as for example they might haue a writ De essend' quiet' de tallagio, the effect whereof was (i) Si Th. filius Ranulphi terram suam teneat per seruitium militare, sicut Domino Regi monstrauit, tunc nullum ab eodem Thoma capiant tallagium nec pro eo dando ipsum distringant, vel homines suos qui per consimile seruitium teneant. And this agreeth with the ancient Charter of King Henrie the first, before mentioned, which hee made on the day of his Coronation for the restitution of the Ancient Lawes. (k) Militibus qui ꝑ loricas terras suas defendunt & deseruiunt terras Dominicarum carucar' suarum quietas ab omnibus gildis, & omni opere &c. concedo.) and the reason thereof is there yeelded, Sicut tam magno grauamine alleuati sint

(f) Bract. vbi supra. Fleta lib. 3. cap. 14.
(g) Britton. fol. 187. Bract. in. vbi supra.
(h) Carta Hen. primi. Mat. Paris. Mirror. cap. 2. §. 17.
(i) Rot. claus. 19. H. 3. m. 22.
(k) Carta H. 1. in libro rub. fol. 41. in Sccario.

son baron & luy poient enter ē la terre & ouste le seignior, car ceo est hors de cas de le dit estatute, entant que le Seignior ne poit tender mariage a luy que est marie, &c. Car deuant le dit estatute Westm̄. 1. tiel issue female que fuit deins age de 14. ans, al tēps de mort son auncester, & puis que el auoit accomplish lage de 14 ans, sans ascun tender de mariage per le Seignior a luy, tiel heire female donque puissoit enter en le terre, & ouste le seignior sicome appiert per le rehersall & parolx de le dit statute, issint que le dit Statute fuit fait en tiel cas, tout pur laduantage de Seigniors come il semble. Mes uncore ē touts foits est entendue per les parolx de m̄ le Statute que le Seignior nauera les deux ans apres les, 14. ans, come est auantdit, mes lou tiel heire female soit deins lage de 14. ans, nient marie al temps de mort s̄ auncester.

heire female, and then her husband and shee may enter into the Land, & oust the Lord, For this is out of the case of the said statute insomuch as the Lord cannot tender mariage to her which is maried &c. For before the said statute of W. 1. such issue female which was within the age of 14. yeares at the time of the death of her ancestor, & after she had accomplished the age of 14. yeares, without any tender of mariage by the Lord vnto her, such heire Female might haue entred into the land, and ousted the Lord as appeareth by the rehearsall and words of the said statute, so as the said statute was made (as it seemeth) in such case altogether for the aduantage of Lords. But yet this is alwayes intended by the words of the same Statute, that the Lord shall not haue these two yeares after the 14. yeares as is aforesaid, but where such heire female is within the age of 14. yeares, and vnmarried at the time of the death of her ancestor.

sint, ita equis & armis se bene instruant vt apti & parati sint ad seruitium meum, & defensionem Regni mei. But these Priuiledges and Quittances are discontinued, and the charge remayneth.

(l) Glanuil. lib. 7. cap. 9. 10. Fleta lib. 1. cap. 8 & 9. & lib. 3. cap. 16. 17. &c. Bracton. lib. 2 cap. 16. Mirror. cap. 5. §. 2. Britton. 162.

It is called commonly in (l) our Bookes seruitium militare, &c. or seruitium militis. And this seruice was created and prouided for the defence of the Realme, to performe which seruice the heires are not accounted in Law able till the age of one and twentie yeares. Therefore during their minoritie, the Lord shall haue the custodie of them, not for benefit only, but that the Lord might see, that they bee in their young yeares taught the deeds of Chiualrie, and other vertuous and worthy Sciences.

(m) Fortescue cap. 44.

(m) Si hæreditas teneatur per seruitium militare, tunc per leges infans ipse, & hæreditas eius, &c. per Dominum fœdi illius custodientur, &c quis, putas, infantem talem in artibus bellicis quos facere, ratione tenuræ suæ, ipse astringitur Domino fœdi sui, melius instruere poterit, aut velit, quam Dominus ille, cui ab eo seruitium tale debetur, & qui maioris potentiæ & honoris æstimatur, quam sunt alij amici propinqui tenentis sui? Ipse namque vt sibi ab eodem tenente melius seruiatur diligentem Curam adhibebit, & melius in hijs eum erudire expertus esse censetur quam reliqui amici iuuenis, &c. & rectera non minimum erit Regno accommodum, vt incolæ eius in armis sint experti, nam audacter quilibet facit, quod se scire ipse non diffidit.

(n) Lamb. fol. 135. 4.

(n) Amongst the Lawes of Saint Edward the Confessor, it is thus prouided. Debent enim vniuersi liberi homines, &c. secundum fœdum suum, & secundum tenementa sua arma habere, & illa semper prompta conseruare ad tuitionem Regni, & seruitium Dominorum suorum iuxta preceptum Domini Regis explendum & peragendum. And William the Conquerour confirmed that Law in these words. Statuimus & firmiter præcipimus, vt omnes Comites, & Barones, & Milites, & seruientes, & vniuersi liberi homines totius

Regni

regni nostri prædicti habeant & teneant se semper in armis & in equis vt decet, & oportet, & quod sint semper prompti & parati ad servitium suum integrum nobis explendum & peragendum cum semper opus adfuerit secundum quod nobis debent de feodis & tenementis suis de jure facere, &c. Out of these two Lawes the studious and learned reader will gather divers notable things. And therefore if after the Lord hath the wardship of the body and the land, the Lord doth release to the infant his right in the Seigniorie, or the Seigniorie discendeth to the infant, he shall be out of ward both for the body and the land, for he was in ward in respect he was not able to doe those services which he ought to doe to his Lord, which now are extinct, and Cessante causa, cessat causatum? And our Author saith, that the tenure by Knights service draweth unto it ward, Marriage, &c. so as there must be a tenure continuing. As if the Conusor in a statute Merchant be in execution, and his land also, and the Conusee release to him all debts, this shall discharge the execution, for the debt was the cause of the Execution, and of the continuance of it till the debt be satisfied, therefore the discharge of the debt which is the cause, dischargeth the execution which is the effect.

See W.1.*ca*.48. *the second part of the Institutes*.

20.*Ass*.p.7.

¶ *Et trait a luy gard, marriage, & releife*. So as regularly there be Sixe incidents to Knights service, (viz.) two of honour and submission, as Homage and Fealtie. And foure of profit, viz. Escuage, whereof he hath treated before, Ward (.i. Wardship of the land) Marriage, and Reliefe; of all which our Author hath spoken. But there be other incidents to Knights service besides these, (a) as Aide pur faire fits chivalier, & aide pur file marier, &c. which at the Common Law were uncertaine, and were called rationabilia auxilia, because if they were excessive and unreasonable in the judgement of the Court where they were questioned, they ought not to be paide: But now aswell in the Kings case, as in the case of the subiect, they are by Acts of Parliament reduced to certaintie which are worthy your reading.

(a) *Grand Cust.de Norm. ca*.35. *Regist.orig.fo*.87. *Glanvil,lib*.9. *ca*.8.35. *Fleta lib*.2.*cap*.40.& *lib*.3. *ca*.14. *Mirror ca*.1.§.3. *Britton fo*.55.& 90. *F.N.B*. 82.*b W*.1.*ca*.35.25.*E*.3. *ca*.11.11.*H* 4.34.5.*E*.3.11. *Vid. Sect*.110.

¶ *Gard*, or Ward, in Latyne Custodia, and hereof the Lord is called Gardian, Custos, and the minor is called a ward or one in ward. (b) And albeit (as our Author saith) Knight service draweth with it ward, &c. yet by custome the heire of him that holdeth in Socage may be in ward.

(b) 8 *H*.3. *Prescript*. 38. *P.sch*.21.*E*.1.*Coram rege Rot*.43 *Nota pro Hibernia Prior del St. Trinity de Dublins case*.

¶ *Marriage*. Maritagium, betokeneth not only the copulation of man and wife in marriage, but also (as in this place here) the interest of the Gardian in bestowing of a ward in marriage, which the Law gave to the Lord not for his benefit only, but that he should match him vertuously, and in a good family without disparagement as shall be said hereafter, which is the principall foundation of his estate.

(c) *Vid. Sect*.112.

¶ (c) *Reliefe*. Relevium, is derived from the Latyne word Relevare; for so (d) ancient Authors say and give this reason, Quia hæreditas quæ jacens fuit per antecessoris decessum, relevatur in manus hæredum, & propter factam relevationem facienda erit ab hærede quædam prestatio que dicitur relevium. And in Domesday it is called relevamentum and relevatio.

(d) *Bracton lib*.2.*ca*.36. *fo*.84.*Fleta lib*.1.*ca*.10. & *lib*.3.*ca*.16.17. *Britt.ca*.69.70. *Glanv.l.lib*.9.*ca*.4. & *lib*.7.*ca*.9. *Ockam de differentiis rel.vierum*.

The reliefe of a whole Knights fee is five pound, and so according to that rate. And this reliefe was as some hold certaine by the Common Law,* but the reliefe of Earles and Barons were incertaine, and therefore were called relevia rationabilia but the statute of Magna carta, cap.2 limits them in certaine, and mentioneth also a Knights fee. But I reade in the booke of Domesday, Quod Tainus vel miles regis dominicus moriens pro relevamento dimittebat regi omnia arma sua & equum vnum cum sella & alium sine cella, quod si essent ei canes vel accipitres præstabantur regi, vt si vellet, acciperet.

(*) *Ockam. ubi supra. Bracton lib*.2 *fo*.85.

Since Littleton wrote (e) there is a good Law made against fraudulent Feoffments, Gifts, Grants, &c. contrived of fraude to hinder or defraude Lords, &c. of their Reliefes and Herriots amongst other things for the exposition of which statute reade the Authorities quoted in the margent. And it is to be observed that the words of the said Act of 13.Eliz. are, (bee it therefore declared, ordeyned, and enacted) and therefore like cases and in semblable mischiefe shall bee taken within the remedy of this Act by reason of this word (declared) whereby it appeareth what the Law was before the making of this statute.

(e) 13.*Eliz.ca*.5. 17.*E*.3.*Reliefe* 3. 7.*E*.3.*ib*.11.*lib*.3.*fo*.80.&c. *Twynes case*. *Lib*.5.*fo*.60.*Goochs case*. *Lib*.6.*fo*.18. *Pakemans case*. *lib*.10.*fo*.56.*b*. *See also the statutes of* 3.*H*.7. *ca*.4.& 50.*E*.3.*ca*.6. *Vid Mich*.12.& 13.*Eliz*. *Dier* 295.

¶ *Son heire male*. (f) For regularly by the Common Law the heire shall not be in ward unlesse he clayme as heire by discent. The statute of Merton, De hijs qui primogenitos feoffare solent; (g) Did helpe Feoffments by collusion in certaine cases. And Britton saith that Robert de Walrand a sage of the Law did advise the great Lords of the Realme to make the said statute, which when it was past the same Act tooke his first effect in the heire of Walrands owne heire, whereof Britton maketh a speciall remembrance. But now (h) by the statutes of 32.and 34.H.8. of wills, he which holdeth lands by Knights service may by Act executed in his life time, or by his last will in writing dispose two parts as by the said Acts appeareth. If hee dispose all by act executed, then it shall stand good against the heire, so

(f) *Britton*.168. *Fleta.lib*.1.*ca*.9. (g) *Merton ca*.6. *Bract.fo*.85.*Britt.fo*.65. 9.*H*.4.6.4.*H*.7.*ca*.17. 27.*H*.8.7.89. *Partridges case,pl.com*.83. (h) 32.*H*.8.*ca*.1. 34.*H*.8.*ca*.5.

(i) Li. 3. fo. 25. 26. in Butlers case. Li. 6. fo. 75. in Sir George Cursons case. Li. 8. fo. 163. Mights case. Eod. lib. fo. 171. in Vigil Parkers case.
(k) Mir. ca. 1. §. 3.

so as nothing shall discend vnto the heire. But in case of a Deuise by his last will, a third part shall discend to the heire, though all be deuised away: if the Tenant leaue a third part to discend, then the deuise is good for the residue. (i) But these things require so many diuersities grounded vpon euident reasons, and are so plainely expressed in my Commentaries, as they (being verie long) shall not need to be repeated here. (k) And that the tenure by Knights seruice draweth to it Ward, Marriage, and Reliefe, is of great antiquitie, for so it was in the time of King Alfred.

¶ *Quant tiel tenant mort*. Here Littleton speaketh not of a dying seised by the Tenant, for in many cases the heire shall be in ward, albeit the Tenant died not seised, &c. nor in the homage of the Lord. As if the Tenant maketh a feoffement in fee vpon condition, and the feoffor dieth, after his death the condition is broken, the heire within age entreth for the condition broken, he shall be in ward, and yet the feoffor had no estate or right in the land at the time of his death, but onely a condition, and which was broken after his decease. (k) But because the condition restoreth the tenant to the land in nature of a discent, (for he shall be in by discent) by the same reason shall it restore the Lord to the wardship, seeing now (as Littleton saith) the heire of his Tenant is within age, and not able to doe him seruice, and no default in the Lord to barre him of his wardship.

(k) 39. E. 3. 36. tit. Gard 92. 33. E. 3. gard 162. 11. H. 7. 12. 19. E. 3. Gard 114. 18. ass. 18. 40. Ass. 36. 20. El. 362. 4. H. 6. 16. b. F. N. B. 143. 6. H. 4. 4. a.
(l) 7. H. 4. 12. 11. H. 7. 12. 22. E. 4. 7. 6. 40. E. 3. 43. 4. M. 136. 15. E. 4. 10, 11.

(l) And so I doe take it, that if the heire within age recouer in a Dum non fuit compos mentis, or Formedon en discender, or remainder as heire, or such like, the heire shall be in ward, for these be stronger cases than the former, for here a right doth discend to the Demaundant, which right being by course of Law restored to the possession of the heire within age, by consequence the Lord is to haue the wardship of him, but in the case of the condition, no right at all discended to the heire, as hath beene said.

33. E. 3. Gard 162.

And so if tenant in tayle, the remainder in fee, maketh a feoffement in fee, and dieth leauing the issue in taile within age, if the feoffee infeoffe the issue in taile, whereby hee is remitted, hee shall be in ward to the Lord: for as he is restored to the title of the land as heire, so is the Lord restored to his title of wardship as Lord of the Fee. And as to this purpose herein I take no difference betweene a right of action and a right of entrie discending, when by action the right of the land is lawfully recouered by the heire within age, to his Tenant, and albeit hee dyed not in his homage, yet there was a right of homage, and no default or laches was in the Lord, or act done by him to preiudice himselfe thereof.

11. H. 7. 12.

But if one leuis a fine executorie (as sur grant & render) to a man and his heires, and he to whom the land is granted and rendred, before execution dieth, his heire being within age entreth, he shall not be in ward, for his Ancestor was neuer tenant to the Lord: and so there is a manifest diuersitie betweene this and the other cases. Et sic de cæteris.

13. El. Dyer 298.

But if the Tenant maketh a feoffement in fee of lands holden by Knights seruice, to the vse of the feoffee and his heires, vntill the time that the feoffor pay to the feoffee or his heires a hundred pounds, for the which a time and place is limitted, the feoffee dieth, his heire within age, the Lord shal haue the wardship of the bodie of the heire, and of the lands of the feoffee, conditionally, for he cannot haue a more absolute interest in the wardship, than the heire hath in the tenancie: and therefore if the feoffor pay the mony at the day and place, and entreth into the land, in this case both the wardship of the bodie and lands is deuested, because the Lord had no absolute interest in neither of them, but doth depend vpon the performance or not performance of the condition.

(l) 12. H. 4. 16. per Thirning.

(l) So if the Conusor of a fine executorie of lands holden by Knights seruice, dieth his heire within age, the Lord shal haue the wardship of the bodie and land: but if the Conusee entreth, the heire is disherited, and the Lord hath lost the whole benefit of his wardship.

(m) 41. E. 3. 225.
(n) 15. E. 4. 11.

If the Disseisee dieth, his heire being within age, (m) the Lord shall haue the wardship of the heire of the bodie of the Disseisee. (n) But put the case that in that case the Disseisor dieth seised, and his heire within age, the Lord may seise the wardship of his heire also, and of the land also: but the doubt is, whither the heire of the Disseisee shall after the discent to the heire of the Disseisor, continue in ward, for that after the discent the heire of the Disseisor is become his lawfull tenant, and the heire of the Disseisee is not tenant vnto him vntil he hath recouered the land.

(o) 14. H. 8. 5. 4. H. 7. cap.
(p) 41. E. 3. 26. tit. Auowrie. 264. 20. H. 6. 9. 48. E. 3. 8. b. 10. E. 3. 26. 31. E. 3. tit. Gard. 116. 18. E. 3. 7. 14. H. 4. 38. 1. H. 5. Grant 43. 5. E. 4. 3. 7. E. 4. 27. 15. E. 4. 13. 2. E. 2. Auow. 181.

If Cesty que vse before the Statute of 27. H. 8. had died, his heire within age, the Lord (o) should haue the wardship of his heire: and if the feoffee had died, his heire within age, the Lord should haue had the wardship of his heire also, and so a double wardship for one and the same land, the one by the Statute of 4 H. 7. the other by the Common law.

(p) Tenant by Knights seruice maketh a gift in taile, the remainder in fee, Tenant in taile maketh a feoffement in fee, and dieth, his heire within age, the Lord shall haue the wardship of him: and if the Feoffee dieth, his heire within age, the Lord shall haue the wardship also of his heire, and of the land.

If

If Tenant by Knights seruice maketh a gift in taile, and the Donee maketh a feoffement in fee, and the donee dieth his heire within age, the Donor shall haue the wardship of him, because he is his tenant in right. (q) But if the Feoffee dieth, his heire within age, the Donor shall not haue the wardship of his heire, but the Lord paramount, because he is tenaunt in fait to him, neither shall the donor auow vpon the Feoffee or his heyre, for the seruices due vnto him, because he must in his auowrie shew the reuersion in fee to be out of him by the feoffement, and consequently the seruices incident to the reuersion are also out of him, but he shall auow vpon the Donee and his issues: and thus are all the bookes that seeme to be at variance, either answered or reconciled.

(q) *So was it holden Tr.18.El. in Com. Banc per Cur. Which myselfe heard and cited in Sir Tho. Wyats case.*
(r) *So was it resolued in Sir Tho. Wyats case. vt supr.*

(a) *La terre tenus de luy, &c.* Littleton here speaketh of Lands holden of a Subiect: for if a man hold land of the King by Knights seruice in Capite, and other lands of other lords, and dieth his heire within age, the King shall haue the wardship of all the lands by his Prerogatiue: and this was due to the King by the Common Law, the fees of certaine excepted, as in the Statute of Prærogatiua Regis cap.1. appeareth

(a) *Glanuil.li.7.c.10. Bract.li.2.fo.85,86,87. Brit.li.3.ca.2. Flet.l.1.c.10. 9.H.3. Prerog.25.21.H.3. ib.26. Rot. Finium.6.Iohan. Stat. Prerog. Reg.cap.1.*

But if a man holdeth lands of the King by Knights seruice, as of an Honour or Mannor, &c. (b) in that case the King shall onely haue the lands holden of him, and not of any other. Yet by reason of tenures of the King by Knights seruice, of certaine honours, (while they were in the Kings hands) the King (as some haue said) had (as it were by prescription) his Prerogatiue, viz Raleigh hage nec bonony and Peverel, and so of lands holden by Knights seruice of the Duchie of Lancaster in the countie Palatine.

(b) *Bract.vb.supr. Mag.carta ca.31.1.E.6.c.4.5.E.3.5. 47.E.3.21.29 H.8.br.tit. Liuery 58.28.H.8.ib.55.*

(c) When an heire hath bin in ward to the King by reason of a tenure in Capite, after his full age he must sue liuerie, which is halfe a yeares profit of his lands holden. But if he bee of full age at the time of the death of his Ancestor, then he shall pay for lands in possession a whole yeares profit for Primer seisin: but if it be of a reuersion expectant vpon an estate for life, as tenant in Dower, Tenant by the Curtesie, or Tenant for life, then he shall pay but the moity of one yeares profit.

(c) *Lib.8.fo.172. Hales case. 38.H.8.Br.tit. Liuerie 60. Vi. Sect.154.*

(d) If the heire be in ward by reason of a tenure of an Honour or Mannor (except as before) he shall not sue liuerie, but an Ouster le maine cum exitibus, albeit he neuer made tender. (e) And if he be of full age, the King shall haue no Primer seisin, but Reliefe. But where the tenure is in Capite, there the King shall haue the meane profits vntill the tender be made, and if the tender be made, and not duly pursued, the King shall also haue all the meane profits.

(d) *1 El Dy.168.*
(e) *32.H.8.tit. Liu.Br.62.*

(f) He that holdeth of the King by Socage in chiefe, and dieth, his heire of full age, the King shall haue liuerie and Primer seisin onely of the lands so holden, and not of the lands holden of others. (g) But if the heire of such a Tenant in Socage in chiefe, be within the age of fourteene at the death of his Ancestor, he shall neither sue liuerie, nor pay Primer seisin, either then or any time after: and the reason thereof is, for that the custodie of his bodie and lands in that case, belong to the Prochein amy, as Gardein in Socage. (h) Neither shall the King haue Primer seisin of Lands holden in Burgage, (as some haue sayd) for that it is no Tenure in Capite.

(f) *38.H.8. Liuer. Br 60. 45.E.3.11.35.H.6.52. Stanf.13.b.*
(g) *20.El.Dy 362. F.N.B.259.b.*
(h) *F.N.B.263.7.E.4.17. Stanf. Prer.13. Br. tit. Liu 64*

Note, there is a generall liuerie, and a speciall liuerie: A generall liuerie hath two properties:

First, it is full of charge to the heire, for he must find an office in euerie Countie where he hath land, or else he cannot sue a generall liuerie, and hee must sue out his writ of Ætate probanda, &c.

(i) The second propertie is, that it is full of danger: First, It concludeth the heire for euer after to denie any Tenure found in the Office. Secondly, If Liuerie be not sued of all and of euerie parcell which the King ought to haue, whither it be found in the office, or not found (for a generall liuerie could not be sued by parcels) the liuerie is void, and the King may reseise the lands, and be answered of the meane profits. So it is if the Office be insufficient, or the Processe whereof the Liuerie was made be insufficient, or the like, the King shall reseise, as is aforesaid. (a) Therefore for the ease of the heire, and for auoyding of such danger, the heire for the most part sueth out a speciall liuerie, which containeth a beneficiall pardon, and saueth the sayd charges, and preuenteth the said conclusion, and the other dangers, which being of grace, and not of right, as the generall liuerie is, the King may well and iustly take more for a special liuerie, than for a generall, for the causes aforesaid; but euer with such moderation as the heyre may chearefully go through therewith.

(i) *46.E.3.33.47.E.3.21. 21.H.6.28.b.33.H.6.50. 29.Ass.8.Pl.Com. Countee of Leic.case.44.E.3.1.& 25. 12 R.2.Liu.28.2.H.7.fo.12.*
(a) *1.H.4.6.b.37.H.8.Estop.Br.218.7.E.6 ib.222. Scurfields case. Tr.8.Ia.in cur. Ward.23.El.Dy.377. 28.H.8.Br.tit. Liuery 56.*

Note that a liuerie is in nature of a restitution, which is to bee taken fauourably: for if liuerie be made of a mannor cum pertinentijs, the heire shall thereby haue the aduowson appendant, otherwise it is in Grants by Letters Patents.

41.E.3.5.5.E.6.27.ass.48. Pl.Com.252.20.El.Dy 360.

Since the time that Littleton wrote (c) there is a Court of Wards and Liueries erected by Authority of Parliament concerning the order of the Kings wards, &c. to be holden before the Master of the Wards, and the Councell of that Court appointed by those Acts. This hath

(c) *32.H.8.46.33.H.8.c.21.*

made such a manifold alteration, as were too long here to be inserted, & doth belong to another Treatise mentioned in the Epistle of the iurisdiction of Courts, where it were necessary, that the true iurisdiction of that Court should be set downe, a matter of no great difficultie, seeing it began so late by Authority of Parliament. And since Littletons time, (d) there is a right profitable Statute made concerning the finding of Offices and other things, not only concerning the Kings wards, or their rights and possessions, but some other prouisions very beneficiall for the subiect, in all to the number of 12. (e) First that such persons as hold for tearme of yeares, or by copy of Court Rolle, or haue any Rent, common or profit apprender out of any lands found in any office, wherby the King is intituled to the wardship of the Lands or Tenements, or to the forfeiture of the Lands or tenements vpon attainder of treason, felony, præmunire, or any other offence, yet may they haue, hold, enioy, and perceiue their seuerall estates, interests and proffits, although they be not found in the office. And this being a beneficiall Law the estates of Tenant by statute staple, Merchant, and elegit, & Executors that hold lands for payment of debts are taken to be within the benefit of the clause: (f) and so is a doubt in 14. Eli. Dier cleered.

(d) 2. E. 6. ca. 8.

(e) 4. E. 4. 23. 33. H. 8. tit. entre congeab. Br. 125.

(f) 14. Eliz. Dier fo. 319.

2. Where it is found, that the heire is of fewer yeares than in truth hee is, hee shall not bee concluded hereby, (g) but euery such heire at his very full age may prosecute a Writ of ætate probanda, and sue his Liuery or ouster le maine: in which case he had no remedy by the Common Law, but the King may trauerse such an Office found.

(g) 5. Mar. Dier. 136.

(a) 3. Where one person or more be found heire, where another person is heire, the partie grieued had no remedy.

4. Or where one person or more be found heire in one County, and another person or persons found heire in another County, there could haue beene no interpleading.

5. Or if any person be vntruly found by office Lunaticke, or ideot, or dead, the party grieued may trauerse the said office; and you may reade in Kens case how the office shall be trauersed vpon this Act.

(b) 6. Where it is vntruly found by office that any person attainted of Treason, Felony, or Præmunire is seised of any lands, &c. the party grieued hauing iust title of freehold, shall haue his trauers or Monstrans de droit (without being driuen by this double matter of Record to his petition of right as he was before this Statute, which is much more speedy then the petition; for vpon the petition there be foure Writs of search, and euery one must haue 40. dayes before the serning, and now but two Writs of search.

(a) 24. E. 3. 31. 38. 9. H. 6. 18. 12. E. 4. 16. 30. Ass. 28. lib. 4. fo. 56. & 60. Sadlers case. Stanf. prerog. 58. b. 52. 5. E. 4. 4. 16. E. 4. 4. 1. H. 7. 14. 2. H. 7. 12. 4. H. 7. 15. 8. H. 7. 11. F. N. B. 262. 12. R. 2. Liuery 28. F. N. B. 233. Lib. 7. fo. 44. 45. Kens case.
(b) 4. E. 4. 23. 10. H. 6. 19. Lib. 4. fo. 56. &c. Sadlers case. 32. H. 8. entre Conge. Br. 125. 14. E. 3. ca. 14.

7. Where an office is found by these words or the like quod de quo vel de quibus tenementa predicta tenentur, iuratores pred' ignorant, or holden of the King per quæ servitia iuratores ignorant, it shall not be taken for any immediate tenure of the King in chiefe, but in such cases a melius inquirendum to be awarded as hath beene accustomed of old time. This branch hath beene well (d) expounded, for if the first Office finde a tenure of the King per que servitia, &c. yet if vpon the Melius inquirendum the tenure be found of a subiect, the first office hath lost his force per sensum huius statuti, and need not be trauersed, and the Melius, &c. is in nature of the Diem clausit extremum or mandamus, &c. and this was but a declaration of the auncient Common Law, as by the words of the Statute (as hath beene accustomed of old) it appeareth; but if vpon the melius it be found againe as vncertainely as before is said, then it is in iudgement of Law a tenure in Capite, and so it was before the making of this Act, and so are the bookes that speake hereof to be intended; but if vpon the melius a tenure be found of the King Vt de manerio per que servitia, &c. it shall be taken for Knights seruice.

(c) Vid. lib. 6. fo. 6. Wheelers case.

(d) 12. Eliz. Dier fo. 292. a. Lib. 8. fo. 168. Paris Stoughters case.

13. Eliz. Dier. 306. 4. H. 6. 13. 10. H. 4. 2. b.

8. Where it is found that Lands, &c. are holden of the King immediately where in truth they are holden of a common person and not of the King immediatly, and that the heire is within age, such heire within age shall haue his trauerse, &c. which he could not haue had by the Common Law.

9. The meane Lords of whom the lands are holden which the King hath by his prerogatiue during the minority of the heire shall receiue and take such Rents as are due vnto them by the hands of such of the Kings officers as receiue the proffits of the same lands, where before that Act, the Lords vsed to spare the Rents due, &c. during the Kings possession, and after Liuery sued, charged the heire with all the arrerages.

10. There is a prouision for offices found before the statute or before the 20. day of March next after the Act.

11. A speciall clause is that a Scire fac' shall be awarded vpon euery trauers by force of this Act, and where the partie was put to his petition, there vpon the trauers there shall bee two Writs of search granted.

12. And lastly, if iudgement shall be giuen against the King vpon a trauerse by vertue of this Act, all former rights appearing of Record are saued to the King. But albeit these points are most necessary to be knowne, yet let vs now returne to Littleton.

Littleton warily and materially (treating of a common person) saith tenus de luy holden of him, for he shall haue nothing in ward but that which is holden of him. But the King by his prerogatiue

15. E. 4. 12. 46. E. 3. 12. 21. H. 6. 11. 3. H. 7. 5.

prerogatiue shall not only haue such lands and tenements which (as hath beene said) the heire of his Tenant by Knights seruice in capite holdeth of others, but such inheritances also as are not holden at all of any, as Rent charges, Rent secke, Faires, Markets, Warrens, Annuities, and the like; and so is the Law cleerely holden at this day, as it hath beene resolued; and so experience teacheth, that the King by his prerogatiue giuen to him by the ancient Common Law shall haue those inheritances not holden, and so the Quære made by (o) Stanford is cleered and made without question.

(o) Stanf.prær.fo.8.

The Law is changed since Littleton wrote in many cases both for the marriage of the body, and for the wardship of the lands, and a farre greater benefit giuen to the Lords then the Common Law gaue them, and some aduantage giuen to the heires, which before they had not, which shall be touched briefly.

If the Father had made an estate for life or a gift in tayle of lands holden by Knights seruice to his eldest sonne, or other heire apparant within age, the remainder in fee to any other, and died, the heire should not haue beene in ward, for this was out of the statute of Merlebridge: But at this day the heire shall be in that case in ward for his body, and a third part of his land

Marlebridge, ca.1. pl.com.82. 27.H.6.10. 33.H.6.14.

(a) So if the father had infeoffed his eldest sonne within age and a stranger and the heires of the sonne, and died, the sonne should haue beene out of ward; but at this day he shall bee in ward for his body, and for a third part of his moitie. (b) So if the father had infeoffed any of his younger sonnes or others for the making of his wife a ioynture, or for the aduancement of his daughters, or for the payment of his debts, and after infeoffe or conuey the the land to his heire and died, his heire within age, his heire should not haue beene in ward, because hee was bound by the law of nature and nations to prouide for them, but now in all these cases the heire shall be in ward for his body, and a third part of the land, and all this groweth by construction vpon the Statutes of 32 and 34.H.8 (c) But if either the eldest sonne, or any of the younger sonnes purchase lands of his father which are holden by Knights seruice, bona fide for the reasonable value, this is out of those statutes, and the heire shall neither bee in ward nor pay Primer seison.

(a) 31.E.3. Collusion 29. 33.H.6.14.
(b) 33.H.6.14 27.H.6.7. Lib.6.fo.76.77. Sir George Cursons case. 10.Eliz 260. 3.Eliz.193. 20.Eliz.361. 19.Eliz 276. 5.Marie.158.
(c) Lib.8.fo.83. Leonard Loueys case.

And in all the cases abouesaid (for example) if a Feoffment be made to the vse of his wife for life, or to the vse of any of his younger sonnes for life, or to the vse of some persons for life for payment of debts, and vpon all these estates a remainder is limitted ouer, if the wife or Tenant for life die in the life of the father, (d) or if it be conueyed to the vse of the wife or younger children in fee, or fee taile, or in fee for payment of debts, and these lands are conueyed away in the life time of the father, after the decease of the father no wardship, &c. accrueth by force of any of the said Statutes, for such estates must continue till the title of wardship doe growe.

(d) Lib.2.fo.91. Binghams case. lib 6. vbi supra.84. Lib.8 fo.165. Digbyes case.

(e) If the father conuey his lands holden by Knights seruice either of the King or of any meane Lord to his middle sonne in taile, the remainder to the youngest sonne in fee and dieth the eldest being within age, and the King or Lord seize the body and two parts of the land, if the middle brother die without issue, the King or the Lord shall not haue any benefit of the statute against him in remainder, for the statute was once satisfied and the statute extendeth not to him in remainder.

(e) 14.Eliz.Dier 308. 3. Marie Dier.130. Lib.2.fo.93.94. Binghams case, & Northcots case. Lib.10.fo.80.b. Leonard Loueys case.

(f) If there be a grandfather, father, and diuers sonnes, and the grandfather in the life of the father conuey his lands holden by Knights seruice to any of the sonnes, this is out of the statute of 32.H.8. and if the grandfather die, there is neither wardship nor Primer seison due, For the father hath the immediate care of his sonnes, but if the father be dead, then the care of them belong to the grandfather, and then if the granfather conuey any of the lands to any of the sonnes, it is within the said statute: (g) and a conueyance to the vse of any of his collaterall blood, which is not his heire apparant is out of the said statute. And so are conueyances eyther by father, either by father or mother to or to the vse of bastard children out of the statute, for qui ex damnato coitu nascuntur, inter liberos non computentur. And the Preamble speaketh of lawfull generations. If a man seised of lands holden in Socage conuey them to the vse of his wife, or of his children, or payment of his debts and after purchase lands holden by Knights seruice in Capite, and dieth his heire within age, the King shall haue no part of the Socage land. (h) But if in that case he had by his will in writing deuised his Socage lands in fee, and after purchased lands holden in capite, and dieth, the King shall haue so much of the Socage lands as will make a full third part of all. The benefit that grew to the subiect by those Acts of Parliament, were that tenants in Fee simple might deuise their lands by their Last wills in writing in such manner and forme, as by the said Acts appeareth. Also that the father might infeoffe his eldest sonne or other heire lineall or collaterall of his lands holden by Knights seruice, and two parts of the lands shalbe out of ward. And in * Mightes case you shall reade excellent matter of estates made vpon collusion.

(f) Lib.6.fo.77. Sir George Cursons case. 2.Eliz.Dier.181. 8.Eliz.Dier 252.
(g) Lib.10.fo 83. Leonard Loueys case. 18.Eliz.Dier.385.
(h) Leon. Loueys case vbi supra. Butler & Bakers case.lib.3.fo.25.&c.
* Lib.8.fo.163. Mightes case.

And both the Statutes of 32. and 34.H.8. concerning wills and wardships are many wayes preiudiciall to the heires, as taking one example for many. If Tenant by Knights seruice make a feoffment in fee to the use of his wife and her heires, or to the use of a younger sonne and his heires, or wholy for the payment of his debts. In these cases although nothing at all of the lands so holden discend to the heire, but hee is disherited of the same, yet his bodie shall be in ward: but this for a little taste may suffice, more hereof you may reade in my Reports in the seuerall Cases noted in the margent.

Leon. Louezs case. ubi supra. 22. Eliz. Dier. 367.

32. E. 3. gard. 61.

¶ *Pleine age.* **Full age regularly is one and twentie yeares.**

2. H. 5. 4.

¶ *Entendement del ley. Entendement* .i. *intellectus* **the understanding** or intelligence of the Law. Regularly Iudges ought to adiudge according to the common intendement of Law.

10. H. 6. 8. 21. E. 3. 33. a. 27. H. 8.

By intendement of Law euery Parson or Rector of a Church is supposed to be resident on his Benefice, unlesse the contrarie be proued.

Of common intendement one part of a Manor shall not be of another nature then the rest.

Of common intendement a will shall not be supposed to be made by collusion. In facto quod se habet ad bonum & malum magis de bono, quam de malo lex intendit. Lex intendit vicinum vicini facta scire. Nulla Impossibilia aut inhonesta sunt præsumenda, vera autem & honesta, & possibilia. Lex semper intendit quod conuenit rationi. As in this case the Gardeine shall haue the custodie of the land untill the heire come to his full age of one and twentie yeares, because by intendement of law the heire is not able to doe Knights Seruice before that age, which is grounded upon apparant reason. There note that the full age of a man or a woman to alien, demise, let, contract, &c. is one and twentie yeares, the ciuill Law fiue and twentie yeares, for then the Romans accounted men to haue plenam maturitatem, and the Lombards at eighteene yeares.

Vide Britton. fol. 169.

¶ *Si le heire ne soit marie al temps del mort de tiel Auncester, &c. Auncester* **is deriued of the Latine word** antecessor, **and in Law there** is a difference betweene antecessor and prædecessor. For antecessor is applyed to a naturall person, as I. S. & antecessores sui, but Prædecessor is applyed to a bodie Politique or Corporate, as Episcopus London & prædecessores sui. Rector de D. & prædecessores sui, &c.

Glanuill. lib. 7. cap. 1. Mirror. cap. 5. §. 2. Britton. fol. 168. b. 39. H. 6. cap. 2.

¶ *Mes si tiel tenant deuie son heire female esteant del age de* 14. *ans, &c.* **And the reason as I find in Antiquitie, wherefore** the Law gaue the marriage of the heire female if she were within the age of fourteene, and that she should not marrie her selfe, was pur ceo que les heires females de nostre terre ne se marieront a nous enemies, & dount il nous couiendroit lour homage prendre, si eux se puissent marier a lour volunt. This is a speciall age for an heire female to bee out of ward, if shee attaine unto it in the life time of her ancester, for at that age she may haue a husband able to do Knights Seruice. A woman hath seuen ages for seuerall purposes appointed to her by Law: as seuen yeares for the Lord to haue aide pur file marier: nine yeares to deserue Dower, Twelue yeares to consent to mariage, untill fourteene yeares to be in ward, fourteene yeares to bee out of ward, if she attained thereunto in the life of her Ancester; Sixteene yeeres for to tender her mariage if she were under the age of fourteene at the death of her ancester, and one and twentie yeares to alienate her Lands, Goods and Chattels.

35. H. 6. 40. Bracton. lib. 2. cap. 37.

34. E. 1 Stat. 3. Glanuil. lib. 7. cap. 9. Dier 5. Marie 162. Bracton. lib. 2. cap. 37. F. N. B. 202.

A man also by the Law for seuerall purposes hath diuers ages assigned unto him, viz. twelue yeares to take the oath of Allegeance in the Torne or Leet. Fourteene yeares to consent to mariage, fourteene yeeres for the heire in socage to choose his Gardein, and fourteene yeares is also accounted his age of discretion. Fifteene yeares for the Lord to haue aide pur faire fitz Chiualer. Under one and twentie to be in ward to the Lord by Knights Seruice. Under fourteene to be in ward to Gardein in Socage. Fourteene to be out of ward of Gardein in Socage, and one and twentie to be out of ward of Gardein in Chiualrie, and to alien his Lands Goods and Chattels.

35. H. 6. 52. tit. gard. 71. Staunford. 3. b. F. N. B. 256. 259. 35. H. 6. 40.

¶ *Mes si tiel heire female soit deins lage de* 14. *ans & nient marie, &c. Le Seignior auera la gard del terre.* **But put case that the Lord cannot** haue the wardship of the Land, as if the Lord before the age of fourteene granteth ouer the wardship of the bodie, in this case the grantee of the bodie cannot enioy the benefit of the two yeares, because he cannot hold ouer the land, and the Lord, which hath the wardship of the Land only should lose the benefit of the two yeares, because he hath the lands only and cannot tender any mariage, therfore in this case the heire female shal enter into her land at her age of 14. yeares. So if a tenant holdeth of one Lord by prioritie, & of another by posterioritie & dieth, his heire female within the age of 14. yeares, the Lord by posterioritie shall haue the lands, but untill her age of 14. yeares, because the mariage belongeth not to him. Also if the Lord marieth the heire female within the two yeares, her husband and shee shall presently enter into the lands. For Cessante causa, cessat effectus: & cessante ratione legis, cessat beneficium legis.

Britton. fol. 169. 35. H. 6. 52.

It

If the Lord tender a conuenable mariage to the heire within the two yeares, and shee marie else where within those two yeares, the Lord shall not haue the forfeiture of the mariage, for the Statute giueth the two yeares only to make a tender. *35.H.6.52.35.H.6.tit gard. 71. Lib.6.fol.71. the Lord Darcies Case.*

¶ *Et si le seignior deins les dits 2. ans ne luy tender tiel mariage, &c. donque el al fine del dits 2. ans poet enter, & ouste le seignior.* This is so euident, as it needeth no explication.

¶ *Mes si tiel heire female soit marie deins lage de 14. ans en la vie son Ancester, & son ancester deuie il esteant deins age de 14. ans le seignior nauera la gard forsque de la terre iesque al age de 14. ans &c.* Note, albeit the heire female be maried at the age of twelue yeares in the life of her ancestor, (at which age shee may consent to Matrimony) to a man of full age, that is able to doe Knights Seruice, yet if the Ancestor die before her age of fourteene, the Gardein shall haue the Land vntill her age of fourteene, because (as hath beene said) that is the time appointed by the Common Law. And so if the heire male be married in the life of the Ancestor at his age of fourteene yeares, and the Ancestor dieth, the Lord shall haue the Land vntill the ward commeth to the age of one and twentie. *F.N.B.143.*

¶ *Car ceo est hors del case del dit statute, intant que le seignior ne poet tender mariage a luy que est marie.*

Natura non facit vacuum, nec lex supervacuum. The Law doth neuer enforce a man to doe a vaine thing.

And where the said Statute of W.1. giueth vnto the Lord the said two yeares, thereby is implyed, that if he dieth within the two yeares, his Executors or Administrators shall haue the same. For when the Statute vesteth an interest in the Lord, the Law giueth the same to his Executors or Administrators. Then put case, That a Lord hath the wardship of the bodie and land of an heire female, and maketh his Executor and dieth before her age of fourteene yeares, whether the Executor shall haue the two yeares, because the Executor is not Lord. But I take it, the Executor hauing the wardship of the bodie and land, shall in that case haue the two yeares, for that they were vested in the Lord. *27.H.8.3. 11.E.3.Executors 77. 4.E.3.55. 28.Ass.p.7.*

It is further prouided by the said Statute, that if the Lord tender a Conuenable marriage to the heire female, within the said two yeares, and the heire female refuseth, then the Lord shall hold the land vntill her age of one and twentie yeares, and further vntill he hath leuied the value of her mariage. But if the Lord doth not tender a mariage within the two yeares, he shal lose the value of the mariage, and content himselfe with the two yeares value. *31.Ass.p.26. Lib.6 fol.71. L.Darcies case.*

¶ *Car deuant le dit statut &c. sicome appiert per le rehersall & parols de le dit statute.* Nota, the rehearsall or preamble of the Statute is a good mean to find out the meaning of the statute, and as it were a key to open the vnderstanding thereof. The tender of a mariage to an heire female before the age of fourteene is void, which must be vnderstood where the Lord may hold the land for the said two yeares, for then the statute appointeth the time of the tender, but where the Lord cannot haue the two yeares, he may tender a mariage to the heire female at any time after the age of twelue and before fourteene, for so he might haue done at the Common Law. *35.H.6.52.gard.71. 35.H.6.52.gard.71. Lib.6 fo.71. Lord Darcies case Britton.169.*

Sect. 104.

¶ Nota que le plein age de male & female solonque le common parlance, est dit lage de 21. ans. Et lage de discretion est dit lage de 14. ans, car a tiel age le enf. que est marie deins tiel age a vn feme, puit agreer

Note that the full age of male and female according to common speech is said the age of 21. yeares. And the age of discretion is called the age of 14. yeares, For at this age, the Infant which is maried within such age to a wo-

¶ Of full age, which is the age of one and twentie, and of the age of discretion, which is the age of fourteene somwhat hath beene spoken before. But now to the point of agreement or disagreement in this case. The time of agreement, or disagreement, when they marrie infra annos nubiles, is for the woman at 12. or after, and for the man, at fourteene, or after, and there need no new mariage, if they so agree, but disagree they cannot *5.Mar.gard.Br.pl.vltimo. 39.E.3.32.33.prer.reg cap.6. Tr.24.Eliz. Rot.842. in bank le roy Banisters case.*

not before the said ages, and then they may disagree and marie againe to others without any diuorce: and if they once after giue consent, they can neuer disagree after. If a man of the age of fourteene marie a woman of the age of ten, at her age of twelue he may aswell disagree, as she may, though he were of the age of consent, because in contracts of Matrimonie either both must be bound, or equall election of disagreement giuen to both, and so è conuerso, if the woman be of the age of consent, and the man under.

a tiel mariage, ou disagreer.

man, may agree or disagree to such mariage.

Sect. 105.

CEt si la gardeine en chiualrie marie un foits le garde deins lage de 14. ans, a un feme, & puis sil al age de 14. ans disagree a le mariage, il est dit per ascuns, que lenfant nest pas tenuz per le ley destre auterfoits marie per son gardeine pur ceo que le gardeine auoit un foits le mariage de luy, & pur ceo il fuit hors de son garde, quant al garde de son corps. Et quant il auoit un foits le mariage de luy & un foits fuit hors de son garde, il nauera plus auant le mariage de luy.

AND if the gardeine in Chiualrie doth once marie the Ward within his age of 14. yeares to a woman, & if afterward at his age of 14. yeares he disagree to the mariage, it is said by some, that the Infant is not tied by the Law, to bee againe maried by his Gardein, for that the Gardein had once the mariage of him, and because hee was once out of his ward, as to the ward of his bodie. And when hee had once the mariage of him, and hee was once out of his wardship, he shall no more haue the mariage of him.

13.E.1.gard.137. Britton.fol.169.acc. Glanvil.lib.7.cap.12. 27.H.6.gard.118.

CIt is a maxime in law. Quod Dominus non maritabit minorem in custodia sua nisi semel, And another saith, Si semel legitimè nupt' fuer', &c. postmodum non tenebuntur sub custodia dominorum esse. Albeit this mariage is de facto, and not de iure, and though the disagreement dissolueth it ab initio, yet the Lord shall neuer haue the mariage of him.

27.H.6.gard.118.

And so if the Gardein marieth his ward to a woman, and after the mariage is dissolued by reason of a precontract, yet the Gardein shall neuer haue the mariage of the ward againe.

27.H.6.gard.118.

But if one rauisheth a ward from the Lord, and marieth him within the age of consent, in that case if the Lord taketh again his ward, and hee at the age of consent disagreeth to the mariage, the Lord shall haue the mariage of him, for hee neuer had it before.

F.N.B.143.

So likewise, if the Ancestor marieth his heire apparant infra annos nubiles, and dieth his heire within age, the ward disagreeth, the Gardein shall haue the wardship of him. The same Law it is in the same case, if the wife dieth before the age of consent, the Lord shall haue the mariage of the heire.

7.H.6.11.

(a) 30.E.1.gard.156. 12.E.1.gard.138. 21.E.3.19. 20.E.3.gard.41. Temps E.1.ibidem.128. 35.H.6.45. 7.H.6.11. Vide prerogat.Regis cap.6. 13.H.3.gard.147. Staunf.prær.26.27. (b) 27.H.6.gard.118. F.N.B.143.m. 19.E.3.iudgement 123. 45.E.3.16. (c) 47.E.3.tit.action sur le statut.38. and the Bookes abouesaid.

And so note a diuersitie when the ward is maried by the Ancestor or by a Rauisher, and when by the Gardein himselfe. (a) For if the Ancestor marie his heire apparant infra annos nubiles and dieth: In this case if the mariage be dissolued by disagreement, either of the ward or of his wife, the Gardein shall haue the mariage of him (b) And so it is if a Rauishor marie a ward infra annos nubiles, and the mariage is dissolued vt supra, the Gardein shall haue the mariage. If the heire male in ward of the age of ten yeares be maried without the consent of the Lord, he may tender unto the heire infra annos nubiles a mariage, albeit he be so maried. and if he refuse and agree to the former mariage, the Lord shall haue the forfeiture of his mariage, as it hath beene holden, [redacted] But otherwise it is (c) (saith Littleton) where the Gardein himselfe marieth the ward, vt supra, And the reason of the diuersitie is, because in this case the Gardein had once the mariage of him, but so had not he in either of the other cases, and it is a maxime in Law Quod Dominus non maritabit pupillum nisi semel.

It appeareth vpon consideration of all the bookes aforesaid that where the Ancestor marrieth his heire apparant within the age of consent, and dieth, the enfant still being within the age of Consent, the Lord may take the infant (if he will) into his possession, in respect the infant may disagree to the marriage, and if the infant be deteyned from him, he shall recouer him in a writ of Rauishment of Ward, and thereupon haue the infant deliuered to him. (d) But if the Ancestor marrieth his heire apparant infra annos nubiles, and dieth his heire being infra annos nubiles, and after age of Consent the heire agreeth to the marriage, neither the King nor the Lord shall haue the marriage, for now it is a marriage ab initio, and there neede no other marriage.

(d) 7.H.6 11. adiudge in the booke at large.

Section 106.

EN mesme le maner est, si le gardein luy marie, & la feme deuie esteant lenfant deins lage de xiiii. ans, ou xxi.

IN the same manner it is if the gardian marry him & the wife die the infant being within the age of 14. yeares or 21.

This Littleton addeth because hee spake in the case next before of a disagreement by the infant, here hee saith, that if the wife die, the infant being within the age of consent.

Sect. 107.

EEt que tiel enfant poit disagreer a tiel mariage, quant il vient al age de xiiii. ans, il est proue per les parolx del statute de Merton Cap.6. que issint dit.

ANd that such infant may disagree to such marriage, when he comes to the age of 14. yeares, it is proued by the words of the statute of Merton cap.6. which saith thus:

De dominis qui maritauerint illos quos habent in custodia sua, villanis, vel alijs, sicut burgensibus vbi disparagentur, si talis hæres fuerit infra 14. *annos, & talis ætatis quod matrimonium consentire non possit, tunc si parentes illi conquerantur, dominus amittat custodiam illam vsque ad ætatem hæredis, & omne commodum quod inde receptum fuerit conuertatur ad commodum hæredis infra ætatem existent', secundum dispositionem parentum propter dedecus ei impositum. Si autem fuerit* 14. ans & vltra, *quod consentire possit, & tali matrimonio consenserit, nulla sequatur pœna.*

Et issint est proue p mesme le estatute, que nul disparagement est mes lou celuy que est en garde est marie deins lage de xiiii. ans.

And so it is proued by the same statute, that there is no disparagement but where hee which is in Ward is maried within the age of 14. yeares.

L*Estatut de Merton.* So called because the Parliament was holden at Merton.

Et que tiel enfant poit disagreer, &c. il est proue, &c. Note the time of disagreement is set downe by act of Parliament, and so obserued by Littleton, who seekes no other proofe therein then by the Law of England.

Merton. ca.6.

Vbi disparagentur. Disparagement, disparagatio commeth of the verbe disparage, and that of dispar, and ago.

Now it is necessary to bee vnderstood what disparagements there be for the which the heire may refuse.

And of such disparagements there be foure kindes. The first propter vitium animi, as an ideot, non compos mentis, a Lunatique, &c. The second propter vitium sanguinis, as first a Villeine, 2. Burgensis. 3. The sonne or daughter of a person attainted of treason or felony, [illegible] pardoned, for the blood is corrupted. 4. A Bastard. 5. An Alien or the childe of an Alien. Burgensis is a man of trade, as an Haberdasher, a Draper

Bracton lib.2.fol.91. Britton fol.169. Fleta lib.1. cap.12. Mirror ca.2.§.17. Rot. Parl.18.E.1.fo.9. The daughter of Neuil maried to the sonne of Tho: of Weyland after his attainder.

Draper or the like, (and this agreeth with the Ciuill Law, Patricij cum plebis matrimonia ne contrahant.) Whereof Glanuill speaketh thus. Si vero fuerit filius burgensis ætatem habere tunc intelligitur, quando discrete sciuerit denarios numerare, & pannos vlnare & alia paterna negotia similiter exercere.

The third propter vitium corporis, as first de membris, hauing but one hand, one foot, one eye, &c. Secondly, deformitie, as to looke a squint, a criple, halt, lame, decrepit, crooked, &c. Thirdly, Priuation, as blind, deafe, dumbe, &c. Fourthly, Disease horrible, as Leprosie, Palsy, Dropsey, or such like diseases. Fiftly, great and continuall infirmitie, as a Consumption and such like. Sixtly, Impotencie to haue children in respect either of age past children, or so tender yeares as there is too great disparitie, or for naturall disabilitie or impediment or such like. Seuenthly, Defloured of her Virginitie.

1.E.6.cap.13.

The fourth kind of disparagement was propter iacturam priuilegij, &c. as to marie the heire to a widow, whereby he should by reason of the Bigamie haue lost the benefit of his Cleargie, whereby he might saue his life, but now the exception of Bigamie in that case is ousted by the (d) Statute. And Littleton saith that there bee many other disparagements which are not specified in the said Statute, for those two mentioned are put but for examples. In a word it must be competens maritagium absque disparagatione.

(d) Vide Sect.109. F.N.B.149.

¶ *Si talis heres fuerit infra 14. annos, & talis ætatis quod matrimonio consentire non possit, &c.* Note albeit the ward where hee is disparaged may disagree at his age of fourteene yeares, yet the Law doth so abhorre the odious dealing of the Gardein, to whom the custodie of the heire is committed, and his horrible profanation of honorable mariage, the only ligament of mens Inheritances as it inflicteth a great punishment vpon the Lord in this case, albeit the mariage bee not perfect, but auoidable by disagreement.

¶ *Tunc si parentes illi conquerantur.* Littleton in the next Section expoundeth these words in this manner, viz. Si parentes conquerantur, .i. Si parentes inter eos lamententur, quæ est tant a dire, que si les Cosens de tiel infant ont cause de faire lamentation ou complaint pur le hont fait lour Cosen issint disparage, quel est in manner vn hont a eux. Parens est nomen generale ad omne genus cognationis. See more of this in the next Section.

¶ *Dominus amittat custodiam illam vsque ad ætatem hæredis & omne commodum quod inde receptum fuerit conuertatur ad commodum hæredis, &c.* Here followeth the penaltie.

First, amittat custodiam, that is, the whole benefit of the wardship. But in this case if the Gardein hath granted the wardship of the Land to another bona fide, and after, the heire is disparaged, the Grantee shall not forfeit his interest, for the Statute is (Dominus amittat custodiam.)

Secondly, Et omne commodum quod inde receptum fuerit conuertatur ad commodum hæredis secundum dispositionem parentum. These words are expounded by Littleton which needeth no further explanation: Now where readers vpon this Statute, haue put a case, that if the Tenant hath issue a daughter, his wife enseint with a sonne and dieth, the Lord doth disparage the daughter before the age of twelue yeares, the sonne is borne, the daughter disagrees, the sonne dieth, the daughter within the age of fourteene, she shall be in ward againe. This case is not warranted by this Statute, for this Statute extends not to the heires female.

Vide the second part of the Institutes. Merton cap.5.6. 35.H.6.53.

If the Tenant make a Lease to A. for life, the remainder to B. in fee, the Tenant for life surrenders vpon condition, B. dieth his heire within age, the Lord disparages the heire, Tenant for life entreth for the condition broken and dieth, the heire shall be out of ward, for that he claymeth as heire to one man. But if after the disparagement, lands discend from another ancestor to the ward so disparaged, he shall be in ward for those Lands.

If two Joyntenants be of a ward, and the one disparageth the heire, both shall lose the wardship, for the words be & omne commodum, &c.

¶ *Si autem fuerit 14. annorum & vltra, &c. nulla sequatur pœna.* By which it appeareth (as Littleton obserueth) that there is no disparagement but where the ward is maried within the age of fourteene.

Britton. fol.169.acc.

Section 108.

9.H.3.

¶ *Estatute de magna Charta.* Though it be in forme of a

¶ Nota que il soloit estre question, coment ceux

Note, it hath beene a question how these words shall bee pa-

parolx serront entendes, Si parentes conquerantur, &c.*Et il semble a ascuns q̃ consideront lestatute de Magna Charta que voit, Quod hæred' maritentur absque disparagatione, &c. Sur quel cel Statute de Merton sur tiel point est foundue, Que nul action poit estre pris sur cel Statute, entant que il ne fuit unques view ne oye, q̃ ascun action fuit port sur cel Statute de Merton p cel disparagement enuers le gardeine pur cest matter auandit, &c. Et si ascun action puissoit estre prise sur tiel matter, il serra entendue ascun foits estre mise en vre. *Et nota que ceux parolx, serront entendes, Si parentes conquerantur, id est si parentes inter eos lamententur, que est taunt adire, que si les cousins de tiel enfant ont cause de faire lamentation ou complaint enter eux pur le hont fait a lour Cousin issint dispavage, quel est en maner un hont a eux, donques puit le pro-

vnderstood, (*Si parentes conquerantur.*) *And it seemeth to some who considering the statute of *Magna carta*, which willeth, *Quod hæredes maritentur absque disparagatione, &c.* Vpon which, this statute of *Merton* vpon this point is founded, That no action can be brought vpon this statute, insomuch as it was neuer seene or heard that any action was brought vpon the statute of *Merton* for this disparagement against the gardian for the matter aforesaid, &c. And if any action might haue beene brought for this matter, it shall bee intended that at some time it would haue beene put in vre. *And note that these words shall bee vnderstood thus, *Si parentes conquerantur, id est si parentes inter eos lamententur*, which is as much to say, as if the cousins of such infant haue cause to make lamentation or complaint amongst themselues for the shame done to their cousin so disparaged, which in manner is a shame to them, then may the next

Charter, yet being granted by assent and authoritie of Parliament Littleton here saith it is a statute. (Vid. lib. 8. the Princes case.)

This Parliamentary Charter hath diuers appellations in Law; Here it is called Magna Carta, not for the length or largenesse of it (for it is but short in respect of the Charters granted of priuate things to priuate persons now adayes being (Elephantinæ cartæ) but it is called the great Charter in respect of the great weightinesse & weighty greatnesse of the matter contained in it in few words, being the fountaine of all the fundamentall Lawes of the Realme, and therefore it may truely be said of it, that it is magnum in parvo. It is in our bookes called Carta libertatum et comunis libertas Angliæ or libertates Angliæ. Carta de libertatibus, magna carta, &c. And well may the Lawes of England be called libertates, quia liberos faciunt. Magna fuit quondam magnæ reverentia Cartæ. (*Bracton*, 414. & 291. *Fleta lib.* 2. *cap.* 48. & *lib.* 3. *cap.* 3. *Mirror, cap.* 2. §. 18. *Britton fol.* 177. *b.*)

This statute of Magna Carta, is but a Confirmation or restitution of the Common Law, as in the statute called Confirmatio cartarum, Anno 25 E. 1. it appeareth by the opinion of all the Justices; and in 5. H. 3. tit. Mord. 53. Magna Carta is there vouched, for there it appeareth that King Iohn had granted the like Charter of renouation of the ancient Lawes. (25. *E.* 1.) (5. *H.* 3. *Mord.* 53. *Math. Paris*, 246. 276. 248.)

This statute of Magna carta hath beene confirmed aboue 30. times; and commanded to be put in execution. By the statute of 25. E. 1. ca. 2. iudgements giuen against any points of the Charters of Magna Carta or Carta de foresta are adiudged voide: And by the statute of 42. E. 3. ca. 3. if any statute be made against either of these Charters it shall be voide. (25. *E.* 1. *ca.* 2.) (42. *E.* 3 *ca.* 3.)

Sur lestatute de magna carta lestatute de Merton est foundue sur tiel

tiel point, viz. Quod hæredes maritentur absque disparagatione.

Foundue, So as Magna Carta is the foundation of other Acts of Parliament. This Act extendeth as well to females as to males.

Nul action poet estre prise sur cel statute, intant que il ne vnques fuit view ou oye, &c. Et si ascun action puissoit estre prise sur cest matter il serra intend a ascun foits estre mise in vre.

Hereby it appeareth how safe it is to be guided by iudiciall presidents the rule being good, Periculosum existimo quod bonorum virorum non comprobatur exemplo.

chein cousine a que lenheritage ne puit discender, enter & ouster le gardein en chiualry. Et sil ne voile, vn auter cousin del enfant poit ceo faire, & les issues & pfits pzender al vse del enfant, & de ceo render accōpt al enfant, quant il vient a son plein age: ou autermt lenfant deins age poit enter luy mesme, & ouster le gardein, &c. Sed quære de hoc.

Cousin to whom the inheritance cannot discend, enter and ouste the gardein in Chiualrie. And if he will not, another cousin of the infant may doe this, and take the issues & proffits to the vse of the infant and of this to render an accoūt to the infant whē hee comes to his full age: or otherwise the infant within age may enter himselfe and ouste the gardein, &c. *Sed quære de hoc.*

And as vsage is a good interpreter of Lawes, so non vsage where there is no example is a great intendment, that the Law will not beare it: for saith Littleton, If any action might haue beene grounded vpon such matter, it shall be intended that sometime it should haue beene put in vre. Not that an Act of Parliament by non Vser can be antiquated or lose his force, but that it may be expounded or declared how the Act is to be vnderstood.

*Vid. Petitiones coram domino rege in Parliamento, fo.*3.18.*E.*1.

39.*H.*6.39.*per Ashton.* 6.*Eliz. Dier*,229. 23.*Eliz. Dier. Nullum breue de errore de iudicio in* 5.*part. quia nullum breue reperitur.* 3.*E.* 3.50.11.*H.*4.7.& 38.

Si parentes conquerantur. Of this sufficient hath beene said before.

Si les Cousins. Here Littleton expoundeth parents to be his cousins, vnder which name of cousins Littleton includeth vncles and other cousins, who when the father is dead are in loco parentum.

*Vid. Le statute de Merlebridge, ca.*17. *In custodia parentum.*

Ont cause a faire lamentation, &c. Note if they haue cause to make lamentation, it sufficeth though they neuer complaine.

Pur le hont fait a lour cousin. For when their cousin is disparaged in his marriage, it is not only a shame and infamy to the heire, but in him to all his blood and kindred.

Donques poet le procheine cousin a que le enheritance ne poet discender enter & ouster le gardein in chiualrie.

This is worthy the obseruation for the words of the statute are generall Secundum dispositionem parentum, and the construction thereof shall be according to the reason of the Common Law, for the next cousin to whom the inheritance cannot discend shall enter and oust the gardian, and shall be in place of a gardian, as it is in case of a gardian in socage.

Et sil ne voille, vn auter cousin del enfant poet ceo faire. Still pursuing the reason of the Common Law in case of gardian in Socage.

Et les issues & proffits prender al vse del enfant, &c. This is so euident as it needeth no explication.

Ou auterment lenfant deins age poet enter luy mesme & ouste le gardein. If none of the cousins aforesaid will enter, then the heire himselfe may enter. In all which the reason of the Common Law is pursued. But what if the heire be disparaged and the next of kin doth enter, and when the heire commeth to 14 he agreeth to the marriage, yet shall not this giue any aduantage to the Lord, for that he had lost the wardship before.

Sect. 109.

¶ Of this sufficient hath beene said before.

¶ ITem mults auters diuers disparagemts y sont, que ne sont specifies en mesme lestatute. Come si lheire que est en gard est marry a vn que nad forsque vn pee, ou forsque vn maine, ou que est deforme, decrepite, ou ayant horrible disease, ou graund & continual infirmity: Et (si soit heire male) si soit marry a feme que est passe lage denfanter. Et mults auters causes de disparagements sont Sed de illis quære car il est bon matter daprender.

ALso there be many and diuers other disparagements, which are not specified in the same statute. As if the heire which is in Ward be married to one which hath but one foot, or but one hand, or which is deformed, decrepit, or hauing some horrible disease or great and continuall infirmity. And (if he be an heire male) if hee be married to a woman past the age of childebearing. And there be other causes of disparagement, but inquire of them, for it is a good matter to vnderstand.

Sect. 110.

¶ ET des heires males que sont deins lage de 21. ans apres le mort lour auncester nient marries, en tiel cas le Sir auera le mariage de tiel heire, & auera temps & space de tender a luy couenable mariage sans disparagement deins le temps de 21. ans. Et est ascauoir, que lheire en tiel case poit eslier sil voit estre marry ou non, mes si le Sir que est appel gardein en chiualry a tiel heire tender couenable mariage deins lage de 21. ans sans disparagement, & lheire ceo refuse, & ne soy marie deyns le dit age,

ANd of heires males which bee within the age of 21. yeares after the decease of their Ancestor and not married, In this case the Lord shall haue the mariage of such heire, and hee shall haue time and space to tender to him couenable mariage without disparagement within the said time of 21. yeares. And it is to bee vnderstood, that the heire in this case may chuse whither hee will be married or no, but if the Lord which is called gardian in chiualry tenders to such heire couenable mariage within the age of 21. yeares without dispa-

¶ *DE tender a luy couenable mariage, &c.* But it is in the election of the Lord whether for the single value the Lord will tender a mariage or no, for he shall haue the single value without any tender.

Lib. 6 fo. 70 Lo. Darcies case.
Vid. Britton, fol. 169.

And of this there needeth no other explication. The value of the mariage of such an heire is according to the valuation by lawfull triall or as much as another had before offered to giue for the same without fraude and couyn.

Merton, cap. 6.
18. E. 3. 18.

¶ *Le heire en tiel case poet eslier sil voet este marie, ou non, &c.* And so on the other side though there be a tender made of a couenable mariage without disparagement, yet the heire may refuse, for in euery mariage there

donques le gardeine aũra l'value del mariage del tiel heire male, mes ſi tiel heire luy mẽ marie deins lage de 21. ans encounter la volunt le gardein en chiualrie donqz le gardein aũa le double value del mar per force de leſtat d Merton auantdit come en mẽ leſtat eſt compriſe pluis a pleine.

ragement, & the heire refuſeth this, and doth not marrie himſelfe within the ſaid age, then the Gardein ſhall haue the value of the mariage of ſuch heire male, but if ſuch heire marieth himſelf within the age of 21. yeares againſt the will of the Gardein in Chiualrie, then the Gardein ſhall haue the double value of the Marriage by force of the Statute of *Merton* aforeſaid, as in the ſame Statute is more fully at large compriſed.

there muſt bee a free conſent.

¶ *Si tiel heire.* That is, if ſuch an heire to whom a tender hath been made by the Lord, and by whom a refuſall haue beene made, if ſuch an heire afterwards marieth another within age, he ſhall forfeit double the value, but if hee before any tender marieth himſelfe within age, hee ſhall pay but the ſingle value of the mariage.

Neither the ſingle value nor the double value ſhall bee recouered againſt the heire, but after his full age, but for both theſe the Lord hath a double remedie: viz. an Action as is aforeſaid, or the Lord may retaine the land after full age for his ſatiſfaction of both, with this difference that in the caſe of the ſingle value the taking of the profits ſhall not be accounted parcell of the value but as a gage or pledge till the heire doe ſatiſfie him of the ſingle value, but in caſe of the double value, the perception of the profits ſhall be taken in ſatiſfaction of the double value, for the Statute of Merton which giueth the forfeiture ſaith, Dominus teneat terram, &c. per tantum tempus quod inde percipere poſſit duplicem valorem maritagii, which words (quod inde, &c.) proueth that the taking of the profits ſhall goe in ſatiſfaction: but in caſe of the ſingle value, vntill the heire doth ſatiſfie the Lord of the ſame.

Stat. de Merton, cap. 6. 2. E. 2. acc. ſur leſtat. 43. 3. E. 2. ibid. 27. 16. E. 3. ibid. 14. 18. E. 3. 18. Temps E. 1. acc. ſur leſtat. 43. E. 3. 21. 27. H. 8. 4. Statut. de Merton, cap. 7. 35. H. 6. tit. gard. 71. Lib. 6. fol. 72. Lord Darcies caſe.

No forfeiture of mariage is giuen by the ſaid Statute of Merton, of an heire female, as appeareth by the ſaid Act, neither at the Common Law could the Lord haue holden the land of the heire female after fourteene yeares for the value.

Section 111.

¶ Item diuers tenants teignont de lour Seignior p ſeruice de chiualer, & vncore ils ne teignont per Eſcuage, ne paieront eſcuage come ceux que teignont de lour Seigniors per caſtle garde, ceſtaſcauoire, a garder vn tower del caſtle lour Seignior, ou vn huis ou vn auter lieu del caſtle per reaſonable garniſhment, quant lour Seigni-

ALſo diuers Tenãts hold of their Lords by Knights ſeruice, and yet they hold not by Eſcuage, neither ſhall they pay Eſcuage. As they which hold of their Lords by Caſtleward, that is to ſay, to ward a tower of the Caſtle of their Lord, or a doore or ſome other place of the Caſtle vpon reaſonable warning, when their Lords heare that the enemies wil come,

Lib. 4. fol. 88. in Lutterels caſe. Lib. 6. fol. 20. a. Gregories caſe. 19. R. 2. gard. 195.

¶ *Per Caſtle gard. Wardum caſtri, ſeu caſtle gardum, ſeu caſtri-gardum.* He that holdeth by Caſtle-gard, holdeth by Knights Seruice, but not by Eſcuage, for Eſcuage is due when the King maketh a Voyage Royall out of this Realme (as hath been ſaid) and the Tenant maketh default, but Caſtle gard is to be done within the Realme, & without any Voyage royall.

Alſo a certaine tearme is appointed for the Seruice of the Tenant that holdeth by Eſcuage, but no certaine terme by Law for him that holdeth by Caſtle gard. Vide in the Title of Grand Seriantie Sect. Hereof come

ors oyont que enemies voylent vener ou sont venus en Engleterre. Et en plusors auters cases home poit tener per seruice de chiualer, & uncore il ne tient per escuage, ne papera escuage, sicome serra dit en le tenure per Graund Serieanty. Mes en touts cases ou home tient p seruice de chiualer, tiel seruice trait al seignior gard & mariage.

or are come in England. And in many other Cases a man may hold by Knights Seruice, and yet hee holdeth not by Escuage nor shall pay Escuage, as shall bee said in the tenure by Grand Seriantie. But in all Cases where a man holds by Knights Seruice, this Seruice draweth to the Lord ward and mariage.

Castellani, or Constabularij castri, for Keepers or Constables of a Castle.

Vide Mag. Cart cap. 19. 20. W. 1. cap. 7. Bract lib. 5. fol. 363. Fleta lib. 2. cap. 43.

¶ *A garder vn tower del Castle, &c.* A Tower, or a Doore, or a Bridge, or a Sconce, or some other certaine part of the Castle, for the tenure must be certaine. And this may be done by the Tenant himselfe or his Deputie.

Magna Cart. cap. 20.

¶ *Del Seignior.* for it cannot bee of a Castle of another.

Lord and Tenant by Castle gard, the Lord granteth ouer his seigniory to another, (a) the Castle gard is gone because the Grantee hath not the Castle. (b) For the same reason it is, that if one holdeth of mee as of my Manor of D. by fealtie and suite of Court, if I graut ouer the seruices of this Tenant, the suite is gone because the Grantee hath not the Manor. (c) But if the Castle be wholy ruinated, Si Castrum sit penitus dirutum, yet the tenure remayneth by Knights Seruice, and it goeth in benefit of the Tenant, as to the garding of the Castle untill it be reedified. But ward and Mariage belongeth to the Lord in the meane time. For Littleton in the end of this Section putteth it for a generall rule in all cases where a man holdeth by Knights Seruice, it draweth ward and Mariage.

(a) Temp. E. 2. tit. Ass. 399. 31. E. 3. tit. Ass. 441.

(b) 17. E. 3. 65. 72. 4. E. 3. 42.

(c) Lib. 4. fo. 88. Luttrels case. 3. H. 8. Bendloes, Capels case. 4. E. 3. 55.

If the Tenant make default in garding of the Castle, the Lord may distraine for it, and recouer satisfaction in damages.

¶ *Per reasonable garnishment.* This warning must bee giuen by the Lord or some other for him, and the Tenant need not to stirre untill he haue such warning.

¶ *Enemies.* Which is to be understood of any manner of enemies whatsoeuer. And though Littleton speakes of enemies, yet it seemeth that to keepe a Castle in time of Insurrection and Rebellion (albeit in proprietie of speech Rebels are no enemies) is a tenure by Knights Seruice. Vide Hill 8. E. 1. Midd. Rott 86.

¶ *Voilent vener.* For preparation is to be made upon warning before the enemie be come indeed into England. This appeareth to be in time of hostilitie and warre, or for preparation therefore. But a tenure to keepe a Castle in time of peace only is no Knights Seruice.

If the Tenant by Castle gard doe serue the King in his warre, hee shall bee discharged against the Lord according to the quantitie of the time that he was in the Kings host.

Fleta speaketh of an old word called Wardwite and (saith he) significat quietanciam misericordiæ in casu quo non inuenerit quis hominem ad Wardam faciendam in Castro.

Fleta lib. 1. cap. 42.

Sect. 112.

¶ ET si un tenant que tient de son seignior per seruice de entier fee de chiualer morust, son heire donques esteant de plein age .s. de 21. ans,

AND if a Tenant which holdeth of his Lord by the seruice of a whole Knights fee dieth, his heire then being of full age s. of 21. yeares, then

¶ R *Eleife, releuium.* This word is deriued from the originall before.

Vide Sect. 103.

Nota, Releife (a) is no seruice but an improuement of the seruice, or an incident to the seruice, for the which the Lord may distreine but cannot haue an Action of Debt, but

(a) Temps E. 1. releife. 13. 41. E. 3. 22. 4. E. 2. auowrie. 210. 7. H. 6. 13. 22. H. 8. Rot. 528. 34. E. 1. auowrie. 238.

Donque le Seignior auera C. s. pur reliefe, & del heire celuy que tient per le moitie dun fee de chiualer L. s. & de celuy que tient per l'quart part d' fee dun chiualer 25. s. & sic que pluis, pluis, & que meins, meins.	the Lord shall haue C. s. for a reliefe, and of the heire of him which holds by the moitie of a Knights fee 50. s. and of him which holds by the fourth part of a Knights fee 25. s. and so he which holds more, more, and which lesse, lesse.

but his Executors or Administrators may haue an Action of Debt, and cannot distraine.

(b) Stat. de 1. E. 2. de militibus. Vide lib. 9. fol. 124. Anth. Lowes case.

And it (b) is to be vnderstood that fœdum militis, a Knights Fee, consisteth of twentie pound land, and hee payeth for his reliefe for a whole Knights fee, the fourth part of his fee viz. fiue pound, and so according to the rate.

Baronia, a Baronie, or a Barons Fee consisteth of thirteene Knights fees, and the third part of a Knights fee which amounteth to foure hundred Markes per annum, and the Baron for an entire Baronie payeth for his reliefe an hundred Markes, which is the fourth part of the value of his Baronie.

Comitatus, an Earledome, or an Earles fee consisteth of a Baronie, and the third part of a Baronie, which includeth twentie Knights fees amounting to foure hundred pound land per annum, and he payeth for his reliefe for an entire Earldome the fourth part of his reuenue, and that is a hundred pound. All which appeareth by the Statute of Magna Charta, cap. 2. made in the ninth yeare of Henrie the third, at which time there was neither Duke, Marquesse nor Viscount in England as before is said. But there be Presidents in the Exchequer that a Dukedome consisting of two Earledomes, viz. eight hundred pound land by the yeare payeth two hundred pound, and a Marquesse consisting of two Baronies, viz. eight hundred Markes land per annum, and of an Earldome and a halfe payeth two hundred Markes for his reliefe. What the Viscount should pay in certaine I haue not heard. Before the making of the Statute of Magna Charta the King had rationabile releuium of Noblemen, and it was not reduced to any certaintie, yet ought it to haue beene reasonable and not excessiue.

Glanuil. lib. 9. cap. 4. 6. Bracton. lib. 2. fol. 83. Britton. fol. 178. Ockam. 42. F. N. B. 83. 256. Fleta lib. 3. cap. 17. Magna Charta cap. 2.

I haue seene the Record of a Charter made in 20. H. 6. to Henry Beauchampe, Earle of Warwicke, whereby he was created King of the Ile of Wight, to him and the heires males of his bodie, his reliefe was incertaine, and not limited by the Statute of Magna Charta.

It is to be obserued that the words of the Statute of Magna Charta, be Hæres Comitis de Comitatu integro & hæres Baronis de Baronia integra, &c. Now what an entire Earledome, and an entire Baronie is hath beene declared before.

Vide Bracton fol. 84. 14. H. 4. in recordo longo. 10. H. 7. 19. 20. E. 3. Ass. 122. tit. auowrie 126. 18. Ass. pl. vltimo. 22. E. 3. 8.

It is also to be obserued that at and before the Statute of Magna Charta, all Earledomes and Baronies were deriued from the Crowne, and were holden by the King in Capite, and and the King would not suffer them to be deuided, or seuered. And such entire Earledomes, and entire Baronies are within the Statute, but at this day Earles and Barons are without such Earledomes and Baronies of the Kings gift in chiefe. For at the Creation of an Earle he hath sometimes an Annuitie granted vnto him, & sometime nothing, so as such Earles and Barons so created are cleerely out of the Statute of Magna Charta, and are to pay such reliefes as other men that hold of the King in Capite. For as the heire of a Knight shall not pay reliefe vnlesse he hath a Knights fee, &c. so neither the Earle nor Baron shall pay any reliefe by this Statute, vnlesse he hath an Earledome, &c. or Barony, &c.

16. E. 3. Eschange 2. 46. E. 3. forfeiture 18.

¶ *Son heire de pleine age .s. de 21. ans.* And yet in some case the heire shall pay reliefe when he was within age at the time of the death of his Ancestor. As if a man holdeth lands of the King by Knights Seruice in Capite, and of a common person other lands by Knights Seruice, and dieth his heire being within age, the King hath all in ward by his Prerogatiue vntill the full age of the heire. In this case the heire shall pay reliefe to the other Lord, for that the King had the wardship of bodie and lands. And the Lord vpon euery Discent ought to haue either wardship or Reliefe.

24. E. 3. 24. 26. H. 8. 32. H. 8. cap. 2. in fine.

But if there be Lord and Tenant by Knights Seruice, and the Tenant dieth, his heire being within age, the Lord wayueth his wardship as he may, and taketh himselfe to his Seigniorie, in this case the Lord shall not haue reliefe at his full age because hee might haue had the wardship of the bodie and land. Lord and Tenant of two Manors by diuers tenures by Knights Seruice, the Tenant is disseised of the one, and the Disseisor dieth seised, and the Tenant dieth seised of the other his heire within age, the Lord seised the bodie and lands of that Manor and after the heire at his full age recouereth the other Manor against the heire of the Disseisor, he shall pay reliefe for that Manor, and so one Lord of the heire of one Tenant shall haue both wardship during his minoritie and reliefe at his full age.

1. E. 3. 6. Pl. Com. 229. 33. E. 3. tit. gard. Statham.

¶ *Son heire.* (k) And yet the successor of a Bishop or Abbot may pay reliefe by prescription or grant.

If the tenant infeoffeth his heire apparant by collusion, and dieth, (l) his heire of full age it is a question in our bookes, whether he shall haue reliefe either by the Common Law, or by the Statute of Marlebridge.ca.6. But now the statute (m) of 13.Eliz,ca 5. hath cleered that question, and that the Lord shall haue reliefe where the conueyance is made to any person by collusion, &c.

(k) 3.E.3.13.76. 8.R.2.reliefe, 14. 3.H.4.2. 2 E.3. Auowrie.124.
(l) 39.E.3.tit. Reliefe 24.E.3 24.E.3.Reliefe 11. Bracton lib.2.85.
(m) 13.Eliz.ca 5.

Section 113.

This is euident, and needeth no explanation.

¶ ITem home poit ten son tre de son Sňr per le seruice de deux fees de chiualer, & donque lheire esteant de pleine age al temps de mort son auncestre paiera a son Sňr x.l. pur reliefe.

ALso a man may hold his land of his Lord by the seruice of two Knights fees,& then the heire being of full age at the time of the death of his Ancester shall pay to his Lord x.pound for reliefe.

Sect. 114.

¶ NOta si soit aiel, pier, & fits,& sa mere morust viuant le pier de le fits & puis laiel que tient sa terre p seruice de chiualer morust seisie, & sa terre discendist al fits la mere, come heire al aiel q est deins age: en cest cas la Sňr auera le garde de la terre, mes nemy le garde del corps del heire,pur ceo que nul serra en gard de son corps a ascun Sňr viuant son pier pur ceo que le pier durãt son vie auera le mariage de son heire apparant, & nemy le Sňr. Autermint est ou le pier est mort viuant la mere, lou le terre tenus en chi-

NOte, if Grandfather, father and sonne, and the mother dieth liuing the father of the sonne, and after the grandfather which holds his land by Knights seruice dieth seised, and his land discend to the sonne of the mother as heire to the grandfather who is within age: In this case, the Lord shall haue the Wardship of the land,but not of the body of the heire, because none shall be in ward of his body to any Lord,liuing his father,for the father during his life shall haue the mariage of his heire apparant, & not the Lord.Otherwise it is where the father dieth liuing the mother,

¶ *Fitz.* Yet the father shall haue the mariage of his Daughter if she bee his heire apparant, and Littletons reason extendeth to the Daughter,for that (saith he) the father shall haue the wardship of his heire apparant, within which words the Daughter is included, so long as she continueth heire apparant.

¶ *Le seignior auera le gard del terre.* Note that albeit in this case the Law doth giue the custody of the body of the father, and barreth the Lord thereof, yet the Lord shall haue the wardship of the Land by force of the tenure at the first creation thereof. And so it is if the father marieth his heire within age and dieth, yet the Lord shall haue the wardship of the land.

¶ *Viuant son pier.* This doth not extend to any collaterall heire, but only to the sonne or daughter being heire apparant, for albeit a man shall haue an action of trespasse, Quare consanguineum & hæredem cæpit,and albeit the words be Cujus maritagium ad ipsum pertinet, because the well bestowing of his

Fleta lib.1. ca.14. 16.E.3.disseisin 6. 31.E.1.gard 154. 8.E.2.tresp.235. F.N.B.243. Ambrosia Gorges case. lib.6.fo.22.

9 E 2.18.E.3.25.29.Ass.35. 29.E.3.37. 31.E.3.barr.237

ualry discendist al fits de part son pier, &c.

where the land holden in chiualry discends to the son on the part of the father, &c.

32.E.3.Gard 32.30.E.3.17. 31.H.6.55.12.H.4.16. F.N.B.143.31.E.3.Br.357 9.E.4.53.

his heire apparant in mariage is a great establishment of his house, yet that is to be vnderstood as against a wrong doer but not against a gardian in Chiualrie, and the mother shall haue the like writ for taking away of her sonne and heire apparent: and yet the mother shall not barre the Lord by Knights seruice, of his wardship of the bodie, as Littleton heere saith, Qui tamen ex filia tua nascitur in potestate tua non est, sed patris eius.

V.Flet.l.1.c.6.Sec W.2.c.35

¶ *A ascun seignior*. Put the case there is Lord, & Feme Tenant by Knights seruice of a Carue of land, the Feme maketh a feoffement in fee vpon condition, and taketh the Lord to husband, and haue issue a sonne, the wife dieth, the issue entreth for the condition broken, the Lord entreth into the land as Gardeine by Knights seruice, and maketh his Executors, and dieth: in this case the Executors shall haue the wardship of the land during the minoritie of the heire, but not the wardship of the bodie, for albeit the Lord seemeth to haue a double interest in the wardship of the bodie, one as Lord, and another as father, yet as Father, and not as Lord in iudgement of Law, he shall haue the wardship of the bodie of his son and heire apparent, in respect of nature, which was before any wardship in respect of Seigniories by Knights seruice began, and that wardship by reason of nature cannot be waiued, and claime made in respect of the Seigniorie. And the Executors of the father shall not haue such a wardship which the Testator had as father, neither can such a wardship be forfeited by outlawrie, because it is due to the father in respect of priuitie of nature.

33.H.6.55.Li.7.fo.13. in Caluins case. V.Flet.li.1.ca.12.§.cum Patr.de feodo, &c.

¶ *De son heire apparent*. And therefore if the father be attainted of felonie, &c. then cannot the sonne or daughter be an heire apparent, because the bloud is corrupted betweene them, and consequently in the life of the father, his sonne in that case shall be in ward.

A woman seised of lands in fee holden by Knights seruice, taketh husband an Alien, and hath issue, and the wife dieth, the issue shall be in ward, and the father shall not haue the custodie of him, for that in the eye of the Law he is not his heire apparent, as Littleton heere speaketh.

Sect. 115.

This Section is an addition to Littleton, and therefore I passe it ouer, and the rather, for that the said Statute of 4. H.7. is become of no force, for that by the Statute of 27.H.8. cap.10. all vses are transferred into possession.

C* NOta, si home soit seisie de Terre que est tenus per seruice de Chiualer, & fait feoffment en fee a son vse, et morust seisie del vse, son heir deins age, et nul volunt per luy declare, le Seignior auera Briefe de droit de gard de corps et del Terre sicome Tenant vst deuie seisie del demesne. Et si le heire soyt de pleine age al temps del morant son ancestor, vn tiel case il payera reliefe sicome il fuissoit seisie del demesne. Et cest per lestatut de anno 4.H.7.cap.17.

NOte, if a man be seised of land which is holden by Knights seruice, and maketh a feoffement in fee to his own vse, and dieth seised of the vse, his heire within age, and no will declared by him, the Lord shall haue a Writ of Right of the wardship of the bodie and land, as if the tenant had died seised of the demesne. And if the heire bee of full age at the time of the decease of his Ancestor, in this case he shal pay reliefe, as if he had bin seised of the demesne. And this is by the statute of 4.H.7.cap.17.

Sect. 116.

NOta, il y ad Gardein en droit en Chiualrie, et Gardein en fayt en Chiualrie. Gardein en droit en Chiualrie est, lou le Seigniour per cause de son Seigniorie, est seisie de gard de Terres & del heyre, vt supra. Gardein en fayt en Chiualrie est, lou en tiel case le Seigniour apres son seisin graunt per fait ou sauns fayt le Gard des Terres, ou del heire ou dambideux a vn auter. Per force de quel grant le Grauntee est en possession, donque est le Grauntee appel Gardeine en Fait.

NOte, there is Gardeine in right in Chiualrie, and Gardeine in Deede in Chiualrie. Gardeine in Right in Chiualrie is, where the Lord by reason of his Seigniorie is seised of the Wardship of the Lands, and of the heire, *vt supra*. Gardeine in Deede in Chiualrie is, where in such case the Lord after his Seisin grants by Deed, or without Deede, the Wardship of the Lands, or of the Heire, or of both, to another, by force of which grant the Grauntee is in possession, then is the Grauntee called Gardeine in Fait, or Gardeine in Deede.

¶ HEre Littleton diuideth Gardeine in Chiualrie, into Gardein in Right, and Gardeine in Fait. And this is euident, and needeth no explanation.

¶ *Per fait ou sauns fait.* Heere Littleton affirmeth, That the wardship of the bodie may bee graunted ouer without Deed, and herein note a diuersitie betweene an originall Chattell of a thing that properly lieth in grant, and a Chattell derived out of a Freehold of any thing that lieth in grant. As for example, if a man maketh a Lease for yeares of a Villeine, this cannot be done without deed, neither can the Lessee assigne it ouer without Deed, because it is derived out of a Freehold that lieth in grant: but the wardship of the bodie is an originall Chattell, during the minoritie, derived out of no Freehold, and therefore as the Law createth it without deed; so it may be assigned ouer without Deed.

12.E.3.tit.Grant 59.7.E.3.63. 26.E.3.65.28.E.3.96 14.E.3.Act.sur Lest.17. 25.E.3.40.31.E.3.Vouch.5 46.E.3.25.10.E.4.16. 12.H.4.19.5.H.7.17.36. 22.El.Dyer 371.35.H.8. Br.tit.Grant 85.

A Corporation aggregate of many cannot make a Lease for yeares without Deed, in respect of the quality of the Incorporation, but that Lessee may assigne it ouer without Deed.

36.H.8.tit.Grant B.125. 22.H.6.34.19.H.6.33.

If an Aduowson be holden by Knights seruice, and the Tenant dieth, his heire being within age, the Lord cannot grant the wardship of the Aduowson without Deed, because it is derived out of an Inheritance that lieth in grant, and passeth not by Liuerie: for, Ius præsentandi est incorporale, and so (albeit there be diuersitie of opinion in our bookes) is the Law taken at this day.

24.E.3.69.70.5.E.3.58. 43.E.3.15.5.H.7.36. 14.H.7.16.15.H.8.8.

Bract.366.368.246.43 E.3.1.6. 5.H.7.37.11.H.6.4. 6.H.7.3.18.H.8. 26.Eliz.Dyer 323.

Chap. 5. *Sect.* 117.

Socage.

TEnure en ſocage eſt, lou le tenant tient de ſon ſeigni or ſon tenement p certeine ſeruice p̄ touts maners de ſeruices, iſſint que les ſeruices ne ſont pas ſeruices de chyualer: Sicõe lou home tient ſon t̃re de ſon ſeignior p fealtie ⁊ p certeine rent p̄ touts maners de ſeruices, ou lou home tient p homage ⁊ fealtie ⁊ cert̃ rent pur touts maners de ſeruices, ou lou il tiẽt p homage ⁊ fealty p̄ touts maners de ſeruices, car homage p ſoy ne fait pas ſeruice de chĩr.

TEnure in Socage, is where the Tenant holdeth of his Lord the tenancie by certaine ſeruice for all manner of ſeruices, ſo that the ſeruice be not Knights ſeruice: As where a man holdeth his land of his Lord by Fealty and certaine rent for all manner of ſeruices: or elſe where a man holdeth his land by homage, fealty, and certaine rent, for all manner of ſeruices, for Homage by it ſelfe maketh not Knights ſeruice.

*Mirror ca.*1.§.3.

4.*H.*7.*ca.*19.
*Lib.*4.*Terringhams caſe fo.*39.& 4 *H.*7.*ca.*12.

TEnure in *Socage.* Agriculture or Tillage is of great account, in Law, as very profitable for the Common Wealth, wherein the goodneſſe of the habit is beſt knowne by the priuation, For by laying of Lands, vſed in tilth, to paſture, ſixe maine inconueniences doe daily encreaſe. Firſt, Idleneſſe, which is the ground and beginning of all miſchiefes. 2. Depopulation, and decay of townes, for where in ſome townes 200. perſons were occupied, and liued by their lawfull labours, by conuerting of tillage into paſture, there haue beene maintained but two or three heardmen: And where men haue beene accounted ſheepe of Gods paſture, now become ſheep-men of theſe paſtures. 3. Huſbandry, which is one of the greateſt commodities of the Realme, is decayed. 4. Churches are deſtroyed, and the ſeruice of God neglected by diminution of Church liuings, (as by decay of tythes, &c.) And 5. Iniury and wrong done to Patrons and Gods miniſters. 6. The defence of the Land againſt forraine enemies enfeebled and impayred, the bodyes of Huſbandmen being more ſtrong and able, and patient of cold, heate, and hunger, then of any other.

(a) 20.E.3.*Admeſurement*.8
14.*Aſſ.*21. 24.E.3.25.
* *Mirror.*
*Bracton fo.*217. *Fleta. lib.*2. *ca.*41. *Regiſt. orig.*97.
*Ockam.*38.39. 4.E.3.2.a.
18.E.2.*tit. action ſur leſtat.*45. *Temps E.*1.
Auowry 230.
29.E.3.16.17.
*Cic. lib.*1.*offic.*

The two conſequents that follow of theſe inconueniences, are firſt the diſpleaſure of Almighty God, and ſecondly the ſubuerſion of the Pollicie and good Gouernment of the Realme, and all this appeareth in our bookes. And the Common Law (a) giueth errable land (which anciently is called Hyde & gaine) the preheminencie and precedencie before meadowes, paſtures, woods, mines, and all other grounds whatſoeuer: and * aueria carucæ the beaſts of the plow haue in ſome caſes more priuiledge than other cattle haue. And amongſt the Romans Agriculture or tillage was of high eſtimation, inſomuch as the Senators themſelues would put their hand to the plow, and it is ſaid, That neuer proſpered tillage better, then when the Senators themſelues plowed (ſuch force hath the example of ſuperiors) whereof three famous Romanes in their ſeuerall kindes ſpake.

Omnium rerum ex quibus aliquid exquiritur nihil agricultura melius, Nihil vberius, nihil dulcius, nihil libero homine dignius.

*Virgil. lib.*1.*Georg.*

O fortunatos nimium, ſua ſi bona norunt
Agricolas, quibus ipſa procul diſcordibus armis
Fundit humo facilem victum iuſtiſſima tellus.

Seneca in Epiſt.

Nullum laborem recuſant manus quæ ab aratro ad arma transferuntur, &c. fortior autem miles ex confragoſo venit, ſed ille vnctus, & nitidus in primo puluere deficit. But now let vs peruſe our Authors words.

¶ *Socagium.* Littleton in this chapter Section 119. fetcheth this word from the originall. Socagium idem est quod seruitium socæ, & soca idem est quod caruca. s. vn soke ou vn carue.

And Bracton agreeth herewith. Dicitur socagium (saith he) à socco & inde tenentes dicuntur Socmanni (b) eo quod deputati sunt tantummodo ad culturam. And Benerth signifieth the seruice of plough and cart. It is to be obserued that in the booke of (c) Domesday, Land holden by Knights seruice was called Tainland, and land holden by Socage was called Reueland, which appeareth in that there it is said, Hæc terra fuit terra regis Edwardi Taineland sed postea conuersa est in Reueland. And in that booke they that held in Socage were called by seuerall names, as Sochemanni or Sokemanni, which still continueth, sometime * Coleberti. i. qui tenent in liberum socagium per redditum, and sometime they are called Radchenestres. i. liberi homines, qui tamen arabant, herciabant, falcabant, & metebant, &c. And here it appeareth how necessary it is, that words be fetched from their originalls, and our Author est verus Etimologus both in this and in many other places in his (d) three bookes. And it is to be obserued once for all, that the legall termination of (agium) in composition signifieth seruice or dutie; as homagium the seruice of the man, Escuagium, seruitium scuti, (e) Socagium seruitium socæ, hidagium the dutie to be paid for a hide or plough-land, and so of cornagium, coragium, carnagium, cariagium, burgagium, villenagium, guidagium, (which one discribeth thus) quod datur alicui vt tuto conducatur per loca alterius, and the like.

Bracton lib. 2. fo. 77.
(b) Glanuil, lib 7. ca. 9. & 11. & lib. 9. ca. 4. Fleta lib. 1. ca. 8. & lib. 3. ca 14. & 16. Britton fo. 154.
(c) Domesday. Herefordsc. Vid. deuant, Sect. 1. Sutu. Wendesford. Wescestersc.
** Mich. 10. E. 3. Coram rege Willes in Thesaur.*
(d) For etimologies vid. Sect. 95. 154. 164. 204. 234. 267. 268. &c.
(e) Fleta lib. 3. ca. 14. Bracton. lib 2. ca. 16. Britton fo. 164.
(f) Mirror, ca. 2. §. 18.

¶ *Issint que les seruices* (f) *ne sont pas seruices de Chivaler.* And in the next Section he saith, and euery tenure, that is not a Tenure in Chiualry is a tenure in Socage, Ex donationibus autem feoda militaria, vel magnam Seriantiam non continentibus oritur nobis quoddam nomen generale quod est sokagium. Here Littleton speaketh of Tenures of common persons, for grand Seriantie is not Knights seruice, and yet it is not a tenure in Socage, as shall be said hereafter. Also here he meaneth temporall seruices, and not Frankalmoigne as by the examples he put is manifest, and as in his proper place shall appeare more at large. Also here Littleton speaketh of Socage largely taken, and so called ab effectu, that is, all tenures that haue the like effects and incidents belonging to them, as Socage hath, are termed tenures in Socage, albeit originally seruice of the plow was not reserued: as if originally a Rose, a paire of guilt Spurres, a Rent, and such like were reserued, or that the Tenants in Condemnatos vltrices manus mittant vt alios suspendio, alios membrorum detruncatione, &c. puniant, these are said to be tenures in Socage ab effectu, for that there shall be like Gardein in Socage, like Reliefe, and such other effects and incidents as a tenure in Socage hath, and are so tearmed to distinguish the same from Knights seruice. Nay, the worst Tenure that I haue read of, is of this kinde, as to hold lands to be Vltor sceleratorũ condemnatorum, vt alios suspendio, alios membrorum detruncatione vel aliis modis juxta quantitatem perpetrati sceleris puniat, (that is) to be a Hangman or Executioner. It seemeth in ancient times such officers were not Voluntaries, nor for lucre to be hired, vnlesse they were bound thereunto by Tenure. And so note that some Tenures in Socage are named à causa, and some and the greater part ab effectu.

Fleta, vbi supra.
Ockam, cap. quà per formam consuetudinem, &c.
Ockam fo. 31. a. & b.

¶ *Car homage de soy ne fait seruice de chiualer.* But it is a presumption that where homage is due, that the land is holden by Knights seruice, as hath beene said.

Sect. 118.

¶ ITem home poit ten̄ de son s̄ir pur fealty t̄m, et tiel tenure est tenure en socage. Car chescun tenure que nest pas tenure in chiualry, est tenure en socage.

ALso a man may hold of his Lord by fealty only, and such tenure is tenure in socage: for euery tenure which is not tenure in chiualrie is a tenure in Socage.

Of this sufficiently hath beene said before.

Sect. 119.

¶ ET il est dit, que la cause pur que tiel tenure est dit & ad le nosme de tenure en socage,

ANd it is said that the reason why such tenure is called, and hath the name of tenure in Socage,

¶ *Tempsde memory* Time of memorie is when no man aliue hath had any proofe prœfe to the contrarie, nor haue any Conusance to the contrarie, as shall bee hereafter said in his proper place. And of necessitie this change hereafter spoken of must be before time of memorie, for within time of memorie, the seruices of the Plough cannot be changed into money by consent of the Tenant, and the desire of the Lord, &c. into an annuall Rent, neither by release or confirmation or other conueyance as long as the Seigniorie remaine as shall bee said in his due place.

Cap. burgage. Sect. 170.

Mirror. cap. 2 §. 18. *Vide* 19. *E.* 2. *auowrie*. 224. 3. *E.* 2. *accom. sur lest.* 24. 30 *E.* 3. 24. 20. *E.* 3. *auowrie* 124. 39. *E.* 3. 17. 39. *Ass. p.* 3. 30. *Ass.* 1.

Cap. confirmation. Sect. 539.

¶ *Deuoient vener oue lour Sokes.* The Plough is named propter excellentiã, but the Sicle and the Sythe for the reaping in Haruest and such like are also included. For as Carucata terræ, a plough land, may containe Houses, Milles, Pasture, Medow, and Wood &c. as perteining to the Plough, so vnder the seruice of the Plough all seruices of Tillage or Husbandry are included.

4. *E.* 3. 161. 6. *E.* 3. 283.

¶ *Vncore le nosme de Socage demurt.* Although the cause wherupõ the name of Socage first grew bee taken away, yet the name remaine (as it hath beene) and is vsed to distinguish this tenure from a tenure by Knights Seruice. Nomina si nescis, perit cognitio rerum

est ceo; Quia socagium idem est quod seruitium socæ, & soca idem est quod caruca, s. vn soke ou vn carue. Et en ancient temps deuant le limitation de temps de memorie grand part de les tenants que tyendront de lour Seigniors per socage, deuoient vener oue lour sokes, chescun de les dits tenants pur certein iours per an pur arer & semer les demesnes le Seignior, & pur ceo que tielx ouerages fueront fait pur le viuer & sustenance de lour Seigniors, ils fueront quits enuers lour Seigniors de touts maners de seruices, &c. Et pur ceo que tielx seruices fueront faits oue lour sokes tiel tenure fuit appel tenure en socage. Et puis apres tiels seruices fueront changes en deniers, per consent des Tenants & per desire des Seigniors, s. en vn annual rent, &c. Mes vncore le nosme de Socage demurt, & en diuers lieux les tenants vncore font tiels seruices oue lour sokes a lour Seigniors, issint que touts maners de tenures que ne sont pas tenures per seruice de chiualer, sont appels tenures en socage.

is this, becauſe *Socagium, idem eſt, quod ſeruitium Soca*, and *Soca, idem eſt quod caruca, &c.* A Soke or a Plough. In ancient time before the limitation of time of memorie, a great part of the tenants which held of their Lords by Socage, ought to come with their Ploughes, euery of the ſaid Tenants for certaine dayes in the yeare to plow and ſow the Demeſne of the Lord. And for that ſuch Workes were done for the liuelihood and ſuſtenance of their Lord, they were quit againſt their Lord of all manner of ſeruices, &c. And becauſe that ſuch ſeruices were done with their Ploughes, this tenure was called Tenure in Socage. And afterward theſe ſeruices were changed into money by the conſent of the Tenants, and by the deſire of the Lord, *viz.* into an annuall rent, &c. But yet the name of Socage remayneth, and in diuers places the Tenants yet doe ſuch ſeruices with their Ploughes to their Lords, ſo that all manner of Tenures which are not Tenures by Knights Seruice, are called tenures in Socage.

rerum: Et nomina si perdas certè distinctio rerum perditur. Therefore the names of things (as Littleton here teacheth) are for avoyding of confusion diligently to be obserued.

Section 120.

¶ Item si home tient de son Seignior per escuage certaine, s. en tiel forme quant lescuage curge & est assesse per Parliament a greinder summe ou meinder summe, que le tenant paiera a son Seignior forsque demy. marke pur escuage, & nient pluis ne meins, a quel graund summe, ou a quel petite summe que lescuage courge &c. tiel tenure est tenure en Socage, & nemy seruice de chiualrie. Mes lou le summe que le tenant paiera pur lescuage est non certain, s. lou il poit estre que le somme que le tenant paiera pur lescuage a son Seignior poit estre a vn foits le greinder & a auter foits le meinder, solonque ceo que est assesse &c. donques tiel tenure est tenure per seruice de chiualer.

Also if a man holdeth of his Lord by eſcuage certaine .s. in this manner, when the eſcuage runneth, and is aſſeſſed by Parliament to a greater or leſſer ſumme, that the Tenant ſhall pay to his Lord but halfe a Marke for Eſcuage, and no more nor leſſe, to how great a ſum, or to how little the eſcuage runneth, &c. Such tenure is tenure in Socage, and not Knights Seruice, but where the ſumme which the tenant ſhall pay for Eſcuage is vncertaine, .s. where it may bee that the ſumme that the tenant ſhall pay for eſcuage to his Lord may be at one time more, and at another time leſſe according as it is aſſeſſed, &c. ſuch tenure is tenure by Knights Seruice.

¶ E*scuage certeine.* Is not in rei veritate seruitium Scuti, which is to bee done by the body of man, but it is seruitium Crumenæ, of money which is to be drawne out of the Purse, and that is in effect a Tenure in Socage; wherein it is to be obserued that the seruice of payment of money is the more base and lesse profitable, for the Commonwealth in this case, and hereof somewhat hath beene said before in the Chapter of Escuage, Sect. 98. 99.

If a man hold by Homage, Fealtie, and Escuage, s. by an halfe penny when escuage runs at fortie shillings, this is a tenure in Socage and no Knights Seruice for two causes. *15. E. 2. tit. avowrie 215. 31. E. 1. Ass. 441. 26. Ass. 66. 5. E. 3. 6.*

First, It is Socage tenure because of the certaintie for to the tenure in socage, certa seruitia doe euer belong, so as the Husbandman may the rather liue in quiet. *5. E. 4. 128. Vide Rot. Parl. 4. E. 3. nu. 19. Clauerings case excellently resolued in Parliament. Hill. 3. E. 2. coram Rege. Rot. 34. Agnes. Frowiks case.*

Secondly, Escuage is to bee paid at euery time when it is assessed, and here it is not to bee paid but when it amounteth to fortie shillings.

Sect. 121.

¶ Item si home tient sa terre pur paier certaine rent a son seignior pur Castle-garde, tiel tenure est tenure en socage:

Also if a man holdeth his Land to pay a certaine rent to his Lord for Caſtle-gard, this tenure is tenure in ſocage, but where

¶ Herein the difference standeth thus, If a rent be paid for Castle-gard it is cleere a socage tenure, as it is *Vide Sect. 88. 89.*

Vide lib. 4. fol. 88. in Lutterels case. 19. R. 2. gard. 195. 26. Ass. 66 F. N. B. 83. 256. Lib. 6. fol. 20. Gregories case.

is agreed in Lutterels Case according to Littletons opinion, but if a summe in grosse or other thing be voluntarily paid or given by the Tenant, and voluntarily received by the Lord in lieu of Castle-gard, yet the tenure by Knights Seruice remayneth. Vide Sect. 88. 89.

Mes lou le tenant doit p luy m̄, ou p vn auter faire Castle-garde, tiel tenure est tenure per seruice de chiualer.

the tenant ought by himselfe or by another to doe Castle-gard, such tenure est tenure by Knights Seruice.

Section 122.

¶ It is called Rent Seruice, because it is accompanied with some corporal seruice, as Fealtie at the least, in respect whereof the Lord may distraine for it of common right. See more of this matter in the Chapter of Rents.

¶ Item en touts cases lou le tenant tient del Seignior a paier a luy ascun certeine rent, cel rent est appelle rent seruice.

ALso in all cases where the tenant holdeth of his Lord to pay vnto him any certaine rent, this rent is called Rent Seruice.

Sect. 123.

¶ *En tiels tenures en Socage.* If a man bee seised of a Rentcharge, Rent secke, common of pasture, and such like Inheritances, which doe not lie in tenure, and dieth his heire within age of 14. yeares. In this case the heire may chose his Gardein, but if he bee of such tender yeares as hee can make no choice then (if the father hath made no disposition of the custodie of the childe) it were most fit that the next of kinne to whom the Land cannot discend should haue the custodie of him. And whosoeuer taketh the rent, the heire shall charge him in an account. But if he hold any Land in Socage, In that Case the

Vide le statute de 4. & 5. Ph. & Marie cap. 8.

¶ Item en tielx tenures en socage si le t ad issue & deuie son issue esteãt deins lage d 14. ãs, donques le prochine amy del heir a q̄ lheritage ne poit discẽdr auer la gard d la terr & del heir iesq al age del heir d 14. ans, & tiel Gardein est appelle gardein en socage. Car si la terre descẽdist al heire de pt le pier donques la mere, ou auter procheine cosen de pt le mere auera la garde. Et si terre discendist al heire de part la mere, donques le pier ou le prochein amy de part de pier auera le garde de tielx terr̄s ou tenemẽts. Et quant lheire vient al age de 14. ans compleat, il poit enter & oustre le Gardein en Socage, &

ALso in such tenures in Socage if the Tenant haue issue and die, his issue being within the age of 14. yeares, then the next friend of that heire to whom the inheritance cannot discend shall haue the Wardship of the Land and of the Heire vntill the age of 14. yeares, and such Gardeine is called Gardeine in Socage. For if the land discend to the heire of the part of the father, then the mother, or other next Cousin of the part of the mother shall haue the Wardship. And if land discend to the heire of part of the mother, then the father or next friend of the part of the father shall haue the Wardship of such Lands or Tenements.

De-

occupier la terre luy mesm sil voit. Et tiel Gardeine en socage ne prendra ascuns issues ou profits de tielx terres ou tenements a son vse demesne, mes tantsolement al vse & profit del heire, et del ceo il rendra accompt al heire quant pleast al heire apres ceo que lheire accomplish lage de xiiii. ans. Mes tiel Gardein sur son accompt auera allowance de touts ses reasonable costs et expences en touts choses, &c. Et si tiel gardein maria lheire deins xiiii. ans, il accomptera al heire, ou a ses executors de value del mariage, coment que il ne prist riens pur le value del mariage, pur ceo que il serra rette sa folly demesne, que il luy voiloit marier sans prender la value del mariage, sinon que il luy maria a tiel mariage que est tant en value come le mariage del heire, &c.

And when the heire cometh to the age of 14. years complete he may enter and oust the Gardian in socage, and occupie the land himselfe if hee will. And such gardian in socage shal not take any issues or profits of such lands or tenemēts to his own vse, but only to the vse & proffit of the heire, and of this he shal render an account to the heire when it pleaseth the heire after hee accomplisheth the age of 14. yeares. But such gardein vpon his account shal haue allowance of all his reasonable costs and expences in all things, &c. And if such gardein marry the heire within age of 14. yeares hee shall account to the heire or his Executors of the value of the mariage, although that hee tooke nothing for the value of the mariage, for it shall bee accounted his owne folly, that he would marry him without taking the value of the marriage, vnles that he marrieth him to such a mariage that is as much worth in value as the mariage of the heire.

Gardian in socage shall take into his custody as well Rent charges, &c. as the land holden in Socage because hee hath the custody of the heire.

¶ *Si le tenant adisseisie & devie.* The same Law it is if the Tenant hath no issue, but a brother or cosin within age of 14 yeares at the time of his death. (a) Also this doth extend aswell to issue female as to issue male. (a) 19. R. 2. Ascéins, 132.

¶ *Deins lage de 14. ans.* Of this sufficient hath beene spoken in the next preceding chapter.

¶ *Donques le procheine Amy del heire a que le enheritance ne poet discender.* The next friend of the heire, &c. Here Amy or friend is taken for the next of blood, so as the effect of it is, that the next of blood to whom the inheritance cannot discend, whereby affinitie without blood is excluded. Glanvil, lib. 7. cap. 11. Bricton, 163. Fleta lib. 1. cap. 9. Stat. de Hibernia, tit. Partition.

¶ *Le procheín.* The next.

(b) If there be two or three brethren, and the youngest holdeth land in Socage and hath issue and dieth his issue within age of 14. yeares both the Uncles are in equall degree, and yet the eldest shall be Gardein, because in equall degree the Law preferreth him. (b) Vid. 30. Ass. 47. (c) And yet if lands holden in Socage be giuen to a man and the heires of his body, and he dieth, his heire within age, the next cosin of the part of the father albeit he be worthier shall not bee preferred before the next cousin of the part of the mother, but such of them as first seaseth the heire shall haue his custody: (c) Plowd. Com. [illegible] But if lands bee giuen in Frankmariage, and the Donees haue issue and die their issue within age of 14. yeares, the next of kinne of the part of the mother shall haue the custody of the body, and not the next of kinne of part of the father albeit he first seased him, because the mother was the cause of the gift. 47. H. 3. Gard 146. If a man bee seised of lands holden in Socage of the part of his father, and of other lands holden in Socage of the part of his mother, and dieth his issue being within the age of 14. yeares, In this case such of

the next of Kin of either side as first happeth the bodie shal haue him, but the next of bloud of the part of the father shall enter into the lands of the part of the mother, and the next of Kinne of the part of the mother, shall enter into the lands of the part of the father.

(d) F.N.B.139.b. Regist. (e) 7.E.3.46.16.E.3.c.52 21.E.3.8.31.E.3.Enfant 9. 17.E.2. Account 121. 26.E.3.63.10.H.6.14. F.N.B.118. (f) Bract. li.2. fo.88. (h) Flet. li.1.ca.10.

(d) If A. be Gardein in Socage of the bodie and lands of B. within the age of fourteene yeares, A. shall be Gardein in Socage per cause de Gard. But an Infant within age, that (e) is not in the custodie of another, cannot be Gardein in Socage, because no writ of accompt lieth against an Infant. And herewith agreeth Bract. (f) and yeeldeth this reason, Alium regere non potest, qui seipsum regere non nouit. And Fleta saith, (h) That minor minorem custodire non debet, alios enim præsumitur male regere qui seipsum regere nescit: And by like reason an Ideot, a man non compos mentis, a Lunaticke, a man surdus & mutus, or surdus & mutus, or a Leaper remoued by a writ de Leproso amouendo, cannot be a Gardein in Socage, but in a case of Gard per cause de Gard, there lieth an Action of Account against A. in the case abouesaid.

(i) Lib. Rub. cap.70. (k) Glanv. li.7.ca.11. (l) Pl. Com Carrels case. (m) Lit. li.1.fo.2,3. (n) Bract. li.2.fol.87. Brit. fo 163.b. Fle. li.1.c.10. 28.E.1.Stat.1. Fortesc.c.40.

¶ *A que le heritage ne poet descender.* (i) Nullus hæredipetæ suo propinquo vel extraneo periculosa sane custodia committatur. Note (k) this word (Poet) may or can. (l) And therefore this doth not onely exclude an immediate discent, but all possibilitie of discent. As if a man hath issue two sons by seueral Venters, & hauing lands holden in Socage of the nature of Burgh English, dieth, the yonger brother wi*t*hin age of 14. yeres, (m) the elder brother of the halfe bloud shall not haue the custodie of the land, because by possibilitie the elder may inherit the land, for if the yongest die without issue, & the land discend to an Uncle, the elder brother of the halfe bloud may be heire vnto him: & herewith do agree our antient Authors: (n) Hæres sokmanni sub custodia capitalium Dn̄orum non erit, sed sub custodia consanguineorum suorū propinquiorū, hoc est, eorū qui coniuncti sunt iure sanguinis, & non iure successionis, ex parte quorum non discendit hæreditas, & regulariter verum est, quod nunquam remanebit aliquis in custodia alicuius, de quo haberi possit suspitio, quod velit ius clamare in ipsa hæreditate, & vnde si plures sint filiæ & hæredes & tenere debeant in socagio, nulla debet esse in custodia alterius.

(o) Fortesc. vb. supr. Statut. de Homagio capiendo, temps E.1.

(o) And this is contrarie to the Ciuile Law; for, Leges Ciuiles impuberum tutelas proximis de eorum sanguine committunt, agnati fuerint, siue cognati, vnicuique, videlicet, secundum gradum & ordinem qui in hæreditate pupilli successurus est. But this the Law of England saith, Est quasi agnum lupo committere ad deuorandum.

¶ *Donques la mere.* Note, albeit Land cannot discend to the mother from her sonne, (as hath beene said) because Inheritance cannot ascend, yet here it appeareth by Littleton, That she is next of bloud, for none (as hath beene said) can be Gardeine in Socage, but the next of bloud, and the like is to be said of the Father, as hereafter next appeareth.

¶ *Donques le Pier.* By this it appeareth, That the Father in case of a tenure in Socage shall be gardein in Socage, & shal not haue the custodie of his eldest sonne, in respect of his paternall naturall custodie, (as he shall haue in case of a Tenure by Knights seruice, as before it appeareth) but as Gardeine in Socage: and the reason of the diuersitie is, for that in the case of a tenure in Socage, the father must by Law be accountable to the Sonne both for his mariage, as also for the profits of his Lands, which he should not be if he had the custodie of his eldest sonne in this case as his father, in respect of nature, and the act a Law neuer doth any man wrong.

But no Lord or other person in respect of any tenure by Knights Seruice or otherwise shal haue the custodie of any child that is heire apparant to his father, but the father only during his life, as hath beene said before.

It is to be obserued, that in the Lawes of England, there are three manner of Gardeinships, viz. by the Common Law, by the Statute Law, and Custome. By the Common Law there are foure manner of Gardians, viz. Gardein in Chiualrie, whom Littleton hath described before Section 103. &c. Gardein by nature, as the Father of the eldest sonne of whom Littleton hath spoken Section 114. Gardein in Socage treated of by Littleton in this Section, and Gardein per cause de nurture, all frequent in (a) our Bookes. By the Statute, that is, in 4 & 5 Phil. & Mariæ, of women children, and that is in two manners, either of the father or mother without assignation, or of any other to whom the father shall appoint the custodie, either by his last will, or by any Act in his life time, whereof you shall reade at large (b) in Ratcliffes Case in my Reports.

(a) 8 E.3.43. 8.E.4.5. (b) Lib.3 fol.57. Ratcliffes case. (c) 32.E.3. gard.32. 8.R.2. gard.166.

(c) Lastly, by Custome, as of Orphans by the custome of the Citie of London, and of other Cities and Boroughes.

¶ *Tant solement al vse & profit del heire.* And therefore Gardein in Socage shall not forfeit his interest by outlawrie or attaindor of felonie or Treason because he hath nothing to his owne vse, but to the vse of the heire.

Also

Also if the mother be Gardian in Socage, and taketh husband, and dieth; the husband shall not haue this custody by Suruiuour, because the wife had it en auter droit in the right of the heire.

Tl. Com.

A Gardian in Socage shall not (d) present to a benefice in the right of the heire because hee cannot be accomptable therefore, for that he can make no benefit thereof, for the Law doth abhorre simony or any corrupt Contract for benefices, and therefore in that case the heire shall present himselfe, and Britton speaking of these Gardians said well, Les queux gardeins sont pluis serjants que gardeins, (that is) which gardians are rather seruants then Gardians.

(d) 8.*E*.2. *presentment* 10. 7.*E*.39. 27 *E*.3.89. 29.*E*.5.5. *F N B* 33. 31.*E*.3. *Estoppel*, 345. *Britton* 163.164. *Fleta lib*.1.*cap*.10.

¶ *Il rendra account, &c. apres que lheire ad accomplishe lage de* 14. *ans.* This point hath beene much controuerted in our bookes, and the causes of the doubts haue beene, first vpon the words of the statute of (e) Merlebridge, ca. 17. 2. Upon the originall writ of Account against the Gardein in Socage. The words of the statute be Cum ad legitimam ætatem peruenerit sibi respondeat, &c. and legitima ætas, (f) lawfull age, is xxi. yeares. 2. Also the writ of Accompt reciteth the said statute, Quare cum de communi consilio regni nostri prouisum sit quod custodes terrarum & tenementorũ quæ tenentur in Socagio hæredibus terrarum & tenementorum illorum cum ad plenam ætatem pervenerint reddant rationabilem compotum. (g) whereupon it is gathered that no action of account did lye against the Gardein in Socage at the Common Law, vntill the heire bee of his lawfull age of 21. yeares. But as to the first (legitima ætas) as the statute (h) speaketh) or plena ætas (as the writ doth render it) are to be vnderstood secundum subiectam materiam, that is of the heire of Socage land whose lawfull and full age as to the custody or Gardeinship is 14. And as to the recitall of the statute, (i) it is euident that an action of Account did lye against Gardein in Socage at the Common Law. And that the statute was made in affirmance or declaration of the Common Law for the statute speaketh only De custodia parentum that is of a Gardein in right, but yet an action of Account lyeth against him that occupieth the land as Gardein, albeit he be not of the blood (as hereafter shall be said.) And vpon consideration had of the said statute and of all the bookes, it was adiudged in the Court of Cõmon Pleas, Pasch. 16. Eliz. rot. 436. according to the opinion of Littleton, that the heire after the age of 14. yeares shall haue an action of Account against the Gardein in Socage, when he will at his pleasure, and so is an ancient question well resolued.

(e) *It is called the statute of Merlebridge because the Parliament in* 52.*H*.3 *was holden there.*
(f) 16.*E*.3. *writ* 100. 18 *E*.3.55.77. 29.*E*.3.5. *v d*.32.*E*.3.*Gard*.31. *F.N.B*.118. 6.*E*.3.38.
(g) 16.*E*.2. *Account* 120. 17.*E*.2.*ibid*.121.
(h) 2 *E*.2. *Account* 14.*E*.3 *Ibid*. 3.*Mar*.137. *Kelwey* 131.
(i) 18.*E*.2.*Auowry* 220.
Pasch.16.*Eliz*.*Rot*.436. *in communi banco*.

Britton was of opinion that the statute of Marlebridge which gaue the Capias in Account, extended to Gardein in Socage, for he wrote before the statute of W.1. ca 11. But later bookes haue ouer-ruled this point, that no Capias lyeth against Gardein in Socage, for the statute extendeth to Bailifes only; Neither doth the statute of W.2. extend to gardein in Socage, for that speaketh only De seruientibus, balivis, camerarijs, & receptoribus.

Mirror, *ca*.2.§.17. *Britton*.*fo*.163.*b*. *Fleta lib*.2.*ca*.64. 18.*E*.2. *Auowrie* 220. 17.*E*.3.59.*Merlbr*.*ca*.23. *W*.2.*ca*.11.

¶ *Mes tiel gardein sur son account auera allowance de touts ses reasonable costs & expences en touts choses.* **And this is due to all accountants** by the Common Law, and so it is declared by the said statute of Merlebridge, Saluis ipsis custodibus rationabilibus misis suis.

The statute of Merlbr. intended by Littl. ... *ca*.17.

¶ *Allowance.* **What other allowances shall the gardein haue?**

If the Gardein receiue the Rents and profits of the lands, and be robbed of the same, whether shall he be discharged thereof vpon his Account? and it seemeth, that if he be robbed without his default of negligen ce hee shalbe discharged thereof. As if a Bailife of a Mannor or a Receiuer, or a Factor of a Merchant or the like accountant be robbed, hee shall be discharged thereof vpon his account and seeing the Gardein shall be charged as Bailife after the heires age of 14. and be discharged vpon his account, if he be robbed, Pari ratione if hee bee robbed before the age of 14. But otherwise it is of a Carrier, for he hath his hire, and thereby implicitely vndertaketh the safe deliuery of the goods deliuered to him, and therefore he shall answer the value of them if he be robbed of them. Note the diuersity and so it was resolued * in the Kings bench.

41.*E*.3.3. 22.*Ass*.41. 22.*E*.3.*Account* 111. 29.*Ass*.28. 3.*H*.7 4.*b*. 6.*H*.7.12. 10.*H*.7.25. 10.*H*.6.21. 2.*E*.4.15. *Doct*.& *Stud*.*ca*.38.*fo*.130.
* *Hill*.38.*Eliz*. *inter Woodliefe & Curties*.

So it is if goods be deliuered to a man to be safely kept; and after those goods are stolne from him, this shall not excuse him, because by the acceptance he vndertooke to keepe them safely, and therefore he must keepe them at his perill.

So it is if goods be deliuered to be one to be kept, for, to be kept, and to be safely kept, is all one in Law, But if the goods be deliuered to him to be kept, as hee would keepe his owne, there if they be stolne from him without his default or negligence, he shalbe discharged. So if goods be deliuered to one as a gage or pledge, and they be stolne, he shall be discharged, because he hath a property in them, and therefore he ought to keepe them no otherwise then his owne; but if he that gaged them, tendred the money before the stealing, and the other refused to deliuer them, then for this default in him he shall be charged.

29.*Ass*.28.

If A. leaue a chest locked with B. to be kept, and taketh away the Key with him, and acquainteth

8.*E*.2.*tit*.*Detinue* 59.

quainteth not B what is in the Chest, and the Chest together with the goods of B. are stolne away, B. shall not be charged therewith, because A. did not trust B. with them as this case is. And that which hath beene said before of stealing, is to be understood also of other like accidents as shipwracke by sea, fire by lightning, and other like inevitable accidents. And all these cases were resolued and adiudged in the Kings bench.* And by these diuersities are all the bookes concerning this point reconciled.

* *Pasch.*43. *Eliz. inter Southcote & Bennet in detinue.*

Note, Reader it is necessary for any that receiueth goods to be kept, to receiue them in this speciall manner, viz. to be kept as his owne, or to keepe them at the perill of the owner. But now is Littleton to be further heard.

¶ *Et si tiel gardein maria le heire deins* 14.*ans, &c.* For if hee marry the heire after 14. hee is out of his custody, and no account shall be made therefore.

¶ *Il accountera a luy.* Hee shall account for the mariage of the heire, viz for so much as any man bona fide had offered for the mariage or would giue in mariage unto him.

¶ *Ou a ses Executors.* Note that an infant of the age of 14. may make his will (as some hereupon haue collected) but the meaning of Littleton is, that if after his mariage he accomplish his age of 18. yeares at what time he may make his Testament, and constitute executors for his goods and chattells. and the words are so to be understood as may stand with Law and reason. Note, Executors could not haue an action of Account at the Common Law in respect of the priuitie of the account, but the statute of W.2.ca 23. hath giuen the action of account to executors the statute of 25.E.3.ca.5. to Executors of Executors, and the statute of 31.E.3.ca.11. to Administrators.

7.E.3.61. 19.E.3.*account* 56. 38.E.3.7. 31.E.3.*tit. Account*, 57.

¶ *Que il voile luy marier sans prender le value.* So as the Gardein shall not account only for that which hee shall receiue in this case, but for which hee might receiue.

3.E.3.10. 45.E.3.*Account*.40. 2.R.2.*Ibid.* 45. 6.R.2.*Account* 47.

¶ *Si non que il luy marier a tiel mariage que est tant en value, &c.* This needeth no explanation.

If the heire in Socage be rauished out of the custody of the Gardein and the rauisher marrieth the heire, the Gardein shall haue a Writ of rauishment of ward, and recouer the value of the mariage, &c. and shall account to the heire for the same.

*Hill.*3.E.2. *Coram Rege, Rot.* 34. *Agnes Frowicke case* F.N.B.139.I. & 140. 26.E.3.65.1.E.3.19.20.

And the Gardein in Socage is bounden by Law, that the heire bee well brought up, and that his euidences be safely kept.

The Grandmother of the sonne and heire of John Berneuill who held the Mannor of Totington in the County of Midd. in Socage recouered the heire in a Rauishment of ward against Simon Cheuin which had married the stepmother of the heire, and by rule of the Court the plaintife Pro nutritura hæredis, & pro custodia euidentiarum invenit plegios.

*Trin.*1.H.5 *Coram Rege Rot.*1.*Midd.*

Section 124:

¶ *ET si ascun auter home que nest pas procheine amy, &c.* If a stranger entreth into the lands of the infant within age of 14. and taketh the profits of the same, the infant may charge him as Gardein in Socage. And this doth well agree with the Writ of account against a Gardein in socage, for the words be, Idem B. prefato A. rationabilem compotum suum de exitibus

19.E.2.*Avowry*, 221. 39.E.3.16. 41.E.3.*Account* 35. 49.E.3.10. 18.E.3.77. 28.*Ass.p.*11. *Pl Com.*542. 6.E.3.38.F.N.B.118.

¶ ET si ascun auter home q̃ nest procheín amy, occupie les terres ou tenemẽts del heire come gardeine en Socage, il serra compell de render accompt al heire, auxi bien sicõe il fuissoyt procheín amy: car il nest pas plee pur luy en briefe Daccompt adire, que il nest procheine amie, &c. mes il respondra ꝛ quel

AND if any other man, who is not the next friend, occupies the lands or tenements of the heire as Gardein in Socage, he shall be compelled to yeeld an account to the heire as well as if hee had beene next friend, for it is no plea for him in the Writ of Account to say that he is not the next friend, &c. but hee shall answer

il ad occupie les terres ou tenements come gardeine en socage ou nemy. Sed Quære, si apres ceo que le heire ad accomplish lage de 14. ans, & Gardeine en socage continualment occupia la terre tanque lheire vient a plein age s. 21. ans, si le heyre a son plein age auera action Daccompt enuers le gardeine de temps que il occupia apres les dits 14. ans, come enuers Gardeine en Socage, ou enuers luy come son baylife.

whether hee hath occupied the lands or tenements as Gardein in Socage or no. But *quare*, if after the heire hath accomplished the age of 14. yeares, and the Gardein in Socage, continually occupieth the land vntill the heire comes to full age, s. of 21. yeares, if the heire at his full age shall haue an action of Account against the gardein, from the time that he occupied after the said 14. yeares, as gardein in Socage, or against him as his Bailife.

provenientibus de terris & tenementis suis in N. quæ tenentur in socagio & quorum custodiam idem B. habuit dum pred: A. infra ætatem fuit vt dicitur And true it is that in iudgement of Law he had the custody of the lands: and hee is called Tutor alienus, and the right Gardein in Socage tutor proprius, and it is no plea for him to denie that he is Procheine amy, but he must answer to the taking of the proffits as Littleton here saith.

13.E.3.*Account* 77. 22.E.3.11. 41.E.3.*Account*.35. 10.H.7.7. 4.H.7.6.b. 7.H.7.9.a.

¶ *Sed quære, &c.* This Quære came not out of Littletons quiuer for it is euident that after the age of 14 yeares he shall be charged as Bailife at any time when the heire will, either before his age of 21 yeares or after.

6.R.3.38. 32.E.3.*Account* 60. 7.E.4. F.N.B.118.

Sect. 125.

¶ Item si gardein en chiualrie face ses executors & deuy, le heire esteant deins age, &c. les executors aueront le garde durant le nonage, &c. Mes si Gardein en Socage face ses executors, & deuy, le heire esteant deins lage de 14. ans, ses executors naueront pas le garde, mes vn auter procheine amy, a que le heritage ne poyt my discend, auera la garde, &c. Et la cause de diuersitie est, pur ceo que Gardeine en

ALso if Gardein in Chiualrie makes his executors and die, the heire being within age, &c. the Executours shall haue the Wardship during the nonage, &c. but if the Gardeine in Socage make his Executours & die, the heire being within the age of 14. yeares, his Executors shall not haue the Wardship, but another the next friend, to whom the Inheritance cannot discend, shall haue the Wardship, &c. And the reason of this diuersitie is be-

¶ *A Son proper vse.* A Tenant holdeth Land of a Bishop by Knights Seruice which Signiorie the Bishop hath in the right of his Bishopricke, the Tenant dieth his heire within age, the Bishop either before or after seisure dieth, neither the King nor the Successor of the Bishop shall haue the Wardship, but his Executors. For albeit the Bishop hath the Signorie in auter droit, yet the Wardship being but a Chattell hee hath in his owne right, and a Chattell cannot go in the succession of a sole Corporation, vnlesse it bee in the case of the King.

7.R.2.bre.634. 40.E.3.14. 2.H.4.19. 10.Eliz.Dier.277.

7.H.4.41. 44.E.3.42.

And yet if a Bishop haue an Aduowson, and the Church become void, and the Bishop die, neither the Successor nor the Executors shall present, but the King because it is but a Chose in action. And so it is in case where the King hath wardship, but that

24.E.3.26. 44.E.3. F.N.B.33. *See more of this in the chapter of Warranty. Sect.*

that is a prerogatiue that belongeth to the King, to prouide for the Church being void, for where the Tenure by Knights Seruice is of a common person, the Executours of the Tenant shall present where the auoydance fell in the life of the Tenant.

31. E. 3. accompt. 57. 19. E. 3. ibid. 156. 48. E. 3. 2. 2. H. 4. 13. F. N. B. 117. 39. H. 6. 5. 4. E. 4. 25. 43. E. 3. 21. Lib. 11. fol. 89.

¶ *Le heire est sauns remedie, &c.* For albeit in an Action of account against a Gardeine in Socage, &c. the Defendant cannot wage his Law, yet in respect of the priuitie of the matters of account, and the discharge resting in the knowledge of the parties thereunto, an action of account neither lieth against the Executors of the accountant, nor at the Common Law for the Executors of him to whom the account is to be made as is aforesaid but that is holpen by Statute, (*) It hath beene attempted in Parliament to giue an action of account against the Executors of a Gardeine in Socage, but neuer could be effected.

chiualrie ad le garde a son proper vse, & Gardein en Socage nad le garde a son vse, mes al vse del heire. Et en cas lou le Gardeine en Socage deuy deuant ascun accompt fait per luy al heire, de ceo le heire est sans remedie, pur ceo que nul briefe daccompt gist enuers les Executors si non pur le Roy solement.

cause the Gardeine in Chiualrie hath the Wardship to his owne vse, and the gardein in Socage hath not the Wardship to his owne vse, but to the vse of the heire. And in this case where the Gardein in Socage dieth before any account made by him to the heire, of this the heire is without remedy for that no writ of acconnt lieth against the Executours, but for the King only.

* Rot. parl. 50. E. 3. nu. 123.

(a) Pl. Com. 321. Keylwey 131. Lib. 11. fol. 89.

¶ *Si non pur le roy solement.* (a) The reason of this is because the Kings treasure is the sinewes of warre, and the honour and safetie of the King in time of peace, firmamentum belli, & ornamentum pacis, and therefore the death of the partie shall not barre the King of his treasure due unto him upon the account, because it is intended that the King was busied about the publike for the good of the Common-wealth, and had not leisure to call his accountant to make his account, and nullum tempus occurrit Regi. Littleton speaketh of the Kings Prerogatiue but twice in all his Bookes, viz. here and Sect. 178. and in both places as part of the Lawes of England. Prærogatiua is (b) derived of præ. i. ante, and rogare, that is to aske or demand beforehand, whereof commeth prærogatiua, and is denominated of the most excellent part, because though an Act hath passed both the Houses of the Lords and Commons in Parliament, yet before it be a Law, the Royall assent must be asked or demanded and obtained, and this is the proper sence of the word. But legally (*) it extends to all Powers, Preheminences and Priuiledges, which the Law giueth to the Crowne, whereof Littleton here speaketh of one. Bracton lib. 1. in one place calleth it libertatem, in another Priuilegium Regis. (c) Britton (d) (following W. 1.) Droit le Roy. (e) Registr. ius Regium, and ius Regium Coronæ, &c.

Vide Sect. 178. Stanf. prar. 32. (b) Fortescue. fol. 45. Rot. Parliam. 1. H. 4. nu. 188. Pl. Com. 236. Stanf. pl. cor. 162. b. Stanf. prar. 1. a. b. & 10. b. (*) Stanf. prar. 5. 10.

(c) Westm. 1. cap. 50. (d) Britton. fol. 27. (e) Regist. fol. 61. &c.

Sect. 126.

43. E. 3. barre 294. 9. E. 4. 36. Bract. lib. 2. fol. 35. Glanuil. lib. 9. cap. 4.

¶ *Certeine rent.* A Tenant holdeth of his Lord certaine Lands in Socage to pay yearely a paire of gilt Spurs or fiue shillings in money at the Feast of Easter. In this case the rent is incertaine, and the tenant may pay which of them he will at the said Feast, and likewise the tenant may pay which of them he will for reliefe, but if hee pay it not when he ought, then may the

¶ Item le seignior de que la terre est tenus en Socage apres le mort son tenant, auera reliefe en tiel forme. Si le tenant tient per fealtie & certain rent, a paier annualment &c. si les termes de paiment

Also the Lord of whom the Land is holden in Socage after the decease of his Tenant shall haue reliefe in this manner. if the Tenant holdeth by fealtie, and certaine Rent to pay yearely, &c. if the tearmes of

son

sont a payer per deux termes del an, ou per quater termes dl an, le Seignior auera del heire son tenant tant come le rent amount que il paya p an. Sicome le tenāt tient de son seignior per fealtie & x. s. de rent, payable a certaine termes del an, donques lheire paiet al Seignior x. s. pur reliefe, ouster les x. s. que il paiera pur le rent.

payment bee to pay at two tearmes of the yeare, or at foure termes in the yeare the Lord shall haue of the heire his Tenant, as much as the Rent amounts vnto which he payeth yearly. as if the Tenant holds of his Lord by fealtie, and ten shillings Rent payable at certaine termes of the yeare, then the heire shall pay to the Lord ten shillings, for reliefe, beside the ten shillings which he payeth for the Rent.

Lord distreine for which of them he will. But if the tenure be to attend on his Lord at the Feast of Christmasse, or to pay ten shillings, there the reliefe must bee ten shillings, because the other cannot be doubled, & sic de similibus.

¶ *A paier annuelment.* If the tenant holdeth of his Lord by fealty and to pay euery two or three yeare tenne shillings, albeit this be no Annuall Rent, yet shall hee pay ten shillings for reliefe, & sic de similibus.

But it is to be noted, that beside reliefe whereof Littleton here speaketh, there belongeth to a tenure in socage of common right, aide for the making of his eldest Sonne a Knight at the age of fifteene yeares, & to marie his daughter at the age of seuen yeares. *Vide Sect.* 103. F.N.B 82. *West.* 1. *cap.* 35. 25. E. 3. *stat.* 5. *cap.* 11.

En mesme le manner est, si home soit seisie de certeine terre que est tenus en Socage, & fait feoffement en fee a son vse & morust seisie del vse (son heire del age de 14. ans, ou pluis) & nul volunt per luy declare, le Seignior auera reliefe del heire, sicome auant est dit; Et cest per le statute de Anno 19. Henrici 7. cap. 15.

In the same manner it is, if a man be seised of certain land which is holden in Socage, and maketh a feoffment in fee to his owne vse, and dieth seised of the vse (his heire of the age of 14. yeares or more) and no will by him declared, the Lord shall haue reliefe of the heire as afore is said. And this by the Statute of 19. Henrie 7. cap. 15.

This is an addition to Littleton, wherefore I omit it the rather for that the Statute of 19. H. 7. is for the cause aboue mentioned become of none effect.

Section 127.

¶ ET en tiel cas apres la mort le Tenant, tiel reliefe est due al Seignior maintenant, de quel age que le heire soit, pur ceo que tiel Seignior ne poit auer le garde de corps ne de terre

AND in this Case, after the death of the tenant, such reliefe is due to the Lord presently, of what age soeuer the heire bee, because such Lord cannot haue the wardship of the bodie, nor of the land of the heire.

¶ M*Aintenant*, and as Littleton saith, he ought not to attend the payment of his reliefe according to the dayes of payment, but he ought to haue his reliefe presently, and for the same he may incontinently distraine after the death of the Tenant. 16. H. 7. 4. 18. E. 3. 26. p. 18. *Bracton. lib.* 2. *fol.* 85. *debit heres vna vice* (*) *additum suum vnius anni duplicatum.* Britten. *fol.* 178. *acc.* *Fleta lib.* 1. *cap.* 8.

And therefore in the case aforesaid, where the Tenant holdeth by the Rent of fiue shillings, or a paire of gilt

le heire. Et le Seignior en tiel case ne doit attendre a le payment de son reliefe, solonques les termes & iours de paiment de rent, mes il doit auer son relief maintenant, & pur ceo il poit incontinẽt distraine apres le mort son tenant, pur reliefe.

And the Lord in such case ought not to attend for the payment of his reliefe, according to the termes and dayes of payment of the rent, but hee is to haue his reliefe presently, and therefore he may forthwith distreine after the death of his Tenant for reliefe.

Spurres, if the heire bee not presently (that is as presently as conueniently may, all due circumstances considered) after the death of his Ancestor readie upon the land to pay reliefe, the Lord may distraine for which of them hee will, and if the tenant tendred either of them according to the Law, and none for the Lord was readie there to receiue it, yet the Lord may distreine for that which was tendred at his pleasure.

45.E.3.19. 35.H.6.52. 20.Eliz. Dier 361. Stanford, p ar. 13.b. F.N.B. 256. 259.

¶ *De quel age que le heire soit.* And yet it appeareth in our Bookes that in this case the King in Case of a tenure in Socage in chiefe shall not haue primer seisin unlesse the heire be of the age of fourteene yeares at the death of his Ancestor, for if he be under that age he is in the gard and custodie of his prochein amy.

But otherwise it is in case of a common person, as here it appeareth. And where in some impressions these words be added (issint que il passa lage de 14. ans) those words are added and are against Law, and no part of Littletons worke.

Section 128.

¶ EN Mesme le Maner est lou le tenant tient de son Seignior per fealtie, & un li. de Peper, ou Cummin, & le tenant morust, le seignior auera pur relief un lib. de Cummin, ou un lib. de Peper, ouster le cõmon rent. En mesme le maner est lou tenant tient a payer per an certaine number de Capons, ou de gallines, ou un paire de gaunts; ou certaine bushels de frument, & hmodi.

IN the same manner it is, where the Tenant holdeth of his Lord by fealtie, and a pound of Peper or Cummin, and the Tenant dieth, the Lord shall haue for reliefe a pound of Cummin, or a pound of Pepper besides the cõmon rent. In the same manner it is where the Tenant holdeth to pay yeerely a number of Capons or Hennes, or a paire of Gloues, or certaine bushels of Corne or such like.

¶ *Vn lib. de pepper ou cumyn.* Here it is to bee obserued that the Lord may reserue Pepper or any other things that be exotica, forreigne, of the growth of outlandish Countries, or beyond Sea, aswell as of the growth of England, where, by Nauigation the life of euery Iland is imployed. And where Littleton here putteth his case in the disiunctiue, if the tenant doth hold by fealtie and one pound of Pepper or a pound of Cummin, hee shall pay for reliefe a pound of Pepper, or a pound of Cummine ouer and besides the rent. But if the tenant holdeth of his Lord by doing of certaine worke dayes in haruest, or to attend at Christmasse or such like hee shall not double the same, for of Corporall seruice or labour or worke of the tenant, no reliefe is due, but where the tenant holdeth by such yearely rents or profits, which may be paid or deliuered, whereof Littleton hath put his examples, and by them is manifestly proued that corporall seruice, worke, or labour shall not be doubled in this Case.

¶ *Ou certaine bushels de frument.* Here it appeareth that the reliefe of bushels of Corne is to be paid presently though the tenant die in winter before Corne be ripe.

Note

Note, here are examples put of fiue natures: 1. Aromatorum exoticorum, of spices or drugs of outlandish growth. 2. Granorum, of Corne of English growth. 3. Auium villaticarum, of Powltry, as Capons, Hens, &c. 4. Artificiorum, of handicrafts as a paire of Gloues generally either of Outlandish or English. 5. Aut similiū, or such like (that is) like of Outlandish growth or of English growth, or of Poultrie, or of Artifices Outlandish or English, and like herein that they may be paid or deliuered to the Lord euery yeare or euery second or third yeare, &c.

Sect. 129.

¶ MEs en ascun case le seigniour doit demurrer a distreiner pur son reliefe iesque a certaine temps. Sicome le tenāt tient de son seignior pur vn Rose, ou p vn bushel de Roses, a paier al feast de Natiuitie de Saint John Baptist, si tiel tenant deuie en yuer, donque le Sn̄r ne poit dist̄ p̄ son reliefe tāque al tēps q̄ les Roses p le course del an poiēt auū lour cresser, &c. & sic de similibus.

BVt in some case the Lord ought to stay to distreine for his reliefe vntill a certaine time. As if the tenant holds of his Lord by a Rose, or by a bushell of Roses to pay at the feast of St. *Iohn* the *Baptist* if such tenant dieth in Winter, then the Lord cannot distreine for his reliefe vntill the time that Roses by the course of the yeare may haue their growth, &c. and so of the like.

¶ *Per le course del an.* Lex spectat naturæ ordinem, the Law respecteth the order and course of nature, Lex non cogit ad impossibilia. The Law compells no man to impossible things. The argument ab impossibili is forcible in Law, Impossibile est quod naturæ rei repugnat. And here is to be obserued that Littler. puts a diuersity betweene Corne and Roses, for Corne will last, and therefore the tenant must deliuer the Corne presently before the time of growth (as before is said) and so of Saffron and the like, but Roses or other flowers that are fructus fugaces, cannot be kept, and therefore are not to be deliuered till the time of growing, neither is the tenant driuen by Law artificially to preserue Roses, for the Law in these cases respecteth nature, and the course of the yeare as Littleton here saith, Et ars naturam imitatur, & sic de similibus.

Sect. 130.

¶ ITem si ascun voile demand, pur q̄ home poit tener de son seignior p fealty tantsolemēt p̄ touts maners des seruices, entant que quant le tenāt ferra fealtie, il iurera a son Seignior q̄ il ferra a son Sn̄r touts maners des seruices dues, & quant il ad

ALso if any will aske, why a man may hold of his Lord by Fealty only for all manner of seruices, insomuch as when the tenant shall doe his fealty, he shall sweare to his Lord, that hee will doe to his Lord all manner of seruices due, and when hee hath done fealty in

¶ *QVant le tenant ferra fealty, il iurera a son Seignior, &c.* Here it appeareth that the doing of the Fealtie is both a performance of his seruice, and of his oath also when it is done for that no other seruice is due. And that one oath of fealty is taken of all that hold, and is not to be changed for any noueltie or nicety of inuention, for Iudges anciently and continually haue suppressed innouations and would in no case change the ancient Common Law.

31.E.3.tit.Gager deliuerance,5.
38.E.3.1.42.Ass.p.12.
4.E.3.ca.5.
18.E.3.ca.4.& 6.
4.H.4.ca.2. 2.H.4.fo.28.

¶ Il

See of this in the Chapter of Fee simple Sect.4.

See more of this in the Chapter of Warrantie, Sect.

W.2.ca.33. Flet.li.2.ca.43. & li.5.ca.34 32.H.8.ca.24.

¶ *Il convient que il doit faire a son Seigniour ascun seruice.* For there can be no Tenure without some Seruice, because the Seruice maketh the Tenure.

¶ *Son escheat de la terre.* Eschaeta is deriued of this word Eschier quod est accidere: For an escheat is a casuall profit quod accidit Domino ex euentu & ex insperato, which happeneth to the Lord by chance, and vnlooked for. And of this word Eschaeta, commeth Eschaetor, an Escheator, so called, because his office is to inquire of all casuall profits, and them to seise into the Kings hands, that the same may be answered to the King.

Lands may escheat to the Lord two manner of wayes: one by Attainder, the other without attainder. By Attainder in three sorts: First, Quia suspensus est per collum. Secondly, Quia abiurauit Regnum. Thirdly, Quia vtlegatus est, without attainder, as if the tenant dies without heire.

¶ *Ou per case auter forfeiture.* As if the Land bee aliened in Mortmaine, or when Littlet wrote, if the Tenaunts had erected Crosses vpon their houses or tenements, in preiudice of the Lords, that the Tenaunts might claime the priuiledge of the hospitlers to defend themselues against their Lords, they had forfeited their Tenances. But since Littleton wrote, the Hospitlers are dissolued, and consequently that forfeiture is gone.

¶ *Ou profit.* As Reliefe, Aid pur file marrier, aid pur faire fitz chiualer, and the like.

fait fealtie en tiel case nul auter Seruice est due. A ceo il poyt estre dit, Que lou vn Tenant tient sa Terre de son Seignior, il couient que il doit fait a son Seignior ascun Seruice, car si le Tenaunt ne ses heires deuoyent faire nul manner de Seruice al Seignior ne a ses heires, donque per long temps continue il serroit hors de memorie & de remembrance, le quel la terre fuit tenus per le seignior, ou de ses heires, ou nemy, & donques pluis tost & pluis redimént voilont hões dire que la terre nest pas tenus del Seignior ou de ses heires, q̃ auterment: Et sur ceo le Seignior perdra son Escheat de la terre, ou per case auter forfeiture ou profit que il poet auer de le terre. Issint il est reason que le Seignior & ses heires ont ascun Seruice fayt a eux, pur prouer & testifier que la terre est tenus de eux.

this case no other Seruice is due. To this it may bee sayd, That where a Tenant holds his land of his Lord, it behooueth that hee ought to doe some seruice to his Lord: For if the Tenant nor his heires ought to doe no manner of Seruice to his Lord nor his heires, then by long continuance of time it would grow out of memorie, whether the Land were holden of the Lord, or of his Heires, or not, and then will men more often and more readily say, That the Land is not holden of the Lord, nor of his Heires, than otherwise: And hereupon the Lord shall lose his Escheat of the Land, or perchance some other forfeiture or profit which he might haue of the Land. So it is reason that the Lord and his heyres haue some Seruice done vnto them, to prooue and testifie, That the Land is holden of them.

Sect. 131.

¶ ET pur ceo q̃ fealtie est incident a touts manners de tenures, forspris le Tenure en Frankalmoigne, (si cõe sera dit en le tenure ð Frankealmoigne) & pur ceo que le Seignior ne voiloit al cõmencement del Tenure auer ascun auter seruice forsque Fealtie, il est reason que home poet tener de son Seignior per fealtie tantsolement. & quaunt il ad fait son fealtie, il ad fait touts ses seruices.

AND for that fealtie is incident to all manner of Tenures, but to the Tenure in Frankealmoigne, (as shall be said in the Tenure of Frankalmoign) and for that the Lord would not at the beginning of the Tenure haue any other seruice but Fealtie, it is reason that a Man may hold of his Lord by Fealtie onely, and when hee hath done his Fealtie, he hath done all his Seruices.

¶ *Fealtie est incident.*

Of Incidents there bee two sorts, *viz.* seperable, and inseperable.

Seperable, as Rents incident to reuersions, &c. which may be seuered, inseperable, as fealtie to a reuersion or tenure which cannot be seuered: for as all lands and Tenements within England are holden of some Lord or other, and either mediately or immediately of the King, so to euerie tenure at the least, fealtie is an inseperable incident, so long as the Tenure remaines; and all other Seruices, except Fealtie, are seuerable. But where the tenure is by Fealtie only, there is no reliefe due for the cause abouesaid.

Section 132.

¶ ITem si vn home lesse a vn auter pur terme ð vie certaine terres ou tenemẽts sauns parler de ascun rent rendð a le Lessor, vncore il ferra fealtie a le Lessor, pur ceo que il tient de luy. Auxy si vn lease soit fait a vn hõe pur terme de ans il est dit que le Lessee ferra Fealtie a le Lessor, pur ceo que il tient de luy. Et ceo est proue bien per les parols del brief de Wast, quaunt le Lessour ad cause de porter Briefe de Wast enuers luy, le quel Briefe dira, que le Lessee tient les Tenements de le Lessor pur terme de ans,

ALso if a man letteth to another lands or tenemẽts for terme of life, without naming any rent to bee reserued to the Lessor, yet he shall doe fealtie to the Lessor, because he holdeth of him. Also if a Lease bee made to a man for terme of yeares, it is said that the Lessee shall doe fealtie to the Lessor, because he holdeth of him. And this is wel prooued by the words of the writ of Wast, when the Lessor hath cause to bring a writ of Wast against him, which Writ shall say, That the Lessee holds his Tenements of the Lessour for terme of yeares. So the

¶ *Si vn hõe lesse pur terme de vie sauns parler de rent, &c. il ferra fealtie, &c.* *V. Sect. 214.*

And the reason is, Because there is a Tenure, & fealtie (as hath beene said) is incident to al manner of tenures, & it is to bee noted, that the law for the suretie of

40.E.3.34. 9.H.6.41. 10.H.6.13 9.E.4.1. 21.E.4.29. 5.H.5.12. 5.H.7.11.

V.id.Sect.84.

of the Lord, that his Tenant ſhall be faithfull and loyall to him doth create ſuch a ſeruice, as the Tenant ſhall be bound thereunto by oath.

¶ *Auxi ſi leaſe ſoit fait pur ans, &c. le leſſee ferra fealty.* For there alſo is a tenure betweene them. And Littletons opinion in this caſe is holden for good Law at this day.

¶ *Et ceo eſt proue bien per les parols del breiſe. &c.* Nota, the originall writs (are as it were) the foundations and grounds of the Law, and as it appeares here by Littleton are of great authoritie for the proofe of the Law in particular caſes.

¶ *Pur ceo que il nad ſuer eſtate.* Therefore Tenant at will ſhall not doe Fealty (as hath beene ſaid before) becauſe the matter of an oath muſt be certaine: the reſt of this Section needs no explication.

iſſint le briefe proua vn tenure enter eux. Mes celuy q̃ eſt tenãt a volunt ſolonq; le courſe del common ley, ne ferra fealty, p̃ ceo que il nad aſcun ſuer eſtat. Mes auterment eſt de tenant a volunt ſolonq; le cuſtome del mannor, p̃ ceo que il eſt oblige pur faire fealty a ſon Sñr pur deux cauſes: Lun eſt p̃ cauſe del cuſtome: lauter eſt, pur ceo q̃ il priſt ſon eſtate en tiel forme pur faire a ſon Sñr fealty.

Writ proues a tenure betweene them. But he which is Tenant at will according to the courſe of the Common Law ſhall not doe Fealtie, becauſe hee hath not any ſure eſtate: but otherwiſe it is of Tenant at will according to the cuſtome of the Mannor, for that he is bound to doe fealtie to his Lord for two cauſes, the one is, by reaſon of the cuſtome, and the other is for that he taketh his eſtate in ſuch forme to doe his Lord fealty.

Bract.lib.2.ca.5.& lib.4.ca.1. Britton fo.164.165. Mirror ca.2. §.18. Glanuil.lib.7.ca.1.& lib.12.ca.3.& 25. Fleta,lib.3.ca.5.

21.H.7.39. 29.E.3.14.

40.E.3.29. 8.H.6.23. 7.E.4.12. 12.H.8.8.

¶ *VN Abbe, Prior, ou auter hõe de religion ou de ſaint eſgliſe.* It is to be obſerued, that of Eccleſiaſticall perſons ſome bee regular, and ſome bee ſecular. They bee called regular becauſe they liue vnder certaine rules, and haue vowed three things: true obedience, perpetuall chaſtity and wilfull pouerty. And when a man is profeſſed in any of the orders of Religion, he is ſaid to bee home de religion, a man of religion or religious. Of this ſort be all Abbots, Priors and others of any of the ſaid order regular. Secular are perſons Eccleſiaſticall, but becauſe they liue not vnder certain rules of ſome of the ſaid orders, nor are Voluntaries,

¶ TEnant en frankalmoigne, eſt lou vn Abbe ou Prior ou vn auter hõe de religion, ou d̃ ſaint Egliſe, tiẽt de ſon Sñr en frankalmoigne, q̃ eſt adire en Latin in liberam eleæmoſinam. Et tiel tenure commencẽ adeprimes en auncient temps en tiel forme; Quant vn home en auncient temps fuit ſeiſie d̃ certain terres ou tenements en ſon demeſne come de fee,

TEnãt in Frãkalmoigne, is where an Abbot or Prior, or another man of Religion, or of holy Church, holdeth of his Lord in Franke almoigne: that is to ſay in Latin *in liberam Eleemoſynam*, that is, in free almes. And ſuch tenure began firſt in old time when a man in old time was ſeiſed of the lands or tenements in his demeſne as of Fee, and of the ſame land infeoffed

A

& de mesmes les terres ou tenements enfeoffa vn Abbe & son Couent, ou vn Pryor, &c. a auer & tener a eux & lour successors a touts iours en pure & perpetual almoigne, ou en frankalm ou per tielx parols; A tener de le grantor, ou de le feoffor, & de ses heires en frankalmoigne: en tiels cases les tenements sont tenus en frankalmoigne.

an Abbot and his couent, or Prior and his Couent, to haue and to hold to them and their successors in pure and perpetuall almes, or in Frank almoigne, or by such words, to hold of the grauntor, or of the lessor and his heires in Free almes: In such case the tenements were holden in Frankalmoigne.

they are for distinction sake called secular, as Bishops, Deanes and Chapters, Archdeacons, Prebends, Parsons, Vicars, and such like. All which Littleton here includeth vnder these generall words, De saint Eglise, of holy Church and none of these are in Law said to be homes de religion or religious.

Where Littleton saith (infeoffa vn Abbe & son couent) his meaning is that the Abbot only is infeoffed, for he is only a parson capable and the Couent are dead persons in Law, and haue power of assent only, and that they thereunto assent. But since Littleton wrote, all Abbeys, Priories, Monasteries, and other religious houses of Monkes, Canons, Friers, and Nunnes, &c. haue bin dissolued, & their possessions giuen to the Crowne. *See the statutes of 27. H. 8. not printed but in the abridgement 31. H. 8. cap. 13. & 32. H. 8. ca. 24. &c. Vid. Sect. 530.*

The Ecclesiasticall state of England, as it standeth at this day (which is necessarie for our student to know) is deuided into two Prouinces, or Archbishopricks, (viz.) of Canterbury, and of Yorke. The Archbishop of Canterbury is stiled, Metropolitanus & primas totius Angliæ; And the Archbishop of Yorke Primas Angliæ. Each Archbishop hath within his Prouince suffragan Bishops of seuerall Diocesse. The Archbishop of Canterbury hath vnder him within his Prouince, of ancient foundations, viz. Rochester his principall Chaplaine, London his Deane, Winchester his Chancellor; Norwich, Lincolne, Ely, Chichester, Salisbury, Exeter, Bathe and Wells, Worcester, Couentry and Lichfield, Hereford, Landaffe, St. Dauid, Bangor, and St. Assaphe, & foure founded by King H. 8. erected out of the ruines of dissolued Monasteries (that is to say) Gloucester, Bristowe, Peterborow, and Oxford. The Archbishop of Yorke hath vnder him foure, (viz.) the Bishop of the County palatine of Chester newly erected by King H. 8. and annexed by him to the Archbishopricke of Yorke, of the County palatine of Durham, Carlile, and the Isle of Man annexed to the Prouince of Yorke by H. 8. but a greater number this Archbishop anciently had, which time hath taken from him. The extent of euery Diocesse you may elsewhere reade, the which for breuitie I here omit. All the said Archbishopricks, and Bishopricks of England were founded by the Kings of England to hold by Barony as hereafter shall be said.* And euery Archbishop and Bishop hath his Deane and Chapter, whereof more shall be said hereafter. The Archbishop of Canterbury hath the precedencie, next to him the Archbishop of Yorke, next to him the Bishop of London, and next to him the Bishop of Winchester, and then all other Bishops of both Prouinces after their ancientnesse. *Math. Parker de vitis Archiepiscoporum. Linwood. Camden Britania. Vid. Rot. Parliam. anno 36. H. 8. 1. E. 6. 5. E. 6. &c. Westminster also was newly erected a Bishopricke by H. 8. but by Queene Mary it was restored to be an Abby, and by Queene Eliz. created a Deanry Collegiate. Chester had beene anciently a Bishops sea and long since translated to Couentry. 33. H. 8. ca. 31. Camden vbi supra. 26. H. 8. first fruites and tenths. Vid Sect. 137. * Lib. 3. fo. 73. Deane and Chapt. of Norwich case. Vid. Sect. 134. 201. 31. H. 8. ca. 10.*

Euery Diocesse is deuided into Archdeaconries, whereof there be 60. and the Archdeacon is called oculus Episcopi, and euery Archdeaconry is parted into Deanries, and Deanries againe into Parishes, Townes and Hamlets. And thus much for the better vnderstanding of our Author, and how the state Ecclesiasticall standeth at this day, shall suffice. *Vid. more hereof, Sect. 180. 528. 648. &c.*

Frnkalmoigne, que est a dire en Latyne, in liberam Eleemosinam. In English in free Almes. There is an officer in the Kings house called Eleemosinarius vulgarly called the Kings Almner (whose office and dutie is excellently discribed in ancient Authors) viz. Fragmenta diligenter colligere & est diligenter distribuere singulis diebus egenis, ægrotos, & leprosos, incarceratos, pauperesque viduas, & alios egenos vagosque in patria commorantes charitatiue visitare; item equos relictos, robas, pecuniã, & alia ad Eleemosinã largita recipere, & fideliter distribuere, debet etiam regem super Eleemosinæ largitione crebris summonitionibus stimulare, præcipue diebus sanctorũ, & rogare ne robas suas, quæ magni sunt pretij, histrionibus, blanditoribus, accusatoribus, seu menistrallis, sed ad Eleemosinæ suæ incrementũ jubeat largiri. *Fleta lib. 2. ca. 23.*

All Ecclesiasticall persons may hold in Frankalmoigne be they Secular or Regular, & no lay person can hold in Frankalmoigne. This adiectiue (liber) doth distinguish many things in Law from others, as here libera Eleemosina are words appropriated to this case, and doth distinguish it from a tenure by diuine seruice, liberum tenementum, from a tenure in villenage, or by Copyhold or base tenure, liberum fœdum franke fee, from a tenure in ancient Demeane, liberum *Vid. Sect. 1. Bracton lib. 4. ca. 37. 38. Britt. ca. 32.*

Britton. cap. 66. Bracton. lib. 4. F.N.B. 150. Bract. lib. 4. fol. 288. 247. 292. Britton. fol. 245. Fleta. lib. 5 cap. 21. Fortescue cap. 26. 24. E. 3. 34. 43. E. 3. consi. ir. 11. 27. Ass. 59. Stanf. 173. Vide Sect. 199. Fleta. lib. 1. cap. 47.

berum maritagium, from other estates taile, libera firma, franke ferme, when an estate is changed from Knights Seruice to Socage, liberum socagium, from a tenure by seruice in Chiualrie. Francus bancus to distinguish it from other Dowers, for that it commeth freely without any act of the husbands, or assignement of the heire. Libera lex, to distinguish men, who enjoy it, and whose best and freest birthright it is, from them, that by their offence haue lost it, as men attainted in an attaint, in a conspiracie vpon an Indictment, or in a Premunire, &c. And so of libera capella, francus plegius, frankpledge, libera chasea, free Chase, liber burgus, liber aper, liber taurus, and the like. But in a matter (some will say) of curiositie, this shall suffice, and yet seeing, it tends to the better vnderstanding (others say) it is tolerable.

Glanvil. lib. 7. cap. 1. fol. 44. 45. acc. Britton. cap. 66. fol. 164. Bract. lib. 2. cap. 5. & 10. N.N.B. 211.

By the ancient Common Law of England, a man could not alien such lands as he had by discent without the consent of his heire, yet he might giue a part to God in free Almoigne, or with his daughter in free mariage, or to his seruant in remuneratione seruitij. Our old Bookes described Frankalmoigne thus, when Lands or Tenements were bestowed vpon God, (that is) giuen to such people as are consecrated to the seruice of God. In our ancient Bookes these gifts of deuotion were called Churchesset, or Churchseed, quasi semen Ecclesiæ, but in a more particular sence, it is described thus. Certam mensuram bladi tritici significat, quam quilibet olim sanctæ Ecclesiæ die sancti Martini tempore tam Britonum quam Anglorum contribuerunt: plures tamen Magnates post Romanorum aduentum illam contributionem secundum veterem legem Moisi nomine primitiarum dabant prout in breui Regis Knuti ad summum Pontificem transmissum continetur, in quo illam contributionem Churchsed appellant quasi semen Ecclesiæ.

Fleta lib. 1. cap. 42.

¶ *Et tiel tenure.* For albeit neither fealtie nor any other temporall seruice is due, yet it is a tenure.

7. E. 4. 12. 33. H. 6. 6. 7. 39. H. 6. 29. (a) Mortmaine. Britton. fol. 32. & 90. Bracton. lib. 2. cap. 5. Fleta. lib. 3. cap. 5.

¶ (a) *En ancient temps.* That is to say before the statutes of Mortmayne, viz. Magna Charta, cap. 36. & 7. E. 1. de religiosis, &c. and before the Statute of Quia emptores terrarum, as shall be hereafter in his proper place said in this Chapter.

11. H. 7. 12.

¶ *Enfeoffa vn Abbe & son Couent, &c.* Albeit the Couent bee dead persons in Law, and the Abbot only capable (as before is said) yet if the feoffement be made to an Abbot and Couent, the feoffement is good, and the state vesteth only in the Abbot. And note a man may infeoffe an Abbot, a Bishop, a Parson, &c. or any other sole bodie politique by deed or without deed in free Almes, and so may a gift in frankmariage be made without deed also: but if Lands be giuen to a Deane and Chapter, or any other Corporation aggregate of many, there the gift must be by deed.

39. H. 6. 30. b.

Vide Litt. in the Chapter of Fee simple, Sect. 1. 2.

¶ *A auer & tener a eux & a lour successors.* For in case of an Abbot or Prior and Couent regularly a Fee Simple doth not passe without these words (Successors) for the diuersitie standeth thus betweene a Corporation aggregate of many capable persons, and a sole Corporation. As if Lands be giuen to a Deane and Chapter, they haue a fee simple without these words (successors) for that the bodie neuer dies, but if Lands be giuen to a Bishop, Parson, or any other sole Corporation, who after their deceases haue a succession, there without these words (Successors) nothing passeth vnto them but for life. But of Corporations aggregate of many there is a diuersitie when the head and bodie both are capeable, as in the case of Deane and Chapter, and when one as hath beene said is only capeable, as in case of Abbot or Prior and couent, but yet out of the generall rules the case of Frankalmoigne is excepted as hereafter shall be said. Also Lands must bee giuen to a Corporation aggregate of many by Deed, but to a sole Corporation it may be granted without Deed

39. H. 6. 30.

Bracton lib. 2. cap 10. Potest donatio fieri in liberam Eleemosinam Ecclesijs Cathedralibus, Conuentualibus, Parochialibus & viris religiosis.

35. H. 6. 56. 7. E. 4. 11. Vide Bracton. lib. 2. cap. 10.

¶ *En pure & perpetuall almoigne.* Here it appeareth that a tenure in Frankalmoigne may be created without this word (libera) for pura implyeth as much.

35. H. 6. 56. 7. E. 4. 11. Bract. vbi supra. 44. E. 3. 24.

¶ *Ou en Frankalmoigne.* But one of these words either pura or libera, must be vsed or else it is no tenure in Frankalmoigne.

20. H. 6. fol. 36.

¶ *Ou per ceux parolx a tener de le grantor ou feffor & ses heires en Frankalmoigne.* Here it appeareth that by these words a fee simple passeth without these words (Successors) albeit it be in case of a sole Corporation. For as in case of a gift in Frankmariage, an Estate taile passeth to the Donees without words of heires of their two bodies, as hath beene said in the Chapter of Fee taile, so in case of a gift in Frankalmoigne (which may be resembled to a diuine mariage) a Fee simple passeth, as hath beene said, though it be in case of a sole Corporation without this word (Successors.) And besides grants in Frankalmoigne are ancient Grants as hath beene said, and therefore shall bee allowed as the Law was taken when such Grants were made.

38. E. 3. 4. a. 14. H. 6. 12. 10. H. 7. 13. 16. H. 7. 9. 18. E. 3. conusans. 39. 33. H. 6. 22. 17. E. 3. 51. 6. E. 3. 54. &c. Tr 5. E. 3 Rot. 4. in Seaccario. The Prior of Dunstables case.

Sect.

Sect. 134.

¶ EN Mesme le Manner est, lou terres ou tenements fueront grant en ancient temps a vn Deane & Chapter, & a lour successors, ou a vn Parson dun Esglis, & a ses successors, ou a ascun auter home de saint Esglis, & a ses Successors en frankalm si il auoit capacitie dapprendre tiels grants ou feoffements &c.

IN the same manner it is where Lands or tenements were granted in ancient time to a Deane and Chapter & to their Successours, or to a Parson of a Church & his successors, or to any other man of holy Church, and to his successours in Frankalmoigne, if hee had capacitie to take such graunts or feoffements, &c.

¶ *EN Mesme le Manner, &c.* Here Littleton hauing put an example of bodies incorporate aggregate of many whereof the head is only capable now putteth examples, both of bodies incorporate, aggregate of many (all being capable and of sole Corporations of Seculer persons.

¶ *Deane. Decanus* is deriued of the Greek word *δέκα* that signifieth Ten, for that hee is an Ecclesiasticall Secular Gouernour, and was anciently ouer ten Prebends or Canons at the least in a Cathedrall Church, and is head of his Chapter.

¶ *Chapter. Capitulum est Clericorum congregatio sub vno Decano in Ecclesia Cathedrali.* And Chapters be twofold, viz. the Ancient, and the later. And the later be also of two sorts, first, those which were translated or founded by King Henry the Eight, in place of Abbots and Couents, or Priors and Couents, which were Chapters whiles they stood, and these are new Chapters to old Bishopricks. Secondly, where the Bishopricke was newly founded by Henry the Eight (as Chester, Bristow, &c.) there the Chapters are also new. There is a great diuersitie betweene the commings in of the ancient Deane, and of the new. For the ancient come in in much like sort as Bishops doe: for they are chosen by the Chapter by a conge de eslier as Bishops be, and the King giuing his Royall assent, they are confirmed by the Bishop. But they which are either newly translated or founded, are Donatiue, and by the Kings Letters Patents are installed, which are matters necessary to be knowne.

¶ *Sil auoit capacitie a prender.* For Ecclesiasticall persons haue not capacitie to take in succession, vnlesse they be bodies Politique, as Bishops, Archdeacons, Deanes, Parsons, Vicars, &c. or lawfully incorporate by the Kings Letters Patents or prescription, as Deanes and Chapters, Colledges, &c. But a Colledge of religious persons, Chauntrie Priests, and such like, that are not lawfully incorporated, but only consist in vulgar reputation haue no capacitie to take succession, therefore Littleton added materially (sic ad capacitie à prender.)

Sect. 135.

¶ ET tiels que teignont en frankalmoigne sont oblige de droit deuant dieu de fair orisons, praiers, mess. & autres diuine seruices pur les almes de lour grantor ou feoff. & pur les almes de lour heires

AND they which hold in Frankalmoigne, are bound of right before God, to make Orisons, Prayers, Masses, and other diuine Seruices for the soules of their Grantor or Feoffor, and for the soules of their heires

¶ IN this Section there appeareth a diuision of Tenures, that is to say, some be spirituall, and some be temporall. And of spirituall some be incertaine, as tenures in Frankalmoigne, and some be certaine, as tenure by diuine Seruice. Againe diuine seruice certaine is two fold, either spirituall as Prayers to God, or temporall, as distribution of almes to poore people.

queux sont mortes, & pur le prosperitie & bon vie & bon salute de lour heires q̄ sont en vie. Et pur ceo ils ne ferront a nul tēps ascun fealtie a lour Seignior, pur ceo q̄ tiel diuine seruice est meliour pur eux devant Dieu que ascun feasans de fealtie, & auxi pur ceo que ceux parolx (Frankalm̄) excludе le Seignior dauer ascun terrein ou temporall seruice, mes dauer tantsolement diuine & spirituall seruice destre fait pur luy, &c.

which are dead, and for the prosperitie and good life and good health of their heires which are aliue. And therefore they shall doe no fealty to their Lord, because that this diuine Seruice is better for them before God then any doing of fealtie, and also because that these words (Frankalmoigne) excludeth the Lord to haue any earthly or temporall Seruice, but to haue only Diuine and Spirituall Seruice to bee done for him, &c.

¶ *Oblige de drois.* That is they are compellable by the Ecclesiasticall Law to doe it, and therefore it is said that they are bound of right, for want of remedy, and want of right is all one, and the Common Law (as here it appeareth) taketh knowledge of the Ecclesiasticall Law in that behalfe.

¶ *De faire Orisons, Prayers, Messes, & auters Diuine Seruices.* Since Littleton wrote, the Lyturgie or Booke of Common Praier and of Celebrating Diuine Seruice is altered; this alteration notwithstanding, yet the tenure in Frankalmoigne remaineth, and such Prayers and diuine Seruice shall be said and celebrated as now is authorised, yea, though the tenure be in particular, as Littleton (a) hereafter saith, viz. A Chaunter vn messe, &c. ou a Chaunter vn placebo & dirige, yet if the tenant saith the Prayers now authorised it sufficeth. And as Littleton (b) hath said before in the case of Socage the changing of one kind of temporall services into other temporall services, altereth neither the name nor the effect of the tenure: so the changing of spirituall services into other spirituall services, altereth neither the name nor effect of the tenure. And albeit the tenure in Frankalmoigne is now reduced to a certaintie contained in the Booke of Common Prayer, yet seeing the originall tenure was in Frankalmoigne, and the change is by generall consent by authoritie of Parliament, (c) whereunto every man is partie, the tenure remaynes as it was before.

(a) *Vide Sect.137.*

(b) *Vide Sect.119.*

(c) *2.E.6.cap.1.5.& 6.E.6.cap.1. 1.Eliz cap.2.*

¶ *Ne ferront ascun fealtie.* Herein Tenant in Frankalmoigne differeth from a Tenant in Frankmariage, for tenant in Frankmariage shall doe fealtie, as hath beene said in the Chapter of Fee taile, but tenant in Frankalmoigne, shall not doe any, or any other thing, but deuota animarum suffragia.

¶ *Tiel diuine seruice est melieur per eux.* And it is also said in our Bookes (d) Que Frankalmoigne est le pluis haute seruice, and this was confessed by the Heathen Poet.

(d) *33.H.6.6. 13.E.1.tit. count.de voucher.118.*

——fuit hæc sapientia quondam
Publica priuatis secernere, sacra profanis.

And certaine it is, that Nunquam res humanæ prosperè succedunt vbi negliguntur diuinæ.

Section 136.

¶ Et si tiels que teignont lour tenements en frankalmoigne ne voilōt ou faillont d̄ faire tiel

And if they which hold their Tenemēts in frankalmoigne will not or faile to do such diuine seruice (as

¶ *Le Seigniour ne Poet eux distreiner pur cest non feasant, &c.*

¶ *Distreine.* The

Di-

diuine seruice (cõe est dit) le s͞nr ne poit eux distrainer p̄ cel non fesant, &c. pur ceo que nest mis en certaine quelx seruices ils doient fait, mes l' s͞nr de ceo poit complaine a lour ordinarie ou visitour, luy preyant que il voiloit mitter punishment & correction d ceo, & auxy de prouider q̄ tiel negligence ne soit pluis auāt fait, &c. Et lordinary ou visit de droit ceo doit faire, &c.

is said) the Lord may not distrain them for not doing this, &c. because it is not put in certeyntie what seruices they ought to do: but the Lord may complaine of this to their Ordinary or visitour praying him that he will lay some punishment and correction for this, & also prouide that such negligēce be no more done &c. And the ordinary or Visitor of right ought to doe this, &c.

word Distresse is a French word, in Latyn it is called districtio siue angustia; because the cattell distreyned are put into a streight, which we call a pownd.

¶ *Pur ceo que nest mise in certaine queux seruices ils doient faire.* It is a Maxime in Law that no distresse can bee taken for any seruices that are not put into certaintie (e) nor can bee reduced to any certaintie for Id certum est quod certum reddi potest; for (f) oportet quod certa res deducatur in iudiciū; & vpon the auowrie, Damages cannot be recouered for that, which neither hath certaintie nor can be reduced to any certainty, and yet in some cases there may bee a certainty in vncertainty, as a man may hold of his Lord to (*7.E.3.38.*) there all the sheepe depasturing within the Lords Mannor, and this is certaine enough, albeit the Lord hath sometime a greater number, and sometime a lesser number there, and yet this incertaintie being referred to the Mannor which is certaine, the Lord may distraine for this vncertaintie. Et sic de similibus.

(e) 35.H.6.37. *Br. tit. office* 4. 8.E.3.3.56. 20.E.3. *Auowrie* 131. (f) *Bracton fol.* 230. & 328.

¶ *Poet complayner.* (That is) to complaine in course of Iustice, according to the Ecclesiasticall Law.

¶ *A lour ordinarie.* Ordinarius, and so he is called (g) in the Ecclesiasticall Law, Quia habet ordinariam jurisdictionem in jure proprio, & non per deputationem; the name we haue anciently taken from the Canonists, and doe apply it only to a Bishop or any other that hath ordinary iurisdiction in causes Ecclesiasticall; In this case of Littleton it is to be obserued that the Law doth appoint euery thing to be done by those, vnto whose office it properly appertaineth, and forasmuch as it belongeth to the office of the Ordinarie in this case to see diuine seruice said, and to compell them to doe it by Ecclesiasticall censures, therefore complaint is to be made vnto him. Here and in the next Section it appeareth, that for deciding of Controuersies, and for distribution of Iustice within this Realme, there bee two distinct iurisdictions, the one Ecclesiasticall limitted to certaine spirituall and particular cases (of the one whereof our Author here speaketh) and the Court wherein these causes are handled is called Forum ecclesiasticum. The other iurisdiction is secular and generall, for that it is guided by the common and generall Law of the Realme, Quæ pertinet ad coronam & dignitatem regis, & ad regnum in causis & placitis rerum temporalium in foro seculari. So as in this case put by our Author, the Lord hath remedy for his diuine seruice (albeit they issue out of temporall lands) in foro ecclesiastico, by the Ecclesiasticall Law, otherwise the Lord should be without remedy. Yet the Common Law, to the intent that Ecclesiasticall persons might the better discharge their dutie in celebration of diuine seruice, and not to bee intangled with temporall businesse, hath prouided, that if any of them be chosen to any temporall office hee may haue his Writ De clerico infra sacros ordines constituto non eligendo in officium, &c and thereof be discharged.

(g) *Mirror.ca.*5.§. *Bracton lib.*5.*fo.*405.&c. *Fleta lib.*2.*ca.*50.&.55. & *lib* 6.*ca.*38. *Britton, fo.*69.70. *W.*2.*ca.*19. 17.E.2.*bre.*822.*Regist.*141 *Lindwood, tit. de Constitut. cap extet.* *Bracton.lib.*5.*ca.*2. *fo.*400, & 401. *and the other Authors abouesaid.* *Regist.orig.*187.

¶ *On Visitor.* That is, where the King or any of his Progenitors is Founder of the house, there the Ordinary regularly shall not visit them, but the Chancelour of England is appointed by Law to be Visitor of them, or where a speciall Visitor is appointed vpon the foundation, the complaint must be made to the Visitor.

27.E.3.84.85.*Regist.*40. F.N.B.42.10.*Eliz. Dier.* 273. 16.E.3.*bre.*660. 21.E.3.60. 6.H.7.13. 8.*Ass.*29. *Brooke tit. Premunire* 21.

¶ *De droit doit ceo faire.* De droit, of right, (that is to say) he ought to doe it by the Ecclesiasticall Law in the right of his office.

And here is implied a Maxime of the Common Law, that where the right, as our Author here speaketh is spirituall, and the remedy therefore only by the Ecclesiasticall Law, the conusans thereof doth appertaine to the Ecclesiasticall Court.

*Sect.*137.

Sect. 137.

2. E. 3. 27, 28.

¶ *PEr certaine Diuine Seruice destre fait, sicome a chaunter vn messe, &c. ou de distribuer en Almoign, &c.* Here be the two parts aboue mentioned, of diuine Seruice, and for this Diuine seruice certaine, the Lord hath his remedie, as here it appears by our Author in foro seculari: for here it appeareth, that if the Lord distreyne for not doing of diuine Seruice, which is certain, hee shall vpon his Auowrie recouer dammages at the Common Law, that is, in the Kings Temporall Court, for the not doing of it. And if issue be taken vpon the performance of the Diuine Seruice, it shall be tried by a Jurie of twelue men, because albeit the Seruice be Spirituall, yet the dammages are temporall, and so is the Seigniorie also.

38. H. 6. 26, 27.

And here is implied another Maxim of the Law, that where the Common or Statute Law giueth remedie, in foro seculari, (whether the matter be Temporall or Spirituall) the Conusans of that cause belongeth to the Kings Temporall Courts only, vnlesse the iurisdiction of the Ecclesiastical Court be saued or allowed by the same statute, to proceed according to the Ecclesiasticall Lawes.

2. E. 6. ca. 13. versus finem. 13. E. 3. ca. 5. 11. H. 7. ca. 8. 1. El. ca. 2. 13. El. ca. 1. 23. El. ca. 1. 1. Ia. c. 11. & 12.

¶ *Ou de distributer en almoigne al cent pours homes.* Here note that the Almes & Reliefe of poore people being a worke of charitie, is accounted in Law diuine Seruice, for what herein is done to the Poore for Gods sake, is done to God himselfe.

¶ *Poet distrein, &c.* Here (&c.) includeth many

CMEs si vn Abbe ou Prior tient de son Seignior per certain diuine Seruice en certaine destre fait, sicome a chaunter vn messe chescun vendredie en le Semaine pur les Almes, vt supra, ou chescun an a tiel iour a chaunter placebo & dirige, &c. ou de trouer vn chapleine de chanter messe, &c. ou de distributer en Almoign al cent poures homes cent deniers a tiel iour, en tiel case, si tiel Diuine Seruice ne soit fayt le Seignior poet distreyner, &c. pur ceo que le Diuine Seruice est mise en certaine per lour Tenure, que le Abbee ou Prior deuoit faire. Et en tiel case le Seignior auera Fealtie, &c. come il semble. Et tiel Tenure ne passe dit Tenure en Frankalmoigne, eins est dit Tenure per Diuine Seruice, car en Tenure en Frankalmoigne nul mention est fait dascun manner de Seruice, car nul poet tener en Frankealmoigne

BVt if an Abbot or Prior holds of his Lord by a certaine diuine Seruice, in certaine to be done, as to sing a Masse euerie Fryday in the weeke, for the Soules, *vt supra*, or euerie yeare at such a day to sing a *Placebo & Dirige*, &c. or to find a Chaplaine to sing a Masse, &c. or to distribute in almes to an hundred poore men an hundred pence at such a day. In this case if such Diuine Seruice bee not done, the Lord may distreyne, &c. because the Diuine Seruice is put in certaine by their Tenure, which the Abbot or Prior ought to doe. And in this case the Lord shal haue Fealtie, &c. as it seemeth. And such Tenure shall not bee said to bee Tenure in Frankealmoigne, but is called Tenure by Diuine Seruice: For in Tenure in Frankealmoigne, no mention is made of any manner of Seruice: For none can hold in Frankealmoigne, if there be expressed any manner

moigne, si soit expresse ascun maner de certain seruice que il doit faire, &c.

of certaine Seruice that he ought to doe, &c.

excellent things, as when, where, and what may bee distreined, of al which there is a tast giuen in their proper places.

¶ *En tiel case le Seignior auera fealtie, &c. come semble.* For as it hath beene said, Fealtie is incident to euerie Tenure sauing the Tenure in Frankalmoigne, and where the Lord may distreyne, there is Fealtie due. And Britton calleth this Tenure (by Diuine Seruice) Aumone, and not libera Eleemosina. And saith he, Tenure en aumone est terre ou tenement que est done a aumone, dount ascun seruice est retenue al feoffor. Brit. fo. 164.

¶ *&c.* And here (&c.) implieth, Distresse, Escheat, and the like.

¶ *Et tiel Tenure nest passe dit Tenure en Frankalmoigne, eins est dit tenure per Diuine seruice, &c.* And therefore our old Booke diuided Spirituall Seruice into Free almes, (which was free from any limitation of certaintie) and almes, because the Tenants were bound to certaine diuine Seruices. 33. H. 6. Brit. ca. 66.

¶ *Sil soit expresse ascun manner de certaine seruice.* This holdeth where the certaintie is reserued vpon the originall Grant. If lands were giuen to hold In libera Eleemosina reddendo, a rent, it seemeth the reseruation of the rent to be void,* because it is repugnant and contrarie to the former grant in libera Eleemosina. 13. E. 1. Count de Vouch. 118. *13. H. 4. tit. Mesne 74. 30. E. 3. 30. 19. E. 2. Auowrie 224. 32. E. 1. Taile 31. 26. Ass. 66. 4. H. 6. 17.

Vide Triñ 4. E. 3. and F. N. B. 231. f. That an Abbot or Prior that hold in Frankalmoigne, shall not be charged with a Corodie. Also lands holden in Frankalmoign cannot (l) be antient Demesne, in respect of charges incident thereunto. Trin. 4. E. 3. F. N. B. 231 f. 15 E. 3. Corody 4. 11. Ass. 12. 50. Ass. Pl. 6. (l) 12. E. 1. ant. Dem. 39. 8. E. 3. 5.

¶ *Que il doit faire, &c.* Here by (&c.) is understood Temporall or Spirituall Seruice, also which he ought to doe corporally, or render or pay.

There were within this Realme of England one hundred and eighteene Monasteries, founded by the Kings of England, whereof such Abbots and Priors as were founded to hold of the King per Baroniam, and were called to the Parliament by Writ, were Lords of Parliament, and had places and voyces there: And of them there were twentie seuen Abbots, and two Priors, as by the Rolles of Parliament appeare. But since our Author wrote, all these (as hath beene said) are dissolued. King* Stephen did found the Abbey of Feuersham in Kent, Et dedit Abbati & Monachis, & successoribus suis Manerium de Feuersham Com Kanc', simul cum Hundredo, &c. tenendum per Baroniam, &c. Who albeit he held by a Baronie, yet because he was neuer (that I (m) find) called by Writ, he neuer sate in Parliament. * For example, Rot. Parl. 5. H. 8. & 21. H. 8, &c. (m) Claus. Pas 30. E. 1. ew. togethis foundation is so pleaded.

All the Archbishops and Bishops of England haue bin founded by the Kings of England and doe hold of the King by Baronie (as before hath beene said) and haue beene all called by Writ to the Court of Parliament, and are Lords of Parliament: As (amongst many) taking one notable Record, (o) Mandatum est omnibus Episcopis qui conuenturi sunt apud Gloucestriam, die Sabbathi in Crastiñ Sanctæ Katherinæ, firmiter inhibendo quod sicut Baronias suas quas de Rege tenent, diligunt, nullo modo præsumant consilium tenere de aliquibus quæ ad Coronam Regis pertinent, vel quæ personam Regis, vel statum suum, vel statum concilij sui contingunt, sciturі pro certo, quòd si fecerint, Rex inde se capiet ad Baronias suas. Teste Rege apud Hereford, 23. Nouemb. &c. And the Bishopricks in Wales were founded by the Princes of Wales: and the Principalitie of Wales was holden of the King of England, as of his Crowne: and when the Prince of Wales committed Treason, Rebellion, &c. the Principalitie was forfeited, and the Patronages of the Bishops annexed to the Crowne of England, so as the King is to haue Pensions for his Chaplaines, and Corodies for his Vadelets of them, as of Bishops founded by himselfe. And vide Mich. 10. H. 4. Rot. 60. Wallia coram Rege, that the iudgement was giuen accordingly against the Bishop of Saint Dauids, in Wales, Per Iusticiarios de vtroque Banco & alios de perito concilio Domini Regis. And the Bishops of Wales are also called by Writ to Parliament, and are Lords of Parliament as bishops of England be. (o) Ex Rot. Pat. de anno 18. H. 3. M. 17. 10. H. 4. fo. 6. b.

Section 138.

Item si soit demand, si tenñ en frankmariage ferra fealtie a le donñ ou a

Also if it bee demanded, if tenant in frankmariage shall doe fealtie to the do-

Le quel serra inconuenient, &c. An argument drawne from an inconuenience is forcible in Law as hath beene obserued V. Sect. 87. 139. 201. 269. 440. 478. 665. 722.

ued before, and ſhall bee often hereafter. Nihil quod eſt inconveniens eſt licitum. And the Law that is the perfection of reaſon cannot ſuffer any thing that is inconuenient.

* 40.Aſſ 27.

Littleton fo.50.b. 42.E.3.5. 28.E.3.395. 20.H.6.28.

It is better ſaith the Law to ſuffer a miſchiefe (that is particular to one) then an inconuenience that may preiudice many. See more of this after in this chapter.

Note the reaſon of this diuerſitie betweene Frankalmoigne and Frankmarriage ſtandeth vpon a maine Maxime of Law, that there is no land, that is not holden by ſome ſeruice ſpirituall or temporall, and therefore the Donee in Frankmariage ſhall doe Fealty, for otherwiſe hee ſhould doe to his Lord no ſeruice at all, and yet it is Frankmariage, becauſe the Law createth the ſeruice of Fealty for neceſſity of reaſon, and auoyding of an inconuenience. But tenant in Frankalmoigne doth ſpirituall and diuine ſeruice which is within the ſaid Maxime and therefore the Law will not compell him to doe any temporall ſeruice. See the next Section.

¶ *Et enconter reaſon.* And this is another ſtrong argument in Law. Nihil quod eſt contra rationem eſt licitum. For reaſon is the life of the Law, nay the Common Law it ſelfe is nothing elſe but reaſon, which is to be vnderſtood of an artificiall perfection of reaſon gotten by long ſtudie, obſeruation and experience and not of euery mans naturall reaſon, for nemo naſcitur artifex. This legall reaſon eſt ſumma ratio. And therefore if all the reaſon that is diſperſed into ſo many ſeuerall heads were united into one, yet could hee not make ſuch a Law as the Law of England is, becauſe by many ſucceſſion of ages it hath beene fined and refined by an infinite number of graue and learned men, and by long experience growne to ſuch a perfection for the gouernment of this Realme, as the old rule may be iuſtly verified of it Neminem oportet eſſe ſapientiorem legibus: No man (out of his owne priuate reaſon) ought to be wiſer than the Law, which is the perfection of reaſon.

ſes heires deuant le quart degree paſſe, &c. il ſemble que cy: Car il neſt pas ſemble quant a cel entent a tenant en frankalmoigne, pur ceo que tenant en frankalmoigne ferra, p cauſe de ſa tenure, diuine ſeruice pur ſon Sñr come deuant eſt dit, & ceo il eſt charge a fait p la ley del ſaint eſgliſe, & pur ceo il eſt excuſe & diſcharge de fealtie, mes tenant en frankemariage ne ferra pur ſon tenure tiel ſeruice, & ſil ne ferra fealtie, donqz il ne ferra a ſon Seignior aſcun mãner de ſeruice, ne ſpiritual ne temporal, le quel ſerroit inconuenient & encount reaſon que home ſerra Tenant deſtate denheritance, a vn auter & vncore l Sñr auera nul maner de ſeruice de luy, & iſſint il ſemble que il ferra fealtie a ſon Sñr deuant le quart degree paſſe. Et quãt il ad fait fealty il ad fait touts ſes ſeruices.

nor or his heires before the fourth degree be paſt, &c. it ſeemeth that he ſhall, for he is not like as to this purpoſe to tenant in frankalmoigne, for tenant in frankalmoigne by reaſon of his tenure ſhall doe diuine ſeruice for his Lord, (as is ſaid before) and this hee is charged to doe by the Law of holy Church, and therefore he is excuſed and diſcharged of fealty, but tenant in frankmariage ſhall not doe for his tenure ſuch ſeruice, and if he doth not fealty, he ſhall not doe any manner of ſeruice to his Lord neither ſpiritual nor temporall, which would be inconuenient, and againſt reaſon, that a man ſhall be tenant of an eſtate of inheritance to another, and yet the Lord ſhall haue no manner of ſeruice of him. And ſo it ſeemes he ſhall doe fealtie to his Lord before the fourth degree be paſt. And when hee hath done fealtie, he hath done all his ſeruices.

Sect. 139.

¶ Et si vn Abbe tient de son Sñr en frankalm, et Labbe et le couent south lour common seale alien mesmes les tenements a vn seculer home en fee simple, en ceo cas le seculer home ferra fealtie a l'Seignior, pur ceo que il ne poit tener de son Sñr en frankalmoigne. Car si le seignior ne doit auer de luy fealty, donque il auera nul manner d' seruice que serroit inconuenient, ou il est Sñr, & le tenement est tenus de luy.

AND if an Abbot holdeth of his Lord in frankalmoign, and the Abbot and Couent vnder their cōmon seale alien the same tenements to a secular man in fee simple. In this case the secular man shall doe fealtie to the Lord, because hee cannot hold of his Lord in frankealmoigne, for if the Lord should not haue fealty of him hee should haue no manner of seruice which should bee inconuenient where he is Lord, and the tenements be holden of him.

¶ This case is worthy of great obseruation for hereby it appeareth, that albeit the Alienors held not by fealty nor any other terrene seruice but only by spirituall seruices and those incertaine, yet the alienee shall hold by the certaine seruice of Fealty (and of this opinion is Littleton in our bookes agreeable with former Authoritie) for the Law createth a new temporall seruice out of the Land to be done by the Alienee wherewith the Abbot was not formerly charged for the auoyding of an inconuenience, viz. that the Feoffee should doe no manner of seruice, and consequently the land should bee holden of no man, wherein it is to bee remembred that (as hath been said before) all the lands and tenements in England in the hands of any subiect are holden of some Lord or other, and that euery tenant must doe some kinde of seruice. And that all Lands and Tenements are holden either mediatly or immediatly of the King, for originally all lands and tenements were deriued from the Crowne. And it is to be obserued that when the Law createth any new tenure, it is the lowest, (viz. Tenure in Socage) and with the least seruice that can be done, and neerest to the freedome of the former seruice, as in this case a Tenure in Socage by Fealty only is created by the Law, which is the lowest and least seruice the Law can create, because Fealty is incident to euery tenure except Tenure in Frankalmoigne, for if it should Create any other seruice it must create Fealty also. And the Law according to equitie and Iustice giueth this Fealtie to the Lord of whom the land was before holden in Frankalmoigne. And lastly that the Law so abhorreth an inconuenience, as it Createth out of the Land a new seruice for auoyding thereof. It appeareth by our bookes that a Seigniory in Frankalmoigne may bee granted ouer, and consequently the Tenant shall hold of the Grantee by Fealty only, and therefore Britton said well, that no seruice could be demanded of a Tenant in Frankalmoigne tant come les terres remaine en les maynes les feoffees.

31.E.3. Cessavit 22. 33.H.6.67. 21.E.4.11. lib.9.fo.123. Anth. Lowes case.

Lib.9.fo.123.in Anth. Lowes case.

41.Ass. Pl.6.

Britton 164 b.

Sect. 140.

¶ Item si home graunta a cel iour a vn Abbe, ou a vn Prior terres ou tenements en frankalmoigne, ceux parolx (frākalmoigne) sont

ALso if a man grant at this day to an Abbot or to a Prior, lands or tenements in Frankalmoigne, these words (frākalmoigne) are voide, for it is or-

¶ *Ordeine per lestatute.* Here it appeareth by the authoritie of Littleton, that this is a Statute, and yet the King alone speaketh, viz. Dominus Rex in Parliamento suo, &c. ad instantiam magnatum regni sui concessit prouidit & statuit.

Vide lib. 8. the Princes case.

But because it is Dominus Rex in Parliamento, &c. concessit, it is as much in this case being an ancient statute as Dominus Rex authoritate Parliamenti concessit. Secondly, It is amongst other acts of Parliament entred into the Parliament Roll, and therefore shall bee intended to bee ordained by the King, by the consent of the Lords and Commons in that Parliament assẽbled. Thirdly, It is a generall Law whereof the Judges may take knowledge, and therefore it is to bee determined by them whether it bee a statute or no. Now for the divers formes of Acts of Parliament, you may reade them in the Princes Case vbi supra.

¶ *Quia emptores terrarum.* This statute is called so, because the statute beginneth with these words, Quia emptores terrarum.

¶ *Nul poet aliener, &c. terres in fee simple de tener de luy mesme.* This is iustly inferred vpon the Statute, but the letter of the Statute is that Feoffatus teneat terram illam de capitali Domino, &c. So as by the authoritie of Littleton, he that citeth a Statute is not bound to recite the very words thereof so long as he misseth not of the substance and necessary consequence thereupon, and yet the safer way is to vouch the words of a Law as they be.

13.E.3. tit. release 33. 27.H.8. F.N.B. 211. I.

¶ *Granta per licence mesme les tenements, &c.* Here Littleton speaketh of a licence or a dispensation within the said Statute of Quia emptores terrarum (and mentioneth no other Statute) which may bee done by the King and all the Lords immediate and mediate, for it is a rule in Law, Alienatio licet prohibeatur, consensu tamen omnium, in

voides, pur ceo que il est ordeine per lestatute que est appelle; Quia emptores terrarum (que lestatut fuit fait, Anno 18. Ed.1.) que nul poit aliener ne graunter terres ou tenements en fee simple, a tener de luy mesme. Issint si hõe seisie de certaine tenements quex il tiẽt de son Seignior per seruice de chiualer, & a cel iour il &c. granta per licẽce mesmes les tenements a vn Abbe, &c. en Frankalmoigne, Labbe tiendra immediatment mesmes les tenemẽts per seruice de chiualer de mesme le seignior, de q̃ son grauntor tenoit, & ne tiendra my de son grant en frankalmoigne, p cause de mesme lestatut, issint que nul poit tener en frankalmoigne, si non q̃ soit per title de prescription, ou per force de graunt fait a ascun d̃ ses predecessors, deuant q̃ mesme le statute fuit fait. Mes le roy poit doner terres ou tenements en fee simple, a tener en Frankalmoigne, ou per auters seruices, car il est hors de cas del estatute.

dained by the Statute which is called, *Quia emptores terrarũ* which was made *Anno* 18. *E.* 1.) that none may alien nor grant Lands or Tenements in Fee simple to hold of himselfe. So that if a man seised of certaine tenements which hee holdeth of his Lord by Knights Seruice, & at this day he &c. grãteth by licence the same tenements to an Abbot, &c. in Frankalmoigne, the Abbot shall hold immediately the Tenements by Knights seruice of the same Lord of whom his grantor held, and shall not hold of his grantor in Frankalmoigne, by reason of the same Statute. So that none can hold in Frankalmoigne, vnlesse it bee by title of prescription, or by force of a grant made to any of his Predecessours before the same statute was made: but the King may giue Lands or Tenements in Fee simple to hold in Frankalmoigne, or by other seruices, for he is out of the case of that Statute.

quorum fauorem prohibita est, potest fieri, and quilibet potest renunciare iuri pro se introducto: and the licence of Lords immediate, and mediate in this case shall enure to two intents, viz. to a dispensation both of the statute of *Quia emptores terrarum*, and of the Statutes of Mortmaine, as Littleton here implyeth, because their deeds shall be taken most strongly against themselues. But it is a safe and good policie in the Kings licence to haue a non obstante also of the Statutes of Mortmaine, and not only a non obstante of the Statute of Quia emptores terrarum. But it appeareth by Littleton (which is a secret of Law) that there needeth not any non obstante by the King of the Statutes of Mortmaine, for the King shall not be intended to be misconusant of the Law, and when he licenceth expressely to alien to an Abbot, &c. which is in Mortmaine, he needs not make any non obstante of the Statutes of Mortmaine, for it is apparant to be granted in Mortmaine, and the King is the head of the Law, and therefore Præsumitur Rex habere omnia iura in scrinio pectoris sui, For the maintenance of his grant to be good according to the Law, for which cause of purpose Littleton maketh no mention of any licence in Mortmaine. Dispensatio est mali prohibiti prouida relaxatio vtilitate seu necessitate pensata.

43. Ass. Pl. 19. 9. E. 4. b. 11. Pl. Com. 502. 503. Grendons case. Vid. lib. 10. 25. 26. 31. & 110. Vide S. 686.

¶ *Labbe tiendra, &c. per seruice de chiualer.* For although by the death of the Abbot there is neither ward, Mariage, nor reliefe due, yet he holdeth by Knights Seruice, albeit the Lord cannot haue the fruit of it, and if he with the consent of the Couent alien, the land ouer to a man and his heires, there is the ward, Mariage, and Reliefe reuiued. But by prescription (as it hath beene said) the successor of an Abbot may pay reliefe. An Abbot or Prior, &c. that holdeth Lands by Knights Seruice, albeit hee ought not in respect of his profession to serue in warre in proper person, yet must he find a sufficient man conueniently arrayed for the warre to supply his place. And if he can find none, then must he pay Escuage, &c. for his profession doth not priuiledge him, but that the Kings seruice in his warre must be done that belongeth to his tenure.

Little. fol. 20. a. 8. R. 2. releife 14. 3. H. 4. 2. a. Vide Littel. fol. 20.

Nota (Reader) since Littleton wrote a man might either in his life time, or by his last will in writing, (m) giue Lands, Tenements, &c. to any spirituall bodie Politicke or Corporate, to be holden of himselfe in Frankalmoigne, or by Diuine Seruice, as by the statute of 1. & 2. Phil. & Mariæ (which indured for twenty yeares) appeareth, which statute since that time hath beene fauourably and benignely expounded.

(m) 1. & 2. Ph. & Mar. ca. 8. Mich. 8 & 9. Eliz. Dier. fol. 255.

¶ *Issint que nul poet tener en Frankalmoigne si non que sont per title de prescription, &c.* It is to be understood, that a man seised of lands may at this day giue the same to a Bishop, Parson, &c. and their successors in Frankalmoigne, by the consent of the King and the Lords mediate and immediate of whom the Land is holden, for the rule is Quilibet potest renunciare iuri pro se introducto.

12. E. 4. 4. 27. H. 8. 2. E. 2. auowrie 185.

So if an Ecclesiasticall Parson hold lands by fealtie and certaine Rent, the Lord at this day may confirme (n) his estate, to hold to him and to his successors in Frankalmoigne, for the former Seruices bee extinct, and nothing is reserued but that he holds of him, and so hee did before.

(n) 4. E. 3. 21. 22. E. 3. 15. 38 H. 6. 25. Litt. cap confir. mat. 1 3.

¶ *Mes le roy poet, &c. car il est hors de case del statute.*

It is cleere that the King is out of the case of the Statute, for the Statute is Quod feoffatus teneat terram illam, &c. de capitali Domino feodi, &c. and this cannot bee intended of the King, who is superior to all and inferiour to none, but where the King is bound by Acts of Parliament, and where not, Vide lib. 11. fol. 66. Magdalen Colledge Case.

Lib. 11. fol. 66. Magdalen Colledge Case.

Section 141.

Et nota q̃ nul poit tener terres ou tenements en frankalmoigne, forsprise del grantor, ou de ses heires. Et pur ceo il est dit, que si soit Seignior, mesne & tenant, & le tenant est vn Abbe que tient

And note that none may hold lands or tenements in frankalmoigne, but of the Grauntour, or of his heires. And therefore it is said, that if there be Lord, Mesne, and Tenant, and the tenant is an Abbot which

¶ *Forsprise del grantor ou de ses heires.* The tenure in Frankalmoigne is an incident to the inheritable bloud of the grantor, and cannot be transferred nor forfeited to any other, no more then a Foundership of a house of Religion, which is intended to bee in Frankalmoigne, or homage ancestrell, or the writ of Contra formam feoffamenti, or the writ of

14. E. 3. tit. Mesne 7. 14. H. 3. tit. disclaymer B. 33. 15. E. 3. confirm. 8. 27. H. 8. 6. Tempe E. 1. garr. 90 45. E. 3. 23. 47. H. 3. garr. 99. 11. H. 4. 52. 14. H. 4. 5. 10. H. 7. 11. 28. Ass. 33. 18. E. 3. 18. 22. E. 3. 18. Corody broke. 5. 22. H. 6. 50. 4. E. 2. auowry 101. 202. 19. E. 3. ibidem 122. 11. E. 3. ibid. 100. 30. H. 6. 7. 33. H. 8. Dier 51. F. N. B. 16. F. N. B. 21. e.

Contra

Contra formam collationis,
15.E.3 confirm. 8. or any other incident to their inheritable bloud. But it is no incident inseperable for the Lord may release to the Tenant in Frankalmoigne, and then the tenure is extinct, and he shall hold of the Lord Paramont by fealtie, as in the case of Littleton, Sect. 139.

¶ *Ou de ses heires.* Here (or) hath the sence of (and.) for a man cannot at this day grant lands in taile and reserue a Rent to his
Vide 15.E.4. heires, and exclude the grantor himselfe, for the heire cannot take any thing in the life of the Ancestor, neyther can the heire take any thing by discent when the Ancestor himselfe is secluded. But if a man had granted Lands at the Com-
33.E.3.tit. Annuitie 52. 3.Ass.Pl.8.&c. mon Law to hold of his heires, these words (to hold of his heires) are void, and he shall hold of the grantor as he held ouer, which he should haue done, if hee had made no reseruation at all.

And albeit Littleton sayth that no man can hold lands in Frankalmoigne, but of the grantor or his heires, yet might an Abbót by assent of his Couent, or a Bishop with assent of his Chapter, and such like by licence as is aforesaid, haue giuen lands in Frankalmoigne, to hold of them and their Successors, and as Littleton himselfe agreeth; the King may giue Land in Frankalmoigne. In which case the land shall be holden of him his heires and successors.

¶ *Et pur ceo est dit si soit Seignior, mesne & tenant, & le tenant est un Abbe, &c.* **By this it appeareth that if the Seigniory be transferred** by act in Law to a stranger, and thereby the priuitie is altered, that the tenure in Frankalmoigne is changed to a tenure in Socage by fealtie, aswell as it appeareth before when the Seigniory or Tenancy is granted to another, and the Law in this case also createth a new fealty wherewith the Land was not charged before.

¶ *Donques le mesnaltie deuendra per escheat al dit Seignior Paramont.*
2.E.4.46. This new tenure created by Law shall vpon the Escheat drowne the Seigniorie, for alwayes
7.E.4.12.a. the Seigniory neerer to the land drownes the Seigniory, that is more remote of, and yet the Lord in this case to whom the Mesnalty is escheated, shall hold by the same seruices that he held before the Escheat.

de son mesne en fraũkalmoigne, si le mesne deuy sans heire, donque le mesnaltie deuiendra per escheate al dit Seignior Paramont, & Labbe adonque tient de luy immediate per fealtie tantum, & ferra a luy fealtie, pur ceo que il ne puit tener de luy en Frankalmoigne, &c.

holdeth of his Mesne in frankalmoigne, if the Mesne die without heire, the Mesnaltie shall come by Escheat, to the said Lord Paramont, and the Abbot shall then hold immediatly of him by fealtie only, & shall do to him fealtie, because hee cannot hold of him in frankalmoigne, &c.

Sect. 142.

¶ *Home de Religion.* And yet this case extendeth to all Ecclesiasticall persons that hold in Frankalmoigne, be they secular or regular, for the mesne ought to acquite all of them,
(a) Pl.Com 306.b. in Shermingtons case. 33.H.6.6. 39.H.6.29. 14.E.3.mesne 7. for they be bound (a) to make prayers for their founder or his heires, and in consideration of those prayers, the founder, &c. is bound to pay to the chiefe Lord all Rents and seruices issuing out of that Land, as it appeareth by that which followeth.

¶ *De luy acquiter.*

¶ Et nota q̃ lou tiel hõe de religion tient ses tenements de son Sñr ẽ frankalmoigne son Sñr est tenus p la ley de luy acquiter de chescun mãner ð seruice, que ascun Sñr paramount de luy voet auer ou demander de mesmes les tenements, et sil ne

And note that where such man of religion holds his tenements of his Lord in frankalmoigne, his Lord is bound by the law to acquite him of euery manner of seruice which any Lord paramont will haue or demand of him for the same tenements, and if he doth not acquite

luy aquita pas, mes suffra luy destre distraine, &c. donques il auera envers son seignior un briefe de Mesne, & recouera envers luy ses damages & ses costes de son suit, &c.

him, but suffereth him to bee distreyned, &c. hee shall haue against his Lord a Writ of Mesne, and shall recouer against him his damages and costs of suit, &c.

Acquiter is compounded of ad, and the old verbe, quietare, and signifieth in Law (b) to discharge, or keepe in quiet, and to see that the tenant be safely kept from any entries or other molestation for any manner of seruice issuing out of the land to any Lord that is aboue the Mesne. (c) And hereof commeth (d) acquitall, and quietus est, (that is) that hee is discharged; and he that is discharged of a felony, &c. by iudgement, is said to be acquited of the felony, acquietatus de felonia; and if he be drawne in question againe, he may plead (e) auterfoits aquite. And therefore if such a Tenant, as Littleton here speaketh of, be distrained by any Lord paramount, the Mesne (to keepe the Tenant quiet) may put his beasts in the pownde, in stead of the beasts of the Tenant.

There be three kinds of Acquitalls. 1. An acquitall by Deede. 2. An acquitall by Prescription. 3. An aquitall by Tenure: And by Tenure foure manner of wayes. 1. By owelty of seruices, for seruice acquites seruice. 2 Tenure in Frankalmoigne, whereof Littleton here speaketh. 3. Tenure in Frankmarriage. 4. Tenure by reason of Dower.

¶ *De chescun manner de seruice.* (f) And yet not of seruices only as Homage, Fealty, Rent workes and other seruices, but also of improuement of seruices, as if he be distreyned for reliefe, * Aide pur file marier, aide pur faire fitz chivaler, &c. Also for Suite seruice to a hundred, (g) but for suite reall in respect of resiance within any Hundred, Leete or Turne the Mesne shall make no acquitall, for that is in respect of his person and resiance.

¶ *Breife de mesne.* Breue de medio, A writ of mesne, so called by reason of the words of the writ of Mesne, which are, Vnde idem A qui medius est inter C & præfatum B. A, which is mesne betweene C. that is the Lord paramont, and B. that is the tenant paravaile. And note that there be 6. writs in Law that may be maintained quia timet, before any molestation, distresse, or impleading, as a man may haue his writ of Mesne (whereof Littleton here speakes) before he be distreyned. 2. A Warrantia cartæ before he bee impleaded. 3. A Monstrauerunt before any distresse or vexation. 4. An Audita quærela before any Execution sued. 5. A Curia claudenda before any default of inclosure. 6. A Ne iniuste vexes before any Distresse or molestation, and these be called Breuia anticipantia, writs of preuention.

¶ *Et recovera vers luy ses damages.* It is to be knowne that there be two seuerall iudgements in a writ of Mesne, one at the Common Law, another by the statute of W. 2 ca. 9 At the Common Law he shall haue iudgement to recouer his acquitall and if he be distreyned or damnified his damages and costs; And the processe at the Common Law was Summons, Attachment and Distresse infinite in the same Countie where the writ is brought. * The iudgement by the said statute of W. 2. is a forjudger of the Mesnaltie, and that in two seuerall cases, one vpon Processe giuen by the said statute, viz. Summons, Attachement and Grand distresse, and if he commeth not, and the writ be returned he shall be forjuged: the other case is where the Tenant recouereth his acquitall in a writ of Mesne, if hee be not acquited afterwards, he shall haue a writ of Distringas Ad acquietandum against the same Mesne, and if he commeth not, he shall be forjudged by his default of the mesnaltie, and so if he commeth, and it be found against him by Verdict he shall be forjudged: but Forjudger in that case is not giuen against his heire for that the statute speaketh only of the mesne and not of his heires. And the iudgement in case of forjudgement is, quod T, (le Mesne) Amittat servitia de A. (le tenant) de tenementis prædictis, & quod omisso prædicto T. prefat' R. (le seignior paramount) modo sit attendens & respondens per eadem servitia per quæ T. tenuit. The said statute in case of forjudgement doth not binde a Feme couert, and yet if such a iudgement be giuen against a Baron and feme it is not voyde but erronious, and to be reuersed in a writ of error, and so a forjudgement against a Tenant in taile shall binde the issue in taile in an Auswrie vntill he reuerseth it by error. If two ioyntenants bring a writ of Mesne, and the one is summoned, and seuered, the other cannot forjudge the Mesne, for he ought to be attendant to the Lord paramount, as the mesne was, and that cannot he be alone. And so it is if there be two ioyntenants Mesnes, and in a writ of Mesne brought against them, one maketh default, and the other appeares, there can be no forjudger.

(b) *Fleta lib. 2. ca. 43. Britton fo. 58. 59. Vid. hereafter in this Sec. in breife de Mesne.*

(c) *Vid. Sect. 142. 540.*
(d) *8. E. 2. Corone, 424. 20. E. 2. Ibid. 232. Stanf. Pl. Corone, 105.*
(e) *4. E. 3. 35. 17. E. 3. 44. 7. H. 4. 18. 34. H. 6. 47. 13. E. 4. 6. F. N. B. 136. Lib. 9. fo. 110. 111. in Treshams case.*

3. E. 3. 14. 77. 5. E. 3. 11. 4. H. 6. 28. 39. E. 3. 19. 11. H. 4. 52. 12. H. 4. 9. 14. H. 4. 17. F. N. B. 136. b. h. 39. H. 6. 30. 33. H. 6. 7. F. N. B. 135. m. 4. E. 4. 35. 12. H. 4. 9. 28. E. 3. 95 17. E. 3. 39.
(f) *39. H. 6. 31. a. 9. E. 4. 27. F. N. B. 136. m. 17. E. 2. Mesne. 5. E. 3. 49.*
* *Bracton lib. 2. fol. 84.*
(g) *4. E. 3. 42.*

For this Writ see the Register fol. and F. N. B. fol. 135. Mirror ca. 2 §. 13. Bracton lib. 2. fol. 84. Britton fol. 58. Fleta lib. 2. ca. 43. Westm. 2. cap. 9.

W. 2. ca. 9. Vid. lib. 8 fol. 134. Mary Shepleys case.

* *Bracton, lib. 2. fol. 84. Fleta lib. 2. cap. 43.*

46. E. 3. 31. 18. E. 2. tit Mesne. F. N. B. 136. 2. H 4 7. 17. E 3. Contra formã Collat. 1. F. N. B. 121.

[illegible]. 3. 41. tit. Mesne 18. 9. E. 2. ibid. 67. 14. E. 2. ibid 70. Lib. 9. fol. 73. b. Doct. Husseys case.

If

If the Tenant be disseised, and the Disseisor in a writ of Mesne forjudge the meane, this shall not bind the Disseisee. And so if the Mesne be disseised, and a forjudgement is had against the Disseisor, this doth not bind the Disseisee, for the words of the said Statute are, Quando tenens sine præiudicio alterius quam medio attornare se potest capitali Domino.

But if the daughter, the sonne being in venter sa mere, be forjudged, it shall bind the son that is borne afterwards, because he had no right at the time of the forjudgement. And so if the tenant enter in Religion, and his heire forjudgeth the Mesne, and then the Auncestor is deraigned, he shall be bound causa qua supra. If there be Lord, Prior, Mesne and Tenannt, the Mesne cannot be forjudged, because he alone can doe nothing to the preiudice to the disherison of his Church; And the like Law is of a Bishop, Parson, and the like.

19. E. 3. Judgm. 117.

W. 2. ca. 9.

No foreiudgment can be but when there is but one meane betweene the Lord distreyning, and the Tenant, because the Tenant upon the forjudgement cannot bee attendant to the Lord distreyning, in respect there is a meane betweene them, and so the said Statute provideth for in expresse termes.

Nota, the Plaintife in the writ of Mesne may chuse either Processe at the Common Law, or upon the said statute of W. 2. Fore-Judgement is called Forisjudicatio, and hee that is forjudged, Forisjudicatus. And Bracton hath this writ, Rex Vicecomiti, &c. & non permittas quod A. capitalis Dominus feodi illius habeat custodiam hæredis quia in Curia nostra forisjudicatur de custodia, &c. Fleta calleth it, Abiudicationem, and thereupon commeth abiudicatus; for hee saith, Post Proclamationem, &c. factam abiudicetur medius de feodo & seruitio suo.

50. E. 3. 23. F. N. B. 137. Bract. li. 4. 256. b. Brit. f. 58. b. Flet. li. 2. ca. 43.

Chap. 7. Homage Auncestrel. Sect. 143.

Tenure p homage auncestrel est, lou vn Tenant tient sa Terre de son Seignior per homage, & mesme le Tenant & ses Auncestors que heire il est ont tenus mesme le Terre del dit Seignior, & de ses auncestors que heire le Seigniour est, de temps dont memorie ne court per homage, & ont fait a eux homage. Et ceo est appel Homage auncestrel, per cause de continuance que ad este per title de Prescription en le Tenancie en le sanke le Tenant, & auxy en le Seigniorie

Tenãt by homage Auncestrel is, where a tenant holdeth his land of his lord by homage, and the same Tenaunt and his Auncestours whose heire hee is, haue holden the same land of the same lord, and of his Auncestors whose heire the Lord is, time out of memorie of man, by Homage, and haue done to them Homage. And this is called Homage Auncestrell, by reason of the continuance which hath beene by title of Prescription in the Tenancie in the bloud of the Tenant, and also in the Seigniorie in

¶ *Per title de Prescription en le Tenancie en le sanke le tenant, & auxy en le Seignior en le sanke le Seignior.* Here Littletõ doth not define what Homage auncestrell is, but putteth an example in one case. For in the 146. Section it appeareth, that bloud is not alwayes necessarie on the Lords side. In this example here put, there must be a double prescription both in the bloud of the Lord and of the Tenant, and therefore I thinke there is little or no land at all at this day holden by Homage auncestrel.

9. H. 3. Vouch. 277. 47. H. 3. Garr. 99. Temps E. 1. Gar. 90. 4. E. 2. Vouch. 245. 45. E. 3. 43. 11. H. 4. 52. 4. H. 6. 25.

And hereof it is said, Autant est le Seignior tenus a son homage, come le homage a son Seignior forsque solement en reuerence. And herewith agreeth Bracton, Est tanta & talis connexio per homagium inter Dominum & tenentem, quod tantum debet Dominus tenenti quantum tenens Domino præter solam reuerentiam.

Brit. fo. 170. a.

Bract. fo. 78. Glanv. li. 9. ca. 4, 5, 6.

¶ *Treit a luy garranty.*

rie en le sanke le Seignior. Et tiel Seruice de Homage Ancestrell trait a luy garrantie, cestascauoir, que le Seignior que est en vie & ad receiue le homage de tiel Tenant, doit garranter son Tenant quant il est impleade de la terre tenus de luy per Homage Ancestrel.

the bloud of the lord. And such seruice of Homage Auncestrell draweth to it, warrantie, that is to say, that the Lord which is liuing, and hath receiued the Homage of such Tenant ought to warrant his Tenant when he is impleaded of the land holden of him by Homage Auncestrell.

Hereby appeareth what a reuerend respect the Law hath to ancient Inheritances continued in the bloud of the Lord, and of the Tenant, for in this example put, if the continuance hath not beene in the bloud of both sides, no warrantie belongeth to Homage Ancestrell, but if ancient continuance hath beene on both sides, (m) then such Homage Ancestrell draweth to it warrantie, so as ancient continued Inheritance on both parties hath more priuiledge and account in Law, then Inheritances lately or within memory acquired.

Vide Britton vbi supra. 14.H.6.25. 18.H.6.2.b. Glanuill lib.9.cap.4.5.& 6. 9.H.3.Voucher 277. 47.H.3.Voucher 270.271. 43.E.3.3.a.

See the second part of the Institutes vpon the 6.chapter of the statute of Bigamis.

If the Lord grant the seruices of his Tenant by Homage Ancestrel, the Tenant shall not be compelled in a per quæ seruitia to atturne, vnlesse the Conusee will grant in Court to warrant the Land vnto him. *18.H.6.2.b. per Newton.*

If the Tenant vouch by force of this warrantie in Law, it is a good counterplea, that the Tenant (or any one of his Ancestors) recessit de seruitio suo & fecit seruitium suum. A. B. sine aliqua coactione propria voluntate. *9.H.3. voucher 277.*

¶ *Et ad receiue homage de tiel tenant.* (a) So as before homage receiued, the Tenant could not absolutely bind the Lord to warrantie, and therefore of ancient time there lay (b) a writ De homagio capiendo, for the Tenant against the Lord to compell him to receiue his homage for the benefit of his warrantie. Which writ you shall read in Bracton and (c) Britton and the Processe and manner of triall thereupon, and the same you shall find in 47.H.3.

(a) 9.H.3.Voucher 277. Temps E.1.Gar.90. 45.E.3.23. (b) Glanuil lib.9.cap.4.5. et lib.1.cap.3. Bracton lib.2.fol.83. (c) Britton fol.172.173. 47.H.3.garrantie 99.

Sect. 144.

¶ Et auxy tiel seruice per homage auncestrel trait a luy acquital. s. que le Sr̃ doit acquiter le Tenant enuers touts auters Sr̃s paramont luy de chescun manner de seruice.

AND also such seruice by homage ancestrell draweth to it acquitall, s. that the Lord ought to acquite the Tenant against all other Lords paramont him of euery manner of seruice.

¶ *Treit a luy acquitall.* Of acquitall somewhat hath beene said in the Chapter of Frankalmoigne. *Sect.142.& 540.*

Section 145.

¶ Et il est dit, q̃ si tiel tenant soit empleð p vn Præcipe quod reddat, &c. & il vouche a garrantie son seignior, q̃ vient eins p proces, & demanda del tenãt que il ad de luy lier a

AND it is said that if such tenant be impleaded by a *Præcipe quod reddat, &c.* and vouche to warranty his Lord who commeth in by processe & demands of the tenant what he hath to binde

¶ VN *Præcipe quod reddat.* This is vnderstood of the Kings writ directed to the Sherife of the County where the land lyeth, whereby the Sherife is authorised to command the Tenant of the land to yeeld the same to the Demandant, and of these words of the writ (Præcipe quod reddat) the writ is so called. Writs of

*Regiſt.*159.

of Præcipe be of foure kindes, Præcipe quod reddat, Præcipe quod faciat, Præcipe quod permittat, & Præcipe quod non permittat, &c. as appeareth by the Regiſter.

*(d) Mir.ca.*5.§.1.& 5. *Bract.li.*5.*fo.*380,381. *Brit.ca.*75.*de Gar.Vouch. Flet.li.*6.*c.*23,24 25,26.& *optime. Lamb.Explic.Verb. Aduocare.*

Et il vouche a garrantie. A voucher, in Latyn vocatio, or aduocatio is a word of art made of the Verbe Voco, and is in (d) the vnderſtanding of the Common Law, when the Tenant calleth another into the Court that is bound to him to warrantie, that is, either to defend the right againſt the Demandant; or to yeeld him other land, &c. in value, and extendeth to lands or tenements of an eſtate of freehold or inheritance, and not to any chattel reall, perſonall, or mixt, ſauing only in caſe of a Wardſhip granted with warrantie (as ſhalbe ſaid more at large in the chapter of warranties) for in the other caſes concerning chattels, the partie, if hee hath a warrantie, ſhall not vouche, but haue his action of Couenant, if he hath a Deed, or if it bee by parol, then an action vpon his caſe, or an action of Deceipt, as the caſe ſhall require. Now ſeeing that one Latyn, French or Engliſh word can haue this particular ſignification, therefore the common Lawyer (that I may ſpeake once for all) is driuen, as the profeſſors of other liberall ſciences vſe to doe, to vſe ſignificant words framed by art which are called vocabula artis, though they be not proper to any language. Hee that boucheth is called the Vouchor vocans, and he that is vouched is called Vouchee Warrantus.

(e) V. Reg. Ind for all theſe Iudiciall writs.

*(f) V. Vet. N. B.*179.186. 39.*E.*3.28,14.*H.*6.7. 17.*E.*3.41.3.*H.*4.4. 11.*H.*4.72.45.*E.*3.19. *F.N.B.*134,135.

(e) The proces whereby the Vouchee is called, is a ſommonea ad warrantizandum, whereupon if the Sherife returneth that the Vouchee is ſummoned, and hee make default, then a (f) Magnum cape ad valentiam is awarded, when if he make default againe, then iudgement is giuen againſt the Tenant, and he ouer to haue in value againſt the Vouchee, If the Vouchee doe appeare and after make default, then Parvum cape ad valentiam is awarded, and if he make default againe, then iudgement as before. But if the Sherife returne, that the Vouchee hath nothing, then after writs of Alias and plures, a writ of ſequatur ſub ſuo periculo ſhalbe awarded, and if the like returne be made, then ſhall the Demandant haue iudgement againſt the Tenant, but he ſhall not haue iudgement to recouer in value, becauſe the Vouchee was neuer warned. And it appeareth that he hath nothing: but in the grand Cape ad valentiam, it appeareth, that he hath aſſetts, and his making default after ſummons is an implied confeſſion of the warranty. And it is called a ſequatur ſub ſuo periculo, becauſe the Tenant ſhall loſe his land

garranty, & il mre coment il & ſes aunceſters q̃ heire il eſt, ount tenus ſa terre del vouchee & de ſes aunceſters, de temps dont memorie ne curt. Et ſi l'ſeignior que eſt vouche ne auoit reſceiue pas homage del tenant ne daſcun de ſes aunceſters, le ſeignior (s'il voit) poit diſclaimer en le ſeigniorie & iſſint ouſte le tenant de ſon garrantie. Mes ſi le Sñr q̃ eſt vouch ad receiue homage de le Tenant, ou de aſcun de ſes aunceſters, donques il ne diſclaimera, mes il eſt oblige p̃ la ley de garranter le tenant, & donq; ſi le tenant perd ſa t̃re en default del vouchee il recouera en value enuers le vouchee de terres & tenements que le vouchee auoit al temps de le voucher, ou vnques puis.

him to warranty, and hee ſheweth how hee & his anceſtors whoſe heire hee is, haue holden their land of the Vouchee and of his anceſtors time out of minde of man. And if the Lord which is vouched hath not receiued homage of the tenant, nor of any of his anceſtors, the Lord (if hee will) may diſclaime in the ſeigniory, and ſo ouſte the tenant of his warranty, but if the Lord who is vouched hath receiued homage of the tenant, or of any of his anceſtors, then he ſhall not diſclaime, but hee is bound by the Law to warrant the tenant, and then if the tenant loſeth his land in default of the Vouchee, he ſhall recouer in value againſt the vouchee of the lands and tenements which the vouchee had at the time of the voucher, or any time after.

land without any recõpence in value, unlesse he upon that writ can bring in the vouchee to warrant the land unto him: and if at the Sequat sub suo periculo, the tenant and the Vouchee make default, and the Demandant hath judgement against the Tenant, and after brings a Scire fac: to have execution, the Tenant may have a Warrantia Cartæ, and if he were impleaded by a stranger; he may vouche againe, but if hee had judgement to recover in value, he shall never have a Warrantia cartæ, or vouche againe, for by this judgement to recover in value, he hath benefit of the warrantie. And you shall finde in bookes a recovery with a single Voucher, and that is when there is but one Voucher; and with a double Voucher, and that is when the Vouchee voucheth over, and so a treble Voucher, &c. Againe, you shall finde there also a forreine Voucher, and that is when the Tenant being impleaded within a particular jurisdiction (as in London or the like) voucheth one to warranty and prayes that he may be summoned in some other county out of the jurisdiction of that Court: this is called a forreine Voucher, but might more aptly be called a voucher of a forreiner de forinsecis vocatis ad Warrantizandum. Note, that by the Civill Law every man is bound to warrant the thing that he selleth or conveyeth, albeit there be no expresse warranty, but the Common Law bindeth him not, unlesse there be a warrantie, either in Deede or in Law for Caveat emptor, as shalbe said more at large in the chapter of warrantie in the third booke.

Glan. ca. 12. *F.N.B.* 6. *e.*

¶ *Le Seignior (s'il voet) poet disclaymer* (u) *en le Seigniorie. Disclaimer, disclamare*, **is compounded of** de **and** clamo, **and signifieth utterly to** renounce the Seigniorie.

Brit. 174.

(a) Note there be divers kinds of Disclaymer, that is to say, a Disclaymer in the tenancie; a Disclaymer in the bloud; and a Disclaymer in the Seigniory; whereof Littleton here putteth his case.

(b) But if the tenant in Frankalmoigne bring a writt of Mesne against his Lord, the Lord cannot disclayme in the Seigniorie, because he cannot hold of any man in Frankalmoigne, but of his Donor and his heires. And so note a diversity betweene a Tenure in Frankalmoigne, whereby Divine Service is maintained, and Homage Ancestrell which respecteth Temporall Service. But if the Lord will not disclayme in the Seigniory, in the case of Homage Ancestrell, then albeit he hath not received Homage, he shall warrant the land.

(a) 47. *H.* 3. *Disclaim.* 35. 16. *H.* 7. 1. 20. *E.* 2. *tit. Nuper ob.* 14. *F.N.B.* 197. & 151. *b.* 45. *E.* 3. 19. 21. *E.* 3. 50. *E.* 3. 23. &c.
(b) 14. *H.* 3. *tit. Disclaim. b.* 33

¶ *Si le Seignior que est vouche ad receive homage, &c. il ne disclaymera.* Therefore it is good for the Tenant, to the intent to oust the Lord of his Disclaymer, in his voucher to alledge, that the Lord hath taken homage of him, and if he alledge it not, and the Lord offer to disclayme, the Tenant may counterplead the same by acceptance of Homage, and the reason that the Lord cannot disclayme in that case is, for that hee hath accepted his humble and reverent acknowledgement to become his man of life and member and terrene honour, and to be faithfull and loyall to him for the Tenements which he holds of him, and against the acceptance hereof the Lord cannot disclayme.

47. *H.* 3. *Disclaim.* 35. *V. Bract. l.* 4. 252. *b.* 16. *H.* 7. 1 *Brit.* 173, 174.

¶ *Que il avoit al temps del voucher.* **Hereby it appeareth, that the** Tenant shall not be driven to recover in value only those Lands which the Lord had from that Ancestor which created the Seigniory, for that were in manner impossible, for that the Seigniory must be created before time of memory, and the first Creation of the Seigniory did not create the warranty, but the continuance of both sides time out of minde created the warranty. And that is, the reason that a writ of Annuity shall not (c) lye against the heire by prescription because it cannot be knowne, whether he hath any land by discent from the said Ancester, that first granted the Annuity. And here is a point worthy of observation that in the case of Homage Ancestrell, (which is a speciall warranty in Law) by the Authority of Littleton, the lands generally that the Lord hath at the time of the Voucher shall be liable to execution in value, whether he hath them by discent or purchase. But in the case of an expresse warrantie the heire shall be charged but only for such lands as he hath by discent from the same Ancestor, which created the warrantie.

(c) 49. *E.* 3. 5. *b.* 10. *E.* 4. 10. *b.* 19. *H.* 6. 74. 37. *H.* 6. 19. 5. *H.* 7. *F.N.B.* 152.

Note, what priviledge this ancient warrantie (created by operation of Law) hath more then the expresse warrantie. And so you may observe, that in this case, firmior & potentior est operatio legis quam dispositio hominis.

¶ *Al temps de voucher ou unques puis.* **This is evident and worthy** of diligent observation, viz that the lands of the Vouchee shall be lyable to the warranty, that the Vouchee hath at the time of the Voucher; for that the Voucher is in lieu of an action, and in a Warrantia cartæ, the land which the Defendant hath at the time of the writ brought, shall be lyable to the warranty.

Upon a Judgement in Debt, the Plantife (d) shall not have Execution, but only of that land, which the Defendant had at the time of the Judgement, for that the Action was brought in respect of the person and not in respect of the land. But if an Action of Debt bee brought

28. *E.* 1. *Vouch.* 291. 9. *Ed.* 2. *War. Car.* 20. 19. *Fines* 127. 29. *E.* 3. 3. 18. *E.* 3. 1. 2. *H.* 4. 10. 23. *E.* 3 *Recou. in valu.* 3. 16. *E.* 3. *Vouch.* 85. 19. *Edw.* 3. *Vouch.* 24. 22. *E.* 3. *Fitz. Nat. Bre.* 134. *f.*
2. *H.* 4. 14. 42. *E.* 3. 5. 42. *ass.* 17 9. *E.* 2 *tit. Exe cut.* 249.

againſt the heire, and he alieneth, hanging the writ, yet ſhall the Land which he had at the time of the originall Purchaſe be charged, for that the Action was brought againſt the heire in reſpect of the land. (e) If a man be Nonſuit, the land only which hee had at the time of the amerciament aſſeſſed ſhall be charged, and not that which hee had at the finding of the pledges. For the amerciament is not in reſpect of the land, but of his want of proſecution, which was a default in his perſon. But the iſſues of a Iuror ſhall be leuied vpon the Feoffee, albeit they were not loſt before the feoffment, becauſe he was returned and ſworne in reſpect of the land. Note the diuerſitie.

(e) 22. *Aſſ. pl.* 32.

If a man giue lands in fee with warrantie, and bind certaine lands ſpecially to warrantie, the perſon of the Feoffor is hereby bound, and not the Land, vnleſſe he hath it at the time of the Voucher

32. *E.* 1. *Voucher* 292.

Sect. 146.

CE Ceſt aſcauoir, que en cheſcun cas ou le Seigniour poit diſclaimer ē ſon ſeigniorie per la ley, & de ceo voit diſclaim̄ en Court de Record, ſon ſeigniorie eſt extinct, & le tenant tiendra del Seignior procheine paramont le ſeignior que iſſint diſclaime. Mes ſi vn Abbe ou Prior ſoit vouch per force de homage anceſtrel, &c. comment que il ne vnque priſt homage &c. vncore il ne poit diſclamer en tiel cas, ne en nul auter cas, car ils ne poient anienter ou deueſter choſe de fee que ad eſte veſtue en lour meaſon.

AND it is to bee vnderſtood, that in euery caſe where the Lord may diſclaime in his Seigniorie by the Law, and of this hee will diſclaime in a Court of Record his Seigniorie is extinct, and the Tenant ſhall hold of the LORD next Paramount to the Lord which ſo diſclaimeth. But if an Abbot or Prior bee vouched by force of Homage Anceſtrell, &c. albeit that hee neuer tooke homage, &c. yet hee cannot diſclaime in this caſe nor in any other caſe, for they cannot take away or deueſt a thing in fee which hath beene veſted in their houſe.

Vide Britton. fol. 58. 110.

C *Son Seigniorie eſt extinct, & le tenant tiendra de Seignior prochein paramount, &c.* Here two things are to be obſerued, First, that by this diſclaymer in the Seigniory, the Seigniory is (f) extinct in the Land.

(f) 45. *E.* 3. 7. 22. *E.* 4. 35.

Secondly, That after the Diſclaymer the Tenant ſhall hold of the next Lord Paramount by the ſame ſeruices, as the meſne ſo diſclayming held before.

Vide Sect. 143.

C *Si vn Abbe ou prior ſoit vouch &c. vncore, &c. vncore il ne poet diſclaimer, &c.* Here it appereth of the Lords ſide, that continuance of bloud is not neceſſary, but yet there muſt bee priuity of ſucceſſion time out of mind in one politique body for if that bodie, be once diſſolued, though a new bee founded of the ſame name, and all the poſſeſſions be granted to them, yet the Homage Anceſtrell is gone. But if a Prior and Couent bee tranſlated Concurrentibus hijs quæ in iure requiruntur to an Abbot and Couent, or to Deane and Chapter, there the Homage Anceſtrell remaines, for though the name bee changed, yet the body was neuer diſſolued, but in effect it remayneth ſtill. If the body Politique were founded within time of memory, there cannot be Homage Anceſtrell, for that continuance faileth, and though Anceſtor is euer properly applyed to a naturall body, yet it is called Homage Anceſtrell when the tenure is of a body Politique, for that it is Anceſtrell of the Tenants ſide: but on the other ſide an Abbot or Prior cannot hold by Homage Anceſtrell, for as appeareth by Littletons examples, it muſt euer be Anceſtrell of the Tenants ſide. And where Littleton putteth his caſe of an Abbot or Prior, the ſame Law is of a Biſhop, Deane, Archdeacon, Prebend, Parſon, Vicar, and the like. Another thing here to be obſerued is, that an Abbot or Prior cannot diſclayme &c. for regularly it is true, Quod meliorem conditionem Eccleſiæ ſuæ facere poteſt Prælatus, deteriorem nequaquam, and againe, Eccleſiæ ſuæ conditionem meliorem facere poſſunt

14. *H.* 6. 12. 2. *H.* 6. 9. 38. *Aſſ. p.* 22. 37. *Aſſ.* 6. *Lib.* 3. *fol.* 73. *&c. Deane and Chapter de Norwich caſe.*

poſſunt ſine conſenſu, deteriorem non poſſunt ſine conſenſu. And therefore an Abbot, Prior, Biſhop, Deane, Archdeacon, Prebend, Parſon, Vicar, or any other ſole Corporation that is ſeiſed in auter droit cannot diſclayme, becauſe as Littleton ſayth, they alone cannot deueſt any fee which is veſted in their Houſe or Church. For the wiſdome of the Law would neuer truſt one ſole perſon with the diſpoſition of the Inheritance of his Houſe or Church. But an Abbot, and Prior had their Couent, the Biſhop his Chapter, the Parſon and Vicar their Patron and Ordinary, and the like of other ſole Corporations, without whoſe aſſent they could paſſe away no Inheritance.

40.E.3.27. 5.E.4.1. 6.E.3.51.52.
10.E.4.2.4. 21.H.7.20.

¶ *Ils ne poient anienter ou deueſter choſe de fee, &c.* These general words haue certaine exceptions for in a quo Warranto at the ſuite of the King againſt a Biſhop, Abbot, or Prior for Franchiſes and Liberties, if the Biſhop, Abbot, or Prior diſclaime in them, this ſhould bind their Succeſſors. If an Abbot or Prior had knowledged the Action in a Writ of Annuity this ſhould haue bound the Succeſſour, becauſe hee cannot falſifie it in an higher action, and there muſt be an end of Suites, Expedit Reipublicæ vt ſit finis litium. But if the Abbot leuie a fine, or acknowledge the action in a Præcipe quod reddat, the Succeſſor ſhall be bound pro tempore, but he may haue a Writ of Right, and recouer the Land.

8.E.3.51.52.
38.E.3.33. 16.E.3.tit. Abbot.13. 19.E.3.tit. Abbot.12. 7.R.2. Abbot.7. 12.H.4.11. 20.H.6.fo vltimo. 4.H.7.2. 2.H.4.6.

¶ *Per force de Homage Anceſtrell, &c.* Here (&c.) implyeth or by any other warranty (l) as by the reaſon which our Authour here yeeldeth, appeareth.

¶ *Choſe de fee.* (k) For if in an Action of Debt vpon an Obligation againſt an Abbot, the Abbot acknowledgeth the Action, and dieth, the Succeſſor ſhall not auoyd Execution though the Obligation was made without the aſſent of the Couent, for he cannot falſifie the recouerie in an higher Action: Et res iudicata pro veritate accipitur, and this is but a Chattell. And ſo it is of a Statute or Recogniſance, acknowledged by an Abbot or Prior.

34.Aſſ.p.7. 14.E.4.tit. Abbot.B. 8.E.3.28. 12.H.8.7.
(l) 12.H.8.7.
(k) 7.R.2.tit. Abbot.7. See the Bookes next aboue.

Sect. 147.

¶ ITem ſi home que tient ſon terre per homage anceſtrel, alien a vn auter en fee, le alienee ferra Homage a ſon ſeignior, mes il ne tient de ſon Seigniour per Homage Aunceſtrel, pur ceo que le tenancie ne fuit continue en le ſanke de les aunceſters lalienee, ne lalienee nauera iames garrantie de la terre de ſon ſeignior pur ceo que le continuance del tenancie en le tenant et a ſon ſank per lalienation eſt diſcontinue. Et ſic vide, que ſi le tenant que tient la terre per homage anceſtrell de ſon Seig-

ALſo if a Man which holds his land by Homage Anceſtrell, alien to another in fee, the alienee ſhall doe homage to his Lord, but hee holdeth not of his Lord by homage anceſtrell; becauſe the Tenancie was not continued in the bloud of the Anceſtors of the alienee, neither ſhal the alienee haue warrantie of the land of his Lord, becauſe the continuance of the tenancie in the Tenant, and to his bloud by the alienation is diſcontinued. And ſo ſee, that if the tenant which holdeth his Land of his Lord

¶ *Alien a vn auter en fee.* For hereby the priuity of the eſtate is altered and the continuance of it in the bloud of the Tenant is diſſolued. But if the Tenant maketh a Leaſe for life, or a gift in taile, this is a continuance of the priuitie and eſtate in the Tenant in reſpect of the reuerſion that remayneth in him: for the fee, whereof Littleton here ſpeaketh was not out of him. But if the Tenant maketh a feoffment in fee vpon condition, and dieth his heire performeth the condition, and reentreth the homage anceſtrell is deſtroyed in reſpect of the interruption of the continuance of the priuity and eſtate, and this caſe was put and not denied in the argument of (m) of the Caſe betweene the Lord Cromwell and Andrewes, Mich.14. & 15.Eliz. which I my ſelfe heard and obſerued. As if Ceſty que vſe had made a feoffment in fee vpon condition and entred for the condition broken hee ſhould haue detained the Land againſt

(m) 1. Mich.14. & 15.Eliz.
5.H.7.

nior, alien en fee, coment que il repriſt eſtate de lalienee arrere en fee, il tient la terre p homage, mes nemy per Homage aunceſtrell.

by homage anceſtrell alieneth in fee, though hee taketh an eſtate againe of the alienee in fee, yet he holds the lād by homage, but not by homage anceſtrell.

gainſt the Feoffees for euer, for that the eſtate and priuitie was for the time taken out of the Feoffees, and thereby diſſolued for euer. But if the Land were recouered againſt the tenant upon a faint title, and the Tenant recouer the ſame againe in an action of higher nature, there the Homage Anceſtrell remaines, for the right was a ſufficient meane for the continuance: ſo it is if he had reuerſed it in a Writ of Error. (n) If the alienee be impleaded in Littletons caſe and vouche the alienor that held by Homage Anceſtrell, albeit hee commeth in by fiction of Law to many purpoſes in priuitie of his former eſtate Yet to this purpoſe he cannot come in as Tenant by Homage Anceſtrell, becauſe of the diſcontinuance of the eſtate and priuitie, and as Littleton ſayth, the Tenancie was not continued in the bloud. (o) and Britton ſaith, Et come aſcun nequedent ſoit Vouche per homage, & le Seigniour tende de auerrer que le tenement dount il vouche fuit tranſlate hors del ſanke del primer purchaſer per feoffment ou per aſcun auter tranſlation: en tiel caſe ſoit le tenant charger de voucher ſon feoffor ou ſes heires.

(n) *5.E.3.11. per Cantrel.*

(o) *Britton.fol.170.a.*

38.E.3.20. 11.H.4.22. 17.E.3.47.59.73.74. 26.E.3.56. 18.E.3.56. 16 E.3.Voucher.87. 18.E.3.30. 44.E.3. Litt.fol.169.

Coment que il repriſt eſtate del alienee en fee, &c. For the cauſe aforeſaid in reſpect of the interruption of the priuitie and continuance of the eſtate. And herewith agreeth our Bookes in Caſes of Warranties in Deed or Warranties in Law. See more of this in the Chapter of Warranties.

Sect. 148.

ITem il eſt dit, que ſi home tient ſa terre de ſon ſeignior per homage & fealty, & il ad fait homage & fealty a ſon ſeignior, & le ſeignior ad iſſue fits & deuy, & le ſeigniory diſcendiſt a le fits, en ceo cas le Tenant que fiſt homage al pere ne ferra homage al fits, pur ceo que quant un tenant ad fait un foits homage a ſon Seignior il eſt excuſe pur terme de ſa vie de faire homage a aſcun auter heire del ſeignior, mes uncore il ferra Fealtie al fits & Heire le Seignior, coment que il fiſt Fealty a ſon Pere.

ALſo it is ſaid that if a man holds his land of his Lord by Homage and Fealty, and hee hath dȯne homage and fealtie to his Lord, and the Lord hath iſſue a ſonne and dies, and the Seigniorie diſcendeth to the ſonne, in this caſe the Tenant which did homage to the father ſhal not doe homage to the ſonne, becauſe that when a tenant hath once done homage to his Lord, hee is excuſed for terme of his life to doe homage to any other heire of the Lord, but yet he ſhal do fealty to the ſonne and heire of the Lord, although he did fealty to his father.

NE ferra homage al fitz: If A. holdeth of B. as of the Manor of Dale, whereof B. is ſeiſed in taile. B diſcontinueth the eſtate taile, and taketh backe an eſtate in Fee ſimple. A. doth homage to B. B. dieth ſeiſed, the iſſue in taile entreth, A. ſhall doe homage againe to the heire in taile of B. becauſe hee is remitted to the eſtate taile, and the ſtate in fee that his father had, in reſpect whereof the homage is done is vaniſhed, and the heire in taile is in of a new eſtate, in reſpect whereof hee ought to doe a new homage. (p) But regularly it is true which Littleton ſayth, that when a Tenant hath done once homage to his Lord, he is excuſed for terme of his life to make homage to any other heires of the Lord. But he ſhall doe fealtie to his ſonne, albeit he hath done fealtie to the father.

(p) *Britton.175.176.*

Sect. 149.

¶ Item si le Sñr apres l'homage a luy fait per son tenant grant le seruice de son tenant per le fait a vn auter en fee, & le tenant atturna, &c. donque le tenant ne serra my compel de faire homage, mes il ferra fealtie, coment que il fist fealtie deuant a le grauntor. Car fealtie est incident a chescun atturnement del tenant, quant le seigniorie est graunt. Mes si ascun home soit seisie dun mannor, & vn auter hõe tient de luy la terre come del manor auandit per homage, le quel tenant ad fait homage a son Sñr q̃ est seisie del mannor, si apres vn estrange port Præcipe quod reddat enuers le Sñr del manor & recouera le manor enuers luy, et suist execution, en cest case le tenant ferra auterfoits homage a celuy q̃ recouera le manor, coment q̃ il fist homage deuant, p̃ ceo que lestat celuy que receiuoit le primer homage, est defete per le recouerie, et ne girra en la bouche le tenant a fauxer ou defeater le recouerie que fuit enuers son Seignior. Et sic vide diuersitatem en

ALso if the Lord after the homage done vnto him by the tenant, grant the seruice of his Tenant by Deed to another in fee, and the Tenant atturneth, &c. the Tenant shall not bee compelled to doe homage, but he shall doe fealty, although he did fealty before to the grantor. For fealty is incident to euery atturnement of the tenant, when the seigniorie is granted But if any man bee seised of a mannor, and another holds of him the land as of the Mannor aforesaid by homage, which tenant hath done homage to his Lord who is seised of the Mannor, if afterwards a stranger bringeth a *Præcipe quod reddat* against the Lord of the Mannor, and recouereth the Mannor against him, and sues execution, In this case the tenant shall againe do homage to him which recouered the mannor, although he had done homage before, because the estate of him which receiued the first homage is defeated by the recouery, and it shall not lye in the power of the tenant to falsifie or defeate the recouerie which was against his lord. And so see a

¶ *Item si le Sñor, &c. grant le seruice de son tenant per fait, &c.* Note a diuersitie when the Lord alieneth the seigniorie, and when the tenant alieneth the tenancie, for when the Tenant hath done homage, & the seigniory is transferred to another either by the act of the partie as alienation, or by act in Law, as discent, yet the tenant shall not iterat homage, as he shall do fealty, but when the Tenant doth homage, and alieneth the tenancy, there is a new Tenant, which neuer did homage, and therefore he ought to doe homage to the Lord albeit his Alienor had done it before. And it is to be obserued that none shall doe * homage but the Tenant of the land to the Lords of whom it is holden, and therfore if homage bee due to bee done by the Tenant, if the Tenant alieneth the land to another, the Alienor cannot be compelled to doe homage.

Brit.176.

13.E.1.tit.Per que Seruitia, 22. & tit.Gar.91.

8.E.4.19.b.

¶ *Attorne, &c.* Here by (&c) is to be vnderstood that albeit hee pay his rẽt, perform his Annual seruices and doe Fealtie which is a part of homage,

ceo case lou home vient a le Seigniorie per recouerie, & lou il vient per discent ou per graunt al Seigniorie.

diuersitie in this case, where a man commeth to a Seigniorie by recouerie, and where he commeth to the same by discent or grant.

homage, yet homage he shall not doe.

¶ *Mes si ascun home soit seisi dun Mannor, &c.* Here it appeareth, that the case of the recouerie of the Seigniorie differeth from the alienation of the Lord, which is his owne act, or the discent of the Seigniorie to the heire, which is an act in Law. And the reason of this diuersitie is, for that by the recouerie, the state of him that receiued the homage, is defeated, for it shall not lie in the mouth of the Tenant, to falsifie, or to frustrate or defeat the recouerie which was against his Lord of the Mannor or Seigniorie, for that the Tenant had nothing therein, and euery man by Law ought to meddle in such cases with that which belongeth vnto him, which is worthy of obseruation concerning falsifying of recoueries.

Vide Sect. 551. 33.E.3. auowrie 255. 37.H.6.33. 39.H6. 34. 7.H7.11. Doct. & Stud. fol. 43. 28.H.8.Dier.41

Note that to falsifie, in legall vnderstanding is to prooue false, that is, to auoyd, or as Littleton here saith, to defeat, in Latine, fallare, seu falsificare, (i.) falsum facere.

7.H.8.cap.4.

But since Littleton wrote, it is recited by Act of Parliament, That whereas diuers, &c. haue suffered recoueries against them of diuers Mannors, &c. for the performance of their wils, for the suretie of their wiues ioyntures, &c. and the recouerors had no remedie to compell the Freeholders and Tenants, &c. to attorne vnto them, nor could by order of Law attaine to the rents, seruices, &c. that Act doth giue the recouerors power to distreyne and auow, whereupon many haue thought, that this doth impugne Littletons case of the Recouerie. But distinguendum est: Littleton intendeth his case either vpon a recouerie by title, (for hee saith, that the state of the Tenant in the recouerie is defeated) or without any consent vpon pretence of title, which is all one, for the Tenant cannot falsefie, and the Lord should auow as one that came in of a former title. And Littleton hath good authoritie in Law to warrant (a) his opinion, and the Statute of 7 H 8. extendeth to common recoueries had by consent and agreement, as appeareth by the Act it selfe, which then was, and yet is a common assurance and conueyance, whereof the Law taketh notice, and whereupon (as appeareth by the Act, an vse might bo limitted. So as it is apparant, that such recouerors came in meerely vnder the state of the Lord, &c. and had no remedie (as the Statute saith) to compell the Freeholders and Tenants to atturne, and without atturnement, could neither distreyne nor auow; wherefore this Statute gaue recouerors remedie to distreyne, and a forme to auow and iustifie, which they had not before, as it appeareth by the Doctor and Student, who liued at that time: The bodie of the Act is, That such recouerors may distreyne and make auowrie, &c. as those persons against whom the sayd recouerie is, should haue done, &c, if the same recouerie had not beene had, and haue like remedie, &c.

(a) 39.H.6.22. 37.H.6.38 35.H.6.22.

28.H.8.Dier.41.

If a man had made a lease for yeares to begin at Michaelmas, reseruing a rent, and before Michaelmas he had suffered a common recouerie, the recouror should distreyne for that Rent, which the Lessor before the recouerie could not. But if the recouerie had not beene had, then he might haue distreyned, and so it is within the Statute: but if a fine had beene leuied of a Mannor, and before atturnement the Conusee had suffered a common recouerie, the recouerор should not distreyne, &c. because the Conusee against whom the recouerie was had, could not.

But this Act extended onely to Distresses and Auowries for Rents, Seruices, and Customes, and gaue also a forme of a Quare impedit. But vpon this Statute it was holden, That the recouror could not haue an Action of Debt against the Lessee for yeares, nor an Action of wast against Tenant for life or yeares, and therefore remedie was prouided in these cases, by the Statute of 21.H.8.

21.H.8.cap.15.

Section 150.

Item si vn Tenant que doit per son Tenure fayre a son Seignior Homage, vient a son Seignior, & dit a luy

Also if a Tenant which ought by his Tenure to doe his Lord Homage, commeth to his Lord, and saith vnto him, Sir, I

¶ *Vient a son seigniour.* The tenant ought to seeke the Lord to doe him homage, if the Lord be within England, for this seruice is personall as well of the Lords side, as of the Tenants side, for Law requi-

luy, Sir, ieo doy a vous faire homage pur les Tenements que ieo teigne de vous, & ieo sue icy prist a vous faire homage pur mesmes les Tenements, pur que ieo vous pry, que ore ceo voiles receiuer de moy.

ought to doe homage vnto you for the Tenements which I hold of you, and I am here readie to doe homage to you for the same Tenements, and therefore I pray you, that you would now receiue the same from mee.

reth order and decencie. And therefore Bracton saith, Et sciendum, Quod ille qui homagium suum facere debet, ob tentu reuerentiæ quam debet Domino suo, adire debet Dominum suum vbicunque inuentus fuerit in Regno, vel alibi si possit comodè adiri, & non tenetur Dominus quærere suum tenentem, & sic debet homagium ei facere. And the same Law it is for Fealtie, and the diuersitie betweene these seruices, and the rent is because that these are personall, and the rent may be payd and receiued by other, and therefore a tender of the rent vpon the land is sufficient.

Bracton fol. 80. a. And Britton fol. 171. agreeth herewith.

Sect. 151.

¶ Et si le Seigniour adonques refusa de ceo receiuer, donque apres tiel refusal le Seigniour ne poet distreiner le Tenant pur le homage aderere, deuant que le Seignior requiroit le Tenant de faire a luy homage, & l'Tenant a ceo faire refusa.

And if the Lord shall then refuse to receiue this, then after such refusall the Lord cannot distreyne the Tenant for the homage behind, before the Lord requireth the Tenant to doe homage vnto him, and the Tenant refuse to doe it.

¶ And the reason hereof is, for that when the Tenant hath done his endeauour and dutie to offer his corporall seruice, and the Lord refuseth the same, or doe not accept his seruice vpon his tender thereof, (which is a refusall in Law) then the Law in respect of the Lords fault, requireth, that before the Lord can distrein for it, that he doth require the tenant to doe that seruice, and if he either refuse to doe it, or doe it not when he is required, it is a refusall in Law.

Vid. Bracton fo. 83. Britton 171. 172. 21. E. 3. 24. 21. Ass. p. 73. 20. E. 3. Avowrie 223. 45. E. 3. 9. 7. E. 4. 4. 21. E. 4. 17. 20. H. 6. 31.

Sect. 152.

¶ Item home poit tener sa terre per homage auncestrel, et per Escuage, ou per auter seruice de Chiualer, auxibien sicome il poyt tenir sa terre per homage auncestrel en Socage.

Also a man may hold his land by homage Auncestrell, and by Escuage, or by other Knights Seruice, as well as hee may hold his land by homage Auncestrell in Socage.

¶ So as Homage Auncestrel may belong as well to a Tenure by Escuage or Knights seruice, as to a Tenure in Socage, or to a tenure in nature of Socage, whereof there hath bin spoken in the chapter of Socage.

Chap.8. Grand Serieantie. Sect.153.

TEnure per graund serieantie est lou vn home tient ses terres ou tenements de nostre Sire le Roy per tiels seruices que il doit en son proper person faire al Roy, come de porter le banner de nostre seignior le Roy, ou sa lance, ou de amesner son hoste, ou destre son Marshal, ou de porter son espee deuant luy a son coronement, ou destre son sewer a son coronement, ou son Caruer, ou son Butler, ou destre vn de ses Chamberlains de le resceit de son Eschequer, ou de faire auters tiels seruices &c. Et la cause que tiel seruice est appell grand serieantie est, pur ceo que il est pluis grand & pluis digne seruice que est le seruice en le tenure descuage. Car celuy que tyent per Escuage nest pas limite per sa tenure de faire ascun pluis especial seruice que ascun auter que tient per escuage doit faire. Mes celuy que

TEnure by grand Serianctie is where a man holds his lands or tenements of our Soueraign Lord the King by such seruices as hee ought to doe in his proper person to the King, as to carry the Banner of the King, or his Lance, or to lead his Army, or to be his Marshall, or to carry his sword before him at his Coronation, or to bee his Sewer at his Coronation, or his Caruer, or his Butler, or to be one of his Chamberlaines of the receipt of his Exchequer, or to do other like seruices, &c. And the cause why this seruice is called grand Serieanty is, for that it is a greater and more worthy seruice, than the seruice in the tenure of Escuage. For he which holdeth by Escuage is not limitted by his tenure to doe any more especiall seruice, then any other which holdeth by Escuage ought to doe, but hee which holdeth by grand

Tenure per grand Serieantie. Serieantie cometh of the French word (Sergeant) i. Satelles, and (a) Serjeantia idem est quod servitium. And it is called (b) Magna Serieantia or serianteria, * or Magnum servitium, great seruice aswell in respect of the excellency and greatnesse of the person to whom it is to be done, (for it is to be done to the King only) as of the honour of the seruice it selfe, and so Littleton himselfe in this Section saith, that it is called Magna serieantia or Magnum servitium, because it is greater and more worthy than Knights seruice, for this is Re vera, servitium regale, and not Militare only Fleta saith, Magna autem serieantia dici poterit, cum quis ad eundem cum rege in exercitu cum equo co-operto vel huiusmodi ad patriæ tuitionem fuerit feoffatus.

(a) Glanvil lib.9.ca.4.
(b) Bracton lib.2.35. & 84.85. lib.1 ca.10.
* Fleta, lib.1.cap.10.lib.2. ca.9, in fine.
(c) Britton, cap.66. fol.164.165.
Ockam cap. quod non absoluitur.
45.E.3.25. per Finchden.
* Fleta, vbi supra.

De nostre seignior le roy. This tenure hath seuen speciall properties. 1. To bee holden of the King only. 2. It must bee done when the Tenant is able in proper person. 3. This seruice is certaine and particular. 4. The reliefe due in respect of this tenure differeth from Knights seruice. 5. It is to bee done within the Realme. 6 It is subiect to neither, Aid pur faire fitz chiualeir or file marier. And 7. it payeth no Escuage.

Bracton, lib.2.84.
11.H.4.34.
10.H.4. Avowrie, 267.
F.N.B.83.
10.H.6. anc. demesne, 11.

Come de porter le banner de nostre seignior le roy ou de amesner son host. This great seruice to the King may (as it appeareth hereby) concerne the Warres and matters Militarie, for some grand Ser-

23.H.3. stat. Gard Stat. de Ward & relevio. 28.E.1.

tient p grand Serieanty doit fait un especial ſuice al Roy, que il que tient per eſcuage ne doit faire.

Serianty ought to doe ſome ſpeciall ſeruice to the King which he that holds by Eſcuage ought not to doe.

...ieanties are to be done in the time of warre for the ſafety of the Realme, and ſome in time of peace, for the honour of the Realme.

Ou deſte ſon Marſhall. * If the King giueth lands to a man to hold of him to be his Marſhall of his hoſt, or to be Marſhall of England, or to be Conſtable of England, or to be high Steward of England, * Chamberlaine of England and the like, theſe are grand Serieanties, and theſe & ſuch like grand Serieanties are of great and high iuriſdiction, and ſome of them concerne matters militarie in time of warre and ſome ſeruices of honour in time of peace. And this is to be obſerued that though there were diuers Lords Marſhalls of England before the raigne of (z) R.2. yet King R.2. created Thomas Mowbrey Duke of Norfolke, and firſt Earle Marſhall of England Per nomen comitis Mariſchalli Angliæ.

Ou de porter ſon eſpee, &c. ou deſte ſon ſewer a ſon Coronement, &c. Theis and ſuch like grand Seriantles at the Kings Coronation are ſeruices of honour in time of peace.

Deſte vn de ſes Chamberlaines, &c. ou de faire autiels ſeruices. It is alſo a Tenure by grand Seriantie to hold (a) by any office to be done in perſon concerning the receipt of the Kings treaſure, Quia theſaurus regis reſpicit regem & regnum; And cenſus regius eſt anima Reip. ſo it is Firmamentum belli, & Ornamentum pacis.

Milites camerarij dicuntur, quia pro camerariis miniſtrant, and concerning their office, this is the effect as Ockam (b) ſaith, Officium camerariorum in recepta conſiſtit in tribus, Scilicet claues arcarum, &c. baiulant, pecuniam numeratam ponderant, & per centenas libras in forulas mittunt. But diſcontinuance in effect hath worne out their office. And yet they continue their name, and keepe the keyes of the Treaſurie where the Records doe lye.

And another ſaith, Camerarius dicitur a camera, quia camera eſt locus in quem theſaurus recolligitur, vel conclaue in quo pecunia reſeruatur, So as camerarius in legall ſignification eſt cuſtos regij cenſus: and Willielmus de Bellocampo comes Warwici (held) officium camerarij in Scaccario.

Or by any office concerning the Adminiſtration of Juſtice, quia juſticia firmatur ſolium.

It appeareth by an ancient Record (c) that Varianus de ſancto Petro tenuit de domino rege in capite medietatem ſeriantiæ pacis per ſervicium inveniendi decem ſervientes pacis ad cuſtodiendam pacem in Ceſtria.

See Ockam of the inſtitution and ancient order of the Exchequer; Dier 4. Eliz. 213. the Uſherie of the Exchequer holden by grand Seriantie.

Tiels ſeruices, &c. Here by (&c.) is to be vnderſtood other like ſeruices not expreſſed, as partly appeareth by that which hath beene ſaid, viz. to bee Steward of England, Conſtable of England, Chamberlaine of England, and other honorable ſeruices whereof more ſhall be ſaid in this chapter.

Ou vn eſpeciall ſeruice al roy. That is to ſay, that this great ſeruice be ſpecially ſet downe, for it may conſiſt of diuers branches, as to goe with the King in his warre in the foreward, and to returne in the rereward. And alſo to pay Rent, &c. but yet it muſt be certaine and particular.

* Fleta lib. 1. cap. 10. 11. Eliz. Dier 285. Camden Brit. 286. 287.
* Ockam cap. officium conſtabularii.
(z) Pat. rot. patent. de anno 20. R. 2.
(a) Vid. 51. H. 3. ſtatu. 5. 10. E. 3 ca. 11. 14. E. 3. ca. 14. 26. H. 8. ca. 2. 34. & 35. H. 8. ca. 16. 11. E. 4. fo. 1. Pl. Com. 207. 208.
(b) Ockam cap. qui ſit Scaccarium.
Geruaſi Tilburienſis in libro nigro ſub cuſtodia camerariorum.
Rot. clauſ. 8. E. 1. Membr. 1.
Ex lectura Marrowe.
(c) Ex Inquiſitione poſt mortem Vriani de Sancto Petro, 4. E. 2. Ceſtr.
Vid. 7. Aſſ. 12. 7. E. 3. 57.
23. H. 3. gard. 148.

Section 154.

Item ſi tenant q̃ tient per eſcuage morust ſon heire eſteant de pleine age, ſil tenoit per vn fee de chiualer, le heire ne paiera forſq; C.s. pur reliefe, come eſt ordeine per l' ſtatute de Magna Carta, cap. 2. Mes ſi celuy que tient de roy per grand

Also if a tenant which holds by Eſcuage dieth his heire being of full age, if hee holdeth by one Knights fee, the heire ſhall pay but a C.s. for reliefe, as is ordained by the ſtatute of *Magna Carta, cap.* 2. But if hee which holdeth of the King by grand Serieanty

Seriantie morust, son heire esteant de plein age, le heire paiera al Roy pur reliefe le value de les terres ou tenements per an (ouster les charges & reprises) queux il tient del Roy per grand Serieantie. Et est ascauoir, que Serieantia en Latin, idem est quod seruitium, & sic Magna Serieantia, idem est quod magnum seruitium.

dieth, his heire being of full age, the heire shall pay to the King for reliefe one yeares value of the lands or tenements which hee holdeth of the King by Grand Serieantie ouer and besides all charges and reprises. And it is to be vnderstood, that *Serieantia* in Latine, is the same *quod seruitium*, and so *Magna Serieantia* is the same *quod magnum seruitium*.

11.H.4.72.b. ¶ *Paiera al Roy pur releife le value de ses terres, &c.* And herewith agreeth 11.H.4.72.b.

¶ *Serieantia idem est quod seruitium.* Hereby it appeareth that the explanation of ancient words and the true sence of them are requisite, and to bee understood per verba notiora.

Section 155.

¶ *Tenãts per escuage doient faire lour seruice hors del Roialme.*

3.N.B.83.F. For hee that holdeth by Cornage or Castle-gard holdeth by Knights Seruice, & is to doe his Seruice within the Realme, but hee holdeth not by Escuage, and therefore Littleton materially said Tenant per Escuage, and not tenant by Knights Seruice.

¶ *Pur le greinder part.* For to beare the Kings Banner, or his Lance, or to lead his Host, and to be his Marshall, &c. may be aswell without the Realme, and therefore Littleton said (for the greatest part.)

¶ Item ceux que teignont per escuage doient faire lour seruice hors de roialme mez ceux que teignont per graund serieantie, pur le greindr part doient faie lour seruices deins le Roialme.

Also they which hold by Escuage, ought to doe their Seruice out of the Realme, but they which hold by Grand Serieantie (for the most part) ought to do their Seruices within the Realme.

Sect. 156.

4.H.5.cap.7.
22.E.4.cap.8.
Camden.in Britannia.

¶ *En le marches de Scotland. Marches* is either a Saxon word and signifieth, limites bourdours, or an English word, viz. Markes. Nota, for that it lyeth neere to Scotland, it is said in the Marches of Scotland, and yet the Land

¶ Item il est dit, que en le Marches de Scotland, ascuns teignont de Roy per Cornage, cestascauoir, pur ventier vn cornu, pur garner hões de pais quant ils oyent que le Scottes ou auters enemies veignont ou voilent enter en Engleterre, quel seruice est graund

Also it is said that in the Marches of Scotland some hold of the King by Cornage that is to say, to winde a horne to giue men of the Countrie warning when they heare that the Scots or other enemies are come or will enter into England, which seruice is grand Seriantie.

graund Serieãty. Mes si ascun tenant tient dascun auter Seignior que de Roy per tiel seruice de Cornage, ceo nest pas grande Serieanty, mes est seruice de chiualer, & trait a luy garde & mariage, car nul poit tener per grand Serieanty si non de Roy tant solemẽt.

But if any tenant hold of any other Lord then of the King by such seruice of Cornage, this is not grand Seriantie, but it is Knight Seruice. And it draweth to it Ward and Marriage, for none may hold by grand Seriantie, but of the King only.

whereof Littleton here speaketh, lieth in England.

¶ *Per Cornage. Cornagiũ* is derived (as cornuare also is) à cornu, and is as much (as before hath beene noted) as the seruice of the Horne. It is also called in old bookes Horngeld.

Note a tenure by Cornage of a common person is Knights Seruice, of the King it is Grand Seriantie, so as the Royall dignitie of the person of the Lord maketh the difference of the tenure in this case. And I find that there were Cornicularij amongst the Romans, & dicti fuerunt cornicularij quia cornu faciebant excubias militares, and Magna Seriantia is appropriated only to this tenure.

23.H.tit.gard.148. 8.E.3.66. in fine. 16.E.3.auowrie 90. F.N.B.83.

Sect. 157.

¶ Item home poit veier Anno 11. H. 4. que Cokayne adonque chiefe Baron deschequer, vient en le common banke, portãt ouesques luy la Copie dun recorde in hæc verba; Talis tenet tantam terram de domino Rege per Serieantiam, ad inueniendum vnum hominem ad guerram vbicunque infra quatuor Maria, &c. Et il demaunda sil fuit graund Serieãty ou petite Serieantie. Et Hanke, adonques disoit, que il fuit graunde Serieantie, pur ceo que il ad seruice a faire p corps dun home, & sil ne purra trouer nul home a faire l' seruice pur luy, il Mesme doit faire. Quod alij

ALso a man may see in *Anno* 11.*H.* 4. that *Cokayne* then Chiefe Baron of the Exchequer came into the Common Place, and brought with him the Copie of a Record in these words. *Talis tenet tantam terram de Domino Rege per Serieantiam ad inueniendum vnum hominem ad guerram vbicunque infra quatuor Maria, &c.* And hee demanded if this were Grand Seriantie, or petite Seriantie. And *Hanke* then said, that it was Grand Seriantie, because hee had a Seruice to do by the bodie of a man, and if he cannot find a man to doe the seruice for him, hee himselfe ought to doe it. *Quod alij Iusticiarij concesse-*

¶ E*T sil ne purra trouer nul home a faire le seruice pur luy, &c.* Hereby it appeareth that Tenant by Grand Seriantie, may in some Cases make a deputie, and therefore the diuersitie is, that where the Grand Seriantie is to bee done to the royall person of the King, or to execute one of those high and great Offices, there his Tenant cannot make a Deputie without the Kings Licence, and therefore Littleton hath said before that such seruices are to bee done in proper person. But he that holdeth to serue him in his warre within the Realme or by Cornage may make a Deputie.

11.H.4.72. 24.E.3.32. Vide Hil.8.E.1. Middle inter Placita de Banco. Sir Iohn Moyses Case.

11.H.4.72.

(*) Iohannes de Archier qui tenet de Domino Rege in capite per Seriantiæ archerie, &c. in Comitatu Glouc. hæres in custodia.

(*) Claus. 18.H.3.M.5.

¶ *Infra quatuor Maria.* That is within the Kingdome of England, and the Dominions of the same Kingdome.

Rot.Escaetor. 41.H.3.m.23. Stephen Haringdons case.

Now it is good to bee seene what persons that hold by Grand Seriantie may doe and performe that honourable seruice in person, and who ought not to be receiued thereunto

(a) 1.R.2.Rot.clauſ.m.45.

unto, but ought to make a ſufficient Deputie. At the Coronation of (a) King R. 2. John Willſhire Citizen of London exhibited his Petition to the high Steward of England in his Court, that where the ſaid John held certaine lands in Hayden in the Countie of Eſſex, of the King by Grand Serjantie, viz. to hold a Towell when the King ſhould waſh his hands before dinner the day of his Coronation, &c. and prayed that he might bee accepted to doe this Office of Grand Serjantie, the iudgement followeth. Et quia apparet per record' de Scaccario Domini Regis in Curia monſtrat' quod prædicta tenementa tenentur de Domino Rege per ſeruitium prædictum. Ideo dictus Iohannes admittitur ad ſeruitium ſuum huiuſmodi faciendum per Edmondum Comitem Cantabrigiæ deputatum ſuum, & ſic idem Comes in iure ipſius Iohannis Manutergium tenuit quando Dominus Rex lauabat manus ſuas dicto die Coronationis ſuæ ante prandium.

Iuſticiarij cõceſſerunt. (Cokaine) Donque doit le tenant en ceo cas paier reliefe al value del terre per an? Ad quod non fuit reſponſum.

runt. Then ſaith *Cokayne*, ought the Tenant to pay reliefe to the value of the land by the yeare? *Ad quod non fuit reſponſum.*

By which Record it appeareth that the ſaid John Willſhire being of his qualitie, and hauing not any dignitie, could not do and performe this high and honourable ſeruice to the Royall perſon of th' King, but did make an honourable Deputie who performed it in his right which is worthy of obſeruation.

Vide 1.R.2.*memb*.45.

At the ſame Coronation William Furneuall exhibited his Petition in the ſame Court, That where he held the Mannor of Farnham, in the Countie of Buck. with the Hamlet of Cere in the ſame Countie, by the ſeruice to find to the King at his Coronation a Gloue for his right hand, and to ſupport the Kings right hand the ſame day, whiles he held in his hand the Verge Royall, the iudgement followeth. Qua quidem Petitione debite intellecta & facta publica proclamatione ſi quis clameo ipſius Willielmi in ea parte contradicere vellet, nemineque ei contrariante, conſideratum fuit, quod idem Willielmus aſſumpto per eum primitus ordine militari, ad ſeruitium prædictum admitteretur faciendum, & poſtmodo (videlicet) die Martis proximo ante Coronationem prædictam Dominus Rex ipſum Willielmum apud Kenington honorifice præfecit in militem, & ſic idem Willielmus ſeruitium ſuum prædictum, dicto die Coronationis iuxta conſiderationem prædictam perfecit & in omnibus adimpleuit. By which it appearth, that a Knight is of that dignitie, that he may performe this high and honourable ſeruice in his owne perſon, and although this William Furneuall was diſcended of an honourable Family, yet before he was created Knight he could not performe it.

And Sir Iohn de Argentine Chiualier performed the ſeruice of Grand Serjantie, to bee the Kings Cup-bearer at the ſame Coronation.

(m) *Vide* 1.R.2.m.45.

(m) Anne, which was the wife of Sir Iohn Haſtings Earle of Pembroke who held the Mannor of Aſhley in Norfolke of the King by Grand Serjantie, viz. to performe the Office of the Napery at his Coronation, was adiudged to make a Deputie, becauſe a woman cannot doe it in perſon, and thereupon ſhe deputed Sir Thomas Blount Knight, who performed the ſame in her right. Iohn ſonne and heire of Iohn Haſtings Earle of Pembroke, exhibited in the ſame Court his Petition, ſhewing that by his tenure he was to carrie the great Spurres of Gold before the King at his Coronation, &c. The Iudgement is, Audita & intellecta billa prædicta pro eo quod dictus Iohannes eſt infra ætatem, & in cuſtodia Domini Regis quanquam ſufficienter oſtenditur per recorda, & euidentias, quod ipſe ſeruitium prædictum facere deberet. Conſideratum extitit, quod eſſet ad voluntatem Regis, quis dictum ſeruitium iſta vice in iure ipſius Iohannis faceret, & ſuper hoc Dominus Rex aſſignauit Edmundum Comitem Marchiæ ad deferendum dicto die Coronationis prædicta calcaria in iure præfati heredis, ſaluo iure alterius cuiuſcunque. Et ſic idem Comes Marchiæ Calcaria illa prædicto die Coronationis coram ipſo Domino Rege deferebat.

Vide 1.R.2.m.45.

By which it appeareth, that the heire before he hath accompliſhed his age of one and twentie yeares, cannot performe this great and honourable ſeruice, but during his minoritie the King ſhall appoint one to performe the ſeruice.

Section 158.

46.E.3.15.a. per Finchden.

CHere Littleton ſaith that hee that holds by Grand Serjantie, doth hold by Knights

CET nota que touts q̃ teignont de Roy p grand

AND note that all which hold of the King by Grand

Ser-

Serieanty, teignont de Roy per seruice de chiualrie, & le Roy p ceo auera garde, mariage, & reliefe, mes le Roy nauera de eux Escuage, sils ne teignont de luy per Escuage.

Seriantie, hold of the King by Knights Seruice, and the King for this shall haue Ward, Mariage and Reliefe, but hee shall not haue of them Escuage, vnlesse they hold of him by Escuage.

Seruice which is so said of the effects. And therefore Littleton doth adde that the King shall haue ward, Mariage, and Reliefe, which are the effects of Knights Seruice, &c.

Sometimes in ancient records, Seruitium Militare, is called Seruitium Haubericum, or Seruitium Brigandinum, or Seruitium Loricatum. And a Haubert or Brigandine signifieth a Coat of Male.

Chap. 9. Petit Serjeantie. Sect. 159

Tenure per petit serieantie, est lou home tient sa terre de nostre Seignior le Roy, de render al Roy annuelment vn arke, ou vn espee, ou vn dagger, ou vn cuttel, ou vn launce, ou vn paier de Gants de ferre, ou vn paire de Spoures dore, ou vn sete, ou diuers setes, ou de render auters tiels petit choses touchants le guerre.

Tenure by petie Serianty is where a man holds his Land of our Soueraigne Lord the King, to yeeld to him yeerely a Bow, or a Sword, or a dagger, or a Knife, or a Lance, or a paire Gloues of Male, or a paire of gilt Spurres, or an Arrow, or diuers Arrowes, or to yeeld such other small things belonging to Warre.

De nostre seignior le roy. And so Littleton concludeth this chapter that a man cannot hold by grand Serieanty or petite Seriantie, but of the King, and of the King as of his person, and not of any honour or Mannor. And it is to bee obserued that regularly a Tenure of the King as of his person is a Tenure in Capite so called κατ' ἐξοχήν propter excellentiam, because the head is the principall part of the body, and hee that holdeth of any common person as of his person he in truth holdeth in Capite, but againe κατ' ἐξοχήν it is only in common understanding applied to the King, and that Seigniory of a common person is called a Tenure in grosse, that is by it selfe, and not lincked, or tyed to any Mannor, &c.

Britton, fol 164. Bracton, lib. 2. fol. 35. Fleta lib. 2. cap. 9. Ockam cap. quid de auibus oblatis.

And this Tenure of the King in Capite, is said (a) to be a Tenure of the King as of his Crowne, that is as he is King. (b) And therefore if one holdeth land of a common person in grosse as of his person, & not of any Mannor, &c. and this Seigniory escheateth to the King (yea though it be by attainder of treason) he holdeth of the person of the King, and not in Capite, because the originall tenure was not created by the King. And therefore it is directly said that a Tenure of the King in Capite is when the land is not holden of the King as of any Honor, Castle or Mannor, &c. But when the land is holden of the King as of his Crowne.

(a) *Bracton, lib. 2. fo. 87.*
(b) *3. E. 3. tenures. B. 94. 30 H. 8. 43. 28. H. 8. Liuery. B. 57. 29. H. 8. ibid. 58. 6. H 8. Dier, 58. Vid Lestatut de 1. E. 6. ca. 4. F. N. B. 5. K.*

Note that an Honor is the most noble Seigniorie of all others, and originally Created by the King, but may afterward be granted to others. See for the creation of an Honor. 31. H. 8. ca. 5. 32. H. 8. cap. 37. 38. 37. H. 8. cap. 18.

And it is to be obserued that a man may hold of the King in capite, or of his Crowne aswell in Socage as by Knights seruice.

¶ *De render al Roy annuelment vn arke, ou vn espee, &c.* As grand Sericantie must be done by the body of a man, So petite Serieanty hath nothing to doe with the body of a man, but to render some things touching warre, as a bowe, a sword, a dagger, a knife, a launce, a paire of gantlets of iron, or shafts and such like.

Magna Carta, cap. 27.

It is to be obserued that grand Serieantie or Knights seruice is not in law called Liberum seruitium, as Socage, is but per feodum vnius militis, &c but to finde the King so many Ships for

Regist. fo. 2. F. N. B. fo. 1.

for his passage is called liberum seruitium, and therefore it is said, Per liberum seruitium ad Inueniendum nobis quinque naues ad transitum nostrum ad mandatum nostrum. And therefore cleerely such a Tenure is neither Grand Serieantie, nor Knights Seruice, because nothing is to be done by the bodie of any man, nor in that case, touching Warre, but Ships to be found. And this is the reason that Littleton yeeldeth of the examples he doth here put: because that such a Tenant by his Tenure ought not to goe, nor to doe any thing in his person touching Warre. And herewith agreeth Bracton, Ex paruis Serjeantijs quæ non respiciunt Regem, nec Patriæ defensionem nullum competere debet maritagium nec custodiam, &c.

Bract.li.2.fo.35.

9.H.3.Gard.145.

If a man holdeth land of the King, to find an horse of such a price, and a Saddle and a bridle by fortie days, or any other time when the King goeth with his Armie against Wales, this is Petite Serieantie, and no Grand Serieantie for the cause aforesaid.

Section 160.

CEt tiel seruice nest forsque Socage en effect, pur ceo que tiel Tenant per son Tenure ne doit aler ne fayre ascun chose en son proper person, touchant le guerre mes de render & paier annualment certaine choses al Roy, sicõe home doyt payer vn Rent.

And such Seruice is but Socage in effect, because that such Tenant by his Tenure ought not to goe nor doe any thing in his proper person touching the war, but to render & pay yearly certaine things to the King, as a man ought to pay a Rent.

¶ Tiel seruice nest forsque Socage, &c. But as it hath beene sayd, the dignitie of the person of the King, giueth the name of Petit Serjeantie, which in case of a common persõ should be called plain socage ab affectu: for it shal haue such effects or incidents as belong to Socage, and neither ward nor marriage, &c. for they belong to Knights Seruice.

9.H.3.Gard.145.

Mag.Chart ca.28.
Vid.Sat.de Wardu & Relcuiis. 28.E.1.

Of this Tenure the great Charter in the person of the King saith thus, Nos non habebimus custodiam hæredis, &c. occasione alicuius paruæ Serjeantiæ quam tenet de nobis per seruitium reddendo nobis cultellos, sagittas, &c.

Section 161.

CEt nota que hõe ne poyt tener per graund Serjeantie, ne per petit Serjeanty, si non de Roy, &c.

And note that a man cannot hold by grãd Serjeantie, nor by petite Serjeantie, but of the King, &c.

¶ Of this sufficient hath beene sayd before, sauing that parua Serjeantia is only appropriate to this Tenure.

Vid.Sect.1.

Chap.10. Tenure en Burgage. Sect.162.

CTenurẽ en Burgage est, lou auntient Burgh est, de que le Roy est Seignior, &

¶ Tenure in Burgage is where an antiẽt Burrough is, of the which the king is lord,

Burgage, in Latyne Burgagium, is derived of this word Burgus, which is Vicus, Pagus, or Villa, a Towne, and it is called a Burgh, because it sendeth Burgesses to Parliament.

Bracton lib.3.Tract.2.
Britton fol.164.
Mirror.cap.2.§.18.
Lib.10 fol.123.124. The Maior of Lynne Case.
40.Ass.p.27. 43.E.3.32.
21.E.4.53. & 54.
21.H.7.15. 2.E.3.cap.3.

(b) Bracton lib.3.fol.124.
Fleta lib.1.cap.47.

Of Burghs some be incorporate, and some not, and some be walled, and some not. (b) It

ceux

ceux que ont Tenements deins le Burgh teignont del Roy lour Tenemẽts que chescun Tenant pur son Tenement doit payer al Roy un certain Rent per an, &c. Et tiel Tenure nest forsque Tenure en Socage.

and they that haue tenements within the Burrough, hold of the King their tenements, that euerie Tenant for his Tenement ought to pay to the King a certaine rent by yeare, &c. and such Tenure is but Tenure in Socage.

was in former times taken for those Companies of ten Families, which were one anothers pledge, and therfore a Pledg in the Saxon tongue a Borhoe, whereof (some take it) that a Burgh came, whereof also commeth headborough, or Borowhead, Capitalis Plegius, a Chiefe Pledge, viz. the chiefe man of the Borhoe, whom Bracton calleth Frithburgus, and hereof also commeth Burghbote, which as Fleta saith, signifieth Quietanciam reparationis murorum ciuitatis aut Burgi.

Euerie Citie is a Burgh, but euerie Burgh is not a Citie, whereof more shall be said hereafter. And the termination of this word Burgagium, (as before hath beene noted) signifieth the seruice whereby the Burgh is holden. And of this word (Burgh) two antient and noble Families take their names, viz. de Burgo, and de Burgo caro, Burchier.

¶ *De que le Roy est Seignior.* But it may be holden of another as by that which immediatly followeth appeareth. F.N.B. 64.d.

Sect. 163.

CEt mesme le manner est, lou un auter Seigniour Espiritual ou Temporall, est Seignior de tiel Burgh, & les Tenants de Tenements en tiel Burgh teignont de lour seignior a payer, chescun de eux un annual Rẽt.

AND the same manner is, where another Lord Spiritual or Temporall is Lord of such a Burrough, and the Tenants of the Tenements in such a Burrough hold of their Lord, to pay each of them yearely an annuall Rent.

¶ This is euident, and needeth no explanation, onely this by the way is to be obserued, That Bishops being Lords of Parliament, haue not beene called Lords Spirituall so lately, as some haue imagined. 16.R.2.ca.5. 1.H.4.ca.3.&c.

Section 164.

CEt est appel tenure en Burgage, pur ceo que les Tenements deins le Burgh sont tenus del Seigniour del Burgh per certaine rent, &c. Et est ascauoire que les antient villes appel Burghs

AND it is called Tenure in Burgage, for that the Tenemẽts within the Burrough be holden of the Lord of the Burrough by certaine rent, &c. And it is to wit, that the antient Townes called Burroughs, bee the

¶ P*er certaine Rent, &c.* By (&c.) here is implied fealtie, or other seruice, as to repaire the house of the Lord, &c.

¶ *Les antient Villes appel Burghes.*

So as a Burgh is an antient Towne holden of the King or any other lord, which sendeth Burgesses to the Parliament.

And it is to be obserued, that Burgh and Burie haue all one signification, as Canterburie, Burie Saint Edmond, Sudburie, Salisburie, Banbury, Heytesbury, Malmesburie, Shaftesbury,

sont les pluis ancient villes que sont deins Engleterre, car ceux villes q̄ ore sont cities, ou counties, en auncient temps fueront burghes, & appelles burges, car de tielx auncient villes, appelles Burghes, veignont les Burgesses al Parliament, quant le Roy ad summon son parliament.

most ancient towns that be within England, for the Townes that now bee Cities or Counties, in old time were Boroughes, and called Boroughs, for of such old Townes called Boroughes, come the Burgesses of the Parliament, to the Parliament, when the King hath summoned his Parliament.

Shaftesbury, Teukesbury, and others send Burgesses to the Parliament, Vide pro Villis, Parochijs & Hamlettis postea, Sect. 171.

¶ *Cities*. Ciuitas, whereof commeth the word Citie. A Citie is a Borough incorporate, which hath, or haue had a Bishop and though the Bishopricke bee dissolued, yet the Citie remayneth.

Lamb. fo. 125.

In the time of William the Conquerour it is declared in these words, Item nullum mercatum, vel forum sit, nec fieri permittatur nisi in ciuitatibus regni nostri, & in Burgis clausis & muro vallatis & castellis, & locis tutissimis, vbi consuetudines regni nostri, & jus nostrum comune, & dignitates coronæ nostræ quæ constitutæ sunt à bonis prædecessoribus nostris deperire non possunt, nec defraudari, nec violari, sed omnia rite, & per judicium & justitiam fieri debent: & ideo castella & burgi & civitates sunt & fundatæ & edificatæ scilicet ad tuitionem gentium, & populorum regni, & ad defensionem regni, & idcirco observari debent cum omni libertate & integritate, & ratione. So as by this it appeareth that Cities were instituted for three purposes: First, Ad consuetudines regni nostri, & jus nostrum commune & dignitates coronæ nostræ conseruand'. 2. Ad tuitionem gentium & populorum regni. And thirdly, Ad defensionem regni. For conseruation of Lawes, whereby euery man enioyeth his owne in peace: for tuition and defence of the Kings subiects, and for keeping the Kings peace in time of sudden vprores, And lastly for defence of the Realme against outward or inward hostility.

Mirror, cap. 2 §. 18. Britton, fo. 87.

Civitas & vrbs in hoc differunt, quod incolæ dicuntur civitas, vrbs verò complectitur ædificia, but with vs the one is commonly taken for the other. Villeins sont coultivers de fiefe demurrants in villages vpland, car de ville est dit villen, & de Boroughes Burgesses, & de cities, citizens.

Mich. 7. R. 1. Rot. 1. (which was in anno Dom. 1195.) in 42 Ass. of darreine presentment for the Church of St. Peters in Cambridge.

Euery Borough encorporate that had a Bishop within time of memory is a Citie, albeit the Bishopricke be dissolued, as Westminster had of late a Bishop, and therefore it yet remaines a Citie. The Burghe of Cambridge, an ancient Citie, as it appeareth by a iudiciall Record (which is to be preferred before all others) where Mos civitatis Cantabrigiæ is found by the oath of 12. men the recognitors of that assise, which (omitting many others) I thought good to mention, in remembrance of my loue and dutie Almæ Matri Academiæ Cantabrigiæ.

There be within England two Archbishopricks, and 23. other Bishopricks therefore so many Cities there be, and Cambridge and Westminster being added, there are in all 27. Cities within this Realme, and may be more, then at this time I can call to memory

It is not necessary that a City be a County of it selfe, as Cambridge, Elye, Westminster, &c are Cities, but are no Counties of themselues, but are part of the Counties where they be.

¶ *Counties*, or Shires, the one taken from the French, the other from the Saxon, in Latyn Comitatus. Counties are certaine circuits or parts of the kingdome, into the which the whole Realme was diuided for the better gouernment thereof, so as there is no land, but it is within some County. And euery of them is gouerned by a yearly officer which we call a Shireue. Which name is compounded of these two Saxon words Shire and reue, (i) præpositus or præfectus comitatus; but hereof more hereafter in his proper place shalbe spoken. There be in England 41. Counties, and in wales twelue.

Lib. 10. fo. 123. 124. Vide Devant, Sect. 97.

¶ *Veignont les Burgesses al Parliament, &c.* Parliament is the highest, and most honourable and absolute Court of Justice of England consisting of the King, the Lords of Parliament, and the Commons. And againe, the Lords are here deuided into two sorts, viz. Spirituall and Temporall; And Cōmons are deuided into three parts, viz into Knights of Shires or Counties, citizens out of Cities, and Burgesses out of Boroughs. The words of the writ to the Shriffe for the election being, Duos milites gladijs cinctos magis idoneos, & discretos comitatus tui, & de qualibet civitate comitatus tui duos ciues, & de

qualibet

quolibet Burgo duos Burgenses de discretioribus, & magis sufficientibus, &c. All which haue voyces, and suffrages in Parliament; You shall reade in the Parliament Rolls that (as hath beene said) there is Lex & consuetudo parliamenti, quæ quidem lex quærenda est ab omnibus, ignorata à multis, & cognita à paucis. Of the members of this Court some be by discent, as ancient Noble men, some by Creation, as Nobles newly created, some by succession, as Bishops, some by Election, as Knights, Citizens, and Burgesses.

Vid Sect. 3.

It is called Parliament because euery member of that Court should syncerely and discreetly Parler la ment for the generall good of the Cōmon wealth. Which name it hath also in Scotland, and this name before the Conquest was vsed in (a) the time of Edward the Confessor, William the Conquerour, &c. It was anciently before the Conquest called Michel Sinoth michel gemote, alsa Witenage mote, that is to say, the great Court or meeting of the King and of all the wise men, sometime of the King with the counsell of his Bishops, Nobles, and wisest of his people. This Court the Frenchman calleth Les Estates, or Lassemble des Estates.) In Germany it is called a Diet: for those other Courts in France that are called Parliaments, they are but ordinary Courts of Iustice, and (as Paulus Iouius affirmeth) were first established by vs.

4.H.8.cap.8.
(a) *Treatise de modo tenend. Parliam. 21.E.1 fo.60.a. Iohannes de Rupicella tempore regis Iohannis. Poll.Virgil.lib.3.tempore H.1. W.1. 3.E.1.in the title.*

The King of England is armed with diuers councells, one whereof is called Commune concilium, and that is the Court of Parliament, and so it is legally called in writs and iudiciall proceedings Commune concilium regni Angliæ. And another is called (b) Magnum concilium: this is sometime applied to the vpper house of Parliament, and sometime out of Parliament time to the Peeres of the Realme, Lords of Parliament, who are called Magnum concilium regis, for the proofe whereof take one (c) Record, for many in the fift yeare of King H.4. at what time there was an exchange made betweene the King, and the Earle of Northumberland, whereby the King promiseth to deliuer to the Earle lands to the value, &c. Per aduice & assent des estates de son realme & de son Parliament (parensi que Parliament soit devant le feast de St.Lucy) ou auterment per advice de son graund councell, & auters estates de son Realme, que le Roy ferra assembler devant le dit feast, in case que le Parliament ne soit. And herewith agreeth the Act of Parliament in 37 E.3.cap 18. where it is said, before the Chancellour, Treasurer, and great Councell. Thirdly, (as euery man knoweth) the King hath a priuie Councell for matters of state, (as for example) (d) Henricus de bello monte Baro de magno & de privato consilio regis juratus; and many others before and after. The fourth Councell of the King are his Iudges of the Law for Law matters, and this appeareth frequently in our (e) bookes, and must be intended, when it is spoken generally by the Councell it is to bee vnderstood Secundum subiectam materiam, for example if it be legall, then by the Kings Councell of the Law, viz. his Iudges.

(b) *Bracton, lib.1.ca.2. Regist.280.*
(c) *27.Aug.5.H.4.*
(d) *In Dorso Claus. 16.E.2.M.5.*
(e) *43.Ass.15 27.H.6.5. 1 R.3.11 Regist.191.122. 123. 4.E.3.2.39 E.3.35. 3.Ass.15.19.E.3. iudgement 174.*

Now for the Antiquitie of this high Court of Parliament, whereof Littleton here speaketh; It appeareth that diuers Parliaments haue beene holden long before and vntill the time of the Conquerour, which be in print, and many more appearing in ancient Records and Manuscripts. (f) Le Roy Alfred assembler' ses Comities, &c & ordeina pur vsage perpetual que deux foitz per an ou pluis sovent pur mister in temps de peace se assemblerent a' Londres a Parlementer sur le guidament del people de Dieu, & coment soy garderent de pecher, viueront en quiet, & receiueront droit per vsages & sanits judgements per ceste estate se fieront plusors ordinances per plusors Roys iesque a temps le Roy que ore est, que fuit le Roy E.1. The conclusion of that great Parliament holden by King Ethelstan at Gratcly is very remarkeable, which I haue seene in these words: All this was enacted in that great Synod or Councell at Gratcly; whereat was the Archbishop *Wolfehelme* with all the Noblemen and wise men which King *Ethelstan* called together.

W.1.ca.1. Lastat de templar. 16.R.2.stat. de Præmunire. See the same published by Mr. Lambert.
(f) *Mirror.ca.1.§.2.*
Vid. Statutes de 4.E.3. ca.14. & 36.E 3.ca.10.

There haue beene in the time of, and since, the Conquest in the raignes of H.1. King Stephen, H.2. R.1 King Iohn, H.3. &c. 280. Sessions of Parliament, and at euery Session diuers Acts of Parliament made, no small number whereof are not in print.

Mirr.ca.2.§.4.7 10.14. cap.4.de defaults. & cap.de Homicide.cap.1 §.13.ca 4 de Pagns. Ockam quod cum Ven. Math.Pariss.212.213.

The iurisdiction of this Court is so transcendent, that it maketh, inlargeth, diminisheth, abrogateth, repealeth and reuiueth Lawes, Statutes, Acts and Ordinances concerning matters Ecclesiasticall, Capitall, Criminall, Common, Ciuill, Martiall, Maritine and the rest. None can begin, continue or dissolue the Parliament but by the Kings authority. Of which Court it is said (a) Que il est de tresgrand honor & Iustice, de que nul doit imaginer chose dishonorable. (b) Habet rex curiam suam in concilio suo in Parliamentis suis, presentibus prælatis, comitibus, baronibus, proceribus, & alijs viris peritis vbi terminatæ sunt dubitationes judiciorum, & novis injurijs emersis nova constituuntur remedia, & vnicuique iustitia prout meruerit retribuetur ibidem. But this properly doth belong to the Iurisdiction of Courts, and therefore this little taste hereof shall suffice.

(a) *Pl.Com.398.b. Doctor & Stud.ca.55.fo.164.*
(b) *Fleta lib.2.ca.2. Fortescue de laudibus legum Angliæ. Bracton, lib.1.ca.2.*

Sect. 165.

¶ Item, p̄r greinder part tielx burghes ont diuers customes & vsages que nont pas auters villes. Car ascuns burghes ont tiel custome, q̄ si home ad issue plusors fits & morust, le puisne fits enheritet touts les tenements que fuer a son pere deins m̄ le burgh come heire a son pere per force de custome. Et tiel custome est appel Burgh English.

ALso for the greater part such Boroughes haue diuers customes and vsages, which bee not had in other towns, for some Boroughes haue such a custome, that if a man haue issue many sonnes and dyeth, the youngest son shall inherit all the tenements which were his fathers within the same Borough as heire vnto his father, by force of the custome, the which is called Borough English.

¶ *Customes & vsages.* Consuetudo, is one of the maine triangles of the Lawes of England, those Lawes being deuided into Common Law, Statute Law and Custome. Of which it is said, * that Consuetudo quandoque pro lege servatur, in partibus vbi fuerit more vtentium approbata, & vicem legis obtinet, longęvi enim temporis vsus & consuetudinis non est vilis authoritas (c) Longa possessio (sicut jus) parit jus possidendi, & tollit actionem vero domino.

(*) *Bract.lib.1.ca.3.fol.2.*

(c) *Idem lib.2.fol.52.*

Of euery custome there be two essentiall parts, Time and Vsage, Time out of minde, (as shall be said hereafter) and continuall and peaceable Vsage without lawfull interruption.

¶ *Que nont pas auters villes.* It is necessary to bee knowne what customes may bee alledged in an vpland towne which is neither Citie nor Borough, * In an vpland towne, that is neither in Citie nor Borough, such a Custome to deuise lands cannot be alledged. Neither in an vpland towne can there be a custome of Borough English or Gauelkinde, but these are customes which may be in Cities or Boroughes. (d) Also if lands be within a Mannor, Fee, or Seigniory, the same by the custome of the Mannor, Fee, or Seigniory may be deuisable, or of the nature of Gauelkinde or Borough English. * But an vpland Towne may alledge a custome to haue a way to their Church, or to make By-lawes for the reparations of the Church, the well ordering of the Commons and such like things. And it is to bee obserued, that in speciall cases a custome may be (e) alledged within a Hamlet, a Towne, a Burgh, a Citie, a Mannor, an Honour, an Hundred, and a Countie: but a custome cannot be alledged generally within the kingdome of England, for that is the Common Law.

(*) 44 *E.3.33.* 40.*Ass.4.27.41.21.E.4.54* 43.*E.3.32.*

(d) 21.*E.4.53.54.*

(*) 21.*E.4.54.* 15.*E.4.29.* 11.*H.7.14.* 44.*E.3.18.* 21.*H.7.40.*

(e) *Bract.lib.4.271.* 34.*E.1.detinue 60.* 17.*E.2.detinue 58.* 3.*E.3.dett.156.* 30.*E.3.25* 39.*E.3.6.9.10.* 31.*E.3.render 6.* 17.*E.3.27* 21.*E.4.28.* 22.*E.4.8.* 7.*E.3.51.* 39.*E.3.23.* 34.*H.8.Dier.54* *F.N.B.122.* 5.*E.3.tresp.13.*

¶ *Le puisne fits enheritera.* And yet by some customes the youngest brother shall inherit, for Consuetudo loci est obseruanda.

¶ *Touts les terres ou tenements:* Either in fee simple, fee taile, or any other inheritance. If lands of the nature of Borough English be letten to a man and his heires during the life of I.S. and the Lessee dieth, the youngest sonne shall enioy it.

¶ *Borough English;* So called because this custome was first, (as some hold) in England.

Vide Glanuil.lib.7.cap.3.9.

Sect. 166.

¶ Item, en ascun burghes per le custome feme auera pur sa dower touts les tenements q̄ fueront a sa baron, &c.

ALso in some Boroughes by custome, the wife shall haue for her dower all the tenements which were her husbands.

¶ AND this is called Frank banke, Francus bancus. Consuetudo est in partibus illis, quod vxores maritorum defunctorum habeant francum bancum suum de terris Sockmannorum tenent' nomine dotis.

Bract.lib.4.tract.6 ca.13. *F.N.B.150.e.* *Pl.Com.413.*

¶ *Que fueront a sa baron, &c.* Here is implied by (&c.) that in some places the wife shall haue the moity of the lands of her husband so long as she liues vnmaried, as in Gavelkinde. And of lands in Gauelkinde a man shall be Tenant by the Curtesie without hauing of any issue. In some places the widow shall haue the whole; or halfe Dum sola & casta vixerit, and the like. (l) F.N.B. 150. 10. E. 3. aide. 129.

Sect. 167.

Item, en ascuns burghes per le custome hõe poit deuiser per son testament ses terres & tenements que il ad en fee simple deins mesme l'burgh al temps de s morant, & per force de tiel deuise, celuy a que tiel deuise est fait, apres le mort le deuisor poit enter ẽ l's tenements issint a luy deuises, a auer & tener a luy solonque la forme & effect del deuise, sans ascun liuerie d' seisin destre fait a luy, &c.

ALso in some Boroughs by the custome, a man may deuise by his Testament his Lands and Tenements which hee hath in Fee simple within the same Borough at the time of his death, and by force of such deuise, hee to whom such deuise is made after the death of the deuisor, may enter into the Tenements so to him deuised, to haue & to hold to him after the forme & effect of the deuise, without any liuerie of seisin thereof to bee made to him, &c.

DEuiser. This is a French word and signifieth sermocinari to speake, for testamentum est testatio mentis, & index animi sermo. So as a deuiser per son testament, is to speake by his Testament what his minde is to haue done after his decease.

Per son testament. Testamentum est (m) duplex 1. in scriptis. 2. nuncupatiuum seu sine scriptis. And in some Cities and Boroughs Lands may (n) passe as chattels by will nuncupatiue or paroll without writing. Re-uera (o) terminatum est quod potest legari vt catallum tam hæreditas quam perquisitum per Barones London, & Burgenses Oxon. ideo verum est quod in Burgis non iacet assisa mortis antecessoris. But in Law most commonly, Vltima voluntas in scriptis, is used where Lands or Tenements are deuised, and testamentum when it concerneth chattels.

(m) Vide Sect. 586.
(n) Britton. fol. 164. 212. b.
(o) Bract. lib. 4. fol. 272. Fleta lib. 5. cap. 5. & lib. 2. cap. 50.

¶ *Ses terres ou tenements.* And by the same custome he may deuise a Rent out of the same Lands and Tenements.

¶ *Que il ad en fee simple.* For Lands in taile are not deuisable by will, and therefore he in this place necessarily added (que il ad en fee simple) and purposely omitted the same in the clause concerning Borough English, because there an estate taile is included. 4. E. 3. 53. 7. H. 6. 1. 14 H. 8. 5. 22. Ass. 78. Abbr. Ass. 118. b. 4. E. 2. mordanc. 39. 49. E. 3. 17. F. N. B. 196. 21. H. 6. 38. a. 7. E. 2. ti. mordanc.

¶ *Poet enter.* Note the custome of a Citie or Borough concerning the deuise of lands is, Quod liceat vnicuique ciui siue burgensi, &c. eiusdem ciuitatis siue burgi tenementa sua in eadem ciuitate siue burgo in testamento suo in vltima voluntate sua, tanquam catalla sua legare cuicunque voluerit, &c. (p) Now if a man deuiseth either by speciall name or generally, goods or chattels reall or personall, and dieth, the deuisee cannot take them without the assent of the Executors. But when a man is seised of lands in fee, and deuiseth the same in fee, in taile, for life, or for yeares, the deuisee shall enter, for in that case the Executors haue no medling therewith. And in the case of a deuise by will of lands, whereof the Deuisor is seised in fee, the freehold or interest in Law is in (q) the Deuisee before hee doth enter, and in that case nothing (r) (hauing regard to the estate or interest deuised) discendeth to the heire. But if the heire of Deuisor entreth and holdeth the Deuisee out, hee may either enter as Littleton here saith, or haue his writ called ex graui quærela, and this writ (without any particular vsage) is incident to the custome to deuise, for otherwise, if a discent were cast before the deuisee did enter, the deuisee should haue no remedie. After an actuall possession this writ lyeth not, for then the deuisee may haue his ordinary remedie by the Common Law.

F. N. B 199. Regist. in ex graui Querela.
(p) 2. H. 6. 16. 27. H. 6. 8. 2. E. 4. 13. 21. E. 4. 21. 4. H. 7. 16.
(q) 4. Mar. Br. tit. deuise 49.
(r) Regist. fol. 244. 39. Ass. pl. 6. 3. E. 3. deuise 12. 29. Ass. 31. 34. E. 3. ut form. don. Pl. post emo. 30. H. 8. deuise 28. F. N. B. 198. 199. &c. Britton. fol. 212. b.

(s) 27.H.8.cap.10. Britton,fol.212.78.b.164. Vide. bere in this Section. 32.H.8.ca 2. 34.H.8.cap.5. (t) Vide lib.3.fol.25. &c. in Butler & Bakers case. Lib.6.fol.16. & 76. Lib.8.fol.84.85. Lib.9.133. Lib.10.82.83.84. Lib.11. fol.24. Lib.1.fol.25.a. (u) Dier 4. & 5.Ph. & Mar.155.an.6.Eliz.Dalison. Pasch.20.Eliz. betweene Barker and his wife plaintiffe and William Long defendant in a Writt of partition. Bendloes adiudged.

And well said Littleton that Lands and Tenements were deuisable in Burghes by custome, for that (s) at the Common Law no Lands or Tenements were deuisable by any last will and Testament, nor ought to be transferred from one to another, but by solemne liuerie of seisin, matter of record, or sufficient writing, but as Littleton here saith, that by certaine priuate customes in some Burghes they are deuisable. But now since Littleton wrote by the Statutes of 32. and 34. H.8. Lands and Tenements are generally deuisable by the last will in writing of the tenant in fee simple, whereby the ancient (t) Common Law is altered, whereupon many difficult questions, and most commonly disherison of heires (when the Deuisors are pinched by the messengers of death) doe arise and happen. But (u) these Statutes take not away the custome to deuise, whereof Littleton speaketh: for though Lands deuisable by custome be holden by Knights Seruice, yet may the Owner deuise the whole Land by force of the custome, and that shall stand good against the heire for the whole. But the deuise of lands holden by Knights Seruice by force of the Statutes is utterly void for a third, and the same shall discend to the heire. If he hath any Lands holden by Knights Seruice in Capite, and Lands in Socage, he can deuise but two parts of the whole, but if he hold Lands by Knights Seruice of the King, and not in Capite, or of a meane Lord, and hath also Lands in Socage, he may deuise two parts of his Land holden by Knights Seruice, and all his Socage lands. If he holds any Land of the King in Capite, and by Act executed in his life time he conueyeth any part of his Lands to the vse of his wife, or of his children, or payment of his debts, though it bee with power of reuocation, hee can deuise by his will (x) no more, but to make vp the Land so conueyed two parts of the whole. And if the Lands so conueyed amount to two parts or more, then hee can deuise nothing by his will. But if hee hath land only that is holden in Socage, then he may deuise by his will all his Socage lands; so as it is apparant that the benefit of the Lords was more carefully prouided for, then the good of the heire. But if a man holding some Land of the King by Knights Seruice in Capite, conuey two parts of his Land to the vse of his wife for life, now (as hath beene said) hee can deuise no part of the residue, but yet he may by his will deuise the reuersion of the two parts so conueyed to his wife: for the intention of the Act is to giue power to dispose two parts intirely.

(x) Lib 6.fol.17.18. Sir Edw. Cleres case. Lib.3.fol.34.b. Butler & Bakers case.

Lib.10.fol.80 81. Leon.Loueyes case.

Leon.Loueyes case, & Butler & Bakers case. Vbi supra.

If the Deuisor leaue a full third part of the Land immediatly to discend in Fee simple or in taile, he may deuise the other two parts in Fee simple if a third part be not left, it shall be made vp according to the Act. But hereditaments that are not of any yearely value, as bona & catalla felonum & fugitiuorum, waifes, estrayes, and the like can neither be left to discend for any part of the third part, or deuised as part of the two parts. But yet if such Franchises of vncertaine value be holden of the King in Capite, they shall restraine the deuise of all his lands and make it void for a third part. So it is if a man hath a reuersion expectant vpon an estate taile dry & fruitles holden of the King by Knights Seruice in Capite, yet that shall restraine him to deuise but two parts of his lands only. And where the Statute speakes of a remainder, it is to be intended only of such a remainder, as may draw ward & Mariage by the Common Law. As if a reuersion vpon a state for life be granted to one for life, the remainder in fee, during the life of the grantee for life it is not within the Statute, but if he dieth this is such a remainder, as is within the Statute, although it be dry and fruitlesse. If a gift in taile or a lease for life be made, the remainder in fee, this remainder in fee is not within the Statute. But if a man hath Lands holden by Knights Seruice in Capite in possession, reuersion, or remainder, and also seised of Socage Land, and deuise by his will all his lands, and after he selleth away the Capite Land, or that land is recouered from him, the will is good for the whole Socage land. The values both of the third part, and the two parts of the lands shall be taken as they happen to be at the time of the death of the Deuisor, for then his will takes effect.

Leon. Loueyes case. Vbi supra, fol.81.

Lib.8.fol.84.85. Sir Richard Pexhals case. Lib.3.fol.33. Butler & Bakers case.

He that holds by Knights Seruice in chiefe deuiseth by his will a Rent, common or other profit as shall amount to the value of two parts out of all his Lands, this Rent issueth only out of the two parts, & the third part is free of it. And if he hath lands holden by Knights Seruice, & not in Capite, he may charge two parts of the Knight Seruice Land as is aforesaid, and all his Socage Land, &c. And if he hath only Socage Land, hee may by his will charge it at his pleasure, so as the Kings end Lords third part is free, and the heires two parts charged, and this is only only by force of the Statute of 34 H.8.

Lib.6.fol.17.18. in Sir Edw. Cleres case.

If a man make a feoffment in fee of his Lands holden by Knights Seruice to the vse of such person and persons, and of such estate and estates, &c. as he shall appoint by his will, in this Case by operation of Law, the vse and state vests in the Feffor, and he is seised of a qualified fee. In this case, if the Feoffor limit Estates by his will, by force, and according to his power, there the vses and estates growing out of the feoffment are good for the whole, and the last will is but directorie. But in that case if the Feoffor had deuised the land (as Owner thereof) without any reference to the feoffment and power thereby giuen then taking effect by the will, it is void for a third part. But if he had formerly conueyed two parts to the vse of his wife, &c. and after deuised the residue by his will without any reference to his power by the

feoffee

feoffment, yet this will ſhall enure to declare the vſe vpon the feoffement, becauſe hee had no power as Owner of the Land to deuiſe any part of it. But if the feoffement had beene made to the vſe of his laſt will, although he deuiſeth the Land with reference to the feoffment, yet it taketh effect only by the will, and not by the feoffement. All which and many other points of intricate and abſtruſe learning you ſhall more largely reade in my Reports.

¶ *Sauns aſcun liuerie de ſeiſin deſte fait a luy, &c.* For in his life time Liuery of ſeiſin could not be made becauſe his will is ambulatorie till his death, and no eſtate paſſeth during his life, neither can Liuery be made after his deceaſe, for then it commeth too late. 40.Aſſ.38.

Here (&c.) implyeth that the deuiſe is good without any Atturnement of any Leſſee or Tenant.

Section 168.

¶ Nota coment que home ne poit granter ne doner ſes tenements a ſa feme, durant le couerture, pur ceo que ſa feme & luy ne ſont forſque vn perſon en ley, uncore per tiel cuſtome il poit deuiſer per teſtament, ſes tenements a ſa feme, a auer & tener a luy en fee ſimple, ou en fee taile, pur term de vie ou pur terme des ans, pur ceo que tiel deuiſe ne priſt effect forſque apres la mort le deuiſor, car touts deuiſes ne preignont effect forſque apres la mort le deuiſor. Et ſi home fait a diuers temps diuers teſtaments, & diuers deuiſes, &c. uncore le darrein deuiſe & volunt faitz luy eſtoiera, & lauters ſont voides.

ALſo though a man may not grant nor giue his tenements to his Wife during the couerture, for that his Wife and hee bee but one perſon in the Law, yet by ſuch cuſtome hee may deuiſe by his Teſtament his tenements to his wife, to haue and to hold to her in Fee ſimple, or in Fee taile, or for tearme of life, or yeares; for that ſuch deuiſe taketh no effect, but after the death of the Deuiſor. And if a man at diuers times make diuers Teſtaments, and diuers deuiſes, &c. yet the laſt deuiſe and will made him, ſhall ſtand and the other are voyd.

¶ *Home ne poet graunter ne doner ſes tenements a ſa feme, &c.* This opinion is (a) cleere, for by no conueyance at the Common Law a man could during the couerture either in poſſeſſion, reuerſion or remainder, limit an eſtate to his wife. But a man may by his deed couenant with others to ſtand ſeiſed to the vſe of his wife, or make a Feoffement or other Conueyance to the vſe of his wife, and now the ſtate is executed to ſuch vſes by the Statute (b) of 27.H.8. for an vſe is but a truſt and confidence, which by ſuch a meane might be limited by the huſband to the wife. But a man cannot couenant with his wife to ſtand ſeiſed to her vſe, becauſe he cannot couenant with her for the reaſon that Littleton here yeeldeth. (a) 4.H.7. (b) 27.H.8.cap.10.

¶ *Durant le couerture.* That is during the continuance of the Marriage. For to couer in Engliſh is Tegere in Latine, and is ſo called, for that the wife is ſub poteſtate viri, and ſhe is diſabled to contract with any without the conſent of the huſband. (c) Omnia quæ ſunt vxoris ſunt ipſius viri, non habet vxor poteſtatē ſui ſed vir. Bract.lib.2.ca.15.

¶ *Vn perſon en ley.* Vir & vxor ſunt quaſi vnica perſona quia caro vna, & ſanguis vnus, res licet ſit propria vxoris, vir tamen eius cuſtos, cum ſit caput mulieris. Idem lib.5.tract.5.cap.25.

If Ceſtey que vſe had deuiſed, that his wife ſhould ſell his land, and made her executrix and died, and ſhe tooke another huſband, ſhe might ſell the land to her huſband, for ſhe did it in auter droit, and her huſband ſhould be in by the deuiſor. 10.H.7.20.

¶ *Per teſtament.* Teſtamentum is (as is ſaid before) teſtatio mentis, and is fauourably to be expounded according to the meaning of the Teſtator. In contractibus

tractibus benigna, in testamentis benignior, in restitutionibus benignissima interpretatio facienda est.

(d) 4.E.2.Tit.Deuise 23. (e) 44. Ass.p.36. 44.E.3 33 18.E.3.8. (f) Britton 264.

¶ *A son feme.* And Littleton himselfe yeeldeth the reason, (d) because the deuise doth not take effect till after the decease of the deuisor. And in some (e) places the custome is generall, that he may deuise any lands, &c. In some (f) places Lands only which the Deuisor purchased. In some place that he may deuise any estate, in some places for life only, &c.

But albeit the last will doth not take effect untill after his decease, yet if a Feme Couert bee seised of Lands in fee, she cannot deuise the same to her husband, because at the making of her will she had no power being sub potestate viri to deuise the same, and the Law intendeth it should be done by coertion of her husband.

2.H.5.8. 2.R.3 22.

¶ *Diuers testaments.* For Voluntas testatoris est ambulatoria vsque ad mortem (as hath beene said before) and the latter will doth countermand the first. And it is truly said that the first grant, and the last will is of greatest force.

¶ *Diuers deuises, &c.* Hereby (&c.) is to bee understood aswell deuises of Chattels reall or personall, as of freehold and inheritance. Also that in one will where there be diuers deuises of one thing the last deuise taketh place. Cum duo inter se pugnantia reperiuntur in testamento vltimum ratum est.

Sect. 169.

¶ ITem p tiel custome hõe poyt deuiser per son testament que ses Executors poyent aliener & vender ses tenemẽts que il ad en Fee simple, pur c̃tain summ̃ de money a distributer p̃ son alme. En cest cas, coment que le deuisor deuie seisie de les tenements, et les tenements discẽdont a son heire: uncore les executors apres l' mort lour testator, poient vender les tenẽts issint a eux deuises, & ouste l' hẽ, & ent fait feoffmt, alienation, & estate p fait, ou sãs fait a eux a q̃ux l' vend est fait. Et issint pois veier icy un cas ou hõe poit fair loial estat, & uncor il nauoit riens en les

ALso by such custome a man may deuise by his Testament, that his Executours may alien and sell the Tenements that he hath in Fee simple, for a certaine sum, to distribute for his Soule: In this case though the deuisor die seised of the tenemẽts and the tenements discend vnto his heire, yet the executors after the death of the testator may sell the tenemẽts so deuised thẽ, & put out the heire, and thereof make a feoffement, alienation, and estate by Deed, or without deed, to them to whom the sale is made. And so may yee here see a case where a Man may make a lawfull estate,

¶ *QVe ses executors poent aliener ou vender ses tenements.* And that which in Littletons time a man might doe by custome in some particular places he may now doe by the Statutes of 32. & 34. H 8 generally.

* 32.H.8.cap.2. 34.H.8.cap.5.

¶ *Les Executors apres le mort lour testator poient vender.* Here it appeareth, that the Executors hauing but a power, (as Littleton putteth the case) to sell, they must all ioyne in the sale. Then put the case that one dieth, it is regularly true, that being but a bare authoritie, the suruiuors cannot sell. But if a man deuiseth his land to A. for terme of life, and that after his decease, his lands shall be sould by his executors generally, (as Littleton here putteth his case) and make three or foure Executors, and during the life of A. one of the Executors dieth, and then A. dieth, the other two or three Executors may sell, because the land could not be sould before, and the Plurall number of his Executors remaine. But if they had beene named by their names, as by I.S. I.N. I.D. and I. G. his Executors,

49.E.3.16. 29.Ass.17. 39.Ass.17. 9.H.6.24. 15.H.7.12.21. 14.H.8.6. 30.H.8. Tit.Deuise Br.31. 2.Eliz. Dier 177.

les Tenements al temps del estate fait. Et le cause est, pur ceo que la custome & vsage ad este tiel. Quia consuetudo ex certa causa rationabili vsitata priuat communem Legem.

& yet hee hath naught in the Tenements at the time of the estate made: and the cause is, for that that the custome & vsage is such. *For a custome vsed vpon a certain reasonable cause depriueth the cõmon law.*

then in that case the suruiuors could not sell the same, because the words of the Testator could not be satisfied; * I my self knew this case adiudged*: A special verdict was found, that A. was seised of certaine lands in fee, and deuised the same in taile, and if the Donee died without issue, that his said land should bee sould by his sonnes in Law, (he in truth hauing fiue sons in Law) one of his sonnes in Law died in the life of the Donee, and after the Donee died without issue, and then the foure of the sonnes in Law sould the land, and it was adiudged that the sale was good, because they were named generally by his sonnes in Law, and the Lands could not be sould by them all. And the words of the Will, in a benigne interpretation are satisfied in the plurall number, albeit they had but a bare authoritie: but if they had bin particularly named, it had beene otherwise. But if a man deuiseth lands to his Executors to bee sould, and maketh two Executors, and the one dieth, yet the suruiuor may sell the land, because as the state, so the trust shall suruiue; and so note the diuersitie betweene a bare trust, and a trust coupled with an interest. In both those cases the Executors may (a) sell part of the land at one time and part at another as they may find purchasers.

Hill.26.El. inter *Vincent & Lee in the Kings Bench.*

39.Ass.p.17. 4.Eliz.Dier 210. 23.Eliz.Dier 371. Pasch.32.Eliz.Ro.1307. in Communi Banco. and so resolued in Vincents case.

(a) Lib.1.fol.173.in Digges case. (b) 21.H.8.cap.4.

In Littletons case admit that one Executor had refused to sell, then (as the Law stood when Littleton wrote) it was cleare that the others could not sell, but now by the statute (b) of 21.H.8 it is prouided that where lands are willed to be sold by Executors, that though part of them refuse, yet the residue may sell. And albeit the Letter of the Law extendeth only where Executors haue a power to sell, yet being a beneficiall Law, it is by construction extended where lands are deuised to Executors to be sold. Yet in neither of those cases, albeit one refuse, can the other make sale to him that refused, because he is party and priuie to the last will, and remaine Executor still. Mine aduice to them that make such deuises by will is, to make it as certaine as they can, as that the sale be made by his Executors or the Suruiuors or suruiuor of them, if his meaning be so, or by such or so many of them, as take vpon them the probate of his will, or the like. And it is better to giue them an Authority then an estate, vnlesse his meaning be they should take the profits of his lands in the meane time, and then it is necessary that he deuiseth, that the meane profits till the sale shalbe assets in their hands, for otherwise they shall not be so. But hereof thus much shall suffice.

Tr.27.H.8. in the Common Place. Seriant Bendloes report.

¶ *Et ent faire feoffment*. For albeit the Executors in this case haue no estate or interest in the land, but only a bare and naked power, yet this Feoffment amounteth to an alienation, to vest the land in the Feoffee, as it appeareth here, and the Feoffee shalbe in by the Deuisor.

40.E.3.16. 38.Ass.3. 39.Ass.17. 13.E.3.deuise.3. 14.H.8.10. 15.H.7.12.b.

¶ *Per fait ou sauns fait*. And therefore if by the custome a man deuiseth that a Reuersion or any other thing that lyeth in Grant shall bee sold by the Executors, they may sell the same without Deede for the Vendee shall be in by the Deuisor, and not by the Executors as hath beene said.

19.H.6.

¶ *Consuetudo ex certa causa rationabili visitata priuat communem legem.* Quia consuetudo contra rationem introducta potius vsurpatio quam consuetudo appellari debet. Consuetudo præscripta & legittima vincet legem.

¶ *Priuat communem legem*. For no custome or prescription can take away the force of an Act of Parliament, and therefore Littleton materially speaketh here of the Common law.

4.E.4.4. 11.H.4.7. 39.H.6.39. 7.H.6.1.a. 9.H.6.56. 8.H.7.4. 8.Eliz.Dier.247.

Sect. 170.

¶ **Et nota q̃ nul custome est allowable, mesq̃ tiel custome q̃ ad este vse**

And note that no custome is to bee allowed, but such custome as hath bin vsed

¶ *Prescription*. Prescription is a title taking his substance of vse and time allowed by the Law, Præscriptio est titulus ex vsu & tempore substantiam capiens

capiens ab authoritate legis. In the Common Law a prescription which is personall is for the most part applied to persons being made in the name of a certaine person and of his Ancestors or those whose estate he hath, or in bodies politique, or Corporate, and their predecessors, for as a naturall body is said to haue Ancestors, so a body politique or corporate is said to haue predecessors. And a custome which is locall is alledged in no person, but laid within some Mannor or other place. As taking one example for many, I.S. seised of the mãnor of D. in fee prescribeth thus: That I.S. his Ancestors, and all those whose estate hee hath in the said Mannor haue time out of minde of man had and vsed to haue Common of pasture, &c. in such a place, &c. being the land of some other, &c. as pertaining to the said Mannor. This properly we call a prescription. A custome is in this manner. A Copyholder of the Mannor of D. doth pleade, that within the same Mannor, there is and hath beene such a custome time out of minde of man vsed, that all the Copyholders of the said Mannor haue had and vsed to haue common of pasture, &c. in such a waste of the Lord parcell of the said Mannor, &c. where the person neither doth or can prescribe, but alledgeth the custome within the Mannor. But both to customes and prescriptions, these two things are incident inseparable, viz. possession, or vsage: and Time Possession must haue three qualities, it must be long, continuall, and peaceable, Longa, continua, & pacifica: for it is said, Transferuntur dominia sine titulo & traditione, per vsu captionem, s. per longam, continuam, & pacificam possessionem. Longa .i. per spatium temporis per legem definitum, of which hereafter shall bee spoken. Continuam dico ita quod non sit legittime interrupta.

12.E.4.1 2. Marie, Br. Prescr.100. 6.E.6.Dyer 71. 14.Ed.3. Bar.277 43.E.3.32. 7.H.6.26. 22.H.6.14. 16.E.2 tit.Prescript.53. 45.Ass.8. 40.Ass.27.41. 21.E.4.53.54.

Bract.fo,51,52.

per title de prescription, s. ð temps dont memorie ne curt. Mes diuers opinions ont este ð temps dont memorie, &c. & ð title p prescription, q̃ est tout vn en ley. Car ascuns ont dit que temps de memorie serra dit ð temps de limitation en vn briefe ð droit, scilicet de temps le Roy R. le i. puis le conquest, come est done per le statute de Westminster 1. pur ceo que le briefe de droit est le pluis hault briefe en sa nature que poit estre, & per tiel briefe hõe poit recouer son droit de la possession son auncestors de pluis auncient temps que home purroit p ascun briefe per l' ley, &c. Et entant que il est done p le dit estatute que en briefe de droit nul soit oye a demander de le seisin son auncestors de pluis longe temps q̃ de temps le Roy R. auantdit, issint ceo est proue q̃ continuance de possession, ou auters customes, & vsages vses puis le dit temps, est le title de prescriptiõ, &c. & hoc certum est. Et auters

ont

by title of prescription, that is to say, from time out of minde. But diuers opinions haue beene of time out of minde, &c. & of title of prescription, which is all one in the law. For some haue said, that time of minde should bee said from time of limitation in a Writ of right, that is to say, from the time of King *Richard* the first after the Conquest, as is giuen by the statute of Westminster the first, for that a writ of right is the most highest Writ in his nature that may be. And by such a writ a man may recouer his right of the possession of his Ancesters, of the most ancient time that any man may by any writ by the Law, &c. And in so much that it is giuen by the said Estatute, that in a writ of right none shall be heard to demãd of the seisin of his ancestours of longer time, than of the time of King Richard aforesaid, therefore this is prooued, that continuance of possession, or other customes & vsages vsed after the same time is the title

ont dit, q̃ bien & veritye est, que ſeiſin & continuance puis le dit limitation, est vn title de preſcription, come est auantdit, & per cauſe auandit. Mes ils ont dit, que il y auxy vn auter title de preſcription, que fuit a la common ley deuant aſcun eſtatute de limitation de briefe, &c. & ceo fuit lou vn cuſtome, ou vn vſage, ou auter choſe ad eſte vſe de temps dont memorie des homes ne curt a la contrarie. Et ils ont dit, que il eſt proue per l'pleder, lou home voit pleder vn title de preſcription de cuſtome il dirra q̃ tiel cuſtome ad eſte vſe, *de tempore cuius contrariũ memoria hominũ non exiſtit*, & c'eſt autant a dire, quãt tiel matter eſt pleé, q̃ nul home adonq; en vie ad oye aſcun proofe a l'contrarie, ne auoit aſcun conuſans a l'contrarie. Et entãt que tiel title de preſcription fuit a le common ley, & nient ouſte par aſcun eſtatute, *ergo*, il demurt come il fuit a le common ley, & le pluis toſt, entant que la dit limitation de briefe d' droit eſt de cy long tẽps paſſe, *Ideo de*

of preſcription, and this is certaine. And others haue ſaid, that well and truth it is, that ſeiſin and continuance after the limitation, &c. is a title of preſcription, as is aforeſaid, and by the cauſe aforeſaid. But they haue ſaid that there is alſo another title of preſcription that was at the Common law, before any eſtatute of limitation of writs, &c. And that it was where a Cuſtome or vſage, or other thing hath beene vſed, for time whereof minde of man runneth not to the contrary: And they haue ſaid that this is proued by the pleading: where a man will pleade a title of preſcription of cuſtome, hee ſhall ſay that ſuch cuſtome hath beene vſed from time whereof the memory of men runneth not to the contrary, that is as much to ſay, when ſuch a matter is pleaded, that no man then aliue hath heard any proofe of the contrary, nor hath no knowledge to the contrary, and inſomuch that ſuch title of preſcription was at the Common Law, and not put out by an eſtatute, *Ergo*, it abideth as it was at the Cõmon Law, and the rather, inſomuch that the ſaid limitation of a writ of Right, is of ſo long time paſſed, *Ideo quære de hoc.* And

Pacificam dico, quia ſi contentioſa fuerit, idem erit quod prius, ſi contentio fuerit iuſta. Vt ſi verus dominus ſtatim cum intruſor vel diſſeiſor ingreſſus fuerit ſeiſinam, nitatur tales viribus repellere, & expellere, licet id quod inceperit perducere non poſſit ad effectum dum tamen cum defecerit diligens ſit ad impetrandum & proſequendum; Longus vſus nec per vim, nec clam, nec precario, &c. *Idem fo.*222.*b.*

If a man preſcribeth to haue a Rent, and likewiſe to take a Diſtreſſe for the ſame; it cannot bee auoyded by pleading, that the Rent hath beene alwayes paid by compulſion, albeit it began by wrong. 13.*E.*4.6.

Vn title de preſcriptiõ. Seeing that preſcription maketh a title, it is to be ſeene, firſt to what things a man may make a title by preſcription without Charter. And ſecondly, how it may be loſt by interruption.

For the firſt, as to ſuch Franchiſes and Liberties as cannot be ſeiſed as forfeited, before the cauſe of forfeiture appeare of Record, no man can make a Title by preſcription becauſe that preſcription being but an Vſage in pais, it cannot * extend to ſuch things as cannot bee ſeiſed nor had without matter of Record: as to the goods and chattels of Traitors, felons, felons of themſelues, fugitiues, of thoſe that be put in exigent, Deodands, Conuſance of

31.*H.*6 *Preſcrip.*44. 21.*E.*4.6. 1.*H.*7.23. 9.*H.*7.11.20. 7.*H.*6.45. 6.*E.*3.32.42. 45.*E.*3.2. 2.*E.*4.26.

(*) *Fleta li.*1.*cap.*25. *Brit. fo.*6.& 15. 44.*aſſ.p.*8 49.*E.*3.3.*Stãf.Pl.C.r.*21.51 *Lib.*5.*fo.*109.110.*Li.*9.*f.*29

of pleas, to make a Corporation, to haue a Sanctuarie, to make a Coroner, &c. to make Conseruators of the peace, &c.

hoc quære. **Et plusors auters customes & vsages ont tiels auncient burghes.**

many other customes and vsages haue such ancient boroughes.

(e) 22.E.3.Coron.241. 9.H.7.11.20. 18.H.6.prescr.45. 11.H.4.10. 21.H.7.33. 9.E.4.12. 39.E.3.35. 46.E.3.16. 11.H.6.25. F.N.B.91. 1.H.7.24. Stanf.pl.Cor.38. 44.E.3.4. 22.E.4.43.44. 3.E.3.Brook prescr.57. 44.Ass.pl. (*)8.H.6.16. (f) 12.E.4.16. 32.H.6.25. 12.Eliz. Dier.288.289.

(e) But to Treasure Trove, waifes, Estraies, wrecke of Sea, to hold Pleas, courts of Leets, Hundreds, &c. Infange thiefe, Outfange thiefe, to haue a Parke, warren, Royall fishes, as Whales, Sturgions, &c. Faires, Markets, Franke foldage, the keeping of a Goale, Tolle, a Corporation by prescription, and the like, a man may make a Title by vsage and prescription only without any matter of record, (*) Vide Sect.310. where a man shall make a Title to lands by prescription.

But it is to bee obserued (f) that although a man cannot as is aforesaid prescribe in the said Franchise to haue Bona & catalla proditorum, felonum, &c. yet may they and the like be had obliquely or by a meane by prescription; For a County palatine may be claimed by prescription, and by reason thereof to haue Bona & catalla proditorum, felonum, &c.

11.E.3.tit.issue 40.

As to the second, by what meanes a Title by prescription, or Customs may be lost by interruption; It is to be knowne that the Title being once gained by prescription or custome cannot be lost, by interruption of the possession for 10. or 20. yeares, but by interruption in the right, as if a man haue had a Rent or Common by prescription, vnity of possession of as high and perdurable estate is an interruption in the right.

15.E.3.tit.iudgement 133. 14.E.3.ibid.155.

In a Writ of Mesne the Plaintife made his title by prescription, that the Defendant and his Ancestors had acquited the Plaintife and his Ancestors, and the Terre-tenant time out of minde, &c. the Defendant tooke issue, that the Defendant and his Ancestors had not acquited the Plaintife and his Ancestors & the Terre-tenant, and the Jury gaue a speciall verdict, that the Grandfather of the Plaintife was enfeoffed by one Agnes, and that Agnes and her Ancestors were acquited by the Ancestors of the Defendant time out of minde before that time, since which time no acquitall had beene; and it was adiudged and affirmed in a Writ of error, that the Plaintife should recouer his Acquitall, for that there was once a title by prescription vested, which cannot be taken away by a wrongfull Cessor to acquite of late time, and albeit the verdict had found against the letter of the issue, yet for that the substance of the issue was found, viz. a sufficient title by prescription, it was adiudged both by the Court of Common pleas, and in the Writ of error by the court of Kings bench for the Plaintife, which is worthy of obseruation. So a modus decimandi was alledged (*) by prescription time out of minde for tithes of Lambes, and thereupon issue ioyned, and the Jury found that before 20. yeares then last past there was such a prescription, and that for these 20. yeares he had paid tithe Lambe in Specie, and it was obiected first that the issue was found against the Plaintife, for that the prescription was generall for all the time of prescription, and 20. yeares faile thereof. 2. That the party by payment of tythes in Specie had waiued the prescription or custome. But it was adiudged for the Plaintife in the prohibition, for albeit the Modus decimandi had not beene paid by the space of 20. yeares, yet the prescription being found, the substance of the issue is found for the Plaintife. And if a man hath a Common by prescription, and taketh a Lease of the land for 20. yeares, whereby the common is suspended, after the yeares ended, hee may clayme the common generally by prescription, for that the suspensation was but to the possession, and not to the right; and the inheritance of the common did alwayes remaine, and when a prescription or custome doth make a title of inheritance (as Littleton speaketh) the partie cannot alter or waiue the same in pais.

(*) Mich.43.& 44.Eliz. in a prohibition betwne Nowell pl. and Hicks Vicar of Edmonton defendant in the Kings Bench.

(e) Bract.fol.314.

¶ *Temps dont memory, &c. & de title per prescription que est tent vn en ley.* **So as the time prescribed or defined by Law is, time, whereof** there is no memory of man to the contrarie. (e) Omnis quærela, & omnis actio iniuriarum limitata infra certa tempora.

¶ *Temps de limitation.* **Limitation as it is taken in Law is a** certaine time prescribed by Statute, within the which the demandant in the action must proue himselfe or some of his Ancestors to be seised.

(f) Regist.158. Bract.fol.373. 5.Ass.p.2. 34.H.6.40. (g) Stat.de Mert. 20.H.3.ca.8. (h) West.1.an.3.E.1.ca.38. Vide W.2. 13.E.1.ca.46. (i) Mirror.ca.5.§.1.

¶ *En briefe de droit.* **In (f) ancient time the limitation in a Writ** of Right was from the time of H.1. whereof it was said, à tempore Regis Henrici senioris. After that by the Statute of (g) Merton the limitation was from the time of H.2. and by the Statute (h) of W.1. the limitation was from the time of R.1. And this is that limitation that Littleton here speaketh of. Whereof in the Mirror in reproofe of the Law it is thus said, (i) Abusion est de counter cy longe temps dount nul ne poet testmoigner de vien & de oyer que ne dure my generalment ouster 40. ans.

Time

Time of limitation is two fold, First, in Writs, and that is by divers Acts of Parliament. Secondly, To make a title to any Inheritance, and that (as Littleton here saith) is by the Common Law.

Glanuil.lib 13.*ca.* 3.& 34. *Mirror.ca.* 5.§.4. *Fleta.lib.*2.*ca.* 38.& *li.*4.*ca* 5 *Britton.fol* 79 82. *Bracton.lib.*2 *fol* 52.& *fol.* 179.253.373.

Limitation of times in Writs are provided by the said Statute of Merton, and after by the said Statute of W.1. which Littleton here citeth, and which was in force when hee wrote, but is since altered by a profitable and necessary Statute (k) made Anno 32.H.8. and by that Act, the former limitation of time in a Writ of Right is changed and reduced to threescore yeares next before the Teste of the Writ, and so of other actions as by the Statute at large appeareth. But it is to be observed, that this Act of 32.H.8. extendeth (l) not to be a Formedon, in the Discender, nor to the Services of Escuage, Homage, and Fealtie, for a man may live above the time limited by the Act, neither doth it extend to any other service which by common possiblitie may not happen or become due within sixtie yeares, as to cover the hall of the Lord, or to attend on his Lord when he goeth to warre or the like, nor where the seisin is not traversable or issuable, neither doth it extend to a Rent created by Deed, nor to a Rent reserved upon any particular estate, for (m) in the one case the Deed is the title, and in the other the reservation, nor to any Writ of Right of Advowson, Quare impedit, or Assise of Darreine presentment (for there was a parson of one of my Churches that had beene Incumbent there above fiftie yeares, and died but lately) or any Writ of Right of ward, or ravishment of ward, &c. but they are left as they were before the Statute of 32.H.8. But hereof thus much for the better understanding of Littleton shall suffice.

(k) 32.*H.*8.*ca.*2. *See the second part of the Institutes. Merton.ca.*8.

(l) *Mich.*10 & 11.*Eliz. Dier.*278. *Fitzwilliams case.*

*Lib.*4.*fol.*10.& 11. *Bevils case.*

(m) *Lib.*8.*fol.*65. *Sir Williams Fosters case.*

1.*Mar.Parliam.*2 *ca* 5. *Vide* 17.*E.*3.11. *Pl.Com.*371.*b.*

¶ *De temps le Roy, R.*1. **And that was intended from the first day** of his raigne, for (from the time) being indefinitely doth include the whole time of his Raigne, which is to be observed.

Vide 34.*H.*6.36.

¶ *Briefe de droit*, breue de recto, **a Writ of Right so called, for that** the words in the Writ of Right are, Quod sine dilatione plenum rectum teneas.

¶ *Title de prescription al common ley, &c. de temps dont memorie des homes ne curge al contrarie.* Docere oportet longum tempus, & longum vsum illum, viz. qui excedit memoriam hominum, tale enim tempus sufficit pro iure.

*Bract.lib.*4.*fol.*230. *Fleta lib.*4.*cap.*24.

¶ *Ascun proofe al contrarie.* **For if there bee any sufficient proofe** of Record or writing to the contrary, albeit it exceed the memory, or proper knowledge of any man living, yet is it within the memory of man: for memorie or knowledge is two fold. First, By knowledge by proofe, as by Record or sufficient matter of writing. Secondly, By his owne proper knowledge. A Record or sufficient matter in writing are good memorials for Litera scripta manet. And therefore it is said, when we will by any Record or writing commit the memory of any thing to Posteritie, it is said tradere memoriæ. And this is the reason that regularly a man cannot prescribe or alleage a Custome against a Statute, because that is matter of Record, and is the highest proofe and matter of Record in Law. But yet a man may prescribe against an Act of Parliament when his Prescription or Custome is saved or preserved by another Act of Parliament.

28.*Ass.*25. 38.*Ass.*18. 45.*E.*3.26. 5.*H.*7.10. 8.*H.*7.7. 11.*H.*7.21. *Dier* 23.*Eliz.*273.

There is also a diversitie betweene an Act of Parliament in the negative and in the affirmative, for an affirmative Act doth not take away a custome as the Statutes of Wils of 32. and 34.H.8. doe not take away a Custome to devise Lands, as it hath beene often adiudged. Moreover, there is a diversitie betweene Statutes that be in the negative, for if a Statute in the negative be declarative of the ancient Law, that is in affirmance of the Common Law, there aswell as a man may prescribe or alledge a custome against the Common Law, so a man may doe against such a Statute, for as our Author saith, Consuetudo, &c. priuat communem legem. As the Statute of Magna Charta provideth, that no Leet shall be holden but twice in the yeare, yet a man may prescribe to hold it oftener, and at other times, for that the Statute (n) was but in affirmance of the Common Law.

*Magna Charta cap.*35.

(n) 6.*H.*7.2. 8.*H.*7.34. 12.*H.*7.18. 31.*H.*6.*lect.*11. 18.*H.*6.13.

So the Statute (o) of 34.E.1. provideth that none shall cut downe any trees of his owne within a Forest without the view of the Forester: but inasmuch as this Act is in affirmance of the Common Law, a man may prescribe to cut downe his woods within a Forest without the view of the Forester. And so was it adiudged in 16.Eliz. in the Exchequer by Sir Edward Sanders Chiefe Baron, and other the Barons of the Exchequer, as Sir Iohn Popham Chiefe Iustice of the Kings Bench reported to me.

(o) 34.*E.*1.*tit.forest. Rast.* 1.*E.*3.*cap.*2.

In the Eire of the Forest of Pickering before Willoughby, Hungerford and Hanburie, Iustices Itinerants there, Anno 8.E 3. I reade (p) a clayme made by Henry de Percy, Lord of the Mannor of Semor within the said Forest, the Foresters, Verderours, and Regarders found his clayme to be true, viz. Quod prædictus Henricus de Percy, & omnes antecessores sui tenentes

(p) *Itin. Pickering. anno* 8. *E.*3.*Rot.*38.

tes manerium prædictum à tempore quo non extat memoria & sine interruptione aliquali tenuerunt prædictum manerium cum pertinentijs extra regardum Forestæ, & habuerunt Woodwardum portantem arcum & sagittas ad præsentandum præsentanda de venatione tantum, &c. & habuerunt in boscis suis de Semere forgeas, & mineras, & amputârunt, dederunt, & vendiderunt boscum suum infra manerium prædictum sine visu forestariorum pro voluntate sua, & fugarunt, & ceperunt Vulpes, Lepores, Capriolos, &c. sicut idem Henricus Percy superius clamat. which clayme by prescription, and found as is aforesaid, the Justices doubted only of two points. The first, forasmuch as the said Mannor was within the limits of the Forest, it should not only be Contra assisam Forestæ, for his Woodward to beare Bow and Arrowes, where by Law he ought to beare but an Hatchet and no Bow nor Arrowes within the forest, but also de facili cedere possit in destructionem ferarum, &c. and therefore doubted whether it might be clayned by prescription. Their second doubt was concerning fugationem, & captionem Capriolorum in boscis suis prædictis, eo quod est bestia venationis Forestæ, & transgressores inde conuicti finem facerent vt pro transgressione venationis, and for that difficultie, the clayme was adiourned into the Kings Bench. But of the other parts of the Prescription no doubt at all was made: and the like had beene allowed in the same Eire, as in the case of Thomas Lord Wake of Lydell, and of Gilbert of Acton, in the same Eire, Rot.37. and of others.

¶ *Il est proue per le pleader.* Note one of the best arguments or proofes in Law is drawne from the right entries or course of pleading, for the Law it selfe speaketh by good pleading, and therefore Littleton here saith, It is proued by the pleading, &c. as if pleading were ipsius legis viua vox.

Entant que tiel title per prescription fuit al comon ley &c. Note all the prescriptions that were limited from a certaine time were by Act of Parliament, as from the time of H.1. which was the first time of limitation set downe by any Act of Parliament, and so from the Raigne of R.1. &c. But this Prescription of time out of memory of man was (as Littleton here saith) at the Common Law, and limited to no time. Also here is implyed a maxime of the Law, viz. That whatsoeuer was at the Common Law, and is not ousted or taken away by any Statute remayneth still.

¶ *Common ley.* The Law of England is deuided, as hath beene said before into three parts; the Common Law, which is the most generall and antient Law of the realme; of part whereof, Littleton wrote, 2. Statutes or Acts of Parliament; and 3. particuler Customes (whereof Littleton also maketh some mention) I say particuler, for if it be the generall Custome of the realme, it is part of the Common Law.

The Common Law hath no controller in any part of it, but the high Court of Parliament, and if it be not abrogated or altered by Parliament, it remaynes still as (Littleton here saith) The Common Law appeareth in the Statute of Magna Charta and other ancient Statutes (which for the most part are affirmations of the Common Law) in the originall writs in iudiciall Records, and in our Bookes of termes and yeares, Acts of Parliament appeare in the Rolls of Parliament, and for the most part are in print. Particular customes are to be proued.

Section 171.

¶ ITem, chescun Burgh est un ville, mes ney e conuerso. Plus serra dit de custome en le tenure de villenage.

ALso euery Borough is a Towne but not *è conuerso:* more shall bee said of custome in the tenure of villenage.

¶ *Ville.* Villa quasi vehilla quod in eam conuehantur fructus. And it is called Vicus, because it is prope viam. Villa est ex pluribus mancionibus vicinata & collata ex pluribus vicinis. If a Towne be decayed so as no houses remayne, yet it is a Towne in Law. And so if a Borough bee decayed, yet shall it send Burgesses to the Parliament, as old Salisbury and others doe. It cannot bee a Towne in Law, vnlesse it hath, or in time past hath had a Church and celebration of Diuine Seruice, Sacraments and Burials: what alteration hath beene made in Townes, heare what a great Lawyer saith, In Anglia Villula tam parua inueniri non poterit, in qua non est Miles, Armiger, vel Paterfamilias, &c. magnis ditatus possessionibus, nec non liberi tenentes alij & valecti plurimis suis patrimonijs sufficientes, &c. And it appeareth by Littleton, that a Towne is the genus, and a Borough is the species, for he saith that euery Borough is a Towne, but euery Towne is not a Borough. Et sub appellatione Villarum continentur Burgi & Ciuitates.

Vide Linwood verbo vicus. Bracton.lib.5.fol.434. & lib.4.fol.211. Fortescue cap.29. 7.E.6. fines leuie de terre. Br.91.

34.E.1. quare.Imp.187.

Fortescue cap.29.

Fortescue cap.34.

Berewica, or Berewit in Domesday signifieth a Towne, Hæ Berewicæ pertinent ad Berchley. (Et sic recitat plus quam viginti villas.) *Domesday. Glouc.*

There be in England and wales eight thousand, eight hundred and three Townes, or there abouts.

See more De villis, parochijs & Hamlettis in the ancient Authors of the Law, and plentifully in our other bookes. But let us now heare what Littleton saith. *Bract. ubi sup. Flet. l. 4. c. 15. & lib. 6 ca. 49. But fo 124. & 274. &c.*

Chap.11. Villenage. *Sect.172.*

¶ Tenure en Villenage est plus propermẽt quant un villein tient de son Sñr a que il est villein, certaine terres ou tenemẽts solonq; l'custome del manor, ou autERment a la volunt son Seignior, & de faire a son seignior villein seruice: Come de porter & de carier le fime le Sñr hors del Citie ou del Manor son Seignior iesques a l'terr son Seignior, en gisant ceo sur le terre, & huiusmodi. Et ascuns franke homes teignont lour tenements solonq; le custome del certaine manors per tiels seruices. Et lour tenure auxy est appell tenure en villenage, & uncore ils ne sont pas villeines: Car nul tre tenus en villenage, ou villeine terre, ne ascun custome surdant de la tre, ne unques ferra

Tenure in villenage is most properly when a Villeine holdeth of his Lord, to whom he is a villeine, certaine lands or tenements according to the custome of the Mannor, or otherwise at the will of his Lord, and to doe to his Lord villeine seruice: As to carry and recarry the dunge of his Lord out of the Citie, or out of his Lords Mannor, vnto the land of his Lord, and to spread the same vpon the land, and such like. And some free men hold their tenements according to the custome of certaine Manors by such seruices. And their tenure also is called Tenure in villenage, and yet they are not villeines. For no land holden in villenage or villein land, nor any custome arising out of the land, shall euer make a free man villeine, but a

¶ *Tenure en Villenage.* Villeine is the French word Vilaine, and that A villa quia villæ adscriptus est, for they which are now called Villaini of ancient times were called Ascriptitij, and in the Common Law hee is called Nativus, quia pro maiore parte natus est seruus, and this is hee which the Civilians call servus. (a) Theyn in the Saxon tongue is Liber, and Then servus. Theme (sometime written Theame corruptly) is an old Saxon word, and signifieth Potestatem habendi in nativos sive villanos cum eorum sequelis, terris, bonis & catallis. But Teame sometime corruptly written Theam is of another signification, for it is also an old Saxon word, (b) and signifieth where a man cannot produce his Warrant of that which he bought according to his Voucher.

¶ *Villenage.* Villenagium, (as in like cases hath beene said when the termination is in Age) is the seruice of a bondman, And yet a free man may doe the seruice of him that is bound. And therefore a tenure in Villenage is twofold, one where the person of the Tenant is bound, and the tenure seruile, the other where the person is free, and the tenure seruile. (c) Serva terra liberos de sanguine existentes, villanos facere non potest. And therefore it is said (d) Est enim ratio & regula generalis in istis duobus casibus quod liber homo nihil libertatis propter personam

Lib. Rub. 76. & 77. Glan. li. 5. ca. 1. & 2. &c. Vide Bract. li. 1. ca. 6, &c. Brit. fo. 77. & 67. 82. 97. 98. 125. 126. 147. Flet. li. 1 c. 3. Flet. li. 2 cap. 44. Idem lib 4. ca. 11, & 12. Mir. ca. 2. §. 18. Ockam.

(a) *Flet. li. 1. ca. 24.*

(b) *Vide Lamb. inter Leges Sancti Edw fo. 132. nu 25.*

(c) *Hil. 29. E. 1. coram Rege Ebor. in Thesaur.*

(d) *Bract. li. 4. fo. 170.*

personam suam liberam confert villenagio, nec liberum tenementum è contrario mutat statum aut conditionem villani. And againe, (e) Villenagium vel seruitium nihil detrahit libertati, habita tamen distinctione vtrum tales sint villani, & tenuerunt in villano socagio de dominico Domini Regis. And againe, (f) Tenementum non mutat statum liberi non magis quam serui, poterit enim liber homo tenere purum villinagium faciendo quicquid ad villanum pertinebit, & nihilominus liber erit, cum hoc faciat ratione villenagii, & non ratione personæ suæ, & ideo poterit quãdo voluerit villenagium deserere, & liber discedere nisi illaqueatus sit per vxorem natiuam ad hoc faciendũ ad quam ingressus fuit in villenagium, & quæ præstare poterit impedimentum, &c. And againe, (g) Purum villenagium est a quo præstatur seruitium incertum & indeterminatum vbi scire non poterit vespere, quale seruitium fieri debet mane, viz. vbi quis facere tenetur quicquid ei præceptum fuerit. And another saith to the same intent, Ceux ne scauoient le vespere de quoy ils seruer en la Matyn. (h) Fuerunt in Conquestu liberi homines qui libere tenuerunt tenementa sua per libera seruicia, vel per liberas consuetudines, & cum per potentiores eiecti essent postmodum reuersi receperunt eadem tenementa sua tenenda in Villenagio, faciendo inde opera seruilia sed certa & nominata, &c. & nihilominus liberi, quia licet faciunt opera seruilia, cum non faciunt ea ratione personarum, sed ratione tenementorum, &c.

(e) Idem lib. 1. ca. 6. Brit. c. 31 & 66. Flet li. 1. ca. 3.

(f) Bract. fo. 26. 43. E. 3. 5. act.

(g) Bract. li. 4. fo. 208. Brit. ca. 31.

(h) Bract. li. 1. fo. 7.

franke home villein. Mes vn villein puit faire franke terre deste villein terre a son Sñr. Sicome lou vn villeine purchase terre en fee simpl', ou en fee taile, le Seignior del villein poet enter en la terre, & ouste le villeine & ses heires a touts iours, & puis le Seigniour (s'il voloit) puit lesser mesme la terre, a le Villein a tener en Villenage.

Villeine may make free land to be Villein land to his Lord. As where a Villeine purchase land in fee simple, or in fee taile, the Lord of the Villeine may enter into the land, and out the Villeine and his heires for euer: And after, the Lord (if he will) may let the same land to the Villein, to hold in Villenage.

How Villenage or seruitude began, and for what cause, it is said, (i) Ab homine, & pro vitio introducta est servitus, sed libertas à Deo hominis est indita naturæ, quare ipsa ab homine sublata semper redire gliscit, vt facit omne, quod libertate naturali priuatur. And another saith, (k) That the condition of Villeines from freedome vnto bondage, of antient time grew by constitutions of Nations, (l) Fiunt etiam serui liberi homines captiuitate de iure gentium; And not by the Law of Nature, as from the time of Noahs Floud forward, in which time all things were common to all, and free to all men alike, and lived vnder the Law Naturall, and by multiplication of people, and making proper and priuate those things that were common, arose battells. And then it was ordained by constitution of Nations, That none should kill another, but that he that was taken in battell, should remaine bond to his taker for euer, and to doe with him, and all that should come of him, his will and pleasure, as with his beast, or any other Chattell, to giue, or to sell, or to kill: And after it was ordained for the crueltie of some Lords, That none should kill them, and that the life and members of them, as well as of freemen, were in the hands and protection of Kings, and that he that killed his Villeine, should haue the same iudgement as if he had killed a Freeman. Thereupon they were called, Serui, quia seruabantur a Dominis & non occidebantur, & non a seruiendo. He is called, Nativus a nascendo, quia plerumque natus est servus: And he is called Villanus, for that he doth his Villeine seruice in Villis.

(i) Fortesc. ca. 42.

(k) Brit. ca. 31.
(l) Bract. li. 1. ca. 6.
Flet. li. 1. ca. 3. & ca. 5.
Mir. ca. 2 §. 18.

Est autem libertas naturalis facultas eius quod cuique facere libet nisi quod de iure, aut vi prohibetur. Seruitus est constitutio de iure gentium qua quis Domino alieno contra naturam subjicitur. And againe, (m) Et tout soyt que touts creatures duissont este franks solonque le Ley de nature, per constitution nequidant, & fait de homes sont auters creatures enseruies sicome est dit beasts en Parkes, pissons en seruors, & oyseaux en cages.

Bracton Lib. 1. cap. 6.
Britton cap. 31. & vbi supra.
Fleta Lib. 1. cap 2. & 3.
(m) Mirror cap. 2. §. 18.

(n) This is assured, That bondage or seruitute was first inflicted for dishonouring of parents: for Cham the father of Canaan (of whom issued the Canaanites) seeing the nakednesse of his father Noah, and shewing it in derision to his brethren, was therefore punished in his sonne Canaan, with bondage. And herewith agreeth the Diuine, Ante Vini inuentionem inconcussa libertas: non esset hodie seruitus si ebrietas non fuisset.

(n) Mirror cap. 2. §. 18.
Genesis 9. vers. 20. 21. &c.

Ambrose.

¶ *Hors del citie ou del Mannor, &c.* This is false printed, for the

originall

originall is, Hors del scite del Mannor, and so would it be amended at the Impressions of the Bookes hereafter.

¶ *Et ascuns frank homes teignent, &c.* This is apparant enough, especially vpon that which hath beene said. *Mirror ca.2.§.18. Acc.*

¶ *Ou vn Villeine purchase terre en fee simple.* Yet the Villeine may purchase some kind of Inheritances in fee simple, which the Lord of the Villeine cannot haue. As if a Villeine purchase a Common sauns nomber, the Lord shall not haue it, for the Lord may surcharge the same, which should be a preiudice to the Terre-tenant, and the same law of a Corodie in certaine granted to a Villeine, and such like Inheritances. And therefore Littleton materially sayd, Purchase terre: when the Villeine hath an estate of any thing certaine, the Lord shall haue it as a rent granted to the Villeine, Commons certaine, Estouers certaine, and such like. (o) But that which lieth in action as a warrantie made to the Villeine, his heires, and Assignes, the Lord shall not take aduantage of by Voucher, because it is in lieu of an action, neither shall the Lord take aduantage of any Obligation or Couenant, or other thing in Action made to the Villeine, because they lie in priuitie, and cannot be transferred to others. *Mirror cap.2. §.18.* *22.Ass.p.37.* *(o) Doctor & Stud.cap.43.*

(p) If a man be Lessee of a Villeine for life, for yeares, or at will, and the Villeine purchaseth lands in fee, if the Lessee entreth into the Lands, he shall hold the lands as a perquisite to him and his heires for euer. But if a Bishop hath a Villeine in the right of his Bishopricke, and he purchaseth lands, and the Bishop entreth, the Bishop shall haue this Perquisite to him and his successors, and not to him and his heires, for the Law respecteth the qualitie, and not the quantitie of his estate. So if Executors haue a Villeine for yeares, and the Villeine purchase lands in fee, and the Executors enter, they shall haue a fee simple, but it shall be assets. *(p) L.5.E.4.61.18.E.3.29. 21.H.6.37. Bro.tit.Vil.90.*

¶ *Fee taile.* By this it is apparant, that if lands be giuen to a Villeine, and to the heires of his bodie, the Lord may enter and put out the Villeine and the heires of his bodie, for, Quicquid acquiritur seruo acquiritur Domino. And in this case the Lord gaines a fee simple determinable vpon the dying of the Villeine, without heire of his bodie, and the absolute fee simple remaineth still in the Donor. And if the Lord enter, and after infranchise the Donee, and after the Donee hath issue, yet that issue shall neuer haue remedie either by Formedon or entrie, to recouer this Land, by force of the Statute of Donis Conditionalibus, for that Statute giueth remedie to the issues of the Donee that haue capacitie and power to take and retaine such a gift. And the title of the Lord remaines as it did at the Common Law, for the Statute restraineth acts done onely by the Tenant in taile. And so it is, if lands be giuen to an alien, and to the heires of his bodie, vpon office found, the land is seised for the King, afterwards the King makes the Alien a Denizen, who hath issue and dieth, the King shall detaine the land against the Issue. *15.E.4.9.b. Pl.Com. 555. in Walsinghams case.*

Section 173.

¶ ET nota, si feoffment soit fait a certaine person ou persons en fee al vse dun villeine, ou si vn villeine, oue auters persons soient enfeoffes al vse le villeine, quel estate que le villeine ad en le vse, en fee Taile, pur terme de vie, ou dans, le Seignior del villeine poit enter en touts ceux terres & tenements, sicome le villein vst este sole seisie del demesne. Et cest per Lestatute de Anno 19.H.7.cap.15.

¶ AND note, if a feoffement be made to a certaine person or persons in fee, to the vse of a Villeine; or if a Villeine with other persons, be infeoffed to the vse of the Villein, what estate soeuer that the villeine hath in the vse, in fee taile, for terme of life or yeares, the Lord of the Villein may enter into all those lands and tenements, as if the Villeine had been sole seised of the Demesne. And this is giuen by the statute of *Anno 19.H.7.ca.15.*

¶ This is an addition to Littleton, and the Statute of 19 H.7.ca.15. therein mentioned, for the cause that hath beene aforesaid, hath lost his force.

Sect. 174.

(q) 15. E. 3. tit. aid. 33. Bracton, lib 2. fo. 26. Mirror, cap. 2. §. 18.

See more of this after in this chapter, Sect. 194.

(r) Fleta, lib. 3. cap. 13. Mirror cap. 2. §. 18.

A Paier vn fine pur le mariage, &c. (q) And this villeine and seruile tenure is called in old bookes Marchetum or merchet Marchetum verò pro filia dare non competit libero homini inter alia propter liberi sanguinis priuilegium, &c. And this is true De Communi jure, sed modus & conventio vincunt legem. And as Littleton here saith, it is the folly of a such a free man to take such Mannors, Lands or Tenements to hold of the Lord by such bondage. And yet this doth not make such a free man a villeine, (r) Quia hujusmodi præstationes fiunt ratione tenementi & non ratione personæ in donatione comprehensæ & reservat', non enim vnum & idem est, sed longe aliud, tenere libere, & per liberū servitium, &c. for the signification of this word, vide Sect. 194 & 74 & 441.

MEs si ascun franke home voile prender ascun tres ou tenements a tener de son Sr̄ p tiel villein seruice, s. a payer vn fine a luy pur le mariage de ses fits ou files, donq; il paiera tiel fine pur le mariage, & nient obstant que il est le follie de tiel frank home de prender en tiel form̄ terres ou tenements a tener de la seignior per tiel bondage, uncore ceo ne fait le franke home villeine.

BVt if a free man will take any lands or tenements to hold of his Lord by such villeine seruice, *viz.* to pay a fine to him for the marriage of his sonnes or daughters, then hee shall pay such fine for the mariage, yet notwithstanding though it be the folly of such free man to take in such forme lands or tenements to hold of the Lord by such bondage, yet this maketh not the free man a villeine.

Sect. 175.

Lib. Rub. cap. 76. 77. Bracton, lib. 1. cap. 6. Bract. fol. 77.

(s) Bract. lib. 1. cap. 6. Fleta, lib. 1. cap. 3. 8. Ass. P. 13. 11. Ass. 12. 24. Ass. 1. 73. Ass. 1. 17. E. 3. 78. 79. 27. E. 3. 89. 18. E. 4. 25. 27. H. 8. 7. b. Le statute de 17. E. 3. ca. 17. (t) 17. E. 3. 23. 11. H. 4. 26. 37. H. 6. 21. Dier. Mich. 7. & 8. Eliz. 242. Pl. Com. 79. &c. (u) Glanuel. lib 9. cap. 8. Bracton, lib. 3. fo. 156. Britton, fo. 121. (w) Lib. 6. fo. 11. & 12. in Ieutlemans case.

CHescun villeine ou est villeine per title de prescription, &c. Euery villeine is either by prescription or confession Servi autem nascuntur aut fiunt. By prescription, either regardant to a Mannor, &c. or in grosse. In grosse either by prescription or by granting away a villeine that is regardant or by confession. (s) Fit etiam servus liber homo per confessionem in curia Regis fact'.

ITem chescun villeine, ou est vn villeine p title de prescription, cestascauoir, q̄ il & ses auncestors ont este villeines ō temps dont memorie ne curt, ou il est villein per son confession demesne en Court de Record.

ALso euery villeine is either a villeine by title of prescription, to wit, that hee and his Ancestors haue beene villeines time out of minde of man, or hee is a villeine by his owne confession in a Court of Record.

En court de Record. Record is deriued of the Latyn word Recordor, that is to keepe in minde as the Poet saith, Si rite audita recordor And therefore a Record or Inrolment is a memoriall or monument of so high a nature, (t) as it importeth in it selfe such an absolute verity, as if it be pleaded, that there is no such Record, it shall not receiue any tryall by Witnesse, Jury or otherwise, but only by it selfe, (u) And euery Court of Record is the Kings Court, albeit another may haue the profit, wherein if the Judges doe erre, a Writ of error doth lye. (w) But the County Court, the Hundred court, the court Baron, and such like are no courts of Record, and therefore the proceedings therein may be denied, and tryed by Jury, and vpon their judgements a Writ of error lyeth not, but a Writ of false judgement

ment for that they are no Courts of record, because they cannot hold plea of debt or trespasse if the debt or damages doe amount to 40. shillings, or of any trespasse Vi & armis.

Monumenta quæ nos recorda vocamus ſunt veritatis & vetuſtatis veſtigia.

Sect. 176.

¶ MEs ſi frank home ad diuers iſſues, & puis il confeſſe luy m deſtre villein a vn auter en Court de Record, vncore les iſſues que il auera deuant le confeſ. ſont franks, mes les iſſues que il auera apres le confeſſion ſerront villeines.

BVt if a free man hath diuers iſſues, and afterwards he confeſſeth himſelfe to be a villaine to another in a Court of Record, yet thoſe iſſues which he hath before the confeſſion are free, but the iſſues which hee ſhall haue after the confeſſion ſhall be villaines.

This is ſo euident as it needeth no explication.

Section 177.

¶ ITem, ſi le villein purchaſe fee & alien la terre a vn auter deuant que le ſeignior enter, donques le Seignior ne poit enter, car il ſerra adiudge ſon follie q̃ il nentra pas quant la terre fuit en le maine le villein. Et iſſint eſt dez biens ſi le villein achate biens, & eux vend ou done a vn auter deuant que le Seignior ſeiſiſt les biens, adonques le ſeignior ne poit eux ſeiſer. Mes ſi le ſeignior deuant aſcũ tiel vender ou done, viẽt deins la ville la ou tielx biens ſont, & la ouertment enter les vicines claima les biens et ſeiſiſt parcel

ALſo if a Villaine purchaſe land and alien the land to another, before that the Lord enter, then the Lord cannot enter, for it ſhall bee adiudged his folly, that hee did not enter when the Land was in the hands of the Villaine. And ſo it is of goods: If the Villaine buy goods & ſell or giue them to another, before the LORD ſeiſeth them, then the Lord may not ſeiſe the ſame: but if the Lord before any ſuch ſale or gift, commeth into the Towne where ſuch goods be, and there openly amongſt the neighbors clayme the goods, and ſeiſe part of the goods in the name of ſeiſin

¶ IN this caſe before the Lord doth enter, hee hath neither Ius in re nec ius ad rem, but only a poſſibilitie of an eſtate, which eſtate hee muſt gaine by his entrie, and therefore if the Villaine doth by way of preuention alien before the Lord doth enter the Lord is barred of the poſſibilitie which he had to the Land for euer (a) Si autem ſeruus vẽdiderit feodum quod ſibi & hæredibus perquiſiuerit antequam Dominus ſeiſinam inde ceperit valet donatio & Dominus ſibi ipſi imputet, quod tantum expectauit. But (b) if the Villaine of the King purchaſeth Land and alieneth before the King (vpon an office found for him) doth enter, yet the King after office found ſhall haue the Land, Quia nullum tempus occurrit Regi, as Littleton himſelfe ſaith in the next Section. And yet after office found the King ſhall not haue the meane profits becauſe the title is by the ſeiſure.

(a) *Fleta, lib.* 3. *ca.* 13. *Britton, fol.* 98. *a.* 19. *E.* 2. *Dower* 171.

(b) 35. *E.* 3. *tit. Villenage* 22. 9. *H.* 6. 21. *per Balington.* 12. *H.* 7. 12.

¶ *Purchaſe terre.*

The like Law is of Seigniories, Aduowſons, Reuerſions, Remaynders, Rents, Commons certaine; and ſuch like certaine Inheritances, wherein the Villaine hath

des biens en nosme de seisin de touts les biens q̃ le villeine ad ou auer poit &c. Ceo est dit bon seisin en ley, et le occupation que le villeine ad apres tiel claime en l'z biens, serra pris en le droit le Seigniour.

of all the goods which the Villaine hath or may haue, &c. this is a good seisin in law, and the occupation which the Villaine hath after such clayme in the goods shall bee taken in the right of the Lord.

hath any estate or interest. If the Villaine purchase Land either in Fee simple, Fee taile, or for life, if the Villaine doth alien before the Lord doth enter, he doth preuent the Lord. But yet the issue of the Villaine shall recouer the Land intayled in a Formedon, and then the Lord may enter.

¶ *Alien la terre.* Alien commeth of the Verbe Alienare, id est, alienum facere vel ex nostro dominio in alienum transferre, siue rem aliquam in Dominium alterius transferre. If a freeman hath issue and afterward by confession becommeth bond, and purchase Lands in fee, and before the Lord enter hee dieth seised, and the Land discends to his issue which is free, in this case the Lord shall not enter vpon the heire, and yet this is a discent and no alienation. The like Law it is if the land so purchased by the Villaine doth eschcate to the Lord of the Fee before any entry made by the Lord of the Villaine, so as the act of the Law that is the discent or escheat may aswell preuent the Lord of his entrie, as the act of the partie by alienation.

If a Villaine be disseised before the Lord doth enter, the Lord may enter into the Land in the name of the Villaine, and thereby gaine the Inheritance of the land, but if there bee a discent cast, so as the entrie of the Villaine be taken away, then the Villaine must recontinue the estate of the land by iudgement and execution, before the Lord of the Villaine can enter, and this word alien doth not only extend to alienations of land in deed, but also to alienations in law, as if the Villaine purchase land and dieth without heire, and the land escheate, or if there be a recouery against the Villaine in a Cessauit or the like.

¶ *Et issint est des biens, &c. Biens,* bona includes all chattels aswell reall as personall. Chattels is a French word, and signifieth goods, which by a word of art we call Catalla. Now Goods or Chattels are either personall or reall, personall as horse and other beasts, housholdstuffe, Bowes, weapons, and such like, called personall because for the most part they belong to the person of a man, or else for that they are to be recouered by personall actions. Reall, because they concerne the realitie, as tearmes for yeares of Lands or Tenements, Wardships, the interest of tenant by Statute Staple, by Statute Merchant, by Elegit and such like.

Bona diuiduntur in mobilia & immobilia, mobilia rursum diuiduntur in ea quæ se mouent, & quæ ab alijs mouentur: but by the Common Law, no estate of Inheritance or Free-hold is comprehended vnder these words bona or catalla. And it is to be obserued, that as the title of the Lord to his villains lands beginneth by his entrie, so his title to the goods beginneth by the seisure of them. And here againe it is to bee obserued, that where our Author in this branch concerning goods vseth these words (sell or giue) that the same extendeth aswell to gifts in Law as gifts in deed. And therefore if a neife hath goods, and taketh Baron by this gift in Law by force of the Marriage, the Lord is barred. And so it is if a Villaine make his Executors and dieth, by this gift in law the Lord is barred as shall be said hereafter.

3.H.4.15. 46.E.3.barre 217. Doct. & Stud. cap. 43. fol. 139. 22.E.3.6. Baldwyn Freuils case.

¶ *Et claime les biens & seisist parcel des biens.* For a claime only of the goods of the Villaine is not sufficient in Law, but he must seize some part in the name of all the residue, as here it appeareth, or that the goods be within the view of the Lord, for the claime and his view amount to a seizure, as the clayme of a Ward being present by word is a sufficient seisure, albeit the Gardeine layeth no hands of him. See hereafter Sect. 321. And so note a diuersitie betweene a clayme of Lands or Tenemens, and goods. (c) In an Action of trespasse or detinue brought by the Villaine, a release made to the defendant by the Lord is a good barre, for that amount to a seisure and grant, If the Villaine doth buy goods and make his Executors and dieth before the Lord doth seize them, the Executors shall detaine them against the Lord of the Villaine

(c) 18.H.6.23.b. per Ascough. 3.H.4.16. 46.E.3. barre 217.

¶ *Ad ou auer poet, &c.* Here (&c.) doth imply an excellent point of learning, for that such a claime doth not only vest the goods which the Villeine then hath, but also which he after that shall acquire and get. But otherwise it is of lands of freehold or Inheritance, for there such a generall entrie or clayme extends only to the lands the Villeine hath

at

at that time, and not to any other which he shall purchase after, as by our Author in this Section may iustly be collected.

Sect. 178.

MEs si le Roy ad un villein que purchase terre, & alien deuant que le roy entra, uncore le roy poit enter en que maines que la terre deuiendra. Ou si le villein achata biens, & eux vendist deuant que le roy seisist les biens, uncore le roy poit seiser les biens en que maines que les biens sont, Quia nullum tempus occurrit Regi.

BVT if the King hath a Villeine who purchases Land, and alien it before the King enter, yet the King may enter into whose hands soeuer the land shal come. Or if the villeine buyeth goods and sell them before that the King seizeth them; yet the King may seize these goods in whose hands soeuer they bee. Because *Nullum tempus occurrit Regi.*

SI le roy ad villein, &c. This is euident vpon that which hath beene said before.

Vide Sect. 125. Vide Stanford prær. fol. 32 a.

¶ *Ou si tiel villeine achata biens &c.* If the Kings Villeine acquire any goods or chattels, the propertie of them is in the King before any seisure or office, and it is well said of an ancient Author, (d) Al roy quant al droit, de la corone ou a franch estate ne poet nul temps occurre, and another (e) speaking in the person of the King saith, Nul temps nest limit quant a mes droits.

35. E. 3. tit. Villenage 22.

(d) Mirror cap. 3.

(e) Britton. fol. 88. Bract. lib. 1. quæ res Domini possint.

Sect. 179.

ITem si home lessa cert terre a un auter pur terme de vie sauant le reuersion a luy, & un villeine purchase del lessor le reuersion; en cest cas il semble que le seignior del villeine poit maintenant veñ a la terre, & claime le reuersion come le Seignior le dit villeine, & per cel claime le reuersion est maintenant en luy. Car en auter forme il ne poit vener a le reuersion. Car il ne poit enter sur le tenant a terme de vie. Et sil doit demurrer tanque apres le mort le tenant a terme

ALso if a man let certaine land to another for terme of life sauing to himselfe the reuersion, and a villeine purchase of the lessor the reuersion: In this case it seemeth that the Lord of the villeine may presently come to the land and claime the reuersion as the Lord of the said villeine, and by this claime the reuersion is forthwith in him. For in other forme or manner he cannot come to the reuersion. For hee cannot enter vpon the Tenant for life. And if hee should stay vntill after the death of the Tenant for

¶ *PVit maintenant vener a la terre.*

For hee cannot claime the reuersion but vpon the Land, and hee by his comming vpon the Land for that purpose is no trespassor, because the Law giueth him power to claime the reuersion, lest hee should bee preuented, and claime hee cannot vnlesse hee commeth to the Land. So likewise if the villeine purchase a Seigniorie, rent, Common or any other freehold or Inheritance out of any Lands or Tenements of another, the

de vie, donques per cas il viendra trope tarde. Car perauent le villeine voile granter ou aliene le reuersion a vn auter en le vie le tenant a terme de vie, &c.

life, then perchance hee should ccme too late. For peraduenture the villeine will grant or alien the reuersion to another in the life of the Tenant for life, &c.

Vide 41.E.3.tit. Audita querela.18. 12.H.4 tit. Execution. 28.F.N.B.104. 2.H.7.15.b.

the Lord may lawfully come to the Land to make his claime to the seigniorie, rent or other profit out of the Land. But if the villeine purchase a Seigniorie or a rent [illegible], or other inheritance issuing out of the Land of the Lord himselfe, it is said that the Seigniorie Rent common or such other Inheritance is extinguished in the Lords possession without any claime.

¶ *Grant.* Here must be intended an attornment, for after the grant and before attornment the Lord may claime the reuersion.

¶ *En la vie del tenant per vie, &c.* Hereby, (&c.) is included tenant in taile, tenant pur auter vie, tenant by Statute Marchant, Staple, Elegit, and for yeares, for during all these estates the Lord may claime the Reversion aswell as in case of the Tenant for life.

Section 180.

¶ EN Mesme le maner est, lou vn villein pchase vn Aduowson dun esgl̃ plein dun incumbẽt, le Seignior del villein poit vener al dit esglise, & claime le dit aduowson, & per cel claim̃ ladvowson est en luy. Car sil doit attẽdre tanq; apres le mort lencumbent, & adonque a presenter son clerk a le dit esglise, donque en le meane temps le villeine poit aliener le aduowson, & issint ouste le Seignior de son presentment.

IN the same manner it is, where a villeine purchases an Aduowson of a Church full of an Incumbent, the Lord of the villeine may come to the said Church, and claime the said Aduowson, and by this claime the Aduowson is in him. For if hee will attend till after the death of the Incumbent, and then to present his Clarke to the said Church, then in the meane time, the villeine may alien the Aduowson, & so oust the Lord of his presentment.

23.H.14.b.

¶ ADuowson. Aduocatio so called because the right of presenting to the Church was first gained by such as were Founders, Benefactors, or Maintayners of the Church, viz. ratione fundationis, as where the Ancestor was founder of the Church, or ratione donationis, where he endowed the Church, or ratione fundi as where hee he gaue the soile whereupon the Church was built, and therefore they were called Aduocati: they were also called Patroni, and thereupon the Aduowson is called Ius Patronatus. And in one word Aduowson of a Church is the right of presentation or collation to the Church. Aduocatus est ad quem pertinet ius aduocationis alicuius Ecclesiæ, vt Ecclesiam nomine proprio non alieno possit præsentare. Every Church is either presentatiue, collatiue, donatiue or electiue. Vide Section 645.648.

Fleta.lib.5.cap.14.

24.E.3.30. 25.E.3.47. 38.E.3.9. 44.E.3.3. 9.H.6.31. 22.H.6.27. 21.E.4.34.b. Vide Sect.648.

¶ *Plein dun incumbent.* If the Church bee presentatiue, the Church is full by admission and Institution against any common person, but against the King it is not full untill induction.

10.H.6.7.

¶ *Incumbent*, commeth of the verbe incumbo, that is to be diligently resident, id est, obnixe operam dare, and when it is written encumbent it is falsely written, for it ought to be Incumbent, as Littleton doth here. And therefore the Law doth intend him to bee resident on his Benefice.

¶ Le

¶ *Le Seignior del villeine poit vener al eglise & claime le dit advowson.* Note albeit the Advowson is a thing incorporeall, and not visible, yet because the principall dutie of the Presentee of the Patron is to be done in the Church the clayme of the Lord of the Villeine must be made there, and by that clayme the inheritance of the Advowson shall be vested in the Lord, for every clayme or demand to devest any estate or interest must bee made in that place which is most apt for that purpose.

¶ *Apres la mort del incumbent.* Nota, a Church presentative may become voide five manner of wayes, viz. by death whereof Littleton here speaketh. 2. By creation. 3 By resignation. 4. By deprivation. 5. By cession as by taking [redacted] a [redacted] benefice incompatible. *Doct & Stud. lib. 2. ca. 31. 5. E. 3. 180. 10. E. 3 482. 25. E. 3. 49 9 E. 3. 462. 11. H. 4. 37. 59. & 76. 41. E. 3. 5. F. N. B. 31. 32.*

¶ *Et adonques a presenter son Clerke al dit eglise, &c.* A presentation is derived A presentando, quia presentare nihil aliud est quam præsto dare, seu offerre. And Littleton here briefely expresseth the effect of a presentation, for it is the act of the Patron offering his Clerke to the Bishop of that Diocesse to be instituted to such a Church in these or the like words directed to the Bishop, Præsento vobis A.B. Clericum meum ad Ecclesiam de Dale, &c. This may be done aswell by word, as by writing, and if it be by writing it is no Deede, for the presentation is of the Clerke, and the direction to the Bishop, so as this writing is in nature of a Letter to the Bishop: and this is the reason that the King himselfe may present by word as elsewhere is said. A Villein at this day purchaseth an Advowson in fee, the Church becomes voyde, the Lord for 100. pound given by A.B. Clerke presents him to the Church, and his Clerke is admitted, instituted and inducted, yet this gaineth not the Advowson to the Lord. (d) And so it is in that case if any on the behalfe of A.B had given or contracted with the Lord in consideration of any valuable thing to present A B. to the said Church, albeit it had beene without the consent or knowledge of A.B. yet it should not have vested the Advowson in the Lord. But this was not Law when Littleton wrote. (e) But now by the statute of 31. Eliz. the presentation, admission, institution and induction in both the said cases and in the like are made voide, where before the said statute they were but voydable by deprivation. And if a man present by usurpation to a benefice by reason of any corrupt contract, agreement, &c. that presentation, and the institution and induction thereupon are voyde, for that act extends to all Patrons aswell by wrong as by right; but where any presents by usurpation, the rightfull Patron and not the King shall present, for otherwise every rightfull Patron may lose his presentation. And such an incumbent that commeth in by reason of any such corrupt agreement is so absolutely disabled for ever after to be presented to that Church, as the King himselfe, to whom the Law giveth the title of Presentation in that case, cannot present him againe to that Church, for the Act being made for suppression of symonie, and such corrupt agreements so binds the King in that case, as he cannot present him that the Law hath disabled, for the words of the Act be, Shall thereupon and from thenceforth be adjudged a disabled person in Law to have or enjoy the same benefice. (f) And the partie being disabled by the Act of Parliament, (which being an absolute and direct Law) cannot be dispensed withall by any grant, &c. with a Non obstante, as it may be, when any thing is prohibited Sub modo as upon a penaltie given to the King. And the said Act doth not only extend to benefices with cure, but to Dignities, Prebends, and all other Ecclesiasticall livings.

(d) Adiudge in communi banco. Mich. 41 & 42 El. inter Baker & Rogers.
(e) Adiudged in the Kings bench. Mich 13 Ia. in a quare Imp: brought by the King against the Bishop of Norwich, Thomas Cole & Robert Secker Clerke for the Vicarage of Haverell in Suff.
(f) Pl. Com. 502. 27. H. 8. 2. H. 7 6. 11. H. 7 11. 13. H. 7 8. b. 11. H. 4. 76. 5. E. 3. 29. F. N. B. 211. E.

¶ *Clerke.* Clericus is twofold, Ecclesiasticus (which Littleton here intendeth) and he is either secular, or regular, so called because he is Servus & hæreditas domini: and Laicus, and in this sence is signified a Pen-man, who getteth his living in some Court or otherwise by the use of his pen. *4. H. 4. ca. 12.*

Note if the Church becommeth voide, albeit the present avoydance be not by Law grantable over, yet may the Lord of the Villeine present in his owne name, and thereby gaine the inheritance of the Advowson to him and his heires for albeit it be not grantable over, yet it is not meerely a Chose in action, (g) for if a Feme covert be seised of an Advowson, and the Church becommeth voide, and the wife dieth the husband shall present to the Advowson, (h) but otherwise it is of a bond made to the wife, because that is meerely in action.

(g) 14. H. 4. 12. 38. E. 3. 35. 13. E. 3. 9. quare. imp. 57.
(h) 43. E. 3. 10. 39. E. 3. 5. 4. H. 6. 5.

Section 181.

¶ Item il y ad villein regard, & villeine en gros.

Also there is a villeine regardant, and a villein in grosse.

¶ *Villein regardant.* Hee is called regardant to the Manor, because he hath the charge to *8. H. 7. 4.*

to be all base or villenous services within the same, and to gard and keepe the same from all filthis or loathsome things that might annoy it, and his service is not certaine, but hee must haue regard to that which is commanded unto him. And thereupon hee is called Regardant, A quo præstandum seruitium incertum & indeterminatum, vbi scire non poterit vespere, quale seruitium fieri debet mane, viz. vbi quis facere tenetur quicquid ei præceptum fuerit, As before hath beene obserued. And Littleton sayeth hereafter, That no other thing is said to be regardant but onely a Villeine: (l) Yet in old Bookes it was sometimes applied to Seruices.

Bract.li.2.fo.26. Mir.ca.2. §.18.

Vid.Sect.184.

(l) 20.E.3.tit.Vse 30.

¶ *Ingrosse*, is that which belongs to the person of the Lord, and belongeth not to any Mannor, Lands, &c.

villein regardant est sicome home est seisi dun Mañ a que un villein est regardãt, & celuy que est seisie del dit mañ, ou ceux q̃ estat il ad en mesm le mannor ount este seises de le dit villein & de ses Auncestors, come villeins & niefs regardants a mesme le mannor de temps dont memorie ne curt. Et villeine en grosse est, lou un hõe seisie dun Mannor a que un villeine est regardant, & il graunt mesm le villein p son fait a un auť, donq̃s il est villein en grosse, & nemy regardant.

A villein regardant is, as if a man be seised of a Mannor, to which a villeine is regardant, and he which is seised of the said Mannor, or they whose estate he hath in the same Mannor, haue beene seised of the Villein & of his Ancestours as villeins & niefs regardant to the same mannor time out of memory of man. And villein in grosse is, where a man seised of a Mannor wherunto a villein is regardãt, & granteth the same villein by his Deed to another, then he is a villein in grosse, and not regardant.

Sect. 182.

Mir.ca.2.§.18.

¶ This needeth no explanation. but to adde the saying of an antient Author, Seruage de home est subiection, issuant de cy grand antiquitie, que nul franke coppe poet estre troue per humane remembrance.

¶ Item si un hõe & ses Ancestors que hẽe il est, ount este seisies dun villein et de ses ancestors, come des Villeins en grosse, de tẽps dont memorie ne curt, tiels sont Villeines en grosse.

ALso if a man and his Ancestours whose heire he is, haue beene seised of a Villeine, and of his Auncestors as of Villeines in Grosse, time out of memorie of man, These are Villeines in Grosse.

Sect. 183.

Vi.Sect.441.294.174.74.
(l) Bract.li.5.Tract.5.ca.28.

(m) Glan.li.ca.1.

¶ OF *fine*. In Latyne, Finis. (l) Ideo dicitur finalis concordia, quia imponit finem litibus, & est exceptio peremptoria. (m) Finis est amicabilis compositio & finalis concordia ex consensu & licentia

¶ Et hic nota, que tiels choses q̃ ne poient este grants, ne aliẽs sans fait ou fine, home que voile auer tiels choses per pre-

AND heere note, that such things which cannot be granted nor aliened without Deed or Fine, a man which will haue

preſcription, ne poet autrement preſcriber forſque en luy, & en ſes Auncestors que heire il eſt & nemy per ceux parols, en luy & en ceux que eſtate il ad, p̄ ceo q̃ il ne poet auer lour eſtate ſans fait ou auter eſcripture, le quel couient deſte monſtre a le court, ſi il voile auer aſcun aduantage de ceo. Et pur ceo que le grant & alienation dun villeine en gros ne giſt ſās fait ou auť eſcriptuř, hōe ne poit p̄ſcriber ē vn villein ē gros ſās mōſtrās d̄ſcriptuř, ſinon en ſoy meſme que claime le villeine, & en ſes Anceſtors que heire il eſt, Mes d̄ tiels choſes que ſont regardants ou appendāts a vn mannor, ou a auters terres & Tenements home poet preſcriber que il et ceux que eſtate il ad, queux fueront ſeiſies de le Mannor, ou de tiels terres & Tenements, &c. ont eſte ſeiſies de tiels choſes come regardants ou appendants a l' mannor, ou a tiels tres & tenements, de temps dont memorie, &c. Et la cauſe eſt, pur ceo que tiel Manor,

ſuch things by preſcription, cānot otherwiſe preſcribe, but in him and in his Auncestors whoſe heire hee is, and not by theſe words, In him & them whoſe eſtate hee hath, for that he cānot haue their eſtate without Deed or other Writing, the which ought to bee ſhewed to the Court, if hee will take any aduantage of it. And becauſe the grant and alienation of a villeine in groſſe, lieth not without Deed or other Writing, a man cannot preſcribe in a Villein in groſſe, without ſhewing forth a Writing, but in himſelfe which claims the Villeine, and in his Aunceſtours whoſe heire hee is. But of ſuch things which are regardant or appending to a Mannour, or to other lands and tenements, a man may preſcribe, that hee and they whoſe eſtate hee hath who were ſeiſed of the Mannour, or of ſuch lands and Tenements, &c. haue bin ſeiſed of thoſe things, as regardant or appendant to the mannor or to ſuch lands & tenements time out of mind of man: And the

Domini Regis, vel eius Iuſticiariorum. (n) Talis concordia finalis dicitur eo quod finem imponit negotio, adeo vt neutra pars litigant̄ ab eo de cætero poterit recedere. Of the ſeuerall parts of a Fine, and many incidents to the ſame, you ſhall read in my Reports

¶ *Que eſtate, &c.*

Quorū ſtatum, as much to ſay, whoſe eſtate he hath. Here Littleton declareth one excellent rule, (o) That a man cannot preſcribe in any thing by a que eſtate, that lyeth in grant, and cannot paſſe without Deed or Fine, but in him and his Aunceſtors he may, becauſe he comes in by diſcent, without any conueyance. Neither can a man plead a que eſtate in himſelfe, of any thing that cannot paſſe without Deed, (p) but in another he may, as in barre of an auowrie, the Plaintife may plead, a que eſtate in the ſeigniorie in the auowant. But Littletons words are to bee obſerued, (Home que voile auer tiels choſes per preſcription) Therefore (q) when a thing that lieth in graunt is but a conueyance to the thing claimed by preſcription, there a que eſtate may bee alledged of a thing that lieth in grant, as a man may preſcribe, that he and his Anceſtors, and all thoſe whoſe eſtate hee hath in an Hundred, haue time out of mind, &c. had a Leet, &c. this is good, &c.

(r) Regularly the Plaintife ſhall not intitle him by A que eſtate, but hee muſt ſhew how he came by it, but after Auowrie made, the Plaintife ſhall plead a que eſtate, becauſe he is now become as a Defendant.

(ſ) A man may plead, A que eſtate of a tenure in taile, or of an eſtate for life, ſo as he auerreth the life of them, but he cannot plead a que eſtate, of a Leaſe for yeares, or at will.

(t) A Diſſeiſor, Abatour, Intruder, Recoueror, or any other that commeth in the poſt, ſhall

(u) *Lib. 9. cap. 3. Statut. de Modo leuandi Fines. Pl Com. 357.*

Lib. 5. fol. 38. Toyes caſe.

(o) *22. Aſſ. 53. 23. Aſſ 6. 12. H. 7. 10. 18.*

(p) *39. H. 6. 8. 18. E. 4. 23.*

(q) *11. H. 4. 89. 19. R 2. Action ſur le caſe 51. 13. E. 3. Br. 674.*

(r) *9. E 4. 3. 6. 29. Aſſ. 19. 2. H. 6 10. 48. E. 3. Tit, 33. 3. H. 28.*

(ſ) *41. Aſſ 2. 40. Aſſ. 28. 2. H. 4. 20. 15. E. 4. 1. 5. H. 7. 39. 18. E. 4. 10. 7. E. 6. Tit. Que eſtate Br. 31. 27. H. 6. 3. 7. El. Dyer 238.*

(t) *22. H. 6. 34. 6. E. 4. 12. 31. H. 8. Que eſtate Br 48. 39. H. 6. 14. 9. H. 6. Eſtop. 25*

(u) 11.H.4.81.27.H.6.32. 9.E.4.3. 2.E.6.111.que estate, 8.1.E.6.que estate, Br.49.

shall plead a que estate.

(v) A que estate must bee alledged in the Tenant or Defendant himselfe, and not in one in the meane conveyance from whom hee claymeth and yet some bookes be to the contrary.

ou tres & tenements, poyent passer per alienation sans fait, &c.

reason is for that such manor or lands and tenements may passe by alienation without deed,&c.

¶ *Le quel covient deste monstre al court.* The reason whereof a Deede that is pleaded ought to be shewed to the Court is, because every Deede must prove it selfe to have sufficient words in Law whereof the Court must adiudge, and also to bee proved by others as by witnesses or other proofe if the Deede be denied which is matter of fact.

¶ *Per alienation sauns fait,&c.* Here by (&c.) is implyed, that whatsoever passeth by Livery of seisin either in Deede or in Law, may passe without Deede, and not only the Rents and services parcell of the Mannor shall with the demeanes, as the more principall and worthy passe by Livery without Deede, but all things regardant, appendant, and appurtenant to the Mannor as incidents or adiuncts to the same shall together with the Mannor passe without Deede, all which, as here it appeareth, and else-where is said, shall passe without saying Cum pertinentijs.

Section 184.

¶ R*egardant*, *Vide Sect.* 181.

¶ *Appendants.* Appendant is any inheritance belonging to another that is superiour or more worthy. In law it is called Pertinens quasi invicem tenens holding one another, a word indifferent both to things appendant and things appurtenant, the quality and nature of the things doe make the difference, but regardant (as our Author saith) is only applied to a villeine.

Vide Sect.1.

(w) 5.Ass.p.8.H.7.4.5. 28.H.8.Dier.30.b. Pl. Com.381.F.N.B. fo.181.

(w) Appendants are ever by prescription, but appurtenants may be created in some cases at this day. As if a man at this day grant to a man and his heires common in such a moore for his beasts levant or couchant upon his mannor, or if he grant to another common of Estovers or turbary in fee simple to be burnt or spent within his mannor, by these grants these Commons are appurtenant to the mannor, and shall passe by the grant thereof. In the civill Law it is called Adjunctum.

E Cest ascavoir, que nul chose est nosme regardant a un mannor, &c. forsque villein, mes certeine auters choses come aduowson & comon de pasture, &c. sont nosmes appendants al mannor ou al tres & tenements, &c.

AND it is to be understood that nothing is named regardant to a mannor,&c. but a villeine, but certaine other things as an aduowson, & common of pasture,&c. are named appendant to the mannor or to the lands and tenements,&c.

(x) 43.Ass.p.10. 43.E.3.22.

(x) If A. be seised of a mannor whereunto the franchise of waife and stray and such like are appendant, and the King purchaseth the mannor with the appurtenances, now are the royall Franchises reunited to the Crowne, and not appendant to the Mannor, but if he grant the mannor in as large and ample manner as A. had, &c. it is said that the Franchises shall bee appendant (or rather appurtenant) to the Mannor.

(y) Hill & Granges case. Pl.Com.168.

Concerning things appendant & appurtenant, two things are implied. (y) First that prescription (which regularly is the mother thereof) doth not make any thing appendant or appurtenant, unlesse the thing appendant or appurtenant agree in quality and nature to the thing whereunto it is appendant or appurtenant, as a thing corporeall cannot properly bee appendant to a thing corporeall, nor a thing incorporeall to a thing incorporeall. But things incorporeall which lye in grant as Advowsons, Villeines, Commons and the like, may bee appendant to things corporeall, as a Mannor house or lands, or things corporeall to things incorporeall, as lands to an Office.

(z) 1.H.7.24.Pl.Com.169.

(a) 5.Ass.9.

(b) 10.E.3.5.37.H.6.34. 26.H.8.4.lib.4.fo.36.37. in Tirringhams case.

(z) But yet (as hath beene said) they must agree in nature and quality, for (a) common of Turbary or of Estovers cannot be appendant or appurtenant to land, but to a house, to be spent there. (b) Nor a Leete that is temporall, to a Church or Chappell which is Ecclesiasticall. Neither can a Nobleman, Esquire, &c. clayme a seate in a Church by prescription

tion as appendant or belonging to land, but to a house, for that such a seat belongeth to the house in respect of the inhabitancie thereof, and therefore if the house bee part of a Mannor, yet in that case he may clayme the seate as appendant to the house for the reason aforesaid.

Secondly, that nothing can be properly appendant or appurtenant to any thing unlesse the principall or superiour thing bee of perpetuall subsistance and continuance, for example. An Aduowson, that is said to be appendant to a Mannor, is in rei veritate appendant to the Demesnes of the Mannor, which are of perpetuall subsistance and continuance, and not to Rents or seruices, which are subiect to extinguishment and destruction.

5.E.6. Dier.70.b.

An Aduowson is appendant to the Mannor of Dale, of which Mannor the Mannor of Sale is holden, the Mannor of Sale is made parcell of the Mannor of Dale by way of Eschcat, the Aduowson is only appendant to the Mannor of Dale.

And where it is said that a chamber may be parcell of a Corody, and passe by the name of the Corody which may be extinguished, there he that hath the Corody hath but his habitation in the chamber, as a Fellow of Trinity Colledge in Cambridge hath in his chamber, or as one that had a Corody and a chamber in an house of Religion, he had but his habitation only. As for Offices of fee whereunto land may appertaine they are of perpetuall subsistance, either being in esse, or in that they are grantable ouer.

31.H.6.15.b.

Note that an Aduowson at one turne may be appendant, and at another Turne in grosse, as if the Mannor be deuided betweene Coperceners, and euery one hath a part of the Mannor without saying any thing of the Aduowson appendant, the Aduowson remaines in copercenarie, and yet in euery of their turnes, it is appendant to that part which they haue; and so it is if they make composition to present against common right, yet it remaines appendant. But if upon such a partition an expresse exception be made of the Aduowson, then the Aduowson remaines in Copercenarie and in grosse, and so are the bookes reconciled.

13.E.2.quar.Imp.170. 43.E.3.35. 13.E.3.quar.Imp.58. 17.E.3.38. 9.Eliz.Dier.259.7.E.3.20. 19.E.3.quar.Imp.59. 35.H.6.32.33.38.H.6.9. 2.H.7.5.

¶ *Comon de pasture.* (c) Communia, It commeth of the English word Common, because it is common to many, and thereupon, and accordingly is here called by Littleton Common of pasture, for that the feeding of beasts in the land wherein the Common is to be had belongs to many.

(c) Glanvill, lib.13.ca.36. Bract. lib.4.ca.19, & 40. Brit.cap.55.56.57. Fleta, lib.4.ca.19. Mirror.ca.5 §.3.

(d) There be foure kindes of Common of pasture, viz. Common appendant which is of common right, (and therefore a man need not prescribe for it) for beasts commonable (that is) that serue for the maintenance of the plough, as horse and oxen to plow the land, and for kine and sheepe to compester the land, and is appendant to arrable land.

(d) 20.E.3.Admesurement, 8. Temps E.1.Common 24.17. E.2.ibid.23.4.H.6. 22.H.6.

(e) The second is Cōmon appurtenant that is for beasts not commonable, as swine, goates, and the like. (f) If a man purchase part of the land wherein Common appendant is to bee had, the Common shalbe apportioned, because it is of common right, but not so of a Common appurtenant, or of any other Common of what nature soeuer. But both Common appendant and appurtenant, shalbe apportioned by alienation of part of the land to which Common is appendant or appurtenant, and for Common appurtenant one must prescribe.

(e) 37.H.6.34. 26.H.8.4. F.N.B.181.

(f) Lib.4.fo.37.38. &c. Turninghams case.

(g) The third is Common per cause de vicinage, which differeth from both the other Commons, for that no man can put his beasts therein, but they must escape thither of themselues by reason of vicinity, in which case one may Inclose against the other, though it hath beene so used time out of minde, for that it is but an excuse for trespasse.

(g) Lib.8.fo.78.79. W.Wildes case.

The last is Common in grosse, which is so called for that it appertaineth to no land, and must be by writing or prescription. Of Common appendant, appurtenant, and in grosse, some bee certaine, that is for a certaine number of beasts, some certaine by consequent, viz. for such as be leuant and couchant upon the land, and some be more incertaine, as common sans number in grosse, and yet the Tenant of the land must common or feed there also.

There bee also (h) diuers other Commons as of Estouers, of Turbary, of Pischarye, of digging for Coles, Mineralls and the like (i) If Common appendant bee claymed to a Mannor, yet in rei veritate it is appendant to the Demesnes and not to the seruices, and therefore if a Tenancie escheate, the Lord shall not encrease his Common by reason of that (k) If a man clayme by Prescription any manner of Common in another mans land, and that the owner of the land shall be excluded to haue Pasture, Estouers or the like, this is a prescription or custome against the Law, to exclude the owner of the soyle, for it is against the nature of this word Common, and it was implyed in the first graunt that the owner of the soyle should take his reasonable profit there, as it hath beene adiudged. * (l) But a man may prescribe or alledge a custome to haue and enioy Solam vesturam terræ, from such a day till such a day, and hereby the owner of the soyle shall be excluded to pasture or feede there, and so hee may prescribe to haue Seperalem pasturam, and exclude the owner of the soyle from feeding there. Nota diuersitatem. (m) So a man may prescribe to haue Seperalem piscariam in such a water, and the owner of the soyle shall not fish there, but if hee clayme to haue Communiam piscariæ, or Liberam piscariam, the owner of the soyle shall fish there, and all this hath beene

(h) Fleta ubi supra.

(i) 18.E.3.fo.43.

(k) 15 E.2.Prescript.51. 12.H.8.fo.2.

** Pasch. 26.Eliz. in the Kings Bench, inter White & Shirland in Com.Oxon. Vid. Sect.1.& 2.*

(l) Vid.3.E.3.29,30. 4.E.3.7. 46.E.3.23. 15.E.2.Prescript.51.

(m) 20.H.6.4. 10.H.7.24. Temps E.1.Assise 422.

(*) Inter Chinery & Fishen in le Common Banke in replevin & Mich. 29. & 30. Eliz. inter Shirland & White in Com. Oxon. Et inter Foisson & Craithrode eodem termino in Essex.
(n) 19. H. 6. 33.
(o) Vide Sect. 541.

beene resolved. (*) And therefore it is necessary for every man by learned advice to pleade according to the truth of his case for Parols sont plea.

(n) A man seised of land whereunto common is appendant, and is disseised, the Disseisee cannot use the common untill he entreth into the land whereunto it is appendant, (o) But if a man be disseised of a Mannor whereunto an Advowson is appendant, hee may present unto the Advowson before he enters into the Mannor, and the reason of this diversitie is because in the case of the common it should be a prejudice to the Tenant of the soile. For if the Disseisee might doe it the Disseisor also might put on his Cattle, which should be a double charge to the Tenant, but not so of the Advowson.

Sect. 185.

Item si home voile en Court de record soy conuster destre villein, que ne fuit villein adevant, tiel est villeine en grosse.

Also if a man will acknowledge himselfe in a Court of Record to bee a Villeine, who was not a villeine before, such a one is a Villeine in grosse.

Bract. lib. 1. cap. 6.
Britt. fol. 78.
Fleta lib. 1. cap. 3. 43. E. 3. 4. b.
19 E. 2. tit. vill. 34.
18. E. 4. 29.
(p) 19. H. 6. 32. 26. Ass. 62.
37. Ass. 17.
11. H. 4. 16. in Appeale.

This is intended in some action brought against him that made such confession, (p) or where hee is brought into Court by course of Law, for if he commeth into the Court extraiudicially and not by any due course of Law, such confession is without warrant of Law and bindeth not the partie, because the Court had no warrant to take it. But if a Præcipe be brought against one he may confesse himselfe villeine to an estranger, and that he holds the Land in villenage of him, and this is good and shall bind him. And if in that case the demandant reply, that hee the day of his writ purchased was a free man, and thereupon issue is taken, and hee is tried to bee free yet he shall remayne villeine to the stranger in respect of his confession.

41. E. 3. tit. vill. 6.
19. H. 6. 32. b.

If a Writ of Nativo habend' be brought against one, and the Plantiffe as he ought offereth in his Count to prove the villenage by the Cousins and Kindred of the Defendant, and thereupon produceth the Uncles of the Defendant who upon examination confesse themselves to be villeines to the Demandant, this confession being entred of Record, doth so bind, that albeit they were so free before, they and the heires of their bodies are by this confession bond and Villeines for ever, for the Uncles came in by due course of Law in an Action depending in Court.

Sect. 186.

Item home que est villein est appelle villein, & feme que est villein est appelle nyefe: Sicome home que est utlage est dit utlage, & feme que est utlage est dit waive.

Also a man which is a villein is called a Villeine, and a woman which is Villein, is called a Neife. As a man which is outlawed, is called outlawed: and a woman which is outlawed, is called Waived.

Niefe. Or Naife is in Latine naturalis, seu nativa, because for the most part Niefs are bond by Nativitie.

F. N. B. 161. a.
Regist. 132. & 277.
Britton. fol. 20.
Bract. lib. 3. tract. 2. ca. 12. 13
Fleta lib. 1. cap. 28.
3. H. 5. tit. utlawrie Statham.

¶ *Feme que est utlage est dit waive.*

Waive, Wauiata and not utlegata or exlex, for that women are not sworne in Leets, or Tornes, as men which be of the age of 12. yeares or more be, and therefore men may be called utlegati, id est, extra legem positi, but women are Waiviatæ, id est, derelictæ, left out or not regarded, because they were not sworne to the Law, wherein it is to be noted that of ancient time a man was not said to bee within the Law, that was not sworne to the Law, which is intended of the Oath of Alleagiance in the Leet.

Regist. orig. 132.

And the Outlawrie of a woman is legally called Waiviaria mulieris.

Sect. 187.

¶ ITem si vn Villein, prent frank feme a feme, & ad issue enter eux, lissues serront Villeines. Mes si niefe prent franke home a sa baron, lour issues sert franke.

* Et cest contrarie a le ley ciuill, car la est dit, Partus sequitur ventrem.*

ALso if a Villeine taketh a freewoman to wife, and haue issue betweene them, the issues shall be Villeines. But if a Niefe taketh a freeman to her husband, their issue shall be free.

* This is contrarie to the Ciuill Law, for there it is said, *Partus sequitur ventrem.* *

¶ Circulus totum alimentum à stipite capit poma tamen edit sua. The science takes all his nourishment from the stocke, and yet it produceth his own fruit.

Fortescue cap.42. Glanuill.lib.5.cap.6. Hill.29.E.1. coram Rege Eborum in Thesaur.

(q) Si quis de seruo patre natus sit & matre libera pro seruo reddatur occisus in ea parte, quia semper à patre, non à matre generationis ordo texitur, si pater sit liber & mater ancilla pro libero reddatur occisus. (r) Lex Angliæ nunquam matris sed semper patris conditionem imitari partum iudicat.

(q) Lib.rub.cap.77.

(r) Fortescue vbi supra.

(s) The husband and wife are all one person in Law, and the Niefe marrying a freeman is infranchised during the couerture, and therefore by the Common Law of England, the issue is free.

(s) Herewith agreeth Britton fol.78.b.

(t) Si mulier serua copulata sit libero, &c. quod partus habebit hæreditatem, & mater nullam dotem, quia mortuo viro suo libero redit in pristinum statum seruitutis nisi hæres ei dotem fecerit de gratia. And when a bondman marrieth a free woman, they are all one person in Law, and Duæ animæ in carne vna, and vxor subiecta est viro, & sub potestate viri.

(t) Bract.lib.4.fol.198.b. Idem lib 1.ca 6. Mirror.cap.2.§.18.

(u) Obseruatur in Com' Cornubiæ de tali consuetudine, quæ talis est quod si liber homo ducat natiuam aliquam in vxorem ad liberum tenementum & liberum thorum, si ex ea duæ procreantur filiæ, vna erit libera & altera villana, quia ibi partiti sunt pueri inter liberum patrem & Dominus vxoris villanæ.

(u) Bract.lib.4.fol.271.

(x) Qui vero procreantur ex natiua vnius, & natiuo alterius, proportionabiliter inter Dominos sunt diuidendi.

(x) Glanuill.lib.5.cap.6.

¶ *Et ceo est contrarie al ley ciuil.* For true it is that by that Law Partus sequitur ventrem, aswell where a free man takes a bond woman to wife, as where a bond man takes a free woman to wife. In the first case the issue is by the Ciuill Law bond, and in the other free, both which Cases are contrarie to the Law of England: but this is no part of Littleton, and therefore we in this manner passe it ouer.

Fortescue ca.42.

Section. 188.

¶ ITem nul bastard poit estre villein, si non que il voile soy conuster estre villeine en court de record, car il est en ley quasi nullius filius, pur ceo que il ne poit enheriter a nulluy.

ALso no bastard may be a villeine, vnlesse hee will acknowledge himselfe to bee a villeine in a Court of Record, for he is in law, *quasi nullius filius*, because he cannot be heire to any.

¶ *NVllius* (a) *filius.*

Cui pater est populus, pater est sibi nullus, & omnis,
Cui pater est populus, non habet ille patrem.

(a) Vide Sect.199. 13.E.1.tit.villen.36.

(b) Some hold that the Bastard of a niefe shall bee a villeine. (c) And others hold that if a villeine hath a Bastard by a woman, and after marieth the woman, that this Bastard is a villeine, but the law is contrarie in both cases, for in both cases, the issue by the Common Law is a Bastard, and consequently, quasi nullius filius, as Littleton here saith. (d) Though a Bastard be a reputed sonne, yet is he not such a sonne in consideration whereof an vse can bee raysed for the reason that Littleton here yelds, because in iudgement of Law he is Nullius filius. (e) And for

(b) Bract.lib.1.fol.5.a. Fleta lib.1.cap.3. Britton,fol.78. (c) 39.E.3.34. 43.E.3.4. Britton.vbi supra.

(d) 23.Eliz. Dier.374.

(e) 13.Eliz.Dier.296.

14.Eliz.Dier.313. 18.Eliz.Dier.345.

for the same reason where the Statute of 32.H.8. of Wills speaketh of Children, bastard children are not within that Statute, and the bastard of a woman is no child within that Statute where the mother conveys Lands vnto him.

(f) Trin.18.E.1.Rot.61. Bedf. coram Rege.

(f) It was found by verdict that Henrie the sonne of Beatrice which was the wife of Robert Radwell deceased, was borne per vndecim dies post vltimum tempus legitimum mulieribus constitutum. And thereupon it was adiudged, Quod dictus Henricus dici non debet filius prædicti Roberti secundum legem & consuetudinem Angliæ constitut'. Now Legitimum tempus in that case appointed by Law at the furthest is nine moneths, or fortie weekes, but shee may be deliuered before that time, which iudgement I thought good to mention. And this agreeth with that in Esdras. Vade & interroga prægnantem, si quando impleuerit nouem menses suos ad huc poterit matrix eius retinere partum in semetipsa? & dixi, non potest Domine.

4.Esdras 4.41. Vide Tancirell. noua reperta, pag.485.&c.

Sect. 189.

¶ Item chescun villein est able & franke de suer touts mañers dactions enuers chescun person, forspris enuers son Seignior a que il est villein. Et vncore en certein choses il poit auer action enuers son Seignior. Car il poit auer enuers son Seignior vn action dappeal ď mort son pere, ou dauters de ſs auncesters que heire il est.

Also euery Villein is able and free to sue all manner of Actions against euery person, except against his Lord to whom he is villeine: and yet in certain things he may haue against his Lord an Action, for hee may haue against his Lord an action of appeale for the death of his father, or of his other Ancestors whose heire he is.

(g) Bract.lib.4.fol 196. Britton cap.49.fol.125.

¶ *Chescun Villeine est able & franke de suer,&c.* (g) In an Action brought by a villeine. Versus non Dominum, non valebit ei exceptio, quia est seruus alienus ex quo nihil ad ipsum verum liber sit an seruus. (h) And it is to bee obserued, that hee that hath but a particular estate in a villeine, as tenant for life or for yeares shall disable the villeine if he brings an action against him, but the Lessor shall not (as it is said) disable him, (i) Examinatio villenagii non tenet, nisi ex ore veri Domini fuerit pronunciata.

(h) 14.E.4.6.b. 15.E.4.32. 20.E.3. tit Villein 10. 38.E.3.21.

(i) Fleta lib.2.cap.4.

¶ *Appeale.* Appellum commeth of the French word Appeller, that signifieth to accuse, or to appeach. An Appeach. (k) An Appeale is an accusation of one vpon another with a purpose to attaint him of felonie by words ordained for it.

(k) Brito cap.22.fol.38. Bracton. lib.1.fol.6.

¶ *De mort* (l) for a villeine shall not haue an appeale of robberie against his Lord, for that he may lawfully take the goods of the villeine as his owne. (m) And if in an Appeale of death it be found for the Plaintiffe, he is enfranchised for euer. Hinc enim est quod eo ipso sunt huiusmodi Domini seruos suos amissuri cum de iniurijs fuerint conuicti. And there is no diuersitie herein whether he be a villeine regardant, or ingrosse although some haue said the contrarie.

(l) 18.E.3.32. 11.H.4.93. 1.H.4.6. 29.H.6.tit. Corone 17.
(m) Fleta li.1.ca.5.1.H.4.6

Section 190.

¶ Auxi vn Niefe que est rauie per sa seignior, poit auer vn appeale de rape enuers luy.

Also a Niefe that is rauished by her Lord, may haue an Appeale of Rape against him.

(n) Mirror.ca.1.§.12. Cap.3.de rape. & cap.4.de homicide.

¶ *Rape.* (n) raptus is when a man hath carnall knowledge of a woman by force and against her will.

¶ *Appeale de rape.* By the generall puruiew of the Statutes, (*) that giue the Appeale of Rape, the Niefe shall haue an Appeale of Rape against the Lord. (o) And it seemeth by the ancient Authors of the Law, that this so hainous an offence was seuerely punished by losse of eyes and priuie members, but of old time it was felony which you may reade at large in the second part of the Institutes W.1.cap.13.

(*) W.1.ca.13. W.2.ca.35. 6.R.2.ca.6. 11.H.4.cap.13. 1.E.4.cap.1.
(o) 29.H.6.tit.Coron.17. Bract.lib.3.fol.147.

(p) And

(p) And this word Rape which our Author here vseth is so appropriated by Law to this case, as without this word (Rapuit) it cannot be expressed by any Periphrasis or circumlocution, for Carnaliter cognovit eam or the like will not serue.

(p) 9.E.4.26. *Mirror*, ca.1.§.13.

Section 191.

¶ AUxy si vn villeine soit fait executor a vn auter, & le Sñr del villeine fuit en dette a le testator en vn certeine summe dargent que nest my paie, en ceo case le villeine come executor de le testator auera action de det enuers son seignior, pur ceo q̃ il ne recouera le debt a son vse demesne, mes al vse le testator.

ALſo if a villeine be made executor to another, and the Lord of the villeine was indebted to the teſtator in a certaine ſumme of money which is not paid, In this caſe the villeine as executor of the teſtator ſhall haue an action of debt againſt his Lord, because hee ſhall not recouer the debt to his own vſe, but to the vſe of the teſtator.

¶ Of this matter sufficient hath beene spoken in this chapter before. The villeine shall haue an action as Executor against his Lord, and it is no plea for the Lord, to say that the Plaintife is his villeine, for hee shall not bee enfranchised by the vser of this action, because hee hath it by a gift in Lawe to the vse of the Testator and not to his owne vse.

21.E.4.50.a.

Sect. 192.

ITem le Sñr ne poit prender hors del possession de tiel villein q̃ est executor les biens le mort, & sil face, le villeine cõe executor auera action de trespasse de mesmñs les bñs issint prises enuers son Sñr, & recouera damages al vse le testator. Mes en touts tielx cases, il couient que la Sñr que est defendant en tielx actions face protestation, q̃ le plaintife est son villein, ou autrement le villeine serra enfranchise, co-

ALſo the Lord may not take out of the poſſeſſion of ſuch villeine who is Executor of the goods of the deceaſed, and if he doth, the villeine as execntor ſhall haue an action for the ſame goods ſo taken againſt his Lord, and ſhall recouer damages to the vſe of the teſtator. But in all ſuch caſes, it behoueth that the Lord which is defendant in ſuch actions maketh proteſtation that the plaintife is his villein, or otherwiſe the villeine ſhall bee infran-

¶ *LE Seignior ne poet prender hors del possession*, &c. Of this also sufficient hath beene said before.

¶ *Et recouera damages al vse del testator.* (q) Note damages recouered by the Executor in an action of trespasse shall bee assets, and yet they were neuer in the testator. And so it is in other like cases as by our bookes it appeareth.

(q) 21.E.4.4.b. 11.H.6.35.b. 3.H.6.2. 2.H.4,21. 1.H.4.6.

(r) If an Executor hath a villeine for yeares, and the villeine purchases lands in fee the Executor entreth, he shall haue the whole fee simple, but because he had the villein in auter droit, viz. as Executor to the vse of the dead it shall be assets in his hands. Note a diuersitie betweene the quantitie of the estate and the qualitie of it, for the Law respecteth not the quantity of the estate, for not only

(r) *Doct. & Stud.* Brooke tit. *Villenage*, 70.

(s) Tenant

(s) L.5.E.4.61.
(t) 21.H.6.37.

(s) Tenant in taile and Tenant for life of a villeine shall haue the perquisite of the villeine in fee, but (t) Tenant for yeares and Tenant at will also shall haue it in fee.

ment que le matter soit troue p̄ le Sñr, & encounter l' villein, come est dit.

chised although the matter bee found for the Lord, & against the villeine as it is said.

(u) 41.E.21.
(w) 18.E.3.29.

But the Law respecteth the qualitie, for in what right he hath the Villeine, in the same right shall he haue the perquisite, as in the case of the Executor aboue said, and in the case of the Bishop (u) that hath the Villeine in right of his Church, he shall haue the perquisite in the same right.

(w) So if a man hath a Villeine in the right of his wife, he shall haue the perquisite also in her right. But if the purchase be after issue had, then the Baron shal haue the perquisite to him and his heires, because by the issue hee is intituled to bee Tenant by the Curtesie in his owne right.

Vi. Sect. 193.
(x) Pl. Com. 276.b. In Greisbrokes case.

¶ *Protestation*. (x) Protestatio **is an exclusion of a conclusion, that a** partie to an Action may by pleading incurre, or it is a safegard to the partie which keepeth him from being concluded by the plea he is to make, if the issue be found for him: but in this case without a protestation, albeit the issue be found for the Lord, the Villeine shall be enfranchised, as it appeareth hereafter in this Section.

Sect. 193.

Britt. fol. 79. 125.b. 126.a.

¶ C*Eo serra trie en le le Countie, &c.* Be tried, that is as it is intended by the verdict of xii. men, that is called in Law a triall triatio.

(a) 7.E.3.50. 26.E.3.73. 38.E.3.34. 40.E.3.36. 43.E.3.4.31. 44.E.3.36. 47.E.3.26. 22.H.6.52. 35.H.6.12. 39.H.6.24. Vide Sect. 534.

(a) In this case the Law doth fauour the villeine in the issue, for otherwise by the rule of Law in like cases hee ought to answer to the speciall matter, viz. to the regardancy, but in fauour of liberty hee may reply that hee is free and of free estate, and consequently this issue concerning the person shall bee tried where the writ is brought. (b) The like law it is, if issue bee ioyned vpon the Ideocy of the Plaintife or Defendant it shall bee tried where the writ is brought because it concerneth the person.

(b) 2. Mar. Dier. 112.

¶ *In fauorem libertatis*. **It is common**ly said that three things be fauoured in Law, Life, Liberty, Dower.

(c) Fortescue, ca. 42.

(c) Impius & crudelis iudicandus est qui libertati non favet: Angliæ iura in omni casu libertati dant favorem.

Tryall is to finde out by due examination the truth of the point in issue or question betweene the parties, where-

¶ ITem si villeine suist vn actiō de trespasse, ou vn auter action enuers son Sñr en vn Countie, & le Sñr dit q̄ il ne serra respondus, pur ceo q̄ il est son villein regardant a son manor en auter County, & le Plaintife dit que il est franke & de franke estate, & nemy villeine, ceo serra trie en le Countie lou le Plaintife auoit conceiue son action, & nemy en l' county lou le manor est, & ceo est in fauorem libertatis, **& pur cel cause vn estatute fuit fait** an. 9. R. 2. cap. 2. **le tenor de quel ensuist en tiel forme. Item pur la ou plusors villeins, & Neifes, sibien des graundes Seignîors**

ALso if a villeine sueth an action of trespasse or any other action against his Lord in one Countie, and the Lord saith that he shall not bee answered because hee is his villeine regardant to his mannor in another County, & the plaintife saith that hee is free, and of a free estate, and not a villein, this shall bee tried in the Countie where the Plaintife hath conceiued his action, and not in the County where the mannor is, and this is in fauour of liberty. And for this cause a statute was made *anno* 9. *R*. 2. *ca*. 2. the tenor whereof followeth in this forme. Also for that where many villeins & neifs,

ors, come des auters gentes, sibñ espirituals come temporals sensuent, deins cities, villes, & lieux enfranchise, come en la citie de Londres, & auters semblables, & feignont diuers suits enuers lour Sñrs, a cause de eux fait franks per le respõs de lour Sñrs: Accorde est & assentus, q̃ les seigniors, ne auters, ne soyent my forbarres de lour villeines per cause de lour respons en ley. Per force de quel estatute, si ascun villeine voylloit suer ascun maner de action a son vse demesne en ascun Countie, ou il est fort a trier enuers son Seignior l' Sñr poyt eslyer de pleader que le plaintife est son villeine, ou de faire protestation que il est son villein, & de pleder son auter matter en barre. Et sils sont a issue, & lissue soit troue pur le Sñr, donqz l' villein est villeine come il fuit deuant per force de mesme lestatute. Mes si le issue soit troue pur le villeine, donque le villeine est franke, pur ceo que le

aswell of great Lords as of other men aswell of spirituall and temporall flye and goe into Cities, Townes and places franchised as into the Citie of London and other like places, and feyne diuers suites against their Lords because they would make themselues free by the answer of their Lords. It is accorded and assented, that Lords nor others shall not be forebarred of their villeins by reason of their answer in Law. By force of which statute if any villeine will sue any manner of action to his owne vse in any County where it is hard to trie against his Lord, the Lord may choose whether he wil plead that the plaintife is his villeine, or make protestation that hee is his villeine, and plead his other matter in barre. And if they be at issue, and the issue be found for the Lord, then the villeine is a villeine as hee was before by force of the same statute. But if the issue bee found for the villeine, then the villeine is free, because that the Lord tooke

upon iudgement may bee giuen. And as the question betweene the parties is twofold, so is the triall thereof: for either it is questio iuris, (and that shall be tried by the Judges either upon a Demurrer, speciall verdict or exception, for Cuilibet in sua arte perito est credendum: & quod quisque norit in hoc se exerceat, and it is commonly and truly said, Ad questionem iuris non respondent iuratores;) or it is quæstio facti. And the triall of the fact is in diuers sorts whereof a light touch is giuen before, Sect. 102. of these a triall by xii. men (here intended by Littleton) is the most frequent and common; And some few rules of Law, are necessary here to be remembred (for the better understanding of the bookes of Law hereafter) where and from what place, viz. De quo viceneto, out of what neighbourhood the Jury shall come, a necessary point to bee knowne, for if there bee a mistryall, (that is) if the Jury commeth out of a wrong place, or returned by a wrong officer and giue a verdict, iudgement ought not to bee giuen upon such a verdict. (d) Wherein the most generall rule is, that euery tryall shall be out of that Towne, Parish, or Hamlet, or place knowne out of the towne, &c. within the Record, within which the matter of fact issuable is alledged, which is most certaine and neerest thereunto, the Inhabitants whereof may haue the better and more certaine knowledge of the fact: as if the fact be alledged in quadam platea vocat' Kingstreet in civitate Westm. in com' Midd. in this case the Visne cannot come out of Platea, because it is neither Towne, Parish, Hamlet, nor place out of the neighbourhood whereof a Jury may come by Law; but in this case it shall not come out of Westminster but out of the Parish of St. Margaret, because that is the most certaine. But

Vid. Sect. 234.

Vid. Sect. 102.

Vid. Sect. 234. more of this matter.

(d) 3.E.3.73. 20.H.6.30. 7.H.4.27. 9.H.5.8. 8.H.6.34. 7.H.6.27. 17.E.3.56. 43.E.3.5. 47.E.3.6. 34.H.6.1.

therein also it is to bee noted, that if it had beene alledged in Kingstreet in the parish of St. Margaret in the County of Middlesex, then should it haue come out of Kingstreet, for then should Kingstreet haue been esteemed in law a town:

Seignior ne prist al commencement pur son plee que le villein fuit son villeine, mes ceo prist per protestation, &c.

not at the beginning for his Plee that the villeine was his villeine, but tooke this by protestation. &c.

(e) 4.E.3.30. 8.E.3.68. 39.H.6.13. *Brooke pleading* 61.
(f) 4.E.4.41. 5.E.4.20. 22.E.4.2. 35 H.6.30. 22.H.6.47. lib.1.162. *Digges case. lib.* 11.fo.25. lib.6.fo.14.
(g) 1.E.3.8. 7 H.6.38.
(h) 22.E.4.tit.visne F.27. 6.H.7.3 b 11.H.2.7.22.b. 9.E.4 3.a. 2.E.4.26. 39.H 6.tresp.93. 4.E.3.30.

(e) for whensoeuer a place is alledged generally in pleading (without some addition to declare the contrary as in this case it is) it shall be taken for a Towne. (f) And albeit Parochia generally alledged is a place incertaine, and may, (as we see by experience) include diuers Townes, yet if a matter be alledged in Parochia, it shall be intended in Law that it containeth no more Townes then one, vnlesse the party doth shew the contrary. (g) But when a parish is alledged within a City, there without question the Visne shall come out of the parish, for that is more certaine then the City.

(h) If a trespasse be alledged in D, and nul tiel ville is pleaded, the Jury shall come out De corpore comitatus, but if it be alledged in S. and D. and nul tiel ville de D. is pleaded, the Jury shall come out de Viceneto de S. for that is the more certaine. So if a matter be alledged within a Mannor, the Jury shall come de Viceneto manerij, but if the Mannor bee alledged within a towne, it shall come out of the towne, because that is most certaine, for the Mannor may extend into diuers townes. And all these points were resolued by all the Judges of England vpon conference betweene them in the Case of Iohn Arundel Esquire indited for the death of William Parker. *

* Lib.6 fo.14. *Arundels case.*
(i) 45.E.2.5.a. 46.E.3.6. & 7. *Gernons case.* 18.E.3.58. 11.H.4.56.b.57. 17.E.3.36.b 39. Ass.10. 38. Ass.30. 35. Ass.7.

(i) In a reall action where the Demandant demands land in one County, as heire to his father, and alledge his birth in another County, if it bee denied, that he is heire, it shall not be tryed where the birth was alledged, but where the land lyeth, for there the Law presumes it shal be best knowne who is heire. But if the Demandant make himselfe heire to a woman, for that is the surer and more certaine side and the mother is certaine, when perhaps the father is incertaine, and therefore there it shall be tried, where the birth is alledged, because they haue more certaine conusance then where the land lyeth. And so it is where generally bastardy is alledged, the tryall shall be in like case Mutatis mutandis. (k) If a man pleade the Kings Letters patents, and the other partie pleade Non concessit, it shall not be tryed, where the Letters patents beare Date, for they cannot be denyed, but where the land lyeth.

(k) *Mich.31. & 32.Eliz. Rot.365. in the Kings bench inter Edan & Franklyne adiudge.* 3.Mar. Dier.129. 18.Eliz. Dier.355. 17.Eliz. Dier.342.

Euery tryall must come out of the neighbourhood of a Castle, Mannor, Towne or Hamlet, or place knowne out of a Castle, Mannor, Towne or Hamlet, as some forrests and the like, as before and by the Authorityes thereupon quoted appeareth.

Euery plea concerning the person of the Plaintife, &c. shall be tried where the Writ is brought as it appeareth before.

When the matter alledged extendeth into a place at the Common Law and a place within a Franchise, it shall be tryed at the Common Law.

(l) 8.E.4.24. 9.H.6.46.47. 21.H.6.4. 18. Ass.7. 30.E.3.16.17. 7.E.4.31. 27.H.8.30. 11.H.4.68.
(m) 15.E.4.25.b 9.H.6.46 26.E.3. 7.E.4.31. 39.E.3.16.17.

(l) In an action against two, the one pleads to the Writ, the other to the action, the plea to the Writ shall be first tryed, for if that be found, all the whole Writ shall abate, and make an end of the businesse

(m) In a plea personall against diuers Defendants, the one Defendant pleades in barre to parcell, or which extendeth only to him that pleadeth it, & the other pleades a plea which goeth to the whole, the plea that goeth to the whole, (that is) to both Defendants shall be first tried, and of this opinion was Litleton in our bookes, for the tryall of that goeth to the whole, and the other Defendant shall haue aduantage thereof, for in a personall action the discharge of one is the discharge of both. As for example, if one of the Defendants in trespasse pleade a release to himselfe, (which in Law extends to both) and the other pleades not guiltie (which extends but to himselfe) or if one pleade a plea which excuses himselfe only, and the other pleads another plea, which goeth to the whole, the plea which goeth to the whole shall bee first tried, for if that be found it maketh an end of all, and the other defendant shall take aduantage hereof, because the discharge of one is the discharge of both; but in a plea reall it is otherwise, for euery Tenant may lose his part of the land; (n) as if a Præcipe be brought as heire to his father against two, and one pleade a plea which extendeth but to himselfe, and the other pleads a plea which extends to both as bastardie in the Demandant, & it is found for him, yet the other issue shall be tryed, for he shall not take aduantage of the plea of the other, because one ioyntenant may lose his part by his misplea. (o) But where an issue is ioyned for part, and a Demurrer for the residue, the Court may direct the tryall of the issue, or iudge the Demurrer first at their pleasure.

(n) 9.H.6.46. 39.E.3.16.17.
(o) *Lib.10.fo.54. and the bookes there cited.*
(p) *Mich.21. et 22.Eliz. Dier* 367. *Lib.5.fo.36.b. Bainhams case* 39.E.3.2.b. 44.E.3 6. 11 H.6.13. *Lib.5. fo.40. Dormers Case.*

(p) If a Venire fac. be awarded to the Coroners where it ought to be to the Shiriffe or the Visne commeth out of a wrong place, yet if it be Per assensum partium, and so entred of Record,

it

it shall stand, for Omnis consensus tollit errorem. And thus much of these excellent points of learning: and if you desire to know the institution and right use of this tryall by 12. men, and of the antiquitie thereof, and more of this matter, reade the 234. Section hereafter which is worthy of your observation.

Vid. Sect. 234.

¶ *Estatute.* Or statute, This commeth of the Latyn word Statutum, which is taken for an Act of Parliament made by the King, the Lords and Commons, and is devided into two branches generall and speciall. This statute here mentioned is a generall statute, and is darkely and obscurely penned,

Vid. 25. E. 3. ca. 18. F N. B. 77. e. 26. E. 3. 73.

¶ *Et sils sont a issue.* (q) Issue, exitus, a single, certaine, and materiall point issuing out of the allegations or pleas of the Plaintife and Defendant consisting regularly upon an affirmative and negative to be tried by twelve men, And it is twofold, a speciall issue, as here in the case of Littleton, or generall, as in trespasse, not guilty: in assise, nul tort, nul disseisin, &c. And as an issue naturall commeth of two severall persons, so an issue legall issueth out of two severall allegations of advers parties.

(q) Vid. Sect. 41. 4. 7. H. 6. 43. 9. E. 4. 36. 36. H. 6. 15. 5. E. 4. 26. 11. H. 4. 79.

And to make our bookes more easie to be understood concerning this point, it is good to set downe some necessary rules (amongst many other) concerning ioyning of issues. An issue being taken generally referreth to the Count, and not to the Writ: As in an Account the Writ chargeth him generally to be his receiver, the Count chargeth him specially to be his receiver by the hands of T. the Defendant pleadeth that he was never his receiver in manner and forme, &c. this shall referre to the count, so as he cannot be charged but by the receipt by the hands of T.

7. E. 3. 34.

(r) A speciall issue must be taken in one certaine materiall point which may bee best understood, and best tryed.

(s) An issue shall not be taken upon a negative pregnant, which implyeth another sufficient matter, but upon that which is single and simple, as Ne dona pas per le fait, imply a gift by parol, therefore the issue must be Ne dona pas modo & forma.

(t) An Issue ioyned upon an Absque hoc, &c ought to have an affirmative after it: two affirmatives shall not make an issue, unlesse it be lest the issue should not be tried.

(u) Some issues bee good upon matter affirmative and negative, albeit the affirmative and negative be not in precise words, as in debt for rent upon a lease for yeares, the Defendant pleades that the Plaintif had nothing at the time of the Lease made, the Plaintif replyeth that he was seised in fee, &c. this is a good issue.

(w) Where the issue is ioyned of the part of the Defendant, the entry is Et de hoc ponit se super patriam, but if it be of the part of the Plaintife, the entrie is Et hoc petit quod inquiratur per patriam.

(x) There be some negative pleas, that bee issues of themselves, whereunto the Demandant, or Plaintife cannot reply, no more then to a generall issue which is Et prædictus A similiter. As if the Tenant doe vouche, and the Demandant counterplead that the Vouchee or any of his Ancestors had any thing, &c. whereof he might make a Feoffment, hee shall conclude, Et hoc petit quod inquiratur per patriam, & prædictus tenens similiter. So in a Fine pleaded by the Tenant, &c. the Demandant may say, Quod partes finis nihil habuerunt, & hoc petit quod inquiratur per patriam & præd' tenens similiter. And so in a Writ of Dower, the Tenant plead Vnques seisie que dower, he shall conclude, Et de hoc ponit se super patriam, & pred'. petens similiter, and so in many other cases, and of this opinion was Littleton in our bookes. (y) A man leaveth his wife enseint with a childe, issue shall not be taken that she was not enseint by her husband on the day of his death, for Filiatio non potest probari, but the issue must bee whither she was enseint the day of his death.

(r) 20. E. 3. Issue 31. 22. Ed. 4. 28. 8. E. 3. 8. 9. H. 6. 18. 38. E. 3. 33.
(s) 21. H. 6. 9 b. 16. E. 4. 5. 24. E. 3. 32. 33. 75. 31. E. 3. Issue 17. 13. E. 3. F. 27. 21. E. 3. 49. 30. E. 3. 8. 10. E. 3. 32. 22. E. 3. 13. 18. E. 3. Issue 35. 5. H. 7. 8. 31. Ass. 25. 2. E. 4. 4. 8. 2. H. 4. 23. 38. H. 6. 22. 40. E. 3. 5. 5. E. 3. 24.
(t) 18. El. Dyer 253. 22. Hen. 6. 19. 32. H. 6. 23. 2. R. 3. 5. H. 7. 5. 11. H. 4. 79.
(u) 2. H. 7. 4. 5. H. 7. 12. 26. 11. H. 4. 83. 6. E. 4. 6. b. 26. H. 8. Dyer 6. in Formedon. 28. H. 8. Dyer 31. 18. Hen. 6. 8. 9. 15. E. 4. 32. 32. H. 6. 23. 7. H. 6. 27. 43. Ass. 49. E. 4. 36. Pl. Com. 172. a. 36. H. 6. 15.
(w) 26. H. 8. 3. 18. El. Dyer 353.
(x) 22. H. 6. 57. 59. 33. H. 6. 21. 3. H. 7. 9. 12. E. 4. 13. 17. E. 3. 53. 77. 78. 22. E. 3. 16. 17. 24. E. 3. 30. 40. E. 3. 19.
(y) 41. E. 3. 11. b.

(z) A protestation avayleth not the partie that taketh it, if the issue be found against him, and therefore if the issue be found for the villeine, he is infranchised for ever. And yet in some speciall case albeit the issue be found against him that maketh the protestation, yet he shall take benefit of his protestation, (*) as if a man entreth into warrantie, and taketh by protestation the value of the land, albeit the plea be found against him, yet the protestation shall serve him for the value.

(z) 10. E. 4. Protest. 5. 10. E. 4. 12. 32. Ass. 9. 30. E. 3. 14. 9. H. 6. 59. Vid. Sect. 192.
** 30. E. 3. 14.*

Section 194

¶ Item le Seignior ne poet mayhemer son villeine. Car s'il maihema son villein,

Also the Lord may not mayme his villeine. For if hee mayme his villeine,

¶ *Mayhemer,* (a) or Mehaigner, A French word of which commeth Mayhim, mahemium (id est) membri mutilatio, and

(a) Stamf. li. 1. ca. 41. Glanvil. lib. 14. ca. 7. Bract. lib. 3. fol. 144, 145. Brit. cap. 25. fol. 48, 49. Flet. li. 1. ca. 38.

il ſerra de ceo endite a le ſuit le Roy, & ſil ſoit de ceo attaint, il ſerra pur ceo vn grieuous fine & ranſome al Roy. Mes il ſemble que villeine nauera pas per le ley vn appeal de Mayhem enuſs ſon Sñr, Car en appeale de Mayheme home recouera forſqz damñs, & ſi le villeine en ceo cas recoũa damñs enuers ſon ſeignior, & ent auoit execution, le Sñr poit prender ceo que le villeine auoit en execution de le villiene, & iſſint le recouerie voide, &c.

he ſhall of that be indicted at the Kings ſuit. And if hee be of that attainted, he ſhall for that make grieuous Fine and ranſome to the King. But it ſeemeth that the Villeine ſhall not haue by the Law any Appeale of Mayhem againſt his Lord, for in Appeale of Mayhem a man ſhal recouer but his dammages. And if the Villeine in that caſe recouer dammages againſt his Lord, and hath thereof execution, the Lord may take that the Villeine hath in execution from the Villeine, and ſo the recouery is void, &c.

Mirror.cap.1.§.9.

and membrum eſt pars corporis habens deſtinatam operationem in corpore. Mayhemium vero dici poterit vbi aliquis in aliqua parte ſui corporis effectus ſit invtilis ad pugnandum. And the Law hath ſo appropriated this word Mayhem, which our Author here vſeth, to this offence, as mayhemauit cannot be expreſſed by any other word, as mutilauit, truncauit, or detruncauit, or the like.

Vide Sect.1.

¶ *Il ſerra indite*, or rather endite, and ſo is the originall, for it commeth of the French word enditer, and ſignifieth in Law an accuſation found by an Enqueſt of 12. or more vpon their Oath, and the accuſation is called Indictamentum. And as the Appeale is euer the ſuite of the partie, ſo the enditement is alwayes the ſuit of the King, and as it were his declaration. (b) Some deriue it from the Greeke word ἰνδείκνυμι to accuſe.

(b) Lamb.Iuſt.of Peace.

¶ (c) *Nauera &c. Appeale de mayhem.* Becauſe in that Appeale he ſhall recouer but damages, which the Lord after execution might take againe, and ſo the iudgement inutile and illuſory, and Sapiens incipit à fine. And the Law neuer giueth an action where the end of it can bring no profit or benefit to the Plaintife. But here it is to be obſerued that albeit the partie grieued can haue no action for the Mayhem, yet at the Kings ſuite hee ſhall be puniſhed therefore, for the reaſon hereafter expreſſed in this Section. (d) And in ancient time there were Appeales de plagis & de impriſonamento, but they are out of vſe and turned to actions of Treſpaſſe.

(c) Vide 1.H.4.6.b.

(d) Fleta lib.1.cap 40. Britt.cap.25. Bract.145. Mirror cap.3.

¶ *Fine*, finis. Here fine ſignifieth a pecuniarie puniſhment for an offence, or a contempt commited againſt the King, and regularly to it impriſonment appertayneth. And it is called finis becauſe it is an end for that offence. (e) And in this caſe a man is ſaid Facere finem de tranſgreſſione, &c. cum Rege, to make an end, or fine with the King for ſuch a tranſgreſſion. It is alſo taken for a ſumme giuen by the tenant to the Lord for concord, and an end to bee made. (f) It is alſo taken for the higheſt and beſt aſſurance of Lands, &c.

(e) Regiſt.Iudic.25. Lib.8.fol.59.Beechers caſe.

(f) Vide Sect.74.174.441.

Here it is good to ſee what a fine differeth from an amerciament. (g) Amerciament in Latine is called miſericordia, for that it ought to be aſſeſſed mercifully, and this ought to bee moderated by affeerement of his equals, or elſe a Writ De moderata miſericordia, doth lie: and thereof Glanuill ſaith thus. (h) Eſt autem miſericordia Domini Regis qua quis per iuramentum legalium hominum de viceneto eatenus amerciandus eſt, ne aliquid de ſuo honorabili contenemento amittat.

(g) Lib.8.fol.59. Beechers Caſe. F.N.B.76.

(h) Glanvill.lib.9.cap.11. Magna Charta cap.14. Fleta lib.2.cap.43.& 60.& lib.1.cap.43. Bract.lib.3 fol.116.

(i) The cauſe of an amerciament in plea reall, perſonall or mixt (where the King is to haue no fine) is for that the Tenant or Defendant ought to render the demand (as hee is commanded by the Kings Writ) the firſt day: which if he do, he ſhall not be amerced (ſo as for the delay that the Tenant or Defendant doth vſe he ſhall be amerced. (k) And albeit the amerciament cannot be impoſed, nor the King fully intitled thereunto vntill iudgement be giuen, becauſe by the iudgement the wrong is diſcerned, yet a pardon before iudgement, after iudgement giuen, ſhall diſcharge the partie, becauſe the originall cauſe, viz. the delay, &c. is pardoned. (l) What then if a Præcipe be brought againſt an Infant, and hanging the plea, he commeth of full age?

(i) 22.E.3.1.& 2. 14.E.3.amerciam.16. 8.R.2.ibid.26.&c.

(k) Pl.Com.401.Coles caſe. 37.H.6.21. Lib.5.fol 49.Vaughans caſe.

(l) Vaughans caſe vbi ſupra. Beechers caſe vbi ſupra.

he shall be amerced for the delay after his full age. So likewise if the Demandant or Plantiffe bee Nonsuit or Judgement giuen against him, hee shall bee likewise amerced pro falso clamore.

(m) And for the payment of this amerciament the Demandant or Plantiffe, &c. shall find pledges, and those Demandants or Plantiffes, that shall find no pledges, (as the King, the Queene, an Infant, &c.) shall not be amerced. And therefore when such are Demandant or Plantiffe, the writ shall not say, Si Rex, &c. fecerit te securum de clamore suo prosequendo.

(n) If a writ doe abate by the Act of the Demandant or Plantiffe, or for matter of forme, the Demandant or Plantiffe shall be amerced, but if it abate by the Act of God, as by the death of one where there is two or the like, there shall be no amerciament. And to an amerciament, imprisonment belongeth not, as it doth to a fine or ransome. If you desire to reade more of fines and amerciaments. Vide lib.8.fol.38.39. &c. Greslyes case. & lib.11. fol 43.44. Godfreyes case.

(m) F.N.B.31.f.47.C. & 101.a. Bract.lib.4 fol.254. 17.E.3.75. 18.E.3.2. Br.tit.amerciam.53. 43.Ass.45.&c.

(n) Lechers case lib.8.f.60.b.

(o) It is to be knowne that Wit, Wita, is an old Saxon word, and signifieth an amerciament, as Fledwite an amerciament for fleeing or being a fugitiue, and so is Flemiswite, Blodwite an amerciament for drawing of bloud. Ferdwite concerning warfare, and so Letherwite, Childwite, Wardwite and the like. Sometime it signifieth forfeiture, sometime freedome, or acquitall.

(o) Fleta lib.1.cap.43. Stat.de exposit.verborum.

(p) And Bote is also an ancient Saxon word, and sometime signifieth amerciament, or compensation, as Theltbote Manbote, or freedome from the same, as Brigbote, Castlebote, Burghbote.

(p) Lamb.explication of Saxon words. Leges Inæ.cap.19.

Wera or Were (q) sometime signifieth amerciament or compensation, but properly Wera Anglice idem est in Saxonis lingua vel pretium vitæ hominis appretiatum. Which & the like words you shall often reade in ancient Charters.

(q) Lamb. vbi supra & Fleta lib.1.cap.43.

¶ *Ransome.* (r) Redemptio is here taken for a grand summe of money for redeeming of a great Delinquent from some heynous crime, who is to bee captiuate in prison vntill he payeth it, some hold it to amount to his whole estate, and others hold that ransome is a treble fine. (s) But in Legall vnderstanding a fine and ransome are all one, for vpon the Statute of Merlebridge cap 3 vpon these words, Non ideo puniatur Dominus per Redemptionem. (t) The Tenant shall not haue (where the Lord distreyneth within his fee where nothing is behind) an Action of Trespasse, quare vi & armis against his Lord, for therein the Lord should be punished by redemption, that is by fine, and in that action the fine is very small. And this is manifest by many Authorities in all succession of ages: and this appeareth by our Author in this place, for he saith, Il serra pur ceo vn greiuous fine & ransome. Where fine and ransome must of necessitie in his opinion be taken for all one: for if the fine and ransome were diuers, then should the partie, that mayhemed the Villeine pay two summes, one for a fine, and another for a ransome, which neuer was done. And aptly a redemption and a fine is taken to bee all one, for by the payment of the fine hee redeemeth himselfe from imprisonment, that attendeth the fine, and then there is an end of the businesse.

(r) Dier.6.Eliz.232.

(s) See the second part of the Institutes Merlebr.cap.3.

(t) 5.H.7.10. 48.E.3.5.6. 41.E.3.26. 44.E.3.13. 2.H.4.4. 11.H.4.78. 1.H.6.6. 9 H.7.14. 8.E.4. 15.10.E.4.7. 20.E.4.3. 21.E.4.3. Mich.17.& 18. Eliz. Beuels case lib.4.fol.11. & lib.9.fol.76. Combs case.

It signifieth properly a summe of a money paid for the redemption of a captiue, and is compounded of re and emo, that is to redeeme or buy againe. And it is to be knowne, that (u) by the ancient law of England, if the Defendant in an Appeale of Mayhem had bin found guiltie, the iudgement against the Defendant had beene, that hee should lose the like member, that the Plantiffe lost by his meanes; as if the Plantiffe had lost an hand, the Defendant also should lose one, & sic de cæteris: In respect whereof the writ said, (w) Felonicæ mayhemauit, for that the Defendant should lose a member.

(u) 40.Ass.9. Mirror cap.4. & ca.5.§.18. Britton cap.25 fol.48. Bract.lib.3 fol.144. 145. Fleta lib.1.cap.38.

(w) Bracton.vbi supra. Britton cap.3.fol 77 b.

Alwayes at the Common Law, when the Defendant should lose life or member, the writ said Felonice, &c. And now albeit the Law be changed (for at this day, the Plantiffe shall, as our Author saith, recouer but damages) yet the writ of Appeale saith still Felonice.

Note the life and members of euery subiect are vnder the safegard and protection of the King, for as Bracton (x) saith, Vita & membra sunt in potestate Regis. And therewith agreeth a notable Record, Pasch.19.E.1. coram Rege Rot.36. Northt. vita & membra sunt in manu Regis, to the end that they may serue the King and their Countrie when occasion shall be offered. May, the Lord of the Villeine for the cause aforesaid cannot mayheme the Villeine, but the King shall punish him for mayming of his subiect (for that hereby hee hath disabled him to doe the King Seruice) by fine, ransome, and imprisonment vntill the fine and ransome bee paid. So as there is a manifest diuersitie betweene a ransome and an amerciament. For ransome is euer when the law inflicteth a corporall punishment by imprisonment, (& so is also a fine) but otherwise it is of an amerciament as hath bin said. And (y) Ancients haue said that Ransome nest forsque redemption de paine corporell per fine des deniers. This offence of mayhem is vnder all felonies deseruing death, and aboue all other inferior offences, so as it may be truly said of it, that it is, Inter crimina maiora minimum, & inter minora maximum. And in my Circuit in Anno 11. Iacobi Regis in the Countie of Leicester one Wright a young strong and lustie

(x) Bract.lib.1.fol.6. Pasch.19.E.1.coram Rege Rot.36.Northt.

(y) Mirror.cap.5.§.1.& 3.

Rogue to make himselfe impotent thereby to haue the more colour to begge or to bee relieued without putting himselfe to any labour, caused his companion to strike off his left hand, and both of them were indited, fined, and ransomed therefore, and that by the opinion of the rest of the Iustices for the cause aforesaid.

¶ *Voyde, &c.* Here by (&c.) is implyed a maxime in Law, Quod inutilis labor & sine fructu non est effectus legis. And againe, Non licet, quod dispendio licet. And Sapiens incipit à fine, and Lex non præcipit inutilia. (z) Therefore the Law forbiddeth such recoueries whose ends are vaine, chargeable and vnprofitable.

(z) *Vide Sect.273. & 578.*

Sect. 195.

¶ Item si vn Villein soit demandant ē action real, ou plaintife en action p̄sonal, euers son sñr, si le Sñr voile plede en disabilitie de son p̄son, il ne poit faire pleine defence, mes il defendera forsq; tort & force & demandera iudgement sil serra respondus, & monstre son matter maintenant, comt il est son villein, & dd̄era iudgment sil serra respondue.

ALso if a Villeine bee demandant in an action real, or plaintiffe in an action personall against his Lord, if the Lord will plead in disabilitie of his person, he may not make plaine defence, but he shall defend but the wrong and the force, and demand the iudgment if he shall be answered, and shew his matter by and by how he is villeine, and demand iudgement if he shall be answered.

¶ D*Emaundant*, petens, Is hee which is Actor in a reall action, because hee demandeth Lands, &c. And Plaintif, querens in actions personals and mixt, quia quæritur de iniuria, &c. Tenant, tenens in reall actions, and defendant, defendens in actions personall and mixt.

3. Lev. 181 North vs Hoyle
1. Salk 217. Ferrer vs Miller.

¶ *Defence.* Commeth of the word defendo, so called of the manner of the pleading, viz. prædict' A.B. defendit vim & iniuriam, &c.

For example in a personall action brought by A. against C. D. the defence is, & prædictus C. D defendit vim & iniuriam quando, &c. & damna, & quicquid quod ipse defendere debet, &c.

In this defence there bee three parts to bee considered; First, when he defendeth the wrong and the force, this hath a double effect, viz to make himselfe partie to the matter, and this is the reason, that the Defendant in this and the like actions can plead no plea at all before he makes himselfe partie by this part of the defence, as it appeareth here by Littleton, that (a) if the Defendant will plead in disabilitie of the person of the Plaintiffe he must first make himselfe partie by this first part of the defence. Neither can he plead to the iurisdiction of the Court without this part of the defence. Secondly, (b) By the defence of the Damages, he affirmeth that the Plaintiffe is able to sue, and (vpon iust cause) to recouer Damages. Thirdly, And by the last part, viz. and all that which he ought to defend, when and where he ought, he affirmeth the iurisdiction of the Court; Et sic de similibus. And of such necessitie is it for the Tenant or Defendant to make a lawfull defence, as (c) albeit he appeareth and pleades a sufficient barre without making defence, yet iudgement shall be giuen against him.

(a) 40.E.3.36. 14.H.6.18 35.H.6.12. 1.E.4.15.

(b) 29.E.3.23. 8.H.6.3.

(c) 36.H.6. iudgement 58.

(d) If Villenage be pleaded by the Lord in an Action reall, mixt or personall, and it is found that he is no Villaine, the bringing of a Writ of Error is no enfranchisement, because thereby he is to defeat the former iudgement, and if in the meane time, the Plantiffe or Demandant bring an action against the Lord, he need make no protestation, so long as the Record remaynes in force, for at that time he is free, but the Lord shall be restored to all by a Writ of Error.

(d) 18.E.4.6. & 7.

Section 196.

¶ Item 6. maners de homes y sont queux, sils suont ac-

ALso there are sixe mãner of mē who if they sue, iudgement

¶ V*N est lou Vileine suist action &c.* Littleton here

(e) *Bract.lib.5.fol.421. Britton.cap.49.fol.125. Mirror.cap.2.§.18.*

tion

tion, iudgement poit estre demaund sils serrõt respondus, &c. Un est, lou villeine suist action enuers son Seignior, come en le cas auantdit.

may bee demanded, if they shall bee answered, &c. One is where a Villeine sueth an Action against his Lord, as in the case aforesaid.

rehearseth .6. kind of disabilities of the person, disabling him to sue any action reall, personall or mixt.

13 H.4. Suerty, 12. agarden (l all disablo.

Sils serrõt respondus. This is the legall conclusion of the plea, when the plea is in disabilitie of the person. And of the verbe respondere came responsalis often used in the ancient Authors of the Law. (f) Responsalis was he, that was appointed by the Tenant or Defendant, in case of extremitie and necessitie to alleage the cause of the parties absence, and to certifie the Court vpon what triall, he will put himselfe, viz. the Combate or the Countrie. So as his power was more then the Essoinor which casteth an Essoigne only to excuse the absence of the partie, as an estranger which casteth a protection, doth. For by the Common Law, the Plaintife or Defendant, Demaundant or Tenant could not appeare by Attornie without the Kings speciall Warrant by Writ or Letters Patents, but ought to follow his Suite in his owne proper person (by reason whereof there were but few Suites) (g) Abusion est a reteiner attorny sans breue de la Chancerie. And therefore Bracton saith truly (h) Attornatus hæc omnia facere potest (that is, plead all manner of pleas) Est igitur magna differentia inter Attornatum & Responsalem. So as the statutes that giue the making of Attorneys, haue worne out Responsales. Now what manner of men Attorneys ought to be, or rather what they ought not to be, heare what Antiquity hath said, (i) Attorneyes poient estre touts ceux aux queux ley voile suffer, fems ne point este Attorneyes, ne ensans, ne serfs, ne nul que est en gard ou autrement faut de foy, ne nul criminous, ne nul essoigne, ne nul que nest a le foy le Roy, ne nul que ne poet eite Counter, &c.

(f) Bract. lib.4.fo.212.b. & lib.5.fo.349. Fleta, lib 6.ca 11. Glanuill lib 11.ca.1. Britton ca.126. Vid W.1.ca.43. F.N.B.25.C. Regist.9.

(g) Mirr.ca 5.§.

(h) Bracton, vbi supra.

(i) Mirror, ca.2.§.21.

Section 197.

LE ii. est lou vn home est vtlage sur action de det, ou Trespas, ou sur auter act, ou Indictment, le tenant ou defendant poit monstre tout le matter de record, & lutlagarie, & demaunde iudgement sil sert respondue, pur ceo que il est hors de la ley de suer ascun action durant le temps que il soit vtlage.

THe 2. is, where a man is outlawed vpon an Action of debt or trespasse, or vpon any other action or indictment, the Tenant, or the Defendant may shew all the matter of Record and the outlawrie, and demand iudgement if he shall bee answered, because he is out of the Law to sue an action during the time that he is outlawed.

LE 2. est (k) lou vn home est vtlage, &c. But these generall words receiue a distinction, viz. (l) if an Executor or an Administrator sueth any action, Utlary in the Plaintife shall not disable him, because the suite is In auter droit, that is in the right of the Testator, and not in his owne right. And for the same reason, (m) a Maior and Comminalty shall haue an action, though the Maior bee outlawed. (n) In a Writ of Error to reuerse an Utlary, Utlary in that suite, or at any strangers suite shall not disable the Plaintife, because if he in that action should be disabled, if he were, Outlawed at seuerall mens suites, he should neuer reuers any of them. (o) In an Attaint outlary in the Plaintife cannot be pleaded in disability of the person (p) Outlary in Chester or Durham shal not disable the Plaintife in any Court at Westminster, &c. (q) Minor vero & qui infra ætatem 12. annorum fuerit, vtlagari non potest, nec extra legem poni, quia ante talem ætatem, non est sub lege aliqua nec in decenna. (r) He that is abiured the realme may be disabled, for that hee is extra legem, and yet he is not properly outlawed.

(k) Bracton lib.5.fo.421. Britton ca.22.fo.39. Mirror, ca.1. de Exceptions a provors, ca.4. de faults punishable.

(l) 21.E.4.49.b. 21.H.6.30.b. 14.H.6.15.

(m) 12.E.4.fo.12.

(n) 7.H.4.40.

(o) 23.H.8.ca.3, 2.H.7.7.

(p) Mirror, cap.3.acc. 12.E.4.16. 33.H.6.ca 2.

(q) Bract lib.3.fo.125. 3.H.5. Vtlagary.11. 38.E.3.5.

(r) Britton fo.39.

Monstre tout le matter de record. Here note two things, first by this word (Monstre) that (s) when any man pleads an Utlary in disability of the person, that hee

(s) 20 E.2. Corone 232. 19. Ass.p.10. 3.H.6.15.b. 37.H.6.23. 5.H.7. 6. Eliz. Dier 228. F.N.B.244 Stanf.pl.coron.105.

he must shew forth the Record of the Outlawrie, maintenant sub pede sigilli, (because the Plea is but dilatorie) vnlesse the Record be in the same Court. But if he plead an Outlawrie in barre, if it be denied, he shall haue a day to bring it in.

(t) 28. Ass. 49. 12. E. 3. Vtlagarie 3. M. 4. & 5. El. Dyer 222. 38. E. 3. 13.

Secondly, (t) before the Defendant can disable the Plaintife, the Outlawrie must appeare of Record, and the Iudgement after the quinto exactus giuen by the Coroners in the Countie Court, is not sufficient, vntill the Writ of Exigent be returned, and the Outlawrie appeare of Record: which is manifest by Littletons owne words, (viz.) Matter de Record, whereof see more hereafter, Sect. 503.

It is to be obserued, That there be two kind of appearances before the Quinto exactus, to auoyd the Outlawrie, viz. an Apparance in deed, that is, to render himselfe, &c. And the other is by an apparance in Law, (u) that is, by purchasing a Supersedeas out of the Court where the Record is, which is an apparance of Record: and therefore though it bee not deliuered to the Sherife before the quinto exactus, yet it shall auoyd the Outlawrie, and so are the Bookes that speake hereof to be intended.

(u) Tr. 44. El. in Com. Banc. inter Mere & Dolburie. 33. H. 6. 1. 11. H. 4. 34. Dyer 3. El. 192. 5. El. 223. 4. H. 4. le 1. case. 8. H. 4. f. 7. 37. H. 6. 17. 33. E. 3. Err. 77. 21. H. 6. 20.

(w) 33. H. 6. 19. b. &c.

(x) 44. E. 3. 27.

(w) If a man be outlawed at the suit of one man, all men shall take aduantage of this personall disabilitie. And so it is in case of Alien nee, and of Excommengement: but otherwise it is in case of Villenage, for that disabilitie is onely giuen to the Lord.

¶ *Duraunt le temps que il est vtlage.* (x) **If the Defendant plead** an Outlawrie in the Plaintife, in disabilitie of his person, and the Plaintife after that Plea pleaded, purchase a Charter of Pardon, because the Charter hath restored him to the Law, the Defendant shall answer. So note, the disabilitie abateth not the writ, but disinableth the Plaintife, vntill he obtaineth a Charter of Pardon, and so it appeareth here by Littleton.

(y) 9. El. Dyer 262. 7. H. 4. 4. b. Stanf. Pl. Coron. 188. Lib. 5. fo. 109. in Foxleyes case. 28. E. 3. 92. 29. Ass. p. 47. 63. 32. H. 6. 5.

¶ *Iudgement s'il serra respondue.* (y) **If the ground or cause of the** Action be forfeited by the Outlawrie, then may the Outlawrie be pleaded in barre of the Action, as in an Action of Debt, Detinue, &c. But in reall Actions, or in personall, where dammages be incertaine, (as in Trespasse of Batterie, of Goods, of breaking his Close, and the like) and are not forfeited by the Outlawrie, there Outlawrie must be pleaded in disabilitie of the person.

(z) Mir. ca. 1. §. 3. & ca. 3. & 4. sæpe ca. 5. §. 1.

(*) Flet. li. 1. ca. 27. Bract. li. 5. fo. 421. Brit. fo. 20. b.

(a) Mir. ca. 4. §. defaults punissable.

(b) Lamb. fol. 128.

(c) 2. Ass. T. 3. 2. E. 3. tit. Coron. 148.

(z) And it is to be obserued, That in the raign of King Ælfred, and vntill, and a good while after the Conquest, no man could haue beene outlawed but for Felonie, the punishment whereof was death: but now the Law is changed, as it appeareth by that which hath beene sayd; and hereby you shall vnderstand old Bookes and Records which say, That an outlawed man had Caput Lupinum, because he might be put to death by any man, as a wolfe that hatefull beast might. (*) Vtlagatus & waiuiata capita gerunt Lupina, quæ ab omnibus impunè poterunt amputari, merito enim sine Lege perire debent, qui secundum legem viuere recusant. And another saith, (a) Vtlage pur felonie teigne leu pur loup, & est criable Woolfeshered, pur ceo que loupe est beast hay de touts gents, & de ceo en auant list al ascun de le occire ou foer del loup dont custome soloit este de Porter les testes al chiefe lieu del countie, ou de la Franchise, & soloit leu auoire d'un marke del Countie pur chescun teste de vtlage & de loupe. And this agreeth with the Law before the Conquest, (b) Vtlagatus lupinum gerit caput, quod Anglicè, Woolfeshead dicitur, & hæc est lex communis & generalis de omnibus vtlagatis. (c) But in the beginning of the raigne of King Edward the third, it was resolued by the Iudges, for auoyding of inhumanitie, and of effusion of Christian bloud, That it should not bee lawfull for any man but the Sherife onely, (hauing lawfull warrant therefore) to put to death any man outlawed, though it were for Felonie, and if he did, he should vndergoe such punishments and paines of death, as if he had killed any other man; and so from thenceforth the Law continued vntill this day. (Nota, Woolfeshead, and Wulferfod is all one)* And after in Bractons time, and somewhat before, Processe of Outlawrie was ordained to lie in all Actions that were Quare vi & armis, which Bracton calleth Delicta, for there the King shall haue a Fyne. But since, by diuers Statutes, Processe of Outlawrie doth lie in Account, Debt, Detinue, Annuitie, Couenant, Action sur le Statute de 5. Rich. 2. Action sur le Case, and in diuers other Common or Ciuile Actions. But now let vs heare what Littleton will say vnto vs.

* Bract. li. 5. fo. 421. 8. H. 6. 9. b. 40. E. 3. 5. 35. H. 6. 6. 40. E. 3. 2.

Sect. 198.

(a) Bract. li. 5. fo. 415. 427. Mir. ca. 1. §. 3. ca. 5. §. 1. & ca. 3. except. a prouers. Flet. li. 6. ca. 47. Brit. fo. 29. 13. E. 3. Bre 677. 25. Ed. 3. de Natiu vltra mare. 31. E. 3. Cosinage 5. 42. E. 3. 2. 9. E. 4. 7.

¶ *ALien.* (a) Alienigena is deriued from the Latyne word Alienus, and according

CLE 3. est, vn Alien que est nee hors de la ligeance nostre

THe third is, an Alien which is born out of the ligeance of

nostre Seignior le Roy, si tiel alien voile suer vn Action reall ou personall, le Tenant ou Defendant poit dire que il fuit nee en tiel pais, que est hors d{e} la ligeance le Roy, & demaund iudgement si il serra respondue.

our soueraigne Lord the King, if such alien wil sue an Action reall or personal; the Tenãt or Defendãt may say, That hee was borne in such a Countie which is out of the Kings Allegeance, and aske Iudgement, if he shall be answered.

to the Etymologie of the word, it signifieth one borne in a strange Countrie, vnder the obedience of a strange Prince or Countrie, (And therefore Bracton saith, That this exception; Propter defectum Nationis, should rather be, Propter defectum Subiectionis) or as Littleton saith, (which is the surest) Out of the liegeance of the King. Note, here Littleton saith not, Hors del Realme, but Hors de liegeance; for he may be borne out of the Realme of England, yet within the liegeance. And he that is borne within the Kings Liegeance is called sometime a Denizen, quasi deins nee, borne within, and thereupon in Latyne called Indigena, the Kings Liegeman, for Ligeus is euer taken for a naturall borne Subiect. But many times in Acts of Parliament, Denizen is taken for an Alien borne, that is intranchised or denizated by Letters Patents, whereby the King doth grant vnto him, (b) Quod ille in omnibus tractetur, reputetur, habeatur, teneatur, & gubernetur, tanquam ligeus noster, infra dictum Regnum nostrum Angliæ oriundus, & non aliter, nec alio modo. But the King may make a particular Denization: (c) As he may grant to an Alien, Quod in quibusdam Curijs suis Angliæ audiatur vt Anglus, & quod non repellatur per illam exceptionem quod sit alienigena & natus in partibus transmarinis, to enable him to sue onely. The seuerall sences of which word must be gathered, ex antecedentibus, adiunctis, & consequentibus, and they that take him in that sence, deriue the word from Donaison (i.) Donatio, because his freedome is giuen vnto him by the King.

11.H.4.26. 14.H.4.19,20. 3.H.6.55. 22.H.6.38. Stanf.Pl.Cor.197.a. Lib.7.fo.1. Caluins case. Pl.Com.268.per Sanders. Vid.Sect.1.439,440,441.

(b) 9.E.4.f.8. Pl.Com.130.b.

(c) Rot Parl.22.E.1. Elias de Dauboute.

There is another kind, and that is an Alien naturalized, and that must be by Act of Parliament. And this Alien naturalized to all intents and purposes, is as a naturall borne subiect, and differeth much from denization by Letters Patents, for if he had issue in England before his denization, that issue is not inheritable to his father: but if his father be naturalized by Parliament, such issue shall inherit. So if an issue of an Englishman be borne beyond Sea, if the issue be naturalized by Act of Parliament, he shall inherit his fathers lands; but if hee be made Denizen by Letters Patents, he shall not, and many other differences there bee betweene them.

¶ *Ligeance*, à Ligando, **Being the highest and greatest obligation** of dutie and obedience that can be. Liegeance is the true and faithfull obedience of a Liegeman or Subiect, to his Liege Lord or Soueraigne. Ligeantia est vinculum fidei, ligeantia est legis essentia.

Vid. Caluins case, vbi supra.

Ligeantia domino Regi debita est duplex:

- *Perpetua.*
  - 1 Originaria, siue naturalis, siue nata, (d) and this is alwayes absolute and incident inseperable, nemo patriam in qua natus est exuere, nec ligeantiæ debitum eiurare possit.
  - 2 Data, aut per denizationem, aut per naturalizationem (vt supradictum est) & ista ligeantia per denizationem potest esse sub conditione.
- *Temporanea, aut*
  - Localis, quia quilebet alienigena qui in hoc Regno sub protectione Regis degit, Domino Regi ligeantiã debet. And if he be indicted of high Treason, the Inditement shall say, (e) Contra Ligeantiæ suæ debitum, & ideo dicitur temporanea & localis, quia non durat nisi quousque infra Regnum moratur.
  - Limitata, As when one is made Denizen for life or in taile, (f) but one cannot be naturalized either with limitation for life, or in taile, or vpon condition: for that is against the absolutenesse, puritie, and indelibilitie of naturall Allegeance.

(d) 13.El.Dyer f.300.b. Doctor Stories case.

(e) 3.& 4.P.& M.Di.144 Li.7.fo.6.&c.Caluins case.

(f) 9.E.4.7. Caluins case vbi supra.

* An Abbot, Prior, or Priors Alien, shall haue Actions reall, personall, or mixt, for any thing concerning the possessions or goods of his Monasterie here in England, though he bee an Alien borne out of the Kings Liegeance, because he bringeth it not in his owne right, but in

** 13.E.3.bre.264.20.E.3.Anuitie 24.17.E.3.21.40.E.3.10. 27.Ass.48. 14.H.4.37. 22.E.4.44. 21.H.7.7. Stanf Prar.54.Lestat.de Carl.sta.35.E.1.*

the right of his Monastery, and not in his naturall but in his politique capacitie.

(h) Bracton, 426.427,430. 8.E.3.51.5.E.2.Aiel.8. 13.E.3.Bre.677. 22.E.3.14.20. 21.E.3. Cosinage,5. 42.E.3.2. 13.E.4.9.11.H.4.26. 9.E.4.7.19.E.4.7.20.E.46 13.E.4.9.10. 32.H.6.23. 38.H.8 Br.Denizen.10. 1.E.6.Nonhab.Br.13.& .62. Vid.4.H.3.Dower 179. 6.E.3.263.31.H.6.ca.4. Liure de Entries in eiect.7. 6.H.8.Dior.2.6.H.7.15. * 29.E.3.Br.Denizen,15.

¶ *Reall ou personall.* (h) In this case the Law doth distinguish betweene an Alien that is a subiect to one that is an enemy to the King, and one that is subiect to one that is in league with the King, and true it is that an Alien enemie, shall maintaine neither reall nor personall action Donec terræ fuer' communes, that is untill both Nations bee in peace; but an Alien that is in league shall maintaine personall actions, for an Alien may trade and traffique, buy and sell, and therefore of necessity he must be of ability to haue personall actions, but he cannot maintaine either reall or mixt actions. An Alien that is condemned in an information shall haue a writ of error to relieue himselfe, Et sic de similibus.

* If an Alien be made a Prior or Abbot, the plea of Alien nee shall not disable him to bring any reall or mixt action concerning his house, because he is in auter droit, as before is said

Vid. Stanf. Pl.Cor.197.a.

¶ *Hors del ligeance nostre seignior le Roy.* Here Littleton doth not say, out of the Realme or beyond the Sea, (as he doth Sect,439.440.441.677.) But out of the Ligeance; for (as hath beene said before) a man may be borne out of the Realme, viz. of England, as in Ireland, Jersey, and Gerney, &c. and yet seeing hee is not borne out of the Ligeance of the King, as Littleton here speaketh he is no Alien. But hereof there is so much, and so plentifully spoken in our bookes, and especially in the case of Caluyn vbi supra, as this shall suffice.

(i) Liure de Entries Alien.1.

¶ *Et demaund iudgement sil serra respondue.* So as the Tenant or Defendant shall neither plead Alien nee to the writ or to the action, but in disability of the person, as in case of villenage and outlawrie before. (i) And Littleton is to bee intended of an Alien in league, for if hee be an Alien enemy the Defendant may conclude to the Action.

Section 199.

¶ LE 4. est, un hõe q̃ p iudg. done enuers luy sur un briefe de Præmunire facias, &c. est hors de protection le Roy, si il suist ascun action, & le Tenant ou le Def. msta tout le record enuers luy, il poit demaund iudgement sil serra respondu, car la ley le Roy, & les bres le Roy, sont les choses per queux home est protect & aide, & issint durant le temps que home en tiel cas est hors de la protection le Roy, il est hors de estre aide ou ptect per le ley le Roy, ou per bre le Roy.

THE 4. is, a man who by iudgement giuen against him vpon a writ of *Præmunire facias, &c.* is out of the Kings protection, if hee sue any action, and the tenant or defendant shew all the Record against him, hee may aske iudgement if hee shall be answered, for the Law & the Kings writs be the things by which a man is protected and holpen, and so during the time that a man in such case is out of the Kings protection, hee is out of helpe and protection by the Kings Law, or by the Kings writ.

For Statutes; Vid.35.E.1. Stat.de Carlile. 25.E.3.ca.22.25.E.3. statut.de prouisors.27.E.3.c.1 38.E.4.ca.3.2.R.2.ca.12. 3.R.2.ca.3. 12.R.2.ca.5. 16.R.2.ca.5. 2.H.4.ca.3. & 4.6.H.4.ca.1.24.H.8. ca.12.25.H.8.ca.19.20. 26.H.8.ca.16. 1.Eliz.ca.1. 5.Eliz.ca.1. 13.Eliz.ca.1. 2.8. 27.Eliz.ca.2. 39.Eliz.ca.18.

For Presidents. Vid.Mich. 29.E.3.coram Rege in Thesaur. Pasch.44.E.3 Ibid. Melbernes Case. Mich.38.H.6.ibid. the case of Richard Beauchamp and others. Hill, 25.H.8. Coram Rege. The Case of Nicke Bishop of Norwich. Trin.36.H.8.Rot.9. Coram Rege, The Case of the Bishop of Bangor. Mich.26.& 27 Eliz. Coram Rege, Perrot against D. Benance and others. Booke of Entries, fo.429.& 430 & ibid. Mich.9.H.7.fo.23.

¶ PRæmunire. Some hold an opinion that the writ is called a Præmunire, because it doth fortifie Iurisdictionem iurium regiorum Coronæ suæ of the Kingly Lawes of the Crown against forreine iurisdiction, and against the usurpers upon them, as by diuers Acts of Parliaments appeare. But in truth it is so called of a word in the writ; for the words of the writ bee Præmunire facias præfatum A.B. &c. quod tunc sit coram nobis, &c. Where Præmunire is used for præmonere, and so doe diuers interpreters of the Ciuill and Cannon Law use it, for they are præmuniti that are præmoniti. By the statutes before quoted in the margent you shall perceiue what statutes were made before Littleton wrote, and what haue beene ordained since to make offences in danger of a Præmunire.

Bookes Cases. 21.E.3.40.b. 18.H.6.6. 9.E 4.2.35.E 3.7.24.H.8. tit. Præmunire,16.10.H.4.12. 27.E.3.84.6.H.7.14. 44.E.3.36.

¶ *Hors del protection le roy.* The iudgement in a Præmunire is that the Defendant shalbe from thence forth out of the Kings protection, and his lands and tenements, goods and chattels

forfeited

forfeited to the King, & that his body shall remaine in prison at the Kings pleasure. So odious was this offence of Præmunire, that a man that was attainted of the same might haue bin slain by any man without danger of Law, because (k) it was prouided by Law, that a man might doe to him as to the Kings enemy, and any man may lawfully kill an enemie. But Queene Elizabeth and her Parliament * liking not the extreame and inhumane rigor of the Law in that point did prouide that it should not be lawfull for any person to slay any person in any maner attainted in or vpon any Præmunire, &c. Tenant in taile is attainted in a præmunire, he shall forfeit the land but during his life, for albeit the statute of 16.R.2.ca.5 enacteth, that in that case their lands and tenements, goods and chattells shall be forfeit to the King, that must bee vnderstood of such an estate as he may lawfully forfeite, and that is during his owne life. And these generall words doe not take away the force of the statute De donis conditionalibus, but he shall forfeite all his Fee simple lands, states for life, goods and chattells, and so was it resolued in Trudgins case.

*11.H 7.tit.Præmunire,F.5. 17.H 7. Iustice Spilmans in Turberuiles case. Kelwey,fo.195. Doct. & Stud. Lib.2.cap.32. Brooke,tit Præmunire,21. Temps.E.6.Bishop Barloes case. (k) 24.H.8.Brooke:Coron 196 * 5.Eliz.ca.1.*

Hill,21.Eliz. Trugins case resolued per les Iustices. 7.H.4.20.Simon Beuerleys case.

¶ *Car la ley le Roy & les briefes le Roy, &c.* There bee three things as here it appeareth wherby euery subiect is protected, viz. Rex, Lex, & Rescripta regis, the King, the Law and the Kings writs. The Law is the rule, but it is mute; The King iudgeth by his Iudges, and they are the speaking Law, Lex loquens. The processe and the execution which is the life of the Law consisteth in the Kings writs. So as he that is out of the protection of the King cannot be aided or protected by the Kings Law, or the Kings writ, Rex tuetur legem, & lex tuetur jus. (l) Besides men attainted in a Præmunire, euery person that is attainted of high treason, petit treason, or felony is disabled to bring any action for hee is * Extra legem politus, and is accounted in Law Ciuiliter mortuus.

*(l) 4.E.4.8. 1.E.4.1.6. 30.E.3.4. 8.Eliz. Dier.245. *. Mich.9.E.3. coram rege, Rot 84.Warw.*

It is to be vnderstood that there is a generall protection of the King, whereof Littleton here speaketh, and this extends generally to all the Kings loyall subiects, Denizens and Aliens within the Realme, whose offences haue not made them vncapable of it as before it appeareth, And there is a particular protection by writ, which is one of the Kings writs that Littleton here speaketh of. This particular protection is of two sorts, one to giue a man an immunity or freedome from actions or suites, the second for the safety of his person seruants and goods, lands and tenements whereof he is lawfully possessed from violence, vnlawfull molestation or wrong. The first is of right and by Law, the second are all of grace (sauing one) for the generall protection implyeth as much. Of the first sort some are Cum clausula (volumus) so called because the writ hath this word (volumus) in it, viz. Volumus quod interim sit quietus de omnibus placitis & querelis, &c. And the other a protection Cum clausula (nolumus) so called for the like reason. Of protections Cum clausula (volumus) for staying of pleas and suites there be foure kindes, viz. Quia profecturus (so called by reason they are part of the words of the writ) 2. Quia moraturus (so named for distinction for the like cause) 3. Quia indebitatus nobis existit of the matter. 4. When any sent into the Kings seruice in warre is imprisoned beyond sea. The former are for staying of actions and suites in generall. The third is for staying of suites of the subiect for debts & duties due by the Kings debtor to them. Of the fourth you shall reade hereafter in this place. For the former two, these nine things are to be obserued First, for what cause they are to be granted. 2. for what persons they are allowable. 3. A threefold time is to be considered, viz. the time of the purchase of them, the time of the continuance of them, and the time when they shall be cast. 4. In what place the seruice is to be performed. 5. In what actions these protections are allowable. 6 Under what seale and to whom they are directed. 7. Who is to allow, or disallow of them. 8. By whom they are to be cast and in what manner. 9. How vpon iust cause they may be repealed or disallowed. I must but point at these matters to make the studious reader capable of them and referre him to the bookes and other Authorities at large being excellent points of learning. As to the first, it is of two natures, the one concerne seruices of war as the Kings souldier, &c. the other wisedome and councell, as the Kings Ambassador or Messenger Pro negotijs regni, both these being for the publique good of the Realme, priuate mens actions and suites must be suspended for a conuenient time, for, Iura publica anteferanda privatis, and againe, jura publica ex privatis promiscue decidi non debent. (a) And the cause of granting of the protection must be expressed in the protection, to the end it may appeare to the Court that it is granted Pro negotijs regni & pro bono publico, (b) or as some others say, Pur le common profit del realme. And Britton saith Nostre seruice, sicome estre en nostre force, & le defence de nous & de nostre people, &c. * A man in execution in salua custodia shall not be deliuered by a Protection.

Prote-ction { Generall. Particular. Of the Generall, vid lib.7. Caluyns case per totum.

(a) 39.H.6.39. 3.H.6. tit. Protection.2. 13.R.2. ca.16.

*(b) Mirror, cap.3.§. Britton, fo.281. Fleta lib.6. cap.7.8. &c. Bracton * 5 Marie Dier, 162.*

(c) To the second these Protections are not allowable only for men of full age, but for men withing age, and for women, as necessary attendants vpon the Campe, and that in three cases, Quia lotrix, seu nutrix, seu obstetrix.

(c) 19.H.6.51. 30.E.3.21 F.N.B.28.l.11.E.3 Rot pat 3.part for the Countesse of Warw.

(d) Corporations aggregate of many are not capable of these two protections either Profecturæ, or Moraturæ because the Corporation it selfe is inuisible, and resteth only in

(d) 30.E.3.1. 21.E.4.36. 21.E.3.97.

consideration of Lawe. (e) Protection for the Husband shall serue also for the wife.

(f) Albeit the Vouchee, Tenant by resceit, prier in aide or garnish be no parties to the writ, yet before they appeare a Protection may be cast for them, because when the Demandant grants the Vouchor or receit in iudgement of Law they are made priuie, but if the Demandant counterplead the Vouchor or resceit, then vntill it be adiudged for them, and so priuie in Law, a Protection cannot be cast for them. And so it is of the garnishee, a protection may be cast for him at the day of the retorne of the Scire fac: (g) No Protection can bee cast for the Demandant or Plaintife, because the Tenant or Defendant cannot sue a resommons, or a re-attachment, but the Plaintife only that sued out the sommons or Attachment, &c. must sue also the resommons or re-attachment. And so it is of an Actor in nature of a Plaintife, &c. as the Garnishee after appearance, and an auowant, and the like. (h) An officer of the Kings resceit or any other officer in any Court of Record, whose attendance is necessary for the Kings seruice or administration of Iustice being sued, cannot haue a Protection cast for him.

(i) In euery action or plea reall or mixt against two (where a Protection doth lye) a protection cast for the one doth put the plea without day for all. So it is in debt, detinue and account. But in trespasse, or any Action in nature of trespasse, which is in law seuerall where euery one may answer without the other, there a Protection cast for the one shall serue for him only, vnlesse they ioyne in pleading, or if they plead seuerall pleas, and one Venire facias is awarded against all, there a Protection cast for one, shall put the plea without day for all, and therefore in former times, the Plaintife vsed to sue out seuerall Venire fac' in those cases for feare of a protection, &c.

(k) As to the threefold time, First, a Protection profecturæ regularly must not be purchased hanging the plea, but this fayleth when he goeth in the Kings seruice in a Voyage royall, and that is twofold, either touching warre, and that only is when the King himselfe or his Lieutenant, that is prorex goeth, or when any goeth in the Kings Ambassage Pro negotio regni, or for the marriage of the Kings daughter or the like, this also is called a Voyage royall. But a protection Moratur may be purchased, and cast pendente placito.

(l) Regularly a protection cannot be cast, but when the partie hath a day in Court, and when if he made default, it should saue his default: therefore when Execution is to be granted against body, lands or goods, no protection can be cast because the Defendant hath no day in Court. If a protection be cast at the Nisi prius for one, if before the day in banke it be repealed by Innotescimus, yet because it was once well cast, it shall saue his default, but if the protection be disallowed, either for variance, or that it lay not in the action or the like, there it shall turne to a default.

If a man hath a protection, and notwithstanding pleade a plea, yet at another day of continuance, after that a protection may be cast, so at a day after an Exigent, but after appearance he cannot cast a protection in that terme vntill a new continuance be taken.

(n) Thirdly, No protection either Profecture or Morature, shall indure longer, then a yeare and a day next after the teste or date of it. And so it is of an Essoigne de seruice le Roy. If a protection beare teste 7. die Ianuarij And haue allowance pro vno anno, the resummons, re-attachement or regarnishment may be sued 8. Ianuarij the next yeare, and yet that is the last day of the yeare.

And where Britton treating of an Essoigne beyond the Græcian Sea in a Pilgrimage, &c. saith thus, (o) Ascun gent nequident se purchasent nous letters de protection patents durable a vn an ou a 2. ou a 3. ans, & ialameyns font attorneys generals, ausi per nous letters patents: & ceux font bien & sagement, car nul grand Seignior ne chiualier de nostre realme ne doit prender chemyn sauns nostre conge, car issint poet le realme remainer disgarny de fort gente.

Three things are hereupon to be obserued, First, that this was a protection of grace, whereof more shall be said hereafter. Secondly, that it was for safetie of the great men of the realme, and that they should make generall Attornies, so as no actions, or suits should be therby stayed. Thirdly, (by the way) that great men could not passe out of the Realme without the Kings licence. (p) A protection granted to one, &c. vntill he returned from Scotland, was disallowed for the incertaintie of the time.

(q) To the fourth, the protection aswell Morature as Profecture must bee regularly to some place out of the Realme of England, and that must be to some certaine place, as super salua custodia Caliciæ, &c. and not to Carlisle or Wales, which are within the Realme, or to the like. But it may be to Ireland or Scotland, because they are distinct Kingdomes, or to Callice, Aquitaine, or the like, but a protection, Quia moratur super altum mare will not serue, not only, because (as some thinke) that mare non moratur, but for the incertaintie of the place, and for that a great part of the Sea is within the Realme of England.

(r) To the fifth. In some Actions, Protections shal not be allowed by the Common Law, and in some actions they are ousted by Act of Parliment, Actions at the Common Law, as all Actions that touch the Crowne as Appeales of Felonie, and appeales of Mayhem. (s) So

Where

(e) 35.H.6.3.43.E.3.23. 48.E.3.7. 4.H.5. protection. 107.
(f) 45.E.3.protect.37.3.H.6 18 30.8.H.6.16.9.H.6.36. 40 E.3.18.32 E.3.protect. 54.21.E.3.14.H.4.16. 45.E.3.tit.protect.40. 14.E.3.protect.66.
(g) 24.E.3.26. 47.E.3.5. 5.H.5.5 38.E.3.1.F.N.B. 28.g.20.R.2.protect.106. 22.H.6.28 9.H.6.36. 43.E. 3.36.17.E.3.24.25.E.3.43 24.E.3.26.13.E.3.protection.71.14.E.3.ibid.65.63. 20.E.3.ibid.84.
(h) 7.H 4.3.a.
(i) 19.E.3.protect.80.81. 32.E.3.ibid.55.16.E.2.ibid. 77.13.E.3.ibid.70.41.E.3. ibid.95.41.E.3.32.42 E.3.9. 5.H.5.7.3.H.4.15.2.R.2. protect.45.43.E.3.ibid 31. 2.H.6.22.21.H.6.41. 38.E. 3.12.7.H 6.21. 33.E.3.protect.116.4.H.4.4. 29.E.3. 41.45.E.3.24.28.11.E.4.7. F.N.B.28.k.
(k) 3.H.6.protect.2.39.H. 6.39.44.E.3.12.13.R.2.ca. 16.3.H.4.16.11.H.4.7. 7.E.4.27.28.H.6.1. 17.H.6.protect.56. 10.E.3.54.13.E.3.amerciament 18.Lib.7.fol.7.8.Caluins case.13.R.2.cap.16.
(l) 4.H.6 22.17.E.3.76. 33.E.3.tit.protect.115. 34.E.3.ibid.124.27.E.3.79 29.E.3.protect.85.88.. 2.E. 4.15.19.E.3.protect.82.79. 13.E.3.ibid.72.9.E.3.21. 3.H.6.55.4.H.6.22. 11.H. 6.14.14.H.6.22.21.H.6.10 27.H.6.4.28.H.6.1.35.H.6 58.44.E.3.2.16.48.E.3.8. 7.H.4.5.14.H.4.23. 27.E.3.78.
(m) 22.E.3 4.16.E.3. protect.47. 44.E.3 16..3E.3 amerciament.18. 34.E.3. Protection.123.
(n) 39.H.6. 39.F.N.B. fol.28. Fleta.lib.6.cap.8. Temps E.1.grand cape 26.
(o) Britt fo.282.283.& 280. Fleta lib.6.ca.8.accord.
(p) 1.E.3.25.
(q) Lib.7.fol.8. Caluins case. 7.E.4.29. F.N.B.38.e.g.h. 7.H.4.14.19.H.6.35. 38.H.6.3.32.H.6.3.R.2. Rot.Parliam.nu.21. 22.E.4 protect.18. 8.R.2.ibid.125. 11.H.4 57. Regist.indic.14. 36.H.6.tit.protect.27. 6.R. 2.ibid.14.Regist.orig.88.sape.
(r) Bract.lib.5.139.140. Britton.181. Fleta lib.6.cap. 7.8.&c. 14.E.2.protect.109 34.E.3.ibid.122. 19.E.3. ibid.78.33.E.3.ibid.99. 21.E.3.13.
(s) 10.H.6.protect.105.

where the King is sole partie no protection is to be allowed in like manner in à decies tantum, where the King and the subiect are Plaintifes, but in late Acts of Parliament Protections in personall actions are expresly ousted. A Protection may be cast against the Queene the Consort of the King.

In a Writ of Dower vnde nihil habet, no Protection is allowable, because the Demaundant hath nothing to liue vpon. Otherwise it is in a Writ of right of Dower. Likewise in a Quare impedit, or assise of Darreine presentment a Protection lieth not, for the eminent danger of the laps. Neither lieth a Protection in an Assise of Nouel disseisin, because it is festinum remedium, to restore the Disseisee to his freehold, whereof he is wrongfully and without iudgement disseised. (u) In a quare non admisit, a Protection is not allowable because it is grounded vpon the quare impedit, and the like in a Certificate vpon an assise for the like reason, and sic de similibus. A Protection, quia profecturus, is not allowable (as hath beene said) in any Action commenced before the date of the Protection, vnlesse it bee in a Voyage Royall. (w) An Infant is vouched, and at the Pluries venire fac, a Protection was cast for the Infant, and disallowed, because his age must be adiudged by the inspection of the Court.

(t) 39.H.6.39. 43.E.3.6.& 32.27.H.6.1 F.N.B.28. 17.E.3.23.lib.4.fol.35.Bonions case. Bract.lib.5.fol. 139.140.

(u) 13.E.3.tit.protection.52 12.E.3.ibid.69. 31.E.1.ibid.112.

(w) 19.E.2.protect.111. 32.E.3.ibid.54.

(x) By Act of Parliament no protection shall be allowed in an attaint. (But at the Common Law a Protection for one of the petite Jurie had put the plea without day for all) nor in an Action against a Gaoler for an escape, nor for victuals taken or bought vpon the voyage or seruice, nor in Pleas of Trespasse, or other contract made or perpetrated after the date of the same Protection.

(x) 23.H.8.cap.3. 34.E.1. protection 38. 7.H.4.cap.4. 1.R.2.cap.8.

(y) In a Writ of Error brought by an Infant vpon a fine leuied, the Plantife sued a Scire facias against the Conusee, for whom a Protection was cast, and the Court examined the age of the Plaintife, and by inspection adiudged him within age, and recorded the same, and then allowed the Protection, and this can bee no mischiefe to the Plaintife, whereupon it followeth, that albeit the Plaintife dieth afterwards before the fine be reuersed, yet after his age adiudged and recorded) his heire shall in that case reuerse the fine for the nonage of his Ancestor. (a) And so it was resolued in the case of Kekewiche in a Writ of Error brought by him by the opinion of the whole Court of the Kings Bench, otherwise it is, if the Plaintife dyeth before his age inspected.

(y) 21.E.3.24.31.E.3. protect.97.l.5.E.4.50 35.H.6. 43.46. 8.E.4.8. 17.E.3.22. 13.E.3 protect.73.

(a) Pasch.12.Ia.Regis, in the Kings Bench.

(b) Note in iudiciall writs, which are in nature of Actions, where the partie hath day to appeare and plead, there a Protection doth lie, as in writs of Scire facias vpon Recoueries, Fines, Judgements, &c. albeit by the Statute of W.2. Essoignes and other delayes be ousted in Writs of Scire facias, yet a Protection doth lie in the same. So it is in a Quid Iuris clamat and the like. But in writs of Execution, as habere facias seisinam, Elegit, Execution vpon a Statute, Capias ad satisfaciendum, Fieri facias and the like, there no Protection can bee cast for the Defendant, because he hath no day in Court, and the Protection extendeth only ad placita & querelas, and must be allowed by the Court, which cannot bee but vpon a day of appearance.

(b) 13.E.3.protect.72.Fleta. lib.2.cap.12. 40.E.3.18. 48.E.3.18.19.37.H.6.32. 21.E.4.19.15.H.7.8.47.E.3 5.17.E.3.68.14.E.3. protect.64.W.2.cap.45.

(c) In a writ of Disceit brought against him that obtained and cast a Protection vpon an vntrue surmise in delay of the Plaintife, that Protection is allowable. In an Action brought vpon the Statute of Labourers a Protection doth lie, & sic de similibus.

(c) 20.E.3.protect.83.

(d) To the sixth, no writ of Protection can be allowed, vnlesse it bee vnder the great Seale, (*) and it is directed generally.

(d) 35.H.6.2.Artic.super Cart.6.46.E.3.petition 19.

(*) Lib.2.fol.17. Lanes case. Lib.8 fol.68. Trallops case. 20.H.6.25. 2.E.4.4. 38.H.6.23.

(e) To the seuenth, the Courts of Justice where the Protection is cast, are to allow, or disallow of the same, bee they Courts of Record or not of Record, and not the Sherife, or any other Officer or Minister.

(e) 43.E.3.protect.96.

(f) To the eighth, the Protection may be cast either by any stranger, or by the partie himselfe, an Infant, Fem Couert, a Monke or any other may cast a Protection for the Tenant or Defendant: and this difference there is when a stranger casteth it, and when the Tenant or Defendant casteth it himselfe. (g) For the Defendant or Tenant casting it, hee must shew cause wherefore he ought to take aduantage of the Protection, but an estranger, need not shew any cause, but that the Tenant or Defendant is here by Protection.

(f) 21.E.4.18.

(g) 38.H.6.23.

(h) As to the ninth, A Protection may be auoyded three manner of wayes: First, vpon the casting of it before it be allowed. Secondly, by repeale thereof after it bee allowed: by disallowing of it many wayes, as for that it lyeth not in that Action, or that he hath no day to cast it, or for materiall variance betweene the Protection and the Record, or that it is not vnder the great Seale, or the like. (i) Thirdly, After it be allowed by Innotescimus, as if any tarrie in the Countrie without going to the seruice for which hee was retained, ouer a conuenient time after that he had any Protection, or repaire from the same seruice, vpon information thereof to the Lord Chancellor, he shal repeale the Protection in that case by an Innotescimus. But a Protection shall not be auoyded by an auerment of the partie in that case, because the Record of the Protection must be auoyded by matter of as high nature.

(h) 44.E.3.12.47.E.3.6.

(i) 13.R.2.ca.16.11.H.4.70 7.H.6.22.22.H.6.50. 30.H.6.3.19.H.6.35. 21.E.4.20.1.H.6.6.42.E.3 9.44.E.3 2.39.E.3.4.5. 20.E.3 protect.86. 34.E.3.ibid.119.

(k) 44.E 3.4.18.47.E.3.6. 34.E 3.protect.119. 28.H.6. 3. 34.H.6.22, 30.H.6.3. 32.H.6.4.

(k) There is a clause in the Protection to this effect. Præsentibus minime valituris, si contingat ipsum, &c. à custodia castri prædicti recedere. Or si contingat iter illud non arripere, vel infra illum terminum à partibus transmarinis redire. Whereupon there be two conclusions to be observed.

First, That though the Protection be allowed by the Court for a yeare, yet if it be repealed by an Innotescimus, that the resommons or Re-atatchment shall be granted upon the Repeale within the yeare, for the Protection that was allowed had the said clause in it. And of that opinion be our latter Bookes, and the repeale by Innotescimus should serue for little purpose, if the Law should not be taken so.

Secondly, That albeit hee that had the Protection either Morature or Profecture, returne into England, and haply be arrested and in Prison, yet if he came ouer to prouide Munition, Habiliments of warre, victuals or other necessaries, it is no breach of the said conditionall clause, nor against the Act of 13 Richard.2. for that in iudgement of Law comming for such things as are of necessitie for the maintenance of the warre, moratur, according to the intention of the Protection and Statute aforesaid. And thus much of the two first Protections, Cum clausula volumus, Profecture and Morature.

(l) Registrum.281.b. F.N.B.28.b. 33.H.8.ca.29.in the preamble 41.E.3.tit.execution 38 18.E.3.ibid.56.27 E 3.83 b. 4.E.4.16.3.Eliz Dier.197. Rot.Pat.27.E.3.part.1.m.2 (m) 25.E.3.cap.19.

(l) As to the third Protection Cum clausula volumus, the King by his Prerogatiue regularly is to be preferred in payment of his dutie or debt by his Debtor before any subiect, although the Kings Debt or dutie be the latter, and the reason hereof is, for that Thesaurus Regis est fundamentum belli & firmamentum pacis. And thereupon the Law gaue the King remedie by Writ of Protection to protect his Debtor, that hee should not bee sued or attached untill he paid the Kings debt, but hereof grew some inconuenience, for to delay other men of their suits, the Kings Debts were the more slowly paid. And for remedie thereof (m) it is enacte, by the Statute of 25 E.3. that the other Creditors may haue their actions against the Kings Debtor, and to proceed to Iudgement, but not to Execution unlesse hee will take upon him to pay the Kings Debt, and then he shall haue Execution against the Kings Debtor for both the two Debts.

(n) 41.E.3.15. 17.E.3.73. 29.E.3.13. 4.E.4.16.

This kind of Protection hath (as it appeareth) no certaine time limited in it. But in some cases the subiect shall be satisfied before the King, (n) for regularly whensoeuer the King is intitled to any fine or dutie by the suite of the partie, the partie shall bee first satisfied, as in a Decies tantum. And so if in an Action of Debt, the Defendant denie his Deed, and it is found against him he shall pay a fine to the King, but the Plantife shall be first satisfied, and so in all other like case. And so it is in Bils preferred by subiects in the Starchamber there costs and dammages (if any be) shall be answered before the Kings fine as it is daily in experience.

(o) Regist. sæpe. F.N.B.28.C. (p) Vide lib.7.fol.8.9. Caluins case.

The fourth Protection, Cum clausula volumus, is when a man sent into the Kings Seruice beyond Sea is imprisoned there, so as neither Protection, Profecture, or Morature, will serue him, and this hath no certaine time limited in it, (o) whereof you shall reade at large in the Register and F N B.

(q) Register.280 &c. F.N.B.29.A.B.C.D.E. F.G.H. Register.280. Statut de 14.E.3. F.N.B.30.A.

(p) Now are we at length come to Protections, Cum clausula Nolumus, All which sauing one are of grace, and as hath beene said are implyed under the generall Protection, for as Fitzherbert sayth euery loyall subiect is in the Kings Protection. Of these Protections of grace, you shall not reade much in our yeare Bookes, because they stayed no Actions or Suites (q) of the diuers formes, of these you shall reade at large in the Register, and F. N. B. which were too long and needlesse to be here recited.

The Protection Cum clausula nolumus, that is of right is that euery spirituall person may sue a Protection for him and his goods, and for the fermors of their lands and their goods, that they shall not be taken by the Kings Purueyor, nor their carriages or chattels taken by other Ministers of the King, which writ doth recite the Statute of 14.E.3.

Of these Protections I cannot say any thing of mine owne experience, for albeit Queene Elizabeth mayntayned many warres, yet she granted few or no Protections, and her reason was, that he was no fit subiect to be imployed in her seruice, that was subiect to other mens actions, lest she might be thought to delay Iustice.

Section 200.

Entre & professe en Religion.

Lev. est, un home q̃ est enter & professe en religion: Si tiel suist

THe fifth is, where a man is entred and professed in Religion, if

suist vn action, le tenant ou defendant poit monstrer, que tiel est enter en religion en tiel lieu, en lorder de Saint Benet, & la est moigne professe, ou en lorder des Friers preachers, ou minors, & la est frere professe, & issint des auters orders de religion, &c. & demaundera iudgement sil serra responde. Et la cause est, pur ceo que quant vn home entra en religion, & est professe, il est mort en ley, & son fits ou auter cousin maintenant luy enheritera auxybien sicõe il fuit mort en fait. Et quant il entra en Religion il poit faire son testament, & ses executors, les queux executors aueront vn action de det due a luy deuant lentre en Religion, ou auter action que executors poient auer sicome il fuit mort en fait. Et sil ne fait ses executors quant il entra en religion, donques Lordinarie poit committ ladministration de ses biens a auters homes, sicome il fuit mort en fait.

such a one sue an action, the Tenant or Defendant may shew that such a one is entred into Religion in such a place, into the Order of Saint *Benet*, and is there a Monke professed, or in the Order of Friers, Minors and Preachers, & is there a brother professed, and so of other Orders of Religion, &c. and aske iudgement if hee shall bee answered, and the cause is this, that when a man entreth into Religion, and is professed, hee is dead in the Law, and his Sonne or next Cousin incontinent shall inherit him, as well as though hee were dead indeed, and when he entreth into Religion, hee may make his Testament and his Executours, and they may haue an action of debt due to him before his entry into Religion, or any other action that Executors may haue, as if he were dead indeed. And if that hee make no Executours when he entreth into Religion, then the Ordinarie may commit the Administration of his goods to other, as if he were dead indeed.

(a) It is to be obserued that a mã doth enter into Religion at his first comming, and liueth vnder obedience, but hee is not professed till a yeare be past, or some time of probation. And he is said to be professed when he hath taken the habit of Religion, & vowed three things, Obedience, wilfull Pouertie & perpetuall Chastitie. And therefore our Author saith here enter & professe.

(a) Br. & lib. 5. fo 415. 421. Britt. ca. 22 fo. 39. Fleta, lib. 6. ca. 41. 5. E. 2. tit. Nonabil. 26. 3. H. 6. 24. 1. E. 3. 9. 7. H 4. 2. Doctor & Stud. 141. 21. R. 2. iudgement, 263. 11. R. 2. ibid. 107.

¶ *En Lorders des Freres Preachers, ou* (b) *Minors.* It appeareth in our Bookes that of Friers there were foure Orders, viz. Minors, Augustins, Preachers and Carmelites, and the Franciscani, Capuchini, and Obseruantes are included vnder the title of Minors, and they were called Obseruants, because they bee not Conuentuall or ioyned together in a Brotherhood, but liue separately, and bound themselues to obserue more strictly the rights of their Order. (c) Cum quis semel se religioni contulerit renuntiat omnibus quæ seculi sunt, habita distinctione, vtrum habitum probationis susceperit, vel habitum professionis.

(b) 4. H. 4. ca. 17. 25. H. 8. ca 12.

(c) Bracton, fo. 421. b.

¶ *Il est mort en ley.* Ciuiliter mortuus, or mortuus seculo. (d) There is a death in deede, and there is a ciuill death or a death in Law, Mors ciuilis and mors naturalis, as here it appeareth, and therefore to oust all scruples, Leases for life are euer made during the naturall life, &c. If the father enter into Religion, then shall his sonne and heire haue an assise of Mordancester and the Writ shall say, (e) Si W. pater, &c. die quo obijt habitum religionis assumpsit, in quo habitu professus fuit vt dicitur.

(d) Bracton, fo. 301. 426. Britton, fo. 226. 250. 251. Fleta, lib. 6. ca. 41.
(e) F.N.B. 196. 5. E. 4. 3.

¶ *Auxibien*

¶ *Auxibien come il fuit mort en fait.* **But yet to three purposes,** profession, that is, the ciuile death, hath not the effect of a naturall death.

First, This ciuile death shall neuer derogate from his owne grant, nor be any meane to auoyd it. And therefore if Tenant in Taile maketh a feoffement in fee, and entreth into Religion, his issue shal haue no Formedon during his life, because that should be in derogation of his own Grant, and be a meane to auoyd the same.

(f) 32. E. 1. *Dower* 176. 31. E. 3. *Collusion* 29. 33. E. 3. *Entre congeable* 52. 21. E. 4. 14.

(f) Secondly, It shall neuer giue her auaile, without whose consent hee could not haue entred into Religion, and therefore his wife after his ciuile death shall not bee endowed, vntill his naturall death. But if the wife, after her husband hath entred into Religion, alien the Land which is her owne right, and after her husband is deraigned, the husband may enter and auoid the alienation.

Thirdly, It shall not worke any wrong or preiudice to a stranger that hath a former right, and therefore if the Disseisor entreth into Religion, and is professed, so as the land discends to his heire, yet this discent shall not tolle the entrie of the Disseisee.

(g) 5. E. 4. 3. a.
(h) 18. H. 6. 33. *per Fortesc.*

(g) A woman cannot be professed a Nunne during the life of her husband: but some doe hold a diuersitie, (h) that ante carnalem copulam, the husband or wife may enter into Religion without any consent, but post carnalem copulam neither of them can without consent of other.

(i) 31. E. 3. *Collusion* 29.
(k) 34. E. 3. *Garranty* 71. *Vid. the Chapter of Warrantie, Sect.*

(i) But if a man holdeth lands by Knights seruice, and is professed in Religion, his heyre within age, he shall be in ward. (k) If I be disseised, and my brother releases with warranty, and is professed in Religion, and the warrantie discendeth vpon me, this warrantie shall binde me, because I am his heire, and such Inheritance as my brother had shall discend vpon mee.

(l) 21. R. 2. *Iudgm.* 263.

(l) And if one Ioyntenant be professed in Religion, the land shall suruiue to the other. If a man or a woman be professed in Religion in Normandie, or in any other forreine part, such a profession shall not disable them to bring any Action in England, because it wanteth triall, but they must be professed in some house of Religion within this Realme, for that may be tried by the Certificate of the Ordinarie, so as of forreine professions the Common Law taketh no knowledge.

(m) 10. E. 3. 511. 14. E. 3. *Executors* 87. 5. H. 7. 25. 21. H. 6. 30. 3. H. 6. 24.

(m) And yet in some case one that is professed in Religion within the Realme shall haue an Action, as if he be made an Executor, or if he be an Administrator, he shal maintaine an Action not in his owne right, but in right of the Dead.

(n) 44. E. 3. 9. *Nonability* 3. 14. H. 8. 16.

(n) If a Monke be made a Bishop, or a Parson, or a Vicar, he shall haue an Action concerning his Bishopricke, Parsonage, or Vicarage, & sic de similibus.

(o) 2. H. 4. 7. 8. H. 5. 6. 7. E. 4. 30. 44. E. 3. 4. 20. E. 3. *Vill.* 10. & *Nonabilitie* 9. 49. E. 3. 4.
(*) *Bract. fo.* 415, 416, 429. *Mir. c.* 2. §. 14. 14. H. 4. 37. b. 5. H. 7. 26. *Vid. Sect.* 296. 14. E. 4. 36.
(p) *Mir. vb. supra.*
(q) 22. *Ass.* 87. 21. E. 3. 41, 42. 22. E. 3. 2. 37. H. 6. 8. 32. H. 6. 36. *Bract. l.* 5. *f.* 416, 429. 13. E. 3. *Bre.* 261. 22. *Ed.* 3. 2. 38. H. 6. 7. b. 24. E. 3. 34. b. 45. 7. R. 2. *Nonability* 3, 9.

(o) And if a Monke be Farmer of the King, yeelding a rent, he shall haue an Action concerning that Farme. And albeit Littleton speaketh generally of one that is professed in Religion, yet must it not be vnderstood of the Soueraigne or Head of the religious house, as of the Abbot, Prior, or the like, (*) for albeit they be professed in Religion, yet by the policie of the Law, they are persons able to purchase, and to implead, and to be impleaded, to sue, and to be sued for any thing that concernes the house of Religion, for otherwise the house might be preiudiced, and other men also of their lawfull Actions. And this is the antient Law of England, as it appeareth in these words, (p) Des biens des gents de Religion appent laction al Chiefe en son nosme pur loy & son Couent. But what if a Monke, &c. were beaten, wounded, or imprisoned, &c. Doth the Law giue no remedie therefore? yes verily, (q) for in that case the Abbot and the Monke shall ioyne in an Action against the wrong doer, and if the writ be, Ad damnum ipsius Prioris, the writ is good; and if it be ad damnum ipsorum, it is good also. Also if a Monke be by conspiracie falsely and maliciously indicted of Felonie and Robberie, and afterwards is lawfully acquited, his Soueraigne and he shall ioyne in a writ of conspiracie and the like. And where Littleton speaketh of a man that is professed in Religion, the same Law is of a Nunne, sanctimonialis mutatis mutandis.

(r) 4. H. 3. *Br.* 766.
(s) 2. H. 4. *f.* 7. a.

(r) A wife is disabled to sue without her husband, as much as a Monke is without his Soueraigne, and yet we read in bookes, that in some cases a wife hath had abilitie to sue and be sued without her husband: (s) For the wife of Sir Robert Belknap, one of the Iustices of the Court of Common Pleas, who was exiled or banished beyond sea, did sue a writ in her owne name, without her husband, he being aliue, whereof one sayd, Ecce modo mirum, Quod fœmina fert Breue Regis non nominando virum coniunctim robore Legis.

(t) 10. E. 3. 53.

(t) King Edward the third brought a Quare impedit against the Ladie of Maltravers, and shee pleaded that she was Couert of Baron; whereunto it was replyed for the King, that her husband the Lord Maltrauers, was put in exile for a certaine cause, and she was ruled to answer.

(u) 1. H. 4. 1. b.

(u) King Henrie the fourth brought a writ of ward against Sibel B. who pleaded that she was Couert Baron, &c. Whereunto it was replied for the King, that her husband for a crime that he had committed against the King and the Peeres, was relegate or exiled into Gascoigne, there to remaine vntill he obtained the Kings grace: And Gascoigne chiefe Iustice, Ex assensu sociorum, awarded, that she should answer.

Sir Th. Egerton Lord Chancellor, in his argument which he published apart by himselfe in

Caluins case De Post-Natis, demanded what former President there was for the warrant of the Ladie Belknaps case in 2 H.4.7. which occasioned me to search, and upon search I found that the like Iudgement had bin giuen before at the Parliament holden in Cro Epiph', An. 19. Edw 1. where the case was, That Thomas of Weyland being abiured the Realme for Felonie, in the yeare before, Margerie de Mose his wife, and Richard sonne of the sayd Thomas, exhibited their petition of Right into the Parliament, for the Mannor of Sobbu, wherein her husband had but an estate for life ioyntly with her, & the inheritance in Richard the son by Fine. The Earle of Gloucester, Lord of the Fee, (who claiming the land by Escheat, had taken the possession thereof) alledged, Quod non fuit iuri consonum quod aliqua fœmina intraret in aliquas terras viuente marito suo, eo quod præfatus Thomas abiurauit Regnum & adhuc viuit, & asseritidem Comes nunquam huiusmodi casum accidisse & inde petit post multas allegationes quod possit prædictum manerium tenere vt eschaetam suam, super quo per ipsum Dominum regem præceptum fuit, quod tam Iustic' sui de vtroque Banco quam cæteri de Regno suo tam milites quam Seruientes in legibus & consuetudinibus Angliæ experti mandarentur, quod essent coram Rege & eius Consilio, &c. ad certiorandum ipsum Regem qualiter & quomodo in casu isto fuerit procedendum, & qualiter temporibus præteritis & antecessorum suorum in casibus consimilibus fieri consueuit, & interim scrutantur Recorda de consimilibus, vbi recitantur duo vel tres consimiles casus. Et quia licet prius non videbatur aliquibus iuri consonum fuisse quod vxor in vita viri secundum sanctam Ecclesiam, qualitercunque deliquisset quoad forum Regni, non posset nec deberet a viro suo seperari, & sic quicquid foret in possessione vxoris, conuerteretur in potestatem viri sui, & hoc manifeste imminueret contra consuetudinem Regni. Et etiam quia quidam dubitabant quod de possessionibus & bonis vxoris vir possit aliqualiter sustentari. Tamen coram Consilio Domini Regis vocatis Thesaurar' & Baronibus & Iusticiarijs de vtroque Banco concordatum est, quod prædicta Margeria rehabeat talem seisinam, &c secundum purportum finis prædict. &c. patet etiam consimile exemplum tempore Henrici patris regis. I haue cited this solemne resolution the more at large, because there be many excellent things to be obserued in it: so as by that which hath beene sayd, it plainly appeareth, that this opinion concerning the habilitie of the wife of a man abiured or banished, was not first hatched by the Iudges in Henrie the fourths time. And here is to be obserued, that an abiuration, that is a deportation for euer into a forreine Land, like to Profession, (whereof our Author speaketh here) is a ciuile death, & that is the reason that the wife may bring an Action, or may be impleaded during the naturall life of her husband. And so it is, if by Act of Parliament the husband be attainted of Treason or Felonie, and sauing his life, is banished for euer, as Belknap, &c. was, this is a ciuile death, and the wife may sue as a Feme sole. And hereby you may vnderstand your Bookes which treat of this matter. But if the husband by Act of Parliament, haue iudgement to be exiled but for a time, which some call a Relegation, that is no ciuile death. And in 8.E.2. an Abiuration is called a diuorce betweene the husband and wife. Sed opus est interprete, for by Law no Subiect can be exiled or banished his Countrie, whereby he shall perdere patriam, but by authoritie of Parliament, or in case of Abiuration, and that must be vpon an ordinarie proceeding of Law, as it was in this case of Weyland.

Pl. in Parliamento 19.E.1.

Note the antient triall of difficult matters in Law.

The great authoritie of Iudiciall Records and Presidents.

A solemne resolution of the Law in this point.

8.E.2 Coron.425.

So resolued in Parliament, vpon the making of the Statute of 35.El ca.1.

Exilium Hugonis de Spencer patris & filii tempore E.2.

Another example we haue in our Bookes to this effect: If the husband had aliened the Land of his wife, and after had committed felonie and beene abiured the Realme, the wife shall haue a Cui in vita in his life time, agreeable with the sayd resolution in Parliament, for that the abiuration was a ciuile death.

31.E.1. Cui in vita 31.

See in the Register, a woman was banished out of the Towne of Calice for adulterie, by the Law or custome of that place, and there appeareth Carta pardonationis pro muliere bannita. Sed nos non habemus talem consuetudinem.

Regist. fo.312.b.

(a) But by the Common Law, the wife of the King of England is an exempt person from the King, and is capable of lands or tenements of the gift of the King, as no other Feme couert is, and may sue and be sued without the King, for the wisedome of the Common Law would not haue the King (whose continuall care and studie is for the publique, & circa ardua Regni) to be troubled and disquieted for such priuate and pettie causes: so as the wife of the King of England is of abilitie and capacitie to grant and to take, to sue and be sued as a Feme sole by the Common Law.

(b) And such a Queene hath many prerogatiues, as she shall find no pledges, for such is her dignitie, as she shall not be amerced.

The Queene nor the Kings sonne are restrained by the Statute of 1.H 4. cap.6. concerning grants by the King.

(c) In a Quare impedit brought by her, some say that Plenartie is no plea, no more than in the case of the King.

(d) If any Baliffe of the Queenes bring an Action concerning the Hundred, he shall say, In contemptum Domini Regis & Reginæ.

(a) Vide in my Preface to the sixt booke, This was Law before the Conquest
10.E.3.27.b.508. 30.E.3.5. 18.E.3.1. 22 E.3.21. 49.E.3.4. 49.Ass.8. 11.H.4.67. 14.Ed.3.Voucher 110. 20.E.3.Nonabil.9. 31.E.3.Quar.Imp.146. 3.H.7.14.29. H.6.2. 28 H.6.13. 7.H.7.7.a. 26.H.6.Aid le Roy 24. Flet.l.2.ca.63.in Fine. Pl.Cro.231.Staunf.Prer.10.b.
(b) 8.E.3.2.33.E.1.Briefe 916. F.N.B.101.a.
(c) 18.E.3 32.24.E.3.35.75.
(d) 32 E.3.Br.346. 9.E.3.33.

The Queene shall pay no Tolle.

(e) F.N.B. 235. A.

(e) If the Tenant of the Queene alien a certaine part of his tenancie to one, and another part to another, the Queene may distraine in any one part for the whole as the King may doe; but other Lords shall distreyne but for the rate, and therefore where the Queene so distreyneth, there lyeth a writ De onerando pro rata portione. (f) The writ of right shall not be directed to the Queene no more then to the King, but to her Bailife, otherwise it is when any other is Lord.

(f) F.N.B. 1. F.

(g) 14 E. 3. *Voucher*, 110. 21. E. 3. 53. 22. E. 3. 3. b. 17. E. 3. 65. 10. E. 3. 17. 5. E. 3. 4. 15. E. 3. *Aide del Roy* 66. 10. E. 3. 18. 26. H. 6. *Aide le Roy* 24. (h) 21. E. 3. 13. 34. E. 3. *Protect.* 122. 11. H. 4. 67. b. (i) 30. E. 3. 5. (k) *Lestat. de* 25. E. 3. *de Proditionibus.* (l) *Rot. Parliam.* 8. H. 6. nu. 9.

(g) In case of aide prier of the Queene, it is Domina regina inconsulta, and the cause of the aide prier shall not be Counterpleaded no more than in the Kings case. And see where the aide shalbe granted of the King and Queene, and where of the Queene only, and she of the King. (h) But a Protection shall be allowed against the Queene, but not against the King, neither shall the Queene be sued by petition but by a Præcipe. (i) The Queene is not bound by the statute of Merlebridge for driving a Distresse into another County.

(k) If any doe compasse the death of the Queene, and declare it by any overt fact, the very intent is treason, as in the case of the King.

(l) No man may marry the Queene Dowager without the Kings licence. But let us now returne to Littleton.

(m) 4. E. 4. 25. 6. E. 4. 4. 45. E. 3. 10. a. 18. E. 4. 19. 22. H. 6. 5. 5. H. 7. 25. b.

¶ *Il poet faire son testament & ses executors, &c.* (m) If A. be bound to the Abbot of D. A. is professed a Monke in the same Abby and after is made Abbot thereof, he shall have an action of debt against his owne Executors.

(n) Pl Com. 280. 281. Greistrokes case.

¶ *Donques lordinary poet commit administration, &c. sicome il fuit mort en fait.* (n) Note the statute of 31. E. 3. ca. 11. that giveth actions to the Administrators speaketh of a man that dies intestate, which by the Authority of Littleton extendeth aswell to a civill death as to a naturall.

Sect. 201.

(a) Bracton, lib. 5. fo. 415. 426. 427. Fleta lib. 6. ca. 44. Britton, ca. 49. fo. 125.

¶ *Excommenge, excommunicatus, excommunicatio.* (a) Sicut quis poterit habere lepram in corpore, ita & in anima. Excommunicato interdicitur omnis actus legitimus, ita quod agere non potest nec aliquem convenire, licet ipse ab alijs possit conveniri.

Excommunicatio est nihil aliud quam censura a Canone vel judice Ecclesiastico prolata & inflicta priuans legitima communione Sacramentorũ, & quandaque hominum.

* F.N.B. 64. F.

* It is deuided into the greater and the lesser. Minor est per quam quis à Sacramentorum participatione conscientia vel sententia arceatur. Maior est quæ non solum à Sacramentorum verum etiam fidelium communione excludit, & ab omni actu legittimo separat & dividit, but either of them both disableth the party.

(b) Bracton, 426. b. act.

(b) Cum excommunicato autem nec orare nec loqui nec palam, nec abscondite, nec vesci, licet exceptis quibusdam personis. But every Excom-

¶ LE vi. est, lou un home est excommenge per la ley de saint Esglise, & il suist un action real ou personal, le tenant ou defend. poit plede que celuy que suist est excommenge, & de ceo covient mitter lettr̃ de Levesque south son seale, tesmoignant lexcommengemẽt, & demaundera iudgemẽt sil serra respondue, &c. Mes en cest cas si le demandant ou plaintife ceo ne poit dedire, le brẽ nabatera my, mes le iudgement serra, que le tenant ou defendant aler̃ quite sans

THe vi. is, where a man is excõmunicated by the law of holy Church, & he sueth an action reall or personall, the tenant or defendant may pleade that he that sueth is excõmunicated & of this it behoues him to shew the Bishops letters vnder his seale, witnessing the excõmunication & ask iudgement if he shal be answered, &c. but in this case if the demandãt or plaintife cannot deny it, the writ shall not abate, but the iudgement shall be, that the tenant or defendant shall goe quite without day, for

tour, pur ceo q̄ quant le demandant ou plaintife ad purchase les letters de absolution, & ceux sont monstres a le court, il poit aū vn resommons, ou reattachment sur son original, solonque la nature de son bre. Mes en les auters v. cases le bre abatera, &c. si le matter mise ne poit estre dedit.

this, that when the demandant or plaintife hath purchased his letters of absolution, and shewed them to the Court, he may haue a resummons or a reattachment vpon his originall, after the nature of his writ, &c. But in the other cases the writ shall abate, &c. if the matter shewed may not bee gainsaid.

munication disableth not the partie. (c) If Balifes and Commons or any other Corporation aggregate of many bring an Action, Excommengement in the Bailiffes shall not disable them, for that they sue and answer by Attorney, otherwise it is of a sole Corporation. But if Executors or Administrators be excommunicated, they may bee disabled, because they which conuerse with a person excommunicate are excommunicate also. (d) If a Bishop be defendant an (excommunication by the same) Bishop against the Plaintife shal not disable him, and it shall be intended for the same cause, if another be not shewed.

(c) 30.E.3.15. 42.E.3.13. 21.H.6.30. 21.E.4.49.

(d) See Artic. Cleri. ca.7. 5.E.3.8. 8.E.3 70. 9.H.7.21. 10.H.7.8. & 9. 18.E.3.58. 28.E.3 97. 16.E.3. Excom. 5. 20.E.3. ibid. 9. 3.H.4.3.

Letter del euesque desouth son seale. (e) None can certifie excommengement but only the Bishop, vnlesse the Bishop be beyond sea or in remotis, or one that hath ordinary iurisdiction, and is immediate Officer to the Kings Courts. As t. e Archdeacon of Richm or the Deane and Chapter in time of vacation. (f) But in ancient time euery Officiall or Commissary might testifie Excommengement in the Kings Court, and for the mischiefe that ensued thereupon it was ordained by Parliament, that none should testifie Excommengement but the Bishop only.

(g) If a Bishop certifie, that another Bishop hath certified him that the partie which is his Diocesan is Excommunicated, this Certificat vpon anothers report is not sufficient (h) If the Bishop of Rome, or any other hauing forreine Authority doth excommunicate any subiect of this Realme, and certifieth so much vnder his seale of Leade, this shall not disable the party. For the Common Law disalowes all Acts done in disability of any subiect of this Realme by any forraine power out of the Realme, as things not authentique whereof the Judges should giue allowance. (i) If the Bishop certifieth the Excommunication vnder seale, albeit he dyeth, yet the Certificate shall serue (k) Si quis innodatus fuerit per excommunicationes diuersas pro diuersis delictis, & profert litteras absolutionis de vna sententia non erit absolutus quousque de omnibus alijs absoluatur.

(e) Bracton lib.5. fo.425.b. 12.E.4.15. 20.H.6.17. 20.E.3 Excommengement 20. 33.E.3. ibid. 29. 44.E.3. ibid 23. 11.H.4.14. F.N.B.64.65.239. 7.E.4.14. 8.H.6.3. Registr.67.

(f) 11.H.4.62. in Debt.

(g) 33.E.3. Excom. 29. F.N.B.65.

(h) 16 E.3 Excom. 4. 31.E.3. ibid. 4. & 6. 30. Ass. 9. F.N.B.64. 4.H.7.15. 12.E.4.15. 14.H.4.14.

(i) 14.E.3. Excom. 8. 8.E.2. ibid. 26.

(k) Hill. 14.E.3. Coram Rege, London in Thesaur.

Euesque. Episcopus, a Bishop is regularly the Kings immediate Officer to the Kings Court of Justice in causes Ecclesiasticall, And all the Bishopricks in England are of the Kings foundation, and the King is Patron of them all, (l) and at the first they were donatiue, and so it appeares by our bookes, and by Acts of Parliament and by History, and that was Per traditionem anuli & pastoralis bacculi. i. the crosier. And King Henry the first, being perswaded by the Bishop of Rome to make them electiue by their Chapter or Couent refused it. (m) But King Iohn by his Charter acknowledging the custome and right of the Crowne in former times, yet granted De communi concensu Baronum, that they should be eligible, which after was confirmed by diuers Acts of Parliament, And afterward the manner and order aswell of election of Archbishops and Bishops, as of the Confirmation of the election, and Consecration (n) is enacted and expressed in the statute of 25 H.8. But by the statutes of 31.H.8. and 1.E.6. they were made donatiue by the Kings Letters patents, both which statutes are repealed, and the statute of 25.H 8. doth yet remaine in full force and effect.

(l) 17.E.3. fo.40. 25.E.3. cap. de Prouis. 25.H.8. ca.20. lib.3. fo.73. le case de Deane & Chapter de Norwich Matt. Par. pag. 62. Vid. Sect. 133. 134.

(m) Rot. Patent. 15. January 17. Regis Iohannis. Matt. Par. pag 252. 35.E.1. Lestat. de Carlisle. 25.E.3. Lestatut. de Prouis. 13.R.2. ca.2.

(n) 25.H.8. ca.20.

And where Littleton saith, that the Bishop vnder his seale must testifie, &c. it is to bee knowne, (o) that none but the Kings Courts of record, as the Court of Common pleas, the Kings bench, Justices of Gaole deliuery, and the like can write to the Bishop to certifie bastardy, mulierty, loyaltie of Matrimony and the like Ecclesiasticall matter: for it is a rule in Law, That none but the King can write to the Bishop to certifie, and therefore no inferiour Court, as London, Norwich, Yorke, or any other Incorporation can write to the Bishop, but (p) in those cases the plea must be remoued into the Court of Common pleas, and that Court must write to the Bishop, and then remaund the Record againe. And this was done in respect of the honour and reuerence which the Law gaue to the Bishop being an Ecclesiasticall Judge

(o) 2.E.3. Corone, 160. 8.E.3.59. 24.E.3.33. 44.E.3.28. 8.R.2. Conusans, 88.

(p) 41.E.3. 42.E.3. fo.6. 18.E.3.61. 14.H.4.25. 3.H.4.12. Regist. 7.4. F.N.B.6.E.

and a Lord of Parliament, by reason of the Baronie which every Bishop hath. And this was the reason (a) a Quare Impedit did lye of a Church in Wales in the County next adioyning, for that the Lordships Marchers could not write to the Bishop, (b) neither shall conusance be granted in a Quare Impedit, because the inferiour Court cannot write to the Bishop. And herewith agreeth Antiquitie. (c) Nullus alius preter regem potest episcopo demandare inquisitionem faciendam. (d) And another speaking of loyaltie of marriage, Nec alius quàm rex super hoc demandaret episcopo, quod inde inquireret, episcopus alterius mandatum quam regis non tenetur obtemperare; and therewith agreeth Britton also.

(a) 8.E.3.59.36.H.6.33. tit. *Quar. Imp.* Brooke 109. 35.H.6.30. 11.H.6.3. 14.E.3.33.
(b) 15.E.3.*Conusans* 41. *Surmise* 24. 40.E.3.2. *Vide Sect.*134.
(c) *Bract. lib.*3.106.
(d) *Fleta lib.*5.*cap.*24. *Britton. fol.* 248.b.

¶ *Le Briefe nabatera, &c.* Abater is a French word, and signifieth Destruere or Prostruere to destroy or prostrate. And Abatement de briefe is a prostration or overthrowing of the writ.

¶ * *Alera quite sauns iour, &c.* That is to goe quiet without any continuance to any certaine day, and therefore the Defendant is not bound to any certaine attendance, untill the party purchaseth his Letters of absolution, and the reattachment or resommons be sued, the entrie of which award is Ideo loquela prædicta remaneat sine die quousque, &c.

(*) *Bract. lib.*5.*fol.*425. 11.R.2.*Excom.*25.13.E.4.8 3.*Assp.*12.
*Vide Sect.*671.

¶ *Iour.* Dies (e) in legall understanding is the day of appearance, of the parties or continuance of the plea. And you shall understand that first in reall actions there are, dies communes, common dayes, whereof you shall reade in divers ancient Statutes.

(e) 51.H.3.*cap.*1.&2. *Marlebr. ca.*12. 32.H.8.*ca.*21

(f) Also in all Sommons upon the originall there must bee fifteene dayes after the Sommons before the appearance. (g) But if the originall be returned tarde and Sommons alias goeth forth, there must bee nine Returnes betweene the Teste and the returne. And so in other iudiciall processe in reall actions, saving if Conusans bee demanded to bee holden within his Mannor, there processe shall be awarded from three weekes to three weekes.

(f) *Articul. super Cart. ca.*15 28.E.1.
(g) 8.H.6.20.30.H.6.35. 8.Eliz.*Dier.*252.

And before the Statute of Articuli super cartas, in all Sommons and Attachements in plea of Land there shall be contained the tearme of fifteene dayes. (q) And it appeareth aswell by the Statute, as by the ancient Authors of the Law, who wrote before the Statute, that this was the ancient Common Law: and the reason of these long dayes given in reall actions was (the recovery being so dangerous) that the Tenant might the better provide him both of answere and of proofes, (*) but by consent they may take other then common dayes.

(q) *Mirror. cap.*2.§.19. *Bract. lib.*5.*fol.*334.& *lib.*4. *fol.*255. *Britton. fol.*279.b. *Fleta. lib.*6.*cap.*6.12.E.4.15.
(*) 11.H.6.23.15.E.3. *iour.*23. 21.E.3.29.15.*Ass.* *Britton. fol.*10.b.

And it is not amisse to note what the ancient Law was in proceeding against a man for his life. And therefore heare what Britton saith, Sur le presentment de cest felony (under which hee includeth also Treason) voilons nous (for he wrote in the Kings name) que trestous ceux que ent sert' endites, face le Viscont hastiment prender, & sauement lour corps en prison garder & que ilz sont menes devant nous, ou devant nous Iustices: & pur ceo que nulluy ne soit disgarnis de lour respons, voilons que ceux que issint soient prise que ilz eynt temps de purveyer lour respons 15. iours an meyns silz le prient, & en dementiers soient safement gardes: (r) Vide Fortescue of this matter. And see the Mirror that in some cases the partie convicted had fortie dayes, or at least thirtie dayes to shew some matter to disturbe (that is to arrest) Iudgement, which now I know is gone in desuetudinem and great expedition is now made in pleas of the Crowne concerning the life of man. Sed de morte hominis nulla est cunctatio longa.

(r) *Fortescue in libro de laudibus legum Angliæ.* *Mirror. ca.*4.§. *Sept choses disturbent iudgement mortels.*

(s) And the use of the Kings Bench at this day is, that if the offence be committed in another Countie then where the Bench sits, and the Inditement be removed by Certiorari, there must be fifteene dayes betweene every processe and the returne thereof, but if it be committed in the same Countie where the Bench sit they may proceed de die in diem, but so they will doe rarely: but let us returne againe to the Common Pleas.

(s) *Lib.*9.118.b. *Zanchers case.*

Secondly, There is a day called dies specialis, (a) as in an Assise in the Kings Bench or Common Pleas, the Attachement need not be 15. dayes before the appearance. Otherwise it is before Iustices assigned, but generally in Assizes, the Iudges may give a speciall day at their pleasure, and are not bound to the common dayes, (*) and these dayes they may give aswell out of terme as within. So upon an imparlance the Court may give any speciall or particular day, but that must be in the tearme time, and likewise in a Scire facias, upon a fine or a recovery in a recovery in a reall action, because it is a writ of Execution, and so it is in a per que servitia and the like and in all iudiciall writs, in processe against an Infant to iudge of his age, or where the husband prayeth in aid of his wife, or in a pone at the suite of the Defendant there need not bee fifteene dayes. Also after Demurrer in Law the Court may give what day they will. (b) And it is worthy the noting, that if in an Assise the parties be adiorned to Westm. usque 15. Pasche, there they be not demaundable till the fourth day, but if it be adiorned usque diem Lunæ, or Diem Martis, there the parties are demaundable on that day.

(a) *Artic. super cart. ubi supra.* F.N.B.177.e.11.*Ass.*30. 12.*Ass.*4.22.*Ass.*79. 3.H.6. *Assise* 2.9.E.4.5.a.27.E.3. 1.2.W.1 *cap. ultimo.*
(*) F.N.B.177.D.7.*Ass.* 7.14.*Ass.*4.24.E.3.31. 39.E.3.20 9.E.4.18. 12.E. 4.15.8.H.5.*Error.*87.
12.E 4.15.
(b) 41.E.3.*Iour.*16. 8.E.4. 4. 1.H.6.4. 27.*Ass.*33.

Thirdly, (c) There is a day of grace, dies gratiæ, or a day of courtesie, the name doth shew of what kind it is, and regularly this day is granted by the Court, at the Prayer of the De-

(c) 3.E.2.*avowrie.*188. 15.E.3.*iour.*26.22.E.3.20. 1.E.3.4.*lib.*9.*fol.*49. *Countee de Salops case,* 33.H.6.42.

maundant or Plantife in whose delay it is, and neuer at the prayer of Tenant or Defendant. But it is worthy of obseruation (d) that a day of grace is neuer granted where the King is partie by Aide prayer of the Tenant or Defendant, nor where any Lord of Parliament or Peere of the Realme is Tenant or Defendant. (e) And sometime the day that is 4. die post is called dies gratiæ, for the very day of returne is the day in Law, and to that day the Judgement hath relation, but no default shall be recorded till the fourth day be past, vnlesse it be in a Writ of right, where the Law alloweth no day, but only the day of returne. This day is sometims called dies amoris, and sometime a dies datus, but it were too long to enumerate all. This shall be sufficient to giue the Reader a taste to vnderstand the residue concerning this matter.

(d) 14. E. 3. iour. 24. 15. E. 3. ibid. 21. 22. E. 3. 9. 27. E. 3. 88.
(e) 22. E. 4. iour. 39. 18. E. 3. ibid. 20. 38. E. 3. 20. 9. Ass. 21. 21. E. 3. 13. 41. E. 3. ibid. 16. 33. H. 6. 42. 34. H. 6. 27. 10. Eliz. Dier. 267. 39. H. 6. 29. 24. E. 3. 28. 24. E. 3. breue 556. Bract. lib. 5. fol. 367.

(f) There is also a day of appearance in Court by the Writ, and by the Roll, by Writ when the Sherife returns the Writ. By the Roll, when he hath a day by the Roll, and the Sherife returne not the Writ, there the Defendant to saue himselfe from corporall paine as by imprisonment, or to preuent the losse of issues, or to saue his freehold or inheritance may appeare by the day he hath by the Roll.

(f) 21. E. 3. 43. 3. H. 6. 2. a. 22. H. 6. 20. 3. E. 4. 15. 6. E. 4. 7. E. 4. 15. 8. E. 4. 18. 3. H. 7. 8. 10. H. 7. 11. b. 27. H. 8. 14. Lib. 11. 40. 17. E. 3. 2. 11. Eliz. Dier. 286.

(g) Note, it is said commonly that the day of Nisi prius, and the day in banke is all one day, that is to be vnderstood as to pleading, but not to other purposes.

(g) 21. H. 6. 10. 20. 4. H. 6. 9. 40. E. 3. 31.

There are dies iuridici (which (h) Britton calleth temps discouenables) and dies non iuridici: dies iuridici (except it be in Assises) are only in the tearme. (i) And there be also in the tearme dies non iuridici. As in all the foure tearmes the Sabbath day is not dies iuridicus, for that ought to be consecrated to Diuine Seruice. Also in Michaelmasse Tearme the Feasts of All Saints and of All Soules: in Hillarie Tearme, the Purification of the blessed Virgin Marie, and in Easter Tearme the Feast of the Ascention are not dies iuridici, but set apart by the ancient Judges and Sages of the Law for Diuine Seruice. For Trinitie Tearme (which sometime had seuen dayes of returne, and was as long as Michaelmasse Tearme is now: but for auoyding of infection in that hot time of the yeare, and that men might not be letted to gather in Haruest, three returnes (since Littleton wrote) viz. Crastino Sancti Iohannis Baptistæ, Octabis Sancti Iohannis Baptistæ, and 15. Sancti Iohannis Baptistæ, are by the Statute of 32. H. 8. cut off and become dies non iuridici) And in those dayes the Feast of Saint John the Baptist was not dies iuridicus And the said Statute called, Dies Communis in Banco, is in diuers points (since Littleton wrote) altered, as by the said Statute appeareth. And in ancient time respect and reuerence was had by Law to certaine times, as it appeareth (k) by the Statute of W. 1. cap. 5. which hath a short but an excellent preamble. viz. Et pur ceo que grand charitie serra de faire droit a touts in tout temps, ou mestior serroit: purueu est per assentment des prelates, que Assises de nouel disseisin, mortdauncester, & darreine presentment fuissent prises en le Aduent, en septuagesime, & en Quaresine, auxibien come (le home) prent lenquestes, & ceo pria le Roy, as Euesques.

(h) Britton. fol. 134. a.
(i) Mirror cap. 3. §. exception de temps & cap. 5. §. 1.
32. H. 8. cap. 21.
(k) W. 1. cap. vltimo.

(l) This Statute is expounded in Bookes, which I haue only added, to the end the studious Reader might vnderstand the Bookes that darkly speake of this matter, and bee ignorant of nothing, that belongs to the vnderstanding of any part of the Law. Now Aduent is a moneth before the Feast of the Natiuitie of our Sauiour Christ, so called, de Aduentu Domini in carne. Septuagesima beginneth euer on the Sabbath Day, and is the third Sabbath before Shrouesunday, so called because it is the 70. day before the Feast of Easter. Sexagesima is the second Sabbath before Shrouesunday so named, because it is the 60. day before Easter, and so of Quinquagesima, and Quadragesima (m) whereof you shall reade in Acts of Parliament, and ancient Authors. Now as there bee dies iuridici, so there bee horæ conuenientes, whereof the Mirror saith (n) abusion que len tient pleas per dimenches (id est, Sabbaths) ou per auters iours defeudus, ou deuant le soliel leuy, ou noctantre, ou en dishonest lieu.

(l) 7. Ass. p. 7. 14. Ass. 5. F. N. B. 177. &c. Britton. fol. 134. b.
(m) W. 1. cap. 51. fait anno 3. E. 1. Britton. fol. 134. cap. 53.
(n) Mirror lib. 5. §. 1.

(o) Furthermore there are (as ancient Authors terms them) dies solaris aut dies lunaris secundum quod Deus diuisit lumen à tenebris, ex quibus duobus diebus efficitur vnus dies qui dicitur artificialis ex die præcedente & nocte subsequente, qui constat ex 24. horis.

(o) Bract. lib. 4. fol. 264. Britton. fol. 209.

But we at this day retayning the same method doe differ in words. For wee say, Dierum alij sunt naturales, alij artificiales, dies naturalis constat ex 24. horis, & continet diem Solarem & noctem, and therefore in Inditements of Burglarie, and the like wee say in nocte eiusdem diei. Iste dies naturalis est spatium in quo Sol progreditur ab Oriente in Occidentem, & ab Occidente iterum in Orientem. Dies artificialis siue Solaris incipit in ortu Solis, & desinit in occasu, and of this day the Law of England takes hold in many cases. Now diuers Nations beginne the day at diuers times. The Iewes, the Chaldeans and Babylonians beginne the day at the rising of the Sunne, the Athenians at the fall, the Vmbri in Italie beginne at midday, the Egyptians and Romans from midnight, and so doth the Law of England in many cases. Of all which you shall reade plentifull matter in our Bookes, and in my Reports which by this short instruction you shall the better vnderstand.

Gen. cap. 1. vers. 4. 5.

(p) There is also Annus minor and maior. The lessor yeare consisteth of 365. dayes and sixe houres, whereby in euery fourth yeare, there is dies excrescens, which makes that yeare to

(p) Bract. lib. 5. fol. 359. Britton. fol. 209. a.

(q) 17.Eliz.Dier.345.
(r) 21.H.3.stat.de anno bissextili.
(s) Lib.6.fol.62.Catesbyes case.

haue in rei veritate 366. dayes, and that is called annus maior. (q) A quarter of a yeare containeth by legall computation 91. dayes, and halfe a yeare containeth 182. dayes for the odde houres in legall computation are rejected, and by (r) the Statute de anno bissextili it is prouided, Quod computentur dies ille excrescens & dies proxime præcedens pro vnico die, so as in computation that day excrescent is not accounted. A moneth mensis is regularly accounted in Law 28. dayes, and not according to the Solar moneth, nor according to the Kalender, (s) vnlesse it bee for the account of the laps in a quare impedit. There is mensis Solaris, and mensis Lunaris. Solaris est 12. pars anni, viz. spatium 30. dierum, horarum 10. & minutorum 30. & Lunaris est spatium 28. dierum.

(t) Bract.lib.5.fol.425. Britton.ca.74.lib 7 fo.29.30

Resommons ou re-attachement. These are Writs that the Demaundant or Plantife after he hath obtained his Letters of absolution may sue out to bring the Tenant or Defendant againe into Court to haue day, to make answere unto him. (t) And these Writs doe lie in all cases when the plea is discontinued or put without day either in this case or in case when the Demaundant or Tenant hath his age, or for the non venue of the Iustices, or in case of a Protection or Essoine de seruice le Roy &c. Of these Writs there be two sorts, viz generall and speciall, whereof you may see Presidents, and reade more at large in the case of discontinuance of Processe in my Reports, and need not here to be inserted.

Sur son originall. This is intended of his originall Writs, or of that which is in stead of an originall Writ. But note that in the other fiue cases the Writ shall abate, and in the case of Excommengement the Writ shall not abate, but the plea to bee put without day untill the Plantife purchase his Letters of absolution, and sue out his resommons or re-attachement.

(u) Bract.lib.5.fol.421.
(x) Britton fol.39.& 88.
(y) Fleta lib.6.cap.39. 22.E.3.indorss. claus.20. part.nu.14. F.N.B.234.Register.

In ancient times more persons seemed to be disabled then these sixe recited by Littleton. As first he that was a Leaper, and by the Writ De leproso amouendo was propter contagionem morbi prædicti (as the Writ sayth) & propter corporis deformitatem (as others say) to be remoued from the societie of men to some solitary place, and thereupon (u) it is said, Datur etiam exceptio tenenti, ex persona petentis peremptoria propter morbum petentis incurabilem & corporis deformitatem, vt si petens leprosus fuerit, & tam deformis quod aspectus eius sustineri non possit, & ita quod à communione gentium sit separatus, talis quidem placitare non potest, nec hæreditatem petere. (x) And herewith Britton agreeth treating of disabled men, as men outlawed, abiured the Realme, attainted of Felonie, &c. addeth ne mesel, custe de common gents.

(y) And Fleta sayth, Competit etiam ei exceptio propter lepram manifestam vt si petens leprosus fuerit & tam deformis quod à communione gentium merito debet separari, talis enim morbus petentem repellit ab agendo.

And if these ancient Writers be understood of an appearance in person, I thinke their opinions are good Law, for they ought not to sue nor defend in proper person but by Atturny, for they are separated à communione gentium propter contagionem morbi & deformitatem corporis.

(a) Cambden.in Leicestershire.verbo.Burton.
(b) Leuit.cap.13.verse 44.45.46. Numeri cap.5.verse 1.2.4. Regum.cap.15.
(c) Bract.l.5.420.421. Britton.fol.39. Fleta lib.6.cap.37.
(d) 33.H.6.18. F.N.B.27.G.
(e) 27.H.8.11. 40.E.3.16. 20.E.4.2. F.N.B.27.H.

Before the Conquest this disease was not knowne in England. For Master Camden writing of Burton Lazers in Leicestershire sayth, (a) Primis Normannorum temporibus collecta per Angliam stipe nosocomium hoc constructum ferunt, quo tempore lepra (quæ à nonnullis Elephantiasis) grauissime vi contagionis per Angliam serpsit. And it is called Morbus Elephantiasis, because the skinnes of Leapers are like to Elephants. (b) And the Law of England for the remouing of the Leapers from the societie of men to some solitarie place is grounded upon Gods Law.

(c) Also there was a time when Ideots, Madmen, and such as were deafe, and dumbe, naturally were disabled to sue, because they wanted reason and understanding, (tales enim non multum distant à brutis) but at this day they all may sue, for the suite must bee in their name, but it shall be followed by others. (d) And note, that when an Ideot doth sue or defend, he shall not appeare by Gardeine or Porcheine Amy, or Atturney, but he must be euer in person, (e) but an Infant or a Minor shall sue by Porcheine Amy, and defend by Gardeine but now let us heare what Littleton will say unto us.

Section 202.

(a) Mirror cap.2.§.18. Doct.& Stud.fol.141. 4.E.4.25.per Danby. 27.Ass.pl.49.

Chaplein (a) secular, Is he that is Infra sacros ordines, but he is not regular, (that is) liueth not under certaine rules,

Item si un villein est fait un chapleine seculer, uncore son seignior poit luy seiser

Also if a villeine be made a secular Chaplaine, yet his Lord may seise him as

seiser cōe son villeine, & seisie les biens, &c. Mes il semble que si le villein enter en Religion, & est professe, que le Sn̄r ne poit luy prender ne seiser, pur ceo que il est mort en ley, nient pluis q̄ si vn frank hōe prent vn niefe a sa feme, le Seignior ne poit prendre ne seiser la feme de le baron. Mes son remedy est dauer vn action envers le baron pur ceo que il prist sa niefe a feme sans son licence & volunt, &c. Et issint poit le Sn̄r auer action envers le soueraign del meson que prist & admittast son villein destre professe en mesme le meason sans licence & la volunt le Seignior, & recouera ses damages a la value de le villein. Car celuy que est professe Moigne serra vn Moigne, & come vn Moign serra pris pur terme de sa vie natural, sinon que il soit deraigne per la ley de saint Esglise. Et il est tenus per son Religion de gard son cloister, &c. Et si le Sn̄r luy puissoit prender hors de sa meason, donques

his villeine, and seise his goods, &c. But it seemeth that if the villeine enter into Religion, and is professed that the Lord may not take nor seise him, because hee is dead in Law, no more then if a freeman taketh a neife to his wife the Lord cannot take nor seise the wife of the husband, but his remedy is to haue an action against the husband, for that hee tooke his niefe to wife without his licence and will, &c. And so may the Lord haue an action against the soueraigne of the house which takes and admitteth his villeine to bee professed in the same house, without the licence and leaue of the Lord, and hee shall recouer his damages to the value of the villeine. For he which is professed a Monke shalbe a Monke, and as a Monke shall be taken for terme of his naturall life, vnlesse hee be deraigned by the law of holy Church. And he is bound by his Religion to keepe his Cloyster, &c. And if the Lord might take him out of his house,

nor hath vowed those three things aboue specified.

¶ (b) *Enter en religion & est professe.* That is intended (as hath beene said) when hee is regular and profest vnder certaine rules, as to become one of the foure orders of Friers (that is to say) Freres minors, Augustines, Preachers, or Carmelites, or become a Monke, Cannon or Nunne, &c. Qui ad viuendum regulariter se astringunt, siue sunt Monachi, siue Canonici, regulares, siue sanctimoniales. For all these are regular and Votaries, and are dead persons in Law, but so are not the secular persons, as Prebends, Parsons, Vicars, &c.

And therefore it is holden in our bookes, (c) that if a secular Priest taketh a wife and hath issue and dieth, the issue is lawfull and shall inherite as heire to his father, &c. for (as it was then holden) the mariage was not voide, but voydable by diuorce, and after the death of either partie no diuorce can bee had.

But if a man marrieth a Nunne, or a Monke marrieth, these mariages were holden voide and the issues bastards, because (as it was then holden) the marriage was vtterly voide; for that the Nunne and the Monke (as Littleton here saith) were dead persons in Law. And that is the reason yeelded by Littleton, wherefore a villeine being professed in religion cannot bee seised by the Lord, because hee is dead in Law, and yet his blood or bondage is not thereby altered, but his person in respect of his profession only priuiledged. (d) In Decretalibus statutum est quod nullus episcopus spurios aut seruos donec à dominis suis fuerint manumissi ad sacros ordines promouere præsumat. But notwithstanding his person is priuiledged till hee be disgraded. And so it is holden in

(b) *Britton. cap. 31. fo. 79. Doctor & Student. fo. 142.*

4. H. 4. ca 17.

(c) 22. H. 7. 39. *19. H. 7. tit. bastardy. 33. 5. E. 2 tit. Nonability, 26. 47 E. 3. Casuals.*

(d) *Glanuill, lib. 5. ca. 5. Britton fo. 79. & 82.*

(e) *Fleta lib.* 2. *cap.* 44. *Briton. vbi supra.*

our old bookes. (e) If a villeine be made a Knight for the honour of his degree, his person is priuiledged, and the Lord cannot seize him vntill he be disgraded. Nullam villem personam ratione spuriũ, vel seruilis conditionis ad militiæ strenuitatis ordinem promoueri licebit sed cum à Dominis suis petantur vt natiui ipsis primo degradatis statim ad iudicium procedatur

il ne viueroit cõe vn mort person, ne solonqz son Religion, le quel serroit inconuenient, &c.

then he should not liue as a dead person, nor according to his religion, which should be inconuenient, &c.

(f) F.N.B. 78 b. 30. E. 1. *tit. Villen.* 46. 33. E. 3. *ibid.* 21. 18. E. 2. *ibid.* 30. 46. E. 3. 6. 4. E. 4. 25. 1. H. 4. 6. 13. E. 1. *Villen.* 36. 18. *Ass.* 10. *Doct. & Stud.* 141. *Mirror. cap.* 2. §. 18. *acc.*

¶ *Si vn frank home prent vn niefe.* (f) Some haue holden that by this marriage the wife shall be free for euer, but the better opinion of our Bookes is, that she shall be priuiledged during the couerture only, vnlesse the Lord himselfe marrieth his Niefe, and then some hold, that she shall be free for euer.

If a Niefe be regardant to a Mannor, and she taketh a freeman to husband by licence of the Lord, and the Lord maketh a feoffment in fee of the Mannor, the husband dieth, the Feoffee shall not haue the Niefe but the Feoffor, for that during the marriage shee was seuered from the Mannor. And so is the Booke 29. Ass. (which is falsly printed) to be vnderstood.

(g) 16. H. 3. *nuper obiit* 17. 8. H. 3. *breue* 789.

(g) If two Coperceners be of a Villeine, and one of them taketh him to husband, she and her husband shall not haue a nuper obijt against her Copercener, but after the decease of her husband she shall.

(h) *Vide Britton fol.* 82. *Fortescue cap.* 43. 46. E. 3. 6 a.

(i) 7. R. 2. *tit. barre* 240.

(k) *Britton. fol.* 82. b.

¶ (h) *Mes son remedie est dauer vn action vers le Baron, &c.* Albeit marriage is lawfull, yet when it worketh a preiudice to a third person, an action in this Case lyeth against the husband to the value of his losse. And albeit hee did not know her to bee a Niefe, yet the action lyeth against him, for hee must take notice thereof at his perill, (i) vnlesse she be out of the seruice of the Lord and vagarant, and then if one not knowing her to bee a Niefe marrieth her, some say that in that case no action lyeth against the husband. (k) And likewise the Lord shall haue an action against those that were the meanes to make the Villeine a Knight.

31. H. 6. *cap.* 5. 12. H. 7. *ca.* 7. 11. H. 4. 5. b.

¶ *Soueraigne*, Præcipuus, Chiefe, as here, soueraigne del meason is the Chiefe of the house.

31. H. 8. *cap.* 29.

¶ *Si non que il soit deraigne.* This word (deraigne) commeth of the French word desrayer, or deraigner, that is to say, to displace or to turne one out of his order, and hereof commeth deraignment a displacing, or turning out of his order. So when a Monke is derained, he is degraded and turned out of his Order of Religion, and become a lay man.

40. *Ass.* 27. *per Finchden.*

¶ *Le quel serra inconuenient.* Ab inconuenienti is a good argument in Law, as Littleton often obserueth. And here Littleton concludeth that the Lord cannot take a Monke out of his house, for that it should be inconuenient, which Littleton here sheweth, for diuers reasons, and therefore vnlawfull. And the inconuenience is, that where a man of Religion should liue according to his profession in Religion, by the taking of him out hee should not

¶ *Si le Seignior luy puissoit prender, &c.* By this it appeareth, that if a man detayneth a Villaine in his house, the Lord of the Villaine may take him out of the house, for here the impediment wherefore the Lord could not take him out of the house, was for that the Villaine was a Monke professed. And so in case of the wardship here next following.

Section 203.

¶ B*Riefe de rauishment de garde.* This writ is giuen by the Statute of W. 2. cap 35. in verbis conceptis, the wordes of which writ bee that the defendant, Talem hæredem cujus maritagium ad ipsum A.

¶ EN mesme le maner est, si soit gardeine en chiualrie de corps & de terre dun enfant deins age, si lenfant quant il

¶ IN the same manner it is, if there be a Gardein in Chiualrie of the bodie & land of an infant within age, if the infant

il vient al age de 14. ans entra en Religion, & est professe, le garden nad auter remedie (quant a le garde de le corps) forque bře de rauishment de gard enuers le Soueraigne de le meason. Et si ascun esteant de plein age, que est cosin & hře del enfant enter en l terre, le gardein nad ascun remedie quant al garde d la tre, pur ceo que lentrie del hře lenfant est congeable en tiel case.

when he comes to the age of 14. yeares entreth into Religion, and is profest, the gardein hath no other remedy (as to the wardship of the body) but a writ of rauishment *de gard* against the soueraigne of the house. And if any being of full age who is cosin and heire of the enfant entreth into the land, the gardein hath no remedy as to the wardship of the land, for that the entry of the heire of the infant is lawfull in such case.

pertinet, &c, rapuit & abduxit &c. contra pacem. Now Rapere signifieth properly to take away by violence and force. And when the Soueraigne tooke and admitted the ward into his house to bee professed, this in iudgement of Law is a Rauishment of the ward, and as it appeareth in our bookes before the said statute, there lay a generall action of trespasse in that case. Lib. 9. Dettor Husseys case. fol. 72.

Apres lage de 14. ans, &c. Our Author mentioneth this age because it is prohibited by the statute of 4. H. 4. that no childe shall be receiued into any house of religion before that age without consent of his parents and gardeins, &c. 4 H. 4. cap 17.

Le gardein nad ascun remedy, &c. Here it appeareth that by the profession of the ward, the Lord loseth the wardship of the land, because he is Civiliter mortuus, a dead man in law and cannot hold any inheritance, neither can the gardein continue the wardship of the land, because by the ciuill death of the ward the inheritance is discended to another, who is either to be in ward, or pay reliefe. So as in this case the gardein hath Damnum, but it is Absque iniuria, because he loseth the wardship of the land by act of Law, viz the discent thereof to another, and therefore the Law giueth to him no remedy in this case, neither by any formed writ, nor by action upon his case, for Littletons words are generall, (he hath not any remedie.)

Sect. 204.

Item, en mults diuers cases le Sñr poit faire manumission & enfranchisement a son villein. Manumission est proprement, quant le Sñr fait un fait a son villein de luy enfranchiser Per hoc verbũ (Manumittere) quod idem est quod extra manum, vel extra potestatem alterius ponere. Et pur ceo que per tiel fait le villein

ALso in many and diuers cases the Lord may make manumission and enfranchisement to his villein. Manumission is properly when the Lord makes a deed to his villeine to enfranchise him by this word (*Manumittere*) which is the same as to put him out of the hands and power of another. And for that that by

Manumission. (l) Manumittere quod idem est quod extra manum vel potestatem ponere. (l) Glanvil lib. 5. cap. 5. Britton, fol 78. &c. 82. 97. 110. Fleta lib. 3. cap. 13. & lib. 2. ca. 44.

Quia quamdiu quis in seruitute est, sub manu & potestate domini sui est.

Qui in potestate domini sui est, in manu domini sui esse dicitur, sed postquam Manumissus est, ab illo liberabitur; ergo dicitur quasi extra manum, id est, extra potestatem domini sui missus. And here is to bee noted (as in many other places is obserued) what regard Littleton hath to the true Etimologies of words.

(m) *Enfranchisement.* (Hereby Littleton (m) Mirror ca. 2. §. 18.

son explaneth Manumission) & is derived from the French word Franchise; that is, Liberty, and in the Common Law it hath divers significations, sometimes the incorporating of a man to be free of a Company or body politique, as a free man of a Citie, or Burgesse of a burroughe, &c. sometimes to make an Alien a Denizen, and here to manumise a villeine or bond man.

est mis hors de la main & de la poier son Seignior, il est appell Manumission. Et issint chescun maner de enfranchisement fait a un villein poit estre dit Manumission.

such deed the villeine is put out of the hands and of the power of his Lord, it is called Manumission. And so every manner of infranchisement made to a villein, may bee said to be a Manumission.

So as this word (Enfranchisement) is more generall then Manumission, for that is properly applyed to a villeine, and therefore every Manumission is an infranchisement, but every Infranchisement is not a Manumission. (n) There be two kindes of Manumissions, one expresse, and the other implied. Expresse, when the villeine by deed in expresse words is manumised and made free, the other implyed by doing some act, that maketh in judgement of Law the villeine free, albeit there be no expresse words of Manumission or Enfranchisement. (o) If a villeine be manumised, albeit he become ingratefull to the Lord in the highest degree, yet the Manumission remaines good: and herein the Common Law differeth from the Civill Law, for, Libertinum ingratum leges civiles in pristinam redigunt servitutem, sed leges Angliæ semel manumissum semper liberum judicant, gratum & ingratum.

(n) Mirror, cap. 2. §. 18.

(o) Fortescue, ca. 46.

There be also some cases where the villeine shall be priviledged from the seisure of the Lord, albeit he be not absolutely manumised or infranchised. Sometimes Ratione loci, (p) as if a villeine remaine in the ancient demeane of the King a yeare and a day without clayme or seisure of the Lord, the Lord cannot have a Writ of Nativo habendo or seise him so long as hee remaines and continues there, and the reason of this was in respect of the service hee did to the King in plowing and tillage of the demeanes and other labours of husbandry for the Kings benefit. And herewith agreeth old bookes (q) which say that this immunity was sometime granted by common consent to the King for his profit, and for the helpe or ease of his villeines.

(p) 39. E. 3. 6. b. F. N. B. 79. a.

(q) Glanvil, lib. 5. ca. 5. Fleta lib. 1. ca. 44. Britt. fo. 79. Mirror, ca. 2. §. 18.

(r) If a villeine be a Priest of the Kings Chappell, the Lord cannot seise him in the presence of the King, for the Kings presence is a priviledge and protection for him. Sometime Ratione professionis, (s) as if a villeine be professed a Monke, or a Neife a Nunne, as hath beene said. (t) Sometime (as some hath said) Ratione dignitatis, as if the villeine be made a Knight, &c. Sometime Ratione matrimonii, as if a Neife marry a free man she is priviledged during the mariage, but not absolutely enfranchised, for if her husband die she is Neife againe, unlesse the Lord himselfe marieth the Neife, and then she is enfranchised for ever as hath been said before. And it shall not bee amisse to observe the wisedome of our Ancients with what solemnity (for more suretie therof) Manumissions were made: Qui servum suum liberat, in Ecclesia vel mercato vel comitatu vel hundredo coram testibus & palam faciat, & liberas ei vias, & portas conscribit apertas, & lanceam & gladium vel que liberorum arma in manibus ei ponat. Our Author having spoken of an expresse manumission, here followes infranchisements in Law.

(r) 27. Ass. p. 49.
(s) Glanvil lib. 5. cap. 5.

(t) Britton, ubi supra.

Lib. Rub. cap. 78.

Section 205.

FOr when the Lord enableth the villein to have an Action against him as for debt or Annuity, &c. or giveth to the villein a certaine and fixed estate in Lands, Tenements, or hereditaments as a Lease for yeares, this amounteth to an infranchisement not only during the years but for ever, (u) and albeit the Lease be made to the villein without Deed yet it is an infranchisement for ever.

(u) 50. E. 3. tit. vil. 25. 11. H. 7. 13.

CAuxi si le Seignior fait a son villein un Obligation de certeine somme darget ou grant a luy per son fait un annuity, ou lessa a luy per son fait terres ou tenements pur terme des ans, le villein est enfranchise.

ALso if the Lord maketh to his villeine an Obligation of a certaine somme of money or granteth to him by his Deed an Anuuity, or lets to him by his Deed lands or tenements for terme of yeares, the villeine is enfranchised.

Sect. 206.

A Vtry ſi le Sñr fait vn feoffement a ſon villein daſcun terres ou tenemẽts per fait, ou ſans fait, en fee ſimple, fee taile, ou pur terme de vie, ou ans, & a luy liuera ſeiſin, ceo eſt vn enfranchiſement.

ALſo if the Lord maketh a feoffment to his villeine of any lands or tenements by Deed or without Deed, in fee ſimple, fee taile, or for terme of life or yeares, and deliuereth to him ſeiſin, this is an enfranchiſement.

This is euident and agreeth with our bookes. Vit. 24. E. 3. 32. 12. H. 3. tit. Vill 42.

Section 207.

MEs ſi le Sñr fait a luy vn leaſe des terres ou tenements, a tener a volunt le Sñr, per fait, ou ſans fait, ceo neſt aſcun enfranchiſemẽt pur ceo q̃ il nad aſcun manner ō certainty ne ſuertie de ſon eſtate, mes le Sñr luy poit ouſter quant il voylet.

BVt if the Lord maketh to him a leaſe of lands or tenements, to hold at will of the Lord by deed or without deed, this is no enfranchiſement for that, that hee hath no manner of certaintie or ſuretie of his eſtate, but the Lord may ouſt him when hee will.

PEr fait. So as a Deed made to a villeine by the Lord is no infranchiſement, when the Deede transferreth no certaine or fixed eſtate, but reuocable at the Lords will. If the Lord releaſe to his villein all his right in Blacke acre, and the villeine is not thereof ſeiſed, this is no infranchiſement becauſe it is voide and can giue no cauſe of action. If the Lord attorneth to his villeine, this is no infranchiſement, 11. H. 7.

Section 208.

A Vtry ſi l Sñr ſuiſt enuers ſon villein vn Præcipe quod reddat, ſil recouer, ou ſoit nonſue apres appearance, ceſt vn manumiſſion, pur ceo q̃ il puiſſoit loyalmẽt enter en la terre ſans tiel ſuit. En meſme le manner eſt, ſil ſuiſt enuers ſon villein vn action ō dett ou dac count, ou de couenãt,

ALſo if the Lord ſueth againſt his villein a *Præcipe quod reddat*, if hee recouer or bee nonſuite after appearance, this is a manumiſſion, for that hee might lawfully haue entred into the land without ſuite. In the ſame manner it is, if hee ſue againſt his villeine an action of debt, or account, or of couenant, or of

SI Seignior ſuiſt enuers ſon villeine vn Præcipe quod reddat, &c. ceo eſt vn manumiſſion. And the principall reaſon hereof is, for that by this ſuite hee enableth the villeine to be a perſon able to render him the land by courſe of law where the Lord without any ſuch ſuite might haue entred. (w) But if Tenant in tayle be of a Mannor whereunto a villein is regardant, and enfeoffeth the villeine of the Mannor and dyeth, the iſſue ſhall haue a formedon againſt the villeine, and after the recouery of the manor he ſhall ſeiſe the villein. (w) 24. E. 3. Diſcont. 16. Vid. Britton 78. & 126.

ou de Trespasse, ou de huiusmodi, ceo est vn enfranchisement, pur ceo que il puissoit emprison le villein, & prender ses biens sans tiel suit. Mes si le seignior suist son villeine per appeale de felony, ou il fuit endict de ceo deuant, ceo ne enfranchisera pas le villein coment que le matter de lappelle soit troue encounter le seignior, pur ceo que le Seignior ne puissoit auer le villein destre pendue sāns tiel suit. Mes si le villeine ne fuit endict de mesme le felonie, deuant lappeale sue enuers luy, & puis est acquite de cest felonie, issint que il recouera dammages enuers son seignior pur le faux appeal, donques le villeine est enfranchise, pur la cause de le iudgement de dammages a luy destre don enuers son seignior. Et plusors auts cases & matters y sont, per queux vn villeine poit estre enfranchise enuers son Seignior, &c. Sed de illis quære.

Trespasse, or of such like, this is an infranchisement, for that he might imprison the villeine, and take his goods without such suite. But if the Lord sue his Villeine by appeale of Felonie, where he was indited of the same before, this shall not enfranchise the Villeine, albeit that the matter of appeale bee found against the Lord, for that the Lord could not haue the Villeine to bee hanged without such suite. But if the Villeine were not indited of the same Felonie, before the appeale sued against him, and afterward is acquited of this Felony, so as he recouer dammages against his Lord for the false appeale, then the Villeine is infranchised, because of the iudgement of dammages to bee giuen vnto him against his Lord. And many other Cases and matters there bee by which a Villeine may bee enfranchised against his Lord, &c. But enquire of them.

And the reason is for that he could not seise the Villeine till he had recouered the Mannor which was the principall, and at the time of the writ brought, he was no Villeine.

The Tenant infeoffes the Villeine of the Lord, and an estranger vpon collusion, in this case although the Lord may enter vpon the Villeine for the moytie, yet may hee haue a writ of Ward against them both without infranchisement of the Villeine, for if the Lord should enter vpon the Villeine, then should his Seigniorie be suspended, and then could not he haue a writ of Ward against the oother.

The Lord vpon a writ of Couenant brought by the Villeine, leuies a fine to his Villeine of Land which is ancient Demesne, the Lord of whom the Land is holden reuerseth the fine in a writ of Disceit, albeit the Authoritie and Iurisdiction of the Court is disproued, and that the Lord of the Villeine shall bee restored to the Land giuen by the fine, yet is it an enfranchisement, for that he answered to the writ of Couenant, and the fine was voydable, and not voyde, and therefore being once an enfranchisement, it cannot bee auoyded by the reuersing of the fine.

¶ *Soit non sue (id est) non est prosecutus breue suum*, for by the Law the Plaintife bee first Agent at euery continuance, and therefore the Record sayth, quod petens seu querens (naming them) obtulit se, who if hee bee called, and make default, then he is said to be Nonsuit, id est, non est prosecutus, &c.

By Littleton here it appeareth that there is a Nonsuite before appearance at the returne of the writ, or after appearance at some day of continuance. (x) The difference betweene a Nonsuit and a Retraxit on the part of the Demandant or Plaintife is this. A Nonsuite is euer vpon a demand made when the Demandant or Plaintife should appeare, and hee makes default. A Retraxit is euer when the demandant or Plaintife is present in Court (as regularly

(x) *Lib.*8.*fo.*58.62. *Bechers case.* 3.*H.*6.13.*Brooke tit. Nonsuit* 1. 8.*H.*6.7. 50.*E.*3.12.

gularly he is euer by intendement of Law vntill a day be giuen ouer; vnlesse it be when a verdict is to be giuen, for then he is demandable.) And this is in two sorts, one Priuatiue, and the other Positiue, Priuatiue, as vpon demand made, that he make default, and depart in despite of the Court, and then the entrie is, (y) Et postea eodem die deuenit ad barram prædict tenens, & præd' petens tunc solenniter exactus non venit, sed à secta sua prædicta in contemptum Curiæ se retraxit, ideo consideratum est, &c. Positiue, as when the entrie is; Et super hoc idem querens dicit, quod ipse non vult vlterius placitum suum prædictum prosequi; sed abinde omnino se retraxit, &c. ideo, &c. Another forme thereof is, quod idem querens fatetur se (seu cognouit se) vlterius nolle prosequi versus prædict. defend. &c. de placito prædicto. (z) A departer in despight of the Court is on the part of the Tenant, and is, when the Tenant or Defendant after appearance and being present in Court vpon demand makes departure in despight of the Court, and then the entrie is, Et prædict' tenens seu defendens licet solenniter exactus non reuenit, sed in contemptum Curię recessit & defaltam fecit, ideo, &c. It is called a Retraxit, because that word is the effectuall word vsed in the entrie, as before it appeareth, and it is euer on the part of the Demandant or Plaintife. (a) Another difference betweene a Retraxit and a Nonsuite is; that a Retraxit is a barre of all other Actions of like or inferiour nature: Qui semel actionem renunciauit amplius repetere non potest. But regularly a Nonsuite is not so; but that he may commence an action of like nature, &c. againe. For it may bee, that hee hath mistaken somewhat in that action, or was not prouided of his proofes, or mistaking the day or the like. But yet for some speciall reasons, Nonsuite in some actions is peremptorie.

In a Quare impedit, if the Plaintife bee Nonsuite after appearance, the Defendant shall make a title, and haue a writ to the Bishop (b) and this is peremptorie to the Plaintife, and is a good barre in another quare impedit, and the reason is for that, the Defendant had by iudgement of the Court a writ to the Bishop, and the Incumbent that commeth in by that writ shall neuer be remoued; which is a flat barre as to that presentation, and of this opinion is Littleton in our Bookes. And the same Law, and for the same reason it is in the case vpon a discontinuance.

(c) In a writ De Natiuo habendo, Nonsuit after appearance is peremptorie, for thereby the Villein is infranchised. And so it is if two be Plaintifes in a Natiuo habendo, if one be nonsuit this is the Nonsuite of both, and no sommons and seuerance doth lie in that case, albeit it be a reall action. And this is in fauorem libertatis, for in a Libertate probanda, Nonsuite after appearance is not peremptorie, neither is the Nonsuite of the one, the Nonsuite of both.

(d) Nonsuite in an appeale of Murder, Rape, Robberie, &c. after appearance is peremptorie, and this is in fauorem vitæ, for if the Defendant be acquited, and take out processe vpon the Statute of W.2. against the Abettors, or if he purchase his originall writ, for that cause he may be Nonsuite.

(e) If the Plaintife in an appeale of Mayhem be Nonsuite after appearance it is peremptorie for the writ saith, Felonice maihemauit, and therefore the Nonsuite is peremptorie.

(f) In an Attaint if the Plantife after appearance be Nonsuite, it is peremptorie, and the reason is for the faith that the Law giues to the verdict, and for the terrible and fearefull iudgement that should be giuen against the first Iurie if they should be conuicted, and therefore vpon the Nonsuite, the Plaintife shall be imprisoned, and his pledges amerced. But if the processe in an Attaint be discontinued, the Plaintife may haue another writ of Attaint, because vpon the Nonsuite there is a iudgement giuen but not vpon the discontinuance. Note, it is truely said that Exceptio probat regulam, for these cases excepted stand vpon their speciall and particular reasons, and fall not within the generall reason of the rule. It is a generall rule, that Nonsuite before appearance is not peremptorie in any case, for that a stranger may purchase a writ in the name of him that hath cause of action, as shall be said hereafter in this Section.

(g) In reall or mixt actions the Nonsuite of one Demandant is not the Nonsuite of both, but he that makes default shall be summoned and seuered, but regularly in personall actions, the Nonsuite of the one is the Nonsuite of both, vnlesse it be in certaine particular cases.

(h) In personall actions brought by Executors there shall bee Sommons and seuerance because the best shall be taken for the benefit of the dead. And so it is in an action of Trespasse as Executor for goods taken out of their owne possession. Like Law in account as Executors by the receit of their owne hands.

(i) In an Audita querela concerning the personaltie, the Nonsuite of the one is not the Nonsuite of the other, because it goeth by way of discharge and freeing of themselues, and therefore the default of the one shall not hurt the other.

(k) In a Quid iuris clamat, the Nonsuite of the one is the Nonsuite of both, because the Tenant cannot attorne according to the grant.

(l) Some actions follow the nature of those actions whereupon they are grounded as the writs of Error, Attaint, Scire facias, and the like. If a reall action be brought by seuerall Præcipes against two or more, if the Demandant bee Nonsuite against one, he is Nonsuite a-

(y) *Tr.5 H.6. Rot.320. In Com. Banco.*

(z) *F.N.B.78.f. & 108.d. 19.E.2. Villen.31.*

(a) *Lib.8. vbi supra.*

(b) *5.E.3.35. 2.H.5. 31.H.6.15. 22.H.6.44,45. 33.H.6.1.55. 19.E.4.9. 21.E.4.2.b. &c. F.N.B.38.k. Lib.7.fo.27.b. Sir Hugh Portmans case.*

(c) *6.E.2. Vil.26. 12.E.2. ibid.28. 19.E.2. ibid.31. F.N.B.78.e. 4.E.2. Nonsuit 29.*

(d) *9.H.4.1.12. Stamf. Pl.Cor. 148.a. & 171.c. 22.Ass.97. Fitz.Cor.184. 22.E.3.6. 47.E.3.16. 7.H.7.5. 40 E.3. Dem 77. 17.E.2. Coron.386. 3.E.2. Action sur Lest.28.*

(e) *43.Ass.39. 40.Ass.10.*

(f) *32.Ass 13 19 Ass 13. 20.E.3 att int 42.22.E.3.7. F.N.B.108.d.*

(g) *11.H.6.23.35. F.N.B 35.b. 19.E.3.tit. Seuer.14.3.E.2. Nonsuit 18. 19.E.3. Seuer.16.12.E.3.ib. 38.E.3.9. 29.H.6.45. 38.E.3.35. 41.E.3. Nonsuit 10. 45.E.3.10. 2.H.4.2.*

(h) *42.E.3.13.48 E.3.14. 28.H.6.3.11.E.2. Seuer.26. 13.E.3.ib.15. 18.E.3.ib.28. 5.E.3.ibid.20. 7.E.3.12.*

(i) *15.E.3. Seuer.23. Lib.6.fo 25. Ruddocks case.*

(k) *20.E.3. Seuerance 17.*

(l) *47.E.3.6.b. 47.Ass.3. 29.Ass.34. 7.H.4.45. 34.H.6.31. 25.H.6.19. 29.E.3.37. Lib.6. vb. supra. 22.H.6.42. 4 E.4.33. 19.E.2. Nonsuit 32. 18.E.3. ibid.31. 20.E.3.ib.26 27. 19.E.3. ibid.12. 3.E.3. ibid.17. 38.E.3.9. 20.H.6.45. 44.E.3.16. 19.E.3. Seuerance 16.*

gainst all, for as to the Demandant it is but one writ under one Teste. Note, Severance is twofold, viz. by Sommons ad sequendum simul, and that is when one of the Demandants or Plaintifes never appeared, and by award of the Court of Nonsuit without any sommons, and that is after appearance.

(m) 6. R. 2. Nonsuit 13. 25. H. 8. Nonsuit Br. 68. 20. H. 7. 5.

(m) The Kings Maiestie cannot bee Nonsuite, because in iudgement of Law hee is ever present in Court, but the Kings Attorney, Qui sequitur pro Domino Rege, may enter an ulterius non vult prosequi, which hath the effect of a Nonsuite, but in an information by an Informer, qui tam, &c. the Informer may be Nonsuited.

(n) 2 H. 4. ca. 7. 3. E. 3. 21. 47. E. 3. 1, 2. 3. E. 4. f. 11.

(n) At the Common Law upon every continuance or day given over before iudgement, the Plaintife might have beene Nonsuited, and therefore before the Statute of 2. H. 4 after verdict given if the Court gave a day to be advised, at that day the Plaintife was demandable, and therefore might have beene Nonsuite, which is now remedied by that Statute.

(o) 9. H. 5. 5. 8. R. 2. Nonsuit 34.

(o) But after Demurrer in Law ioyned, if the Court doth give a day over, at that day the Demandant or Plaintife is demandable, and therefore may be Nonsuite, for that is not holpen by any Statute.

(p) 1. H. 7. 1. 21. E. 3. 32. Lib. 11. fo. 39. 41. Metcalfes case.

(p) And after an award to account, the Plaintife may be Nonsuite, and so note a diversitie betweene an Interlocutorie award of the Court, and a finall iudgement.

By these few instructions you shall the more easily understand the Bookes of tearmes and yeares, and other authorities of Law. And here (to returne to Littleton) it is to bee noted, that albeit the Lord be Nonsuite, yet the infranchisement of the Villeine doth remayne for that grew by the appearance to the writ, and cannot be taken away by the Nonsuite subsequent. So it is if the writ doe abate, yet the infranchisement remaynes.

(q) 7. H. 4. 8. 11. H. 4. 13. 9. E. 4. 23. 7. H. 4. 8. 4. 7. H. 7. 6. b. 5. H. 7. 15.

¶ (q) *Apres apparance*, for otherwise a stranger may purchase a writ in his name, and therefore Littleton materially added these words, after appearance.

¶ *Præcipe*. There bee three kind of Præcipes. 1. A Præcipe quod reddat, whereof Littleton here speaketh. 2. A Præcipe quod permittat, and 3. A Præcipe quod faciat, whereof you may reade plentifully in the Register, and Fitzherberts natura brevium, and belongs not properly to this Treatise.

¶ *Account*. Of this sufficient hath beene said before.

Vid. Sect. 748. Lib. 4. fo. 80. Nokes case. F. N. B. 145.

¶ *Covenant*. Conventio. Hereof there bee two kinds, viz. a Covenant personall, and a Covenant reall: and a Covenant in Deed, and a Covenant in Law.

(r) W. 2. cap. 12. 22. Ass. p. 39. 33. H. 6. 2. 14. H. 7. 2. 40. Ass. 18. 40. E. 3. 42.

(s) Kelway. 134.

¶ *Ou il fuit endite de ceo*. (r) For if the Villeine be not first indited of it, then upon the acquitall of the Villeine, the Villeine shall recover dammages against the Lord by the statute of W. 2. (r) quia multi per malitiam, &c. and consequently shall be enfranchised. But if the Villeine be formerly indited of the felony, then though the Villeine be acquited upon the Appeale, he shall recover no dammages against the Lord. For wheresoever the Lord giveth to the Villeine a iust cause of action hee is enfranchised. (s) And therefore if the Lord kill his Villeine his sonne and heire shall have an appeale, and thereby his heire shall bee enfranchised, because the offence of the Lord gave to the heire a iust cause of action against the Lord.

Sect. 209.

Item si Seignior dun manor voile prescriber, que il ad estre custome deins son manor de temps dont memory ne curt, que chescun Tenant deins mesme le mannor, que maria sa file a ascun home sans licence de le seignior del mannor

Also if the Lord of a Mannor will prescribe that there hath beene a custome within his Mannour, time out of minde of man, that every Tenant within the same Mannor, who marieth his Daughter to any man without licence of the Lord of the

(a) 10. E. 3. 23. Roger de Vales Case. 15. E. 3. ayde. 33.

(b) 34. H. 6. 15. a. per Litt.

¶ *Que il ad estre Custome, &c.* Here some may obiect that such a Custome may have a lawfull beginning for Littleton in the beginning of this Chapter, Sect. 174 alloweth that (a) a freeman may take lands of the Lord to bee holden of him, that is to pay a fine for the marriage of his Sonne or Daughter, and therefore (b) some have thought that such a Custome generally within the Mannor should bee good. But the

nor, ferra fine, et ont faire fine al Seignior del mannor pur le temps esteant, cest prescription est void. Car nul doit faire tiels fines forsque tantsolement villeins. Car chescun franke home poit frankement marier sa file a que pleist a luy & sa file. Et pur ceo que cest prescription est encounter reason, tiel prescription est voyd.

Mannour, shall make fine, and haue made fine to the Lord of the Mannor for the time being, this prescription is voyd: For none ought to make such fine but onely Villeines. For euery free man may freely marrie his daughter to whom it pleaseth him and his daughter: and for that this prescription is against reason, such prescription is voyd.

answer is, that though it may be so in a particular case vpon such a speciall reseruation of such a fine vpon a gift of land, yet to claime such a fine by a generall custome within the Mannor, is against the freedome of a Freeman that is not bound thereunto by particular Tenure. But a custome may be alledged within a Mannor, (b) That euery tenant (albeit his person bee free) that holdeth in bondage, or by natiue Tenure, the freehold being in the Lord, shall pay to the Lord for the marriage of his daughter without licence, a Fine: and it is called Marchet, as it were a Chete or fine for marriage. And here Littleton saith, that none ought to pay such fines but Villeines, (that is) either Villeines of bloud, or freemen holding in Villenage or base Tenure. So note a diuersitie betweene a freeholder and a free man holding in Villenage: Villeines vse to pay to their Lords in acknowledgement of their bondage for their seuerall heads, and thereupon it is called Cheuage Cheuagium, of the French word Chiefe, as it were the seruice of the head. Of which Bracton saith, (c) Chiuagium dicitur recognitio in signum subiectionis & dominij de capite suo. And sometimes it is written Chiuage, but more properly Chiefage. (d) Cheuagium signifieth also a great Misprision for any subiect to take summes of money, or other gifts yearely in name of Cheuage, because they take vpon them to be their chiefe heads or Leaders.

(b) 43.E.3.5. 14.H.6.15.

(c) Bracton lib.1.cap.10. Britton fol.79.b.

(d) 27. Ass. 44.

¶ *Pur ceo que cest prescription est encounter reason ceo est voyd.* This containes one of the maximes of the Common Law, viz. that all customes and prescriptions that be against reason, are voyd.

Sect. 210.

MEs en le County de Kent, ou tres & tenements sont tenus en Gauelkind la ou per le custome & vse de temps dont memorie ne curt, les fitz males doient ouelment enheriter, ceo custome est allowable, pur ceo que il estoit oue ascun reason, pur ceo que chescun fitz est auxy graunde gentle home come leigne fitz est,

BVt in the County of Kent where lands and tenements are holden in Gauelkinde, there where by the custome and vse out of minde of man the issues male ought equally to inherite, this custome is allowable, because it standeth with some reason, for euery sonne is as great a gentleman as the eldest sonne is and perchance will grow

¶ *EN (e) le County de Kent.* For that in no Countie of England lands (f) at this day bee of the nature of Gauelkind of common right, sauing in Kent onely. But yet in diuers parts of England, within diuers mannors and Seigniories the like custome is in force.

(e) *Vide Lestatute de Consuetudinibus Kanciæ ann* 21.E.1. 2.E.3.12.3.E.3.21.38. 23. *Ass.* pl.12. 8.E3.42.6.

(f) Vide *Mirror cap.* 1.§.3.

¶ *En Gauelkinde*, that is, Gaue all kind: for this custome giueth to all the sons alike.

¶ *Les fitz males inheriter.* And this is the generall custome extending to sonnes. But yet (g) by custome when one brother dieth without issue, all the other

(g) 23. *Ass.* pl.21.

other brethren may inherit.

¶ *Chescun fitz est auxy grand gentlehome come leigne fitz est.* By this it appeareth, that Gentrie and Armes is of the nature of Gauelkind, for they descend to all the sonnes, euerie sonne beeing a Gentleman alike. Which Gentrie and Armes doe not descend to all the brethren alone, but to all their posteritie: but yet Iure primogenituræ, the eldest shall beare as a badge of his birthright, his fathers Armes without any difference, for that as Littleton saith Sectione he is more worthie of bloud; but all the yonger brethren shal giue seuerall differences, & additio probat minoritatem, and (h) hæreditas inter masculos iure ciuili est diuidenda.

(h) Fortescue cap. 40.

& per case a pluis graunde honor & valour cressera sil auoit rien p ses ancesters, ou autermēt, peraduenture il ne puissoit tielment cresser, &c.

to greater honour and valour if he hath any thing by his ancestors, or otherwise peraduenture hee would not encrease so much, &c.

¶ *Ou auterment peraduenture il ne puissoit tielment cresser.* The reason of this is rendred by the Poet:

Horace.

Haud facile emergunt quorum virtutibus obstat
Res angusta domi. ———

31. H. 8. ca. 3. V. 18. H. 6. ca. 1.

But now by the Statute of 31. H. 8 a great part of Kent is made descendable to the eldest sonne, according to the course of the Common Law, for that by the meanes of that custome, diuers antient and great Families after a few discents came to verie little or nothing.

In plures quoties riuos deducitur amnis,
Fit minor, ac vnda deficiente, perit.

Sect. 211.

V. Sect. 165.

¶ PEr *custome appel Burgh English.* Of this custome Littleton hath spoken before in the chapter of Burgage. And in our bookes there is a speciall kind of Borough English, (i) as it shall descend to the yonger sonne, if he be not of the halfe bloud, and if he be, then to the eldest sonne.

(i) 32. E. 3. tit. Age 81.

(k) Mich. 10. Ia. Eliots case in Briefe de Faux iudgement.

(k) Within the Mannor of B. in the Countie of Berks, there is such a custome, That if a man haue diuers daughters, and no sonne, and dieth, the eldest daughter shall onely inherit; and if hee haue no daughters, but sisters, the eldest sister by the custome shall enherit, and sometime the yongest. And diuers other customes there be in like cases. And herewith agreeth Britton, who saith, (l) De terres des ancienes demeynes soit vse solonque le antient vsage del lieu, dount en ascun lieu le tient leu pur vsage: que le heritage soit departable entre touts les enfants freres & sores, & en ascun lieu que le eigne auera tout, & en ascun lieu que le puisne frere auera tout.

(l) Brit. 187. b.

Item, lou per custome appel Burgh English en ascun Burgh, le fits puisn̄ inherita touts les tenements, &c. cē custome estoit oue asc̄ certaine reason, pur ceo que le fits puisne (sil fault pere & mere) per cause de son iuuentute poit le pluis meins de touts ses freres luy mesme aider, &c.

ALso where by the Custome called Burrough English, in some borow the yongest son shall inherit al the Tenements, &c. this Custome also stands with some certaine reason, because that the yonger sonne (if he lacke father and mother) because of his yong age, may least of all his bretheren helpe himselfe, &c.

¶ *Pur cause de son iuuentute poet le pluis meins de touts ses freres luy mesme aidre, &c.* Here by (&c.) are implied those causes wherefore a youth is lesse able to ayd himselfe, &c. Which the Poet briefely and pithily expresseth thus:

Imberbis

Imberbis Iuuenis tandem Custode remoto,
Gaudet Equis, Canibusque & Aprici gramine Campi,
Cereus in vitium flecti, Monitoribus asper,
Vtilium tardus prouisor, prodigus æris,
Sublimis, cupidusque, & amata relinquere pernix. — *Horat.*

And againe, no liuing creature more infirme than Man:

Nil homine infirmum, tellus animalia nutrit.
Inter cuncta magis. ——— — *Homer.*

Sect. 212.

¶ MEs si home voil prescriber, que si ascuns aūs fueront sur les demesnes de son mannor la dammag̃ feasants, que le Seignior del mannor pur le temps esteant, ad vse eux de distreyner, & le distresse retayne tanque fine fuit fait a luy pur le dammag̃ a sa volunt, cest prescription est void, pur ceo que il est encounter reason, que si tort soit fait a vn home, que il de ceo serr̃ son Judge demesne: Car per tiel voy sil auoit dammages forsque al value dun mail, il puissoit asseser & aũ pur ceo C.l. que seroit encounter reason. Et issint tiel prescription, ou ascũ aut̃ prescription vse (si ceo soit encounter reason) ceo ne doit estre allow deuaunt Judges: Quia malus vsus abolendus est.

BVt if a man wil prescribe, that if any catel were vpō the demeanes of the Mannor, there doing dammage, that the Lord of the Mannor for the time beeing hath vsed to distreyne them, and the distresse to retaine till fine were made to him for the dammages at his will, this prescription is voyd: because it is against reason, that if wrong bee done any man, that hee thereof should be his owne Iudge, for by such way, if hee had dammages but to the value of an halfepeny, he might assesse and haue therefore C. li. which should bee against Reason. And so such prescription, or any other prescription vsed, if it bee against Reason, this ought not, nor will not be allowed before Iudges, *Quia malus vsus abolendus est.*

¶ *Est encounter reason que si tort soit fait a vn home, que il de ceo serra son iudge demesne.* For it is a Maxime in Law, Aliquis non debet esse iudex in propria causa. * And therefore a fine leuied before the Bayliffes of Salop, was reuersed, because one of the Baillifes was partie to the fine, quia non potest esse iudex & pars. — *10.E.3.23. 4.E.3.14. 7.E.3.24. 38.E.3.18. 2.H.3.4. 3.H.4. 8.H.6.19. 5.H.7.9.b.* — * *Hil.4.H.4.Coram Rege Salop.*

¶ Malus vsus abolendus est: And euerie vse is euill, that is (as our Author saith) against reason; Quia in consuetudinibus non diuturnitas temporis, sed soliditas rationis est cōsideranda.

And by this rule cited by our Author at the Parliament holden at Kilkenny in Ireland, Lionel Duke of Clarence beeing then Lieutenant of that Realme, the Irish customs called there the Brehon Law, (for that the Irish call their Judges, Brehons) was wholly abolished, for that (as the Parliament sayd) it was no Law, but a lewd custome, & malus vsus abolendus est. — *An.40.E.3 at Kilkenny.* — *The Brehon Law.* — *Vid. Sect. 265.*

But our Student must know, That King Iohn in the twelfth yeare of his raign went into Ireland, and there by the aduice of graue and learned men in the Lawes whom hee carried with him, by Parliament de communi omnium de Hibernia consensu ordained and established, that Ireland should bee gouerned by the Lawes of England, which

which of many of the Irish men, according to their owne desire, was ioyfully accepted and obeyed, and of many the same was soone after absolutely refused, preferring their Brehon Law before the iust and honourable Lawes of England. Rex, &c. Baronibus, militibus, & omnibus libere tenentibus L. Salutem; Satis vt credimus vestra audiuit discretio, quod quando bonæ memoriæ Iohannes quondam Rex Angliæ pater noster venit in Hyberniam, ipse duxit secum viros discretos & legis peritos, quorum communi consilio, & ad instantiam Hybernensium statuit & præcepit leges Anglicanas in Hybernia, ita qnod leges easdem in Scripturas redactas reliquit sub sigillo suo ad Scaccarium Dublin.

Rot. pat. 11. H. 3. Lib. 7. fo. 22. b. Calvyns case.

Rex Comitibus, Baronibus, militibus, & liberis hominibus & omnibus alijs de terra Hiberniæ salutem. Quia manifestè esse dinoscitur contra coronam & dignitatem nostram & consuetudines & leges regni nostri Angliæ quas bonæ memoriæ Dominus Iohannes Rex pater noster, de communi omnium de Hybernia consensu, teneri statuit in terra illa quod placita teneantur in curia Christianitatis de aduocationibus Ecclesiarum & capellarum vel de laico feodo vel de catallis quæ non sunt de testamento vel matrimonio. Vobis mandamus prohibentes quatenus huiusmodi placita in Curia Christianitatis nullatenus sequi præsumatis in manifestum dignitatis & Coronæ nostræ præiudicium, scituri pro certo, quod si feceritis, dedimus in mandatis Iusticiario nostro Hyberniæ, Statuta curiæ nostræ in Anglia contra transgressiones huius mandati nostri cum Iusticia procedat, & quod nostrum est exequatur. In cuius, &c. Teste Rege apud Winchcomb, 28. die Octobris, anno regni nostri 18. Et mandatum est Iusticiario Hyberniæ, per literas clausas quod prædictas literas patentes publice legi & teneri faciat.

Rot. patent. 18. H. 3. M. 17. N. 21.

Rex, &c. pro communi vtilitate terræ Hyberniæ, & *pro Vnitate terrarum*, prouisum est, quod omnes leges & consuetudines quæ in regno Angliæ tenentur, in Hybernia teneantur, & eadem terra eisdem legibus subiaceat, ac per easdem regatur, sicut Iohannes Rex cum illic esset, statuit & firmiter mandauit. Ideo volumus, quod omnia breuia de communi iure quæ currunt in Anglia similiter currant in Hybernia sub nouo sigillo Regis: In cuius, &c. Teste me ipso apud Woodstocke. Wherein it is to be obserued, That vnion of Lawes is the best meanes for the vnitie of Countries. * Vna vt eadem lex esse debet tam in Regno Angliæ quam Hyberniæ. (m) Terra Hyberniæ inter se habet Parliamentum & omnimodas curias prout in Anglia, & per idem Parliamentum facit leges & mutat leges, & illi de eadem terra non obligantur per statuta in Anglia, quia hij non habent Milites Parliamenti.

Rot. Patent. 30. H. 3.

** Trin. 13. E. 1. Coram Rege in Thesaur. in longo placito. (m) 2. R. 3. fo. 12. In camera stellata. 1. H. 7. 3.*

By an Act of Parliament (called Poynings Law) holden in Ireland in the tenth yeare of Henrie the seuenth, it is inacted, That all statutes made in this Realme of England before that time, should be of force and be put in vre within the Realme of Ireland, which (though it be by way of digression) is not vnnecessarie for our Student to know, But now let vs heare our Author.

CHAP. 12. Of Rents. Sect. 213.

Some haue deuided Rents into foure kindes, viz. Rent seruice, Rent charge Rent distreynable of common right (whereof somewhat shall be said in this chapter) and Rent secke.

¶ *Rent.* In Latyn (Redditus, (a) by some Dicitur à redeundo, quia retro it, & quotannis redit. * And others say it is deriued of reddere, for that the Rent is reserued out of the proffits, of the land, and is not due till the tenant or Lessee take the proffits, for reddendo inde or soluendo, or reseruando inde, or the like, (b) is as much to

*(a) Fleta, lib. 3. ca. 14. Britton, ca. 41. Mirror, ca. 2. §. 16. Pl. Com. 132. b. *Lib. 10. 148. Clunscase.*

(b) Pl. Com. 138. 139 &c. In Brownings & Bestons case. 38. H. 6. 34.

¶ Troys maners de Rents y sont, cestascauoir, Rent seruice, Rent charge, & Rent secke: Rent seruice est lou le tenant tient sa terre de son Sn̄r p fealtie, & certain Rent, ou per homage, fealtie, & certain Rent, ou p auts seruices & certain Rent: & si rent seruice

Three manner of rents there bee, that is to say, Rent seruice, Rent charge, and Rent secke. Rent seruice is, where the tenāt holdeth his land of his Lord by fealtie, and certain rent, or by homage, fealty, and certaine rent, or by other seruices, and certaine rent, and if rent seruice at any day that

Soit a ascun iour (que doit estre pay) adere, le Seignior poit distrainer pur ceo de common droit.

it ought to bee payed, bee behinde, the Lord may distraine for that of common right.

say as the Tenant or Lessee shall pay so much out of the profits of the lands, for Reddere nihil aliud est quam acceptum aut aliquam partem eiusdem restituere. Seu reddere est quasi retro dare, and hereof commeth Redditus for a Rent.

Here note for the better understanding of ancient Records, Statutes, Charters, &c. Gabel, or Gauell, gablum, Gabellũ, Gabellettũ, Galbellettum, and Gauillettũ, Doe signifie a Rent, Custome, Dutie, or seruice, yeelded or done to the King or any other Lord, as Wallingford continet 276. Hagas i. domos reddentes 9. liberas de gablo. i. de redditu. And Oxford, hæc vrbs reddebat pro theolonio & Gablo regi 20. l. & Sextarios mellis, cometi Alpharo 10. libras. And this is the legall signification thereof.

Domesday. Statutum de gauilletto anno 10. E. 2.

¶ *Rent seruice.* It is called a Rent seruice, because it hath some Corporall seruice incident unto it, which at the least is fealtie, as here it appeareth.

¶ *Sa terre.* (c) A Rent seruice cannot be reserued out of any inheritance but such as is manurable whereinto the Lord may enter and take a distresse, as in Lands and Tenements, Reuersions, remainders, and as some haue said, out of the herbage of lands, and regularly not out of any inheritances incorporeall, or that lye in grant. (d) By act of Law one rent or seruice may issue out of another, as if A before the statute of Quia emptores terrarum had giuen lands to B to hold to him by fealtie, and ten shillings rent, and B. had made a feoffment in fee to C. &c. whereby there was a Mesnalty created, in this case C. should hold of B. either by the same seruices the Law created, or such as he specially reserued and B. did by operation of Law hold those seruices of A by fealty and ten shillings rent, that is to say, rent and seruice out of rent and seruic, and if the rent be behinde, the Lord paramount may distreine upon the land for his rent, for both Mesnalty and Seigniory doe issue out of the land, the Mesnaltie immediatly, and the Seigniory mediatly, which is worthy of due consideration and obseruation.

Vid Sect. 21°.
(c) 44. E. 3. 45. lib. 5. fo. 4. Seignior Mountioy's case. 9. Ass. 24. 30. Ass 5. 17. E. 3. 75. Lib 7. fo 23. Buts case. Pl. Com. 39.
(d) 3. H. 6. 21. 5 H 7. 36. 21 H. 7. 39. 1. H. 4. 82. 10. H. 6. 12. 19. E. 3. tit Gard 40. 21. H. 6. 11.

¶ *Certaine rent.* (e) For the Rent must be certaine, or which may be reduced to a certaintie, for Id certum est, quod certum reddi potest (f) Continetur carta reddendo inde annuatim ad tales terminos vel faciendo inde talia seruitia, vel tales consuetudines, quæ omnia debent esse certa & in carta expressa, &c. But of this I haue spoken, Sect. 136. And the rent may aswell be in delivery of Hens, Capons, Roses, Spurres, Bowes, Shafts, Horses, Hawkes, Pepper, Comine, Wheat, or other profit that lyeth in render, office, attendance, and such like: as in payment of money. (g) But a man upon his feoffment or conueyance cannot reserue to him parcell of the Annuall profits themselues, as to reserue the vesture or herbage of the land or the like, for that should be repugnant to the grant, Non debet enim esse reseruatio de proficuis ipsis, quia ea conceduntur, sed de redditu nouo extra proficua.

(e) Britton, fo. 100. a.
(f) Fleta, lib. 3. ca 14.
(g) 38. H. 6. 38. a.

¶ *Poet distreine pur ceo.* For where there is fealtie, &c. incident to the rent, there is a distresse incident also thereunto (h) But it is to bee understood that for a rent or seruice, the Lord cannot distreyne in the night, but in the day time, and so it is of a rent charge: but for Damage feasaunt one may distreine in the night, otherwise it may be the beasts will be gone before he can take them.

(h) Mirror. ca. 2. §. 16. 10. E. 3. Avowry 237. 11. H. 7. 5.

¶ *De comon droit.* Of common right, (i) that is by the common Law, so called because the Common Law is the best and most common birth-right, that the subiect hath for the safegard and defence not only of goods, lands, and reuenues, but of his wife and children, his body, fame and life also. So as the meaning of Littleton in this particular case is, that the Lord may distreine for this rent of common right, that is, by the Common law without any particular reseruation or prouision of the partie. And it is to be obserued that the Common Law of England sometime is called right, sometime common right, and sometime Communis iustitia. In the graund Charter, the Common Law is called right, rectum. Nulli vendemus, nulli negabimus aut differemus iustitiam vel rectum. In the statute of W 1. cap. 1. it is called Common droit. En primes voet le roy, & commande que le peace de St. Esglise & de la terre soit bien garde & maintaine en touts points, & que common droit soit faits a touts auxibien aux poures, come aux riches saunce regard de nulluy, which agreeth with the ancient law in the time of King Edgar, Porro autem has populo quas seruet proponimus leges, primum publici iuris beneficio quisquam fruitur, idque ex æquo & bono siue is diues siue inops fuerit jus redditur. And Fleta saith, Item quod pax Ecclesiæ & terræ inuiolabiliter obseruetur, & quod communis iusticia singulis pariter exhibeatur. And all the Commissions & Charters for execution of Iustice, are Facturi quod ad iustitiam pertinet secundum legem & consuetudinem Angliæ. So as in

(i) W. 1. ca. 1. 2. H. 4. ca. 1. 7. H 4. ca. 1. 4. H. 8. ca. 8.
Lamb. fo. 78. inter Leges Reges Edgari. Fleta, lib. 1. ca. 29.

truth Justice is the daughter of the Law, for the Law bringeth her forth. And in this sence being largely taken, aswell the statutes and customes of the Realme, as that which is properly the Common law is included within Common droit. Littleton in this his Treatise nameth Common droit sixe times.

Vid. Sect. 214. 216. 226. 252. 331.

Sect. 214.

¶ CEEst home voyloit doner terres ou tenements a vn auter en taile, rendant a luy certain Rent p an, il de cõmon droit poit distreiñ pur le rent aderere, coment que tiel done fuit fait sans fait, pur ceo que tiel Rent est Rent seruice. En mñ le maner est, si leas soit fait a vn hõe pur terme de vie, ou dauter vie, rendant al lessor certaine Rent, ou pur terme de ans rendant certaine Rent.

AND if a man will giue Lands or Tenements to another in the taile, yeelding to him certaine rent by the yeare, hee of common right may distraine for the rent behind, though that such gift was made without deed, because that such Rent is Rent Seruice: In the same mãner it is, if a lease be made to a man for life or the life of another rendring to the Lessor certaine Rent, or for tearme of yeares rendring Rent.

35. H. 6. 34.

¶ *Sauns fait.* For it is a rule in Law that a rent Seruice may bee reserued without Deed.

Vid. Sect. 131. 132.

¶ *En mesme le manner si lease soit fait, &c.* For these be Rents Seruices, because fealtie is incident to these Rents, for (as it hath beene said before) a Lessee for life or yeares shall doe fealtie. And if a man make a Lease at will, reseruing a Rent, the Lessee shall not doe fealtie, and yet the Lessor shall distraine for the rent of common right.

¶ *Rendant*, commeth of the word reddo, .i. rem pro re dare, and signifieth yeelding or repaying, but of this I haue spoken before in this Chapter. Sect. 213.

Section. 215.

¶ MEs ẽ tiel cas ou home sur tiel done ou lease voile reseruer a luy rent seruice, il couiẽt que le reuersiõ de les terres & tenemñts soit en le donor ou lessor, car si home voile fair feoffement en fee, ou voile doner terres en taile, le remaindre oustre en fee simple sans fait, reseruant a luy certaine rent, tiel reseruãt est void, pur ceo que nul reuersion remaine en le donor, & tiel tenant tient

BVt in such case where a man vpon such a gift or Lease will reserue to him a Rent seruice, it behoueth that the reuersion of the Lands and Tenements be in the Donor or Lessor. For if a man will make a feoffment in fee, or will giue Lands in taile, the remainder ouer in fee simple without Deed, reseruing to him a certaine Rent, this reseruation is void, for that no reuersion remaines in the Donor, and such

¶ *Reuertion.* Reuersio commeth of the Latine word reuertor, and signifieth a returning againe, and therefore reuersio terræ est tanquam terra reuertens in possessione donatori siue hæredibus suis post donum finitum, &c. as in the cases that Littleton here hath put.

¶ *Il couient que le reuersion, &c. soit en le donor ou lessor, &c.* This is not to be vnderstood only of a reuersion immediatly expectant vpon the gift or lease. For if a man maketh a gift in tayle, the remaynder in tayle reseruing a rent, and keepe the reuersion in himselfe, this is a Rent Seruice.

¶ *Reseruant.* Reseruar commeth of the Latine

tient la terre immediatm de l' seignior de que son donor tenoit, &c.

tenant holds his Land immediately of the Lord of whom his Donor held, &c.

word Reseruo, that is to prouide for store. As when a man departeth with his land, hee reserueth or prouideth for himselfe a rent for his owne liuelihood. And sometime it hath the force of sauing or excepting: So as (k) sometime it serueth to reserue a new thing, viz. a Rent, and (l) sometime to except part of the thing in esse that is granted.

(k) 8.E.4.48. 26.*Ass.Pl.66.* (l) 35.*H.6.34.*

And it is to be vnderstood that in the case of the gift in tayle, lease for life or yeares, the fealtie is an incident inseparable to the reuersion, so as the Donor or Lessor cannot grant the reuersion ouer, and saue to himselfe the fealtie or such like seruice, but the Rent he may except, because the Rent although it be incident to the reuersion yet it is not inseparably incident. If a man maketh a gift in tayle without any reseruation, the Donee shall hold of the Donor by the same seruices that he held ouer. (m) But otherwise it is of an Estate for life or yeares, for there if he reserueth nothing, he shall haue fealtie only which is an incident inseparable to the reuersion, as hath beene said.

(m) *Litt.fol.4. Old tenures* 5. 38.*E*.3.7. 33.*H.6.7.*

Le remaindre ouster en fee simple sans fait. Here it appeareth that if a man maketh a gift in taile, the remainder in fee without Deed, (n) the remainder is good, and passeth out of the Donor by the liuerie of seisin, and so it is of a lease for life or yeares the remainder ouer in fee for the particular estate and the remainder to many intents and purposes, make but one estate in iudgement of Law. Vide Sect 60.

(n) 40.*E*.3.10. 10.*E*.4.1. 12.*E*.4.16. 15.*E*.4.18. 18.*E*.4.12. 18.*H*.8.4. 3.*H*.7.13. *F.N.B*.219. 11.*H*.4.39. 38.*E*.3.36. 44.*E*.3.8.

Remaindre, In legall Latine is remanere comming of the Latine word remaneo, for that (o) it is a remainder or remnant of an estate in Lands or Tenements expectant vpon a particular estate created together with the same at one time as in the cases here of Littleton appeareth.

(o) *Lib.2.fol.51. Cholmelies case.*

Section 216.

ET ceo est per force de lestatute de Quia emptores terrarum, car deuaunt le dit estatute si hōe fesoit vn feoffement en fee simple, per fait ou sans fait, rendant a luy & a ses heires certaine rent, ceo fuit rent seruice, & pur ceo il puissoit distreine de common droit, & sil fuit nul reseruation dascun rēt ne d ascū seruice, vncore le feoffee tenust del feoffor per autiel seruice que le feoffer tenust oustre d son Seignior procheine Paramont.

AND this is by force of the Statute of *Quia emptores terrarum*, for before that Statute, if a man had made a feoffment in fee simple by deed or without deed yeelding to him and to his heires a certaine rent, this was a rent seruice, and for this hee might haue distrained of common right. And if there were no reseruation of any Rent nor of any Seruice, yet the Feoffee held of the Feoffor by the same Seruice as the Feoffor did hold ouer his Lord next Paramount.

QVia emptores terrarum.

Hereof is spoken before in the chapter of Frankalmoigne Sectione 140.

Per fait ou sans fait, &c. For all rent Seruices may bee reserued without Deed (as hath beene said) and as it appeareth here.

And at the Common Law if a man had made a feoffment in fee by Parol he might vpon that feoffment haue reserued a Rent to him and his heires because it was a rent seruice, and a tenure thereby created.

Et sil fuit nul reseruation, &c. le feoffee tenust del feoffor per autiels seruices, &c. This is euident and agreeth with our Bookes (*) that in this case the Law created the tenure, wherein it is to be obserued how the Law regardeth equitie and equalitie without any prouision or reseruation of the partie,

(*) *Brittonfol*.100. 2.*E*.3.33. 25.*E*.3.*gard*.21. 49.*E*.3.10. 22.*Ass.Pl*.53. 7.*H*.4.14. 23.*E*.3.*auowrie*.253. 4.*H*. *Littl.cap.taile. Sect.*

Ipsæ etenim leges cupiunt vt iure regantur.

Section 217.

Mes si home per fait endent a cel iour, fait tiel done en fee taile, le remainder ouster en fee, ou lease a terme de vie, le remainder ouster en fee, ou vn feoffment en fee & per m lendenture il reserue a luy, & a ses heires vn certaine rent & que si le rent soit aderere, q̃ bien lirroit a luy & a ses heirs a distreiner, &c. tiel rent est rent charge, pur ceo que tielx terres ou tenements sont charges oue tiel distresse per force de le scripture tantsolement, & nemy de common droit. Et si tiel home sur fait endent reserua a luy, & a ses heires certain rent sans ascun tiel clause mise en le fait, que il poit distreine, donque tiel rent est rent secke, pur ceo que il ne poit vener de auer le rent, si ceo soit deuy per meane de distresse, & sil ne fuit vnques en cest cas seisie de la rent, il en sans remedie, come serra dit apres.

BVt if a man by deed indented at this day maketh such a gift in fee taile, the remainder ouer in fee, or a lease for life, the remainder ouer in fee, or a feoffement in fee, and by the same indenture hee reserueth to him and to his heires a certaine rent, and that if the rent be behind, that it shall be lawfull for him and his heires to distreine, &c. such a rent is a rent charge, because such Lands or Tenements are charged with such distresse by force of the writing only, and not of common right. And if such a man vpon a deed indented reserue to him and to his heires a certaine rent without any such clause put in the deed, that hee may distreine then such rent is rent secke, for that hee cannot come to haue the rent if it be denied by way of distres. And if in this case hee were neuer seised of the rent, he is without remedie, as shall be said hereafter.

Britton. fol. 100. Fleta lib. 3. cap. 14. Vide Sect. 370.

Per fait indent. It cannot bee a Deed indented, vnlesse it be actually indented, for albeit the words of the Deed bee Hæc Indentura, &c yet if it be not indented in Deed it is no Indenture, but if the Deed bee indented, albeit the words of the deed be not hæc Indentura, yet it is an Indenture.

(p) 8.E.4.8. 13.H.7.22. 35.H.6.34. 20.E.4.13. 17.E.3. 12.H.4.17.

And it is holden that (p) if a feoffment in fee bee made by Deed poll reseruing a Rent this reseruation is good, for when the Feoffee accepts the Deed and Liuerie of the land he agreeth to the rent, and the rent is reserued by the words of the Feoffor, and not by the grant of the Feoffee, but of this more hereafter. In the meane time it is to bee noted, that of ancient time a Deed indented was called Charta cyrographata, or Charta communis, because each partie had a part. And a Deed poll was called Charta de vna parte (q) Chartæ autem de pura donatione de simplici penes donatorium & eius hæredes debet remanere, communes vero duplicari debent ita quod quilibet habet partem suam. Vel si vna sit tantum, tunc in æqua manu communis amici vtriusq; ponatur saluo custodiend' dum cuilibet partiũ necesse fuerit exhibẽdũ.

(q) Fleta lib. 3. cap. 14. Britton. fol. 100.

Reseruant a luy. (r) Note, it is a maxime in Law that the rent must be reserued to him from whom the state of the Land moueth, and not to a stranger. (s) But some doe hold that otherwise it is in the case of the King.

(r) 12.E.2. Feffments 8. 18.E.2. Ass. 381.

(s) 35.H.6.36.

Et tiel rent est rent charge. It is called a Rent charge, because the Land for payment thereof is charged with a distresse. If it be to the whole value of the Land, or to the fourth part of the value, then the rent is called a fee farme. Here Littleton putteth his Case, and so did hee in the

Old tenures. Britton. cap. 66. 164. F.N.B. 210. Brac. 86.

re if the Difference
... rent service & rent Charge
... in one holding ye Land
fealty & certain rent, and
other holding by rent
... in the Deed ~~Sponsor~~
... cum potestate Distringendi.
if holding by certain rent
it imply fealty.
no Distress
rent seck

the next Section before, of a clause of distresse generally granted. (t) A man granted a rent out of certaine land, pro concilio impenso & impendendo, To have and to hold to him and to his Assignes for terme of his life, payable at foure Feasts in the yeare, and for default of payment upon demand, it should be lawfull for him to distreyne, the Grantee granted the rent over: the Assignee after one of the dayes demanded the rent, and distreyned, and the distresse adiudged lawfull, for he needs not make a demand at any of the dayes, as in the case of re-entrie, but he may demand it when hee will, for it is onely to entitle him to his remedie for his meere dutie.

(t) *Li.7.fo.28.b. Maunds case H.43.El in Com Banco, Rot. 1108, inter Maund & Gregorie. M.40.& 41.El.in Com.Banco inter. Stanij & Road. 28.El,Dyer 348.*

¶ *Distreyne, &c.* Here by (&c.) is implied what things are distreynable, which elsewhere is expressed at large. Also where the distresse is to be taken in the same land, and in some other, which with many differences is set downe in his proper place.

Vi.Sect.221.

¶ *Il serra sans remedie.* Note that upon a reservation of a Rent upon a feoffement in fee by deed indented, (w) the feoffor shall not have a Writ of Annuitie, because the words of reservation, as Reddendo, soluendo, faciendo, tenendo, reseruando, &c are the words of the Feoffor, and not of the Feoffee, albeit the Feoffee by acceptance of the state, is bound thereby.

(w) *33.E.3.Annuitie 52. 1.H.4.5. 26.Ass.Pl.66. 21.E.4.*

And where Littlet. putteth his case, when a reservation is made upon an estate that passeth by liverie, the same Law it is, if a man at this day doe bargaine and sell his land by deede indented and inrolled according to the Statute, a rent may be reserved thereupon, for albeit an use had onely passed by the Common Law, yet now by the Statute of 27.H 8 cap.10. the use and possession passe together, and so it was adiudged. * And so it is of a grant of a reversion or remainder, and any other conveyance of Lands or Tenements, whereby any estate doth passe.

* *Mich.39.& 40.El in Com. Banc. inter Wickes & Tillerd.*

Sect. 218.

¶ Aussy si home seisie de certain terre graunt per un fait polle, ou per indenture un annual rent issuant hors de mesme la terre a un auter en fee ou en fee taile, ou pur terme de vie, &c. ouesque clause de distresse, &c. donques ceo est rent charge. Et si le graunt soit sans clause de distres, donques il est Rent secke. Et nota, que Rent secke idem est quod redditus siccus, pur ceo que nul distres est incident a c. quod redditus siccus.

Also if a man seised of certaine land, grant by a Deede poll, or by Indenture, a yearely rent to be issuing out of the same land, to another in fee, or in fee taile, or for terme of life, &c. with a clause of distres &c. then this is a rent charge, and if the Graunt bee without clause of distresse, then it is a Rent secke. And note that Rent Secke *idem est quod redditus siccus*: For that no distresse is incident vnto it.

¶ *Seisie de Terre.* (x) Note that a rent cannot be granted out of a Pischarie, a Common, an Advowson, or such like incorporeall inheritances, but out of lands or tenements whereunto the Grantee may have recourse to distreyne, or which may be put in view to the recognitors of an Assise, as hath beene said before in this chapter. And though it be out of lands or tenements, (z) yet it must be out of an estate that passeth by the conveyance, (as by all Littletons examples appeareth) and not out of a right: As if the Disseisee release to the Disseisor of land, reserving a rent, the reservation is voyd: Et sic de similibus.

(x) *32.E.3 tit.Scir.fac 100. 40.E.3. Pl.Com.139.*

Vid.Sect.213.

(z) *10.E.4.3.b. 33.H.6.5. 50.E.3.9. 8.E.4.8. 5.Ed.3. Fines 1.9.E.3.7. 46.E.3.27. 21.H.6.8. Tempt E.1.Ass.428*

¶ *Grant per fait.* * Also a man may have a Rent by prescription.

19.E.3.Title 34.

¶ *Rent secke* idem est quod redditus siccus. This needs no explanation, for Littleton expounds it himselfe.

Sect. 219.

ITem ſi home granta per ſon fayt vn rent charge a vn auter, & le rent eſt arere, le grantee poet eſlier ſil voet ſuer vn briefe de Annuitie de ceo envers l' grantor ou diſtreyner pur le rent arrere, & l' diſtreſſe retaine tanqȝ il ſoit de ceo pay, mes il ne poit faire ne auer ambideux inſemble, &c. Car ſil recouer per briefe Dannuitie, donques la terre eſt diſcharge, de le diſtreſſe, &c. Et ſil ne ſuiſt Briefe de Annuitie, mes diſtreine pur les arrerages, & le Tenant ſuiſt ſon Replegiare, & donques le grantee auowa le priſel de le diſtreſſe en la Terre en Court de Record, donques eſt la terre charge, & la perſon del grantor diſcharg̃ d' Action d' Annuity.

ALſo if a man grant by his Deed a Rent charge to another, and the rent is behind, the Grantee may chuſe whither he will ſue a writ of Annuitie for this againſt the Grantour, or diſtreine for the rent behind, and the diſtreſſe detaine vntill hee bee payd, but he cannot do or haue both together &c. for if he recouers by a Writ of Annuitie, then the Land is diſcharged of the diſtreſſe, &c. And if he doth not ſue a Writ of Annuitie, but diſtreine for the arrerages, and the Tenant ſueth his Repleuin, and then the Grantee auow the taking of the diſtreſſe in the land in a Court of Record, then is the land charged, and the perſon of the Grantor diſcharged of the Action of Annuitie.

¶ RENT Charge. Here it appeareth by Littleton, that this Prima facie is a Rent charge, whereof in this Chapter ſhall be ſpoken more at large.

And ſo it is of a Rent Secke.

¶ *Home grant.* Put caſe that A be ſeiſed of lands in fee, and he and B. grant a Rent charge to one in fee, this Prima facie is the grant of A. and the confirmation of B. but yet the Grantee may haue a writ of Annuitie againſt both. (a) Two men grant an annuitie of twentie pounds per annum, to another, although the perſons be ſeuerall, yet he ſhall haue but one Annuitie: but if the grant be, Obligamus nos & vtrumqȝ noſtrum, the Grantee may haue a writ of Annuitie againſt either of them, but hee ſhall haue but one ſatiſfaction.

(a) 16. E. 2. tit. Annuity 47. Vid. Sect. 314.

¶ *Briefe de Annuitie* is a writ for the recouerie of an Annuitie. (b) An Annuitie is a yearely payment of a certaine ſumme of money, granted to another in fee for life or yeares, charging the perſon of the grantor onely. (c) But not onely the Grantee, but his heire and his and their Grantee alſo ſhall haue a writ of Annuitie. (d) But if a Rent charge be granted to a man and his heires, he ſhall not haue a writ of Annuitie againſt the heire of the Grantor, albeit he hath Aſſets, vnleſſe the grant be for him and his heires.

(b) Doct. & Stud. ca. 3. 17. El. Dyer 344. b. 45. E. 3. Executor. 72.

(c) 3. E. 6. Dyer 65. And Sergeant Bendloes reporteth, That ſo was the opinion of the Court.

(d) 2. H. 4. 13. Dyer 17. El. 344. b.

¶ *Poet eſlier.* The Grantee hath election to bring a writ of Annuitie, and charging the perſon onely to make it perſonall, or to diſtreyne vpon the land, and to make it reall.

But if a man grant a Rent charge to a man and his heires, and dieth, and his wife bring a writ of Dower againſt the heire, the heire in barre of her Dower, claimes the ſame to be an Annuitie, and no Rent charge, yet the wife ſhall recouer her dower, for hee cannot determine his election by claime, but by ſuing of a writ of Annuitie (as Littleton ſaith) neither can the heire haue after the endowment an Annuitie for the two parts, for that ſhould not be according to the deed of grant, for either the whole muſt be a rent charge, or the whole an Annuitie. But Littleton is to be vnderſtood with ſome limitation: (e) for of a rent granted for oweltie of partition, a writ of Annuitie doth not lie, becauſe it is of the nature of the land diſcended. Alſo of

(e) 29. Aſſ. p. 23.

ſuch

such a rent as may be granted without deed, a writ of Annuitie doth not lie, though it be granted by Deed

(f) And here is to be noted, That here is no election giuen of two seuerall things, as if the grant were of an Annuitie, or a Robe yearely, &c. for there the Grantor had election at the day to deliuer which he would. But here is two remedies giuen for one yearely summe, and consequently the Grantee shall at any time haue election to take which of the remedies he will, for in all cases where seuerall remedies be giuen, the partie to whom the Law giueth the remedies, it giueth him withall election to take which of the remedies he will.

(f) *Sir Rowland Heywards case, li.2. fo.36. 28.E.3.98. 41.E.3.10.a. 2.H.4.12. 6.H.4.10. 36.H.6.10. 9.E.4.46. 21.E.4.55.b. 1.E.5.1. F.N.B.121.*

¶ *Mes il ne poet faire ou auer ambideux ensemble.* **For then he should** recouer one thing twice, which should be a double charge to the Grantor.

Note, as to elections, these diuersities following:

Lib.2.fo.36,37. in Sir Rowland Heywards case.

First, when nothing passeth to the Feoffee or Grantee before election to haue the one thing or the other, there the election ought to be made in the life of the parties, and the Heire or Executor cannot make election. But when an estate or interest passes immediately to the Feoffee, Donee, or Grantee, there election may be made by them, or by their Heires or Executors.

Secondly, when one and the same thing passeth to the Donee or Grantee, and the Donee or Grantee hath election in what manner or degree he will take this, there the interest passeth immediately, and the partie, his heires, or Executors, may make election when they will.

Thirdly, when election is giuen to seuerall persons, there the first election made by any of the persons shall stand.

Fourthly, In case an election be giuen of two seuerall things, alwayes he which is the first agent, and which ought to doe the first act, shall haue the election: As if a man granteth a Rent of twentie shillings, or a robe to one and to his heires, the Grantor shall haue the election, for he is the first Agent, by payment of the one, or deliuerie of the other. So if a man maketh a Lease, rendring a rent or a robe, the Lessee shall haue the election causa qua supra, and with this agree the bookes in the * margent. (g) But if I giue vnto you one of my horses in my Stable, there you shall haue the election, for you shall be the first Agent by taking or seisure of one of them. And if one grant to another twentie loads of Hazill, or twentie loads of Maple to bee taken in his wood of D. there the Grantee shall haue election, for he ought to doe the first act, s. to fell and take the same.

** 9.E.4.36.b. 13.E.4.4.b. 15.E.4.6.b. 11.E.3. Annuitie 27. 11.Ass.p.8. 29.ass.55. 3.E.3.tit.Ass.175. 43.E.3.tit Barre 194.*

(g) *2 H 7.23.a.*

Fiftly, when the thing granted is of things annuall, and are to haue continuance, there the election remaineth to the Grantor, (in case where the law giueth to him election) as well after the day, as before, otherwise it is when the things are to be performed vnica vice. And therefore if I grant to another for life, an Annuitie or a Robe at the feast of Easter, and both are behind, the Grantee ought to bring his writ of Annuitie in the disiunctiue, for if hee bring his writ of Annuitie for the one onely, and recouer, this iudgement shall determine his election for euer; for he shall neuer haue a writ of Annuitie afterwards, but a Scire facias vpon the sayd iudgement. Which reason Fitzherbert in his Natura Breuium not obseruing, held an opinion to the contrarie. But if I contract with you to pay vnto you twentie shillings or a robe at the Feast of Easter, after the Feast you may bring an Action of Debt for the one or for the other.

9.E.4.36. 13.E 4.4. and the other aboue said Bookes.

Sixtly, The Feoffee by his act and wrong may lose his election, and giue the same to the Feoffor: As if one infeoffe another of two acres, To haue and to hold the one for life, and the other in taile, and he before election maketh a feoffement of both, in this case the Feoffor shall enter into which of them he will, for the act and wrong of the Feoffee.

¶ *Sil recouer en Briefe de Annuitie donques est la terre discharge de distresse.* **Here is to be obserued, That this determination of the** election of the Grantee must be by action or suit in Court of Record; (h) for albeit the Grantee distreyne for the Rent, yet he may bring a writ of Annuitie and discharge the land. And Littleton putteth his case here surely vpon a Recouerie in a Writ of Annuitie. (i) But if the Grantee doth bring a writ of Annuitie, & at the returne thereof appeare and count, this is a determination of his election in Court of Record, albeit he neuer proceedeth any further. (k) As if a wife be endowed ex assensu patris, and the husband dieth, the wife hath election either to haue her Dower at the Common Law, or ex assensu patris, if she bring a writ of Dower at the Common Law, and count, albeit she recouer not, yet shall she neuer after claime her Dower ex assensu patris.

(h) *17.El.Dyer 344.b.*

(i) *F.N.B.152.a. 5.H.7.33.b.*

(k) *12.E.2.Dower 158.*

(l) So if the Grantee bring an Assise for the rent, and make his plaint, hee shall neuer after bring a writ of Annuitie. But the purchasing of a writ of Annuitie, and entrie of it in Court of Record, or of an assise, is no determination of the election, because an estranger may purchase a writ in the name of the Grantee, and enter it of Record, but if the Grantee appeare thereunto, &c. then this doth amount to a determination of his election, as hath beene sayd,

(l) *10.E.4.17.*

Glanuill.lib.12.ca.12. Merlbr.ca.21. W.1.ca.16.17. W.2 ca 39. Fleta,lib.2.ca.40.

¶ *Son replegiare.* Littleton spake immediatly before of Vn briefe Dannuity, but here he saith, Son replegiare, because goods may be repleuied two manner of wayes, viz by Writ, and that is by the Common Law, or by the pleinte, and that is by the statutes for the more speedy hauing againe of their cattell and goods. A Replegiare lyeth, as Littleton here teacheth vs, where goods are distreyned and impounded, the owner of the goods may haue a Writ De Replegiari facias, where by the Sherife is commanded, taking sureties in that behalfe, to redeliuer the goods distreyned to the owner, or vpon complaint made to the Sherife he ought to make a Repleuy in the Countrey. Replegiare is compounded of Re, and plegiare, as much as to say, as to redeliuer vpon pledges or sureties; and in the statute of Merlebridge, Deliberare is vsed for Replegiare. (m) And the Sherife ought to take two kinde of pledges, one by the Common Law, and they be Plegij de prosequendo, and another by the statute, viz. Plegij de retorno habendo. Vide Sect.58. what things may lawfully be distreyned, whereupon a Replegiare may be sued. The formes of the Writ you shall reade in the Register and F.N.B. *

Merlbr.ca.21 21.H.6.Returne de Vic.17 (m) W.2.ca.2. Fleta lib.4.ca.5. 4.H.6.15.

* *Regist.F.N.B.68.*

(n) 3.E.3.74. 6.H.4.2.& 39. 9.H.6.39. 20.H.6.19. (o) 33.E.3.Replen.43. 42.E.3.18. 9.H.6.25. F.N.B.69.F. 6.H.7.9. 19.E.3.Repl.32. (p) 42.E.3.18. 11.H.4.17.23. 47.E.3.12. 48 E.3.20. 7.H.4.17.

(n) It is a generall rule that the Plaintife must haue the property of the goods in him at the time of the taking. (o) But yet if the goods of a villeine be distreyned, the Lord of the villeine shall haue a Repleuy, because the bringing of the Repleuy amounts to a clayme in Law and vests the property in the Plaintife. But in that case if the goods of the villeins be taken by a trespasse the Lord shall haue no Repleuy, because the villeine had but a right.

(p) But there is two kinde of properties, a generall propertie, which euery absolute owner hath, and a speciall propertie as goods pledged or taken to manure his lands or the like, and of both these a Replegiare doth lye.

Marlbr.ca.22.

And albeit it be prouided by the Statute of Marlebridge, cap 22. quod vicecomes post querimoniam inde sibi factam ea sine impedimento vel contradictione eius qui dicta aueria ceperit deliberare possit, &c. (q) Yet where the Defendant claymes property, the Sherife cannot proceed, for it is a rule in Law, that propertie ought to be tryed by Writ. And therefore in that case where the tryall is by pleint, the Plaintife may haue a Writ De proprietate probanda directed to the Sherife to trie the propertie, and if thereupon it be found for the Plaintife, then the Sherife to make deliuerance, (for so be the words of the Writ) and if for the Defendant, he can no further proceed, but that is but an enquest of office, and therefore if thereby it bee found against the Plaintife, yet he may haue a Writ of Repleuy to the Sherife, and if he returne the claime of propertie, &c. yet shall it proceed in the court of Common pleas where the propertie shall be put in issue and finally tried, And the Sherife may take a pleint vpon the said act out of the County, and make repleuyn presently, for it should be inconuenient for the owner to forbeare his cattell till the County day.

(q) 30.E.3.22. 31.E.3. Replen.35 & 4. 7.H.4 26.28. 31.H.6. Prop.Prob.5. 1.E.4.9. 21.E.4 64. 2.Eliz.Dier, 173. 21.E.4.68.

(r) 5.E.3.38. 11.H.4.4. 17.E.2.Propr.Prob.6.

(r) It is to be noted that a man cannot clayme property by his Bailife or seruant, and the reason is for that if the clayme fall out to be false he shall be fined for his contempt, which the Lord cannot be vnlesse he maketh clayme himselfe, for Nemo punitur pro alieno delicto.

34.H.6.47.

In a speciall case a man may haue a Repleuyn of goods not destreyned, as if the Mesne put in his cattell in lieu of the cattell of the tenant parauaile, that he is bound to acquite, he shall haue a repleuyn of those cattell that neuer were distreyned.

31.E.3.Gagedeliuer 5.

If a man by his Deede grant a Rent with clause of distresse, and grant further, that hee shall keepe the goods distreyned against gages and pledges, vntill the Rent bee payd, yet shall the Sherife Repleuy the goods distreyned, for it is against the nature of such a Distresse to be irrepleuisable, and by such an entention the currant of Repleuyns should be ouerthrowne to the hindrance of the Common wealth, and therefore it was disallowed by the whole Court, and awarded that the Defendant should gage deliuerance, or else goe to prison. And Bracton is of the same opinion, for he saith, Eodem modo de via obstructâ, per breue quod iusticiet propter communem vtilitatem, ne transeuntes ire diu impediantur, quia hoc esset commune damnum, & in hoc vicecomes & Iusticiarij faciant sicut super detentionem aueriorum contra vadium plegij, propter communem vtilitatem, ne animalia diu inclusa pereant, which in mine opinion is an excellent point of learning.

Bracton,lib.4.fo.233.a & b.

28.E.3.92. 3.H.4.12. 34.H.6.37. 2.E.4.23.

If the beastes of diuers seuerall men be taken, they cannot ioyne in a Repleg. but euery one must haue a seuerall Repleuyn: And so in a Repleuyn it is a good plea to say that the property is to the Plaintife and to a stranger, and where there be two Plaintifes, that the propertie is to one of them.

Regist.fo.133. Bract.fo.121. & 154. W.1.ca 11. Fleta,lib.2. ca.2.F.N.B.66.b.

There is also a Writ De homine replegiando. But Littleton is ready to giue you further instruction, therefore heare him.

¶ *Et auowa le prise, &c. en court de record.* Here it appeareth that an auowry in Court of Record which is in nature of an action is a determination of his election before any iudgement giuen. And this is a good proofe of that which hath beene formerly said of the Writs of Annuity and Assise.

Electio

Electio semel facta & placitum testatum non patitur regressum. 21.H.6.24. *per Newton.* 27.H.6.4.

Quod semel placuit in electionibus amplius displicere non potest.

If a Rent charge be granted to A. and B. and their heires, A. distreyneth the beasts of the Grantor and he sueth a Replevin, A. avoweth for himselfe and maketh conusance for B. A. dyeth and B. surviveth, B. shall not have a Writ of Annuity, for in that case, the election and avowry for the Rent of A. barreth B. of any election to make it an Annuity, albeit he assented not to the avowry.

But here is another diversity to be observed betweene the case aforesaid of the grant of the Rent where he (as hath beene said) may make it either reall or personall, and when a man may have election to have severall remedies for a thing that is meerely personall or meerely reall from the beginning. As if a man may have an action of account or an action of debt at his pleasure, and he bringeth an action of account and appeare to it, and after is Nonsuite, yet may he have an action of debt afterwards because both actions charge the person. The like Law is of an Assise and of a Writ of entrie in the nature of an Assise and the like. 28.E.3.98.b. 27.E.3.89.b.

Sect. 220.

¶ Item, si home voile q̃ un auter aueroit un rent charge issuant hors de sa terre, mes il ne voile q̃ sa person soit charge en ascun maner p briefe dannuitie, donques il poit auer tiel clause en la fine de son fait. Prouiso semper, quod præsens scriptum, nec aliquid in eo specificatum, non aliqualiter se extendat ad onerandum personam meam, per breue, vel actionem de annuitate, sed tantummodo ad onerandum terras, & tenementa mea de annuali redditu predict', &c. Donques la terre est charge, & le person del grantor discharge.

Also if a man would that another should haue a Rent charge issuing out of his land but would not that his person bee charged in any manner by a Writ of Annuity, Then hee may haue such a clause in the end of his deed. Prouided alwaies that this present writing nor any thing therein specified shal any way extend to charge my person by a Writ or an action of Annuity, but only to charge my lands and tenements with the yearely rent aforesaid, &c. Then the land is charged and the person of the grantor discharged.

¶ By this Section it appeareth, that when in a generall grant, the Law doth give two remedies, that the Grantor may provide that the Grantee shall not use one of them and leave the partie to the other. But where the Grantee hath but one remedy, there that remedy cannot be barred by any proviso, for such a proviso should be repugnant to the Grant. 28.H.8.Dier.9.b.

¶ *De annuali redditu, &c.* Hereby (&c.) and the consequent of this Section be implyed divers excellent points of learning, viz. If a man by his Deede granteth a Rent charge out of the Mannor of Dale (wherein the Grantor hath nothing) with such a proviso that it shall not charge his person albeit the repugnancie doth not appeare in the Deed yet the proviso taketh away the whole effect of the Grant, and therefore is in iudgement of Law repugnant, for upon the matter it is but a grant of an Annuity, provided that it shall not charge his person, for which cause our Author putteth his case of a Rent charge issuing truly out of land. *So it was resolved by the Iustices in H.8. as Iustice Spilman reporteth.* 9.H.6.53.

But if a man by his Deede grant a Rent charge out of land, provided that it shall not charge the land albeit the Grantee hath a double remedy (as hath beene said) yet the Proviso is repugnant, because the land is expresly charged with the Rent, but the Writ of Annuity is but implyed in the Grant, and therefore that may be restrained without any repugnancie, and sufficient remedie left for the Grantee, for which cause our author putteth his case of the restraint of bringing a Writ of Annuity. And yet in some case where there is a Prouiso in the Deed that the grantee shall not in any sort charge the person of the Grantor generally, notwithstanding the person of the Grantor shall be charged: As if a man grant a Rent charge out of certaine lands to another for life with such a Prouiso, the Rent is behinde, the Grantee dyeth, the Executors of the Grantee shall haue an action of debt against the Grantor, and charge his person for the arrerages in the life of the Grantee, because the Executors haue no other remedy against the Grantor for the arrerages, for distreyne they cannot, because the estate in the Rent is determined, and the Prouiso cannot leaue the Executors without remedy, as appeareth by that which hath beene said. And therefore our Author putteth his case of a Rent charge continuing. And here is to be obserued that this word (Prouiso) hath diuers operations, sometime it worketh a qualification or limitation, and so it is taken here and often in our bookes: Somtime a Condition, and sometime a Couenant, whereof you shall reade more hereafter, Sect.320.

6.Eliz. Dier 217.

¶ *En le fine de son fait.* Here Littleton putteth his case of one Deed, but though the grant be generall, and want such a Prouiso, yet may the Grantee by another Deed by way of Defeasance grant that he shall not charge the person of the Grantor, and that if he bring a Writ of Annuity, that the Rent shall cease

32.Ass.p.1. Vide Sect.384.

¶ *Nec aliquid in eo specificatum non aliqualiter se extendat, &c.* Here is to be obserued a double negatiue, Nec, and Non, which in Grammaticall construction amounteth to an affirmatiue, for Negatio destruit negationem & ambo faciunt affirmatiuum, yet the Law that principally respecteth substance, doth iudge the Prouiso to be a negatiue according to the intent of the parties, and not according to Grammaticall construction, to the end the Prouiso may take effect, and the like you shall finde hereafter in Littleton. * Mala Grammatica non vitiat cartam. Here our Author putteth his case of one Grantor, put then the case, that A. and B. being ioyntenants of lands in fee by their Deede grant a Rent charge out of those lands, prouided that the Grantee shall not charge the person of A. In this case if the Grantee bringeth a Writ of Annuity, he must charge the person of B. only.

** Lib.3.44. de condic. Sect.362.*

Sect. 221.

¶ Item, si home fait tiel fait en tiel maner, que si A. de B. ne soit annuelment pay al feast de Noel pur terme de sa vie xx.s. de loyal mony, que adonques bien lirroit a m̄ cestuy A. de B. a distreiner pur ceo en le manor de F. &c. ceo est bone rent charge, pur ceo que le manor est charge oue le rent per voy de distres, & uncore la person de celuy que fait tiel fait, est discharge en tiel case de action dannuitie, pur ceo que il ne granta per son fait ascun

Also if one make a Deed in this manner, that if *A.* of *B.* be not yearely payed at the feast of Christmasse for terme of his life xx.s. of lawfull money, that then it shall be lawfull for the said *A.* of *B.* to distreyne for this in the manner of *F.* &c. this is a good rent charge, because the Mannor is charged with the rent by way of distresse, & yet the person of him which makes such deed is discharged in this case of an action of Annuitie, because hee doth

¶ *Que si A. de B.* Here wanteth words to preceade these, viz. que il grant al *A.* de *B.* &c. que si *A.* de *B.* &c. as it appeareth in the originall & so it appeareth in the close of this Section, viz Mes granta tantsolemēt que il poet distreyner. Also without such a grant the clause should be imperfect.

¶ *Pur ceo que le mannor est charge oue le rent per voy de distresse.* And yet no Rent is expresly granted out of the Mannor. But by the grant that hee shall distreyne for such a yearely summe of money in iudgement of Law the Mannor is charged with the Rent, but the person of the Grantor cannot be charged because he expresly granteth no Rent, for that would charge his person, but that the Grantee should distreyne, &c. which only chargeth the land.

¶ *Que*

Annuitie a le dit A. de B. mes granta tantsolement, que il poit distrainer pur tiel Annuitie, &c.

not grant by his Deed any Annuitie to the said *A.* of *B.* but granteth only that he may distreine for such Annuitie, &c.

¶ *Que il poet distreine pur tiel Annuitie, &c.* **Here by** (&c.) **many points worthy of obseruation are implyed, viz. if a man seised of Lands in fee, bindeth his goods and Lands to the payment of a yearely Rent to** A. de B. **this is a good Rent charge with power to distraine, albeit, there be no expresse words of charge, nor to distraine. Or in these words,** Obligo Manerium meum de C. & omnia bona in dicto Manerio existent' A. de B. in annuo redditu de xx. s. ad distringend' per Baliuum Domini Regis pro redditu prædicto **By this grant a Rent charge issueth out of the Mannor, and where the words bee** ad distringendum per Baliuum Domini Regis, **this is for the aduantage of the Grantee. And therefore the Kings Baily should be but his Minister to distreine for his Rent, and that which he may do by his seruant he may do by himselfe, or by any other of his seruants.**

18. Ass. p. 1. 18. E. 3. 32. 3. Ass. 7. 3. E. 3. 12. 10. Ass. 24. 31. Ass. p. 17. 33. Ass. Annuitie 52. 16. E. 3. grant. 64.

If a man by Deed grant a Rent of fortie shillings to another out of his Mannor of Dale, **to haue and to perceiue to him and his heires, and grant ouer by the same Deed, that if the Rent be behind, that the Grantee shall distreine in the Mannor of** Sale **(be the Mannor of** Sale **in the same Countie or in another Countie, and bee this grant by one Deed or diuers Deedes) the Rent is only issuing out of the Mannor of** D, **and it is but a paine, that hee shall distreine in the Mannor of** S. **but both the Mannors are charged, the one with the Rent, & the other with a distresse for the rent, the one issuing out of the Land and the other to bee taken vpon the Land. And whereas our Author puts his case of a grant for life. So it is if I grant to you, that you and your heires, or the heires of your bodie shall distreine for a Rent of fortie shillings within my Mannor of** S **this by construction in Law shall amount to a grant of a Rent, out of my Mannor of** S. **in Fee Simple or Fee Taile for if this shall not amount to a grant of a Rent, the grant shall bee of little force or effect if the Grantee shall haue but a bare distresse and no Rent in him. For then hee shall neuer haue an Assise of this, &c. And this is the reason, that it is so often ruled and resolued, (*) that this amount to a grant of a Rent** per **construction of Law,** Vt res magis valeat, **and all this is necessarily implyed in the (**&c.**) and in this case the Grantee shall not haue a Writ of Annuitie as our Author sayth. And whereas our Author putteth his case where the distresse is to be taken in the same Land out of which the Rent by construction of Law is issuing, hereby is implyed that if a Rent be granted, out of the Mannor of** D. **and the Grantor grant ouer, that if the Rent bee behind, the Grantee shall distreine for the same rent in the Mannor of** S. **this is but a penaltie in the Mannor of** S. **for three causes:**

Lib. 7. fol. 23. 24. in Butts Case.

(*) 3. E. 3. 12. 3. Ass. p. 7. 14. Ass. p. 14. 16. E. 3. tit. grant 64. 8. E. 3. 32. 26. Ass. 38. 30. Ass. 12. 46. E. 3. 18. 32. 8. H. 4. 19. 9. H. 6. 9. 22. H. 6. 11.

First, The Law needs not to make construction that this shall amount to a grant of a Rent for here a Rent is expresly granted to bee issuing out of the Mannor of D. **and the parties haue expresly limited out of what land the Rent shall issue, and vpon what Land the distresse shall be taken, and the Law will not make an exposition against the expresse words and intention of the parties when this way stands with the rule of the Law.** Quoties in verbis nulla est ambiguitas, ibi nulla expositio contra verba expressa fienda est.

Secondly, If in this case this shall amount to a grant of a Rent out of the Mannor of S. **then the Grantor shall be twice charged. For if the Grantee bringeth a Writ of Annuitie this shall extend only to the Mannor of** D. **For vpon the grant of a distresse in the Mannor of** S. **no Writ of Annuitie lyeth, because the Mannor of** S. **is only charged, and not the person of the Grantor as to this; and for this cause the bringing of the Writ of Annuitie cannot discharge the Mannor of** S. **of any Rent: and so the Law by construction against the words and the intention of the parties shall doe iniurie to the Grantor to charge him twice.**

Thirdly, If in such case the Mannor of S. **in which the distresse is only limited, shall bee in another Countie, then it hath beene often adiudged, that the Rent shall not issue out of the same, but the distresse shall be as a meane, and remedie to compell the Tenant of the Land to pay the Rent. And it was said, that there was no diuersitie in reason, that the Law in construction shall make the Rent to be issuing out of this when it lyeth in the same Countie, and not when it lyeth in seuerall Counties for the words in both cases are all one, and there is no reason to say that he shall fayle of a recouerie by Assise. And the Bookes in** 1. Ass. p. 10 **and** 1. E. 3. 21. **and other Bookes doe not say that the Rent issueth in this case out of both, but that the Land in which the distresse shall be taken is charged, and this is true, for it is charged with the distresse. And inasmuch as it was charged with the distresse, their opinion was that the Tenants of both of them shall be named in the Assise. And the opinion of** Finchden **in** 41. E. 3. 13 **was affirmed to bee good Law, That if the Mannor of** D. **out of which the Rent is granted be recouered by an elder Title, that all the Rent is extinct, but if the Mannor of** S. **in which the distresse is limited, be euicted, yet all the Rent remayns.* So if the grantee purchase parcell of the Mannor of** S. **the Rent is not extinct, for that the Rent issueth only out of the Man-**

Vide Bulwars case. Lib. 7 fol. 3. 1. Ass p. 10. 1. E. 3. 21.

Vide 9. E. 3. 13. 31. Ass. 27. 17. E. 4. 6. 10. Ass. 4. 10 E. 3. 18. 2. E. 2. Ass. 36 Cor. 1. Ass. 10. 3. Ass. 7. 32. H. 6. 27. 22. Ass. 66. 31. Ass. 27. 29. E. 3. Assise 366. 41. E. 3. 13. per Finchden.

**Vide 17. E. 4. 6. semblable case Vide Sect. prox. sequen.*

nor of D. And it is said that if a man grant a Rent out of three Acres, and grant over, that if the Rent be behind, that he shall distreine for the Rent in one of the Acres, this Rent is entire and cannot be a Rent secke out of two Acres, and a Rent charge out of the third Acre, and therefore it is a Rent secke for the whole, and yet he shall distreine for this in the third Acre. So if a Rent be granted to two and to their heires out of an Acre of Land, and that it shall be lawfull for one of them and his heires to distreine for this in the same Acre, this is a Rent secke, for insomuch as they stand joyntly seised of one intire Rent, it cannot be as to the one a Rent secke, and as to the other a Rent charge, and this distresse is as an appurtenant to the Rent: and therefore if he which hath the Rent dieth, the survivor shall distreine, and if both grant over the rent to another, he shall distreine for this. But if a man grant a rent out of Blacke Acre to one and to his heires, and grant to him that he may distreine for this in the same Acre for terme of his life, this is a Rent charge for his life, and a Rent secke after, diversis temporibus. Otherwise it is if the distresse be limited for certaine yeares in the same Land, there this remaynes a Rent secke intirely, for that the fee and the freehold is secke in such case.

If a man seised of Lands in fee, and possessed of a tearme for many yeares grant a Rent out of both for life, in tayle or in fee, with clause of distresse out of both, this Rent being a Freehold doth issue only out of the freehold, and the lands in lease are only charged with a distresse. But if he had granted the Rent only out of the Lands in lease for terme of the life of the Grantee, this had issued out of the tearme, and the Land had beene charged during the tearme if the Grantee lived so long.

22.H.6.20.b. If a man be seised of twentie Acres of Land, and grant a Rent of twentie shillings percipiend' de qualibet acra tre meæ (that is) out of every one Acre of my Land, this is a severall grant out of every severall Acre, and the Grantee shall have twentie pounds in all.

A. doth bargaine and sell land to B. by Indenture, and before inrollment they both grant a Rent charge by Deed to C. and after the Indenture is inrolled some have said, that this Rent charge is avoyded, for say they it was the grant of A. and by the inrollment it hath relation to the delivery, which (say they) shall avoyde the grant, notwithstanding the confirmation of the other which had nothing in the Land at that time. But the grant is good, and after the inrollment by the operation of the Statute, it shall be the grant of B. and the confirmation of A. But if the Deed had not beene inrolled, it had beene the grant of A. and the confirmation of B. and so quacunque via data the grant is good.

Sect. 222.

¶ Item, si home ad un rẽt charge a luy & a ses heires issuant hors de certein terr̃, sil purchase ascun parcel de cel a luy, & a ses heires, tout le rent charge est extinct, & lannuitie auxy, pur ceo que rent charge ne poit per tiel maner estre apportion. Mes si home que aver rent service, purchase parcel de la terre dont le rent est issuant, ceo nextiendra tout mes pur le parcel, car rent service en tiel cas poit

Also if a man hath a Rent charge to him and to his heires issuing out of certaine land, if hee purchase any parcell of this to him and to his heires, all the Rent charge is extinct, and the Annuitie also, because the Rent charge cannot by such manner bee apportioned. But if a man which hath a Rent Service purchase parcell of the land out of which the Rent is issuing, this shal not extinguish all, but for the parcell. For

¶ Extinct. Commeth of the Verbe Extinguere, to destroy or put out, and a Rent is said to bee extinguished when it is destroyed and put out.

¶ Apportion. This commeth of the word Portio quasi partio, which signifieth a part of the whole, and Apportion signifieth a Division or Partition of a Rent, common, &c. or a making of it into parts.

(a) Doct. & Stud. lib. 2. cap. 16. 21. H. 7. 2. 21. E. 3. 58.

(a) The reason of this extinguishment is because the Rent is intire, and against common right, and issuing out of every part of the Land, and therefore by purchase of part it is extinct in the whole and cannot bee (b) apportioned, but by act in Law it may, as hereafter shall be said. (c) If the Grantee of a Rent charge purchase parcell of the Land, and the Grantor by his Deed

(b) 30. Ass. 12. 9. Ass. 22.

(c) 46. E. 3. 32. 14. Ass. Ass. 14. 26. Ass. 38.

poit estre apportion solonque le value de la terre. Mes si un tient sa terre de son Seignior per le service de render a son Seignior annuelment a tiel feast un chival, ou un esperon dor ou un Cloue, Gylofer & huiusmodi, si en tiel cas le Seignior purchase parcel de la terre, tiel service est ale, pur ceo que tiel service ne poit estre sever, ne apportion.

a Rent Seruice in such case may be apportioned according to the value of the Land. But if one holdeth his land of his Lord by the seruice to render to his Lord yearely at such a Feast a Horse, a golden Speare, or a Cloue, Gilliflower, and such like, if in this case the Lord purchase parcell of the Land, such Seruice is taken away, because such seruice cannot be seuered nor apportioned.

reciting the said purchase of part granteth that hee may distreyne for the same Rent in the residue of the land, this amounteth to a new grant, and the same Rent shall bee taken for the like Rent or the same in quantity. And so it is (d) if a man by Deede granteth a Rent charge out of his land to a man for life, and granteth further by the same Deede that hee and his heires may distreyne in the land for the same Rent, this amounteth to a new grant of a Rent in fee simple. (d) 8.H.4.19.

But yet a Rent charge by the act of the partie may in some case be apportioned. As if a man hath a Rent charge of xx. shillings, he may release to the Tenant of the land x. shillings or more or lesse, and reserue part, for the Grantee dealeth only with that which is his owne, viz the Rent, and dealeth not with the Land as in case of purchase of part. And so was it holden in the Common place, Hill.14 Eliz. which I my selfe heard and obserued. So (e) if the Grantee of an Annuity or Rent charge of xx pound grant, x. pound parcell of the same Annuity or Rent charge, and the Tenant attorne, hereby the Annuity or Rent charge is deuided. Hill.14.Eliz. (e) 9.H.6.12.53. F.N.B.152.D.E.

And (f) when the Rent charge is extinguished by his purchase of part of the land, hee shall neuer haue a Writ of Annuity, because it was by the grant a Rent charge, and he hath discharged the land of the Rent charge by his owne act by purchase of part. And therefore he cannot by Writ of Annuity discharge the land of the distresse as Littleton hath before said. But if the Rent charge be determined by the act of God or of the Law, yet the Grantee may haue a Writ of Annuity. As if Tenant for another mans life by his Deed grant a Rent charge to one for 21. yeares, Cesty que vie dieth, the Rent charge is determined, and yet the Grantee may haue during the yeares a Writ of Annuity for the arrerages incurred after the death of Cesty que vie, because the Rent charge did determine by the act of God and by the course of Law, Actus legis nulli facit iniuriam. The like Law is if the land out of which the Rent charge is granted be recouered by an elder title, and thereby the Rent charge is voyded, yet the Grantee shall haue a Writ of Annuity, for that the Rent charge is auoyded by the course of Law, and so it was holden in Wards Case aboue remembred against an opinion Obiter in 9.H.6 42.a. (f) 14.E.4.4. 22.E.4. Le darrein case.51. 7.H.6. 9.H.6.1. 5.H.7.33 Wards case cited in lib.2. In Heywards case, fo.36. 9.H.6.42.a.

¶ *Car rent seruice in tiel case poet estre apportion.* **Whether this apportion was at the Common Law or by the force of the Statute of** Quia emptores terrarum, hath beene a question in our bookes. * And it appeareth by Littleton that it was so at the Common Law, for when he citeth any thing prouided by any statute, he citeth the statute, as he hath done this very act before. 2. Littleton speaketh here indefinitely of Rent seruice, and there be diuers kindes of Rent seruices which are not within that statute, and yet such Rent seruices are apportionable by the Common Law, as if a man maketh a Lease for life or yeares reseruing a Rent, and the Lessee surrender part to the Lessor the Rent shall be apportioned. So if the Lessor recouereth part of the land in an action of waste, or entreth for a forfeiture in part the Rent shall be apportioned. * Brooke tit. apportionment 28. 18.E.3.49. 22.Ass.52. 3.Ass.18. 18 E.2. Ann.wiste,218. Vid. lib.6.fo.1.2. in Bruertons case. Vid. lib.8.fo.105.106. in Talbots case.

(g) So likewise if the Lessor granteth part of the reuersion to a stranger the Rent shall be apportioned for the Rent is incident to the reuersion. (h) So it is if Tenant by Knights seruice by his last will and testament in writing deuiseth the reuersion of two parts of the lands the Deuisee shall haue two parts of the Rent. (g) 14.H.8.12. Vid lib.8.fo.79. in Wildes case. Pasch.39.Eliz. Rot.233. So it was adiudged inter Collins & Harding.

And these cases are in mine opinion rightly adiudged against a sudden opinion in Hill.6 & 7.E.6 reported by Serieant Bendlowe to the contrary. Note what inconuenience should follow if by the seuerance of the reuersion the Rent should be extinct. (h) Trin.43.Eliz. Rot.243. inter West & Lassels & Hill. 42.Eliz. Rot.108. in Communi banco inter Ewer & Moyle.

¶ *Purchase parcell de la terre.* **This is intended of a fee simple,** for

(i) 32.H.8.tit. Extinguishment Br.48. 11.Ed.3.Cessavit 21. 17.E.3.57.a.

for if there be a Lord and Tenant of 40 acres of Land by fealty and xx. shillings Rent,(i) if the Tenant maketh a gift in taile, or a Lease for life or yeares, of parcell thereof to the Lord, in this case the rent shall not be apportioned for any part, but the rent shall be suspended for the whole: for a Rent service (saith Littleton) may be extinct for part, and apportioned for the rest, but a Rent service cannot be suspended in part by the act of the partie, and in Esse for other part. So it is if the Lessor enter upon the Lessee for life or yeares into part, and thereof disseise or put out the Lessee, the rent is suspended in the whole, and shall not be apportioned for any part. And where our bookes* speake of an apportionment in case where the Lessor enters upon the Lessee in part, they are to be understood where the lessor enters lawfully, as upon a surrender, forfeiture, or such like, where the rent is lawfully extinct in part. And yet by Act in Law a Rent service may be suspended in part, and in esse for part. * As when the Gardeine in Chivalrie entreth into the land of his Ward within age, now is the Seigniorie suspended: but if the wife of the Tenant be endowed of a third part of the Tenancie, now shall she pay to the Lord the third part of the rent. *. And so it is if the Tenant give a part of the Tenancie to the father of the Lord in Taile, the father dieth, and this descends to the Lord, in this case by Act in Law the Seigniorie is suspended in part and in esse for part, and the same Law is of a Rent charge.

** 21.E.4.29. 9.E.4.1. 7.H.6.26. 4.H.7.6.b. 11.E.3.Cessavit 21.*

** 33.E.3.Dever 138.*

** 30.Ass.p.12.*

** 27.E.3.88.*

Likewise a Segniorie may be suspended in part by the act a stranger: * As if two Joyntenants or Coparceners be of a Seigniorie, and one of them disseise the Tenant of the land, the other Joyntenant or Coparcener shall distreine for his or her moitie.

Concerning the apportionment of Rents, there is a difference betweene a grant of a Rent, and a reservation of a Rent: for (k) if a man be seised of two acres of land, of one in Fee simple, and of another in Taile, and by his Deed grant a rent out of both in fee, in taile, for life, &c. and dieth, the land intailed is discharged, and the land in fee simple remaines charged with the whole rent, for against his owne grant he shall not take advantage of the weakenesse of his owne estate in part. (l) But if he make a gift in taile, a lease for life or for yeares of both acres, reserving a rent, the Donor or Lessor dieth, the Issue in taile avoydeth the gift or lease, the rent shall be apportioned, for seing the rent is reserved out of and for the whole land, it is reason that when part is evicted by an elder title, that the Donee or Lessee should not be charged with the whole rent, but that it should be apportioned ratably, according to the value of the land, as Littleton here saith.

(k) 12.H.4 17. 17.Ed.2. Dever 164. 30.Ass.p.12.

(l) 20.H.6.3. 9.E.4.1.4. 35.H.8.Dyer 56. 7.E.6. Dyer 82. 9.E.3. 6.H.4.17.

(m) Doct.& Stud.li.2.c.17

(m) If a man grant a Rent charge out of two acres, and after the Grantee recovereth one of the acres against the Grantor by a title paramount, the whole rent shall issue out of the other acre: but if the recoverie be by a faint title by Covine, then the rent is extinct for the whole, because he claimeth under the Grantee.

If a man infeoffeth B. of one acre in fee upon condition, and B. being seised of another acre in fee, granteth a rent out of both acres to the feoffor, who entreth into the one acre for the condition broken, the whole rent shall issue out of the other acre, because his title is paramount the grant. But if a man maketh a lease for life of Blacke acre and White acre, reserving two shillings rent, upon condition that if the Lessee doth such an act, &c that then he shall have Fee in Black acre, the Lessee performes the condition, albeit now by relation he hath the fee simple ab initio, yet shall the rent be apportioned, for that the reversion of one acre whereunto the rent was incident, is gone from the Lessor, and so note a diversitie betweene a rent in grosse, and a rent incident to a reversion, concerning the apportionment ther of. And yet in some cases a rent charge shall not be wholly extinct, where the Grantee claimeth from and under the Grantor. As if B. maketh a lease of one acre for life to A and A is seised of another acre in fee, A. granteth a rent charge to B. out of both acres, and doth wast in the acre which he holdeth for life, B recovereth in wast, the whole rent is not extinct, but shall bee apportioned, and yet B. claimeth the one acre under A. And so it is if A. had made a feoffement in fee, and B. had entred for the forfeiture, the rent is wholly apportioned, and is not wholly extinct: and the reason hereof is, for that it is a maxime in Law, That no man shall take advantage of his owne wrong, Nullus commodum capere potest de iniuria sua propria: And therefore seeing the wast and forfeiture were committed by the act and wrong of the Lessee, hee shall not take advantage thereof to extinguish the whole rent: and the whole rent cannot issue onely out of the other acre, because the Lessor hath the one acre under the estate of the Lessee, and therefore it shall be apportioned. * If the King give two acres of land of equall value to another in fee, fee taile, for life or yeares, reserving a rent of two shillings, and the one acre is evicted by a title paramount, the Rent shall be apportioned.

** Dyer Mich. 7.& 8.Eliz. Manuscript. The Earle of Huntingdons case. Vid.F.N.B.234.b. Briefe de Onerando, pro rata porc.*

¶ *Mes si un home tient sa terre, &c. per service de render annuelment, &c. un Chival ou un Esperon dor, &c. si en tiel case le Seignior purchase parcel del terre, tiel service est ale.*

¶ *Chival.*

¶ *Chiual.* Nota, In Latyne Destrarius is a great horse, or horse of seruice, of the French word Destrier. Palfridus, a horse to trauell on, of the French word Palfray: And Runcinus, a Nagge, (you shall often read of them in Records) it commeth of the Italian word Roncino. But admit that parcell of the land holden by such entire seruice come to the Lord by discent, whether shall the entire seruice wholly remaine, or bee extinct? and it is holden that in some case it shall be extinct for the whole, as Suit seruice, and such other entire annuall Suit seruices: But if the seruice be, to render yearely at such a feast a horse, or the like, and the Tenant infeoffe the father of the Lord of part, which discends, yet the Feoffor shall hold by a horse, because the seruice was multiplied, and each of them, viz. the Feoffor and the Feoffee held by a horse.

Anno 6.R.1.Rot.5. Watt, Bruertons case lib.6.fo.2. 34.Ass.15. 35.H.6.Exec 21 Tlo.Com.72.40.E.3..40. 5.E 2.Tit. Auowrie 206.

A. hath common of pasture sauns nombre, in twentie acres of land, and ten of those acres descendto A. the Common sauns nombre is entire and incertaine, and cannot be apportioned, but shall remaine But if it had beene a Common certaine, (as for ten Beasts) in that case the Common should be apportioned. And so it is of Common of Estouers, of Turbarie, of Pischarie, &c. and yet in none of these cases, the discent, which is an act in Law, shall worke any wrong to the Terre tenant, for he shall haue that which belongeth to him, for the act in law shall worke no wrong.

If three Joyntenants hold by an entire yearely rent, as a horse, or of a graine of wheat, and the Tenant cesse by two yeares, and the Lord recouer two parts of the land against two of them, and the third saues his part by tendring of the rent, &c. and finding suretie, albeit the lord come to the two parts by lawfull recouerie, grounded vpon the default and wrong of the two Joyntenants, yet shall the entire annuall rent be extinct.

F. N. B. 209. 40.E.3.40

If the Tenant holdeth by Fealtie and a bushell of wheat, or a pound of Comyn, or of Peper, or such like, and the Lord purchaseth part of the land, there shall be an apportionment, as well as if the rent were in money: and yet if the rent were by one graine of wheat, or one seed of Comyn, or one Pepper corne, by the purchase of part, the whole should be extinct. But if an entire seruice be pro bono publico, as Knights seruice, Castle gard, Cornage, &c. for the defence of the Realme, or to repaire a bridge or a way, to keepe a Beacon, or to keepe the Kings Records, or for aduancement of iustice and peace, as to aid the Sheriff, or to be Constable of England, though the Lord purchase part, the seruice remaines. So it is if the tenure be Pro opere deuotionis siue pietatis, as to find a Preacher, or to prouide the ornaments of such a Church: or pro opere charitatis, as to marrie a poore Virgin, or to bind a poore Boy Apprentice, or to feed a poore man. And so note a diuersitie betweene these cases, and entire seruices for the priuate benefit of the Lord.

Vid. Litt. Cap. Tenant in Common 71.b. Lib.6.fo.1.2.i. Bruertons case Lit.f.49. 11.H.7.12.b. 24.H 8. Tenures 53. Brooke 35.H.6.6. 11.El.Dy.28 9. 16.E.3.Auowrie 93.

Section 223.

Mes si vn hõe tient sa terre dun auter, per Homage, Fealtie, & Escuage, & per certaine rent, si le Sñr purchase parcel de la tr, &c. en tiel cas l' rent sera apportion, come est auantdit, mes vncore en cest case l' homage & fealtie dmurront entier a le Sñr, car le Seignior auera le homage & fealtie de son tenant pur le remnant de les

BVt if a man hold his land of another by Homage, fealty, and Escuage, and certaine Rent, if the Lord purchase part of the land, &c. in this case the rent shall be apportioned, (as is aforesayd) but yet in this case the Homage and Fealtie abide entire to the Lord: For the Lord shall haue the Homage and Fealtie of his Tenant for the rest of the Lands and Tenements

¶ P*Vrchase parcel del ter', &c.* Here by this &c. is implied, that the reasons wherfore homage & fealtie remain & are not extinct in this case, are, First, because it can be no losse to the Tenant, as it might in the case of an horse or other entire seruice, for there it may be the remnant is not sufficient in value to pay it. Secondly, there is no land but it must be holden by some seruice or other, and Homage and Fealtie are the freest and least chargeable seruices to the Tenant.

Bruertons case, vbi supra.

5.E.2.Auowrie 206.

¶ *Pur ceo que tiel seruices ne sont passe annual seruices &c.* This is Ratio vna, but not vnica, as it appeareth by that which

terres et tenem̃ts tenus de luy, come il auoit adeuant, pur ceo que tiels seruices ne sont passe annuals seruices, et ne poyent estre apportion, mes lescuage poit, & serra apportion solonque lafferance et rate de la terre, &c.

holden of him, as hee had before, because that such seruices are no yearely seruices, and cannot bee apportioned, but the Escuage may and shall bee apportioned according to the quantitie and rate of the land, &c.

Bruertons Case lib. 6. Talbots Case lib. 8. fo. 104. 8. H. 7. 11.

hath beene sayd. If there be Lord and Tenant by Fealtie and Herriot seruice, and the Lord purchase part of the land, the Herriot seruice is extinct, (and yet it is not annuall, but to be paid at the death of the Tenant) because it is entire and valuable.

¶ *Solonque lafferance & rate de la terre, &c.* Here is by this (&c.) implied, That in some case where it is entire and valuable, and not annuall, it shall not (as hath beene sayd) be extinguished by purchase of part, *as Knights seruice which is to be performed by the bodie of a man, if the Lord purchase part, yet the tenure by Knights seruice remaines for the residue, Quia pro bono publico, & pro defensione regni, but the Escuage shall be apportioned, as here Littleton saith, because that is for the benefit of the Lord, and yet it is casuall, and not annuall. And where our Author speaketh of Seruices, it is implied, that a Herriot custome, though it be entire, valuable, and not annuall, by the purchase of part shall not be extinct. On the other part, when the tenure is by an entire seruice, and the tenant alien part of the tenancie, in what cases the rent shall be multiplied (that is) where the Feoffor and the Alienee shall pay the entire rent seuerally, (for regularly it holdeth, that quæ in partes diuidi nequeunt, solida à singulis præstantur) and where not, you may read at large in my Reports.*

(*) 7. E. 3. 29. Talbots Case lib. 8. fo. 104.

(*) Bruertons Case lib. 6. fo. 1. 2. Talbots Case lib. 8. fo. 104

And by this (&c.) is also implied, that the apportionment shall not be according to the quantitie of the land, but according to the qualitie or value thereof, as by that which hath been sayd appeareth.

Section 224

Item, si home ad vn rẽt charg̃, & son pier purchase parcel de les Tenements charges en fee, & morust, & cel parcel descend a son fits, q̃ ad l' rẽt charg̃, ore cel charge sẽt apportion solonque le value de la tt̃ come ẽ auantdit d̃ Rent seruice, pur ceo que tiel portion de la terre purchase per la piere, ne vient al fits per sõ fait demesne, mes per discent & ꝑ course del Ley.

Also, if a man hath a Rent charge, and his father purchase parcell of the Tenements charged in fee, and dieth, and this parcel descends to his sonne, who hath the Rent charge, now this charge shall bee apportioned according to the value of the land, as is aforesaid of Rent seruice, because such portion of the land purchased by the Father, commeth not to the sonne by his owne fact, but by discent and by course of law.

5. E. 2. Auowrie 200. 21. E. 3. 38 b 34. Ass. 15. Tit. Apportionment. 8. 28. 9. Ass. 22.

¶ Note heere a diuersitie, when the grantee of a Rent charge commeth to a part of the land charged by his owne act, and when by the course of Law.

30. Ass. Pl. 19.

¶ *Purchase parcel de les Tenements charges en fee.* And so it is if the Tenant giueth to the father of the Grantee part of the land in Taile, and this descend to the Grantee, the rent shall bee apportioned, and so by act in Law a Rent charge may bee suspended for one part, and in esse for another.

34. Hen. 6. 41. b.

And so it is, if the father be Grantee of a rent, and the son purchase part of the land charged, and the father dieth, after whose death the rent descends to the son, the rent shal be appotioned, and so it is if the Grantee grant the rent to the tenant of the land, and to a stranger, the rent is extinct but for a moitie.

If

If a man hath issue two Daughters and grant a Rent charge out of his land to one of them and dyeth the Rent shall be apportioned, and if the Grantee in this case enfeoffeth another of her part of the land, yet the moity of the Rent remaineth issuing out of her sisters part, because the part of the Grantee in the land by the discent was discharged of the Rent. But in all these cases where the Rent charge is apportioned by act in Law, yet the writ of Annuity fayleth, for if the Grantee should bring a writ of Annuity he must ground it upon the grant by Deede, and then must he as it hath beene said bring it for the whole. *9. Ass. 22.* *5.R.2. Annuity 21.*

Annua nec debitum Iudex non seperat ipsum.

Also in respect of the realty the Rent is apportioned, but the personalty is indivisible, and by act in Law shall not be devided. If Execution be sued of body and lands upon a statute Merchant or staple, and after the inheritance of part of those lands discend to the Conusee all the Execution is avoyded, for the dutie is personall and cannot be devided by act in Law. *Pl. Com. 72.* *35.H.6. tit. Execut. 21.* *15.E.4.5.*

¶ *Ne vient al fitz per son fait demesne mes per discent & per course del ley.* If the father within age purchase part of the land charged, and alieneth within age and dyeth, the sonne recovereth in a writ of Dum fuit infra aetatem, or entreth: In this case the act of Law is mixt with the act of the partie, and yet the Rent shall be apportioned, for after the recovery or entry the sonne hath the land by discent.

So it is in case the sonne recovereth part of the land upon an alienation by his father, Dum non fuit compos mentis, the Rent shal be apportioned for the cause aforesaid.

A man seised of lands in a fee taketh wife, and maketh a Feoffment in fee, the Feoffee grants a Rent-charge of x pound out of the land to the Feoffor and his wife, and to the heires of the husband, the husband dieth, the wife recovereth the moity for her Dower by the custome, the Rent charge shalbe apportioned, and she may distreyne for five pound which is the moity of the Rent. In which case two notable things are to be observed. First, albeit the Dower bee by relation or fiction of Law above the Rent, yet when the wife recovereth her Dower, she shall not have her entire Rent out of the residue, for a relation or fiction of Law shall never worke a wrong or charge to a third person, but In fictione iuris semper est Equitas. Secondly, that albeit her owne act doe concurre with the act in Law, yet the Rent shalbe apportioned. *5.E.2. Annuity, 206.* *Lib. 3 fo. 29. in Butler et Bakers case.*

Section 225.

¶ ITem, si soit Sñr & tenant, & le tenãt tient de s̃ Seignior per fealtie & certaine rent, & le Sñr grant le rent p s̃ fait a un auter, &c. reseruant a luy le fealty, & le tenant atturna al grantee de l' rent, ore tiel rent est rent seck a le grantee, pur ceo que les tenements ne sont tenus del grantee de le rent, mes sont tenus del Seignior q̃ reserue a luy fealtie.

ALso if there bee Lord and tenant, and the tenant holds of his Lord by fealtie and certaine rent, and the Lord grants the rent by his deed to another reseruing the fealty to himselfe, and the tenant attures to the grantee of the rent, now this rent is rent secke to the grantee, because the tenements are not holden of the grantor of the rent, but are holden of the Lord who reserued to him the fealtie.

¶ *ET le Seignior grãta le rent, &c.* So it is if the Lord release the Rent to the Tenant saving the fealty, the Rent is extinct. But if there be Lord and Tenant by Fealty and Rent, and the Lord by his Deed reciting the tenure release all his right in the land saving his said Rent, the Seigniories remaines and hee shall have the Rent as a rent service, and the fealtie incident to it, for the said Rent is as much to say as the Rent service whereunto fealty is incident. *12.E.4.11. 9.E.3.1. 40.E.3.22.b. 13.E.3. tit. Releases 36.*

And so it is if the Lord hath issue two daughters and dieth, and upon partition the fealty is allotted to the one and the Rent to the other, she shall have the Rent as a Rent secke. *17.E.3.72.b.*

If there bee Lord of a Mannor and Tenant by fealtie, Suit of Court and Rent, the Lord grant the fealty saving to him the suite of Court and Rent, the saving is good for the Rent but not for the suite to Court, because the Gran- *17.E.3.72.b.*

tee can keepe no Court, and there is no tenure of the Grantor, and therefore the suite of Court is lost and perished in that case.

If the Donee hold of the Donor by fealty and certaine Rent, and the Donor grant the services to another, and the Tenant atturne, some haue said the rent shall not passe because the rent cannot passe but as a Rent seruice being granted by the name of seruices, and the fealty cannot passe because as hath beene said the fealty is incident inseparable to the reuersion. But it seemeth that the rent shall passe as a Rent secke because at the time of the grant it was a Rent seruice in the Grantor, and therefore there be words sufficient to passe it to the Grantee, and it is not of necessity that it shalbe a Rent seruice in the hands of the Grantee.

If there be Lord and Tenant by fealty and certaine rent, and the Lord by Deed grant the rent in fee sauing the fealty, and grant further by the same Deede that the Grantee may distreine for the same rent in the tenancie, albeit a Distresse were incident to the rent in the hands of the Grantee, and although the Tenant attorne to the grant, yet cannot the Grantee distreyne, for the Distresse remaines as an incident inseparable to the Seigniory, for then the Tenant should be subiect to two seuerall distresses of two seuerall men. And so it is if the Lord in that case grant the Rent in tayle or for life, sauing the fealty, and further grant that the Grantee may distreine for it, albeit the reuersion of the rent be a Rent seruice, yet the Donee or Grantee shall haue it but as a Rent secke, and shall not distreyne for it.

7.E.3.2.b. Fitz Warens case. 7.E.3.2.3. Adiudged.

It is to be obserued that where a Rent seruice is become a Rent secke by seuerance of the same from the Seigniory, that now the nature of the rent is changed, for if the Grantee purchase part of the land the whole rent shall be extinct. And whereas in an Assise for a Rent seruice all the Tenants of the land need not to be named, but such as did the disseisin: Yet in Assise for the Rent secke which sometimes was a Rent seruice, all the Tenants must bee named, as in case of a Rent charge, albeit he were disseised but by one sole Tenant, * but if the Lord of a Mannor release the fealty to his Tenant sauing the rent, or that a Mesnalty become a rent by surplusage, those that are now Secke (and sometime were seruice) are part of the Mannor, but a Rent charge cannot be part of a Mannor.

31. Ass. 31. 17. Ass. 10. 12 Ass. pl. 10. F.N.B. 178. D. 32.H.6.3.b. 4.E.2. Ass 440 38.H.8. Dier 31.

(*) 31. Ass. 23. 22. Ass. 53.

Attorne, &c. Of Attornement shall be hereafter said in his proper chapter and place.

Sect. 226.

IN mesme le manner est lou home tient sa terre per homage, fealtie, & certaine rent, si le Snr grant la rent, sauant a luy le homage, tiel rent apres tiel grant est rent secke. Mes la ou terres sont tenus per homage, fealty, & certein rent, si le Snr voit granter per son fait le homage de son tenant a vn auter, sauant a luy le remnant de les seruices, & le tenant atturna a luy, solonque le forme del graunt, en cest case le tenant tiendra

IN the same manner, where a man holds his land by homage, fealty and certaine rent, if the Lord grant the rent, sauing to him the homage, such rent after such grant is rent secke. But there where lands are holden by homage, fealty, and certaine rent, if the Lord will grant by his deed the homage of his tenant to another, sauing to him the remnant of his seruices and the tenant atturne to him according to the forme of the grant, in this case

Si le Seignior voet granter per son fait le homage, &c. It is to be obserued that where the Seigniory is by homage, fealty and rent, (a) if the Lord grant away the Homage, the Fealty shall passe, for fealty is an incident inseparable to Homage (b) & cannot by any sauing in any grant be seperated from it, for homage cannot be sole or alone, but the rent (though it be not saued) shall not passe in that case because the rent is not incident to homage. And so it is if there be Lord and Tenant by fealty and rent, & the Lord grant ouer the fealty without any sauings, the rent passeth not, but fealty hath an incident inseperable belonging to it, which by no sauing can bee separated, and that is a Distresse, for as Littleton saith here, a seruice cannot be secke (that is) without some

(a) 40.E.3.22 per Curiam.

(b) 44.E.3.19.20. 39.H.6.25. 29. Ass. pl. 20. 26. Ass. p. 38.

tiendra sa terre del grantee, & le Seignior que grantast le homage, nauera forsque le rent come rent seck, & ne unques distreynera pur le rent, pur ceo que homage, ne fealtie, ne escuage, ne poit estre dit seck, car nul tiel seruice poit estre dit seck. Car celuy que ad ou doit auer homage, ou fealtie, ou escuage de sa terre poit per common droit distreiner pur ceo sil soit adererere, car homage, fealtie, & escuage sont seruices, per queux terres ou tenements sont tenus, &c. & sont tiels que en nul maner poient estre prises forsque come seruices, &c.

the tenant shall hold his land of the grantee, and the Lord who granted the Homage shal haue but the rent as a Rent seck, & shall neuer distrain for the rent, because that homage nor fealty nor escuage cannot bee said secke for no such seruice may be said secke. For he which hath or ought to haue homage, fealty, or escuage of his land may by common right distreine for it, if it bee behind. For Homage, Fealtie, and Escuage are Seruices by which Lands or Tenements are holden, &c. and are such seruices as in no manner can bee taken but as Seruices, &c.

distresse belonging to it, for then it were not a seruice and so of Homage and Escuage.

¶ *Terres en tenements sont tenus, &c.* By this (&c.) and out of this Section it may bee collected that if (c) there bee Lord and Tenant by Fealtie and Rent, the Annuall Rent which is a profitable Seruice is of higher and more respect in law then the Fealtie, and therefore by the grant of the Rent the Fealtie shall passe as an incident thereunto, but it is an incident separable, and therefore may bee by a sauing, as Littleton hath said, be separated from it. And so when the tenure is by Fealtie and Rent, and the Rent be recouered, the Fealtie shal includedly bee recouered. (d) And where the tenure is by Homage, Fealtie and Rent, by the recouerie of the Rent with the appurtenances vpon a former right, the Homage and Fealtie also shall bee restored by necessitie and indulgence of the Law, for seeing the law giueth no Præcipe for the Homage and Fealtie, but for the Rent only, reason would that by the recouerie of the Rent, the whole entire Seigniorie shall be inclusiuely restored in that case. But if the recouerie be without title there the Rent is recouered as a Rent secke, for that worketh no more then a grant, (*) but by the recouerie of a Mannor whether it be by title or without Title, Homage, Fealtie and all other Seruices parcell of the Mannor are recouered. And albeit Fealtie cannot bee deuided from Homage by grant (as hath beene said) yet by extinguishment it may: (e) As if there be Lord and Tenant by Homage, Fealtie, and Rent, and the Lord release the Seigniorie and Seruices, or all his right in the Land sauing the Fealtie and Rent, or sauing the said Rent, or if hee by expresse words release the Homage sauing the Fealtie and Rent, there the Fealtie and Rent remayne, for the Homage is extinct. And so note a diuersitie betweene a Grant and a Release in that Case. But so long as Homage continues the Fealtie cannot be deuided from it.

(c) 44.E.3.19. 26.Ass.38. 29.Ass.p.20. 9.E.3.2. 39.H.6.24.25. 27.H.8.20. 8.E.4.28.

(d) Temps H.8. Br. tit. incidents.24. 44.E.3.19. 29.Ass.20. 39.H.6.24.25.

(*) Vide Sect.149.

(e) 9.E.3.1.

¶ *Forsque come seruices, &c.* Here is implied a diuersitie betweene these corporall seruices of Homage, Fealtie and Escuage, which cannot become secke or dry, but make a tenure whereunto Distresses, Escheats, and other profits be incident, And other corporall seruices, as to plough, repaire, attend and the like, and all Rents whatsoeuer, for they may become secke or dry and make no tenure.

Sect. 227.

¶ Mes autrement est de rent que fuit un foits rent seruice, pur ceo que quant

BUt otherwise it is of a Rent which was once Rent Seruice, because when it is seuered

¶ Et le Seignior ne poet grant tiel rent oue distres, come est dit. (f) For the

(f) 7.E.3.2.3.

the distresse is an incident inseparable to the fealtie as hath beene said
(g) 7.E.4.11. (g) and therefore a release of distresse is void.
8.H.7.4.5.

¶ *Incident.* Incidens a thing appertayning to or following another as a more worthie or principall, whereof you see here, and in divers other places of Littletons examples. And of incidents some be separable, and some inseparable, as hath beene said.

il est seuer per le grant le Seignior de les auters seruices, il ne poit estre dit rent Seruice, pur ceo que il ne ad a ceo fealtie, que est incident a chescun manner de rent seruice, & pur ceo est dit rent secke, & le seignior ne poit grant tiel rent oue distresse, come est dit.

by the grant of the Lord from the other seruices, it cannot bee said Rent Seruice, for that it hath not fealtie vnto it, which is incident to euery manner of Rent Seruice, and therefore it is called Rent seck. And the Lord cannot grant such a Rent with a distresse, as it is said.

Sect. 228.

¶ *Sauant a luy le reuersion, &c.* By this word (&c.) is to be obserued
(h) 41.E.3.16. (h) that this Rent reserued is a Rent Seruice, and hath fealtie incident to it, and both Rent and fealtie are incident to the reuersion, viz.
(i) 12.E.4.3. 32.H.8.tit. Patents Br. 26. Ass. 66. 48.E.3.9.b. Doct. & Stud. lib. 2. cap. 9. (i) the Rent incident to the Reuersion separably, but the fealtie incident to the Reuersion inseparably, but by the grant of the Rent, the fealtie in this case shall not passe because the fealtie is inseparably incident to the Reuersion, but the Grantee shall haue the rent as a rent secke. Also by this (&c) is implyed an attornement of the tenant, for without that, although by the grant the Rent is turned to a Rent secke, so as the tenant cannot bee charged with any distresse, yet to the passing thereof, there must bee an attornment.

¶ Item si hōe lessa a vn auter terres pur terme de vie, reseruant a luy certain rent, s'il grant le rent a vn auter p son fait, sauant a luy le reuersion de la terre issint lesse, &c. tiel rent nest forsque rent seck, pur ceo que l' grantee nad riens en le reuersion del terre, &c. Mes s'il grant le reuersion del terre a vn auter pur terme de vie, & le tenant atturne, &c. donques ad le grantee le rent come rent seruice, pur ceo q̄ il ad le reuersion pur terme de vie.

ALso if a man let to another lands for tearme of life reseruing to him certaine rent, if hee grant the rent to another by his Deed sauing to him the Reuersion of the land so letten, &c. such Rent is but a Rent seck because that the grantee had nothing in the Reuersion of the land, &c. but if he grant the Reuersion of the land to another for tearme of life, and the tenant attorne, &c. then hath the grantee the Rent as a Rent seruice, for that he hath the reuersion for tearme of life.

¶ *Attorne, &c.* Here is implyed by this (&c.) an attornment in the life of the Grantee, and other incidents to an attornment whereof you shall reade at large in the Chapter of Attornment.

¶ *Donques ad le grantee le rent come rent seruice pur ceo que il ad le reuersion pur terme de vie.* And the reason hereof is because the Rent is incident to the Reuersion as hath beene said, and (as Littleton saith here) passeth away by the grant of the Reuersion, as with the Superior without saying, Cum pertinentijs, &c. for the Reuersion cannot be seck: But by the grant of the Rent the Reuersion doth not passe.

Sect.

Sect. 229.

¶ ET iſſint eſt a entendue q̃ ſi home dona terrez ou tenements en le taile, rendant a luy & a ſes heires certaine Rent, ou leſſa terre pur terme de vie, rendant certaine rent, ſil granta le reuerſion a vn auter &c. & le tenant atturna, tout le rent & ſeruice paſſe per ceſt parol (reuerſion) pur ceo que tiel rent & ſeruice en tiel cas ſont incidents a le reuerſion, & paſſont per le grant de le reuerſion. Mes coment que il granta le rent a vn auter, le reuerſion ne paſſa my per tiel grant, &c.

AND ſo it is to be intended, that if a man giue Lands or Tenements in taile, yeilding to him and to his Heires a certaine rent, or letteth Land for tearme of life rendring a certaine rent, if hee grant the Reuerſion to another &c. and the Tenant atturne, all the Rent and Seruice paſſe by this word (Reuerſion) becauſe that ſuch Rent and Seruice in ſuch caſe are incident to the Reuerſion, and paſſe by the grant of the Reuerſion. But albeit that hee granteth the rent to another, the Reuerſion doth not paſſe by ſuch grant, &c.

¶ THis needs no explication, but is euident by that which hath formerly beene ſaid, ſauing by this (&c.) in the end is implyed the old rule, That the incident ſhall paſſe by the grant of the principall, but not the principall by the grant of the incident, Acceſſorium non ducit, ſed ſequitur ſuum Principale.

Section 230.

¶ ISſint nota le diuerſitie. Et iſſint eſt tenus P. 21. E. 4. Mes il eſt adiudge, Anno 26. Lib. Aſſiſarum, ou les ſeruices del tenãt en taile fueront grants, q̃ c̃ fuit bone grant, nient obſtant que le reuerſion demurt. ¶

SO note the diuerſitie. And ſo it is holden, *P.* 21. *E.* 4. But it is adiudged 26. of the Book of Aſſiſes, where the ſeruices of tenant in taile were granted, that this was a good grant, notwithſtanding that the Reuerſion remayne. ¶

¶ THis is added to Litleton. And therefore as I haue done heretofore, and ſhall doe hereafter in like caſes I paſſe it ouer. And the caſe here cited in 26. Aſſ. p. 66. was contra opinionem multorum, and afterwards that Judgement was reuerſed by writ of Error, for that the Seruices remayned with the Reuerſion as incidents inſeparable.

Section 231.

¶ ITem ſi ſoit ſeignior, meſne, & tenant, & le tenant tiẽt del meſne per ſeruice de v. s̃. & le meſne tient ouſter per ſeruice

ALſo if there bee Lord, meſne and tenant, and the tenant holdeth of the meſne by the ſeruice of fiue ſhillings, & the meſne

¶ S*I ſoit Seignior, meſne & tenant, &c. ſi le Seignior Paramont purchaſe le Seigniorie en fee, &c.*

(k) Some haue ſaid that (k) 20. E. 3. *Auowrie*. 126.

in

de xij. d. si le Seignior paramont purchase le tenancie en fee, donques le seruice de le mesnaltie est extinct, pur ceo que quant le Seignior paramont ad le tenancie, il tient de son Seignior procheine paramont a luy, & sil doit tener ceo de luy que fuit mesne, donques il tiendra vn mesme tenancie immediate de diuers Seigniors, per diuers seruices, que serroit inconuenient, & la ley voit plus tost suffer vn mischiefe que vn inconueniencie, & pur ceo le Seigniory del mesnaltie est extinct.

holdeth ouer by the seruice of 12. pence, if the Lord Paramont purchase the tenancie in fee, then the seruice of the mesnaltie is extinct, because that when the Lord Paramont hath the tenancie, he holdeth of his Lord next Paramont to him, & if he should hold this of him which was Mesne, then hee should hold the same tenancie immediately of diuers Lords by diuers Seruices which should be inconuenient, and the Law will sooner suffer a mischiefe then an inconuenience, & therefore the Seigniorie of the Mesnaltie is extinct.

2. E. 2. tit. Exting. 6. 26. H. 6. ibid. 7.

in this case it were reason, that by the purchase of the Lord paramount, his Seigniorie should bee onely extinct, and that hee should become tenant to the Mesne, and the Mesne to hold ouer as the Lord paramount held. But that cannot be, for that one man cannot be both Lord and Tenant, nor one land immediately holden of diuers lords.

(l) 7. Ass. 2. 9. E. 3. 29.

(l) If the Tenant infeoffe the Lord Paramount and his wife and their heires, in this case the Mesnaltie is but suspended, for if the wife suruiue, both Mesnaltie & Seigniorie are reuiued.

It is sayd, that if there bee Lord Mesne and Tenant, each of them by Fealtie and sixe pence, the Lord confirme the state of the Tenant, to hold of him by Fealtie and three pence, that the Mesnalty is extinct.

(m) 4. E. 3. 39. See for this hereafter in the Chapter of Confirmation, Sect.

(m) And so in the same case, if the Tenant bee an Abbot, and the Lord confirme his estate to hold of him in Frankalmoigne, the Mesnaltie is extinct.

(n) 8. H. 6. 24.

(n) So it is if the Lord release to the Tenant, for whither the Lord purchase the Tenancie, or the Tenant the Seigniorie, the Mesnaltie is extinct. And albeit the Mesne grant the Mesnaltie for life, and then the Lord release to the Tenant, both the reuersion and the estate for life are drowned.

(o) 4. & 5. P. & M. Dy. 154.

(o) So if there be Lord and Tenant, and the tenant make a gift in taile, the remainder to the King, the Seigniorie is extinct.

Vid. Sect. 138, 139.

¶ *Que serra inconuenient.* Here it appeareth, That Argumentum ab inconuenienti is forcible in Law, as hath beene sayd before, and shall bee often obserued hereafter.

(p) 13. H. 4. 3. 40. Ass. p. 27. 12. R. 2. Vauch. 81.

¶ (p) *Le ley voet pluis tost suffer mischiefe que inconuenience.* Lex citius tolerare vult priuatum damnum, quam publicum malum. Here be two Maximes of the Common Law:

First, That no man can hold one and the same land immediately, of two seuerall Lords.

Secondly, That one man cannot of the same land be both Lord and Tenant. And it is to be obserued, That it is holden for an inconuenience, that any of the Maximes of the law should be broken, though a priuate man suffer losse: for that by infringing of a Maxime, not onely a generall preiudice to many, but in the end a publique incertaintie and confusion to all would follow. And the rule of law is regularly true, Res inter alios acta alteri nocere non debet. Et factum vnius alteri nocere non debet, which are true with this exception, vnlesse an inconuenience should follow, as our Author here teacheth vs.

Sect. 232.

¶ [I] *Lauera le iiij. s. come Rent Secke.*

MEs entant que le tenant tenus

BVt in as much as the Tenant holds

nust del mesne p v. s. & le mesn̄ tenust forsque per xij. d. issint que il auoit pluis en aduantage p iiij. s. que il payast a son Seignior, il auera les dits iiij. s. come Rent Seck annuelment de le Seignior que purchase le Tenancie.

of the Mesne by fiue shillings, & the Mesne hold but by twelue pence, so as hee hath more in aduantage by foure shillings, than he payes to his Lord, hee shall haue the sayde foure shillings as a rent Secke yearely of the lord which purchased the Tenancie.

(q) And yet he shall distreyne for it, for seeing the fealtie is extinct, the Law reserues the distresse to the rent, for, as it hath beene sayd in the like case, seeing the fealtie is extinct, the distresse by Act in Law may be preserued, *Quia quando lex aliquid alicui concedit, concedere videtur & id sine quo res ipsa esse non potest.* (r) And therefore if a man maketh a lease for life, reseruing a rent, and bind himselfe in a statute, and hath the rent extended and deliuered to him, he shall distreyne for the rent, because he commeth to it by course of Law. (r) 13. H. 4. Audita querela 237.

(s) But if a Rent seruice be made a Rent secke by the grant of the Lord, the Grantee shall not distreyne for it, for that the distresse remaines with the fealtie. (t) If there be Lord, Mesne and Tenant, and the mesnaltie is a Mannor hauing diuers freeholders, and the Lord purchase one of the Tenancies, and there is a rent by surplusage, this rent albeit it be changed into another nature, (as hath beene sayd) is parcell of the Mannor. But yet by purchase of part of the land, the whole rent is extinct, albeit the Law did preserue it. (s) 28. E. 3. 93. (t) 51. Ass. 23. 22. Ass. 53. 2. H. 6. 14.

Sect. 233.

ITem si hōe que ad Rent Secke est vn foits seisi dascun parcel de le Rent & apres l' Tenant ne voit payer l' rent aderere, ceo est son remedie, il couient de aler per luy ou per auts, a les terres ou tenements dont l' rent est issuant, & la demaund les arerages dl rent, & si le Tenant denia ceo de payer, cest denier est vn disseisin d le rent. Auxy si l' tenant ne soit adonq̄s prist a payer, ceo ē vn denier que est vn disseisin de rent. Auxy si l' Tenant ne nul auter home soit demurrant, sur les terres

ALso if a man which hath a Rent secke be once seised of any parcell of the rent, and after the Tenant will not pay the rent behind, this is his remedie, hee ought to goe by himselfe or by others, to the lands or Tenements, out of which the rent is issuing, and there demand the arrerages of the rent, and if the tenant denie to pay it, this deniall is a disseisin of the rent. Also if the tenant be not then readie to pay it, this is a deniall, which is a disseisin of the rent. Also if the Tenant nor any other man bee remai-

¶ *Seisin*, or Seison is common as well to the English, as to the French, & signifies in the Common Law, Possession, whereof Seisina a Latyne word is made, and Seisire a Verbe.

¶ *Dascun parcel.* (u) A seison of parcel, is a sufficient seison in Law, to haue an Assise of the whole rent. (u) 5. E. 4. 2.

Concerning the generall learning of seisons, you may read Lib 4. Beuils case, fol. 8. lib. 5. fol. 98. lib. 6. fol. 57. lib. 7. fol. 24. 29. lib. 9. fol. 33. And many authorities of Law there cited, but sufficient is said here to explaine Littleton. T. 18. E. 1. coram Rege Nott. in Thesaur.

¶ *A les Terres, &c.* (w) For a demand of the tenant out of the land is not sufficient: but if there bee a house and land, a demand on the land is sufficient, but for a condition broken, it ought to be at the house, as hath beene said before. (w) 49. E. 3. 24. b. 14. E. 4. 4. Pl. Com. 71.

¶ *Arere.* This word Arere, is to bee obserued, for it is not necessary that the grantee of the rent should demand it at the very time when it becommeth due, but at any time after it is sufficient, for this is not like a demand of a rent upon a condition, because that is penall and overthroweth the whole state and (x) therefore the time of demand must bee certaine, to the end the Lessee, Donee, or Feoffee may bee there to pay the rent, but a demand of a Rent secke or Rent charge is but only a formall meane to recouer that which is due, (y) and therefore in that case it may bee demanded after it is behinde at any time whether the Tenant be present or no for remedies for rights are euer fauourably extended.

(x) 29. Ass. 51. 8 H.6.11. Lib. de Entries 79. b.

(y) Mich. 41. E.3. coram Rege adiudg. accordingly.

ou les tenemẽts pur payer le rent quaunt il demaund les arrerages, ceo est vn dñi=er en ley & vn disseisin en fait, & de tiels disseisins il poit auer Assise de Nouel disseisin, enuers l' tenant, & recouera le seisin del rent, & ses arrerages & ses dammages, & les costages d̃ s̃ bt̃ & d̃ s̃ plee, &c. Et si ap̃s tiel recouery & execution ewe le rent soyt autfoits a luy denie, donque il auera vn redisseisin, & recouera ses double dammages, &c.

ning vpon the lands or tenements to pay the rent when hee demandeth the arrerages, this is a deniall in law, and a disseisin in deed, and of such disseisins he may haue an Assise of *Nouel disseisin* against the Tenant, and shal recouer the seisin of the Rent, and his arrerages, & his dammages, & the costs of his writ & of his plea, &c. And if after such recouery & execution had, the rent be again denied vnto him, then hee shall haue a redisseisin, and shall recouer his double dammages &c.

Ceo est vn denier en ley. For wheresoeuer there is a lawfull demand of a rent, and the same is not paid whether the Tenant be present or absent, yet this is a denyall in Law, albeit there bee no words of denyall. It appeareth here that the demand must be made upon the land, and albeit the Tenant nor any for him be there yet must the Grantee demand it, because without a demand there can be no denier in Deede, or in Law.

(z) Vid. Bract. li. 4. fo. 161. 162. 204. Brit ca. 42. 43. &c f. 83. 106. 114. 115. 118. Mir. ca. 2. §. 1. * Flet. li. 4. ca. 1. Bra. vbi supra

Disseisin. (z) Disseisina, is a putting out of a man out of seisin and euer implyeth a wrong. But dispossessing or eiectment is a putting out of possession, and may be by right or by wrong, * Omnis disseisina est transgressio, sed non omnis transgressio est disseisina, & si eo animo forte ingrediatur fundum alienum, non quod sibi vsurpet tenementum, vel iura, non facit disseisinam, sed transgressionem, &c. quærendum est a iudice quo animo hoc fecerit, &c. And of Ancient time a Disseisine was defined thus, Disseisin est vn personel trespasse de tortious ouster del seisin.

Mirror, cap. 2. § 15. Bract. in lib. 4. cap. 4. Britton, cap. 44. 45. &c. Fleta, lib. 4. ca. 5. & 2. & 3.

Mirror, cap. 2. §. 15.

Assise de nouel disseisin. Assisa nouæ disseisinæ. Assisa properly commeth of the Latyn word Assidio, which is to associate or set together, So as properly Assise is an association or sitting together. And the writ whereby certaine persons are authorised & called together is called Assisa nouæ disseisinæ; so as Assisa is but Cessio. But because Cessio is but a generall word, therefore in this since assisa is used in Law for a particular Cession by force of the Writ De assisa noue disseisinæ, and accordingly it was anciently said Assise in vn case nest auter chose que cession des Iustices, and it is called Assisa nouæ disseisinæ, for that the Justices of Eire before whom these Assises were taken in their proper Counties did ride their Circuits from 7. yeares to 7. yeares, and no Disseisin before the Eire if it were not complained of in the Eire could be questioned after the Eire, and therefore a Disseisin committed before the last Eire was called an ancient Disseisin, and a Disseisin after the last Eire was called a new Disseisin or Noua disseisina. Assisa also signifieth a Jury of their sitting together, and also a Cession of Parliament as Littleton hereafter in this chapter sheweth.

Et recouera le seisin del rent. Here, and by the (&c.) in the end of this Section is implyed, that our Author intendeth his case, where the rent issueth out of lands in one County, for if a man be seised of two acres of land in two severall Counties, and maketh a Lease of both of them reseruing two shillings rent in this case, albeit severall Liuerpes be made at severall times, yet is it but one entire rent in respect of the necessitie of the case, and he shall distreyne in one County for the whole, and make one Avowrie for the whole. But he shall haue severall Assises in confinio comitatus, and in either Countie shall

make

make his pleynt of the whole rent, but there shall be but one Patent to the Iustices. (a) And this Assise in confinio comitatus is giuen by the statute of 7. R. 2. cap. 10. for no Assise lay, in that case at the Common Law, but the party might distreine. (b) But for a common of pasture, of Turbarie, of Pischarie, of Estouers and the like in one Countie, appendant or appurtenant to land in an other Countie, an Assise in confinio comitatus, did lye at the Common Law (c) and so it is of a Nusans done in one County, to lands lying in another Countie, the like Assise did lye at the Common Law.

(a) 10. Ass. pl. 4. 18. Ass. p. 1. & 18. E. 3. 32. 22. H. 6. 9. 10.
(b) F. N. B. 180. a.
(c) F. N. B. 183. k.

(d) And albeit the Counties doe not adioyne, but there be 20. Counties meane betweene them, yet the Assise in confinio comitatus doth lye, and the Iustices shall sit betweene the said Counties. (e) And where it is said before of two Counties, the like law it is if the same extend into more Counties.

(d) 5. E. 4. 2.
(e) F. N. B. 180. d.

(f) If a man hold diuers Mannors or lands in diuers seuerall Counties by one tenure and the Lord is deforced of his seruices, he shall haue seuerall writs of Customes and seruices, for euery Countie one writ returnable at one day in the Court of Common pleas, and thereupon count according to his case by the Common Law.

(f) 30 E. 1. tit. Diuit. F. N. B. 151. m.

(g) But if the Tenant in that case doe cease, the Lord shall not haue seuerall writs of Cessauit vt supra, for the writ of Cessauit is giuen by Statute * and the forme and manner of the writ therein prescribed, and thereupon it is holden in our bookes that in that case a Cessauit doth not lye.

(g) 18. Ass. pl. 1.
* W. 2. cap. 21.

¶ (h) *Il auera vn redisseisin & recouera ses double damages, &c.* Here by this (&c.) is also to be understood, that a writ of Redisseisin is giuen by the statute of Merton * (so called because the Parliament was holden at Merton in Anno 20. H. 3.) the Letter whereof is, Item si quis fuerit disseisitus de libero tenemento & coram Iusticiarijs itinerantibus seisinam suam recuperauerit per assisam nouę disseisinæ vel per recognition' eorum qui fecerint disseisinam, & ipse disseisitus, per vicecomitem seisinam suam habuerit, si ijdem disseisitores postea post iter Iusticiariorum vel infra de eodem tenemento iterum eundem conquerentem disseisiuerint, & inde conuicti fuerint, statim capiantur, &c. But the double damages are giuen by the statute of W. 2. cap. 26.

(h) Bracton. fo. 236. Britton, 133. 246. Fleta, lib. 4. cap. 29. Merton, cap. 2. §. 15. Regist. 206. 207.
* Mirror, cap. 3. W. 2. c. 46.
Vide Sect. 234.
Vid Regist. 206. b.

And Littleton in few words hath made a good exposition of this statute for where the statute saith Disseisitus de libero tẽto Littleton expounds it, to extend to a Rent secke or Rent charge, albeit, as hath beene said, they be against common right, yet a man hath a freehold in them, (k) And he that granteth Omnia tenementa sua, a Rent charge or a Rent secke doth passe.

(i) 40. Ass. 23 ar.
(k) 14. E. 4. 4. 11. H. 6. 22.

Coram Iusticiarijs itinerantibus, &c. saith the statute. But Littleton speaketh generally and so is the statute to be intended before any other Iustices that haue authority to take Assises, and Iustices Itinerant are set downe but for an example which is worthy of the obseruation (l) being a penall Law.

(l) Fitz. N. B. 189. b.

Recuperauerit per assisam, &c. saith the statute, here assisa is taken for the verdict of the Assise as Littleton hereafter in this chapter expoundeth the same. Vel per recognitionem, &c. or by confession Then the question is what if the recouery were vpon a demurrer or by pleading of a Record and failer of it, or by any other manner. And seeing Littleton speaketh generally it must be understood of all manner of recoueries in an Assise of nouel disseisin; And so it is confirmed by the statute of W. 2. ca. 26.

¶ *Recouerie.* Recuperatio **commeth of the Verbe** Recuperare, i. ad rem per iniuriam extortam siue detentam per sententiam Iudicis restitui. And Recuperatio in the Common Law, is all one with Euictio in the Ciuill Law, which is, Alicuius rei in causam alterius abductæ per iudicem acquisitio.

¶ *Et execution ewe,* Per vicecomitem seisinam habuerit, **saith the** Statute, but Littleton speaketh generally, (Et execution ewe) And execution had, so as whether it be by the Sherife or by the partie, so as execution or possession be had, it sufficeth.

¶ *Execution,* Executio, **And signifieth in Law, The obtaining** of actuall possession of any thing acquired by iudgement of Law, or by a fine executorie leuied, whether it be by the Sherife, or by the entrie of the partie, whereof you shall read more hereafter.

Vide sect. 504.

Note, it appeareth here by Littleton, That (m) the recouerie in a former writ must bee in Assise of Nouel Disseisin, wherein these words (Tiel recouerie) are to be obserued. And therefore if in a writ of Right close in antient Demesne, the Demandant maketh his protestation, to sue in the nature of Assise of Nouel Disseisin, and after is redisseised, he shall not haue a writ of Redisseisin, because the first recouerie was not by writ of Assise of Nouel Disseisin. (n) And so it is if the recouerie were in Assise of Fresh force by Bill, according to the custome of some Citie or Burrough, also in antient Demesne there be no Coroners.

(m) 14. E. 2. tit. Red ss. 9. F. N. B. 189 g.
(n) 14. E. 3. tit. Red ss. 8. Vide the 2. part of the Institutes Stat. de Merton ca. 3.

Si ijdem disseisitores, saith the Statute. (o) So as it must be the same Disseisors: but here

(o) 9. H. 4. 5. F. N. B. 189. c. 23. Ass. pl. 7.

Iidem is taken for non alij: And therefore if the recouerie in the Assise were against two Disseisors, and one of them redisseise him againe, he shall haue a Redisseisin against him, for hee is not alius. But if the recouerie had beene against one, and he and another redisseise the Plaintife, he shall not haue a Redisseisin, for here is alius, and he cannot haue a Redisseisin against the former Disseisor alone, because he is Ioyntenant with another. (p) For Ioyntenancie in a Writ of Redisseisin is a good plea, and a stranger shall not be subiect to double imprisonment and double dammages.

(p) 33.*E*.3.*redisseisin*.7.

(q) 9.*H*.4.5.*F*.*N*.*B*.188.*E*.

(r) *F*.*N*.*B*.188.*E*. *Regist*. 9.*H*.4.5.

(q) If a recouerie be had against a woman in an Assise of Nouel Disseisin, and the Plaintife recouereth and hath execution, the woman taketh husband, and both of them redisseise the Plaintife, he shall not haue a Redisseisin, because the husband is alius. (r) And yet if a Feme recouer in an Assise, and after take Baron, and they are redisseised, the husband and wife shall haue a Redisseisin, because the husband ioyneth for conformitie, and it is in the right of his wife who was disseised before, so in effect it is idem disseisitus & idem conquerens.

If two Coparceners be disseised, and recouer in an Assise, if after they make partition, and after they be seuerally disseised, they shall haue seuerall Redisseisins, and so it is of ioyntenants for they be Iidem conquerentes & non alij. Also a Redisseisin doth lie against the disseisor which doth redisseise, and against another to whom he made feoffment after the second disseisin, for otherwise the redisseisor might preuent the Plantife of his redisseisin. But in an Assise against A. and B. A. is found Disseisor, and B. Tenant, and the Plaintife doth recouer, and after he which was found Tenant disseises the Plaintife, he shall not haue a redisseisin, because hee did disseise him but once.

F. *N*. *B*. 188.*G*.

De eodem tenemento, saith the Statute. If the Plaintife be redisseised of parcel of the Tenement formerly recouered, he shall haue a redisseisin.

If the Mesne recouereth a Rent when it is a Rent Seruice, and after the rent becommeth a Rent Secke by surplusage, and doth redisseise him of the Rent, he shall haue a redisseisin, for the substance of the Rent remaynes though the qualitie be altered.

(s) 26.*H*.6.*tit*. *Aide* .77.

(s) If tenant in speciall taile recouereth in Assise, and after becommeth Tenant in taile after possibilitie of issue extinct, and then is redisseised hee shall haue a redisseisin. For albeit the state of Inheritance be altered, yet the same freehold remaineth.

8.*E*.3.*tit*.*Redisseisin*.6. *F*.*N*.*B*.189.*F*.

If a man recouer Land in an Assise of nouel disseisin, whereunto there is a common appendant or appurtenant, and after is redisseised of the common, hee shall haue a redisseisin of the common, for it was tacitely recouered in the Assise.

Section 234.

ET memorandum que cest nosme Assise, est nomen æquiuocum car ascun foits est prise pur un Iurie, car le commencement de le Record de Assise de nouel disseisin issint commencera: Assisa venit recognitura, &c. quod idem est quod Iurata venit recognitura, &c. Et la cause est, pur ceo que per le briefe de Assise, il est command a la Uicont, Quod faceret duodecim

AND *memorandum*, that this name Assise is *nomen Equiuocum*, for sometimes it is taken for a Iurie, for the beginning of the Record of an Assise of *Nouel disseisin* beginneth thus. *Assisa venit recognitura, &c.* which is the same, as *Iurata venit recognitura*. And the reason is for that by the Writ of Assise it is commanded to the Sherife, *Quod faceret duodecim liberos & legales homi-*

ÆQuiuocum. For the better understanding hereof, Of these there be two kinds, viz. Æquiuocum, Æquiuocans; and Æquiuocum Æquiuocatum.

Æquiuocum Æquiuocans est pluriuocum; Polysemus, a word of diuers seuerall significations.

Æquiuocum æquiuocatum est vniuocum, that is to say, reduced to a certaine signification as here in Littletons example, Assisa est nomen æquiuocum æquiuocans, for sometime it signifieth a Iurie, sometime the writ of Assise, and sometime an Ordinance or Statute.

Now Assise, Iurata is Æquiuocum Eqniuocatum, and so is breue de Assisa nouæ disseisinæ, and Assisa panis, &c. euen as Canis est nomen æ-

duodecim liberos & legales homines de vicineto, &c. videre tenementum illud, & nomina illorum imbreuiare, & quod summoneat eos per bonos summonitores, quod sint coram Iusticiarijs, &c. parati inde facere recognitionem, &c. **Et pur ceo que per tiel original, un panel per force de mesme le briefe deuoit estre returne, &c. il est dit en l'commencement del Record en le Assise,** Assisa venit recognitura, &c. **Auxy en briefe de droit il est communement dit, que le tenant luy poit mitter en Dieu & grand Assise, &c. Auxy il y ad un briefe en le** Register, **que est appel briefe** de Magna Assisa eligenda. **Issint est ceo bien proue que cest nosme Assise,** aliquando ponitur pro Iurat'. **Et ascun foits il est prise pur tout le breife dassise, & solonque cel entent il est pluis propearment, & pluis communement prise, sicome** Assise de Nouel disseisin **est prise pur tout l'breue de** Assise de Nouel disseisin. **Et en mesme le maner Assise de**

nes de vicineto, &c. videre tenementum illud, & nomina illorum imbreuiare, & quod summoneat eos per bonos summonitores, quod sint coram Iusticiarijs, &c. parati inde facere recognitionem, &c. And because that by such an originall, a pannell by force of the same Writ ought to be returned, &c. it is said in the beginning of the Record in the Assise. *Assisa venit recognitura, &c.* Also in a writ of Right it is commonly said that the Tenant may put himselfe on God and the great Assise. Also there is a Writ in the Register which is called a Writ, *De magna Assisa eligenda:* So as this is well proued that this name Assise, sometimes is taken for a Iury, and somtimes it is take for the whole Writ of Assise, and according to this purpose it is most properly and most cōmonly taken, as an Assise of *Nouel disseisin* is taken for the whole Writ of Assise of *Nouel disseisin.* And in the same manner an Assise of Common of Pasture is taken for the whole Writ of Assise

quiuocum, Canis latrabilis, Canis marinus, Canis Calestis sunt æquiuoca æquiuocata.

¶ *Assise de nouel disseisin.* **Note** (a) **there bee foure** Assises. Viz. **this Writ, an Assise of** Mordancester, **of** Darreine præsentment, **and of** Vtrum.

(a) *Bracton. lib. 4. fol.* 160. *Britton. cap.* 42 *fol.* 105. 134. *F.N.B. Fleta lib.* 4 *ca.* 5. *&c. Mirror. cap.* 2. §. 13.

¶ *Vicount.* Vide Sect. 248. verbo *(Shireue.)*

¶ *Quod faciat* 12. *liberos & legales homines de Viceneto, &c.*

(b) **Albeit the wordes of the writ be** duodecim, **yet by ancient course the sherife must returne** 24 **and this is for expedition of Iustice, for if 12. should only be returned, no man should haue a full Iurie appeare, or be sworn in respect of challēges, without a** Tales, **which should bee a great delay of tryals. So as in this case vsage & ancient course maketh Law. And it seemeth to mee, that the Law in this case delighteth her selfe in the number of 12. for there must not only be 12.** Iurors **for the triall of matters of fact,** (c) **but 12.** Iudges **of ancient time for triall of matters in Law,** in the Exchequer Chamber. **Also for matters of State there were in ancient time twelue** Counsellors of State. **He that wageth his Law must haue** eleuen others with him **which thinke he sayes true. And that** number of 12. **is much respected** in holy Writ, **as** 12. Apostles, 12. Stones, 12. Tribes, **&c.**

(b) 1. *H.* 7. 2.

(c) *Vide pl. com. in proœmio.*

Iosua 4. *Genes.* 49.

(d) **Hee that is of a Iurie must be** liber homo, **that is not only a freeman, and not bound but also one that hath such freedome of mind as he stands indifferent as hee stand vnsworne. Secondly, hee must bee** legalis. **And by the Law euery Iuror that is returned for the triall of any issue or cause ought to haue three properties.**

(d) 9. *E.* 4. 16.

(*) **First,**

common de pasture est pris pur tout le briefe dassise de common de pasture, & Assise de mortdauncester est prise per tout le bre dassise de Mortdancester & Assise de darraine presentmēt est prise per tout le breue dassise de darraine presentment. Mes il semble que le cause pur q̄ tiel briefes al commencemēt fueront appels Assises fuit pur ceo que p chescun tiel briefe il est commande al viscont, Qd' summoneat xij. le quel est a tant adirᵉ, que doit summoner vn Jurie. Et ascun foits Assise est prise pur vn ordinance, s. pur mitter certaine choses en certaine rule & disposition, sicome ordinance q̄ est appel Assisa panis & Ceruitiæ.

of Common of Pasture. And Assise of *Mortdauncester*, is taken for the whole Writ, of Assise of *Mortdauncester* and Assise of *Darreine præsentment*, is taken for the whole Writ of *Darreine præsentment*. But it seemes that the reason why such Writs at the beginning were called Assises, was for that by euery such Writ it is commanded to the Sherife, *Quod summoneat* 12. which is as much to say, that hee ought to sommon a Iurie. And sometime Assise is taken for an Ordinance, to wit, to put certaine things into a certaine rule and disposition, as an Ordinance which is called *Assisa panis & Ceruitiæ*.

(*) *Artic. super Cart. cap. 9. Regist. 178. 8. E. 3. 30.*

(*) First, hee ought to bee dwelling most neer to the place where the question is moued.

Secondly, hee ought to bee most sufficient both for vnderstanding, and competencie of estate.

Vide Sect. 102. 193.

9. H. 6. 37.

Thirdly, hee ought to bee least suspitious, that is to bee indifferent as hee stands vnsworne, and then hee is accounted in Law Liber & legalis homo, otherwise he may be challenged and not suffered to be sworne. The most vsuall triall of matters of fact is by 12. such men, for ad questionem facti non respondent Iudices. And matters in Law the Judges ought to decide and discusse, for Ad questionem iuris non respondent Iuratores.

(e) *Vide Artic. super Cart. ca. 9. Fortescue ca. 25. & ca. 29.*

(f) *Glanuil. lib. 2. cap. 14. 15. Bracton. lib. 3. fol. 116. a.*

(g) *Lamb. verbo Centuria.*

(h) *Lamb. fol. 91. 3.*

(e) For the institution and right vse of this triall by 12. men, and wherefore other Countries haue them not, and this triall excels others. See Fortescue at large, cap. 25. & c. 29. (f) And in ancient time they were 12. Knights. This triall of the fact per duodecim liberos & legales homines is very ancient, for heare what the Law was before the Conquest. (g) In singulis Centurijs comitia sunto, atque liberæ conditionis viri duodeni ætate superiores vnà cum præposito sacra tenentes juranto, &c. Nay, the tryall in some cases, Per medietatem linguæ (as we speake) was as ancient (h) Viri duodeni iure consulti, Angliæ sex; Walliæ totidem, Anglis & Wallis ius dicunto, and of ancient time it was called, duodecim virale iudicium.

Now seeing we are iustly occasioned, and the rather for the (&c.) herein, to speake of a challenge to Jurors, to make the studious Reader capable of the vnderstanding of the Bookes of Law concerning this matter, It shall be necessarie to say somewhat of challenges; and first what a Challenge is.

(a) *W. 2. cap. 32. Vide Stat. de 12. E. 2. de essoin. calumniandis. Fleta lib. 1. cap. 32. Britton. fol. 6. a. 12. a. 118. & 134. 12. Ass. 10.*

(b) *Bract. lib. 3. fol. 137.*

(c) *Bracton. lib. 4. fol. 257. Vet. N. B. fol. 76.*

Challenge is a word common aswell to the English as to the French, and sometime signifieth to clayme, and the Latine word is vendicare, sometime in respect of reuenge to challenge into the field, and then it is called in Latine vindicare or prouocare. Sometime in respect of partialitie, or insufficiencie, to challenge in Court persons returned on a Jurie. And seeing there is no proper Latine word to signifie this particular kind of challenge, they haue framed a word anciently written (a) Chalumniare, and Columpniare, and Calumpniare, and now written Calumniare and hath no affinitie with the Verbe Calumnior or Calumnia which is deriued of that, for that is of a quite other sence signifying a false accuser, & in that sence (b) Bracton vseth Calumniator to be a false accuser: but it is deriued of the old word Caloir or Chaloir, which in one signification is to care for, or foresee. And for that to challenge Jurors is the meane to care for or foresee, that an indifferent tryall be had, it is called Calumniare, to challenge, that is to except against them that are returned to be Jurors, & this is his proper signification (c): But

some-

(c) sometimes a Summons, *Somonitio* is said (d) to be *Calumniata*, and a Count to be challenged, but this is improperly. And forasmuch as mens lives, Fames, lands, and goods are to be tryed by Jurors, it is most necessary that they be *Omni exceptione maiores*, and therefore I will handle this matter the more largely.

A Challenge to Jurors is two fold, either to the Array, or to the Polls: to the Array of the principall Pannell, and to the Array of the *Tales*. And herein you shall understand, that the Jurors names are ranked in the Pannell one under another, which order or ranking the Jurie is called the Array, and the Verbe, to array the Jurie, and so we say in common speech, *Battaile array*, for the order of the battaile. And this Array we call *Arraiamentum*, and to make the Array, *Arraiare*, derived of the French word *Arroier*, so as to challenge the Array of the Pannell, is at once to challenge or except against all the persons so arrayed or impanelled, in respect of the partialitie or default of the Sherife, Coroner, or other Officer that made the returne.

And it is to be knowne, that there is a principall cause of challenge to the Array, and a challenge to the favour: principall, in respect of partialitie, as first if the Sherife or other Officer be of (a) kindred or affinitie to the Plaintife or Defendant, if the affinitie continue. (b) Secondly, If any one or more of the Jurie bee returned at the denomination of the partie, Plaintife or Defendant, the whole Array shall be quashed. So it is if the Sherife returne any one, that he be more favourable to the one than to the other, all the array shall be quashed. (c) Thirdly, if the Plaintife or Defendant have an Action of Batterie against the Sherife, or the Sherife against either partie, this is a good cause of challenge. So if the Plaintife or Defendant have an Action of Debt against the Sherife, (but otherwise it is if the Sherife have an Action of Debt against either partie) or if the Sherife have parcell of the land depending upon the same title, (d) or if the Sherife or his Baylife which returned the Jurie, be under the distresse of either partie, or if the Sherife or his Baylife be either of Councell, Atturney, Officer in Fee or of Robes, or servant of either partie, Gossip, or Arbitrator in the same matter, and treated thereof. (e) And where a Subiect may challenge the array for unindifferencie, there the King being a partie, may also challenge for the same cause, as for Kindred, or that he hath part of the land, or the like: and where the array shall be challenged against the King, you shall read in our Bookes.

(f) By default of the Sherife, as when the array of a Pannell is returned by a Baillife of a Franchise, and the Sherife returne it as of himselfe, this shall bee quashed, because the partie should lose his challenges. But if a Sherife returne a Jurie within a Libertie, this is good, and the Lord of the Franchise is driven to his remedie against him.

If a Peere of the Realme or Lord of Parliament be Demandant or Plaintife, Tenant or Defendant, there must a Knight be returned of his Jurie, be he Lord Spirituall or Temporall, or else the Array may be quashed: but if he be returned, although hee appeare not, yet the Jurie may be taken of the residue. And if others be ioyned with the Lord of Parliament, yet if there be no Knight returned, the Array shall be quashed against all. (h) So in an Attaint there ought to be a Knight returned of the Jurie.

(i) And when the King is partie, as in travers of an Office, he that traverseth may challenge the Array, as hereafter in this *Section* shall appeare: And so it is in case of life, and likewise the King may challenge the Array, and this shall be tried by Triers according to the usual course. (k) The Array challenged on both sides shall be quashed.

(l) And if two estrangers make a Pannell, and not in favourable manner for the one partie or the other, and the Sherife returnes the same, the Array was challenged for this cause, and adiudged good.

(m) If the Baylife of a Libertie returne any out of his Franchise, the Array shall bee quashed, as an array returned by one that hath no Franchise shall be quashed.

Challenge to the Array for favour: (n) He that taketh this, must shew in certaine the name of him that made it, and in whose time, and all in certaintie: this kind of challenge beeing no principall challenge, must be left to the discretion and conscience of the Triers, as if the Plaintife or Defendant be Tenant to the Sherife, this is no principall challenge, for the Lord is in no danger of his Tenant, but *e converso* it is a principall challenge, but in the other hee may challenge for favour, and leave it to triall. So affinitie betweene the sonne of the Sherife and the daughter of the partie, or *e converso*, or the like, is no principall challenge, but to the favor: but if the Sherife marrie the daughter of either partie, or *e converso*, this (as hath been sayd) is a principall challenge, or the like. (o) But where the King is partie, one shall not challenge the Array for favour, &c. because in respect of his allegeance he ought to favour the King more. But if the Sherife be a Vadelect of the Crowne, or other meniall servant of the King, there the challenge is good, and likewise the King may challenge the Array for favour.

Note, upon that which hath beene sayd it appeareth, That the challenge to the Array is in respect of the cause of unindifferencie or default in the Sherife or other Officer that made the returne,

(a) 12. *Ass.* 36.26. *Ass.* 31. 3.E.4.12. 31. *Ass.* 7. 29. *Ass.* 2. 22.E.4.2.12.E.3. *Chall.* 114. 21.E.3.5.b. 3.H.7.5. *Pl. Com.* 73. 15.H.7.9. 7.E.6. *Dier* 78. 12.H.6. *Chall.* 159.
(b) 21.E.4.74. 49.E.3.1. 15.E.3.43. 22.E.3.12. 9.E.4.46. 8.H.5.5. 28. *Ass.* 22. 41.E.3. *Chall.* 99.
(c) 11.H.4.26. 22.E.4.1. 38.E.3.25. 38.H.6.6.
(d) 44.E.3.5. & 38. 44. *Ass.* 23. 22.E.4.1. 3 H.6.39. 15.H.7.9.b. 27. *Ass.* 28. 7.H.7.10. 26. *Ass.* 56. 22. 20.H.6.34. 33. *Ass.* 12. 45. *Ass.* 1. 9. *Ass.* 8. 8. *Ass.* 23. 7.E.3.56. 21.H.7.38. 2.H.4.13. 44.E.3.43. 20.H.6.39. 44. *Ass.* 18. 7.H.6.24. 17.E.2. *Chall.* 168. 4.E.4.11.
(e) 4.H.7. 44.E.3.38. 38. *Ass.* 19. 22.E.4. *Chall.* 63. *Stanf.* 162.c.
(f) 39. *Ass.* 2. 17.E.3.50. 17. *Ass.* 11. 30 *Ass.* 5. 8. *Ass.* 3.
(g) 13.E.3. *Chall.* 115. *Br. Enquest.* 100. *Lib.* 6. *fo.* 54. *Countesse de Rutlands Case. Plo. Com.* 117. 27.H.8.22. 4.Eliz. *Dier* 208. 8.Eliz. *Dier* 246. 14.Eliz. *Dier* 318. 10.Eliz. *Dier* 265.b.
(h) 17.E.2. *Attaint* 69.
(i) 32.E.4. *tit. Chall.* 63. *Stamf. Pl. Cor.* 19. *Ass.* 6.b. 4.H.7.8. 44.E.3.38.
(k) 8.H.4.22.
(l) 6.R.2. *Chal.* 102. 13.E.3. *ibid.* 108.
(m) 32.E.3. *Chal.* 110.111. 32. *Ass.* 6. 38. *Ass.* 13.
(n) 34.H.6. *Chall.* 69. 8.H.4.22. 27. *Ass.* 20. 22.E.3.12. *Vid.* 26. *Ass.* 21. 38.H.6.9. 7.H.6.25. 19.H.6.48. 20.H.6.38. 20.E.4.2. 22.E.4. *Chal.* 62.
(o) 22.E.4. *Chal.* 63. 4.H.7.8.

returne, and not in respect of the persons returned, where there is no vnindifferencie or default in the Sherife, &c. for if the challenge to the Array be found against the partie that takes it, yet he shall haue his particular challenge to the Polls.

In some cases a challenge may be had to the Polls, and in some cases not at all. Challenge to the Polls is a challenge to the particular persons, and these be of foure kinds, that is to say, Peremptorie, Principall, which induce Fauour, and for default of Hundredors.

(p) 1.H.5.Chal.162. 9.H.5.7. 15.E.4.32. 14.H.7.7.19. Dial.& Stud. lib.2. Fortescue cap.27. 3.H.7.2. 2.R.3.13. 32.H.5.26.17.Ass.6. 37.H.6.8. 22.H.8.ca.14. 33.H.8.tit.Chal.Br.217. 33.H.8.ca.23. 1 & 2.P.& M.ca.10. 32.H.6.26. 14.H.7.14. Stanf.Pl.Cor. 137,138. * Hil.1.Ia.R.

(p) Peremptorie, this is so called, because he may challenge peremptorily vpon his owne dislike, without shewing of any cause, and this onely is in case of Treason or Felonie, in fauorem vitæ, and by the Common Law the prisoner vpon an Endictment or Appeale, might challenge thirtie fiue, which was vnder the number of three Juries, but now by the Statute of 22 H.8. the number is reduced to twentie in petite Treason, Murder and Felonie, and in case of high Treason, and misprision of high Treason it was taken away by the Statute of 33. H.8. but now by the Statute of 1.& 2. Phil.& Mariæ, the Common Law is reuiued, for any Treason, the Prisoner shall haue his Challenge to the number of thirty fiue, and so it hath beene resolued * by the Justices vpon conference betweene them in the case of Sir Walter Raleigh and George Brookes. But all this is to bee vnderstood when any subiect, that is not a Peere of the Realme is arraigned for Treason or Felonie; But if hee bee a Lord of Parliament and a Peere of the Realme, and is to bee tried by his Peeres, he shall not challenge any of his Peeres at all, for they are not sworne as other Jurors bee, but find the partie guiltie or not guiltie vpon their faith or allegiance to the King, and they are Judges of the Fact, and euery of them doth seperately giue his iudgement beginning at the lowest. But a subiect vnder the degree of Nobilitie may in case of Treason or Felonie challenge for iust cause as many as he can, as shall be said hereafter.

9.E.4.27.

In an Appeale of death against diuers they pleade not guiltie, and one ioynt Venire facias is awarded, if one challenge peremptorily, he shall bee drawne against all. Otherwise it is of seuerall Venire fac.

Note, that at the Common Law before the Statute of 33.E.1. the King might haue challenged peremptorily without shewing cause, but only that they were not good for the King, and without being limited to any number, but this was mischieuous to the subiect, tending to infinite delayes and danger. And therefore it is enacted, (q) Quod de cetero licet pro Domino Rege dicatur quod iuratores, &c. non sunt boni pro Rege: non propter hoc remaneant inquisitiones, &c. sed assignent certam causam calumniæ suæ, &c. Whereby the King is now restrained.

(q) 33.E.1. Ordinatio de Inquisitionibus. Stanf. Pl. Cor. 162.

Principall, so called because if it be found true, it standeth sufficient of it selfe without leauing any thing to the conscience or discretion of the Triors. Of a principall cause of challenge to the array, we haue said somewhat alreadie, now it followeth with like breuitie to speake of principall Challenges to the Polles, (that is) seuerally to the persons returned.

Principall challenges to the Poll may be reduced to foure heads: First, Propter Honoris respectum, For respect of Honour; Secondly, Propter Defectum, For want or default; Thirdly, Propter Affectum, For Affection or partialitie; Fourthly, Propter Delictum, For Crime or Delict.

Lib.6.fo.52,53. Countesse de Rutlands case. 48.E.3.30. 48.Ass.6.35.H.6.46. 22.Ass.24. F.N.B.165.d. & 166.Regist.179.

First, Propter Honoris respectum, As any Piere of the Realme, or Lord of Parliament, as a Baron, Viscount, Earle, Marquesse, and Duke, for these in respect of Honour and Nobilitie, are not be sworne on Juries; and if neither partie will challenge him, he may challenge himselfe, for by Magna Charta it is prouided, Quod nec super eum ibimus, nec super eum mittemus nisi per legale iudicium parium suorum, aut per legem terræ. Now the Common Law hath diuided all the subiects into Lords of Parliament, and into the Commons of the Realme. The Pieres of the Realme are diuided into Barons, Viscounts, Earles, Marquesses & Dukes: The Commons are diuided into Knights, Esquires, Gentlemen, Citisens, Yeomen, and Burgesses, and in iudgement of Law, any of the sayd degrees of Nobilitie are Pieres to another. As if an Earle, Marquesse, or Duke be to be tried for treason or felonie, a Baron or any other degree of Nobilitie is his Pier. In like manner, a Knight, Esquire, &c. shall bee tried per Pares, and that is by any of the Commons, as Gentlemen, Citisens, Yeomen, or Burgesses, so as when any of the Commons is to haue a trial either at the Kings suit, or betweene partie and partie, a Piere of the Realme shall not be impanelled in any case.

(a) Lib.7.f.18. Caluins case. Li.10.fo.104.14.H.4.19.b. (b) Bract.fo.185. Brit.f.135 Flet.b.4.ca.8. 26. Ass.28. 3.H.6.39 9.E.4.26.b. 21.H.6.20. 10 H.7.20. (c) Vid.Sect.464.38.ass 19. 17.Ass.15. 4.H.6.28. 9.H.5.5. 10.H.6.7.8.18. 2.H.7.1.10.H.7.14. 19.H. 6.9. 7.H.6.25.40.44. 12.E.4.13. 3.H.4.4. (*) 9.H.6.Chal.27.9.H.7.1

Secondly, Propter Defectum,

1 Patriæ, (a) as Aliens borne.

2 Libertatis, (b) as Villeines or Bondmen, and so a Champion must be a Freeman.

3 Annui census, i. liberi tenementi. (c) First, what yearely Freehold a Juror ought to haue that passeth vpon triall of the life of a man, or in a plea reall, or in a plea personall, where the debt or dammage in the Declaration amounteth to fortie Markes, Vid Sect.464. (*) Secondly, this Freehold must be in his owne right, in Fee simple, fee taile, for terme of his owne life, or for another mans life, although it be vpon condition, or in the right of his wife out of antient Demesne, for freehold within antient demesne will not serue, but if the debt or dammage amoun-

teth

reth not to fortie Markes, any Freehold sufficeth. (d) Thirdly, he must haue freehold in that Countie where the cause of the Action ariseth, and though he hath in another, it sufficeth not. (e) Fourthly, if after his returne he selleth away his land, or if Cesty que vie, or his wife dieth, or an entrie be made for the condition broken, so as his freehold be determined, he may be challenged for insufficiencie of Freehold.

(d) 19.H.6.9. 17.Ass.15.
(e) 12.H.7.4. 21.H.6.38. 7.H.4.1.

4 Hundredorum: First, by the Common Law in a plea reall, mixt, and personall, there ought to be foure of the Hundred (where the cause of Action ariseth) returned for their better notice of the cause, for Vicini vicinorum facta præsumuntur scire. But now since Littleton wrote, (f) in a plea personall if two Hundredors appeare, it sufficeth, and in an Attaint, (g) although the Jurie is double, yet the Hundredors are not double. Secondly, (h) If he hath either freehold in the Hundred, though it be to the value but of halfe an acre, or if he dwell there, though he hath no freehold in it, it sufficeth. (i) Thirdly, if the cause of the Action riseth in diuers Hundreds, yet the number shall suffice, as if it had come out of one, and not seuerall hundredors out of each hundred. (k) Fourthly, if there be diuers Hundreds within one Leet or Rape, if hee hath any Freehold, or dwell in any of those Hundreds, though not in the proper Hundred, it sufficeth. (l) Fiftly, if the Jurie come de corpore Cômitatus, or de proximo hundredo, where the one partie is Lord of the Hundred, or the like, there need no Hundredors bee returned at all. (m) Sixtly, if a Hundredor after he be returned, sell away his land within that Hundred, yet shall he not be challenged for the Hundred, for that this notice remaines, otherwise as hath been sayd for his insufficiencie of Freehold, for his feare to offend, and to haue lands wasted, &c. which is one of the reasons of Law, is taken away. (n) Seuenthly, he that challengeth for the Hundred, must shew in what hundred it is, and not driue the other partie to shew it. Eighthly, his challenge for the hundred is not simplicitèr, but secundum quid for though it bee found that he hath nothing in the Hundred, yet shall not he be drawne, but remaine præter H. that is, besides for the Hundred, and albeit he dwelleth or haue land in the Hundred, yet must he haue sufficient Freehold.

(f) 27.Eliz.cap.6.
(g) 7.H.4.47.
(h) 16.E.4.7.4.Mar.Br. Chall.216. 21.E.4.74.75. 9.H.6.66.
(i) 20.H.6.23.4. Mar.Br. Chall.216.
(k) 10.H.6.5. 12.H.4.14. 19.E.4.5.
(l) 37.H.6.11. 25.E.3.43.
(m) 21.H.6.38. 12.H.7.4.
(n) 7.Eliz.Dier.231.

3 Propter affectum: And this is of two sorts, either working a Principall challenge, or to the Fauour. And againe a principall challenge is of two sorts, either by Judgement of Law without any Act of his, or by Judgement of Law vpon his owne Act.

Bract.fol.185. Britt.fol.134.135. Fleta lib.4.c.p.8. 21.E.4.11.12.

And it is said that a principall challenge is, when there is expresse fauour or expresse malice. First, without any Act of his, as if the Juror bee (a) of bloud or kindred to either partie, Consanguineus which is compounded ex Con. & sanguine, quasi eodem sanguine natus, as it were issued from the same bloud, and this is a principall challenge, for that the Law presumeth that one Kinsman doth fauour another before a stranger, (b) and how farre remote soeuer he is of kindred, yet the Challenge is good. And if the Plaintife challenge a Juror, for kindred to the Defendant, it is no Counterplea to say that hee is of Kindred also to the Plaintife, though hee be in a neerer degree, For the words of the Venire facias forbideth the Juror to be of kindred to either partie.

(a) Britton.fol.135.
(b) Mirror.cap.3.de ordinance dattaine. Bracton, Britton, Fleta } vbi supra.

(c) If a body Politique or Incorporate, sole or aggregate of many, bring any action that concernes their body Politique or Incorporate, if the Juror be of kindred to any, that is, of that bodie, (although the body Politique or Incorporate) can haue no kindred, yet for that those bodies consist of naturall persons, it is a principall Challenge. (d) A Bastard cannot bee of kindred to any, and therefore it can be no principall Challenge. And here it is to be knowne that Affinitas, Affinitie hath in Law two sences. In his proper sence it is taken for that Neerenesse that is gotten by marriage, Cum duæ cognationes inter se diuisæ per nuptias copulantur & altera ad alterius fines accedit & inde dicitur Affinis In a larger sence Affinitas is taken also for Consanguinitie and Kindred, as in the Writ of Venire facias, and other where. (e) Affinitie or Alliance by Marriage is a principall Challenge, and equiualent to Consanguinitie when it is betweene either of the parties, as if the Plaintife or Defendant marry the Daughter or Cousin of the Juror, or the Juror marry the Daughter or Cousin of the Plaintife or Defendant, and the same continues or issue be had. But if the Sonne of the Juror hath married the Daughter of the Plantife, this is no principall Challenge, but to the fauour, because it not betweene the parties, much more may be said hereof, sed summa sequor fastigia rerum.

14.Eli.Dier.319. 21.E.4.75 40.Ass.20.Pl Com.f.l. 41.E.3.Chall.99. 21.E.4.75
(c) 7.E.4.4. 17.E.4.7. 21.E.4.20. 28.H.6.10. 28.Ass.18. 34.Ass.6.
(d) 41.E.3.Chall.99. 41.E.3.9. 26.H.6.Chall.163.
(e) Mirror, Bracton, Britton, Fleta } vbi supra. 3.E.4.14. 21.E.3.5.41. 43.E.3.Chall.93. 43.Ass.25 26. 22.E.4.3. 14.H.7.2. 15.H.7.9.

(f) If there be a Challenge for Cosinage, hee that taketh the Challenge must shew how the Juror is Cousin. But yet if the cosinage, that is the effect and substance be found, it sufficeth, for the Law preferreth that which is materiall before that which is formall.

(f) 19.H.8.7. 28.H.8. Dier.37. 1.Maria Dier 91. 2.Eliz.ibid.177.

(g) If the Juror haue part of the Land that dependeth vpon the same Title.

(g) Bracton, Britton, Fleta } vbi supra. Mirror vbi supra.

(h) If a Juror be within the hundred, Leet or any way within the Seigniory immediately or mediately, or any other distresse of either party, this is a principall Challenge. But if either party be within the distresse of the Juror this is no principall Challenge but to the fauour.

(h) 9.H.6.tit.Chall.27. 38.E.3.25. 22.E.4.Chall.61. 4.H.6.25. 3.H.6.39.36.H.6 Chall.46. 22.E.4.1. 27.Ass. 28. 22.E.3.12.

(i) If a witnesse named in the Deed be returned of the Jurie it is a good cause of Challenge of him. (k) So it is if one within age of one and twenty be returned, it is a good cause of Challenge.

(i) 23.Ass.11.
(k) Mirror vbi supra.

(l) 8.H.5.10. 33.H.6.1. 10.H.6.24. 7.H.4.11. 18.E.4.12. 21.E.4.74. 11.R.2.tit. Challenge 106. 27.Ass.13.
(m) 43.E.3.Chall.93. 8.H.5.10.

2. (l) Upon his own Act, as if the Juror hath given a verdict before for the same cause, albeit it be reversed by Writ of Error, or if after verdict, Judgement were arrested. So if hee hath given a former verdict upon the same Title or matter though betweene other persons. (m) But it is to be observed, that I may speake once for all, that in this and other like cases, hee that taketh the Challenge must shew the Record if he will have it take place as a principal Challenge, otherwise he must conclude to the favour, unlesse it be a Record of the same Court, and then hee must shew the day and tearme.

(n) Mirror. ubi supra. Britton. fol. 12. 11.Ass.36. 8.H.4.2. 7.E.4.4. 12.Ass.26. 19.Ass. 6. 40.Ass.10. 25.E.3.cap.3.
(o) 40.Ass.20. 2.H.4.15. 10.H.6.Chall.40. 7.H.6.49. 19.H.6.66. 4 E.4.11. 7.E.4.4.
(p) 20.H.6.39. 9.E.4.46. 35.H.6. 19.H.6. 3.H.6. 24. 7.H.7.10.
(q) Lib.9.fol.71. Peacocks Case.
(r) Mirror, Bracton, Britton — ubi supra. 12.Ass.36. 26.Ass.56. 28.Ass 16. 31.Ass 7. 44.Ass.18.
(s) 13.H.4.13. 11.R.2. Chall.164.
(t) Bracton, Fleta — ubi supra. 44.E.3.5.38. 44.Ass.23. 8.E.3.25. 43.E.3.31. 22.E.4.1. 38.H.6.6. 43.E.3. Chall.93. 11.H.4.26. 11.H.6.15. 32.E.3.Chall.189. 24.E.3.37. 39.Ass.2. 20.Ass.11. 43.Ass.46.
(u) 17.Ass.15.
(w) 8.E.3.39. 20.H.6.39. 33.H.8. Dier.48.
(x) 22.Eliz. Dier.367. Bracton, Britton, Fleta — ubi supra.
(y) 49.E.3.1.
(a) 9.E.4 6. 21.E.4.31. 22.E.4.3. 14.H.6.2. 30.E.4 2. 3.H.7.5. 22.Eliz. Dier. 367.

(n) So likewise one may be challenged, that he was Inditor of the Plaintife or Defendant eyther of Treason, Felony, Misprision, Trespasse, or the like in the same cause.

(o) If the Juror be Godfather to the Child of the Plaintife or Defendant, or è converso, this is allowed to be a good Challenge in our Bookes.

(p) If a Juror hath beene an Arbitrator chosen by the Plaintife or Defendant in the same cause, and have beene informed of, or treated of the matter, this is a principall Challenge. Otherwise if he were never informed nor treated thereof, and otherwise if he were indifferently chosen by eyther of the parties, though he treated thereof. But a (q) Commissioner chosen by one of the parties for examination of witnesses in the same cause, is no principal cause of Challenge for he is made by the King under the great Seale, and not by the party as the Arbitrator is, but he may upon cause be challenged for favour.

(r) If hee bee of Counsaile, Servant, or of Robes, or Fee, of either party it is a principall Challenge.

(s) If any after he be returned doe eate and drinke at the charge of either party, it is a principall cause of Challenge, otherwise it is of a Trior after he be sworne.

(t) Actions brought eyther by the Juror against eyther of the parties, or by eyther of the parties against him, which imply malice or displeasure, are causes of principall Challenge, unlesse they be brought by Covyn eyther before or after the returne, for if Covin be found, then it is no cause of Challenge; other Actions which doe not imply malice or displeasure, are but to the favour.

(u) In a cause where the Parson of a Parish is partie, and the right of the Church commeth in debate, a Parishioner is a principall Challenge. Otherwise it is in debt, or any other Action where the right of the Church commeth not in question.

(w) If eyther party labour the Juror and give him any thing to give his verdict, this is a principall Challenge. But if eyther party labour the Juror to appeare & to doe his conscience, this is no Challenge at all, but lawfull for him to doe it.

(x) That the Juror is a fellow Servant with eyther party, is no principall Challenge but to the favour.

(y) Neyther of the parties can take that Challenge to the Polls, which he might have had to the Array.

(a) Note if the Defendant may have a pincipall cause of Challenge to the array, if the Sherife returne the Jury, the Plaintife in that case may for his one expedition alledge the same, and pray Processe to the Coroners, which hee cannot have, unlesse the Defendant will confesse it, but if the Defendant will not confesse it, then the Plaintife shall have a Venire facias to the Sherife, and the Defendant shall never take any challenge for that cause, and so in like cases. But on the part of the Defendant any such matter shall not be alledged, and Processe prayed to the Coroners, because he may challenge the Jury for that cause, and can bee at no preiudice.

(b) Mirror cap. 3. dordinance dattiant. Bract. lib.4. fol 185. Britt. fol. 134. 135. Fleta lib. 4. cap.8. 7.H.6.25.
(c) 9.H.7.3. 10.H.7.20. 3.H.7.2. 10.E.4.12. 15.E.4 18. 12.Ass.23.

(b) Challenge concluding to the favour, when either partie cannot take any principall Challenge, but sheweth causes of favour, which must bee left to the conscience and discretion of the Triors upon hearing their evidence to find him favourable or not favourable. But yet some of them come neerer to a principall Challenge then other. (c) As if the Juror be of kindred, or under the distresse of him in the Reversion or remaynder, or in whose right the Avowrie or Justification is made, or the like: These be no principall Challenges, because he in Reversion, Remaynder, or in whose right the Avowrie or Justification is not partie to the Record, otherwise it is if they were made parties by Aide, Resceipt, or Voucher, and yet the cause of favour is apparant; so it is of all principall causes, if they were party to the Record. Now the causes of favour are infinite, and thereof somewhat may bee gathered of that which hath beene said, and the rest I purposely leave the Reader to the reading of our Bookes concerning that matter. For all which the rule of Law is, that hee must stand indifferent as hee stand unsworne.

(d) 6.R.2.Chall.141. 19.Ass.6. 38.Ass 22 11.R.2 Chall.165. 4.H.5.ibid.153.

(d) The subiect may challenge the Polles, where the King is party. And if a man be outlawed of Treason or Felony, at the suite of the King, and the party for avoyding thereof alledgeth imprisonment or the like, at the time of the Outlawrie, though the issue be ioyned upon a collaterall point, yet shall the party have such Challenges, as if hee had beene arraigned upon the crime it selfe, for this by a meanes concerneth his life also.

4. Propter

¶ *Propter delictum.* (c) As if the Iuror bee attainted or conuicted of treason, or felony, or for any offence to life or member, or in attaint for a false verdict, or for periury as a witnesse, or in a conspiracie at the suite of the King, or in any suite (either for the King, or for any subiect) be adiudged to the Pillory, tumbrell, or the like, or to be branded, or to be stigmatique, or to haue any other corporall punishment whereby he becommeth infamous (for it is a maxime in law Repellitur à sacramento infamis) these and the like are principall causes of challenge. So it is if a man be outlawed in trespasse, debt or any other action, for he is Exlex, and therefore is not legalis homo. And old bookes haue said that if he be excommunicated, he could not be of a Iury.

(c) *Mirror* *Bracton* *Britton* *Fleta* } *Vbi supra.* 11.*H*.4.41. 12.*H*.4.10. 33.*H*.6.21.

(f) See the statutes of W.2. and Artic. supra cartas, what persons the Sherife ought to returne on Iuryes, And see F.N.B. breue de non ponendis in Assisis & iuratis, and the Register in the same writ. And see there what remedy the party hath that is returned against Law.

(f) *W* 2.*ca*.38. *Artic. super cart ca*.9. F.N.B.165. & 166. *Regist*.

It is necessarie to be knowne the time when the challenge is to be taken. (g) First hee that hath diuers challenges must take them all at once, and the Law so requireth indifferent trialls, as diuers challenges are not accounted double. (h) Secondly, if one be challenged by one party, if after he be tried indifferent, it is time ynough for the other party to challenge him. (i) Thirdly after challenge to the Array, and triall duely returned, if the same party take a challenge to the polles, he must shew cause presently. (k) Fourthly, so if a Iuror be formerly sworne, if he be challenged he must shew cause presently, and that cause must rise since he was sworne. (l) Fiftly, when the King is party, or in an appeale of felony, the defendant that challengeth for cause, must shew his cause presently. Sixtly, If a man in case of treason or felony challenge for cause, and he be tried indifferent, yet hee may challenge him peremptorily. Seuenthly, a challenge for the Hundred must bee taken before so many bee sworne, as will serue for hundredors, or else he looseth the aduantage thereof.

(g) 9.*E*.4.16 10.*H*.5.9. 37.*H*.6.8. 3.*H*.6.38. *Brooke tit chall*.8. 7.*H* 5.40. 14.*H*.7 5.6.
(h) 9.*E* 4.16. 27.*H*.8.2.
(i) 43.*E*.3. *Chal*.93. 20. *E*.3.*ibid*.116. 22.*E*.4 *ibid*.61 7.*H*.4 41. 3.*El Dower* 201.
(k) 22.*E*.4.1. 9.*H*.5.6.
(l) 1.*H*.5.10. 38.*Ass*.22.

8 (m) In a writ of Right, the grand Iury must be challenged before the foure knights before they be returned in Court, for after they be returned in Court, there cannot any challenge be taken vnto them,

(m) 7.*H*.4.20. 15.*E*.4.1.

9 Nota (n) The Array of the Tales shall not bee challenged by any one party, vntill the Array of the principall be tried; but if the plaintife challenge the Array of the principall, the defendant may challenge the Array of the Tales. After one hath taken a challenge to the polle, he cannot challenge the Array.

(n) 9 *E*.4.27. 9.*H*.5.11. 34.*Ass*.6.13.*E*.3. *Chal*.108

Now it is to bee seene how challenges to the Array of the principall Pannell, or of the Tales, or of the polles shall be tried, and who shall bee triors of the same, and to whom processe shall bee awarded.

1 (o) If the plaintife alledge a cause of challenge against the Sherife, the processe shall be directed to the Coroners, if any cause against any of the Coroners, processe shall bee awarded to the rest, if against all of them, then the Court shall appoint certaine Elisors or Elisors (so named ab eligendo) because they are named by the Court, against whose returne no challenge shall be taken to the Array, because they were appointed by the Court, but hee may haue his challenge to the polles. (p) Note if processe be once awarded for the partialitie of the Sherife, though there be a new Sherife, yet processe shall neuer be awarded to him; for the entry is ita quod vicecomes se non intromittat. But otherwise it is, for that he was tenant to either partie or the like.

(o) 18.*E* 4.8.
(p) 15.*H*.7.9. 14.*H*.7.31. 18.*E*.43.

(q) 2 If the Array be challenged in Court, it shall be tried by two of them that be impanelled to be appointed by the Court; for the triors in that case shall not exceed the number of two, vnlesse it be by consent. But when the Court names two for some speciall cause alledged by either partie, the Court may name others, if the Array be quashed, then processe shall be awarded, vt supra.

(q) 29.*Ass*.3. 19.*H*.6.48. 21.*H*.6.*Chal* 38.33.*H*.6.21 4.*E*.4.17.43.*E*.3.*Chal*.95. 2.*R*.2. *ibid*.101. 34.*Ass*.6. 27.*Ass*.28. 43 *Ass*.26.

(r) If a pannell vpon a Venire facias be returned, and a Tales, and the Array of the principall is challenged, the triors, which trie and quash the Array, shall not trie the Array of the Tales, for now it is as if there had beene no appearance of the principall pannell, but if the triors affirme the Array of the principall, then they shall trie the Array of the Tales. If the plaintife challenge the Array of the principall, and the defendant the Array of the Tales, there the one of the principall, and the other of the Tales shall trie both Arrayes. For other matter concerning the Tales, see (s) in my Reports matters worthy of obseruation. (t) When any challenge is made to the polles, two triors shall bee appointed by the Court, and if they trie one indifferent, and he be sworne, then he and the two triors shall trie another, and if another be tried indifferent, and he be sworne, then the two triers cease, and the two that bee sworne on the Iurie shall trie the rest. (v) If the plaintife challenge ten, and the defendant one, and the twelfth is sworne, because one cannot trie alone, there shall be added to him one challenged by the plaintife and the other by the defendant. When the triall is to be had by two Counties, the manner of the triall is worthy of obseruation, and apparant in our (w) bookes. (x) If the foure knights in the writ of Right be challenged they shall trye themselues, and they shall choose the

(r) 9.*E*.4.46. 19.*H* 6.48. 34.*Ass*.6. 7.*E*.6. *Dyer*.78. 9.*H*.5.11.
(s) *Lib*.10.*fo*.104.105. *Denbawds case*.
(t) 19.*H* 6.9. 22.*E*.4. *Chal*.61.62.
(u) 7.*H*.4.41.
(w) 11.*H*.4.61.48.*E*.3.30 11.*H*.4.63.
(x) 22.*E*.3.18.39.*E*.3.3.

(y) 49.*E*.3.1.2.

(z) 2.*H*.4.14. 4.*E*.4.1. 10.*E*.3.32. 22.*Ass*.28.31. 21.*H*.6.56. 16.*Ass*.1. 5.*E*.5.35.36.

the graund Assise, and trie the challenges of the parties. (y) If the cause of challenge touch the dishonour or discredit of the Juror, he shall not bee examined upon his oath, but in other cases he shall be examined upon his oath, to informe the triors. (z) If an inquest be awarded by default, the defendant hath lost his challenge, but the plaintife may challenge for iust cause, and that shall be examined and tried.

Wheresoever the plaintife is to recover per visum iuratorum, there ought to bee sixe of the Jury that have had the view, or knowen the land in question, so as he be able to put the plaintife in possession if he recover.

(a) 8.*H*.5.*tit.Chall*.167. 2.*H*.4.3. 34.*E*.3.*Chall*.175. 21.*H*.6.56. 8.*E*.4.3. 16.*E*.4.1.
* *Bracton, lib*.4.*fo*.185.

In a Proprietate probanda, and a writ to enquire for wast, the parties have been received to take their challenges. (a) But passing over many things touching this matter, I will conclude with the saying of * Bracton, Plures autem aliæ sunt causæ recusandi iuratores de quibus ad præsens non recolo, sed quæ iam enumeratæ sunt, sufficiant exempli causa. And so let us returne to Littleton.

¶ *De visneto, &c.* It should be Viceneto: Vicenetum is derived of this word Vicinus and signifieth Neighbourhood, or a place neere at hand or a Neighbour place. And the reason wherfore the Jury must be of the neighbourhood, is for that Vicinus facta vicini præsumitur scire, all which is implied in this word (&c.)

¶ *Quod summoneat eos, &c.* Summoneo is compounded of Sub & moneo, & Euphoniæ gratia it is said summoneo, to warne or sommon, as in this case the Sherife must warne or summon the Recognitors of the Assise to appeare before the Justices of Assise, &c. And it is truly said (b) that in this case Legittimam summonitionem recipere, in propria persona vbicunque inuentus fuerit in comitatu in quo fuerit res petita, qui quidem sinon inveniatur sufficit, si ad domiciliũ fiat, dũ tamen alicui de familia sua manifeste fuerit relata, &c.

(b) *Bracton lib*.5.*fo*.333.334. *Mirr.cap*.2.§.19. *Fleta lib*.6.*ca*.6. *Britt.ca*.121.

¶ *Per bonos summonitores.* Here two things are to bee observed. First, that the summoners must be Boni (id est) fide digni vt valeant legittimum testimonium perhibere, cum inde per Iusticiarios fuerint requisiti. (c) And another saith, Fems, ne serfs, ne ensans, ne nul ensamys, ne nul que nest fife tenant, ne poet este bone summoner. 2. It is spoken in the plurall number Per bonos summonitores, and therefore there must bee two at the least. Nec sufficit quod summonitio fiat per vnum tantum, &c. necesse est igitur quod per duos ad minus fiat, &c. There is also a summons of a tenant in a reall action, whereof, and of Pernors and Veiors you shall reade (d) plentifully and plainely in our bookes, whereunto being matter of course I referre you.

(c) *Bracton*, *Britton*, *Fleta*. } *Vbi supra.*
Bracton, *Britton*, *Fleta*, *Mirror* } *Vbi supra.*
(d) *Regist.iudicial*.1.2.107. 43.*E*.3.32. 24.*E*.3.35. 3.*E*.3.48. 50.*E*.3.16. 8.*H*.6.1.*b*. *F.N.B*.97.
(e) *Mirror*, *Bracton*, *Britton*, *Fleta* } *Vbi supra.*

Item Summonitionum alia est Generalis, alia Specialis, whereof you shall finde excellent matter in our (e) old bookes, where you shall also reade at large De Sũmonitione, Præsummonitione, & Resummonitione.

¶ *Facere recognitionem.* Cognitio is knowledge, or knowledgement or opinion, and Recognition is a serious acknowledgement or opinion upon such matters of fact as they shall have in charge, and thereupon the Jurors are called Recognitores assisæ, Vid. Sect. 233 Recognitio taken for the confession of the Tenant.

¶ *Pannell* is an English word, and signifieth a little part, for a Pane is a part, and a Pannell is a little part (as a Pannell of wainscot, a Pannell of a saddle, and a pannell of Parchment wherein the Jurors names be written and annexed to the writ. And a Jury is said to be impannelled, when the Sherife hath entred their names into the pannell, or little peece of Parchment in Pannello assisæ.

Register 223.

¶ *Briefe de droit.* Breue de Recto, Writs of right be of two natures 1. a writ of Right, whereof Littleton here speaketh, which is the highest writ of all other reall writs whatsoever, and hath the greatest respect, &c. and the most assured and finall iudgement, and therefore this writ is called a writ of Right right, and this in (f) old bookes is called Dreit dreit, and this writ Est darrein remedie de touts recoueries enter touts ordres des pleas, and the Jury in this writ is called Magna assisa or magna Iurata, as Littleton here saith. 2. Writs of Right in their nature, as the Rationabile parte, and Ne iniuste vexes.

(f) *Bracton Lib*.5.*fo*.372. *Britton fol*.117. *Fleta lib*.6.*ca*.1. *Glanuil lib*.1.*c*.4.5.& *lib*.2.*ca*.7. *lib*.12.*cap*.1

¶ *De Recto.* Rectũ, is a proper and significant word for the right that any hath, and wrong or Injury, is in French aptly called Tort, because Injury & wrong is wrested or crooked, being contrary to that which is right and streight. Now the Law that is Linea recta est index sui & obliqui And Britton * saith that Tort a la ley est contrarye, and as aptly for the cause aforesaid is injury in English called wrong. And Iniuria is derived of In and ius, because it is contrary to right, so as A faire tort is facere tortum, and Fleta saith, (g) Est autem ius publicũ & priuatũ quod ex naturalibus præceptis aut gentium, aut ciuilibus est collectum, & quod in iure scripto ius appellatur, id in lege Angliæ rectum esse dicitur. And in the (h) Mirror and other places of the law it is called, Droit, as droit defend the Law defendeth.

* *Britton, fo*.116. *Fleta lib*.2 *ca*.1.
(g) *Fleta.lib*.6.*ca*.1.
(h) *Mirror, ca*.2.§ 16. & *cap*.5.§.2.

¶ *En le register.* Register, is a most ancient booke of the common

Law

Law, and it is twofold, viz. Registrum breuium originalium, and Registrum breuium iudicialium. It is a French word and signifieth a memoriall of writs. Sometimes the Register of originall writs is called Registrum cancellariæ, because all originall writs doe issue out of the Chancery, as Extra officinam Iustitiæ, for the antiquity and estimation of which booke, I referre the reader to the Epistle before the tenth part of my Commentaries.

13.E.1.ca.24. Pl.Com.228.b.

¶ *Magna Assisa eligenda*, **Is a iudiciall writ to the Sherife to** returne foure lawfull Knights before the Iustices there upon their oathes to returne twelue Knights of the Vicenage to trie the Mise in a writ of Right.

¶ *Assise de common de pasture, &c.* **Of what things an** Assise **of** Nouel disseisin lay at the Common Law, and of what by the statute, you may reade at large in my (k) Reports in Iehu Webbes Case, where the Authorities of Law are plentifully cited, and they and the statute well explaned. But since Littleton wrote, a man may haue (l) an Assise of Nouell disseisin, Assise of Mordanc, or any Præcipe quod reddat, Quod ei deforceat, writs of Dower, or other writs originall, as the case shall require of Tythes, Pencions or other Ecclesiasticall or Spirituall profit, if he be disseised, deforced, wronged, or otherwise kept, or put from the same, which by the Lawes and Statutes of the Realme are made temporall, or admitted to be or abide in temporall hands, so as by the said Act a Lay man hauing tythes or offerings may either sue for the substraction or with-holding of the same in the Ecclesiasticall Court, or at the Common law at his election. And seeing no speciall writ is giuen * by the statute; the partie must haue a generall writ of Assise de lebero tenemento, and make a speciall plaint, But his Præcipe must be Quod reddat omnes & omnimodas decimas maiores, mixtas, & minutas, infra Dale quoquo modo crescen' contingen' ac annuatim renouan', or the like, according to his case. (m) But neither Assise nor any Præcipe did lye of them as of Tythes or any other Ecclesiasticall dutie at the Common Law for the Assise brought of the Tenth part of all manner of Corne growing in C. acres of land after the Tythes of the Parson taken was a Lay profit Apprender, and no Ecclesiasticall dutie.

(k) Lib. 8. fo. 45.
(l) 32. H. 8. ca. 7.
* 7. E. 6. Dier. 83. &c.

But Tythes or other Ecclesiasticall duties, that came to the Crowne by the statutes (n) of 27. H. 8. 31. H. 8. 37. H. 8, and 1. E. 6. are by those statutes and this of 32. H. 8. and of 1 and 2. Ph. & Mariæ in the hands of Lay men temporall inheritances and shall be accounted Assets; and husbands shall be Tenants by the Curtesie, and wiues endowed of them, and shall haue other incidents belonging to temporall inheritances, only this Ecclesiasticall quality they haue, that the owner or possessor thereof may sue for the subtraction of the same in the Ecclesiasticall Court.

(m) 44. E. 3. 5. Vid. Regist. 165. Vid le briefe de indicauit. W 2. ca. 5. Consimili in casu. fe offatis ca. Vltimo. Bracton, lib. 5. fo. 402. Britton, fo. 260. Regist. fo. 15. 4. E. 3. 27. 29. 16 E. 3. quare Imp. 147. Vid 2 H 3. tit Grant. 89.
(n) 27. H. 8. of Monasteries not printed. 31. H. 8. ca 13. 37. H 8. ca. 4. 1 E. 6. ca 14. 1. & 2. Ph. & Mar. ca. 8. 2 E. 3. ca. 13.

But by another (o) statute, remedy is giuen aswell to the Lay person, as to the Ecclesiasticall person for subtraction of all manner of prediall Tythes, and he shall recouer the treble value if they be not iustly deuided or set forth, an) albeit the treble value be not expresly giuen to the proprietarie of the Tythes, yet forasmuch as he is the partie grieued, & he hath the propertie and interest in the tythes, the treble value is giuen to him, & whensoeuer a statute giueth a forfeiture or penalty against him which wrongfully detaineth or dispossesseth another of his duty or interest, in that case he that hath the wrong shall haue the forfeiture or penaltie, & shall haue an action therefore upon the statute at the Common Law, and the King shall not haue the forfeiture in that case. And so it was (p) adiudged in the Exchequer upon conference with other Ia)ges in an information for the treble value for not setting out of tythes in Iclington in the County of Cambr. And if the proprietarie will sue for such subtraction of tythes in the Ecclesiasticall Court, then he shal recouer but the double value by the expresse words of the Act, wherein it is to be obserued, that the act of Parliament doth giue a temporall remedy at the Common lawe to Parsons and Vicars and other Ecclesiasticall persons for an Ecclesiasticall dutie, and to Lay men proprietaries of tythes the like remedy, but as it hath beene said, they haue election either to sue for the treble value at the Common Law, or for the double value in the Ecclesiasticall Court, or for subtraction of tythes there also.

(o) 2. E. 6. ca. 13.
(p) Pasch. 29. Eliz. betweene the Queene and Wood in the Exchequer, and so it was resolued by all the Iudges upon conference, Mich. 4. Ia. Regis.

¶ *Assise de Mordancester*. Assisa mortis antecessores. (q) **This writ a** man may haue after the decease of his immediate Ancestor, as where his father, mother, brother, sister, uncle or aunt die seised of any lands and an estranger abate, &c.

(q) Britton, fo. 178. 179. &c. Bracton, lib. 4. tract. 3. per to um, fo. 252. &c. Mirror, ca. 2. § 15. F.N.B. 114. &c.

¶ *Assise de darreine presentment*. Assisa vltimæ præsentationis, **whereof** you shall reade (r) plentifully in our bookes.

(r) Britton, ca. 90 fo. 222. Bract. lib 4. fo. 238. Mirror ubi supra. F.N.B. 195. Regist. orig. 30.

To these may be added Assisa vtrum or Iuris vtrum (s) which is the highest writ a Parson, Vicar, &c. can haue for the recouering of the Glebe land, &c. in right of his Church. But it may be demanded wherefore these originall writs, are called by the speciall name of Assises more then other originall writs, and here Littleton yeeldeth the reason, because that by these writs, it is commanded to the Sherife Quod summoneat 12 which is as much to say, as to sommon a Iury. So as in these cases, there is a Iury returned the first day, and they are to

(s) Bracton, fo. 285. 286. Britton, ca 95. fo. 234. Mirror, ubi supra. F.N.B. 48. 49.

appeare as soone as the Defendant. And because by these writs a Jury is to be returned the Law calleth them Assises, Ab effectu, because an Assise (which in this sence signifieth a Jury) is to be returned. But besides the signification of the writ * of Assise whereof Littleton here speaketh, it signifieth the whole proceeding upon the writ.

* Mag. Chart ca. 12. And W. 2. ca. 25.

In other originall writs regularly no Jury is to be returned before the appearance of the parties and an issue ioyned betweene them, and therefore these other originalls are not called Assises.

¶ *Pur vn ordinance.* Here Assisa signifieth, an Ordinance, &c. Ordinance, Ordinatio is derived of the verbe Ordinare, To ordaine or set in order. And note, an Act (r) of Parliament (as Littleton here prooveth) is an Ordinance, for it sets downe orders which are to be kept as Lawes: and so is Ordinatio Forestæ, Ordinatio de Inquisitionibus, and Ordinatio contra Seruientes, and other Statutes many times called Ordinances, and it is said almost in everie Act of Parliament, Be it therefore ordained, &c. by authoritie of this Parliament, or the like. But e converso everie Ordinance is not a Statute, as that of 8. H. 6. cap. 29 for everie statute must be made by the King, with the assents of the Lords and Commons, and if it appeare by the Act, that it was made by two of them onely, it is no statute.

(r) 19. H. 3. Juris utrum 16. 39. E. 3. 1. 7. 42. E. 3. 38. 29. E. 3. 7. Regist. orig. 189 33. E. 1. 5. R. 2. ca. 2. Vid. li. 8. le Princes case.

The example put by Littleton, is Assisa panis & ceruitiæ, (s) This Ordinance was made at a Parliament holden anno 51. H. 3. and the like Ordinance was made, entituled Assisa ceruitiæ, which you may see in old Magna Charta fol. 57. b. (t) And so Assisa de Clareden, which was in 10. H. 2. and Assisa Forestæ, ordained in anno 14. E. 1. and such like. And aptly an Ordinance of Parliament Antiquitie hath called an Assise, for that an Act of Parliament doth ordaine such a certaine order, as nothing can be done more or lesse by right. (u) And Fleta saith, Et habet rex in potestate sua, vt leges & consuetudines & assisas in regno suo prouisas & approbatas & iuratas, &c. Where Assises are taken for statutes, which are the effects of the Sessions of Parliament.

(s) Mir. ca. 1. §. 13. & ca. 4 de Articles de Eire. Bract. li. 3. fo. 136. (t) Stanf. fo. 118. Mir. ca. 2. §. 15. Hoveden 313. Regist. orig. 279. (u) Flet. li. 1. ca. 17.

De ponderibus & mensuris, Of weights and Measures is a most necessarie learning to bee knowne, and dayly in use, but it belongeth not to this Treatise. In some other (if God so please) somewhat shall be sayd of them.

Section 235.

¶ *ET le tenant attorna.* Here it appeareth that an Attornament (that is an Agreement to the grant) is no seisin of the rent.

¶ *Il ne ad ascun remedie, &c.* Which is as much to say, as hee hath not any remedie either at the Common Law, or in any Court of equitie, which is worthie of observation.

See more of this in the Chapter of Attornment Sect. 565.

¶ *Voile doner al grantee vn denier, ou vn maile, &c. en nosme de seisin de rent, &c.* Here it is to be observed, that payment of any money in name of seisin of the rent, before any rent become due, is a good seisin of the rent to have an Assise when it is due, and that which is given in the name of seisin of the rent, worketh his

¶ Item si soit seignior & Tenant, & le Seignior granta le rent son tenant per son fait a vn auter, sauant a luy les seruices, & l' Tenant atturna, ceo est vn Rent Secke, come est dit adeuant. Mes si l' rent a luy soit denie al prochein iour de payment, il ny ad ascun remedie, pur ceo que il auoit d' ceo ascun possessiō. Mes si le Tenant quaunt il atturna al grantee, ou apres, voile doner al grantee vn denier, ou vn maile, &c. en nosme

ALso if there bee Lord and Tenant, and the Lord granteth the rent of his Tenant by Deed to another, sauing to him the other seruices, and the Tenant atturneth, that is a Rent secke, as it is aforesaid But if the rent be denied him at the next day of payment, hee hath no remedie, because that he had not thereof any possession. But if the Tenant when he atturneth to the Grauntee, or afterwards, wil giue a penie or a halfe-penie to the Grauntee in

nosme de seisin de le rent, donques si apres a le procheine iour de payment le rent a luy soit denie, il auer Assise de Nouel Disseisin. Et issint est lou hõe granta per son fait vn annual rẽt issuant hors de sa terre a vn auter, &c. si le Grantor adonques ou apres paya al Grantee vn denier, ou vn maile en nosme de seisin de le rent, donques si apres al procheine iour de payment le rent soit denie, le Grantee poet auer assise, ou autrement nemy, &c.

name of Seisin of rent, then if after at the next day of payment the Rent bee denied him, hee shall haue an Assise of *Nouel Disseisin*. And so it is, if a man graunt by his Deed a yearely Rent issuing out of his land, to another, &c. if the Grauntour then after pay to the Grauntee a penie or an halfe-pennie in name of Seisin of the Rent, then if after the next day of payment the Rent bee denied, the Grauntee may haue an Assise, or else not, &c.

effect to giue season, and yet is no part of the rent, nor shal be abated out of the rent: but you shall read more hereof hereafter, Sect. 565.

¶ *Vn denier, ou vn maile, &c.* Heere by this (&c.) is implied, that so it is of the gift of a Sheep, or an Oxe, or a Ring, or a paire of Gloues, or a pound of Pepper, or of any valuable thing.

¶ *Issint si home grãt per son fait vn annual rent issuant hors de son terre a vn auter, &c.* By this (&c.) is implied, that the grant and deliuerie of the Deed is no seisin of the rent: and that a seisin in law, which the Grantee hath by the grant is not sufficient to maintaine an Assise, or any other reall Action, but there must be an actuall Seisin.

Sect. 236.

¶ Item de Rent secke, home poet auer Assise de Mortdancester, ou Briefe de Ayel, ou de Cosinage, & touts auters manners dactions Reals, come la case gist, sicome il poet aver dascun auter rent.

ALso of Rent secke a Man may haue an Assise of *Mortdauncester*, or a Writ of *Ayel* or *Cosinage*, and all other manner of Actions realls, as the case lieth, as hee may haue of any other Rent.

¶ B*riefe de Ayel.* Breue de Auo. This Writ lieth where the Grandfather or Grandmother was seised of any land in fee the day that he died, and an estranger abate, the heyre shall haue this Writ. (w) And if the great Grandfather, Besaiel, Proavus, or great Grandmother Besaieles Proauia, be seised, as is aforesayd, and die, &c. the heire shall haue a Writ De Basaiel, proauo, or besaiels, proauia, &c.

Bract. li. 2 fo 67. Brit cap. 89. & c. 76. Flet. li. 5. c. 7, 8. &c. F.N.B. 221.

(w) 6. E. 3. 34. 7. E. 3. 46. Regist. 226. F.N.B. 221. a. b. Brit. ca. 76.

¶ *Briefe de Cosinage.* Breue de Consanguinitate. (a) This Writ lieth where the great Grandfathers father, Tritavus, (id est) tertius avus, or abavus, (id est) avus aui was seised as is aforesayd, or where grandfathers or grandmothers mother, &c. vt supra. And so it is of the seisin of the brother of the grandfathers grandfather, &c.

(a) Bract. li. 2 fo 67. Brit. ca. 89. & ca. 76. Flet l. 5. ca. 7, 8. F.N.B. 221.

¶ *Rent secke.* And so it is of a Rent charge to all respects.

¶ *Et touts auters manners dactions reals.* Hereupon some haue gathered, that a man shall haue a Writ of Right of a rent seck, or of a rent charge, albeit they be against common right. But that which hath beene sayd by Littleton of an Assise of Mortdauncester, a Writ of Ayel, Cosinage, and other Actions realls, is to be vnderstood after Seisin had by some of the Ancestors of the Demandant, for without an actuall seisin, or a seisin in Deed, none of these are maintainable.

15. E. 2. Hors de son fee 27. 3. E. 3. 35. 4. E. 3. Droit 31. F.N.B. 6. 14. E. 4. 6. Diuersitie des Courts 117. 33. E. 3. Judgm. 252.

Section 237

¶ Rescous. Rescussus is here described by Littleton: It is an antient French word comming from Rescourrer, (id est) Recuperare, that is, to take from, to rescue, or recouer. Rescous is a taking away, and setting at libertie against law, a distresse taken, or a person arrested by the Processe or course of Law. And all is one, as the point of the Disseisin to rescue, the distresse after it is taken, and before hand to resist and withstand the taking of it; but yet it is no Rescous untill it bee distreyned. And therefore you may make fixe Disseisins of a Rent seruice: Rescous of a distresse, resistance to distreyne, Repleuin, Inclosure, Counterpleading of the title, and vouching of a Record, and failing. If the Tenant rescue the distres, and after is disseised of the Tenancie, yet the Assise lieth against him, for the disseisin done of the Rent by the Rescous.

18.E.3.3. 44.E.3.20.b. 20.H.7.1.a. 21.H.7.40.a. F.N.B.102.b. 6.H.6. Disseisin 9. 4.E.2. Ass.43. 8.E.1. ibid. 416. W.2.cap.6. 12.H.7. Kelway 30.

¶ *Pur son rent arere.* Here Littleton decideth an antient question in our Books, (p) viz. That the rent must be behind, or else the Tenaunt may make Rescous: for if no rent be behind when the Distresse is taken, how can the Rescous amount to a disseisin of the rent when none is due? And so it is, if the Tenaunt resist the Lord to distreyne, when there is no rent behind, this can be no disseisin of the rent for the cause aboue sayde, and this (as it appeareth by Littleton) holdeth as well in case of a rent seruice betweene Lord and Tenant, as in case of a Rent charge, &c. And so I heard Sir Christopher Wray Chiefe Justice say, That he had adiudged it: And that which the Tenant may doe when there is no rent behind, may a stranger doe, if his beasts be distrained. If the Tenant tender the rent to the Lord when he is to take the distresse, if notwithstanding the Lord will distreyne, the Tenant may make rescous. If the rent of the Lord be behind, and the Lord distreyne the Cattell of the Tenant in the highway within his fee, the Tenant may make Rescous,

(p) 6.R.2. Rescous 10. 40.E.3.33. 31.E.3. Rescous 17. 22.H.6.2.b. 6.E.4.11.b. 7.E.4.20. 5.E.4.8. 34.H.6.47. F.N.B.102.E. 2.H.4.21.16. 4.E.6. Distres Br. 24. 39.E.3.35. 39.H.6.7 Lib.4.fo.11. Bevills Case. 8.H.4.1.

7.E.4.24.

17.E.3.43. Vide 111. Rescous 14.

¶ Item, sont trois causes de Disseisin de Rent Seruice, s. Rescous, Repleuin, & Enclosure: Rescous est, quaunt le Seignior en la terre tenus de luy distrein p̃ s̃ rent arere & le distres d̃ luy soit rescous: ou si le seignior vient sur la terre, & voile distreyner, & le Tenant ou aut home ne luy voile suffer, &c. Repleuin est, quant le Seignior ad distreyne, et Repleuin soit fait d̃ les distresse per Brief, ou per Plaint. Enclosur est, si les Terres ou les Tenements sont issint encloses, que le Seignior ne poyt vener deins les tres ou tenements pur distreyñ. Et la cause pur que tiels choses issint faits sont disseisins al Seignior, est pur ceo que per tiels choses le Seignior est disturbe de le meane per que il doit auoire & vener a son rent, s̃, de le distresse.

ALSO there bee three causes of Disseisin of Rent Seruice, that is to say, Rescous, Repleuin, and Enclosure: Rescous is when the Lord distraineth in the land holden of him, for his rẽt behind, if the distresse be rescued from him, or the Lord come vpon the land, and will distreyne, and the Tenant or another man wil not suffer him, &c. Repleuin is, when the Lord hath distrained, and Repleuin is made of the distresse by writ or by Plaint. Enclosure is, if the lands and tenements bee so enclosed, that the lord may not come within the Lands and tenements for to distreyne. And the cause why such things so done be Disseisins made to the Lord, is for this, that by such things the Lord is disturbed of the meane by which he ought to haue come to his rent, s. of the distresse.

scous, for that it is defended by Law to distreine in the high way. And by the same reason if the Lord will distreyne aueria carucæ, where there is a sufficient distresse to bee taken besides, or if the Lord distreyne any thing that is not distreynable eyther by the Common Law, or by any Statute, the Tenant may make rescous.

Note, there is a Rescous in Deed and a Rescous in Law: of a Rescous in Deed somewhat hath already beene spoken. A Rescous in Law is when a man hath taken a distresse, and the cattle distreyned as he is driuing of them to the Pownd goe into the House of the Owner, if hee that tooke the distresse demaund them of the Owner, and hee deliuer them not, this is a Rescous in Law, and so of the like.

3.E.3 *Rescous*.12.

And euery word of Littleton is materiall, for he sayth;

¶ *En la terre tenus de luy* And therefore if the Lord distreine out of his fee in Lands not holden of him, the Tenant may make rescous, vnlesse it bee in some speciall Cases.

As if the Lord come to distreine Cattle which hee seeth then within his fee, and the Tenant or any other to preuent the Lord to distreine, driue the Cattle out of the fee of the Lord into some place out of his fee, yet may the Lord freshly follow, and distreyne the Cattle, and the Tenant cannot make rescous, albeit the place wherein the distresse is taken, is out of his fee, for now in iudgement of Law the distresse is taken within his fee, and so shall the writ of of Rescous suppose.

44.E.3.20.6.R.2.*Rescous* 11 11.H.7 4.21.H.7.40.34.H.6.18.16.E.4.10.*lib.9 fol.22 in case de auowrie.*

But if the Lord comming to distreyne had no view of the Cattle within his fee, though the Tenant driue them off purposely, or if the Cattle of themselues after the view goe out of the fee, or if the Tenant after the view remoue them for any other cause, then to preuent the Lord of his distresse, then cannot the Lord distreyne them out of his fee, and if he doth, the Tenant may make rescouse.

If a man come to distreyne for Damage Feasant, and see the beasts in his soyle, and the Owner chase them out of purpose before the distresse taken, the Owner of the soyle cannot distreyne them, and if he doth the Owner of the Cattle may rescue them, for the beasts must be Damage Feasant at the time of the distresse, and so note a diuersitie.

16.E.4.10.2.E.2.*auowrie*. 182.*lib.9. vbi supra.*

There is a diuersity (a) betweene a warrant of Record, and a Warrant, or an Authoritie in Law, for if a Capias be awarded to the Sherife to arrest a man for Felony, albeit the party be innocent, yet cannot he make rescous. But if a Sherife, will by authority which the Law giueth him, arrest any man for Felony which is not guiltie, he may rescue himselfe.

(a) 14.H.7.30.*tit. Iustice de Peace*.9.

¶ *Replevin*, (b) Is deriued of Replegiare **to redeliuer to the Owner** vpon pledges or suretie.

(c) Also to counterplead the Plaintife in an Assise by which hee is delayed, maketh him that pleadeth it a Disseisor. Otherwise it is, if he had pleaded Nul torr, &c.

(b) *Britton fol*.108. *Fleta lib*.4.*cap*.1. *Mirror.cap*.2.§.15.
(c) 24.*Ass*.3.29.*Ass*.32. *Fleta lib*.4.*cap*.1. *Britton fol*.108.

¶ *Encloser*, Is here also described, and need no other explication, for the Lord cannot (d) breake open the gates, or breake downe the Inclosures to take a distresse, and therefore the Law accounts it a disseisin. But all these are intended by Littleton to be disseisons after an actuall seison had, and when the Rent is behind, otherwise none of these are disseisons at all.

(d) 10.E.3.9 49.E.3.14. 7.E.3.3 11.H.7.28.8.*Ass*. 18.10.E.4.2.

But wherefore should a Rescous of the distresse by the party himselfe, or a Repleuine which is a redeliuery of the distresse by the Sherife by the course of Law to the partie be any disseisin of the Rent Seruice? Littleton doth here yeeld the true reason, because that by the Rescue, and by the suing of the Repleuyn, the Lord is disturbed of the means by the which he ought to haue and come to his Rent, viz of the distresse.

Bracton lib 4.*fol*.161.204. *Britton fol*.108. *Fleta lib*.4.*cap*.1.

And so it is of an Incloser, for hee that disturbes a man of the meane disseiseth him of the thing it selfe. (e) As the turning of the whole streame that runnes to a Mill is a disseisin of the Mill it selfe.

So it is if a man be disturbed to enter and manure his Land, (f) this is a disseisin of the Land it selfe: For Qui adimit medium dirimit finē And qui obstruit aditum destruit cōmodum. (g) And therefore where it is said that a man shall not bee punished for suing of writs in the Kings Court, be it of right or wrong, it is regularly true, but it fayleth in this speciall case of the writ of Repleuy for the cause aforesaid. (h) But Denier is no disseisin of a Rent Seruice without rescous or resistance.

(e) 9.*Ass*.19. *Mirr.ca*.2.§.15. *Britt.fol*.108.114.118.141.
(f) 26.*Ass*.17.3.E.4.2.*per Littl*. 40.E.3.14 b.
(g) F.N.B 42.g.22.E.3.15 43.*Ass*.40. 43.E.3.20.*fauer iudg*.10.8.E.4.15.*per Moyle*. 2.R.3.19.
(h) 3.E.3.75. 8.H.6.11.

Sect. 238.

Britton ubi supra. Fleta lib. 4. cap. 21.

Sont 4. causes de disseisin de Rent Charge. And you may adde a fifth, viz. Resistance to Distreyne, Counterpleading and Vouching a Record and fayler thereof, as hath beene said before.

14.E.4.4.35.H.6.7.3.Ass.8 10.E.3.9.40.E.3.24 3.H.6. 35.3.E.3.75.29.Ass.51. 39.Ass.4.40.Ass.2.13 E.1. Assise 404.3.Ass.8.8.H.6.11 18.E.3.Assise78.

Denier. Deniall is a disseisin of a Rent Charge, aswell as of a Rent secke, alb it he may distreyne for the Rent Charge, aswell as for a Rent Service. Nota, That when Bookes say that a detayner of a Rent Charge or Secke is a Disseisin, it must be intended upon a demand made.

If there bee two joyntenants, and the grantee of a Rent Charge distreyne for the Rent, and one of them make Rescous, they are both di..eisors, for a distresse for the rent is a demand in Law, and then the Non-payment is a denyall and a disseisin, but he that made the Rescous is only the Disseisor with force.

ET sont 4. causes de disseisin de rent charge, scilicet, Rescous, Repleuin, Enclosure, & Denier, car Denier est un disseisin de Rent charge, come est auantdit de rent Seck.

AND there bee foure causes of disseisin of a Rent Charge. *scz.* Rescous, Repleuin, Incloser, & Deniall. For Denyall is a disseisin of a Rent Charge, as is said before of a Rent Secke.

Section 239.

49.E.3.15.29. Ass 5. 36. Ass 7 10.E.3. 19.33.H. 6.35. 35.H.6.7.b.

The reason wherefore Inclosure is a disseisin of a Rent Secke, is because the Grantee cannot come upon the land to demand it.

ET deux sont causes de disseisin de Rent Seck, cestascauoir, denier & enclosure.

ANd there be two causes of disseisin of a Rent Secke, that is to say, denyall and inclosure.

Section 240.

(*) Fleta lib. 1. cap. 42. 49.E.3.14.49.Ass.5. 29.Ass.49.

Forstalla. (*) Forestallamentum, signifieth Obtrusionem viæ vel impedimentum transitus, &c.

Oue force & armes. Vi & armis.

(i) Vide Sect. 431.

Force, vis in (i) the Common Law is most commonly taken in ill part, and taken for unlawfull violence, for Maxime paci sunt contraria vis & iniuria. And therefore Britton said well, speaking in the person of the King, Nous volous que touts gents pluis vseant iudgement que force. Arma. Armes in the Common Law signifieth any thing that a man striketh or hurteth

ET il semble que il y ad un auter cause de disseisin de touts les trois seruices auantdits, cestascauoir, si l'seignior soit en alant a la terre tenus de luy pur distreyner pur le Rent arere, & le Tenant ceo oyant, luy encounter, & luy forstala la voy ouesque force & armes, ou luy manace en tiel forme que il ne osast vener

AND it seemeth that there is another cause of disseisin of all the three seruices aforesaid, that is, if the Lord is going to the Land holden of him for to distreine for the Rent behind, and the Tenant hearing this, encountreth with him, forestalleth him the way with force and armes, or menaceth him in such forme, that

vener a sa terre pur distreiner, pur son rent arere pur doubt de mort, ou mutilation de ses members, ceo est vn disseisin, pur ceo que le Seignior est disturbe de le meane per que il doit vener a son rent. Et issint est si per tiel forstalment ou manace, celuy que ad vn rent charge ou rent secke est forstalle, ou ne osast vener a la terre a demaunder le rent arere, &c.

hee dare not come to the land to distreine for his rent behinde, for doubt of death, or bodily hurt, this is a disseisin, for that that the Lord is disturbed of the meane whereby hee ought to come to his rent. And so it is if by such forestalling or menacing, hee that hath rent charge, or rent secke is forestalled, or dare not come to the land to aske the rent behinde, &c.

withall; (k) Omnes illos dicimus armatos qui habent cum quo nocere possunt. Telorum autem appellatione omnia in quibus singuli homines nocere possunt accipiuntur. Sed si quis venerit sine armis & ipsa concertatione ligna sumpserit, fustes & lapides, talis dicetur vis armata, sed si quis venerit cum armis, armis tamen ad dejiciendum non vsus fuerit, & deiecerit, vis armata dicitur esse facta, sufficit enim terror armorum vt videatur armis deiecisse. And Armorum quedam sunt tuitionis (& quod quis ob tutelam corporis sui vel sui juris fecerit, juste fecisse videtur) quædam pacis & Iustitiæ, quædam perturbationis, pacis & iniuriæ; quædam vsurpationis rei alienæ. Againe, Armorum quædam sunt moluta, & quædam quæ faciunt Brusuram, &c. Arma moluta plagam faciunt, sicut gladius, bisacuta & huiusmodi, ligna verò & lapides Brusuras orbes, & ictus, &c. To conclude this, it is truly said, that Armorum appellatione non solum scuta & gladij & galeæ continentur, sed & fustes & lapides, as the Poet saith:

(k) *Bracton lib. 4. fol. 162. et lib. 3. fo. 144. Fleta lib. 4. cap. 4.*

Iamque faces & saxa volant, furor arma ministrat.

Virgill 1. Æneid.

Sed vim vi repellere licet, modo fiat moderamine inculpatæ tutelæ non ad sumendam vindictam, sed ad propulsandam iujuriam.

¶ *Pur doubt de mort & mutilation de ses members.* For it must not be Vagus & vanus timor, sed talis quæ cadere possit in virum constantem, & non in hominem vanum & meticulosum, talis enim debet esse metus qui in se continet mortis periculum & corporis cruciatum. Littleton here saith it must be for feare of death, * or mutilation of members Et nemo tenetur exponere se infortunijs & periculis. And therefore a forestallment with such a menace is a disseisin, not only (saith Littleton) of a Rent seruice, but also of a Rent charge and Rent secke. These be all the disseisins of a rent that our Author speakes of. See hereafter (l) where a disseisin shall be by way of admittance of the owner of the Rent. And Littleton doth adde the binding reason in case of Forestalment, because the Lord is disturbed of the meane by which he ought to come to his rent, whereof there hath beene spoken sufficient before, aswell in case of the Rent charge and Rent secke, as of the Rent seruice,

Bracton lib. 2 16 Britton fo. 19. et 88. Fleta lib. 3. cap. 7.

(*) *See of this in the Chapter of Discents 49. E. 3. 14. 49. Ass. 5. 29. Ass. 47. &c.*

(l) *Vide Sect. 589.*

¶ *&c.* Of the (&c.) in the end of this Section, and what is implied therein, sufficient hath beene spoken before.

Now hath Littleton spoken of remedies for the recouery of the arrerages of rents. But since Littletons time a right profitable statute * in the 32. yeare of H.8. hath beene made for the recouery of arrerages of rents in certaine cases where there lay no remedy at the Common Law, and giueth further remedy in some cases where at the Common Law there was some remedy, which Statute hath beene well and beneficially expounded, and hereupon eight things are to be obserued. First, when Littleton wrote, the Heires, Executors or Administrators of a man seised of a Rent seruice, Rent charge, Rent secke, or Fee farme in fee simple or fee taile had no remedy for the arrerages incurred in the life of the owner of such rents: But now a double remedy is giuen to the Executors or Administrators for payment of debts, &c. viz. either to distreine, or to haue an action of debt.

(*) *32. H. 8. cap. 37.*

2. That the preamble of the statute concerning Executors or Administrators of Tenant for life is to be intended of Tenant pur auter vie so long as cestuy que vie liueth, who are also holpen by the said double remedy: but after the estate for life determined, his Executors or Administrators might haue had an action of debt by the Common Law, but they could not haue

Lib. 4. fo 49. 50. a. Ognells Case 40. E. 3. Execution 98. 45. E. 3. ibid. 71. 9. H. 6. 43. 14. H. 8. 20. 19. H. 6. 43. 34. H. 6. 20. 32. E. 3. Det. 9. 9. H. 7. 17. 19. E. 3. Iurisdiction 22.

(m) 23.*Eliz.Dier*.375.

distreyned, which now they may doe by force of this statute, for in that point it addeth (m) an other remedy, then the Common Law gaue.

3. If a man make a Lease for life or liues, or a gift in tayle reseruing a rent, this is a Rent seruice within this statute.

26.*E*.3.64. 11.*H*.4.*fo.vltimo. Ognels case.vbi supra. & lib*.7.*fo*.39.*b. Lillingstons case.*

4 The distresse is the more plaine and certaine remedy, then the action of debt, for the action of debt must be brought against them that tooke the profits when the rent became behinde or against their Executors or Administrators; but the distresse may be taken vpon the land, be it either in the Tenants owne hands or in the hands of any other that claymes by or from him, (that is by interpretation vnder him) by purchase, gift or discent, and these words, Clayming only by and from him, are to be vnderstood clayming only from or vnder him by purchase, gift or discent, and not paramount or aboue him, as the Lord by escheate clayme th not vnder the tenant by purchase, gift, or discent, but by reason of his seigniory which is a title paramount.

5. If there be Lord and Tenant, and the rent is behinde, and the Lord grant away his Seigniory, and dyeth, the Executors shall haue no remedy for these arrerages, because the grantor himselfe had no remedy for them when he dyed in respect of his grant, and the statute is (in like manner as the Testator might or ought to haue done) Et sic de similibus, for the act giueth no remedy when the Testator himselfe hath dispenced with the arrerages or had no remedy when he dyed.

6. If the Tenant make a Lease for life the remainder for life, the remainder in fee, the Tenant for life payes not the rent due to the Lord, the Lord dyeth, the Tenant for life dyeth, the Executors cannot distreyne vpon him in remainder, because he claymes not by or from the Tenant for life. And so it is of a reuersion for the cause aforesaid. But if a man grant a Rent charge to A. for the life of B. and letteth the lands to C. for life, the remainder to D. in fee, the rent is behinde by diuers yeares, B. dyeth, and after C. dyeth, A. may distreyne D. in remainder for all the arrerages, by the latter branch of the Statute of 32.H.8. and this diuersitie riseth vpon the seuerall pennings of the former branche and of this later, which you may reade in the statute it selfe, and so expounded and adiudged (o) in Edridges case, and the latter clause giueth the lesser estate the greater remedy.

(o) *Lib*.5.*fo*.118. *Edridges case.*

* 40.*E*.3.3.*b*. 11.*H*.4.85. 14.*E*.4.4. 20.*H*.7.1.*a*. 28.*H*.8.*Dier* 24.
(p) 34.*E*.1. *Auowrie* 233. *F.N.B*.122. 10.*H*.6.11. 11.*H*.6.8. *Mich*.32.*H*.8. *Rot*.429. *Leakes case. Ognels case vbi supra.* 3.*E*.3.*Debt* 157.
(q) *W*.1. *ca*.36. *F.N.B*.82.122.

7. For the Arrerages of a Nomine pœnæ, and for reliefe, or for ayde, Pur faire fits chiualer, or Pur file marier this statute * giueth no remedy, For, for the arrerages of the Nomine pœnæ, the Grantee himselfe may haue an action of debt, and consequently his Executors or Administrators, and yet the Nomine pœnæ as an incident to the rent shall discend to the heire: For reliefe the Lord cannot haue an action of debt but distreyne, but his Executors by (p) the Common Law shall haue an action of debt, for it is no rent but a casuall improuement of seruices for the said Aides, if the Lord doth leuy them, the sonne and the daughter respectfully shall haue an action of debt against the Executors or Administrators of the Lord, and if they haue nothing, then against the heire, but this is by the statute (q) of W.1. Note that all manner of arrerages of rents issuing out of a Freehold or inheritance whether they be in money or corne, cattell, fowle, pepper, Comyn, victuall, spurres, gloues, or any other profit to be deliuered or yeelded, & whether they be annuall or euery 2.3. or 4. yeares, &c. or the like are within this statute, but worke dayes, or any corporall seruice or the like are not within this statute.

8. A feme sole is seised of a rent in fee, &c. which is behinde and vnpaid she taketh husband, the rent is behinde againe, the wife dyeth, the husband by the Common Law should not haue the arrerages growne due before the mariage, but for the arrerages become due during the couerture the husband might (r) haue an action of debt by the Common Law, but now this statute * by a particular clause giueth the husband the arrerages due before mariage, and the said double remedy for the same, and that he may distreyne for the arrerages growne due during the couerture, so it giueth him that which he could not haue before, and further remedy for that, which the Common Law gaue him, and so it hath beene (s) adiudged.

(r) 26.*E*.3.64 10.*H*.6.11.
* 32.*H*.6.25.*F.N.B*.121.

(s) *Hill*.17.*Eliz*.*Rot*.457. *inter Sharpe & Pole. Vid. Ognells case vbi supra.*
(t) 19.*E*.3.*Iurisdiction* 22.

The Bishop of (t) Norwich had the first fruits of all the Clergie within the Diocesse at euery auoydance, the Church became voyde, & another Parson became Incumbent, who payd the Bishop parcell of his First fruites according to the taxation of the Church, and for the rest hee had a day giuen vnto him to pay it, the Bishop dyed, the residue was not payd, whereupon his Executors brought an action of debt, and it is adiudged that no action doth lye, because it is a meere spirituall thing and no lay contract, and therefore the Court had no iurisdiction to hold plea of it. I haue beene the longer in the exposition of the said Statute, for that it is a generall case, and doth concerne most part of the Subiects of England.

* *
*

Finis libri secundi.

THE

THE THIRD BOOKE of the first part of the Institutes of the LAWES of ENGLAND.

CHAP. I. *Of Parceners.* *Sect.241*

¶ PArceners sont en deux maners, cestascauoir, Parceners solonque le course del Common ley, & Parceners solonque custom. Parceners solonque le course del cõmon ley sont, lou hõe ou feme seisie de certaine terres ou tenements en fee simple, ou en taile, nad issue forsque files et deuie, et les tenements discendont a les issues, et les files entront en les terres ou tenements issint

PArceners are of two sorts (to wit) Parceners according to the course of the Common Law, and Parceners according to the custome. Parceners after the course of the Common Law are where a man or woman seised of certaine lands or tenements in fee simple or in taile, hath no issue but daughters & dieth, & the tenements discend to the issues, and the daughters enter into the lands or tenements

¶ OUr Author having treated in his two former bookes, first of estates of Lands and tenements, and in his second booke of Tenures whereby the same haue beene holden: Now in his third booke doth teach vs diuers things concerning both of them, as first the qualities of their estates. 2. In what cases the entry of him that right hath, may bee taken away. 3. The remedies, and in what cases the same may be preuented, or auoyded. 4. How a man may be barred of his right for euer, and in what cases the same may be preuented or auoyded. For the first he hauing spoken of sole estates deuideth the quality of estates into Indeuided, & Conditionall. Indeuided, into coparcenary, ioyntenancy and tenancy in common. Coparcenary into parceners by the Common

discendus a eux, dōques els sont appels Parceners, & quaunt a files els sont forsque vn heire a lour ancestor. Et els sont appel Parceners, pur ceo que per le briefe que est appel Briefe de Participatione facienda, **la ley eux voet cohert que partitiō serr fait ent eux. Et si sont deux files as queux les terres discendont, donque els sont appels deux Parceners. Et si sont trois files, dōque els sont appels trois Parceners, Et si quater files, quater Parceners, & issint ouster.**

so discended to them, then they are called Parceners, and bee but one heire to their Ancestour. And they are called Parceners, because by the Writ which is called *Breue de participatione facienda*, the Law will constraine them, that partition shall bee made among them: and if there bee two daughters to whome the land discendeth, then they bee called two Parceners, and if there be three daughters, they bee called 3 parceners, and foure daughters, 4 parceners, and so forth.

Common Law, and Parceners by the Custome, and hee beginneth his third booke with Parceners claiming by discent, which comming by the act of Law, and right of bloud, is the noblest and worthiest meanes whereby lands doe fall from one to another. Conditionall, into conditions expresse or in deed, and Conditions in Law. Conditions in deed, into Gages, which he diuideth into Vadia mortua, and Vadia viua. Vadia mortua, so called because either money or land may bee lost: and Viua, because neither monie nor land can be lost, but both preserued. Then speaketh he of Discents, whereby the entrie of him that right hath may be taken away.

Vid. Sect. 385.

And next to that, of the remedie how to preuent the same, viz by continual claim. Then he teacheth, how a man hauing a defeasible or an imperfect estate, may perfect and establish the same by three meanes, viz. By Release, By Confirmation, and Attournement, where that is requisite. Hauing spoken of a Discent, being an Act in Law which taketh away an entrie, he doth then speake of a discontinuance, the act of the partie, whereby the entrie of them that right haue shal be taken away. And next vnto that he teacheth, in what case the same may be auoyded by Remitter. After he had treated of discents and discontinuances, which take away entries, but barre not Actions. Lastly, he setteth forth the learning of Warranties, (a curious and cunning kind of learning I assure you) whereby both Entrie, Action, and Right may be barred, & the remedies how they may be preuented before they fall, & in what cases they may be auoyded after they be fallen. And thus haue you an account of the thirteene seuerall Chapters of his third booke. And now his method being vnderstood, let vs heare what our Author will say vnto vs concerning Parceners.

¶ *Et quant a files els sont forsque vn heire a lour* (a) *ancester.* This is false printed, for the originall is, Et quanque files els sont, els sont parceners, et sont forsque vn heire a lour auncester.

¶ *Parceners.* (b) Ius discendit quasi vni hæredi propter iuris vnitatem, sicut sunt plures filiæ, &c. & vbi omnes simul & in solidum hæredes sunt, plures cohæredes sunt quasi vnum corpus, propter vnitatem iuris quod habent. Whereupon it followeth, that albeit where there be two Parceners, (c) they haue moities in the lands descended to them, yet are they both but one heire, and one of them is not the moitie of an heire, but both of them are but vnus hæres.

(a) *Bract. li. 2. fo. 66. 71, &c. & 76, &c. & Li. 5. fo. 443. Brit. fo. 58. 112 128. 183. 184. 185. 189. 193. Flet. li. 5. ca. 9. li. 6. ca. 47. Glanu. li. 7. ca. 3. & li. 13 c. 11*
(b) *Bract. li. 2. fo. 66. 76. Flet. vb. sup. Brit. vb. sup. & Statute de Hibernia.*
(c) *Vid. Sect. 8. ver. finem.*

And it is to be obserued, that there is a diuersitie betweene a discent, which is an act of the Law, and a purchase, which is an act of the partie. (d) For if a man be seised of lands in fee, and hath issue two daughters, and one of the daughters is attaynted of felony, the father dieth, both daughters being aliue, the one moitie shall discend to the one daughter, and the other moitie shall escheat.

(d) *Flet. li. 5. ca. 9. Flet. li. 6. ca. 47.*

But if a man make a lease for life, the remainder to the right heires of A. beeing dead, who hath issue two daughters, whereof the one is attainted of Felonie, in this case some hath said that the remainder is not good for a moitie, but voyd for the whole, for that both the daughters, should haue beene (as Littleton saith) but one heire.

A man

A man makes a gift in taile, reseruing two shillings rent to himselfe during his life, and if he die his heire within age, then reseruing a rent of twentie shillings to his heires for euer, he dieth hauing issue two daughters, the one of full age, the other within age, in this case the Donee shall hold by Fealtie onely, insomuch as the one daughter as well as the other is his heire, and both of them (as Littleton saith) make but one heire, ergo his heire is not of full age, neither is his heire in that case of full age. But if the reseruation had beene, And if he die, his heire neither being within age, nor of full age, &c. in this case the reseruation had beene good; and if it doth not begin in his next heire, it shall neuer begin as this case is, for that the precedencie is not performed. (e) But yet if one of them be of age, and the other within age, she shal haue her age and other priuiledges and aduantages that an heire within age shall haue, and when they are demandants, for the nonage of the one, the Paroll shall demurre against them both. (f) Sunt autem plures participes quasi vnum corpus in eo quod vnum ius habent, & oportet quod corpus sit integrum, & quod in nulla parte sit defectus. And when the right heire doth claime by purchase, he must be (say they) a compleat right heire in iudgement of Law. And therefore if lands be giuen to a man and to the heires females of his bodie, and he hath issue a sonne and a daughter, and dieth, the daughter shall haue the land by discent, but if a remainder be limitted to the heires females of the bodie of I.S and he hath issue a sonne and a daughter, his daughter shall neuer take it by purchase, for that she is not heire female of the body of I.S. because he hath a sonne.

(e) *Temps E.1. Age* 128. 8.*E.*2. *Iudgment* 240. 10.*E.*3 7.44.*E.*3. *Age* 47.26.*Ass.*65. 13.*E.*3. *Age.*51. 28.*Ass.*12. 29. *Ass.*25,57. 34 *H.*6.4. *Ass.*17.
(f) *Fleta lib.*5.*ca* 9. *et Lib.*6. *Cap.*47.

If a man giue lands to another, and to the heires males of his bodie, vpon condition, that if he die without heire female of his bodie, that then the Donor shal re-enter, this condition is vtterly voyd, for he cannot haue an heire female, so long as he hath an heire male.

And as they be but one heire, and yet seuerall persons, so haue they one entire freehold in the land, as long as it remaines vndiuided in respect of any strangers Præcipe. (g) But betweene themselues to many purposes they haue in iudgement of Law seuerall Freeholds, for the one of them may infeoffe another of them of her part, and make liuerie. (h) And this Coparcenarie is not seuered or diuided by Law, by the death of any of them, for if one die, her part shal discend to her issue, and one Præcipe shall lie against them, for they shall neuer ioyne as heires to seueral Auncestors in any Action Auncestrell but when one right discends from one Auncestour: and then propter vnitatem Iuris, though they be in seuerall degrees from the common Auncestor, yet shall they ioyne. But the issues of seuerall Coparceners, because seuerall rights discend, shall neuer ioyne as heires to their mothers, and yet when they haue [severally] recouered, a writ of Partition lieth betweene them.

(g) 10.*E.*4. 17.*E.*3.46.
(h) 37.*H.*6.8. 19.*H.*6.45.
*Vid. Sect.*313.

For exanple, (i) If a man hath issue two daughters, and is disseised, and the daughters haue issue and die, the Issues shall ioyne in a Præcipe, because one right discends from the Auncestor, and it maketh no difference whether the common Auncestor being out of possession, died before the daughters, or after, for that in both cases they must make themselues heirs to the Grandfather which was last seised, and when the Issues (k) haue recouered, they are Coparceners, and one Præcipe shall lie against them. And likewise if the Issues of two Coparceners which are in by seuerall discents, be disseised, they shall ioyne in Assise. But in the same case, if the two daughters had beene actually seised, and had beene disseised, after their deceases the Issues shall not ioyne, because seuerall rights discended to them from seuerall Auncestors: and yet when they haue seuerally recouered, they are Coparceners, and one Præcipe lieth against them, and a release made by one of them to the other is good. And so note a diuersitie inter discensum in capita, & in stirpes.

(i) 7.*E.*3.30.34. 48.*E.*3.14. 24.*E.*3.13. *F.N.B.*221. 35.*H.*6.23. 27 *E.*3.89. 31.*H.*6.14.*b.*
(k) 37.*H.*6 8. 9.*E.*4.13.*b* 42.*E.*3.16.17.

And the Statute of Gloucester cap.6. made Anno 6.Edw.1 speaketh, Si home murge, &c. If a man dieth: so as that Statute extendeth not but where one dieth, and hath diuers heires, whereof one is sonne or daughter, brother or sister, nephew or neece, and the others bee in a further degree, all their heires from henceforth shall haue their recouerie by writ of Mortdauncestor. And this seemeth to me to be the Common Law, for Bracton who writ before this statute, saith, (l) In casu cum sit assisa mortis antecessor coniungenda cum consanguinitate, non erit postea recurrendum ad præcipe de Consanguinitate, sed ad assisam mortis, quia persona quæ propinquior est, & facit Assisam, & trahit ad se personam & gradum remotiorem vt vbi potius procedat assisa quam præcipe quia id quod est magis remotum, non trahit ad se quod est magis iunctum, sed è contrario in omni casu. And herewith agreeth the most of our (m) Bookes: and two Coparceners shall haue a writ of Ayel, and by their count suppose the common Auncestor to be grandfather to the one, and great grandfather to the other.

(l) *Bract. in lib.*4.254.*b.* *Britton fol.*181.182.& 178.204. *Fleta lib.*5.*cap.*1. *et* 2. &9. *in fine.*
(m) 19.*E.*3.*Tit.Ioindre in Action* 31. 7.*E.*3.30.*et* 34. 27.*E.*3 89. 48.*E.*3.14. 24.*E.*3.13. *F.N.B.*221. *Register.* *Vide* 32.*E.*1. *Ioindre in Actiō* 34. 13.*E.*3.*ibidem* 29. *Temps E.*2.*ib.*35. 30 *E.*1.*ibid.*36. 25.*H.*6.23.

I haue beene the longer herein, for that this Inheritance of Coparceners is the rarest kind of Inheritance that is in the Law.

Furthermore it is to be obserued, That herein also in case of Coparceners, (n) sometimes the discent is in Stirpes, (viz) To Stockes or Roots, and sometimes in Capita, To Heads: As if a man hath Issue two daughters and dieth, this discent is in Capita, (viz) that euerie one shall inherit alike, as Littleton here saith. But if a man hath Issue two daughters, and the

(n) *Bracton lib.*2.66. *Britton cap.*71. *Fleta lib.*5.*cap.*9.*et* 6.*cap.*47.

the eldest daughter hath issue three daughters, and the youngest, one daughter, al these foure shal inherit, but the daughter of the yongest shall haue as much as the three daughters of the eldest, Ratione stirpium, and not Ratione capitum, for in iudgement of Law euerie daughter hath a seuerall Stocke or Root.

Also if a man hath issue two daughters, and the eldest hath issue diuers sonnes and diuers daughters, and the youngest hath issue diuers daughters, the eldest sonne of the eldest daughter shall onely inherit, for this discent is not in Capita, but all the daughters of the yongest shal inherit, and the eldest sonne is Coparcener with the daughters of the yongest, and shal haue one moitie, (viz.) his mothers part: so that men discending of daughters may be Coparceners, as well as women, and shall ioyntly implead and be impleaded, as is aforesayd.

(o) 26.E.2. Nuper ob. 141 F.N.B. 197. 7.E.3.13.

(o) If there be two Coparceners, and the one bring a Rationabili parte, or a Nuper obijt against the other, the Defendant claime by purchase, and disclaime in the bloud, the Plaintife shall haue a Mortdauncester against her as a stranger for the whole.

* Bract. li.2. fo.66.71. &c. Brit. ca.71. Flet. li.5. ca.9.

¶ *Parceners sont en deux manners.* Here Littleton doth diuide Parceners, and herewith doe agree the antient bookes of Law.*

¶ *Et ils sont appels Parceners, &c.* Parceners, Participes, Et dicuntur Participes, quasi partis capaces, siue partem capientes, quia res inter eas est communis ratione plurium personarum. This Tenancie in the antient bookes of Law is called Adæquatio, and sometime Familia hirsciscunda, an Inheritance to be diuided, and many times Parceners are called Coparceners.

(p) Regist. Orig. 76. 316. Regist. Iud. 80. B. vbi sup. Flet. vbi sup. Bract. vbi sup. & Li.5. fo.443.b.

¶ Breue de Participatione facienda. This is false printed, and should be, De Particione facienda, a Writ whereby the Coparceners are compelled to make partition. Item est alia Actio mixta, quæ dicitur Actio Familiæ hirciscundæ, & locum habet inter eos qui communem habent hæreditatem, &c. Et locum habet vt videtur, inter Cohæredes, vbi agitur de proparte sororum, vel inter alios vbi res inter partes & Cohæredes diuidi debeat, sicut sunt plures sorores, quæ sunt quasi vnus hæres, vel inter plures fratres, qui sunt quasi vnus hæres ratione rei quæ diuisibilis est inter plures masculos, &c.

¶ *Des terres & tenements.* It is to bee considered of what Inheritances daughters shall be Coparceners, and how and in what manner partition shal be made betweene them. Wherein it is to be obserued, That of Inheritances some be entire, and some be seuerall: againe, of entire, some be diuisible, and some be indiuisible. And here it appeareth by Littleton, That Parceners take their appellation, because they are compelled to make partition by Writ of Particione facienda; where note, That Littleton alloweth well to find out the true deriuation of words, as often hath beene and shall be obserued.

If a Villeine discend to two Coparceners, this is an entire Inheritance, and albeit the Villeine himselfe cannot be diuided, yet the profit of him may be diuided, one Coparcener may haue the seruice one day, one weeke, &c. and the other another day or weeke, &c. and for the same reason a woman shall be endowed of a Villeine, as before it appeareth in the Chapter of Dower. Likewise an Aduowson is an entire Inheritance, (q) and yet in effect the same may be diuided betweene Coparceners, for they may diuide it to present by turnes.

(q) 13.E.2. tit. Quar. Imp. 170. 17.E.3.38. Flet. li.5. c.9. Mir. ca.2. §.17.
(r) 44.E.3. tit. Partic. 6. & tit. Auowrie 75. 2.H.6.

A Rent charge is entire, and against common right, (r) yet may it be diuided betweene Coparceners, and by Act in Law the Tenant of the land is subiect to seuerall distresses, and partition may be made before seisin of the rent.

Entire Inheritances not diuisible, we finde diuers in our bookes, and some Inheritances that are diuisible, and yet shall not be parted or diuided betweene Coparceners, as hereafter shall appeare.

(s) 2.E.2. tit. Dower 123.
(t) 17.E.2. Nuper obiit 12. 16 E.2. ibid. 12. 5. Mariæ Dyer 153.

(s) If a man haue reasonable Estouers, as Housebote, Heybote, &c. appendant to his freehold, they are so entire as they shall not be diuided betweene Coparceners. (t) So if a Corodie incertaine be granted to a man and his heires, and he hath Issue diuers daughters, this Corodie shall not be diuided betweene them, but of a Corodie certaine, Partition may bee made.

(u) 17.E.3.72.
(w) 13.E.2. Quare Impedit 170. Fleta lib.5. cap.9.
(x) Mich. 24 et 25. Eliz. inter Comitem de Huntingdon et Seignior Mountioye.

(u) Homage and Fealtie cannot be diuided betweene Coparceners. (w) So a Pischarie incertaine, or a Common sauns nombre cannot be diuided betweene Coparceners for that would be a charge to the Tenant of the Soile. (x) The Lord Mountjoy seised of the Mannor of Canford in fee, did by Deed indented and inrolled, bargaine and sell the same to Browne in Fee, in which Indenture this clause was contained, Prouided alwayes, and the sayd Browne did couenant and grant to and with the sayd Lord Mountjoy, his heirs, and assignes, that the Lord Mountioy, his heires and Assignes might dig for Ore in the lands (which were great wasts) parcell of the sayd Mannor, and to dig turfe also for the making of Allome. And in this case three points were resolued by all the Iudges. First, that this did amount to a grant of an Interest and Inheritance to the Lord Mountjoy, to digge, &c. Secondly, That notwithstanding

ding this grant. Browne his heires and assignes might digge also, and like to the case of Common Sauns nomber. Thirdly, that the Lord Mountioy might assigne his whole interest to one, two, or more, but then if there be two or more, they could make no diuision of it, but worke together with one stocke, neyther could the Lord Mountioy, &c. assigne his interest in any part of the wast to one or more, for that might worke a preiudice and a surcharge to the Tenant of the Land, and therefore if such an incertaine Inheritance discendeth to two Coparceners, it cannot be deuided betweene them

Vide 5. Maria Dier 153.

But then it may be demanded, what shall become of these Inheritances. The answere is, that it appeareth in our Bookes that regularly (y) the eldest shall haue the reasonable Estouers, Common, Pischary, Corody incertaine, &c. and the rest shall haue a contribution, that is, an allowance of the value in some other of the Inheritance, and so of the like. But what if the common Auncester left no other Inheritance to giue any thing in allowance, what contribution or recompence shall the yonger Coparceners haue. It is answered, that if the Estouers or Pischary or Common be incertaine, then shall one Coparcener haue the Estouers, Pischary, or Common, &c for a time, and the other for the like time: as the one for one yeere and the other for another, or more, or lesser time, whereby no preiudice can grow to the Owner of the soyle. Or in case of the Pischary, the one may haue one fish, and the other the second, &c. or one may haue the first draught, and the second the second draught, &c. And if it be of a Parke, one may haue the first Beast, and the second, the second, &c. And if of a Mill, one to haue the Mill for a time, and the other the like time, or the one, one toll dish, and the other, the second, &c. And this appeareth to bee the ancient Law, for it is said. (z) Sunt aliæ res hæreditariæ quæ veniunt in partitionem quæ cum diuidi non possunt conceduntur vni, ita quod aliæ cohæredes alibi de communi hæreditate habeant ad valorem sicut sunt viuaria Piscariæ, parci, vel saltem quod partem habeant pro defectu, sicut secundum piscem tertium vel quartum, vel secundum tractum, tertium vel quartum. Item in parcis secundam, tertiam aut quartam.

(y) 2.E.2. dower 123. 13.E. 2. quar. Imp. 170. Fleta vbi supra. Vide Mirror. ca. 2 §. 17

(z) Bracton lib. 2. 76. Britton cap. 71. 72. Fleta lib. 5. cap. 9.

But now let vs turne our eye to Inheritances of Honour and Dignity. And of this there is an ancient Booke Case (*) in 23. H. 3. tit. partition 18 in these words. Note, if the Earledome of Chester discend to Coperceners it shall bee deuided betweene them aswell as other Lands, and the eldest shall not haue this Seigniory and Earledome entire to her selfe, Quod nota, adiudge per totam Curiam. By this it appeareth that the Earledome (that is, the possessions of the Earledome) shall bee deuided, and that where there bee more Daughters then one, the eldest shall not haue the Dignity and Power of the Earle, that is to be a Countesse. What then shall become of that Dignity. The answere is, (a) that in that case the King who is the Soueraigne of Honour and Dignity, may for the incertainty conferre the Dignity vpon which of the Daughters he please. And this hath beene the vsage since the Conquest as it is said.

(*) 23. H. 3. tit. partition 18.

(a) 3. H. 3. tit. prescription.

But if an Earle that hath his Dignity to him and his heires dieth, hauing issue one Daughter, the Dignity shall discend to the Daughter, for there is no incertainty, but only one Daughter, the Dignity shall discend vnto her and her Posterity as well as any other Inheritance, and this appeareth by many Presidents, and by a late Judgement giuen in Sampson Leonards Case, who married with Margaret the only sister and heire of Gregorie Fines Lord Dacre of the South, and in the case of William Lord Ros.

But there is a difference betweene a dignity or name of Nobility and an Office of Honour. For if a man hold a Mannor of the King to be high Constable of England, and dye hauing issue two Daughters, the eldest daughter taketh husband, he shall execute the Office soly, and before marriage it shall be exercised by some sufficient Deputy, and all this was resolued by all the Judges of England, in the case of (b) the Duke of Buckingham. But the dignity of the Crowne of England is without all question descendible to the eldest daughter alone and to her posterity, and so hath it beene declared by Act of Parliament. (*) For Regnum non est diuisibile. And so was the Discent of Troy.

(b) 11. Eliz. Dier 285. the Duke of Buckinghams Case.

(*) 25. H. 8. cap. 22.

Præterea sceptrum Ilione quod gesserat olim,
Maxima natarum Priami———

Virgil. 1. Æneid.

(b) If a Castle that is vsed for the necessary defence of the Realme discende to two or more Coparceners, this Castle might bee diuided by Chambers and Roomes as other Houses bee, but yet for that it is Pro bono publico & pro defensione Regni, it shall not be diuided, for as one sayth, Propter ius gladij diuidi non potest. And another saith, (*) Pur le droit del espee que ne soeffre diuision en auenture que la force del realme ne defaille pax taunt. But Castles of habitation for priuate vse, that are not for the necessary defence of the Realme ought to bee parted betweene Coparceners aswell as other Houses, and wiues may thereof bee endowed, as hath beene said in the Chapter of Dower.

(b) Bracton lib. 2. fol. 76. Fleta lib. 5. cap. 9.

(*) Britton 186. 187.

Vide Sect. 39.

If there be two Coparceners of certaine Lands with warrantie, and they make partition of the Land, the warranty ſhall remayne, becauſe they are compellable, to make partition. (c) But otherwiſe it was of Joyntenants at the Common Law, as ſhall bee ſaid hereafter in his proper place. (d) Thomas de Eberſton ſeiſed of the Mannor of Eberſton, within the Forreſt of Pickering, had kept time out of mind, a Woodward for keeping of the woods parcell of that Mannor, and had the barke of all the Trees felled in the ſaid woods by any of the Forreſters of that Forreſt as belonging to his Mannor (which he could not haue without a Preſcription.) Thomas of Eberſton infeoffed two of the ſaid Mannor, betweene whom partition was made, ſo as one of them had the owne halfe in ſeueralty, and the other the other halfe. Robert Wyerne afterwards had the one halfe, and Thomas Thurniſe the other, and they in the Eyre of Pickering claymed to keepe a Woodward within the ſaid woods, and the barke aforeſaid, and the truth hereof and the vſage being ſpecially found by the Forreſtors, Verderors, and Regardors, Willoughbie, Hungerford, and Hanburie, Juſtices Itinerants within that Forreſt gaue iudgement as followeth. Ideo conſideratum eſt quod prædict' Robertus & Thomas habeant Woodwardum & Corticem in boſco prædicto de quercubus prædictis ſibi & hæredibus ſuis imperpetuum. Saluo ſemper iure, &c.

(c) 29. *E.* 3. *garan'* 1070.
(d) *Itin. Pickering.* 8. *E.* 3. *Rot.* 34.

Sect. 242.

¶ Auxy ſi home ſeiſie de tenements en fee ſimple, ou en fee taile, deuy ſauns iſſue de ſon corps engender, & les tenements diſcendont a ſes ſoers, els ſont Parceners, come eſt auantdit. Et en meſme le maner, lou il nad pas ſoers, mes les tenements diſcendont a ſes aunts, els ſont Parceners, &c. Mes ſi home nad forſque vn file, el ne poit eſtre dit Parcener, mes el eſt appelle file & heire, &c.

ALſo if a man ſeiſed of Tenements in Fee ſimple or in Fee-tayle, dieth without iſſue of his bodie begotten, and the Tenements diſcend to his Siſters, they are Parceners as is aforeſaid. And in the ſame manner, where he hath no Siſters but the Lands diſcend to his Aunts, they are Parceners, &c. But if a man hath but one Daughter, ſhe ſhall not be called Parcener, but ſhee is called Daughter and Heire, &c.

¶ *Ou en fee taile.* This muſt be intended of an eſtate taile made to the Father and to the heires of his body, for otherwiſe if the ſtate Tayle were made to a man and to the heires of his body, his ſiſters cannot inherit. And not only Daughters ſhall be Coparceners, but Siſters, Aunts, great Aunts, &c.

¶ *File & heire, &c.* Here by (&c.) is implyed Siſter and heire, Aunt and heire, great Aunt and heire, and ſo vpward.

Sect. 243.

¶ By this Section, and the (&c.) in the end of it. It is to be vnderſtood that there are two kind of partitions betweene Coparceners, the one in deed or expreſſe, and the other in Law or Implicite. Of partitions in deed or expreſſe, ſome bee voluntary whereof Littleton enumerates foure Manners, and one compulſary, that is by Writ of Partition.

¶ Ceſt aſcauoir, que partition enter parceners poit eſtre fait en diuers maners. Un eſt, quant els agreeont de faire partition, & font partition de les Tenements, ſicome ſi ſoient deux parceners

AND it is to bee vnderſtood, that partition may be made in diuers manners. One is when they agree to make partition, and do make partition of the tenements. As if there bee two Parceners to deuide between them

a

a deuider enter eux les Tenements en deux parts, chescun part per soy en seueraltie, & d'egal value. Et si sont 3. Parceners a deuider les tenements en trois parts per soy en seueraltie, &c.

the tenements in two parts, each part by it selfe in seueraltie, and of equall value. And if there bee three Parceners, to deuide the tenements in three parts by it selfe in seueraltie, &c.

The first partition in deed betweene Coparceners, is that which Littleton here speaketh of, viz. Quant els agreont & font partition de les tenements, &c. chescun part per soy en seueralty & de egall value, &c. If Coparceners make partitions at full age, and vnmarried, and of sane memorie of Lands in Fee simple, it is good & firme for euer, albeit the values bee vnequall, but if it be of lands entayled, or if any of the Parceners bee of non sane memorie, it shall bind the parties themselues but not their Issues vnlesse it be equall. Or if any be Couert, it shall bind the husband, but not the wife or her heires. Or if any be within age it shall not bind the Infant as shall be said more fully hereafter. The second partition followeth in the next Section. And here the (&c.) implyeth further, that if there be foure Parceners, then foure parts, If fiue, fiue parts and so forth. It further implyeth, that all this must be in seueralty; whereof and with what limitations this is to be vnderstood it hath beene declared before. *Vide Sect.*241.

Section. 244.

Vn auter partition est, a eslier per agreement enter eux, certeine de lour amies, de faire partitiō des terres ou tenemēts en le forme auantdit. Et en tiels cases apres tiel partition, le eigne file prymerment eslie-ra vn des partes issint diuides, que el voit auer pur sa part, & donques la second file porcheine apres luy auter part, & donques l'tierce soer auter part, donques le 4. auter part, &c. si issint soit que soient plusors soers, &c. si ne soit autrement agree enter eux. Car il poit estre agree enter eux, que vn auera tiels tenemēts, & vn aut' tiels tenemēts, &c. sans ascū tiel primer election, &c.

ANother Partition there is, *viz.* to choose by agreement betweene themselues certaine of their Friends to make partition of the Lands or Tenements in forme aforesaid. And in these Cases after such partition, the eldest Daughter shall choose first one of the parts so deuided which she will haue for her part, and then the second Daughter next after her another part, and then the third Sister another part, then the fourth another part, &c. if so bee that there be more Sisters, &c. vnlesse it bee otherwise agreed betweene them. For it may be agreed betweene thē that one shall haue such Tenements, and another such Tenements, &c. without any primer election.

Donques le 4. auter part, &c. here the (&c.) implyeth the fifth after, and after her the sixt, and so forth. 31. *Ass.*26.

Car il poet estre agree inter eux que vn auera tiels tenements, & vn auter tiels tenements, &c.

Here by this (&c.) is imployed diuers rules of Law prouing the conclusion of Littleton in this Section. viz. modus & conuentio vincunt legem. Pacto aliquid licitum est, quod sine pacto non admittitur. Quilibet potest renunciare iuri pro se introduct' But with this limitation that these Rules extend not to any thing, that is against the Common wealth, or common right. For conuentio priuatorum non potest publico iuri derogare.

Sect. 245.

* Bract. lib. 2. 77. Fleta, lib. 5. ca. 9. Britton, ca. 72.

ENitia pars. It is called in old bookes * Æisnetia which is derived of the French word Eisne or eldest, as much to say as the part of the eldest, for Bracton saith, Quod Eisnetia semper est præferenda propter priuilegium ætatis, sed esto quod filia primogenita relicto nepote vel nepte in vita patris vel matris decesserit, præferenda erit soror antenata tali nepoti vel nepti quantum ad Eisnetiam quia mortem parentum expectant. And herewith agreeth Fleta also, Quod nota, whereby it appeareth that Ænitia pars is personall to the eldest, and that this prerogatiue or priuiledge discendeth not to her issue, but the next eldest after shall haue it, (f) And here is a diuersity to be obserued betweene this case of a partition in deede by the act of the parties, (for there the priuiledge of election of the eldest daughter shall not discend to her issue) And where the law doth giue the eldest any priuiledge without her act, there that priuiledge shall discend. As if there be diuers Coparceners of an Aduowson * & they cannot agree to present, the Law doth giue the first presentment to the eldest, and this priuiledge shall discend to her issue, nay her Assignee shall haue it, and so shall her husband that is Tenant by the Curtesie haue it also.

(f) 45. E. 3. fines 41. 49. E. 3. quar. imp. 59. 18. E. 2. ibid. 176. 5. H. 5. 10. 38. H. 6. 9. Doct. & Stud. 116. 117. Vid. Bracton. 238. 249. * 5. H. 7. 8. 34. H. 6. 40. 11. H. 4. 54. 20. E. 3. quar. Imp. 63. 34. E. 3. Ibid. 198. 15. E. 3. Dar. Presentment 11. 19. E. 3. 20. 21. 21. E. 3. 21. F. N. B. 32.

ET la part que leigne soer ad est appelle en Latin Enitia pars. Mes si les parceners agreeont, que leigne soer ferra partition de les tenements en le forme auantdit, & si ceo el fait, donque il est dit que leigne soer eslier pluis darreine pur sa part, & apres chescun de ses soers, &c.

AND the part which the eldest sister hath is called in Latyn *Enitia pars*. But if the parceners agree that the eldest sister shall make partition of the tenements in manner aforesaid, and if she doe this, then it is said that the eldest sister shall choose last for her part, and after euery one of her sisters, &c.

Donques il est dit leigne soer eslier pluis darreine, &c. By this and the &c. in the end of this Section is implyed the rule of Law is Cuius est diuisio, alterius est electio. And the reason of the Law is for auoyding of partiality.

Ipsæ etinim Leges cupiunt vt Iure regantur.

which might apparantly follow if the eldest might both diuide and choose. Now followeth the third partition in Deede.

Sect. 246.

VN auter partition ou allotment est, sicome soient quater parceners & apres le partition de les terres fait, chescun part del terre soit per soy solement escript en vn petit escrouet, & soit couert tout en cere, en le maner dun petit pile, issint que nul poit veier lescrouet, & donque soient les 4. piles de cere mis en vn bonet a garder, en les maines dun indifferent home, &

ANother partition or allotment is, as if there be foure parceners and after partition of the lands be made, euery part of the land by it selfe is written in a little scrowle, and is couered all in waxe in manner of a little ball, so as none may see the scrowle, and then the 4. balls of waxe are put in a hat to bee kept in the hands of an indifferent man, and then the eldest daughter shall first

donqs leigne file primerment mettra sa maine en le bonnet, quel prendra un pile de cere ovesque lescrouet deins m le pile pur sa part, & donque le second soer mettra sa maine en le bonnet & prendra un auter, le tierce soer le 3. pile, & le 4. soer le 4. pile, &c. & en ceo cas covient chescun de eux luy tener a sa chance & allotment.

put her hand into the Hat and take a ball of waxe with the scrowle within the same ball for her part, And then the second sister shall put her hand into the hat and take an other, the 3. sister the 3. ball, and the 4. sister the 4. ball. And in this case every one of them ought to stand to their chance and allotment.

Quære – if the eldest would relinquish her certain Choice & leave it to chance ——

Allotmēt. Of this partition by Lots ancient Authors * write that in that case Coparceners *Fortunam faciunt iudicem*: And Littleton here tearmeth it chance, for in the end of this Section he saith, that in this case every of them ought to hold her selfe to her chance, & of this kinde of division you shall reade in holy Scripture, where it is said, *Dedi vobis possessionem quam diuidetis sorte.*

* Fleta lib. 5. ca. 9. Bracton, lib. 2. 75. Britton ca. 72. Vid. Numbers, ca. 26. verse 54. 55. & ca. 33. verse 54. Of division by lots.

The &c. in the end of this Section implyeth that if there be more coparceners there must be more balls according to the number of the parceners.

Sect. 247.

Item, un auter partition il y ad, sicome sont quater Parceners, & ils ne voilent agreer a partition destre fait enter eux, donque lun poit aver bre De partitione facienda **envers les auts trois: ou deux de eux poient aver bre** De partitione facienda **envers les auters deux, ou trois de eux poient aver bre** De partitione facienda **envers le quart, a lour election.**

Also there is another partition, As if there bee foure parceners, and they will not agree to a partition to bee made betweene them, then the one may haue a Writ of *Partitione facienda* against the other three, or two of them may haue a Writ of *Partitione facienda* against the other two, or three of them may haue a Writ of *Partitione facienda* against the fourth at their election.

Here followeth the fourth Partition in Deede. Littleton hauing spoken of voluntary Partitions, or Partitions by consent, Now he speakes of a Partition by the compulsorie meanes of Law where no Partition can bee had by consent. Now of what inheritance partition may bee made by the Writ of *Partitione facienda* may partly appeare by that which hath beene said. Moreouer it is to be obserued that the words of the Writ *De partitione facienda* be * *Quod cum eædem A. & B. insimul & pro indiuiso teneant tres acras terræ cum pertinen', &c.* And note that this word (*Tenet*) in a Writ doth alwayes imply a Tenant of a freehold. And therefore (g) if one Coparcener maketh a Lease for yeares, yet a Writ of Partition doth lye. But if one or both make a Lease for life, a Writ of Partition doth not lye betweene them, because *Non insimul & pro indiuiso tenent*, they doe not hold the freehold together, and the Writ of partition must be against the Tenant of the freehold. (h) If one Coparcener disseise another during this disseisin a Writ of partition doth not lye betweene them for that *Non tenent insimul & pro indiuiso.*

* 3. E. 3. 47. 48.

(g) 21. E. 3. 57. F. N. B. 62. g. 28. H. 6. 2. 11. H. 4. 3. 4. H. 7. 10. b.

(h) 4. H. 7. 9. 11. Ass. 23.

But there be other Partitions in deede then here hath beene mentioned. (i) For a Partition made betweene two Coparceners that the one shall haue and occupie the land from Easter untill the first of August only in severalty by himselfe, and that the other shall haue and occupie the land from the first of August untill the Feast of Easter yearely to them and their heires, this is a good partition. Also if two Coparceners haue two Mannors by discent,

(i) Temps. E. 1. Partition 21. F. N. B. 62. I.

and they make partition, That the one shall haue the one Mannor for one yeare, and the other the other Mannor for this yeare, and so alternis vicibus to them and their heires, this is a good Partition. The same Law is if the partition bee made in forme aforesayd, for two or more yeares, and each Coparcener haue an estate of Inheritance, and no Chattell, albeit either of them alternis vicibus haue the occupation but for a certaine terme of yeares.

Of Partitions in Law, some be by act in Law without iudgement, and some be by iudgement, and not in a Writ de Particione facienda. And of these in order.

(k) 36.H.6.7.

(k) If there be Lord, three Coparceners Mesnes, and Tenant, and one Coparcener purchase the Tenancie, this is not onely a partition of the Mesnaltie, being extinct for a third part, but a diuision of the Seigniorie Paramount, for now he must make seuerall Auowries.

(l) 37.H.6.8.43.E.3.1.

(l) If one Coparcener make a Feoffement in fee of her part, this is a seuerance of the Coparcenarie, and seuerall Writs of Præcipe shall lie against the other Coparcener and the Feoffee.

(m) 17.E.3.14.15.

(m) If two Coparceners be, and each of them taketh husband and haue Issue, the wiues die, the Coparcenarie is diuided, and here is a partition in Law.

(n) 12.E.3.Iudgm.162. 7.ass.10.7.E.3.49.10.ass.17 12.Ass.5.17.10.E.3.40.43. 28.Ass.35.21.Ass.18. 20.E.3.Ass.62. 3 E.3.48 b. 19.H.6.45.7.H.6.4.3.Ed.4.10.
** Bract.li.4.fo.216.b.*
(o) 3.E.3.48.21.R.2.tit. Nuper ob.22. 4.H.7.10. 30.E.1.Nup.ob.18. F.N.B.9.b.
** Brit.fo.112.a.*
(p) Li.6.fo.12.& 13. Morrices case,accorde.

(n) If two Coparceners be, and one disseise the other, and the Disseisee bringeth an Assise, and recouer, it hath beene sayd, That she shall haue iudgment to hold her moitie in seueralty. And this seemeth (say they) verie antient, and thereupon vouch Bracton, * Si res fuerit communis locum haberi, poterit communi diuidendo iudicium. And (o) so (say they) if the one Coparcener recouer against another in a Nuper obijt, or a Rationabili parte, the iudgement shal be, That the Demandant shall recouer and hold in seueraltie. But Britton is to the contrarie, for he saith, * Et si ascun des Parceners soit enget ou disturbe de sa seisin per ses auters Parceners, vn, ou plusors, al disseisee viendra assise per seuerall pleint sur ses Parceners & recouera, mes nemy a tener en seueraltie, mes en common solonque ceo que auant le fist, &c. (p) And this seemeth reasonable, for he must haue his iudgement according to his Plaint, and that was of a moitie, and not of any thing in seueraltie, and the Sherife cannot haue any warrant to make any partition in seueraltie or by Meets and Bounds.

Section 248.

CEt quãt iudgement sera done sur tiel brief, le iudgment serra tiel q̃ partition serra fait enter les parties, & que le Vicount en son proper person alera a les terres & tenements, &c. & que il per l' serement de xij. loyalx homes de son Bayliwicke, &c. serra partition enter les parties, et que lun part de mesmes les Terres & Tenements soient Assignes al plaintif, ou a lun des plaintifs, et vn auter part a vn auter Parcener, &c. nient feasant

And when iudgement shal be giuẽ vpon this Writ, the iudgment shal be thus, That partition shall be made between the parties, & that the Sherife in his proper person shall go to the lãds and tenements, &c. & that hee by the otah of 12 lawful men of his Bailiwicke, &c. shall make partition betweene the parties, & that the one part of the same Lands & tenements shall bee assigned to the pl', or to one of the plaintifs, & another part to another parcener, &c. not making mention in the

Bract.fo.66.&c. Brit.71.&c. Brit.ca.72 Flet.li.5.ca.9.

Note the first iudgment in a Writ of Partition, whereof Litleton here speaketh, is, Quod partitio fiat inter partes prædictas de tenementis prædictis, cum pertinentijs, after which Judgement, by this &c. viz. Tenements, &c. is implied, That a Writ shall be awarded to the Sherife, Quod assumptis tecum 12. liberis & legalibus hominibus de Viceneto tuo, per quos rei veritas melius sciri poterit, in propria persona tua accedas ad tenementa prædicta cum pertiñ, & ibidem per eorum sacrament̃ in præsentia partium prædictarum per te præmuniend' si interesse voluerint, prædicta tenementa cum pertiñ per sacrament̃ bonorum & legalium hominum prædictorum habito respectu ad verum valorem earundem in duas partes equales partiri & diuidi, & vnam partem partium illarum, &c.

The last &c in this Section is euident.

Ockam cap. Quid sit liber iudiciarius. 40.E.3.45.9.ass.2.8.ass.35. 49.E.3.2.Regist. F.N.B.16.

Iudgement, Iudi-

fant mention en le iudgement, de leigne ſoer pluis q̃ d puiſn̄.

Iudgement, of the eldeſt ſiſter, more than of the youngeſt.

cium eſt quaſi iuris dictum, ſo called, becauſe ſo long as it ſtands in force, pro veritate accipitur, and cannot bee contradicted: And thereupon Antiquitie called that excellent Booke in the Exchequer, Domeſday, Dies Iudicij, Sicut enim diſtricti & terribilis examinis illa nouiſſima ſententia nulla tergiuerſationis arte valet eludi, &c. ſic ſententia eiuſdem libri inficiari non poteſt, vel impune declinari ob hoc nos eundem librum iudiciarium nominamus, &c. quod ab eo ſunt, & prædicto iudicio non licet vlla ratione diſcedere. By Littleton it appeareth, That the formes of Iudgements, pleas, and other legall proceedings, doe conduce much to the right vnderſtanding of the Law, and of the reaſon thereof, as here Littleton rightly collecteth, vpon the forme of the iudgement that the Sherife ſhall deliuer to them ſuch parts as he thinkes good, and that the eldeſt Coparcener ſhal haue no election when partition is made by the Sherife. And it is to be obſerued, that there be two Iudgements in a Writ of Partition: Of the former Littleton ſpeaketh in this place, And when partition is made by the oath of twelue men, and aſſignement and allotment thereof, and ſo returned by the Sherife, then the latter iudgment is, Ideo conſideratum eſt, quod partitio prædicta firma & ſtabilis imperpetuũ teneatur, and this is the principall iudgement. (q) And of the other before this be giuen, no Writ of Error doth lie. (q) *Lib.11.fol.40. Hill.39.Eliz. Rot.327.in Banke le Roy, inter Ant. Countes de War. et le Seignior Berkley.*

¶ *Shireue* is a word compounded of two Saxon words, viz. Shire, and Reue. Shire, Satrapia, or Comitatus, commeth of the Saxon Verbe Shiram, i. Partiri, for that the whole Realme is parted and diuided into Shires: And Reue is Præfectus, or præpoſitus; ſo as Shireue is the Reue of the Shire, Præfectus Satrapiæ, Prouinciæ, or Comitatus. And he is called Præfectus, becauſe he is the chiefe Officer to the King within the Shire; for the words of his Patent be, Commiſſimus vobis cuſtodiam Comitatus noſtri de, &c. And he hath a threefold cuſtodie, triplicem cuſtodiam, viz. Firſt, Vitæ Iuſtitiæ, for no ſuit begins, and no Proceſſe is ſerued but by the Sherife. Alſo he is to returne indifferent Iuries for the triall of mens liues, liberties, lands, goods, &c. Secondly, Vitæ legis, hee is after long ſuits and chargeable, to make execution, which is the life and fruit of the Law. Thirdly, Vitæ Reipublicæ, He is Principalis Conſeruator pacis within the Countie, which is the life of the Commonwealth, Vita Reipublicæ pax.

He is called before Sect.234. Viſcount, in Latyne, Vicecomes, i. Vice Comitis, that is, in ſtead of the Earle of that Countie, who in antient time had the regiment of the Countie vnder the King. For it is ſayd in the Mirror,* That it appeareth by the ordinance of antient Kings before the Conqueſt, That the Earles of the Counties had the cuſtodie or gard of the Counties, and when the Earles left their cuſtodies or gards, then was the cuſtodie of Counties committed to Viſcounts, who therefore (as it hath beene ſayd) are called Vicecomites, and Ockam cap. Quid centuſ, &c. Porro Vicecomes dicitur, quod vicem Comitis ſuppleat *Vide the ſecond part of the Inſtitutes W.1.cap.10.* *(*) Mirror cap.1.§.3.* *Ockam cap. Quid Centus. &c.*

Marculphus ſaith, This office is, Iudiciaria dignitas. Lampridius, That it is Officium dignitatis. Forteſcue ſaith, Quod Vicecomes eſt nobilis officiarius. And ſee there, and obſerue well his honourable and ſolemne election and creation at this day. But to confirme all that hath bin ſaid touching this point, and to conclude the ſame, among the Lawes of Edward the Confeſſor I find it thus recorded, Verum quod modo vocatur Comitatus olim apud Britones temporibus Romanorum in Regno iſto Britanniæ vocabatur conſulatus, & qui modo vocantur Vicecomites tunc temporis Vice conſules vocabantur; ille vero dicebatur viceconſul qui conſule abſente ipſius vices ſupplebat in iure & in foro. Herein many things are worthie of obſeruation: Firſt, for the antiquitie of Counties. Secondly, That which wee called Comitatum, the Romanes more Latinely called Conſulatum. Thirdly, whom the Saxons afterwards called (as hath beene ſayd) Shireue or Earle, the Romans called Conſul. Fourthly, That the Sherife was deputy of the conſul or earle, & therfore the Romans called him Viceconſul, as we at this day cal him Vicecomes. Fiftly, That the Sherife in the Romans time, and before, was a Miniſter to the Kings Courts of Law & Iuſtice, & had then a Court of his own, which was the County Court, then called Curia Conſulatus, as appeareth by theſe words, Ipſius vices ſupplebat in iure & in foro. Sixtly, That this Realme was diuided into Shires and Counties, and thoſe Shires into Cities, Burroughs, and Townes, by the Brittains. So that King Ælfreds diuiſion of Shires and Counties, was but a renouation or more exact deſcription of the ſame. Laſtly, the conſequence that will follow vpon theſe things being ſo antient, (as in the time of, and before the Romans) the ſtudious Reader will eaſily collect. And afterwards, fol 135 amongſt the Lawes of the ſame King it appeareth, That thoſe whom the Saxons ſometimes called (and now we call) Ældermen, or Eorles, the Romans called Senatores, Et ſimiliter olim apud Britones temporibus Romanorum in regno iſto Britanniæ vocabantur ſenatores qui poſtea temporibus Saxonũ vocabantur Aldermani, non propter ætatem, ſed propter ſapientiam & dignitatem cum quidam adoleſcentes eſſent iuriſperiti tamen & ſuper hoc experti. *Forteſcue cap.24.* *12.R.2.cap.4.* *Lambert fol.129.12.* *Caſar poliebro Huntingdon polidor inter leges. Malmucii. Hooker lib.2.*

De son Baylivvicke. It appeareth before, that the Enquest must be De vicineto, of the place where the lands doe lie, and not generally de Baliua tua. By this it appeareth, That the Sherife is Balivus, and his Countie called Baliua, and therefore it is good to be seene, what Balivus originally signified, and whereof it is derived.

Flet. lib. 2. cap. 67.

Baylife is a French word, and signifies an Officer concerning the administration of Iustice of a certaine Province, and because a Sherife hath an office concerning the administration of Iustice within his Countie or Bayliwicke, therefore he calleth his Countie, Baliua sua, for example, when he cannot find the Defendant, &c. he returneth, Non est inuentus in Baliua mea.

Bracton lib. 3. tract. 2. cap. 33. nu. 3. Idem lib. 3. fo. 121. b.

I haue heard great question made, what the true exposition of this word Balivus is. In the Statute of Magna Charta cap. 28. the letter of that Statute is, Nullus Balivus de cætero ponat aliquem ad legem manifestam nec ad iuramentum simplici loquela sua sine testibus fidelibus ad hoc inductis. And some haue sayd, That Balivus in this statute signifieth any Iudge, for the Law must be waged and made before the Iudge. And this Statute (say they) extends to the Courts of common Pleas, Kings Bench, &c. For they must bring with them Fideles testes, &c. and so hath been the usage to this day.

Bract. li. 3. 156. b. Brit fo. 56. Flet. li. 2. ca. 63.

But I haue perused a verie antient and learned reading upon this Statute, and the Reader taketh it, That at the Common Law before this Statute, he that would make his Law in any Court of Record, must bring with him Fideles Testes. And this opinion herein is warranted by Glanuile, who wrote in the raigne of Henrie the second. But the Reader holdeth, That in the Courts which were not of Record, as the Countie Court, the Hundred Court the Court Baron, &c. there the Def. without any faithfull witnesses, might before this Stat. haue made his Law: for remedie whereof this Act was made, and therefore (saith he) the statute extendeth to the Iudges of such Courts as are not of Record. In 10. H. 4. it is holden, That if a Lord that hath a Franchise in a Leet, doth not enquire of things enquirable, and punish them, the Sherife shall enquire in his Turne, Et si le Vicount ne fare en son Torne, le Baylie le Roy enquirer quant il vient, ou autrement serra inquise per Iustice en Eire. Where Baylie le Roy is understood Iustice le Roy. And in the Mirror * it is holden, That the Statute doth extend to euerie Iustice, Minister of the King, Steward, &c. and all comprehended under this word Baylife.

Glanu. li. 1. ca. 9.

10. H. 4. 4.

* Mir. ca. 5. §. 2. Vi. Bract. fo. 409. Flet. li. 2. ca. 63. 56.

The chiefe Magistrates in divers antient Corporations are called Baylifs, as in Ipswich, Yarmouth, Colchester, &c. And Baylife in French, is Dicecetes Nomarcha, in English, a Baylife or Gouernor. But of this thus much shall suffice.

Sect. 249.

Brit. fo. 185. b. acc. Bract. l. 2. fo. 71. &c. Flet. li. 5. ca. 9.

ET de la partition que le Vicount ad issint fait, il ferra notice as Iustices south son Seale, & les Seales de chescun de les 12. &c. Et issint en ceo case poies veier que leigne soer navera my la primer election, mes le Vicount luy assignera sa part que el auera, &c. Et poit estre que le Vicount doit assigner primerment un part a le plus puisne, &c. & darreinement al eigne, &c.

AND of the partition which the Sherife hath so made, hee shall giue notice to the Iustices vnder his Seale, and the seales of euerie of the 12. &c. And so in this case you may see, that the eldest sister shall not haue the first election, but the Sherife shall assigne to her her part which shee shal haue, &c. And it may be that the Sherife will assigne first one part to the youngest, &c. and last to the eldest, &c.

South son Seale, &c. Note, the partition made and deliuered by the Sherife and Iurors, ought to bee returned into the Court vnder the Seale of the Sherife, and the seals of the twelue Iurors, for the words of the Iudiciall writ of Partition, which doth command the Sherife to make partition, are, Assumptis tecum 12. &c. (so as there must be twelue) & partitionem inde, &c. scire facias Iusticiarijs, &c. sub sigillo tuo, & sigillis eorum per quorum sacramentum partitionem illam feceris, &c. And this is the reason wherfore in this case the partition which they make upon oath, ought to be returned under their Seales: and the reason of that is for the more strengthening of the partition by the 12. and that the Sherife should not returne what partition he would. Now after all this, this (&c.) viz.12.&c. doth imply, that the principall iudgement upon the partition so returned is, Ideo consideratum est per Curiam quod partitio firma & stabilis imperpetuum teneatur, the latter two (&c.) are euident. *Lib.11.fol.40.in Metcalfes Case*

Section 250.

¶ ET nota q̄ partition per agreement parenter parceners, poit estre fait per la ley enter eux, auxibien per parol sans fait, come per fait.

AND note that partition by agreement betweene Parceners may bee made by Law betweene them, aswell by paroll without Deed, as by Deed.

¶ Here it appeareth that (r) not only Lands and other things that may passe by Liuerie without Deed, but things also that doe lie in grant, as Rents, Commons, Aduowsons and the like that cannot passe by grant without Deed, whether they be in one Countie or in seuerall Counties may be parted and deuided by Paroll without Deed. (s) But a partition betweene Ioyntenants is not good without Deed, albeit it be of Lands and that they bee compellable to make partition by the Statutes of 31.H.8.cap.10. and 32.H.8 cap 32 because they must pursue that Act by Writ, de partitione facienda, & a partition betweene ioyntenants without Writ remayns at the Common Law which could not be done by Paroll. And so it is and for the same reason of Tenants in Common. But if two Tenants in Common be, & they make partition by Paroll, & execute the same in seueralty by Liuerie this is good, and sufficient in Law. And therefore where Bookes say, that Ioyntenants made partition without Deed, it must be intended of Tenants in common, and executed by Liuerie.

(r) 3.E.4.9.10. 9.E.4.38. 11.H.4.2. 9.H.4. Partition 13. 21.E.3.38.

(s) Vide Sect.290. 3.H.4.1. 19.H.6.25. 28.H.6.2. 3.E.4.9.10. 47.E.3.22. 47.Ass.8. 19.H.6.1. 17.E.3.46. 30.Ass.8. Lib.4.fol.73. Li.6.fol.12.13. 2.H.7.5. Dier 18.Eliz.358. 31.H.8.Dyer 46. 2 Eliz. Dyer 179. 28.H.8.Dyer 29. 1.Mar.Dyer 98.

Nota, betweene Ioyntenants there is a twofold priuitie, viz in estate and in possession, betweene Tenants in Common, there is priuitie only in possession, and not in estate, but Parceners haue a threefold priuitie, viz. in estate, in person, and in possession.

Section 251. & 252.

¶ ITem si deux meases discendont a deux Parceners, & lun mease vault per an 20. s. lauter forsque 10. s. per an, en cest cas partition poit estre fait enter eux en tiel forme, cestascauoir, que un parcener auera lun mease, & que lauter parcener auera lauter mease, & celuy que auer le mease, que est de value de 20 s. & ses heires, payerent un annual rent

ALso if two Meses discend to two Parceners, and the one Mease is worth twenty shillings *per annum*, and the other but ten shillings *per annum*. In this case partition may bee made betweene them in this manner, to wit, the one Parcener to haue the one Mease, and the other Parcener the other Mease. And she which hath the Mease worth 20. shillings *per annum*, and her heires shal pay

¶ P*Er parol.* Nota, here (t) a Rent may be granted for oweltie of partition without Deed, euen as a Rent in case of a Lease for yeares, for life, or a gift in taile may bee reserued without Deed, and so may a Rent be assigned to a woman out of the Land whereof shee is Dowable, &c. without Deed, but albeit an exchange for Lands in the same Countie may be without Deed, yet (u) a Rent granted for egaltie of the same exchange cannot be without Deed, and the cause of the difference is apparant, for Coparceners are in by discent, and compellable to make partition.

¶ *Le Rent, &c.* (w) The same Law is of Common of Estouers, or a Corodie, or a Common

(t) 8.E.3.16. 21.Ass.p.1. 21.E.3.38. 11.H.4.3.61. 45.E.3.21. 2.H.6.14. 21.H.6.11. 1.Mar.Dyer 91.

of Pasture, &c. or a way granted vpon the partition by the one Coparcener to the other. All which and the like albeit they lye in grant, yet vpon the partition may they be granted without deed.

¶ *Issuant hors de mesme le mease, &c.* (x) For if it bee granted out of other Lands then discended to the Coparceners then there must be a Deed. (z) But if the Rent be granted generally (out of no land in certaine) for oweltie of partition, pro residuo terræ, it shall bee intended out of the purpartie of her that granteth it.

(x) 1. Marie Dier 91.

(z) 29. Ass. 23. 29. E. 3. 9. b. Pl. Com. 34.

(a) If there bee three Coparceners and they make partition, and one of them grant twentie shillings per annum out of her part to her two sisters, and their heires, for Egalitie of partition, the Grantees are not ioyntenants of this Rent, but the Rent is in nature of Coparcenary, and after the death of the one Grantee, the moity of the rent shall discend to her issue in course of Coparcenary, and not suruiue to the other, for that the Rent doth come in recompence of the Land, & therefore shall ensue the nature thereof, and if the grant had beene made to them two of a Rent of twenty shillings, viz. to the one ten shillings, and to the other ten shillings, yet shall they haue the Rent in course of Coparcenary, and ioyne in action for the same.

(a) 15. H. 7. 14. 29. Ass. 23. 29. E. 3. 9. b.

de v. s. issuant hors de mesme le mease a lauter parcener, & a ses heires a touts iours, pur ceo que chescun de eux auoit owelty en value.

a yeerely rent of fiue shillings, issuing out of the same Mease to the other Parcener and to her heires for euer, because each of them should haue equalitie in value.

Sect. 252.

CE tiel partition fait per parol est assets bone, & mesme le Parcener q̃ auera le rent & ses heires, purront distreiner de common droit, pur le rent en le dit mease de le value de 20. s. si le rent de 5. s. soit aderere en ascun temps en quecunque mains q̃ mesme le mease deuiendra, coment que ne fuit vnques ascun escripture de ceo fait enter eux d̃ tiel rent.

AND such partition made by paroll is good enough, and that Parcener who shal haue the rent and his heires may distreine of common right for the Rent in the said mease, worth twentie shillings, if the rent of 5. shillings be behind at any time, in whose hands soeuer the same mease shall come, although there neuer were any writing of this made betweene them for such a rent.

(b) If one Coparcener be married, and for oweltie of partition the husband and wife grant a Rent to the other two out of the part of the Fem Couert, this partition being equall, shall charge the part of the Fem Couert for euer.

(b) 29. Ass. 23. 29. E. 3. 9. 17. E. 3. 10.

(c) If two Coparceners by Deed indented alien, both their parts to another in fee, rendring to them two and their heires a Rent out of the Land, they are not ioyntenants of this Rent, but they shal haue the Rent in course of Coparcenary, because their right in the Land out of which the Rent is reserued, was in Coparcenary.

(c). 38. E. 3. 26. b.

¶ *Purront distreiner de common droit, &c.* That is, (e) in this case the Law doth giue a distresse, lest the Grantee should be without remedie, for the which vpon the partition she hath giuen a valuable recompence in Land, which discended, &c. And so in the case of Dower aboue mentioned.

(e) 1. Marie Dyer 91. 8. E. 3. 16. and other the Bookes abouesaid.

Sect. 253.

¶ *Terres & Tenements, &c.* here (&c.) implyeth a Caution, viz. that they bee such Lands

CEn mesm̃ l' maner est, de touts maners de terres & tenements

IN the same manner it is of all manner of Lands and Tenements, &c. lou tiel rent est reserue a vn, ou a diuis Parceners sur tiel partition &c. Mes tiel rent nest pas rent seruice, mes est rent charge de cómon droit ewe & reserue pur egaltie de partition.

ments, &c. where such rent is reserued to one or to diuers parceners vpon such partition, &c. but such rent is not Rent seruice but a rent charge of common right had and reserued for egaltye of partition.

and tenements out of which a Rent for egaltye of partition may be granted, whereof sufficient hath beene said before.

¶ *Reserue al vn.* Here reseruation is taken for a grant, and if it be vsed vpon the partition, doth amount in this case to a grant, which is worthy the obseruation.

Sect. 254.

¶ ET nota, que nulles sont appelles parceners p le common ley, mes females, ou les heires de females que veignont a terres & tenements per discent. Car si soers purchase terres ou tenements, de ceo ils sont appelles ioyntenants, & nemy parceners.

AND note that none are called parceners by the Common law, but females or the heires of females which come to lands or tenements by discent: for if sisters purchase lands or tenements of this they are called ioyntenants and not parceners.

This needes no explanation.

Sect. 255.

¶ [ITem si deux Parceners de terre en fee simple, font partition enter eux, & la part de vn vault pluis q̄ le part d' lauter, si els fueront al temps de la partition de pleine age s. de 21 ans, donq̄ la partition, touts dits demurrera, & ne serra vnques defeat. Mes si les tenements (dont els font partition) soyent a eux en fee taile, & le part que lun ad est

ALso if two parceners of land in fee simple make partition between themselues, and the part of the one valueth more then the part of the other, if they were at the time of the partition of full age, s. of 21. yeares; then the partition shall alway remaine and bee neuer defeated. But if the tenements (whereof they make partition) be to them in fee taile, and the part of the one

¶ *DOnques le partition touts dits demurrera, &c.* Hereby it appeareth that the inequality of the value shall not impeach a partition made of lands in fee simple betweene Coperceners of full age, no more then it shall doe in case of an exchange.

9. H. 6. 5. and other the bookes aboue-said.

¶ *Ils sont concludes durant lour vies.* This inequall partition doth so conclude the parceners themselues, as she that hath the vnequall part shall not auoyde it during her life.

¶ *Concludes.* This word is deriued of Con and Claudo, and in this sence signifieth to close or shut vp her mouth that shee cannot speake to the contrary.

Husband & wife tenants

meilleur en annual value, que est la part de lauter, coment q̃ els sont concludes durant lour vies a defeater la partitiõ, uncore si le parcener q̃ ad le meinder part en value ad issue & deux, lissue poit disagreer a la partition, & enter et occupier ẽ cõmon lauter part que fuit alotte a sa Aunt, & issint lauter poit enter & occupier en common lauter part alotte a sa soer, &c. sicome nul partition ust este fait.

is better in yearly value then the part of the other, albeit they bee concluded during their liues to defeate the partition, yet if the parcener which hath the lesser part in value hath issue and die, the issue may disagree to the partition, and enter and occupie in common the other part which was alotted to his Aunt, and so the other may enter and occupie in cõmon the other part allotted to her sister, &c. as if no partition had beene made.

11.Ass.p.23.

in speciall tayle of certaine lands in fee haue issue a daughter, the wife dyeth, the husband by a second wife hath issue another daughter both the daughters enter (where the eldest is only inheritable) and make partition, the eldest daughter is concluded during her life to impeach the partition, or to say that the youngest is not heire, and yet she is a stranger to the taile, but in respect of priuity in their persons the partition shall conclude, for a partition betweene meere strangers in that case is voide, but the issue of the eldest shall auoide this partition as issue in taile.

See after the Chapter of Garr.

(g) 51.E.3.34.35. 2.Er. Bastardie 19. 11.Ass.23. 30.Ass.7. 17.E.3.59.

(g) I.S. seised of Lands in fee hath issue two daughters, Rose and Anne, bastards eigne, and Mulier puisne and dieth. Rose and Anne doe enter and make partition. Anne and her heires are concluded for euer.

Section 256

Item si deux parceners de tenemẽts ẽ fee preigne barons, et els et lour barons font partition enter eux, si la part lun est meinder en annual value q̃ la part lauter, durant les vies lour barons la partition estoyera en sa force. Mes coment que il estoyera durant les vies les barons, uncore apres la mort le baron, celuy feme q̃ ad le meinder part poit enter en le part sa soer

Also if two parceners of lands in fee take husbands, and they and their husbands make partition betweene them, if the part of the one bee lesse in value then the part of the other during the liues of their husbands the partition shall stand in its force. But albeit it shal stand during the liues of their husbands, yet after the death of the husband, that woman which hath the lesser part may enter into

Els & lour barons. Here it appeareth that the wife must be partie to the partition, and so are the books * to be intended that speake of this matter.

(*) 42.Ass.22. 8.E.4.4. 9.E.3.38. 15.E.4.20.F.N.B 62. 20.Ass.23.9.H.6.5. 43.Ass.14.

Et defeatera le partition. Note the partition shall not be defeated for the surplusage only to make the partition equall, but here it appeareth that it shall be auoyded for the whole. But of this more shall be said hereafter in this chapter, Sectione 264. (h) And though the partition be vnequall, yet is not the partition voyde, but voydable, for if after the decease of the husband, the wife entreth into the vnequall part, and agreeth thereunto, this shall binde, and therefore Littleton

(h) Vid.2.E.2.Cui in vita 17.

soer come est auantdit, et defeatera la partition.

her sisters part as is aforesaid, and shall defeate the partition.

vseth the word (Defeatera) which proueth it to bee voydable.

Sect. 257.

¶ MEs si l' partitiõ fait penter les barons fuit tiel, que chescun part al temps dallotment fait, fuit de egall annuall value, donque il ne poit apres estre defeat en tielx cases.

BVt if the partition made betweene the husbands were thus, that each part at the time of the allotment made was of equall yearely value, then it cannot afterwards bee defeated in such cases.

¶ *Perenter les barons.* This is mistaken, for the originall is Parenter eux, that is, betweene the Barons and Fems, and not, as it is here betweene the Barons, therefore this error would be hereafter reformed.

¶ *Al temps del allotment.* Hereby it appeareth, that if the parts at the time of the partition be of equal yearely value, neither the wiues nor their heires shall euer auoyde the same, and the reason hereof is, for that the husbands and wiues were compellable by Law to make partition, and that which they are compellable to doe in this case by Law, they may doe by agreement without processe of Law. If the annuall value of the land be equall at the time of the partition and after become vnequall by any matter subsequent, as by surrounding, ill husbandrie or such like, yet the partition remaines good. *9. H. 6. 5. And other the bookes abouesaid.*

Iudicis officium est vt res ita tempora rerum,
Quærere, quæsito tempore tutus eris.

But if the partition be made by force of the Kings writ, and iudgement thereof giuen, it shall binde the Fem-couerts for euer, albeit the parts be not of equall annuall value because it is made by the Sherife by the oath of twelue men by Authority of Law. And the iudgement is that partition shall remaine firme and stable for euer as hath beene said. (a) But a partition in the Chancery where one Copercener is of full age and sueth Liuery, and one other is within age and hath an vnequall part allotted to her, this shal not binde her at full age, for in a writ directed to the Escheator to make partition there is a Salvo iure; And there is no iudgement vpon such a partition. But if such a partition be equall it shall binde, so that a part of the land holden In Capite be allotted to euery of the Coparceners, for to that end there is an expresse Prouiso in the writ. (b) And this partition may bee auoyded either by Scire fac' in the Chancery, or by a writ De partitione facienda at the Common Law at her full age.

(a) *F. N. B.* 256. 259. 260 261. 262. 263. *9. H. 6. 6.* 21. *E.* 3. 31.

(b) *Vide* 21. *E.* 3. 31.

Sect. 258.

¶ ITem si deux parceners sont, et le puisne esteant deins lage de 21. ans, et partition est fait enter eux, issint que la purpartie que est allot al puisne est de meindre value q̃ la purpartie lauter, en cest case le

ALso if two Coparceners be, and the yongest beeing within the age of twenty one yeres, partition is made betweene them, so as the part which is allotted to the youngest, is of lesse value than the part of the

¶ As before in the case of the Fem-Couert, (c) so it is in the case of the Enfant, for if the partition be equall at the time of the allotment, it shall binde him for euer, because he is cõpellable by Law to make partition, and he shall not haue his age in a Partitione facienda,

(c) 43. *Ass.* 14. *9. H. 6.* 5. 6. 7. *E.* 3. 13. 8. *E.* 3. 34. 10. *H.* 4. 5. 31. *Ass.* 16. 21. *H. 6.* 25.

da, and though the partition be vnequall, and the Enfant hath the lesser part, yet is not the partition voyd, but voidable by his entry, for if hee take the whole profits of the vnequall part, after his ful age the partition is made good for euer. And therfore Littlet. here giueth him a caueat, That in that case he take not the whole profits of his vnequall part, neither shall an vnequall partition in the Chancerie bind an Infant as appeareth before. But a partition made by the Kings Writ de Partitione facienda, by the Sherife by the oath of twelue men, and iudgement thereupon giuen, shall bind the Enfant, though his part bee vnequall, Causa qua supra.

le puisne durant le temps de son nonage, et auxy quaunt el vient a pleine age, s. de 21. ans, poit enter en la purpartie a sa soer allot & defeatera la partition. Mes bien soy gard tiel Parcener quant el vient a sa plein age, que el ne preigne a son vse demesne touts les profits des terres ou tenements que a luy fuer allots. Car donques el soy agreea a le partition a tiel age, en quel case la partition estoppera et demurra en sa force: Mes perauenture les profits de la moitie el poit prender, relinquitant les profits de lauter moitie a sa soer.

other; in this case the youngest during the time of her nonage, and also when shee commeth to full age, s. of 21. yeares, may enter into the part allotted to her sister, and shall defeat the partition: but let such parcener take heed when shee comes to her full age, that shee taketh not to her owne vse all the profits of the lands or tenements which were allotted vnto her, for then shee agrees to the partition at such age, in which case the partition shall stand and remaine in it's force: but peraduenture she may take the profits of the moitie, leauing the profits of the other moitie to her sister.

Sect. 259.

*Yl. Sect. 402, 403.

¶ THe Law hath prouided for the safety of a mans or womans estate, that * before their age of twentie one yeares they cannot bind themselues by any Deed, nor alien any land, goods, or chattels.

¶ *Age de 21. ans.* Before this age a man or woman is called an Enfant.

Brit. fo. 65, 66. & 101. Flet. li. 3. ca. 14.

¶ *Fait.* Factum, Anglice, a Deed, and signifieth in the Common Law, an Instrument consisting on three things, viz. Writing, Sealing, and Deliuerie, comprehending a bargaine or contract betweene partie and partie, man or woman. It is called of the Ciuilians, Literarum obligatio.

¶ *Feoffement.* Of this word sufficient hath bin

¶ ET est ascauoir que quant il est dit, que males ou females sont de pleine age, ceo serra entendue de age de 21. ans, car si deuant tiel age, ascun fait ou feoffement, grant, release, confirmation, Obligation, ou auter scripture soit fait per ascun de eux, &c. ou si ascun deins tiel age, soit Baylife ou receiuer a ascun home, &c. tout serue pur nient, & poit estre auoyde. Auxy

AND it is to bee vnderstood, that when it is sayd, That males or females bee of full age, this shall be intended of the age of 21. yeares, for if before such age, any deed or feoffement, graunt, release, confirmation, Obligation, or other writing bee made by any of them, &c. or if any within such age be Baylife or Receiuer to any man, &c. all serue for nothing, and may be auoyded. Al-

Aucun home deuaunt le dit age, ne sera my ture en un Enquest, &c.	So a man before the saydage shall not bee sworne in an Enquest, &c.	sayd before in the first Chapter of the first booke.

¶ *Grant.* Concessio is in the Common law a conueyance of a thing that lies in grant, and not in Liuerie, which cannot passe without Deed, as Aduowsons, Seruices, Rents, Commons, Reuersions, and such like. Of this also sufficient likewise hath beene sayd in the first Chapter of the first booke.

Lib. 3. fol. 63. in Lincolne Colledge Case.

¶ *Release, Confirmation, &c.* Of these shall be spoken hereafter in their proper places and Chapters.

¶ *Obligation* is a word of his owne nature of a large extent, but it is commonly taken in the Common Law, for a Bond containing a penaltie with condition for payment of money, or to doe or suffer some act or thing, &c. and a Bill is most commonly taken for a single Bond without condition.

¶ *Ou auter scripture soit fait per ascun de eux, &c.* Here by this (&c.) is implied some exceptions out of this generalitie, (d) as an Infant may bind himselfe to pay for his necessarie meat, drinke, apparell, necessarie physicke, and such other necessaries, and likewise for his good teaching or instruction, whereby he may profit himselfe afterwards: but if he bind himselfe in an Obligation or other writing, with a penaltie for the payment of any of these, that Obligation shall not bind him. (e) Also other things of necessitie shall bind them, as a presentation to a Benefice, for otherwise the Laps shall incurre against him. Also if an Infant be an Executor vpon payment of any debt due to the Testator, hee may make an acquittance, but in that case a release without payment is voyd, and generally whatsoeuer an Infant is bound to doe by Law, the same shall bind him, albeit he doth it without suit of Law. But of this common learning this little tast shall suffice.

(d) 18. E. 4. 2. 21. H. 6. 31. Lib. 9. fol. 87. Pinchons. Case.

(e) 8. E. 4. 4. 9. H. 6. 5 17. E. 3. 9. 29. Ass. 25. 2. Maria. Dier. 104. 105.

¶ *Baylife ou Receiuer al ascun home, &c.* By this (&c.) many things are implied, as that by Baylife is understood a seruant that hath administration and charge of lands, goods, and Chattels, to make the best benefit for the owner, against whom an Action of Account doth lie for the profits which he hath raised or made, or might by his industrie or care haue reasonably raised or made, his reasonable charges and expences deducted. (f) But one under the age of twentie one yeares shall not be charged in any such account, because by intendment of Law, before his full age he hath not skill and abilitie to raise or make any such improuement and profit.

Fleta Lib. 2. cap. 64. & cap. 67 Brit. fol. 62. 70. Fleta Lib. 2. cap. 64. 41. E. 3. 39. 46. E. 3. Account 40. 2. R. 2. ibidem 45. 6. R. 2 ibid. 3. E. 3. 10.

(f) 13. E. 3. Infant 9. 17. E. 2. Account 121. 21 E. 3. 8 10. H. 4. 14. 2. H. 4. 13. Regist. 135.

An account against a Receiuer, is when one receiueth money to the vse of another, to render an account, but vpon his account he shall be allowed his expences and charges. (g) And therefore a man cannot charge a Baylife as a Receiuer because then the Baylife should lose his expences and charges.

(g) 43. E. 3. 31. 46. E. 3. 3. b. 4. H. 6. 27.

In an account against a Receiuer, the Plaintife must declare by whose hands the Defendant receiued the money, which he shall not doe in the case of a Baylife. (h) But in some case in an Action of Account against one as Receptor denariorum, hee shall haue allowance of his expences and charges, and also shall account for the profit he receiued, or might reasonably receiue, and this was prouided by Law in fauour of Merchants, and for aduancement of trade and traffique.

(h) 30. E. 1. Account 127. 47. E. 3 22. 10. H. 7. 16. Brall. li. 5. fo. 334. Brit. f. 62. Fle. li. 2. c. 64. & 51. 5. E. 3. 1. Lib. Intrat. 17, 18, 19.

As if two ioynt Merchants occupie their stocke, goods, and merchandizes in common to their common profit, one of them naming himselfe a Merchant, shall haue an account against the other naming him a Merchant, and shall charge him as Receptor denariorum ipsius B. ex quacunque causa & contractu ad communem vtilitatem ipsorum A. & B. prouenien' sicut per legem mercatoriam rationabiliter monstrare poterit.

(i) If there be two Ioyntenants or Tenants in Common of lands, and the one make the other his Bailife of his moitie, he shall haue an Action of Account against him as Baylife: And so are the Bookes to be intended, that speake of an Action of Account in that case.

(i) 45. E. 3. 10. 3. E. 3. 27. 39. E. 3. 27. 47. E. 3. 22. F. N. B. 118.

So as there be but three kinds of writs of Account, viz. against one as Gardeine, whereof Littleton hath spoken before in the Chapter of Socage. The second against one as Baylife: And the third, as Receiuer, as here it appeareth. (k) For a man shall not bee charged in an Account as Surueyor, Controller, Apprentice, Reue, or Heyward. And to maintaine an Action of Account, there must be either a priuitie in deed by the consent of the partie, for (l) against a Disseisor or other wrong doer no account doth lie, or a priuitie in Law ex prouisione legis, made by the Law, as against a Gardein, &c. whereof sufficient hath been spoken in the Chapter of Socage.

(k) 13. E. 3. Account 76. 41. E. 3. ibidem 34. 8. E. 3. 46. 8. E. 4. 6. b. F. N. B. 119. d.

(l) 2. Mar. B. Account 89. F. N. B. 117. Pl. Com. 542 2. H. 4. 12. 33. H. 6. 2. 4. H. 7. 6. &c.

¶ Ne

(m) Bracton lib.5. fo.340.b.
(n) 13.E.3. Ley 50.
(o) 26.E.3.63. 2. Maria Dier 104.105.
(p) Vid. devant Cap. de Homage et Cap. de Fealtie Sect. 85.91. Bract.lib.2.fo.124. Britton fo.73.74. et fol.19. Fleta lib.1 cap.27.
(q) 11.H6.40. 1.H.7.25. 15.E.4.2.
(r) 46.E.3.10. 9.E.4.24. 15.E.4.2. 21.H.3.23.

¶ *Ne serra iure en vn Enquest, &c.* By this (&c.) is implied a maxime in Law, (m) Quod minor iurare non potest. For example, (n) An Infant cannot make his Law of Non summons: (o) And therefore the default shall not grieue him, for seeing the meane to excuse the default is taken away by Law, the default it selfe shall not preiudice him. But yet this rule hath an exception, That (p) an Infant when hee is of the age of twelue yeares, shall take the Oath of Allegeance to the King: and this was, as Bracton saith, Secundum leges Sancti Edwardi. But indeed such was the Law in the time of King Arthur, (q) An Infant cannot vpon his oath make his law in an Action of Debt. (r) And the husband and wife of full age for the debt of the wife, before the couerture shall make their Law.

Section 260.

¶ Item si terres ou Tenements soyent dones a vn home en le taile, quel ad tant des terres en fee simple, et ad issue deux files, et deuie, & ses deux files font partition ent eux, issint que la terre en fee simple est allot a le file puisne en allowance des terres & tenements tailes allottes a le file eigne, si apres tiel partition fait, la puisne file alienast sa terre en fee simple a vn auter en fee, & ad issue fits ou file & deuie, lissue poit bien entrer en les Tenements tailes & eux tener & occupier en purpartie ouesque son Aunt. Et ceo est pur deux causes: vn est, pur ceo que lissue ne poit auer ascun remedie de la terre alien per sa mere, pur ceo que la terre fuit a luy en fee simple, & pur tant que il est vn de les heires en taile, & nad my ascun recompence de ceo que a luy affiert de les Tenements tailes, il est reason

ALso if Lands or Tenements be giuen to a man in taile, who hath as much land in fee simple, and hath issue two daughters and die, & his two daughters make partition betweene them, so as the Land in Fee-simple is allotted to the younger daughter, in allowance for the lands and Tenements in Taile allotted to the elder daughter, if after such partition made, the yonger daughter alieneth her land in fee simple, to another in fee, & hath issue a son or a daughter & dies, the issue may wel enter into the lãds in taile & hold and occupie them in purpartie with her aunt. And this is for two causes: one is, for that the issue can haue no remedie for the land sold by the mother, because the land was to her in fee simple, and in as much as she is one of the heirs in taile, & hath no recõpence of that which belongeth to her of the lands in taile, it is reason

¶ *La terre en fee simple est allot a la file puisne.* It is first to be obserued vpon this whole case, That the fee simple Land is allotted to the yongest daughter, and the land entailed to the eldest. This partition Prima facie is good, and herein the partition differeth from the eschange wherein the eschange the estates must bee equall.

But yet this partition by matter subsequent may become voidable, (as Littleton here putteth the case) the eldest Coparcener hath by the partition, and the matter subsequent barred her selfe of her right in the fee simple lands, insomuch as when the youngest sister alieneth the fee simple Lands and dieth, and her Issue entreth into halfe the lands entailed, yet shall not the eldest enter into halfe of the lands in Fee simple vpon the Alienee, for by the alienation, the priuitie of the state is destroyed.

¶ *Le puisne file alien la terre en fee simple, &c.* The same Law it is, if the youngest daugh-

reason que el eit sa purparty de les tenements tailes, & nosmement quant tiel partition ne fait ascun discontinuance.

¶ Mes le contrary est tenus M.10.H.6.s. que le heire ne poit enter sur l'Parcener que ad la terre taile, mes est mis a Formdon.*

that shee hath her portion of the Lands tayled, and namely when such partition doth not not make any discontinuance.

¶ But the contrary is holden *M.10.H.6.* s. that the heire may not enter vpon the parcener who hath the intailed land, but is put to a *Formedon.**

ter had made a gift in tayle, for the Reuersion expectant vpon an estate tayle is of no account in Law, for that it may bee cut off by the tenant in tayle; Otherwise it is of an estate for life or yeares. If in this case the youngest Daughter alien part of the Land in Fee simple, and dieth so as a full recompence for the land entayled discends not to her issue, shee may waiue the taking of any profits thereof and enter into the Land entayled for the Issue in tayle shall neuer bee barred without a full recompence, though there bee a Warrantie in Deed, or in Law discended. If on the other side the eldest Coparcener alien the land entayled and dyeth, her Issue shall haue a Formdon alone for the whole Land entayled, for so long as the partition continueth in force, she is only enheritable to the whole Land entayled.

¶ *Et nad my ascun recompence.* This is intended, as it appeareth of a full recompence.

¶ *Tiel partition ne fait ascun discontinuance.* And the reason thereof is for that it passeth not by Liuery of seisin, but the partition is in truth lesse then a grant, for that it maketh no degree but each Coparcener is in by discent from the common Ancestor. *See more of this in the Chapter of discontinuance. Sectione.*

¶ *Mes le contrary est tenus, &c.* This is no part of Littleton, and is contrary to Law as appeareth by Littleton himselfe, and besides the case intended is not truly vouched, for it is not in 10.H.6. but in 20.H.6. and yet there it is but the opinion of Newton, Obiter, by the way. Vide F. tit. part. 1. *10.H.6.14.*

Section 261.

VN auter cause est, pur ceo que il serra rett la folly del eigne soer que el voit suffer ou agree a tiel partition, ou el puissoit auer si el voile, la moitie de la terre en fee simple, & son moitie des tenements en le taile, pur say pur party, & issint estre sure sans dammage.

ANother reason is for that, it shall be accounted the folly of the eldest sister that shee would suffer or agree to such a partition, where she might if shee would haue had the moity of the Land in Fee Simple, and a moity of Lands entailed for her part; & so to be sure without losse.

¶ *VN auter cause, &c.* This is another reason to proue that by the partition the eldest Daughter hath concluded her selfe as is aforesaid.

¶ *Son moitie des terres en le tayle.* For if a Writ of Partition had beene brought, the eldest should not haue bin compelled to take the whole estate in tayle, for the preiudice that might after ensue, but might haue challenged the one moity of the Lands in Tayle, and another moity of the Lands in Fee simple, and this she might doe ex prouisione legis. But when shee will not submit her to the policie and prouision of the Law, but betake herselfe to her owne policie and prouision, there the Law will not ayde her, as here by Littleton it manifestly appeareth. And so it is in the other case. (*) As if a man be seised of three Mannors of equall value in fee & taketh wife, and chargeth one of the Mannors with a Rent Charge, and dyeth, she may by the prouision of the Law take a third part of all the Mannors and hold them discharged, but if shee will accept the entire Mannor charged, it is holden that she shall hold it charged. *(*) 26.E.3. dower 133. 17.E.2. tit. dower 164. 18.H.6.27.*

Dier.1.Mar.98.

A partition of Lands intayled betweene Parceners, if it bee equall at the time of the partition shall bind the issues in tayle for euer, albeit the one doe alien her part.

But here it may be demanded, that seeing Littleton sayth, that it shall bee taken to bee the folly of the eldest Parcener, &c. what if so be the eldest did not know of the estate tayle eyther in respect of the antiquitie thereof, or for want of hauing of the euidence, or for any other cause, what folly can be imputed to her?

The answer is, That it is presumed in Law, that euery one is Conusant of her right and title to her owne Land; and on the other side it should be arrected great folly in her to be ignorant of her owne title. And therefore the reason of Littleton doth firmely hold.

Section 262.

Auxy si home soit seisie en fee dun carue de terre per iust title, & disseisist vn enfāt deins age dun auter carue, & ad issue deux files, & morust seisi daumbideux carues, lenf. adonques esteant deins age, & les files entront & font partition, issint q̄ lun carue est allotte al purparty lun, come per case al puisne en allowāce dauter carue que est allotte a le purpartie de lauter, si puis lenf. enter en le carue dont il fuit disseisist sur l' possession la Parcener que ad mesme le carue, donques m̄ le Parcener poit entrer en lauter carue que sa soer ad, & tener en Parcenary ouesque luy: Mes si le puisne aliena m̄ la carue a vn auter en fee simple deuant lentrie lenf. & puis lenf. enter sur le possession lalienee, donque

Also if a man bee seised in fee of a carue of Land by iust title, and hee disseise an Infant within age, of an other Carue, and hath issue two Daughters, and dieth seised of both Carues, the Infant being then within age, and the daughters enter and make partition, so as the one Carue is alloted for the part of the one, (as per case to the youngest in allowance of the other carue which is allotted to the purpartie of the other, if afterward the Infant enter into the Carue whereof hee was disseised vpon the possession of the Parcener which hath the same Carue, then the same Parcener may enter into the other Carue which her Sister hath, and hold in Parcenarie with her. But if the yongest alien the same Carue to another in fee before the entry of

Before it appeareth that when the priuitie of the estate is destroyed by the feoffment of one Coparcener, that vpon euiction of a moity by force of an entayle against the other shee shall not enter vpon the alienee. But in this case that Littleton here putteth when the priuity of the state remayneth, and the part of the one is euicted, (*) shee shall enter and hold in Coparcenarie with her other Coparcener, and so it is in the case of an eschange. By reason of the (&c.) in the end of this Section there may two questions bee iustly demanded, what if the whole estate in part of the purpartie of one Parcener be euicted by a title paramont? whether is the whole partition auoyded, for that Littleton here putteth the case that the whole purpartie of the one is defeated?

(*) *15.E.4.3.a.per Littleton. Lib.4.fol.121.122. Bastards Case.*

The second question is whether if but part of the state of one Coparcener bee euicted, as an estate in tayle, or for life leauing a reuersion in the Coparcener, whether that shall auoyde the partition in the whole?

To the first it is answered, that if the whole estate in part of the purparty bee euicted, that shall auoid the partition in the whole, be it of a Mannor, that is entire, or of acres of ground, or the like that bee seuerall, (n) for the partition in that case implyeth for this this purpose both a warranty and a condition in Law, and either of them is entire, and giueth an entry in this case into the whole. And so hath

(n) *13.E.4.3.42.Ass.22.*

que el ne poit enter en lauter Carue, pur ceo que per son alienation el ad luy tout oustrement dismisse dauer ascun pt de les tenements cōe Parcener. Mes si le puisne deuant lentrie lenfant fait de ceo vn leas pur terme dans, ou pur terme de vie, ou en fee tayle, sauant la reuersion a luy, & puis lenfant enter, la parauenture autrement est, pur ceo que el ne soy ceo que fuit en luy, dismisse de tout mes ad reserue a luy le Reuersion & le fee, &c.

the Infant; and after the Infant enter vpon the possession of the Alienee, then she cannot enter into the other Carue, because by her alienation shee hath altogether dismissed her self to haue any part of the Tenements as Parcener. But if the youngest before the entrie of the Infant make a Lease of this for terme of yeares, or for tearme of life, or in Fee Tayle sauing the reuersion to her, and after the Infant enter there peraduenture otherwise it is, because she hath not dismissed herselfe of all which was in her, but hath reserued to her the reuersion, & the fee, &c.

it been lately resolued (o) both in the case of exchange and of the partition.

(o) *Bastards case. Lib.4.fol.121.*

To the second, if any estate of freehold be euicted from the Coparcener in all or part of her purpartie, it shall be auoyded in the whole. As if A. be seised in fee of one acre of land in possession, and of the reuersion of another expectant vpon an estate for life and hee disseise the Lessee for life who makes continuall claym. A. dyeth seised of both Acres, and hath Issue two Daughters, partition is made, so as the one Acre is alloted to the one, and the other Acre to the other, the Lessees enter, the partition is auoyded for the whole, and so likewise hath (p) it beene lately resolued. (q) Yet there is a diuersitie betweene the warrantie, and the condition which the Law createth vpon the partition where one Coparcener taketh benefit of the condition in Law she defeateth the partition in the whole.

(p) *Bastards case, vbi supra.*
(q) *Vide 5.E.3.tit. voucher, 249.*

But when she voucheth by force of the warranty in Law for part, the partition shall not be defeated in the whole, but shee shall recouer recompence for that part. And therein also there is another diuersitie betweene a recouerie in value by force of the warrantie vpon the exchange and vpon the partition: for vpon the exchange he shall recouer a full recompence for all that he looseth, But vpon the partition she shall recouer but the moitie or halfe of that which is lost, to the end that the losse may be equall.

Many other diuersities there be betweene exchanges and partitions, for there are more and greater priuities in case of partition in persons, bloud, and estates, than there is in exchanges; all which were too tedious to rehearse in this place, seeing so much as hath beene said, herein is sufficient for the explanation of the cases of partition which Littleton hath put.

18.E.3.tit. aid 176. 19 H.6.26.

¶ *Donques el ne poet enter en lauter carue, &c.* By this is also approued that which hath beene often said before, that when the whole priuitie betweene Coparceners is destroyed, there ceaseth any recompence to bee expected eyther vpon the condition in Law or warrantie in Law by force of the partition.

¶ *Per son alienation il ad luy tout oustrement dismisse dauer ascun part de les tenements come parcener.* Hereupon it followeth, that if one Parcener maketh a feoffement in Fee, and after her feoffee is impleaded and voucheth the Feoffor, (r) she may haue ayde of her Coparcener to deraigne a warrantie Paramount, but neuer to recouer pro rata against her by force of the warrantie in Law vpon the partition, for Littleton here sayth, that by her alienation shee hath dismissed herselfe to haue any part of the Land as Parcener. And without question as Parcener shee must recouer pro rata, vpon the warrantie in Law against the other Parcener.

(r) *41.E.3.24. 11.H.4.22.23. 14.E.3.aid 24.*

And yet in some case the Feoffee of one Coparcener shall haue ayde of the other Parceners to Deraigne the warranty paramount, and therefore (a) if there bee two Coparceners and they make partition, and the one of them enfeoffes her sonne and heire apparant and dyeth the sonne is impleaded, albeit he be in by the feoffment of his mother, yet shall he pray in ayde of the

(a) *43.E.3.23. Pl.Com. 4.E.3.15. 5.E.3.7. 38.E.3.17. &c.*

(b) 32 E. 1. tit. Aid 178. 3. E. 2. ibid. 163.

the other Coparcener to haue the Warranty Paramount; and the reason (b) of the granting of this aide is for that the warranty betweene the mother and the sonne is by law adnulled, and therefore the Law giueth the sonne albeit he be in by feoffment to pray in aide of the other parcener, to deraigne the Warranty Paramount, wherein is to be obserued the great equity of the Common Law in this case:

Ipsæ etenim leges cupiunt vt iure regantur.

(*) 2. H. 6. 16.

(*) But if a man be seised of lands in fee and hath issue two daughters and make a gift in taile to one of them and die seised of the reuersion in fee which discends to both sisters, and the Donee or her issue is impleaded, she shall not pray in ayde of the other Coparcener either to recouer Pro rata, or to Deraigne the Warranty Paramount, for that the other sister, is a stranger to the state taile whereof the eldest was sole Tenant, and neuer partition was or could be thereof made.

¶ *Mes si le puisne deuant lentrie lenfant fait de ceo vn lease, &c. ou en fee taile sauant le reuersion a luy, &c.* This (vpon that which hath beene said) needeth no explanation. Only this is to be obserued, that albeit it is in the power of tenant in taile to cut off the reuersion, yet if the infant enter before it be cut off, the Law hath such consideration of this reuersion, that shee that loseth it shall enter into her sisters part, and hold with her in Coparcenary for that the priuity betweene them was not wholly destroyed.

Sect. 263.

¶ Item si soient trois ou quater parceners, &c. q̃ font partition enter eux, si le part dun parcener soit defeat p̃ tiel loyal entrie, el poit enter et occupier lauter terres oue touts les auters parceners, et eux compell de faire nouel partition de lauters terres, enter eux, &c.

Also if there be three or foure Coparceners, &c. which make partition betweene them, if the part of the one parcener bee defeated by such lawfull entrie, she may enter and occupie the other lands with all the other parceners, and compell them to make new partition betweene them of the other lands, &c.

¶ *Inter eux, &c.* This (&c.) implyeth that so it is betweene the suruiuing Parceners and the heires of the other, or betweene the heires of Parceners all being dead.

Sect. 264.

¶ Item si sont deux parceners, et lun prent baron, et le baron et sa fem̃ ont issue enter eux, et la feme deuy, et la baron soy tient eyns en le moity com̃ tenant per le curtesie, en ceo cas le parcener q̃ suruesquist, et le tenant per le curtesie bien poient faire partition

Also if there bee two parceners and the one taketh husband and the husband and wife haue issue betweene them and his wife dieth, and the husband keepes himselfe in as tenant by the curtesie, In this case the parcener which surui-

(b) 24. E. 3. 29. 31. E. 3. Brief 339. 9. E. 4. 13. 19. H. 6. 26. 3. H. 6. 26. 3. H. 6. Ass. 1. 37. H. 6. 8. 21. E. 3. 14.

¶ *Le baron soy tient eins cõe tenant per le curtesie.* This is no seuerance of the state in Coparcenary, (b) for the other Coparcener and the Tenant by the Curtesie shall be ioyntly impleaded, for he doth continue the state of Coparcenary as the other Parcener did.

¶ *Vers le tenant*

tition enter eux,&c. Et si le tenant per le curtesie ne voit agreer al partition destre fait, donques le parcener que suruesquist poit auer enuers le Tenant per le curtesie, breife De partitione facienda,&c. et luy cōpeller de faire partition. Mes si le tenant per le curtesie voile auer partition enter eux destre fait, et le parcener que suruesquist ne voit ceo auer, donque le tenant per le curtesie nauera ascū remedy pur auer partition,&c. Car il ne poit auer breife De Partitione facienda, pur ceo que il nest parcener, car tiel breife gist pur parceners tantsolement. Et issint poyes veyer que bre De Partitione facienda gist enuers tenant per le curtesie, et uncore il mesme ne poit auer tiel breife.

ueth, and the tenant by the curtesie may well make partitiō between them,&c. And if the tenant by the curtesie will not agree to make partition then the parcener which suruiueth may haue against the tenant by the curtesie a Writ *De partitione facienda,&c.*& compel him to make partition. But if the tenant by the curtesie would haue partition to be made between them and the parcener which suruiueth will not haue this, then the tenant by the curtesie cānot haue any remedy to haue partition,&c. For hee cannot haue a writ of *Partitione faciēda*, because he is no parcener. For such a Writ lyeth for parceners only. And so you may see that a writ of *Partitione fac'* lyeth against tenant by the curtesie, and yet he himselfe cannot haue the like Writ.

per le Curtesie briefe de partitione facienda,&c. Here by the &c. is impyed that albeit that the Tenant by the Curtesie be an estranger in blood yet the (c) Writ De partitione fac. clearly lyeth against the tenant by the Curtesie, because hee contiueth the estate of Coparcenary.

(c) 3.E.3.47. 9.E.5.13. 16.E.3. Aid 129. 19.E.3. ibid.144.

If two Coparceners be, and one doth alien in fee they are Tenants in common, and seuerall writs of Præcipe must be brought against them, and yet the Parcener shall haue a writ of partition against the Alienee at the Cōmon Law, which is a farre stronger case then the case put of Tenant by the Curtesie. 28.E.3.5.

Tiel briefe gist pur Parceners tantsolement. Hereby it appeareth that neither the Tenant by the Curtesie, nor (much lesse) the Alienee of a Coparcener shall haue a Writ of Partitione fac' at the Common Law, for Littleton saith here, that such a Writ lyeth only for Parceners, * but it may be brought by a Parcener against strangers as it appeareth before. But a Nuper obijt and a Rationabile parte doe lye only betweene two Coparcener on both sides.

(*) 3.E.47.48.

If three Coparceners be and the eldest doth purchase the part of the youngest, the eldest hauing one part by discent, and the other by purchase shall haue a Writ of Partition at the Common Law against the other middle sister; Et sic de similibus And so it is in a farre stronger case, if there be three Coparceners and the eldest taketh husband, and the husband purchase the part of the youngest the husband for his part is a stranger and no Parcener, and yet he and his wife shall haue a writ of partition against the middle sister at the Common Law, because he is seised of one part in the right of his wife who is a Parcener.

Dier 1. Maria 98.

F. N. B. 52. Regist.

Pur auer Partition,&c. Here by this (&c) is included all others that be strangers in blood, whether they come to their estates by Purchase or by act in Lawe. Since Littleton wrote; by the Statutes (d) one Joyntenant or Tenant in common may haue a Writ of Partition against the other, and therefore at this day the Alienee of one Parcener may haue a writ of Partition against the other Parcener, because they are Tenants in common: and the like had beene attempted in former Parliaments (*) but preuailed not untill these later Statutes.

(d) 31.H.8.cap.1. 32 H.8. cap.32. Vid. Sect.290.

(*) Rott. Parl. 1.R.2 nu.82.

(e) The Tenant by the Curtesie shall haue a writ of Partition upon the Statute of 32.H.8.

(e) Brooke tit. Partition 41.

32.H.8.ca.32. for albeit he is neither Joyntenant nor Tenant in Common; for that a Præcipe lieth against the Parcener and Tenant by the Courtesie as hath beene sayd, yet hee is in equall mischiefe as another Tenant for life.

(f) Mich.7. et 8. Eliz. Bendloes inter Wotton et Cooke. Dyer 3. Maria 128.A. et 7.Eliz.243.

(f) If there be three Coparceners and a stranger purchase the part of one of them, he and one other of the Coparceners shall not ioyne in a writ of partition, neither by the Common Law, nor by force of the statute, for the words of the Preamble of the statute be (And none of them by the Law doth or may know their seuerall parts, &c. and cannot by the lawes of this Realme make partition thereof, without other of their mutuall assents, &c.)

Now in this case the one of the Plaintiffes, viz. the Parcener may haue a writ of Partition at the Common Law, and the other Parcener being a purchaser may haue it by the stat. and therefore they shall not ioyne in one Writ.

Chap.2. Parceners by Custome. Sect.265.

¶ Parceners per le custome sont lou hõe seisie en fee simple, ou en fee taile de terres ou tenements q̃ sont de tenure appel Gauelkind deins l' Coũtie de Kent, & ad issue diuers fits & deuie, tielx terres ou tenements discenderõt a touts les fits per le custome, & ouelment enheriterõt & ferront ptition enter eux per le custome, sicome females ferront, & bre de Partitione facienda gist en ceo cas, sicome enter females, mes il couient en la Declaration de faire mention d le custom. Auxy tiel custome est en auters lieux Dengleterr. Et auxi tiel custome est en North Gales, &c.

Parceners by the Custome are, where a man seised in Fee simple, or in Fee tayle of Lands or Tenements which are of the Tenure called Gauelkind within the Countie of Kent, and hath issue diuers sonnes and die, such Lands or Tenements shall discend to all the sons by the Custome, and shal equally inherit and make partition by the custome, as females shall doe, and a writ of Partition lieth in this case as between females, but it behooueth in the Declaration to make mention of the Custome. Also such Custome is in other places of England, and also such custome is in North-Wales, &c.

See before all the Auntient Authours of the Law concerning Gauelkind vbi supra. Lambert verbo Terra exscripta.

(g) 5.E.4.8.b. 11.E.4.56.b. 2.2lo. Com.129.b. in Bucklers Case. Vi.Sect.8. versus finem.

(h) Berochescire. Hereford.

(i) Lamb. verbo Welshmen. Siluester Giraldus.

¶ Mes il couient en le Declaration de faire mention de le custome. Well said Litl. (g) That he in his Declaration must make mention of the Custome, as to say, That the land is of the Custome of Gauelkind, but hee shall not prescribe in it. And so is it of Burgh English, and these two varie in that point from other Customes, for the Law, when they are generally alledged, taketh knowledge of these two.

In (h) Domesday it is thus sayd, Duo fratres tenuerunt in paragio quisque habuit aulam suam, & potuerint ire quo voluerint.

¶ Auxy tiel custome est en auters lieux Angleterre. Of this sufficient hath beene said before.

¶ North Gales. Wales, Wallia, It commeth (i) of the Saxon word Wealh which signifieth Peregrinus, or exter', for the Saxõs so called them, because in troth they were strangers to them, being the remaine of the old and antient Brittons, a wise and warlike Nation inhabiting in the west part of England. These men haue kept their proper Language for aboue these thousand yeares past, and they to this day call vs Englishmen, Saisons, (that is) Saxons. And the like custome as our Author heere saith was in North wales, was also in Ireland, for there the Lands also (which is one marke of the antient Brittons) were of the nature of Gauelkind: but where by their Brehon Law the Bastards ſta rds inherited with their legitimate ſons, as to the Baſtards that cuſtome was aboliſhed. And agreing with Littleton in this poynt, ſee an old Statute.* Aliter vſitatum eſt in Wallia, quam in Anglia, quo ad ſucceſſionem hæreditatis, eo quod hæreditas partibilis eſt inter hæredes maſculos, à tempore cuius non extitit memoria partibilis extitit, Dominus Rex non vult quod conſuetudo illa abrogetur, ſed quod hæreditates remaneant partibiles inter conſimiles hæredes ſicut fieri conſueuit, & fiat partitio illius ſicut fieri conſueuit

Vid. Sect. 212.
** Stat. Wallia, an. 12 E. 1.*

¶ *Parceners per le Cuſtome, &c.* Well ſayd Littleton, By the Cuſtome, for ſonnes are Parceners in reſpect of the cuſtome of the Fee or Inheritance, and not in reſpect of their perſons, as daughters and ſiſters, &c. be. (h) Et ſunt participes quaſi partem capientes, &c. ratione ipſius rei quæ partibilis eſt, & non ratione perſonarum, quæ non ſunt quaſi vnus hæres, & vnum corpus, ſed diuerſi hæredes, vbi tenementum partibile eſt inter plures cohæredes petentes qui diſcendunt de eodem ſtipite & ſemper ſolent diuidi ab antiquo.

(h) Bract. li. 5. fo. 428. Brit. ca. 71. Flet. lib. 5. cap. 9.

Sect. 266.

¶ ITem il y ad auter partic quel eſt dauter nature et dauter forme que aſcuns des partitions auauntdits ſont. Sicome home ſeiſie de certaine Terres ē fee ſimple, ad iſſue deux files et leigne eſt mary, et le piere done parcel de ſes terres a le baron oue ſa file en frankmariage, et moruſt ſeiſie ō le remnant, le quel remnant eſt de pluis greinder value per an, q̄ ſont les Terres dones en Frankmariage.

ALſo there is another partition which is of another nature, and of other forme, then any of the partitions aforeſaid be. As if a man ſeiſed of certaine Lands in Fee-ſimple, hath iſſue two daughters, and the eldeſt is married, and the father giueth part of his Lands to the husband with his daughter in Frankmarriage, and dieth ſeiſed of the remnant, the which remnant is of a greater yerely value than the lands giuen in Frankemarriage.

¶ *Dona parcel de ſes terres a le Baron oue ſa file en frankmarriage.* Here it appeareth, That a gift in frankmarriage may be made after marriage, as hath beene ſayd in the Chapter of Fee tayle.

¶ *Le quel remnant eſt de pluis greinder value per an, &c.* Admit that the lands giuen in Frankmarriage are of greater value than the lands diſcended in Fee ſimple, Shall the other ſiſter haue any remedie againſt the Donees? it is plaine ſhe ſhall not, becauſe it is lawfull for a man to diſpoſe of his owne lands, at his will and pleaſure.

Sect. 267.

¶ EN cel caſe le baron ne le feme auera riens pur lour purpartie de le dit remnant, ſinon que ils voile mitter lour tres dones en frankmariage en Hotchpot oueſque le rem-

IN this caſe neither the husband nor wife ſhall haue any thing, for their purpartie of the ſayd Remnant, vnleſſe they wil put their lands giuen in Frankemarriage, in *Hotchpot*, with the remant of the

¶ *EN cel caſe le Baron ne le Feme auera riens pur lour purpartie, &c.* (i) This gift in Frankmarriage ſhall Prima facie be intended a ſufficient aduancement, and therfore the remnant ſhall diſcend to the other Coparcener, only with this prouiſion in Law, Tacite annexed, that if the donees

(i) 8. H. 3. breue 880. 34. E. 1. nuper Obiit 15. adiudge 4. E. 3. 49. 10. Aſſ p. 14. Vid. 10. E. 3. 38. et 30. Aſſ 7 Bract. Lib. 2. fol 77. Lib. 5. fol. 428. Britton ca. 72 Fleta Lib. 6. cap. 47.

nant de la terre ouesque sa soer. Et si issint ils ne voilent fayre, donques le puisne poet tener & occupier m le remnanc, & prendra a luy les profits tantsolement. Et il semble que cest parol (Hotchpot) est en English, A Pudding, car en tiel Pudding nest communement mise vn chose tantsolemt, mes vn chose ouesque auts choses ensemble. Et pur ceo il couient en tiel case de mitter les Terres dones en frankmariag, ouesque les auters terres en Hotchpot, si le Baron & sa feme voilent auer ascu pt en les auts tres.

land with her sister. And if they wil not doe so, then the youngest may hold and occupie the same remnant, and take the profits onely to her selfe. And it seemeth that this word *(Hotchpot)* is in English, A Pudding, for in this Pudding is not commonly put one thing alone, but one thing with other things together. And therefore it behooueth in this case to put the lands giuen in Frankemarriage with the other Lands in *Hotchpot*, if the husband and wife will haue any part in the other Lands.

nees will put the Land into Hotchpot, then she shall out of the remnant make vp her part equall, but the Donees must doe the first act, and in the meane time the whole fee simple land discends to the other. And this is warranted heere by Littleton, viz. That the Donees shall haue nothing for the purpartie of the remnant, vnlesse they will put their lands giuen in Frankemarriage, in Hotchpot, so as the Donees must doe the first act, and more expressely after in this Chapter, where he directly saith, That the other Sister shall enter into the remnant, & them to occupie to her owne vse, vnlesse the husband and wife will put the Lands giuen in Frankemarriage, into Hotchpot. And herewith agreeth Fleta, who saith, Cum dicat tenens excipiendo, quod non tenetur petenti respondere quia A. participem habet, &c. replicari poterit a petente quod prædict A. tenet quandam partem in maritagium de communi hæredit, nec vult illud in partem ponere. And here are three things (that I may speake once for all) to be obserued. First, That in this speciall case where there be two daughters, one of them onely shall inherit the lands in fee simple. Secondly, That in this case there lieth no writ of Partition, because non tenent insimul & pro indiuiso. Thirdly, If the Parcener to whom the land in fee simple discended, will not put the lands in Hotchpot, then may the Donees enter into the fee simple lands, and hold them in Coparcenarie with her.

And it seemeth by our old Bookes, (k) That by the antient Law there was a kind of resemblance hereof concerning goods. Si autem post debita deducta & post deductionem expensarum quæ necessariæ erunt, id totum quod hunc superfuerit diuidatur in tres partes, quarum vna pars relinquatur pueris si pueros habuerit defunctus. Secunda, Vxori si superstes fuerit, & de tertia parte habeat testator liberam disponendi facultatem: si autem liberos non habeat, tunc medietas defuncto, & alia medietas vxori: si autem sine vxore decesserit liberis existentibus, tunc medietas defuncto, & alia medietas liberis tribuatur: si autem sine vxore & liberis, tunc id totū defuncto remanebit. And by the Law before the Conquest it * was thus prouided, Siue quis in curia, siue morte repentine fuer intestat mortuus, dominus tamen nullam rerum suarum partem (præter eam quæ iure debetur) herioti nomine sibi assumito, verum eas iudicio suo vxori liberis & cognatione proximis iustè pro suo cuique iure distribuito.

(k) Glanuill Lib.7.cap.5. Bracton Lib.2.fol.60. Fleta Lib.2.cap.5. Magna Carta cap.18.3. F.N.B.222. 30.E.3.25. 31.E.3.Resp.60. 31.Ass.14. 17.E.2.Detinew 17.E.3.17. 1.E.2. Detinew 56. 31.H.8.tit. Rationab.parte. Bonorum.6.

** Lamb.f.119.68.*

(l) Regist.142. 34.E.1. Detinew 60. 1 E.4.6. 7.E.4.21. 43.E.3. 38.

But it appeareth by the Register, (l) and many of our Bookes, That there must be a custome alledged in some Countie, &c. to inable the wife or children to the writ De rationabili parte bonorum, and so hath it beene resolued in Parliament. (m) But such children as bee reasonably aduanced by the father in his life time with any part of his goods, shall haue no further part of his goods, for the words of the writ be, Nec in vita patris promoti fuerunt.

(m) 3.E.3.Detinew. 156. 40.E.3.18.

Note, the custome of London is, That if the father aduance any of his children with any part of his goods, that shall barre them to demand any further part, vnlesse the father vnder his hand, or in his last will doe expresse and declare, That it was but in part of aduancement, and then that child so partly aduanced, shall put his part in Hotchpot, with the Executors and widow, and haue a full third part of the whole, accounting that which was formerly giuen vnto him as part thereof. And this is that in effect, which the Ciuilians call Collatio bonorum.

¶ Ee

¶ *Et il semble que cest Parol (hotchpot) est en English*, a Pudding, *&c.* Littleton both here and in other places searcheth for the signification of words, in all Arts a thing most necessary, for ignoratis terminis ignoratur & ars vide for Etymologies, Sect. 95. 119. 135. 154. 164. 201. 234. &c.

¶ *Hutspot* or *Hotspot*, is an old Saxon word, and signifieth so much as Littleton here speakes. And the French vse Hotchpot for a commixtion of diuers things together. It signifieth here metaphorically in partem positio. In English we vse to say Hodgepodge, in Latine Farrago or Miscellaneum.

Vide Britt cap. 72. 4. E. 3. 49. 6. E. 3. 30. 10 E. 3. 38, 24. E. 3. 27. F. N. B. 262. Regist. 320. Fleta lib. 6. ca. 47. Mich. 10. E. 1, coram Rege Hereford. in the same.

The residue of this Section needeth no explication.

Sect. 268.

¶ ET cest terme (Hotchpot) nest forsque vn terme similitudinarie, & est a tant adire, cestascauoir, de mitter les terrs en Frankmarriage & les auters terres en fee simple ensemble, & ceo est a tiel entent de conuster le value de touts les terres, s. de les terres dones en Frankmarriage, & de le remnant que ne fueront dones, & donques partition serra fait en le forme que ensuist. Sicome mittomus que home soit seisie de 30. acres de terre en fee simple chescun acre de value de 12. d. per an, & que il ad issue deux files, & lun est couert de baron, & le pier dona 10. acres de les 30. acres a le baron, oue sa file en Frankmarriage, & morust seisie de l'remnant, donques lauter soer entra en le remnant, s. en les 20. acres, & eux occupier, a son vse demesne sinon que le baron et sa feme voile mitter les 10. acres dones en Frankmarriage, oue les 20. acres en Hotchpot, cestascauoir, ensemble, & donque quant le value de chescun acre est conus cestascauoir, que chescun acre vault per an, & est assesse, ou enter eux agree, que chescun acre vault per an 12. d. donques le partition serra

AND this tearme (*Hotchpot*) is but a tearme similitudinary, & is as much to say, as to put the lands in Frankmarriage, and the other Lands in Fee simple together, and this is for this intent, to know the value of all the Lands *scz.* of the Lands giuen in Frankmarriage, and of the remnant which were not giuen, and then partition shal be made in forme following. As put the case that a man be seised of 30. Acres of Land in Fee simple, euery Acre of the value of 12. pence by the yeare, and that hee hath issue two Daughters, and the one is Couert baron, and the Father giues 10. Acres of the 30. Acres to the Husband with his Daughter in Frankmarriage, and dyeth seised of the remnant, then the other sister shall enter into the remnant, *viz.* into the 20. Acres, and shall occupie them to her owne vse, vnlesse the husband and his wife will put the 10. Acres giuen in Frankmarriage, with the 20. Acres in Hotchpot, that is to say, together and then when the value of euery Acre is knowne, to wit, what euery Acre valueth by the yeare, and is assessed or agreed betweene them, that euery Acre is worth by the yeare 12. pence. Then the partition shall be

serra fait en tiel forme, cestascavoir le baron & sa feme averont oustre les 10. acres dones a eux en Frankmarriage 5. acres en severaltie de les 20. acres & lauter soer avera le remnant, s. 15. acres de l's 20. acres pur sa purpartie, issint que accomptant les 10. acres que le baron & sa feme ount per le done en Frankmarriage, et les auters 5. acres de les 20. acres, le baron et sa feme ont autant en annual value, que lauter soer ad.

made in this manner, *viz.* the Husband and Wife shall haue besides the 10. acres giuen to them in Frankmarriage 5. Acres in seueraltie of the 20. Acres, and the other sister shall haue the remnant, *sciz.* 15. Acres of the 20. Acres for her purpartie, so as accounting the 10. Acres which the Baron and Fem haue by the gift in Frankmarriage, and the other 5. Acres of the 20. Acres, the husband and wife haue as much in yearly value as the other sister.

Bract. lib. 2. fol. 77. lib. 5. fol. 428. Britt. c. p. 72. & Fleta lib. 6. cap. 47. 4. E. 3. 49. 10. E. 3. 37. (n) 10. E. 3. 37. 10. Ass. 14. 4. E. 3. 49. (o) 29. Ass. 23.

¶ AND herewith in expresse tearmes agreeth Bracton, Britton, and Fleta, and all the books abouesaid and many others. And it is worthy the obseruation (n) that after this putting into Hotchpot, and partition made, the Lands giuen in Frankmarriage, are become as the other Lands which discended from the common Ancestor, and of these Lands if she be impleaded (o) she shall haue aide of the other Parcener as if the same Lands had discended. So the Coparcener that hath a Rent granted to her for owelty of partition, as is aforesaid, hath the Rent, as if it had discended to her from the common Ancestor.

Section 269.

¶ ET issint touts foits sur tiel partition, les terres dones en Frankmarriage demurgent a les donees & a lour heires solonq; le forme de le done. Car si lauter Parcen̄ avoit riens de ceo que est done en Frankmarriage, de ceo ensueroit inconveniens, & chose encounter reason, que la ley ne voit suffer. Et la cause pur que les terres dones en Frankmarriage serront mis en Hotchpot, est ceo, quant home done terres ou tenements en Frankmarriage oue sa file, ou oue auter cosin, il est entendus per la ley que tiel done fait per tiel Parol (Frankmarriage) est vn avancement, & pur avancement de sa file, ou de son auter cosin, & nosmement quant

AND so alwayes vpon such partion the Lands giuen in Frankmarriage remayne to the Donees and to their heires according to the forme of the gift, for if the other Parcener should haue any of that which is giuen in Frankmarriage: of this would ensue an inconuenience, and a thing against reason, which the Law will not suffer. And the reason why the Lands giuen in Frankmarriage shal bee put in Hotchpot, is this when a man giueth Lands or Tenements in Frankmarriage with his Daughter, or with his other Cousin, it is intended by the Law that such gift made by this word (Frankmarriage) is an aduancement, and for aduancement of his Daughter, or of his Cousin, and namely, when

quant le donor et ses heyres naueront ascun rent ne seruice de eux, sinon que soit fealty, tanque le quart degree soit passe, &c. Et pur tiel cause la ley est que el auera riens de les auters terres ou tenemẽts discendus, a lauter parcener, &c. sinon que el voille mitter les terres dones ẽ frankmariage en Hotchpot, come est dit. Et si el ne voille mitter les terres dones en frankmariage en Hotchpot, donque el nauera riens del remnant pur ceo que serra entendu per la ley que el est sufficientment auance, a que auancemẽt el soy agree & luy tient content.

the donor and his heires shall haue no rent nor seruice of them but fealty vntill the fourth degree be past. And for this cause the Law is that she shall haue nothing of the other lands or tenements discended to the other parcener, &c. vnlesse shee will put the lands giuen in frankmariage in Hotchpot as is said. And if she will not put the lands giuen in frankmariage in Hotchpot, then she shall haue nothing of the remnant, because it shall be intended by the Law, that she is sufficiently aduanced, to which aduancement shee agreeth and holdes her selfe content.

¶ *De ceo ensueroit enconuenience & chose encounter reason que la ley ne voet suffer.*

Quod est inconueniens aut contra rationem non permissum est in lege. Hereby it appeareth, as it hath beene often noted, (o) that an argument ab inconuenienti aut ab eo quod est contra rationem, is forcible in Law. (p) Nihil enim quod est inconueniens est licitum. *Regula.* (*) *Vid. Sect.* 138. 139. 231. 440. 478. 488. 722. (p) 40. *Aff.* 27.

¶ *Tanque le 4. degree soit pas, &c.* Hereby (&c.) is implyed how the degrees shall be accounted, whereof sufficient hath beene said before. *Sect.* 20.

Sect. 270.

¶ Mesm la ley est perenter les heires de les donees en frankmariage, et les auters parceners &c. si les donees en frankmariag deuiõt deuãt lour auncester, ou deuant tiel partition, &c. quant a mitter en Hotchpot, &c.

THe same Law is between the heires of the donees in frankmariage, and the other parceners, &c. if the donees in frankmariage die before their ancestor or before such partition, &c. as to put in Hotchpot, &c.

¶ By these three (&c.) in this Section is implied that if either the Donees die before the Ancestor, or suruiue the Ancestor and die before such a partition, or if the Donees and all the Parceners die before such partition vpon the putting into Hotchpot, their issues shall haue the same benefit to put the lands into Hotchpot, for that benefit is heritable, and discendible to the issues.

Sect. 271.

¶ Et nota que dones en frankmariage fueront per

ANd note that gifts in frankmariage were by the Cõmon

¶ *Continue, &c.* By this (&c) is to be vnderstood that before the Statute it was a fee simple, and

la common ley deuant le Statute de Westm̃ second, et tout temps puis ad este vse et continue, &c.

Law before the Statute of Westm. second and haue beene alwayes since vsed and continued, &c.

(q) 12.*H*.4.11. 31.*E*.3.*Gard* 116.

since the statute a fee taile. So as it is true, that (q) the gifts doe continue (as our Author here saith) but not the estates. For the estate is changed as at large appeareth in the Chapter of estates in taile. And albeit our Author here saith that such gifts haue beene alwayes since vsed and continued, yet now they be almost growne out of vse, and serue now principally for Moote cases and questions in Law that therupon were wont to rise.

Sect. 272.

¶ Item, tiel mitter en Hotchpot, &c. est lou les auters terres ou tenements q̃ ne fuerent dones en frankmariage discendont de les donors en frankmariage tantsolement, car si les terres discenderont a les files per le pier le donor, ou per le mere le donor, ou per le frere l' donor, ou auter ancestor, et nemy per le donor, &c. la autrement est, car en tiel cas el a quel tiel done en frankmariage est fait auera sa part sicome nul tiel done en frankmariage vst este fait, pur ceo q̃ el ne fuit auancé per eux, &c. eins per vn auter, &c.

Also such putting in Hotchpot, &c. is where the other lands or tenements which were not giuen in frãkmariage discend from the donors in frankmariage only, for if the lands shall discend to the daughters by the father of the donor, or by the mother of the donor, or by the brother of the donor or other ancester, and not by the donor &c. there it is otherwise, for in such case, shee to whom such gift in frankmariage is made shal haue her part as if no gift in frankm: had beene made because that she was not aduanced by them, &c. but by another, &c.

¶ The lands giuen in frankmariage, & the lands in Fee simple must moue from one and the same Ancester, for the lands giuen in Frankmariage are in respect of the aduãcement accounted in Law as hath beene said, as if the same had discended from the same Ancestor who died seised of the fee simple lands, and there is no reason to barre the Donee of her full part of the fee simple lands that discended from another Ancestor from whom she had no such aduancement.

¶ *Nemy per le donor, &c.* Here (&c.) implieth no more but that Donor that made the gift of Frankmariage, the other two (&c.) in this Section neede no explanation.

Sect.273.

¶ Item, si home seisie de 30 acres de terre chescun acre de ouel annual value etant issue deux files cõe est auantdit, et dona 15. acres de

Also if a man bee seised of 30. acres of land euery acre of equall annuall value, and haue issue two daughters as aforesaid, and giueth 15. acres

¶ By this Section & the (&c.) Herein some haue gathered that the value of the lands shall be accounted as they were at the time of the gift in

ceo a le baron oue sa file en frankmariage, & morust seisie de les auters 15. acres, en cest case lauter soer auera les 15. acres issint discẽdus a luy sole, et le baron et sa feme ne mitteront en tiel cas les 15. acres a eux dones en frankmariage en Hotchpot, pur ceo q̃ les tenemẽts dones ẽ frankmariage sont de auxy grand et de bone annual value, come les auters terres discendus, &c. Car si les terres dones en frankmariage sont de tant egal annual value, que le remnant sont, ou de pluis value, en vaine et a nul entent tielx tenemẽts dones en frankmariage serra mis en Hotchpot, &c. pur ceo que el ne poit riens auer de les auters terres discendus, &c. car si el auoit ascun parcel de les tenements discendus, donques el auera pluis de annual value que sa soer &c. que la ley ne voit, &c. Et sicome est parle ẽ les cases auantdits de deux files ou de deux parceners, en m̃ le maner est en semblabł cas lou sont plusors soers ou plusors parceners, solonq; ceo q̃ł case & ł matter est, &c.

hereof to the husband with his daughter in frankmariage, and dies seised of the other 15. acres. In this case the other sister shall haue the 15. acres so discended to her alone, and the husband and wife shall not in this case put the 15. acres giuen to them in frankmariage into Hotchpot, because the tenements giuen in frankmariage are of as great and good yearely value as the other lands discended, &c. for if the lands giuen in frankmariage bee of equall or of more yearely value then the remnant, in vaine and to no purpose shall such tenements giuen in frankmariage bee put in Hotchpot, &c. for that shee cannot haue any of the other lands discended, &c. for if shee should haue any parcell of the lands discended, then she shall haue more in yearly value then her sister, &c. which the Law will not, &c. And as it is spoken in the cases aforesaid of two daughters or of two parceners; in the same manner it is in like case where there are more sisters or more parceners according as the case and matter is, &c.

Frãkmariage, but it is cleere that the value shall bee accounted as it was at the time of the partition, for if the Donor purchase more land after the gift, or if the land giuen in Frankmariage be by the act of God decayed in value, or if the remnant of the lands in fee simple be improued after the gift, or è conuerso the Law shall adiudge of the value as it was at the time of the partition (vnlesse it bee by the proper act or default of the parties) as hath beene said before in the former Chapter. And some haue collected vpon this Section that the reuersion in fee of the lands giuen in Frankmariage shall only discend to the Donee, for otherwise the other sister shal haue more benefit, then the Donee which should bee against the reason of our Author.

¶ *In vaine & a nul entẽt, &c.* For it is a maxime in Law Lex non præcipit inutilia, quia inutilis labor stultus.

Regula. Vid. Sect. 194. 378. Lib. 5. fo. 89.

Sect. 274.

ET est ascauoire, que Terres ou tenemēts dones en frankmariage ne serra mise en Hotchpot, forsque ou Terres discende en fee simple, car de terre discendus en fee taile Partition serra fait, sicome nul tiel done en frākmarriage vst este fait.

AND it is to be vnderstood, that Lands or Tenements giuen in Frankmarriage shall not bee put in *Hotchpot* but where Lands discend in Fee simple, for of Lands discended in Fee taile partition shall bee made, as if no such gift in Frankemarriage had been made.

31.*Ass.*pla.14.

¶ FOr of Lands intailed, the Donee in Frankmarriage shall haue as much part as the other Coparcener, because ouer and besides the Land giuen in Frankmarriage, the Issue in Taile claimeth per formam doni, and both of the Parceners must equally inherit by force of the gift, & voluntas Donatoris, &c. obseruetur.

Sect. 275.

¶ ITem nuls Terres serra mise en Hotchpot oue auts sinon terres que fueront done en frankmariage tantsolement: Car si ascun Feme ad ascuns auters terres ou tenemēts per ascun auter done en le tayle, el ne vnques mittera tiel Terre issint done en Hotchpot, mes el auera sa purpartie de le remnāt discendus, &c. s. a tant que lauter Parcener auera de mesme le remnant.

ALso no Lands shall bee put in *Hotchpot* with other Lands, but Lands giuen in Frankmarriage onely: for if a woman haue any other Lands or Tenements by any other gift in taile, she shall neuer put such Lands so giuen in *Hotchpot*, but she shall haue her purpartie of the remnant discended, &c. *(videlicet)* as much as the other Parcener shall haue of the same remnant.

13.*E.*2.*tit.Taile* 26. 6.*E.*3.30.*b.* 4.*E.*3.49. 50.

¶ FOr if the Ancestor infeoffeth one of his daughters of part of his Land, or purchase lands to him and her and their heires, or giueth to her part of his lands in Taile special or generall, she notwithstanding this shall haue a full part in the remnant of the lands in Fee simple, for the benefit of putting, &c. into Hotchpot, is onely appropriated to a gift in Frankmarriage, (quia maritagium cadit in partem) which shall be (as is aforesayd) accounted as parcell of his aduancement.

Bract.*li.*2.*fo* 77.

Sect. 276.

¶ ITem vn auter Partition poet este fait inter parceñs, que variast de les Partitions auantdits. Sicome y sōt trois Parceners, & le puisñ voet auer partition, & les auts deux ne voillont, mes voilent tener en parcenarie ceo que a eux affiert

ALso another partition may be made betweene Parceners, which varieth from the Partitions aforesayd. As if there bee three Parceners and the youngest will haue partition, and the other two will not, but will hold in parcenarie that which to them belon-

ert sans partē, en cē case si vn pt soit alot en seūalty al puisne soer solonqȝ ceo que el doit auer, donques les auters poient tener le remnant en parcenarie, & occupier en common sans partition si els voilent, & tiel partition est assets bone. Et si apres leigne ou le mulnes Parcener voile fayre partition inter eux, d̄ ceo que ils teignont ils teignont, ils poient ceo bien faire quant a eux pleist. Mes lou partition serra fait per force de Briefe de Partitione facienda, la autrement est car la couient que chescun Parcener auera sa part en seueraltie, &c.

geth, without partition: in this case if one part be allotted in seueraltie to the youngest sister, according to that which shee ought to haue, then the others may hold the remnant in parcenarie, and occupie in Common without Partition, if they will, and such partition is good enough. And if afterwards the eldest or middle parcener will make partition betweene them of that which they hold, they may well do this when they please. But where partition shall bee made by force of a Writ of *Partitione facienda*, there it is otherwise, for there it behoueth that euerie parcener haue her part in seueraltie, &c.

¶ Pluis serr̄ dit des parcen̄s en le Chapter de Joyntenants, & auxy en le Chapter de Tenāts in Common.

More shall bee said of parceners in the Chapter of Ioyntenants, and also in the Chapter of Tenants in Common.

¶ Here it is to be obserued, That this partition is good by consent, for Consensus tollit errorem, but if it be by the Kings Writ, then euerie Parcener must haue his part. And here you may see that modus & conuentio vincunt legem. — 24 H.3.tit.Partic.19. Regula.

¶ *En seueraltie, &c.* Here by this (&c.) is implied another kind of seueraltie than our Author hath mentioned, and that is, That the one Parcener shall haue the land in seueraltie from the feast of Easter, vntill the gule of August, (that is, the first of August) and the other in seueraltie from thence vntill the feast of Easter, or the like, & sic alternis vicibus to them and their heires imperpetuum, whereof sufficient hath beene spoken before.

Chap.3. Of Ioyntenants. Sect.277.

¶ Joyntenn̄ts sont, sicome home seisie de certain Terr̄s ou Tenements, &c. & enfeoffe deux, trois, quater, ou plusors, a auer & ten̄ a eux pur term de lour vies, ou a terme dauter vie, p force de quel feoffm̄t ou lease ils sont sei-

Ioyntenants are, as if a man bee seised of certaine Lands or Tenements, &c. and infeoffeth two, three, foure, or more, to haue and to hold to them for term of their liues, or for terme of anothers life, by force of which feoffement or

¶ This agreeth not with the Original, for it should bee, Ioyn̄ sont sicōe hōe seisie de certaine terres ou tenements, &c. & ent enfeoffe deux ou trois, ou quater, ou plusors a auer & tener a eux & a lour heires ou less. a eux pur terme de lour vies, ou pur terme dauter vie, per force de quel feoffement, ou lease, &c. The error may easily bee perceiued by that which is in print, viz. By force of which feoffement or lease, &c. ergo there must bee — Brast li.4 fo.262. Brit ca.35.& fo 112. Flet.lib.3.ca.4.10. & li.6.cap.47.

sies, tiels sont Ioyntenants.

lease they are seised, these are Ioyntenants.

be feoffment and lease spoken of before.

There be also Ioyntenants by other conueyances than Littlet. here mentioneth as by Fine, Recouerie, Bargaine, and Saile, Release, Confirmation, &c. So there be diuers other limitations than Littleton heere speaketh of: As if a Rent charge of ten pounds be granted to A. and B. to haue and to hold to them two, viz. to A. vntill he be married, and to B vntill he be aduanced to a Benefice, they bee Ioyntenants in the meane time, notwithstanding the seuerall limitations: and if A die before marriage, the rent shall suruiue, but if A. had married, the rent should haue ceased for a moitie, & sic è conuerso on the other side.

Littleton hauing spoken of one kind of Tenants pro indiuiso, viz. of Parceners, commeth now to another, viz. Ioyntenants, and first of Ioyntenants of Freehold. If an Alien and a subiect purchase lands in fee, they are ioyntneants, & the suruiuorship shall hold place, Et nullum tempus occurrit Regi, vpon an office found.

7.E.4.29. 11.H.4.26.

¶ *Ioyntenants*, So called because the lands or tenements, &c. are conueyed to them ioyntly, coniunctim feoffati, &c. or, qui coniunctim tenent, and are distinguished from sole or seuerall Tenants, from Parceners, and from Tenants in Common, &c. and antiently they were called Participes, & non hæredes. And these Ioyntenants must ioyntly implead and ioyntly be impleaded by others, which propertie is common betweene them and Coparceners, but Ioyntenants haue a sole qualitie of suruiuorship, which Coparceners haue not. Littleton hauing now spoken of Parceners and of Ioyntenants of right, doth next speak of Ioyntenants by wrong.

Plow.lib.6.10 47.
Bract.lib.5.fol.435.a.

Section 278.

ITem si deux ou trois, &c. disseisont vn auter dascun terres ou Tenements a lour vse demesne: donques les Disseisours sont Ioyntenants. Mes sils disseisõt vn auter al vse dun de eux, donques ils ne sont Ioyntenants, mes celuy a que vse le disseisin est fait est sole tenant, & les auters nont riens en le tenancie, mes sont appels coadiutors a le disseisin, &c.

ALso if two or three &c. disseise another of any lands or tenements to their owne vse, then the disseisors are Ioyntenants. But if they disseise another to the vse of one of them, then they are not Ioyne-Tenants, but he to whose vse the Disseisin is made, is sole Tenant, and the others haue nothing in the Tenancie, but are called Coadiutors to the Disseisin, &c.

¶ IT is to bee obserued, That some Disseisours, be Tenants of the land and some be no Tenants of the Lands, and of both these kinds Littleton here speaketh.

¶ *&c.* In the first &c. nothing is implied but foure or fiue, or more, but in the latter (&c. many things be to be vnderstood, as of Disseisors that be no Tenants, some are Coadiutors, whereof Littleton here speaketh, some Councellors, Commanders, &c. when the disseisin is not to bee done to any of their vses. Also if A. disseise one to the vse of B. who knoweth not of it, and B. assent to it, in this case till the agreement A. was Tenant of the land, and after agreement B. is Tenant of the land, but both of them be Disseisors: for omnis ratihabitio retrotrahitur et mandato equiparatur. And it is worthie of the obseruation, and implyed also in the latter (&c.) that seeing Coadiutors, Councellors, Commanders, &c. are all Disseisors, that albeit the Disseisor which is Tenant dieth, yet the Assise lieth against the Coadiutor, Councellor, Commander, &c. and Tenant of the land, though he be no disseisor.

50.E.3.2. 27.Ass.14.
14.Ass.13. 8.Ass.p.30.
10.E.3.47. 10.Ass.22.
21.H.8.tit.Disseis.b.77.
38.Ass.21. 27.Ass.30.
12.E.4.9. 7.E.4.7.b.
38.ass.7. 21.H.7.35.
29.Ass.59. 21.H.8.25.
35.H.6.61. 21.E.4.46.
15.E.4.15. F.N.B.179.g.

(a) 50.E.3.2.

(a) The Demandant and others in a Præcipe did disseise the Tenant to the vse of the others, and the Writ did not abate, for the Demandant was a Disseisor, but gained no tenancie in the land, for that he was but a Coadiutor.

A man disseiseth Tenant for life to the vse of him in the reuersion, and after he in the reuersion agreeth to the disseisin, it is said, That he in the reuersion is a Disseisor in fee, for by the disseisin made by the stranger, the reuersion was diuested, which (say they) cannot bee reuested by the

agreement

agreement of him in the Reuersion, for that it maketh him a wrong doer; & therefore no relation of an estate by wrong can helpe him.

¶ *Coadiutor.* Coadiutor est qui auxiliatur alteri, and is deriued a coadiuuando. Anglicè, a fellow helper.

Sect. 279.

¶ ET nota q̃ disseisin est proprement lou vn home entra ẽ ascun terres ou tenements lou son entre nest pas congeable, & ousta celuy que ad Franktenement, &c.

AND note that disseisin is properly where a man entreth into any Lands or Tenements where his entry is not congeable, & ousteth him which hath the Freehold, &c.

¶ This description of a disseisin and the (&c.) in this place is vnderstood only of such Lands and Tenements whereinto an entry may bee made, and not of Rents, Commons, &c. whereof sufficient hath beene said before in the Chapter of Rents, and so in effect Littleton described it before the Edition of his Booke. And note here that euery entry is no disseisin, vnlesse there bee an ouster also of the Freehold. And therefore Littleton doth not set downe an entrie only but an ouster also, as an entry and a claymer, or taking of profits, &c.

3. E. 4. 2. 34. *Ass.* 11. 12. 26. *Ass.* 17. 41. *Ass.* 10. 24. E. 3. 31. *Pl. Com.* 8. *Parson de Hony Lane.* 7. *Ass.* 10. 11. *Ass.* 25. 12. E. 3. *tit. Ass.* 88. 45. *Ass.* 7. 9. *Ass.* 19. 39. *Ass.* 1. 18. E. 3. *Ass.* 174.

Now as there be Ioyntenants by disseisin, so are there Ioyntenants by Abatement, Intrusion, and Vsurpation, all which are included in the latter, &c.

Sect. 280.

¶ ET est ascauoir que la nature de ioyntenancie est q̃ celuy que suruesquist auera solement lentier tenancie solonq; tiel estate que il ad, si le ioynture soit continue, &c. Sicome si trois Ioyntenants sont en Fee simple, & lun ad issue & deuie, vncore ceux que suruesquont auont les tenements entier, & lissue nauera riens. Et si le 2. ioyntenant ad issue & deuie, vncore le tierce que surnesquist auera les tenemẽts entier, & eux auera a luy & a ses

AND it is to be vnderstood, that the nature of ioyntenancie is, that hee which suruiueth shall haue only the entire tenancie according to such estate as he hath, if the ioynture be continued, &c. As if three ioyntenants bee in Fee Simple, and the one hath issue, and dyeth, yet they which suruiue shall haue the whole tenements, and the issue shall haue nothing. And if the two ioyntenants hath issue and dye, yet the third which suruiueth shall haue the whole tene-

¶ *SI le ioynture soit continue, &c.*

Here by this (&c.) many points of Learning are to bee obserued, as that it is proper to ioyntenants only to haue Lands by Suruiuor, for no Suruiuor of other Tenants pro indiuiso shall haue the whole by Suruiour, but only ioyntenants, and this is called in Law Ius accrescendi. Omnes feoffati sunt simul habendi & tenendi nec totum nec partem separatam nec per se, sed vt quilibet eorum totum habeat cum alijs in communi, & cum vnus moriatur non discendit aliqua pars hæredi morientis nec seperata nec in cõmuni ante mortem omnium sed pars illa communis per ius accrescendi accrescit superstitibus de persona ad personam vsque ad vltimum superstitem. But although Suruiuorship bee proper to Ioyntenants, yet it is not proper quarto modo (that is) omni, soli & semper, for there may bee

Bracton lib. 4. fol. 262. b. Britton cap. 35. Fleta lib. 3. ca. 4. & ca. 10. 49. E. 3. fol. 5. 6

heires a touts iours Mes autrement est de Parceners. Car si trois parceners sont, & deuant ascun partition fait lun ad issue & denie, ceo que a luy affiert discendra a sez coheires issint q̃ ils aueront ceo per discent, & nemy per suruiuor, come ioyntenants aueront, &c.

ments to him and to his heires for euer, but otherwise it is of Parceners, for if three Parceners bee, and before any partitiõ made the one hath issue and dyeth, that which to him belongeth shall discend to his issue, and if such Parcener die without issue, that which belongeth to her shal discend to her coheires so as they shall haue this by discent & not by suruiuour, as Ioyntenants shall haue, &c.

Ioyntenants, though there be not equall benefit of Suruiuor on both sides. As if a man letteth Lands to A. and B. during the life of A. if B. dyeth A. shall haue all by the Suruiuor, but if A. dyeth B. shall haue nothing.

Two or more may haue a Trust or an Authoritie committed to them ioyntly, and yet it shall not suruiue. But herein are diuers diuersities to be obserued: First, there is a diuersitie betweene a naked Trust or an Authoritie, and a Trust or Authoritie ioyned to an estate or interest. Secondly, there is a diuersitie betweene Authorities created by the partie for priuate causes, and Authoritie created by Law for execution of Iustice. As for example, (b) if a man deuise that his two Executors shall sell his Land, if one of them dye the Suruiuor shall not sell it, but if he had deuised his Lands to his Executors to be solde there, the Suruiuor shall sell it, which diuersitie is implyed by our Author, for hee sayth, that he, that suruiueth shall haue the entire Tenancie.

If a man make a letter of Atturney to two, to doe any act, if one of them dye, the Suruiuor shall not doe it, but if a Venire facias be awarded to foure Coroners to impannell and returne a Iury, and one of them dye, yet the other shall execute and returne the same.

If a Charter of feoffement (c) be made, and a Letter of Atturney to foure or three ioyntly and seuerally to deliuer seisin, two of them cannot make liuery, because it is neither by them foure or three ioyntly, nor any of them seuerally: but if the Sherife vpon a Capias directed to him make a warrant to foure or three ioyntly or seuerally to arrest the Defendant, two of them may arrest him, because it is for the execution of Iustice (d) which is pro bono publico, and therefore shall be more fauourably expounded, then when it is only for priuate, and so hath it beene adiudged, Iura publica ex priuato promiscuè decidi non debent.

Et deuie. Note there is a naturall death and a ciuill death, and Littletons Case is to be intended of both, and therefore (e) if two Tenants be, and one of them entreth into Religion, the Suruiuor shall haue the whole.

b) 39. Ass. p. 17. 30. H. 8. tit. deuise B. Dyer 3. Eliz. 190. 49. E. 3. 16. 2. Eliz. Dyer 177. 23. Eliz. Dyer 371. 4. Eliz. Dyer 210. 10. H. 4. 2. & 3. 14. H. 4. 34. 39. H. 6. 42. 31. Ass. 20. 33. H. 8. ioynt. Br. 62. 30. H. 8. condition Br. 190. (c) 38. H. 8. Dyer 62. 37. H. 8. fol. 6.

(d) Pasch. 45. Eliz. in the Kings Bench betweene King Hobbes.

(e) 21. R. 2. iudgment. 263.

Sect. 281.

CE Et come le suruiuor tient lieu enter iointenants, en mesme le maner il tient lieu enter eux queux ont ioynt estate ou possession oue auter de chattel real ou personal. Sicome si leas de terres ou tenements soit fait a pluisors pur terme des ans, celuy q̃ suruesquist de les lessees auera les tenements a luy entier, durant l'terme, per force de mesme le leas. Et si vn chiual ou vn auter

AND as the suruiuour holds place betweene ioyntenants, in the same manner it holdeth place betweene them which haue ioynt Estate or Possession with another of a Chattell, reall or personall. As if a Lease of Lands or Tenements bee made to many for tearme of yeares, hee which suruiues of the Lessees, shall haue the Tenements to him only during the terme by force of

ter chattel personall sont done a plusors, celuy que suruesquist auera le chiual solement.

the same lease. And if a Horse, or any other chattell personall be giuen to many, hee which suruiueth shall haue the Horse only.

¶ HEreby it is manifest that Suruiuor holdeth place, regularly aswell betweene Ioyntenants of Goods and Chattels in possession or in right, as Ioyntenants of Inheritance or Freehold.

¶ *Chattell*, or Catell, whereof commeth the word used in Law (f) Catalla and is as Littleton here teacheth twofold, viz. reall and personall, and putteth examples of both.

(f) Regist. Origin. 139. 144. Bract. lib. 2. 39. H. 6. 35. Stanford. Pr. 45.

Section 282.

¶ EN mesme le maner est de debts & duties &c. car si vn obligation soit fait a plusors pur vn debt, celuy q̃ suruesquist auera tout le det ou dutie. Et issint est dauters Couenants & Contracts, &c.

IN the same manner it is of debts and duties, &c. for if an Obligation be made to many for one debt, hee which suruiueth shall haue the whole debt or dutie. And so is it of other Couenants and Contracts, &c.

¶ NOw hee speaketh of Debts, Duties, Couenants, Contracts, &c.

¶ *Dets & Duties, &c.* Here by force of this (&c.) an exception is to bee made of two ioynt Merchants, for the Wares, Merchandizes, Debts, or Duties that they haue as ioynt merchants or Parteners shal not suruiue, but shall goe to the Executors of him that deceaseth, and this is per legem Mercatoriam, which (as hath beene said) is part of the Lawes of this Realme for the aduancement and continuance of Commerce and Trade which is pro bono publico, for the rule is, That Ius accrescendi inter Mercatores pro beneficio commercij locum non habet.

F. N. B. 117. E. 38. E. 3. 7.

And to the latter (&c.) in this Section the like exception must be made.

Section 283.

¶ ITem, ascũs iointenants poient estre que poient auer ioint estate, et estre iointenãts pur terme de lour vies, et vncore ils ont seuerall enheritances. Sicõe terres soient dones a deux homes et a lez heires de leur deux corps engendres, en cest case les donees ont ioint estates pur terme de lour deux vies, et vncore ils ont

ALso there may bee some ioyntenants which may haue a ioint estate, & be ioyntenants for terme of their liues, & yet haue seuerall inheritances. As if lands be giuen to two men and to the heires of their two bodyes begotten, In this case the donees haue a ioint estate for terme of their two liues, and yet they haue seuerall inheritances, for if one of

¶ *ILs ont ioynt estate pur terme de lour deux vies, &c.* Note, albeit they haue seuerall Inheritances in tayle, and a particular estate for their liues, yet the Inheritance doth not execute, and so breake the Ioyntenancie, but they are ioyntenants for life, and tenants in Common of the Inheritance in tayle.

Vide Sect. 296.

¶ *Sicome home & fem poient auer, &c.* Here a diuersitie is implyed, when the estate of Inheritance is limited by one conueyance, as

Vide Westcotes case. Lib. 2. fol. 60. 61.

as in this case it is, there are no severall estates to drowne one in another, But when the states are devided in severall conveyances their particular estates are distinct and devided, and consequently the one drownes the other: As if a Lease be made to two men for terme of their lives, and after the Lessor granteth the reversion to them two, and to the heires of their two bodyes the ioynture is severed, and they are Tenants in common in possession. And it is further implied that in this case of Littleton there is no division betweene the estate for lives, and the severall inheritances, for in this case they cannot convey away the inheritances after their decease, for it is devided only in supposition and consideration of Law, and to some purposes the inheritance is said to be executed, as shall bee said hereafter.

Vid. 12. E. 4. 2. b.

If a man make a Lease for (f) life, and after granteth the reversion to the Tenant for life, and to a stranger and to their heires, they are not ioyntenants of the reversion, but the reversion is by act of Law executed for the one moitie in the Tenant for life, and for the other moity he holdeth it still for life the reversion of that moitie to the grantee.

(f) 39. H. 6. 2. b.

And so it is, if a man maketh a lease (g) to two for their lives, and after granteth the reversion to one of them in fee, the ioynture is severed, and the reversion is executed for the one moity, and for the other moity there is Tenant for life the reversion to the Grantee.

(g) Wiscots case, ubi supra.

If Lessee for life granteth his estate to him in the reversion and to a stranger, the ioynture is severed, and the reversion executed for the one moitie by the act of Law.

Ibidem. 7. H. 6.

severall inheritances, car si lun des donees ad issue, et deux, lauter que survesquist avera tout p le survivor pur terme de sa vie, et si celuy que survesquist auxy ad issue, et deux, donques l'issue del un avera lun moitie, et lissue del auter avera lauter moitie d la terre, et ils tiendront la terre enter eux ē common, et ne sont pas iointenāts, mes sont tenants en common. Et la cause pur q̄ tielx donees en tiel cas ont ioint estate pur terme de lour vies, est p̄ ceo que al commencement les tres fuerōt dones a eux deux, les queux parolx sās pluis dire font ioint estate a eux pur terme de lour vies. Car si home voit lesser tre a un auter p fait ou sāns fait, nient feasant mention q̄l estate il averoit, et de ceo fait liverie de seisin, en ceo case le lessee ad estate pur terme de sa vie, et issint entánt que les terres fueront dones a eux, ils ont ioint estate pur terme de lour vies: & la cause pur q̄ ils averont several enheritances est ceo, entant que ils ne poiēt aūs p nul possibi-

the Donees hath issue and die, the other which surviueth shall haue the whole by the suruiuor for terme of his life, and if he which suruiueth hath also issue, and die, then the issue of the one shall haue the one moity, and the issue of the other, shall haue the other moity of the land, and they shall hold the land betweene them in Cōmon, and they are not ioyntenants but are tenants in common. And the cause why such Donees in such case haue a ioynt estate for terme of their liues, is, for that at the beginning the lands were giuen to them two, which words without more saying make a ioynt estate to them for terme of their liues. For if a man will let land to another by deed or without deed, not making mention, what estate hee shall haue, and of this make liuery of seisin, in this case the lessee hath an estate for terme of his life, and so in as much as the lands were giuen to them, they haue a ioynt estate for terme of their liues, & the reason why they shall haue seuerall inhe-

lity vn heire enter eux ingender, sicome hõe et fem poient auer, &c. donqz la ley voet que lour estate et lour enheritance soit tiel cõe reason voet, solonqz la forme et effect des parolx del done, et ceo est a les heires q̃ lun engendra de son corps p ascun de ses femes, & a les heires q̃ lauter engendra d̃ son corps p asc̃ de ses femes, &c. Issint il couient p necessitie de reason que ils aueront seueralx enheritances. Et en tiel cas si lissue dun des donees apres la mort des donees deuie, issint q̃ il nad ascun issue en vie de son corps engẽdre, donqz le donor ou son heyre poit enter en la moitie come en son reuersion, &c. coment q̃ lauť des donees ad issue en vie, &c. Et la cause est, que entant q̃ les enheritãces sont seueral, &c. le reuersion de eux en ley est seueral, &c. et le suruiuor del issue del auter ne tiendra pas lieu dauer lentierť.

ritances is this; inasmuch as they cãnot by any possibility haue an heire between them ingendred, as a man and woman may haue, &c. the Law will that their estat and inheritance be such as is reasonable, according to the forme and effect of the words of the gift, and this is to the heires which the one shall beget of his body by any of his wiues, and to the heires which the other shall beget of his body by any of his wiues, &c. So as it behoueth by necessity of reason that they haue seueral inheritances. And in this case if the issue of one of the donees after the death of the donees dy, so that he hath no issue aliue of his body begotten, then the donor or his heire may enter into the moity as in his reuersion, &c. although the other donee hath issue aliue, &c. and the reason is, Forasmuch as the inheritances bee seueral, &c. the reuersion of them in Law is seuerall, &c. and the suruiuor of the issue of the other shall hold no place to haue the whole.

If a man maketh a Lease for life and granteth the reuersion to two in fee, the Lessee granteth his estate to one of them, they are not ioyntenants of the reuersion, for there is an execution of the estate for the one moity, and an estate for life, the reuersion to the other of the other moity.

Here Littleton hath well resolued a doubt, for of ancient time it hath beene said (h) That when lands haue beene giuen to two women, and to the heires of their two bodyes begotten (which case our Author putteth in the next Section) that the husband hauing issue should be Tenant by the Curtesie liuing the other sister, for that as some held the inheritance was executed, and that the sisters were Tenants in Common in possession, and consequently the husband to be Tenant by the Curtesie, which he could not be if the women had a ioynt estate for terme of their liues; and likewise it was said (i) that the issue of the one should recouer the moity in a Formdone liuing the other sister. But, Verba sunt hæc, and Littleton grounding himselfe vpon good Authority in Law hath cleered this doubt.

(h) 17.E.3.51.78. 18.E.3.39. 50.E.3. Starhom. en done. 50.E.3. Feoffments & fait.97.

(i) 44.E.3. taile 13. 8.Ass.33. 24.E.3.29. 7.H.4.16. Corbets Case. lib.1. fo.8. 84.6. 4.Maria Dier 145. See before in the chapter of Ten. by the curtesie Sectione.

¶ *Nient feasant mention quel estate il aueroit.* Here Littleton addeth materially (not making mention of what estate) for (k) if in the premisses lands be letten, or a rent granted, the generall intendment is, that an estate for life passeth, but if the Habendum limit the same for yeares or at will, the Habendum doth qualifie the generall intendment of the premisses: And the reason of this is, for that it is a maxime in Law, That euery mans grant shall be taken by construction of Law most forcible against himselfe. Quælibet concessio fortissimè contra donatorem interpretanda est, which is so to be vnderstood that no wrong be thereby done, for it is another maxime in Law Quod legis constructio non facit iniuriam: And therefore if Tenant for life maketh a Lease generally, this shall bee taken by

(k) Pl. Com. in Throgkmortons case.

Regula.

construction

construction of Law, an estate for his own life that made the Lease, for if it should be a lease for the life of the Lessee, it should be a wrong to him in the reuersion. And so it is if Tenant in taile make a Lease generally, the Law shall construe this to bee such a Lease as hee may lawfully make, and that is for terme of his owne life; for if it should be for the life of the Lessee, it should be a discontinuance, and consequently the state which should passe by construction of law should worke a wrong.

(1) 8. E. 3. 427. tit. Feoffem. & Faits 73. 30. H. 8. tit. Ioynt. Br. 53. Dyer fo. 361. Pl. Com. 160.

Et issint entant que les terres fueront dones a eux ils ount ioynt estate pur lour vies. **This is plaine, but with this exception, Unlesse the** Habendum doth otherwise limit the same. And therefore if a Lease be made (1) to two, Habendum to the one for life, the remainder to the other for life, this doth alter the general intendment of the premisses, and so hath it beene oftentimes resolued. And so it is if a Lease be made to two, habendum the one moitie to the one, and the other moitie to the other, the habendum doth make them Tenants in Common, and so one part of the Deed doth explaine the other, and no repugnancie betweene them, Et semper expressum facit cessare tacitum.

Bracton.

Per nul possibilitie. **Here it is to be obserued, That where the** Grant is impossible to take effect according to the Letter, there the Law shall make such a construction as the gift by possibilitie may take effect, which is worthie of obseruation. Benignæ faciendæ sunt interpretationes cartarum propter simplicitatem Laicorum, vt res magis valeat quam pereat.

Issint il couient per necessitie de reason. **The reason of the Law is** the life of the Law, for though a man can tell the Law, yet if he know not the reason thereof, he shall soone forget his superficiall knowledge: but when he findeth the right reason of the law, and so bringeth it to his naturall reason, that he comprehendeth it as his owne, this will not onely serue him for the understanding of that particular case, but of many other. For Cognitio legis est copulata & complicata: And this knowledge will long remaine with him, all which is plainely implied by the words, and (&c.) of our Author in this Section.

Et en tiel case si lissue dun des Donees apres la mort des Donees deuie issint que il nad ascun issue en vie de son corps engendres, donques le Donor ou son heire poet enter en le moitie. **This is mistaken in the imprinting, and va**rieth from the originall, which is, Si lun Donee ou lissue dun des Donees apres la mort des Donees deuie, issint que il nad ascun issue, &c. For it is euident, that if the one Donee himselfe dieth without issue, the Inheritance doth reuert for a moitie, and after the decease of the other Donee, the Donor may enter into that moitie, and whether the Issue of the one Donee dieth without Issue at any time either in the life of the other Donee, or after his decease, it is not materiall, for whensoeuer no issue is remaining of the one Donee, so as the state taile is spent, the Donor may after the decease of the suruiuing Donee, enter into that moitie.

Aristot. 1. Metaphis.

Et la cause est, que entant que les inheritances, &c. Littleton **in this** Chapter hath often sayd, Et la cause est, which is worthie of obseruation, for then we are truly sayd to know any thing, when we know the true cause thereof: Tunc vnumquodque scire dicimur cum primam causam scire putamus: Scire autem proprie est rem ratione & per causam cognoscere.

Virg. 1. Georg.

Fœlix qui potuit rerum cognoscere causas.

And therefore all Students of Law are to applie their principall indeauour to attaine thereunto, all which is implied by the words and seuerall &c. in this Section.

Here the cause of the entrie of the Donor into a moitie in this case is, That in as much as the Inheritance is seuerall, the reuersion is seuerall. Therefore upon the seuerall determination of the estats in taile, the Donor may enter, and the Law reuiueth a reuersion to bee expectant upon the particular estate, because the Donor or Lessor or their heyres after euerie determination of any particular estate, doth expect or looke for to enioy the Lands or Tenements againe.

Dyer 14. El. 309.

Le reuersion de eux en ley est seuerall, &c. **Hereby, and by this** (&c.) is implied, That upon one ioynt or entire gift or Lease there is one ioynt or entire reuersion, and upon seuerall gifts or Leases there be seuerall reuersions. And this is to be understood of the reuersion in the Donor or his heires. But albeit the gifts or Leases be seuerall, yet if the Donors or Lessors grant the reuersion to two or more persons and their heires, they are Ioyntenants of the reuersion. And so it is of a Remainder: and therefore if a gift [illegible] two men and the heires of their two bodies begotten, the remainder to them two and their heires, they are Ioyntenants for life, Tenants in Common of the state taile, and Ioyntenants of the

fee

fee simple in remainder, for they are Ioynt purchasers of the Fee simple, and the remainder in fee is a new created estate, but the reuersion remaining in the Donor, or his heires, is a part of his antient Fee simple.

Sect. 284.

¶ En tiel sicome est dit de males, en mesme le manner est lou terre est done a deux females, & a les heires de lour deux corps engendres.

And as it is sayd of Males, in the same manner it is where land is giuen to two females, and to the heires of their two bodies engendred.

¶ If a man giueth Lands to two men and one woman, and the heires of their three bodies begotten, In this case they haue seuerall Inheritances, for albeit it may be sayd, that the woman may by possibilitie marry both the men one after another, yet first she cannot marrie them both in præsenti, and the Law will neuer intend a possibilitie vpon a possibilitie, as first to marrie the one, and then to marrie the other. Secondly, the forme of the gift is, To the heires of their three bodies, which is not possible, and therefore they shall haue seuerall Inheritances. And so it is, if a gift be made to one man and to two women, mutatis mutandis. In the same manner, if a gift in taile be made to a man and his mother, (m) or to a man and his sister, or to him and his Aunt, &c. in this and like cases, albeit the gift is made to a man and a woman, yet they haue seuerall inheritances, because they cannot marrie together, and are within the rule and reason of our Author. 44.E.3.tit.Taile.13. (m) 18.E.3 39. 7.H.4.18.

Sect. 285.

Item si terres soyent dones a deux, & a les heirs de lun de eux, ceo est bone Joynture, & lun ad franktenement, & lauter ad fee simple: Et si celuy que ad le fee deuie, celuy que ad le franktenement auera lentiertie per le suruiuor pur terme de sa vie. En mesme le manner est, lou tenements sont dones a deux & les heires del corps dun de eux engendres, lun ad franktenement, & lauter ad fee taile, &c.

Also if lands be giuen to two and to the heires of one of them, this is a good Ioynture, and the one hath a Freehold, and the other a fee simple: And if he which hath the fee dieth, he which hath the freehold shal haue the entiertie by suruiuour for terme of his life. In the same manner it is, where tenements bee giuen to the heires of the body of one of them engendred, the one hath a freehold, & the other a fee taile, &c.

¶ By this Section, and the (&c.) in the end of it, they are Iointenants for life, and the Fee simple or estate taile is in one of them, and because it is by one and the same conueyance, they are Iointenants, and the Fee simple is not executed to all purposes, as hath been said before.

If a fine bee leuied to two, (n) and to the heires of one of them, by force whereof hee is seised, he that hath fee dieth, and after the Ioyntenant for life dieth, and an estranger abates, in this case the heire may either suppose the fee simple executed, and haue an assise of Mortdauncester, the words of which writ be, Si R. pater fuit seisitus die quo obijt in dominico suo vt de feodo, which cannot bee sayd of him that hath but a remainder expectant vpon an estate for life, but in respect that he is seised of a fee simple, and of a ioynt estate in possession, the words in the writ be true, That he was seised in Dominico suo vt de feodo. Likewise the heire may haue a Writ of Right, which also in some sort prooues the fee simple executed, or the heire may haue a Scire facias to execute the fine, by which the heire supposeth that (n) 42.E.3.9.10. 11.H.4.55. 31.E.3.Scire Facias 19. 29.H.8.Mord.B.59. 4.E.3.37. F.N.B.196.& 219. 4.E.3.Itinere Derby. 24.E.3.70.

that the fee was not executed, or hee may maintaine a writ of Intrusion where the heire maketh the like supposition, and shall terme it a Remainder. And yet when land is given to two and to the heires of one of them, he in the remainder cannot grant away his fee simple, as hath beene sayd.

Sect. 286.

¶ *Claimer riens per discent de son compaignion, &c.* By which (&c.) is implied, That so it is if one Joyntenant acknowledge a Recognisance or a Statute, or suffreth a iudgment in an action of Debt, &c. and dieth before execution had, it shall not bee executed afterwards. But if execution be sued in the life of the Conusor, it shal bind the suruiuor, and it is further implied, That both in the case of the Charge and of the Recognisance, Statute, and iudgement, if he that chargeth, &c. suruiue, it is good for euer.

F.N.B. 204. E. 297. 7.H.6.2. 13.H.7.22. 10 E.3.34. 17.R.2.tit. Charge 15. 5.H.5.8. Vide Sect. 289.

And so it is (o) if a man bee possessed of certain lands for term of yeares in the right of his wife, and granteth a Rent charge, and dieth, the wife shall auoyd the charge, but if the husband had suruiued, the charge is good during the terme.

(o) 9.H.6.52.

If a Villeine purchase lands, and bind himselfe in a Recognisance, if the Lord enter before execution, the Lord shall auoyd the same, as it hath been sayd.

(p) 8 E.3.tit. Execution Statutes.

But otherwise it is if he had made a Lease for yeares, for the reason that Littleton here yeeldeth in this Section.

If two Joyntenants bee of a terme, (q) and the one of them grant to I.S. that if

(q) 14.H.8.22. Pl. Com. 263.b. in Dame Hales Case.

¶ ITem si deux jointenaunts sont seises destate en Fee simple, & lun graunt un rent charge per son fait a un auter hors de ceo, que a luy affiert, en cest case durant la vie le Grantor, le rent charge est effectuall: Mes apres son decesse le grant de le rent charge est void, quant a charger la tre, car celuy que ad la terre per le suruiuor tiendra tout la terre discharge. Et la cause est, pur ceo que celuy que suruesquist clayma & ad la tre per le suruiuor, & nemy ad, ne poet de ceo claymer rien per discent de son compaignion, &c. Mes auterment est de Parceners, car si soient deux Parceners des tenements en fee simpl, et deuant ascun partition fait, lun charge ceo que a luy affiert per son Fait, dun rent charge, &c. et puis morust sans issue, per que ceo que a luy affiert discend a lauter Parcener, en cest case lauter Parcener tiendra la Terre charge, &c. pur ceo que il vient a cel moitie per discent come heire, &c.

ALso if two Ioyntenants be seised of an estate in Fee simple, and the one graunts a Rent-charge by his Deed to another out of that which belongeth to him: in this case during the life of the Grantor, the Rent charge is effectuall, but after his decease the grant of the Rent charge is voyd, as to charge the land, for hee which hath the land by suruiuor, shal hold the whole land discharged. And the cause is, for that he which suruiueth claimeth and hath the land by the suruiuor, and hath not nor can claime any thing by discent from his companion, &c. But otherwise it is of Parceners, for if there be two Parceners of Tenements in Fee simple, & before any partitiõ made the one chargeth that which to her belongeth by hir Deed, with a Rent charge, &c. & after dieth without issue, by which that which belongeth to her discends to the other parcener, in this case the other parcener shall hold the land charged &c. because she came to this moity by discẽt, as heir, &c.

if he pay to him ten pound before Michaelmasse, that then he shall haue his terme, the Grantor dyeth before the day, I. S. payes the summe to his Executors at the day, yet hee shall not haue the tearme, but the Suruiuor shall hold place, for it was but in nature of a communication, but if he had made a Lease for yeares to beginne at Michaelmasse, it should haue bound the Suruiuor.

And where Littleton putteth the case of a Rent charge, It is so likewise implyed, that if one Ioyntenant granteth a Common of Pasture, or of Turbary, or of Estouers, or a Corodie or such like out of his part, or a way ouer the Land, this shall not bind the Suruiuour: for it is a maxime in Law, that Ius accrescendi præfertur oneribus, and there is another maxime, that Alienatio rei præfertur iuri accrescendi.

45.E.3.13. *Vide Sect.289.*

If one Ioyntenat in Fee simple be indebted to the King, and dyeth, (r) after his decease no extent shall be made vpon the Land in the hands of the Suruiuour.

(r) 40.*Ass*.36 50 *Ass*.5. *F.N.B*.149.*q*. *Pl.Com*.321.

If a recouery be had against one Ioyntenant who dyeth before execution, the Suruiuour shall not auoyd this recouery, because that the right of the moitie is bound by it.

If one Ioyntenant in fee, take a Lease for yeares of an estranger by Deed indented and dyeth, the Suruiuour shall not be bound by the Conclusion, because he claymes aboue it, and not vnder it.

Et la cause est pur ceo que celuy que suruesquist clayme & ad la terre per suruiuor, &c. **Here againe** Littleton **sheweth the reason: and the cause** wherefore the Suruiour shall not hold the Land charged, is, for that hee claymeth the Land from the first Feoffor, and not by his companion, which is Littletons meaning when he sayth, (that he claymeth by Suruiuor) For (s) the suruiuing Feoffee may pleade a feoffment to himselfe without any mention of his ioynt Feoffee. And this is the reason, That if two Ioyntenants bee in fee, and the one maketh a Lease for yeares, reseruing a Rent and dyeth, the suruiuing Feoffee (t) shall haue the Reuersion by Suruiuour, but hee shall not haue the Rent because he claymeth in from the first Feoffor, which is Paramount the Rent. If there be two Ioyntenants in Fee, and the one Ioyntenant granteth a Rent charge out of his part, and after releaseth to his ioynt companion and dyeth, he shall hold the Land charged, for that he is out of the reason and cause set downe by Littleton because he claymeth not by Suruiuor, in as much as the release preuented the same. And of this opinion was Littleton himselfe (u) before the Edition of his Booke. But all men agree that if A. B. and C. be Ioyntenants in fee, and A. chargeth his part, and then releaseth to B. and his heires and dyeth, that the (w) charge is good for euer, because in that case B. cannot be in from the first Feoffor, because he hath a ioynt companion at the time of the Release made, and seuerall writs of Præcipe must be brought against them. And albeit the Release of one Ioyntenant to the residue of the Ioyntenants makes no degree in supposition of Law, neyther is there any seuerall estate betweene them, but the estate of him that releaseth is as it were extinguished and drowned in their estate and possession, so as one Præcipe lyeth against them, yet shall they hold the Land charged as is aforesaid. As if tenant for life grant a Rent charge, and after surrendreth his estate to the Lessor, albeit the estate charged be drowned, and the Lessor is not in by him, yet he shall hold it charged.

(s) 14.E.4.1.b. 18.E.3. *breife* 830. 8.E.2.*entrie* 77. 18.E.3.28. 38.E.3.26. 8.H.6.25. *Vide* 46.E.3.77. 35.H.6.39.

(t) *Dyer Mich.* 2.& 3.*Eliz*. 187. *Lib*.1.*fol*.96. *Vide lib*.6.*fol*.78.79.

(u) 33.H.6.5.a. 9.*Eliz. Dyer* 263.

(w) 37.H.8 *tit.alienation Br*.31. 10.E.4.3.b. 40.E.3.41.b. 33.H.6.5. 22.H.6.42.b. *per Pole*. 35.E.3.*release* 43. 33.E.3.*auowrie* 195. 14.H.8.2.

¶ *Mes auterment est de Parceners, Car si sont deux Parceners &c.* **This** is to be intended aswell of Parceners by custome as of Parceners by the Common Law, and here is implyed the reason of the diuersitie, for that the Suruiuor doth clayme aboue the charge, and the heire by discent vnder the charge.

Section 287.

¶ **Item si sōt deux ioyntenants des terres en Fee simple deins vn burgh, lou les terres & tenemēts sont deuisables per testament. & si lun de les dits deux ioyntenants deuise ceo que a luy affiert per son**

Also if there bee two Ioyntenants of Land in Fee simple within a Borough, where Lands and Tenements are deuisable by Testament, & if the one of the said two Ioyntenants deuiseth that which to him be-

¶ *Per son testament, &c.* **Eyther in** writing or nuncupatiue according to the custome.

¶ *Et la cause est pur ceo que nul deuise, poet prender effect mes apres le mort le deuisor & per sa mort tout la terre maintenant deuient per la ley a son compagnion, &c.*

&c. Here both their claymes commence at one instant, and although an Instant. Est vnum indiuisibile tempore quod non est tempus nec pars temporis, ad quod tamen partes temporis connectuntur, and that, Instans est finis vnius temporis, & Principium alterius. Yet in consideration of Law there is a prioritie of time in an instant, as here the Suruiuor is preferred before the deuise, for Littleton sayth, that the cause is that no deuise can take effect till after the death of the Deuisor, and by his death all the land presently commeth by the Law to his companion. Whereby it appeareth, that Littleton by these words, Post mortem & per mortem, though they iumpe at one instant, yet alloweth prioritie of time in the instant which hee distinguisheth by per and post. And the reason of this prioritie is, that the Suruiuour claymeth by the first Feoffor (as hath bin said) and therefore in iudgement of Law his Title is Paramount, the title of the Deuisee, and consequently the deuise void, and the rule of Law is, that, Ius accrescendi præfertur vltimæ voluntati.

Pl. Com. in Fulmerstons case.

testament, &c. & mourust, ceo deuise est voide. Et la cause est pur ceo que nul deuise poit prender effect, mes apres la mort le deuisor. & per sa mort tout la terre maintenant deuient per la ley a son companion, que suruesquist per le suruiuor, le quel il ne claime, ne ad riens en la terre per my le deuisor, mes en son droit demesne p le suruiuor, solonque le course de ley &c. & pur cel cause tiel deuise est voide. Mes auterment est de Parceners seisies des tenements deuisables en tiel case de deuise, &c. Causa qua supra.

longeth by his Testament, &c. and dyeth, this deuise is voide. And the cause is for that no deuise can take effect till after the death of the deuisor: and by his death al the Land presently commeth by the Law to his companion, which suruiueth by the Suruiuor, the which hee doth not clayme, nor hath any thing in the land by the deuisor, but in his owne right by the suruiuor according to the course of Law, &c. and for this cause such deuise is void. But otherwise it is of Parceners seised of Tenements deuisable in like case of deuise, &c. *Causa qua supra.*

Two Fems Ioyntenants of a Lease for yeares, one of them taketh husband, and dieth, yet the terme shall suruiue, for though all Chattels reals are giuen to the husband, if he suruiue yet the Suruiuor betweene the Ioyntenants is the elder title, and after the marriage the feme continued sole possessed, for if the husband dyeth, the feme shall haue it, and not the Executors of the husband, but otherwise it is of personall goods.

2. H. 5. executors 108.

If a man be seised of a house, and possessed of diuers heirelomes, that by custome haue gone with the house from heire to heire, and by his will deuiseth away the heirelomes, this deuise is void, for as Littleton here saith, the will taketh effect after his death, and by his death, the heirelomes by ancient custome are vested in the heire, and the Law preferreth the Custome before the Deuise. And so it is if the Lord ought to haue a Herriot when his Tenant dyeth, and the Tenant deuiseth away all his goods, yet the Lord shall haue his Herriot for the reason aforesaid. And it hath beene anciently said, that the Heriot shall bee paid before the Mortuarie. (x) Imprimis autem debet quilibet qui testauerit, dominum suum de meliore re quam habuerit recognoscere, & postea Ecclesiam de alia meliore, &c. Wherein the Lord is preferred, for that the tenure is of him. This dutie to the Lord is very ancient, for in the Lawes before the Conquest it is said, Siue quis in curia, siue morte repentina fuerit intestat' mortuus, Dominus tamen nullam rerum suarum partem (præter eam quæ iure debetur herioti nomine) sibi assumito.

(x) Fleta lib. 2. cap. 50. Bracton lib. 2. fo. 60. Britton fol. 178.

Lamb. fol. 119. 68.

In the Saxon tongue it is called Heregeat, as much to say (as I take it) as the Lords beste, for Here is Lord, and geat is beste. But let vs returne to Littleton.

¶ *Mes auterment est de parceners seises des tenements deuisable en tiel case, del deuise, &c.* Causa qua supra.

The reason is euident, for that there is no Suruiuor betweene Coparceners, but the part of the one is discendible, and consequently may be deuised.

Section 288.

¶ ITem il est communement dit, que chescun iointenant est seisie de la terre que il tient ioyntment, per my et per tout, et ceo est autant adire, que il est seisie per chescun parcel, et per tout, &c. et ceo est voier, car en chescun parcel, et per chescun parcel, et per touts les terres et tenements il est iointment seisie ouesque son companion.

ALso it is commonly said, that euery ioyntenant is seised of the land which hee holdeth ioyntly *Per my & per tout*, and this is as much to say as he is seised by euery parcel and by the whole, &c. and this is true, for in euery parcell, and by euery parcell, and by all the lands and tenements he is ioyntly seised with his compagnion.

¶ [*Tem est communement dit, &c.* That is, It is the common opinion, and Communis opinio is of good authority in Lawe, A communi obseruantia non est recedendum, which appeareth here by Littleton.

Vid. Sect. 697.

¶ *Per my & per tout.* Et sic totum tenet &, nihil tenet, s. totum coniunctim, & nihil per se separatim. And albeit they are so seised (as for example where there be two ioyntenants in fee) yet to diuers purposes each of them hath but a right to a moity, as to enfeoffe, giue, or demise, or to forfeite or lose by default in a Præcipe. If my villeine (y) and another purchase lands to them two and their heires, I may enter into a moytie.

Vid. Bracton lib. 5. fo. 430. Britton, cap. 35. Fleta, lib. 3. cap. 4. 40. E. 3. 40. 18. E. 2. bre. 831. 35. H. 6. 39. Vid the second part of the Institutes vpon the 6. chapter of the Statute De bigamis. Fleta, lib. 1. cap. 28. 40. Ass. 79. 48. E. 3. 16.

(y) *Vid. 6. E. 3. 4. 7. E. 4. 29. 11. Eliz. Dier. 183*

And where all the ioyntenants ioyne in a feoffment, euery of them in iudgement of Law doe giue but his part. If an Alien and a subiect purchase lands ioyntly, the King vpon office found shall haue but a moitie. And Littleton afterwards in this chapter saith that one ioyntenant hath one moitie in Law, and the other the other moitie. And therefore if two ioyntenants be (z) and both they make a feoffment in fee vpon condition, and that for breach thereof one of them shall enter into the whole, yet he shall enter but into a moitie because no more in iudgement of Law passed from him; and so it is, of a Gift in taile or a Lease for life, &c.

(z) *Pl. Com. in Brownings case, fo.*

Yet euery ioyntenant may warrant the whole, (a) because a man may warrant more then passeth from him

(a) *Vid. the second part of the Institutes vpon the 6. chapter of the Statute of Bigamis.*

If two ioyntenants make a feoffment in fee (b) and one of the Feoffors die, the Feoffee cannot plead a feoffment from the suruiuour of the whole, because each of them gaue but his part, but otherwise it is on the part of the Feoffees, as hath beene said before.

(b) *14. E. 4. 5. and the other bookes abouesaid.*

And where two ioyntenants be, the one of them (c) may make the other his Baliffe of his moitie, and haue an Action of account against him. And one ioyntenant (d) may let his part for yeares or at will to his companion.

(c) *21. E. 3. 60.*

(d) *11. H. 3. 60. 33.*

If two ioyntenants be of certaine lands, and the one of them by Deede indented (e) bargaineth and selleth the lands, and the other ioyntenant dyeth, and then the Deede is inrolled, there shall passe nothing but the moitie which the bargainer had at the time of the bargaine.

(e) *6. E. 6 tit. Faits inroll. 9. Br.*

Sect. 289.

¶ ITem si deux iointenants sont seisies de certain terres en Fee simple, & lun lessa ceo que a luy affiert a vn estranger pur terme de 40. ans, & deuie deuant le term com-

ALso if two Ioyntenants bee seised of certain lands in fee simple, and the one letteth that which to him belongeth to a stranger for terme of fortie yeares, and dieth before the

¶ P*Er force de mesme le dit lease, &c.*

By this (&c.) is implied, That where our Author speaketh of Ioyntenants seised in fee, that so it is if two bee seised for life, and one make a Lease to begin presently, or in

(f) *Vid Sect. 286. & 660. & Sect. 2.*

in futuro, and dieth, this Lease shall binde the suruiuor, as it hath beene adiudged. (g) And if one Ioyntenant grant vesturam terræ, or herbagium terræ, for yeares, and dieth, this shall binde the suruiuor, for such a Lessee hath right in the land. So it is if two Ioyntenants be of a Water, and the one granteth the seuerall Pischarie.

(g) 11.H.4.90. 14.H.8 6. 17.E.4.6.a.9.H.6.52. 21.H.7.29. 14.H.7.4. 18 E.3.Execution 56. 11.El.Dy.285.P.Com.160.a Tempi E.1.Ass.422.20.H.6 4.7.H.7.13.10.H.7.24.

¶ *Lun lessa.* The one letteth. If two Ioyntenants be of an Aduowson, and (h) the one presenteth to the Church, and his Clerke is admitted & instituted, this in respect of the priuity shal not put the other out of possession, but if that Ioyntenant that presenteth dieth, it shal serue for a title in a Quare impedit brought by the Suruiuor. But yet if one Ioyntenant or Tenant in Cōmon present, or if they present seuerally, the Ordinarie may either admit or refuse to admit such a Presentee, vnlesse they ioyne in presentation, and after the sixe moneths hee may in that case present by Laps.

(h) 6.E.3.38,39.52. 7.E.3.20.21. 17.Ed 3.37.b. 22.E.3.9.30.E.3.16. 21.H.4.54.15.E.3.Dar. presentment.11.10 E.4.94. 1.H.7.1.b.2 R.3.Quar.imp. 102. 9.El.Dy.259. 36.H.8.Br.Present. 27.H 8.fo.11. 5.H.7.8. 6.E.4.10.b.Doct.& Stud. 116. 34.H.6.40. 20.E.3. Quar.imp.63. F.N.B.34.V.

But if two or more Coparceners bee, (i) and they cannot agree to present, the eldest shal present, and if her sister doth disturbe her, she shall haue a Quare impedit against her, and so shall the Issue and the Assignee of the eldest, and yet he is tenant in Common with the youngest. And in the same manner the tenant by the Curtesie of the eldest shall present; but if there be foure Coparceners and the eldest and the second present, and the other two present ioyntly or seuerally, the Ordinary may refuse them all, for the eldest did not present alone but shee and one other of her sisters. But now let vs returne to Littleton.

(i) Bract.li.4.fo.238.245. 247.Brit.fo.223.45.Edw.3. Fines 41.18.E.2.Quar.imp. 176.38.H.6.9.19.E.3.ib. 59.5.H.5.10.F.N.B.34.V

mence, ou deins l' tme, en cest case apres son decease le Lessee poet enter et occupier la moitie a luy Lesse durant le terme, &c. coment que le Lessee nauoit vnq̃s possession de ceo en la vie le Lessor, per force de mesme le lease, &c. Et le diuersitie perenter le case de grant de Rent-charge auantdit, et cest case est ceo, car en grãt de Rent charge p ioyntenaunt, &c. les Tenemẽts demurgent touts foits come ils fueront adeuant, sans ceo que ascun ad ascun droyt dauer ascun parcell de les tenements forsque eux mesmes, et les Tenements sont en tiel plyte, come ils fueront deuant le charge, &c. Mes ou Lease est fayt per vn Ioyntenant a vn auter per terme des ans, &c. maintenaunt per force de le Lease le lessee ad droit en mesme la terre, cestascauoir de tout ceo que a son lessour affiert, et dauer ceo per force de mesme le Lease durant son terme. Et ceo est la diuersitie.

term beginneth, or within the terme, in this case after his decease the Lessee may enter and occupy the moitie let vnto him during the terme, &c. although the lessee had neuer the possession therof in the life of the Lessor, by force of the same lease, &c. And the diuersity between the case of a grant of a Rent charge aforesayd, and this case, is this, for in the grant of a Rent charge by a Ioyntenant, &c. the tenements remaine alwayes as they were before, without this that any hath any right to haue any parcel of the tenements but they themselues, and the Tenements are in the same plight as they were before the charge, &c. But where a lease is made by a Ioyntenant to another for terme of yeares, &c. presently by force of the Lease, the Lessee hath right in the same Land, (*videlicet*) of all that which to the Lessour belongeth, and to haue this by force of the same Lease, during his terme. And this is the diuersitie.

Sect. 290.

¶ Item ioyntenāts (sils voilent) poient faic partition enter eux et la partition est assets bon, mes de ceo faire ils ne serront compels per la ley. Mes sils voylent faic partition de lour proper volunt & agreement, le partition estoiera en sa force.

ALſo ioyntenants (if they will) may make partition betweene them, and the partition is good enough, but they ſhall not bee compelled to doe this by the Law, but if they will make partition of their own will and agreement, the partition ſhal ſtand in force.

¶ *Poient faire partition.* But this partition muſt be (k) by Deed as hath beene ſaid before. But ioyntenants for yeares may (l) make partition without Deed.

¶ *Ils ne ſerra compell.* This is true regularly, but by the cuſtome of ſome Cities and Boroughs one ioyntenant or tenant in Common may compell his companion by writ of partition grounded upon the cuſtome to make partition. But ſince Littleton wrote ioyntenants and Tenants in common generally are compellable to make partition by writ framed upon the Statutes (m) of 31. & 32. H. 8. as before hath beene ſaid. And albeit they be now compellable to make partition, yet ſeeing they are compellable by writ, they muſt purſue the Statutes and cannot make partition by Parol, for that remaines at the Common Law. And by Littletons Authority herein it ſeemeth to me that if one ioyntenant or tenant in Common diſſeiſe another, and the Diſſeiſee bring his Aſſiſe for the moitie, that in this caſe, though the Plaintife prayeth it, yet no iudgement ſhall be giuen to hold in ſeueralty, for then at the Common Law there might haue beene by compulſion of Law a partition betweene ioyntenants and tenants in Common, and by rule of Law the Plaintife muſt haue iudgement according to his pleint or demaund.

If two Ioyntenants be (n) of land with warranty, and they make partition by writing the warranty is diſtroyed, but if they make partition by writ of partition upon the Statute, the warrantie remaines becauſe they are compellable thereunto.

(k) *Vi. Sect. 259. 318.*

(l) *18. El. Dyer 350.*

F.N.B. 62. b.

(m) *31. H. 8. ca. 1. 32. H. 8. ca. 32. Vi. Sect. 264. 247. 259. Mich. 16. & 17. El. 1340. Inter Harris & Eden adiudge. acc. 18. El. Dyer 350. b. Vi. before in the Chapter of Partition, many bookes cited concerning this matter. 3. E. 3. 48. F. N. B. 9. b. 7. Aſſ. 10. 7. E. 3. 29. 10. Aſſ. 17. 10. E. 3. 40. 43. 12. Aſſ. 15. 17. 12. E. 3. iudgement 162. 20. E. 3. Aſſ. 62. 28. Aſſ. 35. 23. Aſſ. 10. 7. H. 6. 4. 19. H. 6. 45. 3. E. 4. 10. Vid. Sect. 247. Brist. fo. 112. Lib. 6 fo. 12. & 13. Morrices Caſe.*

(n) *29. E. 3. tit. Gart.*

Sect. 291.

¶ Item si un ioynt estate soit fait de terre a le baron & a sa fem̄ & a un tierce person, en ceo cas le baron et sa fem̄ nont en ley en lour droit forsq; le moity, &c. et le tierce person auera tant come le baron et sa feme ont, s. lauter moity, &c. Et la cause est, pur ceo que le baron et sa feme ne sont forsque un person en

ALſo if a ioynt eſtate be made of land to husband and wife, and to a third perſon, in this caſe the husbād & wife haue in law in their right but the moitie, and the third perſon ſhall haue aſmuch as the huſband and wife, *viz.* the other moity, &c. And the cauſe is, for that the husband and wife are but one perſon in

¶ *Le baron & ſa feme nont en ley en lour droit forſque le moity, &c.* William Ocle and Ioan his wife (o) purchaſed lands to them two and their heires, after William Ocle was attainted of high treaſon for the murther of the Kings father E. 2. and was executed, Ioan his wife ſuruiued him, E. 3. granted the lands to Stephen de Bitterly and his heires. Iohn Hawkins the heire of the ſaid Ioan in a Petition to the King diſcloſeth this whole matter, and upon a Scire facias againſt the Patentee hath iudgement to recouer the lands,

(o) *Mich. 33. E. 3. Coram Rege Salop. in Theſaur.*

ley, et ſont en ſemblable caſe, ſicome eſtate ſoit fait a deux ioyntenants, ou lun ad per force de ioyntur lun moitie en ley, & lauter lauter moitie, &c. En meſme le maner eſt lou eſtate eſt fait a le baron et a ſa feme, et as auters deux homes, en tiel cas le baron et ſa feme nont forſque la tierce part, et les auters deux homes les auters deux parts, &c. Cauſa qua ſupra.

law and are in like caſe as if an eſtate bee made to two ioyntenants, where the one hath by force of the ioynture the one moytie in law, and the other the other moitie, &c. In the ſame manner it is where an eſtate is made to the husband and wife, and to two other men, in this caſe the husband and wife haue but the third part, and the other two men the other two parts, &c. *Cauſa qua ſupra.*

Pluis ſerra dit del matter touchant ioyntenancie, en le chapter de Tenants en common, et tenant per Elegit, et tenant per ſtatute Merchant.

More ſhall bee ſaid of the matter touching ioyntenancy in the chapter of Tenants in Common and tenant by Elegit, and tenant by Statute Merchant.

lands, for the reaſon here yeelded by our Author.

Vi. Sect. 665.

But if an eſtate be made to a man and a woman and their heires before marriage, and after they marry, the husband and wife haue moyties betweene them, which is implied in theſe words of our Author, Baron & ſa feme.

Forſque vn perſon en Ley. Bract. ſaith (p) vir & vxor ſunt quaſi vnica perſona, quia caro vna & ſanguis vnus. It hath bin ſaid, that if a reuerſion bee granted to a man and a woman and their heires, and before attornment they entermarrie, and then attornement is made, That the husband and wife ſhall haue no moities, in this caſe no more than if a Charter of Feoffement be made to a man and a woman, with a Letter of Atturney to make Liuery, they entermarrie, and then Liuerie is made ſecundum formam chartæ, in which caſe it is ſaid, that they haue no moities. But certain it is that if a feoffment were made before the ſtat. of 27. H. 8. of vſes to the vſe of a man (q) & a womã, & their heires, and they entermarrie, and then the Statute is made, if the husband alien it is good for a moitie, for the Statute executes the poſſeſſion according to ſuch qualitie, manner, forme, and condition, as they had in the vſe, ſo as though it veſt during the couerture, yet the Act of Parliament executes ſeuerall moities in them, ſeeing they had ſeuerall moities in the vſe.

(p) *Bract. li.* 5. *fo.* 416. 20. *H.* 3. *Diſſeiſ.* 52. *Lib.* 4. *fo* 68. *Tokers caſe. Pl. Com.* 483. *Nichols caſe.*

(q) 4. *Mar. Dyer* 149. 3. *Mar. Dyer* 1222. 29. *H.* 8. *Dyer* 32.

If an eſtate be made to a Villeine and his wife (r) being free, and to their heires, albeit they haue ſeuerall capacities, viz. the Villeine to purchaſe for the benefit of the Lord and the wife for her owne, yet if the Lord of the Villeine enter, and the wife ſuruiueth her husband, ſhe ſhal inioy the whole land, becauſe there be no moities betweene them.

(r) 40. *Aſſ. p.* 7.

A man makes a Leaſe to A. and to a Baron and Feme, viz. to A. for life, to the husband in taile, and to the Feme for yeares, in this caſe it is ſayd, That each of them hath a third part, in reſpect of the ſeueraltie of their eſtates.

If a Feoffement be made to a man and a woman and their heires with warrantie, (ſ) and they entermarrie and after are impleaded and vouch and recouer in value, moities ſhal not be betweene them, for though they were ſole when the warrantie was made, notwithſtanding at the time when they recouered and had execution, they were husband and wife, in which time they cannot take by moities.

(ſ) *Pl. Com.* 483. *Nichols caſe*

Albeit Baron and Feme (as Littleton here ſaith) be one perſon in Law, ſo as neither of them can giue any eſtate or intereſt to the other, yet if a Charter of Feoffement be made to the wife, the husband as Atturney to the Feoffor may make liuerie to the wife, and ſo a Feme couert that hath power to ſell land by will, may ſell the ſame to her husband, becauſe they are but Inſtruments for others, and the ſtate paſſeth from the Feoffee or Deuiſee.

21. *H.* 7.

If a husband, wife, and a third perſon purchaſe lands to them and their heires, (t) and the husband before the Statute of 32. H. 8. cap. 1. had aliened the whole land to a ſtranger in fee, and died, the wife and the other Ioyntenant were Ioyntenants of the right, and if the wife had

(t) 11. *E.* 3. *Cui in vita* 9. 26. *E.* 3. *ibid.* 36. *E.* 3. *ibid.* 20. 35. *Aſſ. Pl.* 15. 31. *H.* 6. *tit. Ent. Congeable* 54. 19. *H.* 6. 45. *F. N. B.* 193. *k.*

had died, the other Ioyntenant should haue had the whole right by suruiuor, for that they might haue ioyned in a writ of Right, and the discontinuance should not haue barred the entrie of the suruiuor, for that he claimed not vnder the discontinuance, but by title paramount aboue the same, by the first feoffement, which is worthie of obseruation. But if the husband had ma.e a feoffement in fee but of the moitie, and he and his wife had died, their moitie should not haue suruiued to the other.

And for the better vnderstanding of this diuersitie diuers things are worthy of obseruation.

First, That a right of action & a right of entrie may stand in Ioynture, for at the Common law the alienation of the husband was a discontinuance to the wife of the one moitie, and a disseisin of the other, so as after the death of the husband, the wife hath a right of Action to the one moitie, and the other Ioyntenant a right of entrie into the other, but they are Ioyntenants of the right, because they may ioyne in a writ of Right.

Vi. Sect. 302.

Secondly, That a right of Action or a bare right of entrie cannot stand in ioynture with a Freehold or Inheritance in possession, and therefore if the husband make a feoffement of the moitie, this was a discontinuance of that moitie, * and the other Ioyntenant remained in possession of the Freehold and Inheritance of the other moitie, which for the time was a seuerance of the Ioynture, and so are all the bookes which seemed to varie amongst themselues, cleerely reconciled.

** Vi. the Statute of 32. H. 8. c. it is no discontinuance at this day.*

If two Ioyntenants be of a rent, and the one of them disseise the Tenant of the Land, (u) this is a seuerance of the Ioynture for a time, for the moitie of the rent is suspended by vnitie of possession, and therefore cannot stand in Ioynture with the other moitie in possession. And this is to be obserued, That there shall neuer be any suruiuor, vnlesse the thing be in ioynture at the instant of the death of him that first dieth: for the rule is, Nihil de re accrescit ei qui nihil in re quando ius accresceret habet.

(u) Pl. Com. 419 in. Bratchbridges case.

Also if a man deuiseth lands to two, to haue and to hold to the one for life, and the other for yeares, they are no Ioyntenants, for a state of Freehold cannot stand in Ioynture with a terme for yeares: and a reuersion vpon a freehold cannot stand in ioynture with a Freehold and Inheritance in possession, as shall be sayd in the next Chapter. Neither can a Seisin in the right of a politique capacitie, stand in Ioynture with Seisin in a naturall capacitie, as shall be sayd hereafter.

46 E. 3, 21. 19. H. 6. 45. 37. H. 8. 8. 3. E. 4. 10.

If two Femes be ioyntly seised, and they take Barons, and the Barons ioyne in an alienation and die, the wiues are Ioyntenants of the right, and may ioyne in a writ of Right, and yet they may haue seuerall writs of Cui in vita at their election, but when they haue recouered in those seuerall writs, they shall be Ioyntenants againe. But if the Barons had aliened seuerally, this had beene a seuerance of the Ioynture for a time, for the reason abouesaid.

If two Ioyntenants, the one for life, and the other in fee, lose by default, the one shall haue a writ of Right, and the other a Quod ei deforceat, and yet when they haue seuerally recouered, they shall be Ioyntenants againe. So it is if two Ioyntenants be disseised, and an Assise is brought, and the one is summoned and seuered, and the other recouer the moitie, and after another Assise is brought, and he that recouereth is summoned and seuered, and the other recouer, albeit they seuerally recouer, yet they are Ioyntenants againe.

And in all cases where the Ioyntenants pursue one ioynt remedie, and the one is summoned and seuered, and the other recouer, he that is summoned and seuered shall enter with him: but where their remedies be seuerall, there the one shall not enter with the other, till both haue recouered, and the same Law is of Coparceners. If lands (w) be demised for life, the remainder to the right heires, of I. S. and of I. N. I. S. hath Issue and dieth, and after I. N. hath Issue and dieth, the Issues are not Ioyntenants, because the one moitie vested at one time, and the other moitie vested at another time. And yet in some cases there may be Ioyntenants, and yet the estate may vest in them at seuerall times.

Vid. Lit. cap. Remitter, the last case.
10. H. 6. 10. 31. H. 6. tit. Entre congeable. 46. E. 3. 21. b. 3. E. 4. 10. 37. H. 6. 8.
(w) 24. E. 3. 29. 18. E. 3. 38. 38. E. 3.

If a man (x) make a Feoffement in fee to the vse of himselfe and of such wife as hee should afterwards marrie, for terme of their liues, and after he taketh wife, they are Ioyntenaunts, and yet they come to their estates at seuerall times.

(x) 17. El. Dyer Brents case.

And so it is if I disseise one to the vse of two, and the one agrees at one time, and the other at another, yet they are Ioyntenants.

In this Section are three (&c.) the first and second are at large explained before, the last is intended where more parties take than three.

Chap. 4.

CHAP.4. Of Tenants in Common. *Sect.*292.

¶ Tenants en Common ſont ceux, que ont terres ou tenemẽts en Fee ſimple, Fee taile, ou pur terme de vie, &c. les queux ont tielx terres ou Tenements per ſeuerall titles, & nemy per ioynt title, et nul de eux ſcauoit de ceo ſon ſeuerall, mes ils doient per la Ley occupier tiels terres ou tenements en cõmõ, & pro indiuiſo a prender les profits en common. Et pur ceo que ils auiendront a tielx terres ou tenements per ſeuerall titles et nemy per vn ioynt title, et lour occupation et poſſeſſion ſerra p la ley perenter eux en common, ils ſont appels Tenaunts en common. Sicome vn home enfeoffa deux Ioyntenants en fee, et lun de eux alien ceo que a luy affiert a vn auter en fee, ore le alienee et lauter Ioyntenant ſont Tenants en Common, pur ceo que ils ſont eins en tiels Tenements per ſeuerall titles, car lalienee vient eins en la moitie per la feoffement dun des Ioyntenants, et lauter Ioyntenant ad lauter moitie, per force de l primer Feoffement fait a luy, et a ſon compaignion, &c. Et iſſint ils ſont eins per ſeuerall titles, ceſtaſcauoir, per ſeueral Feoffements, &c.

Tenants in Common are they which haue Lands or Tenements in Fee-ſimple, Fee taile, or for terme of life, &c. and they haue ſuch Lands or Tenements by ſeuerall Titles, and not by a ioynt title, and none of them know of this his ſeuerall, but they ought by the Law to occupie theſe Lands or Tenements in common, and *pro indiuiſo*, to take the profits in Common. And becauſe they come to ſuch Lands or Tenements by ſeuerall titles, and not by one ioynt title, and their occupation and poſſeſſion ſhall be by Law betweene them in Common, they are called Tenants in Common. As if a man enfeoffe two Ioynetenants in Fee, and the one of them alien that which to him belongeth, to another in Fee, now the Alienee and the other Ioyntenant are Tenants in Common, becauſe they are in in ſuch tenemẽts by ſeuerall titles, for the Alienee commeth to the moitie by the Feoffement of one of the Ioyntenaunts, and the other Ioyntenaunt hath the other moitie by force of the firſt feoffement made to him and to his Companion, &c. And ſo they are in by ſeuerall Titles, that is to ſay, by ſeuerall Feoffements, &c.

Flet. li. 3. *ca.* 4.

¶ Litleton hauing ſpoken of Parceners which are onely by diſcent, and of Ioyntenants which are onely by purchaſe, and by ioynt title, ſpeaketh now of Tenants in Common, which may be by three meanes, viz. by Purchaſe, by Diſcent, or by Preſcription, as hereafter in this Chapter ſhall appeare.

¶ *On*

¶ *Ou pur terme de vie, &c.* Here (&c.) implyeth pur terme dauter vie, or for tearme of yeares, or for any other fixed Inheritance in the Land.

And here it appeareth, that the essentiall difference betweene Joyntenants and Tenants in Common, is that Joyntenants haue the Lands by one ioynt Title, and in one Right, and Tenants in common by seuerall Titles, or by one Title and by seuerall Rights, which is the reason that Joyntenants haue one ioynt Freehold, and Tenant in Common haue seuerall Freeholds, only this propertie is common to them both, viz. that their occupation is indeuided, and neyther of them knoweth his part in seuerall. *Vide Sect.* 296.

The Example that Littleton putteth in this Section is perspicuous, and needeth no explication.

Sect. 293.

¶ET est ascauoir, que quant il est dit en ascun Lieur, que home est seisie en fee sauns pluis dire, il serra entendue en fee simple, car il ne serra entendue per tiel paroll (en fee) que home est seisie en fee tayle, sinon que soit mis a ceo tiel addition, fee tayle, &c.

AND it is to bee vnderstood, that when it is said in any Booke, that a man is seised in fee, without more saying, it shall bee intended in fee simple, for it shall not bee intended by this word (in fee) that a man is seised in fee tayle vnlesse there be added to it this addition fee tayle, &c.

¶ This is euident and secundum excellentiam, it shall bee taken for the highest and best fee, and that is fee simple. *Vide devant. Sect.* 99.

¶ *Addition in fee tayle, &c.* Here is implyed a maxime in Law, viz. that Additio probat minoritatem, as it is vulgarly said, the younger sonne giueth the difference.

Sect. 294.

¶ITem si 3. ioyntenants sont, & vn de eux alien ceo que a luy affiert a vn auter home en fee, en cest cas lalienee est tenant en common ouesque les auters deux ioyntenants, mes vncore les auters 2. ioyntenants sont seisies des deux parts ioyntment que remayne, & de ceux deux parts le suruiuor enter eux deux tient lieu, &c.

ALso if three Ioyntenants bee, and one of them alien that which to him belongeth to another man in fee. In this case the alienee is Tenant in common with the other two Ioyntenants, but yet the other two Ioyntenants are seised of the two parts which remain ioyntly, and of these two parts the Suruiuor betweene them two holdeth place, &c.

¶ This needeth no explication, only the (&c.) in the end of this Section implyeth that the same Law is where there be more Joyntenants then three.

Section 295.

¶ Item si soient deux Joyntenants en fee, & lun dona ceo que a luy affiert a vn auter en le tayle, & lauter done ceo que a luy affiert a vn auter en le tayle, les donees sont tenants en common, &c.

ALso if there bee two Ioyntenants in fee, and thē one giueth that to him belongeth to another in tayle, and the other giueth that to him belongs to another in tayle, the Donees are Tenants in common, &c.

Vide Sect. 300.

¶ The (&c.) in the end of this Section implyeth, that so it is when a Lease for life, or pur auter vie is made, for in that case also the Lessees are Tenants in common.

Sect. 296.

¶ Si terres sōt dones a 2. homes, &c. Of this sufficient hath been spoken in the Chapter (a) of Joyntenants.

(a) Sect. 285.

¶ Mes si terres sont dones a 2. Abbes, &c. In this case of the two Abbots in respect of their seuerall capacities, albeit the words be ioynt, yet the Law (b) doth adiudge them to be seuerally seised.

(b) 7.H.7.9.b. 16.H.7.15.b. 3.H.7.11. 10.E.4.16.b. 5.H.7.25. 18.E.27. 49.E.3.25.b. Vide Sect. 209.

The (&c.) in the end of this Section implyeth, that so it is of any (c) body Politique or Corporate bee they regular, as dead persons in law (whereof our Authour here speaketh) or Seculer: as if

(c) 4.H.7.45. 18.E.3.27.b.

¶ Mes si terres sont dones a 2. homes, & a les heires de lour deux corps engendres, les donees ount ioint estate pur terme de lour vies, & si chescun de eux ad issue & deuy, lour issues tiendront en common, &c. Mes si terres sont dones, a deux Abbes, sicome al Abbe de Westminster, & al Abbe de S. Albon, a auer & tener a eux & a lour successors, ē cest cas ils ont maintenant al commencement estate en common, & nemy ioynt estate. Et la cause est, pur ceo q̄ chescun Abbe, ou auter Soueraigne, de meason de Religion, deuant que il fuit fait Abbe, ou Soueraigne, &c. il fuit forsq; come mort person en ley, et quant il est fait Abbe, il est come vn home person able en ley tantsolemēt a purchaser et auer terres ou tenements, ou auters

BVt if lāds be giuē to two men, and to the heires of their two bodies begotten, the Donees haue a ioint Estate for tearme of their liues, and if each of them hath issue and die, their issues shall hold in Common, &c. But if lands be giuen to two Abbots, as to the Abbot of *Westminster*, and to the Abbot of Saint *Albons*, to haue and to hold to them and to their Successors. In this case they haue presently at the beginning an estate in Common, and not a ioynt estate. And the reason is for that euery Abbot or other Soueraigne of a house of religion, before that hee was made Abbot or Soueraigne, &c. was but as a dead person in law, and when he is made Abbot, he is as a mā personable in Law only to purchase and haue lands or tenements or other things to the vse of his House, and

auters choses al vse de sa meason, et nemy a son proper vse, come auter seculer home poit, et pur ceo al commencement de lour purchase ils sont tenants en common, et si lun de eux deuie, Labbe que suruesquist nauera my tout per le Suruiuour, mes le successor de Labbe que morust tiendra le moitie en common oue Labbe q̄ suruesquist, &c.

not to his owne proper vse, as another secular man may, and therefore at the beginning of their purchase they are tenants in common, and if one of them die, the Abbot which suruiueth shall not haue the whole by suruiuor, but the Successor of the Abbot which is dead, shall hold the moitie in common with the Abbot that suruiueth, &c.

lands be giuen to two Bishops, to haue and to hold to them two and their Successours: Albeit the Bishoppes were neuer any dead persons in Law, but alwayes of capacitie to take, yet seeing they take this Purchase in their politique Capacitie, as Bishops, they are presently Tenants in Common, because they are seised in seuerall rights, for the one Bishop is seised in the right of his Bishopricke of the one moitie, and the other is seised in the right of his Bishopricke of the other moitie, and so by seuerall Titles and in seuerall Capacities, whereas Joyntenants ought to haue it in one and the same right and Capacitie, and by one and the same ioynt Title. The like Law is if Lands be giuen to two Parsons and their Successors or to any other such like Ecclesiasticall bodies Politique or Incorporate as hath beene said.

If a Corodie be granted to two men and their heires, in this case because the Corodie is incertaine and cannot be seuered; it shall amount to a seuerall grant to each of them one Corodie, for the persons be seuerall, and the Corodie is personall.

Sect. 297.

ITem si terres soient dones a vn Abbe, & a vn Secular home, A auer & tenir a eux, s. al Abbe, & a ses successors, & al Secular home a luy & a ses heires, donques ils ount estate en cōmon, Causa qua supra.

ALso if lands bee giuen to an Abbot and a Secular man, to haue and to hold to them, *viz.* to the Abbot and his Successors, and to the Secular man, to him and to his heires, They haue an estate in common, *Causa qua supra.*

¶ AND so it is if lands be giuen to the Parson of Dale, and to a Lay man, to haue and to hold to them, that is to say, to the Parson and his Successors, and to the Lay man and his heires, they are presently Tenants in Common for the causes abouesaid. So of a Bishop, &c. Et sic de similibus.

F.N.B.40.I. 16.E.3.Ioindre in action 27. 16. ... p.1. 2.R.3.16.7.H.7.9. 13.H.9.14.

If Lands bee giuen to the King and to a Subiect. To haue and to hold to them and to their heires, yet they are Tenants in Common, and not Joyntenants, for the King is not seised in his naturall Capacitie, but in his Royall and Politique Capacitie, in iure Coronæ, which cannot stand in Joynture with the seisin of the subiect in his naturall Capacitie. So likewise if there bee two Joyntenants, and the Crowne discend to one of them the Joynture is seuered, and they are become Tenants in common. But if Lands bee giuen to A. de B. Bishop of N. and to a Secular man to haue and to hold to them two, and to their heires. In this case they are Joyntenants, for each of them take the lands in their naturall Capacitie.

Pl.Com. in Seig. Barkleys case fol.

If lands be giuen to Iohn Bishop of Norwich and his Successors, and to Iohn Ouerall Doctor of Diuinitie and his heires being one and the same person, he is Tenant in Common (d) with himselfe. But our Authors rules doe not hold in Chattels, Reals or Personals; for if a Lease for yeares be made, or a Ward granted to an Abbot and a Secular man, or to a Bishop and Secular man, or if goods be granted to them, they are Joyntenants, because they take not in their Politique Capacitie.

(d) 13.H.8.14. 16.H.7.15. 9.H.6.25. 45.E.3.25.

Sect. 298.

¶ And the reason is, because they haue seuerall Freeholds and an occupation Pro indiuiso.

Here is to be obserued that the Habendum doth seuer the premisses that Prima facie seemed to be ioynt, for an expresse estate controles an implyed estate, as hath beene said.

¶ Item si terres soient dones a deux a auer, et tener, s. lun moity a lun et a ses heires, et lauter moity a lauter et a ses heires, ils sont tenants en common.

Also if lands be giuen to two to haue and to hold, s. the one moitie to the one and to his heires, and the other moitie to the other, and to his heires, they are tenants in common.

Section 299.

11.Ass.Pl.16.
45.E.3.12. 44.Ass.11.
21.E.4.22.b.

¶ And the like Law is, if the feoffment bee made of a third part or a fourth part, &c. And if there be an Aduowson appendant, they are also Tenants in common of the Aduowson. And albeit it is said that such a feoffment of a moity or third part, &c. is not good without writing, for that (as they say) a man cannot create an vncertain estate in land by Parol, yet is the Law cleere that such a feoffment is good by Parol without writing, and such an vncertaine estate shall passe by Liuery, and so it appeareth in our bookes.

¶ Item si home seisie de certain terres enfeoffa vn auter de le moitie de mesme la terre sans ascun parlance de assignment ou limitation de mesme le moitie ē seueralty al temps del feoffment, donqs le feoffee & le feoffor tiendront lour parts de la terre en common.

Also if a man seised of certaine lands infeoffe another of the moitie of the same land without any speech of assignement or limitation of the same moitie in seueraltie at the time of the feoffment, then the Feoffee and the Feoffor shall hold their parts of the land in common.

21.E.4.22.b.

If a Verdict finde that a man hath Duas partes manerij, &c. in tres partes diuisas,) this shall not be intended to be in Common, but if the verdict be in tres partes diuidendas, then it seemeth that they are Tenants in common by the intendment of the Verdict.

5.E.3.23.67. Temps E 1.Feoffments 115. 34.E.1.quar.imped.179. 10.Eliz.Dier.28. 22.E.3.6.Feoffments 116. 6.E.3.56. 39.E.3.38. 9.E.3.16. 17.E.3.3. 18.E.3.43. 43.E.3.26. 23.Ass.8. 33.H.6.5.a.

But if a man be seised of a Mannor whereunto an Aduowson is appendant, and maketh a feoffment of three acres parcell of the Mannor together with the Aduowson to two. To haue and to hold the one moitie together with the moity of the Aduowson to the one and his heires, and the other moity together with the other moitie of the Aduowson to the other and his heires this cannot be good without Deed, for the Feoffor cannot annex the Aduowson to these three acres, and disanex it from the rest of the Mannor without Deed.

Section 300.

¶ Et est ascauoir, que en mesme le maner come est auantdit de tenants en common, de terres ou tenēts en fee simple, ou en fee taile, en mesme le maner poit estre de

And it is to bee vnderstood that in the same maner as is aforesaid of tenants in common of lands or tenements in fee simple, or in fee taile, in the same

de tenants a terme de vie. Sicome deux ioyntenants sont en fee, & lun lessa a un home ceo que a luy affiert pur terme de vie, et lauter ioyntenant lessa ceo que a luy affiert a un auter pur terme de vie, &c. les deux lessees sont tenants en common pur lour vies, &c.

manner may it be of tenants for terme of life. As if two ioyntenants bee in fee, and the one letteth to one man that which to him belongeth for terme of life, and the other ioyntenant letteth that which to him belongeth to another for terme of life, &c. the said two lessees are tenants in cōmon for their liues, &c.

Vid. Sect. 295. where this is sufficiently explaned before.

Sect. 301.

¶ Item si home lessa terres a deux homes pur terme de lour vies, & lun granta tout son estate de ceo que a luy affiert a un auter, donqs lauter tenant a terme de vie, et celuy a q̄ le graunt est fait sont tenants en common, durant le temps que ambideux les lessees sont ē vie.

¶ Et memorandū, que en touts auters tiels cases, coment que ne sont icy expressement moues ou specifies, si sont en semblabl' reason, sont en semblable ley.

ALso if a man let lands to two men for terme of their liues, & the one grants all his estate of that which belongeth to him to another, then the other tenant for terme of life, and hee to whom the grant is made are tenants in common during the time that both the lessees be aliue.

¶ And *memorandum*, that in all other such like cases although it bee not here expresly moued or specified if they bee in like reason, they are in the like law.

¶ AND so it is if lands be letten to two for terme of their liues, Et eorum alterius diutius viuenti, and one of them graunteth his part to a stranger whereby the ioynture is seuered, and dyeth, here shall be no suruiuour, but the Lessor shall enter into the moity, and the suruiuour shall haue no aduantage of these words Et eorum alterius diutius viuenti for two causes. First, for that the ioynture is seuered. Secondly, for that these words are no more then the Common Law would haue implyed without them, and Expressio eorum quæ tacitè insunt nihil operatur. Hereby it appeareth that in case of Leases for life it is more beneficiall for the Lessor to haue the ioynture seuered then to haue it continue. 30. Ass. 18.

¶ *Si soient en semblable reason sont en semblable ley.* Here Littleton citeth one of the maximes of the Common Law, That wheresoeuer there is the like reason, there is the like Law. Vbi eadem ratio, ibi idem jus, or Vbi eadem ratio, ibi idem jus esse debet, for Ratio est anima legis. And therefore Ratio potest allegari deficiente lege. But it must be Ratio vera & legalis & non apparens. And here it appeareth that Argumentum à simili is good in Law, Sed similitudo legalis est casuum diuersorum inter se collatorum similis ratio, quod in vno similium valet, valebit in altero, dissimilium dissimilis est ratio. Vid. Sect. 1.

Sect. 302.

¶ ITem ſi deux joyntñts ẽ fee ſont, et lun leſſa ceo que a luy affiert a vn auť pur tme de ſa vie, le Tenant a terme de vie durant ſa vie, et lauť Joyntenaunt que ne leſſa paſſe, ſont Tenants ẽ common. Et ſur ceo caſe vn queſtion puit ſurder ſicome en tiel caſe, mittomus que ľ leſſor ad iſſue et duie, viuant lauter Joyntenant ſon companion, et viuant ľ tenant a terme de vie, le queſtion poet eſtre tiel: Si le reuerſion de la moitie que le leſſor auoit diſcẽdra al iſſue le leſſor, ou que lauť joyntenant auera cel reuerſion per le ſuruiuor. Aſcuns ont dit en ceſt caſe, que lauť joyntenant auera cel reuerſion per le ſuruiuor, et lour reaſon eſt tiel, ſ. que quant les joyntenants fueront joyntment ſeiſies en fee ſimple, &c. coment que lun de eux fiſt eſtate de ceo que a luy affiert pur terme de ſa vie, et comt que il ad ſeuer le franktenement de ceo que a luy affiert

ALſo if there bee two Ioyntenaunts in Fee, and the one letteth that to him belongeth to another for terme of his life, the Tenant for term of life during his life, and the other Iointenãt which did not let, are tenants in Common. And vpon this caſe ã queſtion may ariſe, as in ſuch caſe admit that the leſſor hath iſſue and die, liuing the other Ioyntenant his companion, and liuing the Tenant for life, the queſtion may be this, Whether the reuerſion of the moity which the leſſor hath ſhall diſcend to the iſſue of the Leſſor, or that the other joyntenant ſhall haue this reuerſion by the ſuruiuor. Some haue ſaid in this caſe, that the other jointenãt ſhal haue this reuerſion by the ſuruiuor: and their reaſon is this, ſ. That when the Iointenãts were iointly ſeiſed in fee ſimple, &c. although that the one of thẽ make an eſtate of that to him belongeth for term of his life, and although that hee hath ſeuered the

¶ SI deux Ioyntenants en fee, &c.

This needeth no explanation.

¶ *Et ſur ceo caſe vn queſtion poet ſurder, &c.*

Vi. 33. H. 6. 4. b. Here Littleton maketh a queſtion, and ſheweth the reaſons on both ſides, and concludes with a Quære. When Littleton maketh a queſtion, and ſheweth the reaſon on both ſides, the latter is euer his owne, (a) and the better. But Time hath made this queſtion without queſtion, for now all agree, That the jointure is ſeuered for the time, according to the latter opinion here ſet downe in Littleton, whoſe reaſons are vnanſwerable: for many times the change of the freehold makes an alteration or change of the reuerſion. As if Tenant in Taile, or the huſband ſeiſed in the right of his wife, or tenant for life make a leaſe for life of the Leſſee, in euerie of theſe caſes the Leſſour doth gaine a new reuerſion by wrong, as ſhall be ſayd more at large in the Chapter of Diſcontinuance, and if the elder brother grant the reuerſion (expectant vpon a Freehold) for life, it ſhall cauſe poſſeſſio fratris, as hath beene ſayd.

a) V. Sect. 340. 375. 439. 440. 462. 463. 464. 482. 483. 648. 720. 729. vi. Sect. 170.

Vi. Sect. 8. 7. H. 5.

¶ *Per meſme le reaſon le reuerſion que eſt dependant ſur meſme le franktenement eſt ſeuer de le Ioynture, &c.*

7. H. 7. 9. If two Joyntenaunts in fee be, and they both ioyne in a Leaſe to an Abbot and a ſecular man for terme of their liues, here the reuerſion that is dependant vpon ſeuerall freeholds is ſeuered. And ſo it is if they ioine in a Leaſe to two ſecular men, to haue and to hold the one moitie to the

affiert per l'lease, uncore il nad seuer l' fee simple, mes le fee simple demurt a eux ioyntment cōe il fuyt adeuant. Et issint semble a eux, que lauter Joyntenant que suruesquist, auera le reuersion per l' Suruiuour, &c. Et auters ont dit le contrarie, & ceo est lour reason, s. que quaunt lun des Joyntenaunts lessa ceo que a luy affiert a un auter pur terme de sa vie, per tiel Lease le franktenemt est seuer ō le joynture. Et per mesme le reason le Reuersion que est dependant sur mesme le Franktenement, est seuer de le Joynture. Auxy si le Lessour vst reserue a luy un annuall Rent sur le Leas, le Lessor solement aueroit le Rent, &c. le q̄l est un proofe q̄ le reuersiō est solement en luy, et que lauter nad riens en cel reuersion, &c. Auxy si le Tenant a term de vie fuit impleade, &c. & fist default apres default, donques le Lessor serroit de ceo solment receiue a defender son droit, &

freehold of this which to him belongs by the lease, yet hee hath not seuer'd the fee simple, but the fee simple remains to them ioyntly as it was before. And so it seemeth to them, that the other Ioyntenaunt which suruiueth shal haue the reuersion by the suruiuor, &c. And others haue said the contrarie, & this is their reason, s. that when one of the Ioyntenants leaseth that to him belongeth, to another for terme of his life, by such Lease the freehold is seuered frō the joynture. And by the same reason the reuersion which is depēding vpon the same freehold is seuer'd frō the joynture. Also if the lessor had reserued to him an annuall Rent vpon the lease, the lessor onely should haue had the Rent, &c. the which is a proofe, that the reuersion is onely in him, and that the other hath nothing in the reuersion, &c. Also if the Tenaunt for terme of life were impleaded, & maketh default after default, the lessor shall be only receiu'd for this, to defēd

one for life, & the other moity to the other for life, for both these cases are warranted by the authoritie of Littleton.

If two Joyntenants be of a Lease for twentie one yeres, and the one of them letteth his part for certaine yeares, part of the terme, the Joynture is seuered, and suruiuor holdeth not place, for a terme for a small number of yeares is as high an interest, as for manie more yeares, and so was it resolued Hil. 18. El. Reginæ, in Communi Banco, * which I my selfe heard. * Hil. 18. Eliz.

If two Coparceners be in fee, and the one make a Lease for life, this is no seuerance of the Coparcenarie, for notwithstanding the Lord shall make one auowrie vpon them both.

But if two Joyntenaunts be, and one maketh a Lease, this is a seuerance of the joynture, as Littleton here taketh it, and seuerall auowries shal be made vpon them.

¶ *Auxy si le Lessor vst reserue un annual rent, le Lessor solement auera le rent, &c.* But if two Joyntenants make a Lease for life, reseruing a rent to one of them, the rent shall enure to them both, because the reuersion remains in jointure, vnlesse the reseruation be by Deed indented, and then he onely to whom it is reserued shall haue it. But if they make a Lease by Deed indented, reseruing or sauing the reuersion to one of them, that is voyd, because they had the reuersion before, but the rent is newly created. 5 E. 4. 4. 27. H. 8. 16 a. 7. E. 4. 25. 14. Ed. 3. Br. 282.

And so it is if such a Lessee for life should surrender to one of them, it shall enure to them both, for that they haue a ioynt reuersion. But if the Lessee grant his estate to one of them, no part of it shal enure to his Companion, because for the moitie belonging to his Companion, it is in esse 5. E. 4. 4.

in

in him to whom the grant is made, the reuersion to the other in fee.

38.H.6.24.b. 2.R.3. tit. Extinguishment 3.

If two Joyntenants make a Lease for life, the remainder to his Companion in fee, this is a good remainder of his moitie to his Companion.

¶ *Donques le feoffor serra de ceo solement receiue,&c.*

¶ *Receiue*, Receit, Receptio, is in many cases where a person partie to a writ, or an estranger thereunto, to whom a reuersion or remainder appertaineth, shall in default of another person be receiued to defend his or her Freehold or Inheritance, the Law saith, Admittatur, &c. And this admission or receipt is giuen by sundrie statutes, (f) (and this is that which the Ciuilians call, Admissio tertiæ personæ pro interesse.) Et in casibus prædictis duæ concurrunt Actiones: Vna inter petentem & tenentem, & alia inter tenentem ius suum ostendentem & petentem.

(f) W.2.cap.3. 20.E.1. Statute de Defensione Iuris. 13.R.2.cap.16.

¶ *Pur ceo que vn Franktenement ne poet per nature de Ioynture, este annexe a vn reuersion.* And this is the principall reason, and of this sufficient hath beene sayd in the chapter of Joyntenants, Sect. 291.

¶ *&c.* This &c. in the end of this Section, implieth any other heire lineall or colaterall.

son Compaignion en cest case en nul manner serroit receiue, le quel proue le reuersion del moitie destre tantsolement en le Lessor: Et sic per consequens, si le Lessour morust viuant le Lessee pur terme de vie, le reuersion discendra al heire de Lessour, & nemy deuiendra a lauter Joyntenaunt per le suruiuor, Ideo quære. Mes en cest case si celuy Joyntenant que ad le franktenement ad issue et deuie, viuant le lessor & lessee, donques il semble, que mesme lissue avia cest moitie en demesne, et en fee per discent, pur ceo que vn Franketenement ne poet per nature de Joynture estre annexe a vn reuersion, &c. et il est certaine, que celuy que lessa fuit seisie de le moitie en son demesne come de fee, et nul auera ascun iointure en son Franktenement, Ergo ceo discendra a son issue, &c. Sed quære.

his right, and his Companion in this case in no manner shall be receiued, the which proueth the reuersion of the moitie to be onely in the Lessor: & so by consequent if the Lessour dieth, liuing the Lessee for terme of life, the reuersion shall discend to the heire of the Lessour, and shall not come to the other Ioyntenant by the suruiuor, *Ideo quære.* But in this case if that iointenant which hath the Freehold hath issue, & dies liuing the Lessor and the Lessee, then it seemeth that the same Issue shall haue this moitie in Demesne, & in fee by discent, for that a Freehold cannot by nature of Ioynture bee annexed to a Reuersion, &c. And it is certaine, That he which leased was seised of the moitie in his Demesne as of Fee, and none shall haue any Ioynture in his Freehold, therefore this shall discend to his Issue, &c. *Sed quære.*

Sect. 303.

¶ MEs si issint soit q̃ la ley en cest cas est tiel, que si le lessor deuie viuant le lessee, & viuant lauter ioyntenant, que ad le franktenement de lauter moitie, que le reuersion discendra al issue del lessor, donque est le ioynture, & title que ascun de eux poit auer per le suruiuor, & le droit de le ioynture anient, & tout oustrement defeat a touts iours. En mesme le maner est, si celuy ioyntenant que ad le franktenement deuie, viuant le lessor & le lessee si la ley soit tiel que son franktenemēt & fee q̃ il ad en le moity, discendra a son issue, donques le ioynture serra defeat a touts iours.

BVt if it be so that the Law in this case bee such, that if the Lessor dye liuing the Lessee, and liuing the other ioyntenant which hath the freehold of the other moitie, that the Reuersion shall discend to the Issue of the Lessor, then is the Ioynture and title which any of them may haue by the Suruiuour, and the right of the Ioynture taken away, and altogether defeated for euer. In the same manner it is if that ioyntenant which hath the freehold dye liuing the Lessor and the Lessee, if the Law bee so as his freehold and fee which he hath in the moity shall discend to his Issue, then the Ioynture shall be defeated for euer.

¶ *Donque est le ioynture & title, &c. & le droit de le ioynture anient, &c.*

And the reason of this is, for if the ioynture be seuered at the time of the death of him that first deceased the benefit of Suruiuour is vtterly destroyed for euer, as hath beene said (*) afore in the Chapter of Ioyntenants. But in the case aforesaid, if tenant for life dyeth in the life of both the ioyntenants they are ioyntenants againe as they were before.

(*) Vid. Sect. 291.

If two Ioyntenants bee in fee, and the one letteth his part to another for the life of the Lessor & the Lessor dieth, some say that his part shal suruiue to his companion, for by his death the Lease was determined. And others hold the contrary, and their reason is, first, for that at the time of his death the Ioynture was seuered, for so long as he liued the Lease continued. And secondly, that notwithstanding the act of any one of the Ioyntenants there must be equall benefit of Suruiuour as to the Freehold. But here if the other Ioyntenant had first dyed, there had beene no benefit of Suruiuor to the Lessor without question.

Sect. 304.

¶ ITem si 3. ioyntenants sont, & lun relessa p̄ son fait a vn d̄ ses cōpanions tout le droit que il auoit en le terre, donques ad celuy a que le releas est fait le tierc̄ part de les ter-

ANd if three Ioyntenants be, and the one release by his deed to one of his companions all the right which hee hath in the land, then hath hee to whom the release is made the third part of

¶ VPon this case these two things are to be obserued. First, that in this case this Release doth enure by way of mitter lestate, and not (*) by way of Extinguishment, for then the Release should enure to his Companion also, and he is in the Per by him that maketh the Release. (a) But if hee had released to the other two, then had it wrought no degree but

(*) 9. Eliz. Dier 263. 19. H. 6. 17.
(a) 40. E. 3. 41. 13. E. 3. tit. Garr. 35. E. 3. release 43. 22. H. 6. 4. 14. E. 3. Briefe 28. 19. H. 6. 17. 33. H. 6. 5. 28. H. 6. 2. 37. H. 8. Alienation 31. 8. H. 4. 8. 10. E. 4. 3.

but in supposition of Law, for many purposes they to whom the Release is made (as hath beene said) shall bee supposed in from the first feoffor, as they shall deraigne the first Warrantie for the whole.

(b) 9.Eliz.Dier 263. 19.H.6.17.

(b) The second thing to bee obserued is that hee to whom the Release is made hath a fee simple without these wordes (heires) as hath beene touched in the first Chapter of the first Booke, for that hee to whom the Release is, is seised per my, & per tout, of the fee and Inheritance as hath bin said in the Chapter of Ioyntenants. And note the like Law is betweene Coparceners: and further if there be two Coparceners, and the one hath Issue twentie daughters and dyeth, the other may release to any one of the daughters her whole part, albeit she to whom the Release is, hath not an equall part, but for the priuitie and the indeuided estate the Release is good.

But if two Ioyntenants be of twentie Acres, and the one maketh a feoffment of his part in eighteene Acres, the other cannot release his entire part, but only in two Acres, for that the Ioynture is seuered for the residue.

res per force de le dit releas, & il & son companion, teignet les auters deux parts en ioynture. Et quant al tierce part, que il ad per force de releas, il tient cel tierce part oue luy m̃ & son companion en common.

the Lands by force of the said release, and he and his companion shall hold the other two parts in Ioynture. And as to the third part which he hath by force of the release he holdeth that third part with himselfe and his companion in common.

Sect. 305.

¶ This is euident vpon that which hath been said before.

(c) 10.Eliz.Bendloes 9.Eliz.Dier 263.

(c) And it is to bee vnderstood that a Release may enure foure manner of waies, first by way of mitter lestate as here it appeareth. Secondly, by way of mitter la droit. Thirdly, by way of Extinguishment. Fourthly, by way of creation or inlargement of an Estate, as hereafter in this chapter shall appeare.

See more of this in the Chapter of Releases.

10.E.4.3.b. 21.H.6.8.b.

And it is to bee obserued that vpon a release that creates or inlargeth an estate, or enures by way of mitter lestate, a Rent may bee reserued, but not vpõ a release that enureth by way of mitter le droit, or which enures by way of Extinguishment.

The (&c.) in the end of this Section implyeth a diuersitie

¶ Cest ascauoir, q̃ ascun foits vn release prendra effect, & vrera pur mitter lestate de celuy que fist le release, a celuy a que le release en fait, sicome en le cas auantdit, & auxy sicome ioynt estate soit fait a le baron & sa feme, & a la tierce person & la tierce person relessa tout son droit que il ad a le baron, adonque ad le baron la moitie que le tierce auoit, & la feme de ceo nad riens. Et si en tiel case le tierce relessa a la feme nient nosmant le baron en le releas, donques ad la feme le moitie que le tierce auoit &c. & le barõ nad riens de ceo forsq̃ en

And is to bee obserued, that sometimes a deed of release shal take effect, and enure to put the estate of him which makes the release to him to whom the Release is made, as in the case aforesaid, and also, as if a ioynt estate bee made to the husband and wife, and to a third person, and the third person release all his right which hee hath to the husband, then hath the Husband the moitie which the third had, and the wife hath nothing of this. And if in such case the third Release to the Wife not naming the Husband in the Release, then hath the wife the moitie which the

en droit sa feme, pur ceo que en tiel case le release vrera de faire estate a celuy a que le release est fait, de tout ceo que affiert a celuy que fait le release, &c.

third had, &c. And the husband hath nothing of this but in right of his wife, because that in this case the release shall enure to make an estate to whom the release is made of all that which belongeth to him which maketh the release, &c.

between a release which enures by way of mitter lestate (wherof Littleton here speaketh) & a Release that enures by way of Extinguishment; for of a Release enuring by way of Extinguishment made to the husband the wife shall take benefit, or to the wife, the husband shall take benefit, as hereafter shall more at large be said.

Section 306.

¶ Et en ascun cas un releas vrera de mitter tout le droit que il que fait le releas ad, a celuy a que le release est fait. Sicome home seisie de certain tenements est disseisie per deux disseisors, si le disseisee per son fait relessa tout son droit, &c. a un des disseisors, donque celuy a que le releas est fait avera & tiendra touts les tenements a luy solement, et oustera son companion de chescun occupation de ceo. Et le cause est, pur ceo que les deux disseisors fueront eins encounter la ley, et quant un de eux happe le releas de celuy que ad droit dentre, &c. cest droit en tiel cas vestera en celuy a que le releas est fait, et est en tiel plyte, sicome il que avoit droit avoit enter, et luy enfeoffa,

And in some case a release shall enure to put all the right which he who maketh the release hath, to him to whom the release is made. As if a man seised of certaine tenements is disseised by two disseisors if the disseisee by his deed release all his right, &c. to one of the disseisors, then hee to whom the release is made shall haue and hold all the tenements to him alone, and shall oust his companion of euery occupation of this. And the reason is, for that the two disseisors were in against the law, and when one of them happeth the release of him which hath right of entrie, &c. this right in such case shall vest in him to whom the release is made, and he is in like plite, as hee which

¶ Here Littleton pursueth the second part of his diuision, viz. where a release shall enure by way of Mitter le droit.

¶ *Disseisie per deux disseisors, &c.* The like law is, where there bee two ioynt Abators or Intrudors which come in meerely by wrong. But if two men doe vsurpe by a wrongfull presentation to a Church, and their Clarke is admitted, instituted and inducted, and the rightfull Patron releaseth to one of them, this shall enure to them both, for that the vsurpers come not in meerely by wrong, but their Clarke is in by admission and institution which are iudiciall acts. (f) And therefore an vsurpation shall worke a Remitter to one that hath a former right.

(f) *Fitz. N.B. 35. in 11. R. 2. quare Imp. 144.*

¶ *Donques celuy a que le release est fait auera & teignera touts les tenements, &c.* Here by operation of Law presently vpon the deliuery of the release the whole freehold and inheritance is vested in him to whom the release is made, and all the state, that the other Disseisor had wholly deuested; for right and wrong cannot consist together, but the wrongfull estate giueth place to the rightfull. And the reason hereof is for that as hath beene said the disseisor to whom the release was

&c. Et la cause est, pur ceo que il q̄ auoit adeuant estate per tort, s. p disseisin, &c. ad ore per le releas vn estate droiturel.

hath the right had entred & enfeoffed him, &c. And the reason is, for that he which before had an estate by wrong, s. by disseisin, &c. hath now by the release a rightful estate

was made was seised Per my & per tout, whereunto when the right commeth it excludeth the wrong (e) for right which is lawfull, and wrong that is contrary to Lawe cannot stand together.

(e) *Brit. fol. 116. 26. Ass pl. 39. 39. E. 3. 29. 21. H. 6. 41 22. H 6. 22. 7. E. 4. 25. 9. E. 4. 6. 11. H. 7. 12. 20. H. 7. 5. 21. H. 7. 18. 12. E. 4. tit. Discontin. 1. 9. H. 6. 37. 21. H. 6. 52.*

En tiel plite sicome il que auoit droit, auoit enter & luy enfeoffe &c. This (&c.) doth imply that this is true secundum quid, but not simpliciter, for as to the holding out of the ioynt Disseisor it amounts to as much as if hee had entred and enfeoffed him to whom the release is made, but it doth not amount to an entrie and feoffment Simpliciter to all purposes, as shall be said hereafter in his proper place in the chapter of releases.

Sect. 307.

Et e ascun cas vn releas urera per voy dextinguishment, et en tiel case tiel releas aydera la iointenāt a que le releas ne fuit fait, auxybien come luy a q̄ le release fuit fait. Sicome vn home soit disseisie, et le disseisor fait feoffment a deux homes en fee, si le disseisee relessa per son fait a vn de les feoffees, donq̄s cel release urēt a ambideux les feoffees, pur ceo q̄ les feoffees ont estate per la ley, s. per feoffment, et nemy per tort fait a nulluy, &c.

And in some case a release shall inure by way of extinguishment, and in such case such release shall aide the ioyntenant to whom the release was not made aswell as him to whom the release was made. As if a man be disseised and the disseisor makes a feoffment to two men in fee, if the disseisee release by his deed to one of the feoffees, this release shall enure to both the feoffees, for that the feoffees haue an estate by the law, s. by feoffment, and not by wrong done to any, &c.

Here Littleton speaketh of the third kinde of releases. And the reason of this diuersitie (implyed in the (&c.) in the end of this Section) betweene the Disseisors and their feoffees comming in by title and purchase are intended in Law to haue a Warrantie (which is much esteemed in Law) and therefore lest the warranty should be auoyded, the Release shall enure to both the Feoffees in fauour of Purchasors, and so the right and benefit of euery one saued. (f) And in ancient time if the Disseisor had made a Feoffment in fee, or a gift in taile, or a lease for life, and the Feoffee, Donee, or Lessee had continued in seisin quietly a yeare and a day, the entrie of the Disseisee had not beene lawfull upon him, and the reason was for the benefit and safegard of the Warrantie (which was intended by Law) should haue beene destroyed by the entrie. But hereof also more shall bee said in his proper place in the chapter of Releases.

(f) *20. H. 3. Ass. 432. 1. Ass. 13. 9. Ass. 15. 21. Ass. 28. 27. Ass. 68. 32. 29. Ass. 54. 43. Ass. 17. 40. E. 3. 24. 50. E. 3. 21. 3. R. 2. entrie cong: 38. 13. E. 3. tit. Ass. 9. 12. Ass. 20*

Sect. 308.

En mesme le maner est, si le disseisor fait vn lease a vn hōe pur term̄ de sa vie, le remainder

In the same manner it is if the disseisor maketh a lease to a man for terme of his life the re-

der ouster a vn auter en fee, si le disseisee relessa a le tenant a terme de vie tout son droit,&c. cel release urera auxybien a celuy en le remainder, come a le tenant a terme de vie. Et la cause est, pur ceo que le tenant a terme de vie vient a son estate per course de ley, & pur ceo cel release urera, et prent effect per voy dextinguishment de droit de celuy que relessa,&c. Et per cel release le tenant a terme de vie nad pluis ample ne greinder estate, que il avoit devant le release fait a luy, et le droit celuy que relessa est tout oustermcnt extinct. Et entant que cest release ne poit enlarge lestate de le tenant a terme de vie, il est reason que cel release urera a celuy en le remainder,&c.

¶ Pluis serra dit de Releases en le Chapiter de Releases.

mainder ouer to another in fee if the disseisee release to the tenant for terme of life all his right,&c. this release shall inure aswell to him in the remainder, as to the tenant for terme of life. And the reason is for that the tenant for life commeth to his estate by course of law, and therefore this release shall enure and take effect by way of extinguishment of the right of him which releaseth,&c. And by this release the tenant for life hath no ampler nor greater estate then hee had before the release made him, and the right of him which releaseth is altogether extinct. And in asmuch as this release cannot enlarge the estate of the tenant for life, it is reason that this release shall enure to him in the remainder,&c.

More shall be said of Releases in the chapter of Releases.

¶ *CEst release urera auxibien a celuy en le remainder, come a le tenāt a term de vie,&c.* Of this and the rest of this Section, for avoyding of repetition, more shall be said in his proper place in the chapter of Releases.

¶ *Tout son droit,&c.* Here by this (&c.) is implyed, title, demand and other words which may transferre the right,&c. Also here is implyed of in or to the land.

Sect. 309.

¶ ITem si soyent deux Parceners, et lun alien ceo que a luy affiert a vn auter, donqs lauter person et lalienee sont Tenants en Common.

ALso if two Parceners be, and the one alieneth that to her belongeth, to another, then the other Parcener and the Alienee are Tenants in Common.

This is evident, and needeth no explication.

Section 310.

¶ ITem nota que Tenaunts en Common poyent estre per titl' de Prescription, sicome lun et ses auncestors, ou ceux que estate il

ALso note that Tenaunts in Common may bee by title of Prescription, as if the one and his Ancestors, or they whose e-

ad & vn moity ont tenus en Common mesme le moitie, oue lauter tenant que ad lauter moitie et oue ses auncestors ou oue ceux que estate il ad Pro indiuiso, de temps dont memorie ne curt, &c. Et diuers auters manners poient faire et causer homes desti Tenaunts en Common, que ne sont icy expresses, &c.

state he hath in one moitie haue holdē in cōmon the same moitie with the other tenāt which hath the other moitie, & with his Ancestors, or with those whose state he hath vndiuided, time out of mind of man. And diuers other manners may make and cause men to be Tenants in Common, which are not here exprest, &c.

11. E. 3. Trans. 213. 13. E. 3. Breife 674. 8. H. 6. 16. b. Lib. Intrat. 23.

¶ Of this, besides Littleton, there is good authoritie in Law, as there is for al his other cases throughout his 3 bookes, but Joyntenants cannot be by prescription, because there is suruiuor betweene them, but not betweene Tenants in Common.

The two (&c.) in this Section are euident.

Section 311.

¶ In this Section we learne two things: First, That in reall Actions, and in Actions also that are mixt with the personaltie, Tenants in Common shal seuer in Action, because they haue seueral freeholds, & claim in by seueral titles, and therefore as they shall be seuerally by others impleaded, so shall they seuerally implead others in all real and mixt Actions, vnlesse it be in case of necessitie for a thing entire, as hereafter in this Chapter shall appeare. And Littleton here putteth the case of the Assise which is mixt with the personaltie, and therefore he needed not to put any case of any Precipe quod reddat, for if it be so in case of Assise A fortiori, in Writs of higher nature, which is necessarily implied in the (&c.) Now of suits that sound in the realtie, and of personal actions Littleton speaketh hereafter in this Chapter. The second thing here to be learned, is the diuersitie betweene Tenants in Common, and Joyntenants, which both of it selfe, and vpon that which hath been sayd, is apparant.

4. E. 4. 18. b.

¶ Item en ascun cas Tenants en common doyent auer de lour possession seueralx Actions, et en ascū cas ils ioyndront en vn Action. Car si sont deux Tenants en common, et ils sont disseisies, ils doyent auer deux Assises, et nemy vn Assise, car chescun de eux couient auer vn Assise de son moitie, &c. Et la cause est, pur ceo que tenants en common fueront seisies &c. per seueralx titles. Mes autrement est de Joyntenants, car si soyent vint Joyntenants, et ils sont disseisies, ils aueront ē touts lour nosmes forsque vn Assise, pur ceo que ils nont forsque vn ioynt title.

ALso in some case tenants in Common ought to haue of their possession seueral Actiōs and in some cases they shall ioyne in one Action. For if two Tenants in Common be, and they be disseised, they must haue two Assises, and not one Assise, for each of them ought to haue one Assise of his moitie, &c. & the reason is, for that the Tenants in common were seised, &c. by seuerall Titles. But otherwise it is of Iointenants, for if twentie Ioyntenants be, and they bee disseised, they shall haue in al their names but one Assise, because they haue not but one ioynt title.

Sect. 312.

¶ ITem si soyent trois Joyntenants, & vn release a vn de ses companiõs tout le droit que il ad, &c. et puis les auters deux sont disseisies de lentiertie, &c. en cest case les deux auters aueront seueralx Assises, &c. en cest forme, s. ils aueront en lour ambideux nosmes, vn Assise de les deux parts, &c. pur ceo que les deux pts ils teignont ioyntment al temps de le disseisin. Et quant a le tierce part, celuy a que le release fuit fait, couient auer de ceo vn Assise en son nosme demesne, pur ceo que il (quaunt a mesme le tierce part) est de ceo Tenant en Common, &c. pur ceo que il vient a cel tierce part per force del Release, et nemy tantsolement per force del ioynture.

ALso if three Ioyntenants bee, and one release to one of his fellowes all the right which hee hath, &c. and after the other two be disseised of the whole, &c. In this case the two others shall haue seuerall Assises, &c. in this manner, s. They shall haue in both their names an Assise of the two parts, &c. because the two parts they held ioyntly at the time of the disseisin. And as to the third part, he to whom the release was made ought to haue of that an Assise in his owne name, for that hee (as to the same third part) is thereof Tenant in Common, &c. because hee commeth to this third part by force of the Release, and not onely by force of the Ioynture.

¶ This is put for an example (which euer doth illustrate the Rule) and is euident of it selfe: and the (&c.) in this Section needeth no further explication.

Sect. 313.

¶ ITem quant a suer des Actions que touchant l'realtie, y sont diuersities perenter parceners que sont eins per diuers discents, & Tenaunts en common. Car si home seisie de certaine terre en fee ad issue deux files et morust, et les files entront, &c. et chescun de eux ad issue vn fits, et deuieront sauns partition fait enter eux, per que lun moity discendist a le fits dun Parcener, & lauter moitie discendist al fits dauter parcener, et ils entront

ALso to the suing of Actions which touch the realty, there be diuersities betweene parceners which are in by diuers discents, and Tenants in Common: For if a man seised of certain land in fee, hath issue two Daughters and dieth, and the Daughters enter, &c. and each of them hath issue a Sonne, and die without partition made between them, by which the one moitie discends to the Sonne of the one Parcener, and the other moitie discend to the

entront et occupiont en common et sont disseisies, en cest case ils auerõt en lour deux nosmes vn Assise et nemy deux Assises. Et la cause est, que coment que ils veignont eins per diuers discents, &c. vncore ils sont Parceners et briefe de Partitione facienda, gist enter eux. Et ils ne sont parceners eyant regard ou respect tant solement a le seisin et possession de lour meres, mes ils sont Parceners pluis eiant respect a lestate que discendist de lour ayel a lour meres, car ils ne poyent estre Parceners si lour meres ne fueront Parceners adeuant, &c. Et issint a tiel respect et consideration, s. quaunt a le primer discent que fuit a lour meres ils ont vn title en parcenarie, le quel fait eux parceners. Et auxy ils ne sont forsque come vn heire a lour common Auncestor, s. a lour ayel de que la terre discendist a lour meres. Et pur ceux causes deuant partition enter eux, &c. il aueront vn Assise coment que ils veignont eins p seueralx discents.

Sonne of the other Parcener, and they enter and occupie in common and be disseised, in this case they shall haue in their two names one Assise, and not two Assises. And the cause is, for that albeit they come in by diuers discents, &c. yet they are Parceners, and a Writ of Partition lieth between them. And they are not Parceners, hauing regard or respect onely to the Seisin and possession of their mothers, but they are parceners rather, hauing respect to the estate which discend from their Graundfather to their mothers, for they cannot be Parceners if their mothers were not Parceners before, &c. And so in this respect and consideration, s. as to the first discent which was to their mothers, they haue a Title in Parcenarie, the which makes them Parceners. And also they are but as one heire to their common Ancestor, s. to their Grandfather, from whom the Land discended to their mothers. And for these causes, before partition betweene them, &c. they shall haue an Assise, although they come in by seueral discents.

Vi. Sect. 241.

This, vpon that which hath beene sayd in * the Chapter of Parceners, is euident: where you may read excellent points of learning, and diuersities concerning this matter, all which are here either expressed or implied, as the studious and diligent Reader will obserue.

Sect. 314.

EN cest case quant a le Rent & liuer de Pepper, ils aueroun deux Assises & quaunt a lesperuer ou le Chiual forsque vn Assise.

But for the better vnderstanding hereof it is to bee knowne, That if two Te-

ITem si sont deux tenants en Common de certaine Terre en fee, et ils doneront cel terre a vn home en le taile, ou lesserõt a vn home pur terme de

ALso if there bee two Tenaunts in Common, of certain Lands in Fee, and they giue this Land to a man in Taile, or let it to one for terme of life, ren-

de vie, rendant a eux annuelment un certaine rent, & un liuer de Pepper, & un esperuer, ou un chiuall, & ils sont seisies de cest seruice, & puis tout le rent est a derere, & ils distreigneront pur ceo, & le tenant a eux fait rescous. En cest cas quant a le rent & liuer de Pepper ils aueront deux Assises, & quant a lesperuer, ou le chiual forsque un Assise. Et la cause pur que ils aueront deux Assises, quant a le rent & liuer de Pepper, est ceo, entant que ils fueront tenants en common en seuerall titles, & quant ils fieront un done en le tayle ou leas pur terme de vie, sauant a eux le reuersion, & rendant a eux certaine rent, &c. tiel reseruation est incident a lour reuersion, & pur ceo que lour reuersion est en common, & per seuerall titles, sicome lour possession fuit deuant, le rent, & auters choses que poient estre seueres, et fueront a eux reserues sur l'done, ou sur le leas, queux sont incidents per la ley a lour reuersion, tiels choses issint reserues fueront de la nature del reuersion. Et entant que l'reuersion est a eux

dring to them yearely a certaine rent, and a pound of Pepper, and a Hawke or a Horse, and they bee seised of this seruice, and afterwards the whole Rent is behind, and they distraine for this, and the tenant maketh Rescous. In this case as to the rent and pound of Pepper they shall haue two Assises, and as to the Hawke or the Horse but one Assise. And the reason why then they shall haue two Assises as to the rent and pound of Pepper is this, insomuch as they were Tenants in Common in seuerall titles, and when they made a gift in tayle or lease for life, sauing to them the Reuersion, and rendring to them a certaine rent, &c. such reseruation is incident to their reuersion, and for that their reuersion is in common and by seuerall titles as their possession was before the rent and other things which may be seuered, and were reserued vnto them vpon the gift or vpon the lease which are incidents by the Law to their reuersion, such things so reserued were of the nature of the reuersion. And in as much as the reuersion is to them in common by seuerall titles, it beho-

nants in Common bee, and they grant a rent of 20. shillings per annum, out of their land, the Grantee shall haue two rents of 20. shillings for that euery mans grant shall bee taken most strongly against himselfe, and therefore they be seuerall grants in Law.

But if they two make a gift in tayle, a lease for life, &c. reseruing twenty shillings rent to them and their heires they shall haue but one 20. shillings, for they shall haue no more then themselues reserued: and the Donee or Lessee shall pay but 20. shillings according to their owne expresse reseruation: And albeit the reseruation of rents seuerable bee in ioynt words, yet in respect of the seuerall Reuersions the Law makes thereof a seuerance. Now for the rent, as namely 20. shillings or a pound of Pepper may bee seuered, the one Tenant in Common may haue an Assise for the moytie of 20. shillings, and the moytie of a pound of Pepper, de medietate vnius libr' piperis, but he cannot haue an Assise of ten shillings, or de dimidio libræ piperis. But for the Hawke or Horse, albeit they be Tenants in Common, they shall ioyne in an Assise for otherwise they should bee without remedie, for one of them cannot make his plaint in Assise of the moytie of a hawke, or of a horse, for the Law will neuer suffer any man to demand any thing against the order of na-

Tr. Com. Hill & Grange cost. 171. Vide Sect. 219.

Vide 16. Ass. Pl. 1. 16. E. 3. Ioyndre en action. 27.

ture

Regula. Vide Sect.129.
(l) Lib.5.fol.21. Regula.
Regula.
(*) 3.E.3.19.
38.E.3.35. Regula.

ture or reason, as before, it appeareth by Littleton Section.129 Lex enim spectat naturæ ordinem. Also the Law will neuer enforce a man to demand that which hee cannot recouer, and a man cannot recouer (l) the moytie of a Hawke, Horse or of any other entire thing. Lex neminem cogit ad vana, seu inutilia. But in that case they shall ioyne in Assise, and the reason is, Ne Curia Domini Regis deficeret in iustitia exhibenda, or lex non debet deficere cōquerentibus in iustitia exhibenda. And if they should not ioyne, they should haue damnum & iniuriam, and yet should haue no remedie (*) by Law, which should be inconuenient. But the Law will, that in euery case where a man is wronged and endammaged, that hee shall haue remedie. Aliquid conceditur ne iniuria remaneret impunita quod aliàs non concederetur.

en common per seuerall titles, il couient que le rent, et le liuer de Pepper, queux poient estre seuers, soyent a eux en common, et per seuerall titles, et de ceo ils aueront deux Assises, et chescun de eux en son Assise ferra son pleint de le moitie de le rent, et de le moitie del liuer de Pepper, mes de lesperuer, ou de chiual que ne poyent estre seuers, ils aueront forsque vn Assise, car home ne poit faire vn pleint en Assise de le moitie dun esperuer, ne de le moitie dun chiual, &c. En mesme le maner est dauter rents & dauter seruices que Tenants en Common ount en grosse per diuers titles, &c.

ueth that the rent and the pound of Pepper which may bee seuered, bee to them in common and by seuerall titles. And of this they shall haue two Assises, and each of them in his Assise shal make his plaint of the moytie of the rent, and of the moytie of the pound of Pepper. But of the Hawke or of the Horse which cannot be seuered, they shall haue but one Assise, for a man cannot make a plaint in an Assise of the moytie of a Hawke, nor of the moytie of a Horse, &c. In the same manner it is of other Rents and of other Seruices which Tenants in Common haue in grosse by diuers titles, &c.

(m) 5.H.7.8. 13.E.2. quare imp.170. 33.H.6.11. 6.E.4.10.15.E.3.darr. presentment 10.
(n) 6.H.4.6.7. 45.E.3.10. 30.H.6. Assise 39 18.E.3.56.

(m) And Tenants in Common shall ioyne in a quare impedit, because the presentation to the Aduowson is entire.

(n) Also Tenants in Common of a Seigniory shall ioyne in a Writ of Right of ward, and Rauishment of Ward for the bodie, because it is entire.

If two Tenants in Common be of the wardship of the bodie, and one doth rauish the Ward, and the one Tenant in Common releases to the Rauisher, this shall goe in benefit of the other Tenant in Common, and he shall recouer the whole, and this Release shall not bee any barre to him. And so it is if two Tenants in Common be of an Aduowson, and they bring a Quare impedit, and the one doth release, yet the other shall sue forth, and recouer the whole presentment.

Two Tenants in Common shall ioyne in a detinue of Charters, and if the one be Nonsuit, the other shall recouer.

18.E.3.56.

It is said that Tenants in Cōmon shall ioyne in a Warrantia Chartæ, but seuer in Voucher.

¶ *Moitie de chiual, &c.* Here is implyed or any other entire rent or seruice.

¶ *Per diuers titles, &c.* That is by seuerall titles, and not by one ioynt title as hath beene said,

Section 315.

29.E.3.51. 43.E.3.24. 46.E.3.27. 5.H.4.3. 14.H.4.31. 3.H.6.17. 12.H.6.22. 22.H.6.14. 18.E.4.30. 2.R.3.16. 20.H.7.27. 21.H.7.22. 37.H.6.35. 21.E.4.13.

¶ *AVeront tiels actions personells iointment en touts lour nosmes, &c.* By this

¶ ITem, quant al actiōs personals tenants en common aueront tiels actiōs per-

ALso as to Actions personals Tenants in common may haue such actions per-

psonals ioyntment en touts lour nosmes, sicome de trespas, ou de offence que touche lour tenements en common, sicome de bruser lour measons, de enfreinder de lour closes, de pasture, degaster, & de fouler des herbes, de couper lour bois, de pischer en lour pischarie, & huiusmodi. Et en cest cas tenāts en common aueront vn action ioyntment & recoueront ioyntment lour damages, pur ceo que laction est en le personaltie, & nemy ē l' realty, &c.

sonals ioyntly in all their names as of trespasse, or of offences, which concerne their Tenements in Common, as for breaking their Houses, breaking their Closes, feeding, wasting, and defowling their grasse, cutting their Woods, for fishing in their Pischarie, and such like. In this case Tenants in Common shall haue one Action ioyntly, and shal recouer iointly their damages, because the Action is in the personaltie, and not in the realtie, &c.

it appeareth that Tenants in Common shall haue personal Actions ioyntly. And it is to bee obserued, that where dammages are to bee recouered for a wrong done to Tenants in Common, or Parceners in a personall Action, and one of them die, the Suruiuor of them shall haue the Action, for albeit the propertie or estate bee seuerall betweene them, yet (as it appeareth here by Littleton) the personall action is ioynt.

Et huiusmodi. Hereby is implyed a diuersity betweene a chattle in possession, and a personall Chose in Action belonging vnto them. As if two Tenants in Common be of land, and one doth a trespasse therein, of this action they are Iointenants, and the Suruiuor shal hold place. So it is if two Tenants in Common be of a Mannor, and they make a Baylife thereof, and one of them dieth, the Suruiuor shall haue the Action of Account, for the Action giuen vnto them for the arrerages vpon the Account was ioynt. So it is if two Tenants in Common sow their land & one doth eat the same with his cattle, though they haue the Corne in Common, yet the Action giuen to them for trespasse in the same is ioynt, and shall suruiue. For the trespasse and dammage done to them was ioynt, all which here is implyed by Littleton, who sayth, that they shall haue an Action ioyntly, and the same Law is of Coparceners.

Vide Sect. 319. 320. 321.

22. H. 6. 12. 38. E. 3. 7. 13. E. 3. accompt 126. 45. E. 3. 13. 14. 37. H. 6. 32. 38.

But if two Tenants in Common be of goods, as of an horse, or of any other goods personall, there if one dye, his Executors shall be Tenant in Common with the Suruiuor.

Et nemy en le realtie, &c. If two Tenants in Common bee of an Aduowson, and a stranger vsurpe, so as the right is turned to an action, and they bring a writ of Quare impedit which concernes the realtie, the sixe moneths passe, and the one dyeth, the writ shall not abate, but the Suruiuor shall recouer, otherwise there should be no remedie to redresse this wrong. And so it is of Coparceners, and this is one exception out of our Authors rule.

38. E. 3. 5. 17. E. 3. 11. 3. H. 5. Quare Imp. 71. 14. H. 4. 12. 9. H. 6. 30. 22. H. 4. 14. 37. H. 6. 9. b. 10. Eliz. Dyer 279. F. N. B. 35. 9. E. 3. 36. 37. Pl. Com. Seignior. Barkleys case.

(*) But if three Coparceners recouer land & dammages in an Assise of Mordancester, albeit the iudgement be ioynt, that they shall recouer the land and dammages, yet the dammages being accessory, though they be personall, doe in iudgement of Law depend vpon the Freehold, being the principall which is seuerall. And though the words of the iudgement be ioynt, yet shall it be taken for distributiue. And therefore if two of them dye, the entire dammages doe not suruiue, but the third shall haue execution according to her portion, and this is another exception out of our Authors rule. But if all three had sued Execution by force of an Elegit, and two of them had dyed, the third should haue had the whole by Suruiuor, till the whole dammages be paid

(*) 14. E. 3. Execution 75. 45. E. 3. 3. b.

If the Aunt and Niece ioyne in an Action of waste, for waste done in the life of the other sister, the Aunt shall recouer the dammages only, because the same belongs not by Law to the Niece. And some hold the dammages in that case to be the principall.

45. E. 3. 3. b. 48. E. 3. 14. 11. H. 4. 16. b. 35. H. 6. 23. b. 11. E. 2. Wast. 115.

Section 316.

Item si deux tenants en common font vn lease de lour

Also if two Tenants in Common make a lease of their Te-

lour tenemẽts a vn auter p̃ termẽ des ans, rendant a eux certaine rent annualment durant l' termẽ si le rent soit aderere, &c. les tenants en cõmon auerõt vn action de debt enuers le lessee, et nemy diuers actions, pur ceo que laction est en la personalty.

nements to another for terme of yeares, rendring to them a certaiue Rent yearely during the terme if the rent bee behinde, &c. the tenants in common shall haue an action of debt against the lessee, & not diuers actions, for that the action is in the personalty.

This vpon that which hath beene said is euident.

Sect. 317.

¶ MEs en auowry pur le dit rent ils couient seuer, Car ceo est en le realtie, come le assise est supra.

BVt in an auowry for the said rent they ought to seuer for this is in the realty, as the assise is aboue.

Vid.9.E.3.36.37. Pl.Com. Seignior Barklyes Case.

This being an addition to Littleton albeit it be consonant to Law yet I omit it.

Sect. 318.

¶ ITem, tenants en common poyent bien faire partition enter eux sils voilent, coment q̃ ils ne serront compelles de faire partition per la ley, mes sils font enter eux partition per lour agreement et consent, tiel partition est assets bone, come est adiudge en le liuer dassises.

ALso tenants in common may well make partition between them if they will, but they shall not bee compelled to make partition by the law, but if they make partition betweene themselues by their agreement and consent, such partition is good enough, as is adiudged in the booke of Assises.

* *Vid.Sect*.257 290.247.264

Of this sufficient hath beene said * in the chapter of Parceners and Joyntenants.

(o) 19.*Ass*.p.1. 30.*Ass*.p.8. 47.E.3.22.

¶ *In le liuer Dassises*. This booke is of great Authority in Law, and is so called because it principally conteyneth the proceeding vpon Writs of Assise of Nouel disseisin which in those dayes was Festinum & frequens remedium.

Sect. 319.

¶ ITem, sicome y sont tenants en common de terres et tenements, &c. come est auantdit: En mesme le maner y sont de chattels reals et personals: Sicome lease soit fait de certaine terres a deux homes pur terme de 20. ans, et quant ils sont de ceo

ALso as there bee tenants in common of lands and tenements, &c. as aforesaid. In the same manner there be of chattells reals and personals. As if a lease bee made of certaine lands to two men for terme of 20. yeares, and when they be of this possessed, the

ceo possesses lun de les lessees grant ceo q̃ a luy affiert durant le terme a vn auter, donqz mesme celuy a que l'grant est fait, et lauter tiendront et occupieront en common.

one of the lessees grant that which to him belongeth to another during the terme, then hee to whom the grant is made, and the other shall hold and occupie in common.

¶ G*Rant ceo que a luy affiert.* The same law it is if the one Lessee in this case make a Lease of part of the terme, the second Lessee and the other are Tenants in common as hath beene said in the chapter of Joyntenants. The (&c.) in this Section implyeth other hereditaments whereof men may bee Tenants in common, whereof sufficient hath beene said before. *Vid. Sect.* 315.

Section 320.

¶ Item, si deux ont ioyntmt̃ le gard de corps & de tre dun enfant deins age, et lun de eux granta a vn auter ceo q̃ a luy affiert de m̃ le garde, donque le grantee et lauter que ne granta pas, aueront et tiendront ceo en common, &c.

ALso if two haue ioyntly the wardship of the body & lãd of an infant within age, & the one of them grant to another that which to himselfe belongeth of the same ward, then the grantee, and the other which did not grant shall haue & hold this in common, &c.

¶ Hereby it appeareth, that there may bee Tenants in Common as well of chattells reall entire, as wardship of the body, &c. as of chattels Personal; as a Hawke or a Horse. If two Tenants in common be of a Seigniory, and a Ward fall, they are Tenants in common of the wardship aswell of the body as land. And so it is, if the land it selfe escheat to them, they shall be Tenants in common thereof, and so it is of Parceners. *16. E. 3. tit. 8.*

¶ *En common, &c.* Here (&c.) implyeth any other entire chattell. *Vid: deuant. Sect.* 315.

Section 321.

¶ En mesme le maner est de chateux personals: Sicome deux ont ioyntment per done ou per achate vn chiual ou boefe, &c. et lun grant ceo que a luy affiert de mesme le chiual ou boefe a vn auter: Donqs le grãtee, & lauter que ne granta pas, aueront et possideront tiels chateux personals en cõmon. Et en tiels cases, ou diuers persons ont chateux reals ou personels en common et p diuers titles, si lun de eux morust, les auters q̃ suruesquont, nauera ceo p le suruiuor

IN the same manner it is of chattells personals. As if two haue ioyntly by gift or by buying a horse or an oxe, &c. and the one grant that to him belongs of the same horse or oxe to another, the grantee and the other which did not grant, shall haue and possesse such chattells personalls in common. And in such cases where diuers persons haue chattells real or personall in Common, and by diuers titles, if the one of them dieth the others which suruiue shall not haue this as Suruiuor, but the exe-

uiuor, mes les executors celuy que morust tiendront et occupieront ceo ouesque eux que suruesquont, sicome lour testator fist ou deuoit en sa vie, &c. pur ceo que lour titles & droits en ceo fueront seuerals, &c.

cutors of him which dieth shall hold and occupie this with them which suruiue, as their testator did or ought to haue done in his life time, &c. because that their titles and rights in this were seuerall, &c.

Vid. deuant Sect. 3?5.

This is euident enough, and hereof sufficient hath beene said * before.

Section 322.

¶ IT*em* en le case auant*dit*, sic*om*e deux ont estate en common pur terme dans, &c. lun occupier tout, et mist lauter hors de possession et occupation, &c. donques celuy que est mise hors de occupation auera enuers lauter briefe de Eiectione firmæ, de la moitie, &c.

ALso in the case aforesayd, as if two haue an estate in Common for terme of yeares, &c. the one occupy all, and put the other out of possession and occupation, hee which is put out of occupation, shall haue haue against the other a writ of *Eiectione firmæ* of the moitie, &c.

Sect. 323.

¶ En m*ês*me le maner est, lou deux teignont le gard des terres ou tenements durant le nonage dun enfant, si lun oust a lauter de son possession, il que est ouste auera briefe de Eiectment de gard de le moitie, &c. pur ceo que ceux choses sont chateux realx, & poyent estre apportions et seuers, &c. Mes nul Action de Trespas, cestascauoir, Quare clausum suum fregit, & herbam suam, &c. con-

IN the same manner it is, where two hold the wardship of Lands or Tenements during the nonage of an Enfant, if the one oust the other of his possession, he which is ousted shal haue a Writ of *Eiectment de gard* of the moitie, &c. because that these things are Chattels reals, and may bee apportioned and seuered, &c. but no Action of Trespasse (*videlicet*) *Quare clausum suum fregit, & herbam suam &c. conculcauit, & con-*

¶ P*Vr terme de ans, &c.* For one yeare, halfe a yeare, &c.

¶ *Lun occupy tout & mist lauter hors de possession.* These are words materially added, for albeit one Tenant in Common take the whole profits, the other haue no remedie by Law against him, for the taking of the whole profits is no eiectment. But if he driue out of the land any of the cattell of the other Tenaunt in Common, or not suffer him to enter or occupie the land, this is an eiectment or expulsion, whereupon he may haue an Eiectione firmæ, for the one moitie, and recouer damages for the entrie, but not for the meane profits.

¶ Eiectione firmæ *de la moitie, &c.* Here by this and the other (&c.) in these two Sections, are to be understood diuers diuersities betweene Actions which concerne right and interest, (as of Eiectione firmæ, Eiectment de gard, quare eiecit infra terminum of a Chattell real vpon an expulsion or eiectment) and Actions concerning the bare taking of the profits rising of the Land, or doing of Trespasse vpon the Land, as here by the examples doe appeare, for the right is seuerall, and the taking of the profits in Common. The second diuersitie is betweene

21.*E.*4.11.22.43.*E.*3.24. 45.*E.*3.13. 22.*H.*6.50.58. 8.*H.*6.17. 19.*H.*6.57. 32.*H.*6.16.2.*E.*4.23. 14.*E.*4.8. 18.*E.*4.30. 37.*H.*6.33. 21.*E.*3.29. 12.*Ass.*28. 47.*E.*3.22.*b.* 10.*H.*7.16. *F.N.B.*117.*a.* 17.*E.*2.*Account* 122.

conculcauit & consumpsit, &c. & huiusmodi actiones, &c. lun ne poet auer enuers lauter pur ceo q̄ chescun de eux poet enter et occupier en cōmon, &c. per my et p tout les Terres & tenements queux ils teignōt en common. Mes si deux sont possesses de chattels personalx en cōmō per diuers titles, sicome dun Chiual ou Boef, ou Vache, &c. si lun prent ceo tout a luy hors d' possession dauter, lauter nad nul auter remedie, mes de prender ceo de luy que ad fait luy l' tort, pur occupier en common, &c. quant il poet veier son temps, &c. En mesm̄ le manner est de chattels realx, que ne poyent estre seuers, sicome en le case auantdit, que deux sōt possesse dun gard d' corps dun enfant deins age, si lun prent lenfant hors de possession dauter, lauter nad ascun remedie per ascun action per la ley, mes de prend lenfant hors de le possession daut quaunt il veit son temps.

sumpsit, &c. & huiusmodi actiones, &c. the one cannot haue against the other, for that each of them may enter & occupie in cōmon, &c. *per my & per tout* the Lands and Tenements which they hold in Common. But if two be possessed of Chattells personalls in Common by diuers titles, as of a Horse, an Oxe, or a Cowe, &c. if the one take the whole to himselfe out of the possession of the other, the other hath no other remedie but to take this from him who hath done to him the wrong to occupie in common, &c. when he can see his time, &c. In the same manner it is of Chattels realls, which cannot be seuered, as in the case aforesayd, where two bee possessed of the wardship of the bodie of an Enfant within age, if the one taketh the Enfant out of the possessiō of the other, the other hath no remedie by an action by the Law, but to take the enfant out of the possession of the other when he sees his time.

Chattells realls that are apportionable or seuerable, as Leases for yeares, wardship of lands, interest of tenemēts by Elegit, Statute merchant, Staple, &c. of lands and tenements and Chattells realls entire; as wardship of the bodie, a Villeine for yeares, &c. for if one Tenant in common take away the ward or the Villeine, &c. the other hath no remedie by Action, but he may take them againe. Another diuersitie is betweene Chattells reals and Chattels personalls, for if one Tenant in Common take all the Chattells personals, the other hath no remedie by Action, but hee may take them againe, and herein the like law is concerning Chattells reals entire, and Chattels personall for this purpose. But of Chattels entire, as of a ship, horse, or any other entire Chattell, reall or personall, no suruiuor shall bee betweene them that hold them in Common: And Tenants in Common shall not ioyne in an Eiectione firmæ, nor in a Writ of Eiectment de gard, or a Quare eiecit infra terminum, &c. for that these Actions concerne the right lands which are seuerall. 10.*H*.4.*Tresp.* 198. 11.*H*.4.3. 21.*E*.4.11.12.

If two Tenants in Common be of a Mannor, to the which waife and stray doth belong, a stray doth happen, they are Tenaunts in Common of the same; & if the one doth take the stray, the other hath no remedie by action, but to take him againe. But if by prescription the one is to haue the first beast happening as a stray, and the other the second, there an action lieth if the one take that which pertaines to the other. 13.*E*.3.*Briefe* 674.

If two Tenants in Common be of a Doue house, and the one destroy the old Doues whereby the flight is wholly lost, the other Tenant in common shall haue an Action of Trespasse, Quare vi & armis columbare le pl' fregit & ducentas columbas pretij 40. s. interfecit per quod volatum columbaris sui totaliter amisit: For the whole flight is destroyed, and therefore hee cannot in 47.*E*.3.22.*b*.

haue

barre plead Tenancie in Common. And so it is if two Tenaunts in Common bee of a Parke, and one destroyeth all the Deere, an Action of Trespasse lieth.

4.E.2.Trespas 233.
(c) 1.H.5.1. 2.H.5.3.

(c) If two Tenants in Common be of land, and of Mere stones, pro metis & bundis, and the one take them up and carrie them away, the other shal haue an Action of Trespasse Quare vi & armis against him, in like manner as he shall haue for destruction of Doues.

(d) 13 E.3.Trespas 212. 19.R.2.Br.927. 11.E.3. Trespas 212.Vi.18,H.6.5.
(e) 13.H.7.26.

(d) If two Tenants in Common be of a Folding, and the one of them disturbe the other to erect Hurdles, he shall haue an Action of Trespasse quare vi & armis, for this disturbance.

(e) If two severall owners of houses haue a river in common betweene them, if one of them corrupt the river, the other shall haue an Action upon his case.

(f) F.N.B.127.Reg.163.

(f) If two Tenants in Common, or Jointenants be of an house or mill, and it fal in decay, and the one is willing to repaire the same, & the other will not, he that is willing shal haue a writ de reparatione facienda, and the writ saith, Ad reparationem & sustentationem eiusdem domus teneantur, whereby it appeareth, that owners are in that case bound pro bono publico to maintaine houses and mills which are for habitation and use of men.

17.E.2.tit.Account 22. 8.E.2.Account 115. 30.E.1.Account 127. 45.E.3.10. 47.E.3.22.b. 38.E.3.9. 22.E.3.60. 3.E.3.27. 39.E.27.82. F.Nat.B.118.i. 10.H.7.16. 2.E.4.25.

If one Joyntenant or Tenant in Common of Land maketh his Companion his Baylife of his part, he shall haue an Action of Account against him, as hath beene sayd. But although one Tenant in Common or Joyntenant without being made Baylife take the whole profits, no Action of Account lieth against him, for in an Action of Account he must charge him either as a Guardian, Baylife, or Receiver, as hath been sayd before, which he cannot do in this case, unlesse his companion constitute him his Bailife. And therefore all those Bookes which affirme that an Action of Account lieth by one Tenant in Common, or Joyntenant, against another, must be intended when the one maketh the other his Bailife, for otherwise, never his Baylife to render an Account, is a good plea.

W.2.ca.25.

If there be two Tenants in Common of a Wood, Turbarie, Pischarie, or the like, and one of them doth wast against the will of his companion, his companion shall haue an Action of Wast, and he that did the wast before iudgement, hath election either to take his part in certaintie by the Sherife and the oath of men, &c. or that he grant, That from thenceforth he shal not doe wast but according to his portion, &c. and if he make choice of a certaine place, then the place wasted shall be assigned to him. (g) But this extends not to Coparceners, because they were compellable to make partition by the Common Law: and this, as it is sayd, doth extend as wel to Tenants in Common and Joyntenants for life, as to an estate of Inheritance. But if one Tenant in common, or Joyntenant of a Doue house, destroy the whole flight of Doues, no Action of wast doth lie in that case upon the said Statute, * as some doe hold.

(g) 27.H.8.13.21.E.3.29. 29.E.3.39.3.E.2.Wast.35. F.N.B.59.d. F.N.B.49.i.
* 47.E.3.22. 50.E.3.3.

If lands be giuen to two, and to the heires of one of them, and the tenant for life doth wast, he that hath the Inheritance shall haue no action of Wast by the statute of Gloucester, but upon the statute of W.2. he shall haue an Action of wast. And it is to be knowne, that one Tenant in common may infeoffe his companion, but not release, because the freehold is severall. Jointenants may release, but not infeoffe, because the freehold is joynt, but coparceners may both enfeoffe and release, because their seisin to some intents is joynt, and to some severall.

10.E.4.3.b. 22.H.6.42. 21.E.3.47. 17.E.3.47. 18.E.4.27.28. 3.E.4.

Sect. 324.

¶ Item quant un home voile monstrer un feoffement fait a luy ou un done en le taile, ou un lease pur terme de vie dascun terres ou tenements, la il dirra per force de quel feoffement, done ou leas il fuit seisie, &c. mes lou un voile plead un leas ou grant fait a luy de chattel real ou personal, la il dirra per force de quel il fuit possesse, &c.

¶ Pluis serra dit de tenants en common en le chapter de Releases, et tenant per Elegit.

Also when a man will shew a Feoffement made to him, or a gift in taile, or a lease for life of any lands or Tenements, there hee shall say, By force of which Feoffement, gift, or lease, he was seised, &c. but where one wil plead a lease or grant made to him of a Chattell reall or personall, then he shal say, By force of which he was possessed, &c.

More shall be said of Tenants in Common, in the Chapters of Releases and Tenant by *Elegit*.

¶ *Il fuit seisie, &c.* Seisie is a word of art, and in pleading is onely applied t on Freehold at least; as Possesse for distinction sake is to a Chattell real or personal,

As if B. plead a feoffement in fee, he concludeth, Virtute cuius prædict' B. fuit seisitus, &c. But if he plead a lease for yeares, he pleadeth, Virtute cuius prædictus B. intrauit, & fuit inde possessionatus, and so it is of Chattells personalls.

And this holdeth not onely in case of Lands or Tenements which lie in liuerie, but also of Rents, Aduowsons, Commons, &c. and other things that lie in grant, whereof a man hath an estate for life or inheritance.

Also when a man pleads a lease for life, or any higher estate which passeth by Liuerie, hee is not to plead any entrie, for he is in actuall seisin by the liuerie it selfe. Otherwise it is of a Lease for yeares, because there he is not actually possessed vntill an entrie.

Chap.5. Of Estates vpon Condition. *Sect*.325.

¶ Estates, q̄ homes ount en terr̄s ou tenements sur condition sont de deux maners, scilicet ou ils ont estate sur condition en fait, ou sur condition en ley, &c. Sur condition en fait est, sicome vn home per fait endent enfeoffa vn auter en Fee simple, reseruant a luy & a ses heires annualment certaine rent payable a vn feast, ou a diuers feasts per an, sur condition que si le rent soit aderere, &c. que bien list al feoffor & a ses heires en mesmes les terres ou tenements de entrer, &c. ou si terre soit alien a vn home en fee rendant a luy certaine rent, &c. & sil happa q̄ le rent soit aderere per vn semaigne apres ascun iour de payment de

Estates, which men haue in lands or tenements vpon condition are of two sorts, *viz.* either they haue estate vpon Condition in Deed, or vpon Condition in Law, &c. vpon Condition in Deed is, as if a man by Deed indented, enfeoffes another in fee simple, reseruing to him and his heires yearely a certaine rent payable at one feast or diuers Feasts *per annum*, on condition that if the rent bee behind, &c. that it shall bee lawful for the Feoffor and his heires into the same Lands or Tenements to enter, &c. And if it happen the rent to be behind by a weeke after any day of payment of it, or by a moneth after any day of payment of it, or by halfe a yeare, &c. that then it shall be lawful to the Feof-

¶ *Sur condition.* Littleton hauing before spoken of Estates absolute, now beginneth to intreate of Estates vpon condition. And a Condition annexed to the realtie whereof Littleton here speaketh in the legall vnderstanding est modus an Equalitie annexed by him that hath Estate interest, or right to the same, whereby an Estate, &c. may eyther be defeated, or inlarged, or created vpon an incertaine euent. Conditio dicitur cum quid in casum incertum qui potest tendere ad esse aut non esse confertur.

Glanuill lib. 10 *cap.* 8. *Bracton lib.* 2. *cap.* 5 & 17 & *lib.* 4. *fol.* 213. *Britton cap* 36. & *fol.* 89. 99. 114. 130. 205. 206. 207. 249. *Fleta lib.* 3. *ca* 9. & *lib* 5 *c.* 5. *Mirror cap.* 2. §. 15. & 17.

¶ *Sur condition en fait, quæ est facti,* that is, vpon a condition expressed by the partie in legall termes of Law.

¶ *Ou sur condition en ley, &c.* quæ est iuris, that is, tacitè created by Law without any words vsed by the partie. Againe Littleton subdeuideth Conditions in deed (though not in expresse words) into conditions precedent (of which it is said, Conditio adimpleri debet priusquam sequatur effectus) and conditions subsequent. Againe, of conditions in deed some be affirmatiue, and some in the negatiue; and some in the affirmatiue, which imply a negatiue: some make the Estate, whereunto they are annexed, voidable by entrie or claime, and some make the estate

ceo, ou per vn mois apres ascun iour de payment de ceo, ou per vn demy, &c. que adonques bien lirroit a le feoffor & a les heirs dentrer, &c. En ceux cases si le rent ne soit paie a tiel temps ou devant tiel temps limit & specifie deins les condition compriſes en lendenture, dõques poit l feoffor ou ses heirs entrer en tielx terres ou tenements, & eux en son primer estate auer & tener, & de ceo ouste le feoffee tout net. Et est appelle estate sur condition pur ceo que le state le feoffee est defeasible si l condition ne soit performe, &c.

for and his heires to enter, &c. In these cases if the rent bee not paid at such time or before such time limited and specified with in the Condition cõprised in the Indenture; then may the Feoffor or his heires enter into such Lands or Tenements, and them in his former estate to haue and hold, and the Feoffee quite to ouste thereof. And it is called an estate vpon Condition, because that the state of the Feoffee is defeasible, if the Condition bee not performed, &c.

Estate void *ipso facto*, without entrie or clayme.

Also of conditions in deed, some bee annexed to the rent reserued out of the Land, and some to collaterall acts, &c. some bee single, some in the coniunctiue, some in the disiunctiue, as shall euidently appeare in this Chapter, where the examples of these diuisiõs shall bee explayned in their proper place.

Mirror cap.2.§.15.& 17.

¶ *En ley, &c.* Of conditions in Law more shall be said hereafter in this chapter.

¶ *Sur condition en fait, est sicome vn home per fait indent, &c.* Here Littleton putteth one example of sixe seuerall kinds of conditions. That is, First, of a single condition in Deed. Secondly, of a Condition subsequent to the Estate. Thirdly, a condition annexed to the rent, &c. Fourthly, a Condition that defeateth the Estate. Fiftly, A condition that defeateth not the Estate before an entrie. And lastly, a condition in the affirmatiue, which implyeth a negatiue, (as behind or vnpaid implyeth a negatiue) *viz.* not paid. All which doe appeare by the expresse words of Littleton.

¶ *Rend a luy certaine rent, &c.* Here, by this (&c.) is implyed for life, in tayle, or in fee.

¶ *Et en cest case si le rent ne soit pay a tiel temps, &c. donques poet le feoffor ou ses heires enter, &c.* By this Section, and by the (&c.) therein contayned, sixe things are to be vnderstood.

(b) 40.Ass.11. 20.H.6.30. 31.6.H.7.7. 19.H.6.76. 20.H.6.32. 22.H.6.46. Pl.Com. Kidwelys case fol.70. & Hill & Granges case fol.73.

First, where our Author sayth, Si le rent soit arere, that though the rent bee behind and not paid, (b) yet if the Feoffor doth not demand the same, &c. he shall neuer reenter, because the land is the principall debtor, for the rent issueth out of the Land, and in an Assise for the rent the land shall be put in view, and if the land be euicted by a title paramont, the rent is auoyded and after such euiction the person of the Feoffee shall not be charged therewith, for the person of the Feoffee was onely charged with the rent in respect of the grant out of the Land.

Secondly, The demand must be made vpon the Land, because the Land is the debtor, and that is the place of demand appointed by Law.

Lib.4.fol.72.73. Boroughes case.

If the King maketh a Lease for yeares rendring a Rent payable at his receipt at Westminster, and after the King granteth the Reuersion to another and his heires, the Grantee shall demand the Rent vpon the Land, and not at the Kings Receipt at Westminster, for as the Law without expresse words doth appoint the Lessee in the Kings Case to pay it at the Kings Receipt, so in case of a subiect, the Law appoints the demand to be on the Land.

49.Ass.5. 15.Eliz.Dyer 329

If there be a house vpon the same he must demand the Rent at the house. And hee cannot demand it at the backe doore of the house but at the fore doore, because the demand must euer bee made at the most notorious place. And it is not materiall whether any person be there or no.

(c) Bendloes Trespasse 4.& 5 Ph.& Mar.

Albeit the Feoffee be in the Hall or other part of the House, yet the Feoffor need not (c) but come to the fore doore, for that is the place appointed by Law, albeit the doore be open.

(d) If

(d) If the feoffment were made of a wood only, the demand must be made at the gate of the wood, or at some high way leading through the wood or other most notorious place. And if one place be as notorious as another, the Feoffor hath election to demand it, at which hee will, and albeit the Feoffee be in some other part of the wood readie to pay the Rent, yet that shal not auayle him. Et sic de similibus. (d) 15.*Eliz. Dyer* 325.

Thirdly, And if the Feoffor demand it on the ground at a place which is not most notorious, as at the backe doore of a house &c. and in pleading the Feoffor alleadge a demand of the Rent generally at the house, the Feoffee may trauerse the demand, and vpon the euidence it shall bee found for him, for that it was a void demand.

Fourthly, If the Rent bee reserued to bee paid at any place from the Land, yet it is in Law a Rent, and the Feoffor must demand it at the place appointed by the parties obseruing that which hath beene said before concerning the most notorious place. *Lib.4. Boroughes Case fol.73. Pl.Com.70.*

Fiftly, And all this is to be vnderstood when the Feoffee is absent, for if the Feoffee commeth to the Feoffor at any place vpon any part of the ground at the day of payment, and offer his Rent, albeit they be not at the most notorious place, nor at the last instant the Feoffor is bound to receiue it, or else he shall not take any aduantage of any demand of the Rent for that day.

Sixtly, therfore the place of demand being now knowen, it is further to be knowen what time the Law hath appointed for the same. This partly appeareth by that which hath beene last said. For albeit the last time of demand of the rent is such a conuenient time before the sunne setting of the last day of payment as the money may be numbred and receiued, notwithstanding, if the tender be made to him that is to receiue it vpon any part of the land at any time of the last day of payment, and he refuseth, the condition is saued for that time, for by the expresse reseruation the money is to be paid on the day indefinitely, and conuenient time before the last instant, is the vttermost time appointed by Law to the intent that then both parties should meet together, the one to demand and receiue, and the other to pay it, so as the one should not preuent the other. But if the parties meet vpon any part of the land whatsoeuer one the same day, the tender shal saue the Condition for euer for that time. *Lib.5.fol.114.Wades Case.*

And if the reseruation of the rent be (as here Littleton putteth the case) at certaine feasts with condition that if it happen the rent to be behinde by the space of a weeke after any day of payment, &c. In this case the Feoffor needeth not demand it on the feast day, but the vttermost time for the demand is a conuenient time (as hath beene said) before the last day of the weeke, vnlesse before that the Feoffee meet the Feoffor vpon the land and tender the rent as is aforesaid. *Pl.Com.Hill et Granges case 167.172. 20.H.6.30.31. 6.H.7.3.*

If a rent be granted payable at a certaine day. and if it be behinde and demanded that the Grantee shall distreine for it; In this case the Grantee need not demand it at the day, but if he demand it at any time after he shall distreyne for it, for the Grantee hath election in this case to demand it when he will to inable him to distreine. *Mich.40.& 41. Eliz. inter Stanly & Read. Lib.7.fo.28.Maundes case.*

¶ *Et eux en son primer estate auer, &c.* Regularly it is true that he that entreth for a condition broken shall be seised in his first estate, or of that estate which he had at the time of the estate made vpon condition, but yet this fayleth in many cases. *8.H.7.7.b.*

First in Respect of Possibility. As if a man seised of lands in the right of his wife, maketh a Feoffment in fee by Deed indented, vpon condition that the Feoffee should demise the land to the Feoffor for his life, &c. the husband dyeth the Condition is broken, in this case the heire of the husband shall enter for the Condition broken, but it is impossible for him to haue the estate that the Feoffor had at the time of the Condition made; For therein he had but an estate in the right of his wife, which by the couerture was dissolued. And therefore when the heire hath entred for the Condition broken and defeated the Feoffment, his estate doth vanish and presently the estate is vested in the wife. *4.H.6.2. Lib.8 fo.43,44. Whittinghams case.*

2. In respect of Necessity. If Cesty que vse after the Statute of R.3, and before the Statute of 27.H.8. had made a Feoffment in fee vpon condition, and after had entred for the condition broken. In this case he had but an vse when the Feoffment was made, but now hee shall be seised of the whole state of the land. So that as in the former case, the Ancestor had somewhat at the making of the Condition, and the heire shall haue nothing when he hath entred for the Condition broken, so in this case the Feoffor had no estate or interest in the land at the time of the Condition made, but a bare vse, yet after his entrie for the Condition broken he shall be seised of the whole state in the land, and that also for necessitie, for by the Feoffment in fee of Cesty que vse, the whole estate and right was deuested out of the Feoffees. And therefore of necessitie the Feoffor must gaine the whole estate by his entrie for the Condition broken. *5.H.7.6.4.*

Tenant in speciall taile hath issue, and his wife dieth; Tenant in taile maketh a Feoffment in fee vpon Condition, the issue dieth, the Condition is broken, the Feoffor re-enters, he shall

 haue

haue but an eſtate for life; as Tenant in taile apres poſſibility of iſſue extinct by the re-entry, and yet he had an eſtate taile at the time of the Feoffment, and that alſo for neceſſity.

3. In ſome caſes the Feoffor by his re-entry ſhall be in his former eſtate, but not in reſpect of ſome collaterall qualities. As if Tenant by Homage anceſtrell maketh a Feoffment in fee vpon Condition, and entreth vpon the Condition broken, it ſhall neuer be holden by Homage anceſtrell againe. And ſo it is if a Coppyhold eſcheate be, and the Lord make a Feoffment in fee vpon condition, and entreth for the Condition broken. And the reaſon in both theſe caſes is, for that the cuſtome or preſcription for the time is interrupted.

15.Aſſ.12. Lord and Tenant by fealty and rent, the Lord is in ſeiſin of his rent, the Lord granteth his Seignory to another and to his heires vpon condition, the Tenant attorneth and payeth his rent to the Grantee, the Condition is broken, the Lord diſtreyneth for his rent, and Reſcous is made he ſhall be in his former eſtate, and yet the former ſeiſin ſhall not enable him to haue an Aſſiſe without a new ſeiſin.

8.H.7.7. If Tenant in taile make a Feoffment in fee vpon condition, and dyeth, the iſſue in taile within age doth enter for the Condition broken, he ſhall be firſt in as Tenant in fee ſimple as heire to his father, and conſequently and inſtantly he ſhall be remitted. But if the heire be of full age, he ſhall not be remitted becauſe he might haue had his Formdon againſt the Feoffee, and the entrie for the Condition is his owne act, but more ſhall be ſaid hereof in his proper place in the chapter of Remitter.

2.H.6,4. If a man make a Feoffment in fee of Blacke acre and white acre vpon condition, &c and for breach thereof that he ſhall enter into Blacke acre, this is good.

43.Aſſ.47. 12.E.4.4. 2.H.5.7.b. 39.Aſſ.15. 11.H.5.25. 16.Aſſ.47. If Tenant for life make a Feoffment in fee vpon condition and entreth for the Condition broken, he ſhall be Tenant for life againe, but ſubiect to a forfeiture, for the ſtate is reduced, but the forfeiture is not purged.

Section 326.

En meſme le manner eſt ſi terres ſont dones en le taile, ou leſſes a terme de vie ou des ans, ſur condition, &c.

IN the ſame manner it is if lands be giuen in taile, or let for terme of life or of yeares vpon condition, &c.

Sur condition, &c. This implyeth the ſeuerall kindes of conditions in Deed before ſpecified.

Sect. 327.

Mes lou feoffment eſt fait de certaine terres reſeruant certain rent, &c. ſur tiel condition, que ſi le rent ſoit aderere, que bien lirroit al feoffor, & ſes heires dentrer, et la terre tener tanque ils ſoient ſatisfies ou payes de le rent aderere, &c. En ceſt caſe ſi le rent ſoit aderere, & le feoffor ou ſes heires enter, le feoffee

BVt where a feoffment is made of certaine lands reſeruing a certaine rent, &c. vpon ſuch condition that if the rent bee behinde that it ſhall be lawfull for the feoffor and his heires to enter, and to hold the land vntill hee bee ſatisfied or payed the rent behinde, &c. In this caſe if the rent be behinde, and the feoffor or his

Vid. Sect. 332. 19.E.tit.barre 280. 19.R.2.done rent 10. Pl.com.524.

Et la terre tener tanque ils ſoyent ſatisfies ou paies de le rent aderere, &c. By this it is implyed that if ſuch a feoffment be made reſeruing (b) (for example) 8.markes rent at the feaſt of Eaſter, with ſuch a Condition as is aforeſaid the Feoffor at the feaſt day demands the rent, the Feoffee payeth vnto him 6. markes parcell of the rent, the Feoffor entreth into the lands, and taketh the profits towards ſatiſfaction. Afterwards the Feoffee doth tender the two markes reſidue of the rent to the Feoffor vpon the land who refuſeth it. It

(b) 20.E.3.tit.Couenant 3.

feoffee neſt pas ex-clude de ceo tout net, mes le feoffor auera & tiendra la terre et prendra ent les profits tanque il ſoit ſatisfie de le rent aderere, & quant il eſt ſatisfie, donques poit le feoffee re-enter en meſme la terre, & ceo tener come il tenoit adevant; Car en tiel cas le feoffor auera la terre forſque en maner come pur vn diſtres, tanques il ſoit ſatisfie de le rent, &c. coment que il prendre les profits en le meane temps a ſon vſe demeſne, &c.

heires enter; the feoffee is not altogether excluded from this, but the feoffor ſhall haue & hold the land, and thereof take the proffits, vntill hee bee ſatisfied of the rent behinde, and when he is ſatisfied, then may the feoffee re-enter into the ſame land, and hold it as hee held it before. For in this caſe the feoffor ſhall haue the land but in manner as for a diſtreſſe vntill he be ſatisfied of the rent, &c. though hee take the profits in the meane time to his own vſe, &c.

hath beene adiudgeth that the Feoffee vpon the refuſall may enter into the land, for when the Feoffor is ſatisfied either by perceptiō of the profits or by payment or tender and refuſall, or partly by the one and partly by the other, the Feoffee may re-enter into the land. And this is within the words of Littleton, viz. (Vntill he be ſatisfied.) And albeit the Feoffor had accepted part of his rent, yet hee may enter for the condition broken and reteine the land vntill he be ſatiſfied of the whole. All which is worthy of obſeruation.

Et en tiel caſe le feoffor auera la terre forſque en manner come vn diſtreſſe tanque il ſoit ſatiſfie de la rent. &c. By this it appeareth that the Feoffor by his re-entry, gaineth no eſtate of freehold but an intereſt by the agreement of the parties to take the proffits in nature of a Diſtreſſe. And therefore if a man maketh a Leaſe for life with a reſeruation of a rent and ſuch a condition if he enter for the Condition broken and take the proffits of the land Quouſque, &c he ſhall not haue an action of debt for the rent Arere for that the freehold of the Leſſee doth continue, and therefore the booke (c) that ſeemeth to the contrary is falſe printed, and the true caſe was of a Leaſe for yeares as it appeareth afterwards in the ſame page of the leafe.

(c) 30. E. 3 fo. 7.

But herein alſo a diuerſity worthy the obſeruation is implyed, viz. If a man make a Leaſe for yeares reſeruing a rent with a condition that if the rent be behinde, that the Leſſor ſhall re-enter and take the proffits vntill thereof he be ſatiſfied, there the proffits ſhall be accounted as parcell of the ſatiſfaction, and during the time that he ſo taketh the proffits hee ſhall not haue an action of debt for the rent, for the ſatiſfaction whereof he taketh the proffits. But if the condition be that he ſhall take the proffits vntill the Feoffor be ſatiſfied or paid of the rent, (without ſaying thereof) or to the like effect, there the proffits ſhall be accounted no part of the ſatiſfaction but to haſten the Leſſee to pay it, and as Littleton here ſaith, that vntill he be ſatiſfied he ſhall take the proffits in the meane time to his owne vſe.

30. E. 3. 7. *Vid ſemblable.* 27. H. 8. 4. 43. E. 3. 21. 31. Aſſ. Pl. 26. *Vid le ſtatute de Merton. ca 6. and obſerue theſe words, Quod inde percipere poſſint duplicem valorem, &c.* Et ca. 7 without this word (Inde.)

Sect. 328.

ITem, diuers parols (entre auters) y ſont, queux per vertue de eux meſmes font eſtates ſur condition: vn eſt le parol Sub conditione: Si come A. enfeoffa B.

ALſo diuers words (amongſt others) there bee which by vertue of themſelues make eſtates vpon condition, one is the word (*Sub condic'*) as if *A.* infeoffe *B.* of cer-

HEre in this and the next two Sections Littleton doth put foure examples of words that make conditions in Deed, and firſt Sub conditione. This is the moſt expreſſe and proper condition in deed, and therefore our Author beginneth with it.

Sub conditione. (e) *Mirror Dier* 138. 27. H. 8. 15. 13. H. 4 entr. Cong. 57. 29 Aſſ. 7. 33. Aſſ. 11. 40. Aſſ. 13. *Bracton vbi ſupra. Fleta lib. 4. ca. 9. Britton, cap. 36. & vbi ſupra.*

Tale redditū, &c. This

Vid. Sect. 325.

This (&c.) implieth any other rent or sum in grosse, or any colaterall condition whatsoeuer, either to be performed by the Feoffee, (whereof our Author here putteth his case) or by the Feoffor, and extendeth to all kinds of Conditions in Deede, before specified.

de certaine terre, habendum & tenendum eidem B. & hæredibus suis, sub conditione, quod idem B. & hæredes sui soluant seu solui faciant præfat' A. & hæredibus suis annuatim talem redditum, &c. En cest case sans ascun pluis dire le Feoffee ad estate sur condition.

taine land, To haue & to hold to the said B. and his heires, vpon condition that the sayd B. and his heires do pay or cause to be paid to the aforesayd A. and his heires yearely such a rent, &c. In this case without any more saying the feoffee hath an estate vpon Condition.

Sect. 329.

Prouiso. Vid. Sect. 220. Dier 28. H. 8. fol. 13. 27. H. 8. fol. 14. 15. 13. H. 4. Entre Cong. 57. Seignior Cromwells case. Lib. 2. fo. 71. 72 at large. 35. H. 8. tit. Condition. Br. Lib. 8. 89. Frances case.

Prouiso semper qd' B. soluat, &c.

Our Author putteth his case where a Prouiso commeth alone. And for it is if a man by Indenture letteth Lands for yeres, Prouided alwaies, and it is couenanted and agreed betweene the sayd Parties, That the Lessee should not alien, and it was adiudged that this was a condition by force of the Prouiso, and a couenant by force of the other words.

This word Prouiso shal be also taken as a limitation or qualification, as hereafter in his proper place shall be sayd. And sometime it shal amount to a Couenant. All which do appeare by the authorities in the margent.*

(*) 27. H. 8. 15. &c. Ita quod. Fleta lib. 4. cap. 9. Bracton vbi supra. Britton vbi supra.

For the (&c.) in this Section explanation is made in the Section next before.

Ou fueront tiels, Ita quod. This is the third condition in deed, whereof our Author maketh mention.

Auxy si les parols fueront tielx, Prouiso semper, quod prædict' B. soluat, seu solui faciat præfato A. talem redditum, &c. ou fueront tielx, Ita quod prædict' B. soluat seu solui faciat præfato A. talem redditum, &c. En ceux cases sauns pluis dire, le Feoffee nad estate forsque sur condition, issint que sil ne performast le condition, le feoffor et ses heires poyent entrer, &c.

Also if the words were such, Prouided alwayes that the aforesayd B. do pay or cause to be payd to the aforesayd A. such a rent, &c. Or these, So that the sayd B. do pay or cause to be payd to the sayd A. such a rent, &c. In these cases without more saying the Feoffee hath but an estate vpon condition: So as if he doth not performe the condition, the Feoffor and his heires may enter, &c.

Sect. 330.

6. E. 2. Entrie Cong. 65. 8. E. 2. Ass. 320. adiudged. Quod si Contingat Pasch. 37. Eliz. Rot. 254. inter Sayer et Hares in Com. Banco.

Quod si contingat &c.

This is the fourth condition in Deed set downe by our Author.

Denter, &c. hereby it is euident, That

Item auters parols sont en vn fait queux causant les tenements estre Conditionals. Sicome sur tiel feofment

Also there bee other words in a Deede which cause the Tenements to be conditionall: As if vpon such feofment

ment vn Rent est reserue al Feoffor, &c. et puis soit mitte en le Fait cest parol, Quod si contingat redditum prædict' aretro fore in parte vel in toto, quod tunc benè licebit **a le Feoffor et a ses heyres dentrer, &c. ceo est vn fait sur condition.**

a rent bee reserued to the feoffor, &c. and afterward this word is put into the deed, That if it happen the aforesayd rent to be behind in part or in all, that then it shall be lawfull for the Feoffor and his heires to enter, &c. This is a Deed vpon condition.

some words of themselues do make a Condition, and some other, (whereof our Authour here and in the next Section * putteth an example) do not of themselues make a Condition without a conclusion and clause of Re-entrie: And manie times (Si) makes a Condition, and sometimes a limitation, as hereafter shall be sayd in this Chapter.

* Vi. Sect. 331.

3.H.6.7. Si. Flet. li.4.ca.9. Bract. lib.4. fo.213.b.

In esse potest donationi modus, conditio, siue causa. * Scito quòd (vt) modus est (si) conditio (quia) causa.

* 4. Mar. Dyer 138.b.

Conditio is explained before. Modus is at this day properly taken for a modification, limitation, or qualification, for the which also the Law hath appoynted apt words, and because Littleton speaketh of this also in the end of this Chapter, I will reserue this matter to his proper place; where the Reader shall perceiue excellent matter of learning touching this point.

Bract. vbi supra.

Causa, The cause or consideration of the Grant, and herein there is a diuersitie betweene a gift of lands, and a gift of an annuitie or such like. For example, If a man grant an annuitie pro vna acra terræ, in this case this word Pro sheweth the cause of the Grant, and therefore amounteth to a condition, for if the acre of land be euicted by an elder title, the annuitie shal cease, for cessante causa cessat effectus.

Pro. 24.E.3.34.

And so if an annuitie be granted pro decimis, &c. if the Grantee be vniustly disturbed of the tithes the Annuitie ceaseth. And so it is if an Annuitie be granted pro concilio, and the Grantee refuse to giue councell, the Annuitie ceaseth. So if an Annuitie be granted quod præstaret concilium, this makes the Grant conditionall.

9.E.4.20. 32.E.3. Annu. 30. 14.E.4.4. 15.E.4.2.b. 8.H.6.23. 5.E.2. tit. An. 44. 41.E.3.19. 32.E.1. Annuitie 242. 21.E.4.49. 22.E.4.28. 35.H.6.2. 10.E.3.44. 5.E2. 9.E.4.20. 15.b.4.3.

But if A. pro concilio impenso, &c. make a feoffement or a lease for life, of an acre, or pro vna acra terræ, &c. albeit he denieth Councell, or that the acre be euicted, yet A. shall not re-enter, for in this case there ought to be legall words of condition or qualification, for the cause or consideration shall not auoyd the state of the Feoffee; and the reason of this diuersitie is, for that the state of the land is executed, and the annuitie executorie.

And yet sometime in case of lands or tenements (Causa) shall make a Condition. As if a woman giue lands to a man and his heires, causa matrimonij prælocuti, in this case if shee either marrie the man, or the man refuse to marrie her, she shall haue the land againe to her and to her heires. (e) But of the other side, if a man giue land to a woman and to her heires, causa matrimonij prælocuti, though he marrie her, or the woman refuse, he shall not haue the Lands againe, for it stands not with the modestie of women in this kind, to aske aduice of learned Councell, as the man may and ought: * And the rather for that in the case of the woman shee may auerre the cause, (for the reason aforesaid) although it be not contained in the Deed) yea though the feoffement be made without Deed.

Flet. li.5 ca.34. 34. Ass.1. 40. Ass.13. (e) 5.E.2 Cui in vita 34. tit. Condition Br. 5.H.4.1.

* 12.E.1.1. Feoffments & Faits 114. F.N.B. 205.L. Vid. Sect. 365.

If a man maketh a feoffement in fee, ad faciendum, or faciendo, or ea intentione, or ad effectum, or ad propositum, that the Feoffee shall doe or not doe such an act, none of these words make the state in the land conditionall, for in iudgement of Law they are no words of condition, & so was it resolued, Hil. 18. Eliz. in Com. Banco, in the case of a common person, but in the case of the King the sayd or the like words doe create a Condition, and so it is in the case of a will of a common person, which case I my selfe heard and obserued.

Ad faciend. ea intentione &c. Dyer 138. 7.H.4.22. 31.H.8 tit. Condition 19. Br. Pl. Com. 142. 38.H.6.33. 36.37. Doct. & Stud. li.2. ca.34. 27.H.8 18.a. 32.E.3. Breue. 291.

But for the auoyding of a Lease for yeares, such precise words of condition are not so strictly required as in case of Freehold and Inheritance. (f) For if a man by Deed make a Lease of a mannor for yeares, in which there is a clause (And the sayd Lessee shall continually dwell vpon the capitall Messuage of the sayd Manor, vpon paine of forfeiture of the said term) these words amount to a Condition.

(f) 7.E.6. Dier 79. 28.H.8. Dier 27.a. Sub pœna forisfacturæ.

And so it is if such a clause be in such a Lease, Quod non licebit, to the Lessee, Dare, vendere, vel concedere statum, & sub pœna forisfacturæ, this amounts to make the lease for yeres defeasible, & so was it adiudged in the Court of Common Pleas (c) in Queene Elizabeths time, and the reason of the Court was, That a Lease for yeares was but a Contract, which may begin by word, and by word may be dissolued.

Quod non licebit. 3.E.6. Di. 65.66. 4. Mar. 138 (c) Hill. 40. Eliz. Rot. 1610. inter Browne & Ayer. Vid. Pl. Com. 142. Br. & Bostons case.

Sect. 331.

MEs il est diuersity perenter cest parol (ſi contingat,&c.) et les parols procheine auantdits. Car ceux parolx, Si contingat,&c.) ne valent riens a tiel condition, sinon que il ad ceux parolx subsequents, que bñ list al Feoffor et a ses heirs dentrer,&c. Mes en les cases auãtdits, il ne besoigne per la Ley, de mitter tiel clause,(ſcilicet) que le Feoffor et ses heyres poient entrer,&c. pur ceo que ils poyent faire ceo per force des parols auantdits, pur ceo q̃ ils impreignont a eux mesmes en Ley vn condition, ſcilicet, que le Feoffor et ses heires poyent entrer, &c. Uncore il est communemẽt vse en touts tiels cases auauntdits dẽ mitter les clauses en les faits, ſcilicet, si le rent soit aderere, &c. que bien lirroit a le Feoffor et a ses heires dentre,&c. Et ceo est bien fait, a cel intent, pur declarer et expresser a les lays gents, que ne sont apprises en la Ley, de le manner et le condition de le feoffement, &c. Sicome home seisie de terre, lessa mesme la terre a vn auter per fait indent pur terme des ans rendant a luy certain rent, il est vse de mitter en le fait, que si le rent soit arere al iour de payment, ou per vn semaigne, ou per vn mois, &c. que adonque bien lirroit al Lessor a distreyñ,&c. vncore le lessor poit destreiñ dẽ cõmon droit p̃ le rent arere,&c, coment que tiels parols ne vnque fueront mises en le Fait,&c.

BVt there is a diuerſitie between this word *Si contingat,&c.* and the words next aforeſaid, &c. for theſe words, *Si contingat*, *&c.* is naught worth to ſuch a Condition, vnleſſe it hath theſe words following, That it ſhall be lawfull for the Feoffor and his heires to enter,&c. but in the caſes aforeſayd, it is not neceſſarie by the law to put ſuch clauſe, *ſcilicet*, that the Feoffor and his heires may enter, &c. becauſe they may doe this by force of the words aforeſaid, for that they containe in themſelues a condition, *ſcilicet*, That the Feoffor and his heires may enter,&c. yet it is commonly vſed in all ſuch caſes aforeſayd, to put the clauſes in the Deeds, *ſcilicet*, if the Rent bee behind, &c. that it ſhall be lawfull to the Feoffor and his heires to enter, &c. And this is well done, for this intent, to declare and expreſſe to the Common people who are not learned in the Law, of the manner and condition of the Feoffement, &c. As if a man ſeiſed of Land, letteth the ſame Land to another by Deede indented for terme of yeares, rendering to him a certaine Rent, it is vſed to bee put into the Deed, That if the Rent bee behind at the day of payment, or by the ſpace of a weeke or a moneth, &c. that then it ſhall bee lawfull to the Leſſor to diſtreyne, &c. yet the Leſſor may diſtreyne of common right for the Rent behind,&c. though ſuch words were not put into the Deed,&c.

Ils

¶ I*Lz ne besoigne per la ley de mitter tiel clause, &c.* Quæ dubitationis causa tollendæ inseruntur, Communem legem non lædunt. Et expressio eorum quæ tacite insunt, nihil operatur.

¶ *Per vn moys, &c.* Here albeit the clause of distresse bee added, that if the Rent be behind by the space of a weeke or a Moneth that the Lessor may distreine, yet he may distreine within the weeke or Moneth, because a Distresse is incident of Common right to euery Rent Seruice. And the words bee in the affirmatiue, and therefore cannot restraine that which is incident of Common right.

The other (&c.) in this Section vpon that which hath beene said are euident.

Sect. 332.

¶ Item, si feoffment soit fait sur tiel condition, que si le feoffor paya al feoffee a certaine iour, &c. 40. l. dargent, que adonque le feoffor poit reenter, &c. en ceo cas le feoffee est appell tenant en morgage, que est autant adire en Francois come mortgage, & en Latin, mortuum vadium. Et il semble que la cause, pur que il est appelle mortgage, est, pur ceo que il estoyt en doubt si le feoffor voyt payer, al iour limitte tiel summe ou non: & si il ne paya pas, donque le terre que il mitter en gage sur condition de payment de le money, est ale de luy a touts iours, & issint mort a luy sur condition, &c, & si il paya le money, donqs est le gage mort quant a le Tenant, &c.

ITem, if a feoffment be made vpon such cōdition, that if the Feoffor pay to the Feoffee at a certain day, &c. 40. pounds of money, that then the Feoffor may reenter, &c. In this case the Feoffee is called Tenant in morgage, which is as much to say in French, as mortgage, and in Latine *mortuum vadium.* And it seemeth that the cause why it is called mortgage, is, for that is doubtful whether the Feoffor will pay at the day limited such summe or not, and if he doth not pay, then the Land which is put in pledge vpon condition for the payment of the money is taken from him for euer, and so dead to him vpon condition, &c. And if hee doth pay the money, then the pledge is dead as to the Tenant, &c.

¶ M*Ortgage* is deriued (c) of two French words, viz. Mort, that is, mortuum, and Gage that is vadium, or pignus. And it is called in Latine mortuum vadium, or morgagium. Now it is called here Mortgage, or mortuum vadium, both for the reason here expressed by Littleton, as also to distinguish it from that which is called viuum vadium. Viuum autem dicitur vadium, quia nunquam moritur ex aliqua parte quod ex suis prouentibus acquiratur. As if a man borrow a hundred pounds of another, and maketh an estate of Lands vnto him, vntill hee hath receiued the said summe of the issues and the profits of the Land, so as in this case neyther money nor Land dyeth, or is lost; whereof Littleton hath spoken (d) before in this Chapter) and therefore it is called, Viuum vadium.

(c) *Glanuil. lib. 10. cap. 6. 8. & lib. 13. cap. 26. 27.*

(d) *Vide Sect. 327.*

Sect. 333.

¶ ITem sicome home poit faire feoffment en fee en Mortgage, issint home poit faire done en taile en Mortgage, & un leas pur terme de vie, ou pur terme des ans en Mortgage, & touts tiels tenants sont appels tenants en Mortgage, solonque les estates, que ils ont en la terre, &c.

ALso as a man may make a feoffment in fee in Morgage, so a man may make a gift in Tayle in Morgage, and a Lease for terme of life, or for tearme of yeares in Morgage. And all such tenants are called tenants in morgage according to the Estates which they haue in the Land, &c.

This Section vpon that which hath beene said needeth no further explication.

Sect. 334.

27.H.8.19.b.

Lib.8.fol.91. Frances case.

¶ *QVe le feoffor paiera a tiel iour, &c.* Albeit Conditions bee not favoured, yet they are not alwayes taken litterally, but in this case the Law enableth the heire that was not named to performe the Condition for foure causes.

First, Because there is a day limited, so as the heire commeth within the time limited by the Condition, for otherwise he could not doe it, as shall bee said hereafter in this Chapter.

Secondly, For that the Condition descends vnto the heire, and therefore the Law that giveth him an interest in the Condition, giveth him an abilitie to performe it.

Thirdly, For that the Feoffee doth receive no dammage or preiudice thereby (all these reasons are expressly to be collected out of the words of Littleton.) And these things being observed.

Fourthly, The intent and true meaning of the Condition shall bee performed. And where it is here said, that the heire may tẽder al iour assesse, &c. herein is implyed, that

¶ ITem si feoffment soit fait en mortgage sur condition que le feoffor payera tiel summe a tiel iour, &c. come est enter eux per lour fait endent accorde & limit, coment que le feoffor morust deuãt le iour de payment, &c. uncore si le heire feoffor paya mesme le summe de money a mesme le iour a le feoffee, ou tender a luy les deniers, et le feoffee ceo refusa de receiuer, donque poit l'heire entrer en l' terre, et uncore le condition est, que si le feoffour payera tiel summe a tiel iour, &c. nient feasant mention en le condition

dascun

ALso if a feoffment bee made in morgage vpon condition, that the Feoffor shall pay such a summe at such a day, &c. as is betweene them by their Deed indented, agreed, and limited, although the Feoffor dyeth before the day of payment, &c. yet if the heire of the Feoffor pay the same summe of money at the same day to the Feoffee, or tender to him the money, and the Feoffee refuse to receiue it. Then may the heire enter into the Land, and yet the condition is, that if the Feoffor shall pay such a summe at such a day, &c. not making men-

dascun payment destre fait per son heire, mes pur ceo que le heire ad interesse de droit en l'condition, &c. et lentent fuit forsque que les deniers serront paies al iour assesse, &c. et le feoffee nad pluis dāmage, si il soit pay per l'heire, que s'il fuit pay per le pier, &c. Et pur cest cause, si le heire paya les deniers, ou tendera les deniers a le iour assesse, &c. et l'auter ceo refusa, il poit entrer, &c. Mes si vn estrāgē de sa teste demesne, que nad ascun interesse, &c. voile tender les auantdits deniers al feoffee a le iour assesse, le feoffee nest pas tenus de ceo receiuer.

tion in the Condition of any payment to bee made by his heire, but for that the heire hath interest of Right in the Condition, &c. and the intent was but that the money should bee payed at the day assessed, &c. and the Feoffee hath no more losse if it bee paid by the heire, thē if it were paid by the Father, &c. therefore if the heire pay the money or tender the money at the day limited, &c. and the other refuse it, he may enter, &c. But if a stranger of his own head, who hath not any interest, &c. will tender the aforesaid money to the Feoffee at the day appointed, the Feoffee is not bound to receiue it.

the Executors or Administrators of the Morgagor, or in default of them the Ordinarie may also tender as shall be said (f) hereafter in this Chapter. But what if the Condition had beene, if the Morgagor or his heires did pay, &c. and hee dyed before the day without heire, so as the Condition became impossible, here it is to be obserued, that where the Condition becommeth impossible to be performed by the act of God, as by death, &c. the state of the Feoffee shall not bee auoyded, as shall bee said hereafter in this Chapter. And therefore the Law here inableth the heire (of whom no mention was made in the Condition) to performe the Condition least the Inheritance should be lost, wherein diuers diuersities are worthy of obseruation.

(f) Vide Sect. 337.

First, betweene a Condition annexed to a state in Lands or Tenements vpon a feoffment, gift in tayle, &c. and a Condition of an Obligation, Recognizance or such like. (g) For if a Condition annexed to Lands be possible at the making of the Condition, and become impossible by the act of God, yet the state of the Feoffee, &c. shall not bee auoyded. As if a man maketh a feoffment in Fee vpon Condition, that the Feoffor shall within one yeare goe to the Citie of Paris about the affaires of the Feoffee, and presently after the Feoffor dyeth, so as it is impossible by the act of God that the Condition should bee performed, yet the Estate of the Feoffee is become absolute, for though the Condition be subsequent to the state, yet there is a precedencie before the re-entrie, viz. the performance of the Condition. And if the Land should by construction of Law be taken from the Feoffee, this should worke a dammage to the Feoffee, for that the Condition is not performed which was made for his benefit. And it appeareth by Littleton, that it must not bee to the dammage of the Feoffee. And so it is if the Feoffor shall appeare in such a Court the next Tearme, and before the day the Feoffor dyeth, the Estate of the Feoffee is absolute. (h) But if a man be bound by Recognizance or Bond with Condition that he shall appeare the next Tearme in such a Court, and before the day the Conusor or Obligor dyeth, the Recognizance or Obligation is saued, and the reason of the diuersitie is because the state of the Land is executed and setled in the Feoffee, and cannot bee redeemed backe againe but by matter subsequent, viz. the performance of the Condition. But the Bond or Recognizance is a thing in action, and executorie, whereof no aduantage can be taken vntill there be a default in the Obligor, and therefore in all cases where a Condition of a Bond, Recognizance, &c. is possible at the time of the making of the Condition, and before the same can be performed, the Condition becomes impossible by the act of God, or of the Law, or of the Obligee, &c. there the Obligation, &c. is saued. But if the Condition of a Bond, &c. be impossible at the time of the making of the Condition, the Obligation, &c. is single. And so it is in case of a feoffment in fee with a Condition subsequent, that is impossible, the state of the Feoffee is absolute, but if the Condition precedent bee impossible, no

(g) Pl. Com. 456. Wischet Case. 14. H. 7. 2. 15 H. 7. 1. 14. E. 4. 3. 38. H. 6. 2. 3.

(h) 15. H. 7. 18. 31. H. 6. barre 60. 18. E. 4. 17. 9. Eliz. 262. Dier lib. 5. 22. Laughters case. 38. H. 6. 2.

Fleta lib. 4. cap. 9. & Bracton & Britton vbi supra.

14.H.8.28. 10.H.7.22. 4.H.7.4. 8.E.4.1. 28.H.8.25. lib.5.fo.22. Laughters case & 75. 39.E.35. 17.H.6. Obligat.18. 5.Eliz. Dier 222.

state or interest shall growe thereupon. And to illustrate these by examples you shall understand. If a man be bound in an Obligation, &c. with condition that if the Obligor doe goe from the Church of St. Peter in Westmin. to the Church of St. Peter in Rome within three houres that then the Obligation shall be voide. The Condition is voyde and impossible and the Obligation standeth good.

And so it is if a feoffment be made upon condition that the Feoffee shall goe as is aforesaid, the state of the Feoffee is absolute and the condition impossible and voyde.

* Pl. com. Fullers case 272.

* If a man make a Lease for life upon condition that if the Lessee goe to Rome as is aforesaid that then he shall have a fee, the condition precedent is impossible and voyde, and therefore no fee simple can grow to the Lessee.

35.H.6. tit. barre 262. 37.H.6. barre 60. 2.E.3.9. 9.Eliz. Dier 262. 28.H.8.30.

If a man make a feoffment in fee upon condition that the Feoffee shall re-infeoffe him before such a day, and before the day the Feoffor disseise the Feoffee and hold him out by force untill the day be past, the state of the Feoffee is absolute, for the Feoffor is the cause whereof the condition cannot be performed, and therefore shall never take advantage for non performance thereof. (i) And so it is if A. be bound to B. that I.S. shall marry Ioan G. before such a day, and before the day B marry with Iane, he shall never take advantage of the bond, for that he himselfe is the meane, that the condition could not be performed. And this is regularly true in all cases.

(i) 4.H.7.4. 30.H.8. Dier 42. 11.H.4.57. in protection. 10.H.7.18.

(k) Vid. Bracton, Britton Fleta ubi supra.

But it is commonly holden (k) that if the condition of a Bond, &c. be against law, that the bond it selfe is voyde.

Bracton lib.3.fo.100. 2.H.4.9. 8.E.4.12.b. 2.E.4.2. & 3. 4.H.7.4.b. 10.H.7.22. 14.H.8.28. 42.E.3.6.23.

But herein the Law distinguisheth betweene a condition against Law for the doing of any act that is Malum in se, and a condition against Law (that concerneth not any thing that is malum in se) but therefore is against Law, because it is either repugnant to the state or against some Maxime or rule in Law. And therefore the common opinion is to bee understood of conditions against Law for the doing of some act that is malum in se, and yet therein also the Law distinguisheth. As if a man be bound upon condition that he shall kill I.S the bond is voide.

2.H.4.9.

Pl. Com. Brownings case 133.

But if a man make a feoffment upon condition that the Feoffee shall kill I.S. the state is absolute, and the condition voyde.

If a man make a feoffment in fee upon condition that he shall not alien, this condition is repugnant and against Law, and the state of the Feoffee is absolute (whereof more shall be said in his proper place.) But if the Feoffee be bound in a bond, that the Feoffee or his heires shall not alien this is good, for he may notwithstanding alien if he will forfeit his bond that he himselfe hath made.

7.H.6.43.b. 21.H.6.33. 21.H.7.11. 21.H.7.30. 20.E.4.8. Pl. Com. in Brownings case 133.a. 27.H.8.

So it is if a man make a feoffment in fee upon condition that the Feoffee shall not take the profits of the land this condition is repugnant and against Law, and the state is absolute.

But a bond with a condition that the Feoffee shall not take the profits is good. If a man be bound, with a condition to enfeoffe his wife, the condition is voide and against Law, because it is against a maxime in Law, and yet the bond is good, but if he be bound to pay his wife money that is good. Et sic de similibus whereof there bee plentifull Authorities in our bookes.

Vid. Sect. 325.

¶ *Tender les deniers al iour assesse, &c.* Note hereby is implied that albeit a convenient time before sunne set be the last time given to the Feoffor to tender, yet if he tender it to the person of the morgage at any time of the day of payment, and he refuseth it, the condition is saved for that time.

¶ *Il poet enter, &c.* And so may his heire after his death.

¶ *Mes si estranger de sa teste demesne que nad ascun interesse, &c. voile tender les avandits deniers al feoffee al iour assesse, le feoffee nest pas tenus de ceo receiver.* Nota by this period and the (&c.) it is implyed that if the morgager die, his heire within age of 14. yeares (the land being holden in Socage) the next of kinne to whom the land cannot discend being his gardein in Socage may tender in the name of the heire, because he hath an interest as gardeine in Socage. Also if the heire be within age of 21. yeares, and the land is holden by Knights service, the Lord of whom the land is holden may make the tender for his interest which he shall have when the condition is performed, for these in respect of their interest are not accounted estrangers.

Vid. Sect. 401. Hill. 28. Eliz. in banco Regis Inter Watkins & Aswick Pro terris in Com. Devon. 45.E.3. tit. Release 28. 31.E.1. tit. Annuity 51. 33.H.6.18.

But if the heire be an Ideot, of what age soever, any man may make the tender for him in respect of his absolute disability, and the Law in this case is grounded upon charity, and so in like cases.

36.H.6. tit. barre. 166. 33.E.1. tit. Annuity 51. 33.E.3. iudgement 254.

¶ *Le Feoffee nest pas tenus de ceo receiver.* And note that Littleton saith, that he is not bound to receive it at a strangers hand. But if any stranger in the name of the Morgagor or his heire (without his consent or privity) tender the money and the morgage accepteth it, this is a good satisfaction, and the Morgagor or his heire agreeing thereunto may re-enter into the land. Omnis ratihabitio retro trahitur & mandato equiparatur. But the Morgagor or his heire may disagree thereunto if he will.

Section 335.

ET memorandum que en tiel cas, lou tiel tender de le money est fait, &c. & le feoffee d' receiuer ceo refusa, per que le feoffor ou ses heires entront, &c. donque le feoffee nad ascun remedy dauer l' money per le cōmon ley, pur ceo que il serra rette sa follie que il refusa le money quant un loyal tendre de ceo fuit fait a luy.

AND be it remembred that in such case, where such tender of the money is made, &c. and the feoffee refuse to receiue it, by which the feoffor or his heires enter, &c. then the feoffee hath no remedy by the cōmon law to haue this money, because it shall bee accounted his owne folly that hee refused the money, when a lawful tender of it was made vnto him.

Tender de le money est fait, &c. Here is implyed at the due time and place according to the condition.

Entront, &c. viz. into the lands or tenements.

Donque le feoffee nad ascun remedie dauer le money per le common ley, &c. And the reason is because the money is collaterall to the land, and the Feoffee hath no remedy therefore. 8.E.2.tit.Ass.389. 31.Ass.32.

If an Obligation of an hundred pound be made with condition for the payment of fifty pound at a day, and at the day the Obligor tender the money, and the Obligee refuseth the same; yet in action of debt vpon the Obligation, if the Defendant pleade the tender and refusall, he must also pleade that he is yet ready to pay the money and tender the same in Court. But if the Plaintiffe will not then receiue it but take issue vpon the tender, and the same be found against him, he hath lost the money for euer. 22.H.6.39. 21.E.4.25. 22.E.3.5. Lib.9.fo.79. H.Pytons case.

If a man be bound in 200. quarters of wheate for deliuery of a 100. quarters, if the Obligor tender at the day the 100. quarters, &c. he shall not pleade Vncore prist, because albeit it be the parcell of the condition, yet they be Bona peritura, and it is a charge for the Obligor to keepe them. And the reason wherefore in the case of the Obligation the some mentioned in the condition is not lost by the tender and refusall, is not only for that it is a dutie and parcell of the obligation, and therefore is not lost by the tender and refusall, but also for that the Obligee hath remedy by Law for the same. And in this case, Liberata pecunia non liberat offerentem. 8.E.2.tit.Ass.389.

But if a man make a single bond, or knowledge a Statute or Recognizance & afterwards made a defeasance for the payment of a lesser summe at a day, if the Obligor or Conusor tender the lesser summe at the day, and the Obligee or Conusee refuseth it, he shall neuer haue any remedy by Law to recouer it, because it is no parcell of the summe contained in the Obligation, Statute, or Recognizance, being contayned in the defeasance made at the time or after the Obligation, Statute, or Recognizance. And in this case in pleading of the tender and refusal the party shall not be driuen to pleade, that he is yet ready to pay the same or to tender it in Court: Neither hath the Obligee or Conusee any remedy by Law to recouer the summe contained in the Defeasance, (o) And so it is if a man make an Obligation of 100. pound with condition for the deliuery of Corne or timber, &c. or for the performance of an arbitrement, or the doing of any act, &c. This is collaterall to the Obligation, that is to say, is not parcell of it, and therefore a tender and refusall is a perpetuall barre.

7.H.4.18. 5.Mar Dier.150 21.E.4.25. 22.E.3.5. 33.H.6.2.b. 17.Ass.pl.2. 20.E.4.1.b. 9.H.6.16. 36.H.6.26. 15.E.4.1. 16.H.7.13. 18.E.3.53. 7.E.4.4.b. 19.H.8.12. 27.H.8.1.a. 22.H.6.39.tit.Abatemēt 12. 49.E.3.3. 19.H.6.12. (o) Henry Petons case vbi supra.

But if a man be bound to make a feoffment in fee to the Obligee, and he make a Lease and a release to him and his heires, albeit this be a collaterall condition, yet is it well performed, because this amounts in Law to a feoffment. 31.Ass.25. 11.H.4.33. 1.H.6.8. 1.E.4. 17.E.4.3. Pl.Com. Fogasses case, fo.6.

Money, moneta, Legalis moneta Angliæ. Lawfull money of England eyther of Gold or Siluer, is of two sorts, viz. the English money coyned by the Kings Lib.5.fo.114.115. Wades case. Lib.9.fo.78.

authority, or forraine coyne by Proclamation made currant within the Realme. Coine, cuna dicitur a cudendo, of coyning of money. In French Coine signifieth a corner because in ancient time money was square with corners, as it is in some Countries at this day. Some say that Coine dicitur a κοινος id est, communis, quod sit omnibus rebus communis. Moneta dicitur à monendo, not only because he that hath it, is to be warned providently to use it, but also because Nota illa de authore & valore admonet. Pecunia dicitur a Pecu, beasts, Omnes enim veterum divitiæ in animalibus consistebant, and it appeareth that in Homers time, there was no money but exchange of cattell, &c. *Aristotle Lib.*5.*cap.*8.

Nummus ἀπὸ τοῦ νόμου quia lege fit non natura. Vide * the Statute of 9.H.5 of the noble, halfe noble, and farthing of gold, which is the fourth part of a noble, and that is 20.pence. (*) 9.*H*.5.*Stat*.2.*Cap*.7.

Section 336.

12.E.3.Condic.8. 13.Ed.3. ibid.10. 12.Ass.5.

ET *sil faile de paier les deniers,&c.*

If a man make a feoffment of Lands, To have and to hold to him and his heires, upon condition, That if the Feoffee pay to the Feoffour at such a day twentie pounds, that then the Feoffee shall have the lands to him and his heires; if the condition had not proceeded further, it had beene void, for that the Feoffee had a fee simple by the first words, and therefore the words subsequent are materially added, (And if he faile to pay the money, &c.)

Li.5.fo.96,97.Goodales case.

Le second Feoffee voile tender le summe des deniers,&c.

Albeit the second Feoffee bee not named in the Condition, yet shall he tender the summe, because hee is privie in estate, and in judgement of Law hath an estate and interest in the condition, (as Littleton heere saith) for the salvation of his Tenancie, Vi.Sect.334. And note he that hath interest in the conditiō on the one side, or in the land on the other, may tender.

Li.5.fo.114,115.Wades case.

And it is to bee ob-

Item si feoffment soit fait sur tiel condition, Que si le Feoffee paya al feoffor a tiel iour inter eux limit xx.l. adonques le Feoffee auera la Terre a luy et a ses heires, et sil faile de payer les deniers a le iour assesse, que adonque bien list a le Feoffor ou a ses heyres dentrer, &c. et puis devant le iour assesse, le Feoffee venda la terre a un auter, et de ceo fait feoffment a luy, en cest case si le second Feoffee voile tender le summe de les deniers a le iour assesse a le Feoffor, et le Feoffor ceo refusa, &c. donque le second Feoffee ad estate en la terre clerement sans condition. Et la cause est, pur ceo que le second Feoffee avoit interest en le condition pur saluation d͞ son Tenancie. Et en cest case il semble que si le primer Feoffee apres tiel vender de la Terre, voile tender le money a le

ALso if a Feoffement be made on this condition, That if the Feoffee pay to the Feoffor at such a day between them limitted, twenty pounds, then the feoffee shal haue the Land to him and to his heires, and if he faile to pay the money at the day appointed, that then it shall bee lawfull for the Feoffor or his Heyres to enter, &c. and afterwards before the day appointed the Feoffee sel the Land to another; and of this maketh a Feoffement to him, in this case if the second Feoffee wil tender the sum of money at the day appointed, to the Feoffor, and the feoffor refuseth the same, &c. then the second Feoffee hath an estate in the land cleerely without condition. And the reason is, for that the second Feoffee hath an interest in the cōdition for the safegard of his tenancy: and in this case it seemes, that if the first feoffee after such sale of the land, wil tender the

le iour assesse, &c. a le feoffor, ceo serra assets bone pur saluation destate de le second Feoffee, pur ceo que le primer Feoffee fuit priuie a le condition, & issint le tender de ascun de eux deux est assets bon, &c.

money at the day appointed, &c. to the feoffor, this shall be good enough for the safegard of the estate of the second feoffee, because the first feoffee was priuie to the condition, and so the tender of either of them two is good enough, &c.

serued also, That the feoffee may tender any money that is currant within the Realme, albeit it bee forreine coine, so as it bee currant by Act of Parliament, or by the Kings proclamation, as hath beene said.

¶ *Tender le summe.* The Feoffee may tender the money in purses or bagges, without shewing or telling the same, for he doth that which he ought, viz. to bring the money in purses or bagges, which is the usuall manner to carry money in, and then it is the part of the party that is to receiue it, to put it out and tell it.

¶ *A primer Feoffee.* Here it appeareth, that the first Feoffee may notwithstanding his feoffment, pay the money to the Feoffor, because he is partie and priuie to the Condition, and by his tender may saue the state of his Feoffee, which in all good dealing he ought to doe.

Sect. 337.

¶ Item si feoffement soit fait sur condition, Que si le Feoffor paya certaine summe dargent al Feoffee, adonques bien lirroit a Feoffor et a ses heirs dentrer: en cest case si le feoffor deuie deuant le payment fait, et lheire voile tender al feoffee les deniers, tiel tender est voyd, pur ceo que le temps deins quel ceo doit estre fait est passe, car quant le condition est, que si le feoffor paya les deniers al Feoffee, &c. ceo est tant adire, que si le feoffor durant sa vie paya les deniers al feoffee, &c. et quant le feoffor morust, don-

ALso if a feoffment bee made vpon condition, That if the Feoffor pay a certaine summe of money to the Feoffee, then it shal be lawfull to the feoffor and his heyres to enter: in this case if the feoffor die before the payment made, and the heire will tender to the feoffee the money, such tender is void, because the time within which this ought to bee done, is past. For when the condition is, That if the Feoffor pay the money to the Feoffee, &c. this is as much to say, as if the Feoffor during his life pay the money to the Feoffee, &c. & when the feof-

¶ This diuersitie is plaine and euident, & agreeth with our (a) Books, and yet somwhat shal be obserued hereupon: for here it appeareth, That seeing no time is limitted, the Law doth appoint the time, & that is, during the life of the feoffor. Wherein diuers diuersities are worthy the obseruation:

(a) 14.H.7.31. 15.H.7.1.

First, Betweene this case that Littleton here putteth of the condition of a Feoffment in fee, for the payment of money where no time is limited, and the condition of a Bond for the payment of a summe of money where no time is limitted: for in such a condition of a Bond the money is to be payd presently, that is, in conuenient time. (b) And yet in case of a condition of a bond there is a diuersitie betweene a condition of an obligation, which concernes the doing of a transitorie act without limitation of any time, as payment of money, deliuery of Charters, or the like, for there the condition is to bee performed presently, that is, in conuenient time, & when by the condition of the Obligation the act that is to bee done

by presently or and ye Law intendeth convenient time

44.E.3.9. 33.H.6.45.& 48.b. 4.E.4.20. 9.E.4.22. 15.E.4.30. 21.E.4.38 b. 9.H.7.17.b. 10.H.7.15. 14.H.8.21.a.& 29.b.
(b) Lib.6.fo.30.31. Bothies case. 33.H.6.47.48.

2

ques le temps de le tēder est passe. Mes autrement est lou un iour de payment est limit, et le feoffor devie devaunt le iour, donque poet le heire tender les deniers come est auauntdit, pur ceo que le temps de le tender ne fuyt passe per le mort del feoffor. Auxy il semble que ē tiel case lou le feoffor deuy dvant le iour de payment, si les Executors de le feoffor tendront les deniers al feoffee al iour de payment, cel tender est assets bon. Et si le feoffee ceo refuse les heires de feoffor poient entrer, &c. Et le cause est, pur ceo que les Executors representont l' person lour Testator, &c.

for dyeth, then the time of the tender is past. But otherwise it is where a day of payment is limited, and the Feoffor die before the day, then may the heire tender the money as is aforesaid, for that the time of the tender was not past by the death of the Feoffor. Also it seemeth, That in such case where the Feoffor dyeth before the day of payment, if the Executors of the Feoffor tender the money to the Feoffee at the day of payment, this tender is good enough, and if the Feoffee refuse it, the heyres of the Feoffor may enter, &c. And the reason is, for that the Executors represent the person of their Testator, &c.

done to the Obligee is of his owne nature locall, for there the Obligor (no time being limited) hath time during his life, to performe it, as to make a Feoffment, &c. if the Obligee doth not hasten the same by request.
3. In case where the condition of the Obligation is locall, there is also a diversitie, when the concurrence of the Obligor and the Obligee is requisite, (as in the sayd case of the Feoffment) and when the Obligor may performe it in the absence of the Obligee, as to knowledge satisfaction in the Court of Kings Bench, * although the knowledge of satisfaction is locall, yet because hee may doe it in the absence of the Obligee, he must doe it in convenient time, and hath not time during his life.

(*) *Boothies case, ubi supra.*

Another diversity is, where the condition concerneth a transitory or locall act, and is to be performed to the Feoffee or obligee, and where it is to be performed to a stranger: as if A. be bound to B. to pay ten pounds to C. A. tender to C. and hee refuseth, the Bond is forfeited, as in this Section shall bee said more at large.

Another diversitie is betweene a condition of an Obligation, and a condition upon a Feoffment, where the Act that is locall is to be done to a stranger, and where to the Obligee or Feoffor himselfe. As if one make a feoffment in fee, upon condition that the Feoffee shall infeoffe a stranger, and no time limitted, the Feoffee shall not have time during his life to make the feoffment, for then he should take the profits in the meane time to his owne use, which the Estranger ought to have, and therefore he ought to make the feoffment as soone as conveniently he may, and so it is of the condition of an Obligation. But if the condition be, That the Feoffee shall re-infeoffe the Feoffor, there the Feoffee hath time during his life, for the privitie of the condition betweene them, unlesse he be hastened by request, as shall bee said hereafter.

Boothies case, li. 6. fo. 31. Lib. 2. fo. 79. b Seignior Cromwels case. 44. E. 3. 9. 21. E. 4. 41. 2. E. 4. 3. 4. 19. H. 6. 67. 73. 76. 4. E. 4. 4. b. 26. H. 8. 9. b.

Another diversitie is, when the Obligor or Feoffee is to enfeoffe a stranger, as hath bin said, and when a stranger is to infeoffe the Feoffee or obligee: As if A. infeoffe B. of Blacke Acre, upon condition that if C. infeoffe B. of White Acre, A. shall re-enter. C. hath time during his life, if B. doth not hasten it by request, and so of an Obligation.

7. But in some cases albeit the condition be collaterall, and is to be performed to the Obligee, and no time limited, yet in respect of the nature of the thing, the Obligor shall not have time during his life to performe it. As if the condition of an Obligation be, to grant an annuitie or yeerely rent to the Obligee during his life, payable yearely at the feast of Easter, this annuity or yearely rent must be granted before Easter, or else the Obligee shall not have it at that feast during his life, & sic de similibus, and so was it resolved by the Judges (*) of the Common Pleas in the Argument of Andrews case, which I my selfe heard.

14. E. 3. Det. 138 Li. 2. fo. 80. Seignior Cromwells case.

(*) *Vid. Dyer 14. El. 311.*

8. Lastly, when the Obligor, Feoffor, or Feoffee is to doe a sole act or labour, as to goe to Rome,

Rome, Ierusalem, &c. In such and the like cases, the Obligor, Feoffor, or Feoffee hath time during his life and cannot bee hastened by request. And so it is if a stranger to the Obligation or Feoffment were to doe such an act, he hath time to doe it at any time during his life.

¶ *Si les executors del feoffor tendront, &c.* **So as now it appeareth** that eyther the heire of the Feoffor, or his Executors may (when a day is limited) pay the money, and so also may the Administrator of the Feoffor doe, if the Feoffor dye intestate, (f) and this may the Ordinarie doe if there be neyther Executor nor Administrator, as hath beene said. *Lib 5. fol. 96. 97. Goodales Case.* *(f) Vide Sect. 334.*

¶ *Et le feoffee refuse, les heires del feoffor poient enter, &c.* Nota **a tender** by the Executors or Administrators, and a refusall doth giue the heire of the Feoffor a title of entrie. And hereby this (&c.) is a diuersitie implyed, when a tender and refusall shall giue a third person title of entrie.

If a man be bound to A. in an Obligation with Condition to infeoffe B. (who is a meere stranger) before a day, the Obligor doth offer to enfeoffe B. and he refuseth, the Obligation is forfeit, for the Obligor hath taken vpon him to enfeoffe him, and his refusall cannot satisfie the Condition, because no feoffment is made, but if the feoffment had beene by the Condition to be made to the Obligee, or to any other for his benefit or behoofe, a tender and refusall shall saue the Bond, because he himselfe vpon the matter is the cause wherefore the Condition could not be performed, and therefore shall not giue himselfe cause of action. But if A. be bound to B. with Condition that C. shall enfeoffe D. In this case if C. tender, and D. refuse, the Obligation is saued, for the Obligor himselfe vndertaketh to doe no act, but that a stranger shall infeoffe a stranger. And it is holden in Bookes, (h) that in this case it shall be intended, that the feoffment should be made for the benefit of the Obligee. Some to reconcile the Bookes seeme to make a difference betweene an expresse refusall of the stranger, and a readinesse of the Obligor at the day and place to make performance, and the absence of the stranger: but that can make no difference. I take it rather to bee the error of the Reporter; and the Records themselues are necessary to be seene, for the Law herein is, as it hath beene before declared. *33. H. 6. 16. 17. 36. H. 6. 8. 2. E. 4. 2. 3. 15. E. 4. 5 6. 21. E. 4. 13. 32. E 3. barre 264 7. E 3. 29. 9. H. 17. 17. 10. H. 7. 14. b. 35. H. 8. Dyer 56. lib. 5. fol. 23. Lambes case.* *(h) 8. E. 4. 14. 2. E. 4. vbi supra.*

If I enfeoffe one in fee vpon condition to infeoffe I.S. and his heires, the Feffee tenders the feoffment to I. S. and he refuseth it, the Feoffor may reenter, for by the expresse intent of the Condition, the Feffee should not haue and retaine any benefit or estate in the land, but as it were an instrument to conuey ouer the land. *19. H. 6. 34.*

But in that case if the Condition were to make a gift in tayle to I.S. and he refuseth it, and a tender and refusall is made, there the Feoffor shall not reenter, for that it was intended that the Feffee should haue an estate in the Land. And so it is if a feoffment bee made vpon Condition that the Feoffee shall grant a Rent Charge to a stranger, if the Feoffee tender the grant and he refuseth, the Feoffor shall not reenter, because the Feoffee was to retaine the land, which points are worthy of due obseruation. *2. E 4. Entrie conge. 25.*

Here in the case of Littleton, when the Executors make the tender, and the Feoffee refuseth; albeit the heire be a third person, yet is he no stranger, but hee and the Executors also are priuies in Law.

¶ *Le person del testator, &c.* **This is to bee vnderstood concerning** goods and chattels eyther in possession or in action; and the Executor doth more actually represent the person of the Testator, then the heire doth the person of the Ancestor. For if a man bindeth himselfe, his Executors are bound though they bee not named, but so it is not of the heire: Farthermore, here the Administrators and the Ordinary also are implyed, as before hath beene said.

Sect. 338.

¶ **ET nota que en touts cases de condition de paymēt de certaine summe en grosse, touchant terres ou tenements, si loyall tender soit vn**

AND note that in all cases of condition for payment of a certaine summe in grosse touching lands or tenements, if lawfull tender be once re-

¶ This is to be vnderstood, that hee that ought to tender the money is of this discharged for euer to make any other tender, but if it were a dutie before, though the Feoffor enter by force of the Condition, yet the debt or dutie remayneth. As if A. borroweth a hundred *Vide Sect. sequen.*

foits refuse, celuy q̃ duissoit tender le money est d̃ ceo assouth, & pleinm̃t discharge per touts temps apres.

fused, he which ought to tender the money is of this quite and fully discharged for euer afterwards.

hundred pound of B. and after morgageth land to B. upon Condition for payment thereof. If A. tender the money to B. and hee refuseth it, A. may enter into the Land, and the land is freed for euer of the Condition, but yet the debt remayneth, and may bee recouered by Action of Debt. But if A. without any lone, debt, or dutie preceding infeoffe B. of land upon Condition for the payment of a hundred pounds to B. in nature of a gratuitie or gift. In that case if he tender the hundred pound to him according to the Condition and hee refuseth it, B. hath no remedie therefore, and so is our Author in this and his other cases of like nature to be understood.

Section 339.

ITem si le feoffee en mortgage, deuant le iour de payment que serroit fait a luy face ses executors et deuie, et son heire enter en le terre come il deuoit, &c. il semble en cest cas que le feoffor doit payer le money al iour assesse as executors, et nemy al heire le feoffee, pur ceo que le money al commencemẽt trenchast al feoffee en maner come un dutie, et serra entendue que lestate fuit fait per cause de le prompter de le money per le feoffee, ou pur cause dauter dutie. Et pur c̃ le paym̃t ne serra fait al heire, come il semble. Mes les parols del condition poyent estre tiels, que le payment serra fait al heire, come si le condition fuit, que si le feoffor paya al feoffee, ou a ses heires, tiel summe a tiel iour, &c. la apres la

ALso if the Feoffee in morgage before the day of payment which should bee made to him, makes his Executors and die, and his heire entreth into the land as he ought, &c. It seemeth in this case that the Feoffour ought to pay the money, at the day appointed to the Executors, and not to the heire of the Feoffee, because the money at the beginning trenched to the Feoffee in manner as a dutie and shall be entended that the estate was made by reason of the lending of the money by the Feoffee, or for some other dutie, and therefore the payment shall not be made to the heire, as it seemeth, but the wordes of the Condition may be such, as the payment shall be made to the heire. As if the Condition were, that if the Feoffor pay to the Feoffee or to his heires such a summe at

¶ *PAiera tiel some a tiel iour, &c.* Here is implyed that this payment ought to bee reall and not in shew or appearance. For if it bee agreed betweene the Feoffor and the Executors of the Feffee, that the Feoffor shall pay to the Executors but part of the money, and that yet in appearance the whole summe shall bee paid, and that the residue shall bee repaid, and accordingly at the day and place, the whole summe is paid, and after the residue is repaid, this is no performance of the Condition, for the state shal not bee deuested out of the heire which is a third person, without a true and effectuall payment, and not by a shadow or colour of payment, and the agreement precedent doth guide the payment subsequent.

18. E. 4. fol. 18. Lib. 5. fol. 96. Goodales Case. 39. H. 6. 54. 20. E. 3. Accounts Pl. 70.

And by this Section also it appeareth, that the Executors do more represent the person of the Testator, then the heire doth to the Auncestor, for though the Executor be not named, yet the

la mort le feoffee, sil morust devaunt l'iour limit, l'payment doit estre fait al heir al iour assesse, &c.

such a day, &c. there after the death of the feoffee, if hee dieth before the day limitted the payment ought to be made to the heire at the day appointed, &c.

Law appoints him to receiue the money, but so doth not the Law appoint the heire to receiue the money vnlesse he bee named.

¶ *Doit estre fait al heire al iour assesse, &c.* And here it also appeareth that if the condition vpon the Morgage be to pay to the Morgagee or his heires the money, &c. and before the day of payment the Morgagee dieth, the Feoffor cannot pay the money to the Executors of the Morgagee; For Littleton saith that in this case the payment ought to be made to the heire. *Et in hoc casu designatio vnius personæ est exclusio alterius, & expressum facit cessare tacitum.* And the Law shall neuer seeke out a person, when the parties themselues haue appointed one. But if the condition be to pay the money to the Feoffee his heires or Executors, then the Feoffor hath election to pay it either (m) to the heire or Executors.

Margin: Vid. lib. 5. fo. 96. Goodales case Dier 2. Eliz. 181. 44. E. 3. 1. b.

Margin: (m) 12. E. 3. Condition 8. & 10.

If a man make a feoffment in fee vpon condition that the Feoffee shall pay to the Feoffor his heires or assignes 20. pound at such a day, and before the day the Feoffor make his Executors and dyeth, the Feoffee may pay the same either to the heire or to the Executors, for they are his assignes in Law to this intent. But if a man make a feoffment in fee vpon condition, that if the Feoffor pay to the Feoffee his heires or assignes 20. pound before such a feast, and before the feast the Feoffee maketh his Executors and dyeth, the Feoffor ought to pay the money to the heire, and not to the Executors, for the Executors in this case are no assignees in Law, and the reason of this diuersity is this, for that in the first case the Law must of necessity finde out Assignes, because there cannot be any Assignes in Deed, for the Feoffor hath but a bare condition and no estate in the Land which he can assigne ouer. But in the other case the Feoffee hath an estate in the land which he may assigne ouer, and where there may be Assignees in Deed, the Law shall neuer seeke out or appoint any Assignes in Law. And albeit the Feoffee made no assignment of the estate, yet the executors cannot be Assignees, because Assignes were only intended by the condition to be assignees of the estate, and so was it resolued * Mich. 23. & 24. Eliz by the two chiefe Iustices in the Court of wards betweene Randall and Browne which I obserued.

Margin: 27. H. 8. 2. 3. & 4. Ph. & Mar. 140. a. (*) Mic. 23. & 24. Eliz. in Curia Wardorum. Inter Randal & Browne.

But if the condition be to pay the money to the Feoffee his heires or assignes, and the Feoffee make a feoffment ouer, it is in the election of the Feoffor to pay the money to the first Feoffee or to the second feoffee, and so if the first Feoffee dyeth the Feoffor may either pay the money to the heire of the first Feoffee or to the second Feoffee, for the Law will not enforce the Feoffor to take knowledge of the second feoffment, nor of the validity thereof, whither the same be effectuall or not but at his pleasure, and the First Feoffee and his heires are expresly named in the Condition.

Margin: Vid. 2. Eliz. Dier 181. Pl. Com. Chapmans case 185. 288. Vid. Goodales case. lib. 5. fo. 96. 97. 17. Ass. pl. 2. Goodales case vbi supra.

Sect. 340.

¶ Item sur tiel case de feoffment en Morgage, questiō ad este demaunde en quel lieu le feoffour est tenus de tender les deniers a l' feoffee al iour assesse, &c. Et ascuns ont dit, que sur la terre issint tenus en Morgage, pur ceo que l' cōdition est dependant sur le tre; Et ont dit, q̄

ALso vpon such case of feoffment in Morgage, a question hath beene demanded in what place the feoffor is bound to tender the money to the feoffee at the day appointed, &c. And some haue said, vpon the land so holden in Morgage, because the condition is depending vpon the land. And they

¶ *Item sur tiel case de feoffment en morgage question ad este demande, &c.* Here and in other places that I may say once for all, where Littleton maketh a doubt, and setteth downe seuerall opinions and the reasons, hee euer setteth downe * the better opinion and his owne last, and so he doth here. (n) For at this day this doubt is settled, hauing beene oftentimes resolued, that seeing the money

Margin: (*) Vid. Sect. 170. 302. 375. (n) 8. E. 4. 4. & 14. 11. H. 4. 62. 17. Ass. p. 2. 17. E. 3. 2. 21. H. 7. Keylway 74. 16. Eliz. Dier 327. Lib. 4. f. 73. in Boroughes case. 21. E. 4. 6.

money is a summe in grosse and collaterall to the title of the land, that the Feoffor must tender the money to the person of the Feoffee according to the latter opinion, and it is not sufficient for him to tender it vpon the land: otherwise it is of a rent that issueth out of the land. But if the condition of a Bond, or feoffment be to deliuer twenty quarters of wheate or twenty load of Timber or such like, the Obligor or Feoffor is not bound to carry the same about, and seeke the Feoffee, but the Obligor or Feoffor before the day must goe to the Feoffee, and know where he will appoint to receiue it, and there it must bee deliuered. And so note a diuersitie betweene money, and things ponderous, or of great weight. If the condition of a Bond or feoffment be to make a feoffment, there it is sufficient (b) for him to tender it vpon the land, because the state must passe by Liuerie.

8.E.4.2. 19.R.2. Det.178.

(b) 2. E.4.3.

¶ *Deins le roialm Dengleterre.* For if he be out of the Realme of England, hee is not bound to seeke him or to goe out of the Realme vnto him. And for that the Feoffee is the cause that the Feoffor cannot tender the money, the Feoffor shall enter into the land, as if he had duly tendered it according to the condition.

¶ *Vn especiall corporall seruice al feoffee.* This is a diuersity betweene a Rent issuing out of land, and a Corporall seruice issuing out of land, for it

sil le feoffor soit sur le terre la prest a paier la mony al feoffee a le iour assesse, & le feoffee adonques ne soit pas la, adonques le feoffor est assouth, & excuse de paymēt de l' mony, pur ceo que nul default est en luy. Mes il semble a ascuns que la ley est contrary, & que default est en luy. Car il est tenus d' querer le feoffee sil soit adonques en ascun auter lieu deins le Roialme d' Engleterr. Come si home soit oblige en vn obligation de 20. li. sur condition endorce sur mesm lobligat, que sil paya a celuy a que lobligation est fait a tiel iour 10. li. adonque lobligation de 20. li. perdra sa force, & serra tenus pur nul, en cest cas il couient a celuy que fist obligation de querer celuy a que lobligation est fait, sil soit deins Engleterre, & al iour assesse de tender a luy les dits 10. li. auterment il forfeitera la summe de 20. li comprise deins l' obligation, &c. Et issint il semble en lauter cas, &c. Et coment q̄ ascuns ont dit, que le condition est dependant sur la terre, vncore ceo ne proue q̄ le

haue said that if the feoffor be vpon the land there ready to pay the money to the feoffee at the day set, & the feoffee bee not then there, then the feoffor is quit and excused of the payment of the money, for that no default is in him. But it seemeth to some that the law is contrary, and that default is in him, for he is bound to seeke the feoffee if hee bee then in any other place within the Realm of England. As if a man be bound in an obligation of 20. pound vpon condition endorced vpon the same obligation, that if hee pay to him to whom the obligation is made at such a day 10. pound, then the obligation of 20. pound shall lose his force and bee holden for nothing. In this case it behooueth him that made the obligation to seek him to whom the obligation is made if he be in England, and at the day set to tender vnto him the said 10. poūd otherwise hee shall forfeit the summe of 20. pound comprised within the obligation, &c. And so it seemeth in the other case, &c. And albeit that some haue

le feaſans de le condition deſtre performe, couient eſtre fait ſur la terr, &c. nient plus que ſi le condition fuit que le feoffor ferra a tiel iour, &c. vn eſpecial corporall ſeruice al feoffee, nient noſmant le lieu ou tiel corporal ſeruice ſerra fait, & tiel cas le feoffor doit faire tiel corporal ſeruice al iour limitte al feoffee, en quecunque lieu Dengleterre que le feoffee eſt, ſil voile auer aduantage, del condition, &c. Iſſint il ſembl en lauter cas. Et il ſemble a eux que il ſerroit pluis properment dit, que leſtate de la terre eſt dependant, ſur la condition, que adire, que le condition eſt dependant ſur la terre, &c. Sed quære, &c.

ſaid that the condition is depending vpon the land, yet this proues not that the making of the condition to be performed, ought to bee made vpon the land, &c. no more then if the condition were that the feoffor at ſuch a day ſhal do ſome eſpeciall corporal ſeruice to the feoffee not naming the place where ſuch corporall ſeruice ſhall be done. In this caſe the feoffor ought to doe ſuch corporall ſeruice at the day limitted to the feoffee in what place ſoeuer of England that the feoffee be, if hee will haue aduantage of the condition, &c. ſo it ſeemeth in the other caſe. And it ſeemes to them that it ſhall bee more properly ſaid, that the eſtate of the land is depending vpon the condition, then to ſay that the condition is depending vpon the land, &c. *Sed quære, &c.*

ſufficeth (as hath beene ſaid) that the rent bee tendered vpon the land, out of which it iſſueth. But Homage or any other ſpeciall Corporall ſeruice muſt be done to the perſon of the Lord, and the Tenant ought by the lawe of conuenience to ſeeke him to whom the ſeruice is to bee done in any place within England. *21.E.3.10. 20.H.6.31. 27.E.3.34. 21.Aſſ.13. 7.E.4.4. 21.E.4.17. 20.E. Auowrie 113. 45.E.3.9. 46.E.3. Barre 216.*

If a man be bound to pay twenty pound at any time during his life at a place certaine, the Obligor cannot tender the money at the place when hee will; for then the Obligee ſhould be bound to perpetuall attendance, and therefore the Obligor in reſpect of the incertainty of the time muſt giue the obligee notice that on ſuch a day at the place limitted, hee will pay the money, and then the obligee muſt attend there to receiue it: for if the obligor then and there tender the money, he ſhall ſaue the penaltie of the Bond for euer. *Mich.22. & 23.Eliz. in Banke le Roy which I my ſelfe heard and obſerued. 19.Eliz. Dyer 354. Lib.8.fol.92. in Franceis caſe.*

The ſame law it is if a man make a feoffment in fee vpon condition, if the Feoffor at any time during his life pay to the Feoffee twenty pound at ſuch a place certaine that then, &c. In this caſe the Feoffor muſt giue notice to the Feoffee when he will pay it, for without ſuch notice as is aforeſaid the tender will not be ſufficient. But in both theſe caſes if at any time the Obligor or Feoffor meete the Obligee or Feoffee at the place he may tender the money. *18.Eliz. Dyer 354.*

If A be bound to E. with condition, that C. ſhall enfeoffe D. on ſuch a day. C muſt giue notice to D. thereof, and requeſt him to be on the land at the day to receiue the feoffment and in that caſe he is bound to ſeeke D. and to giue him notice. *2.E.4.3.& 4.*

¶ *De tender.* or Tendre is a word common both to the Engliſh and French, in Latyn Offerre, and in that ſence, and with that Latyn word it is alwayes vſed in the Common Law. Vide Sect.514. the tender of the halfe Marke. And before Sect. 333.334.337.

Sect. 341.

¶ Here the diuersitie appeareth betweene a summe in grosse, and a rent issuing out of the land, as hath been touched before.

¶ *Uncore il poet eslier, s. de relinquisher son entry ou de auer un Assise.*

Here it appeareth, That if the condition be broken for non payment of the rent, yet if the Feoffor bringeth an Assise for the rent due at that time, he shal neuer enter for the condition broken, because he affirmeth the rent to haue a continuance, and thereby wayueth the condition. And so it is if the rent had had a clause of Distresse annexed vnto it, if the Feoffor had distreyned for the rent, for non payment whereof the condition was broken, he should neuer enter for the condition broken, but he may receiue that rent and acquite the same, and yet enter for the condition broken. But if he accept a rent due at a day after, hee shall not enter for the condition broken, because he thereby affirmeth the lease to haue a continuance.

14. E. 3. Entre congeable 45. 24. Ass. 11. 45. Ass. 5. 6. H. 7. 3. 17. E. 3. 73. Pl. Com. 133. 22. H. 6. 57.

¶ Mes si feoffment ẽ fee soit fait reseruant al feoffor vn annuall rent, et pur d'fault de payment vn re-entrie, &c. en cest case il ne besoigne le tenant a tẽder le rent, quaunt il est arere, forsque sur le terre pur ceo que ceo est Rent issuant hors de la Terre, que est Rent secke. Car si le Feoffor soit seisie vn foits d' cest rent, et puis il vient sur la terre, &c. et le rent luy soit denie, il poet auer Assise de Nouel Disseisin, Car coment que il poet entr̃ p cause de le condition enfreint, &c. uncore il poet eslier, s̃, de relinquisher son entrie, ou de auer vn Assise, &c. Et issint est diuersitie quant al tender de le Rent que est issuant hors de la Terre, et del tender dauter summ̃ en grosse que ne passe issuant hors dascun Terre.

But if a feoffement in fee bee made, reseruing to the feoffor a yerely rent, and for default of payment a re-entrie, &c. in this case the Tenaunt needeth not to tender the rent when it is behind, but vpon the land, because this is a Rent issuing out of the Land, which is a Rent Secke. For if the Feoffor bee seised once of this Rent and after hee commeth vpon the Land, &c. and the rent is denied him, he may haue an Assise of *Nouel Disseisin*: for albeit he may enter by reason of the Condition broken, &c. yet hee may choose either to relinquish his entrie, or to haue an Assise, &c. And so there is a diuersitie as to the tender of a Rent which is issuing out of the land, and of the Tender of another Summe in Grosse, which is not issuing out of any Land.

Section 342.

¶ Et pur ceo il serra bone et sure chose pur celuy que voet faire tiel feoffement en mortgage, de mitter vn especial lieu lou les deniers serõt payes, et le pluis especiall que est mis, le

And therefore it wil be a good and sure thing for him that wil make such feoffement in morgage, to appoint an especial place where the money shall be payd, and the more speciall that it bee put, the

le melior est pur le feoffor. Si come A. infeoffe B. a auer a luy et a ses heires, sur tiel condition, Que si A. paya a B. en le Feast de Saint Michael Larchangell procheine a vener en Esglise cathedrall de Paules en Londres deins quater heures procheine deuant le heure de noone de mesme le feast a le Rood loft de le Rood de le North doore deins mesme le Esglise, ou al tombe de S. Erkenwald, ou al huis de tiel Chappell, ou a tiel piller, deins mesme Lesglise que adonque bien list al auantdit A. et a ses heyres dentrer, &c. en tiel case il ne besoigne de querer le feoffee en auter lieu, ne destre en auter lieu, forsque en le lieu comprise en lendenture, ne destre la pluis longe temps, que le temps specifie en mesme lendenture, pur tender ou payer le money a le Feoffee, &c.

better it is for the Feoffor. As if A. infeoffe B. to haue to him and to his heires, vpon such condition, That if A. pay to B. on the Feast of Saint *Michael* the Arch-Angel next comming, in the Cathedrall Church of Saint *Pauls* in London, within foure houres next before the houre of Noone of the same feast, at the Rood loft of the Rood of the North doore, within the same Church, or at the Tombe of Saint *Erkenwald*, or at the doore of such a Chappell, or at such a pillar within the same Church, that then it shall be lawfull to the aforesayd A. and his heires to enter, &c. In this case he needeth not to seek the Feoffee in an other place, nor to bee in any other place, but in the place comprised in the Indenture, nor to bee there longer than the time specified in the same Indenture, to tender or pay the mony to the feoffee, &c.

¶ Here is good councell and aduice giuen, to set downe in Conueyances euerie thing in certaintie and particularitie, for Certaintie is the mother of Quietnesse and Repose, and Incertaintie the cause of variance and contentions: and for obtaining of the one, and auoyding of the other, the best meane is in all assurances, to take councell of learned and well experienced men, and not to trust onely without aduice to a President. For as the rule is concerning the state of a mans bodie, Nullum medicamentum est idem omnibus, so in the state and assurance of a mans Lands, Nullum exemplum est idem omnibus.

¶ *Al Tombe de Saint Erkenwald, &c.* This Erkenwald was a younger sonne of Anna King of the East Saxons, and was first Abbot of Chersey in Surrey, which he had founded, and after Bishop of London, a holy and deuout man, and lieth buried in the South Ile, about the Quire in Saint Pauls Church, where the Tombe yet remaineth that Lit. speaketh of in this place, hee flourished about the yeare of our Lord, 680. The residue of this Section, and the (&c.) are euident.

*Sect.*343.

¶ Item en tiel case lou le lieu de payment est limitte, le Feoffee nest oblige de receiuer le payment en nul auter lieu forsque en mesme le lieu issint

Also in such case where the place of payment is limitted, the Feoffee is not bound to receiue the payment in any other place but in the same place so limitted.

¶ Hereby it appeareth that the place is but a Circumstance. And therefore if the Obligee receiueth it at any other place, it is sufficient, though he be not bound to receiue it at any other place.

And

And ſo it is if the money be to be paid on ſuch a Feaſt, yet if the money be tendred and receiued at any time before the day, it is ſufficient.

limit. Mes vncore ſi il reſceiuſt le payment en auter lieu, ceo eſt aſſets bone, et auxy fort pur le feoffor, ſicome le receit vſt eſte en meſme le lieu iſſint limit, &c.

But yet if hee do receiue the payment in another place, this is good enough and as ſtrong for the feoffor as if the receipt had been in the ſame place ſo limited, &c.

Sect. 344.

3.H.7.4.b.9.H.7.16. 11.H.7.20.21. 19.E.4.1.b. 47.E.3.24. 22.E.4.24. 37.H.6.26.Li.9.fo.78.Peytoes caſe.

12.H.4.23.

* Peytoes caſe vbi ſupra.

HEreupon are many diuerſities worthie of obſeruation.

Firſt, there is a diuerſitie, when the condition is for payment of money, and when for the deliuerie of a Horſe, a Robe, a Ring, or the like: for where it is for payment of money, there if the Feoffee or Obligee accept an Horſe, &c. in ſatiſfaction, this is good; but if the condition were for the deliuerie of a horſe, or robe, there albeit the obligee or feoffee accept money or any other thing for the Horſe, &c. it is no performance of the condition. The like Law is, if the condition bee to acknowledge a Recogniſance of twentie pounds, &c. if the Obligee or feoffee accept twenty pounds in ſatiſfaction of the condition, it is not ſufficient in Law, * but notwithſtanding ſuch acceptance, the condition is broken. And ſo it is of all other colaterall conditions, though the Obligee or feoffee himſelfe accept it.

ITem en tiel caſe de feoffmēt en mortgage, ſi l feoffor paya al feoffee vn chiual, ou hanap dargent, ou vn annuel dor, ou auter tiel choſe en plein ſatiſfaction del money, & lauter ceo receiuſt, c ē aſſets bon & auxy fort ſicome il vſt receiue la ſumme del money, coment que le chiual, ou lauſ choſe ne fuit de vintiſme part del value de ſum de le money, pur ceo que lauter auoit ceo accept en pleine ſatiſfaction.

ALſo in the caſe of Feoffement in Morgage, if the Feoffor payeth to the Feoffee a Horſe or a Cup of Siluer, or a Ring of Gold, or any ſuch other thing in full ſatisfaction of the money, and the other receiueth it, this is good enough, and as ſtrong as if hee had receiued the ſumme of money, though the horſe or the other thing were not of the twētith part of the value of the ſum of mony, becauſe that the other hath accepted it in ful ſatisfaction

4.H 7 4. Dy.35.H.8.56. 27.H.8.1.

Secondly, in caſe when the condition is for payment of money, there is a diuerſitie when the money is to be payd to the partie, and when to an eſtranger: for when it is to bee payd to an eſtranger, there if the ſtranger accept a horſe or any colaterall thing in ſatiſfaction of the money, it is no performance of the Condition, becauſe the Condition in that caſe is ſtrictly to bee performed. But if the condition be, That a ſtranger ſhall pay to the Obligee or Feoffee a ſum of money, there the Obligee or Feoffee may receiue a horſe, &c. in ſatiſfaction.

Lib.5.fo.17.Pinnels caſe.

26.H.6.tit.Barre 37.

Thirdly, where the condition is for payment of twentie pounds, the Obligor or feoffor cannot at the time appointed pay a leſſer ſumme in ſatiſfaction of the whole, becauſe it is apparant that a leſſer ſumme of money cannot be a ſatiſfaction of a greater. But if the Obligee or Feoffee doe at the day receiue part, and thereof make an acquittance vnder his Seale in full ſatiſfaction of the whole, it is ſufficient, by reaſon the Deed amounteth to an acquittance of the whole. If the Obligor or Leſſor pay a leſſer ſumme either before the day, or at another place than is limitted by the Condition, and the Obligee or Feoffee receiueth it, this is a good ſatiſfaction.

30.E.3.23.

Fourthly, Not onely things in poſſeſſion man be giuen in ſatiſfaction, (whereof Littleton putteth his caſe, but alſo if the Obligee or Feoffee accept a Statute or a Bond in ſatiſfaction of the money it is a good ſatiſfaction.

11.R 2.tit.Barre 343.

If the Obligor or Feoffor be bound by condition to pay an hundred Markes at a certaine day,

day, and at the day the parties doe account together, and for that the Feoffee or Obligee did owe twentie pound to the Obligor or Feoffor, that summe is allowed, and the residue of the hundred Markes paid, this is a good satisfaction, and yet the twentie pound was a Chose in action, and no payment was made thereof, but by way of retayner or discharge 37.*H*.6.26. 46.*E*.3.33. 34.*H*.6.17. 12.*H*.8.1.*b*.

¶ *En pleine satisfaction*. Nota, In satisfaction, and in full satisfaction is all one.

Sect. 345.

ITem si home enfeoffa vn auter sur condition, que il et ses heires rendront a vn estrange home & a ses heires vn annuel rent de 20. s. &c. et si il ou ses heires faylont de payment de ceo, que adonques bien lirroit al feoffor et a ses heires de entrer, ceo est bon cōdition, et vncore en cest cas, coment que tiel annuall payment est appelle en lendenture vn annuall rent, ceo nest pas propermẽt rent. Car sil serroit rent, il couient estre Rent seruice, ou rent charge, ou rent secke, et il nest ascun de eux. Car si lestrange fuit seisie de ceo, et puis il fuit a luy denie, il nauera vnque Assise de ceo, pur ceo que il nest pas issuant hors dascun tenements, et issint lestrange nad ascun remedie si tiel annual rent soit aderere en cest cas, mes que le feoffor ou ses heires poient enter, &c. Et vncore si le feoffor ou ses

ALso if a man infeoffe an other vpon Condition, that hee and his heires shall render to a stranger and to his heires a yearely rent of 20. shillings, &c. and if hee or his heires fayle of payment thereof, that then it shall bee lawfull to the Feoffor and his heires to enter, this is a good Condition, and yet in this case, albeit such annuall payment be called in the Indenture a yearely rent, this is not properly a rent. For if it should be a rent, it must bee Rent Seruice, Rent Charge, or a Rent Secke, and it is not any of these. For if the stranger were seised of this and after it were denied him, hee shall neuer haue an Assise of this, because that it is not issuing out of any Tenements, and so the stranger hath not any remedie if such yearely rent be behind in this case, but that the Feoffor or his heires may enter, &c. And yet if the Feoffor or his heires enter for default of pay-

¶ R*Endront a vn estrãge home vn annuel rent, &c.*

This reseruation is meerely void (a) for the reasons hereafter in this Section alleadged by Littleton, and also for that no Estate moueth from the strãger, and that he is not partie to the Deed. (a) *Lib*.8.*fol*.70.71.

And albeit it bee a voyde reseruation, and can be no rent, and the words of the Condition be that if the feoffee or his heires faile of payment of it (that is, of the annual rent) that then, &c. yet it appeareth that the Condition is good, and annuall Rent shall bee taken for an annuall summe of money in grosse, and not in the proper signification thereof, viz. to bee a Rent issuing out of Land, which is to bee obserued, that words in a Condition shall bee taken out of their proper sence, Vt res magis valeat quam pereat, and so in like cases it is holden (b) in our Bookes. (b) 6.*E*.2.*entr*.*cong*.55. *recipere*. 8.*Ass*.34.*reuertere*.

But if A. bee seised of certaine lands, and A. and B. ioyne in a Feoffment in fee reseruing a rent to them both and their heires, and the Feoffee grant that it shall be lawfull for them and their heires to distreine for the

the rent, this is a good grant of a rent to them both, because hee is partie to the Deed, and the clause of distresse is a grant of the rent to A. and B. as it appeareth before in the Chapter of rents. But if B. had beene a stranger to the Deed, then B. had taken nothing. And vpon this diuersitie are all the Bookes (c) with prima facie seeme to vary, reconciled.

(c) 18.E.3. Ass.381. 26.H.8.2. 13.E.2 feoffments & fails 108. 31.Ass.p.31.

Car sil serra rent, il couient estre rent seruice, rent charge ou rent secke, & il nest nul de eux. This is a good Logicall argument à diuisione, & argumentum à diuisione est fortissimum in lege. Littleton vseth this argument else where, where see more of this matter.

heires entront pur default de payment, adonque tiel rent est ale a touts iours. Et issint tiel rent nest forsque vn peine assesse a le tenant et ses heires, que sils ne voilent payer ceo solonque la forme del Indenture, ils perdront lour terre per lentrie del feoffor ou ses heires pur default de payment. Et en cest cas il semble que le feoffee et ses heires doient querer le estranger et heires sils sont deins Engleterre, pur ceo que nul lieu est limit lou le payment serra fait, & pur ceo que tiel rent nest pas issuant hors dascun terre, &c.

ment: then such rent is taken away for euer. And so such a rent is but as a paine set vpon the tenant and his heires, that if they will not pay this according to the forme of the Indenture, they shall lose their land by the entrie of the Feoffor or his heires for default of payment. And in this case it seemeth that the Feoffee and his heires ought to seeke the stranger and his heires if they bee within *England*, because there is no place limited where the payment shall bee made, and for that such rent is not issuing out of any land, &c.

(d) Vide Sect. 381.

Pur default de payment. Note here seeing it is but a summe in grosse, there need no demand of the rent, for Littleton here sayth, that the Feoffee ought to seeke the person of the stranger to pay him the summe of money, because it is a summe in grosse, and not issuing out of the Land.

Section 346.

A Le feoffor donor, &c. ou a lour heires. Hereby it may seeme that if a man make a Feoffment, Gift, or Lease, that (omitting himselfe) hee may reserue a Rent to his heires. But Littleton is not so to bee vnderstood, his meaning is, that eyther the Feoffor, &c. may reserue the Rent to himselfe only, or to himselfe and his heires. And yet it is holden (e) in our bookes that a man may make a Feoffment in fee reseruing a Rent of forty shillings to the Feoffee for tearme of his life, and

(e) 5.E.3.27.28.

ET hic nota deux choses, Un est, que nul rent (que proprement est dit rent) poit estre reserue sur ascun feoffment, done, ou leas, forsque tantsolement al feoffor, ou al donor, ou al lessor, ou a lour heires, & en nul maner il poit estre reserue a ascun estrang

AND here note two things, one is, That no rent (which is properly said a Rent) may be reserued vpon any feoffment, gift, or lease, but only to the Feoffor, or to the Donor, or to the Lessor, or to their heires, and in no manner it may bee reserued to any strange person. But if

person

person. Mes si deux iointenants font vn leas per fait endent, reseruant a vn de eux vn certaine annuall rent, ceo est assets bon a luy a que l'rent est reserue, pur ceo q̄ il est priuie a le lease & nemy estrange a le leas, &c.

two Ioyntenants make a Lease by Deed indented reseruing to one of them a certaine yearely Rent, this is good enough to him to whom the Rent is reserued, for that hee is priuie to the Lease, & not a stranger to the Lease, &c.

after his decease a pound of Comyne to his heires, that this is good.

If a man make a Feoffement in fee reseruing a Rent to him or his heires it is good (f) to him for tearme of his life, and void to his heire. (f) Lib. 5. fol. 111. Mallories case.

¶ *Mes si 2. iointenants font vn lease per fait indent, &c.*

This case being by Deed indented, is euident, and it hath beene touched before, but if that two Ioyntenants without a Deed indented make a Lease for life reseruing a Rent to one of them, it shall enure to them both in respect of the ioynt reuersion. And so it is of a surrender to one of them, it shall enure to them both. 5. E. 4. 4. a 27. H. 8. 16. Vide Sect. 58.

If two Ioyntenants, the one for life, and the other in fee, ioyne in a Lease for life, or a gift in tayle reseruing a Rent, the Rent shall enure to them both, for if the particular estate determine, they shall be ioyntenants againe in possession. But if tenant for life & he in the reuersion ioyne in a Lease for life or a gift in tayle by Deed reseruing a Rent, this shall enure to the Tenant for life only, during his life, and after to him in the reuersion, for euery one grant that which he may lawfully grant, and if at the Common Law they had made a Feoffment in fee generally, the Feoffee should haue holden of the Tenant for life during his life, and after of him in reuersion, and so it was holden (g) in the Kings Bench. Vide Sect. 58. (g) Mich. 36. & 37. Eliz.

Section 347.

¶ LE second chose est que nul entre, ou reentre (que est tout vn) poit estre reserue, ne done a ascun person forsq̄ tantsolement al feoffor, ou al donor, ou al lessor, ou a lour heires, & tiel reentre ne poit estre grant, a vn auter person. Car si home lessa terre a vn auter pur terme de vie per Indenture, rendant al lessor & a ses heires certaine rent, & pur default de payment vn reentry, &c. si apres le lessor per vn fait granta le reuersion de la terre a vn auter en fee et le tenant at terme de vie atturna, &c. si le rent a-

THe second thing is, that no entrie nor reentrie (which is all one) may bee reserued or giuen to any person but only to the Feoffor or to the Donor, or to the Lessor, or to their heires. And such reentrie cannot bee giuen to any other person. For if a man letteth land to another for tearme of life by Indenture rendring to the Lessor and to his heires a certaine rent, and for default of payment, a reentrie, &c. If afterward the Lessor by a Deed granteth the reuersion of the Land to another in fee, and the Tenant for terme of life, attorne, &c. if the rent bee

¶ *Que nul entrie &c.* Here Littleton reciteth one of the maximes of the Common law, & the reason hereof is, for auoyding of maintenance, suppression of right, and stirring vp of suites: and therefore nothing in action, entrie, or reentrie can be granted ouer; for so vnder colour thereof, pretended titles might bee granted to great mē, whereby right might bee trodden downe, & the weake oppressed, which the Common Law forbiddeth, as men to grant before they be in possession.

¶ *Pur default*

pres soit aderere, le grantee de le reuersion poit distreiner pur le rent, pur ceo que le rent est incident a le reuersion, mes il ne poit entrer en la tre, & ouste le tenant, si-come l'lessor puissoit, ou ses heyres, si le reuersion vst este continue en eux, &c. Et en cest case lentrie est tolle a touts temps. Car le grantee de le reuersion ne poit entrer, Causa qua supra. Et le lessor, ne ses heyres ne poyent enter. Car si le lessor puissoit ent, donques il couient que il seroit en son primer estate, &c. & ceo ne poit estre, pur ceo que il ad alien de luy le reuersion.

after behinde, the grantee of a reuersion may distreine for the rent, because that the rent is incident to the reuersion, but hee may not enter into the land and oust the tenant, as the lessor might haue done or his heires, if the reuersion had beene continued in them, &c. And in this case the entrie is taken away for euer, For the grantee of the reuersion cannot enter. *Causa qua supra.* And the lessor nor his heires cānot enter, for if the lessor might enter, then hee ought to be in his former estate, &c. And this may not bee, because hee hath aliened from him the reuersion.

fault de payment vn reentrie, &c. Hereupon is to bee collected diuers diuersities, first betweene a condition that requireth a reentrie, and a limitation that *Ipso facto* determineth the estate without any entrie. Of this first sort no stranger as Littleton saith, shall take any aduantage, as hath beene said. But of limitations it is otherwise. As if a man make a Lease Quousque that is untill I.S. come from Rome, the Lessor grant the reuersion ouer to a stranger. I.S comes from Rome, the Grantee shall take aduantage of it and enter, because the estate by the expresse limitation was determined.

Register 246. Pl. Com. 27. 34. E. 3. Formedon 68. F. N. B. 201. Lib. 10 fo. 36. Marie Portingtons case.

So it is if a man make a Lease to a woman Quamdiu casta vixerit, or if a man make a Lease for life to a widow, Si tam diu in pura viduitate vixerit. So it is if a man make a Lease for a 100. yeares if the Lessee liue so long, the Lessor grants ouer the reuersion, the Lessee dies, the Grantee may enter, Causa qua supra.

2. Another diuersitie is betweene a condition annexed to a freehold, and a condition annexed to a Lease for yeares.

Brooke tit. Condition in Abb. 11. H. 7. Loppeniin de Bromley 10. E. 52. 10. Ass pl. 24. Pl. Com. 136. 11. H. 7. 17. 19. R. 2. Done 10.

For if a man make a gift in taile or a Lease for life vpon condition, that if the Donee or Lessee goeth not to Rome before such a day, the Lease shall cease or be voide, the Grantee of the reuersion shall neuer take aduantage of this condition, because the estate cannot cease before an entrie, but if the Lease had beene but for yeares, there the Grantee should haue taken aduantage of the like condition, because the Lease for yeares Ipso facto by the breach of the condition without any entrie was voyde, for a Lease for yeares may begin without ceremony, and so may end without ceremony: but an estate of freehold cannot begin nor end without ceremonie. And of a voide thing an estranger may take benefit, but not of a voydable estate by entrie.

Pl. Com. 313. 314. in Soulatiwnes case.

¶ *Al feoffor, ou al donor, &c. ou a lour heires, &c.* Here is to be obserued a diuersity betweene a reseruation of a rent and a reentry, for (as it hath beene said) a rent cannot be reserued to the heire of the Feoffor, but the heire may take aduantage of a condition, which the Feoffor could neuer doe. As if I infeoffe another of an acre of ground vpon condition that if mine heire pay to the Feoffee, &c. 20. shillings, that he and his heires shall reenter, this condition is good, and if after my decease my heire pay the 20. shillings, he shall reenter for he is priuie in blood, and enioy the land as heire to me.

15. E. 4. 14. a.

21. H. 7. 18. a.

¶ *Forsque tantsolement al feoffor, &c. ou a lour heires.* Our Author speaketh here of naturall persons for an example, for if a Bishop, Archdeacon, Parson, Prebend, or any other body politique or Corporate, Ecclesiasticall or Temporall make a Lease, &c. vpon condition, his successor may enter for the Condition broken, for they are priuie in right.

And so if a man haue a Lease for yeares, and demise or grant the same vpon condition, &c. and die, his Executors or Administrators shall enter for the condition broken, for they are priuie in right, and represent the person of the dead.

(y) If Cesty que vse had made a lease for yeares, &c. vpon Condition, the Feoffees should not enter for the Condition broken, for they are privie in estate, but, not privie in blood.

(y) 27. H. 8. 1.

Another diversitie is in case of a Lease for yeares, where the condition is that the Lease shall cease or be voide as is aforesaid, and where the condition is, that the Lessor shall re-enter, for there the Grantee as Littleton saith, shall never take benefit of the condition.

And it is to be observed that where the estate or Lease is Ipso facto voide by the condition or limitation, no acceptance of the rent after can make it to have a continuance; Otherwise it is of an estate or Lease voidable by entrie.

Pl. Com. Brownings Case. 136.

Another diversitie is betweene conditions in Deed whereof sufficient hath beene said before, and conditions in Law. As if a man make a Lease for life, there is a condition in Law annexed unto it, that if the Lessee doth make a greater estate, &c. that then the Lessor may enter. Of this and the like conditions in Law which doe give an entrie to the Lessor, the Lessor himselfe and his heires shall not only take benefit of it, but also his Assignee and the Lord by Escheate every one for the condition in Law broken in their owne time. Another diversitie there is betweene the iudgement of the Common Law whereof Littleton wrote, and the Law at this day by force of the statute (*) of 32. H. 8, cap. 34. (a) For by the Common Law no Grantee or Assignee of the reversion could (as hath beene said) take advantage of a re-entrie by force of any Condition. For at the Common Law, if a man had made a Lease for life reserving a rent, &c. and if the rent be behinde a Re-entrie, and the Lessor grant the reversion over, the Grantee should take no benefit of the condition for the cause before rehearsed. But now by the said Statute of 32. H. 8. the Grantee may take advantage thereof, and upon demand of the rent and non-payment he may re-enter. By which act it is provided, that aswell every person which shall have any grant of the King of any reversion, &c. of any lands, &c. which pertained to Monasteries, &c. as also all other persons being Grantees or Assignees, &c. to or by any other person or persons, and their Heires, Executors, Successors and Assignees shall have like advantage against the Lessees, &c by entrie for non-payment of the rent, or for doing of waste or other forfeiture, &c. as the said Lessors or Grantors themselves ought or might have had. Upon this Act divers resolutions and iudgements have beene given which are necessary to be knowne.

(*) 32. H. 8. cap. 34. in le preamble
(a) 26. H. 6. tit. entre cong. 49

1. That the said Statute is generall, viz. (b) that the Grantee of the reversion of every common person aswell as of the King shall take advantage of conditions.

(b) Pl. Com. Hill & Granges case, 175. 176.

2. That the Statute doth extend to Grants made by the Successors of the King albeit the King be only named in the act.

M. 10. & 11. Eliz. 180. Dier. Ibid.

3. That where the Statute speaketh of Lessees that the same doth not extend to gifts in taile.

14. Eliz. Dier 309. Wynters case.

4. That where the Statute speakes of Grantees and Assignes of the reversion, (d) that an Assignee of part of the state of the reversion may take advantage of the Condition. As if Lessee for life be, &c. and the reversion is granted for life, &c. So if Lessee for yeares, &c. be, and the reversion is granted for yeares, the Grantee for yeares shall take benefit of the Condition in respect of this word (Executors) in the Act.

(d) Pl. Com. Kidwellyes case 69.
Vid. Dier Mich. 14. & 15. Eliz. 309.
Vid. 7. E. 3. 54. Simile adiudged in Commun bance in the Lord Dyers time, P. 17. Eliz. Mich. 14. & 15 Eliz. Dier 309. adiudge Winters case.

5. That a Grantee of part of the reversion, shall not (c) take advantage of the Condition, as if the Lease be of three acres reserving a rent upon condition, and the reversion is granted of two acres, the rent shall be apportioned by the act of the parties, but the condition is destroyed, for that it is entire and against common right.

(c) Lib. 5. fo. 54. Knights case.

6 That in the Kings case the condition in that case is not destroyed but remaines still in the King.

Wynters case, vbi supra. Knights case vbi supra.

7 By act in Law a condition may bee apportioned in the case of a common person, as if a Lease for yeares be made of two acres, one of the nature of Burrough English, the other at the Common Law, and the Lessor having issue two sonnes, dieth, each of them shall enter for the condition broken, and likewise a condition shall be apportioned by the act and wrong of the Lessee, as hath beene sayd in the Chapter of Rents.

Lib. 4. fo. 120. Dumpers case.

8. If a Lease for life bee made, reserving a rent upon condition, &c. the Lessor levies a fine of the reversion, he is Grantee or Assignee of the reversion, but without atturnement he shall not take advantage of the Condition, for the makers of the makers of the Statute intended to have all necessarie incidents observed, otherwise it might be mischievous to the lessee.

Resolued in Dukes case Pasc. 30. Eliz. in Commun Banco. Malleries case, lib. 5. fo. 112. b.

9. There is a diversitie betweene a Condition that is compulsarie, and a Power of Revocation that is voluntarie; for a man that hath a power of revocation, may by his owne act extinguish his power of Revocation in part, as by levying of a fine of part, and yet the power shall remaine for the residue, because it is in nature of a limitation, and not of a Condition, and so it as resolved (b) in the Earle of Shrewsburies case in the Court of Wards, Pasch. 39. Eliz. and Mich. 40. & 41. Eliz.

(b) 14. Eliz. Dyer 30.

10. If the Lessor bargaine and sell the reversion by Deed indented and inrolled, the Bargainee is not in the Per by the Bargainor, and yet he is an Assignee within the Statute.

So if the Leſſor grant the reverſion in fee to the uſe of A. and his heires, A. is a ſufficient Aſſignee within the Statute, becauſe he comes in by the act and limitation of the partie, albeit he is in the Post, and the words of the Statute be, To or By, and they bee Aſſignees to him, although they be not by him: but ſuch as come in meerely by act in Law, as the Lord of the Villeine, the Lord by Eſcheat, the Lord that entreth or claimeth for Mortmaine, or the like, ſhall not take benefit of this Statute.

Lib 5.fo.113. Mallories caſe. Lib 8.fol.92. Tranes caſe.

11 If the Leſſor in the caſe before bargaine and ſel the reverſion by Deed indented and inrolled, or if the Leſſor make a feoffement in fee, and the Leſſee re-enter, the Grauntee or Feoffee ſhall not take any advantage of any Condition, without making notice to the Leſſee.

And ſo was it reſolved in Wynters caſe. Mich.14.&15 Eliz. in Common Banco and oftentimes ſince. V. Dyer 309.

12 Albeit the whole words of the Statute be, for non-payment of the Rent, or for doing of waſt or other forfeiture, yet the Grantees or Aſſignees ſhall not take benefit of everie forfeiture, by force of a condition, but onely of ſuch conditions as either are incident to the reverſion, as Rent, or for the benefit of the ſtate, as for not doing of waſt, for keeping the houſes in reparations, for making of Fences, ſcouring of Ditches, for preſerving of woods, or ſuch like, and not for the payment of any ſumme in Groſſe, deliverie of Corne, wood, or the like, ſo as other forfeiture ſhall be taken for other forfeitures like to thoſe examples which were there put, (videlicet) of payment of Rent, and not doing of waſt, which are for the benefit of the Reverſion.

Section 348.

¶ ITem ſi ſoyt Seignior et tenant, & l'tenant fait un tiel leaſe pur terme de vie, rendant a Leſſor et a ſes hẽres tiel annual rẽt, & pur default de payment un re-entrie, &c. ſi apres l' Leſſor morust ſans heire durant la vie le Tenaunt a terme de vie, per que le reverſion devient al Seignior per voy deſcheate, et puis le rent de le Tenaunt a terme de vie ſoit adereré, l' Seignior poet diſtreyner l' Tenant pur le Rent arere: Mes il ne poet enter en la terre per force del condition, &c. pur ceo que il neſt paſſe heire al Leſſor, &c.

ALſo if Lord and Tenant be, and the Tenant make a Leaſe for terme of life, rendring to the Leſſor and his Heyres ſuch an annuall Rent, and for default of payment, a re-entrie, &c. if after the Leſſor dieth without heire during the life of the Tenant for life, whereby the Reverſion commeth to the Lord by way of Eſcheat, and after the rent of the tenant for life is behind, the Lord may diſtreyn the Tenant for the rent behind, but he may not enter into the Land by force of the condition &c. becauſe that he is not heire to the Leſſor, &c.

¶ *AL Seigniour per voy de Eſcheat, &c.*

19.E.3. Reſceit 14.

Note here it appeareth, That the Lord by Eſcheat ſhall diſtreyne for the Rent, and yet the Rent was reſerved to the Leſſor and his heires, but both Aſſignees in Deed and Aſſignees in Law ſhall have the rent, becauſe the Rent being reſerved of Inheritance to him and his heires, is incident to the reverſion, and goeth with the ſame. But if the Rent were reſerved to him and his Aſſignes, and the Leſſor aſſigned over the reverſion, and dieth, the Aſſignee ſhall not have the Rent after his deceaſe, becauſe the Rent determined by his death, for that it was not reſerved to him, his heires, and Aſſignes.

¶ *Mes il ne poet enter en la terre per force del Condition, &c.*

Hereby it appeareth, That at the Common Law neither Aſſignes indeed, nor Aſſignes in Law could have taken the benefit of either entrie or reentrie, by force of a condition.

¶ *Pur ceo que il neſt paſſe heire al Leſſor, &c.*

(f) 21.H.7.18. 17.Aſſ 20. 29.E.3.Gard 113.114. 28.Aſſ.pl.18. Lib.7.fol 7. The Earle of Bedfords caſe.

The Gardein in Chivalrie or in Socage ſhal in the right of the heire take benefit of a Condition by entrie or re-entrie, by the Common Law, and ſo it is here implied.

Section 349.

¶ Item si terre soit graunt a vn home pur terme de deux ans sur tiel condition, que sil payeroit al grantor deins les dits deux ans 40. Markes adonques il aueroit la terre a luy et a ses heyres, &c. en cest case si le Grantee enter per force de le Grant sans ascun liuerie de seisin fait a luy per le Grantor, et puis il paya al Grauntor les 40. Markes deins les deux ans, vncore il nad riens en la terre forsque pur terme de deux ans, pur ceo que nul liuerie de Seisin a luy fuit fait al commencement. Car sil aueroit Franktenement et fee en cest case, pur ceo que il ad performe le condition, donque il aueroit Franktenement per force del prime graunt, lou nul liuerie de Seisin de ceo fuit fait, que serroit inconuenient, &c. Mes si le Grantor vst fait liuerie de seisin al Grantee per force de la Grant, donque aueroit le Grantee le Franktenement et le fee sur mesme le condition.

Also if land bee graunted to a man for terme of two yeares, vpon such condition, That if hee shall pay to the Grauntor within the sayd two yeares fortie Marks, then he shall haue the Land to him and to his Heyres, &c. In this case if the Grantee enter by force of the Grant, without any Liuerie of Seisin made vnto him by the Grauntor, and after he payeth the Grauntor the fortie Markes within the two yeares, yet he hath nothing in the land but for terme of two yeares, because no liuerie of Seisin was made vnto him at the beginning: for if he should haue a freehold and fee in this case, because he hath performed the condition, then he should haue a freehold by force of the first Grant, where no liuerie of Seisin was made of this, which would be inconuenient, &c. but if the Grauntor had made Liuerie of Seisin to the Grantee, by force of the Graunt then should the Grauntee haue the Freehold and the Fee vpon the same condition.

¶ Here sixe things are to be obserued: First, Littleton here putteth an example of a condition precedent. Secondly, That such a Condition which createth an estate may be made by Paroll without Deed. Thirdly, That Liuerie of Seisin in this case must be made before the Lessee enter, (as Littleton here saith at the beginning) for after his entrie liuerie made to him that is in possession is voyd, as hath beene sayd. Fourthly, That if no Liuerie of Seisin be made, that no Fee simple doth passe, although the money be paid. Fifthly, That it is inconuenient, that the Fee simple should passe in this case without liuerie of seisin. Sixtly, That Argumentum ab inconuenienti, is forcible in Law, as often hath been and shall be obserued. See more of this kind of condition in the Section next following. *V. Sect.* 66.

¶ *Et a ses heires, &c.* Here (&c.) implieth an estate in taile, or a Lease for life.

Sect.

Sect. 350.

¶ O*Re il ad fee simple conditionall, &c.* The like is of an Estate in taile or for life. Many are of opinion against Littleton in this case, and their reason is, because the Fee simple is to commence upon a condition precedent, and therefore cannot passe untill the condition be performed: And that here Littleton of a Condition precedent doth (before the performance thereof) make it subsequent: and for proofe of their opinion they auouch many successions of authorities that no Fee simple should passe before the condition performed. 31. E.1.tit. Feoffments & Faits 119. A letteth a Mannor to B. for term of twenty yeres, and the Deed would, That after the terme of twentie yeares that B. and his heirs should hold the sayd Mannor for euer by twelue pounds rent, A. taketh a wife and dieth before the term be past, the wife of A. demands Dower. And there Wavland chiefe Justice saith, That the Fee and the franktenement doth repose in the person of the Lessor untill the terme be past, for before that, the condition is not performed, for if the Lessor had aliened the land before the end of the terme, B. should not recouer by a Writ of Assise, and by the death of the Lessor the chiefe Lord should haue had the wardship

31.E.1.tit.Feoffments & Faits 119.

¶ ITem si terre soit grant a un home pur terme de 5. ans, sur condition, que s'il pay al Grantor deins les deux primer ans 40. Markes, que adonque il aueroit fee, ou autrement forsque pur terme de les v. ans, et liuerie de Seisin est fait a luy pur force de le graunt, ore il ad fee simple conditionall, &c. Et si en ceo case le Grauntee ne paia my al Grantor les 40. Markes deins les primers deux ans, donques immediate apres mesmes les deux ans passes, le fee et le franktenement est, et serra adiudge en le Grantor, pur ceo que le Grantor ne poet apres les dits deux ans maintenant enter sur le Grauntee, pur ceo que le Grantee ad uncore titl per trois ans dauer et occupier la terre per force de mesme le grant. Et issint pur ceo que le condition del part le Grantee est enfreint, et le Grauntor ne poet entrer la Ley mittera le fee et le franktenement en le Grauntor. Car si Grantee en cest case fait wast, donques apres le enfreinder de le condition, &c. et apres les deux

ALso if Land be granted to a man for term of fiue yeares, vpon condition, That if he pay to the Grauntor within the two first yeares fortie Markes, that then he shall haue fee, or otherwise but for terme of the fiue yeares, and liuerie of Seisin is made to him by force of the Grant, now he hath a fee simple conditionall, &c. And if in this case the Grauntee doe not pay to the Grantor the fortie Markes within the first 2 yeares, then immediately after the sayd two yeares past, the fee & the freehold is and shall bee adiudged in the Grauntor, because that the Grauntor cannot after the sayd two yeares presently enter vpon the Grauntee, for that the Grauntee hath yet title by three yeares to haue and occupie the land, by force of the same Grant. And so because that the condition of the part of the Grauntee is broken, and the Grauntor cannot enter, the Law will put the fee and the Freehold in the Grauntor: for if the Grauntee in this case makes Wast, then after the breach of the condition, &c. and after the two

deux ans, le grantor auera son briefe de wast. Et ceo est bone proofe adonque que le reuersion est en luy, &c.

yeares, the Grauntor shall haue his Writ of Waste. And this is a good proofe then, that the reuersion is in him, &c.

of the heire of the Lessor, and by iudgement the wife recouered Dower, for the termor could not haue fee, all which be the words of that Booke.

11. E. 2. tit. voucher 265. I letteth Lands to B for eight yeares, and if the Lessor pay not a hundred Markes to the Lessee at the end of the tearme, that then he shall haue fee: by the non-payment of the money. The fee and franktenement accrueth to him, and before, the Lessee cannot bee impleaded in a Præcipe, neyther shall he vouche. *12. E. 2. tit. voucher 265.*

(x) 7. E. 3. 10. I. letteth certaine lands to N. for the tearme of ten yeares, rendring a hundred shillings by the yeare to him and his heires, and granted by deed, that if he held the lands ouer to him and his heires, that he should render by the yeare twenty pounds, the Lessor during the tearme brought an Action of debt for the rent. And there Herle Chiefe Iustice of the Common Pleas giueth the rule, that during the tearme the Lessee had but for yeares, and therefore the Action of Debt maintenable. *(x) 7. E. 3. 10. Pl. Com. Sayes case 272.*

(y) 44. E. 3. tit. attaint. 22. and 43. Ass. p. 41. D. and A. infeoffe the two Plaintifes in the Assise, they let those lands to S. for tearme of nine yeares vpon Condition, that if the Plaintife in the Assise pay a hundred shillings to S. during the tearme that S shall haue it but for nine yeares, and if they pay it not that S. shall haue fee. S. continueth his estate by one yeare, and after granteth his estate to one H which H. continueth his estate by two yeares, and granted the residue of the tearme to R. and within the tearme of nine yeares the Plaintifes in the Assise pay the hundred shillings to S. R. continueth his possession after the tearme, and infeoffeth D which infeoffeth the Lord Furniuall, against whom and others without any claime or entrie made by the Plaintifes, after the nine yeares ended, hee brought his Assise, and after adiournment recouered. *(y) 44. E. 3. tit. attaint. 22. 43. Ass. p. 41.*

(z) 10. E. 3. 39. & 40. R. doth let certaine lands to I. for tearme of twelue yeares, and in suretie of his tearme he maketh a Charter of the fee vpon Condition, that if hee bee disturbed within the tearme, that he cannot hold the lands vntill the end of the tearme, that then he shall hold the lands to him and his heires for euer, and seisin was deliuered vpon the one Charter and the other. R. within the tearme plowed and sowed the land, and tooke the profits against the will of I. and I. vpon this disturbance had fee and recouered in Assise. *(z) 10. E. 3. 39. 40. 10. Ass. 15. tit. Ass. 161. Pl. Com. Brownings case 135.*

6. R. 2. tit. Quid iuris clamat. 20. If a Lease be made for a tearme vpon Condition, if the Lessee pay a certaine summe within the tearme, that then he shall haue fee, if hee pay the money hee shall haue the fee, but if before the day of payment the Lessor leuieth a fine to another the Lessee ought to attorne by protestation, and if he pay the money, the Conusee shall haue it, and the Conusee shall haue the rent reserued vntill the day of payment, and if Land be letten for tearme of yeares vpon Condition, that if the Lessee be ousted within the tearme by the Lessor, that hee shall haue fee, if hee be ousted, he shall haue fee by the Condition, and notwithstanding hee shall not haue any Assise, but hee must hap possession after the ouster, and of this he shall haue an Assise *6. R. 2. tit. quid iuris clamat 20.*

And generally the Bookes (*) are cited that make a diuersitie betweene a Condition precedent, and a Condition subsequent. *(*) 15. H. 7. 1. a. 14 H. 8. 18. 20. 3. H. 6. 6. b.*

And lastly, they cite Dier, (a) 10. Eliz 281. and in Say and Fullers case; Pl. Com 272. the opinions of Dyer and Browne. *(a) Dyer 10. Eliz. 281. Pl. Com. 272.*

Notwithstanding all this there are those that defend the opinion of Littleton, both by reason and authoritie. By reason for that by the rule of Law a liuery of seisin must passe a present Freehold to some person, and cannot giue a Freehold in futuro, as it must doe in this case, if after liuery of seisin made the Freehold and Inheritance should not passe presently, but expect vntill the Condition be performed, and therefore if a Lease for yeares bee made to beginne at Michaelmas, the remaynder ouer to another in fee, if the Lessor make liuery of seisin before Michaelmas the liuery is void, because if it should worke at all it must take effect presently and cannot expect. *Vide Litt. in the Chapter of Tenants for yeares.*

Secondly, they say that when the Lessor makes liuery to the Lessee, it cannot stand with any reason that against his owne liuery of seisin a Freehold should remayne in the Lessor, seeing there is a person able to take it. But if a man by Deed make a Lease for yeares the remaynder to the right heires of I. S. and the Lessor make liuery to the Lessee secundum formam chartæ this liuery is void, because during the life of I. S. his right heire cannot take (for nemo est hæres viuentis) and in that case the Freehold shall not remayne in the Lessor, and expect the death of I. S. during the tearme, for albeit I. S. die during the tearme, yet the remaynder is void because a liuery of seisin cannot expect.

makes a Charter to the Lessee, and thereby doth grant unto him, that if he pay unto the Lessor a hundred Markes during the tearme, that then he shall have and hold the Lands to him and to his heires.

Pl. Com. in Nichols case 487. In this case, say they, there need no livery of seisin, but doth enure as an executorie grant by increasing of the state, and in that case, without question, the Fee simple passeth not before the Condition performed.

And therefore Littleton warily putteth his case of an estate made all at one time by one Conveyance, and a livery made thereupon.

For Littleton himselfe in the Section before sayth, That in that case without a livery nothing passeth of the Freehold and Inheritance.

(d) 10. E. 3. 54. And this diversitie (say they) is proved by Bookes, and thereupon they cite (d) 10 E 3. 54. in a Writ of Dower, the Tenant vouched to warrantie, the vouchee as to part pleaded that the husband was never seised of any estate whereof she might bee endowed, as to the residue the tenant pleaded that he lessed to the husband in gage upon Condition, that if the Lessor paid ten Markes at a certaine day, that he should re-enter, and if hee fayled of payment, that the Land should remayne to the husband and his heires, which must be intended to be done by one entire Act, and pleaded that he paid the money at the day which is allowed to bee a good plea, Ergo, the Fee simple passe[illegible] by the Livery, otherwise the plea had amounted that the husband was never seised, &c. And say they that it cannot be intended, that the Judges should bee of one opinion in Trinitie Tearme, and of another opinion in Michaelmasse Tearme in the same yeare, and therefore (they hold) their severall opinions, are in respect of the said diversitie of the cases.

(c) 32. E. 3. tit. garr. 30. (c) 32. E. 3. tit garr. 30. A Tenant by the curtesie made a Lease for yeares, & in surety of the tearme, &c. made a Charter in Fee simple, and made Livery according to the Charter (note a speciall mention made of Livery in this case) and issue being taken in an Assise, whether the

Tenant

Tenant by the course se demised in fee, upon the speciall matter found, it was adiudged that a Fee simple passed, and that the heire might enter for a forfeiture, which say they in case of a Livery is an expresse iudgement in the point agreeing with the opinion of Littleton.

(f) 43.E.3.35. in an Action of waste against one in Lands which hee held for teafme of yeares, Belknap pleaded thus for the Defendant, that the Defendant was seised in fee, and infeoffed the Plaintife, &c. and after the Plaintife demised the Land backe againe to the Defendant for yeares upon condition, that if the Defendant paid certaine money, &c. that then the Defendant might retaine the land to him and to his heires, and if not, the Plaintife might enter, &c. and pleaded that the tearme endured, and that the day of payment was not come, and demanded iudgement, if the Plaintife may mayntaine an Action of waste, inasmuch as the Defendant had now a Fee simple, and shewed forth the Indenture of Lease with the condition, (which agreeth with Littletons case) all being done at one time, and by one Deed, and a Livery intended, and with Littletons opinion also. It is true, say they, that Cauendish as counsell with the Plaintife offered to demurre, but never proceeded. (g) Vide 20. Ass. pl.20. (f) 43.E.3.35.

(g) 20. Ass. Pl.20.

Other Authorities they cite, but these (as I take it) are the principall, and therefore for avoyding of tediousnesse, having I feare beene too long upon this point, the others I omit. Only this they adde that Littleton had seene and considered of the said Bookes, and have set downe his opinion where livery of seisin is made upon a Conveyance made at one time, as hath beene said, that he hath Fee simple conditionall.

Benigne lector vtere tuo iudicio, nihil enim impedio. Conditio beneficialis quæ statum construit benigne secundum verborum intentionem est interpretanda, odiosa autem quæ statum destruit stricte secundum verborum proprietatem est accipienda. Lib.8.fo.90. Frances case.

A Lease is made to a man and a woman for their lives upon condition, that which of them two shall first marrie, that one shall have fee, they entermarrie, neyther of them shall have fee, for the incertaintie.

Note if the condition be to increase an estate, (that is to say,) to have fee upon payment of money to the Lessor or his heires at a certaine day, before the day the Lessor is attainted of treason or felony, and also before the day is executed, now is the condition become impossible by the act and offence of the Lessor, and yet the Lessee shall not have fee because a precedent condition to encrease an estate must be performed, and if it become impossible, no estate shall rise.

¶ *Pur ceo que le grantor ne poet enter, &c.* **Regularly when any man** will take advantage of a condition, if he may enter he must enter, and when he cannot enter he must make a clayme, and the reason is for that a free-hold and inheritance shall not cease without entry or clayme, and also the feoffor or Grantor may waive the condition at his pleasure. *Pl.Com. Browning & Bestons case, 133.b.*

As if a man grant an Advowson to a man and to his heires upon condition, that if the Grantor, &c. pay 20. pound on such a day, &c. the state of the Grantee shall cease or bee utterly void. The Grantor payeth the mony yet the state is not revested in the Grantor before a claym, and that clayme must be made at the Church. (d) And so it is of a reversion or remainder of a Rent or Common or the like, there must be a clayme before the state be revested in the Grantor by force of the condition, and that clayme must be made upon the land. *Vid. Littleton cap. Villein.* *(d) Pl.Com. Brownings case, 133.b.*

A fortiori in case of a Feoffment which passeth by Livery of seisin there must be a re-entry by force of the condition before the state be voide. *42.E.3.1.*

If a man bargaineth and selleth land by Deed indented and inrolled with a Prouiso that if the Bargainer pay, &c. that then the state shall cease and be voide, he payeth the money, the state is not revested in the Bargainer before a re-entry, and so it is if a bargaine and sale be made of a Reversion Remainder Advowson, Rent, Common, &c And so it is if lands be devised to a man and his heires upon condition, that if the Devisee pay not 20. pound at such a day, that his estate shall cease and be voyde; the money is not paid, the state shall not bee vested in the heire before an entrie. And so it is of the Reversion or Remainder, an Advowson, Rent, Common, or the like. *Lib.2 fo.50. Sir Hugh Cholmeleys case.*

Quere if ye ... hath any right to the Estate ...

But the said rule hath divers exceptions. First, in this present case of Littleton, for that he can make no entrie, hee shall not be driven to make any clayme to the reversion, for seeing by construction of Law the freehold and inheritance passeth Maintenant out of the Lessor, by the like construction, the freehold and inheritance by the default of the Lessee shalbe revested in the Lessor without entrie or clayme. *Vid. lib.1 fol.174. Digs case. 20.E.4.18.19.*

2. If I grant a Rent charge in fee out of my land upon condition, there if the condition be broken, the rent shall be extinct in my land, because I (that am in possession of the land) neede make no clayme upon the land, and therefore the Law shall adiudge the rent voyde without any clayme. *Pl Com. Brownings case, 133.b. 20.E.4.19.*

3. If a man make a feoffment unto me in fee upon condition that I shall pay unto him 20. poand at a day, &c. before the day I lette unto him the land for yeares reserving a rent, and *20.E.4.19. 20.H 7.4 b.*

after faile of payment the Feoffee shall retaine the land to him and to his heires, and the rent is determined and extinct for that the Feoffor could not enter, nor need not clayme vpon the land for that he himselfe was in possession, and the condition being collaterall is not suspended by the Lease, otherwise it is of rent reserued.

Lib.1.174. Digges case. 4. If a man by his Deed in consideration of fatherly loue, &c. couenant to stand seised to the vse of himselfe for life, and after his decease to the vse of his eldest sonne in taile, the remainder to his second sonne in taile, the remainder to his third sonne in fee with a Prouiso of reuocation, &c. the father doth make a reuocation according to the Prouiso, the whole estate is maintenant reuested in him without entrie or clayme for the cause aforesaid

¶ *Le grantee ad vncore title pur 3.ans.* **By this it appeareth that** albeit the Lessee had Pro tempore a fee simple, yet after that fee simple is deuested out of him, and vested in the Lessor he shall hold the lands for three yeares by the expresse limitation of the parties.

Pl. Com. in Fulmerstons case. 107.b. If a man make a Lease for 40. yeares, the Lessee afterwards taketh a Lease for 20. yeares vpon condition that if he doth such an act, that then the Lease for 20. yeares shall be voide, and after the Lessee breake the condition, by force whereof the second Lease is voide, notwithstanding the Lease for 40. yeares is surrendred, for the condition was annexed to the Lease for 20. yeares, but the surrender was absolute. So it is if a man make a Lease for 40. yeares, and the Lessor grant the reuersion to the Lessee vpon condition, and after the condition is broken, the tearme was absolutely surrendered. And the diuersitie is when the Lessor grants the reuersion to the Lessee vpon condition, and when the Lessee grants or surrenders his estate to the Lessor, for a condition annexed to a surrender may reuest the particular estate, because the surrender is conditionall. But when the Lessor grants the reuersion to the Lessee vpon condition, there the condition is annexed to the reuersion and the surrender absolute.

7.E.4.29. 14.E.4.6. 45.E.3.

8.E.2. Ass. 395. A gardeine in Chiualry tooke a feoffment of the infant within age that was in his ward, and the infant brought an Assise, and the Gardein shall be adiudged a Disseisor which prooueth that the feoffment as against the infant was voide, and yet by acceptance thereof the interest of the Gardein was surrendred.

30.E.3.27. A man maketh a Lease for terme of life by Deede, reserving the first seuen yeares a Rose, and if the Lessee will hold, the land after the seuen yeares, to pay a rent in money, the Lessee will not hold ouer, but surrender his tearme, In this case in iudgement of Law he had but a tearme for seuen yeares. And so it is if a man make a Lease for life, and if the Lessee within one yeare pay not 20. shillings, that he shall haue but a tearme for two yeares if he pay not the money the estate for life is determined, and he shall haue the land but for two yeares.

¶ *Ceo est bone proofe adonques que le reuersion est in luy, &c.* **Here is** implyed that no man can haue an action of waste, vnlesse the reuersion be in him, and by the Authority of our Author the reason of a case, and well applyed is a good proofe in Law.

Section 351.

¶ **MEs en tiels cases de feoffment sur condition, lou le feoffor poit loyalment enter pur le condition enfreint, &c. la le feoffor nad le franktenemēt deuant son entrie, &c.**

BVt in such cases of feoffment vpon condition, where the feoffor may lawfully enter for the condition broken, &c. there the feoffor hath not the freehold before his entrie, &c.

This vpon that which hath beene said is euident and needeth no further explanation.

Sect. 352.

¶ **ITem si feoffment soit fait sur tiel condition, que l'feoffee donera le terre al feoffor,**

ALso if a feoffment be made vpon such condition that the feoffee shall giue the land to

3. Marie 134. Dier 14. Eliz. Dier. 311.b. 2.H.4.5. 44.E.3.9. Lib.2.fo.79.80.81. in Seignior Cromwells case.

¶ *Qve le feoffee donera, &c.* Here is no time limitted, therefore the Feoffee by the Law hath time du-

for, & a la feme del feoffor, a auer & tener a eux, & a les heyres de lour deux corps engendres, & pur default de tiel issue, le remainder al droit heyres le feoffor. En ceo cas si le baron deuy, viuant la feme, deuant ascun estate en le taile fait a eux, &c. donques doit le feoffee per la ley faire estate a la feme cy pres le condition, et auxy cy pres lentent de le condition que il poit faire, cestascauoir, de lesser la terre al fem̃ pur terme de vie sans impeachment de wast, le remainder apres son decease a les heyres de corps sa baron de luy engendres, & pur default de tiel issue, le remainder as droit heires le baron. Et la cause pur que le lease serra en cest cas a la feme sole sans impeachment de wast, est pur ceo q̃ le condition est, q̃ lestate serra fait al baron & a sa feme en taile. Et si tiel estate vst este fait en le vie le baron, donques apres le mort le baron el vst ewe estate ent en le taile: quel estate est sans impeachment de wast; Et issint il est reason, que cy pres que

the feoffor, and to the wife of the feoffor, to haue & to hold to them and to the heires of their two bodyes engendred, and for default of such issue the remainder to the right heires of the feoffor. In this case if the husband dyeth liuing the wife before any estate in taile made vnto them, &c. then ought the feoffee by the law to make an estate to the wife as neere the condition, and also as neere to the entent of the condition as he may make it, That is to say, to let the land to the wife for terme of life without impeachment of waste the remainder after his decease to the heires of the body of her husband on her begotten, and for default of such issue the remainder to the right heires of the husband. And the cause why the lease shall bee in this case to the wife alone without impeachment of waste is for that the condition is, that the estate shall be made to the husband & and to his wife in taile. And if such estate had been made in the life of the husband, then after the death of the husband she should haue

ring his life, vnlesse he be hastened by the request of the Feoffor or the heires of his body, as Littleton saith in the next Section.

¶ *Si le baron deuie, &c.* But in this case if the Feoffee dyeth before any Feoffment made then is the condition broken, because he made not the estates, &c. within the time prescribed by the Law. But if the feoffment be made vpon condition that the Feoffee before the feast of St Michael the Archangell next following giue the land to the Feoffor and to his wife in taile vt supra, and before the day the Feoffee dyeth, the state of the heire of the Feoffee shall be absolute, because a certaine time is limitted by the mutuall agreement of the parties, within which time the condition becommeth impossible by the act of God as hath beene said before, and therefore it is necessary when a day is limited, to adde to the condition, that the Feoffee or his heires doe performe the condition, but when no time is limitted, then the Feoffee at his perill must performe the condition during his life (although there be no request made) or else the Feoffor or his heires may re-enter. 15.H.7.13. 33.H.6.26.27. 9.Eliz. Dier.262. Pl.Com.456. Lib.2.fo.79. Seignior Cromwells case.

¶ *Fait a eux, &c.* Here the (&c.) implyeth according to the condition with the remainder ouer.

¶ *Al feoffor & a la feme, &c.* Here it appeareth that albeit the Feme bee a stranger, yet the Feoffee is not bound to make it within conuenient time, because the Feoffor who is priuy to the condition is to take Joyntly 27.E.3. Dower 135. Seignior Cromwells case, Vbi supra.

ioyntly with her. And so it is if the condition be to enfeoffe the Feoffor and an estranger, the Feoffee hath time during his life vnlesse he be hastened by request. Otherwise it is (as hath beene said) where the condition is to enfeoffe a stranger or strangers onely.

If a man make a feofment in fee, vpon condition that the Feoffee shal make a gift in taile to the Feoffor, the remainder to a stranger in fee, there the Feoffee hath time during his life, as is aforesayd,

home poit faire estate a lentent de condition, &c. q̃ il serroit fait, &c. coment que el ne poit auer estate en taile si come el puissoit auer si le done en le taile vst estre fait a sa baron et a luy en le vie sa baron.

had an estate in taile, which estate is without impeachment of waste. And so it is reason, that as neere as a man can make the estate to the intent of the condition, &c. that it should bee made, &c. albeit she cannot haue estate in taile, as she might haue had if the gift in taile had been made to her husband and to her in the life of her husband, &c.

Seignior Cromwels case vb. sup.

because the Feoffor who is partie and priuie to the condition, is to take the first estate. But if the Condition were to make a gift in taile to a stranger, the remainder to the Feoffor in fee, there the Feoffee ought to doe it in conuenient time, for that the stranger is not priuie to the condition, and he ought to haue the profits presently, as before hath beene sayd.

¶ *De faire estate al feme cy pres le condition, & auxy cy pres lentent del Condition que il poet faire, &c.*

A. infeoffe B. vpon condition that B. shall make an estate in Frankmarriage to C. with one such as is the daughter of the Feoffor; in this case he cannot make an estate in Frankmarriage, because the estate must mooue from the Feoffee, and the daughter is not of his bloud, but yet he must make an estate to them for their liues, for this is as neere the Condition as hee can. And so it is if the Condition be, to make to A. (which is a meere Lay man) an estate in frankalmoigne, yet must he make an estate to him for his life, for the reason heere yeilded by Litleton.

A diuersitie is to be vnderstood betweene conditions that are to create an estate, and conditions that are to destroy an estate: for here it appeareth, That a condition that is to create an estate, is to be performed by construction of Law, as neere the condition as may be, and according to the entent and meaning of the condition, albeit the letter and words of the condition cannot be performed: but otherwise it is of a condition that destroyeth an estate, for that is to be taken strictly, vnlesse it be in certaine speciall cases: and of this somewhat hath beene sayd before in this Chapter.

30. H. 8. tit. Condit. Br. 190. V. 33. H. 8. tit. Ioint. Br. 62.

As if a man morgage his land to W. vpon Condition, that if the Morgagor and I. S. pay twentie shillings at such a day to the Morgagee, that then he shall re-enter, the Morgagor dieth before the day, I. S. payes the money to the Morgagee, this is a good performance of the condition, and yet the letter of the condition is not performed. But if the Morgagor had beene aliue at the day, and he would not pay the money, but refused to pay the same, and I. S. alone had tendred the money, the Morgagee might haue refused it. But if a man make a lease to two for yeares, with a prouiso, If the Lessees die during the terme, the Lessor shall re-enter, one Lessee alien his part and die, the Lessee cannot re-enter, but the Assignee shall enioy the terme so long as the Suruiuor liueth, and the reason is, because the Lease by the prouiso is, Not to cease till both be dead. But in the former case, albeit the Morgagor be dead, yet the act of God shall not disable I. S. to pay the money, for thereby the Morgagee receiues no preiudice: And so it is in that case, if I. S. had died before the day, the Morgagor might haue payd it.

Lib. 2. fo. 79. 80. 81. Seignior Cromwels case. 2. H. 4. 5.

And here is to be obserued a diuersitie when the Feoffee dieth, for then (as hath beene sayd) the condition is broken, and when the Feoffor dieth, for then the state is to bee made as neere the intent of the Condition as may be.

¶ *Al feme pur terme de sa vie sans impeachment de wast.*

Here it appeareth, That this estate for life ought to be without impeachment of wast, and yet if the wife doth accept of an estate for life, without this clause, without impeachment of wast, it is good, because the state for life is the substance of the Grant, and the priuiledge to be without impeachment of wast is colaterall, and onely for the benefit of the wife, and the omission of it onely for the benefit of the heire.

2. H. 4. 5. Seignior Cromwels case vb. supra.

Also if the wife take husband before request made, and then they make request, and the state

is

is made to the husband and wife, during the life of the wife this is a good performance of the condition, albeit the estate be made to the husband and wife: where Littleton saith it is to bee made to the wife, but it is all one in substance, seeing that the limitation is during the life of the wife.

¶ *Sauns impeachment de Wast*, Absque impetione vasti, (that is) without any challenge or impeachment of Wast, and by force hereof the Lessee may cut downe the Trees and conuert them to his owne vse. Otherwise it is if the words were, Sauns impeachment per ascun Action de Wast, for then the discharge extends but to the Action, and not to the Trees themselues, and in that case the Lessor shall haue them. *See in my Reports lib.* 11. *fo* 83. *Lib.* 9 *fo.* 9. *li.* 2. 23.

And it is to be obserued, That after the decease of the husband the state is not to bee made to the wife and the heires of her bodie by her late husband ingendred, and so to haue an estate of Inheritance as she should haue had by suruiuor, if the estate had beene made according to the condition, but onely an estate for life without impeachment of wast, &c. for that by the authoritie of Littleton is not so neere the intent of the condition, as the case that Littleton putteth. But I will search no further into this case, but leaue it to the learned and iudicious Reader.

¶ *Et apres son decesse a les heires del corps le Baron de luy engendres.*

Note here, admit that there were two Issues in taile, the remainder shall presently vest onely in the eldest, and yet if he dieth without Issue, it shall per formam doni vest in the youngest, as hath beene sayd in the Chapter of Estate taile: and so it is tacite proued heere; for otherwise the condition (if there were two issues) could not be performed.

Sect. 353.

¶ ITem en cest case si le baron et la feme ont issue, et deuiont deuant le done en le Taile fait a eux &c. Donques le Feoffee doit faire estate al Issue et a les heires de corps son pere et son mere engendres, et pur default de tiel Issue le remainder a les droit heires le Baron, &c. Et mesm la Ley est en auters cases semblables. Et si tiel Feoffee ne voet faire tiel estate, &c. quaunt il est reasonablement requise per eux que deuoyent auer estate per force de le condition, &c. donque poet le Feoffor ou ses heyres enter.

ALso in this case if the husband and wife haue Issue, & die before the gift in taile made to them, &c. then the feoffee ought to make an estate to the Issue, and to the heires of the bodie of his father and his mother begotten, and for default of such Issue, &c. the remainder to the right heires of the husband, &c. And the same Law is in other like cases: and if such a Feoffee will not take such estate, &c. when he is reasonably required by them which ought to haue the state by force of the Condition, &c. then may the Feoffor or his heires enter.

¶ *Quant il est reasonablement requise per eux queux deuoient auer estate per force de le Condition.*

Note here it appeareth, That the Feoffee hath time during his life to make the estate, vnlesse he be reasonably required by them that are to take the estate. This is to bee intended of parties or priuies, and not of meere strangers, for there (as hath beene sayd) the state must be made in conuenient time.

And concerning the request it is to be knowen, that when the request is made, the partie or priuy must request the feoffee at a time certaine, to be vpon the land, and to make the state according to the condition, for seeing no time certaine is prescribed for the making of the state, and it is incertain when the request shall bee made, such request and notice must be made as hath bin sayd before in this chap. Of this Section, with the (&c.) there needeth not, vpon that which hath been said, any farther explication.

Sect. 354.

¶ ITem si feoffmẽt soit fait sur condition, que le feoffee re-infeoffer plusr͂s hõe͂s a auer et tener a eux et a lour heires a touts iours, et touts ceux que deuoient auer estat͂ moront deuant ascun estat͂ fait a eux, donque doit l' feoffee faire estate al hẽre celuy que suruesquist de eux, a auer & tener a luy et a les heires celuy que suruesquist.

ALso if a Feoffement bee made vpon condition, That if the feoffee shal re-enfeoffe many men, to haue and to hold to them and to their heirs for euer, & al they which ought to haue estate, die before any estate made to them, then ought the feoffee to make estate to the heire of him which suruiues of them, to haue & to hold to him and to the heires of him which suruiueth.

¶ *Que le feoffee re-infeoffera plusors homes.* By the re-feoffment it is implied to be made to the Feoffors, for a feoffement ouer to strangers cannot be sayd a Re-feoffement, and if the feoffement should be made ouer to strangers onely, then as hath beene often sayd, it must bee made in conuenient time.

¶ *Al Heire celuy que suruesquist, a auer & tener a luy & a les heires celuy que suruesquist.* Hereupon questions haue beene made, wherefore the Habendum is not to the heires of the heire, and for what reason it is by Littleton limitted to the heires of the suruiuor. And the cause is, for that if it were made to the heirs of the heire, then some persons by possibilitie should be inheritable to the land, which should not haue inherited if the state had beene made to the Suruiuor and his heires, and consequently the condition broken.

For example, If the Suruiuor tooke to wife Alice Fairefield, in this case if the limitation were to the sonne and his heires, then if the sonne should die without heires of his father, the blood of the Fairefields (being the blood of his mother) should inherit. But if the limitation be to the right heires of the father, then should not the blood of the Fairefields by any possibilitie inherit, for then it is as much as if the state had beene made to the suruiuor and his heires: And therefore these words, (Et à les heires celuy que suruesquist) which many haue thought
vi. Sect. 4. superfluous, are verie materiall. Note well this kind of Fee simple, for it is worthie the obseruation: but sufficient hath beene sayd to open the meaning of Littleton, and therefore I will diue no deeper into this point, but leaue it to the further consideration of the learned Reader.

Section 355.

¶ ITem si feoffmẽt soit fait sur condition, denfeoffer vn auter, ou d' doner en taile a vn aut͂, &c. si le feoffee deuant l' pformance del condition enfeoffa vn estranger, ou fait vn lease pur t͂me de vie, donques poet l' feof-

ALso if a Feoffement be made vpon condition, To enfeoffe another, or to make a gift in taile to another, &c. if the Feoffee before the performance of the Condition, enfeoffe a stranger, or make a Lease for life, then

¶ LIttleton hauing spoken of defaults of performance, or expresse breaches of conditions, speaketh now in what cases the Feoffee in iudgement of Law doth so disable himselfe to performe the Condition: And of disabilities some bee by act of the partie, and some by act in Law.

¶ *Ou a doner en taile a vn auter, &c.* Here is implied an estate for life or for yeares, &c.

for & ses heires enter, &c. pur ceo que il ad luy mesme disable de performer le Condition, entant que il ad fait estate a vn auter, &c.

may the Feoffor and his heirs enter, &c. because he hath disabled himselfe to performe the cōdition in asmuch as he hath made an estate to another, &c.

¶ *Enfeoffe vn Estranger, ou fait vn Lease pur terme de vie.* This is a disabilitie by the act of the partie, for herein the Feoffee hath disabled himself to make the Feoffement or other estate according to the Condition. And to speake once for all, the Feoffee is disabled when he cannot conuey the Land ouer according to the Condition in the same plight, qualitie and freedome as the Land was conueyed to him, for so the Law requireth the same, as shall manifestly appeare hereafter. And here where our Authour speaketh of a feoffment, he includeth an estate taile as well as the fee simple.

13.H.7.23.b. 32.E.3 barre 264.21.Ass.28.38.Ass pl.7.

Section 356.

¶ En mesme le manner est, si le feoffee, deuant le condition performe lessa mesme la terre a vn estranger, pur terme des ans, en cest case le feoffor et ses heires poyent enter, &c. pur ceo que le feoffee ad luy disable de faire estate de les tenements accordant a ceo que estoit en les tenements, quant estate ent fuit fait a luy. Car sil voile faire estate de les tenements accordant a le condition, &c. donques poit le lessee pur terme dans enter & ouste mesme celuy a que le estate est fait, &c. et occupier ceo durant son terme.

¶ IN the same manner it is if the Feoffee before the Condition performed, letteth the same land to a stranger for tearme of yeares, in this case the Feoffor and his heires may enter, &c. because the Feoffee hath disabled him to make an estate of the tenements according to that which was in the tenements when the state thereof was made vnto him. For if hee will make an estate of the tenements according to the Conditi-on, &c. then may the Lessee for yeares enter and ouste him to whom the estate is made, &c. and occupie this during his tearme.

¶ S*i le feoffee deuant le condition performe lessa mesme la terre a vn estranger pur terme des ans, &c.* Here the &c. implyeth a Lease to take effect in futuro aswell as in præsenti, also a Lease for one yeare or halfe a yeare, &c.

The reason of this is euidently set downe before. And againe of disabilities some be by Act in præsenti, whereof Littleton hath put two examples, and some in futuro, whereof now he will speake in the next Section.

Sect. 357.

¶ ET plusors ont dit, que si tiel feoffement soit fait a vn home sole sur mesme le condition, & deuant que il ad per-

AND many haue said that if such feoffment be made to a single man vpon the same Condition, and before hee hath per-

¶ First here is an example of a disability both by act in Law, and in futuro, for by marriage the wife is entitled by Law to Dower, after the death of her husband.

Secondly, It appeareth, that albeit the wife by the marriage is but intitled to haue

(a) 13.H.7.23.b. 34.E.3.dower.127.M.27.E.3 tit.dower 135.28.Ass.Pl.4. 14.H.7.7.6. lib.2.fol.59.b.

forme mesme la condition il prent feme, donques le feoffor et ses heires maintenant poient enter, pur ceo que sil fesoit estate accordant a le condition, et puis morust, donques la feme serra endowe, et poit recouer sa dower per briefe de dower, &c. et issint per le prisel del feme les tenements sont mis en vn auter plite que ne fueront al temps del feoffment sur condition, pur ceo que adonques nul tiel feme fuit dowable, ne serroit dowe per la ley, &c.

formed the same Condition hee taketh wife, then the Feoffor and his Heires maintenant may enter, because, if hee hath made an estate according to the Condition & after dieth, then the wife shall be endowed, and may recouer her Dower by a Writ of Dower, &c. and so by the taking of a wife, the Tenements bee put in another plight then they were at the time of the feoffment vpon Condition, for that then no such Wife was dowable; nor should bee endowed by the Law, &c.

haue dower, & the estate which she is to haue in futuro, viz. after the decease of her husband, yet it is a present cause of entrie. As a Lease for yeares to begin at a day to come is a present disabilitie and cause of reentrie, for that the Land is not in that freedome and plight, as it was conueyed to the Feoffee, and after the state made ouer according to the Condition the land shall be charged therewith.

Iulius Winningtons case.

¶ *En vn auter plight.* Plight is an old English word, and here signifieth not only the estate, but the habit and qualitie of the land, and extendeth to rent charges, and to a possibilitie of Dower. Vide Sect. 289. where Plight is taken for an estate or interest of and in the land it selfe, and extendeth not to a Rent Charge out of the Land.

¶ *A vn home sole.* For if the Feoffee were married at the time of the feoffement, then the Dower can bee no disabilitie, because the Land shall remaine in such Plight as it was at the time of the feoffment made vnto him.

¶ *Donques le feoffor & ses heires maintenant poient enter.* Here it appeareth, that seeing that for this title or possibilitie the Feoffor may presently enter, that albeit the wife happen to die before the husband, so as this title or possibilitie tooke no effect, yet the Feoffor may re-enter, for the Feoffee being disabled at any time though the same continue not, yet the Feoffor may re-enter, for in that case, he that is once disabled is euer disabled. And herein a diuersitie is to be obserued betweene a disabilitie for a time on the part of the Feoffee, and a disabilitie for a time of the part of the Feoffor. For if a man maketh a feoffment in fee vpon condition that the Feoffee before such a day shall re-enfeoffe the Feoffor, the Feoffee taketh wife, and the wife dyeth before the day, yet may the Feoffor re-enter.

So it is if the Feoffee before the day entreth into Religion, and is professed, and before the day is deraigned, yet the Feoffor may re-enter.

21. E. 4. 55. So it is if the Feoffee before the day make a feoffment in fee, and before the day take backe an estate to him and his heires, yet the Feoffor may re-enter.

Albeit in these cases a certaine day be limited, yet the Feoffee being once disabled is euer disabled. And so it is when no time is limited by the parties, but the time is appointed by the Law.

But if a man make a feoffment in fee vpon Condition, that if the feoffor or his heires pay a certaine summe of money before such a day, the Feoffor commit Treason, is attainted and executed, now is there a disabilitie on the part of the Feoffor, for he hath no heire, but if the heire be restored before the day he may performe the Condition, as it was resolued (*) Trin 18. Eliz. in Communi Banco in Sir Thomas Wiats case, which I heard and obserued. Otherwise it is if such a disabilitie had growne on the part of the Feoffee, and the reason of the diuersitie is, for that as Littleton saith, maintenant by the disabilitie of the Feoffee, the Condition is broken, and the Feoffor may enter, but so it is not by the disabilitie of the feoffor, or his heires, for if they performe the Condition within the time it is sufficient, for that they may at any time performe the Condition before the day. And so it is if the feoffor enter into Religion, and before

(*) Trin. 18. Eliz. in Communi Banco in Sir Thomas Wiats case.

the day is deraigned, he may performe the Condition for the cause aforesaid; Et sic de similibus. The (&c.) in this Section are sufficiently explayned.

Sect. 358.

EN mesme le maner est, si le feoffee charge la terre per son fait dun rent charge deuant le performance del condition, ou soit oblige en vn estatute de le Staple, ou statute Merchant, en tielx cases le feoffor et ses heires poyent entrer &c. Causa qua supra. Car quecunque que venust a les tenements per le feoffment de le feoffee, eux couient estre liables, et estre mis en execution per force de lestatute Merchant, ou de statute del Staple, Quære. Mes quant le feoffor ou ses heires, pur l's causes auantdits, aueront enter, come ils deuoyent, come il semble, &c. donques touts tiels choses que deuant tiel entrie puissent troubler ou encumber les tenements issint dones sur condition, &c. quant a mesmes l's tenements sont oulterment defeats.

IN the same manner it is if the Feoffee charge the land by his Deed with a rent charge before the performance of the Condition, or be bound in a Statute Staple or Statute Merchant, in these cases the Feoffor and his heires may enter, &c. *Causa qua supra.* For whosoeuer commeth to the Lands by the feoffment of the Feoffee, they ought to bee lyable, and put in execution by force of the Statute Merchant, or of the Statute Staple. *Quære.* But when the Feoffor or his heires for the causes aforesaid, shall haue entred, as it seemes, they ought, &c. then all such things which before such entrie might trouble or incumber the Land so giuen vpon Condition, &c. as to the same Land, are altogether defeated.

Poyent entrer, &c. And here it is to bee vnderstood, that the grant of the rent charge is a present disabilitie of the Feoffee, and therefore albeit the Grantee doth bring a Writ of Annuitie, and discharge the Land of it, ab initio, yet the cause of entrie being once giuen by the act of the Feoffee, the Feoffor may re-enter. And so it is if the grant of the rent charge were made for life, and the Grantee died, before any day of payment, yet the Feoffor may re-enter. *13.H.7.23.b. 44.E.3.9.b. 26.E.3.73. 20.H.6.34. Iulius Wynningtons case. vbi supra*

The like Law is of any iudgement giuen against the Feoffee wherein debt or dammages are recouered.

Ou soit oblige in vn Statute de la Staple, &c. If the Feoffee be disseised, and after bindeth himselfe in a Statute Staple, or Merchant, or in a Recognizance, or take wife, this is no disabilitie in him, for that during the disseisin, the Land is not charged therewith, neyther is the land in the hands of the disseisor liable thereunto. And in that case if the wife die or the Conusee release the Statute or Recognizance, and after the disseisee doth enter, there is no disabilitie at all, because the Land was neuer charged therewith, and therefore in that case the Feoffee may enter and performe the Condition in the same plight and freedome as it was conueyed vnto him. *Lib. 2 fol. 59. 60. Iulius Wynningtons case.*

And it is to be obserued, that Litl. putteth these cases as examples, for there are some other disabilities implyed, that are not here expressed. *18. Ass. Pl. vltimo. 19.E.3.39. Lib. 2. fol. 80. b. Sir Cromwels case.*

The Lord Clifford did hold his Barony and the Sheriffwicke of Westmerland of the King by Grand Serjeantie in capite, and the King gaue him Licence that he might infeoffe thereof diuers Chaplyns in fee, so that they should giue the same to the Lord Clifford and the heires

males

males of his body the remainder over, &c. the Lord Clifford according to the Licence infeoffed the Chaplyns, and before they made the reconveyance the Lord Clifford dyed, and it was adiudged that the heire might enter for the condition broken. For in this case the Feoffees were bound by Law to haue made the gift in tayle to the Lord Clifford himselfe, albeit he neuer made any request, for otherwise they pursued not the Licence, and if they should make the state to the issue of the Lord Clifford, then might the King seise the Barony, &c. for default of a Licence, and that in default of the Feoffees. And then the same should not be in the same plight and freedome as it was at the time of the feoffment made vpon condition which is worthy of obseruation.

If a man grant an Aduowson vpon condition that the Grantee shall regrant the same to the Grantor in taile. In this case if the Church become voyde before the regrant or before any request made by the Grantor, he may take aduantage of the condition, because the Aduowson is not in the same plight as it was at the time of the grant vpon condition. And so was it resolued, (*) Pasch. 14. Eliz. in comuni banco, betweene Andrews and Blunt, which I heard and obserued, and which my Lord Dier hath omitted out of his report of that case, and therefore the Grantee in that case at his perill must regrant it before the Church become voyde, or else he is disabled, otherwise he hath time during his life if he be not hastened by request.

(*) *Pasch. 14. Eliz. 311. Dier*

44. E. 3. 9.

If the Feoffee suffer a Recouery by default vpon a fayned title, before execution sued the Feoffor may re-enter for this disability. Et sic de similibus.

Sect. 359.

Item, si vn home fait vn fait de feoffment a vn auter, & en le fait est nul condition, &c. & quant le feoffor a luy voyle faire liuerie de seisin per force de mesme le fait, il fait a luy le liuerie de seisin sur certaine condition, en cest cas rien de les tenements passa per le fait, pur ceo que le condition nest comprise deins le fait, & le feoffment est en tiel force sicome nul tiel fait vst este fait.

ALso if a man make a deed of feoffment to another and in the deed there is no condition, &c. & when the feoffor will make liuery of seisin vnto him by force of the same deed, hee makes liuery of seisin vnto him vpon certain condition, in this case nothing of the tenemẽts passeth by the deed for that the condition is not comprised within the deed, & the feoffment is in like force as if no such deed had beene made.

ET en le fait est nul condition, &c. either in Deed or in Law.

Et le feoffment est en tiel force sicome nul tiel fait vst este fait. And the reason hereof is, for that the estate passeth by the Liuery of seisin. And in this case the Feoffor vpon the deliuery of seisin must expresse the state to him and his heires or to the heires of his body, &c.

18. E. 3. 19. 36. 17. *Ass. p.* 20. 8. *H.* 5. 8. 27. *H.* 6.

34. *Ass. pl.* 1.

If an agreement be made betweene two, that the one shall enfeoffe the other vpon condition in surety of the payment of certaine money, and after the Liuery is made to him and his heires generally, the state is holden by some to be vpon condition in asmuch as the intent of the parties was not changed at any time, but continued at the time of the Liuery.

13. E. 3. *tit. Estoppell* 177. 19. E. 3. *ibid.* 184.

If a man make a Charter of feoffment in fee, and the feoffor deliuer seisin for life, the Feoffee shall hold it but for life, but if the Liuery be expresly for life, and also according to the Deed the whole fee simple shall passe because it hath a reference to the Deed.

Sect. 360.

Item si feoffmẽt soit fait sur tiel condition,

ALso if a feoffment be made

Item si feoffment soit fait, &c. And

condition, q̃ le feoffee ne alienera la terre a nulluy, cest condition est voide, pur ceo que quant home est enfeoffe de terres ou tenements il ad power de eux aliener a ascun person per la ley. Car si tiel condition serroit bone donque la condition luy ousteroit de tout le power que la ley luy dona, le quel serroit encounter reason, & pur ceo tiel condition est voide.

vpon this condition that the feoffee shall not alien the land to any, this condition is voide, because when a man is infeoffed of lands or tenements he hath power to alien them to any person by the law. for if such a condition should bee good, then the cōdition should ouste him of all the power which the law giues him, which should bee against reason, & therefore such a condition is voide.

the like Law is of a deuise in fee vpon condition that the Deuisee shall not alien, the condition is voide, and so it is of a grant, release, confirmation or any other conueyance whereby a fee simple doth passe. For it is absurd and repugnant to reason that hee, that hath no possibility to haue the land reuert to him, should restraine his Feoffee in fee simple of all his power to alien. And so it is if a man be possessed of a Lease for yeares, or of a horse, or of any other chattell reall or personall, and giue or sell his whole interest, or propertie therein vpon condition that the Donee or Vendee shall not alien the same, the same is voide, because his whole interest and propertie is out of him, so as he hath no possibility of a Reuerter, and it is against Trade and Traffique, and bargaining and contracting betweene man and man: and it is within the reason of our Author that it should ouster him of all power giuen to him. *Iniquum est ingenuis hominibus non esse liberam rerum suarum alienationem*, and *Rerum suarum quilibet est moderator, & arbitor*. And againe, *Regulariter non valet pactum de re mea non alienanda*. But these are to be understood of conditions annexed to the grant or sale it selfe in respect of the repugnancie, and not to any other collaterall thing, as hereafter shall appeare. Where our Author putteth his case of a feoffment of land, that is put but for an example: for if a man be seised of a Seigniory or a Rent, or an Aduowson or Common or any other inheritance that lyeth in grant, and by his Deede granteth the same to a man and to his heyres vpon condition that he shall not alien, this condition is voide. But some haue said that a man may grant a Rent charge newly created out of lands to a man and to his heyres vpon condition that he shall not alien that, that is good, because the rent is of his owne creation, but this is against the reason and opinion of our Author, and against the height and purity of a fee simple.

21.H.6.34.a. 8.H.7.10.b. 33.Ass.11.24. Doct & Stud.39.124. 13.H.7.23.

Argumentum ex absurdo. Vid. Sect. 722.

A man before the Statute of *Quia Emptores terrarum* might haue made a feoffment in fee, and added further, That if hee or his heires did alien without Licence that he should pay a fine, that this had beene good. And so it is said, that then the Lord might haue restrained the alienation of his Tenant by condition, because the Lord had a possibilitie of reuerter, and so it is in the Kings case at this day because he may reserue a tenure to himselfe.

14.H.4. 13.H.7.23.

21.H.7.8. Lib. 5. 56. Knights case.

If A. be seised of Blacke acre in fee, and B. infeoffeth him of White acre vpon condition that A. shall not alien Blacke acre, the condition is good, for the condition is annexed to other land, and ousteth not the Feoffee of his power to alien the land whereof the feoffment is made, and so no repugnancy to the state passed by the feoffment, and so it is of gifts or sales of chattells realls or personalls.

Sect. 361.

Mes si le condition soit tiel, que le feoffee ne alienera a vn tiel, nosmant son nosme, ou

BVt if the condition be such that the feffee shall not alien to such a one, naming his name, or to any of his

If a feoffment in fee bee made vpon condition that the Feoffee shall not infeoffe I.S. or any of his heires or issues, &c. this is good, for he doth not restraine the feoffee of all his power: the reason here yeilded by our Author

Pl. Com. 77.a. 8.H.7.10.b. 21.E.4.47.a.

a aſcun d ſes heyres, ou de iſſues d vn tiel, &c. ou huiuſmodi les qux conditiõs ne tollent tout la power dalienation del feoffee, &c. donqȝ tiel condition eſt bone.

heires, or of the iſſues of ſuch a one, &c. or the like, which conditions doe not take away all power of alienation from the feoffee, &c. then ſuch condition is good.

Author is worthy of obſeruation. And in this caſe if the Feoffee enfeoffe I.N. of entent and purpoſe that he ſhall enfeoffe I.S. ſome hold that this is a breach of the condition, for Quando al quid prohibetur fieri, directo prohibetur & per obliquum.

10.*H.*7.11.*Dist.* & *Stud.*124. 13.*H.*7.23.

If a feoffment bee made vpon condition that the Feoffee ſhall not alien in Mortmaine, this is good, becauſe ſuch alienation is prohibited by Law, and regularly whatſoeuer is prohibited by the Law, may be prohibited by condition, bee it Malum prohibitum, or malum in ſe. In ancient deeds of feoffment in fee there was moſt commonly a clauſe, Quod licitum ſit donatorio rem datam dare vel vendere cui voluerit exceptis viris religioſis & Iudæis.

*Bracton, lib.*1.*fo.*13.*a.*

Section 362.

ITem, ſi tenemẽts ſoient dones en l'taile ſur tiel condition, que le tenant en le taile ne ſes heyres ne alieneront en fee, ne en le taile, ne pur terme dauter vie, forſqȝ pur lour vies demeſne, &c. tiel condition eſt bone. Et la cauſe eſt, pur ceo que quant il fiſt tiel alienation & diſcontinuance de le taile, il fait le contrarie a lentent le donor, pur que leſtatute de W.2. cap.1. fuit fait, per quel eſtatute les eſtates en le taile ſont ordeines.

ALſo if lands bee giuen in taile vpon condition, that the tenant in taile nor his heires ſhall not alien in fee, nor in taile nor for terme of anothers life but only for their owne liues, &c. ſuch condition is good. And the reaſon is for that when hee maketh ſuch alienation and diſcontinuance of the entaile, hee doth contrary to the intent of the donor, for which the ſtatute of *W.*2. *cap.*1. was made, by which ſtatute the eſtates in taile are ordained.

33.*Aſſ.*11.24. *Lib.*6.40.41. *Mildmayes caſe.* 21.*H.*6.33. 13.*H.*7.23. 21.*H.*7.11.

*Vid. Sect.*220.*&c.*

Note here the double negatiue in legall conſtruction ſhall not hinder the negatiue, viz. Sub conditione quod ipſi nec hæredes ſui non alienarẽt. And therefore the Grammaticall conſtruction is not alwayes in iudgement of Law to be followed.

Forſque pur lour vies demeſne, &c. And yet if a man make a gift in taile vpon condition that hee ſhall not make a Leaſe for his owne life, albeit the ſtate be lawfull yet the condition is good; becauſe the reuerſion is in the Donor. As if a man make a Leaſe for life or years vpon condition, that they ſhall not grant ouer their eſtate or let the land to others, this is good, and yet the grant or Leaſe ſhould bee lawfull. (*) If a man make a gift in taile vpon condition that he ſhall not make a Leaſe for three liues or 21. yeares according to the Statute of 32.H.8. the condition is good, for the Statute doth giue him power to make ſuch Leaſes which may be reſtrained by condition, and by his owne agreement, for this power is not incident to the eſtate, but giuen to him collaterally by the Act according to that rule of Law, Quilibet poteſt renunciare iuri pro ſe introducto.

21.*H.*6.33. 13.*H.*7.23.24. 27.*H.*8.17.19. 31.*H.*8. *Dier* 45.

(*) *Dier*, 33.*H.*8.*fo.*48.49

Quant il fiſt tiel alienation & diſcontinuance del ſtate taile. And therefore if a gift in taile be made vpon condition, That the Donee, &c. ſhall not alien, this condition is good to ſome intents, and voyd to ſome: for as to all thoſe alienations which amount to any diſcontinuance of the ſtate taile, (as Littleton here ſpeaketh) or is againſt the Statute of Weſtminſter 2. the condition is good without queſtion. But as to a common recouerie the condition is voyd, becauſe this is no diſcontinuance, but a barre, and this common

*Vid. Lib.*6.40.41. *Sir Anth. Mildmayes caſe.*

recouerie is not restrained by the said Statute of W. 2. And therefore such a condition is repugnant to the estate taile, for it is to be obserued, that to this estate taile there bee diuers incidents. First, To be dispunished of wast. Secondly, That the wife of the Donee in Taile shall be endowed. Thirdly, That the husband of a Feme Donee after Issue shall be Tenaunt by the Curtesie. Fourthly, That Tenant in taile may suffer a common recouerie: and therefore if a man make a gift in Taile, vpon condition to restraine him of any of these incidents, the condition is repugnant and voyd in Law. And it is to be obserued,* that a collateral warrantie or a lineall with assets in respect of the recompence, is not restrained by the Statute of Donis conditionalibus, no more is the common recouerie in respect of the intended recompence. And Littleton to the intent to exclude the common Recouerie, saith, Tiel alienation & discontinuance, ioyning them together. 22.E.3.19.17.El.343.Dier. (*) 13.H.7.24 b.

If a man before the Statute of Donis conditionalibus, had made a gift to a man and to the heires of his bodie, vpon condition, That after Issue hee should not haue power to sell, this condition should haue been repugnant and voyd. Pari ratione, after the Statute a man makes a gift in taile; the Law tacite giues him power to suffer a common recouerie, therefore to adde a Condition, That he shall haue no power to suffer a common recouerie, is repugnant and voyd.

If a man make a Feoffement to a Baron and Feme in fee, vpon condition, That they shall not alien, to some intent this is good, and to some intent it is voyd: for to restraine an alienation by Feoffement, or alienation by Deed, it is good, because such an Alienation is tortious and voydable; but to restraine their Alienation by Fine is repugnant and voyd, because it is lawfull and vnauoydable. 10.H.7.11. 13.H.7.23. Lib.6. 41.b. in Sir Anthonie Milldmayes case vbi supra.

It is sayd, That if a man infeoffe an Enfant in Fee, vpon condition, That he shall not alien, this is good to restraine Alienations during his minoritie, but not after his full age.

It is likewise sayd, That a man by Licence may giue Land to a Bishop and his Successors, or to an Abbot and his Successors, and ad a Condition to it, That they shal not without the consent of their Chapiter or Couent, alien, because it was intended a Mortmaine, that is, that it should for euer continue in that Sea or house, for that they had it en auter droit, for religious and good vses. Doctor & Student 124.

¶ Lestatute de W. 2. cap. 1. Hereby it appeareth, That whatsoeuer is prohibited by the intent of any Act of Parliament, may be prohibited by condition, as hath been sayd. 10.H.7.11. Doct & Stud. 124. 13.H.7.23.

Section 363.

¶ CAr il est proue per les parols comprises en mesme Lestatute, que la volunt del donor en tiels cases serroit obserue, et quaunt le Tenant en le Taile fait tiel discontinuance, il fait le contrarie a ceo, &c. Et auxy en estates en le taile dascun Tenements, quant le reuersion de fee simple, ou remainder en Fee simple est en auters persons, quaunt tiel discontinuance est fait, donques le fee simpl

FOr it is prooued by the words comprised in the same statute, That the will of the Donor in such cases shall be obserued, and when the Tenaunt in Taile maketh such discontinuance, hee doth contrarie to that, &c. And also in estates in Taile of any Tenements, when the Reuersion of the Fee simple, or the remainder of the Fee simple is in other persons, when such discontinuance is made, then the fee sim-

¶ *QVant le reuersion ou rem' en fee est en auters persons.* Put the case that a Man make a gift in Taile to A. the remainder to him and to his heires, vpon condition that he shall not alien, as to the state taile the condition is good, for such alienation is prohibited, as hath beene said, by the sayd Statute. But as to the Fee simple, some say it is repugnant and voyd, for the reason that Littleton hath yeelded: and therefore some are of opinion, That this is a good Condition, and shall defeat the Alienation for the estate taile onely, and leaue the Fee simple in the Alienee, for that the Condition did in Law extend onely to the state taile, and not to the remainder. 11.H.7.6. 13 H.7.23.24. Dyer 2.& 3 Phil. & Mar. 127.b.

¶ *Encounter le profit*

fit de ses Issues. Hereby it appeareth, That to restrain tenant in taile from alienation against the profit of his issues, is good, for that agreeth with the will of the Donor, and the intent of the Statute*.

(*) 46.E.3.4.

But a gift in Taile may bee made upon condition, That Tenant in Taile, &c. may alien for the profit of his issues, and that hath beene holden to be good, and not restrained by the said Stat. and seemeth to agree with the reason of Littleton, because in that case, Voluntas Donatoris obseruetur, &c. and it must be for the profit of the issues.

en le remainder est discontinue. Et pur ceo que l'Tenant en taile ne fert tiel chose encounter le profit de ses issues & bon droit tiel condition est bon come est auauntdit, &c.

ple in the remainder is discontinued. And because Tenant in Tayle shall doe no such thing against the profit of his issues and good right, such Condition is good, as is aforesayd, &c.

Section 364.

21.H.7.11.

¶ A*Lienont, &c. Et auxy si touts les Issues sont morts, &c.* Note Littleton purposely made parcell of the Condition in the Copulatiue, that the Tenant in Taile should alien, &c. For if a gift in Taile be made to a man and to the heirs of his bodie, and if he die without heires of his body, that then the Donor and his Heires shall re-enter, this is a voyd Condition, for when the issues faile, the estate determineth by the expresse limitation, and consequently the adding of the condition to defeat that which is determined by the limitation of the estate, is voyd, and in that case the wife of the Donee shall be endowed, &c. And therefore Littleton to make the Condition good, added an alienation, which amounted to a wrong, and he restrained not the Alienation onely, (for then presently upon the Alienation the Donor, &c. might re-enter and defeat the estate Taile)

¶ Item home poit doner Terres en taile, sur tiel condition, Que si le tenant en le Taile ou ses heires alienont en fee, ou en taile, ou pur terme dauter vie, &c. et auxy que si touts issues veignants del Tenant en le taile soient morts sans issue, que adonques bien lirroit al Donor et a ses heires de enter, &c. Et per tiel voy le droit de le taile poet estre salue apres discontinuance al issue en le taile, si ascun y soit, issint que per voy dentre del Donor, ou de ses heires le taile ne fuit my defeat per tiel condition: Quære hoc. Et uncore si le Tenant en l'taile en ceo case, ou ses heires font ascun discontinuance, celuy en le reuersion ou ses heires, apres ceo que le taile est determine, pur default de issue, &c. poyent enter en

ALso a man may giue lands in Taile vpon such condition, that if the Tenant in Taile or his heires alien in fee or in taile, or for terme of another mans life, &c. and also that if all the Issues comming of the Tenant in Taile, bee dead without Issue, that then it shall be lawfull for the Donor and for his heires to enter, &c. And by this way the right of the taile may bee saued after discontinuance, to the issue in taile, if there bee any: so as by way of entrie of the Donor or of his heires, the taile shal not bee defeated by such conditiō: *Quære hoc.* And yet if the tenant in taile in this Case, or his Heires, make any discontinuance, he in the reuersion, or his Heyres, after that the Taile is determined for default of Issue, &c. may enter into

en le terre per force de mesme le condition, & ne serront my cohert de suer briefe de formdon en le reuerter.

the Land by force of the same Condition, and shall not bee compelled to sue a Writ of Formedon in the reuerter.

but added, and die without issue, to the end that the right of the estate in tayle might bee preserued, and not defeated by the Condition, but might bee recouered againe by the issue in tayle in a Formedon.

And Littleton expressely saith, that the Donor and his heires after the discontinuance, and after that the estate tayle is determined, may re-enter; which is the intention and true meaning of Littleton in this place. And where it is said in this Section (Quære hoc.) this is added by some that vnderstood not this case, and is not in the originall.

Note, that in a Condition consisting of diuers parts in the coniunctiue, as here in the case of Littleton both parts must be performed, according to the old rule, (a) Si plures conditiones ascriptæ fuerunt donationi coniunctim omnibus est parendum & ad veritatem copulatiue requiritur quod vtraque pars sit vera. But otherwise it is when the Condition is in the disiunctiue, for the same Author in that case sayth; Si diuisim cuilibet; vel alteri eorum satis est obtemperare. Et in disiunctiuis sufficit alteram partem esse veram. What then if the Condition or Limitation be both in the Coniunctiue and Disiunctiue: as if a man make a Lease to the Husband and wife for the tearme of one and twentie yeares, if the Husband and Wife or any Child betweene them so long shall liue, and then the wife dieth without issue, shall the Lease determine, or continue during the life of the Husband? And the answere is, that it shall continue, for the disiunctiue referreth to the whole, and disioyneth not only the latter part as to the Child, but also to the Baron and Fem, so as the sence is, if the Baron, Fem, or any Childe shall so long liue.

(b) And so it is if an vse be limited to certaine persons, vntill A. shall come from beyond Sea, and attaine vnto his full age, or die, if he doe come from beyond Sea, or attaine to his full age, the vse doth cease.

(a) Bracton lib. 2. fol. 19. vide Pl. Com. 76. in Wimbeshes case. & fo. 107. in Fulmerstons case. Bracton vbi supra.

So it was adiudged in Communi Banco pasch. 30. Eliz. inter Baldwyn & Cocke commonly called Impetuous case.

(b) Hill. 35. Eliz. en trespasse per le Seignior Mordant vers George Vaux so adiudged in the Kings Bench.

Section 365.

¶ Item, home ne poit pleder en ascun action, que estate fuit fait en fee, ou en fee taile, ou pur terme de vie, sur condition, s'il ne voucha vn record de ceo, ou monstra vn escript south seale, prouant mesme la condition. Car il est vn cõmon erudition, que home per plee ne defeatera ascun estate d' franktenement per force dascun tiel condition s'non que il monstra le proofe de condition en escript, &c. si-

ALso a man cannot plead in any action, that an estate was made in fee, or in fee tayle, or for tearme of life vpon Condition, if hee doth not vouch a Record of this, or shew a writing vnder Seale, proouing the same Condition. For it is a common learning, that a man by plea shall not defeat any estate of freehold by force of any such Condition, vnlesse he sheweth the proofe of the Condition in writing, &c. vnlesse it bee

¶ EN ascun action. Bee the action reall, personall, or mixt, if a Condition be pleaded to defeat a freehold it is regularly true, that a Deed must be shewed forth (a) in Court. And the reason why the Deed shall bee shewed forth to the Court is; for that to euery Deed there be two things requisite, the one that it be sufficient in Law, and this is called the Legall Part, and therefore the iudgement of that belongeth to the Judges of the Law: the other concernes matter of Fact, as sealing and deliuery, and this belongs to the Jurors. And because euery Deed ought to approue it selfe, and be proued by others too; it must approue it selfe vpon the shewing of it forth in Court in two manners.

First, as to the composition of the words, that it bee suf-

39. E. 3. 22. 4. E. 4. 35. a. 9. E. 4. 25. b. 26. a. 6. H. 7. 8. b. 11. H. 7. 22. b. 7. H. 6. 7. 14. H. 8. 22. b. 28. Ass. p. 8. (a) Lib. 10. fol. 92. Doctor Layfields case. 7. E. 3. 57. 25. E. 3. 41. 41. E. 3. 10. &c.

non que ceo soit en ascuns especiall cases, &c. Mes de chattels reals sicome de leas fait a terme dans, ou de grants de gards fait per gardeins in chiualrie, & huiusmodi, &c. home poit pleder que tiels leases ou grãts fueront faits sur cõdition &c. sans monstre ascun escript de le condition. Issint en mesme le maner home poit faire de dones & grants de chattels personals & de contracts personals, &c.

in some speciall cases, &c. But of Chattels reals, as of a Lease for yeares, or of grants of Wards made by Gardeins in Chiualrie and such like, &c. a man may plead that such Leases or grants were made vpon Conditon, &c. without shewing any writing of the Condition. So in the same manner a man may doe of gifts and Grants of Chattels Personals, and of Contracts personals, &c.

sufficient in Law, and that the Court shall adiudge.

Secondly, of ancient time if the Deed appeared to bee rased or interlined in places materiall, the Judges adiudged vpon their view, the Deed to be voyd. But of latter time, the Judges haue left that to the Jurors to try whether the rasing or interlining were before the deliuerie.

45.E.3.21.a. And there is a difference betweene a rent, and a reentrie, for vpon a gift in taile, or lease for life, a rent may bee reserued without Deed, but a Condition with a reentrie, cannot bee reserued in those cases without deed.

Lib 5. fol 52.53. &c. Pages case, 6.R.2.c.p.4.

¶ *Escript de south seale.* Which Littleton intendeth to be a Deed vnder Seale.

And well said Littleton, A Deed vnder Seale, For though the Deed bee inrolled, yet hee cannot plead the inrolment thereof, though it bee of record. And though it be exemplified vnder the great Seale, (b) yet must he shew forth the Deed it selfe vnder Seale as Littleton here saith, and not the exemplification. And so when Littleton wrote, no Constat or inspeximus, of the Kings Letters Patents were auayleable to be shewed forth in Court, but the Letters Patents themselues vnder Seale. For both the Constat and inspeximus are but exemplifications of the inrolment of the Charters, or Letters Patents: and this appeareth by the resolution of two seuerall (c) Parliaments, one holden in the third and fourth yeare of King Edward the sixt, and the other in the thirteenth yeare of Queene Elizabeth. But now by those Statutes the exemplification or Constat vnder the great Seale of the inrolment of any Letters Patents made since the fourth day of Februarie, Anno 27.H 8 or after to be made, shall be sufficient to be pleaded and shewed forth in Court, aswell against the King, as any other person by the Patentees themselues (whereof there was some doubt (d) conceiued vpon the said Statute of E.6.) and by all and euery other person and persons clayming by from or vnder them. Which Statutes are generall and beneficiall, and especially the Act of 13.Eliz. for that extends not only to Lands, Tenements, and Hereditaments, but to euery other thing whatsoeuer, and ought to be fauourably construed for aduancement of the remedie and right of the subiect.

(b) Vide 32.H.8. in Patents Br. 12.H.7.12. b.

(c) 3.& 4.E.6.cap.4.& 13.Eliz.cap.6.

(d) Dyer.1.Eliz.167.

The difference betweene a Constat, Inspeximus, and a Vidimus you may reade (e) at large in Pages Case. But none of them by Law ought to be had, but only of the inrolment of record, and not of a Deed or any other writing that is not of Record, and no Deed, &c. can be inrolled, vnlesse it be duly and lawfully acknowledged.

(e) Lib.8. fol.8. in the Trinities case. Vide Pages case vbi supra.

33.E.3.gard.162. 20.E.3. dowerin present.13.35.H 6. tit.monstrans des faits 118.

¶ *Si non que soit en ascun especiall cases, &c.* Hereby is implyed that if a Gardein in Chiualrie in the right of the heire entreth for a Condition broken, he shall plead the state vpon Condition without shewing of any Deed, because his interest is created by the Law. And so it is (f) of a Tenant by Statute Merchant or Staple, or Tenant by Elegit.

(f) 30.H.7.5.

Likewise Tenant in Dower shall plead a Condition, &c. without shewing of the Deed. And the reason of these and the like Cases, is for that the Law doth create these estates, and they come not in by him that entred for the Condition broken, so as they might prouide for the shewing of the Deed, but they come to the Land by authoritie of Law, and therefore the Law will allow them to plead the Condition without shewing of it.

5.E.3.37. 11.H.4.83. 35.H.6.tit monstrans des faits 11.b.7.H 6.17.H.5.3. 3.H.6.21. 33.H.6.1. 24.H.8.8.

(f) But

(f) But the Lord by escheat albeit his estate be created by Law shall not plead a Condition to defeate a freehold without shewing of it, because the Deede doth belong vnto him. (f) 35. H. 6. vbi supra.

A Tenant by the curtesie shall not (g) pleade a condition made by his wife, and a re-entry for the condition broken without shewing the Deed, for albeit his estate be created by Law, yet the Law presumeth that he had the possession of the Deedes and Euidences belonging to his wife. (g) 35. H. 6. vbi supra.

(h) But Lessees for yeares and all others that claime by any Conueyance from the partie or iustifie as seruant by Commandement, &c. must shewe the Deede. (h) 14. H. 8. 8. Pl. com. 149.

(i) R. brought an Eiectione firmæ against E. for Eiecting him out of the Mannor of D. which he held for terme of yeares of the demise of C. E. the Defendant pleaded that B. gaue the said Mannor to P. and Katherine his wife in tayle who had issue E. the Defendant, and after the Donees infeoffed C. of the Mannor vpon condition that hee should demise the Mannor for yeares to R. the Plaintife, the remainder to the husband and to the wife, &c. C. did demise the land to R. the Plaintife for yeares but kept the reuersion to himselfe, wherefore Katherine after the decease of her husband entred vpon the Plaintife, &c. for the condition broken, and died, after whose decease the land discended to E. the issue in taile, &c now defendant, iudgement si action, exception was taken against this plea because E. the Def. maintained his entrie by force of a condition broken, and shewed forth no Deed, & the plea was ruled to be good, because the thing was executed, and therefore hee need not shew forth the Deed. Nota the Defendant being issue in taile was remitted to the estate taile. (i) 44. E. 3. 22. See after this chapter. Section 366.

In a Præcipe quod reddat against S. who pleaded that R. was seised, and infeoffed him in Morgage vpon condition of payment of certaine money at a day, and said that R. paid the money at the day, and entred iudgement of the Writ: exception was taken to this plea for that he shewed forth no Deed of the condition, and it was ruled that he need not shew forth the Deed for two causes. 1. That he ought not to shew any Deed to the Demandant because the Demandant is a stranger. 2. It might be when R. paid the money, and the condition performed, that the Deed was redelliuered to R. and thereupon the plea was adiudged good, and the Writ abated. 11. E. 3. tit. Monst. des faits. 175. 45. E. 3. 8.

If land be morgaged vpon condition, and the Morgagee letteth the lands for yeares, reseruing a rent, the condition is performed the Morgagee re-enters, in an action of debt brought for the rent the Lessee shall pleade the condition and the re-entrie without shewing forth any Deede. 45. E. 3. 8. b. Finch.

In an Assise the Tenant pleades a feoffment of the Ancester of the Plaintife vnto him, &c. the Plaintife saith that the feoffment was vpon condition, &c. and that the condition was broken, and pleads a re-entrie, and that the Tenant entred and tooke away the Chest in which the Deed was and yet detaineth the same, the Plaintife shall not in this case be enforced to shew the Deed. 10. H. 4. 9. b. 43. E. 3. Vid. 10. E. 3. 41. Simile in Dower.

If a woman giue lands to a man and his heires by Deede or without generally, she may in pleading auerre the same to be Causa matrimonij prælocuti, albeit she hath nothing in writing to proue the same, the reason whereof see Sect. 330. 12. E. 1. Feoffments & faits, 114. F. N. B. 205. b. 13. R. 2. Monstrans des faits 165. 4. E. 4. 35. &c.

¶ *Mes des chattels realls sicome lease fait a volunt a terme des ans, &c.* This is apparant. 11. H. 7. 22. b. 6. H. 7. 8. 9. E. 4. 25 26. 14. H. 8. 22. b.

Sect. 366.

¶ ITem coment que hōe en ascun action ne poit pleder vn condition que toucha & concerna franktenement sauns monstrer escript de ceo, come est auantdit, vncore home poit estre aide sur tiel condition per verdict de xii. hōes

ALso albeit a man cannot in any action plead a condition which toucheth & concernes a freehold without shewing writing of this as is aforesaid, yet a man may be aided vpon such a condition by the verdict of 12. men taken at large in an assise

¶ *Verdit or verdict de 12. homes.* Veredictum quasi dictum veritatis, as Iudicium est quasi iuris dictum. Et sicut ad quæstionem juris, non respondent juratores, sed judices: sic ad questionem facti non respondent judices sed juratores. For Iurors are to trie the fact, and the Iudges ought to iudge according to the Law that riseth vpon the fact, Lib. 8. fo. 155. Lib. 9. fo. 13. Lib. 11. fo. 10.

prise a large en Assise de Nouel disseisin, ou en ascun auter action, lou les Justices volent prender le verdict de xij. Jurors alarge. Sicome mittomus q̄ home seisie de certaine terre en fee, lessa mesm̄ la terre a vn auter pur terme de vie sans fait, sur condition d̄ render al lessor vn certeine rent, & pur default de paiment vn re-entrie, &c. per force de quel le lessee est seisie come de franktenemēt, et puis l' rent est aderere, p̄ que le lessor enter en la tre, et puis le lessee arraig̃ vn Assise de Nouel disseisin, de la terre envers le lessor, le quel plede q̄ il fist nul tort, ne nul disseisin, et sur ceo, lassise soit prise, en cest case les Recognitors del assise poyent dire et render a les Justices lour verdict alarge sur tout le matter, come adire que le defendant fuit seisie de la terre en son demesn̄ come de fee, et issint seisie mesme la terre lesse al plaintife pur terme de sa vie, rendāt al lessour tiel annuel rent paiable a tiel feast, &c. sur tiel condition, que si le rent fuit aderere a ascun tiel feast a que doit

of *Nouel disseisin*, or in any other action where the Iustices will take the verdict of 12. Iurors at large. As put the case, a man seised of certaine land in fee letteth the same land to another for terme of life without deed vpon condition to render to the lessor a certaine rent, and for default of payment, a re-entrie, &c. by force whereof the lessee is seised as of freehold, and after the rent is behinde, by which the lessor entreth into the land, and after the lessee arraigne an Assise of *Nouel Disseisin*, of the land against the lessor, who pleads that he did no wrong nor disseisin, and vpon this, the Assise is taken; in this case the Recognitors of the Assise may say and render to the Iustices their verdict at large vpon the whole matter, as to say that the defendant was seised of the land in his demesne as of fee, and so seised, lette the same land to the plaintife for terme of his life rendring to the lessor such a yearely rent payable at such a feast, &c. vpon such condition that if the rent were behinde at any such feast at which

fact, for Ex facto Ius oritur.

¶ *Prise alarge.* There be two kindes of verdicts, viz. one generall, and another at large or especiall. As in an Assise of Nouel disseisin brought by A. against B. the Plaintife makes his plaint, Quod B. disseisiuit eũ de 20. acris terræ cum pertinentiis, the Tenant pleades, Quod ipse nullam iniuriam seu disseisinam præfato A. inde fecit, &c. the recognitors of the Assise doe finde Quod prædict. A. iniuste & sine iudicio disseisiuit prædict. B. de prædict. 20. acris terræ cum pertinent. &c. This is a generall verdict. The like law it is if they finde it negatiuely. And Littleton here putteth a case of a Verdict at large or a speciall Verdict, and it is therefore called a speciall Verdict or a Verdict at large, because they finde the speciall matter at large, and leaue the iudgement of Law thereupon to the Court, of which kinde of Verdict it is said, (l) Omnis conclusio boni & veri iudicij sequitur ex bonis & veris premissis & dictis Iuratorum.

(l) *Trin.33.E.1.Coram Rege Nott. in Thesaur.*

And though Littleton here putteth his case of a Verdict at large vpon a generall issue (which in the case hee puts it was necessary for the Tenant to pleade) yet when issue is ioyned vpon some speciall point, the Jury, as shall be said hereafter in this Section may finde the speciall matter, if it be doubtfull in Law, for as much doubt may arise vpon one point vpon the speciall issue as vpon the generall issue. And as a special verdict may be found in Cõmon

43.Ass.31.Stanf.pl.cor. 164.165. 3.E.3.Coron.284. 286.287. 44.E.3.44. 41.E.3.Coron.451.

doit

doit estre pay, donques bien lirroit al lessor dentrer, &c. per force de quel lease le plaintife fuit seisie en son demesne come de franktenement, et que puis apres le rent fuit aderere a tiel feast, &c. per que le lessor entra en le terre sur le possession le lessee et prieroit le discretion de les Justices, si ceo soit un disseisin fait al plaintife ou nemy, donque pur ceo que appiert a les Justices, que ceo fuit nul disseisin fait al plaintife entant que lentrie de le lessour fuit congeable sur luy; les Justices doyent doner iudgement que le plaintife ne prendra riens per son briefe dassise. Et issint en tiel cas le lessor serra aide, et uncore nul escripture unques fuit fait del condition. Car cibien que les Jurors poient auer conusance de le lease, auxybien il poient auer conusance de le condition que fuit declare & rehearse sur le leas.

it ought to bee paid, then it should bee lawfull for the lessor to enter, &c. by force of which lease the plaintife was seised in his demesne as of freehold, and that afterwards the rent was behinde at such a feast; &c. by which the lessor entred into the land vpon the possession of the lessee, and prayed the discretion of the Iustices if this be a disseisin done to the plaintife or not. Then for that it appeareth to the Iustices that this was no disseisin to the plaintife, insomuch as the entrie of the lessor was congeable on him; the Iustices ought to giue iudgement that the plaintife shall not take any thing by his writ of Assise. And so in such case the lessor shall bee aided, and yet no writing was euer made of the condition. For aswell as the Iurors may haue conusance of the lease, they also as well may haue conusance of the condition which was declared & rehearsed vpon the lease.

Pleas, so may it also be found in Pleas of the Crowne, or criminall causes that concerne life or member.

A verdict finding matter incertainly or ambiguously is insufficient and no iudgement shall be giuen thereupon, as if an Executor plead Plein. ment administr., and issue is ioyned thereupon, and the Jury finde, that the Defendant haue goods within his hands to bee administred, but finde not to what value, this is incertaine and therefore insufficient.

40.E.3.15. 20 E.3.amendment.57. 18.E.3.49. in Cessauit. 30.E.3.23. 7.H.4.39.

A Verdict that finde part of the issue, and finding nothing for the residue, this is insufficient for the whole, because they haue not tried the whole issue wherewith they are charged. As if an information of intrusion bee brought against one for intruding into a messuage, and 100. acres of land, vpon the generall issue the Jury finde against the Defendant for the land, but saith nothing for the house, this is insufficient for the whole and so was it twice adiudged. (m) But if the Jury giue a verdict of the whole issue, and of more, &c. that which is more is surplusage, and shall not (a) stay iudgement, for Vtile per inutile non vitiatur, but necessarie incidents required by law the Jury may finde.

17.E.3.47. 18.E.3.48. 22.E.3.1. 18.E.3.56. 15.E.3.Iudgement.58. 2.H.5.3. 7.H.6.5. 7.E.4.24. 28.H.6.10.

(m) Hill.25.Eliz. in a writ of Error betweene Brace and the Queene in the Exchequer chamber. Mich.28 & 29. Eliz. inter Gomersall & Gomersall in account in the Kings bench.

(a) 32.E.3.Cessauit.25.

If the matter and substance of the issue be found, it is sufficient as Littleton himselfe sayeth hereafter.

Vid. Sect.484.485.

Vid. Sect.58. 13.E.3.garr.26 15.E.3.Ass.322. 17.E.3.6. 18.Ass.2. 35.Ass.8.

Estoppels which bind the interest of the Land, as the taking of a Lease of a mans owne land by Deed indented, and the like, being specially found by the Jurie, the Court ought to iudge according to the speciall matter, for albeit Estoppels regularly must bee pleaded and relied vpon by an apt conclusion, and the Jurie is sworne ad veritatem dicendam, yet when they find veritatem facti, they pursue well their oath, and the Court ought to adiudge according to Law. (b) So may the Jurie find a Warrantie being giuen in euidence, though it be not pleaded, because it bindeth the right, vnlesse it be in a Writ of Right, when the Mise is ioyned vpon the meere right.

(b) 1.H.4.6.b. 27.H.8.22.b Pl.Com.515. Lib.4.fo.53. Rawlins case. & ibid. Pledels case. Hill.31.Eliz. betweene Sutton and Dicons in the Common place, the case of the Lease for yeares by Deed indented. 34.E.3.Dico.29.

(c) After

(c) 7.R.2. Corone. 108. Plo.Com.Fremans Case 211. 11.H.4.2. 20.Ass. 12. 16.Ass.16. 22.Ass.23. 5.H.7. 22.

(c) After the verdict recorded, the Jurie cannot varie from it, but before it bee recorded they may varie from the first offer of their verdict, and that verdict which is recorded shall stand: also they may varie from a priuie verdict.

An issue found by verdict shall alwayes be intended true vntill it be reversed by attaint, and thereupon vpon the attaint no *Supersedeas* is grantable by Law.

Pasch. 24.H.8. of the Report of Inst ce Spilman in the Kings Bench. 11.H.4.17. 35.H.6. Examin 17. 29.H.8.37. Dier. 35.H.8.55. 4. et 5. Eliz. 218 14.H.7.1. 20.H.7.3. (d) Pasch.6.E.6. in the Common Place.

If the Jurie after their euidence giuen vnto them at the Barre, doe at their owne charges eat or drinke either before or after they be agreed on their verdict, it is finable, but it shall not auoyd the verdict; but if before they be agreed on their verdict, they eat or drinke at the charge of the Plaintife, if the verdict be giuen for him, it shall auoyd the verdict; but if it be giuen for the Defendant, it shall not auoyd it, *Et sic è conuerso.* (d) But if after they bee agreed on their verdict they eat or drinke at the charge of him for whom they doe passe, it shall not auoyd the verdict.

(e) 11.H.4.16.17. 3.Mar Iurors Br.8. Vide Dier vbi supra.

(e) If the Plaintife after euidence giuen, and the Jurie departed from the Barre, or any for him, doe deliuer any Letter from the Plaintife to any of the Jurie concerning the matter in Issue, or any Euidence or any escrow touching the matter in issue, which was not giuen in Euidence, it shall auoyd the verdict, if it be found for the Plaintife, but not if it bee found for the Defendant, & *sic è conuerso.* But if the Jurie carrie away any writing vnsealed, which was giuen in euidence in open Court, this shall not auoyd their verdict albeit they should not haue carried it with them.

Pasch.6.E.6. vbi supra.

(f) 24.E.3.75.

By the Law of England a Jurie after there Euidence giuen vpon the Issue, ought to bee kept together in some conuenient place, without meat or drinke, fire or candle, which some Bookes (f) call an imprisonment, and without speech with any, vnlesse it be the Baylife, and with him onely if they be agreed. After they be agreed they may in causes betweene partie and partie giue a verdict, and if the Court be risen, giue a priuie verdict before any of the Judges of the Court, and then they may eat and drinke, and the next morning in open Court they may either affirme or alter their priuie verdict, and that which is giuen in Court shall stand. But in criminall cases of life or member the Jurie can giue no priuie verdict, but they must giue it openly in Court. And hereby appeareth another diuision of verdicts, *viz.* a publique verdict openly giuen in Court, and a priuie verdict giuen out of the Court before any of the Judges, as is aforesayd.

21.E.3.18.

A Jurie sworne and charged in case of life or member, cannot be discharged by the Court or any other, but they ought to giue a verdict. And the King cannot be Non-suit, for he is in iudgment of Law euer present in Court: but a common person may be Non-suit.

W.2.cap. 30. 9.H.4.11. 8.E.4.29. 9.H.7.13. 23.H.8 tit.Verdit. Br.85. 11.Eliz. Dier 283.284. 3 E.3. Itinere North 284.286 43.Ass.31. 26 H 8.5. 44 E.3.44. F.tit.Cor.194. 44.Ass.17. 45.E.3.20. Pl.Com.92. 9.H.7.3. Vide Lib.9.12.13. Dowmans Case. And see there many other Authorities. 31.Ass.Pl.21. 10.H.4.0. (m) See more before in this Chapter, Sect.365.

¶ *En Assise de Nouel disseisin ou en ascun auter action, &c.* Here it is to be obserued, That a speciall verdict, or at large, may be giuen in any Action, and vpon any Issue, be the Issue generall or speciall, and albeit there bee some contrarie opinions in our Bookes, yet the Law is now setled in this poynt.

¶ *Per que le Lessor enter.* Here it appeareth that the condition is executed by re-entrie, and yet the Lessor after his re-entrie shall not by the opinion of Littleton, plead the Condition without shewing the Deed, because he was partie and priuie to the condition, for the parties must shew forth the deed, vnlesse it be by the act and wrong of his aduersarie, as hath beene sayd, (m) but an estranger which is not priuie to the Condition, nor claimeth vnder the same, as in the cases abouesayd appeareth, shall not after the Condition is executed in pleading, be inforced to shew forth the Deed: and by this diuersitie all the Books and authorities in Law which seeme to be at variance are reconciled. See also for this matter the Section next following.

10.Ass p.9. 21.Ass.28. 17.Ass.20. 31.Ass.21. 33.Ass.2. 39.E.28.44.E.3. 22. 10.H.4.9. 7.H.5.5. 9.E.4 26. 18.E.4.12. 15.E.4.16.17. 11.H.7.22.

¶ *Les Recognitors del Assise poient dire, &c.* Here it appeareth that the Jurors may find the fact, albeit the Deed be not shewed in euidence, and the rather for that the Condition vpon the Liuerie (as hath beene sayd) is good, albeit there be no Deed at all.

¶ *Et prieront le discretion des Iustices.* That is to say, They (hauing declared the speciall matter) pray the discretion of the Justices, which is as much to say, as That they would discerne what the Law adiudgeth thereupon, whither for the Demaundant, or for the Tenant: so as by the authoritie of Littleton, *Discretio est discernere per legem, quid sit iustum,* that is, to discerne by the right line of Law, and not by the crooked cord of priuate opinion, which the Vulgar call Discretion: *Si à iure discedas, Vagus eris, & erunt omnia omnibus incerta;* and therefore Commissions that authorise any to proceed *Secundum sanas discretiones vestras* is as much to say, as *Secundum legem & consuetudinem Angliæ.*

Lib.10.fo.4. case de Sewers.

¶ *Car cibien come les Iurors poient auer conusance, &c.* Hereby it appeareth, That they that haue Conusance of any thing, are to haue Conusance also of all Incidents and Dependants thereupon, for an Incident is a thing necessarily depending vpon another.

It

If a Deed be made and dated in a forreine Kingdome, of Lands within England; yet if Liuerie and Seisin be made, *secundum formam cartæ*, the land shall passe, for it passeth by the Liuerie. *1.E.3.17. in Graystes case.*

*Sect.*367.

EN mesme le manner est de Feoffement en Fee, ou done en le Taile sur Condition, coment que nul escripture vnque fuit fayt de ceo. Et sicome est dit de verdict a large en Assise, &c. En mesme le manner est en briefe dentre founde sur disseisin, et en touts auts actions, ou les Justices voilent prender le verdict a large p la ou tiel verdict a large est fait, la manner del entrie entire est mis en lissue, &c.

IN the same manner it is of a Feoffement in Fee, or a Gift in Taile, vpon condition, although no Writing were euer made of it. And as it is sayd of a Verdict at large in an Assise, &c. In the same manner it is of a Writ of Entrie founded vpon a disseisin, & in all other Actions where the Iustices will take the Verdict at large, there where such Verdict at large is made, the manner of the whole entrie is put in the Issue, &c.

And it is to bee obserued, That the Court cannot refuse a speciall verdict, if it bee pertinent to the matter put in Issue. See the Section next preceding.

Verdict alarge. It is called a Verdict at large because it findeth the matter at large, and leaues it to the iudgement of the Court: or it is called a speciall Verdict, because it findeth the speciall matter, &c. So as hereby it appeareth, That a Verdict (as hath beene sayd) is two fold, *viz.* a Verdict at large, or a speciall Verdict, (which is all one) whereof Littleton here speaketh; and a generall Verdict that is generally found according to the Issue, as if the Issue be not guiltie, to find the partie guiltie or not guiltie generally, & *sic de cæteris*. There is also a Verdict giuen in open Court, and a priuie verdict giuen out of Court before any of the Judges of the Court, so called because it ought to be kept secret and priuie from each of the parties, before it be affirmed in Court. *See the Section next following* *See the next preceding Section*

Sect. 368.

ITem en tiel case lou Lenquest poit dire lour verdict a large, sils voilent pndre sur eux le Conusance de la ley sur le matter, ils poient dire lour verdict generalment, come est mis en lour charge, come en le case auantdit, ils poient bien dire que le Lessor ne disseisa pas le Lessee, sils voilent, &c.

ALso in such case where the Enquest may giue their verdict at large, if they will take vpon them the knowledge of the Law vpon the matter, they may giue their verdict generally as is put in their charge, as in the case aforesaid they may well say, That the lessor did not disseise the Lessee, if they will, &c.

Although the Jurie, if they will take vpon them (as Littleton here saith) the knowledge of the Law, may giue a generall verdict, yet it is dangerous for them so to doe, for if they doe mistake the Law, they runne into the danger of an Attaint, therefore to find the speciall matter is the safest way where the case is doubtfull.

Sect.

Sect. 369.

¶ Pur ceo que il nad ascũ escripture de ceo. Hereby it also appeareth, That albeit the Condition was executed by re-entrie, yet the lessor cannot plead it without shewing of a Deed. But of this matter sufficient hath beene sayd before in the two next preceding Sections.

¶ *Quel est bone plea en Barre.* In a case where there haue beene some varietie of opinions in our Bookes, Littleton here cleereth the doubt, and that vpon a good ground. For hee himselfe reporteth in our Bookes, That it was holden by all the Justices of England, That a lease for life, the reuersion to the Plaintife, was a good barre in an Assise, and also that a Lease for yeares, the reuersion to the Plaintife, might be pleaded in an Assise: and so of a Feoffement in Fee with warrantie. And herein the diuersitie of pleading is to be obserued, for in the case here put by Littleton of a Lease for life, the Tenaunt shall plead it in Barre. But in a case of a Lease for yeares,

18. E. 4. 10. 12. Ass. 38. 10. Ass. 16. 26. H. 6. Barre 9. 38. Ass. 28. 4. 31. Ass. 26. 39. Ass. 3. 43. Ass. 18. 44. Ass. 3. 18. E. 3. Ass. 77. 32. E. 3. ibid. 97. 18. Ass. 22.

4. Eliz. Dyer 207. 8. Eliz. Dyer 246.

¶ Item en mesme le case si le case fuit tiel, que apres ceo, que le Lessor auoit enter pur default de payment, &c. que le Lessee vst enter sur le lessor et luy disseisist, en cest case si le Lessor arraigne vn Assise enuers le Lessee, le Lessee luy puit barre de lassise. Car il poit pleader enuers luy en bar, coment le Lessor que est Plaintife fist vn lease al Defendant pur terme de sa vie, sauant le reuersion al Plaintife, quel est bone plea en Barre, entant que il conust le reuersion estre al Plaintife, en cest case le Plaintife nad asc matt de luy ayd fors que le condition fait sur le Leas, et ceo il ne poet pleader pur ceo que il nad ascun escripture de ceo. Et entant que il ne poet responder al barre il serra barre. Et issint en cest case poyes veier que home est disseisie, et vncore il nauera Assise. Et vncore si le Lessee soit Plaintife, et le Lessor Defendant il barrera le Lessee per verdict dassise, &c. Mes en cest case lou le Lessee est Defendant, si il ne voit plead le dit plea en Barre, mes plead nul tort, nul disseisin, donqs le lessor recouera per Assise, Causa qua supr.

Also in the same case, if the case were such, That after that; that the Lessor had entred for default of payment, &c. that the Lessee had entred vpon the Lessor, and him disseised; in this case if the Lessor arraigne an Assise against the Lessee, the Lessee may barre him of the Assise: for hee may plead against him in Bar, how the Lessor who is pl. made a lease to the def. for term of his life, sauing the Reuersion to the Pl., which is a good plea in bar insomuch as hee acknowledges the reuersion to be to the Pl. In this case the plaintif hath no matter to ayd himselfe, but the conditiõ made vpon the lease & this he cãnot plead, because he hath not any writing of this: and inasmuch as hee cannot answere the bar he shal be barred. And so in this case you may see that a man is disseised, & yet he shal not haue assise. And yet if the lessee be pl. and the lessor def. he shall bar the lessee by verdit of the Assise, &c. but in this case where the Lessee is def. if he wil not plead the said plea in bar, but plead *nul tort, nul diss.* thẽ the lessor shal recouer by assise, *Causa qua supra.*

yeares, or of an estate of Tenant by Statute or Elegit, the Defendant shall not plead in barre, as to say, Assisa non, &c. but iustifie by force of the Lease, &c. and concludo, & issint sans tort. And if the Tenant of the Freehold be not named, he shall plead, Nul tenant de franktenement nosme en le breife: and in the case of the feoffment with warrantie, hee must relie vpon the warrantie.

Section 370.

¶ Item, pur ceo que tielx conditions sont plus communement mis & specifies en faits endentes, ascun petit chose serra icy dit (a moy fitz) de endenture & de fait Poll concernants conditions. Et est ascauoir, que si lendenture soit bipartite, ou tripartite, ou quadripartite, touts les partes de lendenture ne sont que un fait en ley, & chescun part de lendenture est de auxy grande force et effect, sicome touts les parts ensemble.

AND for that such Conditions are most commonly put and specified in Deeds indented, somewhat shall bee here said (to thee my sonne) of an Indenture, and of a Deed Poll concerning Conditions. And it is to bee vnderstood, that if the Indenture be bipartite, or tripartite, or quadripartite, all the parts of the Indenture are but one Deed in Law, and euery part of the Indenture is of as great force and effect as all the parts together bee.

¶ EN *faits endentes.* Those are called by seuerall names, as Scriptū indentatum, carta indenta, Scriptura indentata, Indentura, Literæ indentatæ. An Indenture is a writing containing a Conueyance, Bargaine, Contract, Couenants or agreements betweene two or more, and is indented in the top or side answerable to another that likewise comprehendeth the selfe same matter, and is called an Indenture, for that it is so indented, and is called in Greeke συμγραφον. *Vid. Sect.* 217.

If a Deed beginneth; Hæc Indentura, &c. and in troth the Parchment or Paper is not indented; this is no Indenture, because words cannot make it indented. But if the deed be actually indented, and there is no words of Indenture in the Deed, yet it is an Indenture in Law, for it may bee an Indenture without words, but not by words without indenting. *Lib.*5.*fol.*20. *Stiles case.*

¶ *En faits indent.* And here it is to be vnderstood that it ought to bee in Parchment or in Paper. For if a writing bee made vpon a peece of wood, or vpon a peece of Linnen, or in the barke of a tree, or on a stone, or the like, &c. and the same bee sealed or deliuered, yet is it no Deed, for a Deed must bee written eyther in Parchment or Paper as before is said, for the writing vpon these is least subiect to alteration or corruption. *14.E.2.Ley 79. 4.E.2. Fines 116. 4.E.2. Ley 68. 2.R.2. Det 4. 27.H.6.9. F.N.B.122.I.*

¶ *Si lendenture soit bipartite, ou tripartite, ou quadripartite, &c.* Bipartite is when there be two parts and two parties to the Deed. Tripartite when there are three parts and three parties, and so of Quadripartite, Quinquepartite, &c.

¶ *Et de fait poll.* A deed poll is that which is plaine without any indenting, so called, because it is cut euen or polled, euery Deed that is pleaded shall be intended to be a Deed poll, vnles it be alleaged to be indented.

¶ *Touts les parts del endenture ne sont que vn en ley.* If a man by deed indented make a gift in tayle, and the Donee dyeth without issue, that part of the Indenture which belonged to the Donee doth now belong to the Donor, for both parts doe make but one Deed in Law. *38.H.6.24.25. 9.H.6.35.33.H.6.34. 9.E.3.18. 9.E.4.18. Pl.Com.134.*

¶ *Et chescun part del Indenture est de auxy grand force, &c.* This is manifest of it selfe, and is proued by the Bookes aforesaid.

It is to be obserued, that if the Feoffor, Donor, or Lessor seale the part of the Indenture belonging to the Feoffee, &c. the Indenture is good; albeit the Feoffee neuer sealeth the Counterpart belonging to the Feoffor, &c.

Section 371.

ET feaſance de Indenture eſt en deux maners. Un eſt de faire eux en le tierce perſon. Un auter eſt de faire eux en le primer perſon. Le feaſance en le tierce perſon eſt come en tiel forme.

Hæc Indentura facta inter R. de P. ex vna parte, & V. de D. ex altera parte, Teſtatur, quod prædictus R. de P. dedit & conceſſit, & hac præſenti carta indentata confirmauit præfato. V. de D. talem terram, &c. Habendum & tenendum, &c. ſub conditione, &c. In cuius rei teſtimonium partes prædictæ ſigilla ſua præſentibus alternatim appoſuerunt. *Vel ſic*: in cuius rei teſtimonium vni parti huius Indenturæ penes præfatum V. de D. remanenti, prædict' R. de P. ſigillum ſuum appoſuit, alteri verò parti eiuſdem Indenturæ penes R. de P. remanenti idem V. de D. ſigillum ſuum appoſuit. Datum, &c.

Tiel Endenture eſt appel endenture fait en le tierce perſon, pur ceo que les Uerbes, &c. ſont en la tierce perſon. Et tiel forme dendentures eſt de pluis ſure feaſance, pur ceo que eſt pluis communement vſe, &c.

AND the making of an Indenture is in two manners. One is to make them in the third perſon. Another is to make them in the firſt perſon. The making in the third perſon is as in this forme.

This Indenture made betweene R. of P. of the one part, and V. of D. of the other part, witneſſeth that the ſaid R. of P. hath granted, and by this preſent Charter indented confirmed to the aforeſaid V. of D. ſuch Land &c. To haue and to hold, &c. vpon Condition, &c. In witneſſe whereof the parties aforeſaid to theſe preſents interchangeably haue put their Seales, Or thus. *In witneſſe whereof to the one part of this Indenture, remayning with the ſaid V. of D. the ſaid. R. of P. hath put his Seale, and to the other part of the ſame Indenture remayning with the ſaid R. of P. the ſaid V. of D. hath put his ſeale. Dated, &c.*

Such an Indenture is called an Indenture made in the third perſon, becauſe the Verbes, &c. are in the third perſon. And this forme of Indentures is the moſt ſure making, becauſe it is moſt commonly vſed, &c.

9.E.3.18. Vide the Bookes afore rehearſed.

ET *le feaſance del Indenture eſt en deux maners, &c.* Here is another of our Authors perfect diuiſions. In this & the next Section following. Littleton doth illuſtrate his meaning by ſetting downe formes and examples which doe effectually teach.

Vide 40.E.3.2. 7.H.7.14. Dier 28.H.8.19 Lib.2.fol. 4.& 5. Godards caſe.

In theſe two formes there are to bee obſerued (amongſt other) three generall parts of the ſame, viz. the Premiſſes, the Habendum, and the In cuius rei teſtimonium But hereof hath beene ſpoken at large, Sect 1.4.& 40. for Littleton ſpeaketh not here of the deliuery, but only of the Context or words of the Deed.

17.Eliz. Dier 342. 1.R.3. 14.H.6.28.Bab. 12.H.4.12. 30.Aſſ.31.

Pur ceo que eſt le pluis communement vſe. Here it appeareth that which is moſt commonly vſed in Conueyances is the ſureſt way. A communi obſeruantia non eſt recedendum, & minime mutanda ſunt quæ certam habuerunt interpretationem. Magiſter rerum Vſus. It is prouided by the Statute of 38.E.3.cap.4. that all penall Bonds in the third

perſon

person be void and holden for none, wherein some of our Bookes (d) seeme to differ, but they being rightly understood, there is no difference at all. For the Statute is to bee intended of Bonds taken in other Courts out of the Realme, and so it appeareth by the Preamble of that Act. And it was principally intended of the Courts of Rome, and so it appeareth by Justice Hankford in 2.H.4. in which Courts Bonds were taken in the third person. So as such Bonds made out of the Realme are void, but other Bonds in the third person, are resolued to be good, as well Indentures in the third person, by the opinion of the whole Court in 8.E.4. (d) 40.E.3.1. 2.H.5.10. 8.E.4.5.

Sect. 372.

¶ LE feasance de Indenture en le primer person est come en tiel forme. Omnibus Christi fidelibus ad quos præsentes literæ indentatæ peruenerint, A. de B. salutem in Domino sempiternam. Sciatis me dedisse, concessisse, & hac præsen' carta mea indentata confirmasse C. de D. talem terram, &c. *Vel sic*: Sciant præsentes & futuri, quod ego A. de B. dedi, concessi, & hac præsenti carta mea indentata confirmaui C. de D. talem terram, &c. Habendum & tenendum, &c. sub conditione sequenti, &c. In cuius rei testimonium tam ego præd' A. de B. quam prædict' C. de D. his Indenturis sigilla nostra alternatim apposuim'. *Vel sic*: In cuius rei testimonium ego præfatus A. vni parti huius Indenturæ sigillum meum apposui, alteri verò parti eiusdem Indenturæ prædict' C. de D. sigillum suum apposuit, &c.

THe making of an Indenture in the first person is, as in this forme. *To all Christian people whom these presents indented shall come, A. of B. sends greeting in our Lord God euerlasting. Know yee mee to haue giuen, granted, and by this my present Deed indented, confirmed to C. D. such land, &c.* Or thus: *Know all men present and to come that I A. of B. haue giuen, granted, and by this my present Deed indented, confirmed to C. of D. such land, &c. To haue and to hold, &c. vpon Condition following, &c. In witnesse whereof, aswell I the said A. of B. as the aforesaid C. of D. to these Indentures haue interchangeably put our Seales.* Or thus: *In witnesse whereof I the aforesaid A. to the one part of this Indenture haue put my Seale, and to the other part of the same Indenture, the said C. of D. hath put his Seale, &c.*

¶ HEre Littleton sets downe three formes of Deeds indented in the first person, Breuis via per exempla, longa per precepta. It is requisite for euery Student to get Presidents and approued formes not only of Deeds according to the example of Littleton, but of Fines, and other Conueyances, and Assurances, and specially of good and perfect pleading, and of the right entries and formes of Judgements which will stand him in great stead: both while he studie, and after when he shall giue councell. It is a safe thing to follow approued Presidents, for Nihil simul inuentum est perfectum. *Vide Sect.371.*

Section 373.

¶ ET il semble que tiel endenture que est fait en le primer person est auxy bone en la ley,

AND it seemeth that such Indenture which is made in the first person is as good in law as the

ley, sicome lendenture fait en le tierce person, quant ambideux parties ont a ceo mise lour seals, car si l'endenture fait en l' tierce person, ou en le primer person, mention soit fait que le grantor auoit mise solement son seale, & nemy le grauntee, donques est lendenture tantsolement le fait le grauntor. Mes lou mention est fait que le grantee ad mis son seale a lendenture, &c. donques est lendenture auxybien le fait le grantee come le fait le grauntor. Issint il est le fait dambideux, & auxy chescun part de lendenture est le fait dambideux parties en tiel case.

Indenture made in the third person, when both parties haue put to this their seales, for if in the Indenture made in the third person, or in the first person, mention be made that the grantor only hath put his seale, and not the grantee, then is the Indenture only the deed of the grantor. But where mention is made that the grantee hath put to his seale to the Indenture, &c. then is the Indenture as well the deed of the grantee as the deed of the grantor. So is it the deed of them both, and also each part of the Indenture is the deed of both parties in this case.

¶ Here is to be obserued, that albeit the words in this Indenture be only the words of the Feoffor, yet if the Feoffee put his Seale to the one part of the Indenture, it is the Deed of them both. And in this speciall case to make it the Deed of the Feoffee, it appeareth by Littleton, that mention must be made in the Deed, that hee hath put to his Seale. for that he is no way made partie to make it, being made in the first person, but only by the clause of putting his Seale thereunto. Otherwise it is of a Deed indented in the third person as before it appeareth, for there he is made partie to the Deed in the beginning. And Littletons rule is true, that euery part of an Indenture is the Deede of both parties, for as it hath beene said both parts make but one Deed in Law in that case.

Sect.374.

¶ *Sur certaine condition, &c.* Here by this (&c.) is implied, that the condition in this case doth extend both to the estate for life, & to the remainder, but by speciall limitation it may extend to euery one of them, and not to the other. And albeit he in the remainder be no partie to the Indenture (the parties thereunto only being the Lessor and the Tenant for life) yet when hee in the remainder entreth and agreeth to haue the lands by force of the Indenture, hee is bound to performe the conditions contained in the In-

¶ Item si estate soit fait p Indenture a vn home pur terme de sa vie, le remainder a vn auter en fee sur certaine condition, &c. & si le tenant a terme d vie auoit mis son seale al part de lendenture, & puis morust, & il que est en le remainder ent en la terre, per force de son remainder, &c. en cest cas il est tenus de performer touts les conditiōs comprise en lenden-

ALso if an estate bee made by Indenture to one for terme of his life, the remainder to another in fee vpon a certaine condition, &c. and if the tenant for life haue put his seale to the part of the Indenture, and after dieth, and he in the remainder entreth into the land by force of his remainder, &c. In this case hee is tied to performe all the conditions comprised

lendenture, sicome le tenant a terme de vie, devoit faire en sa vie, & uncore cestuy en le remainder ne unques enseale ascun part del endenture. Mes la cause est, que entant que il enter et agreea dauer les terres per force del endenture, il est tenus de performer les conditions deins mesme lendenture sil voile auer la terre, &c.

in the Indenture, as the tenant for life ought to haue done in his life time, and yet hee in the remainder neuer sealed any part of the Indenture. But the cause is, for that inasmuch as hee entred and agreed to haue the lāds, by force of the Indenture hee is bound to performe the conditions within the same Indenture if hee will haue the land, &c.

denture. And here is also a diuersitie to be vnderstood that any estranger to the Indenture may take by way of remainder, but he cannot in this case take any present estate in possession, because he is an estranger to the Deede.

If A. by Deed indented betweene him and B. letteth lands to B. for life, the remainder to C. in fee reseruing a rent, Tenant for life dieth, he in the remainder entreth into the lands, he shall bee bound to pay the rent, for the cause and reason before yeelded by Littleton. An Indenture of Lease is ingrossed betweene A. of the one part, and D. and R. of the other part, which purporteth a demise for yeares by A to D and R, A. sealeth and deliuereth the Indenture to D. and D. sealeth the Counterpane to A. But R. did not seale and deliuer it. And by the same indenture it is mentioned, that D. and R did grant to be bound to the Plaintife in 20. pound in case that certaine conditions comprised in the Indenture were not performed. And for this 20. pound A. brought an Action against D. only, and shewed forth the Indenture. The Defendant pleaded, that it is proued by the Indenture that the demise by indenture was made to D. and R. which R. is in full life and not named in the writ, Iudgement of the writ. The Plaintife replyed that R. did neuer seale & deliuer the Indenture, & so his writ was good against D. sole. And there the counsell of the Plaintife tooke a diuersity betweene a rent reserued which is parcell of the Lease, and the land charged therewith, and a summe in grosse, as here the 20. pound is, for as to the rent they agreed that by the agreement of R. to the Lease, he was bound to pay it, but for the 20. pound that is a summe in grosse and collaterall to the Lease, and not annexed to the land, and groweth due only by the Deed, and therefore R. said they was not chargeable therewith for that he had not sealed and deliuered the Deed. But in asmuch as he had agreed to the Lease which was made by Indenture he was chargeable by the Indenture for the same summe in grosse, and for that R. was not named in the writ, it was adiudged that the writ did abate.

50.E.3.22. 3.H.6,26.b.

38.E.3.8.a. 3.H.6.26.b. Vide 45.E.3.11.12.

¶ *Auer la terre, &c.* Here is implyed an ancient maxime of the Law, viz. Qui sentit commodum sentire debet & onus, Et transit terra cum onere.

Section 375.

¶ Item si feoffment soit fait p fait Poll sur condition, & pur ceo que le condition nest pas performe, le feoffor entra & happa la possession de le fait Poll, si le feoffee port un action de cel entrie enuers le feoffor, il ad este question si le feoffor poit pleder le condition per le dit fait Poll encounter le feoffee. Et ascuns ont dit que non, entant que il semble

ALso if a feoffment bee made by deed Poll vpon condition, and for that the condition is not performed, the feoffor entreth and getteth the possession of the deed Poll, if the feoffee brings an action for this entrie against the feoffor, it hath beene a question if the feoffor may plead the condition by the said deed Poll against the feoffee. And some haue said

semble a eux que vn fait Poll, & le propertie de mesme le fait appertient a celuy a que le fait est fait, & nemy a celuy que fist le fait. Et entant que tiel fait ne attient al feoffor, il semble a eux que il ne poit pas ceo pleder. Et auters ont dit le contrarie, et ont monstre diuers causes. Un est, si le case fuit tiel, que en action perenter eux, si le feoffee pleder mesme le fait et monstre est al Court, en cest cas entant que le fait est en Court, le feoffor poit monstrer al court coment en le fait sont diuers conditions destre performes de le part le feoffee, &c, et pur ceo que ils ne fueront performes, il enter, &c. et a ceo il serra resceiue. per mesme le reason quant le feoffor ad le fait en poigne, et ceo monstra a le court, il serra bien resceiue de ceo pleder, &c. et nosment quant le feoffor est priuie al fait, car couient estre priuie al fait quant il fist le fait, &c.

hee cannot, inasmuch as it seemes vnto them that a deed Poll and the property of the same deed belongeth to him to whom the deed is made, and not to him which maketh the deed. And inasmuch as such a deed doth not appertaine to the feoffor. It seemes vnto them that he cannot plead it. And others haue said the contrary, and haue shewed diuers reason, one is, if the case were such that in an action betweene them if the feoffee plead the same deed and shew it to the Court, in this case insomuch as the deed is in Court, the feoffor may shew to the Coutt how in the deed there are diuers conditions to be performed of the part of the feoffee, &c. and because they were not performed, he entred, &c. and to this he shall be receiued. By the same reason when the feoffor hath the deed in hand, and shew this to the court, he shall well be receiued to plead it, &c. and namely when the feoffor is priuy to the fait, for he must bee priuie to the deed when he makes the deed, &c.

(a) Vid. Sect. 170. 302. 340.

HEre the latter opinion is cleere Law at this day, and is Littletons owne opinion (a) as before hath beene obserued.

Ont monstre diuers causes.

Fœlix qui potuit rerum cognoscere causas,
Et ratio melior semper praeualet.

24. E. 3. 73. 45. E. 3. *Monstrans des faits.* 55. (b) 40. *Ass.* 34. lib. 5. 75. b. *Wymarks case.* (c) 12. H. 4. 8. 42. E. 3. 27. *Wymarks case, vbi supra.* 38. H. 6. 2. 41. *Ass.* 29. 12. H. 4. 8. 7. H. 4. 39. 11. H. 4. 73. 45. E. 3. 11. F. N. B. 243.

Entant que le fait est en Court, &c. And herewith do agree (b) many Authorities in Law. (c) And if the Deed remaine in one Court, it may be pleaded in another Court without shewing forth; Qui lex non cogit ad impossibilia.

De part le feoffee, &c. Here also is implyed if the condition bee to be performed on the part of the Feoffor or by a stranger, and it is to be vnderstood that when a Deed is shewed forth to the Court the Deed shall remaine in Court all that tearme in the custody of the Custos breuium, but at the end of the Tearme (if the Deed be not denied) then the Law adiudgeth the Deed in the custody of the partie to whom it belongeth, for a mans euidences are as it were the sinewes of his land. But if the Deed be denied, then the Deed in iudgement of Law remaineth in court vntill the plea be determined. The residue of this Section needeth no explication.

Sect. 376.

¶ Auxy si deux homes font vn trespas a vn auter, le quel release a vn de eux per son fait touts actions personals, & nient obstant il suist action de trespasse enuers lauter, le defendant bien poit monstrer que le trespasse fuit fait per luy et per vn auter son companion, et que le Plaintife per son fait quel il monstre auant relessa a son companion touts actions personals, iudgement si action, &c. Et vncore tiel fait appertient a son companion, et nemy a luy, mes pur ceo que il poit auer aduantage per le fait si voit monstrer le fait al Court, il poit ceo bien pleder, &c. Per mesme le reason poit le feoffor en lauter cas quant il doit auer aduantage per le condition compris deins le fait Poll.

Also if two men doe a trespasse to another, who release to one of them by his deed all actions personalls, and notwithstanding sueth an action of trespasse against the other, the defendāt may well shew that the trespasse was done by him and by an other his fellow, and that the Plaintife by his deed (which he sheweth forth) released to his fellow all actions personalls, and demand the iudgement, &c. and yet such deed belongeth to his fellow and not to him, but because hee may haue aduantage by the deed if hee will shew the deed to the Court, hee may well plead this, &c. by the same reason may the feoffor in the other case when he ought to haue aduantage by the condition comprised within the deed Poll.

¶ *Si deux homes font vn trespasse a vn auter, &c.* Here by this Section it is to bee vnderstood that when diuers doe a trespasse, the same is Ioynt or Seuerall at the will of him to whom the wrong is done, yet if he release to one of them; all are discharged, because his own Deed shall be taken most strongly against himselfe, but otherwise it is in case of appeale of death, &c. as if two men be ioyntly and seuerally bounden in an Obligation, if the Obligee release to one of them; both are discharged, and seeing the Trespassers are parties and priuies in wrong, the one shall not plead a Release to the other without shewing of it forth, albeit the Deede appertaine to the other. *27.E.3.83. 23.E.4.2. 15.E.4.26. 21.E.4.72. 22.E.4.7. 8.H.6.15. 20.H.6.41. 21.H.6. Arbitrement,41. 2.R.3.9.4. 14.H.8.10. 34.H.8.tit.Estrange al fait 2. 3.H.6.18.26.*

If an action of debt vpon an Obligation be brought against an heire, he may pleade in barre a Release made by the Obligee to the Executors. But albeit the Deed belong to another, yet must he shew it forth, for both of them are priuie to the Testator. *13.E.3.tit.Monstrans des faits,43.*

¶ *Per mesme le reason.* Vbi eadem Ratio, ibi idem Ius.

Sect. 377.

¶ Auxy si le feoffee donast ou grātast le fait Poll al feoffor, tiel grant serra bone, et donques le fait & le propertie del

Also if the feoffee granteth the deed to the feoffor, such grant shall bee good, and then the deed and the propertie therof belongeth

¶ *Le property del fait appertient al feoffor.* Hereby it appeareth that a man may giue or grant his Deed to another, and such a grant by Paroll is good. And

And it is also implied, That if a man hath an Obligation, though he cannot graunt the thing in Action, yet hee may giue or grant the Deed, viz. the Parchment and Waxe to another, who may cancell and vse the same at his pleasure.

¶ *Serra plus tost entend que il vient al fait per loyall meane, que per tortious meane.* Omnia præsumuntur legitimè facta, donec probetur in contrarium. Iniuria non præsumitur.

¶ Quære de dubijs. There be three kind of vnhappie men.

1 Qui scit & non docet, Hee that hath knowledge and teacheth not.

2 Qui docet & non viuit, Hee that teacheth and liueth not thereafter.

3 Qui nescit, & non interrogat, He that knoweth not, and doth not enquire to vnderstand. Therefore Littleton saith, Quære de dubijs.

fait appertient al Feoffor, &c. Et quant le Feoffor ad le Fait en poigne, et est plead al Court, il sera plus tost entendue que il vient al Fait per loyal meane, que per tortious meane. Et issint a eux semble que le Feoffor poet bien pleader tiel fait polle que comprent condition, &c. sil ad le fait en poigne. Ideo semper quære de dubijs, quia per rationes peruenitur ad legitimam rationem &c.

to the Feoffor, &c. and when the Feoffor hath the deed in hand, and is pleaded to the Court, it shall be rather intended, That he commeth to the Deed by lawfull meanes, than by a wrongfull mean: & so it seemeth vnto them, That the feoffor may well plead such deed poll which compriseth the condition, &c. if he hath the same in hand. *Ideo semper quære de dubijs, quia per rationes peruenitur ad legitimam rationem &c.*

Infœlix cuius nulli sapientia prodest.
Infœlix qui recta docet, cum viuit inique.
Infœlix qui pauca sapit spernitque doceri.

¶ Quia per rationes peruenitur ad legitimam rationem. For Ratio is Radius diuini Luminis, And by reasoning and debating of graue learned men the darknes of ignorance is expelled, and by the light of legall Reason the Right is discerned, and thereupon Judgment giuen according to Law, which is the perfection of Reason. This is of Littleton here called Legitima ratio, whereunto no man can attaine but by long studie, often conference, long experience, and continuall obseruation.

Certaine it is, That in matters of difficultie the more seriously they are debated and argued, the more truly they are resolued, and thereby new inuentions iustly auoyded.

Inter cuncta leges & percontabere doctos.

Section 378.

¶ *Condition en Ley, &c.* Littleton hauing spoken of Conditions in Deed, now according to his owne diuision commeth to speake of Conditions in law.

¶ *Que ne soit specifie en Escript.* A Condition in Law is that which the Law intendeth or implieth without expresse words in the Deed.

¶ Estates que homes ont sur condition en ley sont tiels estates que ont vn condition per la ley a eux annex, comment que ne soit specifie en escript. Si come home grant per son fait a vn auter lofficce de Par-

Estates which men haue vpon Condition in Law, are such Estates which haue a Condition by the law to them annexed, albeit that it bee not specified in writing. As if a man graunt by his Deed to another the

Parkership de vn park a aver & occupier mesme loffice pur terme de son vie, lestate que il ad en loffice est sur condition en ley, cestascauoir, que le parker bien & loyalment gardera le park, & ferra ceo que a tiel office appertient a faire, ou autrement bien lirroit al grauntor & a ses heires de luy ouste, & de grant a vn auter sil voit, &c. Et tiel condition que est entendus per la ley estre annexe a ascun chose, est auxy fort sicome la condition fuissoit mis en escript.

the office of Parkership of a Parke, to haue and occupie the same office for terme of his life, the estate which he hath in the office is vpon Condition in Law, to wit, that the Parker shall well and lawfully keepe the Parke, and shall doe that which to such office belongeth to doe, or otherwise it shal be lawful to the grātor, & his heires to oust him, and to grant it to another if hee will, &c. And such Condition as is intended by the Law to be annexed to any thing, is as strong as if the Condition were put in writing.

¶ *Que le Parker bien & loyalment gardera le Parke, &c.* Parke, this should be written Parque which is a French word, and signifieth that which we vulgarly call a Parke of the French Verbe Parquer, to imparke, to inclose. It is called in Domesday Parcus. In law it signifieth a great quantitie of ground inclosed, priuiledged for wild beasts of chase by prescription, or by the Kings grant.

The beasts of Parque, or Chase properly extend to the Bucke, the Doe, the Foxe, the Matron, the Roe, but in a common and legall sence, to all the beasts of the Forrest. There bee both Beasts and Foules of the Warren. Beasts, as Hares, Conies, and Roes called in Records (d) Capreoli. Fowles of two sorts, viz. Terrestres and Aquatiles, Terrestres of two sorts. Siluestres and Campestres: Campestres as Partridge, Quaile, Raile, &c. Siluestres, as Phesant, Woodcocke, &c. Aquatiles, as Mallard, Herne, &c. whereof I haue seen this Record. (*) Rex concessit Iohanni de Beuerly Armigero suo quod ipse cum quibuscunque canibus suis ad quascunque bestias, feras Regis in quibuscunque, forestis, parcis suis quotiescunque voluerit venari possit, & quoscunque Falcones possit permittere volare ad quascunque aues de Warrena in quibuscunque riparijs, &c.

(d) Hill. 15. E. 3. coram Rege in Thesaur.

(*) 38. E. 3. rot. patent. part 1. m. 10.

It is resolued (e) by the Justices and the Kings Councell, that Capreoli, id est, Roes, non sunt Bestiæ de foresta, eo quod fugant alias feras. Beasts of Forests, be properly Hart, Hind, Bucke, Hare, Beare and Woolfe, but legally all wild beasts of Venery.

(e) Hill. 13. E. 3. coram Rege in Thesaur.

A Forrest and Chase are not, but a Parke must bee inclosed. The Forrest and Chase doe differ in Offices and Lawes: euery Forrest is a Chase, but euery Chase is not a Forrest. A subiect may haue a Forrest by especiall grant of the King, as the Duke of Lancaster, and the Abbot of Whitbie had.

Vid. Sect. 1.

Ockam cap. quid Regis Foresta saith, Foresta est tuta ferarum mansio non quarumlibet, sed siluestrium, non quibuslibet in locis, sed certis, & adhoc idoneis, vnde Foresta E mutata in O. quasi feresta; hoc est, ferarum statio.

Vide Bract fol 221. & 316. Britton fol. 34. Fleta lib 2. cap. 34. 35.

Pudzeld or Woodgeld is to be free from payment of money for taking of wood in any Forest. But let vs now returne to our Littleton.

In this Section Littleton putteth an example of a Condition in Law annexed to the office of the Keeper of a Parke, but this example must bee vnderstood with a distinction, for if the Parker doth not attend on the Parke one or two, &c. dayes, this is no forfeiture of the Office of Parkership, but if in his default any Deere be killed, and so a dammage to the Lord, that is a forfeiture; for (that it may be said once for all) non-vser of it selfe without some speciall dammage is no forfeiture of priuate Offices, but non-vser of publique Offices which concerne the administration of Justice, or the Common wealth, is of it selfe a cause of forfeiture.

5. E. 4. 15. b. L. 5. E. 4. 26. Pl. Com. 379. 380.

2. H. 7. 13. 39. H. 6. 32. &c.

¶ *Luy ouster sil voit, &c.* Littleton here speaketh of an Ouster by force of a Condition in Law; therefore it is to bee seene in what other cases the Grantor may lawfully oust his Officer.

There is a diuersitie betweene Officers that haue no other profit, but a Collaterall certaine fee, for there the Grantor may discharge him of his seruice, as to be a Bayly, Receiuer, Sur-

18.E.4.8. 31.H.8. grants. Br. 134 34 H.8. ibid. 93. 11. Eliz. Dier. 285.

ueyor, Auditor, or the like, the exercise whereof is but labour and charge to him, but hee must haue his fee: for the maine rule of Law is, That no man can frustrate or derogate from his owne grant to the preiudice of the Grantee. And where albeit the Grantee hath no other profit but his fee, yet that fee is to bee perceiued and taken out of the profits appertayning to the Lord within his Office, for there the Grantor cannot discharge him of his seruice or attendance, for that may turne to the preiudice of the Grantee, if the Grantor will not grant the Office at all. But in all cases where the Officer relinquisheth his Office, and refuseth to attend, he loseth his Office, Fee, Profit and all.

22.H.6.10. 3.6.E.6. Dier 71.

There is another diuersitie where the Grantee besides his certaine fee hath profits and auayles by reason of his Office, there the Grantor cannot discharge him of his seruice or attendance, for that should be to the preiudice of the Grantee. As if a man doth grant to another the Office of the Stewardship of his Courts of his Mannors with a certaine fee, the Grantor cannot discharge him of his seruice and attendance, because he hath other profits and fees belonging to his Office, which he should lose, if he were discharged of his Office. And as in the case which Littleton here putteth of the Office of the Keeper of a Parke, for that hee hath not only his fee certaine, but profits and auayles also, in respect of his office, as Deere Skinnes, Shoulders, &c. But now let vs proceed and see what other particular forfeitures in Law bee of this Office here spoken of by Littleton, and somewhat of Conditions in Law in generall.

15.E.4.3.l. 5.E.4.26. 28.H.8. Bendloes enter Eues. de Londres & Hecton. lib. 9. fol. 50. 95. 96. 99.

(f) Mich. 33.E.1. coram Rege in Thesaur. Leuesque de Durhams case.

And it is to be vnderstood, that if any Keeper kill any Deere without warrant, or fell or cut any Trees, woods, or Vnderwoods, and conuert them to his owne vse, it is a forfeiture of his Office, for the destruction of vert is, by a meane, destruction of Venison. So it is if he pul down the lodge or any house within the Park for putting of Hay into it for feeding of the Deere or such like, it is a forfeiture, and the reason wherefore the Office in these and in like cases shall be forfeited (f) is quia in quo quis delinquit in eo de iure est puniendus.

Pl. Com. 379. a. Sir Henrie Neuils case, 21 E.4.20.93.

As to Conditions in Law, you shall vnderstand they bee of two Natures, that is to say, by the Common Law, and by Statute. And those by the Common Law are of two Natures, that is to say, the one is founded vpon Skill and Confidence, the other without Skill or Confidence: Vpon Skil and Confidence, as here the Office of Parkership, and other Offices in the next Section mentioned, and the like.

Lib. 8. fol. 44. Wittinghams case.

Touching Conditions in Law without Skill, &c. some bee by the Common Law, and some by the Statute. By the Common Law, as to euery estate of Tenant by the Courtesie, Tenant in Tayle after possibilitie of issue extinct, Tenant in Dower, Tenant for Life, Tenant for Yeares, Tenant by Statute Merchant, or Staple, Tenant by Elegit, Gardein, &c. there is a Condition in Law secretly annexed to their Estates, that if they alien in fee, &c. that he in the reuersion or remainder may enter, and sic de similibus, or if they clayme a greater Estate in Court of Record, and the like.

Concerning Conditions in Law founded vpon Statutes, for some of them an entrie is giuen, and for some other a recouery by action: where an entrie is giuen, as vpon an alienation in Mortmaine, &c. and the like. Where an action is giuen, as for waste against Tenant for life and yeares, and the like.

¶ *Et tiel Condition que est entendue per la ley estre annex a ascun chose est auzi fort, &c.* **Here it is worthy the obseruation to take a view of** the diuisions aforesaid in some particular case. As for example. Admit that an Office of Parkership be granted or discend to an Infant or Feme Couert, if the Conditions in Law annexed to this Office which require Skill and Confidence bee not obserued and fulfilled, the Office is lost for euer, because as Littleton saith, here it is as strong as an expresse Condition. But if a Lease for life be made to a Fem Couert, or an Infant, and they by Charter of feoffment alien in fee, the breach of this Condition in Law, that is without Skill, &c. is no absolute forfeiture of their estate. So of a Condition in Law giuen by Statute, which giueth an Entrie only. As if an Infant or a Fem Couert with her husband aliens by Charter of feoffment in Mortmaine, this is no barre to the Infant, or Fem Couert. But if a recouery be had against an Infant or Fem couert in an Action of Waste, there they are bound and barred for euer.

Lib. 8. fol. 44. Wittinghams case.

And it is to be obserued, that a Condition in Law by force of a Statute which giueth a recouery is in some case more strong then a Condition in Law without a recouery. For if Lessee for life make a Lease for yeares, and after enter into the land, and make waste, and the Lessor recouer in an Action of Waste, he shall auoid the Lease made before the waste done. But if the Lessee for life make a Lease for yeares, and after enter vpon him, and make a feoffment in fee this forfeiture shall not auoid the Lease for yeares. Nor in any of the said cases a precedent Rent granted out of the Land shall be auoyded. For if Lessee for life grant a Rent charge, and after doth waste, and the Lessor recouereth in an Action of Waste, he shall hold the Land charged

ged

ged during the life of the Tenant for life, but if the rent were granted after the waste done, the Lessor shall auoid it.

And the reason wherefore the Lease for yeares in the case aforesaid, shall be auoyded, is because of necessitie the Action of waste must be brought against the Lessee for life, which in that case must bind the Lessee for yeares, or else by the Act of the Lessee for life the Lessor should bee barred to recouer Locum vastatum, which the Statute giueth.

If a man hath an Office for life which requireth Skill and confidence, to which Office he hath a house belonging, and chargeth the house with a Rent during his life, and after commit a forfeiture of his Office, the Rent charge shall not be auoyded during his life, for regularly a man that taketh aduantage of a Condition in Law shall take the Land with such charge as he finds it. And therefore Littleton is here to be vnderstood, that a Condition in Law is as strong as a condition in deed, as to auoide the estate or interest it selfe, but not to auoide precedent charges, but in some particular cases as by that which hath beene said appeareth.

There be at this day more conditions in Law annexed to offices then were when Littleton wrote; for example, for offices in any wise touching the administration or execution of Iustice, or Clerkship in any Court of Record, or concerning the Kings Treasure, Reuenue, Account, Customes, Alnage, Auditorship, Kings Surueyor, or keeping of any of his Maiesties Castles, Forts, &c. For if any of these officers bargaine or sell any of the said offices or any Deputation of the same, or take any money or profit, or any promise, couenant, bond or assurance, to haue any money or reward for the same, the person so bargaining or selling, or that shall take any such promise, couenant, bond or assurance shall not only forfeit his estate; but also euery person so buying, giuing or assuring be adiudged a disabled person to haue or enioy the same office or offices, deputation or deputations, &c. And that all such bargaines, sales, promises, couenants and assurances, as be before specified, shall be voide, except as in the said Act is excepted. 3.H.7.ca.12. Auditor, Receiuer, Bailiffe, Keeper of a Castle, Master of the game Keeper or Parker, of any Forrest, Parke, Chase &c. 7.E.6.ca.1. Tresurer, Receiuer Collector, Bailiffe, &c. 5.E.6.ca.16.

Sir Robert Verron Knight being Coferer of the Kings house of the Kings gift, and hauing the receit of a great summe of money yearely of the Kings Reuenue, did for a certaine summe of money bargaine and sell the same to Sir A. I. and agreed to surrender the said office to the King, to the entent a grant might be made to Sir A. who surrendred it accordingly: and thereupon Sir A. was by the Kings appointment admitted and sworne Coferer. And it was resolued by Sir Thomas Egerton Lord Chancellor, then chiefe Iustice and others to whom the King referred the same, that the said office was voyde by the said Statute, and that Sir A. was disabled to haue or take the said office, and that no Non obstante could dispence with this act to enable the said Sir A. for the reason and cause before-mentioned, Sect. 180. And hereupon Sir A. was remoued, and Sir Marmaduke Darell sworne (by the Kings commandement) in his place. And note that all promises, bonds and assurances aswell on the part of the bargainer, as of the bargainee are voyde by the said act. (*) Nulla alia re magis Romana respublica interiit, quam quod magistratus officio venalia erant. Mich. 13. Iacobi Regis. Lib. 3. fo. 83. Colthils case. * Ærod. fo. 353.

(g) Iugurthum going from Rome, said to the Citie, Vade venalis ciuitas, mox peritura si emptorem inuenias. (g) Salust.

Therefore by the Law of England it is further prouided that no Officer or Minister of the King shall be ordained or made for any gift or brocage, fauour or affection, nor that any which pursueth by him or any other, priuily or openly to be in any manner of office, shall bee put in the same office or in any other, but that all such officers shall be made of the best and most lawfull men and sufficient. A Law worthy to be written in letters of gold, but more worthy to be put in due execution. For example, neuer shall Iustice be duly administred, but when the Officers and ministers of Iustice be of such quality, and come to their places in such manner as by this law is required. 12.R.2.ca.2.

¶ *Tiel condition que est entendus per la ley estre annex a ascun chose, est auxi fort sicome la condition fuit mise in escript.* And this accords with that ancient rule; Vtique fortior & potentior est dispositio legis quam hominis. Vid. Sect. 419. 429. 430.

Sect. 379.

¶ En mesme le maner est de grants doffices de Seneschall, Constabular, Bedelary, Bailiwick, ou auters

IN this manner it is of grants of the offices of Steward, Constable, Bedelarie, Bayliwick, or other offices, &c. But if

¶ *Seneschall.* Of this I haue spoken before. 21.E.4.20. Pl. Com. 379.

¶ *Constabularie.* Of this likewise something hath beene spoken before. 8.E.4.6.

Stanf. fo. 142. 32. H. 8. ca. 28.

qui non sit de villa vbi castrum suum situm est, &c. Stanford, fo. 152. Constabularius Turris London, for Custos turris, 32. H. 8. ca. 28. Constable of the Forrest, for the keeper of the Forrest.

¶ *Bedelarye.* **Bedell is derived of the French word** Beadeau, which signifieth a messenger of the Court or under Baylife, in Latyn Bedellus.

And the oath of a Bedell of a Mannor is that he shall duly and truly execute all such Attachements and other Proces as shall be directed to him from the Lord or Steward of his Court, and that he shall present all pound Breaches, which shall happen within his office, and all chattells wayved, and estrayes.

¶ *Baylivvicke.* **Of this sufficient hath beene said before.**

Sect. 380.

¶ Item estates de tres ou tenemēts purront estre sur condition en ley, coment que sur lestate fait, ne fuit ascun mention ou reherſal fait de le condition. Sicome mittomus q̄ vn leas soit fait a le baron et a sa feme, a auer et tener a eux durant l'couerture enter eux, en cest cas ils ont estate pur termē de lour deux vies sur condition en ley, s̄. si vn de deux devie, ou que devorce soit fait enter eux, donque bien lirroit

ALso estates of lands or tenements may bee made vpon condition in law, albeit vpon the estate made there was not any mention or rehersall made of this condition. As put the case that a lease be made to the husband and wife, to haue and to hold to them during the the couerture betweene them. In this case they haue an estate for terme of their two liues vpon condition in law, s. if one of them dy, or that there be a diuorce betweene

¶ HEre Littleton termeth words of limitation to bee Conditions in law; for his first example is;

¶ *Durant le couerture enter eux.* Durante coopertura inter eos This word (Durãte) is properly a word of limitation; as Durante viduitate, or Durante virginitate, or Durante vita, &c. And properly a Condition in Law is as hath beene said where the Law createth the same without any expresse words.

37. H. 6. 17. 3. E. 3. 15. 8. Ass. Pl.

Dum, also maketh a limitation, as if a Lease be made, Dum sola fuerit, or Dum sola & casta vixerit. Dummodo is also a word of limitation as Dum-

lirroit a le lessor et a ses heires dentrer, &c.

them, then it shall bee lawfull for the lessor and his heires to enter, &c.

modo solueret talem redditum. Quamdiu also is a word of limitation, for if a man grant a rent out of the Mannor of D. Quamdiu the Grantor shall bee dwelling vpon the Mannor, this is good, or Quamdiu se bene gesserit.

And so be these words, Donec, Quousque, Vsque ad, Tam diu, Vbicunque.

¶ *Si lun de eux demie, &c.* For if one of them die the couerture is dissolued, and consequently the state determined by the limitation.

¶ *Ou que diuorce soit fait enter eux, &c.* Here is a distinction to be vnderstood: for there be two kinde of diuorces, viz. one a Vinculo matrimonij, * and the other A mensa & thoro. Diuortium dicitur à diuertendo, or Diuortendo quia vir diuertitur ab vxore. Diuorces A vinculo matrimonij are these Causa Præcontractus, Causa Metus, Causa Impotentiæ seu Frigiditatis, Causa Affinitatis, Causa Consanguinitatis, &c. And I reade in an ancient Record Coram Rege Termino Pasch. 30. E. 1. William de Chadworthes case, that he was diuorced from his wife for that he did carnally know her daughter before he married the mother; All which are causes of Diuorce preceding the marriage.

A mensa & Thoro, as Causa Adulterij which dissolueth not the marriage A vinculo Matrimonij, for it is subsequent to the marriage. And the Diuorce that Littleton here speaketh of is intended of such Diuorces, as dissolue the marriage A vinculo matrimonij, and maketh the issue bastard, because they were not Iustæ nuptiæ. And therefore in Littletons case though the husband and wife be diuorced Causa Adulterij, yet the freehold continueth, because the Couerture continueth. And it is further to be vnderstood that many Diuorces that were of force by the Cannon Law, when Littleton wrote, are not at this day in force, for by the Statute of 32. H. 8. ca. 38. it is declared that all persons be lawfull (that is, may lawfully marry) that be not prohibited by Gods lawe to marry, that is to say, that be not prohibited by the Leuiticall degrees.

A man married the daughter of the sister of his first wife, and was drawne in question in the Ecclesiasticall Court for this marriage alledging the same to be against the Cannons, and it was resolued (n) by the Court of Common-Pleas vpon consideration had of the said Statute that the marriage could not be impeached, for that the same was declared by the said Act of Parliament to be good, in asmuch as it was not prohibited by the Leuiticall degrees, Et sic de similibus.

14. E. 2. Grant 92.
37. H. 6. 27.
10. Ass. 4. 6. E. 3. 8. 9. 31. 3. E. 3. 18. Annuity 40. 19. H. 6. 54. Temps E. 1. Annuity 150. 11. Ass. p. 8. 21. Ass. p. 18. 26. E. 3. 63. 7. E. 4. 16. 9. E. 4. 25. 26. 9. H. 6. 39. 14. H. 8. 13.
* 47. E. 3. 27. 39. E. 3. 32. 33. 11. H. 4. 14. 76. Bracton fo. 298. 18. E. 4. 28. 24. H. 8. bastardi Br. 44. 39. E. 1. bastard 21. 22. E. 4. tit. Consultat. 5. 6. E. 3. 249. 25. E. 3. 37.
(*) Vid. Sect. 399.
32. H. 8. ca. 38.
(n) Tr. 2 Iac. Rot. 1031. Richard Parsons case.

Sect.381.

¶ ET que ils ont estate pur terme de lour deux vies, Probatur sic, chescun home que ad estate de franktenement en ascun terres ou tenements, ou il ad estate en fee, ou en fee taile, ou pur terme de sa vie demesne, ou pur terme dauter vie, et per tiel lease ils ount franktenement, mes ils nont p cest grant fee, ne fee taile, ne pur terme dauter vie, Ergo, ils ont estate pur terme de lour vies, mes ceo est sur condition en ley, en le forme auantdit, et en cest cas sils fieront wast, le feoffor auera enuers eux briefe de wast suppo-

AND that they haue an estate for term of their two liues, is proued thus, euery man that hath an estate of freehold in any lands or tenements, either he hath an estate in fee, or in fee taile, or for terme of his own life, or for terme of another mans life, & by such a lease they haue a freehold, but they haue not by this grant fee, nor fee taile, nor for terme of anothers life, *Ergo*, they haue an estate for terme of their owne liues, but this is vpon condition in lawe in forme aforesaid, and in this case if they shal do wast, the feoffor shall

supposant per son breife, Quod tenet ad terminum vitæ, &c. mes en son count il declare coment & en quel maner le leas fuit fait.

haue a writ of waste against them supposing by his writ, *Quod tenet ad terminũ vitæ, &c.* but in his count hee shall declare how, and in what manner the lease was made.

Pl. Com. 561. b. Vi. Sect. 345 simile. ¶ *Probatur sic.* By this argument logically drawne a diuisione, it appeareth, how necessarie it is that our Student should (as Littleton did) come from one of the Uniuersities, to the studie of the Common Law, where he may learne the liberall Arts, and especially Logicke, for that teacheth a man not onely by iust argument to conclude the matter in question, but to discerne betweene truth and falsehood, and to use a good method in his studye, and probably to speake to any Legall question, and is defined thus, Dialectica est scientia probabiliter de quouis themate disserendi, whereby it appeareth how necessarie it is for our Student.

37. H. 6. 27. ¶ *Supposant per son briefe* Qđ tenet ad terminum vitæ, *&c.* This and the rest of this Section is euident and plaine.

Sect. 382.

¶ En mesme l'manner est, si vn Abbe fait vn Lease a vn hõe, a auer et tener a luy durant le temps que l'lessor est Abbe, en cest case le Lessee ad estate pur terme de sa vie demesm, mes ceo est sur condition en ley, s̃, que si labbe resigna, ou soit depose, que bien lirroit a s̃ successor dentrer, &c.

IN the same manner it is if an Abbot make a leas to a man for yeares, to haue and to hold to him during the time that the Lessor is Abbot; in this case the lessee hath an Estate for term of his own life: but this is vpon condition in Law, s. That if the Abbot resigne or be deposed, that then it shall be lawfull for his successor to enter, &c.

Vi. Bract. lib. 5. 414. ¶ *Si vn Abbe.* So it is of a Bishop, arch-Deacon, and other Ecclesiasticall or temporall Bodie Politique or Corporate, or of any Officer or Graduate, or the like.

¶ *Resigne ou soit depose.* And so it is of a Translation and Cession.

Section 383.

¶ Item hõe poit veier en le Liur Dassise, viz. anno 38. E. 3. p. 3. vn pl. Dass. en cest forme que ensuist: s̃, Un Assise de Nouel Disseisin auterfoits fuit port vers A. que pleda al Assise, et troue fuit per verdict, Que

ALso a man may see in the Booke of Assises, *Anno 38. E. 3. p. 3.* a plea of Assise in this form following, s. An Assise of *Nouel Disseisin* was sometime brought against A. who pleaded to the Assise, and it was found by verdict, that

¶ *LIVRE Dassises* is a Booke of the Reports of Cases in the raigne of King Edward the third, and it is called the booke of Assises, because the greatest part of the cases therein are vpon Writs of Assises brought, as hath been said, and which hath beene cited before.

¶ *Deuisa les Tenements a vendre per son Executor.* This must

laun-

launceston le plaintif deuisa ses Tenements a vendre per le Defendant, que fuit son Executor, et de faire distribution des deniers pur son alme: Et fuit troue que maintenant apres la mort le Testator, vn home luy tendist certaine summe de deniers pur les Tenements, mes non pas al value, & que le Executor puis auoit tenus les Tenements en sa main demesne per deux ans, al entent deles vender pluis chier a ascun auter, et troue fuit que il auoit tout temps prist les profits de les Tenements a son vse demesne sans riens faire pur lalme le mort, &c. Moubray Iustice disoit, Lexecutor en tiel case est tenus per la ley a faire le vender a plus tost que il purroit apres la mort son Testator, et troue est que il refuse de faire vender, & issint il auoit vn default en luy, et issint per force del deuise il fuist tenus dammis touts le profits auenants de les Tenements al vse le mort, et troue est que il ad

the Ancestour of the Plaintife deuised his lands to bee sould by the Defendant who was his Executor, and to make distribution of the money for his Soule. And it was found, That presently after the death of the Testator, one tendred to him a certaine sum of mony for the lands, but not to the value, and that the Executor afterwards held the lands in his own hands two yeares, to the entent to sell the same deerer to some other, and it was found that he had all the time taken the profits of the lands to his own vse, without doing any thing for the soule of the deceased, &c. *Moubray* Iustice said, The Executor in this case is bound by the Law to make the sale as soone as hee may after the death of his Testator, and it is found that hee refused to make sale, and so there was a default in him, and so by force of the Deuice he was bound to put all the profits comming of the lands to the vse of the Dead, and it is found that he tooke them to his

be intended to bee of Lands deuisable by Custome, for Lands by the Common law were not deuisable, (as hath beene sayd:) for in this Section is implied a Diuersity, viz. when a man deuiseth that his Executor shall sell the Land, there the lands discend in the meane time to the heire, and vntill the sale bee made, the heire may enter and take the profits. But when the Land is deuised to his Executor to be sould, there the deuise taketh away the discent, and vesteth the state of the land in the Executor, and he may enter and take the profits, and make sale according to the deuise. And here it appeareth by our Author, That when a man deuiseth his Tenements to be sould by his Executors, it is all one as if he had deuised his Tenements to his executors to be sould: and the reason is; because he deuiseth the tenements, whereby hee breakes the Discent.

¶ Mowbray. Iohn Mowbray was a renowned Judge of the Court of Common pleas, and discended of a Noble Familie.

¶ *Lexecutor en tiel case est tenus per la Ley a faire le vender a pluis tost que il purroit apres la mort son Testator, &c.* And the reason hereof is, for that the meane profits taken before the sale, shall not bee Assets, so as he may be compellable to pay debts with the same, and therefore the law will enforce him to sell the lands as soone as hee can, for otherwise hee shall take aduantage of his owne laches: But if a man deuise that his Executor shall sell his land, there hee may sell it at any time, for that hee hath but a bare power, and no profit. And by this case it appeareth, what construction the Law maketh for the speedie payment of debts. And here is to bee obserued, That many

words

Sect. 384.

¶ ET multz auters choses et cases y sont destates sur condition en la Ley, et en tielx cases il ne besoigne dauer monstre ascun fait rehearsant la Condition, pur ceo que la Ley en luy mesme purport l' Condition, &c.

Ex paucis dictis intendere plurima possis.

¶ Plus serra dit de Conditions en le prochein Chapter, en le Chapter de Releases, et en le Chapter de Discontinuance.

AND many other things there are of Estates vpon Condition in Law, and in such cases hee needed not to haue shewed any Deed, rehearsing the condition, for that the Law it selfe purporteth the Condition, &c.

Ex paucis dictis intendere plurima possis.

More shall bee sayd of Conditions in the next Chapter, in the Chap. of Releases, and in the chapter of Discontinuance.

9.E.4.36. ¶ HEreby it appeareth That Limitations which (as hath bin sayd, Littleton termeth Conditions in Law) may be pleaded without Deed, and the reason of our Author is obseruable, because the Law in it selfe purporteth the Condition, whereof somewhat hath beene sayd before: and therefore looke backe to the Conditions in Law, or words of limitation, and withall that a stranger may take aduantage of a limitation, as hath beene sayd.

Vi. Sect. 228. Littleton hauing spoken at large of Conditions in Deed and in Law, somewhat seemeth necessarie to be sayd of defeasances, wherby the state or right of Frehold or Inheritance may bee defeated and auoyded.

Bract. li. 2. fo. 16. 27. Ass. p. 2. 5. E. 3. 42 E. 3. 1. 43. E. 3. 17. 43. Ass. 12. 7. H. 6. 43. 8. H. 6. 23. 32. E. 3. Annuitie 30. 5. E. 3. Annuitie 44. ¶ *Defeasance*, Defeisantia is fetched from the French word De faire, i. to defeat or vndoe, infectum reddere quod factum est. There is a diuersitie betweene Inheritances executed, and Inheritances executorie, as Lands executed by Liuerie, &c. cannot by Indenture of Defeasance be defeated afterwards. And so if a Disseisee release to a Disseisor, it cannot be defeated by Indentures of Defeasance made afterwards, 30. Ass. p. 1. 30. Ass. p. 11. 31. Ass. 32. but at the time of the release or feoffement, &c. the same may be defeated by Indentures of Defeasance, for it is a Maxime in Law, Quæ incontinenti fiunt in esse videntur.

But

But Rents, Annuities, Conditions, warranties, and such like that bee Inheritances Executorie may be defeated by Defeasances made eyther at that time, or at any time after. And so the Law is of Statutes, Recognizances, Obligations, and other things Executory. *20. Ass. pl. 7. 7. E. 4. 29. Browning & Besons case. Pl. Com. 131. 28. H. 8. Dier 6. 27. H. 8. 15. 19. R. 2. done 16. Albanies case lib. 1. 107.*

¶ *Ex paucis dictis intendere plurima possis.*

Verses at the first were inuented for the helpe of memory, and it standeth well with the grauitie of our Lawyer to cite them. By this Verse of our Author, Inferences and Conclusions in like cases are warrantable.

Lastly, somewhat were necessary to be spoken concerning clauses of prouisoes, contayning Power of Reuocation, which since Littleton wrote, are crept into voluntarie Conueyances, which passe by raysing of vses, and executed by the (*) Statute of 27. H. 8. and are become very frequent, and the Inheritance of many depend thereupon. *(*) 27. H. 8. cap. 10.* As if a man seised of Lands in fee, and hauing issue diuers Sonnes by Deed indented, couenanteth in consideration of Fatherly loue, and the aduancement of his Bloud, or vpon any other good consideration to stand seised of three Acres of Land to the vse of himselfe for life, and after to the vse of Thomas his eldest Sonne in tayle, and for default of such issue to the vse of his second Son in tayle, with diuers like remaynders ouer. With a Prouiso that it shall be lawfull for the Couenantor at any time during his life to reuoke any of the said vses, &c. This Prouiso being coupled with an vse, is allowed to bee good, and not repugnant to the former States. But in case of a Feoffement, or other Conueyance, whereby the Feoffee or Grantee, &c. is in by the Common Law, such a Prouiso were meerely repugnant and void.

And first in the case aforesaid, if the Couenantor who had an estate for life doe reuoke the vses according to his power, he is seised againe in fee simple without entry or clayme.

Secondly, he may reuoke part at one time, and part at another.

Thirdly, If he make a feoffment in fee, or leuie a fine, &c. of any part, this doth extinguish his power but for that part, whereas in that case the whole Condition is extinct. But if it be made of the whole, all the power is extinguished. So as to some purposes, it is of the nature of a Condition, and to other, in nature of a limitation. *Lib. 1. fol. 173. 174. Digges case. Lib. 1. fol. 107. Albanies case. Lib. 10. fol. 142. Scropes case. Lib. 7 fol. 12. 13. Sir Francis Englefields case.*

Fourthly, If hee that hath such power of reuocation hath no present interest in the Land, nor by the Cestui que vse of the state shall haue nothing, then his feoffment or fine, &c. of the Land is no extinguishment of his power, because it is mere collaterall to the Land.

Fiftly, By the same Conueyance that the old vses bee reuoked, by the same may new bee created or limited, where the former cease ipso facto by the reuocation, without entrie or clayme.

Sixtly, That these reuocations are fauourably interpreted, because many mens Inheritances depend on the same. And here I may apply the abouesaid verse.

Ex paucis dictis intendere plurima possis.

Chap. 6. Discents que tollent Entries. *Sect. 385.*

¶ Discents, que tollent Entries sont en deux maners, cestascauoir, ou discent est en fee, ou en fee taile: Discents en Fee que tollent entries sont, sicome home seisie de certaine terres ou tenements est

Discents which toll Entries are in two maners, to wit, where the discent is in fee, or in fee taile. Discents in fee which toll entries are, as if a man seised of certaine lands or tenements is by another disseised, and the disseisor hath issue, and dieth of

¶ Discents. This word commeth of the Latin word discendere, id est, ex loco superiore in inferiorem mouere, and in legall vnderstanding it is taken when Land, &c. after the death of the Ancester is cast by Course of Law vpon the heire, which the Law calleth a Discent. And this is the noblest and worthiest meanes whereby Lands are deriued from one to another, because *Mirror, cap. 2. §. 5. Bracton lib. 5. fol. 370. & 434. Britton fol. 115. 215. Vide Sect. 5.*

because it is wrought and vested by the Act of Law, and Right of Bloud, to the worthiest and next of the Bloud and Kindred of the Ancester, and therefore it hath not in the Common Law altogether the same signification, that it hath in the Ciuil Law, for the Ciuilians call him, Hæredem qui ex testamento succedit in vniuersum ius testatoris. But by the Common Law hee is only Heire which succeedeth by Right of Bloud. And this agreeth well with the Etymologie of the word (Heire) to whom the Lands discend, for Hæres dicitur ab hærendo, quia qui hæres est hæret, hoc est, proximus est sanguine illi cuius est Hæres. So as hee that is Hæres, sanguinis est hæres & hærus hæreditatis.

¶ *Discents que tollent entries sont en deux Manners.* Here is an exact and perfect diuision made by our Authour, and withall plaine & perspicuous.

p vn auter disseisie, & le disseisor ad issue & morust de tiel estate seisie, ore les tenements discendont al issue del disseisor per course de la ley come lheire a luy: Et pur ceo que la ley mitte les terres ou tenements sur lissue per force del discent, issint que lissue vient a les tenements per course de ley, & nemy per son fait demesne, lentrie le disseisee est tolle, & il est mis de suer vn briefe Dentre sur disseisin enuers le heire le disseisor, de recouerer la terre.

such estate seised, now the Lands discend to the issue of the disseisor by course of Law, as heire vnto him. And because the Law cast the lands or tenements vpon the issue by force of the Discent, so as the issue commeth to the lands by course of Law, and not by his owne Act, the entrie of the Disseisee is taken away, and hee is put to sue a Writ of Entrie *sur disseisin* against the heire of the Disseisor, to recouer the Land.

Now as a Discent is the worthiest meanes to come to Lands, &c. so hath the Heire more priuiledges, then any that by other order or meanes come to the Lands, &c. as shall appeare hereafter.

(*) *Bracton lib.4.fol.162.& 209. Britton fol.115. Fleta lib.4.cap.2.* (a) *50.E.3.21.1.Ass.13. 30.H.3.Ass.432. 9.Ass.15. 29.Ass.54. 26.Ass.12. 21.Ass.28.43.Assise 17.* (b) *Lamb.explicat.fol.120. 70.*

Nota, In ancient time (*) if the Disseisor had bin in long possession, the Disseisee could not haue entred vpon him. (a) Likewise the Disseisee could not haue entred vpon the Feoffee of the Disseisor, if he had continued a yeare and a day in quiet possession. But the Law is changed in both these Cases, only the dying seised being an Act in Law doth hold at this day, and this seemeth to be very ancient, for this was the Law before the Conquest. (b) Porro autem quam maritus sine lite & controuersia sedem incoluerit, eam coniux & proles sine controuersia possidento, si qua in illum lis fuerit illata viuentem, eam hæredes ad se (perinde atque is viuus) accipiunto.

And one of the reasons of this ancient Law may be, that the heire cannot suddenly by entendement of Law, know the true state of his Title. And for that many aduantages follow the possession and Tenant, the Law taketh away the entrie of him that would not enter vpon the Ancestor, who is presumed to know his Title, and driueth him to his Action against him, that may be ignorant thereof.

11.H.7.12. 40.E.3.24.

¶ *Et morust de tiel estate seisie.* To a Discent that taketh away an entrie, a dying seised is necessary, as here it appeareth, but a man to other purposes may haue Lands by Discent, though his Ancestor died not seised, as hath beene said before.

33.E.3.gard.162.6.H.4.4. 39.E.3.36. 15.E.4.14. F.N.B.143.q. 7.H.4.12.5.2.Ass.p 9. 21.E.3.2.

¶ *Des terres ou tenements.* That is of such tenements as bee corporeall, and doe lie in liuery, and not of Inheritances, which lie in grant, as Aduowsons, Rents, Commons in grosse, and such like which be Inheritances Incorporeall, and yet are included within this word (tenements) For Discents of them doe not put him that right hath to an Action, and the reason of this diuersitie is, for that houses serue for the habitation of men, and Lands to be manured for their sustenance, and therefore the heire after a Discent shall not be molested or disturbed in them by entrie.

¶ *Est pur vn auter disseisie.* The like Law is, of an abatement or intrusion, and of the Feoffees, or Donees, &c.

Upon

Upon the words of Littleton a diversitie may be collected, that if a recovery be had by A. against B. and before execution B. dis seised, this Discent shall not take away the entrie of the Recoveror. But if after execution B. had disseised the Recoveror and died seised this discent shall take away the entrie of the Recoveror within the expresse words of Littleton: and so it is in case of a Fine.

33.*E.*3.*title* 3. *Entrie congé* 51. 45.*E*.3.*quar Imp.* 139. 27.*E*.3.88. 9 *H*.6.49. 21.*H*.6.17. 3.*E*.4.6. 12.*E*.4.19. 3.*H*.7.3. 6 *E* 4. 11.7.*H*.7.15. 5.*H*.7.31. 10.*H*.7.5.*b*.

(n) A recovery is had against Tenant for life, where the remainder is over in fee, Tenant for life dieth, he in remainder entreth before execution, and dieth, the entrie of the recoveror is lawfull, because hee is privie in estate, otherwise it is if the Discent had beene after execution.

(n) 5.*H*.7.2.

A. recovereth an Advowson against B. in a writ of Right, and hath iudgement finall, the Incumbent dieth. B. by usurpation presents to the Church, and his Clarke is admitted and institnted, B. dieth, A. is put out of possession, and the heire of B. is not so bound by the iudgement either in bloud or estate, but he shall present (o) B. levie a fine to A. of an Advowson to him and his heires, after the Church become void. B. present by usurpation, and his Clarke is admitted and instituted, this shall put A. the Conusee out of possession. And the reason of these two cases is for that at the Common Law, every presentation to a Church did put the rightfull Patron out of possession, and did put him to his writ of Right, whether the presentation were by Title or without, and therefore albeit the usurpation were in both the said cases before execution, yet it put the rightfull Patron out of possession. So note a diversitie betweene a recovery of Land, and of an Advowson.

45.*E*.3.*quare Imp*.139.
(o) 8.*E*.2.*quare Imp*.166.

¶ *Lentrie le disseisee est tolle.* Here is one of the priviledges which the Law giveth to the heire by Discent of Houses and Lands.

(p) At the Common Law if the Disseisor, Abator, or Intrudor had died seised soone after the wrong done, the Disseisee and his heires had beene barred of his and their entrie without any time limited by Law, but now by the Statute (q) made since Littleton wrote, it is enacted, that except such Disseisor hath beene in the peaceable possession of such Mannors, Lands, &c. whereof he shall die seised by the space of five yeares next after such disseisin, &c. without entrie or continuall clayme, &c. that there such dying seised, &c. shall not take away the entrie of such person or persons, &c. But after the five yeares the Disseisee must make such continuall clayme as our Author hath taught us, the learning whereof is necessary to be knowne. And it is said that Abators and Intrudors are out of this Statute, because the Statute is penall and extends only to a Disseisor, and that was the most common mischiefe, Et ad ea quæ frequentius accidunt iura adaptantur.

(p) *Lestatw de* 32.*H*.8.*ca*.33 *Vide Sect*.422.416.
(q) 37.*H*.6.1.
Pl. Com,47.*in Wimbesbes case.*

The Feoffee of a Disseisor is out of the said Statute, & remayne at the Common Law. But to a Disseisor the statute is taken favourably for advancement of the ancient right: for whether the disseisin be without force, or with force it is within the Statute. And albeit the Statute speake of him that at the time of such Discent had title of entry, &c. or his heires, yet the successors of bodies Politique or Corporate, so you hold your selfe to a disseisin, are within the remedie of this Statute, for the Statute extended cleerely to the Predecessor, being disseised; and consequently without naming of his Successor extendeth to him, for he is the person that at the time of such Discent had title of entrie.

Mich.4.& 5.*Eliz*. *Dier* 219. *acc*.

But if a man make a Lease for life, and the Lessee for life is disseised, and the Disseisor die seised, the Lessee for life may enter within five yeares, but if he die before hee doth enter, it is said that the entry of him in the Reversion is not lawfull, because his entry was not lawfull upon the Disseisor at the time of the Discent, as the Statute speaketh. But if Lessee for life had dyed first, and then the Disseisor had died seised, he in the Reversion had beene within the remedie of the Statute, because he had title of entry at the time of the Discent, as the Statute speaketh, and so within the expresse letter of the Statute, albeit, the Disseisin was not immediate to him, and the like is to be said of a remaynder, &c.

Vide Pl. Com.47. *ubi supra.*

¶ *Breife dentrie sur disseisin*, Breue de ingressu super disseisinam. Of this writ somewhat shall be said in the next Section.

F.N.B.191.

Section 386.

¶ DIscēts Ētaile que tollēt entries sont, sicome home est disseisie, et

DIscents in Tayle which take away Entries are, as if a man bee disseised, and the

¶ M*orust de tiel estate seisie.*

If a Disseisor make a gift in tayle, and the Donee discontinueth in fee, and disseise the

the Discontinuee, and dyeth seised, this discent shall not take away the entrie of the disseisee for the discent of the fee simple is vanished and gone, by the Remitter, and albeit the issue be in by force of the estate taile, yet the Donee dyed not seised of that estate, and of necessitie there must be a dying seised as hath beene said, which is a point worthy of obseruation, and implyeth many things.

le disseisor dona mesme la terre a vn auter en le taile, & le tenant en le tail ad issue & morust de tiel estate seisie, & lissue enter, en cest case lentre le disseisee est tolle, & il est mis de suer enuers lissue de le tenant en taile vn briefe. Dentre sur disseisin.

disseisor giueth the same land to another in taile, and the tenant in taile hath issue and dieth of such estate seised and the issue enter, in this case the entrie of the disseisee is taken away & he is put to sue against the issue of the tenant in taile a writ of *Entrie sur disseisin.*

¶ *En cest case lentrie le disseisee est tolle.* 9.H.9.24. But if a Disseisor make a gift in taile, and the Donee hath issue and dyeth seised, now is the entrie of the Disseisee taken away, but if the issue die without issue, so as the estate taile which discended is spent, the entrie of the Disseisee is reuiued, and he may enter vpon him in the reuersion or remainder.

15.H.4.8.9. 33.H.6.5.b. per Moyle. 34.H.6.11.a. per Curiam. Vid. Sect. 395.

So if there be Granfather, Father and Son, and the son disseiseth one, and infeoffeth the Grandfather who dieth seised, and the land discendeth to the Father, now is the entrie of the Disseisee taken away; but if the Father dieth seised, and the land descendeth to the Sonne, now is the entrie of the Disseisee reuiued, and he may enter vpon the sonne, who shall take no aduantage of the discent, because he did the wrong vnto the disseisee. But in the case abouesaid some haue said that where after such discent to the Father, he made a Lease to the son for terme of another mans life vpon whom the Disseisee entred, the Sonne brought an Assise and recouered, and the reason that hath beene yeelded is for that the Sonne had not a fee simple which he gained by disseisin, but is a purchaser of the freehold only from the Father, and the discent remaine not purged.. Contrary it were as it is there said if the Sonne were heire to the discent But the booke cited there in Fitzherb. tit. Title Placit. 6 doth not warrant that case, and I hold the Law to be contrary, viz. that the disseisee in that case shall enter vpon the Disseisor, aswell as if the Father had conueyed the whole fee simple to the Sonne, for in that case the discent of the Father is not purged. If a Disseisor make a Lease to an Infant for life, and he is disseised, and a discent cast, the Infant enters, the entrie of the Disseisee is lawfull vpon him. More shall be said of the like matter in this chapter hereafter in his proper place, Sect. 393. 395.

13.E.3. Br. tit. Entrie Cong. 127.

¶ *Breife dentrie sur disseisin.* Breue de ingressu super disseisinam. This writ lyeth only vpon a disseisin made to the Demandant or to some of his Ancestors, and of this writ there be foure kindes; First the writ that lyeth for the Disseisee against the Disseisor vpon a disseisin done by himselfe, and this is called a writ of entrie in the nature of an Assise. The second is a writ of Entrie sur disseisin en le Per whereof Littleton here speaketh, for the heire by discent is in the Per by his Ancester: so it is if the Disseisor make a feoffment in fee, a gift in taile, or a Lease for life, for they are in the Per by the Disseisor. (*) The third is a writ of Entrie Sur disseisin en le Per & Cui, as where A. being the Feoffee of D. the Disseisor maketh a feoffment ouer to B. there the Disseisee shall haue a writ of Entrie Sur disseisin of Lands, &c in which B. had no entrie but by A. to whom D. demised the same, who vniustly and without iudgement disseised the Demandant. These are called Gradus, Degrees which are to be obserued or else the writ is abatable for Sicut natura non facit saltum, ita nec lex.

19.H.6.56. 9.H.5.9.
Bracton. lib. 5. fo. 219.b. & 318. Britton. fo. 264. 265. Fleta lib. 5. cap. 35. 5.E.3.216. (*) 22.E.3.1.b. 7.E.3.25. F.N.B.192.

The fourth is a writ of Entrie sur disseisin in le post, which lyeth when after a disseisin the land is remoued from hand to hand beyond the degrees, and it is called In le Post, because the words of the writ be Post disseisinam quam D. iniuste, &c. fecit, &c. the formes of these writs you shall reade in the Register and F.N.B. and therefore it were needlesse to recite them here. So as a degree is of two sorts, either by act in Law, whereof Littleton here putteth an example of a Discent, or by act of the partie by lawfull conueyance as is aforesaid. But it is to be vnderstood, that at the Common Law, if the lands were conueyed out of the degrees, the Demandant was driuen to his writ of right, in respect of his long possession in so many diuers hands, which the Law doth euer respect and fauour. And therefore by the Statute (a) of Marlebridge the writ of Entrie in le post is giuen, Prouisum est etiam quod si alienationes illæ de quibus breue de ingressu dari consueuit, per tot gradus fiant, per quot breue illud in forma prius vsitata fieri non possit, habeant conquerentes breue ad recuperandā seisinam suam sine mentione

14.H.4.40.
(a) Marlebr. ca. 29. 24.E.3.70.

mentione graduum, adcuiuscunque manus per huiusmodi alienationes res illa deuenerit, per breue originale, & per commune consilium domini regis inde prouidendum, &c.

Now it is necessary to be knowne what doth make a degree. First no estate gained by wrong doth make a degree, and therefore neither Abatement, Intrusion, or Disseisin upon Disseisin doth make a degree. Neither doth every change by lawfull title worke a degree, as if a Bishop or an Abbot, or the like disseise one and die, and his successor is in by lawfull title, for though the parson be altered, yet the right remaines where it was, viz. in the Church, and both of them seised in the same right, viz. in the right of the Church, and therefore in the very case Bracton (b) demands the question An faciunt gradum de Abbate in abbatem sicut de hærede in hæredem? Et videtur quod non magis quam in computatione discensus, quia etsi alternetur persona, non propter hoc alternatur dignitas sed semper manet. And herewith agreeth (c) Fleta.

Bracton, vbi supra. Britton, vbi supra. Fleta vbi supra. 4.E.2.bre.790. 21.H.6.8.

(b) Bracton, lib. 4. fo. 321. 5.E.3.38. 5.E.2. entrie 66. 11.H.4.83.

(c) Fleta, lib. 5. ca. 34. 3.E.3. entrie. 1 r. 22.E.3.7. F.N.B. 191. k.

Also an estate made to the King doth make no degree, and therefore if a Disseisor by Deede inrolled conuey the land to the King, and the King by his Charter granteth it ouer, the Disseisee cannot haue a Writ of Entrie in le per & Cui, but in le Post, for the Kings Charter is so high a matter of record as it maketh no degree.

Also an estate of a Tenant by the Curtesie, or of the Lord by escheate, or of an execution of an use by the statute of 27. H. 8. or by iudgement, or recouery, or of any other that come in in the post, worke no degree. (d) But a tenancie in dower by Assignement of the heire doth worke a degree, because she is in by her husband, but Assignement of Dower by a Disseisor worketh no degree, but is in the Post, as hereafter shall be said in his proper place.

5.E.2. entrie 66. 7.E.3.360.

(d) 36.H.6. dower 30.

When the degrees are past, so as a Writ of entrie in the Post doth lye, yet by euent it may be brought within the degrees againe, as if the Disseisor infeoffe A. who infeoffes B. who infeoffe C. or if the Disseisor die seised, and the land discend to A. and from him to C, now are the degrees past, and yet if C. infeoffe A. or B. now it is brought within the degrees againe.

44.E.3.4.5. 39.E.3.25. 5.H.7.6. 3.H.6.38.

If the Disseisor make a Lease for life, the remainder in fee, Tenant for life dyeth, he in the remainder is in the Per, because he now claimeth immediately from the Disseisor, and both these estates make one degree.

50.E.3.27.

Note there be diuers other Writs of entrie, then a Writ of entrie Sur disseisin whereof Littleton here speakes, as a Writ of entrie Ad terminum qui præterijt, in casu prouiso, in consimili casu, ad communem legem, sine assensu capituli, dum fuit infra ætatem, dum non fuit compos mentis, cui in vita, Sur cui in vita, Intrusion, Cessauit, and the like, and that which hath beene said of one may be applyed to all.

Sect. 387.

¶ Et nota que en tiels discents, que tollent entries, il couient que home morust seisie en son demesne come de fee, ou en son demesne come de fee taile. Car vn morant seisie pur terme de vie, ne pur terme dauter vie, ne vnquez tollent entre.

And note that in such discēts which take away entries, it behoooueth that a man die seised in his demesne as of fee, or in his demesne as of fee taile; for a dying seised for terme of life, or for terme of another mans life doth neuer take away an entrie.

¶ If a Disseisor make a Lease to a man and to his heires during the life of I. S. and the Lessee dieth this shall not take away the entrie of the Disseisee, because he that died seised had but a freehold only, and heires in that case were added to preuent the occupant, for the heire in that case shall not haue his age as it was adiudged in (d) Lambs case.

Dier. 8. Eliz. 253. 7.H.4.46. 8.H.4.15. 17.E.3.48. 11.H.4.42.

(d) Pasch. 26. Eliz. in Communi banco.

But if he in the reuersion disseise his Tenant for life, and dyeth seised, this discent shall take away the entrie of the Tenant for life.

3.H.3. tit. Entr. Cong. 58. F.N.B. 145. m. 9.H.7.25. a.

So it is if there be Tenant for life, the remainder in taile, the remainder in fee, and Tenant in taile disseiseth the Tenant for life and dyeth seised, this shall take away the entrie of the Tenant for life.

9.H.7.25.

But if the Kings Tenant for life be disseised, and the Disseisor die seised, this discent shall not take away the entrie of the Lessee, because the Disseisor had but a bare estate during the life of the Lessee, and Littleton saith, that a discent of an estate for terme of another mans life shall not take away an entrie.

¶ *En son demesne come de fee.* If an infant bee disseised, and the

Sect. 388.

¶ ITem un discent de reuersion, ou de Remainder, ne unques tollent entrie, issint que en tiels cases que tollent entries, per force de discents, il couient que celuy que morust seisie ad Fee et Franktenemt al temps de son morant, ou Fee taile et Franktenement al temps de son morant, ou autrement tiel discent ne tolle entre.

ALso a Discent of a Reuersion or of a Remainder, doth not take away an Entrie. So as in those cases which take away Entries by force of Discents, it behooueth that hee dieth seised of Fee and Freehold at the time of his decease, or of Fee taile and Freehold at the time of his death, or otherwise such discent doth not take away an Entrie.

¶ ANd therefore if a Disseisor make a Lease for yeares, and die seised of the Reuersion, this discent shall take away the entrie of the Disseisee, because hee died seised of the Fee and Franktenement. Like Law it is if the Land be extended upon a Statute, Judgment or Recognisance, and so it is in case of a Remainder.

But if he had made a Lease for life; and die seised of the Reuersion, this discent shall not take away the entrie of the Disseisee, for that though he had the Fee, yet he had not the Franktenement.

Vi. Sect. 392. 393. So it is of a Tenaunt in Taile mutatis mutandis, and note the Law doth euer giue great respect to the Estate of Freehold, though it be but for terme of life.

If a Disseisor make a Lease for terme of his owne life, and dieth, this discent shall not take away the entrie of the Disseisee, for though the Fee and Franktenement discend to the Issue, yet the Disseisor died not seised of the Fee and Franktenement: and Littleton saith, That unlesse he hath the Fee and Franktenement at the time of his decease, such discent shall not take away the entrie.

Sect. 389.

¶ ITem come est dit de Discents que discendont al issue de ceux que moront seisies, &c. Mesme la Ley est lou ils nont ascun issue, mes les tenements discendont al frere, soer, uncle, ou auter cosin de celuy que morust seisie.

ALso as it is sayd of Discents which discend to the Issue of them which die seised, &c. the same Law is where they haue no issue, but the lands discend to the Brother, Sister, Vncle, or other Cosine of him which dieth seised.

¶ BY this it appeareth, that a Discent in the Collaterall Line doth take away an entrie, as well as in the Lineall.

¶ *Morust seisie &c* Here (&c.) implieth Fee simple, or Fee taile.

Sect. 390.

¶ Item ſi ſoit Seignior et tenant, et le Tenant ſoit diſſeiſie, et le diſſeiſor aliena a vn auter en fee, et la lienee devie ſauns heire, et le Seignior enter come en ſon eſcheat en ceſt caſe le Diſſeiſee poet entrer ſur le Seignior, pur ceo que le Seignior ne vient a le Terre per diſcent, mes per voy deſcheat.

Alſo if there bee Lord and Tenant, and the Tenant be diſſeiſed, and the Diſſeiſor alien to another in Fee, and the Alienee die without iſſue, and the Lord enter as in his Eſcheat: In this caſe the Diſſeiſee may enter vpon the Lord, becauſe the Lord commeth not to the Land by Diſcent, but by way of Eſcheat.

¶ *Le Diſſeiſee poet enter ſur le ſeignior, &c.* For albeit the Diſſeiſor die ſeiſed, and the Lord by Eſcheat commeth to the Land by act in Law, yet becauſe the land diſcendeth not to him, the entrie of the Diſſeiſee in reſpect of the Eſcheat ſhall not be taken away. For a dying ſeiſed, and a diſcent, and not a dying ſeiſed and an Eſcheat, doth take away an entrie: for (as hath beene ſayd) the diſcent is the worthier title. But in that caſe, if the Lord by Eſcheat die ſeiſed, and the Land diſcend to his heire, that diſcent ſhall take away the entrie of the Diſſeiſee. So it is if the Diſſeiſor die ſeiſed, and the heire of the Diſſeiſor dieth without heire, the Diſſeiſee cannot enter vpon the Lord by Eſcheat. So as there is a diverſitie as touching the diſcent, when after a diſcent caſt, the Iſſue in Taile dieth without Iſſue, and when after a diſcent the heire in fee ſimple dieth without heire, for he in the Reverſion, or one vpon the eſtate taile claimeth in above the ſtate taile, and the lord by Eſcheat claimeth in vnder the heire in Fee ſimple. 7.H.6.1. 9.H.7.24.b.

Section 391.

¶ Item ſi home ſeiſie de certaine Terre en fee, ou en Fee taile, ſur condition de render certaine rent, ou ſur auter condition, coment que tiel Tenant ſeiſie en fee, ou en fee taile, morust ſeiſie, vncore ſi le condition ſoit enfreint en lour vies, ou apres lour deceaſe, ceo ne tollera pas lentrie del Feoffor, ou del Donor ou de lour heires, pur ceo que le Tenancie

Alſo if a man bee ſeiſed of certain land in Fee or in Fee taile, vpon condition to render certain rent, or vpon other condition, albeit ſuch Tenaunt ſeiſed in Fee or in Fee Tayle, dyeth ſeiſed, yet if the Condition bee broken in their liues, or after their deceaſe, this ſhall not take away the entrie of the Feoffor or Donor, or of their heires, for that the Tenancie is char-

¶ Vpon theſe two Sections is to be obſerved a diverſitie betweene a right, for the which the Law giveth a remedie by Action; and a title for the which the Law giveth no remedie by Action, but by entry onely. For example, The Feoffee vpon Condition in this caſe hath a right to the Land, therefore his entry may be taken away, becauſe hee may recover his right by Action, but the Feoffor or Donor that hath but a Condition, his title of entrie cannot be taken away by any diſcent, becauſe he hath no remedie by Action to recover the Land, and therefore if a Diſcent ſhould take away his entrie, it ſhould barre him for ever. And the Law is all one whether the diſcent were before the condition broken, or after. 33.Aſſ.11.24. 21.H.6.17. 33.Aſſ.11.24.

Alſo

Brooke tit. Mortmaine 6. 47. E. 3. 11. 21. E. 3. 17.

40. Ass. 13.

Also he that hath a title to enter upon a Mortmain, shall not be barred by a discent, because then he should bee without al remedie. And so it is in case where a woman that hath a title to enter, causa matrimonii prælocuti, no discent shall take away her entrie, because she hath but a title, and no remedie by Action.

If a man be seised of lands in fee, and by his last will in writing deviseth the same to another in fee, and dieth, after whose decease the Freehold in Law is cast upon the devisee, the heire before any entrie made by the Devisee, entreth, and dieth seised, this shall not take away the entrie of the Devisee, for if the discent, which is an Act in Law, should take away his entrie, the Law should barre him of his right, and leave him utterly without remedie. And so it is for him that entreth for consent to a ravishment, & so it was resolved in the case of Martyn Trotte of London, (n) Paschæ 32. El. in Com Banco. And accordingly was the opinion of the Court of Common Pleas, (o) Pasch. 1. Ia. Reg. To this may bee added as a like case, the Kings Patentee before he enter, &c. Another reason wherefore a discent shall not take away the entrie of him that hath a title to enter by force of a condition, &c. is, for that the Condition remaines in the same essence that it was at the time of the creation of it, and cannot be devested or put out of possession as lands and tenements may.

(n) Pasch. 32. Eliz. in communi Banco. 7. R. 2. Gerr. Fee. 3. 41. E. 3. 14. per Finchden. (o) Pasch. 1. Iac. Regis in Com. Banco.

est charge oue le condition, et lestate del Tenant est conditionall en quecunque mains que le Tenancie vient, &c.

ged with the Condition, and the state of the Tenant is conditionall, in whose hands soever that the tenancie commeth, &c.

Sect. 392.

Item si tiel tenant sur condic soit disseisie et le disseisor devie ent seisie, & la t're descendist al heire le disseisor, ore le entrie le tenant sur condition, que fuist disseisie est toll: Mes uncore si le condition soit enfreint, donque poet le Feoffor ou le Donor que fierent estate sur condition, ou lour heirs entrer, Causa qua supra.

Also if such Tenant upon Condition be disseised, and the Disseisor die therof seised, and the land discend to the Heyre of the Disseisor, now the entrie of the Tenant upon condition, who was disseised, is taken away. Yet if the Condition be broken, the Feoffor or the donor which made the estate upon condition, or their heirs may enter, *Causa qua supra.*

Section 393.

Devie seisie, &c. viz. in fee simple, or in fee tayle.

Et son heire enter, &c. So as hee hath an actuall fee simple.

De la 3. part de les tenements, &c. id est, in severaltie.

By this Section it appeareth, that an entry being taken away by the Discent, is revived by the endowment, albeit the Tenant in Dower shall have it but for her life. And the cause is, for that although the heire entred, yet

Item si un disseisor devie seisie, &c. & son heire enter, &c. le quel endowa la feme le disseisor de la tierce part de les tenements, &c. En cest cas quant a cest tierce part que est assigne a la feme en Dower maintenant apres ceo que la feme enter, & ad le pos-

Also if a Disseisor die seised, &c. and his heire enter, &c. who indoweth the wife of the Disseisor of the third part of the Land, &c. In this case as to this part which is assigned to the wife in Dower, presently after the wife entreth and hath the possession of the same third

possession de mesme la tierce part, le disseisee poit loyalment enter sur la possession le feme en mesme la tierce part. Et la cause est, pur ceo que quant la feme ad son Dower, el serra adiudge eins immediate per son baron, & nemy per lheire, & issint quãt a le franktenement de mesme la tierce part, le discent est defeate. Et issint poies veir, que deuant le endowmẽt le disseisee ne poit enter en ascun part, &c. & apres le dowment il poit enter sur la fee &c. mes uncore il ne poit enter sur les auters deux parts que lheire le disseisor ad per le Discent.

part, the disseisee may lawfully enter vpon the possession of the wife into the same third part. And the reason is for that when the Wife hath her dower, shee shall bee adiudged in immediately by her Husband and not by the heire. And so as to the Freehold of the same third part, the Discent is defeated. And so you may see that before the endowment the Disseisee could not enter into any part, &c. and after the endowment hee may enter vpon the wife, &c. but yet hee cannot enter vpon the other two parts which the heire of the Disseisor hath by the Discent.

when the wife is endowed she shall not be in by the heire, (a) but immediately by her husband being the Disseisor, which is in for her life by a Title Paramount the dying seised and discent, and therefore in iudgement of Law, the Discent as to the Freehold, and the possession which the heire had is taken away by the endowment; for the Law adiudgeth no meane seisin betweene the husband and the wife. (a) 8.E.2.Entrie 75. 19.E.2.Dower 171. 5.E.2.Entrie 66. 24.E.3.32.40. 38.Ass.Pl.26. 43.E.3.32.45.E.3.9.b. 11.H.4.11. 7.H.5.3. 10.E.3.27.28. 36.H.6.Dower 30.

If there bee Lord, Mesne and Tenant, the Mesne doth grant to the Tenant to acquite him against the Lord and his heires, the Lord dies his wife hath the Seigniorie assigned to her for her dower, and distraines the Tenant; albeit the grant was only to acquite him against the Lord and his heires only, yet because she continued the estate of her husband, and the reversion remayned in the heire, the grant did extend to the wife, which is a notable case. 31.E.1.mesne 55.

If after the dying seised of the Disseisor, the Disseisee abate, against whom the wife of the Disseisor recouer by confession in a Writ of dower, in that case, though the Discent be auoyded as Littleton here saith, yet the Disseisee shall not enter vpon the Tenant in Dower, because the recouerie was against himselfe; but if he had assigned Dower to her in paiis, some say hee should enter vpon her.

A man makes a gift in tayle reseruing twentie shillings Rent, the Donee takes wife, and dieth without issue, the heire entreth and endoweth the wife, shee is so in of the estate of her husband, that albeit the estate tayle be spent, and the rent reserued thereupon determined, yet after she be endowed, she shall be attendant to the heire in respect of the said rent. And so it is of Lord and Tenant, the wife that is endowed, shall be attendant for the due Seruices, but if any seruices be incroached, albeit that incroachment shall bind the heire; yet the wife shall be contributory, but for the seruices of right due. 10.E.3.26.

¶ *Issint poies veir que deuant le dowment, le disseisee ne poet enter, & apres lendowment il poet enter, &c.* The like hath beene said before in this Chapter. Sect 386. where the entry of the Disseisee may be taken away for a time, and by matter ex post facto reuiued againe.

Nota, albeit the Disseisor after a Discent taketh to him but an estate for life; yet when the Disseisee doth enter vpon him, he shall thereby deuest the Reuersion; for the estate of Freehold is that whereupon a Præcipe doth lie, and therefore the entrie of the disseisee is as auaylable in Law, as if he had recouered it in a Præcipe. And so it is if a Disseisor make a Lease for life, and grant the Reuersion to the King, the entrie of the Disseisee vpon the Tenant for life shall deuest the Reuersion out of the King in the same manner, as if the Disseisee had recouered the lands against the Tenant for life in a Præcipe. Vide Sect.302.388. 25.E.3.48.Pl.Com.553.

Sect. 394.

¶ Item, si vn feme soit seisie de terre en fee, dont ieo aye droit & title dentre, si la feme prent baron, & ont issue enter eux, et puis la feme deuie seisie, & apres le baron deuie, et lissue enter, &c. en cest cas ieo poy enter sur le poss. lissue, pur ceo que lissue ne viẽt a les tenemẽts immediate per Discent apres la mort sa mere, &. eins per le mort del pier.

¶ Contrarium tenetur P.9.Hen.7. per tout le court, & M.37. H.6.¶.

ALso if a woman be seised of land in fee, whereof I haue right and title to enter if the woman take husband and haue issue betweene them, and after the wife die seised, and after the husband die, and the issue enter, &c. In this case I may enter vpon the possession of the issue, for that the issue comes not to the lands immediately by Discent after the death of the mother &c. but by the death of the father.

¶ *Contrarium tenetur P.9.H.7. per tout le court, & M.37.H.6.*¶.

¶ *EN cest case ieo poye enter sur le possession lissue, &c.*

Vide 9.H.7.24.& 37.H.6.1.

For here was but a Discent of a Reuersion at the time of the dying seised, for the state of a Tenant by the curtesie, had cõmencement by the hauing of issue, and is consummate by the death of the wife, so as a fee and franktenement did not after the decease of the wife discend to the heire, and albeit the Tenant by the courtesie dieth afterwards, and the franktenement is cast vpon the heire, so as now hee hath the fee and franktenement by Discent, yet because the heire came not to the Fee and Franktenement immediately after the decease of the wife, such a mediate Discent shall not take away the entrie of the Disseisee. On the other side an immediate Discent may take away an entry for a time, and mediately may be auoyded by matter ex post facto as hath beene said. But if a dying seised taketh not away the entry of him that right hath at the time of the Discent, it shall not by any matter ex post facto take away his entry.

See before the Chapter of Homage.

If a Disseisor die without heire his wife priuement enseint with an issue, and after the issue is borne, who entreth into the Land, he hath the Land by Discent, and yet thereby the entry of the Disseisee shall not be taken away, because as Littleton here saith, the issue commeth not to the Lands immediately by Discent after the decease of the Father.

And so it is if a Disseisor make a gift in tayle, the remaynder in fee, and the Donee dyeth without issue leauing his wife priuement enseint with a Sonne, and he in the remaynder enter, and after the Sonne is borne, and entreth into the Land, this Discent shall not take away the entry of the Disseisee, Causa qua supra.

¶ *Contrarium tenetur, &c.* This is an addition, and therefore to be passed ouer. And at this day this case of Littleton is holden for cleere Law.

Sect. 395.

¶ Item si vn disseisor enfeoffa son pier en fee, & le pier morust de tiel estate seisie, per q̃ les tenẽts discendont a l' disseisor come fits et heire &c. en cest case l' disseisee bien poit enter sur le disseisor, nient obstant le discent, pur

ALso if a Disseisor enfeoffe his father in fee, and the father die seised of such estate, by which the Land discend to the Disseisor, as sonne and heire, &c. In this case the Disseisee may well enter vpon the Disseisor notwithstanding the

pur ceo que quant al diſſeiſin, le diſſeiſor ſerra adiudge eins forſque come diſſeiſor, nient obſtant le diſcent, Quia particeps criminis.

diſcent for that as to the diſſeiſin, the diſſeiſor ſhall bee adiudged in but as a diſſeiſor notwithſtanding the diſcent, *Quia particeps criminis.*

Of this ſufficient hath beene ſaid before in this chapter Sect 386. And regularly it is true that albeit a diſcent be caſt, and the entrie of the Diſſeiſee taken away, yet if the Diſſeiſor commeth to the land againe either by diſcent or purchaſe, of any eſtate or freehold which is implied in the (&c.) the Diſſeiſee may enter vpon him, or haue his aſſiſe againſt him, as if no diſcent or meane conueyance had beene, Quia particeps criminis.

15.E.4.23.a. 1? E.4.2. 18.E.4.2?.a. ?? H.6.5.b. 34.H.6 11 12.H.8.9. 24.H.8 3.0. 18 H.?.5. 5.H.7. 29. ?54. 39.E.3.25.26.

Sect. 396.397.

Item ſi home ſeiſie de certaine terre ē fee ad iſſue deux fits, & moruſt ſeiſie, & le puiſne fits entra per abatement en la terre, quel ad iſſue, & de ceo moruſt ſeiſie, et les tenements diſcendōt al iſſue, et l'iſſue entra en la terre, en ceſt caſe le fits eigne, ou ſon heire, poit enter p la ley ſur liſſue del fits puiſne, nient contriſteant le diſcent, pur ceo que quant le fits puiſne abatiſt ē la terre apres le mort ſon pier deuāt aſcun entrie per le fits eigne fait, la ley intendra que il entra enclaymant come heyre a ſon pier, & p̄ ceo que leigne fits claymia per meſme le title, ceſtaſcauoir, come heyre a ſon pier, il & ſes heires poient enter ſur liſſue de puiſne fits, nient obſtant le diſcent, &c. pur ceo que ils clay-

Alſo if a man ſeiſed of certaine land in fee haue iſſue two ſons, and die ſeiſed, and the younger ſonne enter by abatement into the land and hath iſſue, and dieth ſeiſed thereof, and the land diſcend to his iſſue, and the iſſue enters into the land. In this caſe the eldeſt ſonne or his heire may enter by the law vpon the iſſue of the younger ſon notwithſtanding the diſcent, becauſe that when the younger ſon abated into the land after the death of his father before any entrie made by the eldeſt ſonne, the law entend that hee entred clayming as heire to his father. And for that the eldeſt ſonne claimes by the ſame title, that is to ſay, as heire to his father, he and his heires may enter vpon the iſſue of the younger ſon notwithſtādīng the diſ-

En ceſt caſe le fits eigne, &c. poet entrer ſur liſſue del fitz puiſne, &c. And the reaſon hereof is for that the law intendeth the youngeſt ſonne entred clayming the land as heire to his father, and becauſe the eldeſt ſonne claymeth alſo by the ſame title viz as heire to his father, therefore hee and his heires may enter vpon the ſecond ſonne and his heires in reſpect of the priuity of the blood betweene them, and of the ſame clayme by one title, albeit the youngeſt ſonne gained a fee ſimple by his entrie: for Littleton here calleth it an abatement, which proueth the gaining of a fee ſimple.

And it is to bee obſerued that Aſſiſa mortis anteceſſoris non tenet inter coniunctas perſonas ſicut fratres & ſorores, &c. for theſe are priuie in bloud but it lyeth againſt ſtrangers, and then damages are to bee recouered againſt a ſtranger, but not againſt his brother.

Bract.lib.4.fo.261.282.283. Britton fo.180.181. Fleta lib.5.ca.1.2.&c. 20.E.3.Darr.preſent 13. 12.H.3. Mord.pl.vltimo. 13.E.1.Mord.47 29.Aſſ.11.F.N.B.196.b.

Lands were giuen to the huſband and wife, and to the heires of their two bodies they had iſſue a daughter, the wife died, the huſband had iſſue by another wife foure ſons and dyed, the eldeſt ſonne abate

Paſch.3.E.3. Coram Rege Kanc.in Theſaur.

abated and died seised, this discent did take away the entrie of the daughters because they claymed not by one title. And in ancient bookes the eldest sonne is called Hæres propinquus, and the younger sonne Hæres remotus. And albeit the eldest sonne hath issue and dieth, and after his decease the youngest sonne or his heire entreth, and many discents bee cast in his line, yet may the heires of the eldest enter in respect of the privitie of the bloud, and of the same clayme by one title; but if the youngest sonne make a feoffment in fee, and the Feoffee die seised, that discent shall take away the entrie of the eldest in respect the privity of the blood faileth. And admit that the youngest sonne be of the halfe bloud to his brother, yet he is of the whole bloud to his father, and therefore if he entreth and dieth seised, it shall not barre his elder brother of his entrie. But if the eldest sonne entreth, and gaineth an actuall possession and seisin, then the entrie of the youngest is a disseisin. And then a dying seised shall take away the entrie of the eldest, for Possessio terræ must bee Vacua when the youngest sonne enter by abatement as Littleton saith, because hee hath more colour in that case to clayme as heire to his father who last was actually seised. Therefore if after the decease of the father an estranger doth first enter and abate, upon whom the youngest sonne entreth and disseise him and die seised, this discent shall not binde the eldest, for he entred by disseisin and not by abatement.

8.E.2. Ass 380. 40.E.3.24.b. 29.Ass.24.

Vid. Brooke tit. Entrie 27.

If a man be seised of

mont per un mesme title. Et en mesme le maner il serra, si fueront plusors discents de un issue a un auter issue del puisne fits.

cent,&c. because they claime by the same title. And in the same manner it shall be, if there were more discents from one issue to another issue of the younger sonne.

Sect.397.

MEs en tiel case, si le pier fuit seisie de certaine terres en fee, et ad issue deux fits, et devie, et leigne fits enter, & est seisie, &c. et puis le puisne frere luy disseisist, per quel disseisin il est seisie en fee, et ad il est seisie en fee, et ad issue, & de tiel estat morust seisie, donques leigne frere ne poit entrer, mes est mis a son briefe, Dentre sur disseisin, &c. de recoverer la terre. Et la cause est, pur ceo que le puisne frere vient a les tenemēts per tortious disseisin fait a son eigne frere, et per cel tort la ley ne poit entender que il claime come heire a son pier, nient pluis que un estrange person que ust disseisie leigne frere q̄ navoit ascun title. &c. Et issint poyes veier la diversitie, lou le puisne frere enter apres le mort le pier devant ascun entrie fait

BVt in this case if the father were seised of certaine lands in fee, and hath issue two sons and die, and the eldest sonne enter & is seised, &c. and after the yonger brother disseiseth him, by which disseisin he is seised in fee, and hath issue, and of this estate dieth seised, then the elder brother cannot enter, but is put to his Writ of *Entrie sur disseisin,&c*, to recouer the land. And the cause is for that the youngest brother commeth to the lands by wrongfull disseisin done to his elder brother, and for this wrong the law cannot entend that he claimeth as heire to his father, no more then if a stranger had disseised the elder brother which had no title,&c. And so you may see the diuersitie where the younger brother entereth after the death of the father before any entrie made by

per leigne frere en tiel cas, et ou leigne frere enter apres la mort son pier, et puis est disseisie p le puisne frere, lou le puisne fret puis morust seisie.

the elder brother in this case, and where the elder brother enters after the death of his father, and after is disseised by the younger brother, where the younger after dieth seised.

lands of the nature of Burgh English and hath issue two sonnes and die, and the eldest sonne before any entry made by the youngest entereth into the land by abatement and dieth seised, this shall not take away the entrie of the youngest brother. Et sic de similibus. And these and the like cases are all within the reason and rule of our Author. And where our Author speaketh only of an abatement, so it is of an intrusion, For if the father make a Lease for life and hath issue two sonnes and dieth, and the Tenant for life dieth, and the youngest sonne intrude, and dies seised, this discent shall not take away the entrie of the eldest. But if the father hid made a Lease for yeares it had beene otherwise, for that the possession of the Lessee for yeares maketh the actuall freehold in the eldest sonne. And it is to be obserued that the reason of Littleton in this case (for that both brethren hold by one title) holdeth also in many other cases.

If two Coperceners make partition to present be turne, and one of them usurpe in the turne of the other, this usurpation shall not put the other out of possession because they claime by one title. 22.E.4.4.

If two Coperceners be, and they seuerally present to the Ordinary, yet the Church is not litigeous, because they claime all by one title. Doctor. & Stud.ca.30.fo.117

If upon a Writ of Diem clausit extremum, the youngest sonne be found heire, the eldest son had no remedy by the Common Law because they claymed by one title, but otherwise it is if they claime by seuerall titles as it appeareth in our bookes. But this is now holpen by a (*) Statute made since Littleton wrote. 12.E.4.18. (*) 2.E.6. cap.8.

If two persons be in debate for tithes, which amount aboue the fourth part, and one man is Patron of both Churches, no Iudicauit doth lye, for that both incumbents clayme by one and the same Patron, Et sic de similibus. 2.H.7.12.a. See the Section next following.

And where Littleton saith, seised of lands in fee, the same law it is if a man be seised of lands in taile, and hath issue two sonnes Mutatis mutandis.

¶ *Et est seisie, &c.* (That is to say) actually seised either by entrie as Littleton here putteth it, or by possession of the Lessee for yeares or the like.

¶ *Nauoit ascun title, &c.* That is to say, any pretence or semblance of title, as the younger brother here hath, and in many other cases there is a great diuersity holden in our bookes (o) where one hath a colour or pretence of right, and when he hath none at all, whereof you may reade plentifully in our bookes. (o) 2.E.2. bastardy 19. 21.E.3.34. 22 Ass.85. 39.E.3.26. 17.E.3.59. 11.E.3. Ass.88. 21.H.6.14. 11.E.3. Act.3. Vid. Sect. 400. & cap. Garran.

Sect. 398.

¶ EN mesme le maner est, si home seisie de certaine tre en fee ad issue deux files & deuie, leigne file entra en la terre claymant tout la terre a luy, et ent solemẽt prist les profits, et ad issue & morust seisie, per que son issue enter, quel issue ad issue & deuie seisie, & l' second issue enter, *& sic vltra*, uncore le puisne file ou son issue, quant a le moitie poyt enter sur quecunque issue de leigne file, nient obstant tiel discent,

IN the same manner it is, if a man seised of certaine land in fee hath issue two daughters & dieth, the eldest daughter entereth into the land clayming all to her, and thereof only taketh the proffits, and hath issue and dieth seised, by which her issue enter, which issue hath issue and dieth seised, and the second issue enter, *& sic vltra*, yet the younger daughter or her issue as to the moity may enter vpon any issue whatsoeuer of the elder

discent pur ceo que ils claimont per vn mesme title, &c. mes en tiel case si ambideux Soers auoyent enter apres la mort lour Pier, et ent fueront seisies, et puis leigne Soer vst disseisie la puisne Soer de ceo que a luy affiert, et ent fuit seisie en fee et ad issue, et de tiel estate morust seisie, per que les Tenements discendont al Issue del eigne Soer, donque le puisne Soer, ne ses heires ne poient enter, &c. Causa qua supra, &c.

daughter notwithstāding such discent, for that they claime by one same title, &c. but in such case where both sisters haue entred after the death of their father, and were therof seised, and after the eldest sister had disseised the yonger of her part, & was thereof seised in Fee, and hath Issue, and of such Estate dieth seised, whereby the lands discend to the Issue of the elder sister, then the younger Sister nor her heires cannot enter, &c. *Causa qua supra, &c.*

21. *Ass.* 19. 21. E. 3. 7. 27. 32. 26. *Ass.* 2. 27. *Ass.* 68. 36 *ass. p.* 1. 43. E. 3. 19. 4. H. 7. 10. 16. H. 7. 4.

¶ *Claimont tout la terre.* Here it appeareth, That when the one Coparcener doth specially enter, claiming the whole land, and taking the whole profits, that she gaine the one moitie, viz. of her sister by abatement, and yet her dying seised shall not take away the entrie of her sister, whereas when one Coparcener enters generally, and taketh the profits, this shall be accounted in Law the entrie of them both, and no deuesting of the moitie of her sister.

See more of this in the chapter of Warrantie, Sect. 710. 28. *Ass.* 30. *Vi. Sect.* 710.

If one Coparcener enter claiming the whole, and make a Feoffement in Fee, and take back an estate to her and her heires, and hath Issue and die seised, this discent shall take away the entrie of the other sister, because by the Feoffement the priuitie of the Coparcenarie was destroyed.

¶ *Claimont per vn mesme title, &c.* Of this sufficient hath bin said in the next precedent Section.

¶ *Ne poient enter, &c.* Of this there hath beene also spoken in the same Section.

Section 399.

¶ Item si home est seisie de certaine Terre en fee, et ad issue deux fits, et leigne fits est Bastard, et l'puisne frere est mulier, et le Pier deuie, et le Bastard enter enclaimant cōe heire a son pier, & occupia la terre tout sa vie sans ascun entre fait sur luy per l' mulier, et le Bastard ad issue et morust seisie de tiel estate en fee, et

ALso if a man bee seised of certaine Lands in Fee, and hath Issue two Sonnes, and the elder is a Bastard, and the younger *Mulier*, and the father die, and the Bastard entreth claiming as heire to his Father, and occupieth the Land all his life, without any entrie made vpon him by the *Mulier*, and the Bastard hath Issue and dieth seised

Pl. Com. 57. 39. E. 3. *Le dareine case.*

¶ *Seisie en fee.* For this holds not in case of an estate taile.

Li. 8. fo. 101. 102. *Sir Rich. Lechfords case.*

¶ *Mulier, seu filius mulieratus.* *Mulier* hath three significations; First Sub nomine mulieris continetur qualibet Fœmina. Secondly, Propriè sub nomine mulieris continetur Virgo. Thirdly, Appellatione mulieris in legibus Angliæ continetur Vxor. Et sic filius natus vel filia nata ex iusta vxore appellatur in Legibus Angliæ filius mulieratus seu filia mulierata, a sonne mulier, or a daughter mulier, Sicut Bastardus dicitur à Græco verbo Bassaris, i. Meretrix, seu Concubina, quia procreatur ex meretrice seu

Glanu. li. 7. *ca.* 8. *Bract. li.* 5. *ca.* 19. *Brit. ca.* 70.

Vi. Sect. 188.

et la Terre discendist a son Issue, et son Issue enter, &c. En cest case le mulier est sauns remedie, Car il ne poit enter, ne auer ascun Action pur recouerer la Terre, pur ceo que est vn antient Ley en tiel case vse, &c.

of such estate in Fee, and the Land discend to his Issue, & his issue entreth, &c. In this case the *Mulier* is without remedie, for he may not enter, nor haue any Action to recouer the lād, because there is an antient Law in this case vsed, &c.

concubina. In English he is called base borne, and thereupon some say, That a Bastard is as much to say as one that is a Base Naturall, for Aerd signifieth Nature. I read in Fleta, (p) That there be three kind of Bastards, viz, Manser, Nothus, & Spurius, which are described in two old verses,

(p) Flet. lib. 1. ca. 5. r. Sect. 380.

Manseribus scortum, Notho moechus dedit ortum.
Vt seges è spica, sic Spurius est ab amica.

But we terme them all by the name of Bastards, that be borne out of lawfull marriage. By the Common Law, (r) if the husband be within the foure Seas, that is, within the Jurisdiction of the King of England, if the wife hath Issue, no proofe is to be admitted to proove the child a Bastard, (for in that case, Filiatio non potest probari) vnlesse the husband hath an apparant impossibilitie of procreation, as if the husband be but eight yeares old, or vnder the age of procreation, such Issue is Bastard, albeit hee be borne within marriage. (f) But if the Issue be borne within a moneth or a day after marriage betweene parties of full lawfull age, the child is legitimate.

(r) Bract. li. 4. fo. 278. 279. 7. H. 4. 9. 43. E. 3. 19. 41. E. 3. 7. 44. E. 3. 10. 29. Ass. 54. 98. Ass. 24 1. H. 6 7. 19. H. 6. 17. 39. E. 3. 13. (f) 18. E. 4. 28.

¶ *Discendist a son Issue.* For if the Bastard dieth seised without Issue, and the Lord by Escheat entreth, this dying seised shall not barre the Mulier, because there is no discent. If the Bastard enter, and the Mulier dieth, his wife priuement enseint with a sonne, the Bastard hath issue and dieth seised, the sonne is borne, his right is bound for euer. But if the Bastard dieth seised, his wife enseint with a sonne, the Mulier enter, the son is borne, the Issue of the Bastard is barred: for Littleton putteth his case, that there must not onely be a dying seised, but also a discent to his Issue.

¶ *Et son issue enter, &c.* And so it is to be understood, albeit the Mulier after the decease of the Bastard doth enter before the heire of the Bastard, for the discent bindeth, and not the entrie of the heire.

¶ *Le mulier est sans remedie.* Hereby it appeareth, that this discent differeth from other discents, for this discent barreth the right of the Mulier, whereas other discents doe take away the entrie onely of him that right hath, and leaueth him to his Action, but here by the dying seised of the Bastard, his Issue is become lawfull heire. (a) It is holden that if the Mulier be within age at the time of the dying seised, that he shall be barred, because the Issue of the Bastard is in iudgement of Law become lawfull heire, and that the Law doth preferre Legitimation before the priuiledge of Infancie.

Lib. 8 101. 102. Sir Rich. Lechfords case.

(a) 5. E. 2. Discent B. 49. 31. Ass. 18. 22. 33. E. 3. Verdict 48. 36. Ass. 2. Pl. Com. Stowels case. 10. E. 3. 2.

And the reason of this case is, for that Iustum non est aliquem post mortem facere bastardum qui toto tempore vitæ suæ pro legitimo habebatur. And so it seemeth to be, That if a man hath issue a sonne being Bastard eigne, and a daughter, and the daughter is married, the father dieth, the sonne entreth and dieth seised, this shall barre the Feme Couert. And the discent in this case of Seruices, Rents, Reuersions expectant vpon Estates Taile, or for life, whereupon Rents are reserued, &c. shall bind the right of the Mulier, but a discent of these shal not driue them that right haue to an Action.

13. E. 1. tit. Bastardy 28.

14. E. 2. Bastardy 26.

So if the Bastard dieth seised, and his Issue endoweth the wife of the Bastard, yet is not the entrie of the Mulier lawfull vpon the Tenant in Dower, for his right was barred by the discent.

Sir Ric. Lechfords case vb. sup.

If the Bastard eigne entreth into the land and hath Issue, and entreth into Religion, this discent shall barre the right of the Mulier.

20. H. 3. Bastardy 29.

¶ *Ad issue deux fits.* If a man hath Issue such a Bastard as is aforesayd, and dieth, and the Bastard entreth and dieth seised, and the Land discendeth to his Issue, the Collaterall Heyre of the Father is bound as well as where there be two sonnes.

And where our Author speaketh of sonnes, so it is if a man hath Issue two daughters, the eldest being a Bastard, and they enter and occupie peaceably as heires, now the Law in fauour of Legitimation shall not adiudge the whole possession in the Mulier, (who then had the onely right, but in both, so as if the Bastard hath issue and dieth, her issue shal inherit. (b) And in the

Hil. 18. E. 3. cor. Reg. Rot. 144 Ebor.
17. E. 3. 59. F. tit. Bastard. 32
Sir Rich. Lechfords case vb. sup.
See afterwards in the Chapter of Warranties.
(b) 2. E. 3. tit. Bastardie 19.

21.E.3.34.b. 30.Ass.p.7. Sir Rich. Lechfords case vb.sup. (c) Brit.ca.70.

the same case if both daughters enter and make partition, this partition shall bind the Mulier for euer.

(c) And an Assise of Mortdancester lieth not betweene the Bastard and the Mulier in respect of the proximitie of bloud.

10.E.3.Vouch.129. 11.E.3. Age 3. 5.H.7.2. Sir Ric. Lechfords case vb.sup.

And the Bastard being impleaded or vouched shall haue his age.

¶ *Et le Bastard enter come heire a son pier.* If a man hath Issue Bastard eigne and Mulier puisne, and the Bastard in the life of the father hath Issue and dieth, and then the father dieth seised, and the son of the Bastard entreth as heire to his grandfather, and dieth seised, this shall bind the Mulier.

¶ *Pur ceo que est antient Ley en tiel case vse, &c.* As hereafter in our Comment vpon the two next Sections shall appeare by our antient Bookes and the antient Statutes of the Realme. And here is implied how necessarie it is after the example of our Author, to looke into the Antiquitie, than which, nothing is more venerable, profitable, and pleasant.

Section 400.

¶ MEs il ad estre lopinion dascuns, que ceo serra intendue lou l' pier ad vn fits bastard per vn feme, et puis espousa mesm la feme, et apres lespousels il ad issue per mesme la feme vn fits, ou vn file mulier, et puis le pier morust, &c. si tiel Bastard enter, &c. et ad Issue et deuie seisie, &c. donque auera lissue de tiel Bastard le Terre cleerement a luy, come auant est dit, &c. et nemy ascun auter bastard la mere, que ne fuit vnque espouse a son pier, et ceo semble bone et reasonable opinion. Car tiel Bastard nee deuant espousels celebres perenter son pier et sa mere, per la Ley de Saint Esglise est mulier, coment que per la Ley del Terre il est Bastard, et issint il ad vn colour dentrer come heire a son pier, pur ceo que il est per vn ley mulier, &c. s. per la Ley de Saint Esglise. Mes autermt est de bastard que nad ascun maner colour dentre come heire, entant que il ne poet per nul Ley estre dit mulier, car tiel Bastard est dit en la Ley, Quasi nullius filius, &c.

BVt it hath beene the opinion of some, That this shall be intended where the father hath a sonne Bastard by a woman, and after marrieth the same woman, and after the espousels he hath issue by the same woman a son or a daughter, and after the father dieth, &c. if such Bastard entreth, &c. and hath issue and die seised, &c. then shall the issue of such bastard haue the land cleerly to him, as it is said before, &c. and not any other bastard of the mother wch was neuer married to his father, and this seemeth to be a good and reasonable opinion: for such a bastard borne before marriage celebrated between his father and his mother, by the law of holy church is *Mulier*, albeit by the law of the land he is a bastard, & so he hath a colour to enter as heire to his Father, for that he is by one law *Mulier*, s. by Law of Holie Church. But otherwise it is of a Bastard which hath no manner of color to enter as heire, insomuch as he can by no law be sayd to be *Mulier*, for such a Bastard is sayd in the law to be *Quasi nullius filius, &c.*

Mes

Mes ad este lopinion dascuns, &c. And our Author here saith, That this opinion is good and reasonable, for that such a Bastard by the Law of Holy church (*) is a Mulier.

Matrimonium subsequens legitimos facit quoad sacerdotium non quoad successionem propter consuetudinem regni quod se habet in contrarium. Yet the Canon Law holdeth them Legitimate, quoad successionem. At a Parliament holden (q) Anno 20. H. 3. for that to certifie upon the Kings writ, that the sonne borne before marriage is a Bastard, was Contra Communem formam Ecclesiæ, rogauerunt omnes Episcopi Magnates vt consentirent, quod nati ante matrimonium essent legitimi sicut illi qui nati sunt post matrimonium quantum ad successionẽ hæreditariam quia Ecclesia tales habet pro legitimis: Et omnes Comites & Barones vna voce responderunt, Quod nolunt Leges Angliæ mutare, quæ huc vsque vsitatę sunt & approbatæ.

¶ Issint que il ad vn colour dentre, &c. Here it is to obserued, That the Law more respecteth him that hath a Colourable title, though it be not perfect in Law, than him that hath no title at all, as hath beene sayd (r) before.

* Vide Britton fol. 128 b. 166. 203. And the Statute of Merton. 20. H. 3. cap. 19. confirmeth this opinion. Hil. 18. E. 3. coram Rege in Thesau. Ebor.

Bracton. lib. 2. fol. 63.
(q) Statut. de Merton 20. H. 3. cap. 9.
Vide Bract. lib. 5. fo. 416. 417. 10. Ass. pl. 20.

(r) Vide Sect. 397. & cap. garr. Sect.

Section 401.

¶ Mes en le case auantdit, lou le Bastard enter apres la mort le pier, et l' mulier luy ousta, et puis le Bastard disseisist le mulier, et ad issue, et deuie seisie, et lissue enter, donq̃ le mulier poit auer briefe Dentre sur diss. enuers lissue del Bastard et recouera la terre, &c. Et issint poies veir le diuersitie lou tiel Bastard continue la poss. tout sa vie sans interruption & lou le mulier enter & interrupt le possession de tiel bastard, &c.

But in the case aforesaid, where the Bastard enter after the death of the father, and the mulier oust him, and after the Bastard disseise the mulier, and hath issue and dieth seised, and the issue enter, then the mulier may haue a Writ of *Entrie sur disseisin* against the issue of the Bastard, & shall recouer the Land, &c. And so you may see a diuersitie where such Bastard continues the possession all his life without interruption, and where the mulier entreth, and interrupts the possession of such Bastard, &c.

¶ Et le mulier luy ousta. An estranger in the name of the Mulier without his commandement cannot enter upon the Bastard, for that the Bastard may gaine the estate and bar the Mulier. And therefore regularly none shall enter but the Mulier, or some other by his commandement. (And therefore Littleton saith, and the Mulier put him out) no more then in the case (a) of the Lord Awdley: for an estranger of his owne head cannot enter in the name of him that right had to enter within the fiue yeares to auoid the Fine. But in both those cases, first, if the Mulier agree thereunto before the discent of the Bastard; or secondly, he that right hath before the fiue yeares be past do assent thereunto, the clayme is good, and shall auoid the estate of the Bastard, and of the Conusee as it was holden in the Lord Awdleyes Case, Quia omnis ratihabitio retrotrahitur, & mandato equiparatur, and standeth well with the words of the Statute, so that they pursue their title, &c. by way of Action or Entry, and so it is (b) 31. H. 8. to be intended.

But in the case of the Bastard eigne, which is Littletons case, Gardein in Socage, or Gardeine in Chiualrie may enter, for they are no strangers, as in another place is plainly shewed. If an Infant make a feoffment in fee, an estranger of his owne head cannot enter (c) to the vse of the Infant, for the estate is voidable. But where the Infant or a man of full age is disseised, an entrie by a stranger of his owne head is good and vesteth presently the right in the Infant. So it is if Tenant for life make a feoffment in fee, an estranger may enter in the name of him in the Reuersion, and thereby the estate shall be vested in him, Et sic de similibus.

(a) Mich. 38. & 39. Eliz. in the Kings Bench upon euidence by the whole Court.
Vide 31. H. 8. entr. congé. Br. 123.

4. H. 7. cap.

Vide Sect. 334.
(b) 31. H. 8. entr. cong. Br. 123.
(c) Pasc. 39. Eliz. in Cõmuni Banco per Curiam. 10. H. 7. 16. 7. E. 3. 69. 26. E. 3. 62. per Thorp. 45. E. 3. release 28. 11. Ass. 11.

¶ *Lou tiel Bastard continue tiel possession sans interruption.* If the Mulier entreth upon the Bastard, and the Bastard recovereth the Land in an Assise against the Mulier, now is the Interruption avoyded, and if the Bastard dieth seised, this shall barre the Mulier.

2. Ass. 9. If the Bastard eigne after the decease of the father entreth, and the King seiseth the land for some contempt supposed to be committed by the Bastard, for which no Freehold or Inheritance is lost, but only the profits of the Land by way of seisure, and the Bastard die, and his Issue is upon his Petition restored to the possession, for that the seisure was without cause, the mulier is barred for ever, for the possession of the King when hee hath no cause of seisure shall bee adiudged the possession of him for whose cause he seised. But if after the death of the Father the mulier be found heire and within age, and the King seiseth, in that case the possession of the King is in right of the mulier, and vesteth the actuall possession in the mulier, and consequently the Bastard eigne is foreclosed of any right for ever.

And so it is when the King seiseth for a contempt or other offence of the Father or of any other Ancestor, in that case if the Issue of the Bastard eigne upon a Petition be restored for that the seisure was without cause, the mulier is not barred, for the Bastard could never enter, and consequently could gaine no estate in the Land, but the possession of the King in that case shall bee adiudged in the right of the mulier. And it is to bee observed, that the Bastard must enter in vacuam possessionem, and must continue during his life without interruption made by the Mulier.

Pl. Com. Parson de Honylanes case 91. 39. H. 6. 24. 21. H. 6. 9. 1. E. 4. 3. 21. E. 4. 5. 5. E. 4. 60. ¶ *Interrupt le possession del Bastard, &c.* If the Bastard invite the mulier to see his House, and to see Pictures, &c. or to dine with him, or to Hawke, Hunt, or Sport with him, or such like upon the Land discended, & the mulier commeth upon the Land accordingly, this is no interruption because he came in by the consent of the Bastard, and therefore the comming upon the Land can be no trespasse, but if the mulier commeth upon the ground of his owne head, and cutteth downe a tree or diggeth the soyle, or take any profit, these shall be interruptions, for rather then the Bastard shall punish him in an Action of Trespasse, the Act shall amount in Law to an Entry, because he hath a right of Entrie. So it is if the mulier put any of his beasts into the ground or command a stranger to put on his beasts, these doe amount to an Entrie, for albeit in these cases the mulier doth not use any expresse words of Entrie, yet these and such like Acts doe without any words amount in Law to an Entrie, for Acts without words may make an Entrie, but words without an Act (viz.) Entrie into the Land, &c.) cannot make an Entrie (all which interruptions are implyed in the said, &c.) More shall be said hereafter of Interruptions in the Chapter of Continuall Clayme.

Sect. 402.

¶ Item, si un enfant deins age ad tiel cause de entry en ascuns terres ou tenements sur un auter, que est seisie en fee, ou en fee taile de mesme les terres ou tenements, si tiel home que est tielment seisie, morust de tiel estate seisie, et les terres discendont a son issue, durant le temps que lenfant est deins age, tiel discent ne tollera lentry

Also if an Infant within age hath such cause to enter into any Lands or Tenements upon another which is seised in fee, or in fee tayle of the same Lands or Tenements if such man who is so seised, dieth of such estate seised, and the Lands discend to his Issue, during the time that the Infant is within age, such Discent shall not take away the entrie of the

[illegible] ¶ *Si un enfant deins age ad cause denterer.* If a man seised of Lands in fee die, his wife privement enseint with a son, and a stranger abate and die seised, and after the sonne is borne, hee shall bee bound by the Discent, because hee at the time of the Discent had no right to enter, & this is to be gathered upon these words of Littleton, ad cause denterer, which at the time of the Discent he had not.

20. H. 6. 28. & 20. E. 4. 25. 26. 25. E. 4. discent. 30. ¶ *Est eins per Discent, &c.* Here is implyed any other heire collaterall or lineall.

An Infant is accounted in Law (as hath beene often said, (d) untill hee passeth the

(d) Vide Sect. 259. 403.

lentry lenfant, mes que il poit enter sur le issue que est eins per discent, &c. pur ceo que nul laches serra adiudge en un enfant deins age en tiel case.

Infant, but that hee may enter vpon the issue which is in by discent, for that no laches shall bee adiudged in an Infant within age in such a case.

age of 21. yeares, and certaine priuiledges hee hath in respect of his infancie.

Nul Laches serra adiudge en le Infant deins age in tiel case.

And Littleton well added (en tiel case) that is, in case of Discent, for in some other Cases Laches shall preiudice an Infant. As Laches shall be adiudged in an Infant if hee present not to a Church within sixe monethes, for the Law respecteth more the Priuiledge of the Church, that the Cure be serued, than the Priuiledge of Infancie. And so the publique Repose of the Realme concerning mens Freehold and Inheritance shall be preferred before the priuiledge of Infancy in case of a fine where the time begin, in the time of the Ancestor. So non-claime of a Villaine, of an Infant by a yeare and a day, which hath fled to an ancient Demesne, shall take away the seisure of the Infant. And if an Infant bring not an Appeale of the death of his Ancestor within a yeare and a day, he is barred of his appeale for euer, for the Law respects more Libertie and Life, than the Priuiledge of Infancie. And here it is to be obserued, that Littleton putteth his case, that an Infant shall enter vpon a Discent, when a stranger dyeth seised, but hee put it not so before, in the case of the Bastard eigne. B. Tenant in tayle infeoffeth A in fee, A. hath issue within age and dyeth, B. abateth and dyeth seised, the Issue of A. being still within age, this Discent shall bind (e) the Infant, for the Issue in tayle is remitted: and the Law doth more respect an ancient right in this case, than the priuiledge of an Infant that had but a defeasible estate. And it is said (f) that if the King dye seised of Lands, and the Land discend to his Successor, this shall bind an Infant, for that the priuiledge of the Infant in this case holds not against the King.

33.E.3. quar.imp.46.

Pl.Com.372.

(e) 11.E.4 1.2. F.N.B.35.m.

(f) 35.H.6 60.

Sect. 403.

Item, si le baron & sa feme come en droit la feme, ont title & droit denter en tenements que un auter ad en fee, ou en fee taile, et tiel tenant morust seisie, &c. en tiel case lentrie le baron est tolle sur lheire que est eins per discent. Mes si le baron deuie, donque la feme bien poit enter sur lissue que est eins per discent, pur ceo que Laches le baron ne turnera la feme ne ses heires en preiudice ne en dammage

ALso if Husband and Wife, as in right of the wife haue title and right to enter into Lands which another hath in fee, or in fee tayle, and such tenant dieth seised, &c. In such case the entrie of the Husband is taken away vpon the heire which is in by Discent: but if the Husband die, then the wife may well enter vpon the Issue which is in by Discent, for that no Laches of the husband shal turne the wife or her heires to any preiudice, nor losse

SI baron & feme come en droit sa feme ont title & droit dentrer, &c. & tiel tenant morust seisie, &c.

These words are generall, but are particularly to bee vnderstood, viz. when the wrong was done to the wife during the Couerture, for if a Feme sole be seised of Lands in fee, and is disseised, and then taketh husband, In this case the husband and wife, as in the right of the wife, haue right to enter, and yet the dying seised of the disseisor in that case shall take away the entry of the wife after the death of her husband, and the reason is aswell for that shee herselfe when shee was sole, might haue entred and recontinued the possession, as also it shall bee accounted her folly that shee would take such a husband which would not enter before the Discent.

9.H.7.24.a. 2.E.4.25. 7.E.4 7.b. 20.H.6.28.b. 42.E.3.12.

15.E.4 discent.30.

 But

9. H. 7. 24.

But if the woman were within age at the time of the taking of husband, then the dying seised shall not after the decease of her husband take away her Entrie; because no folly can be accounted in her, for that shee was within age when she tooke husband, and after Coverture she cannot enter without her husband, all which is implyed in the said (&c.)

en tiel cas, mes que la fem & ses heirs bien poient enter, lou tiel discent est eschue durant le coverture.

in such case, but that the wife & her heires may well enter where such Discent is eschued during the Coverture.

Vid. Sect. 402.

¶ *Laches le Baron ne turnera la fem, &c. al preiudice, &c.* Laches (signifieth in the Common Law, rechlesnesse or negligence, Et negligentia semper habet infortunium comitem. Here is a diversitie to be observed that albeit regularly no Laches shall bee accounted in Infants or Feme Coverts as is aforesaid, for not Entry or Claymes to avoyde Discents, yet Laches shall be accounted in them for not performance of a Condition annexed to the state of the Land. For if a Fem be infeoffed eyther before or after marriage, reserving a Rent, and for default of payment a re-entrie. In that case the Laches of the Baron shall disherit the wife for ever. And so it is (n) of an Infant his Laches, for not performing of a Condition annexed to a state, eyther made to his Ancestor or to himselfe shall barre him of the right of the Land for ever.

20. H. 6. 28. b.
(n) 31. Ass. p. 17.
42. E. 3. 1. Pl. Com. 55.
10. H. 7. 13. H. 7.

35. H. 6. 41. Pl. Com. 236. b.
Fleta lib. 2. cap. 50.

(o) Le statute de Merton ca. 5

If a man make a feoffment in fee to another reserving a Rent, and if he pay not the Rent within a moneth, that he shall double the Rent, and the Feoffee dieth, his heire within age, the Infant payeth not the Rent, he shall not by this Laches forfeit any thing. But otherwise it is of a Feme Covert, and the reason and cause of this diversitie is, for that the Infant is provided for by the Statute, (o) Non current vsuræ contra aliquem infra ætatem existen' &c. But that Statute doth not extend to a Fem Covert, neither doth that Statute extend to a Condition of a re-entrie, which an Infant ought to performe, for the forfeiture thereof cannot bee called Vsura.

Sect. 404.

¶* Mes la Court tient, lou tiel title est done al feme sole, que puis prent baron, que nentra pas, eins suffer un Discent, &c. la auter est, car serra dit la folly le feme de prender tiel baron que nentre en temps, &c. *

But the Court holdeth where such title is given to a fem sole who after taketh husband which doth not enter, but suffer a Discent, &c. there otherwise it is. for it shall be said the folly of the wife to take such a husband which entered not in time, &c.

9. H. 7. 24.

¶ This is added, and therefore as formerly I have done I meddle not withall, howbeit the opinion is holden for Law, as it appeareth in the Section next precedent.

Section 405.

Pl. Com. fo. 368. b. per Sanders
Lib. 4. fo. 127. 128. Beverleys case. Mirror cap. 1. § 9. ca. 5. § 1. Bracton fo. 165. & 420
Britton fo. 167. b. 217. 66.
Fleta l. 6. ca. 39. Fitz. N. B. 232. b. Staunf. Prer. 33. 34.

¶ Here Litl. explaneth a man of no sound memory to be Non compos mentis. Many times (as here it appeareth) the Latyn word explaneth the true sence, and calleth him not Amens, demens, furiosus, lunaticus, fatuus, stultus, or the like, for Non compos mentis is most sure and legall.

Non compos mentis is

¶ [Item, si home que est de non sane memory, que est adire en Latin, Qui non est cōpos mentis, ad cause dentre en ascuns tiels tenements, si tiel discent vt supra, soit ewe en sa vie, durant le temps que il fuit de non

Also if a man which is of non sane memory, that is to say in Latyn, *Qui non est compos mentis*, hath cause to enter into any such tenements, if such discent, *Vt supra*, bee had in his life during the time that hee was not of sound

non sane memorie, & puis deuia, son heire bien poit enter sur luy que est eins p discent. Et en cest case poyes veier vn cas, q̃ lheire poiet enter, & uncore son ancester que auoit mesme le title ne puissoit enter. Car celuy que fuit hors de sa memorie al temps de tiel discent, sil voile enter apres tiel discent, si action sur ceo soit sue enuers luy, il nad riẽs pur luy a pleder, ou de luy ayder, mes a dire que il fuit de non sane memorie al temps de tiel discent, &c. & a ceo ne serra il resceiue a dire, pur ceo que nul home ᵭ pleine age serra resceiue en ascun plee per la ley a disabler sa person demesñ, mes lheire bien poit disabler le person son auncester pur son aduantage demesne en tiel cas, pur ceo q̃ nul laches poit estre adiudge per la ley en celuy que ad nul discretion en tiel case.

memory, & after dieth, his heire may well enter vpon him which is in by discent. And in this case you may see a case where the heire may enter, and yet his Ancestor which had the same title could not enter. For hee which was out of his memory at the time of such discent if he will enter after such a discent, if an action vpon this be sued against him, he hath nothing to pleade for himselfe or to help him, but to say, that hee was not of sane memory at the time of such discent, &c. And he shall not bee receiued to say this, for that no man of full age shall be receiued in any plea by the law to disable his owne person, but the heire may well disable the person of his Ancestor for his owne aduantage in such case, for that no laches may bee adiudged by the law in him which hath no discretion in such case.

of foure sorts; 1. Ideota which from his natiuity by a perpetuall infirmity is Non compos mentis. 2. Hee that by sicknesse, griefe or other accident wholly loseth his memory and vnderstanding. *Ls. 4. 124. 125. Beuerleys case* 3. A Lunatique that hath sometime his vnderstanding and sometime not, Aliquando gaudet lucidis interuallis, and therefore he is called Non compos mentis so long as he hath not vnderstanding. Lastly, he that by his owne vitious act for a time depriueth himselfe of his memory and vnderstanding, as he that is drunken. But that kinde of Non compos mentis shall giue no priuiledge or benefit to him or his heires. And a discent shall take away the entrie of an Ideot, albeit the want of vnderstanding was perpetuall; for Littleton speaketh generally of a man of non sane memory. So likewise if a man that become Non compos mentis by accident as is aforesaid be disseised and suffer a discent, albeit hee recouer his memory and vnderstanding againe, yet he shall neuer auoide the discent, and so it is a fortiori of one that hath Lucida interualla. As for a drunkard, who is Voluntarius dæmon, hee hath (as hath beene said) no priuiledge thereby, but what hurt or ill soeuer hee doth, his drunkennesse doth aggreuate it; Omne crimen ebrietas & incendit & detegit.

If an Ideot make a feoffment in fee, he shall in pleading neuer auoide it, saying that he was an Ideot at the time of his feoffment, and so had beene from his natiuity. But vpon an office found for the King, the King shall auoide the feoffment for the benefit of the Ideot whose custodie the Law giueth to the King. *39. H. 6. 42. b. Abb. Ass. 89. b. F. N. B. 202. 5. E. 3. 70. Britton ca. 28 fo. 66. 25. Ass. pl. 4. 35. Ass. pl. 10.*

So it is of a Non compos, and so it is of him Qui gaudet lucidis interuallis, of an estate made during his Lunacie: for albeit the parties themselues cannot be receiued to disable themselues, yet twelue men vpon the Office may find the truth of the matter. But if any of them alien by fine or recouerie, this shall not onely bind himselfe, but his heires also. As amongst other things requisite to be knowne, these cases you shall finde at large in my Commentaries whereunto for breuity I referre the reader, Vpon all which bookes there haue beene foure seuerall opinions concerning the alienation or other act of a man that is Non compos mentis, &c. For *32. E. 3. tit. Scire fac. 160. Staunf. Pr. 34. F. N. B. 202. e Beuerleys case lib. 4. 126. 127. 128.*

Vid. Br. tit. Dum fuit infra ætatem. 5.

first some are of opinion that he may auoyde his owne act by entrie or plea. Secondly, Others are of opinion, That he may auoyd it by Writ, and not by plea. Thirdly, Others, That hee may auoyd it either by plea or by Writ, and of this opinion is Fitzherbert in his Natura Breuium vbi supra. And Littleton here is of opinion, That neither by Plea nor by Writ or otherwise, hee himselfe shall auoyd it, but his heire in respect his Ancestor was Non compos mentis, shall auoyd it by entrie, plea, or Writ: And herewith the greatest authorities of our Bookes agree, and so was it resolued with Littleton, in Beuerleys case, (r) where it is sayd, That it is a Maxime of the Common Law, That the partie shall not disable himselfe. But this holdeth onely in Ciuile Causes, for in Criminall Causes, as Felonie, &c. the act and wrong of a mad man shall not be imputed to him, for that in those causes, Actus non facit reum, nisi mens sit rea, and he is Amens (id est) sine mente, without his mind or discretion; and Furiosus solo furore punitur, a mad man is onely punished by his madnesse. And so it is of an Infant untill he be of the age of fourteene, which in Law is accounted the age of discretion.

(r) Lib. 4. fo. 126. 127.

26. Ass. 27. 21. H. 7. 31. Stanford 16 b. 8. E. 2. Coron 412. 414. 351. 22. E. 3. ibid. 224. Beuerleys case vbi sup. a F. N. B. 202. D. 3. H. 7. 2. Vid. 3. E. 3. tit. Entrie Cong. Statham 12. E. 4. 8. 39. H. 6. 4. Abbr. Ass. 89. 39. H. 6. 43.

¶ *Et en cest case poyes veir vn case, &c.* And though Littleton saith, (One case) yet other cases may be found to the same end. For if there be Grandfather, Father, and Sonne, and the Father disseise the Grandfather, and make a Feoffement in Fee, without warrantie, the grandfather dieth, albeit the right discend to the father, he cannot enter against his owne Feoffement, but if he die, the sonne shall enter, and auoyd the estate of the Feoffee

15. E. 4. tit. Discent. 30.

So if the Grandfather be Tenant in Taile, and the father disseise him vt supra, mutatis mutandis.

If Lands be giuen to two and to the heires of one of them, he that hath the Fee simple shall not haue an action of Wast vpon the Statute of Gloucester, against the Joyntenant for life, but his heire shall maintaine an Action of Wast against him, vpon the Statute of Gloucester, so the heire shall maintaine that Action which the Ancestor could not.

Sect. 406.

¶ ET si tiel home de non sane memorie fait Feoffement, &c. il mesm ne poet enter ne auer briefe appell Dum non fuit compos mentis, &c. causa qua supra, Mes apres la mort son vre bien poit enter, ou auer le dit Briefe Dum non fuit compos mentis a son election. Mesme la Ley est lou enfant deins age fait Feoffement, et deuie, son heire poit enter, ou auer vn Briefe de Dum fuit infra ætatem, &c.

AND if such a man of Non sane memorie make a Feoffement, &c. he himselfe cannot enter, nor haue a Writ called *Dum non fuit compos mentis, &c. causa qua supra*: but after his death his Heire may well enter, or haue the sayd Writ of *Dum non fuit compos mentis* at his choice. The same Law is where an Infant within age maketh a feoffment and dieth, his heire may enter or haue a Writ of *Dum fuit infra ætatem, &c.*

¶ F*ait feoffement, &c.* Or any other like conueyance in paijs, but Fines and other assurances of Record are not implied in this, (&c).

¶ *Mesme la ley dun Enfant.* This is true, as to the bringing of a Dum fuit infra ætatem, &c. but without question the Infant in that case might haue entred, as it appeareth in the next Section.

¶ *Briefe* Dum non fuit compos mentis. This Writ (as it appeareth by our Author) lieth for the heire of him that was Non compos mentis, and not for himselfe, but a Dum fuit infra ætatem lieth as well for the Ancestor himselfe after his full age, as for his heire.

Sect.407.

¶ ITem si ieo sue disseisie per vn enfant deins age, le quel aliena a vn auter en fee, et lalienee deuie seisie, et les Tnts discendont a son heire, esteant lenfant deins age, mon entry est tolle, &c.

ALso if I be disseised by an Enfant within age, who alieneth to another in Fee, and the Alienee dieth seised, and the lands discend to his heire being an Infant within age, my entrie is taken away. &c.

Sect.408.

MEs si lenfant deins age ent sur lhée que est eins p discent, come il bien poit pur ceo q̃ mesme le discent fuit durant son nonage, donque ieo bien puisse enter sur le disseisor, pur ceo que p son entrie il ad defeat & antient le discent.

BVt if the Infant within age enter vpon the heire which is in by discent, as he well may, for that that the same discent was during his Nonage, then I may well enter vpon the Disseisor, because by his entrie he hath defeated and taken away the discent.

¶ HEre it appeareth, That the entrie of the Infant is lawfull, and giueth aduantage to the Disseisee to enter also, because the discent, which was the impediment, is auoyded. And it is to be obserued, That if the discent bee cast, the Infant being within age, he may enter at any time of his full age.

Vi. the next Sect. following. 43.E.3. tit. Entr. Cong. Vet.N.B.126.b. F.N.B.198 45.E.3.21.

And so it is if an Infant make a Feoffement, &c. he may enter either within age, or at any time after his full age, and so in both cases may his heire.

Sect. 409.

¶ EN mesme le manner est, lou ieo sue disseisie, et le disseisor fait feoffment en fee sur condit, et le Feoffee mort de tiel estate seisie, ieo ne purroy my enter sur lhée le feoffee: mes si le condition soit enfreint, issint q̃ pur cel cause le Feoffor enter sur lheire, ore ieo bñ puisse enter, pur ceo que quãt le Feoffor ou ses heires entront pur le condition enfreint, le discent est oustermẽt defeat, &c:

IN the same manner it is where I am disseised, and the Disseisor make a feoffmẽt in fee vpon condition, and the feoffee die of such estate seised, I may not enter vpon the heire of the Feoffee, but if the Condition be broken, so as for this cause the feoffor enter vpon the heire, now I may well enter, for that when the Feoffour or his heires enter for the condition broken, the Discent is vtterly defeated, &c.

¶ THe reason hereof is apparant, for Cessante causa cessat causatum. Tenant in Capite maketh a Feoffment in fee to the vse of the Feoffee and his heires, vntill the Feoffor pay an hundred pounds to him or his heires, the Feoffee dieth his heire within age, now hath the King the wardship of the bodie, and is intituled to the gard of the land. But if the Feoffor pay the hundred pounds according to the limitation, the wardship is diuested, both for the body and land, and so it is in case of a condition: for as Littleton here saith, the discent which is the cause of wardshippe, is vtterly defeated. And by these two last cases which Littleton hath here put, it appeareth, That there is no difference where the discent is disaffirmed by a right Paramount, where the state was neuer law-

V. the Sect. next precedent. Dyer 13.Eliz.fo.298,299.

lawfull, (as in the caſe of an Infant, and where the diſcent is affirmed for a time, & the eſtate being lawfull) and after defeated by matter ex poſt facto, by a title of Re-entrie.

Section 410.

Item ſi ieo ſoy diſſeiſie, et le Diſſeiſor ad iſſue et enter en Religion, per force de quel les Tenemēts diſcendōt a ſon iſſue, en ceſt caſe ieo bien puiſſe enter ſ liſſue, et uncore la fuit un diſcent. Mes pur ceo que tiel diſcēt vient al iſſue per fait le pier, ſ., pur ceo que il enter en Religion, &c. et le diſcent ne vient a luy per fait de Dieu, ſ. per mort, &c. mon entre eſt congeable. Car ſi ieo arraigne un Aſſiſe de Nouel Diſſeiſin envers mon Diſſeiſor, coment que il puit enter en religion, ceo ne abatera my mon bř mes mō bř (ē non obſtant) eſtoyera en ſa force, et mon recovery vers luy ſert bon. Et per meſme le reaſon le diſcent que aveigne a ſon Iſſue per ſon fait demeſn, ne tollera moy d mon entrie, &c.

Alſo if I bee diſſeiſed, and the deſſeiſor hath Iſſue and entreth into Religion, by force whereof the lands diſcend to his iſſue, In this caſe I may well enter vpon the Iſſue, and yet there was a diſcent: but for that ſuch diſcent commeth to the Iſſue by the Act of the father, s. for that he entred into Religion, &c. and the Diſcent came not vnto him by the Act of God, (*ſcilicet*) by death, &c. my entrie is congeable: for if I araigne an Aſſiſe of *Nouel diſſeiſin* againſt my diſſeiſor, albeit he after enter into Religion, this ſhall not abate my Writ, but my writ (notwithſtanding this) ſhall ſtand in his force, and my recouerie againſt him ſhall bee good. And by the ſame reaſon the diſcent which commeth to his Iſſue by his own Act, ſhal not take from me my entrie, &c.

Vi. Sect. 200. ¶ *Entre en Religion, &c.* Heere is implied Profeſſion. This diſcent ſhall not barre the entrie of the Diſſeiſee, for that the diſcent commeth by the Deed of the Father, becauſe hee entred into Religion, wherein there is an excellent poynt worthie of obſeruation: For albeit the entrie into Religion make not the diſcent, but the profeſſion, whereof you haue read before Sect. 200. Yet here you may learne by Littleton, That the Law reſpects the originall Act, and that is his entry into Religion, which is his owne Act whereupon the profeſſion followed, whereby the diſcent happned, for, Cuiuſque rei potiſſima pars principium eſt. And againe, Origo rei inſpici debet, whereof you ſhal make great vſe in reading of our Bookes. (*) Here Lit. attributeth the cauſe of the diſcent to his entrie into Religion, which was his owne Act, whereas a diſcent doth not take away an entrie vnleſſe it commeth by death, which, as Littleton ſaith, is the act of God, and no glorious pretext of an Act, no though it bee of Religion, ſhall worke a wrong to a ſtranger that hath right, to barre him of his entrie: But it is ſayd, That in the caſe of the Baſtard eigne and mulier puiſne, ſuch a diſcent ſhall bind the Mulier, as before hath beene ſayd, and ſuch an heire that commeth in by ſuch a diſcent ſhall haue his age.

(*) V. Pl. Com. Dame Hales caſe. 6. E. 3. 41. &c.

10. E. 3. 55.

¶ *Car ſi ieo arraigne un Aſſiſe, &c.* Nota if a man be Tenant or Defendant in a reall or perſonall Action, and hanging the ſuit, the tenant or defendant entreth into Religion, by this the writ is not abated, becauſe it is by his owne Act. And ſo it is of a Reſignation, but otherwiſe it is of a Depoſition or depriuation, becauſe he is expelled by iudgement, and yet his offence, &c. was the cauſe thereof, ſed in praeſumptione Legis iudicium redditur in inuitum.

3. H. 6. 41. 10. H. 6. 10. b. 18. E. 4. 19. 9. E. 4. 25. 52. 7. E. 4. 15. 18. E. 3. 24. 25. E. 3. 39. 46. E. 3. 25. 30. E. 1. Breiſe. 885. Bracton lib. 4. fo. 189. & Lib. 5. fo. 414. 22. R. 2. Breif 936. 15. Aſſ. pl. 8.

¶ *Moy de mon entry, &c.* Here is implied, Or any of my heires.

Sect. 411.

ITem si ieo lesse a vn home certaine terres pur terme de 20. ans. & vn autre moy disseisist, & ousta le termor et deuie seisie, et les tenements discēdont a son heire, ieo ne purroy enter, et vncore l' lessee pur terme dans bien puit enter pur ceo que il p̄ son entry ne ousta lheir q̄ est eins p dis=cēt d le frāktenemēt q̄ est a luy discēd⁹ mes solement claime da=uer les tenemēts pur terme dans, le quel nest pas expulsemēt de le franktenement del heire que est eins per discent. Mes au=terment est ou mon tenant a terme de vie est disseisie, Causa patet, &c.

ALso if I let vnto a man certain lands for the terme of twentie yeares, and another disseiseth me, and oust the termor, and die seised, and the Lands discend to his heire: I may not enter, and yet the Lessee for yeares may well enter, because that by his entrie he doth not ouste the heire who is in by Discent of the Freehold which is discended vnto him, but onely claymeth to haue the Lands for tearme of yeares which is no expulsion from the freehold, of the heire who is in by Discent. But otherwise it is where my Tenant for terme of life is disseised, *Causa patet, &c.*

PVr terme de 20. ans. It is clere that a Discent shall not take away the entry of a Lessee for yeares as our Authour here saith, nor of a Tenant by Elegit, or Tenant by Statute Merchant or such like, as haue but a Chattle and no Freehold, and the reason is for that by their entrie vpon the heire by discēt, they take no Freehold (which as often hath bin obserued is so much respected in Law) from him, but otherwise it is of an estate for life, or any higher estate. And as a Discent of a Freehold and Inheritance shall take away the entry of him that right hath to a Freehold or Inheritance, so a Discent of a Freehold and Inheritance cannot take away the entry of him that hath but a Chattle, for that no Discent can be of the same.

A man seised of an aduowson in fee, grants three auoydances one after another, and after the Church becommeth void, and the Grantor presents, and his Clarke is admitted and instituted, and after the Church becomes void, the Grantee may present to the second auoydance, for hee was not put out of possession thereof, for as the Lessor hauing the Freehold and Inheritance cannot disseise the Lessee for yeares, hauing but a Chattle, that any Discent may be cast to take away his entry as Littleton here sayth: so in the said case the Grantor hath the Franktenement and fee of the Aduowson rightfully, so as he cannot make any vsurpation to gaine any estate, or to put the Grantee so out of possession as he should not present, no more then the Lessee for yeares in this case to enter. Also in respect of the priuitie the vsurpation of the Grantor shall not put the Grantee out of possession for the two latter auoydances. And this was resolued (a) by all the Judges of the Court of Common Pleas, which I my selfe heard and obserued.

(a) Hill. 18. Eliz. in Communi Banco.

Sect. 412.

ITem il est dit, que si home est seisie de tenements en fee per occupation en temps de guerre, & ent morust seisie en

ALso it is said that if a man be seised of lands in fee by occupation in time of warre, and thereof dieth seised in the

PEr occupation en temps de guerre. First, It is necessary to be knowne what shall bee said Time of peace, Tempus pacis, and what shall bee said, Tempus belli, siue guerræ, time of warre, Tempus pacis est quando

Inter brevia de anno 1. E. 3. parte 1. & pasch. 28. E. 3. inter adiudicata coram Rege. lib. 2. fol. 37. in thesaur. Pasch. 39. E. 3. inter adiudicata coram Rege in thesaur. lib. 2. fol. 92.

14. E. 3. tit. scire facias 122. but more fully in the Record at large.

do Cancellaria & aliæ Curiæ Regis sunt apertæ quibus lex fiebat cuicunque prout fieri consueuit. And so was it adiudged in the case of Roger Mortimer, and of Thomas Earle of Lancaster. Vtrum terra sit guerrina necne, naturaliter debet iudicari per recorda Regis, & eorum qui curias Regis per legem terræ custodiunt & gubernant, sed non alio modo.

temps de guerre, et les tenements discendont a son heire, tiel discent ne oustera ascun home de son entry, et de ceo home poit vier en vn plee sur vn breife de Aiel, An. 7. E. 2.

time of warre, and the tenements discend to his heire, such discent shall not oust any man of his entrie, and of this a man may see in a Plea vpon a Writ of Aiel, 7. E. 2.

And therefore when the Courts of Justice bee open, and the Judges and Ministers of the same may by Law protect men from wrong and violence, and distribute Justice to all, it is said to be time of peace. So when by Inuasion, Insurrection, Rebellions, or such like the peaceable course of Justice is disturbed and stopped, so as the Courts of Justice be as it were shut vp, Et silent leges inter arma, then is it said to be time of warre. And the triall hereof is by the Records and Judges of the Court of Justice, for by them it will appeare, whether Justice had her equall course of proceeding at that time or no, and shall not be tryed by Jury.

If a man be disseised in time of peace, and the Discent is cast in time of warre, this shall not take away the entry of the Disseisee.

Bracton. lib. 4. fol. 240.

Item tempore pacis quod dicitur ad differentiam eorum quæ fuerunt tempore belli quod idem est quod tempore guerrino, quod nihil differt à tempore iuris & iniuriæ, est enim tempus iniuriæ, cum fuerunt oppressiones violentæ quibus resisti non potest, & disseisinæ iniustæ.

So as hereby it also appeareth that time of peace is the time of Law and right, and time of warre is the time of violent oppression, which cannot be resisted by the equall course of Law. And therefore in all reall actions the explens or taking of the profits are layed Tempore pacis, for if they were taken Tempore belli, they are not accounted of in Law.

Ingham cap. de nouel disseisin.

Lib. 4 fol. 49. 50. Ognels case.

¶ *Per Occupation.* Occupation **is a word of art, and signifieth a** putting out of a mans Freehold in time of warre, and it is all one with a disseisin in time of peace, sauing that it is not so dangerous as it appeareth by Littleton, and therefore the Law gaue a writ in that case of Occupauit, so called by reason of that word in the writ, in stead of dissesiuit in the Assise of Nouel disseisin, if the disseisin had beene done in time of peace, whereby it appeareth how aptly both in this and in all other places, Littleton thorow his whole Booke speaketh. But albeit Occupatio whereof Littleton here speaketh is vsed only in the said writ and in none other, that I can find or remember, yet hath it beene vsed commonly in Conueyances and Leases to limit or make certaine precedent words, as ad tunc in tenura & occupatione. But occupatio is applyed to the possession, bee it lawfull or vnlawfull; It hath also crept into some Acts of Parliament, as 4. H. 7. cap. 19. 39. Eliz. cap. 1. and others, and occupare is sometime taken to conquer.

¶ *Et de ceo home poet vier in vn plea sur briefe de Aiel, anno 7. E. 2.* Hereby it appeares that ancient tearmes or yeares after the example of Littleton are to bee cited and vouched, for confirmation of the Law, albeit they were neuer printed, and that those yeares, and those specially of E. 1. H. 3. &c. are worthy of the reading and obseruation: a great number of which I haue seene and obserued, which in mine opinion doe giue a great light not only to the vnderstanding and reason of the Common Law, and which Fitzherb. either saw not or were by him omitted, but also to the true exposition of the ancient Statutes, made in those times, yet mine aduice is, that they should be read in their time: for after our Studient be enabled and armed to set on our yeare bookes or reports of the Law, let him reade first the latter reports for two causes: First for that for the most part the latter Judgements and Resolutions are the surest, and therefore it is best to season him with them in the beginning both for the settling of his iudgement, and the reteyning of them in memory. Secondly, for that the latter are more facile and easier to be vnderstood, then the more ancient: but after the reading of them, then to reade these others before mentioned, and all the ancient Authors that haue written of our Law; for I would wish our Studient to be a compleat Lawyer. But now to returne. As it is in case of discent, so it is in case of presentation, for no vsurpation in time of war putteth the right Patron out of possession, albeit the incumbent come in by institution and induction. And time of warre doth not only giue priuiledge to them that be in warre, but to all others within the kingdome, and although the admission and institution be in time of peace, yet if the presentment were in time of warre, it putteth not the right Patron out of possession.

6. E. 3. 41. 7. E. 3. darr. pres. 2. 18. E. 2. quar. imp. 175. F. N. B. 31.

Sect. 413.

¶ Item que nul morant seisie (ou les tenements viendront a un auter per succession) tollera lentre dascun person, &c. Come de Prelates, Abbots, Priors, Deans, ou Parson de esglise, ou de auters corps politike, &c, coment que ils fueront xx, morants seisie, et xx. successors, ceo ne tolle iammes ascun home de son entrie.

¶ Plus serra dit de Discents en le prochein chapter.

Also that no dying seised (where the tenements come to another by succession) shall take away the entrie of any person, &c. As of Prelates, Abbots, Pryors, Deanes, or of the Parson of a Church or of other bodies politique, &c. albeit there were xx. dyings seised, and xx. successors, this shall not put any man from his entrie.

More shall be said of Discents in the next chapter.

¶ *Per succession.* This is in the Common Law applyed only to bodyes Politique or Corporate, which haue succession perpetuall and not to naturall men, as to a Bishop and his successors, an Abbot, Deane, Archdeacon, Prebend, Parson, &c. and their successors, and not to I.S. or any other naturall body and his successors, but to him and his heires. And the Successor of any of these is in the Post and the heire of the naturall man is in the Per, and Succedere is deriued of Sub & cedere.

¶ *Corps politique, &c.* This is a body to take in succession framed (as to that capacity) by pollicie, and thereupon it is called here by Littleton a body politique, and it is also called a Corporation or a body incorporate, because the persons are made into a body and of capacity to take and grant, &c. And this body politique or incorporate may commence and be established three manner of wayes, viz. by prescription, by Letters patents, or by acte of Parliament. Euery body politique or Corporate is either Ecclesiasticall or laye. Ecclesiasticall either regular, as Abbots, Pryors, &c. or Secular, as Bishops, Deanes, Archdeacons, Parsons, Vicars, &c. Lay, as Maior and Communalty, Baylifes and Burgesses, &c. Also euery body Politique or Corporate, is either electiue, presentatiue, collatiue or donatiue. And againe is either sole, or aggregate of many; as you may reade in the third part of my Commentaries. And this body Politique or Corporate, aggregate of many is by the Ciuilians called Collegium or Vniuersitas.

Vid. Sect. 1.

7. E. 3. 25. a. 5. E. 3. 13. & 31.

Lib. 3. fo. 73. in the case of the Deane & Chapter of Norwich.

Chap. 7. Continuall Clayme. *Sect.* 414.

Continuall clayme est la, lou home ad droit et title dentrer en ascuns terres ou tenements dont auter est seisie en fee, ou en fee taile, si cesty que ad title dentrer fait continual claime a les

Continual claim is where a man hath right and title to enter into any lands or tenements whereof another is seised in fee, or in fee taile, if hee which hath title to enter makes continuall claime to the lands or tenements be-

¶ Here our Author first describeth what a continuall clayme is. It is called Continuum clameum, because at the Common Law, it must haue beene made within euery yeare and day, as Littleton here teacheth. And yet if he that right hath maketh claime, and the Tertenant dyeth within the yeare and the day, this claime though it bee but once

Mirror cap. 2. §. 15. & §. 18.
Bracton lib. 5. fo. 435. 436.
Britton 107. b. 126. b.
Fleta lib. 6. cap. 52. 53.
Vid. Sect. 424.

Vid. Sect. 385. 32. H. 8. f. 33.

terres ou tenements deuant le morant seisie de celuy que tient les tenements, donques coment que tiel tenant morust ent seisi, & les terres ou tenements discendront a son heire, uncore poit celuy que auoit fait tiel claime, ou son heire enter en les terres ou tenements issint discendus, per cause de continual claim fait, nient contristiant le discent. Sicome en case que home soit disseisie, & le disseisee fait continual claime a les tenements en la vie le disseisor, coment que le disseisor deuie seisie en fee, & la terre discendist a son heire, uncore poit le Disseisee enter sur la possession le heire, nient obstant le discent.

fore the dying seised of him which holdeth the tenements, then albeit that such tenant dieth thereof seised, and the lands or tenements discend to his heire, yet may he who hath made such continuall claime or his heire enter into the lands or tenements so discended by reason of the continual claim made, notwithstanding the discent. As in case that a man be disseised and the disseisee makes continuall claime to the tenements in the life of the disseisor, although that the disseisor dieth seised in fee and the land discend to his heire, yet may the Disseisee enter vpon the possession of the heire notwithstanding the discent.

Vid.Sect.414.

once * made as hath beene said shall preserue the entrie of him that maketh the clayme.

¶ *Ad droit & title denter.* And yet in some cases a continuall claime may bee made by him that hath right and cannot enter.

Dyer 19.Eliz. Pl. Com.374. 15.H.7.3.4. Iacobins case. 28.H.6.28.

If Tenant for yeares, Tenant by Statute Staple, Marchant, or Elegit be ousted, and he in the reuersion disseised, the Lessor or he in reuersion may enter to the intent to make his clayme, and yet his entrie as to take any profits is not lawfull during the terme. And in the same manner the Lessor or he in the reuersion in that case may enter to auoyde a collaterall warrantie, or the Lessor in that case may recouer in an Assise. And so some haue holden may the Lessor doe in case of a Lease for life to this intent to auoid a Discent or a warrantie.

Vid.Sect.442. 45.E.3.21.

7.H.6.40. Contin. Clayme 1. Dowuclers case. 5.E.4.4.

If the Disseisee make continuall clayme and the Disseisor die seised within the yeares, his heire within age, and by office the King is intitled to wardship, albeit the entrie of the Disseisee be not lawfull, yet may he make continuall clayme to auoide a discent, and so in the like.

¶ *Vncore poet celuy que fait tiel clayme ou son heire enter.* This is to be vnderstood in this manner, that if the father make claime, and the Disseisor dyeth, the Father dyeth, his heire may enter, because the discent was cast in the fathers time, and the right of entrie which the Father gained by his claime shall discend to his heire. But if the Father make continuall clayme, and dyeth, and the Sonne make no continuall clayme, and within the yeare and day after the claime made by the Father the Disseisor dieth, this shall take away the entrie of the Sonne, for that the discent was cast in his time, and the clayme made by the Father shall not auaile him, that might haue claymed himselfe. And of this opinion was Littleton himselfe in our bookes where he holdeth that no continuall clayme can auoide a discent vnlesse it be made by him that hath title to enter, and in whose life the dying seised was. See more of this matter hereafter in this chapter, Sect 416.

Bracton, lib.5.fo.436. Fleta, lib.5.cap.52.53. 22.H.6.37. 9.H.4.5.a. 15.E.4.22.a.

22.H.6.37.

And as here Littleton putteth his case of the Ancestor and heire, so it holdeth in all respects of the Predecessor and Successor.

Sect. 415.

¶ EN mesme le maner est, si tenant a terme de vie alien en fee, celuy en le reuersion, ou celuy en le remainder poit enter sur lalienee, et si tiel alienee deuie seisi de tiel estate sans continual claime fait a les tenements deuant le morant seisi del alienee, & les tenements per cause del morant seisi del alienee, discendont a son heire, donques ne poit celuy en le reuersion, ne celuy en le remainder enter. Mes si celuy en le reuersion ou celuy en le remainder que ad cause dentre sur lalienee fait continual claime a les tenements deuant le morant seisi del alienee, donques tiel hōe poit enter apres la mort lalienee, auxybien come il puissoit en sa vie.

¶ IN the same manner it is, if tenant for life alien in fee, hee in the reuersion or hee in the remainder may enter vpon the alienee. And if such alienee dieth seised of such estate without continuall clayme made to the tenements before the dying seised of the alienee, and the lands by reason of the dying seised of the alienee discend to his heir, then cannot he in the reuersion, nor hee in the remainder enter. But if he in the reuersion or in the remainder who hath cause to enter vpon the alienee make continuall clayme to the land before the dying seised of the alienee, then such a man may enter after the death of the alienee, as well as he might in his life time.

¶ By this it appeareth, that a continuall claime may bee made aswell where the lands are in the hands of a Feoffee, &c, by title, as in the hands of a Disseisor, Abator, or Intrudor by wrong, as before hath beene noted.

Sect. 416.

¶ Item si terr soit lesse a vn home pur terme de sa vie, le remainder a vn auter a terme de vie, le remainder a le tierce en fee, si le tenant a terme de vie aliena a vn auter en fee, & celuy en le remainder pur terme de vie fait continual claime a la terre deuant le morant seisie dalyenee,

ALso if land be let to a man for terme of his life, the remainder to another for terme of life, the remainder to the third in fee, if tenant for life alien to another in fee, and hee in the remainder for life maketh continuall claime to the land before the dying seised of the Alienee, and after the

¶ A*Lien a vn auter in fee.* It is to be obserued that a forfeiture may be made by the alienation of a particular Tenant two manner of wayes, either In Paijs, or by matter of Record.

In Paijs, of lands and tenements which lye in Liuery (whereof Littleton intendeth his case) where a greater estate passeth by Liuery, then the particular Tenant may lawfully make, whereby the reuersion or remainder is deuested, as here in the example that Littleton putteth when tenant for life alieneth in

*Vid. Sect.*581.609.610.611.

et puis lalienee morust seisie, et puis apres celuy en le remainder pur term de vie morust, devaunt ascun entrie fait per luy, en cē cas celuy en le remainder en Fee, poit enter sur heire le alienee, per cause de continuall claim fait per luy que auoit le remainder pur terme de sa vie, pur ceo que tiel droit que il aveoit dentre, alera et remaindera a celuy en le remainder aps luy, entant que celuy en l'remainder en fee ne puissoit pas enter ꝭ lalienee en fee durant la vie celuy en le remainder p̄ terme d̄ sa vie, & pur ceo que il ne puissoit adonqz faire continual claim (car nul poit faire continual claim, mes quant il ad title dentrie, &c.)

alienee dieth seised, & after he in the remainder for life die before any entrie made by him, in this case he in the remainder in Fee may enter vpon the heyre of the Alienee by reason of the continuall claime made by him which had the remainder for life, because that such right as hee had of entrie, shall goe and remaine to him in the remainder after him, in so much as hee in the remainder in Fee, could not enter vpon the Alienee in fee during the life of him in the remainder for life, and for that hee could not then make continuall claime. For none can make continuall claime but when hee hath title to enter, &c.

in fee, which must bee vnderstood of a feoffement, fine, or recouerie by consent.

17. El. Dy. 339. 16. El. Dy. 324. If Tenant for life, and hee in the remainder for life in Littletons case had ioyned in a Feoffement in fee, this had beene a forfeiture of both their estates, because he in the remainder is particeps iniuriæ: And so it is if hee in the remainder for life had entred, and disseised Tenant for life, and made a Feoffement in fee, this had beene a forfeiture of the right of his remainder.

33. E. 3. Deuise 21. 15. E. 4. 9. Vi. Sect. 608. 609. 610. A particular estate of any thing that lies in grant, cannot be forfeited by any grant in fee by Deed. As if tenant for life or yeares of an Aduowson, Rent, Common, or of a reuersion or remainder of land by Deed grant the same in fee, this is no forfeiture of their estates, for that nothing passes therby, but that which lawfully may passe, and of that opinion is Littleton in our Bookes.

35. H. 6. 62. Tr. 32. El. in Informat. de intrusion vers Robinson pur le Manor de Drayton Bassit, foresolued by the Court of Exchequer. But if Tenant for life or yeares, the reuersion or remainder being in the King, make a Feoffement in fee, this is a forfeiture, and yet no reuersion or remainder is diuested out of the King, and the reason is in respect of the solemnitie of the feoffement by liuerie tending to the Kings disherison.

By matter of Record, and that by three manner of wales: First, By alienation. Secondly, by claiming a greater estate than he ought. Thirdly, By affirming the Reuersion or Remainder to be in a stranger.

First, By alienation, and that of two sorts, viz. By alienation diuesting, and not diuesting the reuersion or remainder. Diuesting, as by leuying of a fine, or suffering a common recouerie of lands, whereby the reuersion or remainder is diuested: not diuesting, as by leuying of a fine in fee of an Aduowson, Rent, Common, or any other thing that lieth in grant: and of this opinion is Littleton in our Bookes,* and so note two diuersities: First, betweene a grant by fine which is of Record, and a grant by deed in pais, and yet in this they both agree, That the reuersion or remainder in neither case is diuested. Secondly, Betweene a matter of Record, as a Fine, &c. and a Deed recorded, as a Deed inrolled, for that worketh no forfeiture, because the Deed is the originall.

* 15. E. 4. 9. 31. E. 3. Gr. 62. 14. E. 3. 3. Ann. 117.

15. E. 2. Iudg. 237. 6. E. 3. 49. 9. E. 3. 4. 18. E. 2. Fines 120. 15. E. 4. 29. 36. H. 6. 29. 2. H. 6. 9. 4. El. Dy. 9. H. 5. 14. 22. Ass. 31. 18. E. 3. 28. 16. Ass. 16. Secondly, By Claime, and that may be in two sorts, either expresse or implied. Expresse, as if Tenant for life will in Court of Record claime fee, or if Lessee for yeares be ousted, and bring an Assise, Vt de libero Tenemento. Implied, As if in a Writ of Right brought against him, he will take vpon him to ioyn the mise vpon the meere right, which none but Tenant in fee simple ought to doe. So if Lessee for yeares lose in a Præcipe, and bring a Writ of Error for Error in Processe, this is a forfeiture.

Thirdly

21.E.3.14.a. 5.E.4.2. 24.H.8.Conf.Br.87.b.2.f.55. 55.Bucklers case, 27.E.3.77. 17.E.3.7.a. 39.E.3.16. 29.E.3.24. 5.Ass.5. 5.E.3. Entr. Cong.42. 14.E.3.Receit 135. 3.E.3.32. 24.E.3.68. 1.H.7.

Thirdly, By affirming the reversion or remainder to be in a stranger, and that either actually or passively. Actually, by five manner of wayes. As first, if Tenant for life pray in ayd of a stranger, whereby he affirmes the reversion to bee in him. Secondly, if hee atturne to a grant of a stranger, and there note also a diversitie betweene an Atturnement of Record to a stranger, and an Atturnement in paiis, for an Atturnement in paiis worketh no forfeiture. Thirdly, If a stranger bring a writ of Entrie in casu prouiso, and suppose the reversion to be in him, if the Tenant confesse the Action, this is a forfeiture. 4. if Tenant for life plead couinously to the disherison of him in the reversion, this is a forfeiture. Fiftly, if a stranger bring an Action of wast against Lessee for life, & he plead Nul wast fait, this is a forfeiture: or the like.

3. Mar. Dy. 148.

Passively, As if Tenant for life accept a fine of a stranger, sur conusans de droit come ceo, &c. for hereby he affirmes of Record the reversion to be in a stranger.

Li. 2 fo. 55. Bucklers case.

Littleton here speaketh of the forfeiture of an estate, and it is to be knowne, that the right of a particular estate may be forfeited, and he that hath but a right of a remainder or reversion, shall take benefit of the forfeiture. As if Tenant for life be disseised, and he levie a fine to the Disseisor, he in the reversion or remainder shall presently enter upon the Disseisor for the forfeiture. And so it is if the Lessee after the Disseisin had levied a fine to a stranger, though to some respects, Partes finis nihil habuerunt, yet is it a forfeiture of his right.

13.E.4.4.

Littleton here speaketh of an alienation in fee absolutely, but so it is, if the Lessee make a Lease for any other mans life, or a gift in taile. If A. be Tenant for life, and make a Lease to B. for his life, and B. dieth, and the Lessee re-entreth, yet the forfeiture remaineth.

39.Ass.15. 43.E.3. Entrie Cong.30. 2.H.5.7. 39.E.3.16. 45.E.3.25.

If Tenant for life make a lease for life, or a gift in Taile, or a Feoffement in Fee, upon condition, and entreth for the condition broken, yet the forfeiture remaineth. Littleton speaketh of an estate for life, so it is of Tenant in Taile apres possibilitie, Tenant by the Curtesie, tenant in Dower, or if he hath an estate to him and his heires, during the life of I. S. &c. and of tenant for yeares, Tenant by Statute Merchant, Statute Staple, or Elegit.

Littleton saith, That the alienation in fee is made to another, which must bee intended a stranger, for if it be made to him in reversion or remainder, it amounts to a surrender of his Estate, as at large hath beene spoken in the Chapter of Tenant for life.

By Littleton it appeareth, That Tenant for life may enter for the forfeiture of the first Tenant for life, and that if the Tenant for life in remainder make continuall claime, and the Alienee die seised, then may he enter, and if he die before he doe enter, he in the remainder in fee shall enter because he in the remainder could not make any claime, therefore the right of entry which Tenant for life gained by his entrie, shall goe to him in the remainder, in respect of the privitie of estate: and so it is of him in the reversion in fee in like case, for he is also privie in estate.

If two Joyntenants be disseised, and the one of them make continuall claime and dieth, the survivor shall take benefit of his continuall claime, in respect of the privitie of their estate.

But if Tenant for life make continuall claime, this shall not give any benefit to him in the remainder, unlesse the Disseisor died in the life of Tenant for life, for the cause above said, Sectione 414.

If Tenant in Taile, the remainder in fee with garrantie, have judgement to recover in value, and dieth before execution without issue, he in the remainder shall sue execution, for he hath right thereunto, and is privie in estate.

In the same manner if a Seigniorie be granted by fine to one for life the remainder in fee, the Grantee for life dieth, he in the remainder shall have a Per quæ servitia, for he hath right to the remainder, and is privie in estate. Here also appeareth, That none can make continuall claime but he that hath right to enter.

Sect. 417.

¶ Mes est a veier a toy (mon fits) coment et en quel manner tiel continual claime serra fait, et ceo bien apprender trois choses sont a intender. La 1. chose est, si home ad cause

But it is to be seene of thee (my sonne) how and in what manner such continuall claime shall be made: and to learne this wel, three things are to bee understood. The first thing is, If a man hath

¶ *Si home ad cause dentrer en ascuns terres ou tenements, &c.*

It is not sufficient to tell one generaly what he shold do, but to direct him how & in what manner he shall doe it, as Lit. doth in this place. And here the generall rules of our Author are to be understood, that the entrie of a man to recontinue his Inheritance or Freehold,

This hath beene adiudged Mich. 14. & 15 Eliz. Rot. 1458. in the Earle of Arundells case.

hold must ensue his Action for recouerie of the same. As if three men disseise me seuerally of three seuerall Acres of land, being all in one countie, and I enter in one acre in the name of all the three Acres, this is good for no more but for that Acre which I enter into, because each disseisor is seuerall Tenant of the Freehold, and as I must haue seuerall Actions against them for the recouerie of the land, so myne entrie must bee seuerall.

And so it is if one man disseise me of three acres of ground, and letteth the same seuerally to three persons for life, &c. there the entrie upon one Lessee in the name of the whole, is good for no more than that Acre that he hath in his possession. But if the disseisor had letten seuerally the sayd three acres to three persons for yeares, there the entrie upon one of the Lessees in the name of al the three acres, shall recontinue and reuest all the three acres in the disseisee, for that the disseisee might haue had one Assise against the Disseisor, because he remained Tenant of the Freehold, and therefore one entrie shall serue for the whole.

7. Ass. 18. 12. E. 4. 10. 36. H. 6. 27. 32. Ass. pl. 1.

If one disseise me of one acre at one time, and after disseise me of another acre in the same Countie at another time, in this case myne entrie into one of them in the name of both is good; for that one Assise might be brought against him for both Disseisins.

11. H. 7. 25. Dyer 16. El. 337.

But if I infeoffe one of one acre of ground upon condition, and at another time I infeoffe the same man of another acre in the same Countie upon Condition also, and both the conditions are broken, an entrie into one acre in the name of both is not sufficient, for that I haue no right to the land, nor action to recouer the same, but a bare title, and therefore seuerall entries must be made into the same, in respect of the seuerall conditions. But an entrie in one part of the land in the name of all the land subiect to one condition is good, although the parcels be seuerall, and in seuerall townes. And so note a diuersitie betweene seuerall rights of entrie, and seuerall titles of entrie by force of a condition.

dentre en ascuns terres ou Tenements que sont en diuers Villes deins un mesme Countie, s'il enter en un parcel de les terres ou Tenements que sont en un Ville, en nosme de touts ses terres ou Tenements as queux il ad droit dentre deins touts les Villes de mesme le Countie, per tiel entrie il auera auxy bone possession, et seisin de touts terres ou tenements dont il ad title dentrie, sicome il auoit enter en fait en chescun parcel, & ceo semble grand reason.

cause to enter into any Lands or Tenements in diuers Townes in one same Countie, if he enter into one parcell of the lands or tenements which are in one Towne, in the name of all the Lands or Tenements into the which he hath right to enter, within all the Townes of the same Countie: By such entrie hee shall haue as good a possession and seisin of all the lands and Tenements wherof he hath title of entrie, as if he had entred indeed into euery parcell; and this seemeth great reason.

¶ *Deins mesme la Countie.* For if the lands lie in seuerall Counties, there must be seuerall Actions, and consequently seuerall entries, as hath beene said.

5. H. 7. 7. 4. E. 4. 19. 12. E. 4. 11. a.

¶ *En nosme de tout, &c.* If one disseise me of two seuerall Acres in one Countie, and I enter into one of them generally, without saying, In name of both, this shall reuest onely that acre wherein entrie is made, as hath beene sayd, and that is proued by our Bookes which say, That if I bring an Assise of two acres, if I enter into one hanging the writ, albeit it shall reuest that onely Acre, yet the writ shall abate.

¶ *Dont il ad title dentrie.* Here in a large sence title of entrie is taken for a right of Entrie.

Sect. 418.

¶ Car si home voile enfeoffer vn auter sauns fait de certaine terres ou tenements, que il ad deins plusours villes en vn Countie, & il voile liuerer seisin al feoffee de parcel de tenements deins vn ville en nosme de touts les terres ou tenements que il ad en mesme le ville, & en les auters villes, &c. touts les dits tenemts, &c. passont per force de le dit liuery de seisin a celuy a q̄ tiel feoffement en tiel maner est fait, & vncore celuy a que tiel liuery de seisin fuit fait, nauoit droit en touts les terres ou tenements ē touts les villes, mes per cause d̄ liuery de seisin fait de parcel de les terres ou tenements en vn ville: A multo fortiori il semble bone reason, que quant home ad title denter en les terres ou tenements en diuers villes deins vn m̄ Countie deuāt ascun entry per luy fait, que per lentry fait p̄ luy en parcel de les terres en vn ville en le nosme de touts les terres & tenements as queux il ad title denter deins mesme le countie, ceo vest vn seisin de touts en luy & per tiel entry il ad possession & seisin en fait, sicome il auoit enter en chescun parcel, &c.

¶ For if a man will enfeoffe another without deed of certaine lands or tenements which he hath in many townes in one Countie, and he will deliuer seisin to the feoffee of parcell of the tenements within one Towne in the name of all the lands or tenements which he hath in the same towne, and in other townes, &c. all the said tenements, &c. passe by force of the said liuery of seisin to him to whō such feoffment in such manner is made, and yet hee to whom such liuery of seisin was made hath no right in all the lands or tenements in all the townes but by reason of the liuery of seisin made of parcell of the lands or tenements in one Towne: *A multo fortiori*, it seemeth good reason that when a man hath title to enter into the Lands or Tenements in diuers Townes in one same Countie, before entry by him made, that by the entry made by him into parcell of the lands in one towne, in the name of all the lands and tenements to which he hath title to enter within the same Countie, this shall vest a seisin of all in him, and by such entrie hee hath possession and seisin in deed, as if hee had entred into euery parcell.

¶ This is euident, but here is a diuersitie betweene a feoffment and an entry, for a man may make a feoffment of lands in another Countie, and make liuery of seisin within the view, albeit he might peaceably enter and make actuall liuery, and so may he shew the Recognitors in an Assise, the tenures of lands in another Countie, but a man cannot make an entry into lands within the view where he may enter without any feare (for it is (*) one thing to inuest and another to deuest) as hereafter shall be said in the Section next following. 38.E.3.11. 38.Ass.23. (*) Vide Sect. next following.

¶ *A multo fortiori*. Or à minore ad maius, is an argument frequent in our Author, and in our Bookes, the force of argument in this place standing thus: if it be so in a feoffment passing a new right, much more it is for the restitution of an ancient right as the worthier and more respected in Law, which holdeth affirmatiuely as our Author here teacheth vs. Vide Sect.438.

The three (&c.) in this Section need no explication.

Section 419.

LE second chose est a entender, q̃ si hõe ad title denter en ascuns terres ou tenements, s'il ne osast enter en m̃s les terres ou tenemẽts, ne en ascun parcel de c, p̃ doubt ð battery, ou per doubt de mayhem ou pur doubt de mort, s'il alast & approch aux pres les tenements, come il osast pur tiel doubt, et claime per parol les tenements estre les soens, maintenant per tiel claime il ad vn possession, et seisin ẽ les tenem̃ts, auxybñ come s'il vst enter en fait, coment que il navoit vnque possession ou seisin ð mesme les terres ou teñts devant le dit claime.

THe second thing to be vnderstood is that if a man hath title to enter into any lands or tenements, if he dares not enter into the same lands or tenements, nor into any parcell thereof for doubt of beating, or for doubt of mayming, or for doubt of death, if he goeth and approach as neere to the tenements, as hee dare for such doubt and by word claime the Lands to bee his, presently by such claime hee hath a possession and seisin in the lands, aswell as if hee had entred in deed, although hee never had possession or seisin of the same lands or tenements before the said claime.

Vide the Sect. preceding.

HEre is to bee observed, that every doubt or feare is not sufficient, for it must concerne the safetie of the person of a man, and not his houses or goods, for if hee feare the burning of his houses, or the taking away or spoyling of his goods this is not sufficient, because hee may recover the same or dammages to the value without any corporall hurt. *7.E.4.21. 39.H.6.5.*

Again if the feare do concern the person, yet it must not be a vaine feare, but such as may befall a constant man, as if the adverse partie lye in wait in the way with weapons, or by words menace, to beate, mayhem or kill him, that would enter, and so in pleading must hee shew some just cause of feare, for feare of it selfe is internall and secret. But in a speciall verdict, if the Jurors doe find, that the Disseisee did not enter for feare of corporall hurt, this is sufficient and shall bee intended that they had evidence to prove the same. Talis enim debet esse metus qui cadere potest in virum constantem, & qui in se continet mortis periculum, & corporis cruciatum. Et nemo tenetur se infortunijs & periculis exponere. And it seemeth that feare of imprisonment is also sufficient, for such a feare sufficeth to avoid a Bond or a Deed, for the Law hath a speciall regard to the safetie and libertie of a man. And imprisonment is a corporall dammage, a restraint of libertie, and a kind of captivitie. But see in the second part of the Institutes, W.2 cap 49 a notable diversitie betweene a claime or an entrie into land, and the avoydance of an Act or Deed for feare of battery.

39.E.3.28. 11.R.2.tit.dures 2. 12.H.4.19.20.

Bract.lib.2.f.l.16.b. Britton fol.19.66. Fleta lib.3. cap.7. & lib.2.cap.54.49.E 3 14. 14.H.4.13. 39 Ass.11. 11.H.6.51. 38.H.6.27. 39.H.6.36.5. 20.H.5.28. 4.E.4.17.12.E.47.28.H.6. 8. 41.E.3.9. 11.H.4.6. 8. Ass.25. Vide Sect.434. W.2 cap.49. 13.H.4.dures 20.

Per tiel claime il ad vn possession & seisin, &c. Here is to bee observed, that there bee two manner of Entries, viz. an Entrie in Deed, and an Entry in Law. An entry in deed is sufficiently knowne, an entrie in Law is when such a claime is made as is here expressed, which entry in Law is as strong and as forcible in Law as an entry in deed, and that aswell where the Lands are in the hands of one by title as by wrong. And therefore upon such an entry in Law an Assise doth lie aswell as upon an entry in deed, and such an entry in Law shall avoid a warrantie, &c.

Vide Sect.378. 11.H.6.51.

But here is a diversitie to be observed betweene an entry in Law, and an entry in Deed, for that a continuall clayme of the Disseisee being an entry in Law shall vest the possession and seisin in him for his advantage, but not for his disadvantage. And therefore if the Disseisee bring an assise, and hanging the assise, he make continuall claime, this shall not abate the assise, but he shall recover dammages from the beginning, but otherwise it is of an entry in deed. See more of this matter after in this Chapter, Sect.422.

Vide Sect.442. Pl.Com.93. in Ass.de fresh-force. The Parson of Hony-lanes Case.

Section 420.

¶ ET que la ley est tiel, il est bien proue per vn plee dun assise en le Liuer dass, An.38.E.3.P.32. le tenor de quel ensuist en tiel forme. En le Country de Dorset deuant les Justices troue fuit per verdict dassise, que le plaintife que auoit droit per discent de heritage dauer les tenements mis en plaint, al temps del morant son ancester, fuit demurrãt en le ville ou les tenements fueront, & per parolx claime les tenements enter ses vicines, mes pur doubt de mort il nosa approcher les tenements, mes port lassise, & sur cest matter troue, agard fuit que il recouera, &c.

AND that the Law is so, it is well prooued by a plea of an Assise in the Booke of Assises, *An.* 38.*E*.3.*P*.32. the tenor whereof followeth in this manner. In the Countrie of Dorset before the Iustices, it was found by verdict of Assise, that the Plaintife which had right by discent of Inheritance to haue the tenements put in pleint, at the decease of his Ancestor was abiding in the Towne where the tenements were, and by paroll claimed the tenements amongst his Neighbours, but for feare of death hee durst not approach the tenements but bringeth his Assise, and vpon this matter found, it was awarded that he should recouer, &c.

¶ HEre it appeareth that our Booke Cases are the best proofes what the Law is, Argumentum ab authoritate est fortissimum in Lege. And for proofe of the Law in this particular case, Littleton here citeth a case in 38.E.3. but it is misprinted, for the originall according to the truth is. In the Booke of Assises 38 E.3.p.23 and not placito 32. for there be not so many pleas in that yeare. And after the example of Littleton, Booke Cases are principally to be cited for deciding of cases in question; and not any priuate opinion, Teste meipso. More shall be said of the matter implyed in this Section in the next following. 38.*Ass*.p.23.

Sect. 421.

¶ LA tierce chose est a entender, deins quel temps & per quel temps le claime que est dit cõtinuall claime, seruera & aidera celuy que fist le claime & ses heires. Et quant a ceo est ascauoir, que celuy que ad title dente, quant il voiet faire son claime, sil osast approacher la

THe 3. thing is to know within what time & by what time the claim which is said continuall claime shall serue and aid him that maketh the claime, and his heires. And as to this, it is to be vnderstood, that hee which hath title to enter, when he will make his claime, if hee dare approach the Land then

¶ *COuient a luy daler & approcher auxi pres,&c.* By this it should seeme that by the authoritie of our Author, if the Disseisee commeth as neere to the Land as he dare, &c. and maketh his claime, this should be sufficient, albeit hee be not within the view.

And the great authoritie of the Booke (*) in 9.H.4. (being by the whole Court) is not against this; for that case is put where there is no such feare, as here our Authour mentioneth in him that makes the continuall claime, (*) 9.*H*.4.5.

Sss 2 and

and then hee that makes the continuall claime ought to be within the view of the land, and therefore the authority of this booke, as it is commonly conceiued, is not against the opinion of our Author in the point aforesaid. But then it is further obiected, that the said booke is against another opinion of our Author in this Section, viz. that where there is no feare, &c. hee that maketh a continuall clayme * ought to goe to the land or to parcell thereof to make his claime, and therefore in that case he cannot make a claime within the view of the land.

(*) 11.H.6.51. agreeth with our Author in this point.

terre, donques il conient aler a la terre ou a parcel de ceo, & faire son claime, et s'il nosast approcher la terre pur doubt ou pauour de baterie, ou mayheme, ou mort, donques couient a luy daler & approcher au plus pres come il osast vers la terre, ou parcel de ceo, a faire son claim.

he ought to goe to the land, or to parcell of it, and make his claime, and if hee dare not approch the land for doubt or feare of beating or mayming, or death, then ought hee to goe and approch as neere as hee dare towards the land or parcell of it to make his claime.

To this it is answered, that where a continuall claime shall deuest any estate in any other person in any lands or tenements, there, as it hath beene said, he that maketh the claime ought to enter into the land or some part thereof according to the opinion of our Author: but where the claime is not to deuest any estate, but to bring him that maketh it into actuall possession, there a claime within the view sufficeth, as upon a discent the heire hauing the freehold in law may claime land within the view to bring himselfe into actuall possession, and in that sence is the opinion of Hull and the Court to be intended. Et sic in similibus. But yet the entrie into some parcell in the name of the residue is the surest way.

Vid. Sect. 177.

Sect. 422.

ET si son aduersarie que occupia le terre, morust seisie en fee, ou en fee taile deins l'an et le iour apres tiel claim, per que les tenements discendont a son fits come heire a luy, uncore poit celuy que fist le claime entrer sur le possession le heire, &c.

AND if his aduersary who occupieth the land dieth seised in fee, or in fee taile within the yeare and a day after such claime, whereby the lands discend to his sonne as heire to him, yet may hee which make the claime enter vpon the possession of the heire, &c.

Deins l'an, & le iour. It is to be obserued that the Law in many cases hath limitted a yeare and a day to be a legall and conuenient time for many purposes, As at the Common Law upon a fine or finall iudgement giuen in a Writ of right the partie grieued had a yeare and a day to make his clayme. So the wife or heire hath a yeare and a day to bring an appeale of death. If a Villeine remained in ancient Demesne a yeare and a day he is priuiledged. If a man bee wounded or poysoned, &c. and dieth thereof within the yeare and the day, it is felony. By the ancient Law if the Feoffee of a Disseisor had continued a yeare and a day, the entrie of the Disseisee for his negligence had beene taken away. After iudgement giuen in a reall action, the Plaintife within the yeare and the day may haue a Habere facias seisinam, and in an action of debt, &c. a Capias, Fieri facias, or a Leuari facias. A protection shall bee allowed but for a yeare and a day and no longer, and in many other cases.

Vid. Sect. 385.426. 9.H.4.5. 14.H.4.36. 7.E.3.37. Pl.Com.356. 357.367. Mirror, cap.2. §.18. Britton, fol.45.b. & 126.

But this time of a yeare and a day in case of continuall claime is since our Author wrote altered by the said Statute of 32.H.8.ca.33. as before it appeareth.

Vid. Sect. 385.

Sect. 423.

MEs en cest cas apres lan & le iour que tiel claime fuit fait, si le pere donques morust seisi ademain procheine apres lan & le iour, ou un auter iour apres, &c. donques ne poit celuy que fist le claime entrer: & pur ceo si celuy que fist le claime voit estre sure a touts temps que son entre ne serra toll per tiel discent &c. il couient a luy que deins lan & le iour apres le primer claime fait, de faire un auter claime en le forme auantdit, & deins lan & le iour apres le second claime fait, de faire le tierce claime en mesme le maner, & deins lan et le iour de le tierce claime, de faire un auter claime, & issint ouster, cestascauoir, de faire un claime deins chescun an et iour procheín apres chescun claime fait durant la vie son aduersarie, et donques, a quecunque temps que son aduersarie morust seisi, son entrie ne serra tolle per nul tiel discent. Et tiel claim en tiel maner fait, est pluis communement prise et nosme continual claime de luy que fist le claime.

BVt in this case after the yeare and the day that such clayme was made, if the father then died seised the morrow next after the yeare and the day, or any other day after, &c. then cannot hee which made the claime enter: And therefore if hee which made the claime will be sure at all times that his entrie shall not be taken away by such discent, &c. it behoueth him, that within the yeare and the day after the first claime made, to make another claime in forme aforesaid, and within the yeare and the day after the second claime made, to make the third claime in the same manner, and within the yeare and the day after the third claime to make another claime, and so ouer, that is to say, to make a claime within euery yeare and day next after euery claime made during the life of his aduersarie, and then at what time soeuer his aduersarie dieth seised, his entrie shall not be taken away by any discent. And such claime in such maner made is most commonly taken and named continuall claime of him which maketh the claime, &c.

IT is to be obserued, that the yeare and the day shall be so accounted, as the day whereon the Claime was made shall be accounted one: as for example, If the Claime were made 2. Die Martii, that day shall be accounted for one, for Littleton saith in the Section next before (after the clayme made) and then the yeare must end the first day of March, and the day after is the second day of March. *Vid. Sect.* 385.

See for the Computation of the yeare, De anno bisextili, and of the day naturall and artificiall, and other parts of the yeare, (a) Bracton, (b) Britton, and (c) Fleta excellent matter.

(a) *Bract. fo.* 264. 344. 359.
(b) *Britton, fo.* 209.
(c) *Fleta, lib.* 6. *ca.* 11.
Statute de anno Bisextili.
21. *H.* 3. *Dier* 17. *Eliz.* 345.

Sect. 424.

MEs uncore en le cas auantdit, lou son aduersarie

BVt yet in the case aforesaid, where his Aduersarie dieth

ſarie moruſt deins lan & la iour procheine apres le claime, ceo eſt en ley un continuall claime entant que laduerſarie deins lan & le iour procheine apres meſme la claime moruſt. Car il ne beſoigne a celuy que fiſt ſon claime de faire aſcun auter claime, mes a quel temps que il voet deins meſme lan et iour, &c.

within the yeare and the day next after the claime, this is in Law a continuall claime, inſomuch as his aduerſarie within the yere and the day next after the ſame claime, dieth. For hee which made his claime, needeth not to make any other claime, but at what time hee will within the ſame yeare and day, &c.

Vi.Sect.414.

This is euident.

Section 425.

ITem ſi laduerſary ſoit diſſeiſie deins lan et le iour apres tiel claime, & le diſſeiſor ent moruſt ſeiſie deins lan et le iour, &c. tiel morant ſeiſie ne grieuera my celuy que fiſt le claime mes que il poit enter, &c. Car quecunque ſoit que moruſt ſeiſie deins lan et le iour prochein apres tiel claim fait, ceo ne grieuera my celuy que fiſt le claime, mes que il poit enter, &c. coment que fueront pluſors morant ſeiſie, et pluſors diſcents deins m lan et le iour, &c.

ALſo if the Aduerſarie be diſſeiſed within the yeare and the day after ſuch claim, and the Diſſeiſor thereof dieth ſeiſed within the yeare and the day, &c. ſuch dying ſeiſed ſhall not grieue him which made the claime, but that he may enter, &c. for whoſoeuer he bee that dieth ſeiſed within the yeare and the day after ſuch claime made, this ſhall not hurt him that made the claime, but that he may enter, &c. albeit there were many dyings ſeiſed, and many diſcents within the ſame yeare and day, &c.

HEre it appeareth, That the continuall claime doth not onely extend to the firſt Diſſeiſor in whoſe poſſeſſion it was made, but to any other Diſſeiſor that dieth ſeiſed within the yeare and day after the continuall claime made. And whereas our Author ſpeaketh of a ſecond diſſeiſor, &c. herein is likewiſe implied not onely Abators and Intruders, but the Feoffees or Donees of the Diſſeiſors, Abators, or Intruders, and any other Feoffee or Donee immediate or mediate dying ſeiſed within the yeare and day, of ſuch continuall claime made.

Section 426.

ITem ſi home ſoit diſſeiſie, et le Diſſeiſor moruſt ſeiſie deins lan et l'iour prochein apres le diſſeiſin fait, per que les Tenements diſcendont a ſon heire

ALſo if a man be diſſeiſed, and the diſſeiſor dieth ſeiſed within the yeare and day next after the Diſſeiſin made, whereby the Tenements diſcend to his heire, in this

heire, en cest case lentrie le Disseisee est toll, car lan et le iour que aidroit le Disseisee en tiel case, ne serra pris de temps de titl dentre a luy accrue, mes tãtsolement de temps del claim per luy fait en le manner auauntdit, et pur cel cause il serroit bone p̃ tiel disseisee, pur faire son claime en auxy breue temps que il puissoit, apres le disseisin, &c.

case the entrie of the disseisee is taken away, for the yeare and day which should ayd the Disseisee in such case, shall not bee taken from the time of title of entrie accrued vnto him, but onely from the time of the claim made by him in manner aforesaid. And for this cause it shall be good for such disseisee to make his claime in as short time as he can after the Disseisin, &c.

¶ This in case of a Disseisor is now holpen by the Statute made since Littleton wrote as hath been said; for if the Disseisor die seised within fiue yeares after the Disseisin, though there bee no continuall claime made, it shall not take away the entry of the Disseisee, but after the fiue yeares, there must bee such continuall claime as was at the common Law: But that Statute extendeth not to any Feoffee or Donee of the Disseisor immediate or mediate, but they remaine still at the Common Law, as hath been said. 32. *H.* 8. *ca.* 33. *Vi. Sect.* 385. 422.

Sect. 427.

¶ Item si tiel Disseisor occupia la terre per xl. ans, ou per plusors ans sans ascũ claim fait per le disseisee, &c. Et le Disseisee per petit space deuaunt le mort del Disseisor fait vn claim en le forme auantdit, si issint fortunast que deins lan et le iour apres tiel claime le disseisor morust, &c. lentrie le disseisee est congeable, &c. et pur ceo il serroit bone pur tiel home que ne fist claime que ad bone title dentrie, quant il oyet que son aduersarie gist languisshment, de faire son claime, &c.

ALso if such Disseisor occupieth the lands fortie yeares, or more yeares, without any claime made by the Disseisee, &c. and the Disseisee a little before the death of the Disseisor makes a claime in the forme aforesaid, if so it fortuneth, that within the yeare and the day after such claime, the Disseisor die, &c. the entrie of the Disseisee is congeable, &c. And therefore it shall bee good for such a man which hath not made claime, and which hath good title of entrie, when he heareth that his aduersary lieth languishing, to make his claime, &c.

¶ This is euident enough, and in respect of that which hath been sayd, needeth not to be explained.

Sect. 428.

¶ Item sicome est dit en les cases mises, lou home

ALso as it is said in the cases put where a man hath title

¶ Here title is taken in his large sence to include a right.

¶ *Ascun auter title, &c.*

&c. Here is implied Abators or Intruders, and not onely their Disseisors, but the Feoffees or Donees of disseisors, abators, or Intruders, or any other so long as the entrie is congeable.

ad title dentre pur cause dun disseisin, &c. Mesme la Ley est lou home ad droit dentre per cause de ascun auter title, &c.

of entrie by cause of a Disseisin, &c. the same Law is where a man hath right to enter by cause of another title, &c.

Sect. 429.

¶ Item des dits Presidents poies scauer (mon fitz) deux choses. Un est, lou home ad title dentre sur vn Tenant en le taile, sil fist vn tiel claim a la tre, donques est lestate Taile defeat, car cel claime est come entre fait per luy, et est de mesme le effect en Ley, sicome il fuissoit sur mesmes tenements, et vst entre en mesmes les Tenements come deuant est dit. Et donques quaunt le Tenant en le taile immediate puis tiel claime continua son occupation en les tenements, ceo est vn Disseisin fait de mesmes les tenements, a celuy que fist tiel claime, & sic per consequens, le tenant adonques ad fee simple.

ALso of the sayd foresaying thou mayst know (my sonne) two things. One is where a man hath title to enter vpon a Tenant in Taile, if he maketh such a claime to the land, then is the estate tayle defeated, for this claime is as an entrie made by him, and is of the same effect in Law, as if he had bin vpon the same tenements, and had entred into the same, as before is sayd. And then when the tenant in Tayle immediately after such claime continue his occupation in the lands, this is a Disseisin made of the same Tenements to him which made such claime, and so by consequent the Tenant then hath a Fee simple.

¶ *Presidents.* This should be Precedents, and so is the originall, and this agreeth with the right sence of Littleton.

And here it appeareth, That a continuall claime, which is an entrie in Law, is as strong as an entrie in deed.

Vi. Sect. 630. and 639. &c. ¶ *Title de entrie.* Here Title de entrie is taken in the large sence for right of entrie.

Section 430.

¶ LE second chose est, que auxy souent que il que ad droit dentre fait tiel claime & ceo nient contristeant son aduersary continua son occupation, auxy souent laduersary fait tort & disseisin a celuy que fist le claim. Et pur

THe second thing is, That as often as hee which hath right of entrie maketh such claime, and this notwithstanding his aduersary continue his occupation, so often the Aduersarie doth wrong and Disseisin to him which made the claime.

pur cel cause auxy souent poit celuy que fist m le claime pur chescun tiel tort & disseisin fait a luy, auer vn briefe de trns. Quare clausum fregit, &c. et recouera ses damages, &c.

And for this cause so often may he which makes the same claime for euery such wrong & disseisin done vnto him, haue a Writ of trespasse. *Quare clausum fregit, &c.* and recouer his dammages, &c.

¶ Hereby also it appeareth, that an entry in Law is equiualent to an entry in deed.

¶ *Auera breue de trespasse,* quare clausum fregit *& recouera ses damages.* The Disseisee shall haue an Action of trespasse against the Disseisor, and recouer his dammages for the first entrie without any regresse, but after regresse he may haue an Action of trespasse with a Continuando and recouer aswell for all the meane occupation as for the first entry. And here note that Littleton doth here include costs within dammages, &c.

Sect. 431.

¶ Ou il poit auer vn breife sur le statute le Roy R. le second, fait lan de son raigne 5. suppsant p son breife, que son aduersarie auoit ent en l's terres ou tenements celuy que fist le claime, ou son entry ne fuit pas done per la ley, &c. & per tiel action il recouera ses dammages, &c. Et si le case fuit tiel, que laduersarie occupiast les tenements oue force et armes, ou oue multitude de gents a teps de tiel claime, &c. immediate apres mesme le claime, poit celuy que fist le claime, pur chescun tiel fait auer vn briefe de forcible entrie, et recouera ses treble dammages, &c.

Or hee may haue a Writ vpon the statute of *R.* 2. made in the fifth yeare of his Raigne; supposing by his Writ that his Aduersarie had entred into the lands or tenements of him that made the Clayme, where his entry was was not giuen by the Law, &c. and by this action he shall recouer his dammages, &c. & if the case were such that the aduersarie occupied the tenements with force and armes or with a multitude of people at the time of such claime, &c. immediately after the same claime may hee which made the claim for euery such act haue a Writ of forcible entrie & shall recouer his treble dammages, &c.

¶ This is the statute of 5.R.2.cap.7. 37.*H*.6.35. 34.*H*.6.30. 13.*H*.7.15. 10.*H*.6.14. 2.*E*.4.18. 21.*E*.4.5.74. 13.*E*.2.3. 27.*Ass*.64. 38.*Ass*.9. 44.*E*.3.20. 10.*H*.7.27. *Keylwey* 1.*b*. 5.*R*.2.*c*.7.

¶ *Per tiel action il recouera ses dammages.*

This is to bee understood that hee shall recouer dammages for the first tortious entry, but not for the meane profits in this action though he made a regresse. And here note that also he shall recouer his costs of suite expensæ litis, which Littleton doth include within these words (dammages) &c. 2.*E*.4.24.*b*. 9.*E*.4.4.*b*. 16.*H*.7.6.*a*.

¶ *Dammages,* damna in the Common Law hath a speciall signification for the recompence that is giuen by the Jury to the Plaintife or Defendant for the wrong the Defendant hath done unto him.

¶ *Multitude.* One or more may commit a force, three or more may commit an unlawfull assembly, a riot or a rout. A multitude here spoken of (as some haue said) must be ten or more. Multitudinem decem faciunt. And so (say they) it is said, de grege hominum. But I could neuer read it restrained by the Common Law to any certaine number, but left to the discretion of the Judges.

¶ *Vn briefe de forcible entrie & recouera ses treble dammages.* This

8. H. 6. cap. 9. 3. E. 4. 19. 24. F. N. B. 248. 11. E. 4. 11. b. 6. H. 7. 12. b. 22. H. 6. 37. 19. H. 6. Regiſter. 97. 22. H. 6. 57. F. N. B 247. a

Writ is grounded vpon the ſtatute of 8. H. 6. and lieth either where one entreth with force, or where he entreth peaceably and detayneth it with force or where he entreth by force, and deteineth it by force And in this action without any regreſſe the Plaintife ſhall recouer treble dammages, as well for the meane occupation as for the firſt entry by force of the ſtatute. And albeit he ſhall recouer treble dammages, yet ſhall he recouer coſts which ſhall be trebled alſo.

One may commit a forcible entry as hath beene ſaid, in reſpect of the armour or weapons which he hath that are not vſually borne, or if he doe vſe violence, and threats to the terrour of another. And if three or foure goe to make a forcible entry, albeit one alone vſe the violence, all are giltie of force. If the Maſter commeth with a greater number of ſeruants then vſually attend on him it is a forcible entry, (10. H. 7. 12.)

It is to be vnderſtood that there is a force implyed in Law, as euery Treſpaſſe and Reſcous and Diſſeiſin implyeth a force, and is vi & armis, and there is an actuall force, as with weapons, number of perſons, &c. and when an entry is made with ſuch actuall force, an action doth lie vpon the ſaid ſtatute. See before more of force and armes, Sect. 240. (33. H. 6. 20.)

Section 432.

¶ ITem il eſt a veier, ſi le ſeruant dun home que ad title denter, poit per le commandement ſon Maſter faire continuall claime pur ſon Maſter ou non.

ALſo it is to bee ſeene, if the Seruant of a man who hath title to enter, may by the commandement of his Maſter make Continuall Claime for his Maſter or not.

This needeth no explication.

Section 433.

¶ ET il ſemble que en aſcuns caſes il poit ceo faire, car ſil per ſon commandement vient a aſcun parcel d la terre & la fait claime, &c. en le noſme ſon Maſter, ceſt claime eſt aſſets bone pur ſon Maſter, pur ceo que il fait tout ceo que ſon Maſter couient faire ou deuoit faire en tiel cas, &c. Auxy ſi le Maſter dit a ſon ſeruant, que il ne oſaſt vener a la terre, ne aſcun parcel de la terre, pur faire ſon claime, &c. et que il ne oſaſt approcher pluis procheín a la terre forſque a tiel lieu appell Dale, et commanda ſon ſeruant daler a meſme le lieu de Dale, et la faire vn claime pur luy, &c. ſi le ſeruant iſſint fait, &c. ceo ſemble auxy bone claime pur ſon Maſter, ſicome ſon

ANd it ſeemeth that in ſome caſes he may doe this. For if he by his commandement commeth to any parcell of the Land, and there maketh claime, &c. in the name of his Maſter, this claime is good enough for his Maſter, for that he doth all that which his Maſter ſhould or ought to doe in ſuch caſe, &c. Alſo if the Maſter ſaith to his ſeruant that hee dares not come to the land, nor to any parcell of it to make his claime, &c. and that hee dare approch no neerer to the land then to ſuch a place called Dale, and command his ſeruant to goe to the ſame place of Dale, and there make a claime for him, &c. if the ſeruant doth this, &c. this alſo ſeemeth a good claime for his Maſter, as if his Maſter were

ſon Maſter la fuit & propre perſon, pur ceo que le ſeruant fiſt tout ceo que ſon Maſter oſaſt et deuoit faire per la ley en tiel caſe, &c.

there in his proper perſon, for that the ſeruant did all that which his Maſter durſt, and ought to doe by the law in ſuch a caſe, &c.

HEre it appeareth that where the ſeruant doth all that which he is commanded, and which his Maſter ought to doe, there it is as ſufficient as if his Maſter did it himſelfe for the rule is, Qui per alium facit per ſeipſum facere videtur.

Per commandement. If an infant or any man of full age haue any right of Entrie into any lands, any ſtranger in the name and to the vſe of the Infant or man of full age may enter into the lands, and this regularly ſhall veſt the lands in them without any commandement precedent or agreement ſubſequent. (*) But if a Diſſeiſor leuie a fine, with Proclamation according to the ſtatute an eſtranger without a Commandement precedent or an agreement ſubſequent within the fiue yeares cannot enter in the name of the Diſſeiſee to auoide the Fine. And that reſolution was grounded vpon the conſtruction of the Statute of 4.H.7,cap.24. But an aſſent ſubſequent within the fiue yeares ſhould bee ſufficient; Omnis enim ratihabitio retrotrahitur, & mandato æquiparatur, as hath beene ſaid. 7.E.3.69.a.b. 45.E.3. Releaſe 28. 45.E.3.tit.B. eiſe 389. 26.E.3.62.per.Thorp. 11.Aſſ.p.21. 39.Aſſ.p.18. 10.H.7.12.a. 31.H.8.tit.entr.Cong. & tit.Fauxifier recouery 29. (*) Lib.9 fo.106.a. the Lo.Awdelyes caſe.

Auxi ſi le maſter dit a ſon ſeruant que il ne oſaſt, &c. Here it appeareth that where the ſeruant purſueth the commandement of his Maſter, and doth all that which his Maſter durſt and ought to doe by the Law, this is ſufficient. And although the Maſter feareth more than the ſeruant, or admit that the ſeruant hath no feare at all, yet if hee goeth as farre as his Maſter durſt and as he commanded, it is ſufficient. And this is implied in this Section.

Sect. 434.

AUxy ſi home ſoit cy languiſhant, ou cy decreppte que il ne poit per nul maner vener a le terre, ne a aſcun parcel d'ycel, ou ſi vn recluſe ſoit, q̃ ne poit per cauſe de ſon order aler hors de ſa meaſon, ſi tiel maner de perſon commaunda ſon ſeruant daler et faire claime pur luy, & tiel ſeruant ne oſaſt aler a le terre, ne a aſcun parcel de ceo pur doubt de baterye, mayhem, ou mort, &c. et pur cel cauſe tiel ſeruãt vient auxy pres a la terre come il oſaſt pur tiel

ALſo if a man be ſo languiſhing, or ſo decrepite that he cannot by any meanes come to the land nor to any parcell of it, or if there bee a recluſe which may not by reaſon of his order goe out of his houſe, if ſuch manner of perſon commaunde his ſeruant to goe and make claime for him, and ſuch ſeruant dare not goe to the land nor to any parcell of it for doubt of beating, mayhem, or death, &c. and for this cauſe the ſeruant commeth as neere to the land as he dareth for ſuch doubt

REgularly it is true that where a man doth leſſe then the Commandement or Authority committed vnto him there (the Commandement or Authority being not purſued) the act is voide. And where a man doth that which hee is authoriſed to doe and more, there it is good for that which is warranted, and voide for the reſt, yet both theſe rules haue diuers exceptions and limitation.

For the firſt Littleton here putteth a caſe where the ſeruant doth leſſe then he is commanded, and yet it ſufficeth for that Impotentia excuſat legem, for ſeeing the maſter cannot, and the ſeruant dare not enter into the land, it ſufficeth that he come as neere to the land as he dare.

If a man makes a Letter of Attorney to deliuer ſeiſin to I.S. vpon Condition, and the Attorney deliuereth it abſolute, this is voide: and ſo ſome hold if the warrant be abſolute, and he deliuereth ſeiſin vpon Condition, the 21.H.4 3. 12.Aſſ.24. 26.Aſſ.39.

Liuery is voide.

See before Sect.419.

¶ *Pur battery, mayhem ou mort.* See the second part of the Institutes W.2.cap.49. a diuersity betweene the making of an Entrie or Claime, and the auoydance of an Act or Deede.

¶ *Auterment le master serroit en tresgrand mischiefe.* Argumentum ab inconuenienti est validum in lege, quia lex non permittit aliquod inconueniens. And as hath beene often obserued before, Nihil quod est inconueniens est licitum.

46.E.3.Petition 18.
33.H.6.8.
43.E.3.8.b.30.a.

¶ *Recluse.* Reclusus, Heremita, seu Anachorita, so called by the order of his religion he is so mured or shut up, Quod solus semper sit, & in clausura sua sedet; and can neuer come out of his place. Seorsim enim & extra conuersationem ciuilem hoc professionis genus semper habitat: Note here, albeit the Recluse or Anachorite be shut up himselfe, so as he by his order is not to come out in person, yet to auoide a Discent, he must command one to make claime, and such a Recluse shall alwayes appeare by Attorney in such cases where others must appeare in proper person, Impotentia enim excusat legem.

doubt, et fait l' claim, &c. pur son master il semble que tiel claim pur son Master est assets fort, & bon en ley. Car autermemt son master serroit en tresgrand mischiefe, car il bien poit estre que tiel person q̃ est languishant, decrepite, ou recluse, ne poit trouer ascun seruant que osast aler a la terr̃, ne ascun parcel de cel pur faire le claime pur luy, &c.

and maketh the claim, &c. for his master, it seemeth that such claime for his master is strong enough and good in law. For otherwise his master should bee in a very great mischiefe, for it may well be that such person which is sicke, decrepit, or recluse cannot finde any seruant which dare go to the land or to any parcell of it to make the claime for him, &c.

Sect.435.

¶ MEs si le master d' tiel seruant soit de bone sane, et poit, et osast bien aler a les tenements, ou a parcel de ceo de faire son claime, &c. si tiel Master cõmanda son seruant daler a ascun parcel de la terre a faire claime pur luy, et quant l' seruant est an alant de faire le commandement de son Master, il oye per le voy tielx choses que il ne osast vener a ascun parcel de la terre pur fair̃ le claime pur son Master, et pur cel cause il vient auxy pres la tre come il osast pur doubt de mort, et la fait claime pur son Master, et en le nosme de son master, &c. il semble que le doubt en le ley en tiel case serroit, si tiel claime auailera son Master, ou nemy, pur

BVt if the Master of such seruant bee in good health, and can and dare well goe to the lands or to parcell of it to make his claime, &c. if such Master command his seruant to goe to any parcell of the land to make claime for him, and when the seruant is in going to doe the commandement of his Master, he heareth by the way such things as he dare not come to any parcell of the land to make the claime for his Master, and therefore hee commeth as neere to the land as he dare for doubt of death, and there maketh claime for his master, and in the name of his Master, &c. It seemeth that the doubt in law in such case shall be whether such claime shall auaile his Master

pur ceo que le seruant ne fist tout ceo que son Master al temps de son commandement osast faire, &c. Quære.

or not, for that the seruant did not all that which his Master at the time of his commandement durst haue done, &c. *Quære.*

¶ This continuall claime is voide, for that the seruant doth lesse then that which is expresly commanded, and there is no impotencie or feare in the Master.

Sect. 436.

¶ Item ascuns ont dit que lou home est en prison, et est disseisie, et le disseisor mourust seisie durant le temps que le disseisee est en prison, per que les tenements discendont al heire del disseisour, ils ont dit, que ceo ne noiera my le disseisee que est en prison, mes que il bien poit enter, nient obstant tiel discent, pur ceo que il ne puissoit faire continual claime, quant il fuit en prison.

ALso some haue said that where a man is in prison and is disseised, and the disseisor dieth seised during the time that the disseisee is in prison, whereby the tenements discend to the heire of the disseisor, they haue said that this shall not hurt the disseisee which is in prison, but that he wel may enter, notwithstanding such a discent, because hee could not make continuall claim when he was in prison.

¶ *Quant home est en prison & est disseisi.* For if he bee disseised when hee is at large, and the discent is cast during the time of his imprisonment, this discent shall binde him. Excusatur autem quis quod clameum suum non apposuerit, si tempore litigij in prisona detentus fuerit ita quod venire non possit, nec mittere, quia nulli vertitur in dubium, & vbi eadem ratio & idem jus erit, ideo videtur quòd excusari debet, quis si per vim maiorem, vel per fraudem, extra prisonam detentus fuerit; ita quod venire non possit nec mittere, dum tamen hoc per certa iudicia probari poterit.

9.H.7.24.Pl.Com.360.

Bracton, lib. 5.fol.436. Britton, fol.116.b. Fleta, lib.6.cap.52.53. & lib 6.ca.7. & 14.

¶ *Pur ceo que il ne poet faire continual claime quant il fuit en prison.* Here it is to be obserued by the authority of Littleton that he is not enforced in this case by Law to doe it by his seruant or any other by his warrant or commandement, for things done by deputie are seldome well done, but euery man will see his owne businesse most effectually speeded and performed, and that it may be once spoken for all, the reason that a man imprisoned shall not be bound, in this and the like cases is, for that by the entendment of Law he is kept (as it is presumed in Law) without intelligence of things abroade, and also that he hath not libertie to goe at large to make entrie or claime, or seeke counsell. And so note a diuersity betweene a Recluse who might haue intelligence, and a man in prison.

Pl.Com.360. in Stowells case.

Sect. 437.

¶ MEs lopinion de touts les Iustices. P.11 H.7. fuit, que si le disseisin soit auant lenprisonment, coment que le morant seisie soit; il esteant en le prison, son entrie est tolle.

BVt the opinion of all the Iustices, P.11.H.7. was that if the disseisin bee before the imprisonment, although the dying seised be, he being in the prison, his entry is taken away.

¶ This is of a new addition, and mistaken, for there is no such opinion, P.11, H,7. but it is, 9.H,7.fo.24.b.

¶ Et auxy si tiel que est en prison soit utlage in Action de debt, ou trespasse ou en appeal de Robberie, &c. il reuersera tiel utlagarie enuers luy pronounce, &c.

AND also if hee which is in prison be outlawed in an Action of Debt or Trespasse, or in an Appeale of Robberie, &c. he shall reuerse this outlawrie pronounced against him, &c.

¶ *Il reuersera tiel utlagarie.* Nota, the originall is, Reuersera tiel utlagar per Briefe de Error, and so it would be amended: for Outlawries may be reuersed two manner of wayes, viz. by Plea, or by Writ of Error. By Plea, when the Defendant commeth in upon the Capias vtlagatum, &c. hee may by plea reuerse the same for matters apparant, as in respect of a Supersedeas, Omission of Processe, Variance, or other matter apparant in the Record, and yet in these cases some hold, That in another Terme the Defendant is driuen to his Writ of Error.

But for any matters in fact, as death, imprisonment, seruice of the king, &c. he is driuen to his Writ of Error, unlesse it be in case of Felonie, and there in fauorem vitæ he may plead it.

But albeit imprisonment be a good cause to reuerse an Outlawrie, yet it must be by processe of Law in inuitum, and not by consent or couin, for such imprisonment shall not auoyd the Outlawrie; because upon the matter it is his owne act.

Mirror cap. 3. Britton fo. 21. Fleta lib. 1. cap. 28. & lib. 2. ca. 59. Bracton li. 2. 2. E. 4. 1. 4. E. 4. 10. 21. E. 4. 73. 11 H. 7. 5. 21. H. 6. 50. 9. H. 4. 3. 21. H. 6. Vilary 36. 7. H. 6. 27. 21. E. 4. 88. 22. E. 4. 37. 18. E. 3. Villenage 47. 21. E. 4. 37. 33. H. 6. 45. 16. 44. E. 3. Villein 41. 4. H. 4. 19. 11. H. 4. 34. 3. Eliz. Dyer 192. 2. Eliz. 176. 5. Eliz. ibid. 223. 19 H. 6. 2. 8. H. 6. 37. 37. H. 6. 19.

8. H. 4. 7. 21. H. 7. 13. 10. H. 6. 58. 20. H. 6. 20. 21. H. 6. 55. 22 H. 6. 18. 16 39. H. 6. 1. 33. H. 6. 51. 45 38. H. 6. 33. 21. E. 4. 94. 21. H. 7. 33. 5. H. 7. 1. 12. H. 6. 8. 11. H. 6. 67. 19. 1. E. 4. 2. 27. H. 8. 2. 38. Ass. pl. 17. Vid. Sect. 439.

Section 438.

¶ Auxy si un recouerie soit per default vers tiel que est en prison, il auoidera le iudgement per briefe de Error, pur ceo que il fuit en prison al temps de le default fait, &c. Et pur ceo que tiels matters de Record ne noyent celuy que est en prison, mes que ils serront reuerses, &c. a multo fortiori, il semble que un matter en fait, scilicet, tiel discent ewe quant il fuit en prison ne luy noyera, &c. specialment pur ceo que il ne puissoit aler hors de prison pur faire continuall claime, &c.

ALso if a recouerie bee by default against such a one as is in prison, he shal auoid the iudgement by a Writ of Error, because he was in prison at the time of the default made, &c. And for that such matters of Record shal not hurt him which is in prison, but that they shall bee reuersed, &c. *a multo fortiori*, it seemeth that a matter in fact, s. such discent had when hee was in prison, shall not hurt him, &c. especially seeing he could not goe out of prison, to make continuall claime, &c.

¶ THIS is euident enough.

¶ *Per Briefe derror.* For hee shall haue no Writ of Disceit, because the summons was according to the Law of the land, by Summoners and Veiors, and the land taken into the Kings hand by the Pernor.

¶ *Per default.* Default is a French word, and defalta is legally taken for Non-apparance in Court. There bee diuers causes allowed by Law for sauing a mans default, as first by Imprisonment, whereof Littleton here speaketh. 2. Per inundationem aquarum. 3. Per tempestatem. 4. Per pontem fractum. 5. Per nauigium substractum per fraudem petentis, non enim debet quis se periculis & infortunijs gratis exponere, vel subiacere. 6. Per minorem ætatem. 7. Per defensionem summonitionis per Legem. 8. Per mortem Attornati si tenens in tempore non nouit. 9. Si petens essoniatus sit. 10. Si placitum mittatur sine die. 11. Per Breue de Warrantia Diei. But sicknesse (as one holds) is no cause of sauing a default, because it may be so artificially counterfeited, that it cannot be knowne.

5. E. 3. 50. b. 7. H 6. 38.

Fleta lib. 6 cap. 67. & 24. Vid. W. 2. cap. 48 and the exposition thereof, 2. part Instit. 4. E. 2. Disceit 51.

Bracton Lib. 5. Tract. 3. Fleta li. 6 ca. 7. 14. 3. H. 6. 46. 38. E. 3. 5. 31. H. 6 Barre. 66. 12. H. 4. 13. 50. E. 3. 9. 3. H. 6. 48. 2 H. 4. 8. 5. H. 7. 3. F. N. B. 17. Bracton lib. 4. fol. 367 369. Glan lib. 1. cap 8. 28. H. 6. 11. 4. H. 5. Challenge. 153. Br. Sauer. Def. 45.

¶ *Record*. Recordum **is a memoriall or remembrance in Rolles** of Parchment, of the proceedings and Acts of a Court of Justice which hath power to hold plea according to the course of the Common Law, of reall or mixt Actions, or of Actions quare vi & armis, or of personall Actions, whereof the debt or dammage amounts to fortie shillings, or above, which we call Courts of Record, and are created by Parliament, Letters Patents, or Prescription. *Glanuill lib.8.cap.8. Bracton lib.3.fol.156. Britton in proemio & cap.27.*

It is aptly derived of Recordari, which is to keepe in memorie or record, as it is said, Quod dicere nihil aliud est quam recordari, and in the same sence the Poet useth it, Si rite audita recordor. But legally Records are restrained to the Rolles of such onely as are Courts of Record, and not the Rolles of inferiour, nor of any other Courts which proceed not secundum legem & consuetudinem Angliæ. And the Rolles being the Records or memorialls of the Judges of the Courts of Record, import in them such incontrollable credit and veritie, as they admit no averment, plea, or proofe to the contrarie. And if such a Record be alledged, and it be pleaded, That there is no such Record, it shall be tried onely by it selfe: and the reason hereof is apparant, for otherwise (as our old Authors say, and that truly) there should never be any end of controversies, which should be inconvenient. Of Courts of Record you may read in my Reports: but yet during the Terme wherein any iudiciall act is done, the Record remaineth in the brest of the Judges of the Court, and in their remembrance, and therefore the Rolle is alterable during that Term, as the Judges shal direct, but when that Term is past, then the Record is in the Rolle, and admitteth no alteration, averment, or proofe to the contrarie. *Pl.Com.79.b. Mich.7.& 8. Eliz. Dier 242. 17.E.3.49 37.H.6.21.b. 11.H.4.20 b 21.H.6.34. Error.Br 73. 7.H.7.4. 19.Ass.7. Lib.4. fol.52.in Rawlins Case. Glanuill lib.8.cap.8. Bracton Lib.3.fol.156. Britton cap.27. Lib.6.fol.11.Jentlemans Case. & 30. 45.Lib.7.fol.30. Lib.8.fol.60.b.& 67.a. 7.H.6.28. 19.H.6.9.*

If a Grant by Letters Patents under the great Seale be pleaded and shewed forth, the adverse partie cannot plead Nul tiel Record, for that it appeares to the Court that there is such a record: but in asmuch as it is in nature of a coveiance, the partie may denie the operation therof, therefore he may plead Non concessit, and proue in evidence that the King had nothing in the thing granted, or the like, and so it was adiudged. But to returne to Littleton: what then? Shall a man that is in prison be privileged from Suits or Outlawries? Nothing lesse, for if the Tenant or Defendant bee in prison, hee shall upon motion by order of the Court, bee brought to the Barre, and either answer according to Law, or else the same being recorded, the Law shall proceed against him, and he shall take no advantage of his imprisonment. *18.Eliz. Dier 353. 3.Mar. Dier 129. Pl.Com. 232. Seignior Berkleys case. 16.H.7.11.b. 22.H.8.Record. Br.65. 39.H 6.4. 3.Eliz.Dier 187. Lib.6.fol. 15.Edens Case. Mich.31.et 32.Eliz. Rot.365. In Banke le Roy, inter Eden & Franklyn et Browne. 7.H 6.38. 8.H.6.16.*

¶ A multo fortiori. **Here is an argument**, A minori ad maius, and the force of our Authors argument is this, If a man in prison shall not be bound by a recoverie by default for want of answer in Court of Record in a reall Action, which is matter of Record, (the heigth and strength whereof hath beene somewhat touched) à multo fortiori, a discent in the Countrie, which is matter of deed, shall not for want of claim bind him that is in prison. And as the argument à minori ad maius, doth ever hold (as our Author hath alreadie told us) affirmatively, so the argument à maiori ad minus doth ever hold negatively, as our Author here teacheth us: and the reason hereof is this, Quod in minori valet, valebit in maiori, & quod in maiori non valet, nec valebit in minori. *Vide Section 418.*

¶ *Pur ceo que il ne poet aler hors de prison, &c.* **By this it appeareth**, That a man in prison by processe of Law ought to be kept in salua & arcta custodia, and by the Law ought not to goe out, though it be with a Keeper, and with the leave and sufferance of the Gaoler: but yet imprisonment must be, custodia, & non pœna, for, Carcer ad homines custodiendos, non ad puniendos dari debet.

Section 439.

¶ **EN mesme le manner il semble, lou home est hors du Royalme, en service le Roy, pur besoigne del Royalme, si tiel hõe soit disseisie quant il est en service le Roy, et le disseisor mort seisie, le disseisee**

IN the same manner it seemeth where a man is out of the Realme in the Kings service, for the businesse of the Realme, if such a one be disseised when hee is in service of the King, and the disseisor dieth

¶ *Hors du Roialme.* (id est) extra Regnum, as much to say, as out of the power of the King of England, as of his Crowne of England: for if a man be upon the Sea of England, he is within the Kingdome or Realm of England, and within the ligeance of the King of England, as of his Crowne of England. And yet altum mare is out of the iurisdiction of the common law, *6.R.2. Protect.46. Vide Sect.198.440.441.*

Ret. Pat. { 8. H. 3. 9. H. 3. 15. H. 3.
Temps. E. 1. Auowrie 192.
Rot. Vascon. 22. E. 1. m. 8.
Pat. 23. E. 1. 1. pars Pat.
10 E. 1. 8 E. 2. Coron. 399.
Stamf. Pl. Coron. 51.

Law, and within the iurisdiction of the Lord Admirall, whose iurisdiction is verie antient, and long before the raign of Edward the third, as some haue supposed, as may appeare by the Laws of Oleron, (so called for that they were made by King Richard the first when he was there) that there had beene then an Admirall time out of mind, and by many other antient records in the raignes of Henry the third, Edward the first, and Edward the second, is most manifest.

Vide Section 677.

See hereafter in another case which Littleton put in his Chapter of Remitter, there he saith, Ouster le mere, beyond the sea. This great Officer in the Saxon Language is called, Aen mere al, (i.) ouer all the sea, Præfectus maris, siue classis, archithalassus: and in antient time the office of the Admiraltie was called, Custodia marinæ Angliæ, or Maritinæ Angliæ.

seisee esteant en le seruice le Roy, que tiel discent ne grieueroit le Disseisee, mes pur ceo que il ne puissoit faire continual claime, il semble a eux, que quaunt il vient en Engleterre, il poit enter sur lheir le Disseisor, &c. Car tiel home reuersera vn vtlagary pnounce enuers luy durant le temps que il fuit en le seruice le Roy, &c. Ergo à multo fortiori, auera aid et indempnitie per la Ley en lauter case, &c.

seised, &c. the disseisee being in the K. seruice, that such discent shall not hurt the Disseisee, but for that hee could not make continuall claim, it seemes to thē that whē he commeth into England hee may enter vpon the heire of the Disseisor, &c. for such a man shall reuerse an outlawry pronounced against him during the time that he was in the Kings seruice, &c. Therefore *à multo fortiori* he shal haue aid & indemnitie by the law in the other case, &c.

8. R. 3. Cont. claime 13.
4. E. 3. 46.

And note Littleton saith not, Beyond the sea, or extra quatuor maria, for a man reuera may be infra quatuor maria, and yet out of the Realme of England. But Infra quatuor maria, or extra, is taken by construction to be within the Realme of England, or the Dominions of the same.

But here a question may be demanded, what if a man be out of the Realme, and a Recouerie is had against him in a Præcipe by default, whether shall he auoyd it in a writ of Error, as well as he should doe the Outlawrie, or if he had beene imprisoned at the time of such recouery by default? And it seemeth that he shall not auoid the recouerie, for by that meanes a man might be infinitely delayed of his Freehold and Inheritance, whereof the Law hath so great a regard. And few or none goe ouer, but it is either of their owne freewill, or by suit, for what cause soeuer, and he is not in that case without his ordinarie remedie, either by his Writ of higher nature, or by a Quod ei deforceat. But Outlawrie in a personall Action shall be auoyded in that case, quia de minimis non curat Lex, and otherwise he should be without remedie. See Section 437. and note the diuersitie betweene that case of the imprisonment, and this of beeing beyond sea. And Littleton putteth the case of imprisonment, and omitteth the being beyond sea here: neither haue I seene any Booke to warrant, That he that is beyond sea shall in this case auoyd the recouerie by default.

Bract. li. 5. fo. 436.

¶ *En seruice le Roy.* Bracton sheweth, That the exception of being beyond sea is, quia fuit in seruitio Domini Regis vltra mare, viz apud talem locum, and that case is cleere: but you shal heare the opinion of Bracton in the next Section, where he is not in the seruice of the King.

Sect. 440.

Bract. li. 5. fo. 436. b. & 163.
Brit. fo. 21. 216. 217. Flet. li. 6
ca. 52. 53. 13. H. 4. Triall 6.
9. H. 4. 3. 21. H. 6. Error 27.
33. H. 6. 1. 21. H. 6. 34.
26. H. 8. ca. 18. 5. & 6. E. 6.
ca. 11.

¶ And herewith the antient law of England is agreable with Littleton, and the Law at this day. So as it is Vetus & constans opinio. Excusatur etiam quis qd clameum

¶ Item auters ont dit, que si ascun soit hors du Royalm coment que il ne soit en seruice le Roy, si tiel

Also others haue said, that if a man bee out of the Realme, though hee bee not in the Kings

tiel home esteant hors de le Royalme, est disseisie en terres ou tenements deins le Royalme, & le disseisour deux seisie, &c. le disseisee esteant hors du Royalme, il semble a eux q̃ quant le disseisee vient dins le Royalme, que il poit enter sur lheire le disseisor, & ceo semble a eux per deux causes. Un est, que celuy que est hors du Royalme ne poit aver conusans dl desseisin fait a luy per entendement de ley, nient pluis que chose fait hors du Royalm poit estre try deins l Royalme per le serement de 12. & de compeller tiel home per la ley de faire continuall claime, le quel per lentendement de le ley ne puit auer ascun notice, ou conusance de tiel disseisin, ceo serra inconuenient, & nosmemẽt quant tiel disseisin est fait a luy quant il est hors du Royalme, & auxy le morant seisie fuit quãt il fuit hors du royalm: Car ẽ tiel case il ne poit per nul possibility solonque common presumption faire continuall claime, Mes auter-

Seruice; if such a man being out of the Realme be disseised of Lands or Tenements within the Realme, and the Disseisor die seised, &c. the Disseisee being out of the Realme, it seemeth vnto them, that when the Disseisee commeth into the Realme, that he may well enter vpon the heire of the Disseisor, &c. and this seemeth vnto them for two causes: One is, that hee that is out of the Realme, cannot haue knowledge of the Disseisin made vnto him by vnderstanding of the Law, no more than that a thing done out of the Realme may bee tried within this Realme by the oath of 12. men, and to compell such a man to make continuall claime, which by the vnderstanding of the Law can haue no knowledge or Conisance of such Disseisin made or done, this shall be inconuenient, namely, when such a disseisin is done vnto him, whẽ he was out of the Realme, & also the dying seised was done when hee was out of the realme, for in such case hee may not by

non apposuerit, vt si toto tempore litigij fuit vltra mare quacunque occasione. And this is also agreeable with our yeare Bookes.

Nient pluis que chose fait hors del royalm poet este trie deins le royalm per le serement de 12. And in this rule of Law there is warily and truly put by Littleton, these words (by the oath of 12. men) meaning by a Jury. For by certificate a thing done beyond Sea may bee tried, as Littleton himselfe, Sect. 102. hath set downe. And all matters done out of the Realme of England concerning warre, combate, or deeds of armes shall bee tried and termined before the Constable and Marshall of England, before whom the triall is by witnesses, or by combate, and their proceeding is according to the Ciuill Law, and not by the oath of 12. men, as Littleton here speaketh.

42.E.3.2.& 3. Vide Sect. 102.

1.H.4.cap.14.13.H.4.fol.4. 48.E.3.2.& 3.

This rule here rehearsed by Littleton is worthy of explication. If an alien (for example borne in France) bring a reall Action, and the tenant plead that the Demandant is an alien borne vnder the obedience of the French King, and out of the leigeance of the King of England: shall this case want triall because the matter alleaged is out of the Realme? then by the fiction of this plea no demandant shall recouer, therefore in this case, the Demandant shall reply, that hee was borne at such a place in England within the Kings liegeance, and hereupon a Jury of 12. shall bee charged, and if they haue sufficient euidence that hee was borne in France, or in any other place out of the Realme, then shall they find, that hee was borne out of the Kings alleageance, and if they haue sufficient euidẽce that he was borne in England, or Ireland, or Iernsey or Iersey, or else where within the Kings obedience, they shall find that hee

20. Eg. auerment. 34. 27. Ass. 24. 32. H. 6. 25. 15. E. 4. 15. 7. H. 6. 15. 1. R. 3. 4. 6. H. 7. 6. 7. H. 7. 8. F. N. B. 196. 29. Ass. 11. 13. E. 1. mord. 47. 12. H. 3. ibid. 55. Lib. 7. fol. 26. 27. Caluins case. Lib. 6. fol. 47. Dowdales case.

was

ment serroit si tiel dis-seisee fuit deins le Royalme al temps d le disseisin, ou al temps del morant del disseisour.

possibilitie after the common presumption make continuall claime: But otherwise it should be if the Disseisee were within the Realme at the time of the Disseisin, or at the time of the dying seised of the Disseisor.

was borne within the Kings leigeance. And this hath ever beene the pleading and manner of triall in that case. And so it is in the case that Littleton here putteth, if a man in avoydance of a fine or a discent, alleadge that he was out of this Realme in Spaine, at the time of levying of the fine and at the time of the disseisin and discent, the adverse party may alleadge that hee was at such a place in England, &c. whereupon issue shall bee taken, and then in evidence hee may prove that he was out of the Realme, &c. which upon sufficient evidence the Jurie ought to find. And in both these cases and the like in a speciall verdict the Jury may find that hee was borne beyond Sea, or was beyond Sea at that time, &c.

The statute of 25 E.3. De proditionibus doth declare, that it is Treason by the Common Law to adhere to the enemies of the King within the Realme, or without, if hee bee thereof proveablement attaint of overt fact, and that he shall forfeit all his Lands, &c. A man must not imagine that seeing by the Common Law declared by authoritie of Parliament that adhering to the Kings Enemies without the Realme is high Treason, and that the Delinquent may be attainted thereof, &c. that this should want triall, for then the judgement of the Common Law and declaration of the Parliament should be illusorie, which no well advised man will thinke in a matter of so great consequence. But certaine it is that for necessitie sake the adherencie without the Realme must be alleaged in some place within England. And if upon evidence they shall find any adherencie out of the Realme, they shall find the Delinquent guiltie. But most commonly they indited him (if he had lands) in some countie where his lands did lye, that were to be forfeited, and this as appeareth in our bookes was the Common use. And so it is declared by the Statute (*) of 33.H.8. and that it shall bee tried by 12. men of the Countie where the Kings Bench shall sit, and bee determined before the Justices of that Bench, or else before such Commissioners, and in such shire of the Realme, as shall be assigned by the Kings Majesties Commission, and this Statute for this point remaynes in force at this day, and so it was resolved (a) by all the Judges in my time, viz. in 33.Eliz. in the case of Orurcke. And Anno (b) 34.Eliz. in Sir Iohn Perots case done in Ireland, for that is out of the Realme of England, and the case (c) in Mich.19 & 20.Eliz. was utterly denied, & Sir Christopher Wray himselfe (who is supposed to give his opinion in that case) protested that he never gave any such opinion, but did hold the contrary. When part of the Act, especially the originall is done in England, and part out of the Realme, that part that is to be performed out of the Realme, if issue be taken thereupon shall be tryed here by 12.men, and those 12.men shall come out of the place where the Writ is brought. For example (which ever doth illustrate) it was covenanted by Indenture, by Charter partie, that a Ship should sayle from Blackney Haven in Norfolke, to Muttrel in Spaine, and there remayne by certaine dayes.

5.R.2.triall.54.

(*) 33.H.8.cap.2. Stawnford.pl.cor 90.

(a) 33.Eliz.case Orurcke.
(b) 34.Eliz.case de Sir Iohn Perot.
(c) Mich.19.& 20.Eliz. Dier 360.

48.E.3.3.11.H.7.16. 1.R.3.4.

In an Action of Covenant brought upon this Charter partie, the Indenture was alleaged to be made at Thetford in the Countie of Norfolke, and upon pleading the issue was joyned whither the said Ship remayned at Muttrell in Spaine by the said certaine dayes. And it was adiudged that this issue should be tried at Thetford where the action was brought, because there the contract tooke his originall by making of the Charter partie, and so hath it beene often adiudged in such like case.

Pasch.28.Eliz. in action de covenant inter Evangelist Constantine Pl. & Hughgyn defendant in the Kings Bench. Lib.6.fol.47.Dowdales case. Vide 32.H.6.25. 48.E.3.3.11.H.7.16. 2.E.2.obligation 15.

An Obligation made beyond the Seas may bee sued here in England in what place the Plaintife will. What then if it beare date at Burdeaux in France? where shall it be sued? And answere is made, that it may be alleaged to be made In quodam loco vocat' Burdeaux in France, in Islington in the Countie of Middlesex, and there it shall be tried, for whether there be such a place in Islington or no, is not traversable in that case. These points are neccssary to bee knowne in respect of the varietie of opinions in our Bookes. And of these thus much shall suffice, and now is Littleton worthy to be heard.

Entendement de le ley.

¶ *Per entendement de le ley.* Vide, for intendement of Law. Sect. 99.100.110.293 377 393.406.367.462.463.&c. 439.

Vide Sect.269.

¶ *Ceo serr' inconuenient.* Here also as hath beene often said appeareth, that argumentum ab inconvenienti is strong in Law.

¶ *Auterment est si le disseisee fuit deins le royalme al temps del disseisin, &c.* So as if a man be disseised before he goeth over Sea, or commeth into the Realme againe before the Discent, the Discent shall take away his entrie.

Sect

Section 441.

Vn auter matter ils allegeont pur prouer que deuant lestatute fait en le temps de Roy E. 3. An. 34. cap. 16. de son raigne, per quel estatute nonclaime est ouste, &c. le ley fuit tiel, que si vn fine soit leuy de certaine terres ou tenements, si ascun que fuit estrange al fine auoit droit dauer & recouer mesmes les terres ou tenements, sil ne venust & fist son claime a ceo deins lan & le iour procheine apres le fine leuie, il serra barre a touts iours, Quia dicebat', finis finem litib' imponebat. Et que la ley fuit tiel, il est proue per lestatute de Westminster 2. De donis conditionalibus, lou il est parl' que si fine soit leuie de les tenements en taile, &c. Quod finis ipſo iure ſit nullus, nec habeant hæred', aut illi ad quos ſpect' reuerſio (licet fuerint plenæ ætat', in Anglia, & extra priſonam) neceſſitat' apponere clameum ſuum, &c. Issint ceo

AN other matter they alleadge for a proofe, that before the Statute of King *Edward* the Third, made the 34. yeare of his Raigne, by which ſtatute Nonclaim is ouſted, &c. the Law was ſuch, that if a fine were leuied of certaine Lands or Tenements, if any that was a ſtranger to the fine had right to haue and to recouer the ſame Lands or Tenements, if he came not, and made his claime thereof within a yeare and a day next after the fine leuied, he ſhall be barred for euer, *Quia dicebatur quod finis finem litibus imponebat.* And that Law was ſuch, it is proued by the Statute of Weſt. the 2. *De donis conditionalibus*, where it is ſpoken if the fine bee leuied of Tenements giuen in the taile, &c. *Quod finis ipſo iure ſit nullus, nec habeant hæredes, aut illi ad quos ſpectat reuerſio (licet plenæ ætatis fuerint, in Anglia, & extra priſonam) neceſſitat' apponere claeũ ſuum.* So it is proued,

Here it appeareth, what the Common Law was before the said Statute, for Non-claime upon a fine leuied. But now since Littleton wrote by the Statute of 4. H. 7. fiue yeares after Proclamations made upon the fine are giuen to him that right hath to make his Claime, or pursue his Action, where the Common Law gaue him but a yeare and a day. But this Statute of 4. H. 7. extend only to fines and not to Nonclaime upon a Iudgement in a Writ of right, and therefore the said Statute of 34. E. 3 here cited by Littleton which ousteth Nonclaime only to fines leuied, extendeth not to a iudgement in a Writ of right as this day, and therefore the Common Law in that case remayneth to this day, viz. that claime must bee made within a yeare and a day after iudgement. Also if a fine be leuied without Proclamations, or without so many as the Law requireth, then the Statute of Nonclaime doth extend to such a fine.

34. E. 3. 16.

4. H. 7. cap. 24. *See aſwell this Statute, as the Statute of 32. H. 8. cap. 36. well expounded in my Reports. Lib. 3. fol. 44. 45. & c. caſe del fines per totum. Lib. 1. fol. 96. 97. in Shelleys caſe, lib. 2. fol. 93. Binghams caſe. lib. 8. fol. 100. Leechfords caſe. lib. 9. fol. 139. 140. 141. Beaumonds caſe. lib. 10. fol. 49. b. Lampets caſe & 99. a. lib. 9. fol 105. 106. Margaret Podgers caſe. lib. 5. fol. 124. Saffyns caſe. lib. 10. 96. 97. Seymors caſe lib. 8. fol. 72. Greſleys caſe lib. 11. fol. 69. 71. 78. Pl. Com. in Smith & Stapl. caſe, & in Stowe's caſe & Howels caſe & Glanvil lib. 13. cap. 11. Bract. 435. Fleta lib. 6. cap. 53. Brit. 216.*

Dicebatur finis, quia finem litibus imponebat. Here you may obserue the Etymologie of a fine. And herewith agreeth (a) Antiquitie, Finis ideo dicitur finalis concordia quia imponit finem litibus. And after the example (b) of Littleton it is good to search out the Etymologie or right deriuatiō of words for ignoratis terminis ignoratur & ars, as hath bin often obserued in other places. And the Ciuilians call this iudiciall concord, Transactionem iudicialem de re immobili.

(a) *Glanvil lib. 8. cap. 1. Bract. lib. 5. fol. 435. Fleta lib. 6. cap. 52. 53.*

(b) *Etymologies, &c. Vide Sect. 74. 174. 194. 441. 520. 592.*

Stat de anno 13.E.1.

(c) Pl.Com.Stowells case,359

Bracton.lib.5.fo.436.
Britton,fo.216.b.
Fleta,lib.6.ca.53.

Licet fuerit plenæ ætatis, in Anglia, & extra prisonam. In this Act of 13 E.1. De donis conditionalibus is one omitted who is added in the Statute De modo leuandi fines, viz. & sanæ memoriæ (c) But a Feme-Couert had no priuiledge of non-claime at the Common Law as some haue said, because she had a husband that might make claime for her. But yet Bracton saith, Item excusatur vxor quæ sub potestate viri supposita quod clameum non apposuerit licet mittere possit. And citeth a iudgement in the point, Trin. 4.H.3. in Cusins case But Fleta saith, Excusatur si fuerit vxor alicuius, si fuerit per virum impedita, quod non potuit apponere clameum. Also they in reuersion or remainder expectant vpon any estate of Freehold were barred by the Common Law, and yet they could make no claime, because as hath beene said, it belonged to the particular Tenant, and not to them, because their entrie was not lawfull, which was one of the principall causes of making of the said Statute of 34.E.3.+ which ousted Non-claime. But these cases of Couerture and of them in reuersion and remainder are now without question holpen, and iust prouision made for the sauing of their rights and titles by the said Statute of 4.H.7. as by the said act appeareth. +Explained by 32: Harry 8 Ch: 36:

proue, que si vn estrange home que auoit droit a les tenements, s'il fuit hors de Roialme al temps del fine leuie, &c. nad dammage, coment q̄ il ne fist son claime, &c. coment que tiel fine fuit matter de record. Per greinder reason il semble a eux q̄ vn disseisin & discent q̄ est matter en fait, ne issint trope greeuera celuy q̄ fuit disseisie, quant il fuit hors du Royalme al temps de disseisin, et auxy al temps que le disseisor morust seisie, &c. mes que il bien poit enter, nient contristeant tiel discent.

that if a stranger that hath right vnto the tenements, if hee were out of the Realme at the time of the fine leuied, &c. shall haue no dammage, though that hee made not his claim &c. though that such fine was matter of record: by greater reason it seemeth vnto them that a disseisin & discent that is matter in deed shall not so grieue him that was disseised when he was out of the Realme at the time of that disseisin, and also at the time that the Disseisor died seised, &c. but that he may well enter notwithstanding such discent.

Sect. 442.

ARraigne vn assise. To arraigne the Assise is to cause the Tenant to bee called to make the pleint, and to set the cause in such order as the Tenant may be inforced to answer thereunto, and is deriued of the French word Arraigner, which signifieth to order or set in right place An Arraignement is sometime called an Astitution of the Verbe Astituo compounded of Ad and Statuo, that is to place, or set in order one by another. In the same sence that Littleton here vseth it, it is vsed when an appeale is

ITem, Quære si home soit disseisi, et il arraigne vn Assise enuers le disseisor, et les recognitors de l'assise chaunta pur le plaintife, et les Iustices dassise voyle estre aduises d' lour iudgment, tanq; al procheín assise, &c. Et en le dementiers le disseisor morust seisie, &c. si le dit suit del

ALso inquire if a man be disseised, and he arraigne an assise against the disseisor, and the recognitors of the assise chante for the plaintise, and the Iustices of assise will bee aduised of their iudgements vntill the next assise, &c. and in the meane season the disseisor dieth seised, &c. yet the

del assise serra pris en ley pur le dit disseisee un continual claime, entant que nul default fuit en luy, &c.

said suite of the assise shall bee taken in Law for the disseisee a continuall claime, insomuch that no default was in him, &c.

arraigned, both which are arraigned in French, but entred in Latyn. And it is to bee obserued that Littleton saith here Arraigne vn assise, and saith not that the Tenant is arraigned, and so of the appeale, for these are the suites of the subiect, and no man is said to be arraigned, but meerely at the suite of the King, vpon an Enditement found against him, or other record wherewith he is charged. And there the arraignment of the prisoner is to take order, that he appeare, and for the certainty of the person to hold vp his hand and to plead a sufficient plea to the enditement or other record, whereupon they which follow for the King may orderly proceede.

2.& 3.E.6.ca.24. towards the end. Stanf.pl.cor. 105.C.3.H.7.ca.1.

¶ *Iustices dassise.* **Iustices of Assise are assigned and constituted** by the King of the Iudges and Sages of the Law, and are called Iustices of Assise, for that the writs of Assise of Nouel disseisin, (which in former times were accounted Festina remedia and very frequent and common) were returnable before them to be taken in their proper Counties twice euery yeare at the least, whereupon they had authority to giue iudgement and award seisin and execution: and therefore both for the number of them in times past, and for the greater authority they had then as Iustices of Nisi prius (which was to trie issues onely, except in Quare Impedit, and Assises De darreine presentment, in which cases the Iustices of Nisi prius might giue iudgement) they were denominated Iustices of Assise: And diuers Acts of Parliament haue giuen to them great authority both in Criminall causes and Common pleas. These Iustices of Assise, haue also Commissions of Oier and Terminer, of Goale deliuery, and of the peace, of association, and Si non omnes throughout their whole circuits, so as they are armed with ample, prouident, but yet ordinary iurisdiction, for all their Commissions are bounded with this expresse limitation, Facturi quod ad iustitiam pertinet secundum legem & consuetudinem Angliæ. And in former time according to the originall institution and their Commission both the Iustices ioyned both in Common pleas, and pleas of the Crowne.

Vid. Sect. 514. 233. 234. Magna Carta, 30. W.2.ca.3.30.39. Stat. de Ebor. ca.3.4. Artic. Sup. Cart. ca.10. 4.E.3.ca.11. 7.R.2.ca. 27.E.1. De finibus. ca.4. 28.E.1. de appellatis. 4.E.3.ca.2. 2.H.5.ca.8. 3.H.5.ca.7. 13.H.4.ca.7. North.2.E.3.ca.3. 2.E.3.ca.5. 14.H.6.ca.1. 31.H.6.ca.10. 3.H.7.ca.1. 33.H.8.ca.9. 34.& 35.H.8.ca.14.2.& 3.E.6.ca.24. 1.E.6.ca.7. 2.Mar. Dier. 90. 3.& 4.Eliz. Dier. 205.

¶ *Si le dit suite del assise serra prise en ley, &c. vn continuall claime.* And it is holden at this day that it shall amount to a Claime, for that there was no default in him as Littleton saith. (d) Some haue obiected that if the bringing of an Assise should amount to Continuall claime, and euery Continuall claime made by the Disseisee vest the possession and freehold in him, therefore if bringing the Assise, &c. should amount to a Continuall claime that then the writ should abate. But hereunto it hath beene answered in this Chapter, that a Continuall claime is an entrie by construction of Law for the aduantage of the Disseisee, but not for his disaduantage.

(d) See before in this chapter Sect. 419. Vid. Sect. 416.

In a writ of entrie Sur Disseisin against one, supposing that he had not entred but by S. who disseised him, the Tenant said that S. died seised; and the land discended to him, and prayed his age, the Plaintife counterpleaded his age, for that he arraigned an Assise against S. who died hanging the Assise, and he was ousted of his age, for that the bringing of the Assise amounted to a Claime.

24.E.3.25. 9.E.2. age.141. 15.E.3. Counterplea de gar. 5.

If Tenant in Dower alien in fee with warrantie, and the heire in the reuersion bring a writ of entrie In casu prouiso, &c. and hanging the plea, the Tenant dyeth, the heire shall not be rebutted or barred by this warrantie, for that the Præcipe did amount to a Continuall claime. And herewith agreeth (*) Antiquity; Et si clameum non opposuerit, sufficit tamen si ille vel antecessor suus faciat qd tantundẽ valeat, vt si placitũ mouerit teneñ vel fecerit rem litigiosã, quia sicut plus est facto appellare, quam verbo, ita plus est clameum apponere facto, quam verbo: Et ad hoc facit de termino Sanctæ Trinitatis, Anno regni regis, H.3.15. in com. Hunt: de quadam Guldeburga, cui obiectum fuit, quod clameum non apposuit, & ipsa respondit, quod fecit, quod tantundem valet, quia tempore finis facti implacitauit tenentem per aliud breue, &c.

3.E.3. tit. garranties 62.

(*) Fleta. lib.6. ca.52. Bract. lib.5 fo.436.

If the goods of a Villeine (before any seisure made by the Lord) be distrained, the Lord may haue a Repleuyn, and notwithstanding before the bringing of the writ he had no property, yet the very bringing of the writ doth amount to a clayme of the goods, and vesteth the propertie in the Lord.

33.E.3. Repleuin. 43. 42.E.3.18.b. 9.H.6.25.

¶ *Entant que nul default fuit en luy, &c.* **Hereby it is implied, that** our Author enclined to this opinion, that it should amount to a Clayme, for that no default was in him, Et nemo debet rem suam sine facto aut defectu suo amittere, as the rule is.

Here first it is to bee obserued, that albeit the Freehold and inheritance is in this case in no person but in abeiance or in consideratiō of law, yet an entrie and claime by one that hath no right shall gaine the inheritance by wrong. For here Littleton saith, and of such estate died seised, &c. And so it is in case of a Bishop, Parson, Vicar, Prebend, or any other sole Corporation. And in the statute of Merlebridge it is called an intrusion.

Merlb. ca. 28.

Secondly, that seeing by the death of the Abbot (which is the act of God) no person is able to make Continuall claime, therefore a discent during that time shall not preiudice the successor, for as hath beene said, Impotentia excusat legem. If an vsurpation be had to a Church in time of vacation, this shall not preiudice the successor to put him out of possession, but that at the next auoydance hee shall present.

F. N. B. 34. m. W. 2. ca. 5.

¶ *Nient plus que ils sont able de suer Action, &c.* Here that which hath in this Chapter beene sayd is confirmed, viz. That the entrie or continuall claime must pursue the action.

¶ *Car le Couent nest forsque vn mort person, &c.* This is Ratio vna, but not vnica: for though the rest of the Corporation bee no mort persons, as the Chapter in case of Dean and Chapter, or the commonalty in case of Maior and Commonalty, yet cannot they when there is no dean or maior, make claim, because they haue neither abilitie nor capacitie to take or to sue any Action, as our Author here saith.

¶ *Car en temps de*

Sect. 443.

¶ Item Quære si vn Abbe de vn Monastery morust, et durant l' temps de vacation, vn hōe tortiousemēt enter ē certaine parcel de terre del monastery, claymant la terre a luy et a ses heires, et de tiel estate morust seisie, et la terre discendist a son heir, et puis apres vn est elect et fait Abbe de mesme la Monasterie, si mesm̄ Labbe poit enter sur le heire ou nemy. Et il semble a ascuns que Labbe bien poit enter en ceo cas, pur ceo q̄ le Couent en temps de vacac̄ ne fuit ascun person able de faire continuall claime, car neint pluis que ils sont person abl' ā suer Action, nient pluis ils sont able de faire continnall Clayme, car le Couent nest forsque vn mort corps sauns Teste car en temps de Vacation vn graunt fait a eux, ou per eux est voyd, & en cest case Labbe ne poit auer Briefe Dentre sur Disseisin enuers le

Also inquire if an Abbot of a Monasterie die, and during the time of vacation, a man wrongfully entreth in certaine parcels of land of the Monasterie, claiming the land vnto him and his heires, and of that estate dyeth seised, and the land descendeth vnto his heires, and after that an Abbot is chosen, and made Abbot of the Monastery, a question is, if the Abbot may enter vpon the heire or not. And it seemeth to some, That the Abbot may well enter in this case, for this, that the Couent in time of vacation was no person able to make continuall claime, for no more thā they be personable to sue an Action, no more bee they able to make continuall claime, for the Couent is but a dead bodie without Head, for in time of vacation a Grant made vnto them is voyd, and in this case an Abbot may not haue a Writ of *Entrie* vpon *Disseisin*, against the Heire, for

le heire, pur ceo que il ne fuit unques disseisie, et si Labbe ne puissoit enter en ceo case, donques il serra mis a son Briefe de Droit, &c. le quel serra trope dure pur le meason, per que semble a eux, que Labbe bien poit enter, &c.

Quæras de dubijs legē bene discere si vis: Quære dat sapere, quæ sunt legitima vere.

this, That hee was never disseised. And if the Abbot may not enter in this case, then hee shall bee put vnto his Writ of Right, &c. which shall bee hard for the House. By which it seemeth to them, that the Abbot may well enter, &c.

Quæras de dubijs, Legem bene discere si vis:
Quærere dat sapere quæ sunt legitima vere.

vacation vn Graunt fait a eux on per eux, est void &c. And the reason is, because the bodie politique, which is capable, is not compleat, but wanteth the Head. But this is to bee vnderstood of an immediate Grant, for if during the vacation of the Abbathie of Dale, a Lease for life, or a gift in Taile be made, the remainder to the Abbot of Dale and his successors, this remainder is good, if there bee an Abbot made during the particular estate. a H.7.13.49.*Ass.*26. 34.*E.*3.*Garrantie* 69.

If there be Maior and commonaltie of D. and the Maior dieth, a Grant made to the Maior & Cōmonalty of D. is void for the cause aforesaid, but in that case if a Lease for life be made, the remainder to the Maior and Commonaltie of D. the remainder is good, if there bee a Maior elected during the particular estate.

¶ *Poet enter, &c.* Here by this (&c.) is implied, Or make his continuall claime in such sort as hath beene before expressed.

¶ Quæras de dubijs, Legem bene discere si vis:
Quærere dat sapere quæ sunt legitima vere.

Here Littleton expresseth an excellent meanes to attaine to the reason of the Law, by enquiring of, and conference had with learned men, of doubtfull cases:

Inter cuncta leges, & percunctabere Doctos. Horace.

For as Collatio peperit artes, so Collatio perficit artes: And this must bee continuall, for as knowledge increaseth, so doubts therewith increase also; Crescente scientia, crescunt simul & dubitationes.

And here Littleton citeth verie aptly two Verses, for it is truly said, That Authoritates Philosophorum, medicorum & Poetarum sunt in causis allegandæ & tenendæ: And our Author doth cite a verse for memorie, but it is worthie of memorie.

Chap. 8. Of Releases. *Sect.*444.

¶ **Releases sont en diuers manners, cestascauoir, Releases de tout le droit q̄ home ad en terres ou Tenements, et Releases de Actions personals et reals, et**

Releases are in diuers manners, *viz.* Releases of all the right which a man hath in Lands or Tenements, and Releases of Actions

¶ Here our author beginneth with a diuision of Releases. *Vi. Mir. ca.* 2. §. 17. *V. Brit.* 101. *Bract. li.* 5. *Tract. de Except. & Lib.* 4. *fo.* 318. *b. Fleta lib cap.* 14.

These words must be referred thus: Releases are of two sorts, viz. A release of all the right which a man hath either in lands and tenements, or in Goods and Chattels: or there is a Release of Actions Reall, of or in lands or tenements: or Personall, of or in

Goods

V. Sect. 492.

Goods or Chattels: or mixt, partly in the Realty, and partly in the Personaltie.

¶ *Release*. Relaxatio: Of the Etymologie of this word you haue heard before. Fleta (a) calleth it, Carta de quieta clamantia.

(a) Flet. vb. sup.

¶ Nouerint vniuersi per præsentes, &c. Here Littleton sheweth Presidents of Releases of right: and Presidents doe both teach and illustrate, and therefore our Student is to bee well stored with Presidents of all kinds.

¶ Remisisse, relaxasse, & quietum clamasse. Here Littleton sheweth, That there be 3. proper words of Releas, and bee much of one effect: besides, there is Renũciare, acquietare, & there be many other words of releas, as if the lessor grants to the lessee for life, That he shall be discharged of the Rent, this is a good Release, Vide Sect. 532.

Brall. li. 4. fo. 308. Flet. vb. sup. 9. H. 6. 35. 24. E. 3. 27. 13. H. 4. Entr. congeab. 57.

And it is to bee vnderstood, That there bee Releases in Deed, or Expresse: Releases, whereof Littleton heere hath shewed an example. These Expresse Releases must of necessitie be by Deed. There be also Releases in Law, and they are sometime by Deed, and sometime without Deed. As if the Lord disseise the Tenant, and maketh a Feoffement in fee by Deed or without Deed, this is a release of the Seigniorie. And so it is if the Disseisee disseise the heire of the Disseisor, and make a Feoffement in Fee by Deed or without Deed, this is a release in Law, of the right. And the same Law it is of a right in Action.

27 H. 8. 29. of an vse. 34. H. 6. 44. of an attaint. 3. E. 3. 38. 21. E. 4. 81. Pl. Com. Delameres case.

auters choses. Releases de tout l'droit que homes ont en Terres ou Tenements, &c. sont communement fait en tiel forme ou de tiel effect. *Sect. 444.*

¶ Nouerint vniuersi per præsentes me A. de B. remisisse, relaxasse, & omnino de me & hæredib^9 meis quietum clamasse: *vel sic*, Pro me & hæredibus meis quietum clamasse C. de D. totum ius, titulum, & clameum quæ habui, habeo, vel quouismodo in futur̃ habere potero, de, & in vno messuagio cum pertinentijs in F. &c. Et est ascauoire, que ceux Verbs, Remisisse, & quietum clamasse sont de vn tiel effect, sicome tiels Verbs, Relaxasse.

ctions personalls and realls, & other things. Releases of al the right which men haue in lands & tenements &c. are commonly made in this forme, or of this effect:

Know all men by these Presents, That I A. of B. haue remised, released, and altogether from me and my Heires quiet claimed: or thus, *For mee and my Heires quiet claimed to C. of D. all the right, title, and claim which I haue, or by any meanes may haue, of and in one messuage, with the appurtenances in F. &c.* And it is to bee vnderstood, that these words, *Remisisse, & quietum clamasse*, are of the same effect as these words, *Relaxasse*.

8. E. 4. 3. 21. E. 4. 2.

If the Obligee make the Obligor his Executor, this is a release in Law of the Action, but the dutie remaines, for the which the Executor may retaine so much goods of the Testator.

11. H. 7. 4. 20. H. 7. 29. 8. E. 4. 3.

If the Feme Obligee take the Obligor to husband, this is a release in Law. The like law is if there be two Femes Obligees, and the one take the Debtor to husband.

If an Infant of the age of seuenteene yeares release a debt, this is voyd. But if an enfant make the Debtor his Executor, this is a good release in Law of the debt.

But if a Feme Executrix take the Debtor to husband, this is no release in Law, for that should be a wrong to the Dead, and in Law worke a Deuastauit, which an Act in Law shall neuer worke. And so it was adiudged in the Kings Bench, Mich. 30. & 31. Eliz. in which case I was of Councell.

50. E. 3. 24. 32. E. 3. Tit. Scire fac. 102.

But it is to be obserued, That there is a diuersitie betweene a Release in Deed, and a releas in Law: for if the heire of the Disseisor make a lease for life, and the Disseisee release his right to the Lessee for his life, his right is gone for euer. But if the Disseisee doth disseise the heyre of the Disseisor, and make a Lease for life, by this release, in Law the right is released but during the life of the Lessee: for a release in Law shall be expounded more fauourable, according to the intent and meaning of the parties, than a release in Deed, which is the act of the partie, and shall

shall be taken most strongly against himselfe, and so in the case aforesayd, where the Debtor is made Executor.

¶ Totum ius, titulum, & clameum. **But note, that** Ius **or right** in generall signification includeth not only a right for the which a writ of right doth lie, but also any title or claime either by force of a Condition, Mortmaine or the like, for the which no action is given by Law, but only an entrie.

Section 446.

¶ ITem ceux paroles q̃ sont communement mis en tiels faits de releases, &c. (quæ quouismodo in futurum habere potero) sont sicome voides en le ley, car nul droit passa per un releas, forsque le droit que le relessor ad al temps de le releas fait. Car si soit pier & fits, & le pier soit disseisie, et le fits (viuant son pier) relessa per son fait a le disseisor, tout le droit que il ad, ou auer puissoit, en mesmes les tenements sans clause de garrantie, &c. et puis le pier morust, &c. le fits poit loyalment enter sur la possession le disseisor, pur ceo que il nauoit droit en la terre en la vie son pier, mes le droit discendist a luy per discent apres le releas fait, p̃ le mort son pere, &c.

ALso these words which are commonly put in such Releases, s. (*quæ quouismodo in futurum habere potero*) are as voide in Law, for no right passeth by a Release, but the right which the Releasor hath at the time of the Release made. For if there be Father and Sonne, and the Father bee disseised, and the Sonne (liuing his Father) releaseth by his deed to the disseisor all the right which he hath or may haue in the same tenements without clause of warrantie, &c. and after the Father dieth, &c. the Sonne may lawfully enter vpon the possession of the Disseisor, for that hee had no right in the land in his fathers life, but the right discended to him after the Release made by the death of his Father, &c.

¶ NOte, a man may haue a present right, though it cannot take effect in possession, but in futuro.

As hee that hath a right to a reuersion or remaynder, and such a right hee that hath it, may presently release: But here in the case which Littleton puts where the Sonne release in the life of his father, this release is void (a) because hee hath no right at all at the time of the release made, but all the right was at that time in the Father, but after the decease of the Father, the Sonne shall enter into the Land against his owne Release. (a) *Britton fol. 101. 17. E. 3. 67. 42. E. 3. 21. 10. H. 6. 4. 25. Ass. 7. 27. E. 3. Fitz. Garr. 130.*

The Baron make a Lease for life and dieth, the Release made by the wife of her Dower to him in reuersion is good, albeit shee hath no cause of Action against him in præsenti. *16. E. 3. barre 245. Hoes case 5. part. fol. 70. 91.*

¶ *Sans clause de garrantie.* **For if there** be a warrantie annexed to the release, then the Sonne shall be barred. For albeit the release cannot barre the right for the cause aforesaid, yet the warrantie may rebutt, and barre him, and his heires of a future right which was not in him at that time: and the reason (which in all cases is to be sought out) wherefore a warrantie being a Couenant reall should barre a future right, is for auoyding of circuitie of action (which is not fauoured in Law) as he that made the warrantie should recouer the Land against the *20. H. 6. 29.* Tertenant, and he by force of the warrantie to haue as much in value against the same person: yet is there a diuersitie betweene a warrantie and a Feoffment, (b) for if there be Grandfather, Father, and Sonne, and the Father disseiseth the Grandfather, and make a feoffment *(b) 39. H. 6. 43. 21. E. 4. 81. 15. E. 4. tit. entr. cong. 31. 9. H. 7. 2. b. 2. E. 3. 38.*

10. E. 2. confirmation 24. 8. E. 2. garr. 62. 11. H. 4. 33. 43. E. 3. 17. 42. E. 3. 24. per Finchden. 17. E. 3. 67. Lib. 1. fol. 112. 113. in Albanies case.

in fee, the Grandfather dieth, the Father against his owne feoffment shall not enter, but if he die, his sonne shall enter. and so note a diversitie betweene a Release a Feoffment, and a Warrantie. a Release in that case is voide; a Feoffment is good against the feoffor, but not against his heire, a Warrantie is good both against himselfe and his heires.

And here are three diversities worthy of observation, viz. First, betweene a Power or an Authoritie, and a Right. Secondly, betweene Powers and Authorities themselues. Thirdly, betweene a Right and a Possibilitie.

As to the first, if a Man by his last will deviseth that his Executors shall sell his Land, and dieth, if the Executors release all their right and title in the Land to the heire, this is void, for that they haue neither right nor title to the Land, but only a bare Authoritie, which is not within Littletons case of a Release of a right. And so it is if cesty que vse

15. H. 7. 11.

had devised that his feoffees should haue sold the Land. Albeit they had made a feoffment over yet might they sell the vse, for their Authoritie in that case is not given away by the Liverie.

As to the second there is a diversitie betweene such Powers or Authorities as are only to the vse of a stranger, and nothing for the benefit of him that made the release (as in the case before) and a Power or Authoritie which respecteth the benefit of the Releasor, as in these vsuall powers of revocation, when the feoffor, &c. hath a power to alter, change, determine, or revoke the vses (being intended for his benefit) he may release, & where the estates before were defeasible, he may by his release make them absolute, and seclude himselfe from any alteration or revocation as it hath beene resolved, which diversitie you may reade in (m) Albanies case.

(m) Lib. 1. Albanies case, vbi supra. Lib. 5. Hoes case 70. 71. 10. H. 6. 4.

As to the third, before Judgement the Plantife in an Action of debt releaseth to the baile in the Kings Bench all demaunds, and after Judgement is given, this shall not barre the Plaintife to haue Execution against the bayle, because at the time of the release hee had but a meere possibilitie, and neither Ius in re, nor Ius ad rem, but the dutie is to commence after vpon a contingent, and therefore could not be released presently. So if the Conusee of a Statute, &c. release to the Conusor all his right in the Land, yet afterwards hee may sue Execution, for he hath no right in the land till Execution, but only a possibilitie, and so haue I knowne it adiudged.

25. Ass. p. 7. 27. E. 3. execution 130. pasch. 38. Eliz. Rot. 321. inter Borough & Gray.

Sect. 447.

Item en releases de tout le droit que home ad en certein terres, &c. il covient a celuy a que le releas est fait en ascun cas, que il ad le franktenement en les terres en fait, ou en ley, al temps de releas fait, &c. car en chescun cas lou celuy a que le releas est fait ad franktenement en fait, ou franktenement en ley, al temps del releas, &c. donque le releas est bone.

Also in Releases of all the right which a man hath in certaine lands, &c. it behooueth him to whom the Release is made in any case that hee hath the freehold in the Lands, in Deed, or in Law at the time of the Release made, &c. for in euery case where he to whom the Release is made hath the freehold in Deed or in Law at the time of the Release, &c. there the Release is good.

40. E. 3. 28.

De tout le droit. This must be intended of a bare right, and not of a release of a right, whereby any estate passeth, as to a Lessee for yeares, &c. as shall bee said hereafter. Also it must bee intended of a Release of a right of freehold at the least, and not to a right for any tearme for yeares or chattle reall, as if Lessee for yeares bee ousted, and hee in the reversion disseised, and the Disseisor maketh a Lease for yeares, the first Lessee may release vnto him. All which is implyed in the first &c. Also in some case a release of a right made to one that hath neither freehold in Deed, nor freehold in Law is good and availeable in Law, (c) as the Demaundant may release to the vouchee, and yet the vouchee hath nothing in the land, but the reason of that is for that when the vouchee entreth into the warrantie, he becommeth Tenant to the Demaundant, and may render the Land to him, in respect of the privitie, but an estranger cannot release to the vouchee because In rei veritate, he is not tenant of the Land.

(c) 7. E. 4. 13. 20. H. 6. 29. 9. H. 7. 41. 18. E. 3. 12. 8. H. 4. 5. 5. E. 3. 36. 5. E. 3. 46. Vide Sect. 490. 491.

(d) And

(d) And so it is if the Tenant alien hanging the Præcipe, the release of the Demandant to the Tenant to the Præcipe is good, and yet he hath nothing in the land. (d) 10.E.4.14. 12.*Ass.*p.41.

In time of vacation an Annuity, that the person ought to pay may be released to the Patron in respect of the privity, but a Release to the Ordinary only seemeth not good, because the Annuity is temporall. 8.E.3.21. 46.E.3.6.b. 8.H.6.23. 21.H.7.41.

If a Disseisor make a Lease for life, the Disseisee may release to him, for to such a Release of a bare right there needs no privity as shall be said hereafter. But if the Disseisor make a Lease for yeares, the Disseisee cannot release to him, because he hath no estate of Freehold. And yet in some case a right of Freehold shall drowne in a chattell, as if a Feme hath a right of Dower she may release to the Gardein in Chivalrie, and her right of Freehold shall drowne in the chattle, because the writ of Dower doth lye against him, and the heire shall take advantage of it. And it is to be observed, that by the ancient maxime of the Common Law a Right of entrie, or a Chose in action cannot be granted or transferred to a stranger, and thereby is avoyded great oppression, iniurie and iniustice. Nul charter, nul vende, ne nul done vault perpetualment si le donor nest seisie al temps de contracts de 2. droits. s. del droit de possession, & del droit del propertie. And therefore well saith Littleton, that hee to whom a Release of a right is made must have a freehold. *Mirror.ca.*2.§.17.

For the better understanding of transferring of naked rights to lands or tenements either by Release, Feoffment, or otherwise, it is to be knowne, that there is Ius proprietatis, a right of ownership, Ius possessionis a right of seisin or possession, and Ius proprietatis & possessionis, a right both of propertie and possession: and this is anciently called Ius duplicatum, or Droit droit. For example, if a man be disseised of an acre of land, the Disseisee hath Ius proprietatis, the Disseisor hath Ius possessionis, and if the Disseisee release to the Disseisor, hee hath Ius proprietatis & possessionis. And regularly it holdeth true, that when a naked right to land is released to one that hath Ius possessionis, and another by a meane title recover the land from him, the right of possession shall drawe the naked right with it, and shall not leave a right in him to whom the Release is made. For example, if the heire of the Disseisor being in by discent A. doth disseise him, the Disseisee release to A. now hath A. the meere right to the land. But if the heire of the Disseisor enter into the land, and regaine the possession, that shall draw with it the meere right to the land, and shall not regaine the possession only, and leave the meere right in A. but by the recontinuance of the possession, the meere right is therewith vested in the heire of the Disseisor. *Mirror vbi supra.* *Bracton,lib.*2 *fo.*32. *Britton.fo.*89.121. *Bracton,lib.*5.*fo* 372.

But if the Donee in tayle discontinue in fee, now is the reversion of the Donor turned to a naked right, if the Donor release to the Discontinuee and die, and the issue in taile doth recover the land against the Discontinuee, he shall leave the reversion in the Discontinuee, for the issue in taile can recover but the estate taile only, and by consequence must leave the reversion in the Discontinuee, for the Donor cannot have it against his release: but if the Disseisee enter upon the heire of the Disseisor, and infeoffe A. in fee, and the heire of the Disseisor recover the whole estate that shall draw with it the meere right and leaves nothing in the Feoffee. Nota the diversitie. Another diversitie is observable when the naked right is precedent before the acquisition of the defeasible estate, for there the recontinuance of the defeasible estate shall not draw with it the preceding right. (e) As if the Disseisee disseise the heire of the Disseisor, albeit the heire recover the land against the Disseisee, yet shall hee leave the preceding right in the Disseisee. So if a woman that hath right of Dower disseise the heire, and he recover the land against her, yet shall he leave the right of Dower in her. (e) 5.*Ass.*1. 10.*Ass.*16. 50.*E.*3.7. 4.*E.*3.*Estopp.*133. 30.*Ass* 5. 11.*E.*3.*Entrie*,56. 12.*Ass.*41. 27 *E.*3.84.488.

Another diversity is to be noted, when the meere right is subsequent, and transferred by act in Law, there albeit the possession be recontinued, yet that shall not draw the naked right with it, but shall leave it in him, as if the heire of the disseisor bee disseised, and the Disseisor infeoffe the heire apparant of the disseisee being of full age, and then the Disseisee dyeth, and the naked right discend to him, and the heire of the Disseisor recover the land against him, yet doth he leave the naked right in the heire of the Disseisee. So if the Discontinuee of Tenant in taile infeoffe the issue in taile of full age, and Tenant in tayle die, and then the Discontinuee recover the land against him, yet he leaveth the naked right in the issue. (e) But if the heire of the Disseisor be disseised, and the Disseisee release to the Disseisor upon condition, if the Condition be broken, it shall revest the naked right. And so if the Disseisee had entred upon the heire of the Disseisor, and made a feoffment in fee, upon condition, if he entred for the Condition broken, and the heire of the Disseisor entred upon him, the naked right should be left in the Disseisee. But if the heire of the Disseisor had entred before the Condition broken, then the right of the Disseisee had beene gone for ever. But now let us heare what Littleton saith. 23.H.8.tit. *Restore al action* *Br.*5. 50*E.*3 7. *Vid.Sect.*475.475. 478.487. (e) 38.*E.*3.16. 9.*H.*7.24.

Sect.448.

¶ FRanktenement en ley est, sicome vn home disseisist vn auter, et morust seisie, per q̄ les tenements discendōt a son fits, coment q̄ son fits ne entra pas ē les tenements, vncor̄ il ad vn franktent̄ en ley, quel per force de discent est iect sur luy, et pur ceo vn releas fait a luy, issint esteant seisi de frāktenement en ley, est assets bon, et sil p̄rēt feme issint esteant seisie en ley, coment que il ne vnque enter pas en fait, & morust, son feme serra endow.

FReehold in Law is, as if a man disseiseth another and dieth seised, whereby the tenements discend to his sonne albeit that his sonne doth not enter into the tenements, yet hee hath a freehold in law, which by force of the discent is cast vpon him, and therefore a release made to him so being seised of a freehold in Law is good enough, and if he taketh wife being so seised in law although he neuer enter in deed and dieth, his wife shal be endowed.

¶ HEre Littleton discribeth what a freehold in Law is, for hee had spoken before in many places of freeholds in Deed. This Bracton calleth (a) Ciuilem & naturalem possessionem seu seisinam. The naturall seisin is the freehold in deede, and the Ciuill the freehold in Law.

(a) Bract. lib.4.fo.206.236. Britton, fo.83.b. Fleta, lib.3.ca.15. Vid.Sect.680.

If a man leuie a fine to a man Sur conusance de droit come ceo que il ad de son done, or a Fine Sur conusauce de droit tantum, these be feoffments of Record, and the Conusee hath a freehold in Lawe in him before hee entereth.

42.E.3.20. 10.H.6.14. 17.E.3.78. 2.E.3.33.

Upon an exchange the parties haue neither freehold in Deed nor in Law before they enter, so vpon a partition the freehold is not remoued vntill an entrie.

11.H.4.61. 21.H.7.12.

(g) If Tenant for life by the agreement of him in the reuersion surrender vnto him; he in the reuersion hath a freehold in law in him before he enter. (h) Upon a liuery within the view no freehold is vested before an entrie.

(g) 32.E.3. barre 262. 41.Ass.2. 13.H.4. surrender, 10.

(h) 38.E.3.12.

If a man doth bargaine and sell land by Deed indented and inrolled, the freehold in Law doth passe presently. And so when vses are raised by Couenant vpon good consideration.

If a Tenant in a Præcipe being seised of lands in fee, confesse himselfe to be a Villeine to an estranger, and to hold the land in Villenage of him, the estranger by this acknowledgement is actually seised of the freehold and inheritance without any entrie. But let vs returne to Littleton.

17.E.3.77. 18.E.4.25.

Sect. 449.

¶ ITem en ascuns cases de releases de tout le droit, coment que celuy a que le release est fait nad riens en le franktenement en fait, ne en ley, vncore le release est assets bone. Sicom̄ le disseisor lessa la terre que il ad per disseisin a vn auter pur terme de sa vie, sauant le reuersion a luy, si le disseisee ou son heire relessa al disseisor tout le droit, &c. cel

ALso in some cases of releases of all the right, albeit that he to whom the release is made hath nothing in the freehold in Deede nor in Law, yet the release is good enough. As if the disseisor letteth the land which hee hath by disseisin to another for terme of his life sauing the reuersion to him, if the disseisee or his heire release to the disseisor all the right, &c. this

cel release est bone, pur ceo que celuy a que le releas est fait auoit en luy vn reuersion al temps del release fait.

release is good, because hee to whom the release is made had in law a reuersion at the time of the release made.

HEre Littleton addeth a limitation to the next precedent Section, viz. that a release of all the right may be good to him in reuersion, albeit he hath nothing in the Frehold, because he hath an estate in him. 7.E.4.13. 14.H.4.32.b. 41.E.3.17. 49.E.3.28. Case vlt.

Tout le droit, &c. Or Title, Interest, Demand, or the like, and so it is if he in the reuersion hath an estate for life or in taile in reuersion as in the like case it appeareth in the next Section.

Sect. 450.

EN mesme le maner est, lou leas est fait a vn home pur terme de vie, le remainder a vn auter pur terme de auter vie, le remainder a le tierce en le taile, le remainder a le quart en fee, si vn estranger que droit ad a la terre, relessa tout son droit a ascun de eux en le remainder, tiel releas est bone, pur ceo que chescun de eux ad vn remainder en fait vestue en luy.

IN the same manner it is where a Lease is made to a man for term of life, the remainder to another for terme of another mans life, the remainder to the third in taile, the remainder to the fourth in fee, if a stranger which hath right to the land releaseth all his right to any of them in the remainder, such release is good, because euery of them hath a remainder in Deed vested in him.

HEre is another limitation that a Releas is good to him in the remainder, albeit hee hath nothing in the freehould in possession, because he hath an estate in him, as hath beene said. In both these limitations it is to be obserued, that the state which maketh a man Tenant to the Præcipe is said to be the freehold as here the state of Tenant for life, and not the reuersion in fee. 7.E.4.13. 41.E.3.17. 7.E.3.54.54. 18.E.2. Tit. Entrie 74. 3.E.2.tit. Entrie 7 F.N.B. 207. E.

Sect. 451.

MEs si le tenant a terme de vie soit disseisie, & puis celuy que ad droit (esteant le possession en le disseisor) relesse a vn de eux a que le remainder fuit fait tout son droit, cel releas est void pur ceo que il nauoit vn remainder en fait al temps de releas fait, forsque tantsolement vn droit del remainder.

BVt if the tenant for terme of life be disseised, & afterwards he that hath right (the possession being in the disseisor) releaseth to one of them to whom the remainder was made all his right, this release is voide, because hee had not a remainder in Deed at the time of the release made, but only a right of a remainder.

Forsque tantsolement vn droit del remainder. For a release of a right to one that hath but a bare right regularly is voyde, for as Littleton hath before said, he to whom a release is made of a bare right in lands and tenements must haue either a freehold in Deed or in Law in possession, or a state in remainder or reuersion in fee or fee taile or for life. Vid. Sect. 454.

¶ Et nota, Que chescun releas fait a celuy, que ad vn reuersion ou vn remainder en Fait, seruera et aidera celuy que ad le Franktenement, auxybien come a celuy a que le release fuit fait, si le Tenant auoit le release en son poign de pleader.

And note that euerie Release made to him which hath a Reuersion or a Remainder in Deed, shall serue and ayde him who hath the Freehold, as well as him to whom the Release was made, if the Tenant hath the release in his hand to plead.

Sect. 453.

¶ En mesme le manner est lou vn Release e fait al Tenaunt pur terme de vie, ou al Tenant en le Tail, ceo vrera a eux en le reuersion, ou a eux en le Remainder, auxybien come al Tenaunt de Franktenement, et aueront auxy grand aduauntage de cel, sils ceo poyent monstre.

IN the same it is, where a Release is made to the Tenant for life, or to the Tenant in Tayle, this shall enure to them in the reuersion, or to them in the remainder, as well as to the Tenant of the Freehold, and they shall haue as great aduantage of this, if they can shew it.

¶ By this it appeareth, That as a release made of a right to him in reuersion or remainder, shall ayd and benefit him that hath the particular estate for yeares, life, or estate Tayle, so a release of a right made to a particular Tenant for life, or in Taile, shall ayd and benefit him or them in the remainder. If two Tenants in Common of land graunt a Rent charge of 40.s. out of the same, to one in fee, and the Grantee release to one of them, this shall extinguish but twentie shillings, for that the Graunt in iudgement of Law was seuerall. So it is if two men be seised of seueral Acres, and grant a rent vt supra. But there is a diuersitie betweene seuerall estates in seuerall lands, and seuerall estates in one land, for if one be Tenant for life of lands, the reuersion in fee ouer to another, if they two ioine in a grant of a rent out of the Lands, if the grantee releaseth either to him in the reuersion, or to Tenaunt for life, the whole rent is extinguished, for it is but one rent, and issueth out of both estates, and so note the diuersitie.

¶ *Si le Tenaunt ad le fait en son poigne a pleader.* And so it is in both cases: for albeit hee in the reuersion or remainder is a stranger to the Deed when the release is made to the Tenant, and the Tenant for life or in Taile is a stranger to the Deed, when the Release is made to him in reuersion or remainder, yet seeing they are priuies in estate, none of them in pleading shall take benefit thereof, without shewing the same in Court, which is worthie to be obserued.

H.6.8.

¶ *Sils ceo poient monstre.* The one cannot plead the release made to the other, without shewing of it, for that they are priuie in estate, as hath beene sayd. The residue of these two Sections needs no explication.

Sect.

Section 454.

Item si soit Seignior et tenant, et le Tenaunt soit disseisie, et l'seignior relessa al Disseisee tout le droit que il auoit en l'seigniorie, ou en le terre, cel release est bone, et le Seigniorie est extinct, et ceo est pur cause del priuity, que est perenter le Seigniour, et le Disseisee, car si les auers l'Disseisee soient pris, et de eux le Disseisee suist vn Repleuin enuers le Seignior, il compellera le Seignior dauowrer sur luy, car sil auower sur le Disseisor, donques sur l'matter monstre lauowry abatera car le Disseisee est Tenant a luy en droit et en la Ley.

ALso if there bee Lord and Tenant, and the Tenant be disseised, and the Lord releaseth to the Disseisee all the right which he hath in the Seigniorie or in the Land, this Release is good, and the Seigniorie is extinct: And this is by reason of the priuitie which is betweene the Lord and the Disseisee: for if the Beasts of the Disseisee be taken, and of them the Disseisee sueth a Repleuin against the lord, hee shall compell the Lord to auow vpon him, for if hee auow vpon the disseisor, thē vpō the matter shewen the Auowrie shall abate, for the Disseisee is Tenant to him in right and in Law.

HEreupon may bee collected and obserued two diuersities. First, Betweene a Seigniorie or Rent seruice, and a rent Charge: for a Seigniory or Rent seruice may be released and extinguished to him that hath but a bare right in the Land. And the reason hereof is in respect of the priuitie betweene the Lord and the Tenant in right, for he is not only as tenant to the Auowrie, but if hee die his heire within age, he shall be in ward; and if of full age, hee shall pay reliefe, and if hee die without heire, the Land shall escheat. But there is no such priuitie in case of a Rent-charge, for there the charge only lieth vpon the Land

The second diuersitie is betweene a Seigniorie and a bare right to land: for a Release of a bare right to Land to one that hath but a bare right, is voyd, as hath been sayd. But here in the case of our Author, a release of a seigniorie to him that hath but a right, is good to extinguish the Seigniorie. *Vi. Sect. 451.*

Nota, a Seigniorie, Rent, or Right, either in præsenti, or in futuro, may be released fiue manner of wayes, and the first three without any priuitie. First, To the Tenant of the Freehold in Deed or in Law. Secondly, To him in remainder. Thirdly, To him in the reuersion. The other two in respect of Priuitie, as first, here the Lord releaseth his Seigniorie to the Tenant being disseised, hauing but a right, and no estate at all. Secondly, in respect of the priuitie, without any estate or right, as by the Demandant to the Vouchee, or Donor to the Donee, after the Donee hath discontinued in fee, as appeareth hereafter in this Chapter. *Li. 10 fo 48. Lampets case.* *Sect. 455.*

Per cause de priuitie, &c. See for this word (Priuitie) Sect. 461.

Il compellera le Seignior danowrer sur luy, &c. This is regularly true, but if the Lord hath accepted seruices of the Disseisor, then the Disseisee cannot enforce the Lord to auow vpon him, though his beasts be taken, &c. *20. H. 6. 9 b. 41. E. 3. 26. 48 E. 3. 9. 2. E. 4. 6. a.*

If a man hath title to haue a writ of Escheat, if he accept homage or fealtie of the Tenaunt, he is barred of his writ of Escheat: but if he accept rent of the Tenant, that is no bar to him, for it may be receiued by the hands of a Baylife. (d) But some doe hold, that if there be Lord and Tenant, and the Tenant be disseised, and the Disseisee die without heire, the Lord accepts rent by the hands of the Disseisor, this is no barre to him. Contrarie it is if he auow for the Rent in Court of Record, or if he take a corporall seruice, as homage or Fealtie, for the disseisor is in by wrong: but if the Lord accept the rent by the hands of the heire of the Disseisor, or of his Feoffee, because they be in by title, this shall barre him of his Escheat. Which is to *31. E. 1. Disseit 17. 26. E. 3. 72. 4. H. 6. 21. F. N. B. 144. e. (d) 7. E. 6. tit. Escheat Br. 18*

bee

(c) 7. H. 4. 17. 3. R. 2. Entr. cong. 38. 2. H. 4. 8. 6. H. 7. 9. Vi Sect. 556.

(f) 21. H. 8. ca. 19.

Li. 9. fo. 136. Ascoughs case.

27. H. 8. fo. 4. 32. H. 8. ca. 2. Lib. 9. fo. 36. Bucknals case.

34. H. 8. Auowrie Br. 113. 27. H. 8. 4. & 20. Bucknals case vbi supra.

Li. 9. fo. 22. in case Dauowrie. 44. E. 3. 20. 11. H. 7. 4. 21. H. 7. 40. 34. H. 6. 18. 16. E. 4. 10. 6. R. 2. Rescous 32.

be vnderstood of a discent or feoffement, after the title of Escheat accrued: (c) for if the Disseisor make a Feoffement in Fee, or die seised, and after the Disseisee die without heire, then there is no Escheat at all, because the Lord hath a Tenant in by Title. And when Littleton wrote, the Disseisee in the case here put, should haue compelled the Lord to haue auowed vpon him, as Littleton holdeth. But now this is altered by a latter Stat. of (f) 21. H. 8. for whereas by Fines, Recoueries, Grants, and secret Feoffements, &c. made by Tenaunts to persons vnknowne, the Lords were put from knowledge of their Tenants, vpon whom by order of law they should make their Auowries, &c. It is by that Statute enacted, That if the Lord shall distreyne vpon the Lands or Tenements holden, &c. that he may auow, &c. vpon the same Lands, &c. as in Lands, &c. within his Fee or Seigniorie, &c. without naming of any person certaine, and without making auowrie vpon a person certaine. Vpon which Statute these foure poynts are to be obserued: First, That the Lord hath still election either to auow according to the Common Law, by force of the Statute, by reason of this word (May.) Secondly, Albeit the purview of the Act be generall, yet all necessarie incidents are to be supplied, and the scope and end of the Act to be taken: and therefore though he need not to make his auowrie vpon any person certaine, yet he must alledge Seisin by the Lands of some Tenant in certaine, within fortie yeares. Thirdly, That if the Auowrie be made according to the Statute, euerie Plaintife in the Repleuin or second deliuerance, be he Termor or other, may haue euery answer to the Auowrie that is sufficient; and also haue ayd, and euerie other aduantage in Law, (disclaimer onely except) for disclaime he cannot, because in that case the auowrie is made vpon no certaine person. Fourthly, where the words of the Statute be, If the Lord distreyne vpon the Lands and Tenements holden, yet if the Lord come to distreyne, and the Tenant enchase his Beasts which were within the view, out of the Land holden, and there the Lord distreyne, albeit the distresse be taken out of his Fee and Seigniorie in that case, yet is it within the said Statute, for in iudgement of Law the distresse is lawfull, and as taken within his Fee and Seigniorie, and this Statute being made to suppresse Fraud, is to be taken by Equitie.

Sect. 455.

¶ Item si terre soit done a vn home en Taile, reseruant al Donor et a ses heires vn certaine rent, si le Donee soit disseisie, et puis le Donor relessa al Donee et a ses Heires, tout le droit que il auoit en la Terre, et puis le Donee enter en la terre sur le Disseisor, en cest case le rent est ale, pur ceo que le Disseisee al temps de releas fait, fuit tenant en droit, et en la Ley al Donor, et auowre a fine force couient de estre fait sur luy per le Donor pur le rent aderere, &c. Mes uncore rien de droit d' terres, s. de le droit, de le reuersion passera per tiel Release, pur ceo que le Donee a que le Release est fait, adonque nauoit riens en la Terre forsque tantsolement vn droit, et issint le droit del Terre ne puissoit adonques passer al Donee per tiel Release.

ALso if Land be giuen to a man in Taile, reseruing to the Donor and to his heires a certain rent, if the Donee be disseised, and after the Donor release to the donee and his heires all the right which hee hath in the Land, and after the Donee enter into the Land vpon the Disseisor, in this case the Rent is gone, for that the Disseisee at the time of the Release made, was Tenant in Right, and in Law to the Donor, and the Auowrie of Fine force ought to bee made vpon him by the Donor for the rent behind, &c. but yet nothing of the right of the lands, (scz.) of the reuersion, shall passe by such release, for that the Donee to whom the Release is made, then had nothing in the Land but onely a right, and so the right of the Land could not then passe to the Donee by such Release.

¶ Si

¶ *SI le donee soit disseisie, &c.* This is evident by that which hath beene said. But admit that the Donee maketh a feoffment in fee, and the Donor release unto him and his heires, all the right in the land, this shall extinguish the rent, because the Lord must avow upon him, and yet the tenant in taile after the feoffment hath no right in the land. But the reason is in respect of the privitie, and that the (m) Donor is by necessitie compellable to avow upon him only, for if hee should avow upon the discontinuee, then it should appeare of his owne shewing, that the reversion whereunto the rent is incident should bee out of him, and consequently the avowrie should abate, and so was it (n) resolved Trin. 18. Eliz. in the Court of Common Pleas in Sir Thomas Wiats case, which I heard and observed. And Littleton saith here that in case of the Disseisin of fine force, the avowrie must be made upon the Donee.

Vide Sect. 454. 1. *H.* 5. *tit. grant* 43. 14. *H.* 4. 38. *lib.* 3. *fol.* 29. *lib* 6. 58. *Lampets case ubi supra.*

(m) 10. *L.* 3. 26. 48. *E.* 3. 8. *b.* 31. *E.* 3. *gard.* 116. 5. *E.* 4. 3. 7. *E.* 4. 27. 15. *E.* 4. 13.

(n) *Trin.* 18. *Eliz. Sir Thomas Wiats case in Communi Banco.*

¶ *Uncore riens de droit, &c. de reversion, &c.* Here the diversitie aforesaid betweene the Rent Service, and a bare Right to the land appeareth.

Section 456.

¶ EN mesme le manner est, si leas soit a un pur terme de vie, reservant al lessor et a ses heires certaine rent, si le lessee soit disseisie, et puis lessor relessa al lessee et a ses heires, tout le droit que il ad en la terre, & apres le lessee enter, coment que en cest cas le rent est extinct, uncore rien del droit de la reversion passera, Causa qua supra.

IN the same manner it is, if a lease be made to one for terme of life, reserving to the lessor and to his heires a certaine rent, if the lessee be disseised, and after the Lessor release to the Lessee and to his heires all the right which he hath in the land, and after the lessee entreth, albeit in this case the rent is extinct, yet nothing of the right of the reversion shall passe, *Causa qua supra.*

¶ HEreby the diversity is made apparant betweene a Release of a Rent Service out of Land, and a Release of right to Land in this Section.

Sect. 457.

¶ MEs si soit veray seignior & veray tenant, et le tenāt fait un feoffmēt en fee, le quel feoffee ne unque devient tenant al Seignior, si l' Seignior relessa al feoffor tout son droit &c. cest releas est en tout void, pur ceo q̄ le feoffor ad nul droit en la terre & il nest Tenant en droit al

BUt if there be very Lord & very tenāt, and the tenant maketh a feoffment in fee, the which feoffee doth never become tenant to the Lord, if the Lord release to the feoffor all his right, &c. this release is altogether void, because the feoffor hath no right in the Land, and hee is not Tenant in right to the

¶ *VEray Seignior & veray tenant.* This is to be understood of a Lord in fee simple, and of a Tenant of like estate.

There bee foure manner of avowries for Rents and Services, &c, viz. 1. Super verum tenentem, as in the case here put. 2. Super verum tenentem in forma prædicta, as where a Lease for life, or a gift in taile bee made, the remainder in fee. 3. upon one as upon his tenant by the manor omitting (verie) and this is when the Lord hath a particular estate in the Seignorie, and so shall the Donor

Vide Ascoughes case lib. 9. *fol.* 135. 136. 20. *H.* 6. 9. 2. *H.* 4. 24. 12. *E.* 4. 2. 26. *H.* 6. *avowrie* 17. 9. *Eliz. Dier* 257. 5. *H.* 7. 11. 7. *E.* 4. 24. 20. *E.* 3. *avowrie* 131.

Seignior, mes tant solement tenant quāt al auowry faire, et il ne vnques compellera le Seignior dauower sur luy, car le Seignior auowera sur le feoffee s'il voile.

Lord, but only tenant as to make the auowre, and hee shall neuer compell the Lord to auow vpon him, for the Lord shall auow vpon the feoffee if he will.

vpon the Donee or Lessor vpon the Lessee. 4. Sur le matter en la terre, as within his fee and Seigniorie. As where the tenant by Knights Seruice maketh a Lease for life reseruing a Rent, and die his heire within age, the Gardeine shall auow vpon the Lessee, sc. Super materiam prædictam in terris & tenementis prædictis vt infra feodum & Dominium suum. Now by the Statute the very Lord may auow, as in Lands within his fee and Seigniorie, without auowing vpon any person in certaine.

47.E.3.fol.vltimo. 38.H.6.23.

21.H.8.cap.19.

Here appeareth the diuersitie betweene a Tenant in Taile, and a Tenant in Fee Simple, for albeit Tenant in Taile make a feoffment in fee, yet the right of the Entaile remaine, and shall discend to the Issue in taile. But when the Tenant in fee simple make a feoffment in fee, no right at all remaine of his estate, but the whole is transferred to the Feoffee.

Also the Lord is not compellable in that case to auow vpon the Feoffor, but if hee will as Littleton here saith, he may auow on the feoffee, but so it is not as hath beene said in case of tenant in taile.

Note a diuersity betweene Actions and Acts which concerne the right, and Actions and Acts which concerne the possession only. For a Writ of Customes and Seruices lyeth not against the feoffor, nor a release to him shall extinguish the Seigniory. So if a Rescous be made an Assise shall not lie against the feoffor, and him that made the Rescous, because the feoffee is Tenant, and in Assise, the surplusage incroached shall bee auoyded. For these Actions and Acts concerne the right, but of a seisin, and an auowrie which concerne the possession, it is otherwise. And if the Lord release to the feoffor this is good betweene them as to the possession and discharge of the Arrerages, but the feoffee shall not take benefit of it, for that, as hath been said, it extendeth not to the right. But the feoffor shall plead a Release to the feoffee, for thereby the Seigniorie is extinct, as if Lessee for life doth waste, and grant ouer his estate, and the Lessor release to the Grantee, in an Action of waste against the Lessee, he shall plead the release, and yet he hath nothing in the land. And so in waste shall tenant in Dower or by the Courtesie in the like case, and the vouchee, and the Tenant in a Præcipe after a feoffment made. And so in a Contra formam collationis.

4.E.3.22.7.E.3.8.7.E.4.27 29.H.8.tit. auowry. Br.111. Lib.3.fol.65.66. Pennants case.7.H.4.14.

¶ *Le feoffee ne vnques deueigne tenant.* Nota, here an excellent point of Learning, viz. if there bee Lord and Tenant, and the Rent is behind by diuers yeares, and the Tenant make a feoffment in fee, if the Lord accept the Seruice or Rent of the feoffee due in his time, hee shall lose the Arrerages due in the time of the feoffor, for after such acceptance he shall not auow vpon the feoffor, nor vpon the feoffee for the Arrerages incurred in the time of the feoffor. But in that case if the feoffor dieth, albeit the Lord accept the Rent or Seruice by the hand of the feoffee due in his time, he shall not loose the Arrerages for now the Law compelleth him to auow vpon the feoffee, and that which the Law compelleth him vnto, shall not preiudice him.

9.E.4.6.34.H.6.46. 37.H.6.29.H.8. auowrie.

So it is and for the same reason, if there be Lord, Mesne, and Tenant, and the rent due by the Mesne is behind, and after the Tenant forejudge the Mesne, and the Lord receiue the Seruices of the Mesne which issue out of the Tenancie, he shall not be barred of the Arrerages which issued out of the Mesnaltie, and so if the rent be behind, and the Tenant dieth, the acceptance of the seruices by the hand of the heire shall not barre him of the Arrerages, for in these cases albeit the persons be altered, yet the Lord doth accept the seruices of him which only ought to doe them.

4.E.3.22.47.E.3.4.

But as long as the feoffor liueth the Lord shall not bee compelled to auow vpon the feoffee, vnlesse he giueth the Lord notice, and tender vnto him all the Arrerages.

21.H.8.cap.19.

But now by the Statute the Lord may auow vpon the Lands so holden, as in lands within his Fee or Seigniory without naming of any person certaine to bee Tenant of the same, and without making of any auowrie vpon any person certaine, as hath beene said, which hath much altered the Common Law in the cases abouesaid, for the benefit and safetie of the Lord.

But yet these cases are necessary to bee knowne (for which purpose I haue added them) for that the Lord may auow still at the Common Law if he will.

Sect. 458.

¶ Autrement est lou le veray tenant est disseisie, come en le cas auantdit, car si le veray tenant que est disseisie teigne del Seignior per seruice de chiualer, & morust (son heire esteant deins age) le Seignior auera & seisera le garde del heire, & issint nauera il my le gard del feoffor que fist le feoffment en fee, &c. issint il est graund diuersity enter les deux cases, &c.

Otherwise it is where the verie tenant is disseised, as in the case aforesaid, for if the very tenant who is disseised, hold of the Lord by Knights Seruice and dieth (his heire being within age) the Lord shall haue and seize the Wardship of the heire, and so shall he not haue the ward of the feoffor that made the feoffment in fee, &c. So there is a great diuersitie betweene these two cases.

Of this sufficient hath beene said before.

12.H.4.13. 36.E.3.tit gard. 10. 6.H.7.9. 37.H.6.1. 3[illegible] H.6.27. 7 E.6.tit.gard.

Section 459.

¶ Item si vn home lessa a vn auter son terre pur terme dans, si le lessor relessa al lessee tout son droit, &c. deuant que le lessee auoit enter en mesme le terre per force de mesme le leas, tiel releas est void, pur ceo que le lessee nauoit poss. en la terre al temps del releas fait, mes tantsolement vn droit dauer mesme la terre per force de mesme le leas. Mes si le lessee enter en mesme la terre, & ent eit poss. per force de mesme le leas, donque tiel releas fait a luy per le feoffor, ou per son heire, est sufficient a luy per cause del priuitie, que per force del leas est perenter eux, &c.

Also if a man letteth to another his land for tearme of yeares, if the lessor release to the lessee all his right, &c. before that the lessee had entred into the same land by force of the same lease, such release is void, for that the lessee had not possession in the land at the time of the release made, but only a right to haue the same land by force of the lease. But if the lessee enter into the land, and hath possessiō of it by force of the said lease, then such release made to him by the feoffor, or by his heire is sufficient to him, by reason of the priuitie which by force of the lease is betweene them, &c.

¶ *Deuant que le lessee auoit enter, &c.* For before entry the Lessee hath but *interesse termini*, an interest of a terme and no possession, and therefore a release which enure by way of inlarging of an estate cannot worke without a possession, for before possession there is no reuersion, and yet if a tenant for twentie yeares in possession make a lease to B. for fiue yeares, and B. enter, a release to the first lessee is good, for he had an actuall possession, and the possession of his Lessee is his possession. And so it is if a man make a lease for yeares, the remaynder for yeares, and the first lessee doth enter, a release to him in the remaynder for yeares is good to inlarge his estate.

49.E.3.28. 32.H.6.8. 37.H.6.18. 22.E.4.37. 4.H.7.10. 15.H.7.14.

22.E.4. Surrender 6.

But if a man make a lease for yeares to begin presently, reseruing a rent, if before the lessee doth enter the lessor releaseth all the right that hee hath in the land, albeit this release cannot inlarge his estate, yet it shall in respect of the priuitie extinguish the rent. And so it is if a lease be made to begin at *Michaelmas*, reseruing a rent, and before the day the lessor release all the right that hee hath in the land, this cannot enure to

(b) Mich.39.& 40.Eliz. in Scaccario, betweene Sir Henry Woodhouse and Sir William Paston.

enlarge the estate but to extinguish the rent in respect of the priuitie, as it was resolued (b) in the Exchequer which I obserued.

A man granteth the next auoydance of an Aduowson to two, the one of them may before the Church become voide release to the other, for although the Grantor cannot release to them to encrease their estate, because their interest is future, and not in possession, yet one of them to extinguish his interest may release to the other in respect of the priuity. But after the Church become voide, then such a Release is voide, because then it is (as it were) but a thing in action. And this was resolued (c) by the whole Court of Common pleas, which I my selfe heard and obserued. And by consequent in the case of Littleton, if a Lease for yeares be made to two, albeit the Lessor before they enter cannot Release to them to enlarge their estate, yet one of them may before entrie Release to the other.

(c) Pasch.38.Eliz. in quare impedit per Bennet vers. leuesque de Norwich in Communi banco.

Pl. Com. 423.

¶ *Mes tant solement vn droit,&c.* Which is not so to bee vnderstood that hee hath but a naked right, for then he could not grant it ouer, but seeing hee hath Interesse termini before entrie, he may grant it ouer, albeit for want of an actuall possession he is not capable of a Release to enlarge his estate.

¶ *Mes si le lessee enter en mesme le terre,&c.* This is euident. And herein note a diuersitie betweene a Lease for life, and for yeares, for before the Lessee for yeares enter, a Release cannot be made vnto him, but if a man make a Lease for life, the Remainder for life, and the first Lessee dieth, a Release to him in the remainder and to his heires is good before he doth enter to enlarge his estate, for that he hath an estate of a Freehold in Law in him, which may be enlarged by Release before entrie.

25.E.3.53.31.E.3. Confirmat.14.31.Ass. Pl.13.

And where our Author speaketh only of a Lessee for yeares, the same law it is of a Tenant by Statute merchant or Staple, or Tenant by Elegit or the like.

Sect. 460. & 461.

21.H.6.37.2.E.4.6.b. 7.E.4.27. 8.E.4.16. 29.H.6. Release 6.

¶ By these two Sections is to bee obserued a diuersitie betweene a Tenant at will and a Tenant at sufferance, for a release to a Tenant at will is good, because betweene them there is a possession with a priuity, but a Release to a Tenant at sufferance is voyd because he hath a possession without priuity. As if Lessee for yeares hold ouer his terme,&c. a Release to him is voide for that there is no priuity betweene them, and so are the bookes that speake of this matter to be vnderstood.

¶ * *Sed contrariū tenetur,&c.* This is of a new addition, and the booke here cited ill vnderstood, for it is to be vnderstood of a Tenant at sufferance.

¶ *De sa teste demesne occupia.* Hee doth not say, De sa teste

¶ En mesme le maner est, come il semble, ou lease est fait a vn home, a tener de l'lessor a sa volunt, per force de quel leas le lessee eit possession, si le lessor en cest case fait vn releas al lessee de tout son droit,&c. cest releas est assets bon pur le priuitie que est penter eux, car en vain serra d'faire estate per vn liuerie de seisin a vn auter, lou il ad possession de mesmes les tenements per le leas de mesme celuy deuant,&c.

¶ * Sed contrariū tenetur, P.2.Ed.4. ꝑ touts les Justices.

¶ In the same manner it is as it seemeth, where a Lease is made to a man to hold of the Lessor at his will, by force of which Lease the Lessee hath possession, if the Lessor in this case make a release to the Lessee of all his right,&c. this release is good enough for the priuity which is betweene them, for it shall bee in vaine to make an estate by a liuery of seisin to another where he hath possession of the same land by the lease of the same mā before,&c.

But the contrarie is holden, *Pasch.2.E.4.* by all the Iustices.

Sect. 461.

¶ Mes lou home de sa teste demesñ occupia terrẽs ou tenements a la volunt celuy que ad le franktenement, & tiel occupier ne claima riens forsq; a volunt, &c. si celuy que ad le franktenement voile releaser tout son droit al occupier, &c. tiel Release est voide, pur ceo que nul privity ẽ perenter eux per lease fait al occupier, ne per auter maner, &c.

BUt where a man of his owne head occupieth lands or tenements at the will of him which hath the freehold, and such occupier claimeth nothing but at will, &c. if hee which hath the freehold will release all his right to the occupier, &c. this release is voide, because there is no privity betweene them by the lease made to the occupier, nor by other manner, &c.

demesñ enẽ, &c. so as this is to bee understood of a Tenant at sufferance, viz. where a man commeth to the possession first lawfully, and holdeth over. (m) For if a man entreth into land of his owne wrong, and take the profits, his words to hold it at the will of the owner cannot qualifie his wrong, but hee is a Disseisor, and then the Release to him is good, or if the owner consented thereunto, then hee is a Tenant at will, and that way also the Release is good. But there is a diversity when one commeth to a particular estate in land by the act of the partie, and when by act in Law, for if the Gardein hold over, hee is an abator because his interest came by act in Law.

Vid. Sect. 68.

(m) Temps H. 8. tit. Tenant a volunt, Br. 15. 2. E. 4. 38. 18. E. 4. 25. 39. E. 3. 28. 12. E. 3. Ass. 86. 11. E. 3. ibid. 87. 12. Ass. 21. 13. E. 3. Ass. 92. 28. Ass. 11. 34. Ass. 10. 10. E. 3. 41. 8. E. 3. 63.

Vid. 2. part of the Institutes Marlbr. ca. 16. & 10. E. 4. 9. 10.

¶ *Nul privitye.* Privitie, is a word common aswell to the English, as to the French, and in the understanding of the Common Law is Fourefoulde.

1 As Privies in Estate, whereof Littleton here speaketh, as betweene the Donor and Donee, Lessor and Lessee, which privitie is ever immediate.

2 Privies in Blood, as the heire to the ancestor, or betweene Coparceners, &c.

3 Privies in Representation, as Executors, &c. to the Testator,

And fourthly, Privities in Tenure, as the Lord and Tenant, &c. which may bee reduced to two generall heads, Privies in Deed, and Privies in Law.

Old N. B. 117. 137. Lib. 3. fo. 23. Walkers case. Lib. 4. fo. 123. 124. Vid. Sect. 454.

Sect. 462. & 463.

¶ Item si home enfeoffe autrẽs hõẽs de sa terre sur confidence, et al entent de performer sa darreiñ volunt, et le feoffor occupiast mesme la terre a le voluñt de ses feoffees, et puis les feoffees relessont per lour fait a lour feoffor tout lour droit, &c. ceo ad este un question, si tiel releas soit bon ou non. Et ascũs ont dit, q̃ tiel releas

ALso if a man enfeoffe other men of his land upon confidence, and to the intent to performe his last will, & the feoffor occupieth the same land at the will of his feoffees, and after the feoffees release by their deed to their feoffor all their right, &c. this hath beene a question if such release be good or no. And some haue said, that

¶ HEre is a question moued, and the reasons of both sides shewed, and as it hath beene observed, the latter opinion is the better, being Littletons owne opinion.

12. E. 4. 12. b. 15. E. 4. 9. H. 7. 25. Vid. Sect. 302. 176. 340.

¶ *Il serra entendue per la ley que le feoffor doit maintenant occupie la terre a la volunt de les feoffees.* For intendments of Law mentioned by our Author See the Sections in the margent.

4. E. 4. 8. b. 9. H. 7. fo. ultimo. 15. H. 7. 2. b. 14. H. 8. 9. a.

Sect. 99. 100. 110. 367. 377. 393. 406. 440.

Here is to bee observed the intendment of Law, that when a feoffment is made to a future use, as to the performance of his last will, the feoffees shall bee seised to the use

35. H. 6. Subpoena 22. 15. H. 7. 12. b. 37. H. 6. 36. 11. H. 4. 52. 7. H. 4. 22. 1. Mar. 112. Dier.

est voyd, pur ceo que nul priuitie fuit perenter les Feoffees et lour feoffor, entant que nul Lease fuit fait apres tiel feoffement per les feoffees al Feoffor, a tener a lour volunt. Et ascuns ont dit le contrarie, et ceo p̄ deux causes.

such Release is voyd, because there was no priuitie between the feoffees and their feoffor, in somuch as no Lease was made after such feoffement by the feoffees to the feoffor, to hold at their will: and some haue said the contrarie, and that for two causes.

Sect.463.

VNe est, Que quãt tiel feoffement est fait sur confidence a performer la volunt del feoffor il serra intendue per la Ley, que le Feoffor doit maintenant occupier la terre a la volunt de ses Feoffees, et issint il est tiel manner de priuitie enter eux, sicome hōe fait vn feoffement as auters, et ils incontinent sur le Feoffement, voylent & grãterõt que lour feoffor occupiera la Terre a lour volunt, &c.

ONe is, That when such Feoffement is made vpon confidence to performe the will of the Feoffor, it shall bee intended by the Law, that the feoffor ought presently to occupie the Land at the will of his Feoffees, and so there is the like kind of priuitie betweene them: As if a man make a Feoffement to others, & they immediately vpon the feoffement, will and grant, that their Feoffor shall occupie the Land at their wil, &c.

vse of the Feoffor and of his heires in the meane time.

Ipsę etenim Leges cupiunt vt iure regantur.

And reason would that seeing the Feoffement is made without consideration, and the feoffor hath not disposed of the profits in the meane time, that by construction and intendment of Law the Feoffor ought to occupie the same in the meane time. And so it is
35.H.6.Subpena, 22. 30.H.6.tit. Deuise.
when the Feffor disposeth the profits for a particular time in præsenti, the vse of the Inheritance shall be to the Feoffor and his heires, as a thing not disposed of. Wherein it is to be obserued, That Lands and Tenements conueyed vpon confidences, vses, and trusts, are to be ruled and decided, if question groweth vpon the confidences, vses, or trusts, by the Judges of the Law: for that it appeareth by this and the next Section, they are within the Entendment and construction of the Lawes of the Realme.

And it is to be obserued (as hath beene sayd) that there is a diuersitie betweene a feoffement of lands at this day vpon confidence, or to the intent to performe his last will, and a Feoffment to the vse of such person and persons, and of such estate and estates, as he shall appoynt by his last will, for in the first case, the Land passeth by the will, and not by the Feoffement, for after the Feoffement the Feoffor was seised in Fee simple as he was before, but in the latter Case the will pursuing his power is but a direction of the vses of the Feoffement, and the Estates passe by execution of the vses which were raised vpon the Feoffement, but in both cases the Feoffees are seised to the vse of
Lib.6.fo.17.18.Sir Edward Cleres case.
the Feoffor and his heires in the meane time, and all this and much more concerning this matter hath beene adiudged.

Dillon & Fraynes case, l.1.&c. fol.113.
Note, vses are raised either by transmutation of the estate, as by Fine, Feoffement, Common recouerie, &c. or out of the state of the owner of the Land by bargaine and sale by Deed indented and inrolled, or by couenant vpon lawfull consideration, whereof you may read plentifully in my Reports.

A Feoffee to the vse of A. and his heires, before the Statute of 27.H.8. for mony bargaineth and selleth the Land to C. and his heires, who hath no notice of the former vse, yet no vse passeth by this bargaine and sale, for there cannot be two vses in Esse, of one and the same Land, and seeing there is no transmutation of possession by the Terre-tenant, the former vse can neither be extinct nor altered. And if there could be two vses of one and the same Land, then could

not

not the sayd Statute execute either of them for the uncertaintie. But if A. disseise one to the use of B. and A. doth bargaine and sell the land for money to C. C. hath an use, and here be two uses of one land, but of severall natures, the one, viz. upon the bargaine and sale to be executed by the Statute, and the other not.

But since Littleton wrote, all uses are transferred by Act of Parliament, (c) into possession, so as the case which Littleton here puts is therby altogether altered. Yet it is necessarie to bee knowne what the Common Law was before the making of the Statute, and may serue for the knowledge of the Law in like case. (c) 27. H. 8. ca. 10.

¶ *Incontinent sur le Feoffement.* Quæ incontinenti fiunt in esse vident'.

¶ *A lour volunt, &c.* Here is implyed every tenancie at will is at the will of both parties, as before in his proper place hath beene shewed.

Sect. 464.

¶ Un auf cause ils allegeont, Que si tiel tre vault xl. s. per an. &c. donque tiel feoffor serra iure en assises et en auters enquests en plees realx, et auxy en plees personalls de quel graund sum que les Plaintifes voilent counter, &c. Et ceo est per l' Common ley de la Terre, Ergo ceo est pur un graund cause, et la cause est, que la Ley voet que tiels Feoffors et lour heyres doient occupier, &c. et prender et enioyer touts maner d' profits, issues, et reuenues, &c. sicome les Tenements fuerõt lour mesmes sans interruption de les Feoffees, nient obstant tiel feoffement, Ergo mesme la Ley done priuitie perenter tiels feoffors et

Another cause they alledge, That if such land bee worth fortie shillings a yere, &c. then such Feoffor shall be sworne in Assise and other enquests in Plees realls, and also in Plees personalls, of what great summe soeuer the Plaintife will declare, &c. And this is by the Common Law of the land, *Ergo* this is for a great cause, and the cause is, for that the Law will that such Feoffors and their heyres ought to occupie, &c. and take and enioy all manner of profits, issues, and reuenues, &c. as if the Lands were their own without interruption of the Feoffees, notwithstanding such Feoffement. *Ergo* the same law giueth a priuitie betweene such Feoffors and the Feoffees vpon confidence,

¶ By the Statute of 2. H. 5. cap. 3. Statut. 2. it is enacted, That in three cases he that passeth in an Enquest ought to haue Lands and Tenements to the value of fortie shillings, viz. First, Upon trial of the death of a man. Secondly, in Plea reall betweene partie and partie. And thirdly, In Plea personall, where the debt or the dammages in the Declaration amount unto fortie Markes. And it is worth the noting, That the Judges that were at the making of that Statute did construe it by equitie: for where the Stat. speakes in the disiunctiue debt or dammages, they adiudged that where the debt or dammages amounted to forty marks, that it was within the Statute. Fortescue (f) saith, Vbi damna vel debitum in personalibus Actionibus non excedunt quadraginta Marcas monetæ Anglicanæ hinc non requiritur, quod Iuratores in Actionibus huiusmodi tantum expendere possint: habebunt tamen terram vel redditum, ad valorem competentem, iuxta discretionem Iusticiariorum, &c. And for as much as at the time of the making of this Statute, the greater part of the Lands in England in those troublesome and dangerous times (when that unhappie controuersie betweene the Houses of Yorke and Lãcaster was begun) were in use. And the Statute was made to remedie a mischiefe, that

28. H. 8. Dy. fo. 9. Vi. W. 2 ca. 38. Lestat. de 21. E. 1. de Iuratis ponendis in Assisis, &c.

9. H. 5. fo. 5.

(f) Fortesc. ca. 25.

les feoffees sur confidence, &c. pur quux causes ils ont dit que tiels Releases faits per tiels feoffees sur confidēce a lour feoffor ou a ses heirs, &c. issint occupant la terre, serra assets bon, et cest le melior opinion come il semble, &c.

¶ Quære, car ceo semble nul Ley a cest iour.

&c. for which causes they haue sayd, That such releases made by such Feoffees vppon confidence to their Feoffor or to his heirs, &c. so occupying the Lands, shall bee good enough: and this is the better opinion, as it seemeth.

Quare, for this seemeth no Law at this day.

15.H.7.13.b. 13.H.7.7.b. 5.E.4.7.a.

that the Sherife vse to return simple men of small or no vnderstanding, and therefore the Statute prouided, That hee should returne sufficient men, and albeit in Law the Land was the Feoffees, yet for that they had it but vpon trust and Cesty que vse tooke the whole profits, as our Author here saith, and in equitie and conscience the Land was his, therefore the Judges for aduancement and expedition of Justice, extended the Statute (against the Letter) to Cesty que vse, and not to the Feoffees.

(n) 3.H.6.39. Challeng. 19. 21.H.6.39.

(n) But note if a man hath a Freehold pur terme dauter vie, or is seised in his wiues right, and is returned on a Jurie, yet if after he be returned, Cesty que vie, or his wife die, hee may be challenged, and so it is if after the returne the lands be enfeoffed.

¶ *Et ceo est per le Common Ley.* Here three things are to be obserued. First, That the surest construction of a Statute is by the rule and reason of the Common Law. Secondly, That vses were at the Common Law. Thirdly, That now seeing the Statute (g) of 27.H.8 cap.10. which hath beene enacted since Littleton wrote, hath transferred the possession to the vse, this case holdeth not at this day, but this latter opinion before that Statute was good Law, as Littleton here taketh it.

(g) 27.H.8.ca.10.

¶ *Mesme la Ley done priuitie, &c.* Hereof it followeth, That when the Law giues to any man any estate or possession, the Law giueth also a priuitie and other necessaries to the same: and Littleton concludeth it with an Illatiue, Ergo mesme la ley done priuitie, which is verie obseruable for a conclusion in other cases.

And the (Quære) here made in the end of this Section is not in the Originall, but added by some other, and therefore to be reiected.

27.El.ca.6.

Also since Littleton wrote the sayd Statute of 2.H 5. is altered: for where that Statute limited fortie shillings, now a latter Statute hath raised it to foure pounds, and so it ought to be contained in the Venire facias.

Pl.Com.352.b. in Dalamere case, & 349.b. Li.1.fo.121.122.127.140. in Chudleys case. Li.2 fo 58.78. Li.6.fo.64. Li.7.fo.13.& 33.

Nota, an Use is a Trust or Confidence reposed in some other, which is not issuing out of the land, but as a thing collateral, annexed in priuitie to the estate of the land, and to the person touching the Land, scz. that Cesty que vse shall take the profit, and that the Terre-Tenaunt shall make an estate according to his direction. So as Cesty que vse had neither Ius in re, nor Ius ad rem, but onely a confidence and trust, for which he had no remedie by the Common law, but for breach of trust his remedie was onely by Subpœna in Chancerie: and yet the Judges for the cause aforesayd, made the sayd construction vpon the sayd Statute.

Forteſc.ca.25,26,27.

Now how Jurors shall be returned, both in Common Plees, and also in Plees of the Crowne, and in what manner euidence shall be giuen to them, and how they shall be kept, vntill they giue their verdict, you may read in Forteſcue, and therefore need not to be here inserted.

Sect. 465.

¶ Item Releases solonque le matter en fait, ascun foits ont lour effect per force denlarger lestate celuy, a que le

ALso Releases according to the matter in fact, sometimes haue their effect by force to enlarge the state of him to

Flet li.5.ca.34. 15.H.7.14. 22.E 4.4.

¶ It is a certaine rule that when a Release doth enure by way of enlarging of an estate, that there must bee priuitie of estate, as betweene Lessor and Lessee, Donor and Donee. For if A. make a Lease to B. for life, and the

le releaſe eſt fait. Sicome ieo leſſa certain terre a vn home pur terme des ans, per force de que il eſt en poſſ. & puis ieo releſſa a luy tout le droit que ieo aye en le terre ſans pluis parolx mitter en le fait, & deliuer a luy le fait, donques il ad eſtate forſque pur terme de ſa vie. Et la cauſe eſt, pur ceo que quant le reuerſion ou le remainder eſt en vn home, le quel voile enlarger per ſon releas leſtate le tenant, &c. il nauera pluis greinder eſtate, mes en tiel manner & forme, ſicome tiel feoffor fuit ſeiſie en fee, & volloit per ſon fait faire eſtate a vn en certaine forme, & deliuer a luy ſeiſin ꝑ force ð meſme le fait: ſi en tiel fait de feoffement ne ſoit aſcun parol ð enheritance, donques il ad forſqꝫ eſtate pur terme de vie, & iſſint il eſt en tiels releaſes faits per eux en la reuerſion ou en le remainder. Car ſi ieo leſſa la terre a vn home pur terme ð ſa vie, & puis ieo releſſa a luy tout mon droit, ſauns plus dire ē le releas,

whom the releaſe is made. As if I let certaine Land to one for tearme of yeares, by force whereof hee is in poſſeſſion, and after I releaſe to him all the right which I haue in the land without putting more words in the Deed, and deliuer to him the Deed, then hath hee an eſtate but for tearme of his life. And the reaſon is for that when the reuerſion or remaynder is in a man who will by his releaſe inlarge the eſtate of the Tenant, &c. hee ſhall haue no greater eſtate, but in ſuch manner & forme, as if ſuch leſſor were ſeiſed in fee, and by his Deed will make an eſtate to one in a certain forme, and deliuer to him ſeiſin by force of the ſame Deed: if in ſuch Deed of feoffement there be not any word of Inheritance, then he hath but an eſtate for life, and ſo it is in ſuch Releaſes made by thoſe in the reuerſion or in the remainder. For if I let land to a man for tearme of his life, and after I releaſe to him all my right without more ſaying in the releaſe, his eſtate is not

Leſſee maketh a Leaſe for yeares, and after A. releaſeth to the Leſſee for yeares, and his heires, this releaſe is void to inlarge the eſtate, becauſe there is no priuitie betweene A. and the Leſſee for yeares.

If a man make a Leaſe for twentie yeares, and the Leſſee make a Leaſe for ten yeares, if the firſt Leſſor doth releaſe to the ſecond Leſſee and his heires, this releaſe is void for the cauſe aforeſaid.

For the ſame cauſe, if the Donee in taile make a Leaſe for his owne life, and the Donor releaſe to the Leſſee and his heires, this releaſe is void to inlarge the eſtate.

And as priuitie is neceſſarie in this caſe, ſo priuitie onely is not ſufficient. As if an Infant make a Leaſe for life, and the Leſſee granteth over his eſtate with warranty, the Infant at full age bringeth a Dum fuit infra ætatem, the Tenant voucheth his Grantor, who entreth into warrantie, the demaundant releaſeth to him and his heires; Here is priuitie in Law, and a tenancie in ſuppoſition of Law, and yet becauſe hee in rei veritate hath no eſtate, it cannot enure to him by way of inlargement, for how can his eſtate bee inlarged, that hath not any.

If a Tenant by the curteſie grant over his eſtate, yet he is tenant as to an Action of waſte, Attornement, &c. and yet a Releaſe to him and his heires cannot enure to inlarge his eſtate that hath no eſtate at all.

But if a man make a leaſe for yeares, the remaynder for life, a releaſe by the Leſſor to the Leſſee for yeares, and to his heires, is good for that hee hath both a priuitie and an eſtate, and the releaſe alſo to him in the remaynder for life and his heires is good alſo.

If I grant the reuerſion of my Tenant for life, to another for life, now ſhall not I haue an Action of waſte: but if I releaſe to the Grantee for life and his heires, now hee hath the Fee ſimple, and ſhall

48. E. 3. 18. 26 per Perſey & Finchden.
41. E. 3. 17. a. 7. E. 4. 17.

son estate nest my enlarge. Mes si ieo relessa a luy & a ses heires, donques il ad fee simple, et si ieo relessa a luy & a ses heires de son corps engendres, donques il ad fee taile, &c. Et issint il couient de specifier en le fait quel estate celuy a que le releas est fait auera.

enlarged, but if I release to him and to his heires, then he hath a Fee simple, and if I release to him and to his heires of his bodie begotten, then he hath a fee taile, &c. And so it behoueth to specifie in the Deed what estate hee to whom the Release is made shall haue.

punish the waste done after.

It is further to bee obserued, that to a release that enureth by way of inlargement of the estate, there is not only required priuitie, as hath beene said, and an estate also, but sufficient words in Law to raise or create a new estate.

If a man make a Lease to A. for tearme of the life of B. and after release to A. all his right in the land by this, A. hath an estate for tearme of his owne life, for a lease for terme of his owne life is higher in iudgement of Law, then an estate for tearme of another mans life.

16.H.6. release 45. 22.E.2. release. Sta ham.

If a Fem-Couert be Tenant for life, a release to the husband and his heires is good, for there is both priuitie and an estate in the husband, whereupon the release may sufficiently enure by way of inlargement (a) for by the entermarriage he gaineth a freehold in his wifes right.

(a) 13.H.4.6. Stauf. prer. 7.b. 18.E.4.5.22. Ass. 12. 11.H.7.19. 10.H.6.11.

¶ *Tout le droit.* Vide Sect. 650.

¶ *Pur terme des ans.* So it is if a release bee made to tenant by Statute, Staple, or Merchant, or Tenant by Elegit, as hath beene said, and so likewise to Gardeine in Chiualrie which holdeth in for the value, by him in the reuersion of all his right in the land, by this a freehold passeth for the life of him to whom the release is made, for that is the greatest estate that can passe without apt words of Inheritance.

If a man make a lease for ten yeares, the remainder for twentie yeares, he in the remaynder releaseth all his right to the Lessee, he shall haue an estate for thirtie yeares, for one Chattle cannot drowne another, and yeares cannot be consumed in yeares.

¶ *Mes si ieo release a luy & a ses heires, &c.* Here it is to be obserued that when a release doth enure by way of enlargement of an estate no Inheritance either in Fee simple, or Fee taille, can passe without apt words of Inheritance.

9. Eliz. Dier. 263. 10. Eliz. Bend oct. Litt. lib. 3. fol. 68. 69. 70. b. 130. b.

But there is a diuersitie betweene a release that enureth by way of enlargement of the state and by way of mitter lestate, for when an estate passeth by way of mitter lestate, there sometime there need not any words of Inheritance. As if a ioynt estate be made to the husband and to his wife, and to a third person and to their heires, the third person releaseth all his right to the husband, this shall enure by way of mitter lestate, and not by way of enlargement of the estate, because the husband had a Fee simple, and needeth not to haue any words of Inheritance. So it is if the release had beene made to the wife.

See before in the Chapter of Fee Simple.

(b) 40.E.3.41. 46.E.3. 19.H.6.33. H.6.5. 10.E.4.3.

(b) If there be three Joyntenants, and one release to one of the other all his right, this enureth by way of mitter lestate, & passeth the whole Fee simple without these words (heires.) But if there be two Joyntenants, and the one of them release all his right to the other, this doth not to all purposes enure by way of mitter lestate, for it maketh no degree, and he to whom the release is made shall for many purposes be adiudged in from the first feoffor, and this release shall vest, all in the other Joyntenant without these words (heires.)

10.E.4.3.b. 37.H.8. tit alienation. Br. 31. 8.H.4.8. 40. Ass. 5. 9. Eliz. Dier 263.

But if there be two Coparceners, and the one release all his right to the other, this shall enure by way of mitter lestate and shall make a degree, and without these words (heires) shall passe the whole Fee simple. And it is to bee obserued, that to releases that enure by way of mitter lestate, there must be priuitie of estate at the time of the release.

If two Coparceners be of a rent, and the one of them take the Ter-tenant to husband, the other may Release to her, notwithstanding the rent be in suspence, and it shall inure by way of Mitter lestate, and she may Release also to the Ter-tenant, and that shall enure by way of extinguishment: but if she Release to her sister and to her husband, it is good to be seene how it shall enure.

Vid. Litt. fo. 68. 69.

Littleton hauing now spoken of Releases that enure by way of Enlargement of the estate, and of Releases that enure by way of Mitter lestate, proceedeth to Releases that enure by way of Mitter le droit. So as of that which hath beene and shall be said by our Author of Releases, it appeareth that some doe enure by way of Enlargement of estate, some by way of Mitter lestate, some by way of Mitter le droit, by way of Entrie and Feoffment, and some by Extinguishment.

Sect.466.

¶ Item ascuns foits releases vera de mitter et vester le droit celuy que fait le release, a celuy a que le reles est fait. Sicome un home est disseisi, et il relessa a son disseisor tout le droit que il ad, en cest cas le disseisor ad son droit, issint que lou son estate adevant fuit torcious, ore per tiel releas il est fait loyal et droiturel.

ALso sometimes Releases shall enure de mitter and vest the right of him which makes the Release to him to whom the Release is made. As if a man be disseised, and he releaseth to his disseisor all his right. In this case the disseisor hath his right, so as where before his state was wrongfull, now by this release it is made lawfull and right.

¶ *Et il relessa a son disseisor, &c.* This release so putteth the right of the Disseisee to the Disseisor, that it changeth the quality of the estate of the Disseisor for where his estate was before wrongfull, it is by this Release made lawfull. But how farre and to what respects his estate is changed shall be said hereafter in this Chapter in his proper place.

Sect. 467.

¶ Mes hic nota, que quãt hom̃ est seisi en fee simple, dascun terres ou tenements, et un auter voile releaser a luy tout le droit que il ad en mesmes les tenẽts il ne besoigne de parler de les heires celuy a q̃ le releas est fait, pur ceo que il auoit fee simple al temps de releas fait. Car si releas fuit fait a luy pur un iour, ou pur un heure, ceo serroit auxy fort a luy & ley, sicome il vst releas a luy et a ses heires. Car quant son droit fuit ale de luy a un foits per son releas sans ascun condition

BVt here note, that when a man is seised in fee simple of any lands or tenements, and another will release to him all the right which he hath in the same tenements, he needeth not to speake of the heires of him to whom the release is made, for that he hath a fee simple at the time of the release made, for if the release was made to him for a day or an houre, this shall bee as strong to him in law, as if he had released to him and his heires. For when his right was once gone from him by his release without any con-

¶ *Il ne besoigne a parler de les heires, &c.* And the reason of Littleton hereof is for that the Disseisor hath a fee simple at the time of the Release made And this appeareth by that which hath beene said before, so as regularly he that hath a fee simple at the time of the Release made of a right, &c. needeth not speake of his heires.

¶ *Car si release fuit fait a luy par vn iour, &c.* For the diversity is betweene a Release of part of the estate of a Right, and between a Release of a Right in part of the Land. And therefore Littleton here saith, that a Release of a Right for a day or an houre is of as good force, as if he had released his right to him and his heires. But if a man be disseised of two acres hee may release his right in one of them, and yet enter into the other. Vid.6.E.3.17. 12.E.4.10. Discont.F.29.

¶ *Sans ascun condition,*

tion,&c. &c. a celuy que ad fee simple, il est ale a touts iours.

dition, &c. to him that hath the fee simple, it is gone for euer.

Herein is implied two diuersities, first betweene the quantity of the estate in a Right, and the quality thereof, for albeit the Disseisee cannot release part of the state as hath beene said, yet may he release his right vpon condition as here it appeareth by Littleton, (c) and it agreeth with our bookes.

(c) 4. E. 2. Releas 50. 43. Ass. 12. 17. Ass. 2. 31. Ass. 13. 21. H. 24.

Also here is another diuersitie betweene a right whereof Littleton putteth his case which is fauoured in Law, and a Condition created by the party which is odious in Law, for that it defeateth estates. And therefore if a Condition be released vpon Condition, the Release is good, and the Condition voide.

What things may be done vpon Condition is too large a matter to handle in this place, our Author hauing treated of Conditions before, only to giue a touch of some things omitted there, shall suffice. An expresse Manumission of a Villeine cannot be vpon condition, for once free in that case, and euer free, also an Attornment to a Grantee vpon condition, the Condition is voide because the Grant is once setled. But this is to bee vnderstood of a Condition subsequent, and not of a Condition precedent, for in both those cases the Condition precedent is good. But Letters pattents of Denization made to an Alien may be either vpon Condition subsequent or precedent, and so may the King make a Charter of pardon to a man of his life vpon Condition as is abouesaid.

Rot. Parliamen 18. H. 6. num. 29. Ap. Gwilliams case. 20. E. 3 cap. 2. 3. H. 7 fol. 6.

Sect. 468.

Mes lou home ad vn reuersion en fee simple, ou vn remainder en fee simple, al temps de releas fait, la sil voyle releaser al tenant per terme dans, ou pur terme de vie, ou al tenant en le taile, il couient a determiner lestate que celuy a que le releas est fait auera per force de mesme le releas, pur ceo que tiel releas enurera pur enlarger lestate de celuy, a que le releas est fait.

But where a man hath a reuersion in fee simple, or a remainder in fee simple at the time of the release made, there if hee will release to the tenant for yeares, or for life, or to the tenant in taile, hee ought to determine the estate, which he to whom the release is made shal haue by force of the same release, for that such release shall enure to enlarge the estate of him to whom the release is made.

Of this sufficient hath beene said before.

Sect. 469.

Mes autrement est lou home ad forsque droit a la terre, et nad riens en le reuersion ne en remainder en fait. Car si tiel home relessa tout son droit a vn que est tenant de le franktenement, tout son droit est ale, coment que nul mention soit fait de les heires celuy a que le releas est fait. Car si ieo lessa terres a vn home pur terme

But otherwise it is where a man hath but a right to the land, and hath nothing in the reuersion nor in the remainder in Deed. For if such a man release all his right to one which is tenant of the freehold, all his right is gone, albeit no mention be made of the heires of him to whom the release is made: for if I let lands to one for terme of his life, if I after release

De

de sa vie, si ieo puis releas a luy pur enlarger son estate, il couient q̄ ieo relessa a luy et a ses heires de son corps engender, ou a luy et a ses heires, ou per tiels pols: A auer et teñ a luy et a ses heirs de son corps engendres, ou a les heires males de son corps engendres, ou tiels semblables estates, ou auterment il nad pluis greind estate q̄ il auoit adeuant.

to him to enlarge his estate, it behoueth that I release to him and to his heires of his body engendred, or to him and his heires, or by these words, to haue and to hold to him and to his heires of his body engendred, or to the heires males of his body engendred, or such like estates, or otherwise hee hath no greater estate then hee had before.

¶ A *Vn que est tenant de franktenement.* Here it appeareth that to a Release of a right, made to any that hath an estate of freehold in Deed or in Law no priuitie at all is requisite. As if a Disseisor make a Lease for life, if the Disseisor release to the Lessee, this is good, and directly within the rule of Littleton because the Lessee hath an estate of freehold, albeit there be no priuitie. And so it is if a Disseisor make a Lease to A. and his heires during the life of B, and A. dieth, a Release by the Disseisee to his heire before he doth actually enter is good.

Section 470.

¶ Mes si mon teñ a terme de vie, lessa mesme la terre ouster a vn auter pur terme de vie de son lessee, le remainder a vn auter en fee, ore si ieo relessa a celuy a que mon tenant lessast pur terme de vie, ceo serra barre a touts iours, coment que nul mention soit fait d̄ ses heires, pur ceo que al temps de releas fait ieo auoy nul reuersion, mes tantsolement vn droit dauer la reuersion, car p̄ tiel leas, et le remainder ouster que mon tenant fist en ceo cas, mon reuersion fuit discontinue, &c. A tiel releas vrera a celuy & l' remainder, dauer aduantage de ceo auxibien come al tenant a terme de vie.

But if my tenant for life letteth the same land ouer to another for terme of the life of his Lessee, the remainder to another in fee, now if I release to him to whom my tenant made a Lease for terme of life, I shall bee barred for euer, albeit that no mention bee made of his heires, for that at the time of the release made I had no reuersion, but only a right to haue the reuersion. For by such a release and the remainder ouer which my tenant made in this case my reuersion was discontinued, &c. and this release shall enure to him in the remainder to haue aduantage of it as well as to the tenant for terme of life.

¶ Littleton hauing before spoken of releases which enure by way of Enlargemẽt, by way of Mitter l'estate & by way of Mitter le droit, here speaketh of a release of a right which in some respects enureth by way of Extinguishment, as in this case which Litl: here putteth, the Release to the Lessee of the Lessee doth not enure by way of Mitter le droit, for then should he haue the whole right, but as it were by way of Extinguishment, in respect of him, that made the Release, and that it shall enure to him in the remainder which is a quality of an inheritance extinguished.

extinguished. But yet the right is not extinct in deed, as shall be sayd hereafter in this Chapter.

¶ *Mon reversion fuit discontinue, &c.* Heere Discontinue is in a large sence taken for Divested, though the entrie of the Lessor be not taken away, which is implied in this (&c.)

Section 471.

¶ Car a cel intent le Tenaunt a terme de vie et celuy en le remainder sont sicome un Tenaunt en Ley, et sont sicõe un Tenant fuit sole seisie en son demesne come de fee al temps de tiel release fait a luy, &c.

For to this intent the tenant for term of life, and he in the remainder, are as one Tenant in Law, and are as if one Tenaunt were sole seised in his Demesne as of Fee at the time of such Release made unto him, &c.

¶ *Sont come un Tñt en Ley.* Which is certainly true in this case of Remainder, and so it is also in case of a Reversion, as if a Disseisor make a Lease for life, and the Disseisee doth release all his right to the lessee, this Release shall enure to him in the reversion, albeit they have severall estates, as hath beene sayd, which is implied in this (&c.)

But if a Disseisor make a Lease for life, the remainder in fee, albeit they to some purposes (as here is sayd) are as one Tenant in Law, yet if the Disseisee release the Actions to the Tenant for life, after the death of the Tenant for life, he in the remainder shall not take benefit of this release, for it extended onely to the Tenant for life, as it is holden (a) in Edward Althams case. And in like manner if the Disseisor make a Lease for life, and the Disseisee release all Actions to the Lessee, this inureth not to him in the reversion, and so our Author is to be understood of a Release of Rights, and not of a Release of Actions, to the tenant for life, as to or for the benefit of him in the remainder or reversion.

(a) Li. 8. fo. 148. Edw. Althams case.

Section 472.

¶ Item si hõe soyt disseisie per dux, sil relessa a un de eux, il tiendra son compaignion hors de Terre, et per tiel release il auera le sole possession et estate en la Terre. Mes si un Disseisour enfeoffa deux en Fee, et l'disseisee relessa a lun des feoffees, ceo urera a ambideux de les Feoffees, et la cause de diversity ent ceux deux cases est assets preignant. ¶ Pur ceo

Also if a man bee disseised by two, if hee release to one of them, hee shall hold his Companion out of the Land, and by such Release hee shall haue the sole possession and estate in the Land. But if a Disseisor infeoffe two in fee, and the Disseisee release to one of the feoffees, this shal inure to both the feoffees, & the cause of the diversity between these two cases is pregnant e-

¶ *Si home soit disseisie, &c.* This is to be understood where tenant in Fee simple is disseised and release: for if Tenant for life be disseised by two, and he releaseth to one of them, this shall inure to them both, for he to whom the release is made, hath a longer estate than hee that releaseth, and therefore cannot enure to him alone, to hold out his companion, for then should the Release enure by way of entrie and grant of his estate, and consequently the Disseisor to whom the release is made should become Tenant for life, and the Reversion revested in the Lessor, (b) which strange transmutation and change of estates in this case the Law will not suffer. But if Lessee for yeres be ousted, and he in the rever-

21. H. 6. 41.

(b) 13. E. 4. tit. Discont. F. 29

ceo que ils veignont eins per feoffment, et lauters per tort, &c. enough. For that they come in by feoffment, and the others by wrong, &c.

sion disseised, and the Lessee release to the Disseisor, the Disseisee may enter, for the terme for yeares is extinct and determined. But otherwise it is in case of a Lessee for life, for the Disseisor hath a Freehold whereupon the Release of Tenant for life may enure, but the Disseisor hath no terme for yeares whereupon the Release of the Lessee for yeares may enure.

And so it is if Lessee in Taile be disseised by two, and releaseth to one of them, it shal enure to them both. But if the Kings Tenant for life be disseised by two, and he releaseth to one of them, he shall hold out his Companion, for the Disseisor gained but the estate for life. So if two Joyntenants make a lease for life, and after doe disseise the Tenant for life, and he release to one of them, he shal hold out his Companion, for the Disseisin was but of an estate for life.

If Tenant for life be disseised by two, and he in the reversion and Tenant for life joyne in a Release to one of the Disseisors, he shall hold his Companion out, and yet it cannot enure by way of entrie and feoffement. But if they severally release their severall rights, their severall Releases shall enure to both the Disseisors.

But here in Littletons case, where Tenant in Fee simple is disseised by two, and releaseth to one of them, this for many purposes enureth by way of entrie and feoffement, and therefore he to whom the Release is made shall hold out his companion, and be made sole Tenant of the fee simple. And this holdeth not onely in case of a Disseisin, but also in case of Intrusion and Abatement: but necessarily hee to whom the Release is made must bee in by wrong, and not by Title.

If two men doe gaine an Advowson by usurpation, and the right Patron releaseth to one of them, he shall not hold out his Companion, but it shall enure to them both, for seeing their Clerks came in by admission and institution, which are judiciall acts, they are not meerely in by wrong: for an usurpation shal cause a Remitter, as it appeareth in F.N.B.31.m.

But if a Lease for life be made, the remainder for life, the remainder in fee, and he in remainder for life disseiseth the Tenant for life, and then Tenant for life dieth, the Disseisin is purged, and he in the remainder for life hath but an estate for life. And so note a diversity where the particular estate for life is precedent, and when subsequent. 19.H.6.21.38.H.6.28.Case de Occupant.

Where our Author putteth his case of one disseised, put the case that two Joyntenants in Fee be disseised by two, & one of the Disseisees release to one of the Disseisors al his right, he shal not hold out his companion, because the Release is but of the moitie, without any certaintie. If a man be disseised by two women, and one of them take husband, and the Disseisee release to the husband, this shall enure to the advantage of both the Disseisors, because the husband was no wrong doer, but in a manner in by title.

¶ *Il auera le sole possession & estate.* **If two Disseisors be, and they** make a Lease for life, and the Disseisee release to one of them, this shall enure to them both, and to the benefit of the Lessee for life also: for he cannot by the Release have the sole possession and estate, for part of the estate is in another.

And so it is (as it seemeth) if the Disseisors make a Lease for yeares, and the Disseisee release to one of them, this shall enure to them both, for by the Release he cannot have the sole possession: And it appeareth by Littleton, That he must have the sole possession, and hold his Companion. But the Morgagee upon condition, having broken the Condition, is disseised by two, the Morgagor having title of entrie for the Condition broken, release to the one Disseisor, albeit they be in by wrong, yet the Release shall enure to them both for two causes: First, For that they are not wrong doers to the Morgagor, but to the Morgagee, and by Littletons case it appeareth, That wrong is done to him that made the Release. Secondly, That hee that make the Release hath but a title by force of a Condition, and Littletons case is of a right. Like Law of an entrie for Mortmaine, or a consent to ravishment, &c.

¶ *Mes si un Disseisor infeoffa deux, &c.* **And the reason of this diversitie is,** For that the Feoffees are in by Title, and are presumed to have a Warranty, which is much favoured in Law, and the Disseisors are meerely in by wrong. And the equitie of the Law doth preserve in this case the benefit of the estranger to the Release, comming in by one joynt Title. 21.H.6.41.

¶ *Pur ceo que ils veignont eins per Feoffement, & lauters per Tort.* This is of a new addition, and not in the Originall, and therefore I passe it over.

Sect.

Section 473.

¶ Item si ieo sue disseisie, et mon disseisor est disseisie, si ieo releas a le disseisor de mon disseisor, ieo nauera a unque ass. ne entra sur le disseisor, pur ceo que son disseisor ad mon droit per mon release, &c. Et issint il semble en tiel cas, si soyent xx. disseisors, chescun apres autre, et ieo relessa a le darreine disseisor, celuy disseisor barrera touts les autres de lour actions et lour titles. Et la cause est, come il semble, pur ceo que en mults cases, quant un home ad loyal title dentre, coment que il nentra pas, il defeatera touts mean titles per son releas, &c. Mes ceo nest my en chescun cas, come sera dit apres.

Also if I be disseised, and my disseisor is disseised, if I release to the disseisor of my disseisor, I shall not haue an assise nor enter vpon the disseisor, because his disseisor hath my right by my release, &c. And so it seemeth in this case if there be xx. disseised one after another, and I release to the last disseisor, this disseisor shall barre all the others of their actions and their titles. And the cause is, as it seemeth, for that in many cases when a man hath lawfull title of entrie, although he doth not enter, he shall defeat all meane titles by his release, &c. but this holds not in euery case, as shall be said hereafter.

¶ Here it is to be obserued, that a Release by one whose entry is lawfull to him that is in by wrong, shall purge and take away all meane Estates and Titles. And where our Author first putteth his case of two estates by wrong, and after of twentie Disseisins, all Estates be wrong.

21.H.6.41. 11.H.4.33. 9.H.7.25. 2.E.4.16. 21.E.4.78. 12.Ass.22. *Vide* 3.H.6.38. If A. disseise B. who enfeoffeth C. with warrantie, who enfeoffe D. with warrantie, and E. disseiseth D. to whom B. the first Disseisee releaseth, this doth defeate all the meane Estates and Warranties, because the release of B. is made to a Disseisor, and his Entry is lawfull.

Section 474.

¶ Item si mon disseisor lessa, &c. If the Disseisor make a Lease for life, and the Lessee maketh a feoffment in fee, and the Disseisee releaseth to the Feoffee, the Disseisor shall not enter vpon the Feoffee, for albeit the release to one ioynt feoffee of a Disseisor, as hath beene said, shal not exclude the other, yet a release to the Feoffee of a Tenant for life in this case shall take away the Entry of the Disseisor for the alienation which was made to his Disinheritance, hee hauing

¶ Item si mon disseisor lessa les tenements dont il moy disseisist a un auter home pur terme de vie, et puis le tenant a terme de vie aliena en fee, et ieo relessa al alienee, &c. donque mon disseisor ne poit enter, Causa qua supra, coment que a un foits

Also if my Disseisor letteth the tenements whereof hee disseised mee to another for tearme of life, and after the Tenant for tearme of life alieneth in fee, and I release to the alienee, &c. then my Disseisor cannot enter, *Causa qua supra*, albeit that at one

foits lalienation fuit a son disenheritance, &c.

time the alienation was to his disinheritance, &c.

the Inheritance by disseisin, so as hee could haue no warrantie annexed to it, and tenant for life hath forfeited his estate. But if the entry of the Disseisee were not lawfull, it is otherwise. As if a man make a Lease for life, and the Lessee for life is disseised, and that Disseisor is disseised, and he in the reuersion releaseth to the second Disseisor, the first Disseisor shall enter vpon the second Disseisor, and his entry is lawfull, and if the Lessee for life re-enter, he shall leaue the reuersion in the first Disseisor, and the cause is, for that the entry of the Disseisor at the time of the release made was not lawfull. And the Booke of (m) 9.H.7.25. is to be intended of an Estate tayle *mutatis mutandis*. (m) 9.H.7.25.

If in the case aforesaid, the Disseisor make a Lease for life, and the Lessee infeoffeth two, and the Disseisee release to one of the Feoffees, this shall barre the Disseisor, as hath beene said, but yet he shall not hold out his companion for the cause aforesaid.

Sect. 475.

¶ Item si home soit disseisi, le quel ad fits deins age et morust, et esteant le fits deins age, le disseisor morust seisi, et la terre discendist a son heir, & vn estrang abate, et puis le fits le disseisee quant il vient a son plein age, relessa tout son droit a labator, en cest case lheire le disseisor nauera assise de Mordancester enuers labator mes serra bar, pur ceo que labator ad le droit del fits le disseisee per son reles, et lentrie le fits fuit congeable, pur ceo que il fuit deins age al temps del discent, &c.

Also if a man be disseised who hath a sonne within age and dieth, and the sonne being within age the Disseisor dieth seised, and the land discend to his heire, and a stranger abate, & after the sonne of the Disseisee when hee commeth to his full age releaseth all his right to the abator, in this case the heire of the Disseisor shall not haue an Assise of Mordancester against the abator, but shall bee barred because the abator hath the right of the sonne of the Disseisee by his release, and the entry of the sonne was congeable, for that hee was within age at the time of the Discent, &c.

¶ The reason of this case is for that the entrie of the heire is congeable, and the Abator is in the land by wrong.

¶ *Abate.* Is both an English and French word and signifieth in his proper sence to Diminish, or Take away, as here by his entrie he Diminisheth and Taketh away the Freehold in Law discended to the heire, and so it is said to Abate an account signifying Subtraction or withdrawing, &c. and to Abate the courage of a man. In another sence it signifieth to Prostrate, Beate downe or Ouerthrow, as to Abate Castles, Houses, and the like, and to Abate a writ, and hereof commeth a word of Arte, *Abatamentum* which is an Entry by Interposition. Now the difference inter *Disseisinam, Abatamentum, Intrusionem, Deforciamentum, & Vsurpationem, & Purpresturam*, is this. Vet.N.B.115. Britton cap.51 Bracton lib.4 cap 2. F.N.B.203. f.W.1. cap.17.

A Disseisin is a wrongfull putting out of him that is actually seised of a Freehold. And Abatement is when a man died seised of an estate of Inheritance, and betweene the death and the entry of the heire, an estranger doth interpose himselfe, and abate.

Intrusion first properly (n) is when the Ancestor died seised of any estate of Inheritance expectant vpon an estate for life, and then tenant for life dieth, and betweene the death and the entry of the heire an estranger doth interpose himselfe and intrude. (n) F.N.B.203. Fleta lib.4 cap.30.

Secondly, (o) he that entreth vpon any of the Kings Demesnes, and taketh the profits is said to Intrude vpon the Kings possession. (o) Pl.Com. casu de mynes

(p) F.N.B. 141. f. g. h. Thirdly, (p) when the heire in ward entreth at his full age without satisfaction for his marriage, the Writ saith, quod intruſit.

Deforciamentum comprehendeth not only these aforenamed, but any man that holdeth land whereunto another man hath right, be it by discent or purchase, is said to be a Deforceor. Usurpation hath two significations in the Common Law, one when an estranger that no right hath presenteth to a Church, and his Clarke is admitted and instituted, hee is said to bee an usurper, and the wrongfull act that he hath done is called an Usurpation.

(q) Glanvil. lib. 9. cap. 11. Britton fol. 28. 29. Secondly, when any subiect doth use without lawfull warrant, Royall Franchises, he is said to usurpe upō the King those Frāchises. Purpreſtura or Pourpreſtura a Purpresture (q) Purpreſtura eſt, &c. generaliter quoties aliquid fit ad nocumentū regij tenementi, vel regiæ viæ (vel aquarū publicarum) vel ciuitatis, &c. And because it is properly when there is a house builded, or an Inclosure made of any part of the Kings Demesnes, or of an high way, or a common street or publike water, or such like publike things, it is derived of the French word Pourpris which signifieth an Inclosure, but specially applied, as is aforesaid, by the Common Law.

Sect. 476.

Mes si home soit disseisi, & le disseisor fait feofment sur condition, cestascauoir, de render a luy certaine rent, & pur default de payment un reentre, &c. si le disseisie relessa al feoffee sur condition uncore ceo namēdra lestate le feoffee sur condition, car nient obstant tiel releas, uncore son estate est sur condition sicome il fuit deuant.

¶ Et cum hóc concordat opinio omnium Iuſticiariorum, P. 9. H. 7. ¶.

BVt if a man be diſſeiſed and the diſſeiſor maketh a feoffement vpon condition, *viz.* to render to him a certaine rent, and for default of payment a re-entry, &c. if the diſſeiſee releaſe to the feoffee vpon condition, yet this ſhall not amend the eſtate of the feoffee vpon condition, for notwithſtanding ſuch releaſe, yet his eſtate is vpon condition as it was before.

¶ And with this agreeth the opinion of all the Iuſtices, *Paſch. 9. H. 7.*

9. H. 7. 25. Here the entry of the disseisee is congeable, and yet the release doth not avoid the condition because the feoffee is in by title, as hath beene said, and may haue a warrantie. And herein our Author expresseth a diuersitie betweene a Condition in Law, and a Condition in Deed, for in the case before when the Disseisee releaseth to the Feoffee of the Tenant for life, the Condition in law is taken away, but otherwise it is in this case of a Condition in Deed.

Lib. 1. fol. 147. Mayowes case. But if the Feoffee upon Condition make a feoffment in fee over without any Condition, & the Disseisee release to the second Feoffee, the condition is destroyed by the release before the Condition broken or after. For the state of the second feoffee was not upon any expresse Condition, as Littleton here putteth his case, and he may haue aduantage of the release, because it is not against his owne proper acceptance as Littleton speaketh in the next Section.

But if it be a wrongfull title, such a title is taken away by a release, as if A. disseise B. to the use of C. B. release to A. this shall take away the agreement of C. to the Disseisin, because it should make him a wrong doer, as if the disseisor be disseised, the disseisee releaseth to the second Disseisor, this taketh away the right the first Disseisor had against the second, and a relation of an estate gained by wrong shall neuer defeat an estate subsequent gained by right, against 14. H. 8. 28. per Tort. a single opinion, not affirmed by any other in one of our Bookes.

Section 477.

Et le Disseisor grant un Rent-charge, &c. Here is implyed Commons or any

En mesme le manner est, lou home soit diss. de certein terre, & le disseisor

IN the ſame manner it is where a man is diſſeiſed of certaine lands & the Diſſeiſor,

for grant vn rent charge hors d meſm la terre, &c. coment que apres le diſſeiſee releſſa al diſſeiſor, &c. uncore l'rent charge demurt en ſa force. Et la cauſe en ceux deux caſes eſt ceo, q̃ home nauera aduantage per tiel releas q̃ ſerra encounter ſon proper acceptance, et encounter ſon grant demeſne: & coment q̃ aſcuns ont dit que lou lentre d home eſt congeable ſur vn tenant ſil releaſiſt a meſme le tenant, que ceo auaileroit a l'tenant, ſicome il vſt enter ſur le tenant, et puis luy enfeoffa, &c. ceo neſt pas voier en cheſcun cas. Car en le primer cas de ceux deux auauntdits caſes, ſi le diſſeiſſe vſt enter ſur l'feoffee ſur condition, et puis luy enfeffa, donques eſt le condition tout defeat et auoid. Et iſſint en le ſecond caſe, ſi le diſſeiſſe entraſt et enfeoffa celuy que granta l'rent charg, donques eſt le rent charge anient et auoid; mes il neſt pas void per aſcun tiel releas ſans entry fait, &c.

grant a rent charge out of the ſame land, &c. albeit the Diſſeiſee doth afterwards releaſe to the Diſſeiſor, &c. yet the Rent-charge remaynes in force. And the reaſon in theſe two caſes is this, that a man ſhall not haue aduantage by ſuch releaſe, which ſhall bee againſt his proper acceptance, & againſt his own grant. And albeit ſome haue ſaid, that where the entry of a man is Congeable vpon a Tenant if hee releaſeth to the ſame Tenant, that this ſhall auaile the Tenant, as if he had entred vpon the Tenant and after enfeoffed him, &c. this is not true in euery caſe, for in the firſt caſe of theſe two caſes aforeſaid, if the Diſſeiſee had entred vpon the Feoffee vpon condition, and after enfeoffed him, then is the Condition wholly defeated and auoided. And ſo in the ſecond caſe if the diſſeiſee entreth and enfeoffeth him who granted the Rent charge, then is the Rent-charge taken away and auoided, but it is not void by any ſuch releaſe without entrie made, &c.

other profit out of the lands. And the reaſon is becauſe he ſhal not auoid his owne grant by a releaſe, hee himſelfe hath acquired ſince the grant, but if the Diſſeiſor in that caſe be diſſeiſed, and the Diſſeiſee releaſe to the ſecond Diſſeiſor he ſhall auoid it, as by that which hath beene ſaid, Sect. 473. appeareth. So likewiſe if A. and B. bee ioynt Diſſeiſors, and B. grant a Rent-charge, and the Diſſeiſee releaſe to A. all his right. A. ſhal auoid the Rent-charge becauſe it was not granted by him, and ſo not within the reaſon of our Author.

If there bee two Fems ioynt Diſſeiſors and the one taketh husband, and the Diſſeiſee releaſe to the other, ſhee is ſole ſeiſed, and ſhall hold out the husband and wife.

If two Diſſeiſors be, and they infeoffe another, and take backe an eſtate for life or in fee, albeit they remaine Diſſeiſors to the Diſſeiſee as to haue an aſſiſe againſt them, yet if hee releaſe to one of them hee ſhall not hold out his companion, becauſe their ſtate in the land is by feoffment.

If there be two Diſſeiſors and they be diſſeiſed, and they releaſe to their Diſſeiſor, and after diſſeiſe him, and then the Diſſeiſee releaſe to one or both of them, yet the ſecond Diſſeiſor ſhall re-enter, for they ſhall not hold the land againſt their owne releaſe; for Littleton here ſaith, that they ſhall not auoid their owne grant, and by like reaſon they ſhall not auoid their owne releaſe, & ſic de ſimilibus.

¶ *Come ſil vſt enter ſur le tenant & luy enfeoffe.* Here is another kind of releaſe, viz. a releaſe which enureth by way of entry and feoffment, for if a Diſſeiſee releaſe to one of the Diſſeiſors to ſome purpoſe this ſhall enure by way of entry and feoffment, viz. as to hold out his companion. But as to a Rent-charge granted

ted by him it shall not enure by way of entrie and feoffment, for if the disseisee had entred and enfeoffed him, the Rent charge had beene avoyded. But it is a certaine rule that when the entrie of a man is congeable, and he releaseth to one that is in by title (as hereto the feoffee upon condition is) it shall never enure by way of entrie and feoffment, either to avoide a condition with which he accepted the Land charged, or his owne grant, or to hold out his Companion.

And where it appeareth by our Author that acts done by the Disseisor shall not be avoyded by the Release of the Disseisee. It is to be noted that acts made to the Disseisor himselfe shall not be avoyded by the alteration of his estate by the release of the Disseisee, as if the Lord before the Release had confirmed the estate of the Disseisor to hold by lesser services, the Disseisor shall take advantage of it, and so of Estovers to be burnt in the house, and the like law of a warrantie made unto him.

If the heire of the Disseisor indow his wife Ex aſſenſu patris, and the Disseisee release to the Disseisor, he shall not avoide the indowment, for that is like the case put by Littleton of the Rent-charge.

If an Alien be a Disseisor and obtaine Letters of Denization, and then the Disseisee Release unto him, the King shall not have the land, for the Release hath altered the estate, and it is as it were a new purchase, otherwise it is if the Alien had beene the Feoffee of a Disseisor.

If the Lord disseise the Tenant, and is disseised, the Disseisee release to the second Disseisor, yet the Seigniory is not revived, for betweene the parties the Release enures by way of Entrie and Feoffment as to the land, but not having regard to the Seigniory, and for that the possession was never actually removed or revested from the Disseisor who clayment under the Lord, the Seigniory is not revived. But if the Lord and a stranger disseise the Tenant, and the Disseisee release to the stranger, there the Seigniory by operation of Law is revived, for the whole is vested in the stranger which never claymed under the Lord. And in that case, if the Lord had died, and the land had survived, the Seigniory had beene revived. But if the Lord had disseised the Tenant, and beene disseised by two, and the Disseisee released to one of them, the Seigniory is not revived, because he claymed (as hath beene said) under the Lord.

Sect. 478.

Vid. Sect. 514.

Quel briefe de eux il eſliera, &c. Note many times in one case the Law doth give a man severall remedies, and of severall kindes, as in this case by action and by entrie, by action, either a writ of right, or Dum fuit infra ætatem.

9.E.3.98. 9 E.4.46. 21.E.4.55. 41.E.3.10. 2.H.4.12.

Et puis le Diſſeiſor porta breife de droit, &c. Here it appeareth that there is a great art and knowledge for a man that hath divers remedies to choose his aptest remedie, as in this case, if he bring his writ of right, the Disseisor shall be barred, but if he had entred upon the heire of the Alienee, he should have enjoyed the land for ever. For in that case the heire of the Alienee after such an entrie shall never have a writ of right no more then if the Disseisee entreth upon the heire of the Disseisor, and make a Feoffment in fee, if the heire of the Disseisee

Item si hom̃ soit disseisi pur un enfant, le quel aliena en fee, & alienee devie seisie, et son heire enter, esteant le Disseisor deins age, ore est en election le Disseisour, ď aver un briefe de Dum fuit infra ætatem, ou briefe ď droit envers le heire del alienee, et quel briefe de eux q̃ il esliera, il doit recover per la ley, &c. Et auxi il poit enter en la terre sans ascun recoverie, et en cest case lentre l' Disseisie est toll', &c. Mes en cest cas si le disseisie relessa son droit al heire

ALſo if a man bee diſſeiſed by an infant, who alien in fee, and the Alienee dieth ſeiſed, & his heire entreth, the diſſeiſor being within age, now is it in the election of the diſſeiſor to haue a writ of *Dum fuit infra ætatem*, or a Writ of right againſt the heire of the alienee, and which writ of them hee ſhall chooſe, hee ought to recouer by the law, &c. And alſo he may enter into the land without any recouery, & in this caſe the entrie of the diſſeiſee is taken away,

heire del alienee, et puis l'disseisor porta bre de dreit enuers l'heire dalienee, et il ioyne le mise sur l'mere droit &c. le graunde assise doit trouer per la ley que l'tenant ad pluis mere droit que ad le disseisour, &c. pur ceo que le tenant ad le droit le disseisie per son releas, le quel est pluis ancient et pluis mere droit. Car per tiel releas tout le droit le disseisee passa a le tenant, et est en le tenant. Et a ceo que ascuns ont dit, que en tiel case lou home que ad droit al terres ou tenements (mes son entrie nest pas congeable) sil relessa al tenant tout son droit &c. que tiel releas vrera per voy dextinguishment: Quant a ceo il puit estre dit, que ceo est voyer quant a celuy que relessa, car per son releas il ad luy demise quietment de son droit, quant a son person, mes vncore le droit que il auoit bien poit passer a le tenant per son release: Car enconuenient serroit que tiel ancient droit serroit extinct tout oustrement, &c. Car il est communement dit que

&c. But in this case if the disseisee releas his right to the heire of the alienee, and after the disseisor bringeth a writ of right against the heire of the alienee, and hee ioyne the mise vpon the meere right, &c. the great assise ought to finde by the law that the tenant hath more meere right then the disseisor, &c. for that the tenant hath the right of the disseisee by his release, the which is the most ancient & most meere right: for by such release all the right of the disseisee passeth to the tenant, and is in the tenant. And to this some haue said that in this case where a man which hath right to lands or tenements (but his entrie is not congeable) if hee release to the tenant all his right, &c. that such release shall enure by way of extinguishment. As to this it may bee said that this is true, as to him which releaseth, for by his release he hath dismissed himselfe quite of his right as to his person, but yet the right which he hath may well passe to the tenant by his release. For it should bee inconuenient that such an ancient right should bee extinct altogether,

re-enter he shall detaine the land for euer, and the Feoffee shall not maintaine any Writ of right, for a bare right shall neuer be left in the Feoffee, but shall euer follow the possession; as hath beene said, but if the Disseisee entreth vpon the heire of the Disseisor, and make a Feoffment in fee vpon condition, and entreth for the condition broken before the heire of the Disseisor enter, hee is restored to his right againe. 38.E.3.16. 24.H.8. Restore al primer estate. 5. Vid. Sect. 447.

A man maketh a gift in tayle, the remainder in fee, Tenant in tayle dieth without issue, an estranger intrude, and he in the remainder brings a Formedon, and recouereth by default, and maketh a Feoffment in fee, the Intrudor reuers the recouery in a Writ of disceit and entreth he shall detaine the land for euer, and the Feoffee shall not haue a Writ of right. 9.H.7.24.

And so likewise if a Disseisor die seised, and a stranger abate and the Disseisee release to him, the heire of the Disseisor shall enter and detaine the land for euer. For the right to the possession shall drawe the right of the land to it, and shall not leaue a right in him to whom the release is made, as hath beene said before in the 447. Section. 9.H.7.24.

¶ *Le droit del disseisee passa al tenant, & est en le tenant.* For seeing the Tenant hath the whole fee simple, he is capable of the whole right of the disseisee, and as Littleton here saith, the right is in the Tenant.

¶ *Inconuenient serroit.* Here againe as hath beene often obserued, an argument Ab inconuenienti is forcible in Law, and that Judges by the authority of our Author are to iudge of inconueniences as of things vnlawfull, Vid. Sect. 87. 138. 139. 231. 269. 440. 722.

full, as hereby and by many other places it appeareth.

¶ *Vn droit ne poit pas morier.* Dormit aliquando ius, moritur nunquam. For of such an high estimation is right in the eye of the Law, as the Law preserveth it from death and destruction: troden downe it may be, but never troden out. For where it hath beene said that a release of a right doth in some cases enure by way of extinguishment. It is so to be understood either (as Littleton doth here) in respect of him that makes the release, or in respect that by construction of Law it enureth not alone to him to whom it is made, but to others also who be estrangers to the releaze, which as hath beene said is a quality of an inheritance extinguished.

14.H.8.6.b. As if there be Lord and Tenant, and the Tenant maketh a Lease for life the remainder in fee, if the Lord release to the Tenant for life, the rent is wholly extinguished, and he in the remainder shall take benefit thereof, even so when the heire of a Disseisor is disseised, and the Disseisor make a Lease for life, the remainder in fee, if the first Disseisee release to the Tenant for life, this is said to enure by way of extinguishment, for that it shall enure to him in the remainder, who is a stranger to the Release, and yet in truth the right is not extinct but doth follow the possession, viz the Tenant for life hath it during his time, and he in the remainder to him and to his heires, and the right of the inheritance is in him in the remainder, for a right to land cannot die or be extinct in Deed, and therefore if after the death of Tenant for life the heire of the Disseisor bring a Writ of right against him in the remainder and he ioyne the mise upon the mere right, it shall be found for him, because in iudgement of Law he hath by the said Release the right of the first Disseisee.

droit ne poit pas morier.

&c. for it is commonly said, that a right cannot die.

Sect.479. & 480.

¶ HEre Littleton putteth a diversitie betweene Releases which enure by way of extinguishment against all persons and whereof all persons may take advantage, and Releases which in respect of some persons enure by way of extinguishment, and of other persons by way of Mitter le droit. Or betweene Releases which in Deed enure by extinguishment for that hee to whom the Release is made cannot have the thing released, and Releases which having some quality of such Releases are said to enure by way of extinguishment, but in troth doe not, for that he to whom the Release is made may receive and take the thing released. And here Littletõ putteth cases where Releases doe absolutely enure by extinguishment without exception having respect to all persons, and first of the Lord and Tenant. Secondly of the Rent charge. Thirdly, of the Common of pasture.

14.H.8.fol.5.6. 21.H.7.25. 30.H 6. tit.barre.39. 38.E.3.10.

First of the Lord and Tenant, and the Lord release to

¶ MEs releases q̃ enurera per voy dextinguishmẽt envers touts persons, sont lou celuy a que le releas est fait, ne poit aver ceo que a luy est releas. Sicome si soyent Sñr & tenant, et le Sñr relessa al tenant tout le droit que il ad en la seigniory, ou tout le droit que il ad en le terre, &c. tiel releas va per voy de extinguishment envers touts persons, pur ceo que le tenant ne poit aver service pur prender de luy mesme.

BVt releases which enure by way of extinguishment against all persons, are where hee to whom the release is made cannot have that which to him is released. As if there bee Lord and tenant, and the Lord release to the tenant all the right which hee hath in the seigniory, or all the right which hee hath in the land, &c. this release goeth by way of extinguishment against all persons, because that the tenant cannot have service to receive of himselfe.

Sect.480.

¶ EN mesme manere est de releas fait al Tenant del terre de un rent charge ou common de pasture, &c. pur ceo que le tenant ne poit auer ceo que a luy est relesse, &c. issint tiels releases urera per extinguishment en touts voyes.

IN the same manner is it of a Release made to the tenant of the land of a Rent-charge or Common of pasture, &c. because the tenant cannot haue that which to him is released, &c. so such releases shall enure by way of extinguishment in all wayes.

the Tenant his Seigniory, this must of necessitie enure by way of extinguishment to all men, for the Tenant cannot haue seruice to bee taken of himselfe, nor one man can bee both Lord and Tenant. The second is of a Rent-charge, a man cannot haue land and a rent issuing out of the same land. Thirdly, a man cannot haue land and a Common of pasture issuing out of the same land, *Et sic de cæteris.* For in all these cases and the like he to whom the Release is made cannot haue and enioy the thing that is released. But in the case of the right of land, the Tenant of the land may take and enioy it for strengthening his estate therein

The mesne being a Fem entermarrie with the Tenant perauaile, if the Lord release to the Feme, the Seigniory only is extinct. but if hee Release to the husband, both Seigniory and mesnaltie are extinct. And in this case, if the Lord release to the husband and wife, it is a question how the release shal enure, but it is no question but that a Release may be made to a Mesnaltie or a Seigniory suspended in part of the estate.

But here obserue a diuersity where a Release enureth by way of extinguishment of an inheritance which is in possession and may be granted ouer, and a Release of a right, or an action to lands which cannot be granted ouer. (r) For the Lord may release his Seigniorie to the Tenant of the land for life or in taile, *Et sic de cæteris.* But so cannot one release a right or an action, for if it be released but for an houre, it is extinct foreuer, as hath beene said.

(r) 13.*E.*3.*tit.Extinguishment*, *Brook* 45.*et tit.Voucher F.*120. 30.*E.*3.13. 19.*H.*6 19. 21.*E.*3.33. 38.*Ass.*17.

And two things are to be obserued here, first that by the Release of all the right in the land the Seigniorie is extinct, as well as by the Release of all the right in the Seigniorie, for the Seigniorie issueth out of the land. Secondly, That by the release of all his right in the seigniorie or the land, the whole Seigniorie is extinct without any words of Inheritance. If the Tenancie be giuen to a Lord and to a stranger, and to the heirs of the stranger, the Lord release to his Companion all the right in the land, this Release doth not onely passe his estate in the Tenancie, but extinguisheth also his right in the Seigniorie, and so one Release enures to extinguish seuerall rights in one and the same land.

21.*H.*4.*tit.Release*, 21. 18.*E.*2 *ibid.*5. 26.*H.*8.5. 41.*Ass.*6.

If there be Lord and Tenant by Fealtie and Rent, the Lord granteth the Seigniorie for yeares, and the Tenant atturneth, the Lord releaseth his Seigniorie to the Tenant for yeres, and to the Tenant of the land generally, the whole Seigniorie is extinct, and the state of the Lessee also. But if the Release had beene to them and their heyres, then the Lessee had had the Inheritance of the one moitie, and the other moitie had beene extinct. And the reason of this diuersitie is, because when the Release is made generally, it can enure to the Lessee but for life, because it enureth by way of enlargement of estate, and being made to the Tenant of the Land, it enureth by way of extinguishment, as Littleton here saith, and then there cannot remain a particular estate in the Seigniorie for life. But when the Release is made to them and their heires, each one takes a moitie, the one by way of encreasing of the estate, and the other by extinguishment.

Sect. 481.

¶ ITem de prouer que le graund Assise doit passer pur le demandant en le case auauntdit, jeo aye oye souent la Lecture de Lestatute

ALso to proue that the graund Assise ought to passe for the demandant, in the case aforesaid I haue often heard the reading of the Statute of West.2.

¶ *Eo aye oye souent la Lecture de West.*2. Here it is to be obserued, of what authoritie antient Lectures or Readings upon Statutes were, for that they had fiue excellent qualities: First, They declared what the Common Law

de Westminster second, que commence, In casu quo vir amiserit per defaltam tenementum quod fuit ius vxoris suæ, &c. que a le Common Ley devant mesm Lestatut, si Lease soit fait a vn home pur terme de vie, le remainder ouster en fee, et vn estrange per feint Action vst recouer envers le tenant a tme de vie per default, et puis le Tenant morust, celuy en le remainder navoit ascū remedie devaunt le Statute, pur ceo que il navoit ascun possession del terre.

which begunne thus: *In casu quo vir amiserit per defaltam Tenementū quod fuit ius vxoris suæ, &c.* that at the Common Law before the sayd Statute, if a lease were made to a man for terme of life, the remainder ouer in fee, and a Stranger by feigned Action recouered against the Tenant for life by default, and after the Tenant dieth, he in the remainder had no remedie before the Statute, because hee had not any possession of the Land.

Law was before the making of the Statute, as heere it appeareth. Secondly, They opened the true sence and meaning of the Statute. Thirdly, Their cases were briefe, hauing at the most one poynt at the Common Law, and another vpon the Statute. Fourthly, Plaine and Perspicuous, for then the honour of the Reader was to excell others in authorities, arguments, & reasons for proofe of his opinion, and for confutation of the obiections against it. Fifthly, They read, to suppresse subtill inuentions to creepe out of the Statute. But now Readings hauing lost the said former qualities, haue lost also their former authorities: for now the cases are long, obscure, and intricate, full of new conceits, liker rather to Riddles than Lectures, which when they are opened they vanish away like smoake, and the Readers are like to Lapwings, who seeme to be neerest their nests when they are farthest from them, and all their studie is to find nice euasions out of the Statute. By the authoritie of Littleton antient Readings may be cited for proofe of the Law, but new Readings haue not that honour, for that they are so obscure and darke.

¶ *Lestatute de W.2.* which is the third Chapter.

(a) 24.E.3.35. 28.E.3.96. 18.E.2. Entrie 74. 3.E.2. Entrie 7. 6.E.3.24. 7.E.3. Ent. 62. 7.E.3.54.55 15.E.4.15. F.N.B.217.d. Register 241.

¶ *Le remainder ouster en fee.* Here is to be obserued, That although the Statute speaketh of a Reuersion, (a) yet by the authoritie of Littleton a remainder is within the Statute.

See the Statute of 14. Eliz. ca. 8. which prouideth fully for him in the remainder.

¶ *Feint Action.* Feint is a Participle of the French word Fiendre, which is to feigne or falsly pretend, so as a faint Action is a false Action.

(b) W.2.cap.3.

Vide 34.E.3. Formedon 31. 11.E.3. ibid. 31. 8.E.3.59. F.N.B.217.d. 7.H.7.13.

¶ *Navoit ascun remedie devant Lestatute.* (b) Here it appeareth by Littleton, That if a man maketh a Lease for life, the remainder in fee, and Tenant for life suffereth a Recouerie by default, that he in the remainder should not haue a Formedon by the common Law: for Littleton saith, That he had not any remedie before the Statute. Neither is there any such Writ in that case in the Register, albeit in some Bookes mention is made of such a Writ.

Sect. 482.

¶ Mes si celuy en le remainder vst enter sur le tenant a tme de vie, et luy disseisist, & aps le

BVt if he in the remainder had entred vpon the Tenant for life, and disseised him, and after the Te-

38.E.3.3. Tit. Iuris vtrum 1.

¶ Heere a Disseisin gotten by wrong, and defeated by the entrie of him that right hath, is sufficient to maintaine a Writ of Right against the recouerer in this case, for albeit

le Tenaunt entre sur luy, et aps le tenant a terme de vie, per tiel recouery perde per default & morust, ore celuy en l' remainder bien poit auer briefe de Droit enuers celuy que recouera, pur ceo que le mise serra ioin solement sur le meere droit, &c. Uncore en cest case, le seisin de celuy en le remainder fuit defeat per entrie del tenant a terme de vie. Mes peraduenture ascuns voilent argue et dire, que il nauera brief de Droit en cest case, pur ceo que quant le mise est ioine, il est ioin en tiel manner, s. si le tenant ad plus mere droit en le terre en le manner come il tyent, que le demandant ad en le maner come il demanda, et pur ceo que le seisin del dont fuit defeat per lentry de le tenant a terme de vie, &c. donque il ad nul droit en l' maner come il demaund.

nant enter vpon him, and after the Tenaunt for life by such recouerie lose by default and die, now hee in the remainder may well haue a Writ or Right against him wch recouers, because the Mise shalbe ioined only vpon the mere right, &c. Yet in this case the Seisin of him in the Remainder was defeated by the entrie of the tenant for life. But peraduenture some wil argue and say, That hee shall not haue a Writ of Right in this case, for that when the Mise is ioyned, it is ioyned in this manner, (*scilicet*) if the Tenaunt hath more mere right in the land in the manner as he holdeth, than the demandant hath in the manner as hee demädeth, & for that the seisin of the demädant was defeated by the entrie of the tenant for term of life, &c. he hath no right in the manner as he demandeth.

the Seisin is defeated betweene the Lessee for life, and him in the remainder, yet hauing regard to the Recoueror, who is a meere stranger and hath no title; it is sufficient against him. But otherwise it is against the partie himselfe that defeated the Seisin, and the Law is propense to giue remedie to him that right hath. And where some haue thought, that there is no authoritie in Law to warrant Littletons opinion herein, they are greatly mistaken, for Lit. hath good warrant for all that he hath written. 7. E. 3. 62. 38. E. 3. 37. Tit. lur vtr. 1.

Lands are letten to A. for life, the remainder to B. for life, the remainder to the right heires of A. A dieth, B entreth and dieth, a stranger intrudeth, the heire of A. shall haue a Writ of Right of the Seisin which A. had as Tenaunt for life.

Lands are letten to A. and B. and to the heires of A. A. dieth, a recouerie is had against B. the heire of A. shall haue a Writ of Right of the whole, for euery Ioyntenant is seised per my & per tout.

If lands be giuen in tayle, the remainder to A. in Fee, the Donee dieth without Issue, his wife priuemēt enseint, A. entreth, the Issue is borne and entreth vpon him and dieth without Issue, A. shall haue a Writ of Right, of the Seisin which he had.

If Lands be giuen in taile to A. the remainder to his right heires, A. dieth without Issue, the collaterall heire of A. shall haue a Writ of Right of the seisin of A. 4. E. 3. 16. 17.

And so note a diuersitie betweene a Seisin to cause possessio fratris, &c. for there is required a more actuall seisin; and a Seisin to maintaine a Writ of Right. And hereby also are the (&c.) in this Section explained. 40. E. 3. 8. 42. E. 3. 20. 37. as. 4 24. E. 4. 24. 7. H. 5. 4. 11. H. 4 11.

Sect. [redacted] 483

CA A Ceo poit estre dit, que ceux parols (modo & forma, put &c.) in mults des cases sont parols

TO this it may be said, that these words (*modo & forma prout, &c.*) in many cases are words

parols de forme de pleder, & nemy parols de substance. Car si home port briefe dentre In casu prouiso, del alienation fait per le tenant en dower a son disinheritance, et counta del alienation fait en fee, et le tenant dit, que il ne aliena pas en le manner come le demaundant ad declare, et sur ceo sount a issue, et troue est per verdict, que le tenant alyenast en le taile, ou pur terme dauter vie, le demaundant recouera: uncore lalyenation ne fuit en le manner come le demaundant auoit declare, &c.

of forme of pleading, and not words of substance, for if a man bring a Writ of Entrie *in casu proviso*, of the alienation made by tenant in Dower to his disinheritance, and counteth of the alienation made in fee, and the tenant saith, that he did not alien in maner as the Demandant hath declared, and vpon this they are at issue, and is found by verdict, that the Tenant aliened in taile, or for tearme of another mans life, the Demandant shall recouer, yet the alienation was not in manner as the Demandant hath declared, &c.

(c) 9. H. 6. 1. 40. E. 3. 35. 21. E. 4. 22. F. N. B. 206. g. 40. E. 3. 5. 32. H. 8. issue Br. 80. *Vide Sect. sequent.*

12. E. 4. 4.

¶ Where, Modo & Forma are of the substance of the issue, and where but words of forme, this diuersitie is to be obserued, (c) where the issue taken goeth to the point of the Writ or Action, there Modo & forma, are but words of forme, as here in the Case of the Writ of Entrie in casu prouiso, and so is the (&c.) well explained in this Section. But otherwise it is, when a collaterall point in pleading is trauersed, as if a feoffment be alleadged by two, and this is trauersed Modo & Forma, and it is found the feoffment of one, there Modo & Forma is materiall. So if a feoffment be pleaded by Deed, and it is trauersed Absque hoc quod feoffauit modo & forma, vpon this Collaterall Issue, modo & forma are so essentiall, as the Jury cannot find a feoffment without deed.

Section 484.

Vide Sect. praeced.

10. E. 4. 7. 8. E. 4. 15. 20. E. 4. 3. 21. E. 4. 3. *Merlebr. cap. 3.*

¶ *Troue est per verdict que il tient per fealtie tantum.* Here is another diuersitie to bee obserued, That albeit the issue be vpon a collaterall point, yet if by the finding of part of the issue, it shall appeare to the Court that no such action lieth for the plaintife no more then if the whole had beene found there modo & forma are but words of forme, as here in the case which Littleton putteth of the Lord and Tenant, appeareth.

¶ *Car le matter del issue est le quel il tient de luy ou nemy, &c.*

Here it appeareth, that

¶ Auxy si soient Seignior & tenant, & le tenant tient del Seignior per fealtie solement, et le Seignior distreine le tenant pur rent & le tenant porta briefe de Trespas enuers son Seignior de ses auers issint prises, & le Seignior plede que le tenant tient de luy per fealtie & certain rent, & pur le rent arere il vient a distreiner, &c. & demaunde iudgement de briefe port vers luy, Quare vi & armis, &c. & lauter dit que il ne tient de luy en le maner come il suppose, et sur ceo

Also if there bee Lord and Tenant, and the Tenant hold of the Lord by fealty only, and the Lord distreine the Tenant for rent, and the Tenant bringeth a Writ of Trespasse against his Lord for his cattle so taken, and the lord plead that the tenant holds of him by fealtie and certaine Rent, and for the Rent behind hee came to distreine, &c. and demand iudgement of the Writ brought against him, *Quare vi & armis, &c.* And the other saith, that hee doth not

ceo sont a issue, et troue est per verdict que il tient de luy per fealtie tantum, en cest case le briefe abatera, et uncore il ne tient de luy en le maner come le seignior auoit dit. Car le matter del issue est, le quel le tenant tient de luy ou nemy, car s'il tient de luy, coment que le Seignior distreina le tenant pur auter seruices que ne doit auer, uncore, tiel briefe de Trespasse, Quare vi & armis, &c. **ne gist enuers le Seignior, mes serra abate.**

hold of him in the manner, as he suppose, and vpon this they are at issue, and it is found by verdict that he holdeth of him by fealtie only. In this case the Writ shall abate, and yet hee doth not hold of him in the manner as the Lord hath said, for the matter of the issue is whether the Tenant holdeth of him or no, for if hee holdeth of him, although that the Lord distreine the Tenant for other seruices which hee ought not to haue, yet such Writ of Trespasse, doth not lie against the Lord, but shall abate.

Quare vi & armis, &c. if the matter of the issue be found it is sufficient. And this rule holds in criminall causes. For if A. be appealed, or indicted of Murder, viz. that hee of malice prepensed killed I. A. pleadeth that he is not guiltie modo & forma, yet the Jury may find the Defendant guilty of Man-slaughter without malice prepensed, because the killing of I. is the matter and malice prepensed is but a circumstance. Pl. Com. 101.

In Assise of Darreine presentment, if the plaintife alleadge the auoydance of the Church by priuation, and the Jury finde the voydance by death, the Plaintife shall haue iudgement, for the manner of voydance is not the title of the Plaintife, but the voydance is the matter. 6. E. 3. 41 b. 25. E. 3. 50. 9. H. 7. 3. 13. H. 7. 14. 29. E. 3. 38.

(d) If a Gardeine of an Hospitall bring an Assise against the Ordinary, hee pleadeth that in his visitation he depriued him as Ordinary, whereupon issue is taken, and it is found that he depriued him as Patron, the Ordinary shall haue iudgement, for the depriuation is the substance of the matter. (d) 8. E. 3. 70. 8. Ass. 29. & 39. 9. E. 3. 338. 24. E. 3. 34. 5. H. 4. 2. 7. H. 4. 11. Pl. Com. 92. 3. Mar. Dier. 116. 40. E. 3. 35.

The Lessee couenant with the Lessor not to cut down any trees, &c. & bind himselfe in a bond of forty pounds for performance of Couenants, the Lessee cut downe ten trees, the Lessor bringeth an Action of Debt vpon the bond, & assigneth a breach that the Lessee cutteth downe twentie trees, whereupon issue is ioyned & the Jury find that the Lessee cut downe ten, iudgement shall bee giuen for the Plaintife. For sufficient matter of the issue is found, for the Plaintife. De. 2. & 3. Ph. & Mar. 115. b. Trin. 22. Eliz. Rot. 920. Wilmans case. 48. E. 3. 28. 34. Ass. 3. 30. Ass. 5. 41. E. 3. 28. 33. E. 3. verdict. 47. 22. E. 3. 1. b. 48. E. 3. 48. 31. E. 3. account. 58. 28. Ass. 48.

Sect. 485.

¶ Auxy en briefe de trespasse de batterie, ou des biens emports, s'il le defendant plede de rien culpable, en le mann come le Plaintife suppose, et troue est que le defendant est culpable en auter ville, ou a auter iour que le Plaintife suppose, uncore il recouera.

ALso in a Writ of Trespasse for batterie, or for goods carried away, if the Defendant plead not guiltie, in manner as the Plaintife suppose, and it is found that the Defendant is guiltie in another Towne, or at another day then the Plaintife suppose, yet hee shall recouer.

¶ *EN briefe de trespasse de battery & des biens emports, &c.* Here Littleton speaketh of Actions brought for things transitorie. In which cases the wrong beeing done in one Towne, the Plaintife may not only alleage it in another Towne, as Littleton here saith, but also in another Countie, and the Jurors vpon not guiltie pleaded, are bound to find for the plaintife.

Neither can the assault, batterie or taking of goods, &c. alleadged in another Countie, be trauersed without speciall

Et issint en plusors auters cases, ceux parols, s. en le maner come le demaundant ou l'plaintife ad suppose, ne font ascun matter de substance del issue. Car ẽ briefe de droit, lou le mise est ioyne sur le mere droit, il est a tant a dire, et a tiel effect, s. le quel ad pluis mere droit, le tenant ou le demandant al chose en demand.

And so in many other cases these words, s. in manner as the demandant or the plaintife hath supposed, doe not make any matter of substance of the issue, for in a Writ of right, where the mise is ioyned vpon the meere right, that is as much to say, & to such effect, *viz.* whether the tenāt or demaundant hath more meere right to the thing in demand.

cause of iustification which extendeth to some certaine place, as if a Constable of a towne in another Countie arrest the body of a man, that breaketh the peace, there hee may trauerse the County (but he must not rest there) but all other places sauing in the Towne whereof he is Constable. And so it is of taking of goods, the Defendant iustifie for damage feasant in another Countie he must trauerse as before. But where the cause of the iustification is not restrained to a certaine place that is so locall as it cannot be alledged in any other Towne as in the cases before alledged, and the like, then albeit the action bee brought in a forraine Countie, yet he must allege his iustification in the Countie where the action is brought. As if a man be beaten in the County of Middlesex, and he bringeth his action in the Countie of Buck. the Defendant cannot pleade that the Plaintife assaulted him in the County of Midd. &c. and trauerse the County, but he must pleade his iustification in the County of Buck. for that the cause of his iustification is good in any place. And so it is in case of bailement of goods, and other cases for transitory things, as for example.

Trin. 30. Eliz. in the Kings bench, betweene Inglebert and Iones. And herewith agreeth a iudgement in the Court of Common pleas, Pasch. 38. Eliz. Rot. 1656.

In an action vpon the case the Plaintife declared for speaking of slanderous words which is transitorie, and said the words to be spoken in London, the Defendant pleaded a concord for speaking of words in all the Counties of England, sauing in London, and trauersed the speaking of the words in London: the Plaintife in his replication denied the concord, whereupon the Defendant demurred, and iudgement was giuen for the Plaintife. For the Court said, that if the concord in that case should not be trauersed, it would follow that by a new and subtile inuention of pleading, an ancient principle in Law, (that for transitorie causes of action the Plaintife might alledge the same in what place or Countie he would) should be subuerted, which ought not to be suffered, and therefore the Judges of both Courts allowed a trauerse vpon a trauerse in that case: And the wisedome of the Judges and Sages of the Law haue alwayes suppressed new and subtile inuentions in derogation of the Common Law. And therefore the Judges say in one booke (c) we will not change the Law which alwayes hath beene vsed. And another saith (f) it is better that it be turned to a default, then the Law should be changed, or any innouation made

(c) 38. E. 3. 1.
(f) 2. H. 4. 18.
31. E. 3. Gager deliuer. 5.
(*) 42. Ass. 12. 4. E. 3. ca. 5.
18. E. 3. ca. 1. & ca. 6.
4. H. 4. ca. 2.
(h) Lib. 6. fo. 46. 47. Dowdales case. 3. E. 3. Ass. 446. 27. E. 3. 86. 1. Ass. 16. 3. Ass. 4. 6. Ass. 4. 5. Ass. 7. 18. E. 3. 38. 21. Ass. 8. 29. Ass. 5. 44. E. 3. 6. b. 14. H. 4. 35. 5. H. 5. 2. 10. H. 6. 13. 21. H. 6. 51. 37. H. 6. 2. 7. E. 4. 45. 18. E. 4. 1. 22. E. 4. 19. 13. H. 7. 17. 2. Mar. Br. attaint. 104. 10. Eliz. Dier, 171.
(i) 19. H. 6. 48. 11. H. 6. 16. 43. E. 3. 23. b. 46. E. 3. 3. a. 9. H. 6. 62. 21. H. 6. 27. 14. H. 8. 24. 18. E. 4. 1. 20. H. 6. 2. 34. H. 6. 42. 14. H. 6. 21. 22. 4. H. 6. 13. 33. H. 6. 25. 12. E. 4. 12. 28. H. 8. Dier. 29. 21. E. 4. 19. 80. 27. H. 8. 19. 12. H. 8. 1. 11. H. 4. 65. 19. H. 8. 6.

A man did grant a rent, with a new inuented clause of Distresse, viz. That the Grantee should hold the Distresse against gages and pledges, and yet by the whole Court he shall gage deliuerance, for otherwise by this new inuention all Repleuyes shall be taken away.

(*) See many other new inuentions in derogation of the Common Law disallowed by the Judges and by the Court of Parliament.

(h) Where the Jury is bound to finde aswell locall things in many cases as transitory in other Counties, see at large in my Reports.

By this which hath beene said you shall know the Law as it is now in vse in these cases, and the better vnderstand our (i) bookes when you shall reade them concerning as well locall, as transitory things, wherein you shall finde great variety of opinion in our bookes.

¶ *Si le defendant plead de rien culpable.* **This is a good issue if the** Defendant committed no battery at all, but regularly by the Common Law if the Defendant hath cause of iustification or excuse, then can he not pleade not guilty, for then vpon the euidence it shall be found against him, for that he confesseth the battery, and vpon that issue cannot iustifie it, but he must pleade the speciall matter, and confesse and iustifie the battery.

The like Law is in other cases, and therefore this is a learning necessary to be knowne, for that the losse of most causes dependeth thereupon. As if in battery the Defendant may iustifie the same to be done of the Plaintifes owne assault he must pleade it specially, and must not pleade the generall issue, and so of the like. In trespasse of breaking his close, vpon not guilty

be

he cannot giue in euidence, that the beasts came thorow the Plaintifes hedge, which he ought to keepe, nor vpon the generall issue iustifie by reason of a Rent-charge, Common, or the like. 25.H.8.Br.

In detinue the Defendant pleadeth Non detinet, he cannot giue in euidence, that the goods were pawned to him for money, and that it is not paid, but must pleade it, but he may giue in euidence a gift from the Plaintife, for that proueth, he detaineth not the Plaintifes goods. 22.H.6.33.

(d) So in an action of waste, vpon the plea Nul wast fait, he may giue in euidence any thing, that proueth it no waste, as by tempest, by lightning, by enemies, and the like, but he cannot giue in euidence iustifiable waste, as to repaire the house or the like. (e) If one doth waste, and before the action brought the Lessee repaireth it, and after the Lessor bringeth an Action of waste, and the Lessee plead Quod non fecit vastum, hee cannot giue in euidence the especiall matter. (d) 12 H.8.1. 19.E.3. waste 30. 20.E 3.wast.32. (e) 10.Eliz.Dier,276. 2.Mar.Dier 212.

If two men be bound in a bond ioyntly, and the one is sued alone, he may plead this matter in abatement of the writ, but he cannot plead Non est factum, for it is his Deed, though it be not his sole Deed. (f) See in Whelpdales case, where a man may safely plead Non est factū, and where not, and the former books that treat of that matter well reconciled. (f) Lib.5.fo.119. Whelpdales case. 7.E.4.5.7.E.6.Br. Non est fact.14. 1.H.7.15 14.H.8.28. Pl Com. Diue & Man case.

(g) Upon Plene administrauit pleaded by an Executor Et issint riens inter maines, if it bee proued that he hath goods in his hands which were the Testators, he may giue in euidence, that he hath paid to that value of his owne money, and need not plead it specially. 36 H.8.Dier 59. 2.Mar. Dier 112. 1.Eliz.Dier.167.

In an Assise if the Tenant plead Nul tort nul disseisin, he cannot giue in euidence a Release after the Disseisin, but a Release before the Disseisin he may, for then there is no Disseisin vpon the matter. (g) Hill.10.H.8.Rot.323. in Communi banco. Et Mich. 6.E.6. in Communi banco Bendloes.

In a writ of Right if the Tenant ioyne the Mise vpon the meere right, hee cannot giue in euidence a collaterall warrantie, for he hath not any right by it, and therefore it ought to haue beene pleaded. 7.H.5.9. 6.H.7.10. 34.E.3.Droit.29.

Of this learning you shall reade plentifully in our bookes, and in my Reports. This little taste shall here suffice to make the reader capable of the rest. Regularly whensoeuer a man doth any thing by force of a warrant or authority, he must plead it. 9 E.3.32. 8.E.3.24. 33.E.3.Verdit. 18.H.6.24. 39.H.6.38. 18.E.3.19.

But all that hath beene said must be vnder two cautions. First that whensoeuer a man cannot haue aduantage of the speciall matter by way of pleading, there he shall take aduantage of it in the euidence. For example the rule of Law is, that a man cannot iustifie in the killing or death of a man, and therefore in that case, he shall be receiued to giue the especiall matter in euidence, as that it was Se defendendo, or in defence of his house in the night against theeues and robbers or the like. Pl.Com.81.173. 21 H.7 76 16. Kellwey 21.E.4.11. 22.E.4.45. 13.H.7.13. Stanf.Pl. Cor.15. 22.Ass.55. 37.H.6.21.

Secondly, That in any action vpon the case, Trespasse, Battery, or of false imprisonment against any Iustice of peace, Maior, or Bailife of Citie or Towne corporate, Headborough, Port-reue, Constable, Tithingman, Collector of Subsidie or Fifteene, in any his Maiesties Courts in Westminster, or elsewhere concerning any thing by any of them done by reason of any of their offices aforesaid, and all other in their aide or assistance or by their commandement, &c. they may plead the generall issue, and giue the speciall matter for theire excuse or iustification in euidence. 7.Ia.ca.5.

In an Action of trespasse or other suite against any person for taking of any Distresse or other Act doing by force of the Commission of Sewers, the Defendant in any such Action shall and may make Auowrie, Conusance or Iustification generally, that it was done by authority of the Commission of Sewers for Lotte or Tax assessed by that Commission, &c. and the Plaintife shall reply he did it of his owne wrong without such cause. And both these acts were made for auoyding of prolixity and captiousnesse of pleading tending to the great charge and danger of Officers and ministers of Iustice, &c. Euidence, *Euidentia*. This word in legall vnderstanding doth not only containe matters of Record, as Letters patents, Fines, Recoueries, Inrolments, and the like, and writings vnder seale, as Charters and Deeds, and other writings without seale, as Court Rolles, Accounts, and the like, which are called Euidences Instrumenta, but in a larger sence it containeth also Testimonia, the Testimony of witnesses, and other proofes to be produced and giuen to a Iury, for the finding of any issue ioyned betweene the parties. And it is called Euidence, because thereby the point in issue is to be made euident to the Iury. Probationes debent esse euidentes, (id est) perspicuæ & faciles intelligi. But let vs now returne to Littleton. 23.H 8.ca.5.

¶ *Ou a auter iour que le Plaintife suppose.* (g) **As if the Trespasse** were done the fourth of May, and the Plaintife alledgeth the same to be done the fifth of May or the first of May, when no trespasse was done, yet if vpon the euidence it falleth out, That the Trespasse was done before the Action brought, it sufficeth: and this is warranted by Littleton who speaketh indifinitely, that the Iurie may find the Defendant guiltie at another day than the Plaintife supposeth. (g) 19.H.6.47. 5.E.4.5. 21.E.4.66.

¶ *Et a tiel effect.* **Here is to be obserued, That the Law of Eng-**

land respecteth the effect and substance of the matter, and not everie nicitie of forme or circumstance, Qui hæret in litera, hæret in cortice, & apices iuris non sunt iura.

Section 486.

¶ ITem si home soit disseisie, et le Disseisor devie seisie, &c. et son fits et heire est eins per discent, et le Disseisee enter sur lheire Disseisor, le quel entrie est un disseisin, &c. si lheire port Assise ou Briefe de Entre en nature de Assise, il recouera.

ALso if a man bee disseised, and the disseisor dieth seised, &c. and his sonne and heire is in by discent, and the Disseisee enter vpon the heire of the Disseisor, which entrie is a Disseisin, &c. if the heire bring an Assise or a Writ of Entrie in nature of an Assise, hee shall recouer.

¶ ANd the reason hereof is, for that in the Writ of Right mentioned in the next Section the charge of the grand Assise vpon their Oath is vpon the meere right, and not vpon the possession.

Sect. 487.

¶ MEs si lheire port Briefe de Droit envers le Disseisee il serra barre, pur ceo que quant le graund Assise est iure, lour serement est sur le mere droit, et nemy sur le possession. Car si lheire le Disseisor suist un Assise de Nouel disseisin, ou briefe Dentre en natuř dassise, et recouerast vs le Disseisee, et suist executiō, uncore poit le Disseisee auer brē Dentre en le Per envers luy, de le disseisin fait a luy per son pere, ou il poit auer envers lheire briefe de Droit.

BVt if the heyre bring a Writ of Right against the Disseisee, he shall bee barred, for that when the graund Assise is sworne, their Oath is vpon the meere right, and not vpon the possession: For if the Heyre of the Disseisor sue an Assise of *Nouel disseisin*, or a Writ of *Entrie* in nature of an Assise, and recouers against the Disseisee, and sueth execution, yet may the Disseisee haue a Writ of *Entrie* in the *Per*, against him, for the Disseisin made to him by his father, or he may haue against the heire a writ of Right.

¶ *Car si le heire le Disseisor, &c.* Here is a diversitie to bee obserued concerning that which hath beene sayd, when the possession shall draw the right of the land to it, and when not. And therefore when the possession is first, and then a right
50.E.3.7. commeth thereunto, the entrie of him that hath right to the possession shall gaine also the right, which as before it appeareth in those cases there put, followeth the possession,
V. Sect. 447. and the right of possession draweth the right unto it, but when the right is first, and then the possession commeth to the right, albeit the possession be defeated, (as here in Littletons case it is by the heire of the Disseisor) yet the right of the Disseisee remaineth.

¶ *Briefe Dentrie en*
5. Ass. 1. 10. Ass. 16. *le Per.* A. dieth seised, and the land discendeth to B. his sonne, before he entreth an estranger abateth and dieth seised, B. entreth, against whom the heire of the Abator recouereth in an Assise, B. may haue a Writ of Mortdancester

dancester, and recouer the land against him. And if the Disseisin had beene done to A. &c. then after the recouerie in the Assise B. should haue had a Writ of Entrie in the Per, because the heyre that is in by discent is in the Per.

Sect. 488.

¶ Mes si le heyre doit recouer enuers le Disseisee en le case auantdit, per bre de Droit, donque tout son droit serroit clerement ale, pur ceo que iudgement final serroit done enuers luy, que serroit encounter reason, lou le Disseisee ad le pluis meere droit, &c.

BVt if the Heire ought to recouer against the Disseisee in the case aforesayd by a Writ of Right, then all his right should be cleerely taken away, for that iudgement finall shall bee giuen against him, which should bee against reason where the Disseisee hath the more meere right.

¶ *Iudgement final.* The forme whereof you shall see in the last Section of this Chapter.

¶ *Que serra encounter reason.* Argumentum ab inconuenienti. *V. Sect. 87. &c.*

Section 489.

¶ Et saches mon fits que en briefe de Droit, apres ceo que les quater chiualers ont eslie le grand Assise, donques il nad pluis greindet delay que en vn briefe de Formedon, apres ceo que les parties sont a issue, &c. et si le mise soit ioyne sur le Battaile, donques il ad meind delay.

ANd know (my sonne) that in a Writ of Right after the foure Knights haue chosen the grand Assise, then he hath no greater delay than in a Writ of *Formedon*, after the parties be at issue, &c. And if the Mise bee ioyned vpon bataile, then hee hath lesser delay.

¶ *Battaile.* See for this word in the last Section of this Chapter.

¶ *Issue, &c.* Or Demurrer, which is an Issue in Law.

Sect. 490. & 491.

¶ Item release de tout le droit, &c. en ascun case est bone, fait a celuy que est suppose tenant en Ley, coment que il nad riens en les Tenements. Sicome en Præcipe quod reddat, si le Tenant aliena la terre pendant le briefe, et puis le demaundant relessa a luy

ALso a release of all the right, &c. in some case is good made to him which is supposed Tenant in Law, albeit he hath nothing in the Tenements. As in a *Præcipe quod reddat*, if the Tenaunt alien the land hanging the Writ, and after the Demandant releaseth

luy tout son droit, &c. cel release est bone, pur ceo que il est suppose destre tenant per le suit del Demandant, et uncore il nad riens en la Terre al temps de Release fait.

to him all his right, &c. this Release is good, for that hee is supposed to be Tenant by the suit of the Demandant, and yet hee hath nothing in the land at the time of the Release made.

Sect.491.

En mesme le manner est, si en Præcipe quod reddat le tenant vouche, & le Vouchee ent en le Garrantie, si apres le Demandant relessa al vouchee tout son droit, ceo est assets bone, pur ceo que l'Vouchee apres ceo que il auoit enter en le Garrantie, est Tenant en Ley al Demandant, &c.

IN the same manner it is in a *Præcipe quod reddat*, the tenant vouch, and the Vouchee enters into Warrantie, if afterward the Demand: release to the vouchee al his right, this is good enough, for that the Vouchee after that he hath entred into Warranty is Tenant in Law to the Demandant, &c.

(h) 10.E.4.13. 12.Ass.41. 22.Ass.13.23.E.3.21. 25.E.3.40.38.E.3.10.11 7.E.3.6. 19.E.3.tit.Releas. 34.E.3.tit.Releas, 9.E.4.15.39.H.6.40.17.rs. 24.8.H.7.5.20.Ass.2.14.E.3.Procedendo,4.9.E.3.17. 32 E.3.Quare Impedit 2. Dyer 17.Eliz.341. Sect.447. * Vide ant,Sect.447.

Here it doth appeare, That there is a Tenant in Deed and a Tenant in Law, and Littleton in this and the next Section putteth two examples of Tenants in Law, viz (h) the Tenant to a Præcipe after alienation, and of the Vouchee, whereof somewhat hath beene sayd before.

And it is obseruable, That Littleton saith, That in both cases hee is Tenant in Law to the Demandant, and yet he hath nothing in the Land. And therefore if after the Vouchee hath entred into warrantie, and become Tenant in Law, an Ancestor collaterall of the demandant releaseth to the Vouchee with warrantie, he shall not plead this against the Demaundant, for that the Release by the Estranger is voyd, which besides the authorities before vouched, appeareth by Littleton himselfe, * for he saith, That he is Tenaunt in Law to the Demaundant, whereby he excludeth, that he is Tenant in respect of any estranger.

Section 492.

Item quant al releases dactions reals et personals, il est issint, que ascuns actions sont mixt en le realty et en le personaltie, sicome un action de waste sue enuers tenant a terme de vie, cest action est en le realtie, pur ceo que le lieu waste serra recouer. Et auxy en le per-

Also as to releases of Actions Realls, and Personals it is thus. Some actions are mixt in the realtie and in the personaltie, as an action of wast sued against Tenant for life. This Action is in the Realtie, because the place wasted shall bee recouered, and also in the Personaltie, because

Glanu.li.1.ca.1. Bract.li.3.fo.101. Brit.fo.71. Flet li.1.ca 15.& 16.

Nota, there bee two kind of Actions, viz. one that concern the Pleas of the Crowne, Placita Coronæ, or Placita Criminalia, another that concerne Common Pleas, Placita Communia seu Ciuilia. Of that which concerneth Pleas of the Crowne, Littleton speaketh hereafter in this Chapter. Of Actions concerning Common Pleas,

Mir.ca.2.§.1. Bract.vbi sup. Flet.li.1.ca.1.

Littleton speaketh in this place. And these are threefold (that is to say) Reall, Personall and Mixt. Placitorum aliud personale, aliud reale, aliud mixtum. Or Actionum quædam sunt in

personaltie, pur ceo que treble damages serront recouers p̃ le tortious wast fait p le tenant, & pur ceo en cest action, un releas dactions reals est bon plee en barre, et issint est un releas dactions personals.

treble dammages shall bee recouered for the wrongfull waste done by the Tenant, And therefore in this action a release of actions reals is a good plea in barre, and so is a Release of actions personals.

Rem, quædam in Personam, & quædam mixtæ. And generally. Actio is defined. (i) Actio nihil aliud est quam ius prosequendi in iudicio quod sibi debetur. Or Action nest auter chose que loiall demande de son droit.

(k) And by the release of all Actions, causes of action be released, but within a submission of all actions to arbitrement, causes of action are not contained.

(i) *Vide Sect. 444. Bract. lib. 3. fol. 98. Fleta lib. 1. cap. 15. Mirror cap. 2. §. 1.*

(k) *Lib 8. 153. Alibams case. 35. H. 8. Dier 57. 5. Mar. 217. Vide 36. H. 6. 8. Vide 42. E. 3. 22. 23.*

Tenant pur vie. And so it is if it bee brought against tenant for yeares because it agreeth with the reason of Littleton here rendred, viz that the place wasted shall be recouered, and therefore soundeth in the realtie.

Auxy en le personaltie pur ceo que treble damages serra recouers, which doe sound in the personaltie. Wherefore Littleton concludeth, that in an Action mixt a Release of all actions reals is a good barre, and so is a release of all actions personals.

And here is to be obserued a diuersitie betweene the act of the partie, & an act in Law, for a man by his owne act cannot alter the nature of his action, and therefore if the Lessee for life or Lessee for yeares doe waste, now is an action of waste giuen to the Lessor, wherein he shall recouer two things, viz. the place wasted, and treble dammages; in this case if the Lessor release all actions reals, he shall not haue an Action of waste in the personaltie only. And if he release all Actions personals he shall not haue an Action of waste in the realtie only.

(l) And so it is if the Lessee doth waste, and after surrendreth to the Lessor his estate, and the Lessor accept thereof, the Lessor shall not haue an Action of waste.

(l) *19. H. 6 66. 14. H. 6. 14. 11. R. 2. Waste 99. 14. H. 8. 14 23. H. 8. Br. Waste.*

But by act in Law the nature of the action may be changed, as if a man make a Lease pur terme dauter vie, and the Lessee doth waste, and then Cesty que vie dieth, an Action of waste shall lie for dammages only because the other is determined by act in Law.

And againe, hereupon is another diuersitie to be obserued, that in case when an action is well begun, and part of the Action determineth by act in Law, and yet the like action for the residue is giuen, there the writ shall not abate, but proceed. But where by the determination of part the like action remayneth not for the residue, there the Action well commenced shall abate. As if an Action of waste be brought against tenant, pur terme dauter vie, and hanging the writ Cesty que vie, dieth, the writ shall not abate, but the Plaintife shall recouer dammages only, because if Cesty que vie had died before any action brought the Lessor might haue an action of waste for the dammages: So if an Eiectione firme bee brought, and the tearme incurreth hanging the action, yet the Action shall proceed for dammages only, because an Eiectione doth lie after the tearme for dammages only. But if tenant pur auter vie, bring an Assise, and Cesty que vie dieth, hanging the writ, albeit the writ were well commenced, yet the writ shall abate, because no Assise can be maintainable for dammages only.

11. H 6. 43. 9. E. 4. 50. 24. E. 3. 72. 18 E. 3. 28. 9. H. 6. 30.

So if an Action of waste be brought by Baron and Fem. in remainder, in especiall taile and hanging the writ the wife dieth without issue, the writ shall abate, because euery kind of Action of waste must be ad exhæredationem.

2. H. 4. 22. 6. E. 2. briefe 807.

If a writ of Annuitie be brought, and the Annuitie determineth hanging the writ, the writ faileth for euer, because no like Action can be maintained for the Arrerages only, but for the Annuitie and Arrerages.

34. H. 6. 20. 9. E. 4. 39. 14. H. 7. 31. 18. E. 3. Scire facias 10.

But where dammages only are to be recouered, there albeit by act in Law, the like Action lieth not afterwards, yet the Action well commenced shall proceed, (m) as if a Conspiracie be brought against two, and one of them dieth hanging the writ, it shall proceed.

(m) *22. R. 2. briefe 888. 18. E. 4. 1.*

And in an Assise of Nouell disseisin, a writ of Annuitie, Quare impedit and other mixt Actions, a release of Actions reals is a good Plea, and so it is of a release of Actions personals.

2. H. 4. 13. 9. H. 6. 57.

But if three Joyntenants be disseised, and they arraigne an Assise, and one of them release to the Disseisor all Actions personals, this shall barre him, but it shall not barre the other Plaintife, for hauing regard to them the realtie shall bee preferred, & omne maius trahit ad se minus dignum. (n) And in a writ of ward brought by two, the release of the one shall not grieue the other, but shall enure to his benefit, for he shall recouer the whole ward, and hold his companion out.

30. H. 6. Barre 59.

(n) *30. H. 6. vbi supra. 45. E. 3 fol. 6. 18. E. 3. fol. 56. 21. H 6. 18. a.*

But here a diuersitie is to be obserued betweene reall actions wherein dammages are to bee reco-

recovered at the Common Law, as in an Assise, &c. and reall actions where dammages are not to be recovered by the Common Law, but are given by the (o) Statute, for there a release of all Actions personals is no barre, as in the Writ of Dower, Entrie sur disseisin in le per &c. Mordanc', Aiel, &c.

(o) Merton cap. 1. in dower. Glouc. cap. 1.

Sect. 493.

Et en Quare impedit, un releas dactions personals est bone plee, & issint est un release dactions reals, Per Martin, qd' fuit concessum H. 9. H. 6. 57.*

AND in a *Quare impedit*, a release of Actions personals is a good Plea, and so is a release of Actions reals, *Per Martin. Quod fuit concessum. Hill. 9. H. 6. fol. 57.*

9. H. 6. 57. 21. H. 6. 27. b.

This is an addition to Littleton, which although it be Law, and the Booke truly cited, yet I passe it over. But yet note by the way that a release of Actions personals, is also a good barre in a Quare impedit, because it is an Action mixt.

Sect. 494.

Et mesme le maner est en assise de Novel disseisin, pur ceo que il est mixt en le realtie, et e le personalty. Mes si un tiel ass. soit arraigne enter le disseisor et le tenant, le disseisor bien poit plede un releas dactions personals, pur barrer lass. mes nemy un releas dactions reals, car nul pledera releas dactions reals en ass. forsque le tenant.

IN the same manner it is in an Assise of *Novel disseisin*, for that it is mixt in the realtie and in the personaltie; but if such an Assise be arraigned bee against the Disseisor, and the Tenant, the Disseisor may well plead a release of Actions personals to barre the Assise, but not a release of Actions reals, for none shall plead a release of Actions reals in an Assise, but the tenant.

Le *disseisor bien poet pleder, &c.* Nota, every man shall plead such Pleas as are proper for him, and apt for his defence to be pleaded. (q) As a disseisor that hath nothing in the land may plead a release of actions personals, because dammages are to bee recovered against him, and therefore for his defence hee may plead it, but a release of actions reals hee cannot plead, because he hath no estate in the Land, and none shall plead a release of Actions reals in an Assise, but the tenant of the Land. Et sic de caeteris. But the Tenant in an Assise shall plead a release of Actions personals to the Disseisor, for that Plea prooveth that the Plaintife hath no cause of action against him.

(q) 11. Ass. 9. 18. E. 3. 2. 23. 24. 31. E. 3 quare Imp. 161. 7. E. 3. 5. 9. E. 3. 4. 10. E. 3. 30. 22. E. 3. 2. 13. H. 4. 7. 3. E. 2. quare Imp. 44. 38. E. 3. 30. 31. 5. E. 3. 25. 21. E. 3. 16. 17. 5. H. 7. 34. 8 H. 6. 14. 22. H. 6. 28. 26. 1 H. 7. 34. 27. E. 3. 81. 32 H. 6. 15. b. 17. Ass. 25. 2. H. 7. 14. 13. H. 8 13. 14. 44 E. 3. 12. 46 E. 3. 13. 16. E. 4 11. 24 E. 3 34. 4. E. 4 18. 7. H. 4. 34. 2. R. 3 encumbent 4. 33. E. 3. quare Imp 194.

13. E. 4. 2. a.

If the Disseisee release to the Disseisor all actions reals, and the Disseisor maketh a feoffement in fee, and an Assise is brought against them, the Feoffee shall not plead the release to the Disseisor, for that he is not privie to the release, for a release of actions shall only extend to Privies.

If a Disseisor make a lease for life the remainder in fee, and the Disseisee release all Actions, to the Tenant for life, after the death of Tenant for life, he in the remaynder shall not plead the said release.

If the Disseisee release all Actions to the Disseisor, and die, this doth barre him, but for his heire, for after his decease his heire shall have an Action (r) as some have said. And hereby may appeare a manifest diversitie between a release of a Right, and a release of Actions.

(r) 19. H. 6. 23. a.

Section 495.

¶ Item, en tiels actions reals q̃ couient destre sue enuers le tenant dl franktenement, si le tenant ad vn releas dactions reals del Demandant fait a luy deuant le briefe purchase, et il plede ceo, il est bon plee pur le Demandant adire, que celuy que pleda le plee nauoit rien, en le franktenement al temps del releas fait, car adonque il nauoit cause dauer ascun action real enuers luy.

ALso in such Actions Reals which ought to bee sued against the tenant of the Free-hold, if the tenāt hath a release of actions reals from the Demandant made vnto him before the Writ purchased, and he plead this, it is a good plea for the demandant to say, that hee which plead the Plea had nothing in the Freehold at the time of the release made, for then hee had no cause to haue an Action reall against him.

¶ This is euident enough by that which hath beene said, that a release of all actions reals must be made to him that is Tenant of the Land, because a reall Action must be brought against such a Tenant.

Sect. 496.

¶ Item en tiel cas ou home poet enter en Terres ou Tenements, et auxy poit auer vn Action real de ceo que est done p la Ley enuers le Tenant, si en cest case le Demandant relessa al tenant touts maners de Actions reals, vncore ceo ne tolle le dmandant de son entrie, mes le Demandant bien poit enter nient contristeāt tiel releas pur ceo que nul chose est relesse forsque laction, &c.

ALso in such case where a man may enter into Lands or Tenements, and also may haue an Action reall for this, which is giuen by the Law against the tenant, if in this case the Demandant releaseth to the Tenant all manner of Actions realls, yet this shall not take the Demaundant from his entrie, but the Demaundant may well enter notwithstanding such release, for that nothing is released but the Action, &c.

¶ Poet enter. Here it appeareth, That where a man may enter, a Release of all Actions doth not barre him of his right, because he hath another remedy, viz to enter. And this is agreeable with the authoritis of our (f) Bookes. But where his entrie is not lawfull, there a Release of all Actions is by consequence a barre of his right, because he hath released the mean whereby he might recouer his right. As if the Disseisee release all Actions to the heire of the disseisor, which is in by Discent, he hath no remedie to recouer the land, but yet the disseisee hath a right, for that he hath released his Action, & not his right as shal be said hereafter in the Chapter of Remitter in his proper place. If the heire of the Disseisor make a feoffment in fee to two, and the disseisee releaseth to one of the Feoffees all Actions and hee dieth, the Suruiuour shall not plead this release for the causes abouesaid. And hereby also again appeareth another diuersitie betweene a release of a right, and a release of Actions.

(f) 18.E.3.34. 19.E.3. Title 35.

19.Ass.3. 30.E.3.19.6. 19 H.6.4.6. 21.H.7.23.b. 7.H.6.6.

It is to be obserued when a man hath seuerall remedies for one and the selfesame thing be it reall, personall, or mixt, albeit he releaseth one of his remedies, he may vse the other.

Sect.497.

¶En mesme le maner est de choses personals, sicom home a tort p̄rent mes biens, si ieo relessa a luy touts actions personals, vncore ieo puisse p le ley prender mes biens hors de son possession.

IN the same manner is it of things personall, as if a man by wrong take away my goods, if I release to him all actions personals, yet I may by the Law take my goods out of his possession.

This of it selfe is euident.

Sect. 498.

¶Auxy si ieo ay ascū cause daū breife de Detinue de mes biēs vers vn auter, coment q̄ ieo relessa a luy touts actions personals, vncore ieo puisse per le ley prendre mes biens hors ō son possession, pur ceo que nul droit ō les biens est relesse a luy, mes solement laction, &c.

ALso if I haue any cause to haue a Writ of Detinue of my goods against an other, albeit that I release to him all actions personals, yet I may by the Law take my goods out of his possession, because no right of the goods is released to him but only the action, &c.

Glanuil.lib.10.ca.13.

¶Briefe de detinue. Breue de detentione dicitur a detinendo, because Detinet is the principall word in the Writ. And it lyeth where any man comes to goods either by deliuery, or by finding.

41.E.3.2.

In this writ the Plaintife shall recouer the thing detained, and therefore it must bee so certaine as it may be knowne, and for that cause, it lyeth not for money out of a bagge, or chest, and so of corne out of a sacke and the like, these cannot be knowne from other.

(t) 41.E.3.2. 8.H.6.18. 28.29. 21.E.3.28. 3.H.6.19. 30.H.6.4. 9.H.6.18.

(u) 10.H.6.20. 21.H.6.1. 14.H.6.4. 14.H.4.23.24. 27.

(x) 20.H.6.45. 19.E.3. Seuerance 14. 31.E.3.ib.32. 42.E.3.13. 40.E.3.25.

(t) A man shall haue an action of Detinue of Charters which concerne the inheritance of his land if hee know the certaintie of them, and what land they concerne, or if they be in Bagge sealed, or Chest locked, though he knoweth not the certaintie of them: and it is good pollicie (if possibly he can) in that case to declare of one Charter in especiall, (u) and then the Defendant shall not wage his Law. (x) An action of Detinue for Charters doth sound in the realty, for therein summons and seuerance lyeth, and in Detinue of goods a Capias doth lye, but for Charters in speciall a Capias lyeth not, and yet a Release of actions personals in a writ of Detinue of Charters is a good barre.

Sect. 499.

¶ITem si hom̄ soit disseisie, & le disseisor fait feoffment a diuers persons a son vse, et le disseisor continualment prist les profits, &c. et le disseisee relessa a luy touts

ALso if a man bee disseised, and the disseisor maketh a feoffmēt to diuers persons to his vse, and the disseisor continually taketh the proffits, &c. & the disseisee release

¶Per cause del Statute. That is to say the Statute of 4.H.4. cap.7. and 11 H 6.ca 4.

¶Car sil voet pleder le release generalment. Here it appeareth that when the Statute had giuen the action reall a=

touts actions reals, et puis il suist vers luy vn̄e Dentre en nature dassise p cause de lestatute, pur ceo que il prent les profits, &c. Quære, comēt le disseisor serra aide per le dit releas: car sil voile pleder le releas generalment, donques l' demandāt poit dire q̄ il nauoit riens en le franktenement al temps del releas fait, & sil pleda releas specialment, donques il couient conustr̄e vn disseisin, et donq̄s puit le demandant enter en le tre, &c. p son conusans de l' disseisin, &c. Mes peraduenture p especial pleader il luy poit barr̄ de laction que il suist, &c. coment le demandant poit enter.

to him all actions reals, and after hee sueth against him a Writ of entrie in nature of an assise by reason of the statute, because hee taketh the proffits, &c. *Quare*, how the disseisor shall bee ayded by the said release, for if he will plead the release generally, then the demandant may say that hee had nothing in the freehold at the time of the release made, and if hee plead the release specially, then he must acknowledge a disseisin, and then may the demandant enter into the land, &c. by his acknowledgement of the disseisin, &c. but peraduenture by speciall pleading he may barre him of the actiō which hee sueth, &c. though the demandant may enter.

gainst the pernor of the profits, it enableth him to take and pleade a Release of all actions reals, and yet he hath neither Ius in re, nor ius ad rem, which point is worthy of obseruation for manifestation of the equity of the Law. 3. H. 7. 2.

¶ *Donques il couient conustre vn disseisin, &c.* In a Writ of Dower the Tenant pleaded that before the Writ purchased A. was seised of the land, &c. vntill by the Tenant himselfe hee was disseised, and that hanging the Writ A. recouered against him, &c. iudgement of the Writ, and adiudged a good plea, in which plea the Tenant confessed a Disseisin in himselfe. 15. E. 4. 4 b.

¶ *Donques poit le demandant enter.* So might he haue done in this case that Littleton putteth, albeit the Tenant confessed no disseisin. And therefore it is no preiudice to the Tenant to confesse a disseisin in himselfe, &c and then, as Littleton here holdeth, the action shall be barred.

But the reader is to obserue, that now by the Statute of 27 H 8. ca 10. which execute the possession to the vse, all the Statutes against Cesty q̄ vse, or pernor of the profits haue lost their force. 28. H. 8. Dier. 32. 27. H. 8. ca. 10.

Sect. 500.

¶ [Ceō si home suist appeale de felony del mort son ancester enuers vn auter, coment que lappellant relessa al defendant touts maners dactions reals et psonals ceo ne aidera my le defendāt, pur ceo que cest appeal nest pas

ALso if a man sue an appeale of felony of the death of his ancester against another, though the appellant release to the defendant all manner of actions reall & personall, this shall not aide the defendant for that this appeale is not

¶ OUr Author hauing spoken of Common pleas now treateth of certaine Pleas criminall or Pleas of the Crowne whereof it is said, (a) Item, criminalium alia maiora, alia minora, alia maxima, secundum criminū quantitatem; Sunt enim Crimina Maiora & dicuntur capitalia eò quod vltimum inducunt suppliciū, &c. Minora verò, quæ fustigationem inducunt, vel pœnam pilloralem, vel tumboralem, vel (a) Bracton, lib. 3. fo. 101. b.

action real, entant que lappellant ne recouera ascun realtie en tiel Appeale: Ne tiel appeale nest pas Action personal, entant que le tort fuit fait a son Auncestor, et nemy a luy. Mes sil relessa a le Defendant tout manners Actions, donque il serra bone barre en Appeale. Et issint home poit veyer que release de touts maners dactions, est melior que Releas de Actions reals & personals, &c.

an Action reall, in as much as the Appellant shall not recouer any Realtie in such Appeale; neither is such Appeale an Action personall, in as much as the wrong was done to his Ancestor, and not to him. But if he release to the Defendant all manner of Actions, then it shal be a good barre in an Appeale. And so a man may see that a Release of all manner of Actions is better than a release of Actions reals and personalls, &c.

vel carceris inclusionem, &c.

(b) Flet. li. 1. ca. 15.

(b) Criminalium quædam sententialiter mortem inducunt, quædam vero minime.

(c) Mir. ca. 1. §. 4. & ca. 4. des paines en diuers maners.

(c) De peche est briefe diuision, car est mortal ou venial solonque ceo que appiert es paines. And that crime is called mortall or corporall: mortall, because it deserueth death, and such crimes are called Veniall, as may bee redeemed or satisfied by some other punishment than by death.

(x) Mir. ca. 2. §. 7. Bract. li. 3. fo. 137. Brit. ca. 22. 23. Flet. li. 1. ca. 31. 32. 33.

(y) Glanuill Lib. 7. cap. 9. Et lib. 14. cap. 1. et 3.

¶ *Appeale de Felonie.* (x) Appellum signifieth accusatio, an Accusation, and therefore to appeale a man is as much as to accuse him, and in (y) antient Bookes he that doth appeale is called Accusator, and is peculiarly in legall signification applied to Appeales of three sorts. First, Of wrong to his Ancestor, whose heire male he is, and that is onely of death, whereof our Author here speaketh. The second is of wrong to the husband, and is by the wife onely of the death of her husband to be prosecuted. The third is of wrongs done to the Appellants themselues, as Robberie, Rape, and Mayhem. The word Appellum is deriued of Appeller, to call, because Appellans vocat reum in iudicium. He calleth the Defendant to iudgement, and the Plaintife is called the Appellant.

24. H. 8. ca. 12. 1. El. ca. 1.

¶ *Appeale.* Appellatio is a remoouing of a cause in any Ecclesiasticall Court to a Superior, but of this there needeth no speech in this place.

¶ *De mort.* Appeale of death is of two sorts, of Murder and of Homicide. Murder is when one is slaine with a mans will, and with malice prepensed or forethought. Homicide as it is legally taken, is when one is slaine with a mans will, but not with malice prepensed. Chance-medlie, or Per infortunium, is when one is slaine casually, and by misaduenture, without the will of him that doth the act, whereupon death insueth, but of this no Appeale doth lie. Murder commeth of the Saxon word Mordreu.

Lamb. Expos. verb. Æstimatio. Flet. li. 1. ca. 42. Hned. f. 344.

Were is an old Saxon word sometime written Wera, and signifieth the price of the life of a man, Estimatio capitis, that is, so much as one payd for the killing of a man, by which it appeareth, that such gouernment was in those dayes, as slaughters of men were most rarely committed, as Master Lambard collecteth. And you shall not read of any insurrection or rebellion before the Conquest, when the view of Frankpledge and other antient Lawes of this Realme were in their right vse.

21. H. 6. 16.

¶ *Mes sil release al Defendant touts manners d'actions, &c.* And the reason is, for that then all Actions, as well criminall as reall, personall and mixt, be released. But a release of all Actions reall and personall cannot barre an Appeale of death, because that Release extendeth to common or ciuile Actions, and not to Actions criminall: but releases of all Actions criminall or mortall, or concerning Pleas of the Crowne, are good barres in an Appeale of Death, and so the (&c.) in the end of this Section is well explained.

Sect.

Section 501.

¶ **ITem en appeal de Robberie, si l' defendant voil pleader vn release de lappellant de touts Actions personals, ceo semble nul Plee. Car Action del Appeale, lou lapellee avera iudgement de mort, &c. est pluis hault que Action personal est, et nest pas properment dit Action personal: Et pur ceo si le defendant voiloit plead vn release del appellant de barrer luy dappeale, en cest case il couient dauer vn release de touts maners dappeals, ou touts manners dactions, come il semble, &c.**

ALso in an Appeale of Robberie, if the Defendant will plead a release of the Appellant, of all Actions personalls, this seemeth no Plea: for an Action of Appeale where the Appellee shall haue iudgement of death, &c. is higher than an Action personall is, and is not properly called an action personall, and there if the Defendant will plead a Release of the appellant, to barre him of the Appeale, in this case hee must haue a Release of all manner of Appeales, or all manner of Actions, as it seemeth, &c.

¶ *Robberie.* Roboria **properly is when there is a felonious taking away of a mans goods from his person, and it is called Robberie, because the goods are taken as it were** De la Robe: **from the Robe, that is, from the person: but sometimes it is taken in a larger sence.** 22.*Ass*.39. *W*.1.*ca*.20.

¶ *Iudgement de mort, &c.* **By this** (&c.) **is implied Appeales of Rape, of Arson or Burning, of Felonie or Larcenie, for therein also is iudgement of death, and are within our Authors reason.**

¶ *Come il semble, &c.* **It is to be vnderstood, That first a release of all Actions criminall, mortall, or concerning Pleas of the Crowne. Secondly, A Release of al Actions generally. Thirdly, A release of al Appeales. And lastly, a release of all demands are good barres in all these kind of Appeales.** *V.Sect*.508.

Sect. 502.

¶ **MEs en Appeal de Maihem, vn release de touts manners dactions personals est bone plee en Barre, pur ceo que en tiel Action il ne recouera forsque damages, &c.**

BVt in Appeale of Mayhem a Release of all manner of Actions personals is a good plea in Barre, for that in such an Action hee shall recouer nothing but dammages.

¶ *MAyhem* Mahemium, membri Mutilatio **or** Obtrunçatio, **commeth of the French word** Mehaigne, **and signifieth a Corporall Hurt whereby hee looseth a Member, by reason whereof hee is lesse able to fight; as by putting out his eye, beating out his foreteeth, breaking his scull, striking off his arme, hand or finger, cutting off his leg or foot, or whereby he looseth the vse of any of his said members.** *Mir.ca*.1.§.9. *Glanu.li*.14. *ca*.7. *Bract.li*.3. *Tract*.2.*c*.24. *Brit.fo*.48.*ca*.25. *Flet.li*.1. *ca*.38. *Stanf.Pl.Cor.fo*.38.*b*. 28.*E*.3.94. 8.*H*.4.21.

¶ *Damages, &c.* V.Sect.194.

¶ *Release de touts manners Actions Personalls est bone Plea, &c.* **And the reason is, for that euerie Action wherein dammages onely are recouered by the Plaintife, is in Law taken for an Action personall.** 21.*H*.6.16.

Section 503.

¶ Item si home soit utlage en Action personal per procès sur le Original, et port bre Derror, si celuy a que suit il fuit utlage, voile pleader enuers luy un releas d̄ toutz manners Dactions Personals, ceo semble nul plee, car per le dit Action il ne recouera rien en personaltie forsque tantsolement de reuerser le Utlagarie: mes un Release de Briefe Derrour est bone plea.

Also if a man bee outlawed in an Action personal by processe vpon the Originall, and bringeth a Writ of Error, if hee at whose suit hee was outlawed will plead against him a Release of all manner of Actions personalls; this seemeth no plea, for by the said action hee shall recouer nothing in the personaltie, but onely to reuerse the Outlawrie: But a release of the writ of error, is a good plea.

Vi. li. 11. fo. 39. 41. in Metcalfes case vpon what iudgments and awards a writ of Error doth lie.

¶ *Briefe de Error.* This writ lieth when a man is grieued by any error in the foundation, proceeding, iudgement, or execution, and thereupon it is called Breue de errore corrigendo. But without a iudgement or an award in nature of a iudgment no writ of Error doth lie, for the words of the writ be, Si iudicium redditum sit: and that iudgement must regularly be giuē by iudges of record and in a Court of Record, and and not by any other inferiour Judges in base Courts, for thereupon a writ of false iudgment doth lie. In this case of Utlawrie vpon Processe the iudgement is giuen (in the Countie Court, which is no Court of Record) by the Coroners, (sauing in London iudgment is giuen by the Recorder, and not by the Maior, who is Coroner by the Custome of the Citie:) for after the Defendant is Quinto exactus, and maketh default, the iudgement is, Ideo vtlagetur per iudicium Coronatorum, and in London, Per iudicium Recordatoris: so as by the Outlawrie the Plaintife recouers nothing, but the King taketh the whole benefit thereof, for the Law did intend, That the Defendant would rather appeare and answer the Plaintife, &c. than to forfeit all his Goods and Chattels, Debts and Duties to the King, by his default and contumacie. But Littleton is to be intended, That the Sherife doe returne the Exigent whereby the Outlawrie appeares of Record, or that the Outlawrie be remoued by Certiorari, for before that time that the Outlawrie appeare of Record, the Defendant doth not forfeit his goods, nor the Plaintife can be disabled, nor any writ of Error doth lie in that case. And this is the cause that the goods of Outlawes cannot be claimed by Prescription, because they are not forfeited vntill the Outlawrie appeare of Record Vid. Sect. 197. where it appeareth by Littleton, That the Plaintife cannot be disabled by Outlawrie, vnlesse it appeareth of Record.

Li. 5. fo. 111. Fouleys case. Li. 7. fo. 11. 12. Iemlemās case.

15. El. Dyer 317.

Li. 9. fo. 119. S. Zouches case.

28. Ass. 49. 22. E. 3. Vtlag. 3. 38 E. 3. 13. Mich. 4. & 5. El. Dy. fo. 222. Vi. Sect. 197.

¶ *Car per le dit Action il recouera rien en le personaltie.* Hereupon is to be obserued a diuersitie, when by the writ of Error the Plaintife shall recouer, or be restored to any personall thing, as Debt, Dammage, or the like, for then by the reason that Littleton here yeeldeth, the release of all Actions personals is a good plea, for that the Plaintife is to recouer, or to be restored to something in the personaltie. And so likewise when land is to be recouered, or to be restored in a writ of Error, a Release of all Actions reals is a good barre. But where by a writ of Error the Plaintife shall not be restored to any personal or reall thing, then a release of all Actions reall or personall, is no barre, and therefore Littleton here putteth his case with great caution: If a man (saith he) by Processe vppon the Originall bee outlawed, there in deed he shall be restored to nothing in the personaltie against the Plaintife. But where by the Outlawrie he forfeited all his goods and chattels to the King, he shall be restored to them; also therby he shall be restored to the Law, and to be of abilitie to sue, &c. But if the Pl' in a personall Action recouer any debt, &c. or dammages, and be outlawed after iudgment, there in a writ of Error brought by the Defendant vpon the principall iudgement, a release of all Actions personalls is a good plea. And so it is where a Judgement is giuen in a reall Action, a release of all Actions reals is a good barre in a writ of Error brought thereupon.

1. H. 4. 6.

If

If the Tenant in a reall Action release to the Defendant after recouery his right in the Land, he shall not haue a Writ of Error, for that he cannot be restored to the Land. 9.*H*.6.47.

And so it is if debt, &c. or dammages be recouered in a personall action by false Verdict, and the Defendant bringeth a writ of Attaint, a (a) release of all Actions personals is a good barre of the attaint, for thereby the Plaintife is to bee restored to the debt, &c. or dammages which he lost, the like Law is if a Judgement be giuen vpon a false Verdict in a reall Action, a release of all Actions reals is a good barre in an Attaint. For both the Writ of Error, and the writ of Attaint doe insue the nature of the former Action, &c. (a) 26.*H*.8. 3.*b*.13.*E*.4.1.2. 34.*H*.6 31.35.*H*.6.19. 29.*Ass*.35.47.*E*.3.6. 24.*E*.3.37.

And so it is if a Writ of Audita Querela be brought by the Defendant in the former action to discharge himselfe of an execution, a Release of all actions personalls is a good barre, because hee is to discharge himselfe of a personall Execution.

Mes vn release de briefe de error est bone plea, &c. So as in this speciall case here put by Littleton wherein the Plaintife is to recouer or be restored to nothing against the partie, yet for that the Plaintife in the former Action is priuy to the Record, a release of a Writ of Error to him is sufficient to bar the Plaintife in the Writ of Error of the suit & vexation by the Writ of Error. And so note that an Action reall or personall doth imply a recouery of something in the realty or personaltie, or a restitution to the same, but a Writ implyeth neither of them which is worthy of obseruation.

Section 504.

Item, si home recouer debt ou dammages, & il relessa al defendant touts maners dactions, vncore il puit loialment suer execution per Capias ad satisfaciendum, ou per Elegit, ou Fieri facias, car execution per tiel briefe ne poit estre dit action.

ALso if a man recouer debt or dammages, and hee releaseth to the defendant all manner of Actions, yet hee may lawfully sue Execution by *Capias ad satisfaciendum*, or by *Elegit*, or *Fieri facias*: For Execution vpon such a Writ cannot bee said an Action.

Here appeareth a diuersitie betweene an Action and an Execution. For regularly an Action is said in his proper sence to continue vntill iudgement bee giuen, and after Judgement then doth Processe of Execution begin, and therefore a release of all Actions regularly is (b) no barre of Execution, for the Execution doth beginne when the Action doth end. And therefore the foundation of the first is an originall Writ, and doth determine by the Judgement; and writs of Execution are called Judiciall, because they are grounded vpon the Judgement. *Vide Sect*.233. 8.3.9.4.*E*.3.*Attorney* 18. 33.*H*.6.49. 34.*H*.6.51. (b) 13.*H*.4.*Release* 53. 19.*H*.6.3.26.*H*.6.*Execution* 75.

Per Cap. ad satisfaciendum. This is a iudiciall Writ for the taking of the bodie in Execution vntill he hath made satisfaction, where a Capias ad satisfaciendum lyeth at the Common Law, and where it is giuen by Statute, you may reade at large in my Reports. *Sir William Herberts case lib*.3.*fol*.11.12.

I haue read two ancient Records touching the taking of the body in Execution, whereof to my remembrance, I neuer read any touch in our Bookes, yet will I recite them, and leaue them to the iudicious Reader. William de Walton brought an Action of Trespasse of breaking his Close against Iohn Martin, and vpon not guiltie pleaded, hee was found guiltie and dammages assessed, whereupon iudgement was giuen that the Plaintife should recouer his dammages, Et quod prædictus Iohannes capiatur. And the Record saith; Quod prædictus Iohannes venit coram Domino Rege & reddidit se prisone, & quia constat Curiæ per inspectionem corporis ipsius Iohannis, quod idem Iohannes est talis ætatis quod pœnam imprisonamenti subire non potest, ideo dictum est ei, quod eat inde sine die. The other Record is, That Ellen Allot brought an Appeale of Robbery against Iohn Bockiseleke Clarke, Richard Charta and others who pleaded not guilty, and were not found guilty: Whereupon Judgement was giuen that they should goe quite, Et prædicta Elena pro falso appello suo committatur prisonæ, &c. (for (b) by the Statute she ought to be imprisoned in that case for a yeare.) But the Record saith, Quia eadem Elena prægnans fuit, & in periculo mortis, ipsa dimittitur per manucaptionem, &c. ad habendum corpus vsque Quind. Michaelis &c. *Pasch*.14.*E*.3.*Rot*.106.*coram Rege in Thesaur. Surrey*. *Mich*.41.*E*.3.*Rot*.27. *coram Rege Cornub. in Thesaur*. (b) *W*.2.*cap*.12.

There be certaine maximes in the Law concerning Executions, as taking some in stead of many. Ea quæ in Curia nostra rite acta sunt, debitæ executioni demandari debent. Fatum est latam esse sententiam nisi mandetur executioni. Executio iuris non habet iniuriam. Executio est fructus & finis legis. Iuris effectus in executione consistit. Prosecutio legis est grauis vexatio, executio legis coronat opus. Boni Iudicis est iudicium sine dilatione mandare executioni. Fauorabiliores sunt executiones alijs processibus quibuscunque. But now let vs heare what Littleton saith.

¶ *Per Elegit* **This is also a iudiciall writ, and is giuen by** the Statute either vpon a recouery for debt or dammages, or vpon a Recognizance in any Court. And it is called a Writ of Elegit, for that according to the statute that saith, (c) Sit de cætero in electione illius, &c. sequi breue quod Vicecomes fieri faciat, &c. vel quod liberet ei, &c. The words of the writ be Elegit sibi liberari, &c. And thereupon it is called an Elegit. By this writ the Sherife shall deliuer to the Plaintife, Omnia catalla debitoris, (exceptis bobus & afris carucæ) & medietatem terræ. And this must be done by an inquest to be taken by the Sherife.

(c) W 2 cap.18.

When Littleton wrote, by force of certaine Acts (d) of Parliament, execution might bee had of Lands (besides by force of the Elegit) vpon Statutes Merchant, Statutes Staple, and Recognizances taken in some Court of Record, and since he wrote vpon a Recognizance or Bond taken by force of the Statute (*) of 23.H 8. before one of the Chiefe Iustices, or the Maior of the Staple, and Recorder of London out of Tearme, which hath the effect of a Statute Staple. The manner of the Executions vpon Bodie, Lands and Goods, appeareth in the Statutes quoted in the margent.

(d) 11.E.1.Stat.de Acton Burnell. 13.E.1.de mercatoribus. 27.E.3.cap.22. Vide Fleta lib.2.cap.57.25.E 3.53
(*) 23.H.8.cap.6.

Since Littleton wrote a profitable Statute hath beene made (e) concerning executions of Lands, Tenements and Hereditaments, whereby it is prouided that if after such Lands, &c. be had and deliuered in Execution vpon a iust or lawfull title, wherewithall the said Lands, &c. were liable, tied, or bound at such time, as they were deliuered or taken into execution, shall be recouered, deuested, taken, or euicted out of, or from the possession of any such person, &c. before such times, as the said Tenants by Execution their Executors or Assignes shall haue fully leuied their debt and dammages, for the which the said Lands, &c. were taken in Execution, then euery such Recouerer, Obligee, and Recognisee, shall haue a Scire facias out of the same Court from whence the former Execution did proceed, against such person or persons as the former Ercution was pursued, their heires, Executors or Assignes, to haue Execution of other Lands, &c. liable and to be taken in Execution for the residue of the debt or dammages. Sed opus est interprete.

(e) 32.H.8.cap.5.

Therefore first it is to be knowne, that where the Tenant by Execution hath remedie giuen to him by Law after euiction, there the Statute extendeth not to it, for the Act saith, by reason whereof, the said Recouerors, Obligees and Recognizees, haue beene cleerely set without remedie, &c. and the bodie referreth to the preamble, and the party ought not to haue double satisfaction, one by the former Lawes, and another by this Statute.

Lib.4.fol.66. Fulwoods case.

And therfore if part of the Land, &c. be euicted from the Tenant by Execution, this Statute extendeth not to it, because he should hold the residue, till he be fully satisfied, and he must be contented if all be euicted sauing one Acre to hold that, though it bee but a poore remedie: for no new Execution in that case hee can haue vpon this Statute. Therefore if the Conusee hath remedie in præsenti for part, or in futuro for all, or part, this Statute extendeth not to it.

Secondly, If a man be bound to A. in a Statute of a thousand pounds, and by a latter Statute to B. in a hundred pounds, and B. first extendeth, and then A. extendeth and taketh the Land from B. yet B. shall haue no aide of the Statute, because after the extent of A. B. shall re-enioy the Land, by force of his former Execution.

Thirdly, If the wife of the Conusor recouer Dower against the Tenant by Execution, he shall hold ouer, and shall haue no ayde of this Statute.

Fourthly, If a man put out his Lessee for yeares, or disseise his Lessee for life, and after knowledge a Statute, and Execution is sued against him, and the Lessees re-enter, the Tenant by Execution after the Leases ended, shall hold ouer, and haue no aide of this Statute.

Fiftly, This Statute must not be taken litterally but according to the meaning, therefore where the letter is vntill hee, &c. or his Assignes shall fully and wholly haue leuied the whole debt or dammages: if he hath assigned seuerall parcels to seuerall Assignes, yet all they shall haue the Land, but till the whole debt be paid.

Sixtly, where the words be, for the which the said Lands, &c. were deliuered in Execution, A Disseisor conuey lands to the King who granteth the same ouer to A. and his heires to hold by fealtie, and twenty pound rent, and after granteth the Seigniorie to B. B. knowledgeth a

Statute,

Statute, and Execution is sued of the Seigniory. A. dieth without heire and the Connusee entereth, and is evicted by the Disseisor, he shall have the aide of this Statute, and yet it is out of the letter of the Law, for the Seigniory was delivered in Execution and not the tenancy, but he was Tenant by execution of those lands, and therefore within the statute. But the perquisite of a Villeine being evicted is out of the statute, for he is Tenant in fee simple thereof and not Tenant by execution.

Seventhly, where the words be (delivered and taken in execution) yet if after the Liberate, the Connusee entereth, (as he may) so as the land is never delivered, yet is he within the remedie of this statute, for he is Tenant by execution.

Eighthly, where the statute saith, then every such Recoveror, Obligee, & Recognizee shall, &c. and saith not, their Executors, Administrators or Assignes, but they are omitted in this materiall place, yet by a benigne interpretation, this statute shall extend to them, because they are mentioned in the next precedent clause of the eviction, and the remedie must by construction be extended to all the persons, that appeare by the Act to bee grieved, a point worthy the observation.

Ninthly, where the Statute giveth a Scire fac' out of the same Court, &c. if the Record be removed by Writ of Error into another Court, and there affirmed, the Tenant by Execution that is evicted shall have a Scire fac' by the equity of this Statute out of that Court, because the Scire fac' must be grounded upon the Record, Et sic de similibus.

Tenthly, where the Statute giveth the Scire fac' against such person or persons, &c. that were parties to the first Execution, their Heires, Executors or Assignes, &c. this must not be taken so generally as the Letter is, for if the first Execution were had against a Purchasor, &c. so as nothing was liable in his hands but the Land recovered, if this Land be evicted from Tenant by Execution, no Scire fac' shall be awarded against him, his Heires, Executors or Assignes, but if he hath other lands subiect to the Execution, then a Scire fac' lyeth against him or his Assignes, but not against his Executors, neither in that case can he have a Scire fac' upon this Statute against the first Debtor or Recognizor, because it giveth it only against him, &c. that was partie to the first Execution his Heires, Executors or Assignes. But if there be severall Assignees of severall parcells of lands subiect to the Execution, one Scire fac' upon this Statute shall lye against all the Assignes. Sed est modus in rebus. This little taste shall give a light to the diligent reader, not only to see into the secrets of this Statute, but to others also of like nature.

And by the Statute of 23.H.8. it is provided that the Obligee, &c. shall have in every point against such Recognisor, &c. like Proces, Execution, Commodity and advantage in every behalfe, as hath beene had or made upon the Statute staple, and under such manner and forme, as is for the same Statute staple provided: by force of which branch, if the Tenant by execution by force of the act of 23.H.8. be evicted, he shall have the remedie provided for Tenants by execution upon a Statute staple by the Act of 32.H.8. In like manner by force of that clause of 23.H.8. if the extendors upon a Statute staple, &c. doe extend the lands, &c. at too high a rate, the Obligee may pray, that the Extendors themselves may take the lands, &c. at that rate, &c. by force of the said Statutes of Acton Burnel, and De Mercatoribus. Also no execution shall be sued against the heire within age.

40.E.3.26.b. 44.E.3. 2.H.4.17. 15.H.7.15.

But note that upon a Writ of Elegit the Plaintife cannot make any such prayer, because those ancient Statutes doe extend to a Statute Merchant or a Statute Staple only, and neither to a Recovery of debt or damages, nor to a Recognizance in Court, and so hath it beene resolved. (f)

Nota, it appeareth by the Preamble of the said Act of 32.H.8. and by divers (g) bookes, that after a full and perfect execution had by extent returned and of Record, there shall never be any re-extent upon any eviction: but if the extent be insufficient in Law, there may goe out a new Extent.

(h) If a man have a Judgement given against him for debt or damages, or be bound in a Recognizance and dieth his heire within age, or having two daughters, and the one within age no execution shall be sued of the lands by Elegit during the minority, albeit the heire is not specially bound but charged as Terre tenant (i) and so against an heire within age no execution shall be sued upon a Statute merchant or Staple nor upon the Obligation or Recognizance upon the Statute of 23.H.8. for it is excepted in the Proces against the heire. Neither if the heire within age indow his mother shall Execution be sued against her during his minoritie.

Note, that by the Statute (k) of 27.E.3. the execution of Lands upon a Statute staple is referred to the Statute Merchant, and by the Statute De Mercatoribus no Execution shall be had against the heire, so long as he is within age.

Also since Littleton wrote there is a right profitable Statute (l) made against fraudulent Feoffments, Gifts, Grants, &c. Judgements and Executions, aswell of Lands and Tenements,

(f) Mich. 4. & 5. Ph. & Mar. Bendloes, by all the Iustices of the Common pleas. 15.E.3. Extent. 7.

(g) 15.E.3. Extent. 9. 22.E.3. Recovery in value. 22. 31.E.3. Extent 13. 17.E.3.76. 15.E.3. Scire fac. 115. 7.H.4.19. 22. Ass. 44. 22.E.3. fo. ult. 44.E.3.10. 9.H.7.9. 15.H.7.15. 13. Eliz. Dier 299. 29.H.8. Stat. Merchant Br. 40.

(h) 11.E.3. age 4. 15.E.3. age 95. 24.E.3.28. 29. Ass. 37. 29.E.3.50. 47. Ass. 4. 47.E.3.7. lib. 3. fo. 13. Sir William Herberts case. Brooke, age 33.

(i) Temps E.1. Ass. 402. 417. 16.H.7.6. Livere dener. 545. Brooke, age 33.

(k) 27.E.3. cap. 22.

(l) 13. Eliz. cap. 5. Lib. 3. fo. 80. &c. Twynes case. Lib. 5. fo. 60. Goches case.

Lib.6.fo.18. Pakemans case. Lib.10.fo.56.the Chanc. of Oxfords case. So the statutes of 3.H.7.ca.4. & 50.E.3.ca.6. Mich 12. & 13.Eliz. Dier.295. 18.Eliz.351. Dyer.

ments, as of Goods and Chattels, to delay, hinder or defraud Creditors and others of their iust and lawfull Actions, Suites, Debts, Damages, Penalties, Forfeitures, Heriots, Mortuaries and Releases, for the exposition of which and other Statutes see the Authorities quoted in the Margent.

And it is to be obserued that the words of the said Act of 13.Eliz. are, Be it therefore declared, ordained, and enacted: and therefore like cases in semblable mischiefe shall be taken within the remedie of this Act, by reason of this word (Declared) whereby it appeareth, what the Law was before the making of this Act. But let vs now returne to Littleton.

W.2.ca.18.

¶ *Fieri facias.* This is a Writ mentioned in the said Statute, but is a Writ of execution at the Common Law. And is called a Fieri facias, because the words of the Writ directed to the Sherife be Quod fieri facias de bonis & catallis, &c. and of those words the Writ taketh his denomination.

But note that a Capias ad satisfaciendum, is not mentioned in the said Statute, because no Capias ad satisfac' did lye at the Common Law vpon a Iudgement for debt, &c. or damages, but only when the originall action was Quare vi & armis, &c. But latter statutes haue giuen a Capias ad satisfac' where debt, &c. or damages are recouered, as it appeareth at large (m) in Sir William Herberts case whereunto I referre the reader.

(m) Lib.5.fo.11. Sir William Herberts case.

And it is to be obserued that these three Writs of execution ought to be sued out within the yeare and the day after iudgement, but if the Plaintife sueth out any of them within the yeare, he may continue the same after the yeare vntill he hath execution. And to none of these Writs of Executions the Defendant can pleade, but if he hath any matter since the iudgement to discharge him of Execution, he may haue an Audita querela, and relieue himselfe that way, but plead he cannot. As if the Plaintife after Release vnto the Defendant all Executions, yet in none of these three Writs he shall pleade it, but is driuen to his Audita querela, as hath beene said.

Sect. 505.

¶ MEs si apres lan et iour le plaintife voit suer vn Scire facias, a sacher si le defendant poit rien dire pur que le plaintife nauera execution, donques il semble que tiel releas de touts actions serra bon plee en barr: Mes ascuns ont semble contrary, entant que le briefe de Scire facias est vn bre dexecution, & est dauer executiō, &c. Mes vncore entant que sur mē l' briefe l' defendant poit pleader diuers mattrs puis l' iudgement rendue de luy ouster dexecution, come vtlagary, &c. et diuers auters matters,

BVt if after the yeare and day the plaintife will sue a *Scire facias*, to know if the defendant can say any thing why the plaintife should not haue execution, then it seemeth that such release of all actions shall be a good plea in barre. But to some seemes the contrary, in as much as the writ of *Scire facias* as is a writ of execution, and is to haue execution &c. But yet in asmuch as vpon the same writ the Defendant may plead diuers matters after iudgement giuen to oust him of execution, as outlawry, &c. and diuers other matters, this

¶ *Scire facias.* This is a iudiciall Writ and properly lyeth after the yeare & day after iudgement giuen, and is so called because the words of the Writ to the Sherife be, Quod Scire facias præfat' T. (being the Defendant) Quod sit coram, &c. ostensurus si quid pro se habeat aut dicere sciat, quare, &c. So as by the Writ it appeareth that the Defendant is to be warned to plead any matter in Barre of Execution, and therefore albeit it bee a iudiciall Writ, yet because the Defendant may thereupon plead, this Scire facias is accounted in Law to bee in nature of an action, and therefore (n) a Release of all actions is a good barre of the same, and likewise a Release of Executions is a good barre in a Scire facias, this Writ was gi-

(n) 19.H.6.3.28.E.4.7.

matters, ceo bien poit estre dit action, &c.

may bee well said an action, &c.

uen in this case by the Statute of W. 2. for at the Common Law if the Plaintife had surceased to sue Execution by Fieri facias, or Leuari facias a yeare and a day, he had beene driuen to his new originall.

W. 2. cap. 45. 8. E. 3. 297. 298. 18. E. 3. 33. lib. 3. fol. 12. Sir William Herberts case. Fleta, lib. 2. cap. 12.

¶ *Ceo bien poet estre dit action.* Here it is to be obserued that euery Writ whereunto the Defendant may pleade, be it originall or iuditiall is in Law an action.

Sect. 506.

¶ Et ieo croy, que en vn Scire facias hors duu fine, vn releas de touts maners dactions, est bon plee en barre,

AND I take that in a *Scire facias* vpon a fine, a release of all manner of actions is a good plea in barre.

This vpon that which hath beene said is euident of it selfe.

Sect. 507.

¶ Mes lou home recouera debt ou damages, et est accord perenter eux, que le plaintife ne suet execution, donqz il couient q̄ le plaintife fait vn releas a luy de touts maners dexecutions.

BVt where a man recouereth debt or damages, and it is agreed betweene them that the plaintife shall not sue execution, then it behoueth that the plaintife make a release to him of all manner of executions.

¶ [*L couient.* Albeit Littleton here saith, hee ought or must, &c. yet there bee other words which will release an Execution without expresse words of a release of Execution.

As if a man release all suites the Execution is gone, for no man can haue Execution without prayer and suit, but the King only, and therefore if the King releaseth all suites, it is no barre of his Execution because in the Kings case the Judges ought to award execution Ex officio without any suite, but a release of Executions doth barre the King in that case. And so note a diuersity betweene a release of all actions, and a release of all suites.

19. H. 6. 4. 26. H. 6. Execution 4. lib. 8. fo. 153. Ealthams case. Vid. Brooke tit. Releases 87.

So if the body of a man be taken in Execution, and the Plaintife releaseth all actions, yet shall he remaine in Execution, but if he release all debts or duties he is to be discharged of the Execution because the debt or dutie it selfe is discharged.

26. H. 6. tit. Execution, 7.

In the same manner if Execution be sued vpon a Recognizance by Elegit, and the Conusee by Deed make a Defeasance, that if the Conusor doth such an act, that then the Recognizance shall be voide, by this the Execution is discharged.

20. Ass. p. 7.

So it is if iudgement be giuen in an action of debt, and the body of the Defendant is taken in execution by a Capias ad satisfac' and after the Plaintife releaseth the Judgement, by this the body shall be discharged of the Execution.

26. H. 6. vbi supra.

If the Plaintife after Judgement release all demands the Execution is discharged, as shall appeare by that which next hereafter shall be said.

If A. be accountable to B, and B. releaseth him all his duties, this is no barre in an Action of account, for Duties extend to things certaine, and what shall fall out vpon the account is incertaine; and albeit the Latyn word is Debita, yet Duties doe extend to all things due that is certaine, and therefore dischargeth Judgements in personall actions, and Executions also.

20. H. 6. 6. per Toston.

Section 508.

¶ Item si home relessa a un auter touts manners de demands, ceo est le plus melior release a luy a que le Release est fait que il poet aver, et plus urera a son advantage. Car per tiel release de touts manners de demands, touts maners dactions reals, personals, et Actions dappeale sont ales et extincts, et touts manners de executions sont ales et extincts.

ALso if a man release to another all manner of demands, this is the best release to him to whome the Release is made, that he can haue, and shall enure most to his aduantage. For by such release of all manner of demands, al manner of Actions realls, personalls, and Actions of Appeale, are taken away and extinct, and all manner of executions are taken away and extinct.

¶ T*Outs manners de demands.*

¶ *Demande*, Demandum is a word of Art, and in the understanding of the Common Law is of so large an extent, as no other one word in the Law is, vnlesse it be Clameum, whereof Littleton maketh mention Sect.445. And here is to bee obserued, that there bee two kind of demands or claimes, viz a demand or claime in Deed, and a demand or claime in Law; or an expresse, and an implied demand or claime. Littleton here putteth examples of both, and first he speaketh of Reall Actions, wherein hee that bringeth his Action maketh his demand, and therefore he is properly called a demandant, and hee that defendeth is called Tenant, because he is Tenant of the Freehold of the land.

Lit.Sect.445.Bract.li.1. fo.10 Pl.Com.Stailes case, 359,&c.

Of demands implied, or in Law, Littleton putteth examples: First, Of all Actions personalls. Secondly, Of Appeales, for in both those cases he that bringeth the suit is called Plaintife, and not Demandant, and he that defendeth is called Defendant. Thirdly, Of Executions. Fourthly, Of title or right of Entrie, either by force of a Condition, or by any former right, which meerly is a demand or claime in Law, but otherwise it is in the Kings case. Fiftly, Of a Rent seruice, Rent charge, Common of pasture, &c. which also are meere demaunds or claimes in Law. All which, Littleton here and in the two next Sections following, putteth but for examples, for by the release of all demands other things also be released, as Rents seck, all mixt Actions, a Warrantie which is a Couenant reall, and all other Couenants reall and personall, Estouers, all manner of Commons and profits apprender, Conditions before they be broken or performed, or after, Annuities, Recognisances, Statutes Merchant or of the Staple, Obligations, Contracts, &c. are released and discharged.

38.H.8.tit. Releases Br.9. 6.H.7.15. 19.H.6.3,4. 20. Ass.Pl.5 40.E.3.22.49.E.3 7.b.50. Ass.pl.6.14.H.4.8. 13.R.2.tit.Anuy.89. Lib.8. fo 153. Ed.Althams case. Lit.170.Sect.748.Dyer 5. El.217.

Sect. 509.

¶ Et si home ad title de entry en ascuns terres ou tenements, per tiel Release son title est ale.

¶ Sed quære de hoc, car Fitz-Iames chiefe Iustice de Engleterre tient le contrarie, pur ceo que entre ne poit proprement estre dit demande, P.19.H.8.*

ANd if a man hath title of entry into any Lands or Tenements by such a Release, his title is taken away.

¶ *Sed quare de hoc*, for *Fitz-Iames* chiefe Iustice of England holdeth the contrarie, because an Entrie cannot be properly sayd, a Demaund.

¶ *Title.*

¶ Title. Here Title is taken in the largest sence, including Right also. 34.H.8.tit.Releas.B.9. Chaunceys case. Li.8.fo.153. Ed.Altham case.

¶ * Sed quære,&c. This is an addition, and no part of Littleton, and the opinion here cited cleerely against Law.

Section 510.

¶ Et si home ad Rent seruice ou Rent charge, ou Common de Pasture,&c. per tiel release de touts manners de demaunds fait al Tenaunts de la Terre, dont le seruice ou le rent est issuant, ou en que le Common est, le seruice, le Rent, et le Common est ale et extinct, &c.

And if a man hath a Rent seruice or Rent charge, or Common of Pasture,&c. by such a Release of all manner of demaunds made to the Tenants of the Land out of which the seruice or the rent is issuing, or in which the Common is, the seruice, the Rent and the Common, is taken away and extinct.

This vpon that which hath beene sayd, needeth no further explication.

Sect. 511.

¶ Item si home relessa a vn auter touts manners de quarrels, ou touts controuersies ou debates enter eux, &c. Quære a quel matter et a quel effect tiels parols soy extendont, &c.

Also if a man releaseth to another all manner of quarrels, or all controuersies or debates betweene them, &c. Quære to what matter and to what effect such words shall extend themselues.

¶ Quarrels. Querela, à querendo, this properly concerneth Personall Actions, or mixt at the highest, for the Plaintife in them is called Querens, and in most of the writs it is said Queritur. And yet if a man release all Quereles (a mans deed being taken most strongly against himselfe) it is as beneficiall as al actions, for by it al Actions reall and personal are released. And by the release of all quarrels, all causes of Actions are released thereby, albeit no Action be then depending for the same. 40.E.3.47.b.Ed.Althams Case vbi supra. 35.H.8.Dyer.57. 9.E.4.44. 39.H.6.9.

¶ Quarels, Controuersies, and Debates, are Synonima, and of one signification, Litis nomen omnē Actionē significat, siue in rem, siue in personā sit If a man release omnes loquelas, it is as large as omnes Actiones, for omnis Actio est loquela, and it extendeth as well to Actions in Courts of Record, as base Courts, for the writ of Error sayth, In Recordo & Processu, &c. loquelæ quæ fuit inter, &c. and so the writ of false Judgement saith, Recordari facias loquelam, where the iudgement was giuen in the Countie Court. Omnes exactiones, seem to be large words, for Exactio deriuantur ab exigendo, and Exigere signifieth, to enquire or demand. Lib.8.fol.153. Althams Case 21.H.6.16.a.F.N.B.23.18. 50.Ass.6. 40.E.3.22. 13.R.2.Anowrie 89.

Sect. 512.

¶ Item si home p son fait soit oblige a vn auter en

Also if a man by his Deed bee bound to another in a

¶ Relessa al Obligor touts Actions,&c. The reason

certaine ſumme de money a payer al Feaſt de S. Michael prochein enſuant, ſi l'obligee deuant le dit Feaſt releſſa al Obligor touts Actions il ſerra barre del dutie a touts temps, et uncore il ne puiſſoit auer Action al temps de Releaſe fait.

certaine ſumme of money, to pay at the Feaſt of Saint *Michael* next enſuing, if the Obligee before the ſayd Feaſt releaſe to the Obligor all Actions, hee ſhall be barred of the duty for euer, & yet he could not haue an Action at the time of the Releaſe made.

11.H.4.41.43.

of this caſe is, For that the debt is a thing conſiſting meerely in Action, and therefore albeit no Action lieth for the debt, becauſe it is debitum in præſenti, quamuis ſit ſoluendum in futuro, yet becauſe the right of Action is in him, the releaſe of all Actions is a diſcharge of the debt it ſelfe.

(o) Trin. 2. Ia. in Cōi Banco. inter Middleton & Rinnet. 18.H.6.23.b. Pl.Com.277.278. In Greibrakes Caſe per Weſton.

(o) And ſo may an Executor before probate releaſe an Action, and yet before Probate he can haue no Action, becauſe the right of the Action is in him, and ſo it was adiudged. And ſome ſay, that an Ordinarie may releaſe an Action, and yet he can haue none.

5.Eliz. Dier 217.

Albanys Caſe vbi ſupra.

But if a man by Deed doth couenant to build an houſe or make an eſtate, and before the Couenant broken, the Couenantee releaſeth to him all Actions, Suits, and Querrels, this doth not diſcharge the Couenant it ſelfe, becauſe at the time of the Releaſe, nihil fuit debitum, there was no debt or dutie, or cauſe of Action in being. But in that caſe a Releaſe of all Couenants is a good diſcharge of the couenant before it be broken.

Sect. 513.

Mes ſi home leſſa terre a un auter pur terme dun an, rendant a luy al feaſt d' S. Mich. prochein enſuãt 40. s. & puis deuãt meſm l' feaſt il releſſa al leſſee touts actions unc̃ apres meſme le feaſt il auera acc̃ de Det pur non payment de les 40. s. nient obſtant le dit releas. Stude cauſam diuerſitatis enter les deux caſes.

BVt if a man letteth land to another for a yeare, to yeeld to him at the Feaſt of S. *Mich.* next inſuing 40. s. & afterwards before the ſame Feaſt hee releaſeth to the leſſee all actions, yet after the ſame Feaſt hee ſhall haue an action of debt for the non payment of the 40. s. notwithſtanding the ſaid Releaſe. *Stude cauſam diuerſitatis* between theſe two caſes.

7.H.7.5.a.

Releaſe touts Actions. This releaſe ſhall not barre the Leſſor of his Rent because it was neither debitum nor ſoluendum at the time of the releaſe made, for if the land be euicted from the Leſſee before the Rent become due the Rent is auoyded, for it is to bee paid out of the profits of the land, and it is a thing not meerely in action becauſe it may bee granted ouer.

45.E.3.8.17.H.6.26. 13.H.4. Auowrie 240.

But the Leſſor before the day may acquite or releaſe the Rent.

30.E.3.13.b. 47.E.3.24.

10.E.2. Execution 137. 16.E.2. ibid. 138. 16.E.3. Scire Fac. 4. F.N.B. 267. 9.E.3.7.

But if a man bee bound in a Bond or by Contract to another to pay a hundred pounds at fiue ſeuerall dayes, he ſhall not haue an Action of Debt before the laſt day be paſt, and ſo note a diuerſitie betweene duties which touch the realtie, and the meere perſonaltie. But if a man be bound in a Recognizance to pay a hundred pound at fiue ſeuerall dayes preſently after the firſt day of payment he ſhall haue execution upon the Recognizance for that ſumme, and ſhall not tarrie till the laſt be paſt, for that it is in the nature of ſeuerall Iudgements. And ſo note a diuerſity betweene a debt due by Recognizance, and a debt due by Bond or Contract.

5. Mar. Action ſur le caſe. Br. 108. 3. Mar. Dier. 113. Lib. 4. fo. 94. Slades caſe. Lib. 5. fol. 82. b. Ferders caſe.

And ſo it is of a couenant or promiſe, after the firſt default an Action of Couenant, or an Action upon the Caſe doth lie, for they are ſeuerall in their nature. Laſtly, note a diuerſity betweene Debts and Couenants, or Promiſes.

39.H.6.28.b. 5.E.4.45. 2.H.4.13.12. R.2. Releaſe 29.

If a man hath an Annuity for tearme of yeares, or for life, or in fee, and he before it be behind doth releaſe all Actions, this ſhall not releaſe the Annuity, for it is not meerely in Action, becauſe it may be granted ouer.

Section 514.

Item ou home voile suer briefe de Droit, il couient que il counta del seisin de luy, ou de ses ancestors, & auxy q̃ l' seisin fuit en temps de mesme le Roy come il counta en son count: Car cest vn ancient ley vse, come appiert per l' Report dun plee en le Eire de Nottingham, titulo Droit en Fitzherbert, cap.26. en tiel forme q̃ ensuist. John Barre port son briefe de Droit enuers Reynold de Assington, et demaunda certaine tenements, &c. ou le mise est ioyne en le bank, et originall & le Proces fueront demandes deuant Justices errãts, ou les parties viendront, & les 12. Chiualers fieront lour serement sans challenge des parties destre allowes, pur ceo que election fuit fait per assent des parties, oue les quater Chiualers, & le serement fuit tiel, Que ieo verity dirr, &c. le quel R. de A. ad plus mere droit a tener les tenements que John Barre demanda vers luy per son briefe de Droit, ou John, de

Also where a man will sue a Writ of Right, it behoueth that he counteth of the seisin of himselfe or of his ancestors, and also that the seisin was in the same Kings time, as hee pleadeth in his plea. For this is an ancient Law vsed, as appeareth by the report of a Plea in the Eire of *Nottingham, tit. droit in Fitzherbert, cap.26.* in this forme following. *Iohn Barre* brought his Writ of Right against *Reynold* of *Assington*, and demanded certaine Lands, &c. where the mise is ioyned in banke, and the originall and the Processe were sent before the Iustices errants, where the parties came, and the twelue Knights were sworne without challenge of the parties, to bee allowed, because that choise was made by assent of the parties, with the foure Knights, and the Oath was this. That I shall say the truth, &c. whither *R.* of *A.* hath more mere right to hold the tenements which *Iohn Barre* demandeth against him by his Writ of Right, or *Iohn* to haue

¶ *Il couient que il counta del seisin de luy ou de ses auncestors.* For if neither hee nor any of his Ancestors were seised of the land, &c. within the time of limitation, hee cannot maintaine a Writ of Right, for the seisin of him of whom the Demaundant himselfe purchased the land, &c. auayleth not.

And so it is in a Writ of Right of Aduowson.

¶ *Auxy que le seisin fuit en temps de mesme le roy come il counta.* Hereby it appeareth, that not onely a seisin (as hath bin said) is requisite, but also that the seisin be had in the time of the same king according to his Count.

¶ *Report* commeth of the Latin word reportare, à re, & portó, id est, referre, à re, & fero. And in the Common Law, it signifieth a publike relation, or a bringing againe to memory Cases iudicially argued, debated, resolued, or adiudged in any of the Kings Courts of Iustice, together with such causes and reasons as were deliuered by the Iudges of the same, and in this sence Littleton vseth the word in this place.

¶ *En le Eire de Nottingham.* Eire, Iter. And it signifieth the Court of the Iustices in Eire, and thereupon they were called Iusticiarij Itinerantes, in respect that the Iustices residing at Westm.

For the time of limitation. See the Statute of 32. H. 8. cap. Vide Sect.170.

F. N. B. 30. a. 2. E. 3. 27. Littl. 110. 2.

Westminster were called Iusticiarij residentes, and were much like in this respect to the Iustices of Assise at this day, although for authoritie & manner of proceeding (whereof you shall read (p) in the ancient Authors of the Law) farre different. And as the power of the Iustices of Assises by many Acts of Parliament, and other Commissions increased, so these Iustices Itinerant by little and little vanished away. And it is certaine, that the authority of Iustices of Assises Itinerant through the whole Realme, and the Institution of Iustices of Peace in every Countie being duly performed, are the most excellent meanes for the preservation of the Kings peace and quiet of the Realme of any other in the Christian world.

(p) Mirror cap.2.§.3. & §.15.& cap.4.le office des Iustices en Eire. Glanuil.lib.9.cap.11.lib.8.cap.primo. Britton fol.1.b 9.8.&c. Bract.lib.3. fol.115.&c Fleta lib.1.cap.13.&c. 4.E.3.32.6.E.3.35.23.E.3.21.15.H.7.5. Vide Sect.442.233.234.

¶ *De Nottingham.* This should bee Northampton according to the Originall.

This report whereof Littleton here maketh mention, you shall finde an Abstract of it in 3.E.3. since Littletons time put in print by Fitzherbert when he was Serjeant in 11 H.8. and is not in the Reports or Bookes at large. And yet here it appeareth, that they be of great authoritie, and vouched by Littleton himselfe for the proofe of a mayne point in Law. And hereby it also appeareth how necessary it is to read Records and Pleas reported or recorded, though they were never printed. For those and the like Records are Veritatis & Vetustatis vestigia.

3.E.3.Tit.Droit F.26.

¶ *Tit. droit in* Fitzherbert 26. is

auer eux, sicome il demaund, & pur rien dira que le verity ne dira, sicome moy ayde Dieu, &c. sans dire a lour escient. Et tiel serement serra fait en attaint, et en Battaile, & en ley gager, car eux mittont chescun chose a fine. Mes John Barre counta dl seisin dun Rafe son ancester, en temps le Roy Henry, & Reynolde sur le mise ioyne tendist demy mark pur le temps &c. Et sur ceo Herle Iustice dit al grand assise, apres ceo que ils fueront charges sur le mere droit. Vous gentes, Reynold donast demy marke al Roy pur le temps, al entent que si vous troues q̃ launcester John ne fuit pas seisie en le temps que le demaundant ad count, vous nenquires plus auant del droit, et p̃ ceo vous nous dires, s quel launcester John, Rafe per nosme, fuit seisie en temps le Roy Henry, come il ad count, ou non. Et si vous troues que il ne fuit seisie en cel temps, vous nenquires nient pluis, & si vous troues que il fuit seisie, donques enquires ouster del briefe. Et puis le graund

them as he demandeth and for nothing to let, to say the truth, so helpe mee God, &c. without saying to their knowledge. And the like oath shall bee made in an Attaint and in battaile, and in wager of Law, for these doe bring euery thing to an end. But *Iohn Barre* counted of the seisin of one *Ralfe* his Ancestor in the time of K. *Henry*, and *Reynold* vpon the mise ioyned tendred halfe a marke for the time, &c. And hereupon *Herle* Iustice said to the grãd assise after that they were charged vpon the meere right. You good men, *Reynold* gaue halfe a Marke to the King for the time, to the intent that if you find that the Ancestor of *Iohn* was not seised in the time that the demãdant hath pleaded, you shall enquire no further vpõ the right, and for this, you shall tell vs whether the Ancestor of *Iohn*, (*Ralfe* by name) were seised in K. *Henries* time as he hath pleaded, or not. And if you find that he was not seised in this time you shall enquire no more, and if you find that he was seised, then you shall enquire further of the writ. And after the grand Assise came in with their

graund Assise reuiendroit oue lour verdict, & disont que Rafe ne fuit pas seisie ē temps le Roy H. per que fuit agard, que Reynold tiendroit l's tenements vers luy demandes, a luy & ses heires quites de John Barre & ses heires a remnant. Et John en le mercie, &c. Et le cause pur que ieo aye monstre icy a toy mon fits cest plee, est pur prouer le matter precedent q̄ est dit en briefe de Droit, &c. car il semble per cest plee, que si Reinold nauoit pas tendue dimy mark pur enquirer dl temps, &c. donques le graund Assise duissoit estre charg̃ tantsolement dl mere droit, & nemy del possession, &c. Et issint ḡ touts foits en briefe de Droit, si le possession dont le demandant counta soit en temps le Roy, com̄ il auoit count, donques le charge del grande assise serra tāt-solement sur le mere droit, coment que le possession fuit encounter le ley, come il est dit adeuant en cest Chapter, &c.

verdict, and said, that *Ralfe* was not seised in the time of King *Henrie*, whereby it was awarded that *Reynold* should hold the Tenements demanded against him, to him and his heires quite of *John Barre* and his heires to the remnant. And *John* in mercie, &c. And the reason why I I haue shewd to thee my Sonne this Plea, is, to proue the matter precedent which is said in a Writ of right, for it seemeth by this Plea, that if *Reynold* had not tendred the halfe marke to enquire of the time, &c. then the grand Assise ought to be charged onely to enquire of the meere right; and not of the possession, &c. And so alwayes in a Writ of Right if the possession whereof the demandant counteth bee in the Kings time as hee hath pleaded, then the charge of the grand Assise shall be only vpon the meere right, although that the possession were against the Law, as it is said before in this Chapter. &c.

of a new addition, and therefore though it bee true, yet not to bee allowed.

¶ *Et le originall & le proces fuer' demande deuant Justices Itinerants.* For it is to bee vnderstood, that all Pleas either in the realtie or personaltie that were begunne and not determined before Justices in Eire were adiourned by them into the Court of Comon Pleas. *4.E.3.41. Peuerals case. Mirror, Glanuil, Bracton, Britton, Fleta ubi supra.*

¶ *Les 12. chiualers fieront lour serement sauns challenge, &c. pur ceo que le election fuit fait per assent des parties oue les 4. chiualers.*

Here are foure things to be obserued. *30.E.1. tit. challenge 172. 21.E.4 77. 39.E.3.1. 44.E.3.6. 11.H.6.13.*

First, That omnis consensus tollit errorē, and against his own consent hee cannot challenge the twelue.

Secondly, That the foure Knights Electors of the grand Assise are not to be challenged, for that in Law they bee Judges to that purpose, and Judges or Justices cannot bee challenged. And that is the reason that Noblemen that in case of high Treason are to passe vpon a Peere of the Realme cannot be challenged, because they are Judges of the fact, and the Magna Charta saith, per iudicium parum suorum. *4.E.3.13.* *Magna Charta cap. 29.*

Thirdly, That the twelue before any assent may be challenged before the foure Knights Electors, but after assent or returne of the pannell before the Justices there shall be no challenge to the pannell nor to the polles. *39.E.3.2. 7.H.4.20.* *7.H.4.29.*

Fourthly, If there be not foure Knights for Electors in that Countie, the next to them in that Countie shall be taken. Ne curia Regis deficeret in iustitia exhibenda.

¶ *Sauns dire a lour escient.* And here it appeareth, that where the iudgement is finall, there the Oath of the grand Assise or Jury is absolute and not to their

knowledge,

knowledge, as here in the Writ of Right, in the Attaint, and in wager of Law, for the iudgement in euery of these three is finall.

Vid. Sect. 193.
Registrum.

¶ *Le mise est ioyne.* Mise **is a word of art appropriated only to a** Writ of Right, so called because both parties haue put themselues vpon the meere right to be tryed by grand Assise or by battle: so as that, which in all other Actions is called an Issue, in a Writ of Right in that case is called a Mise. And in this sence Littleton taketh it here. But in a Writ of Right if a Collaterall point is to be tryed, there it is called an Issue: and is deriued of this word (Missum) because the whole cause is put vpon this point. It is also taken for expences, as Misæ & Custagia. And sometime it signifieth a customary grant to the King or Lords Marchers of Wales by their Tenants at their first comming to their Lands.

33. H. 8. ca. 13. 3. E. 6. ca. 36.

10. E. 3. 20. 31. E. 3. droit 11. 22. E. 3. 17. 18. H. 3. droit. 62. 33. E. 3. ibid. 39. Lamb. explicat. verborum verbo Mancusa.

¶ *Tender di marke al Roy.* **Master** Lambard **saith that** Mancusa & Marca Saxonice Mancup. 7. Meatc' Nummus 30. valens denarios. And this Meatc' now called a Marke being an old Saxon word is the cause that England most commonly reckoned by Markes, Libra Saxonice is a pund, a pondo, which is called so vntill this day. Solidus qui apud nos est pars libræ vicesima, denarios per id temporis continebat quinque, nunc duodecim, and Scilling is a Saxon word, and with vs vsed to this day. Penny Saxonicè pennig, Latyne Denarius, but the value of these haue not beene alwayes one.

F. N. B. 31. e. 31. E. 3. droit. 15. 6. E. 3. ibid. 24.

In a Writ of Right of Aduowson brought by the King, the Tenant shall not tender the Dimarke, because Nullum tempus occurrit Regi, and therefore the King shall alleage, that hee or his Progenitor was seised without shewing any time.

Mirror, ca. 1. §. 17. ca. 3. de Attaint. ca. 5. §. 1. Bracton. fo. 288. 289. &c. 292. Britt. fo. 241. 245. 246. &c. Fleta, lib. 5. ca. 21. & 34. Fortescue, ca. 26.

¶ *En attaint.* Attincta, **is a Writ that lyeth where a false Verdict** in Court of Record vpon an issue ioyned by the parties is giuen. And of ancient Writers it is called Breue de conuictione. And is deriued of the principle Tinctus, or Attinctus, for that if the petite Jury be attainted of a false oath, they are stayned with periurie, and become infamous for euer, for the iudgement at the Common Law in the Attaint importeth eight great and grieuous punishments. 1. Quod amittat liberam legem imperpetuum, that is, he shall bee so infamous as shall neuer be receiued to be a Witnesse or of any Jury. 2. Quod forisfaciat omnia bona & catalla sua. 3. Quod terræ & tenementa in manus Domini Regis capiantur. 4. Quod vxores & liberi extra domus suas eijcerentur. 5. Quod domus suæ prostrentur. 6. Quod arbores suæ extirpentur. 7. Quod prata sua arentur, Et 8. Quod corpora sua carceri mancipentur. So odious is periury in this case in the eye of the Common Law, and the seuerity of this punishment is to this end, Vt pœna ad paucos, metus ad omnes perueniat, for there is Misericordia puniens, and there is Crudelitas parcens, And seeing all trialls of reall, personall and mixt actions depend vpon the oath of 12. men, prudent Antiquity inflicted a strange and seuere punishment vpon them if they were attainted of periury.

But since Littleton wrote a Statute hath beene made in mittigation of the seuerity of the Common Law in case when the petite Jurye is attainted, and therefore it is taken by equitye. For where the Statute saith, that the party grieued shall haue an Attaint against the party which shall haue iudgement vpon the Verdict, yet an Attaint shall be maintained vpon that Statute against the Executors of the partie, Et sic de similibus. (a) But see the Statute and Authorityes quoted in the Margent. Only I thought good to obserue three things.

(a) 23. H. 8. ca. 3. 3. Eliz. Dier. 201. 7. E. 6. ibidem. 81. 3. Mar. ibid. 129. 7. Eliz. ibid. 235. 24. H. 8. Br. Attaint 76. 4. Mar ibid. 127. 20. H. 7. 5. 42. E. 3. 26. F. N. B. 107. D.

First, that no Attaint can be maintained vpon this Statute but betweene party and party.

Secondly, that no Conusance can be granted vpon any Attaint, because all Attaints are to be taken eyther before the King in his bench, or before the Justices of the Common place, and in no other Courts, &c.

Thirdly, consider what pleas may be pleaded in an Attaint by force of this Act, and what not.

Mirror. ca. 1. §. 3. ca. 3. §. ca. 5 §. 1. Bracton, lib. 3. 141. b. & fo. 320. 331. Glanuil. lib. 2. cap. 3. 4. 5. Lib. 8. ca. 9. Lib 4. ca. 1. Britt. fo. 40. 42. 43. 81. 175. 190. Fleta lib. 1. ca. 32. & lib. 2. ca. 48. (b) 4. E. 3. 41. 17. E. 3. 19. H. 6. 35. 1. H. 4. 3. 30. E. 3. 20. 29. E. 3. 12. 13. H. 4. 4. Stanf. 174. 178. 17 Eliz. Dier 9. E. 4. 35. 1. H. 6. 6. 3. H. 6. 55. Vid. lib. 9. fo. 32. b. & 33. b.

¶ *En battaile.* Duellum, Monomachia, **And it signifieth in the** Common Law a tryall by single fight, by battaile or combate, Monomachia. (b) And in the Writ of Right neither the Tenant or Demandant shall fight for themselues, but finde a Champion to fight for them: because if either the Demandant or Tenant should be slayne, no iudgement could be giuen for the Lands or Tenements in question. But in an Appeale the Defendant shall fight for himselfe, & so shall the Plaintife also, for there if the Defendant be slayne, the Plaintife hath the effect of his suite, that is the death of the Defendant; the order and solemnity whereof you may reade in our ancient and latter Bookes. And this the Law did institute, when the Tenant failed of his witnesses, or Euidences, or other proofes, and the presumption of Law is, that God will giue victory to him that hath right.

Mirror ca. 4. Del office des Iustices, &c. Glanuill lib. 1. ca. 9. lib. 8. ca. 8.

¶ *Ley gager.* Vadiare legem, **And there is also** Facere legem, **by** making of his Law. That is to take an oath (for example) that he oweth not the debt demanded of him vpon a simple Contract, nor any penny thereof. And it is called Wager of

Law,

Law, because of ancient time he put in surety to make his Law at such a day; and it is called making of his Law, because the Law doth giue such a speciall benefit to the Defendant to barre the Plaintife for euer in that case. (r) But he ought to bring with him eleuen persons of his neighbours that will answ upon their oath, that in their consciences he saith truth, so as he himselfe must be sworne De fidelitate, and the eleuen De credulitate.

Lib. 10. *ca.* 5. *Bracton, lib.* 3. *tract.* 2. *ca.* 37. *& lib.* 5 *fo.* 410. *Britton, fo.* 56. *Fleta lib.* 2. *ca.* 56. 63.

And wager of Law lyeth not when there is a specialty, or Deed to charge the Defendant, but when it groweth by word, so as he may pay or satisfie the party in secret, whereof the Defendant hauing no testimony of witnesses may wage his Law; and thereby the Plaintife is perpetually barred, as Littleton here saith, for the Law presumeth that no man will forsweare himselfe for any worldly thing; but mens consciences doe grow so large (specially in this case passing without impunitie) as they choose rather to bring an Action upon his case upon his promise, wherein (because it is Trespasse sur le case) he cannot wage his Law, then an Action of debt.

(r) *Magna Carta, ca.* 28. *Bracton. lib.* 5. *fo.* 410. *Fleta, lib.* 2. *ca.* 63. *Diuersities des Courts,* 33. *H.* 6. 8.

A man Outlawed or attainted in an Attaint, or upon an inditement of conspiracie, or of periury, or otherwise whereby he become infamous shall not wage his Law.

33. *H.* 6. 32.

A man under the age of 21. yeares shall not wage his Law, but a Feme couert together with her husband shall wage her Law.

11. *H.* 6. 40, 15. *E.* 4. 2.

When the suite is for the King, or for his benefit, as in a Quo minus, the Defendant shall not wage his Law.

32. *H.* 6. 24. 8. *H.* 5. *Ley* 66. 35. *H.* 8. *Ley. Br.* 102.

If an Infant be Plaintife the defendant shall not wage his Law. An Alien shall wage his Law in that language he can speake.

26. *E.* 3. 63. *b.* 21. *H.* 6. 42.

In no case where a Contempt, trespasse, disceite, or iniurie is supposed in the defendant, he shall wage his law, because the law will not trust him with an oath to discharge himselfe in those cases, only in some cases in Dett, Detinue, Accompt, the Defendant is allowed by law to wage his Law.

44. *E.* 3. 32. 18. *E.* 3. 4. 24. *E.* 3. 39.

In an Action of Account against a Receiuor upon a receipt of money by the hand of another person for account render (unlesse it be by the hands of his wife, or of his Commoigne) the Defendant shall not wage his Law, because the receipt is the ground of the Action which lyeth not in priuity betweene the Plaintife and Defendant, but in the notice of a third person, and such a receipt is trauersable. (d) But in an Action of debt upon an Arbitrament, or in an Action of Detinue by the bailement of anothers hand, the Defendant shall wage his Law, because the Debet and the Detinet is the ground of those actions, and the Contract or Bailement though it be by another hand, is but the conueyance and not trauersable. In an action of Accompt against a Bailife of a Mannor, the Defendant cannot wage his Law because it soundeth in the realty. In an action of Debt which concernes the realty, as for Debt, Rent upon a Lease for yeares, or an action of Detinue for detayning an Indowment of a Lease for yeares, the Defendant shall not wage his Law, much lesse for Charters or Deeds which concerne inheritance.

15. *E.* 4. 16. 10. *E.* 4. 5. (d) 33. *H.* 6. 24. 13. *H.* 7. 3. *a.* 22. *H.* 6. 41. 1. *H.* 6. 1 *b.* 8. *H.* 6. 11. 18. *H.* 8. 3. 3. *E.* 3. 28. 11. *H.* 4. 54. 5. *H.* 5. 13. 21. *H* 6. 30. 24. *E.* 3. *Ley* 63. 30 *E.* 3. 19. 9. *E.* 4. 1. 34. *H.* 8. *Ley Gager Br.* 97.

In an action of Debt for a Fine or Amerciament in a Leete, the Defendant shall not wage his Law, because the Leete is a Court of Record, but in an action of Debt for an Amerciament in a Court Baron the Defendant shall wage his Lawe, for that it is no Court of Record.

10. *H* 6. 7. 1. *H.* 7. 25. 6. *Eliz. Bendloes.*

In debt upon an account before Auditors the Defendant shall not wage his Law, and this by construction of the Statute of W 2. ca. 11. which giueth them great authority and faith, Coram Auditoribus, and therefore of an account before one auditor the Law lyeth. So if the Lord before Auditors be found in surplusage, in an action of Debt brought by the Accomptant, the Lord shall not wage his Law by construction also upon this Statute, as an incident rising upon the Accounts.

9. *H.* 5. 3 8 *H* 6. 15. 22. *H.* 6. 35. 38. *H.* 6. 6. 14. *H.* 6. 62. 38. *H.* 6. 6.

In an action of Debt by a Gaoler against the Prisoner for his victuals the Defendant shall not wage his Law, for he cannot refuse the Prisoner, and ought not to suffer him to dye for default of sustenance, otherwise it is for tabling of a man at large.

28. *H.* 6. 4. 19. *H.* 6. 20. 22. *H.* 6. 13. 39. *H.* 6. 18.

In an action of Debt brought by an Attorney for his Fees the defendant shall not wage his Law, because he is compellable to be his Attorney. And so if a seruant be retained according to the Statute of Labourers in an action of Debt for his Salary his master shall not wage his Law, because he was compellable to serue, otherwise it is, if he be not retained according to the Statute.

21. *H.* 6. 4. 38. *H.* 6. 22. 39. *H.* 6. 18.

Wheresoeuer a man is charged as Executor or Administrator, he shall not wage his Law, for no man shall wage his Law of another mans Deed, but in case of a Successor of an Abbot, for that the house neuer dyeth.

3. *H.* 6. 38. 1. *H.* 7. 25. 13. *H.* 7.

In Debt upon a penalty giuen by Statute, the Defendant shall not wage his Law. There is another kinde of wager of Law in a real action, of Non summons, but thereof Littleton speaketh not.

10. *H.* 7. 18.

¶ *Et sur ceo* Herle *Iustice dit, &c.* Hereby it appeareth that it is the

the office of the Judges to instruct the grand Assise or Jury in points of Law, for as the graund Assise or other Jurors are triers of the matters of fact, Ad questionem facti non respondent Iudices, so Ad questionem iuris non respondent Iuratores. And accordingly the Judge in this case directed the grand Assise, viz: if they found that, &c.

Glan. li. 13. ca. 1. & 2. Bracton li. 5. fol. 328

Lib. 5 fol. 85. Tewrius case.

¶ *Per que fuit agard.* **Here are two things to bee obserued.** First the forme of a Judgement finall. Secondly, that a Judgement finall is to be giuen in this particular case. For the forme of the finall iudgement for the Tenant is here expressed, that the Tenant shall hold the Tenements demanded against him, to him & his heirs quite of the Demandant and his heires for euer, and the Demandant in the mercy. Quod tenens teneat terram illam sibi & hæredibus suis in pace versus petentem & hæredes suos in perpetuum.

34. E. 3. Iudgm. 256. adiudge accord 13. H. 4. Iudgm. 245. 10. H. 6. 8. 20. H. 6. 38. b. 21. H. 6. 34. b. 26. H. 8. 8. b. 1. Mar. Dy. 98. Li. 5. fo. 85. Tewrius case. F. N. B. 5. 11. 31.

For the second point seeing the Mise is ioyned vpon the meere right, albeit the Verdict of the Grand Assise be giuen vpon another point, yet iudgement finall shall be giuen. And so it is if the Tenant after the Mise ioyned make default, or confesse the action, or if the Demandant be Non-suite, and yet in none of these cases they of the grand Assise gaue their verdict vpon the meere right.

¶ *Come est auantdit,* Vid. Sect. 478.

Chap. 9. Of Confirmation. *Sect. 515.*

¶ Fait de Confirmation est communement en tiel forme, ou a tiel effect, Nouerint vniuersi, &c. me A. de B. ratificasse, approbasse & confirmasse C. de D. statum & possessionem, quos habeo, de, & in vno mesuagio, &c. cum pertiñ in F. &c.

A Deed of confirmation is commonly in this forme, or to this effect: *Know all Men &c. That I A. of B. haue ratified, approoued, and confirmed to C. of D. the estate and possession which I haue of and in one Messuage, &c. with the Appurtenances in F. &c.*

Bract. li. 2. fo. 32. b. & 58, 59. Brit. 235.

¶ Here first our Authour shewes what a Confirmation is: *Confirmation.* Confirmatio commeth of the verbe * Confirmare, quod est firmum facere, and therefore it is said, That Confirmatio omnes supplet defectus, licet id quod actum est ab initio, non valuit. A Confirmation is a conueyance of an estate or right in esse, whereby a voidable estate is made sure & vnauoydable, or whereby a particular estate is increased.

* Lit pag. sequen.

Bract. li. 2. 58.

Bract. li. 2. fo. 27. 58. 38. H. 6. 34. 37. Pl. Com. Count. de Leicester. case.

A Confirmation doth not strengthen a voyde estate. Confirmatio est nulla vbi donum præcedens est inualidum, & vbi donatio nulla omnino nec valebit confirmatio: for a Confirmation may make a voidable or defeasible estate good, but it cannot worke vpon an Estate that is voyd in Law. Non valet confirmatio nisi ille qui confirmat sit in possessione rei vel iuris vnde fieri debet confirmatio, & eodem modo nisi ille cui confirmatio fit, sit in possessione. And another saith, (c) Confirmare est id quod prius infirmum fuit firmare. Et donationum alia incepta, & defectiua, & post tempus confirmata, confirmatio enim omnem supplet defectum, poterit enim esse in pendenti donec per ratihabitionem hæredis cum ad ætatem peruenerit roboretur.

10. E. 2. Confirm. 24 32. E. 3. 9.

(c) Flet. li. 3. ca. 14. & li. 3. c. 3

44. Ass. 3.

¶ Ratificasse. Ratificare est ratum facere, and is æquipollent to Confirmare, which as hath beene sayd, is firmum facere.

¶ Approbasse commeth of Ad and Probo, which is to make perfect and good.

¶ Confirmasse. Here is to bee obserued, That there bee two kinds of Confirmations, viz Confirmations expresse or in Deed, whereof Littleton hath here put these three examples and Confirmations implied, or in Law, whereof Littleton hereafter speaketh in this Chapter. Quælibet confirmatio, aut est perficiens, crescens, aut diminuens, and of all these Littleton putteth examples in this Chapter. And hereof Fleta saith, Carta autem de confirmatione est illa quæ alterius factum consolidat & confirmat, & nihil noui attribuit, quandoque tamen confirmat & addit.

Li. 9. fo. 142. Beaumonds case. Flet. li. 3. ca. 14.

Sect.

Section 516.

¶ En ascũ case vn fait de Confirmation est bone et auailable, lou en tiel case vn Fait de Release nest passe bone, ne auailable. Sicõe ieo lessa Terre a vn home pur terme de sa vie, le quel lessa mesm̃ la terre a vn auter p̃ terme de xl. ans, per force de quel il est en possession. Si ieo p mon Fait confirme lestate del Tenant a terme dans, et puis le tenant a terme de vie morust durant le terme des ans, ieo ne puis enter en la Terre durant le dit terme.

AND in some case a Deed of Confirmation is good and available, where in the same case a Deede of Release is not good nor auaileable. As if I let land to a man for terme of his life, who letteth the same to another for terme of fortie yeares, by force of which he is in possession: if I by my Deed confirme the Estate of the Tenant for yeares, and after the Tenant for life dieth during the terme of yeares, I cannot enter into the Land during the said terme.

¶ LIttleton in this chapter putteth eight Diuersities betweene a Confirmation and a Release, and thereof for illustration here he putteth two cases in this and the next Section, which vpon that which hath beene sayd in the precedent Chapters, is sufficiently explained. Onely in both these cases this is to bee obserued, That where a Confirmation shall enlarge an estate, there priuitie is required, as well as in the case of the Release, as by many examples which Littleton puts in this Chapter appeareth. And note here is the first case wherein a Release and a Confirmation doe differ: 49.E.3.32. 9 H.6.22. Tit. Release 44

Lessee for life made a Lease for thirtie yeares, and after the Lessor and Lessee for life made a Lease for sixty yeares to another, which Lease for sixtie yeares the Lessor did first confirme, and after the Lessor confirmed the lease for thirtie yeares; and after Tenant for life dyed within the thirtie yeares, and it was adiudged, (d) That the Lease for thirtie yeares was determined by the death of Lessee for life, and that the Lessee for sixtie yeares might enter, for that albeit the Lease for sixty yeares was the latter in time, yet was it of greater force in Law, for that the Lessor who had power to confirme which of them he would, did first confirme the second Lease. (d) Inter Vmpel & Lodge. temp. Reg. Eliz.

In this Chapter is also to be obserued eight Cases, wherein a Release and a Confirmation haue the like operation in Law.

Sect. 517.

¶ VNcore si ieo per mon fait de Release auoy releas al tenant a terme dans en la vie le tenant a terme de vie, cel Release serra voyd, pur ceo que adonqs ne fuit ascun priuity perent moy et le tenant a terme dans, car release nest auaileable al Tenant a terme dans, mes lou est vn priuitie perent luy et celuy q̃ releasast.

YEt if I by my Deed of Release had released to the Tenant for yeares in the life time of the tenant for life, this Release shall be voyd, for that then there was not any priuitie betweene me and the Tenant for yeres: for a Release is not auailable to the Tenant for yeares, but where there is a priuitie betweene him and him that releaseth.

This belongeth to the first diuersitie betweene a Release and a Confirmation.

Section 518.

4. H. 7. 10. by Read. 22. E. 4. 36.

¶ Here is the second diversity betweene a Release and a Confirmation. But if the Disseisor make a Lease for yeares to begin at Michaelmasse, and the Disseisee confirm his estate, this is voyd, because he hath but interesse termini, and no estate in him, whereupon a Confirmation may enure.

¶ En mesme le manner est, si ieo soy disseisie, et le Disseisor fait vn Lease a vn aut pur terme dans, si ieo relessa al termor, ceo est voyde, mes si ieo confirma lestate le termor, ceo est bone & effectual.

IN the same manner it is if I be disseised, and the Disseisor make a Lease to another for terme of yeares, if I release to the Termor this is voyd: but if I confirme the Estate of the Termor, this is good and effectuall.

Sect. 519.

¶ Item si ieo soy disseisie, & ieo confirma lestate le Disseisor, il ad bone et droiturel estate en Fee simple, coment que en le fait de confirmation nul mention est fait de ses heires, pur ceo que il auoit fee simple al temps de Confirmation. Car en tiel case si le disseisee confirma lestate le disseisor, A auer et tener a luy et a ses heires de son corps engendres, ou a auer et tener a luy pur le terme de sa vie, uncore le disseisor ad fee simple, et est seisie en son demesne come de fee, pur ceo que quant son estate fuit confirm, donque il auoit fee simple, et tiel fait ne poit changer son estat sans entry fait sur luy, &c.

ALso if I be disseised, and I confirme the estate of the Disseisor, he hath a good and rightfull estate in Fee simple, albeit in the Deed of Confirmation no mention be made of his heires, because he had Fee simple at the time of the Confirmation. For in such case if the Disseisee confirme the state of the Disseisor, To haue and to hold to him and his heires of his bodie engendred, or to haue and to hold to him for terme of his life, yet the Disseisor hath a Fee simple, and is seised in his Demesne as of Fee, because when his estate was confirmed, hee had then a Fee simple, & such Deed cannot change his estate, without entry made vpon him, &c.

19. H. 6. 22. 6. E. 3. Confirm. 4.

¶ Here is the first case wherein the Release and Confirmation both agree, viz. a Confirmation to a Disseisor in Taile, or for any particular estate, is of the like force as a Release to a Disseisor, during such estate, which in both cases is good for euer. In the same manner it is, if the Disseisor make a gift in taile, and the Disseisee confirme the estate of the donee for the life of the donee, this confirmation enures to the whole estate taile, for a confirmation can make no fraction of any estate, to extend but to part of the estate onely: Et sic de cæteris.

Section 520.

¶ En mesme le maner est, si son estate soit confirme pur terme de un iour ou pur terme dun heure, il ad bon estate en fee simple, pur ceo que son estate en fee simple fuit un foits confirm. Quia confirmare idem est quod firmum facere, &c.

In the same manner it is if his estate bee confirmed for tearme of a day, or for tearme of an houre, hee hath a good estate in fee simple, for this, that his estate in fee simple was once confirmed. *Quia confirmare idem est quod firmum facere, &c.*

¶ Here is the second case wherein the release and Confirmation doe agree. The reason of this is for that the Disseisor hath a fee simple, and therefore if his estate be confirmed but for an houre it is good for ever, because (saith Littleton) Confirmare idem est quod firmum facere.

Nota, a diversitie betweene a bare assent without any right or interest, and an assent coupled with a right or interest; and therefore an Attornement cannot bee made for a time nor upon Condition; *Lib. 5. fol. 81. Fordes case.* but if the person make a Lease for a hundred yeares, the Patron and the Ordinary may confirme fiftie of the yeares, for they have an interest, and may charge in time of vacation. And so if a Disseisor make a Lease for a hundred yeares, the Disseisee may confirme parcell of those yeares but then it must be by apt words, for he must not confirme the Lease or demise or the estate of the Lessee, for then the addition for parcell of the tearme should be repugnant when the whole was confirmed before, but the Confirmation must be of the Land for part of the tearme. So may the Confirmation be of part of the land, as if it be of fortie, he may confirme twentie, &c. So if tenant for life make a Lease for a hundred yeares, the Lessor may confirme either for part of the terme or for part of the Land. But an estate of Freehold cannot be confirmed for part of the estate, for that the estate is intire, and not severall as yeares be.

Sect. 521.

Item si mon Disseisor fait un leas a terme de vie, le remainder ouster en fee, si ieo releas al tenant a terme de vie ceo urera a celuy en le remainder. Mes si ieo confirm lestate de le tenant a terme de vie, uncore apres son decease ieo puis bien enter, pur ceo que riens est confirme forsque lestate le tenant a terme de vie, issint que apres son decease, ieo puis enter. Mes quant ieo relessa

Also if my Disseisor maketh a Lease for life, the remaynder over in fee, if I release to the Tenant for life, this shall enure to him in the remaynder. But if I confirme the Estate of the Tenant for tearme of life, yet after his decease I may well enter, because nothing is confirmed but the Estate of the Tenant for

¶ Here is the third Case wherein the release, and confirmation differ, for the confirmation to the Tenant for life doth not enure to him in the remainder.

And so it is when the severall estates be in one person, as if the Disseisor make a gift in taile the remaynder to the right heires of Tenant in taile, if the Disseisee confirme the estate in tayle, it shall not extend to Fee simple, no more then if the Disseisor had made a gift in taile, the remainder for life, the remainder to the right heires of tenant in taile, this extendeth only to the estate taile, and not

tout mon droit al tenant a terme de vie, ceo vzera a celuy en le remainder, ou en l'reuersion, pur ceo que tout mon droit est ale per tiel releas. Mes en cest cas, si le disseisie confirme lestate & le title celuy en le remainder sans ascun confirmation fait a tenant a terme de vie, le disseisie ne poit enter sur le tenant a term̄ de vie, pur ceo que l'remainder est dependant sur lestate le tenant a terme de vie, & si son estate serroit defeate, le remainder serroit defeate, per lentrie le disseisie, & ceo ne serra reason que il per son entre defeateroit le remainder encounter son confirmation, &c.

life, so that after his decease I may enter. But when I release all my right to the Tenant for life, this shall enure to him in the remainder or in the reuersion, because all my right is gone by such release. But in this case if the Disseisee confirme the estate and title of him in the remainder without any confirmation made to Tenant for life, the Disseisee cannot enter vpon the Tenant for terme of life, for that the remaynder is depending vpon the state for life, and if his estate should bee defeated, the remainder should be defeated by the entry of the Disseisee, and it is no reason that he by his entry should defeat the remainder against his confirmation, &c.

to the remaynder for life, nor to the remaynder in fee. But if the Disseisor make a lease for life to A. & B, and the Disseisee confirme the estate of A, B. shall take aduantage thereof, for the estate of A. which was confirmed was ioynt with B and in that case the Disseisee shall not enter into the Land, and deuest the moitie of B.

If the Disseisor infeoffe A and B, and the heires of B. if the Disseisee confirme the estate of B for his life, this shall not only extend to his Companion, as hath beene said, but to his whole fee simple, because to many purposes hee had the whole Fee simple in him, and the confirmation shall bee taken most strong against him that made it.

Tenant in tayle discontinueth in fee and dieth, the Discontinuee make a lease for life, and granteth the reuersion to the issue, he shall haue a Formedon against tenant for life, for by his Formedon he must recouer estate of Inheritance, and the Lessee for life hath not the Inheritance, but the issue in taile himselfe hath it.

If feoffee vpon condition make a Lease for life, or a gift in taile, and the feoffor release the Condition to the feoffee, he shall not enter vpon the Lessee or Donee, because he cannot regaine his ancient estate.

If the Feoffee vpon Condition make a Lease for life, the remaynder in fee, if the Feoffor release the Condition to the Lessee for life, it shall enure to him in the remaynder, aswell as in the case of the right, or of a Rent, &c.

If a Feme Disseisoresse make a feoffment in fee to the vse of A. for life, and after to the vse of herselfe in taile, and the remaynder to the vse of B. in fee, and then taketh husband the Disseisee, and he releaseth to A. all his right, this shall enure to B, and to his owne wife also, for by the rule of Littleton it must enure to all in the remaynder.

But if A. letteth to B. for life, and B. maketh a Lease to C. for his life, the remaynder to A. in fee. A. releaseth to C. all his right, this is good to perfect the estate of C. for his life. But when C. dieth A. shall bee in of his old estate for his release could not enure to himselfe to perfect his defeasible remaynder, but his ancient right remayneth. And note that in these two cases the fee is deuested, and vested all at one instant, in the same manner, as if tenant in taile make a Lease for life, at the same instant the estate taile is deuested out of the Donee, and the reuersion in fee out of the Donor, and a new fee vested in Tenant in taile. And so if the husband make a Lease for life of his wiues land, he deuesteth his owne estate, that he hath in her right, and the Inheritance of his wife, and at the same instant vesteth a new reuersion in fee in himselfe.

Vide 29. Ass. 17. 30. H. 8. Recou en value Br. 30. 13. E. 3 entr. cong. Br. 127.

¶ *Mes en cest case si le disseisee confirme lestate & title celuy en le remaynder.* Here is the third case wherein the Release and Confirmation

doe

doe agree for the Confirmation made to him in the remaynder shall auayle the Tenant for life, as much as the Release shall. Pl.Com. Delamers case. Vid.Sect.374.

¶ *Pur ceo que le remaynder est dependant, &c.* By this some haue gathered that if a Disseisor make a Lease for life, reseruing the reuersion to himselfe, and the Disseisee confirmeth the state of the Disseisor, that he may enter vpon the Lessee, because the estate of him in the Reuersion dependeth not vpon the state for life as the Remainder, but all is one, for by the Confirmation made to him in the Reuersion, all the right of him that confirmeth is gone, as well as when he maketh it to him in remainder, and he cannot by his entrie auoide the estate of the Lessee for life, but he must auoide the state of the Lessor which against his owne confirmation, he cannot doe, and it hath beene adiudged, that if a Disseisor make a Lease for life, and after leuie a Fine of the reuersion with Proclamations, and the fiue yeares passe, so as the Disseisee is for the Reuersion barred, he shall not enter vpon the Lessee for life.

¶ *Le remainder serra defeat.* It is regularly true, that when the particular estate is defeated, that the remainder thereby shall be also defeated, but it faileth in diuers cases.

For where the particular estate and the remainder depend vpon one title, there the defeating of the particular estate is a defeating of the remainder. But where the particular estate is defeasible, and the remainder by good title, there though the particular estate be defeated the remainder is good. As if the Lessor disseise A. Lessee for life, and make a Lease to B. for the life of A. the remainder to C. in fee, albeit A. re-enter, and defeate the estate for life, yet the remainder to C. being once vested by good title shall not be auoyded, for it were against reason, that the Lessor should haue the remainder againe against his owne Liuery, and this is well warranted by the reason of Littleton in this case. So it is if a Lease be made to an infant for life, the remainder in fee, the Infant at his full age disagree to the estate for life, yet the remainder is good, for that it was once vested by good title, for in both these cases, there was a particular estate at the time of the remainder created. Vid. Pl.Com. Colthirsts case.

If a Lease be made to A. for the life of B. the remainder to C. in fee, A. dyeth before an occupant entreth, here is a remainder without a particular estate, and yet the remainder continueth good. 17.E.3.48.

A rent is granted to the Tenant of the land for life, the remainder in fee, this is a good remainder, albeit the particular estate continued not, for Eo instante, that he tooke the particular estate, Eo instante the remainder vested, and the suspencion in iudgement of Law grew after the taking of the particular estate. 3.E.3.Abb.Ass.

If a man grant a rent to B. for the life of Alice, the remainder to the heires of the body of Alice, this is a good remainder, and yet it must vest vpon an instant. 7.H.4.6.

Sect. 522.

¶ [Item si sont deux disseisors, et le disseisee relessa a vn de eux, il tiendra son compagnion hors de la terre. Mes si le disseisee confirma lestate de lun, sans pluis dire en le fait, ascuns diont que il ne tiendra son compagnion dehors. Mes tiendra ioyntment oue luy. pur ceo que riens fuit confirme forsque

ALso if there bee two disseisors and the disseisee releaseth to one of them, hee shall hold his companion out of the land, but if the disseisee confirme the estate of the one without more saying in the Deed, some say that he shall not hold his companion out, but shall hold ioyntly with him for that nothing was con-

¶ This is the fourth case wherein the release and the confirmation seeme to differ, being made vnto one of the Disseisors.

¶ *Confirme forsque son estate, &c.* Hereby it appeareth that if the Disseisee confirme the estate of the one Disseisor in the lands, To haue and to hold the lands or tenements, or the right of the Disseisee, to him and his heires, hee shall hold out the other Disseisor, and that appeareth by Littleton, first vpon these words (Confirme the state of one) without more saying in the Deed,

Deed, viz. To haue and to hold the Lands, &c. Secondly, the reason of Littleton in expresse words is, for that nothing was confirmed but his estate which was ioynt. Thirdly, the next two Sections make it plaine where the Habendum is added.

son estate que fuit ioynt, &c.

firmed but his estate which was ioynt, &c.

Hereby also it appeareth, that a Release is more forcible in Law then a Confirmation. If the Disseisee and a stranger Disseise the heire of the Disseisor, and the disseisee confirme the estate of his companion, this shall not extinguish his right that was suspended: so as if the heire of the Disseisor re-enter the right of the disseisee is reuiued. And so it is, if the Grantee of a Rent-charge and an estranger disseise the Tenant of the land, and the Grantee confirme the estate of his Companion, the Tenant of the land re-enter, the Rent is reuiued, for the Confirmation extended not to the Rent suspended, otherwise it is of a Release in both cases.

Sect. 523.

¶ ET pur ceo ascuns ont dit, que si deux iointenants sont, et lun confirme lestate lauter, que il nad forsque ioint estat, sicome il auoit adeuant. Mes sil ad tiels parols en le fait de confirmation, a auer et tener a luy et a ses heires touts les tenements dont mention est fait ē le confirmation, donques il ad estate sole en les tenements, &c. Et pur ceo il est bon et sure chose en chescun confirmation dauer ceux parolx; A auer et tener les tenements, &c. en fee, ou en fee taile, ou pur terme de vie, ou pur terme dans, solonque ceo que le cas est, ou le matter gist.

AND for this some haue said that if two ioyntenants bee, and the one confirme the estate of the other, that he hath but a ioynt estate as he had before, but if hee hath such words in the Deed of confirmation, to haue and to hold to him and to his heires all the tenements whereof mention is made in the Confirmation, then he hath a sole estate in the tenements, &c. And therefore it is a good and sure thing in euery confirmation to haue these words, To haue and to hold the tenements, &c. in fee, or in fee taile, or for terme of life, or for terme of yeares according as the case is or the matter lyeth.

¶ AND this Confirmation leaueth the state as it was, and doth not amount to any seuerance of the ioynture as some haue said.

34.E.3.tit. Confirm.

¶ *Mes sil ad tiels parols en le fait, &c.* This is plaine and euident enough.

¶ *Et pur ceo il est bone & sure chose, &c.* This is good counsell and worthy to be followed.

Sect.524.

¶ HEre the diuersity is apparant betweene a Confirmation of the estate for life in the land to haue and to hold the said state in the land to him and his heires, this cannot en-

¶ CAr al entent dascuns, si hōe lessa terre a vn auter pur terme de vie, et puis confirma son e-

FOr to the intent of some, if a man letteth land to another for life, and after confirme his estate which

state que il ad en m̃ la terre, a auer et tener son estate a luy et a ses heires, cest confirmation quant a ses heires est void, car ses heires ne poient auer son estat que ne fuit forsque pur terme de son vie. Mes sil confirma son estate per ceux parols, a auer mesme la terre a luy et a ses heirs, cest confirmation fait fee simple en cest case a luy en la terre, pur ceo que les parols a auer et tener, &c. va a le terre & nemy al estate que il ad, &c.

hee hath in the same land, to haue and to hold his estate to him and to his heires, this confirmation as to his heires is voide, for his heires cannot haue his estate which was not but for terme of his life. But if he confirme his estate by these words, to haue the same land to him and to his heires, this confirmation maketh a fee simple in this case to him in the land, for that the words to haue and to hold, &c. goeth to the land and not to the estate which hee hath, &c.

large his estate, for his estate being but for life, that estate cannot bee extended to his heires. But in that case if he confirme the state for life in the land in the premisses of the Deed and the Habendum is in this sort, To haue and to hold the land to him and his heires, this shall enlarge his estate and create in him a fee simple. 18.E.3.40.

Wherein is to bee noted (c) that the Habendum and the premisses doe in substance well agree together, and that the Habendum may enlarge the premisses but not abridge the same.

(c) Vid. Pl.Com. in Throgmortons case fo. Wrotesleyes case 197.

And seeing that in conveyances, limitations of remainders are usuall and common assurances, it is dangerous by conceipts or nice distinctions to bring them in question, as haue in latter time beene attempted.

¶ *Son estate, Vid. Sect.650.*

Sect. 525.

¶ Item si ieo lessa certaine terre a un fem sole pur term̃ d̃ sa vie, la quel prent baron, et puis ieo confirma lestate le baron et sa feme, a auer et tener pur term̃ de lour deux vies, en cest case le baron ne tient iointment oue sa feme, mes tient en droit de sa feme pur terme de sa vie. Mes cest confirmation urera a le baron per voy de remainder p̃ terme de sa vie, sil suruequist sa feme.

ALso if I let certaine land to a feme sole for terme of her life, who taketh husband, & after I confirme the estate of the husband and wife, to haue and to hold for terme of their two liues. In this case the husband doth not hold ioyntly with his wife, but holdeth in right of his wife for terme of her life. But this confirmation shall enure to the husband by way of remainder for terme of his life, if he suruiueth his wife.

¶ HEre is the fourth case wherein the Release and confirmation doe agree, and in this case it is to be obserued that the Baron hath such an estate in the land in the right of his wife as hee is capable of a confirmation to enlarge his estate, and therefore if the confirmation had beene made of his estate to him alone to haue and to hold the land to him and to his heires, this had beene good to haue conueyed the fee simple to him after the decease of his wife, for if in this case a Release be made to the husband and his heires, this is sufficient to conuey the inheritance of the land to the husband. Vid. Sect. 573. 16.H.6.tit. Release 45. 22.E.3.tit. Release Statham.

¶ *Ne tient iointment oue sa feme.* For two causes, First because the

the wife hath the whole for her life. Secondly, Joyntenants must (as hath beene before sayd in the Chapter of Joyntenants,) come in by one title. But in this case if the Confirmation had beene made to the husband and wife, To have and to hold the land to them two and to their heires, they had beene Joyntenants of the Fee simple, and the husband seised in the right of his wife for her life, for the husband and the wife cannot take by moities during the Coverture. (18.E.3.20.)

If a man letteth land to the husband and wife, to have and to hold the one moitie to the husband for terme of his life, and the other moitie to the wife for her life, and the Lessor confirme the estate of them both in the land, To have and to hold to them and to their heires, by this Confirmation as to the moitie of the husband, it enureth onely to the husband & his heyres, for the wife had nothing in that moitie, but as to the moitie of the wife, they are joyntenants, as hath bin sayd, for the husband hath such an estate in his wives moitie, in her right, as is capable of a Confirmation. But if such a Lease for life be made to two men by severall moities, and the Lessor confirme their estates in the land, To have and to hold to them and to their heires, they are Tenants in Common of the Inheritance, for regularly the Confirmation shall enure according to the qualitie and nature of the Estate which it doth enlarge and increase. (18.Ass.p.3.18.E.3.Confir.17 17.E.3.68.28.E.3.94. 40.E.3. 8.Ass.30.)

If a Lease for life be made to A. the remainder to B. for life, and the Lessor confirms their Estates in the land, To have and to hold to them and their heires, A. taketh one moitie to him and his heires, and therefore of the one moitie he is seised for life, the remainder to B. for life, and then to him and his heires: Of the other moitie A is seised for life, the immediate Inheritance to B. and his heires, because as to the moitie which B. takes, the same is executed: as if the Reversion be granted to Tenant for life, and to a stranger, it is executed for one moytie (as hath beene sayd before) and therefore in this case they are Tenants in Common. (39.H.6.9.)

If lands be given to two men, and to the heires of their two bodies begotten, and the Donor confirmeth their two estates in the land, To have and to hold the land to them two and to their heires: In this case some are of opinion, That they shall be Joyntenants of the Fee simple, because the Donees were joyntenants for life, & (say they) the Confirmation must enure according to the estate which they have in possession, and that was joynt. But others hold the contrarie; for first they say, That the Donees have to some purposes severall Inheritances executed, though betweene the Donees survivor shall hold for their lives. Secondly they say, That when the whole estate which comprehendeth severall Inheritances, is confirmed, the Confirmation must enure according to the severall Inheritances, which is the greater and most perdurable estate, and therefore that the Donees shall be Tenants in Common of the Inheritance in this case.

V.Sect.573. ¶ *Per voy de remainder, &c.* Here some question hath beene made of this terme Remainder, without any cause at all, because in Law it is in nature of a Remainder. For in case of a fine, when a reversion expectant upon an estate for life in A. is granted to B. Et quæ ad ipsum reverti debet post mortem A. præfato B. & hæredibus suis remaneant, &c. and a more colourable exception might be taken against this word Remancant there, than in the case of Littleton. (Pl.Com Colthirst case. Doct. & Stud.ca.21.)

(* 16.H.6.tit.Release 45. (o) 9 E.4.18. (p) 6.E.3 9. (q) 17.E.3.68.b.) It is true, That in * 16 H 6 it is called a Reversion: in (o) 9.E.4. it is called a Remainder: in (p) 6.E.3 it is sayd, That by the Confirmation an estate accrued to the husband for terme of his life. In (q) 17.E.3. the husband, living the wife, shall have nothing but in abeyance after the death of his wife. But lest there should be pugna verborum, which learned and wise men ever avoyd, all doe resolve, That the estate of the husband is good, and that it doth enure by way of increase and inlargement of his estate. And albeit in this case of Littleton, the husband by the Confirmation gaineth an estate for life in remainder, (as Littleton termeth it) yet if the husband doth wast, an Action of wast shall lie against him and his wife, notwithstanding the meane remainder, because the husband himselfe committeth the wast, and doth the wrong: And therefore shall not excuse himselfe for his committing of wast, in respect he himselfe hath the remainder, no more than if a man lesseth to A. during the life of B. the remainder to him during the life of C. if he commit Wast, an Action of wast shall lie against him. (17.E.3.68.b. V.Sir.Ed.Carys case, li. 5.)

Sect. 526.

¶ Mes si jeo lessa al Feme sole terre pur terme dans, le quel prent baron

But if I let land to a Feme sole for terme of yeares, who taketh husband, and af-

(3.E.3.17.b. Pl.Com.418.b. 38.H.6.23. 14.H.4.12. 18.E.3.35 Pl.Com. Dame Hales case. 30.Ass.p.15. 4.H.6.5.7.H.6.1 9.H.6.52 37.Li.Ass. 21.H.7.39. 21.E.4.40.26.H.8.7.) ¶ This is the fifth case wherein the Release and Confirmation doe agree: and it is to bee observed, That Chattels reals, as Leases for yeares, Ward-

baron, et puis ieo confirma lestate le baron et sa feme, a auer et tener la terre pur terme ô lour dux vies: en cest case ils ont ioynt estate en le Franketenement de la terre, pur ceo que la fem̃ nauoit frank-tenement adeuãt, &c.

ter I confirm the estate of the husband and his wife, To haue and to hold the land for term of their two liues: In this case they haue a ioynt estate in the free-hold of the Land, for that the wife had no Freehold before, &c.

ships, and the like, are not giuen to the husband absolutely, (as all Chattels personalls are) by the intermarriage, but conditionally if the husband happen to suruiue her, and he hath power to alien them at his pleasure: but in the mean time the husbãd is possessed of the Chattels reall in her right.

Secondly, That the husband hath such a possession in her right of the Chattel, as is capable of a Confirmation, or of a Release.

Thirdly, That the Confirmation in this case to the husband and wife for their liues, maketh them Ioyntenants for life, because a Chattell of a Feme Couert may bee drowned: and so note a diuersitie betweene a Lease for life, and a Lease for yeares, made to a Feme Couert; for her estate of Freehold cannot be altered by the Confirmation made to her husband and her, as the terme for yeares may, whereof her husband may make disposition at his pleasure.

Section 527.

¶ ITem si mon disseisor granta a vn rent charge hors de la terre dont il moy disseisist, et ieo rehersant le dit grãt confirma mesme le grant, et tout ceo que est comprise deins mesme le graunt, et puis ieo enter sur le Disseisor, Quære en cest case, si le Terre soit discharge de le rent ou nemy.

ALso if my Disseisor granteth to one a Rent charge out of the Land whereof he disseised me, and I rehearsing the sayde Grant, confirme the same Grant, and al that which is comprised within the same grant, and after I enter vpon the Disseisor, *Quære* in this case, if the land be discharged of the Rent or no.

¶ This is the fifth case wherein the Releas and Confirmation doe differ, for a Release to the Grantee in this case (a) were voyd. It is holden by some authoritie since Littleton wrote, That the Disseisee after his re-entrie shall not auoyd the Rent charge against his owne Confirmation: and there a generall rule is taken, that such a thing as I may defeat by my entrie, I may make good by my Confirmation. (a) 11.*H*.7 28. *Li*.1.*fo*.147. *Anne Mayowes case*. 3.*H*.4.10

If the Feoffee vpon Condition grant a Rent Charge in fee, and the Feoffor confirmeth it, and after the Condition is broken, and the Feoffor enter, hee shall not auoyd the Rent charge. And so it is if the heire of the Disseisor grant a Rent charge, and the Disseisee confirmeth it, and after recouer the land, he shall not auoyd the rent: and yet in neither of these cases, his entrie was congeable at the time of the Confirmation. *Li*.1.*fo*.147.148. *Anne Mayowes case*.

Section 528.

¶ ITem si vn parson dun Esglise charge le glebe de son Esglise per son fait, et puis le patron et Lordinarie

ALso if a Parson of a Church charge the Glebe land of his Church by his Deed, and after the patron & Ordinary con-

¶ PArson. Persona in the legall signification it is taken for the Rector of a Church parochiall, and is called Persona Ecclesiæ, because hee assumeth and taketh vpon him the parson of the Church, and is sayd *Glan*.li.13 ca.23.24.25. *Bract*.li.4.ca.285,&c. *Brit*.fo.234.b.&c. *Flet*.li.5. ca.19.20. & li.6 ca.18. *Reg*. *F*.*N*.*B*.48.49.

confirmont mesme le grant, & tout ceo que e comprise deins m l' grant, donques le grant estopera en sa force, solonque l' purport de mesme le graunt. Mes en tiel case couient que le Patron eit Fee simple en lauowson, car s'il nad estate en Lauowson forsque pur terme de vie, ou en le taile, donque l' grant ne estopera forsque durant sa vie, & la vie le Parson que grantast, &c.

firme the same grant, and all that is comprised in the same Grant, then the Grant shall stand in his force, according to the purport of the same Graunt. But in this case it behooueth, that the Patron hath a Fee simple in the Aduowson, for if hee hath but an Estate for life or in taile in the aduowson, then the Graunt shall not stand, but during his life, and the life of the Parson which granted &c.

sayd to be seised in iure Ecclesiæ, and the Law had an excellent end herein, viz That in his person the Church might sue for and defend her right; and also be sued by any that had an elder and better right, and when the Church is full, it is sayd to be plena & consulta of such a one Parson thereof, that is full and prouided of a Parson, that may vicem seu personā eius gerere.

Bra. vbi sup.

Persona Impersonata, Parson Impersonee is the Rector that is in possession of the Church Parochiall, be it presentatiue, or impropriate, and of whom the Church is full.

8. E. 3. 26. 43. 38. E. 3. 4. 3. Mar. Dy. 123.

Here are diuers things to bee noted: First, That the Confirmation is of the grant, which in deed is but a meere assent by Deed to the Grant. And therefore it is holden, That if there be Parson, Patron, and Ordinarie, and the Patron and Ordinarie giue licence by Deed to the Parson to grant a Rent charge out of the glebe, and the Parson granteth the Rent charge accordingly, this is good, and shall bind the Successor, and yet heere is no confirmation subsequent, but a Licence precedent.

7. H. 4. 15.

Secondly, The Ordinarie alone, without the Deane and Chapter, may agree thereunto, either by Licence precedent, or Confirmation subsequent, for that the Deane and Chapter hath nothing to doe with that which the Bishop doth as Ordinarie, in the life time of the Bishop.

(b) 19. El. Dy. 356. 357. 21. H. 6. 9. 33. H. 8. tit Charge Br. 58.

Thirdly, (b) But if the Bishop be Patron, there the Bishop cannot confirme alone, but the Deane and Chapter must confirme also, for the Aduowson or Patronage is parcell of the possession of the Bishopricke, and therefore the Bishop without the Deane and Chapter, cannot make the Grant good but onely during his owne life, after the decease of the Incumbent, either by Licence precedent, or Confirmation subsequent.

See more of these kind of Confirmations in my Reports. Li. 2. 39. & 24. Li. 1. 153. Li. 4. 23. 24. Li. 5. fo. 31. 81. Li. 10. 6. li. 11. 19. li. 6. 34.

A. Parson of D. is Patron of the Church of S. as belonging to his Church, and present B. who by consent of A and of the Ordinarie grant a Rent charge out of the Glebe, this is not good to make the Rent charge perpetuall, without the assent of the Patron of A. no more than the assent of the Bishop who is Patron, without the Deane and Chapter, or no more than the assent of the Patron, being Tenant in Taile or for life, as Littleton saith. And Littleton here saith, That the Patron that confirmes must haue a Fee simple, meaning to make the charge perpetuall. And Littleton after saith, That in the case of the Parson the fee is in abeyance, and seeing the consent of the Patron is in respect of his interest as heire, it appeareth by Littleton, he may consent vpon Condition, otherwise it is of an Attornement because that is a bare assent. Also if the estate of the Patron be conditionall, and he confirmeth, and after the Condition is broken, his Confirmation is voyd.

31. E. 3. Grant. 61. 26. ass. 38. 8. El. Dy. 252. Vi. li. fo. Le case de Deane & Chapter de Norwich.

Fourthly, He that is Patron must be Patron in Fee simple, for if hee be Tenant in Taile, or Tenant for life, his Confirmation or Agreement is not good to bind any Successor, but such as come into the Church during his life. But if the Patron be Tenant in Taile, and discontinue the estate in taile, the Lease shall stand good during the Discontinuance, or if the estate taile be barred, it shall stand good for euer.

But here is to be obserued a diuersitie betweene a sole Corporation, as Parson, Prebend, Vicar, and the like, that haue not the absolute Fee in them, for to their Grants the Patron must giue his consent. But if there be a Corporation aggregate of many, as Dean and Chapter, Master, Fellowes, and Schollers of a Colledge, Abbot or Prior, Couent, and the like, or any sole Corporation that hath the absolute Fee, as a Bishop with consent of the Deane and Chapter, they may by the Common Law make any grant of or out of their possessions, without their Founder or Patron, albeit the Abbot or Prior, &c. were presentable: and so it is of a Bishop, because the whole estate and right of the Land was in them, and they may respectiuely maintaine a Writ of Right.

12. H. 4. 12. 19. E. 3. 7. 9. Eliz. Dyer, 238. 11. H. 6. 9. 10. Eliz. Dyer, 6. E. 3. 10. 2. E. 3. 20. 9. E. 4. 6. 2. H. 4. 11. 38. E. 3. 19. 25. E. 3. 54

If a Bishop hath two Chapters, and he maketh a grant, both Chapters must confirme it or else the Successor shall avoid it. But if one of the Chapters be dissolved, then the Confirmation of the other sufficeth, but it needeth not the Confirmation of the King who is Founder and Patron of all Bishopricks. Temps R. 2. tit. grant 104. 50. E. 3. tit. Assise Statham. 11. Eliz. Dier 282.

And note a diversitie betweene a Confirmation of an Estate, and a Confirmation of a Deed, for if the Disseisor make a Charter of feoffment to A. with a Letter of Attorney, and before Livery the Disseisee confirme the estate of A. or the Deed made to A, this is cleerely void, though Livery be made after. But if a Bishop had made a Charter of feoffment with a Letter of Attorney, and the Deane and Chapter before Livery Confirme the Deed, this is a good Confirmation and Livery made afterwards is good. And so it hath beene adiudged.

The like Law is of a Confirmation of a Deed of grant of a Reversion before Attornement.

In the same manner it is if a Bishop at the Common Law had granted lands to the King in fee by Deed, and the Deane and Chapter by their Deed confirme the Deed of the Bishop, and after the Deed of the Bishop is inrolled, this is good albeit the Confirmation of the Deane and Chapter bee not inrolled, for the assent upon the matter is made to the Bishop.

But this Confirmation that Littleton here speaketh of must bee made in the life, and during the incumbencie of the person, and so in the life of the Bishop, or of any other sole Corporation. But it is to be knowne that Grants made by Parsons, Prebends, Vicars, Bishops, Master and Fellowes of any Colledge, Deane and Chapter, Master or Gardeine of any Hospitall or any having any Spirituall or Ecclesiasticall Living are restrained by (c) divers Acts of Parliament, so as they cannot grant any rent charge, or to make any alienation, or to make any Leases other then such as are mentioned in those Acts which you may reade at large, And the expositions upon the same in my (*) Commentaries. 33. E. 3. Confirm. 22. 31. E. 3 Abbot 10. 21. H. 7. 1. Vide Sect. 393. & 643. (c) 13. Eliz. cap. 10. 1. Eliz. cap. 18. Eliz. cap. 11. 1. Iac. cap. 3. Vid Sect. 593. & 648. (*) Lib. 2 fol. 46. lib. 4. 76. & 120. lib. 5. 9. 6. 14. lib. 6. 37. lib. 7. 8. lib. 11. 67.

Sect. 529.

¶ Item si home lessa terre pur terme de vie, le quel tenant a term de vie charge la terre ove un rent en fee, & celuy en le reversion confirma mesme le grant, le charge est assets bone & effectuall.

Also if a man letteth land for term of life, the which Tenant for life charge the land with a rent in fee, and hee in the reversion confirme the same grant, the charge is good enough and effectuall.

¶ Here is a diversitie to bee observed where the determination of the Rent is expressed in the deed, and when it is implyed in Law. For when Tenant for life granteth a rent in fee this by Law is determined by his death, and yet a Confirmation of the grant by him in the reversion make that grant good forever, without wordes of inlargement, or clause of distresse which would amount to a new grant. And yet if the Tenant for life had granted a Rent to another and his heires by expresse words, during the life of the Grantor, and the Lessor had confirmed that grant, that grant should determine by the death of Tenant for life. 26. Ass. Pl. 38. 45. Ass. Pl. 23 Lib. 1 fol. 147. Anne Maurnes case. 14. Ass. Pl. 14.

Tenant for life upon a Condition grant a Rent in fee, the Lessor confirme the grant, and after the Condition is broken, the Lessor re-enter, he shall not avoid the grant.

Sect. 530.

¶ Item si soit un perpetual chanterie, dont lordinarie nad rien a medler ne a faire, Quære si le patron del chaunte-

Also if there bee a perpetuall Chanterie wherewith the ordinary hath nothing to doe or meddle. Quere if the Patron of

¶ This is meant of a Chauntery Donative wherewith the Ordinary hath not to deale, and by this grant, when Littleton wrote, the Chaunterie should have beene charged for ever, because no other had any interest in this Chanterie Vide Sect. 648.

same

ry, & le Chapleine de mesme le chauntery poient charg l' chauntery oue vn rent charge en perpetuitie.

the Chantery, and the Chapleine of the same Chantery may charge the Chantery with a Rent charge in perpetuitie.

saue only the Patron and Chauntry Priest, and the grant is made Concurrentibus hijs quæ in iure requiruntur. But since Littleton wrote, all, and all manner of free Chappels and Chaunteries perpetuall, whereof Littleton here speakes, are by (a) Acts of Parliament giuen to the Crowne, and the bodies Politike thereof dissolued. See hereafter, Section 648. more at large of all this present Section.

(a) 37. H. 8. cap. 4. 1 E. 6. cap. 14.

Sect. 531.

Item en ascun cas cest verbe Dedi ou cest verbe Concessi, ad mesme leffect en substance, & vrera a mesme lentent, come cest verbe Confirmaui. Sicome ieo sue disseisie dun carue de terre, & ieo face tiel fait; Sciant præsentes, &c. quod dedi a le disseisor, &c. vel quod concessi a le dit disseisor le dit carue, &c. & ieo deliuer tantsolement le fait a luy sauns ascun liuery de seisin del terre, cest vn bone confirmation, & auxy fort en ley, sicome il auoit en le fait cest verbe confirmaui, &c.

Also in some case this verbe *Dedi*, or this Verbe *Concessi* hath the same effect in substance, and shall enure to the same intent, as this verbe *Confirmaui*. As if I bee disseised of a Carue of Land, and I make such a Deed. *Sciant præsentes &c. quod dedi* to the Disseisor &c. or *quod concessi* to the said Disseisor, the said Carue, &c. and I deliuer only the Deed to him without any liuerie of seisin of the land, this is a good cõfirmation, & as strong in Law, as if there had beene in the Deed this verbe *Confirmaui, &c.*

Here Littleton proceedeth according to the former diuision to shew words that in Law doe amount to a Confirmation. And here is to bee obserued, that some words are large and haue a generall extent, and some haue a proper and particular application. The former sort may containe the latter, as Dedi, or Concessi may amount to a grant, a feoffment, a gift, a Lease, a Release, a Confirmation, a Surrender, &c. and it is in the Election of the partie to vse to which of these purposes he will.

Bract. lib. 2. fol. 59. b. 21. H. 6. feoffments & faits 103. 22. H. 6 42. 14. H. 4. 36. 19. H. 6. 44. 7. H. 7. 16. 32. E. 3. briefe 291. Brooke tit. Confirmation, 20. 14. H. 7. 2 37. H. 6. 17. Dier. 8. Eliz. 4. H. 7. 10. 22. E. 4 36. 40. E. 3. 41.

Est autem confirmatio quasi quædam ratihabitio, sufficit tamen quandoque per se, si etiam in se contineat donationem, vt si dicat quis, dedi & confirmaui, licet iuuari possit ex aliqua donatione præcedente.

Bracton. lib. 2. fol. 59. b.

But a Release, Confirmation, or Surrender, &c. cannot amount to a grant, &c. nor a Surrender to a Confirmation, or to a Release, &c. because these bee proper and peculiar manner of Conueyances, and are destined to a speciall end.

Dedi & Concessi, &c. Here is implied that there be more words then Dedi and Concessi, that will amount to a Confirmation, as dimisi. (e) In ancient Statutes and in originall Writs, as in the Writ of Entrie in casu prouiso, in consimili casu ad Communem legem, and many others, this word dimisi is not applied only to a Lease for life but to a gift in taile, and to a State in fee. (f) Also if a man make a Lease to A. for yeares, and after by his Deed the Lessor Voluit quod haberet & teneret terram pro termino vitæ suæ. This is adiudged by this verbe (volo) to be a good Confirmation for terme of his life, Benigne enim faciendæ sunt interpretationes cartarum propter simplicitatem laicorum vt res magis valeat quam pereat.

(e) 32. E. 3. briefe 291. Brooke tit. Confirm. 20. Vide lestate de Glouc. cap. 4. (f) 7. E. 3. 9.

Bracton.

And he to whom such a Deed comprehending Dedi, &c. is made, may plead it as a Grant, as a Release, or as a Confirmation at his election.

14. H. 4. 36. Lib. 5. fol. 15. in Newcomens case.

If a Parson and Ordinary make a Lease for yeares of the Glebe to the Patron, and the

Pa-

Patron by his Deed granteth it ouer, or if the Disseisor granteth a Rent to the Disseisee, and he by his Deed granteth it ouer, and after re-enter, in both these cases one and the same words doe amount both to a Grant, and to a Confirmation in iudgement of Law of one and the same thing, ne res pereat. And so it is if a Disseisor make a Lease for life, or a gift in taile, the remaynder to the Disseisee in fee, the Disseisee by his Deed granteth ouer the remaynder, the particular Tenant attorneth, the Disseisee shall not enter vpon the Tenant for life, or in taile, for then he should auoyd his owne grant, which amounted to a grant of the estate, and a Confirmation also.

Sect. 532.

¶ Item si ieo lessa terre a vn home pur terme dans, per force de quel il est en possession, &c. Et puis ieo face vn fait a luy, &c. Quod dedi & concessi, &c. le dit terre a auer pur terme de sa vie, & deliuera a luy le fait, &c. donques maintenant il ad estate en le terre pur terme de sa vie.

Also if I let land to a man for tearme of yeares, by force whereof hee is in possession, &c. and after I make a Deed to him &c. *Quod dedi & concessi, &c.* the said land to haue for tearme of his life, and I deliuer to him the Deed, &c. then presently he hath an estate in the Land for tearme of his life.

¶ Here is the first Case wherein the Confirmation and the Release doe agree. And is euident and needeth no explication.

Section 533.

¶ Et si ieo die en le fait, a auer & tener a luy & a ses heires de son corps engendres il ad estate en fee taile, & si ieo die en le fait, a auer & tener a luy & a ses heires, il ad estate en fee simple, car ceo vrera a luy per force de confirmation denlarger son estate.

And if I say in the Deed, to haue and to hold to him and to his heires of his bodie ingendred, he hath an estate in fee taille. And if I say in the deed, to haue & to hold to him and to his heires, he hath an estate in fee simple. For this shall enure to him by force of the Confirmation to inlarge his estate.

¶ This also is euident and needeth no explication, sauing that whensoeuer a Confirmation doth inlarge and giue an estate of Inheritance, there ought to bee apt words (as Littleton here expresse them) vsed for the same.

Section 534.

¶ Item si home soit disseisie, et le disseisor deuie seisie, et son heire est eins per

Also if a man be disseised, & the disseisor die seised, & his heire is in by discent,

¶ *Quant al heire del disseisor, &c. les tenements passont per voy de feoffment.* For the

diſcent, et puis le diſſeiſee & lheire le diſſeiſor font iointment vn fait a vn auter en fee et liuery de ſeiſin ſur ceo eſt fait (quant al heire le diſſeiſor, que enſealaſt le fait) les tenements paſſont et vront per meſme le fait per voy de feoffment, et quant al diſſeiſee que enſealaſt meſme le fait, ceo ne vrera ſinon per voy de confirmation. Mes ſi le diſſeiſee en ceſt cas port briefe dentre en le Per et Cui enuers lalienee del heire le diſſeiſor, Quære coment il pledra cel fait enuers le demandant per voy de confirmation, &c. Et ſaches mon fits, que eſt vn des pluis honorables, laudables, et profitables choſes en noſtre ley, de auer le ſcience de bien pleder en actions reals et perſonals, et pur ceo ieo toy counſaile eſpecialment de mitter ton courage et cure de ceo apprender.

and after the diſſeiſee, and the heire of the diſſeiſor make ioyntly a Deed to another in fee, and liuery of ſeiſin is made vpon this, (As to the heire of the diſſeiſor that ſealed the deed) the tenements doe paſſe and enure by the ſame deed by way of feoffment, and as to the diſſeiſee who ſealed the ſame Deed, this ſhall enure but by way of confirmation. But if the diſſeiſee in this caſe brings a writ of entrie in the *Per* and *Cui* againſt the alienee of the heire of the diſſeiſor. *Quære* how he ſhall plead this Deed againſt the demandant by way of confirmation, &c. And know my ſon that it is one of the moſt honorable, laudable & profitable things in our law to haue the ſcience of well pleading in actions reals & perſonals, and therefore I counſaile thee eſpecially to imply thy courage and care to learne this.

the land ſhall euer paſſe from him that hath the ſtate of the land in him. As if Ceſty que vie and his Feoffees after the Statute of 1.R.3. and before the Statute of 27.H.8. cap. 10. had ioyned in a feoffment, it ſhall be the feoffment of the Feoffees, because the ſtate of the land was in him.

21.H.7.34.b. Pl.Com 59.a. in Wimbiſhes caſe.

So it is if the Tenant for life, and he in the remainder or reuerſion in fee ioyne in a feoffment by Deede. The Liuery of the freehold ſhall moue from the Leſſee, and the inheritance from him in the reuerſion or remainder, from each of them according to his eſtate. For it cannot be adiudged by Law, that the feoffment of Tenant for life doth drawe the reuerſion or remainder out of the Leſſor or him in remainder, or doth worke a wrong becauſe they ioyned together.

Pl.Com.59.a. Pl.Com.140.in Brownings caſe. 2.H.5.7. 13.H.7.14. 13.E.4.4.a. 27.H.8.13. M.16 & 17.Eliz.339.

If there bee Tenant for life, the remainder in tayle, the remainder in tayle, &c. and Tenant for life and he in the remainder in tayle leuy a Fine, this is no diſcontinuance or deueſting of any eſtate in remainder, but each of them paſſe that which they haue power and authority to paſſe.

Lib.1.fo.76. Bredons caſe.

A. Tenant for life the remainder to B. for life, the remainder in tayle, the remainder to the right heires of B. A. and B ioyne in a Feoffment by Deed, albeit it may be ſaid that this is the feoffment of A. and the Confirmation of B and conſequently hee in the remainder in tayle cannot enter for the forfeiture during the life of B. But becauſe B ioyned in the Feoffment which was tortious to him in the remainder in taile, and is Particeps criminis, therefore they forfeited both their eſtates, and he in the remainder in taile might enter for the forfeiture. But if he in the reuerſion in fee and Tenant for life ioyne in a Feoffment by paroll, this ſhall be (as ſome hold) firſt a ſurrender of the eſtate of Tenant for life, and then the feoffment of him in the Reuerſion, for otherwiſe if the whole ſhould paſſe from the Leſſee then he in the reuerſion might enter for the forfeiture, and euery mans act (Vt res magis valeat) ſhall be conſtrued moſt ſtrongly againſt himſelfe.

19.Eliz.Dier.339.

And it is to be obſerued that Littleton here putteth a diſcent, ſo as the entrie of the Diſſeiſee is not lawfull, for if the Diſſeiſor and Diſſeiſee ioyne in a Charter of feoffment, and enter into the land, and make Liuery, it ſhall be accounted the feoffment of the Diſſeiſee, and the confirmation of the Diſſeiſor.

Quære

¶ *Quare coment il pledera cest fait, &c.* Hee may pleade the feoffment of the heire of the Disseisor, and the Confirmation of the Disseisee as it hath beene pleaded and allowed.

Lib. 1. fo. 146. 147. Mauwes case.

¶ *Et saches mon fits, que est un de pluis honorable, &c.* Here is to be observed the excellency of good pleading, and Littletons grave advice, that the student should imploy his courage and care for the attaining thereof: which hee shall attaine unto by three meanes; First by reading, Secondly by observation, and thirdly by use and exercise. For in antient time the Serjants and Apprentices of Law did draw their owne pleadings, which made them good pleaders. And in this sence Placitum may be derived A Placendo, quia omnibus Placet.

See my Preface to the 9. Booke of my Reports.

Now seeing good pleading is so honourable and excellent, and that many a good cause is daily lost for want of good and orderly pleading, it is necessary to set downe some few rules (amongst many) of the same, to facilitate this learning, that is so highly commended to the studious reader. For when I diligently consider the course of our bookes of yeares and termes from the beginning of the raigne of E. 3. I observe, that more tangling and questions growe upon the manner of pleading, and exceptions to forme, then upon the matter it selfe, and infinite Causes lost or delayed for want of good pleading. Therefore it is a necessary part of a good common Lawyer to be a good Prothonotary. And now wee will performe our promise.

The order of good pleading is to be observed, which being inverted great prejudice may grow to the partie tending to the subversion of Law. Ordine placitandi servato, servatur & jus, &c.

First in good order of pleading a man must pleade to the jurisdiction of the Court. Secondly to the person, and therein first to the person of the Plaintife, and then to the person of the Defendant. Thirdly to the Count. Fourthly to the Writ. Fiftly to the Action, &c. (a) which order and forme of pleading you shall reade in the ancient Authors agreeable to the Lawe at this day, and if the Defendant misorder any of these, hee loseth the benefit of the former.

The Count must be agreeable and conforme to the Writ, the barre to the Count, &c. and the judgement to the Count, for none of them must be narrower or broader than the other.

A Count or Declaration, which anciently and yet is called Narratio ought to containe two things, (b) viz. Certainty and Verity, for that it is the foundation of the suite, whereunto the Adverse party must answer, and whereupon the Court is to give his judgement: (c) Certa debet esse intentio & narratio, & certum fundamentum, & certa res quæ deducitur in judicium. But it must be understood that there be three kinde of Certainties; First to a common intent, and that is sufficient in a barre which is to defend the party and to excuse him. (d) Secondly a certaine intent in generall, as in Counts, Replications, and other pleadings of the Plaintife, that is to convince the Defendant, and so in Inditements, &c. Thirdly, a certaine intent in every particular, as in Estoppells.

(e) Hee pleadeth a plea in abatement of the Writ (which of ancient times was, and yet is called Breve) or a plea after the latter continuance ought to plead it certainly.

(f) The ancient formes of Counts are to be duly observed, as Cum dimisit, or Cum dedit, and not to say, that he was seised, and demised, &c (And yet if he say so, it maketh not the Count vitious) (g) but in a barre replication or other kinde of pleading, the partie must alledge a seisin in the Lessor or Donor, and ancient formes of pleading are also to be observed.

(h) Counts, or such as be in nature of Counts (as an Avowrie wherein the Defendant is an Actor) need not to be averred, but all other pleas in the Affirmative ought to be averred, Et hoc paratũ est verificare, &c. but pleas meerely in the Negative ought not to be averred, because a negative cannot be proved.

(i) Where there is but one Tenant or one Defendant, he cannot have two such pleas, as each of them doe goe to the whole, but where there are divers, each of them may pleade severall pleas which extend to the whole.

(k) That which is alledged by way of conveyance or inducement to the substance of the matter need not to be so certainly alledged, as that which is the substance it selfe.

(l) Every plea must be direct, and not by way of argument, or rehearsall.

(m) Where a matter of Record is the foundation or ground of the suite of the Plaintife, or of the substance of the plea, there it ought to be certainly and truly alledged, otherwise it is, where it is but conveyance. But the proceedings and sentences in the Ecclesiasticall Courts may be alledged summarily as that a Divorce was had betweene such parties, for such a cause, and before such a Judge, and Concurrentibus hijs quæ in jure requiruntur, for the Judge must be alledged, to the intent the Court may write to him if it be denied.

Good matter must be pleaded in good forme, in apt time, and in due order, or otherwise great advantages may be lost.

(a) *Bracton, lib. 5 fo. 400. Britton, fo. 41. a & 122. Fleta, lib 6. ca. 35. 36. &c. 40 E. 3. 9. b. 17. E. 3 74. 8. E. 3 5. & 9. 35. H. 6. 12.*
(b) *Pl Com. fo. 121, 122. 3. E. 4. 21. Vid. lib. 5. fo. 120. 121.*
(c) *Bracton, lib. 2 fo. 140.*
(d) *Lib 5. 120. 121. Longs case. Pl Com. 56. Wimbishes case.*
(e) *7. H 6. 17. 32. H. 6. 12. 15 Pl Com. 33. b.*
(f) *34. H 6 48. 8 H. 5. 4 b. 21. E. 4. 52 5 E. 3. 15. 30. H. 6. 3. 10. H. 6. 2. 21. H 7 26.*
(g) *48. E. 3, 8. 2. H. 4. 13. 6 H. 4. 2. b. 10. E. 4. 2. F N B. 156. e 11. E 3 Aide 32. 9. H. 6 59. 10 E 4. 4.*
(h) *Pl. Com. Bretts case, 342. 27. H. 8. 27. 27 H 6 9. H. 7.*
(i) *40. E. 3. 31. 32. 33. 41 E. 3. 11. 9 H 6. 46. 27. E. 3. 81. 44. E. 3. 23. 45 E. 3. Double plea, 39. 43. E. 3. 21. 38. H. 6. 29. 37. H. 6 23. 33. H. 6. 51. 15 E. 4. 25. 7 H. 4 12. 41. E. 3. Double plea 78.*
(k) *Pl. Com 81. 11. H. 4. 89 34. H 6. 48. 19. R. 2. Assise for le case 52. 22 E. 3. 19. 30. E 3. 9.*
(l) *5. H 7. 8. 6. E. 4. 2. 21. E. 4. 44. 27. H. 8. 4. 22. H. 6. 17. E. 4. 7. 22. E. 4. 8.*
(m) *Pl. Com 65. a. b & 100. 376. & 410. 22. H. 6, 38 19. H. 6. 49. 37. H. 6. 14. 36. H. 6. 5. 21. E. 4. 54. 11. H. 6 15. 38. H. 6. 23. 42. Ass. 5. 48. E. 3. 11. 4. E 4. 12. 9. E. 3. 46. 21. E. 4. 52. 35. H 6. 35. 10. H. 7. 9. 15. 11. H. 7. 8. 22. E. 3. 2. 34. H. 6. 27. 12. H. 8. 5. 6. 7. E. 4. 32. 9. E. 4. 24. 8. E. 4. 31. 8. Ass. 29. 5. E. 4. 70. 3. E. 4. 1.*

(n) Generall estates in Fee simple may be generally alledged, but the commencement of Estates taile, and other particular estates regularly must be shewed, vnlesse in some cases where they are alledged by way of inducement, and the life of Tenant in Taile, or for life, ought to be auerred.

(o) When any speciall and substantiall matter is alledged by either partie, that ought to be especially answered, and not to be passed ouer by a generall pleading.

(p) The Plea of euerie man shall be construed strongly against him that pleadeth it, for euerie man is presumed to make the best of his owne case: Ambiguum placitum interpretari debet contra proferentem.

(q) Euerie Plea that a man pleadeth ought to be triable, for without triall the cause can receiue no end: Et expedit reipublicæ vt sit finis litium.

(r) The Tenant before his default saued, may plead all Pleas which proue the writ abated, as death, &c. or matters apparant in the Writ, but no Plea, which proue it abateable, as taking of husband, &c.

(s) When a man is authorised to doe any thing by the Common Law, by Grant, Commission, Act of Parliament, or by Custome, he ought to pursue the substance and effect of the same accordingly.

(t) All necessarie circumstances implied by Law in the Plea need not to be expressed, as in the plea of a Feoffement of a Mannor Liuerie and Attornement are implied.

(u) When a Count, Barre, Replication, &c. is defectiue in respect of omission of some circumstance, as time, place, &c. there it may be made good by the plea of the aduerse party, but if it be insufficient in matter, it cannot be salued.

(w) Euerie man shall plead such pleas as are pertinent for him, according to the qualitie of his case, estate, or interest, as Disseisors, Tenants, Incumbents, Ordinaries, and the like.

(x) Surplusage shall neuer make the Plea vicious, but where it is contrariant to the matter before.

(y) That which is apparant to the Court by necessarie collection out of the Record neede not to be auerred.

(a) A man is bound to performe all the couenants in an Indenture: if all the couenants be in the Affirmatiue, he may generally plead performance of all, but if any be in the negatiue, so many he must plead specially (for a negatiue cannot be performed) and to the rest generally. (b) So if any be in the disiunctiue, he must shew which of them he hath performed. So if any are to be done of Record, he must shew that specially, and cannot inuolue that in generall pleading.

(c) In many cases the Law doth allow generall pleading, for auoyding of prolixitie and tediousnesse, and that the particular shall come on the other side.

(d) Pleadings which amount to the generall Issue are not to bee allowed, but the generall Issue is to be entred, Vi. Sect. 10. 485. 499.

(e) Euerie plea ought to haue his proper Conclusion, as a Plea to the Writ to conclude to the Writ, a Plea in Barre to conclude to the Action, an Estoppel to relie vpon the Estoppels, Et sic de similibus.

(f) When the Conclusion of a Plea, Et issint, Et sic, is the affirmatiue, it shall not waiue the speciall matter, for there the special matter is the substance & foundation of the conclusion, and affirmed by the same. But where the conclusion is in the negatiue, there the speciall matter regularly is waiued.

(g) Whensoeuer speciall matter is pleaded, and the Conclusion (Et sic) is to the poynt of the Writ or Action, the speciall matter is waiued.

The names of legall Records are, a Writ, a Count, a Barre, a Replication, a Reioynder, a Rebutter, a Surrebutter, &c.

(h) New and subtill deuices and inuentions of pleading ought not to alter any Principle of Law, whereof you haue heard plentifully before.

The Count or Declaration is an exposition of the Writ, and addeth time, place, and other necessarie circumstances, that the same may be triable, and any imperfection in the Count doth abate the writ.

Pleadings are diuided into Barres, Replications, Reioynders, Surreioynders, Rebutters, and Surrebutters, &c. They are words of Art, and are called Barres, Barræ, so called because it barreth the Plaintife of his Action. Replicationes, à Replicando; Reiunctiones, à Reiungendo, Rebutter, of the French word Rebouter, i. à Repellendo, To put backe or auoyd, and so of Surrebutter.

But each partie must take heed of the ordering of the matter of his pleading, lest his Replication depart from his Count, or his Reioynder from his Barre, & sic de cæteris.

(i) In antient Writers a Bar is called Exceptio peremptoria, a Replication was then called Replicatio, as now it is: a Reioynder, Triplicatio; a Surreioynder, Quadriplicatio, & sic vlterius in infinitum.

(n) 35. H. 6. 35. 21. E. 4. 51. 9. H. 4. 5. 19. H. 6. 73. 5. E. 4. 12. 10. E. 4. 18. 13. H. 7. 18. 36. H. 8. Pleading. Br. 160.
(o) Vi. Sect. 193. 3. H. 6. 47. 41. E. 3. 22. 9. Ass. 9. 22. Ass. 45. 2. E. 3. 42. 13. E. 3. Ane. Demesne 15. 20. E. 3. ib. 45. 7. H. 7. 8. li. 10 Fol. 91. Lib. 11. fol. 10.
(p) 3. H. 7. 3. 26. Ass. 10. 14. H. 4. 4. b. 27. H. 6. 8. b. 21. H. 6. Debt 43. 7. H. 6. 24. 31. 35. H. 6. 48. 47. E. 3. 14. Pl. Com. 46. a. Li. 3. 58. 59. Linc. Col. case.
(q) 22. E. 4. 40. 1. 3. 20. E. 4. 10. 21. E. 4. 35. 22. H. 6. 50.
(r) 40. E. 3. 40. 43. 46. 41. E. 3. 2. 18. E. 3. 16. 26. E. 3. 68. 42. E. 3. 3. 10. 46 6. E. 3. 37. 8. E. 3. 20. 30. E. 3. 60. 14. H. 4. 15. 12. E. 4. 1. 38. E. 3. 28. 7. H. 7. 3.
(s) 10. E. 4. 3. 27. H. 6. 8. H. 7. 13. 9. H. 7. 26. 37. H. 6. 1. 27. H. 8. 13. 21. H. 7. 25. 11. H. 4. 33. Pl. Com. 79. 16. E. 4. 10. 1. H. 7. 33. 20. H. 7. 1. 6. E. 4. 4. 5. 21. E. 4. 54. 22. H. 6. 47. 11. H. 6. 8. 25. E. 3. 50. b. 23. Ass. 7. 2. Eliz. Dier. 184.
(t) Pl. Com. 149. b. & 105. a 37. H. 6. 38.
(u) 18. E. 4. 16. b. 22. E. 4. 2. 76. 5. H. 7. 13. 38. H. 6. 17. 18. 19. 18. E. 3. 34. Pl. Com. 229. b. Lib. 8. 133. Turners case.
(w) 5. H. 7. 34. 5. E. 3. 26. 22. H. 6. 28.
(x) 19. H. 6. 30. 32. Pl. Com. 232. b. et fol. 502. per Dier & 503.
(y) 13. H. 4. 17. 10. E. 4. 18. 33. H. 6. 54. 35. H. 6. 30. 21. H. 7. 32. Bract. li. 3 fo. 154 Pl. Cō. 87. b. 26. H. 6 Gard. 58
(a) 2. H. 7. 15. 4. H. 7. 12. 10. H. 7. 12. 13. H. 7. 19. 26. H. 8. 5. b
(b) Li. 8. fo. 133. Turners case & fo. 120. Benbarns case. Lib. 9. 25. 61. Li. 10. 100.
(c) 12. H. 8. 6. 7. 2. R. 3. 17. 14. E. 4. 7. 9. E. 4. 19.
(d) 44. E. 3. 2. 34. H. 6. 5. 10. H. 6. 6. & 17. 12. E. 4. 11. 14. 14. H. 8. 24. 7. E. 3. 12. 17. E. 3. 44.
(e) 18. H. 6. 33. 22. H. 6. 53. 36. H. 6. 17. 38. H. 6. 18. 25. 5. E. 3. 15. 16. 22. Ass. 33. 2. El. Dy. 184.
(f) Pl. Com. 14. 15. 2. E. 4. 18. 39. E. 3. 14. 32. 33. E. 3. 57. Quar. imp. 25. 18. H. 6. 30. 7. 4. 18. 38. Ass. 14. 24. E. 3. 48. 22. E. 3. 13. 38. H. 6. 25. 32. H. 6. 14. 19. H. 8. 7. 27. H. 8. 12. b.
(g) 7. E. 4. 26. 11. H. 7. 4. 12. H. 7. 6. 33. H. 6. 9. 37. 43.
(h) V. Sect. 485.
(i) Bract. li. 5. fo. 400. Flet. li. 6. ca. 37.

• A departure in pleading is sayd to be when the second Plea containeth matter not pursuant to his former, and which fortifieth not the same, and thereupon it is called *Decessus*, because he departeth from his former Plea, and therefore whensoever the Reioynder (taking one example for all) containeth matter subsequent to the matter of the Barre, and not fortifying the same, this is regularly a departure, because it leaueth the former, and goeth to another matter. As if in an Assise the tenant plead a discent from his father, & giueth a colour, the Demandant intituleth himselfe by a Feoffement from the Tenant himselfe, the Plaintife cannot say, That that Feoffement was vpon Condition, and to shew the Condition broken, for that should bee a cleere departure from his Barre, because it containeth matter subsequent. But in an Assise, if the Tenant pleadeth in Barre, That I.S. was seised and infeoffed him, &c. and the plaintife sheweth, That he himselfe was seised in Fee, vntill by I.S disseised, who infeoffed the Tenant, and he re-entred, the Defendant may plead a release of the Plaintife to I.S. for this doth fortifie the Barre.

[*39.E.3.13.b.39.H.6.15. 6.H.7.8. 21.H.6.32. Pl.Com 105.1.Mar.Dier 95 28.H.8.ibidem.31. 6.H.7.8.3.H.6.Departure.2*]

If a man plead performance of Couenants, and the Plaintife replie, That hee did not such an act according to his Couenant, the Defendant saith, That he offered to doe it, and the plaintife refused it, this is a departure because the matter is not pursuant, for it is one thing, to do a thing, and another to offer to doe it, and the other refused to doe it: therefore that should haue beene pleaded in the former Plea. *Vide* & caue in a *Quare impedit*, what Plea shall bee safely pleaded *in primo placito*.

[*8.El.Dy.253.23.El.Di.371 6.E.3.3.40.E.3.32.43.E.3.11.1.E.4.4.18.E.4.24. 5.H.7.27 8.H.6.11.33.H.6 14.*]

When a man in his former Plea pleadeth an estate made by the Common Law, in the second Plea regularly he shall not make it good by an Act of Parliament. So when in his former Plea he intituleth himselfe generally by the Common Law, in his second Plea hee shall not enable himselfe by a Custome, but should haue pleaded it first.

[*Pl.Com.105.b.Fulmerstons case. 21.H.7.25. 27.H 8.3. 21.H.7.17.37.H.6.5. 38.H.6.25.*]

If a man plead an estate generally, (as for example a Feoffement in Fee) hee in his second Plea shall not maintain it by other matter *tant amount* in Law, as by a Disseisin and Release, or by a Lease and Release, or a gift in Taile in Barre, and in the second Plea a Recouerie in value, for this is a departure: but he in thet case shall count of a gift, and maintaine it in his Replication by a Recouerie in value, because he could haue no other Count.

[*21.H.7.25.1.E 4.4. 3.H.7.5.7.H.7.2.*]

See more of this matter, where the Plaintife varying from time or place alledged in the count of Actions transitorie, shall commit no departure.

[*V.Sect.485.*]

The Plea that containes duplicitie or multiplicitie of distinct matter to one & the same thing, whereunto seuerall answers (admitting each of them to be good) are required, is not allowable in Law. And this rule you see extendeth to Pleas perpetuall or peremptorie, and not to Pleas dilatorie, for in their time and place a man may vse diuers of them, and hereof antient Writers * speake notably; *Sicut Actor vna Actione debet experiri saltem illa durante, sic oportet tenentem vna exceptione, dum tamen peremptoria (quod de dilatorijs non est tenendum) quia si liceret pluribus vti exceptionibus peremptorijs simul & semel sicut fieri poterit in dilatorijs sic sequeretur, quod si in probatione vnius defecerit ad aliam probandam possit habere recursum quod non est permissibile, non magis quam aliquem se defendere duobus baculis in duello, cum vnus tantum sufficiat.*

[*Pl.Com.139.142. * Flet.li.6.ca 35. Bract li.5.fo.400.*]

But where the Tenant or Defendant may plead a generall Issue, there vpon the generall Issue pleaded, he may giue in euidence as many disting matters to barre the Action or right of the Demandant or Plaintife, as he can.

A speciall Verdict may containe double or treble matter, and therefore in those cases the Tenant or Defendant may either make choyce of one matter, and to plead it to barre the Demandant or Plaintife, or to plead the generall Issue, and to take aduantage of all, or hee may plead to part one of the Pleas in Barre, and to another part another Plea, and his conclusion of his Plea shall auoyd doublenesse, and hereby neither the Court nor the Jurie is so much inueigled, as if one Plea should containe diuers distinct matters. And if the Tenant make choyce of one Plea in Barre, and that be found against him, yet he may resort to an Action of an higher nature, and take aduantage of any other matter. And the Law in this poynt is by them that vnderstand not the reason thereof misliked, saying, *Nemo prohibetur pluribus defensionibus vti.*

[*17.E.3.73. 39.H 6.27.*]

And it is worthie of obseruation, That in the raignes of *Edward* the second, *Edward* the first, and vpwards, the Pleadings were plain & sencible, but nothing curious, euermore hauing chiefe respect to matter, and not to formes of words, and were often holpen with a *Quesitum est*, and then the questions moued by the Court, and the answers by the parties were also entred into the Rolle. But euen in those dayes the formes of the Register of originall Writs were then punctually obserued, and matters in Law excellently debated and resolued, and where any great difficultie was, then it was resolued by all the Judges and Sages of the Law (who were for matters in Law called *Concilium Regis*) and their assemblie and resolution was entred into the Rolle. As for example, In the great case in a *Quare impedit*, betweene the King and the Prior of Worcester, concerning an Appropriation, whether it were a Mortmaine, the Record saith, *Ad quem diem venit prædictus Prior per Attornatum suum, &c. Et*

[*Hil 32.E.1.Cor.Reg.in fine Rotul.*]

examinatis & intellectis recordo & processu coram toto concilio tam thesaurario & Baronibus de Scaccario, quam Cancellario, ac etiam Iusticiarijs de vtroque Banco inspecta causa, pro qua, pro Domino Rege dicunt, quod ad ipsum Regem pertinet præsentare, &c. consideratum est, &c. For in those dayes, though the Chancellor and Treasurer were for the most part men of the church, yet were they expert and learned in the Lawes of the Realme:

As for example, in the time of the Conqueror, Egelricus Episcopus Cicestrensis vir antiquissimus, & in Legibus sapientissimus, as elsewhere I haue sayd.

(a) Ockam fo. 17. (a) Nigellus Episcopus Eliensis Hen. 1. Thesaurarius in temporibus suis incomparabilem habuit Scaccarij Scientiam, & de eadem scripsit optime.

(b) Pasch. 5. R. 1. Cor. Rege. (b) Henricus Cant. Episcopus, H. Dunelm̄ Episcopus, Willielmus Eliensis Episcopus. G. Roffens. Episcopus.

(c) 1. H. 3. Rot. pat. Bract. sæpe. (c) Martinus de Pateshul Clericus Decanus diui Pauli London̄ constitutus fuit capitalis Iustic' de Banco, quia in legibus huius Regni peritissimus.

(d) Bract. sæpe. (d) Willus de Raleigh Clericus Iusticiarius Domini Regis.

(e) 8. E. 3. 31. (e) Iohannes Episcopus Carliensis tempore H. 3.

Robertus Passelewe Ep̄us Cicistrensis tempore H. 3.

(f) Rot. pat. 24. H. 3. (f) Robertus de Lexintonio Clericus constitutus capitalis Iustic' de Banco.

(g) Liber eius de Legibus extat script. temp. E. 1. (g) Iohannes Britton Episcopus Hereford.

(h) Rot. Pat. 17. E. 2. (h) Henricus de Stanton clericus, constitutus fuit capitalis Iusticiarius ad placita, with many others. And so were diuers and many of the Nobilitie, who when matters of great difficultie were brought into the vpper house of Parliament by Writ of Error, Adiornnement, or other Parliamentarie course, did by the assistance of the reuerend Judges, who euer attended in that Court, iudge and determine the same as by former and antient Records, and specially by the sayd Record of 5. R. 1. doe manifestly appeare, and therefore the Lords of Parliament were called for those purposes, Concilium Regis, and like to the afore mentioned record there be verie many.

In the raigne of Edward the third, Pleadings grew to perfection both without lamenesse, and curiositie, for then the Judges and Professors of the Law were excellently learned, and then knowledge of the law flourished, the serieants of the Law, &c. drew their owne pleadings, and therfore truly said that reuerent iustice Thirning, in the raigne of H 4. that in the time of Ed. 3. the Law was in a higher degree than it had beene any time before; for (saith he) before that time the manner of Pleading was but feeble in comparison of that it was afterward in the raigne of the same King. (12. H. 4. 3.)

In the time of Henric the sixt the Judges gaue a quicker eare to Exceptions to Pleadings, than either their Predecessors did, or the Judges in the raigne of Edward the fourth, when our Author flourished, or since that time haue done, giuing no way to nice Exceptions, so long as the substance of the matter were sufficiently shewed. And as in the raigne of King Edward the third, by an Act of Parliament * it is prouided, That Counts or Declarations should not abate so long as the matter of the Action be fully shewed in the Declaration and Writ, so since our Author wrote, in the raigne of Queene Elizabeth prouision is made, That after Demurrer the Judges shall giue iudgement according to the right of the cause and matter in Law, without regarding any imperfection, defect, or want of forme in any Writ, Retorne, Plaint, Declaration, or other pleading or course of proceeding whatsoeuer, except such as the partie demurring shall specially shew. In which Act, Appeales and Indictments of Felony, Murder, or Treason concerning mans life, and the forfeiture of his lands and goods, are excepted. An excellent and a profitable Law concurring with the wisedom and iudgment of antient and latter times, that haue disallowed curious & nice exceptions tending to the ouerthrow or delay of iustice, apices juris non sunt jura: yet it is good for a learned professor to make all things plain & perfect, & not to trust to the after aid or amendment, by force of any stat. lest his Clients cause matcheth not therewith; and as it is in Physicke for the health of a mans bodie, so it is in remedies for the safetie of a mans cause. In Law, Præstat cautela quam medela.

* 36. E. 3. ca 15. 46. E. 3. 21. Dy. 299. Li 8 fo. 161. Li. 10. fo. 131.

Li. 10. fo. 88. Pl. Com. 421.

But now let vs returne to our Author.

Section 535. 536. 537.

¶ Item si soyent Seignior et Tenant, mesque le seignior confirma lestate que le tenant ad en les tenements, uncore le Seigniorie entierment demurt a le

Also if there be lord & tenant, albeit the Lord confirme the estate which the Tenaunt hath in the Tenements, yet the Seigniorie remaineth entire to the

a le Seignior come il fuit adeuant.

Lord as it was before.

Sect. 536.

¶ En mesme le manner est, si home ad un rent charge hors de certein terre, & il confirma lestate que le tenant ad en la terre, uncore demurt a le confirmor le rent charge.

IN the same manner is it if a man hath a Rent charge out of certaine Land, and hee confirme the estate which the Tenant hath in the land, yet the Rent charge remayneth to the Confirmor.

Sect. 537.

¶ En mesme le manner est, si un home ad common de pasture en auter terre, sil confirma estate de le tenant de la terre, rien departes de luy de son common, mes ceo nient obstant le common demurt a luy come fuit adeuant.

IN the same manner it is if a man hath common of pasture in other land, if he confirme the estate of the Tenant of the Land nothing shall passe from him of his Common, but notwithstanding this, the Common shall remayne to him as it was before.

¶ Here is the first Case wherein the Release and Confirmation doe differ, for by the release of the Seigniory, Rent charge or Common are extinct. And so these three Sections be evident and need no explication, saving that some doe gather upon these two last Sections and the next ensuing, that a man cannot abridge a Rent charge or common Pasture by a Confirmation as he may doe a Rent Service in respect of the privity betweene the Lord and Tenant, so as (say they) a tenure may bee abridged by a Confirmation, but not a Rent charge or Common: and therefore Littleton beginneth the next Section with an Adverbe adversative, viz. (mes but) &c. But a man may release part of his Rent charge, or Common, &c.

Sect. 538.

¶ Mes si soient Seignior & tenant, le quel tenant tient de son Seignior per le service de fealtie & 20. s. de rent, si le Seignior per son fait confirma lestate le tenant, a tener per 12. d. ou per un denier, ou per un maile, en cest case le tenant est discharge

BVt if there be Lord and Tenant which Tenant holdeth of his Lord by the service of fealtie, and 20. shillings rent, if the Lord by his Deed confirme the estate of the Tenant to hold by 12. pence or by a penny, or by a halfe penny. In this case the Tenant is discharged of all the

¶ AND the reason wherefore no service of another cannot be reserved upon the Confirmation is, because as long as the state of the Land continueth it cannot by the Confirmation of the Lord bee charged with any new service. So as it is evident that the Lord by his Confirmation may diminish and abridge the services, but to reserve upon the Confirmation new services he cannot, so long as the former estate in the Tenancie continueth. And as where a Confirmation doth

28. E. 3. 92. 93. 26. Ass. 37. 6. Eliz. Dier 230. b. 7. E. 4. 25. a. 21. E. 4. 62. per Brian. 10. E. 3. tit. auowrie 100.

inlarge

de touts les auters seruices, & ne rendra rien a le Seignior, forsque ceo que est comprise deins mesme le Confirmation.

other Seruices, and shall render nothing to the Lord, but that which is comprised in the same Confirmation.

inlarge an estate in land, there ought to be priuitie, as hath beene said, so regularly where a Confirmation doth abridge seruices there ought to be priuity also.

And therefore here Littleton putteth his case of Lord and Tenant betweene whom there is priuitie. And therfore if there be Lord, Mesne and Tenant the Lord cannot confirme the estate of the Tenant to hold of him by lesser seruices, but this is void, for that there is no priuity betweene them, and a Confirmation cannot make such an alteration of Tenures.

7.E.3.19. 24.E.3.18.6.

And the case in 4.E.3. maketh nothing against this opinion, for there the case in substance is this, Iohn de Bonuile held certaine Lands of Ralfe Vernon, and before the Statute of Quia emptores terrarum, leuied a Fine of the same lands to the Abbot of Cogsall and his Successors to hold of the chiefe Lord (which was Ralfe Vernon) by the seruices due and accustomed. Ralfe Vernon made a Charter to the said Abbot in these words. Concessi etiam eidem Abbati & successoribus suis relaxaui & quietum clamaui totum ius, &c. quod habeo, vel potero habere in omnibus tenementis quæ idem Abbas habet de dono Iohannis de Bonuile. Tenendum de me & hæredibus meis in puram & perpetuam Eleemosinam. And adiudged that it was a good tenure in Frankalmoigne, which case prooueth nothing that the Lord Paramount may by his Confirmation to the Tenant perauaile extinct the Mesnaltie (as it is abridged by Master Fitzherbert in the title of Confirmation, Pl. 21.) for the immediate Lord did there make the said Charter, and not any Lord Paramount. (And therefore it is euer good to relie vpon the Booke at large, for many times Compendia sunt dispendia, and Melius est petere fontes, quam sectari riuolos.) And of this opinion was Master Plowden vpon good aduisement and consideration.

4.E.3.19.

4 E.3.10. 9.E.3.1. 12.E.4. 11. 16.E.3. fines 4. 6.Eliz. Dier 230.

And here is the seuenth Case wherein the Release and Confirmation doth agree, for if there be Lord and Tenant by Fealtie and twentie shillings rent, the Lord may release all his right in the Seigniory or in the Tenancie sauing fealty and ten shillings rent, but he cannot saue a new kind of seruice, for he may aswell abridge his seruices vpon a Release as vpon a Confirmation. And as there is required priuitie when the Lord abridgeth the seruices of his Tenant by his Confirmation: so must there be also, when the Lord by his Release abridgeth the seruices of his Tenant. And therefore the Lord Paramount cannot release to the Tenant perauaile sauing to him part of his seruices, but the sauing in that case is void.

Briton fol. 57. 177. 40.E.3. 21. 47. 48. 18.E.3.26. 30. Ass. 6. 14.H.4.8.

¶ *Et rendra rien a son Seignior forsque ceo que est comprise, &c.* Which words are thus to be vnderstood, that the Tenant shall not render any more Rent or annuall Seruice to the Lord then is contained in the Deed, but other things notwithstanding the said Confirmation the Tenant shall yeeld to the Lord, as reliefe, ayde pur file marier, and ayde pur faire fitz Chiualer, because these are incidents to the tenure that remayne, and shall not be discharged without speciall words, by the generall words of all other Actions, Seruices and Demands. And so if a man hold of me by Knights Seruice, Rent, Suite, &c. and I release to him all my right in the Seigniory, excepting the Tenure by Knights Seruice, or confirme his estate to hold of me by Knights Seruice only for all manner of Seruices, Exactions, and Demands. Yet shall the Lord haue ward, Marriage, Reliefe, Ayde pur file marier, & pur faire fitz Chiualer, for these be incidents to the tenure that remayne. But it is holden that if a man make a gift in taile by Deed reseruing two shillings rent a luy & ses heires pro omnibus & omnimodis seruitijs exactionibus secularibus & cunctis demandis, if the Donee die his heire of full age, the Donor shall haue no reliefe, because in the originall Deed of the gift in tayle it is expressely limited, that by the Seruice of two shillings Rent he shall be quite of all Demands, (and Reliefe lieth in Demand) and by reason of those words say they there cannot any Reliefe become due, but some doe hold the contrary in that case.

13.R.2. tit. auowrie 89. Nota ꝺ̃cum Fitzh.

Sect. 539.

¶ Mes si le Seignior voile per fait de confirmation, que le tenant en cest cas doit render

BVt if the Lord will by his Deed of Confirmation that the Tenant in this case shall yeeld

render a luy vn esperuer, ou vn rose annualment a tiel feast, &c. cest confirmation est voide, pur ceo que il reserua a luy vn nouel chose que ne fuit parcel de ses seruices deuant la confirmation, et issint le seignior poit bien per tiel confirmation abridger les seruices, per queux le tenant tient de luy, mes il ne poit reseruer a luy nouel seruices.

to him a Hawke or a Rose yearely at such a feast, &c. this confirmation is voyde, because he reserueth to him a new thing which was not parcell of his seruices before the confirmation, And so the Lord may well by such confirmation abridge the seruices by which the tenant holdeth of him, but hee cannot reserue to him new seruices.

This upon that which hath beene said before in the next preceding Section is euident, and needeth no further explication.

Sect. 540.

Item si soit seignior, mesne, et tenant, et le tenant est vn Abbe, que tient de mesne per certaine seruice annualment, le quel nad ascun cause dauer acquitance enuers son mesne, pur porter briefe de Mesne, &c. en cest cas, si le mesne confirma lestate que labbe ad en la terre, a auer et tener la terre a luy et a ses successors en frankalmoigne, &c. en cest cas le confirmation est bone, et adonques labbe tiendra de le mesne en frankalmoigne. Et la cause est pur ceo que nul nouel seruice est reserue car touts les seruices especialment specifies sont extincts, et nul rent est reserue al mesne forsque que labbe tient de luy la terre, et ceo fist il deuant la confirmation, car celuy que tient en frankalmoigne, ne doit faire ascun corporall seruice, issint que per tiel confirmation il appiert, que le mesne ne reserua a luy ascun nouel seruice, mes que les tenements serront tenus de luy come ceo fuit deuant. Et en cest case

ALso, if there be Lord, Mesne, and tenant, and the tenant is an Abbot that holdeth of the mesne by certaine seruices yearely, the which hath no cause to haue acquitance against his mesne for to bring a writ of Mesne, &c. in this case if the mesne confirme the estate that the Abbot hath in the land, to haue and to hold the land vnto him & his successors in frankalmoigne, or free almes, &c. in this case this confirmation is good, and then the Abbot holdeth of the mesne in frankalmoigne: and the cause is for that no new seruice is reserued, for all the seruices specially specified bee extinct, and no rent is reserued to the mesne, but the Abbot shall hold the land of him as it was before the confirmation, for he that holdeth in frankalmoigne ought to doe no bodily seruice, so that by such confirmation it appeareth the mesne shall not reserue vnto him no new seruice, but that the lands shall bee holden of him as it was before, and in this

case labbe auera vn briefe de mesne, sil soit distreint en son default per force de l' dit confirmation, lou per case il ne puissoit auer vn briefe adeuant, &c.

case the Abbot shall haue a writ of Mesne, if hee bee distrained in his default, by force of the said confirmation, where percase hee might not haue such a writ before.

4.E.3.19. 22.E.3.15.b. the Lord Wakes case. 10.E.3.5. 15.E.3. Confirmat.8. 4.E.3.19.20. F.N.B.136.h.& 9. 4.E.4.35 31.E.1. Mesne 55. 11.E.3. Auowrie 100. 22 E.3.18.b. 30.E.3.23. 16.H.3. Auowrie 243.

¶ HEre our Author hauing seene the former Bookes putteth his case that the mesne maketh the Confirmation to hold in Frankalmoigne and not the Lord paramount

¶ *Et en cest case labbe auera breife de mesne.* Here is to be noted, that vpon a Confirmation to hold in Frankalmoigne there lyeth a writ of Mesne, albeit the cause of acquitall begin after the Seignior. And so vpon such a Confirmation the Tenant shall haue Contra formam feoffamenti.

Sect. 541.

¶ Item si ieo sue seisie dun villein come de villeine en gros, et vn auter luy prent hors de ma possession, enclaimant luy destre son villein la ou il nauoit ascun droit dauer luy come son villein, et puis ieo confirma a luy lestate que il ad en mon villeine, cest confirmation semble void, pur ceo que nul poit auer possession de vn home come de villein en grosse, si non celuy que ad droit de luy auer come son villein en grosse. Et issint entant que celuy a que le confirmation fuit fait, ne fuit seisie de luy come de son villeine a le temps de confirmation fait, tiel confirmation est void.

ALso if I be seised of a villeine as of a villeine in grosse, and another taketh him out of my possession, clayming him to bee his villein there where hee hath no right to haue him as his villeine, and after I confirme to him the estate which hee hath in my villeine, this confirmation seemeth to be voide, for that none may haue possession of a man as of a villeine in grosse, but he which hath right to haue him as his villeine in grosse. And so in asmuch as hee to whom the confirmation was made, was not seised of him as of his villeine at the time of the confirmation made, such confirmation is voide.

¶ HEre is to bee obserued a diuersity betweene the custody of the body of a ward within age, and a right of inheritance in the body of a villeine in grosse, for a man may be put out of possession of the custodie of his ward but not of his villeine in grosse no more then a man can be of his prisoner which he hath taken in war.

45.E.3.10. 30.H.6. tit.barre 59. Registrum 102. 1.H.6.cap.5.

Also of things that are in grant, as Rents, Commons, and the like, it is at the election of the party whether hee will be disseised of them or no, as shall bee said after in his proper place. But of a villeine in grosse he cannot at all be disseised. (a) Non valet confirmatio nisi ille qui confirmat sit in possessione rei vel iuris vnde fieri debet confirmatio, & eodem modo nisi ille cui confirmatio fit sit in possessione.

Brooke tit. Property 28.

(a) Bracton lib.2.59.b. 24.E.3.111. discont.16. 42.E.3.18. 40.E.3.17. 43.E.3.4. 9.E.4.38. Dier 10.Eliz. Grenelicecase.

And materially doth Littleton put his case of a Villeine in grosse, for of a villeine regardant to a Mannor, the Lord may be put out of possession, for by putting him out of possession of the Mannor which is the principall, hee may likewise bee put out of possession of the villeine regardant which is but accessory. And by the recouery of the Mannor the villeine is recouered. But if another doth take away my villeine in grosse or regardant he gaineth no possession of him. And this doth well appeare by the writ of Natiuo habendo, for that writ is not brought against any person in certaine (because no man

can

can gaine the possession of him. But the writ is to this effect; Rex vic' Salutem, præcipimus tibi quod iuste & sine dilatione habere facias A.B. natiuum & fugitiuum suum, &c. vbicunque inuentus fuerit, &c. & prohibemus super forisfacturam nostram ne quis eum iniuste detineat; so as detaine him one may, but to possesse himselfe of him, and to dispossesse the Lord he cannot.

And if a man might haue beene dispossessed of a Villeine in grosse, or of a Villeine regardant (vnlesse he be dispossessed of the Mannor also, as hath beene said) the Law would haue giuen a remedy against the wrong doer, as the Law doth in the case of a ward.

Now seeing it doth appeare by our Bookes (a) (and by Littleton himselfe by implication speaking only of a villeine in grosse) that if a man be disseised of the Mannor whereunto the Villeine is regardant, he is out of possession of his villeine, and so an Aduowson appendant, and the like. Hereby (Littleton putting his case of a Villeine in grosse) and by diuers Authorityes a point controuerted in our bookes (*) is resolued, viz. that by the grant of the Mannor without saying Cum pertinentiis, the Villeine Regardant, Aduowson appendant and the like doe passe, for if the Disseisor shall gaine them as incidents to the Mannor, whose estate is wrongfull, A multo fortiori the Feoffee, who commeth to his estate by lawfull conueyance, shall haue them as incidents. But where the entrie of the disseisee is lawfull, he may seise the Villeine regardant, or present to the Aduowson, &c. before he enter into the Mannor, otherwise it is where his entrie is not lawfull, and so are the ancient Authors (b) to be intended.

(a) *Bracton, fo. 243. Britton, fo. 126.*

(*) *9.E.4.38. 3.H.4.13. 18.E.3.44. 16.E.3. Quar. Imp 146. 19.R.2. Itesp.255 19.H.6.33. 21.H.6.9. 33.H.6.33. 5.H.7.36. 38. 10.H.7.9.F.N.B.33.9. 21.H.6.33. per Moyle. 30.E.3.31. 39.E.3.31. 43.E.3.12.*

(b) *Bracton, fo. 242.243. Britton, fo. 126. Fleta, etc.*

Sect. 542.

Mes en cest cas, si tiels parols fueront en le fait, &c. Sciatis me dedisse & concessisse tali, &c. talem villanum meum, cest bone, mes ceo vrera per force et voy de grant et nemy per voy de confirmation, &c.

BVt in this case if these words were in the deed, &c. *Sciatis me dedisse & concessisse tali, &c. talem villanum meum*, this is good, but this shall enure by force and way of grant, and not by way of confirmation, &c.

Here it is to be obserued that a man hath an inheritance in a Villeine, whereof the wife of the Lord shall be endowed as hath beene said, for in him a man may haue an estate in Fee or fee taile for life or yeares. And therefore Littleton is here to bee vnderstood, that in the Grant there were these words (his heires) or else nothing passed but for life, as of other things that lye in Grant.

2.H.6. F.N.B.77.a.b.

24.E.3. Disceit. 16.

Sect. 543.

Et ascun foits ceux verbs Dedi & concessi, vreront per voy dextinguishment del chose done ou grant, sicome vn tenant tient de son seignior per certeine rent, et le seignior granta per son fait a le tenant et a ses heires le rent, &c, ceo vrera a le tenant per voy dextinguishment, car per tel grant le rent est extinct, &c.

ANd sometimes these verbes, *Dedi & concessi*, shall enure by way of extinguishment of the thing giuen or granted, as if a tenãt hold of his Lord by certaine rent, & the Lord grant by his deed to the tenant and his heires the rent, &c. this shall enure to the tenant by way of extinguishment, for by this grant the rent is extinct, &c.

And this grant of the rent shall enure by way of release. *3.E.19. Ass.7.*

Section 544.

¶ EN mesme le maner est, lou vn ad vn rent charge hors de certaine terre, et il graunta al tenant de la terre le Rent charge &c. Et la cause est, pur ceo que appiert per les parols del grant, que le voluut le donor est, que le tenant auera le rent, &c. et entant que il ne puit auer ne perceiuer ascun rent hors de son terre demesne, pur ceo le fait serra intendue et pris pur le pluis aduãtage et auaile pur le tenaunt que puit estre pris, et ceo est per voy dextinguishment.

IN the same manner it is where one hath a Rent Charge out of certaine Land, and hee graunt to the Tenaunt of the Land the Rent Charge, &c. And the reason is, for that it appeareth by the words of the Grant, That the will of the Donor is, That the Tenaunt shall haue the rent, &c. and in as much as hee cannot haue or perceiue any rent out of his owne Land, therefore the Deed shal be intended and taken for the most aduantage, and auaile for the tenant, that it may be taken, and this is by way of extinguishment.

34.H.6. ¶ BUt if the Grantee of the Rent charge granteth it to the Tenaunt of the Land and a stranger, it shall be extinguished but for the moitie: and so it is of a Seigniorie.

Sect. 545.

¶ ITem si ieo lessa Terre a vn home pur terme dans, & puis ieo confirma son estate sans pluis porolx mitter en le fait, per cel il nad pluis greinder estate que pur terme dans, sicome il auoit adeuant.

ALso if I let Land to a man for terme of yeares, and after I confirm his estate, without putting more words in the Deed, by this he hath no greater estate than for terme of yeares, as hee had before.

Sect. 546.

¶ MEs si ieo relessa a luy mon droit que ieo aye en le terre sans plus parols mitter en le fait, il ad estate de franketenement. Issint poyes entend mon fits diuers grands diuersities perenter Releases & confirmations.

BVt If I release to him all my right which I haue in the Land, without putting more words in the Deed, hee hath an estate of Freehold. So thou mayst vnderstand (my sonne) diuers great diuersities betweene Releases and Confirmations.

In these two Sections is the seuenth case wherein a Release and Confirmation do differ.

Sect. 547.

¶ ITem si ieo esteant deins age lessa terre a vn aut pur terme de xx. ans, et puis il graunte l' terre a vn auter p̄ tme de x. ans, issint il granta forsque parcel de son terme, en cest case quant ieo sue de pleine age, si ieo relessa al Grauntee de mon lessee, &c. cest release est voyd, pur ceo que il ny ad ascun priuitie perenter luy et moy, &c. Mes si ieo confirme son estate, donque cest confirmation est bone. Mes si mon Lessee graunta tout son estat a vn aut, donq̄s mō release fait a l' grātee ē bone et effectual.

ALso if I being within age, let land to another for terme of xx. yeres, and after he granteth the land to another for term of x. yeres, so hee graunteth but parcell of his terme: In this case when I am of full age, if I release to the Grantee of my Lessee, &c. this Release is voyd, because there is no priuitie betweene him and me, &c. but if I confirme his estate, then this confirmation is good. But if my lessee grant all his estate to another, then my Release made to the Grantee is good and effectuall.

¶ HEre are two things to be obserued: First, That the Rease of an Enfant in this case is not voyd but voydable. Secondly, this is the eighth case put by Littleton, wherein the Release and Confirmation doe differ. 7.E.4.6 b.18.E.4.8. 9.H.7.24.

Sect. 548.

¶ ITem si home granta vn rēt charge issuant hors de son terre a vn auter pur terme de son vie, et puis il confirma son estate en le dit rent, a auer et tener a luy en fee taile ou en fee simple, cest Confirmation est voyd, quant a enlarger son estate, pur ceo que celuy que confirme nauoit ascun reuersion en le rent.

ALso if a man graunt a Rent-charge issuing out of his Land to another for terme of his life, and after hee confirmeth his estate in the sayd rent, To haue and to hold to him in fee taile or in fee simple, this Confirmation is voyd as to inlarge his estate, because hee that confirmeth hath not any reuersion in the rent.

¶ HEere the Diuersitie is apparant, betweene a rent newly created, and a Rent in esse: which needeth no explication. Only this is to be obserued, That Littleton intendeth his Deed of Confirmation not to containe any clause of Distresse, for otherwise, as to the Confirmation the Deed is voyd, but the clause of Distresse doth amount to a new grant, as in the Chapter of Rents hath beene sayd. 21.E.3.47.15.E.4.8.b. Pl.Com.35.8.H.4.19.

Section 549.

¶ MEs si home soit seisie en fee de Rent seruice ou de Rent

BVt if a man be seised in fee of a Rent Seruice, or Rent Charge,

rent charge, et il grant le rent a un auter pur terme de vie, et le tenant atturna, et puis il confirma lestate de le grantee en fee taile, ou en fee simple, cest confirmation est bone, quant a enlarger son estate, solonque les parols le confirmation, pur ceo que celuy que confirmast al temps de confirmation, auoit un reuersion del rent.

and he grant the rent to another for life, and the tenant attorneth, and after hee confirmeth the estate of the grantee in fee taile, or in fee simple, this confirmation is good, as to enlarge his estate according to the words of the confirmation, for that he which confirmed at the time of confirmation had a reuersion of the rent.

¶ Here is the eight case wherein the Release and Confirmation doth agree, and it is here to be obserued that to the grant of the estate for life Littleton doth put an attornement, because it is requisite, but to the Confirmation to the Grantee of the rent to enlarge his estate, there is none necessary, and therefore he putteth none; but of this more shall be said in the chapter of Attornement, Sect. 556. 575.

Sect. 550.

¶ Mes en cas auantdit lou home graunt un rent charge a un auter pur terme de vie, sil voile que le grantee aueroit estate en le taile, ou en fee, il couient que le fait de grant del rent charge pur terme de vie, soit surrender ou cancell, et donques de faire un nouel fait dautiel rent charge. A auer et perceiuer a le grantee en le taile, ou en fee, &c. Ex paucis plurima concipit ingenium.

BVt in the case aforesaid where a man grant a rent charge to another for terme of life, if he will that the Grantee should haue an estate in taile, or in fee, it behoueth that the deed of grant of the rent charge for terme of life be surrendred or cancelled, & then to make a new Deed of the like rent charge. To haue & perceiue to the Grantee in tayle or in fee, &c. *Ex paucis plurima concipit ingenium.*

Vide Sect. 636.

¶ *Surrender ou cancell.* Note by cancellation of the Deed the rent which lyeth only in grant ceaseth (as here it appeareth) aswell as by the Surrender. And the reason wherefore (if the Grantor make a new grant of the rent, and not enlarge it by way of Confirmation as Littleton must be intended) the Deed should be surrendred or cancelled, is least the Grantor should be doubly charged, viz. with the old grant for life, and with the new grant in fee, or as hath beene said, the Grantor may grant to the Grantee for life and his heires; that he and his heires shall distreine for the rent, &c. and this shall amount to a new grant, and yet amount to no double charge, whereof you may see before in the Chapter of Rents.

Chap.10. Of Attornement. Sect.551.

ATtornement eſt, come ſi ſoit Sñr & tenant, & l' Sñr voile granter p̄ ſon fait les ſeruices d̄ ſ t a vn aut pur terme dans, ou per terme de vie, ou en taile, ou en fee, il couient que l' tenant atturna al grauntee en le vie le grantor, p force & vertue del grant, ou autrement le grant eſt void. Et atturnement eſt nul auter en effect forſq; quant le t ad oye del grant fait p ſ Sñr, q̄ meſme le tenant agreea per parol a le dit grant, ſicome adire a le grauntee, ieo moy agree a le grant fait a vous, &c. ou ieo ſue bien content de le graunt fait a vous, mes le pluis common atturnemt eſt, adire, Sir, ieo atturna a vous per force del dit graunt, ou ieo deueigne vře tenant, &c. ou liuerer al grantee vn denier, ou vn maile ou vn farthing per voy dattornement.

ATtornemēt is, as if there be Lord and tenant, and the Lord will grant by his Deed the ſeruices of his Tenant to another for terme of yeares, or for tearme of life, or in taile, or in fee, the tenant muſt attorne to the Grantee in the life of the Grantor by force and vertue of the grant or otherwiſe the grant is void. And Attornement is no other in effect, but when the Tenant hath heard of the grant made by his Lord that the ſame tenant do agree by word to the ſaid grant, as to ſay to the Grantee, I agree to the Grant made to you, &c. or I am well content with the grant made to you, but the moſt common Attornement is, to ſay, Sir, I attorne to you by force of the ſaid Grant, or I become your Tenant, &c. or to deliuer to the Grantee a pennie, or a halfe pennie, or a farthing by way of Attornement.

ATtornemēt is an agreement of the Tenant to the grant of the Seigniory, or of a rent, or of the Donee in tayle or tenant for life or yeares, to a grant of a Reuerſion or Remaynder made to another. It is an ancient word of art, and in the Common Law ſignifieth a torning or attorning from one to another, wee vſe alſo *Attornamentum* as a Latine word, and *attornare* to attorne. And ſo Bracton (a) vſeth it, *Item videndum eſt ſi Dominus attornare poſſit alicui homagium & ſeruitium tenentis ſui contra voluntatem ipſius tenentis, & videtur quod non.*

Bracton lib 2. fol. 81. Britton fo. 105. b. 176. & 177. Fleta lib. 3. cap. 6.

(a) Bracton lib. 2 fol 81. b. Fleta, Britton vbi ſupra.

And the reaſon why an Attornement is requiſite is yeelded in olde Bookes to bee, *Si Dominus attornare poſſit ſeruitium tenentis contra voluntatem tenentis tale ſequeretur inconueniens quod poſſit eum ſubiugare capitali inimico ſuo, & per quod teneretur Sacramentum fidelitatis facere ei qui eum damnificaré intenderet.*

Bracton lib. 2. fol. 81. b. Britton vbi ſupra.

Il couient que le tenant attorna al grantee en la vie del grantor, &c. And ſo muſt hee alſo in the life of the Grantee, and this is vnderſtood of a grant by Deed. And the reaſon hereof is for that euery grant muſt take effect as to the ſubſtance thereof in the life both of the Grantor and the Grantee. And in this caſe if the Grantor dieth before Attornement, the Seigniory, Rent, Reuerſion, or Remaynder diſcend to his heire, and therefore after his deceaſe

Vide Litt. fol. 118. 11. H. 7. 19.

Lib. 1. fol. 104. 105. Shelleys caſe.

40. Aſſ. 19. 34. H. 6. 7. 20. H. 6. 7.

deceafe the Attornement commeth too late, fo likewife if the Grantee dieth before Attornement, an Attornement to the heire is void, for nothing difcended to him, and if hee fhould take, hee fhould take it as a Purchafor, where the heires were added but as words of limitation of the eftate, and not to take as Purchafors.

34 H.6.7. 20.H.6.9.
Bracton lib.2.fol.81.82. &c.
Lib.6.fol.68. Sir Moyles Finches Cafe.

But if the grant were by fine then albeit the Conufor or Conufee dyeth, yet the grant is good. For by fine leuied the ftate doth paffe to the Conufee and his heires, and the Attornement to the Conufee or his heires at any time to make priuitie to diftraine is fufficient. But all this is to be taken as Littleton vnderftood it, viz. of fuch grants as haue their operation by the Common Law. For fince Littleton wrote if a fine be leuied of a Seigniory, &c. to another to the vfe of a third perfon and his heires, he and his heires fhall diftraine without any Attornement, becaufe he is in by the Statute of 27.H.8.cap.10. by transferring of the ftate to the vfe, and fo he is in by act in Law

27.H.8.cap.16.
Vide Sect.384.

And fo it is and for the fame caufe, if a man at this day by Deed indented and inrolled according to the Statute bargaineth and felleth a Seigniory, &c. to another, the Seigniory fhall paffe to him without any Attornement, and fo it is of a Rent, a Reuerfion, and a Remaynder. So as the Law is much changed, and the ancient priuiledge of Tenants, Donees, and Leffees much altered concerning Attornement fince Littleton wrote.

Lib.6.vbi fupra.
Vide Sect.149.

But if the Conufee of a fine before any Attornement by Deed indented and inrolled, bargaineth and felleth the Seigniory to another, the bargainee fhall not diftreine becaufe the bargainor could not diftreine. Et fic de fimilibus, for nemo poteft plus iuris ad alium transferre quam ipfe habet. Vide Sect.149. Where vpon a recouery, the Recoueror fhall diftreine and auow without Attornement.

49.E.3.4. 34.H.6.8. 6.E.4.13.

A grant to the King or by the King to another is good without Attornement by his Prerogatiue.

¶ *Attornement eſt nul auter en effect, &c.* **It is to be vnderftood** that there be two kind of Attornements, viz. an Attornement in deed or expreffe, and an Attornement in Law or implicite. Of Attornement expreffe or indeed Littleton fpeaketh here, and of Attornement in Law he fpeaketh after in this Chapter. And to both thefe kinds of Attornements there is an incident infeparable, that is, that the Tenant hath notice of the grant for an Attornement being (an agreement or confent to the grant, &c.) he cannot agree or confent to that which he knoweth not. And the vfuall pleading is, to which grant the Tenant attorned. And therefore if a Bayly of a Mannor who vfed to receiue the rents of the Tenants purchafe the Mannor, and the Tenants hauing no notice of the purchafe continue the payment of the Rents to him, this is no Attornement. So if the Lord leuie a fine of the Seigniory, and by fine take backe an eftate in fee, the Tenant continueth the payment of the rent to the firft Conufor without notice of the fines, this is no Attornement. But it is to be knowne that there be two kind of notices, viz. a notice in deed or expreffe, whereof Littleton here fpeaketh, when he fayth, that the Tenant agreeth to the grant, and a notice in Law or implyed, whereof Littleton hereafter fpeaketh in this Chapter.

Lib.2.fol.67.b. Tookers cafe. 13.Eliz. Dyer 302. Tookers cafe vbi fupra.
Lib.2. Tookers cafe vbi fupra.

¶ *Del grant fait per fon Seignior.* **Here is to bee feene when the** thing granted is altered what becommeth of the Attornement.

If there be Lord, Mefne and Tenant, and the Mefne grant ouer his Mefnaltie by Deed, the Lord releafeth to the Tenant whereby the Mefnalty is extinct, and there is a rent by furplufage, an Attornement to the grant of this rent fecke is good, although the qualitie of that part of the rent is altered, becaufe it is altered by act in Law.

If a reuerfion of two Acres be granted by Deed, and the Leffor before Attornement leuie a fine of one of them, and the Tenant attorne, this is good for the other Acre.

(a) 18 E.3.tit. variance 63. 22.E.3.18. Tookers cafe, vbi fupra.

(a) If the Reuerfion be granted of three Acres, and the Leffee agree to the faid grant for one Acre this is good for all three, and fo it is of an Attornement in Law if the reuerfion of three Acres be granted, and the Leffee furrender one of the Acres to the Grantee, this Attornement in a barre fhall be good for the whole reuerfion of the three Acres according to the Grant.

¶ *Et le tenant agrea.* **Hereafter in this Chapter** Littleton **doth** teach what manner of Tenant fhall attorne.

¶ *Agrea per parol, &c.* **And fo hee may and more fafely by his** Deed in writing.

39.H.6.3. Tookers cafe. Vbi fupra.

¶ *Sicome adire a le grantee, &c.* **Here is to be feene to what man**ner of Grantees the Attornement is good. Regularly the Attornement muft bee according to the grant eyther expreffely, or implyedly, Of the firft Littleton hath here fpoken.

In-

Implyedly, as if a reversion be granted to two by Deed, and the Lessee attorne to one of them according to the grant, this Attornement is good, but not to vest the reversion only in him to whom Attornement is made, but it shall enure to both the Grantees, for that is according to the grant, and for that it cannot vest the reversion only in him to whom the Attornement is made. And so it is if one Grantee dieth, the Attornement to the Survivor is good. *Tookers case vbi supra. 11. H. 7. 12.*

If the Lord grant by Deed his Seigniory to A. for life, the remaynder to B. in fee, A. dyeth and then the Tenant attorne to B, this Attornement is void, because it is not according to the grant, for then B should haue a remainder without any particular estate. *20. H. 6. 7.*

If a reversion be granted to a man and a woman, they are to haue moities in Law, but if they entermarrie and then Attornement is had, they shall haue no moities, (and yet by the purport of the grant they are to haue moities,) because it is by act in Law. *Tookers case vbi supra. Pl. Com. 167. 483.*

If a Feme grant a reversion to a man in fee, and marry with the Grantee, this is a good Attornement in Law to the husband. *2. R. 2. tit. Attornement 8.*

If a reversion be granted by Deed to the vse of I. S. and the Lessee hearing the Deed read, or hauing notice of the contents thereof attorne to Cesty que vse, this is an implyed Attornement to the Grantee.

If a reversion be granted for life, the remaynder in tayle, the remaynder in fee, the Attornement to the Grantee for life shall enure to them in the remaynder to vest the remaynder in them. *Temps E. 1. Attorn. 22. 18. E. 47.*

And in those cases if the Tenant should say, that I doe attorne to the Grantee for life, but that it shall not benefit any of them in remaynder after his death, yet the Attornement is good to them all, for hauing attorned to the Tenant for life, the Law (which hee cannot controll) doth vest all the remaynder. And of this more shall be said hereafter in this Chapter.

Littleton here putteth fiue examples of an expresse Attornement, but of them the last is the best, because the eare is not only a witnesse of the words, but the eye of the deliuery of the penny, &c. and so there is dictum & factum. And any other words which import an agreement or assent to the grant doe amount to an Attornement. And albeit these fiue expresse Attornements be all set downe by Littleton, to be made to the person of the Grantee, (b) yet an Attornement in the absence of the Grantee is sufficient, for if he doth agree to the grant eyther in his presence or in his absence, it is sufficient. *(b) Lib. 2. fol. 68. 69. Tookers case. 28 H. 8. tit. Attornement Br. 40.*

Sect. 552.

¶ Item si le Seignior graunt l' seruice de son tenant a vn home, & puis per vn fait portant vn darreine date, il granta mesmes les seruices a vn auter, & l' tenant attorne a le second grantee, ore le dit grauntee ad les seruices, & coment que apres le Tenant voile attorner a le primer grauntee cest clerement void, &c.

Also if the Lord grant the seruice of his Tenant to one man, and after by his Deed bearing a later date hee grant the same seruices to another, and the Tenant attorne to the second Grantee, now the said Grantee hath the seruices, and albeit afterwards the Tenant will attorne to the first Grantee, this is cleerely void, &c.

¶ Here it is to bee obserued, that Littl. expresseth not what estate is granted, and very materially, for if the former grant were in fee, and the latter grant were for life, and the tenant doth first attorne to the second Grantee he cannot after attorne to the first grantee to make the fee simple passe, for that should not be according to the grãt, but in that case the Attornement to the first is countermanded. And so it is if a Reversion expectant vpon an estate for life be granted to another in fee, and after the Grantor before Attornement confirme the estate of the Lessee in tayle, the Attornement to the Grantee for the fee simple is void.

In the same manner, if a Reversion vpon an estate for yeares be granted in fee, and the Lessor confirme the estate of the Lessee for life he cannot afterwards attorne.

11.H.7.19. 2.R.2 vbi supra.

If a Feme sole maketh a Lease for life or yeares reseruing a rent, and granteth the Reuersion in fee, and taketh husband, this is a Countermand of the Attornement.

P.3.Eliz.Bendlowes.

Where our Author putteth his case of the whole reuersion, if two Coperceners bee of a reuersion, and one of them granteth her moity by Fine, the Conusee shall haue a Quid iuris clamat for the moitie.

11.H.7.12.

If in the case that our Author here putteth of seuerall grantees, if the Tenant Attorne to both of them, the Attornement is voide, because it is not according to the Grant. If a reuersion be granted for life, and after it is granted to the same Grantee for yeares and the Lessee attorneth to both Grants it is voide for the incertaintie; A multo fortiori, if the Lord by one Deede grant his Seigniory to I. Bishop of London and to his heires, and by another Deede to I. Bishop of London and to his Successors, and the Tenant attorne to both grants, the Attornement is voide, for albeit the Grantee be but one, yet he hath seuerall capacities, and the grants are seuerall, and the Attornement is not according to either of the Grants.

But if A grant the reuersion of Blacke acre or White acre, and the Lessee attorne to the Grant, and after the Grantee maketh his election, this Attornement is good, for albeit the state was incertaine, yet he attorned to the Grant in such sort, as it was made, and so note a diuersitie betweene one grant and seuerall grants, and obserue in this case an Attornement good in expectation, and yet nothing passed at the time of the Attornement but by the election subsequent.

Section 553.

Item si home soit seisie de vn mannor, quel mannor est parcel en demesne, et parcel en seruice, sil voile aliener cel mannor a vn auter, il couient que per force del alienation, que touts les tenants que teignont del alienor come de son manor, attornerent al alienee, ou autermēt les seruices demurront continualment en lalienor, forprise tenants a volunt, car il ne besoigne que tenants a volunt atturnent sur tiel alienation, &c.

ALso if a man bee seised of a mannor, which mannor is parcell in demesne, and parcell in seruice, if hee will alien this mannor to another, it behooueth that by force of the alienation, all the tenants which hold of the alienor as of his mannor doe attorne to the alienee, or otherwise the seruices remaine continually in the alienor, sauing the tenants at will, for it needeth not that tenants at will doe attorne vpon such alienation, &c.

Temps.E.1.Attornement. 48.E.3.15.

Here it is to bee obserued that when a man maketh a feoffment of a Mannor the seruices doe not passe but remaine in the Feoffor vntill the Freeholders doe attorne, and when they doe attorne the Attornment shall haue relation to some purpose and not to other. For albeit the Attornment be made many yeares after the feoffment, yet it shall haue relation to make it passe out of the Feoffor Ab initio euen by the Liuery vpon the feoffment, but not to charge the Tenants with any meane arrerages or for waste in the meane time, or the like.

If a reuersion of Land be granted to an Alien by Deed, and before Attornement the Alien is made Denizen, and then the Attornment is made, the King vpon office found shall haue the land: for as to the estate betweene the parties it passeth by the Deede Ab initio.

Pasch.5.E.3.Coram Rege. Suffex in Thesaur. 21.E.3.47. 34.E.3.Double plea 24. 42.Ass p 6. 43.Ass p.22. 30.E.3.{29.E.3. 26.E.3. Per quae seruitia 21. 8.H.4.16. 12.H.4. 20.H 6.7. 35.H.6. 9.E.4.33. 13.H.7.14.a. 1.H.7.31. 4.E.6.Attornement,Br.30.

If a man plead a feoffment of a Mannor hee needs not pleade an Attornement of the Tenants, but (if it be materiall) it must be denied or pleaded of the other side.

And vpon consideration had of all the bookes touching this point whether the seruices of the Freeholders doe passe, wherein there haue beene three seuerall opinions, viz. some haue holden that the seruices doe passe in the right by the Liuery as parcell of the Mannor, but not to auow without Attornement as in the case of the Fine. And others haue holden, that they both passe in right and in possession to distreine without Attornement. And the third opinion is, that in this case the said seruices passe neither in possession nor in right, but vntill Attornement remaine

remaine continually in the Alienor as Littleton here holdeth. And so it was resolued Pasch. 15. Eliz. betweene Brasbitch and Barwell according to the opinion of our Author. And I neuer yet knew any of Littletons cases (albeit I haue knowne many of them) to bee brought in question, but in the end the Judges concurred with our Author. Vid. Hill. 14. Eliz. Rot. 508. in Communi banco.

And where our Author speaketh of the Attornement of the Freeholders, if the Lord make a Lease for yeares or for life of a Mannor, and the Freeholders attorne to the Lessee, if after the reuersion of the Mannor be granted, the Attornement of the Lessee for yeares or life shall binde the Freeholders, for by their former Attornement, they haue put the Attornement into the mouth of the Lessee. 9. E. 2. tit. Attornement 18. 19. E. 2. ibid. 19. 21. E. 3. 47. 5. H. 5. 12. b. Vid. Litt. Sect. 549. & 556.

¶ *Forsprise tenant a volunt, &c.* Here is implied Tenant at will or by copy of Court Rolle according to the custome of the Mannor, so as the Freehold and inheritance both of lands in the hands of Tenant at will by the Common Law or by Custome, shall passe both in right and in possession without any Attornement.

Sect. 554.

¶ Item si soient seignior et tenant, et le tenant lessa la terre a un auter pur terme de vie, ou dona la terre en le taile sauant le reuersion a luy, &c. si le Seignior en tiel cas granta son seigniory a un auter, il couient que celuy en le reuersion atturna al grauntee, et nemy le tenant a terme de vie, ou le tenant en le taile, pur ceo que en cest cas celuy en le reuersion est tenant al Seignior, et nemy le tenant a terme de vie, ne le tenant en le tayle.

ALso if there bee Lord and tenant, & the tenant letteth the land to another for term of life, or giueth the land in taile sauing the reuersion to himselfe, &c. if the Lord in such case grant his Seigniory to another, it behoueth that hee in the reuersion attorne to the grantee, and not the tenant for terme of life, or the Tenant in taile, because that in this case he in the reuersion is tenant to the Lord, and not the tenant for terme of life, nor the tenant in taile.

¶ For it is a maxime in Law, that no man shall attorne to any grant of any Seigniory, Rent seruice, Reuersion or Remainder, but hee that is immediatly priuie to the Grantor, and because in this case there is no priuitie betweene the Lord and the Tenant for life, or Donee in taile, but onely betweene the Lord and him in the reuersion, for in this case the Attornement of him in the Reuersion only is good.

¶ *Sauant le reuersion a luy, &c.* That is to say, without limitation of any remainder ouer, and this is but to make his opinion plaine, as to the point that he putteth it.

Section 555.

¶ En mesme le maner est, lou sont seigniour, mesne, et tenant, si le Seigniour voile granter les seruices del mesne, coment que il ne fait ascun mention en son grant del mesne, uncore il couient que le mesne atturna, &c. et nemy le tenant pera-

¶ IN the same manner is it where there are Lord, Mesne and Tenant, if the Lord will grant the seruices of the Mesne, albeit hee maketh no mention in his grant of the Mesne, yet the Mesne ought to attorne, &c. and not the Tenant perauaile, &c.

peravaile, &c. pur ceo q̄ le mesne est tenant a luy, &c.

for that the Mesne is Tenaunt vnto him, &c.

This standeth upon the same reason that the next precedent case did.

Section 556.

¶ Mes autermēt est, lou certaine terre est charge dun Rent charge, ou Rent seck, car en tiel case si celuy que ad le rent charḡ ceo grant a vn auter, il covient q̄ l' tenant del franktenement attourna al Grantee, pur ceo que le franktenement est charḡ ove le rent, &c. et en rent charge nul avowrie doit estre fait sur ascun person pur le distresse prise, &c. mes il avowera le prise bone et droiturel, come en terres ou tenements issint charges a son distresse, &c.

But otherwise it is where certain lād is charged with a Rent charge or Rent secke, for in such case if he which hath the Rent charge grant this to another, it behooveth that the Tenaunt of the freehold attorn to the Grātee, for that the Freehold is charged with the rent, &c. And in a Rent charge no Avowrie ought to be made upon any person for the distresse taken, &c. but hee shall avow the prisel to bee good and rightfull, as in lands or Tenements so charged with his distresse, &c.

¶ Here is to be observed a diversitie betweene a Rent service and a Rent charge, or a Rent secke; for as to the Rent service, no man (as hath beene sayd) can attorne, but he that is privie; so in case of a Rent charge it behooveth that the Tenaunt of the Freehold doth attorne to the Grantee, without respect of any privitie. And therefore the Disseisor onely in the case of a grant of a Rent charge, shall attorne, because he is (as Littleton saith) tenant of the Freehold, but in case of a grant of a Rent service, the Attornement of the Disseisee sufficeth.

21.H.6.9.b.

If there be Lord and Tenant by homage, fealtie, and rent, the Tenant is disseised, the Lord granteth the rent to another; the Disseisee attorneth, this is voyd: but if hee had graunted over his whole Seigniorie, the Attornement had beene good, and the reason of this diversitie is heere given by our Author, for that when the rent was graunted onely, it passed as a Rent secke, and consequently the Disseisor being Terre-Tenant, must attorne. But when the Seigniorie is granted, then the Disseisee in respect of the privitie may attorne.

¶ *Covient que le Tenant del Franktenement, &c.* And therefore if the Tenant of the land charged with a Rent charge or a Rent secke, make a lease for life, and hee that hath the Rent charge or Rent secke granteth it over, the Tenant for life shall attorne, for he is Tenant of the Freehold, according to the expresse saying of our Author, and (as hath beene sayd) there needeth no privitie.

And it was holden by Dyer chiefe Justice of the Court of Common Pleas, and Mounson Justice, in the argument of Bracebridges case abovesayd, & not denied, that if he that hath a rent charge granteth it over for life, & the tenant of the Land attorn thereunto, & after he granteth the reversion of the Rent charge, that the Grantee for life may attorne alone. And that these words of Littleton are to bee understood when a Rent charge or Rent secke is granted in possession: And therewith agreeth 46.E.3. where it appeareth, That the Quid juris clamat in that case, did lie against the Grantee for life.

46.E.3.27.2.H.6.9. Vi.Lit.Sect. 547. & 553.

A man maketh a lease for life, and after grants to A. a Rent charge out of the reversion, A. granteth the rent over, hee in the reversion must attorne, and not the Tenant of the Freehold, for that the Freehold is not charged with the rent, for a Release made to him by the Grantee doth not extinguish the rent. And Littleton is to be understood, that the Tenant of the Freehold

hold must atturne when the Freehold is charged.

¶ *Et en Rent charge nul Auowrie doit estre fait sur ascun person, &c.* This is the reason that Littleton giueth of the difference betweene the Rent seruice and the Rent charge. Now it may be sayd, That this reason is taken away by the Statute of 21.H.8. for by that Statute the Lord needs not auow for any rent or seruice vpon any person in certaine, and then by Littletons reason there needeth no priuitie to the attornement of a seigniorie, for (say they) Cessante causa vel ratione legis cessat lex. As at the Common Law no aid was grantable of a stranger to an Auowrie: because the Auowrie was made of a certaine person, but now the Auowrie being made by the sayd Act of 21.H.8. vpon no person, therefore the reason of the Law being changed, the Law it selfe is also changed, and consequently in an Auowrie, according to that Act, ayd shall be granted of any man, and the like in many other cases, which case is granted to be good Law: but albeit the Lord (as hath beene sayd) may take benefit of the Statute, yet may he auow still at his election vpon the person of his Tenaunt. Also albeit the manner of the Auowrie be altered, yet the priuitie (which is the true cause of the sayd difference) remaineth still as to an Attornement. 21.H.8.cap.19. Vid.Sect.454. 27.H.8.4.b.

Rent charge, &c. **It is to be obserued, to what kind of Inheritances** being granted, an Attornement is requisite. And in this Chapter Littleton speaketh of fiue: First, of a Seigniorie, Rent seruice, &c. Secondly, of a Rent charge. Thirdly, of a Rent secke. And hereafter in this Chapter of two more, viz. of a Reuersion and Remainder of Lands; for the Tenant shall neuer need to attorne but where there is Tenure, attendance, remainder, or payment of a Rent out of land. And therefore if an Annuitie, Common of pasture, Common of Estouers, or the like, be granted for life or yeares, &c. the reuersion may be granted without any Attornement, and albeit sometimes in some of these cases or the like, an Attornement be pleaded, yet it is surplusage, and more than needeth, because in none of them there is any Tenure, Attendance, Remainder, or payment out of land. 21.H.7.2. 1.H.5.1.37.Ass.14.36.Ass. pl.3. 31.H.8.tit. Attornment.Br.59.

Sect. 557.

¶ ITem si soit Seignior et tenant, et le tenant lessa son tenement a vn auter pur terme de vie, le remainder a vn auter en fee, et puis le Seignior granta les seruices a vn auter, &c. et le tenant a terme de vie attorna, ceo est assets bone, pur ceo que le Tenant a terme de vie est tenaunt en cest case al seignior, &c. et celuy en le remainder ne poit estre dit tenant al seignior, quant a cel entent forsque apres la mort le tenant a terme de vie, vncore en cest case si celuy en le remainder morust sans heire, le seignior auera le remainder per voy descheate, pur ceo que coment que le seignior en tiel cas couient dauower sur le tenant a terme de vie, &c. vncore tout lentier tenement quant a touts les estates de franktenement, ou de fee simple, ou auterment, &c. en tiel cas sont ensemble tenus de le seignior, &c.

ALso if there be Lord and Tenant, and the tenant letteth his tenement to another for terme of life, the remainder to another in fee, and after the Lord grant the seruices to another, &c, and the Tenant for life attorne, this is good enough, for that the Tenaunt for life is Tenaunt in this case to the Lord, &c. and he in the remainder cannot be said to be tenant to the Lord, as to this entent, vntill after the death of the tenant for life; yet in this case if hee in the remainder dieth without heire, the Lord shall haue the remainder by way of Escheat, because that albeit the lord in such case ought to auowe vpon the tenant for life, &c. yet the whole entire Tenement, as to all the estates of the Freehold or of Fee simple, or otherwise, &c. in such case are together holden of the Lord, &c.

¶ Mes

¶ * Mes nemy de faire Auowrie sur eux touts ensemble. M.3.H.6.

¶ * But not to make Auowrie vpon them all together. M.3.H.6.

15.E.3. Attorn.10.12.E.4.4 18.H.6.2. 9.E.2.tit. Attorn.18.18.E.4.7. Temps E.1 Attorn.22 Vi.Sect.580.

¶ ET le Tenant a terme de vie attorna, &c. For he that is (as hath beene sayd) priuie and immediately Tenant to the Lord, must attorne: and that is in this case, The Tenant for life, and so of the other side if a Seigniorie be granted to one for life, the remainder to another in fee, the Attornment to the Tenant for life is an Attornment to the remainder also; vnlesse it be that they in the remainder ought to haue acquitall, or other priuiledge, (whereof they should be preiudiced) and then albeit an Attornement bee had to the Tenant for life, and he acknowledge the acquitall, &c. yet after his decease he in remainder shall not distreyne vntill he acknowledge the Acquitall, notwithstanding the Attornment of the Tenant for life.

3.H.6.1. Old Tenures 107. (a) 15.E.4.13 4.

¶ Auera le remainder per voy descheat. For the remainder is holden of the Lord, but not immediately holden, and in this case by the escheat of the remainder the Seigniorie is extinct, for the Fee simple of the Seigniorie being extinct, there cannot remain a particular estate for life thereof, in respect of the Tenure and attendance ouer, and of this opinion is Littleton (a) himselfe in our Bookes. But otherwise it is of a Rent charge, for if that be granted for life, and after he in the reuersion purchase the land, so as the reuersion of the Rent charge is extinct, yet the Grantee for life shall enioy the rent during his life, for there is no Tenure or attendance in this case.

M.3.H.6.1.

¶ * Mes nemy de faire Auowrie, &c. This is added to Littleton, but it is consonant to Law, and the authoritie truly cited.

Section 558.

¶ ITem si soit Seignior et tenant, et le tenant lessa les tenements a vn feme pur terme de vie, le remainder ouster en fee, et la feme prent baron, et puis le seignior granta les seruices, &c. a le baron et ses heires, en cest case le seruice est mis en suspence durant le couerture. Mes si la feme deuie viuant le Baron, le baron et ses heires aueront le rent de ceux en le remainder, &c. et en ceo case il ne besoigne ascun attornement per parol, &c. pur ceo que le baron que doit attorner accepta le fait del graunt de les seruices, &c. le quel acceptance est vn attornment en la Ley.

ALso if there bee Lord and Tenant, and the Tenant letteth the tenements to a woman for life, the remainder ouer in fee, and the woman taketh husband, and after the Lord grant the seruices, &c. to the husband and his heires, in this case the seruice is put in suspence during the Couerture, but if the wife die liuing the husband, the husband and his heires shall haue the rent of them in the remainder, &c. And in this case there needeth no Attornement by parol, &c. for that the husband which ought to attorne, accepted the deed of grant of the seruices, &c. the which acceptance is an attornment in the Law.

5.E.3.42. 15.E.3. Attornment,11.

¶ LE quel acceptance est vn attornement en la Ley, &c. Littleton hauing spoken (as hath beene sayd) of Attornements in Deed or expresse, now commeth to speake of Attornements in Law, or implied, and hauing before set downe fiue expresse Attornments in Deed, doth in this Chapter enumerate 7. Attornments in Law. Heere it is to be vnderstood, That the expresse Attornement of the husband will binde the wife after the

couerture,

couerture, and in as much as this acceptance of the grant is an Attornement in Law without a word of Attornement the Seigniorie shall passe. And this is the first example that Littleton putteth of an Attornement in Law; which amounteth to an expresse Attornement, for that it is an agreement to the grant. 44. E. 3. tit. Fines 37. 12. E. 4. 4.

If the Lord grant his Seigniory to the Tenant of the Land, and to a stranger, and the Tenant accept the Deed, this acceptance is a good Attornement to extinguish the one moity, and to vest the other moity in the Grantee, as hath beene said.

Section 559.

EN m̃ l' manner est, si soyent Seignior & tenant & le tenant prent feme, & puis le Seignior granta les seruices a la feme & ses heirs, & le baron accepta le fait, en cest cas apres la mort le baron, la feme & ses heires aueront les seruices, &c. car per le acceptance del fait per l' baron, ceo est bone attornement, &c. coment que durant la couerture les seruices sont mis ẽ suspence, &c.

IN the ſame manner is it, if there be Lord and tenant, and the Tenant taketh wife, and after the Lord grant his ſeruices to the wife and his heires, & the husband accepteth the deed. In this caſe after the death of the husband the wife and her heires ſhall haue the ſeruices, &c. for by the acceptance of the deed by the husband, this is a good attornement, &c. albeit during the couerture the ſeruices ſhal be put in ſuſpence, &c.

HEre is the second example that Littleton putteth of an Attornement in Law and standeth upon the former reason.

Sont miſe en ſuſpence. Suspence commeth of ſuſpendeo, and in Legall understanding is taken when a Seigniorie, Rent, Profit apprender, &c. by reason of unitie of possession of the Seigniorie, Rent, &c. and of the land out of which they issue are not in eſſe for a time, & tunc dormiunt but may be reuiued or awaked. And they are said to be extinguished when they are gone for euer & tunc moriuntur and can neuer be reuiued, that is when one man hath as high and perdurable an estate in the one as in the other.

Sect. 560.

ITem si soyent Seignior & tenant, & l' tenãt granta les tenements a vn home pur terme d' sa vie, le remainder a vn auter en fee, si le Seignior granta l's seruices a le tenant a terme de vie en fee, en cest cas le tenant a

ALſo if there bee Lord and Tenant, and the Tenant grant the tenemẽts to a man for tearme of his life the remaynder to another in fee, if the Lord grant the ſeruices to the Tenant for life in fee, in this caſe the tenant for tearme of life

HEre is the third case that Littleton putteth of an Attornement in Law. And it is to bee obserued that albeit a grant, as hath beene said, may enure by way of release, and a release to the Tenant for life doth worke an absolute extinguishment, whereof hee in the remaynder shall take benefit, yet the Law shall neuer make any construction against the purport of the grant to the preiudice of any, or against the meaning of the parties as here

here it should, for if by construction it should enure to a release, the heires of the Tenant for life should bee disherited of the rent, and therefore Littleton here sayth, that the heires of the Grantee shal haue the Seigniory after his death. And here is an Attornement in Law to a grant suspended that cannot take effect in the grantee so long as he liueth but shall take effect in his heires by discent for the Inheritance of the Seigniorie was in the tenant for life, and the suspension only during his life.

terme de vie ad fee en les seruices, Mes les seruices sont mis en suspence durant sa vie. Mes les heires le tenant a terme de vie aueront les seruices apres son decease, &c. Et en cest cas il ne besoigne attornement, car per lacceptance del fait de celuy, que doit attourner, &c. est ceo attournement de luy mesme.

hath a fee in the seruices; but the seruices are put in suspence during his life. But the heires of the Tenant for life shall haue the seruices after his decease, &c. And in this case there needeth no Attornement, for by the acceptance of the Deed by him which ought to attorne, &c. this is an Attornement of it selfe.

Section 561.

¶ MEs lou le tenant ad ex grand & haut estate en les tenements, sicome le Seignior ad en le Seigniory, en tiel case, si le Seignior graunta les seruices al tenant en fee, ceo vrera per voy dextinguishment, causa patet.

BVt where the Tenant hath as great and as high estate in the tenements, as the Lord hath in the Seigniory, in such case if the Lord grant the seruices to the Tenant in fee, this shall enure by way of extinguishment, *Causa patet*.

¶ HEre Littleton intendeth not only as great and high an Estate, but as perdurable also, as hath beene said, for a Disseisor or Tenant in fee vpon condition hath as high and great an Estate but not so perdurable an Estate, as shall make an extinguishment.

Sect. 562.

¶ HEre in this case hee in the Reuersion of the tenancy must attorn, because he is the Tenant to the Lord, and yet the Seigniorie shall bee suspended during the life of the Grantee, because hee hath an estate for life in the Tenancie, but his heires shall enioy the Seigniorie by Discent.

¶ *Vncore il ne*

¶ ITem si soyent Seignior & tenant, & le tenant fait vn leas a vn home pur terme de sa vie, sauant le reuersion a luy, si le Seignior granta le Seigniorie a le tenant a terme de vie en fee, en cest case il couient

ALso if there bee Lord and Tenant, and the Tenant maketh a Lease to a man for terme of his life, sauing the reuersiō to himselfe, if the lord grāt the Seigniory to tenant for life in fee. In this case it behoueth that he in the reuer-

ent que celuy en le reuersion attorna al tenant a terme de vie per force de cel grant, ou autrement le grãt est voide, pur ceo que celuy en le reuersion est tenãt al Sñr, &c.

¶* Et uncore il ne tiendra del tenant a terme de vie, durant sa vie, Causa patet.*¶

sion must attorne to the tenant for life by force of this grant, or otherwise the grant is voide, for that hee in the reuersion is tenant to the Lord, &c.

*¶ Yet hee shall not hold of the tenant for life during his life. *Causa patet, &c.*

tient, &c. This is added, and not in the originall and is against Lawe, and therefore to be reiected.

¶ *Tenant al Seignior, &c.* Here is to bee understood a diuersitie when the whole estate in the Seigniory is suspended, and when but part of the estate in the Seigniory is suspended. And in this case the Seigniory is suspended but for terme of life, (a) and therefore as to all things concerning the right it hath his being, but as to the possession during the particular estate the Grantee shall take no benefit of it, therefore during that time he shall haue no Rent, Seruice, wardship, Reliefe, Harriot, or the like, because these belong to the possession, but if the Tenant dieth without heire, the Tenancie shall escheate unto the Grantee, for that is in the right, and yet when the Seigniory is reuiued by the death of the Tenant, there shall be Wardship, as if the Tenant marry with the Seignioresse and dieth, his heire within age, the wife shall haue the wardship of the heire. Also in the case that Littleton here putteth, albeit the seigniory be suspended but for life, yet some hold that he cannot grant it ouer because the Grantee tooke it suspended, and it was neuer In esse in him, but if the Tenant make a Lease for yeares or for life to the Lord, there the Lord may grant it ouer because the Seigniory was In esse in him, and the fee simple of the Seigniory is not suspended, but if the Lord disseise the Tenant, or the Tenant enfeoffe the Lord upon Condition there the whole estate in the Seigniory is suspended, and therefore he cannot during the suspencion take benefit of any Escheat, or grant ouer his Seigniory.

(a) 34. Ass. p. 15.

16. E. 3. tit. Voucher. 88.

5. E. 3. Twoug. case.

Sect. 563.

¶ Item si soient seignior et tenant, et le tenãt tient del Seignior per xx. maners des seruices, et le Seignior granta son seigniory a un auter, si le tenant paya en fait ascun parcel dascun de les seruices al grauntee, ceo est bone attornment, de et pur touts les seruices, comẽt que lentent de le teñ fuit dattourner forsque de cel parcel, pur ceo que le seigniory est entier, coment que ils sont di-

ALso if there bee Lord and tenant, and the tenant holdeth of the Lord by xx. maner of seruices, and the Lord grant his Seigniory to another, if the tenant pay in Deed any parcell of any of the seruices to the Grantee, this is a good Attornement, of and for all the seruices, albeit the entent of the tenant was to attorne but for this parcell, for that the Seigniorie is intire, although there bee diuers man-

¶ HEre it appeareth that an Attornement being made for parcell is good for the whole, for seeing hee hath attorned for part, it cannot bee voide for that, and good it cannot be unlesse it be for the whole; but of this sufficient hath beene said before in this chapter.

¶ *Paya ascun parcell des seruices.* Here is the fourth example of an Attornement in Law, for payment of any parcell of the seruices, is an agreement in Law to the grant.

¶ *Coment que lentent del tenant fuit dattorner, &c.*

4. E. 3. 55. Malmans case. 21. E. 3. 23. 5. E. 4. 2. 22. Ass. 66. 7. H. 4. 10. 35. H. 6. 8. Per Prisott.

40. E. 3. 34.

Quia

10.H.6.

Quia intentio inseruire debet legibus, non leges intentioni. And yet as farre as it may stand with the rule of Law, it is honourable for all Iudges to iudge according to the intention of the parties, and so they ought to doe. And of this somewhat in this Chapter hath beene said before.

uers maners des seruices que le tenant doit faire, &c.

ner of seruices which the tenant ought to doe, &c.

Sect. 564.

48.E.3.24. 3.E.3. Quid iuris clamat. 4.E.3.28.29. 37.H.6.14. per Moyle. 37.E.3.29.

Here is to be obserued that this iudgement in the Scire facias (which is no more but that the Demandant shall haue execution, &c.) is a good Attornement, albeit it is presumed that Iudiciū redditur in inuitum, & that an Attornement in Law of any part is good for the whole. And this is the fift example that Littleton putteth of an Attornement in Law.

Note that in case of a Deede nothing passeth before Attornement as hath beene said; In the case of the Fine, the thing granted passeth as to the state, but not to distraine, &c. without Attornement. In the case of the King the thing granted doth passe both in estate and in priuity to distraine, &c. without Attornement, unlesse it be of Lands or Tenements that are parcell of the Dutchy of Lancaster, and lye out of the County Palatine.

Item si soit Seignior et tenant, et le tenant tient del Sñr per plusors maners des seruices, et l' Sñr granta les seruices a vn auter per fine, si le grantee sua vn Scire facias hors del mesme le fine pur ascun parcel de les seruices, et ad iudgement de recouer, cel iudgement est bone attornement en ley, pur touts les seruices.

ALso if there bee Lord and tenant, and the tenant holdeth of the Lord by many kinde of seruices, and the Lord grant the seruices to another by fine, if the Grantee sue a *Scire facias* out of the same fine for any parcell of the seruices, and hath iudgement to recouer, this iudgemēt is a good attornement in Law for all the seruices.

Sect. 565.

Item si le Seignior dun rent seruice graunta les seruices a vn auter, et le tenant attorna per vn denier, et puis le grauntee distraine pur le rent arere, et le tenant a luy fait rescous, en ceo cas le grauntee nauera assise del rent, forsque briefe de rescous, pur ceo que le doñ del denier per le tenant, ne fuit forsque per voy dattornement, &c. Mes si le tenant auoit done a le grauntee le dit denier, come parcel de le rent, ou vn malle, ou vn farthing per voy de seisin

ALso if the Lord of a Rent seruice grant the seruices to another, and the tenant attorne by a penny, and after the Grantee distraine for the rent behinde, & the tenant make rescous, In this case the grantee shall not haue an Assise for the rent but a writ of rescouse because the giuing of the penny by the tenant was not but by way of attornement, &c. but if the tenant had giuen to the grantee the said penny as parcell of the rent, or a halfe penny or a farthing by way of seisin of the rent then this

seisin del rent, donque ceo est bone attornement, et auxy est bon seisin al grauntee del rent, et donqz sur tiel rescous le grantee auera assise, &c.

is a good attornement, and also it is a good seisin to the Grantee of the rent, and then vpon such rescous the Grantee shall haue an assise, &c.

HEreupon is to be obserued a diuersity betweene money giuen by way of Attornement, and where it is giuen as parcell of the rent by way of seisin of the rent. For albeit the rent be not due before the day, yet a payment of parcell of the rent before hand is an actuall seisin of the rent to haue an Assise. And so it is if he giue an oxe, a horse, a sheepe, a Knife, or any other valuable thing in name of seisin of the rent beforehand, this is good. And therefore a payment in name of seisin is more beneficiall for the Grantee; because that is both an actuall seisin and an attornement in Law, and yet being giuen before the day in which the rent is due, it shall not be abated out of the rent. So, as to giue seisin of the rent, it is taken for part of the rent, but as to the payment of the rent, it is accounted as no part of the rent, and the reason of the diuersity is for that remedies to come to rights or duties are euer taken fauourably. Here also appeareth that there is an actuall seisin, or a seisin in Deede of a rent, whereof (as Littleton here speaketh) an Assise doth lye; and a seisin in Law which the Grantee hath by Attornement before actuall possession.

39.H.6.3.26. 3.E.4.2. Vid. Sect. 235. 25.E.3.44. 49.E.3.15. 37.H.6.39. 49.Ass.p.6. 34.H.6.42. 15 E.3. Execution 63. 40.E.3.22. 28.H.6.6 b. 7.H.4.2. tit. Attourny Br. 57.

Sect. 566.

ITem si sont pluisors Iointenants que teignont per certaine seruices, et le Seignior graunta a vn auter les seruices, et vn de les Iointenants attorna al grauntee, ceo est auxy bon, sicome touts vssent attorne, pur ceo que le seigniory est entier, &c.

ALso if there bee many Iointenants which hold by certaine seruices, and the Lord grant to another the seruices, and one of the Ioyntenants attorne to the grantee, this is as good as if all had attorned, for that the seigniory is entire, &c.

HEre is to be obserued what manner of Tenants shall attorn to the Grant. And first (b) if there two or more Ioyntenants and one of them attorne it is sufficient, for as it hath beene often said, there cannot bee an Attornement in part. And albeit there is great Authority against Littleton, yet the Law hath beene adiudged according to Littletons opinion, as it hath beene in other of his cases when they haue come in question, and as it is of an Attornement; so it is of a seisin, a seisin of a Rent by the hands of one Ioyntenant is good for all, and a seisin of part of the rent is a good seisin of the whole.

(b) 39.H.6.3.26. See Tookers case vbi supra, and the Authorities there cited.

(c) If either the Grantor or the Grantee die, the Attornement is Countermanded, but if the Tenant die he that hath his estate may attorne at any time. If the Tenant grant ouer his estate, his Assignee may attorne.

(c) Vid lib. 4. fol. 8. lib. 6. fol. 57. lib. 9. fol. 34. Vid. 4.H.6.29. 18.E.4.10.

(d) If an Infant hath lands by purchase or by discent he shall be compelled to attorne in a Per quæ seruitia, and no mischiefe to the Infant, for when he commeth to full age hee may disclaime to hold of him, or he may say that he hold by lesser seruices, but there should be a greater mischiefe for the Lord if the Attornement of an Infant should not be good, for hee should lose his seruices in the meane time.

If an Infant be a Lessee he shall be compelled to attorne in a Quid iuris clamat. The Attornement of an Infant to a grant by Deede is good, and shall binde him, because it is a lawfull act, albeit he be not vpon that grant by Deed compellable to attorne. Of Baron and Feme Littleton putteth many cases in this chapter.

(e) A man that is deafe and dumbe, and yet hath vnderstanding may attorne by signes, (f) but one that is not Compos mentis cannot attorne, for that he that hath no vnderstanding cannot agree to the Grant.

What conueyances shall be good without Attornements more shall be said in this Chapter in his proper place.

(d) 42.E.3. Age 33. 26.E.3.62. 37.H.8. tit. Attorne: Br. 26.E.3.62. 28. Ass. 27. 32.E.3. tit. per quæ seruit. 9. 2.E.2. Autorn. 78. 2.E.2. ibid. 77. 18.H.6.2. Lib. 9. fo. 84. 85 Conyes case, 4. Mar. Dier 137. 21.E.3. Age 85. 7.E.2. Age 140. (e) 26.E.3.63. (f) 18.E.3.53.

Sect. 567.

Item ſi home leſſa tenemẽts a terme dans, per force de quel leaſe le Leſſee eſt ſeiſie, et puis le Leſſor per ſon fait granta le reuerſion a auter pur terme de vie, ou en taile, ou en fee, il couient en tiel caſe que le Tenãt a terme dans attorna, ou autrement rien paſſera a tiel grantee per tiel fait. Et ſi en ceſt caſe le tenant a terme dans atturna al Grantee, donque maintenant paſſera le Franketenement al Grauntee per tiel atturnement ſauns aſcun liuerie de ſeiſin, &c. pur ceo que ſi aſcun liuerie de ſeiſin, &c. ſerra, ou beſoigne deſtre fait en cel caſe, donque le tenant a terme dans ſerroit al temps de liuerie de ſeiſin ouſte de ſon poſſeſſion, le quel ſerroit encounter reaſon, &c.

Alſo if a man letteth tenemẽts for terme of yeares, by force of which Leaſe the Leſſee is ſeiſed, and after the Leſſor by his Deed grant the reuerſion to another for terme of life, or in Taile, or in Fee, it behooueth in ſuch caſe that the Tenant for yeares attorne, or otherwiſe nothing ſhall paſſe to ſuch grantee by ſuch deed. And if in this caſe the Tenaunt for yeares attorne to the Grantee, then the Freehold ſhall preſently paſſe to the Grantee by ſuch attornment without any liuerie of ſeiſin, &c. becauſe if any liuerie of ſeiſin, &c. ſhould be or were needfull to bee made, then the Tenant for yeares ſhould be at the time of the Liuery of ſeiſin ouſted of his poſſeſſion, which ſhould bee againſt reaſon, &c.

Here Littleton hauing ſpoken of Graunts of Seigniories and Rent charges, and Rents ſecke iſſuing out of land, here treateth of a Grant of a Reuerſion of land vpon an eſtate for yeares, ſeeing this grant of the Reuerſion muſt be by Deed, and the agreement of the Leſſee for yeares requiſite thereunto, the Freehold and Inheritance do paſſe thereby, as well as by Liuerie of ſeiſin, if it were in poſſeſſion: and the grant of the reuerſion by Deed with the Attornement of the Leſſee, is counteruaile in Law a Feoffment by Liuerie, as to the paſſing of the Freehold and Inheritance.

(g) 6. E. 3. 53. 25 E. 3. 53. Brook. Tit. Attorn. 48. *A terme dans.* (g) And yet a Tenant by Statute Merchant, or Tenant by Statute Staple, or by Elegit, muſt alſo attorne, for the Grantee may haue a Venue facias ad computandum, or tender the mony, &c. and diſcharge the Land, and if the reuerſion be granted by fine, they ſhall be compelled to attorne in a Quid iuris clamat.

30 E. 3. Scir. fa. 101. Dy. 1. 4. And ſo the Executors that haue the land vntill the debts bee payd, muſt attorne vpon the grant of the Reuerſion, although they haue not any certaine terme for yeares.

Sect. 568.

Item ſi Tenements ſoiẽt leſſes a vn home pur terme de vie, ou done en le taile ſauãt le

Alſo if Tenements be letten to a man for terme of life, or giuen in Taile, ſauing the reuerſion, &c. if hee in

Here Linleton, ſpeaketh of a Reuerſiõ expectant vpon an an eſtate for life, or a gift in Taile.

Il couient que le Tenaunt de la Terre at-

le reuerſion, &c. ſi celuy en le reuerſion en tiel caſe granta le reuerſion a vn auter per ſon fait, il couient que le Tenaunt de la Terre attourna al Grantee en la vie le Grantor, ou auterment, le Graunt eſt voyd.

the reuerſion in ſuch caſe grant the reuerſion to another by his Deed, it behooueth that the Tenant of the Land attorne to the Grauntee in the life of the Grantor, or otherwiſe the Graunt is voyd.

torne al Grauntee, &c. Let vs therefore ſpeake firſt of Tenaunt for life: and yet in ſome caſe albeit Tenaunt for life hath granted ouer his Eſtate, yet he ſhall atturne, (a) as if Tenant in Dower or by the Curteſie, grant ouer his or her eſtate, and the heire grant ouer the reuerſion, the Tenant in Dower or by the Curteſie may atturne, becauſe at the time of the Grant made they were attendant to the heyre in reuerſion, and the Grantee cannot be Tenant in Dower, or Tenant by the Curteſie. And if the Reuerſion bee granted by Fine, the Fine muſt ſuppoſe that the Tenant in Dower or by the Courteſie, did hold the land, albeit they had formerly granted ouer their eſtate, and albeit the Reuerſion doth paſſe by the Fine, yet the Quid iuris clamat muſt be brought againſt him that was Tenant at the time of the note leuied. But yet after the reuerſion is granted ouer, the Grantee ſhall not haue any Action of waſt againſt the Tenant in Dower or by the Curteſie, but the Action of waſt muſt be brought againſt their Aſſignee, and not againſt themſelues, for Tenant by the Curteſie or Tenant in Dower cannot hold of any but of the heire: and therefore in reſpect of the priuitie, they ſhall attorne and be ſubiect to an Action of waſt, as long as the reuerſion remaineth in the heire, albeit they haue granted ouer their whole eſtate. And it is worthie of the obſeruation, that if the grantee of the reuerſion doth bring an action of waſt againſt the aſſignee of the tenant by the curteſie, (b) the pl' muſt rehearſe the ſtat. which prooueth that no prohibition of waſt in that caſe lay at the common law, as it did if the heire had brought it againſt the tenant by the curteſie himſelfe: & therfore ſome doe hold, That if the heire do grant ouer the reuerſion, that the attornment of the Aſſignee of the Tenant by the Curteſie, or of Tenant in Dower is ſufficient, becauſe they afterward muſt be attendant and ſubiect to the Action of waſt.

(a) 10. H. 4. tit. Atturne. 16. 11. H. 4. 18. 30. E. 3. 16. 38. E. 3. 23. 18. E. 3. 3. 10. E. 3. Quid iuris clam. 41. 41. E. 3. 18. Temps E. 1. tit. Waſt, 122.

F. N. B. 55. E. Regiſt. fo. 72. 4. E. 3. 26.

(b) Regiſt. 72.

If the reuerſion of Leſſee for life be granted, and Leſſee for life aſſigne ouer his eſtate, the Leſſee cannot attorne, but the attornement of the Aſſignee is good, becauſe (as Littleton here ſaith) it behooueth that the Tenant of the Land doe attorne, and after the aſſignement there is no tenure or attendance, &c. betweene the Leſſee and him in reuerſion. 18. E. 4. 10. b. 26. B. 3. 62.

If Leſſee for life aſſigneth ouer his eſtate vpon Condition, he hauing nothing in him but a Condition ſhall not attorne, but the Aſſignee may attorne becauſe he is Tenant of the land. 5. H. 5. 10.

Section 569.

¶ En meſm̃ l' maner eſt, ſi terre ſoit done en taile, ou leſſe a vn hõe p̃ terme de vie, le remainder a vn aut̃ en fee, ſi celuy en le remainder voile granter ceſt remaind̃ a vn auter, &c. ſi le tenant de la terr̃ atturna en la vie le Grantor, donques l' grant de tiel rem̃ eſt bon, ou auterment nemy.

IN the ſame manner is it if land be granted in taile, or let to a man for term of life, the remainder to another in fee, if he in the rem̃ wil graunt this remainder to another, &c. if the tenant of the land atterne in the life of the Grantor, then the grãt of ſuch a remainder is good, or otherwiſe not.

¶ Littleton alſo ſpeaketh here of an Attornement by tenant in Taile, and true it is that he may attorne, but where the reuerſion is granted by fine, hee is not cõpellable to attorn, becauſe he hath an eſtate of Inheritance which may continue for euer. And ſo it is of a tenant in taile after poſſibilitie of Iſſue extinct, he ſhall not be compelled to attorne for the Inheritance which was once in him. (c) But if Tenannt in taile after poſſibilitie of Iſſue extinct grant ouer his Eſtate, his Aſſignee ſhal be compelled to attorn, becauſe he neuer had but a bare ſtate for life

12. E. 4. 3. 4. 3. E. 4. 12. 43. E. 3. 1. 46. E. 3. 13.

5. H. 5

20. E. 3. Quid iuris clam. 50.

(c) See the Chap. of Tenant in Taile after poſſibilitie of Iſſue extinct. And Ewins caſe there cited to be adiudged.

But

But as to Tenant in Taile note a diuersitie betweene a *Quid iuris clamat*, and a *Quem redditum reddit*, or a *Per quæ seruicia*; for against a Tenant in Taile, no *Quid iuris clamat* lieth, as is aforesayd. But if a man make a gift in taile, the remainder in fee, and the Seigniorie or Rent charge issuing out of the land be granted by Fine, the Conusee shall maintaine a *Per quæ seruicia*, or a *Quem redditum*, and compell him to attorne, for herein his estate of Inheritance is no priuiledge to him, for that a tenant in Fee simple (as his estate was at the Common law) is also compellable in these cases to attorne.

Section 570.

¶ * P. 12. E. 4. Et la est ten' per tout le Court, que Tenant en Taile ne serra arct datturner, mes sil atturna *gratis*, cest assets bone. *

P. 12. *Edw.* 4. It is there holden by the whole Court, that Tenant in Taile shall not be compelled to attorne, but if he will attorne *gratis*, it is good enough.

12. E. 4. 3. 4. ¶ This is added to Littleton, and therefore though it be good Law, and the Books truly cited, yet I passe it ouer.

Section 571.

¶ ITem si terre soit lesse a vn home pur terme dans, le remainder a vn auter p̄ terme de vie, reseruant al Lessour vn certaine rent per an, et liuerie de seisin sur ceo est fait al tenant p̄ terme dans, si cestuy en le reuersion en cest case granta le reuersion a vn auter, &c. et le tenant que est en le remainder apres le terme dans soy attourna, ceo est bone Attournement, et celuy a que cest reuersion est graunt per force de tiel Attournement destreynera le Tenant a terme dans pur le Rent due ap̄s tiel Attornment, coment que le ten̄t a terme dans ne vnques attournast a luy. Et la cause est, p̄ ceo que lou le reu̇sion est dependant sur lestate del franktenem̄t, suffist que le t̄ del franktenem̄t attourna p̄ tiel Grant del Reu̇sion, &c.

ALso if Land bee let to a man for yeares, the remainder to another for life, reseruing to the Lessor a certaine rent by the yeare, and Liuerie of Seisin vpon this is made to the Tenant for yeares, if hee in the Reuersion in this case grant the Reuersion to another, &c. and the Tenant which is in the Remainder after the terme of yeares attorne, this is a good Attornement, and hee to whome this Reuersion is granted, by force of such Attornement shall distreyne the Tenant for yeares for the Rent due after such Attornement, albeit that the Tenant for yeres did neuer attorne vnto him. And the cause is for that where the Reuersion is depending vpon an estate of Freehold it sufficeth that the Tenant of the Freehold doe attorne vpon such a Grant of the reuersion, &c.

¶ S*uffist que le Tenant del Franktenement attorna.* Note Littlet. saith not here, That the Tenant of the Franktenement ought in this case to attorne, but

that

that it sufficeth that he doth attorne. And I heard Sir Iames Dier Chiefe Iustice of the Common Pleas hold, that in this case if the tenant for yeares did attorn it would vest the reuersion, for seing the estate for yeares is able to support the estate for life, he shall binde him in the remaynder by his Attornement in respect of his estate and priuitie.

Pasch. 15. Eliz. in Brabribches Case in Communi Banco.

Sect. 572.

CEt est ascauoir, que lou vn leas a terme dans, ou a terme de vie ou done en taile est fait a ascun home, reseruant a tiel lessor, ou donor, vn certaine rent, &c. si tiel lessor, ou donor, graunta son reuersion a vn auter, & le tenant del terre attourna, le rent passa al grauntee, coment que en le fait del grant de reuersion nul mention soit fait de le rent, pur ceo que le rent est incident al reuersion en tiel case, & nemy è conuerso, &c. Car si home voile graunter le rent en tiel case a vn auter, reseruant a luy le reuersion del terre, coment que le tenant attorna a le grauntee, ceo serra forsque vn rent secke, &c.

AND it is to be vnderstood, that where a lease for yeares or for life, or a gift in taile is made to any man reseruing to such Lessor or Donor a certaine rent, &c. if such Lessor or Donor grant his Reuersion to another, & the tenant of the land attorne, the rent passeth to the Grantee, although that in the deed of the grant of the Reuersion no mention be made of the rent, for that the Rent is incident to the Reuersion in such case, and not *è conuerso, &c.* For if a man will grant the rent in such case to another, reseruing to him the Reuersion of the Land, albeit the Tenant attorne to the grantee, this shall bee but a Rent secke, &c.

Of this Littleton hath spoken before in the Chapter of Rents.

Section 573.

ITem si home lessa terre a vn auter pur term de sa vie & puis il confirma per son fait lestate del tenant a term de vie, le remainder a vn auter en fee, & le tenant a terme de vie accepta le fait, donques est le remainder en fait en celuy a que le remainder est done ou limitte per mesme le fait, car per lacceptance del tenant a term de vie de le fait, ceo est vn agreement de luy, & issint vn attornement en ley. Mes vncore celuy en le remainder nauera ascun action

ALso if a man let land to another for his life, and after hee confirme by his Deed the estate of the Tenant for life, the remaynder to another in fee, and the Tenant for life accepteth the Deed, then is the remaynder in fait in him to whom the remaynder is giuen, or limited by the same Deed. For by the acceptance of the Tenant for life of the deed, this is an agreement of him, and so an Attornement in Law. But yet hee in the remaynder shall not haue any acti-

tion de waste, ne auter benefit per tiel remainder, si non que il auoit le dit fait en poigne, per que l' remainder fuit taile ou graunt a luy. Et pur ceo que en tiel cas l' tenant a term de vie voile p cas reteigner le fait a luy, a cel entent que celuy en le remainder naueroit ascun action d' waste enuers luy, pur ceo que il ne poit vener dauer le fait e sa possession, il serra bone & sure chose en tiel cas pur celuy en le remaynder, que vn fait endent soit fait per celuy que voile faire tiel confirmation, & le remaynder ouster, &c. & que celuy que fait tiel confirmation deliuera vn part del Indenture al tenant a terme de vie, & le auter part a celuy que auera le remainder. Et donque il per monstrance de le part del endenture, poit auer action de wast enuers le tenant a terme de vie, & touts auters aduantages que celuy en le remainder poit auer en tiel case, &c.

on of Waste nor other benefit by such remaynder vnlesse that hee hath the said Deed in hand whereby the remaynder was entayled or granted to him. And because that in such case the Tenant for life peraduenture will retaine the Deed to him to this intent that he in the remaynder should not haue any Action of Waste against him for that hee cannot come to haue the Deed in his possession it will bee a good and sure thing in such case for him in the remaynder, that a Deed indented bee made by him which will make such Confirmation, and the remaynder ouer, &c. and that hee which maketh such Confirmation deliuer one part of the Indenture to the Tenant for life, and the other part to him that shall haue the remaynder. And then he by shewing of that part of the Indenture may haue an Action of Waste against the tenant for life and all other aduantages that he in the remainder may haue in such a case, &c.

Vide Sect. 525. 575.
Vide Pl. Com. in Colthirsts Case. Doct. & Stud. cap. 20. fol. 93. 94.
8. R. 2. in waste in Liure of entrie 17. E. 3. confirmat. 4.

¶ Here Littleton putteth a case of a remaynder whereunto an Attornement is requisite. And this is the first example of an Attornement in Law.

¶ *Remaynder a vn auter, &c.* Of this sufficient hath been said in the Chapter of Confirmation. Sect. 525.

35. H. 6. fol. 8. 14. H. 8. Pl. Com. 149. in Throckmortons case. 45. E. 3. 14. 15. 21. H. 4. 39. 14. H. 4. 31.

¶ *Si non que il auoit le fait en poigne.* And albeit he hath no remedie to come to the Deed during the life of Tenant for life, yet because hee is priuy in estate hee shall not maintaine an Action of waste without shewing the Deed, but when the remaynder is once executed, he shall not need to shew the Deed.

¶ *Il serra bone & suer chose, &c.* Hereby it appeareth how necessary it is to vse learned aduice in a mans Conueyance, for thereby shall bee preuented many questions, and not to follow the aduice of him that is experimented only. For as in Physicke, Nullum medicamentum est idem omnibus, so in Law one forme or president of Conueyance will not fit all cases.

Sect. 574.

¶ Item si deux Joyntenants sont, &c. que leffont lour terr a un auter pur terme de vie, rendant a eux & a lour heires certaine rent per an, en cest case si un des Joyntenants en le reuersion, relessa a lauter Joyntenant en mesme le reuersion, cest releas est bone, & celuy a que le releas est fait, auera solement le rent del tenant a terme de vie, & auera solement un briefe de waste enuers luy coment que il ne unques attorneroit per force de tiel releas, &c. Et la cause est pur le privity que un foits fuit perenter le tenant a terme de vie, & eux en le reuersion.

Also if two Ioyntenants bee who let their Land to another for tearme of life rendring to them and to their heires a certaine yearely rent. In this case if one of the Ioyntenants in the reuersion release to the other Ioyntenant in the same reuersion this release is good, and he to whom the release is made shall haue only the rent of the Tenant for life, and shall only haue a Writ of Waste against him although hee neuer attorned by force of such release, &c. And the reason is for the priuitie which once was betweene the Tenant for life and them in the reuersion.

¶ *Deux Iointenants.* And so it is (as it is here to be understood) albeit there bee three or more Joyntenants, and one of them releaseth to one of the other.

It is true that there is a difference betweene these releases, for the Release in the one case maketh no degree, but hee to whom the Release is made is supposed in from the first Feoffor, and in the other it worketh a degree, and hee to whom the Release is made is in the per by him; yet in neyther of these cases there is requisite any Attornement, for both of them are within Littletons reason (for the privitie, &c.)

¶ *Pur le priuitie, &c.* For if one Joyntenant make a Lease for yeares reserving a Rent and dieth, the Survivor shall not have the Rent, and therefore Littleton here addeth materially for the privity that was betweene the Tenant for life and them in the reuersion. *2 Eliz. Dier. 176.*

And here it is good to bee seene what grantors or others that make Conueyances, &c. are such as their Grants or Conueyances are either good without Attornement; or where the Tenant is no way compellable to attorn. Tenant for life shall not bee compelled to attorne in a quid iuris clamat upon a grant of a reuersion by fine holden of the King in Chiefe without licence, but the reason hereof is not because the Tenant for life might be charged with the fine, for his estate was more ancient then the fine leuied, but because the Court will not suffer a preiudice to the King, and the King may seise the reuersion and rent, and so the Tenant shall be attendant to another. Also it is a generall rule that when the grant by fine is defeasible, there the Tenant shall not bee compelled to attorne. *45. E. 3. 6. b. 13. Eliz. Dier 188. Lib. 3. fol. 86. Iustice Windhams case. 36. H. 6. 24.*

As if an Infant leuie a fine, this is defeasible by writ of Error during his minoritie, and therefore the Tenant shall not be compelled to attorne.

So if the Land be holden in ancient Demesne, and hee in the reuersion leuieth a fine of the reuersion at the Common Law, the Tenant shall not be compellable to attorne, because the estate that passed is reuersible in a writ of Deceit. *5. E. 3. 25. 31. E. 3. Ancient Demesne 16.*

So if Tenant in tayle had leuied a fine, the Tenant should not be compelled to attorne, because it was defeasible by the issue in tayle. *24. E. 3. 25. b. 37. H. 6. 33. 48. E. 3. 23.*

But now the Statutes of 4. H. 7. and 32 H. 8. hauing giuen a further strength to fines to barre the issue in tayle, the reason of the Common Law being taken away, the Tenant in this case shall be compelled to attorne, as it was adiudged (*) in Iustice Windhams Case. *(*) Lib. 3. fol. 86. Iustice Windhams case.*

If an alienation be in Mortmaine the Tenant shall not bee compelled to attorne because the Lord Paramont may defeat it. *17. E. 3. 7. 22. E. 3. 18.*

Sect. 575.

¶ EN mesme le maner, & pur mesme la cause est, lou home lessa terre a vn auter pur terme de vie, le remainder a vn auter pur terme de vie, reseruant le reuersion al lessour, en cest cas si celuy en le reuersion relessa a celuy en le remainder et a ses heires touit son droit, &c. donques celuy en le remainder ad vn fee, &c. et il auera vn briefe de Wast enuers le tenant a terme de vie sans ascun attornement de luy, &c.

IN the same manner, and for the same cause is it, where a man letteth land to another for life, the remainder to another for life, reseruing the reuersion to the lessor, in this case if hee in the reuersion releaseth to him in the remainder and to his heires all his right, &c. Then he in the remainder hath a fee, &c. and hee shall haue a writ of Waste against the tenant for life without any attornement of him, &c.

Vid. Sect. 549. 553. 556.

This needeth no explication.

Section 576. 577.

¶ ITem si home lessa terres ou tenements a vn auter pur terme des ans, et puis il oust a son termour, et ent enfeoffa vn auter en fee, et puis le tenant a terme dans enter sur le feoffee, enclaimant son terme, &c. et puis fait wast, en cest case le feoffee auera per la ley vn briefe de wast enuers luy, et uncore il nattornast pas a luy. Et la cause est, come jeo suppose, pur ceo que celuy que ad droit de auer terres ou tenements pur term dans, ou auterment, ne seroit per la ley misconusant de les feoffments que fueront faits de

ALso if a man lett lands or tenements to another for terme of yeares, and after he oust his termor, and thereof enfeoffe another in fee, and after the tenant for yeares enter vpon the feoffee, clayming his term, &c. and after doth waste, in this case the feoffee shall haue by law a writ of Waste against him, and yet hee did not attorne vnto him. And the cause is as I suppose, for that he which hath right to haue lands or tenements for yeares, or otherwise should not by lawe bee misconusant of the feoffments which were made of and vpon the same

¶ THere haue beene now in all seuen examples, that Littleton putteth of an Attornement in Law, And here he putteth two cases also of a notice in Law. And the reason of both these are here rendred by Littleton. First for the notice Littleton saith that the Lessee shall not by Law be misconusant of the Feoffments that were made of and vpon the same land. And the reason of the Attornement is because the whole fee simple passeth by the Feoffment, and the Lessee by his regresse leaueth the reuersion in the Feoffee which saith Littleton is a good Attornement. The same Law it is of a Tenant by Statute Merchant or Staple, or Elegit. And so it is of a Lease for life, as Littleton here saith, and so it was resolued (c) in Brasbritches case, and after in the Deane of Pauls his case in the

46. E. 3. 30. b. 2. H. 5. 4. 5. H. 5. 12. 34. H. 6. 6. 28. E. 3. 47. 9. H. 6. 10.

(c) Brasbritches case T. 15. Eliz. Deane of Pauls case 30. Eliz.

de et sur mesmes les terres, &c. et entant que per tiel feoffment le tenant a terme dans fuit mis hors de son possession, et per son entre il causast le reuersion destre a celuy a que le feoffment fuit fait, ceo est bon attornement, car celuy a que le feoffment fuit fait, auoit nul reuersion deuaunt que le tenant a terme dans auoit enter sur luy, pur ceo que il fuit en possession en son demesne come de fee, et per lent del tenant a term dans il y ad forsque vn reuersion, quel est per le fait l'ten a term dans, s. per son entrie, &c.

lands, &c. and inasmuch as by such feoffment the tenant for yeares was put out of his possession, and by his entrie he caused the reuersion to bee to him to whom the feoffment was made, this is a good attornement, for hee to whom the feoffment was made had no reuersion before the tenant for yeares had entred vpon him for that he was in possession in his demesne as of fee, and by the entrie of the tenant for yeares, hee hath but a reuersion, which is by the act of the tenant for yeares, s. by his entrie, &c.

Sect. 577.

Mesme la ley est, come il semble, lou vn Leas est fait pur terme de vie, sauant le reuersion al Lessour, si le Lessour disseisist le Lessee, & fait feoffment en fee, si le tenant a terme de vie enter et fait wast, le feoffee auera briefe de waste sans ascun auter attournement, Causa qua supra, &c.

THe same Law is, as it seemeth where a Lease is made for life, sauing the reuersion to the Lessor if the Lessor disseise the Lessee, and make a feoffment in fee, if the tenant for life enter and make waste the Feoffee shall haue a writ of waste without any other attornement, *Causa qua supra, &c.*

Common place. But shall the Lessee in this case whether hee will or no doe an act that amount to an Attornement, viz. by his regresse or else lose the profit of his land? And some doe hold that in that case if the Lessee for life doe recouer in an Assise, this is no Attornement, because hee come to it by course of Law, and not by his voluntary act. And yet in that case as in the case of the fine the state of the reuersion is in the Feoffee. (f) But others doe hold it all one in case of a recouery, and a regresse.

(g) If the Lessor disseise Tenant for life or ouste Tenant for years, and maketh a feoffment in fee, by this the rent reserued vpon the Lease for life or yeares is not extinguished, but by the regresse of the Lessee the rent is reuiued, because it is incident to the reuersion: and so hath it beene adiudged. But if a man be seised of a rent in fee, and disseise the Tenant of the land, and make a feoffment in fee, the Tenant re-entreth, this rent is not reuiued; And so note a diuersity betweene a rent incident to a reuersion, and a rent not incidēt to a reuersiō.

If two ioynt Lessees for yeares or for life bee ousted or disseised by the Lessor, and he enfeoffe another, if one of the Lessees re-enter this is a good Attornement, and shall binde both, for an Attornement in law is as strong as an Attornement in Deed.

34.H.6.7.

(f) 18.E.3.48 b. Lib 6.fo.60.b. Sir Moyle Finches case.

(g) 9 H.6.16. Deane of Pauls case, Vbi supra.

If a man make a Lease for life, and then grant the reuersion for life and the Lessee attorne, and after the Lessor disseise the Lessee for life, and make a feoffment in fee, & the Lessee re-enter, this shall leaue a reuersion in the Grantee for life, and another reuersion in the Feoffee, and yet this is no Attornement in Law of the Grantee for life, because he doth no act, nor assent to any which might amount to an Attornement in Law. Et res inter alios acta alteri nocere non debet. Neither hath the Grantee for life the land in possession, so as he may well be misconusant of the feoffment made vpon the Land, and so out of the reason of Littleton, But yet the reuersion in fee doth passe to the Feoffee.

Section 578.

¶ ITem si leas soit fait pur terme de vie, le remainder a un auter en le Taile, le remaind ouster a les droit heires le tenant a terme de vie. En cest case si le tenant a terme de vie granta son remainder en fee a auter per son Fait, cel remainder maintenant passa per le fait sans ascun Attournment, &c. Car si ascun doit attorne en cest case, ceo serroit le tenant a terme de vie, et en vain serroit que il atturneroit sur s grant demesne, &c.

ALso if a Lease be made for life, the remainder to another in Taile, the remainder ouer to the right heirs of the Tenant for life: In this case if the Tenant for life grant his Remainder in fee to another by his Deede, this Remainder maintenant passeth by the Deede without any Attournement, &c. for that if any ought to attourne in this case, it should be the Tenaunt for life, and in vaine it were that he should attorne vpon his owne Grant, &c.

¶ HEere it appeareth, that where the Ancestor taketh an Estate of Freehold, and after a Remainder is limited to his right Heires, that the Fee simple vesteth in himselfe, as well as if it had beene limited to him and his heires, for his right heires are in this case words of limitation of estate, and not of purchase. Otherwise it is where the Auncestor taketh but an estate for yeares: As if a Lease for yeares be made to A. the remainder to B. in Tayle, the remainder to the right heires of A. there the remainder vesteth not in A. but the right heires shall take by purchase if A. die during the estate Taile, for as the Auncestor and the Heyre are Correlatiua of Inheritances, so are the Testator and Executor, or the Intestate and Administratour of Chattels. And so it is if A. make a Feoffement in Fee to the vse of B. for life, and after to the vse of C. for life or in Taile, and after to the vse of the right heirs of B. B. hath the Fee simple in him as well when it is by way of limitation of vse, as when it is by Act executed.

Vi. Sect. 194. 273. ¶ *En vaine serroit, &c.* Quod vanum & inutile est Lex non requirit. Lex est ratio summa, quæ iubet quæ sunt vtilia & necessaria, & contraria prohibet, and arguments drawne from hence are forcible in Law.

Sect. 579.

¶ ITem si soit Seignior et tenant, et le Tenant tient del Seignior per certaine rent, et service de chiualer, si le Seignior granta les seruices de son tenant per fine, les seruices sont maintenant en le grantee per force del fine, mes uncore le Seignior ne poet pas distreyne pur ascun parcel de les seruices sans attournment: Mes si le tenant deuia (son heire deins age) le Seignior auera le gard del corps

ALso if there be Lord and Tenant, and the Tenant holdeth of the Lord by certaine Rent and Knights seruice, if the Lord grant the seruices of his Tenant by fine, the seruices are presently in the Grantee by force of the Fine: but yet the Lord may not distreine for any parcell of the seruices, without Attornement. But if the Tenant dieth, his heire within age, the Lord shall haue the Wardship

corps del heire, et de ses terres, &c. coment que il ne unques attur-nast, pur ceo que le Seigniorie fuit en le grantee maintenant per force del fine. Et auxy en tiel cas, si le tenant morust sans heire, le Seignior auera les tenements per voy deschear.

of the bodie of the heire, and of his lands, &c. albeit he neuer attorned, because that the Seigniorie was in the Grauntee presently by force of the Fine. And also in such case if the Tenaunt die without Heire, the Lord shall haue the Tenancie by way of Escheat.

¶ HEere Littleton beginneth to shew what aduantages the Conusee of a Fine may take before Attornement, and what not.

(h) First, hee cannot distreyne because an Auowrie is in lieu of an Action, and thereunto priuitie is requisite. So likewise, and for the same cause hee can haue no Action of Wast, nor Writ of Entrie, ad Communem legem, or in Consimili casu, or in casu prouiso, Writ of Customes and Seruices, nor Writ of Ward, &c.

(h) 8.E.3.44. 26.E.3.63. 10.H.6.16.34.H.6.7. 12.E.4.4. 40.E.3.7. 5.H.5.12 48.E.3.15.b. 3.E.2. Droit 33.

But if a man make a Lease for yeares, and grant the reuersion by fine, if the Lessee bee ousted, and the Conusee disseised, the Conusee without Attornement shall maintaine an Assise, for this Writ is maintained against a stranger, where there needeth no priuitie. And such things as the Lord may seise or enter into without suing any Action, there the Conusee before any Attornment may take benefit thereof, as to seise a Ward or Heriot, or to enter into the lands or tenements of a Ward, or escheated to him, or to enter for an alienation of Tenant for life or yeares, or of Tenant by Statute Merchant, Staple, or Elegit, to his disherison.

Sect. 580. 581. 582.

¶ EN mesme le manner est, si hõe granta le reuersion de son tenaunt a terme de vie a un auter per fine, le reuersion passa maintenant al Grantee per force del fine, mes le grantee iammes nauera Actiõ de wast sans atturnment, &c.

IN the same manner it is, if a man graunt the reuersion of his Tenant for life, to another by fine, the reuersion maintenant passeth to the Grantee by force of the fine, but the Grauntee shall neuer haue an Action of Wast withont Attornment, &c.

Sect. 581.

¶ MEs uncore si le Tenant a terme de vie alienast en fee, le grantee poet enter, &c. pur ceo que le reuersion fuit en luy per force del Fine, et tiel alienation fuit a son disheritance.

BVt yet if the tenant for life alieneth in fee, the Grantee may enter, &c. because the Reuersion was in him by force of the fine, and such Alienation was to his disheritance.

¶ IT is sayd in our books, That if Tenant for life haue a priuiledge not to be impeachable of wast, or any other priuiledge, if hee doth attorne without sauing his priuiledge, that hee hath lost it; which is so to bee vnderstood, where he attornes in a Quid iuris clamat brought by the Conusee of a fine, that if he claimeth not his Priuiledge, but attorne generally, his priuiledge is lost, for that the Writ supposeth him to bee but a bare Tenant for life, and by his generall Attornement according to the Writ he is barred for euer to claime any priuiledge but a bare Estate for life. But if vpon a grant of the reuersion by deed, the Tenaunt for life doth attorne, hee loseth no priuiledge, for there can be no conclusion or barre by the Attornement in paijs: and so it is of an Attornement in Law. As if the Lessor disseise the Lessee for life, and make a Feoffement in Fee, and the Lessee re-enter, this is an attornment in law, which shall not preiudice him

40.E.3.7.43.E.3.5. 48.E.3.32.45.E.3.6. 21.E.3.48. 24.E.3.32. 39.H.6.25. F.N.B.136.b.

Sect.

of any priuiledge: so it is if the Lessor leuie a Fine of the reuersion, and the Conusee die without heire, whereby the Reuersion escheateth, in this case the Law doth supply an Attornment, and therefore the Lessee shall lose no priuiledge. But in the Quid iuris clamat, if the Lessee shew his estate and his priuiledge, and is readie, sauing to him his priuiledge, &c. to attorne, hereby either his priuiledge shall bee allowed and entred of record, or he shall not be compelled to attorne: (b) and if the plaintife bee within age, so as hee cannot acknowledge the priuiledge, the tenant shal not bee compelled to attorne vntil his full age, when hee may acknowledge it. But otherwise it is, (as some hold) if a Quid iuris clamat bee brought by Baron and Feme, the priuiledge shall be entred into the Rolle notwithstanding she is a Feme Couert. And in a Per quæ seruicia brought by the Conusee of the Mesne, the Tenant may shew that he held by homage Auncestrell, and sauing to him his Warrantie and acquitall, he is readie to attorne. In the same manner, if the Tenaunt hath any other acquitall, and the Mesne leuie a Fine to one for life, the remainder to another in Fee, the Tenant for life bringeth a Per quæ seruicia, and the Tenant is readie to attorne sauing his acquitall, and the Plaintif acknowledgeth it, and thereupon the tenant attorne, tenant for life dieth; in this case albeit regularly the Attornement to the Tenant for life is an Attornement to him in the Remainder, yet in this case hee in the remainder shall not distreyn, til he hath acknowledged the acquitall, which must be in a Per quæ seruicia brought by him against the Tenant.

(b) 43. E. 3. 9.

45. E. 3. 11. a. Vet. N. B. in Per quæ seruicia. 5. E. 3. Mesne 56. & Per quæ seruicia 16. 37. H. 6. 33. 39. H. 6. 25. 18. E. 4. 7.

Vi. Sect. 557.

Sect. 582.

¶ MEs en cest cas lou le Seignior granta les seruices de son Tenant per fine, si Tenant deuie (son heire esteant de plein age) le Grantee per le fine nauera reliefe, ne vnques distreynera pur reliefe, sinon que il auoit lattornement del Tenaunt que morust, car de tiel chose que gist en distresse, sur que le Briefe de Repleuin est sue, &c. home doit & couient dauower le prisel bon et droiturel, &c. et la couient estre attornment del Tenant, coment que le graunt de tiel chose soit per fine, mes dauer le gard de les terres ou tenements issint tenus durant le nonage lheire, ou de eux auer per voy descheat, la ne besoigne ascun distresse, &c. mes vn entrie en la terre per force de le droit del seigniory que le grantee ad per force del Fine, &c. Sic vide diuersitatem.

BVt in this case where the Lord granteth the seruices of his Tenant by fine, if the Tenant die (his heire being of ful age) the grantee by the fine shall not haue reliefe, nor shall euer distreine for reliefe, vnlesse that hee hath the Attornement of the Tenaunt that dieth: for of such a thing which lieth in Distresse, whereupon the Writ of Repleuin is sued, &c. a man must and ought to auow the taking good & rightful, &c. and there there ought to be an attornment of the tenant, although the graunt of such a thing be by fine. But to haue the wardship of the lands or tenements so holden during the nonage of the heire, or to haue them by way of escheat, there needs no distresse, &c. but an entrie into the land by force of the right of the Seigniorie, which the Grauntee hath by force of the fine, &c. *Sic vide diuersitatem, &c.*

¶ *Alien enfee, &c.* Of this sufficient hath been sayd in the next precedent Section.

¶ *Nauera reliefe, &c.* Of this sufficient hath been said in the next precedent Section.

Sect. 583.

¶ ITem si soit Seignior, mesne & tenant, & le mesne graunta per fine les seruices de son tenāt a vn auter en fee, & puis le grantee morust sans heire, ore les seruices del mesnaltie deuiendront & escheate al Seignior Paramont per voy descheat, & si apres les seruices del mesnaltie sont aderere, en cest cas celuy que fuit Seignior Paramont poit distreiner le tenant, nient obstant que le tenant ne vnques atturnast, et le cause est, pur ceo que le mesnaltie fuit en fait en le grantee per force de le dit fine, & le Seignior Paramont puissoit auower sur le grauntee, pur ceo que il fuit son tenant en fait, coment que il ne serroit a ceo compelle, &c. Mes si le grantor en cest case deuiast sans heire en la vie le grantee, donque il serroit compelle dauower sur le grantee, et auxy entant que le Seigniour Paramont ne claime le mesnaltie per force del graunt fait per fine leuie per le mesne, mes per vertue de son Seigniorie Paramont, s. per voy descheat, il auowa sur le tenant pur les seruices que le mesne auoit, &c. coment que le tenant ne vnques atturna pas.

ALso if there be Lord, Mesne and Tenant, and the Mesne grant by fine the seruices of his Tenant to another in fee, and after the grantee die without heire, now the seruices of the mesnaltie shall come and escheate to the Lord Paramont by way of escheate. And if afterwards the seruices of the Mesnaltie bee behind. In this case hee which was Lord Paramont may distreine the Tenant, notwithstanding that the Tenant did neuer attorne, and the cause is, for that the Mesnaltie was in deed in the Grantee by force of the said fine, and the Lord Paramont may auow vpon the Grantee because in deed hee was his Tenant, albeit hee shall not be compelled to this, &c. But if the Grantor in this case had died without heire in the life of the Grantee, then he should bee compelled to auow vpon the Grantee and also in as much the Lord Paramont doth not claime the Mesnaltie by force of the grant made by fine leuied by the Mesne but by vertue of his Seigniorie Paramount, *viz.* by way of escheat he shall auow vpon the Tenant for the seruices which the mesne had, &c. albeit that the Tenant did neuer attorne.

HEre Littleton putteth a Case where one that claymeth vnder a Conusee by fine may distraine or maintaine any Action, albeit there was neuer any Attornement made to the Conusee or to him that hath his estate. *45.E.3.2. 34.H.6.9. 37.H.6.38. 39.H.6.32. 5.H.7.18. per Curiam.*

And here is a diuersitie betweene an act in Law that giueth one Inheritance in liew of another, and an Act in Law that conueyeth the estate of the Conusee only. Of the former Littleton here putteth an example of the escheat of the Mesnaltie which drowneth the Seigniory Paramont, and therefore reason would that the Lord by this act in Law should haue as much benefit of the Mesnaltie escheated, as he had of the Seigniory that is drowned, and the rather for that the Law casteth it vpon him, and hee hath no remedie to compell the Tenant to *Lib.6.fol.68. Sir Moyle Finches case.*

attorne. Another reason hereof Littleton here preldeth, because the Lord commeth to the Mesnaltie by a Seigniorie Paramont, and therefore there needeth no Attornement (c) As if Lessee for life be of a Mannor, and he surrender his estate to the Lessor there needeth no Attornement of the Tenants because the Lessor is in by a title Paramount. But if the Conusee dieth, and the Law casteth his Seigniory upon his heire by discent, he shall not be in any better estate, then his Ancestor was, because he claymeth as heire meerely by the Conusee.

(c) Temps E. 2. Attorn. 18. 39. H. 6. 38. per Prisot.

So it is (as hath beene said) if the Conusee of a fine before Attornement bargaineth and selleth the Seigniory by Deed indented and inrolled, the Barganee shall not distraine because the Bargainor, from whom the Seigniory moueth, had neuer actuall possession.

Sir Moyle Finches case, vbi supra.

So and for the same reason if a Reuersion be granted by fine, and the Conusee before Attornement disseise the Tenant for life and make a feoffment in fee, and the Lessee re-enter, the feoffee shall not distraine.

Sect. 584.

EN mesme le maner est, lou le reuersion dun tenant a terme de vie soit grant per fine a vn auter en fee, & le grantee apres morust sans heire, ore le Seignior ad le reuersion p voy de escheat. Et si apres le tenant fait wast, le Seignior auera briefe de wast enuers luy, nient contristeant que il ne vnques atturna, Causa qua supra. Mes lou vn home claime per force del graunt fait per le fine, s. come heire, ou com assignee, &c. la il ne distreinera ne auowera, ne auera action de wast, &c. sans Attornement.

IN the same manner it is where the reuersion of a Tenant for life is granted by fine to another in fee, and the grantee afterwards dieth without heire, now the Lord hath the reuersion by way of escheate, and if after the Tenant maketh waste, the Lord shall haue a Writ of Waste against him, notwithstanding that he neuer attorned, *Causa qua supra.* But where a man claimeth by force of the grant made by the fine .s. as heire or as assignee, &c. there hee shall not distraine nor auowe, nor haue an action of waste, &c. without Attornement.

Here Littleton expresseth two diuersities, first betweene an act in law, and the grant of the partie. This case is put of an (d) escheate, which is a meere act in Law, but so it is, when it is partly by Act in Law, and partly by the Act of the partie, as if the Conusee of a Statute Merchant extendeth a Seigniory or Rent, hee shall distreine without any Attornement. If a man make a Lease for life or yeares, and after leuie a fine to A. to the vse of B. and his heires. B. shall distraine and haue an Action of waste albeit the Conusee neuer had any Attornement because the reuersion is vested in him by force of the Statute, and hath no remedie to compell the Lessee to attorne.

(d) 45. E. 3. 2. 34. H. 6. 7. 5. H. 7. 18. per Curiam.

13 H. 4. auowrie 237.

Lib. 6. fol. 68. in Sir Moyle Finches case.

27. H. 8. cap. 10.

And so it is of a bargaine and sale by Deed indented and inrolled, but this is by force of a Statute since Littleton wrote.

Secondly, where he that commeth in by Act in Law is in the per, as the heire of the Conusee, who setteth in his Ancestors seat, Tanquam pars antecessoris de sanguine, and the Lord by escheate, which is an estranger, and commeth in meerely in the Post.

Section 585.

ITem en ancient Boroughs & Cities, lou terres & tenements

ALso in ancient Boroughes and Cities, where Lands and Te-

ments deins mesmes les boroughes et Cities sont deuisable per testament per custome et use &c. si en tiel borough ou citie hōe soit seisie de rent seruice, ou de rent charge, et deuisa cel rent ou seruice a un auter per son testament et mourust, en cest cas celuy a que tiel deuise est fait, poit distreiner le tenant pur le rent ou seruice aderere, coment que le tenant nattorna pas.

nements within the same Boroughes and Cities are deuisable by testament by custome and vse, &c. if in such Borough or Citie a man be seised of a rent seruice, or of a rent charge, and deuiseth such rent or seruice to another by his testament and dieth, In this case he to whom such deuise is made may distreine the tenant for the rent or seruice arere, although the tenant did neuer attorne.

¶ Here doth Littleton put a case where a man may haue a Seigniory, Rent, Reuersion, or Remainder meerely by the act of the party and may distraine, and haue any action without any Attornement, and that is by deuise of lands deuisable by custome when Littleton wrote by the last will and Testament of the owner. 34. H. 6. 6. 5. H. 7. 18. 19 H. 6. 24. 21. H. 6. 38, a. F. N. B. 121. a.

Sect. 586.

¶ En mesme le maner est lou home lessa tiels tenements deuisables a un auter pur terme de vie, ou pur terme dans, et deuisa le reuersion per son testamēt a un auter en fee, ou en fee taile et mourust, et puis le tenant fait wast, celuy a que le deuise fuit fait auera briefe de wast, coment que le tenant ne unque attorna. Et la cause est pur ceo, que la volunt le deuisour fait per son testament serra performe solonque lentent del deuisour, et si leffect de ceo girroit sur lattournement del tenant, donques per case le tenant ne voyle unques atturner, et donques le volunt del deuisor ne serroit unque performe, &c. et pur ceo le deuisee distreinera, &c. ou auera action de wast, &c. sans attournment. Car si home deuisa tiels tenements a un auter per son testament, Habend' sibi imperpetuum, & mourust, et le deuisee enter, il ad fee simple,

IN the same manner is it, where a man letteth such tenements deuisable to another for life, or for yeares, and deuiseth the reuersion by his Testament to another in fee, or in fee taile, and dyeth, and after the Tenant commits waste, he to whom the deuise was made shall haue a writ of waste, although the Tenant doth neuer attorne. And the reason is for that the will of the Deuisor made by his Testament shall bee performed according to the intent of the Deuisor, and if the effect of this should lye vpon the Attornement of the Tenant, then perchance the Tenant would neuer attorne, and then the will of the deuisor should neuer bee performed, &c. and for this the deuisee shall distraine, &c. or he shall haue an action of waste, &c. without attornement. For if a man deuiseth such tenements to another by his testament, *Habend' sibi imperpetuum*, & dieth, and the deuisee

ple, Causa qua supra, uncore si fait de feoffment vst este fait a luy per le deuisor en sa vie de mesmes les tenements, Habend' sibi imperpetuum, et liuery de seisin sur ceo fuit fait, il naueroit estate forsque pur terme de sa vie.

uisee enter, hee hath a fee simple, *Causa qua supra*, yet if a deed of feoffment had beene made to him by the deuisor of the same tenements, *Habend' sibi imperpetuum*, & liuery of seisin were made vpon this hee should haue an estate but for terme of his life.

¶ Both this and the precedent case stand vpon one and the same reason which Littleton here yeeldeth, viz. because that the will of the Deuisor expressed by his Testament shall be performed according to the intent of the Deuisor, and it shall not lye in the power of the Tenant or Lessee to frustrate the will of the Deuisor by denying his Attornement, here Littleton mentioneth a maxime of the Common Law, viz. Quod vltima voluntas testatoris est perimplenda secundum veram intentionem suam, and reipublicæ interest suprema hominum testamenta rata haberi.

Vid. Sect. 167. Bracton. lib. 1. fol. 11. & fo. 60. Fleta. lib. 2. ca. 15. Britton, fol. 78. & fo. 212. b.

¶ *Testament*. Testamentum .i. testatio mentis, which is made nullo presentis metu periculi sed sola cogitatione mortalitatis. Omne testamentũ morte consummatũ.

¶ *Car si home deuisa tiels tenements a vn auter, &c.* Here Littleton putteth a case where the entent of the Testator shall be taken, viz. where a man by deuise shall haue a fee simple without these words heires, and here Littleton putteth the diuersity betweene a will and a feoffment.

41. E. 3. 16. 34. H. 6. 7. 15. H. 7. 12. 19. H. 8. 4.

Now by the Statutes of 32. and 34. H. 8. (as hath beene said in the chapter of Burgage) Lands, Tenements and Hereditaments are deuisable, as by the said Acts doe appeare.

Vid. Sect. 167.

Sect. 587.

¶ Item si home seisie dun mannor quel est parcel en demesñ et parcel en seruice, et ent soit disseisie, mes les tenants que teignont del mannor ne vnques attournant a le Disseisor, en cest cas coment que le Disseisor morust seisie et son heire soit eins per discent, &c. uncore poit le Disseisee distreine pur le rent arere, et auer les seruices, &c. Mes si les tenants viendront al Disseisor, et diont, nous deveignomus vostre tenants, &c. ou auter attournement a luy fesoyent, &c. et puis le Disseisor morust seisie, donque le Disseisee ne poit distreine pur le rent, &c. pur ceo que tout le manor discendist al heire le Disseisor, &c.

Also if a man bee seised of a mannor which is parcell in demesne and parcell in seruice, and is thereof disseised, but the tenants which hold of the mannor doe neuer attorne to the Disseisor. In this case albeit the Disseisor dieth seised, and his heire is in by discent, &c. yet may the Disseisee distreine for the rent behinde, and haue the seruices, &c. but if the tenants come to the Disseisor and say, We become your tenants, &c. or make to him some other attornement, &c. and after the Disseisor dieth seised, then the Disseisee cannot distraine for the rent, &c. for that all the Mannor discendeth to the heire of the Disseisor, &c.

¶ Littleton hauing spoken of estates gained by lawfull conueyances doth now speake of estates gained by wrong. And here putteth a case of a disseisin of a Mannor where it appeareth, that the Disseisor cannot disseise the Lord of the rents or seruices without the

the Attornement of the Tenants to the Diſſeiſor, for ſeeing an Attornement is requiſite to a feoffment and other lawfull conueyances, A fortiori, a Diſſeiſor or other wrong doer ſhall not gaine them without Attornement. The like law is of an Abator and an Intrudor. But albeit the Diſſeiſor hath once gotten the Attornement of the Tenants and payment of their rents, yet may they refuſe afterwards, for auoyding of their double charge. And here the Attornement of the Tenant of a Mannor to a Diſſeiſor of the demeanes ſhall diſpoſſeſſe the Lord of the rents and ſeruices parcell of the Mannor, becauſe both demeanes, rents and ſeruices make but one entier Mannor, and the demeanes are the principall: but otherwiſe it is of rents and ſeruices in groſſe, as in this next Section our Author teacheth vs.

6.H.7.14. 11.H.7.28. 11.H.4.14.a.b.

Sect. 588.589.

¶ Mes ſi vn tient de moy per rent ſeruice, le quel eſt vn ſeruice en groſſe, et nient p[er] reaſon de mon mannor, et vn auter que nul droit ad, claima le rent, et reſceiue et prent meſme le rent de mon tenant per coherciſon de diſtres, ou per auter forme, et diſſeiſiſt moy per tiel prender de rent, coment q̄ tiel diſſeiſor moruſt iſſint ſeiſie ē pernant d̄ rent, vncore apres ſa mort ieo puiſſoy bien diſtreiner le tenant pur le rent que fuit aderere deuant le deceaſe del diſſeiſor. et auxy apres ſon deceaſe. Et la cauſe eſt, pur ceo que tiel diſſeiſor neſt pas mon diſſeiſor forſque a ma election et ma volunt. Car coment que il prent l' rent de mon tenant &c. vncore ieo puiſſoy a touts foits diſtreiner mon tenant pur le rent arere, iſſint q̄ il eſt a moy forſque ſicome ieo voile ſufferer le tenant eſtre per tant de temps arere p̄ paier a moy m̄ le rent, &c.

BVt if one holdeth of mee by rent ſeruice, which is a ſeruice in groſſe, and not by reaſon of my Mannor, and another that hath no right, claimeth the rent, & receiues & taketh the ſame rent of my tenāt by coertion of diſtreſſe, or by other forme, and diſſeiſeth mee by ſuch taking of the rent. Albeit ſuch Diſſeiſor dieth ſo ſeiſed in taking of the rent, yet after his death I may well diſtreine the tenant for the rent which was behinde before the deceaſe of the Diſſeiſor, and alſo after his deceaſe. And the cauſe is, for that ſuch Diſſeiſor is not my diſſeiſor but at my election and will. For albeit he taketh the rent of my tenant, &c. yet I may at all times diſtreine my tenant for the rent behinde, ſo as it is to mee but as if I will ſuffer the tenant to bee ſo long time behinde in payment of the ſame rent vnto me, &c.

Sect. 589.

¶ Car le payment de mon tenant a vn auter, a que il ne doit pas payer, neſt pas diſſeiſin a moy, ne ouſta moy pas de mon rent ſans ma volunt et ma election, &c. Car coment que ieo puiſſoy auer Aſſiſe enuers tiel Pernor,

FOr the payment of my Tenaunt to another to whom hee ought not to pay, is no diſſeiſin to me, nor ſhall ouſt me of my Rent, without my will and election, &c. For although I may haue an Aſſiſe againſt ſuch Pernor, yet this is at my elec-

nor, uncore ceo est a mon election, si ieo voile prender luy come mon disseisor ou non. Issint tiels discents de rents en gros, ne ousteront pas le seignior de distreyner, mes a chescun temps ils poyent bien distreyner pur le rent arere, &c. Et en cest case si apres le distresse de luy que issint torcionsment prist le rent, ieo graunt per mon fait le seruice a vn auter, et le tenant attourna, ceo est assets bone, et les seruices per tiel grant et attournement maintenant sont en le Grantee, &c. Mes auterment est, lou le rent est parcel del Manor, et le disseisor morust seisie del Manor entier, come come en le case procheine auaunt est dit, &c.

ction, whether I will take him as my Disseisor, or no. So such discents of Rents in grosse shall not oust the Lord of his Distresse, but at any time he may well distreyne for the Rent behinde, &c. And in this case if after the distresse of him which so wrongfully tooke the Rent, I graunt by my Deede the Seruice to another, and the Tenaunt attourne, this is good enough, and the seruices by such Grant and Attornement are presently in the Grantee, &c. But otherwise it is where the Rent is parcell of a Mannor, and the Disseisour dieth seised of the whole Mannor, as in the case next before is sayd, &c.

HEre Littleton putteth a diuersitie betweene a Rent seruice parcell of a Mannor, whereof hee had spoken before, and a Rent seruice in Grosse. For a man cannot be disseised of a Rent seruice in Grosse, Rent charge, or Rent secke by Attornement or payment of the Rent to a stranger, but at his Election; for the rule of Law is, Nemo redditum alterius inuito Domino percipere aut possidere potest; and our Author hath before* taught vs, what be Disseisins of Rents seruices, Rents Charges, and Rent seckes, and payment to a stranger is none of them, but at the Lords election, as our Author here saith.

*Vi. Sect. 237. 238. 239. 240.

24.E.3.4. 1.E.5.5. See the Authorities there following in the next Traffe.

Pernor, i. The taker of my rent. But if the disseisee bring an Assise against such a Pernor, then he doth admit himselfe out of possession.

5.E.4.1. 23.H.3.tit.ass.430. 34.E.3.40. 34.16.Ass.p.15. 16.E.3.Release 56. 1.E.5.5. F.N.B.179.E. 15.E.4.8. Flet.li.4.ca.12.

Discents. A discent of a Rent in grosse bindeth not the right owner but that he may distreyne, albeit he admitted himselfe out of possession, and determined his election, as by bringing of an Assise, &c.

If the Tenant of the land pay the Rent to a stranger which hath no right thereunto, and the right owner release to him, this Release is good, because hee thereby admitted himselfe to bee out of possession. But if the Tenant had giuen him any thing in name of Attornement, and the right owner had released to him, this Release had beene voyd, because an Attornement only can be no disseisin of the Rent.

Ieo grant per mon fait, &c. This also prooueth, That the right owner is not out of possession, and that this grant ouer is a demonstration of his election that he is in possession.

Section 590.

ITem si ieo sue seisie dun manor parcel en demesn, et parcel en seruice, et ieo done certaine acres del terre, parcel de demesne de mesme le manor a vn auter

ALso if I be seised of a Mannor, parcell in Demesne, and parcell in Seruice, and I giue certaine acres of the land, parcell of the Demesne of the same Mannour, to

auter en le taile, rendant a moy et a mes heires vn certaine rent, &c. Si en cest case ieo sue disseisie de la Manor, et touts les tenants atturnont et payont lour rents al disseisor, et auxy le dit tenant en le taile paya le rent per moy reserue al Disseisor, et puis le Disseisor morust seisie, &c. et son heire entra, et est eins per discent, vncore en cest case ieo puisse bien distreigner le Tenant en le taile, et ses heires, pur le rent per moy reserue sur le done, scil. auxy bien pur le rent esteant aderere deuant le discent al heire le Disseisor, et auxy pur le rent que happa destre aderere apres mesme le discent, nient obstant tiel morant seisi del disseisor, &c. Et la cause est, pur ceo que quant home dona tenements en le taile, sauant le reuersion a luy, et il sur le dit done reserua a luy vn Rent ou auters seruices, tout le rent et les seruices sont incidents a la reuersion, et quant vn home ad vn reuersion, il ne puissoit estre ouste de son reuersion per le fait dun estrange home, sinon que le tenant soit ouste de son estate et possession, &c. car cy longement que le Tenant en le Taile et ses heirs continuont lour possession per force de mon done, cy longement est le reuersion en moy et en mes heires, et entant que le rent et les seruices reserues sur tiel done sont incidents et dependants al reuersion, quecunque que ad le reuersion, auera mesme le Rent et Seruices, &c.

another in Taile, yeelding to mee and to my Heires a certaine Rent, &c. if in this case I be disseised of the Mannour, and all the Tenaunts attorne and pay their rents to the Disseisor, and also the sayd Tenant in Taile pay the Rent by me reserued, to the Disseisor, and after the Disseisor dieth seised, &c. and his heire enter and is in by Discent, yet in this case I may wel distreyne the Tenant in Taile and his heires, for the rent by me reserued vpon the Gift, *scz.* as well for the Rent being behind before the discent to the heire of the Disseisor, as also for the rent which happeth to be behind after the same discent, notwithstanding such dying seised of the Disseisor, &c. And the reason is, for that when a man giueth lands in Taile, sauing the reuersion to himselfe, and hee vpon the sayd gift reserueth to himselfe a Rent or other Seruices, all the rent and Seruices are incident to the Reuersion, and when a man hath a Reuersion, he cannot be ousted of his Reuersion by the Act of a Stranger, vnlesse that the Tenaunt be ousted of his estate and possession, &c. For as long as the Tenant in Taile and his Heires continue their possession by force of my gift, so long is the reuersion in me and in my Heires: and in as much as the rent and seruices reserued vpon such gift, be incident and depending vpon the reuersion, whosoeuer hath the Reuersion, shall haue the same Rent and Seruices, &c.

Sect. 591.

En mesme le maner est, lou ieo lessa parcel del demesn del manor a un auter pur terme de vie, ou pur terme dans, rendant a moy certaine rent, &c. coment que ieo soy disseisie del manor, &c. et le disseisor morust seisie, &c. et son heir esteant eins per discent, uncore ieo distreiner pur le rent arere vt supra, nient obstant tiel discent. Car quant home ad fait tiel done en taile, ou tiel leas pur terme de vie, ou pur terme dans del parcel de le demesne de un manor, &c. sauant le reuersion a tiel donour ou lessour, &c. et puis il soit disseisie de le manor, &c. tiel reuersion apres tiel disseisin est seuer del manor en fait, coment que ne soit seuer en droit. Et issint poyes veier (mon fits) diuersitie, lou il y ad un Manor parcel en demesne & parcel en seruices, les queux seruices sont parcel de mesme le Manor nient incidents a ascun reuersion, &c. & lou ils sont incidents al reuersion, &c.

IN the same manner is it, where I let parcell of the demesnes of the Mannor to another for terme of life or for terme of yeares, rendering to mee a certaine rent, &c. albeit I be disseised of the mannor, &c. and the disseisor die seised, &c. and his heire bee in by discent, yet I may distreine for the rent arere *vt supra*, notwithstanding such discent, for when a man hath made such a gift in taile, or such a lease for life or for yeares of parcell of the demesnes of a mannor, &c. sauing the reuersion to such donor or lessor, &c. And after he is disseised of the mannor, &c. such reuersion after such disseisin is seuered from the mannor in deed, though it be not seuered in right. And so thou mayest see (my sonne) a diuersitie, where there is a Mannor parcell in Demesne and parcell in Seruices, which Seruices are parcell of the same Mannor not incident to any Reuersion, &c. And where they are incident to the Reuersion, &c.

HEre Littleton putteth a diuersitie betweene Rents and Seruices parcell of a Mannor (whereof hee had spoken before) and Rents and Seruices incident to a Reuersion parcell of a Mannor.

And the reason of this diuersitie is for that as long as the Donee in taile, Lessee for life, or Lessee for yeares are in possession, they preserue the Reuersion in the Donor or Lessor, and so long as the Reuersion continue in the Donor or Lessor, so long doe the Rents and Seruices which are incident to the Reuersion belong to the Donor or Lessor. Neither can the Donor or Lessor be put out of his Reuersion unlesse the Donee or Lessee bee put out of their possession, and if the Donee or Lessee be put out of their possession, then consequently is the Donor or Lessor put out of their Reuersion. But if the Donee or Lessee, make a regresse and regaine their estate and possession, thereby doe they *ipso facto*, reuest the Reuersion in the Donor or Lessor.

(a) 18. *Ass. p.* a. 38. *H.* 6. 33. *Pl. Com. Fulmerstons case* 103. *Lib.* 5. *fol.* 11. 12 25. 19. *E.* 2. *Briefe* 845. 4. *E.* 3. *Briefe* 713.

And here is to be obserued that when a man is seised of a Mannor, and maketh a gift in tayle, or lease for life, &c. of parcell of the Demesne of the Mannor (a) the Reuersion is part of the Mannor and by the grant of the Mannor the Reuersion shall passe with the Attornement of the Donee or Lessee. But if the Lord make a gift in taile, or a lease for life of the whole Mannor, excepting blacke Acre parcell of the Demesnes of the Mannor, and after hee granteth away his Mannor, blacke Acre shall not passe, because during the estate taile or lease for life it is seuered from the Mannor. And so note a diuersitie, that a Reuersion of part may be parcell of a Mannor in possession, but a part in possession cannot be parcell of the Reuersion of a Mannor expectant vpon any estate of Freehold. But if a man make a lease for yeares of a Mannor excepting blacke Acre, and after granteth away the Mannor, blacke Acre shall passe, because the Freehold being entire it remayneth parcell of the Mannor, and one Præcipe of the whole Mannor shall serue. But otherwise it is in case of the gift in taile or lease for life excepting any part, there must be seuerall writs of Præcipe, because the Freehold is seuerall.

Chap.11. Of Discontinuance. *Sect.592.*

¶ Discontinuance est vn ancient parol en la ley, & ad diuers significatiōs, &c. Mes quant a vn entent, il ad tiel signification, s. lou vn home ad alien a vn auter certaine terres ou tenements & morust, et vn auter ad droit de auer mesmes les terres ou tenements, mes il ne poit entrer en eux per cause de tiel alienation, &c.

Discontinuance is an anciēt word in the Law, & hath diuers significations, &c. But as to one intent it hath this signification, *viz.* where a man hath aliened to another certaine lands or Tenements and dieth, and another hath right to haue the same Lands or Tenements, but hee may not enter into them because of such an alienation, &c.

¶ *Discontinuance*, is a word compounded of de and continuo, for continuare is to continue without intermission. Now by addition of de (Euphoniæ gratia dis to it) which is priuatiue, it signifieth an intermission. Discontinuare nihil aliud significat quam intermittere, desuescere, interrumpere. And as our Author saith, (a) it is a very ancient word in Law.

Vide Sect.637.

(a) 8.*H*.4.8.*b*.11.*H*.4.85.*b*.

A discontinuance of estates in Lands or Tenements is properly (in legall vnderstanding) an alienation made or suffered by Tenant in tayle, or by any that is seised in auter droit, whereby the issue in tayle, or the heire or successor or those in Reuersion or Remaynder are driuen to their Action, and cannot enter.

All which is implyed by the discription of our Author, and by the (&c.) in the end of this Section.

I haue added (properly) by good warrant of our Author himselfe, for Sectione 470 he vseth Discontinuance for a deuesting or displacing of a Reuersion, though the entrie bee not taken away.

This Discontinuance consisteth in doing or suffering an Act to bee done, as hereafter shall appeare. And where our Author saith, that it hath diuers significations, there is also a Discontinuance of Processe consisting in not doing, where the Processe is not continued, concerning which there is an excellent Statute made in furtherance of Justice in (b) 1.E.6. and is well expounded in my Reports, and therefore need not here to be inserted.

(b) *Vide, the Statutes of* 1.*E*.6.*ca*.7.*&* 31.*Eliz*.*ca*.1. *Lib*.7.*fol*.30.31.*&c. le case de discontinuance de proces.*

There is another erronious proceeding and that consisteth in misdoing, as when one Processe is awarded in stead of another, or when a day is giuen which is not legall, this is called a miscontinuance & if the Tenant or Defendant make default it is error: but if he appeare, then the miscontinuance is salued, otherwise it is of a Discontinuance. But let vs returne to the Discontinuance of Estates in Lands whereof Littleton doth entreate in this Chapter.

39.*E*.3.7.*a*. 46.*E*.3.30. 37.*H*.6 a 5.26. 9.*E*.4.18. 12.*E*.4.

¶ *Significations.* Here (as in many other places) it appeareth how necessary it is to know the signification of words.

*Vide Sect.*74.174.194. 441.520.

And in this Chapter it appeareth, that when Littleton wrote, the Estate in Lands and tenements might haue beene discontinued fiue manner of wayes, viz. by Feoffment, by Fine, by Release with warrantie, Confirmation with warrantie, and by suffering of a Reconerie in a Precipe quod reddat. And this was to the preiudice of fiue kinds of persons, viz. of Wiues, of Heires, of Successors, of those in Reuersion, and of those in Remaynder. But for Wiues, and their Heires, and for Successors the Law is altered by Acts of Parliament since Littleton wrote, as in this Chapter in their proper places shall appeare.

Section 593.

¶ Si come vn Abbe seisie de certaine terres ou tenements en fee, & alienast mesmes les terres ou tenements a vn auter en fee, ou en fee taile, ou pur terme de vie, & puis labbe morust, son successor ne poit enter en les dits terres ou tenemēts, coment que il ad droit eux auer come en droit de son meason, mes il est mis a son action de recouerer mesmes l's terres ou tenemēts, quel est appelle Breue de ingressu sine assensu capituli, &c.

As if an Abbot be seised of certaine Lands or Tenements in fee, and alieneth the same Lands or Tenements to another in fee or in fee taile or for terme of life, and after the Abbot dieth, his Successor cannot enter into the said Lands or Tenements, albeit hee hath right to haue them as in right of his house, but he is put to his action to recouer the same Lands or Tenements, which is called a Writ, *Breue de ingressu sine assensu capituli, &c.*

¶ Here Littleton putteth an example of a discōtinuance made by one seised in auter droit, as by an Abbot who had a fee simple in the right of his Monastery, and therefore his Alienation without the assent of his Couent had beene a Discontinuance at the Common Law, and had driuen his Successor to a Writ De Ingressu sine assensu capituli.

¶ De Ingressu sine assensu capituli, &c. It is called so because the Alienation was sine assensu capituli, for if it had beene cum assensu capituli, it should haue beene a barre to the successor. And because the successor could not enter, the Common Law gaue him this Writ, and is so called of these words contained in the Writ, which Writ you may reade in the Register & Fitzherberts N.B.

Regist. Orig. fol. 230. F.N.B. 195. Bracton lib. 4. fol. 323. Fleta lib. 5. cap. 34.

And here is to bee noted, that in Law the Couent, albeit they be regular and dead persons in Law, yet are they said in Law to be Capitulum to the Abbot, aswell as the Deane and Chapiter, that be Secular to the Bishop. But it is to bee obserued and implyed in this (&c.) that a sole bodie politique that hath the absolute right in them, as an Abbot, Bishop and the like may make a Discontinuance, but a Corporation aggregate of many as Deane and Chapiter, Warden and Chaplaines, Master and Fellowes, Maior and Comminalty, &c. cannot make any Discontinuance, for if they ioyne, the Grant is good, and if the Deane, Warden, Master, or Maior make it alone where the bodie is aggregate of many it is void, and worketh a disseisin. But now (as hath beene said) by the Statute of 27. H. 8. and 31. H. 8. all the Abbots, Priors, and other Religious persons are so dissolued as there be none remayning this day, and by the Statutes of 1. Eliz. and 13. Eliz cap. 10. and 1. Iac. cap. 3. Bishops and all other Ecclesiasticall persons are disabled to alien or discontinue any of their Ecclesiasticall Liuings, as by the same Acts doth appeare.

21. E. 4. 86.

See more of this matter hereafter in this Chapter. Sect. 648. and before Sect. 528.

Sect. 594.

¶ Item si home seisie de terre come en droit

Also if a man bee seised of Land as in right of his

¶ En droit sa feme, &c. That is to say, in fee simple [illegible] taile,

de

de sa feme, &c. enter & feoffa vn auter, &c. & morust, la feme ne puit enter mes est mis a son action, le quel est appel Cui in vita, &c.

wife, &c. and thereof infeoffe another, &c. and dieth, the Wife may not enter, but is put to her Action, the which is called, *Cui in vita, &c.*

or for life. Here Littleton putteth another case where a man is seised in auter droit, and may make a Discontinuance, as the husband seised in the right of his wife, and therefore the Common Law gave her a Cui in vita, and her heire a Sur cui in vita because they could not enter. But this is altered since our Author wrote by the Statute of 32. H. 8. by the purview of which Statute, the wife and her heires after the decease of her husband may enter into the Lands or Tenements of the wife notwithstanding the alienation of her husband. *Bracton lib. 4. fol. 202. & 22. & 324. Fleta lib. 5. cap. 34. & 36. F. N. B. 193. Regist. 32. H. 8. cap. 28.*

And here is one of the alienations to make a Discontinuance, viz. a feoffment, and where our Author speaketh of a husband seised in the right of his wife, so it is, where the husband and wife are joyntly seised to them & their heires of an estate made during the Coverture, & the husband make a feoffment in fee, & dieth, the wife now may enter within that statute, although it was the Inheritance of them both. And so it is if the feoffment bee made by the husband and wife, (albeit the words of the Statute be by the husband only) for in substance this is the act of the husband only. *Dier 4. & 5. Ph. & Mar. 146. 3. Eliz. Dier 191. Lib. 8. fol. 71. 72. Greneleys case.*

If the husband cause a Precipe quod reddat upon a faint title to bee brought against him and his wife, and suffereth a recoverie without any Voucher, and Execution to bee had against him and his wife, yet this is holpen by the Statute, for this by like construction is the act of the husband, and the words of the Statute be, made, suffered, or done.

If the husband make a feoffment in fee of the Lands, which hee holdeth in the right of his wife, and after they are divorced Causa præcontractus, yet the woman may enter within the purview of that Statute, and is not driven to her writ of Cui ante divortium, as she was at the Common Law, albeit the entrie be by the Statute given to the wife and now upon the matter she was never his lawfull wife. But it sufficeth that she was his wife De facto at the time of the alienation, and where her husband dieth shee cannot bee his wife at the time of the entrie. *Greneleys case, ubi supra.*

If the husband levie a fine with Proclamations, and dieth, the wife must enter or avoid the Estate of the Conusee within five yeares, or else shee is barred for ever by the Statute of 4. H. 7. for the Statute of 32. H. 8. doth helpe the Discontinuance but not the barre, and the Statute speaketh of a fine, and not of a fine with Proclamations. *6. E. 6. Dier. 72. b. 4. H. 7. c. 24.*

If lands be given to the husband and wife, and to the heires of their two bodies, and the husband maketh a feoffment in fee and dieth, the wife is holpen by the said Statute as hath beene said, and so is the issue of both their bodies. Fem tenant in taile taketh husband, the husband maketh a feoffment in fee, the wife before entrie dieth without issue, hee in the Reversion or Remaynder may enter. For first the Reversion or Remaynder cannot bee discontinued in this case because the estate tayle is not discontinued. Secondly, the words of the Statute be Shall not be preiudiciall or hurtfull to the wife or her heires, or such as shall have right title or interest by the death of such wife, but that the same wife and her heires, and such other to whom such right shall appertaine after her decease, shall or lawfully may enter into all such Mannors, Lands, &c. according to their rights and titles therein, by which words the entrie of him in the Reversion or Remaynder in that case is preserved. The husband is Tenant in taile, the remaynder to the wife in taile, the husband make a feoffment in fee, by this the husband by the Common Law did not only discontinue his owne estate taile but his wives remaynder but at this day after the death of the husband without issue, the wife may enter by the said Act of 32. H. 8. If the husband hath issue and maketh a feoffement in fee of his wives Land, and the wife dieth, the heire of the wife shall not enter during the husbands life, neither by the Common Law nor by the Statute. *Greneleys case ubi supra. Pasch. 7. Iac. 8. E. 2. tit. Cui in vita. 26. 34. E. 1. ibidem 30. 10. E. 3. 12. Dier 21. Eliz. 363.*

¶ Cui in vita, &c. Here is also implyed a Sur cui in vita, also for the heire this writ here mentioned in our Author is so called of those words contained in the Writ which you may reade in the Register and Fitzherberts, N. B.

Sect. 595.

¶ Item si tenant en taile de certaine terre ent enfeoffa un auter, &c. et ad issue et morust, son issue ne poit pas enter en la terre coment que il ad title et droit a ceo, mes est mis a son action que est appel Formedon en le discender, &c.

ALso if tenant in taile of certaine land, thereof enfeoffe another, &c. and hath issue and dieth, his issue may not enter into the land albeit he hath title and right to this, but is put to his action which is called a *Formedon in le discender, &c.*

Fleta, lib. 5. ca. 34. F.N.B. 211. 212. Regist.

¶ *Enfeoffa un auter, &c.* Here is implyed, or make a gift in taile or an estate for life. Here Littleton putteth a third example of a Discontinuance made by Tenant in taile so as his issue is put to his Formedon in the Discender, which is given to the issue in taile by the Statute of 13. E. 1. cap. 1. because he cannot enter.

¶ *Tenant en taile.* This extendeth aswell to a woman Tenant in taile as to a man, and was generally good Law when Littleton wrote, but now by the Statute of (d) 11. H. 7. if the woman hath any estate in taile joyntly with her husband, or only to her selfe or to her use in any Lands or Hereditaments of the inheritance or purchase of her husband, or given to the husband and wife in taile by any of the Ancestors of the husband, or by any other person seised to the use of the husband or his Ancestors, and shall hereafter being sole or with any other after taken husband discontinue, &c. the same: every such Discontinuance shall be voyde, and that it shall be lawfull for every person to whom the interest, title, or inheritance, after the decease of the said woman should appertaine, to enter, &c. So as if such a feme Tenant in taile doe make any Discontinuance in fee, in taile, or for life, although it be without warranty, yet this doth not take away the entrie after her death either of the issue or of him in reversion or remainder. This Statute hath beene excellently expounded by divers resolutions and judgements (e) which I have quoted in the margent, and are worthy of due observation.

(d) 11. H. 7. ca. 20. Vid. Sect. 697.

(e) Lib. 3. fo. 10. 51. Sir George Brownes case. eodem lib. fo. 60. &c. Linc. Coll. case. lib. 1. fo. 176. Mildemayes case. Dier 3. & 4. Ph. & Mar. 146 idem 8. Eliz. 248. 17. Eliz. 340. idem 19. Eliz. 354. Idem. 20. Eliz. 362. 27. H. 8. 23. Lib. 5. fo. 79. Fitzh. case. Lib. 8. fo. 71. 72. Graveleys case.

If lands were entayled to a man and to his wife, and to the heires of their two bodyes, and the husband had made a Feoffment in fee and died, and then the wife died, this had beene a discontinuance at the Common Law: for the title of the issue is as heire of both their bodyes, and not as heire to any one of them, and his entrie must ensue his title or action.

¶ *De formedon.* De forma donationis, so called because the Writ doth comprehend the forme of the gift. And there be three kinde of Writs of Formedon, viz. The first in the Discender to be brought by the issue in taile, which clayme by discent Per formam doni. The second is in the Reverter, which lyeth for him in the reversion or his heires or Assignes after the state taile be spent, The third is the Remainder, which the Law giveth to him in the remainder, his Heires or Assignes after the determination of the estate taile, of all which you may reade in the Register and F N.B.

Here Littleton sheweth that the issue in taile shall have a Formedon in the Discender. What other actions Tenant in taile may have, and not have, is good to be seene.

(a) Tenant in taile shall have a Quod permittat.

(b) Tenant in taile shall have a writ of Customes and Services In le debet, & solet, but shall not have it in the Debet only.

(c) In like manner he shall have a Secta ad molendinum in le debet & solet, but not in the Debet tantum.

(d) Tenant in taile shall have a Writ of Entre in consimili casu and an Admesurement, and a Nativo habendo, Cessavit, Escheat, Waste, and the like.

(e) But Tenant in taile shall not have a writ of Right Sur disclaymer, nor a Quo jure, nor a Ne injuste vexes, nor a Nuper obijt, or Rationabile parte, nor a Mordancester, nor a Sur cui in vita, for these and the like none but Tenant in fee shall have: and the highest writ that a Tenant in taile can have is a Formedon.

(a) 4. E. 3. 38. 43. E. 3. 25. 4. E. 4. 25. F.N.B. 124.
(b) 2. E. 2. Droit. 28.
(c) F.N.B. 123.
(d) 21. E. 3. 11. 5. E. 3. 23. 11. H. 4. 49.
(e) 2. E. 3. Droit. 28. 13. H. 7. 24. 5. E. 4. 2. 20. E. 3. Avowry 131. F.N.B. 10. 46. E. 3. tit. Cui in vita, 33.

Section

Section 596. 597.

¶ Item si soit tent en le taile, le reuersion esteant al Donor et a ses heires, si le tenant fait feoffment, &c. et morust sans issue, celuy en le reuersion ne poit enter, mes est mis a son action de Formedon en le reuerter.

ALso if there bee tenant in taile the reuersion being to the Donor and his heires, if the Tenant make a feoffment, &c. and die without issue, hee in the reuersion cannot enter, but is put to his action of *Formedō in le reuerter*.

Sect. 597.

¶ En mesme le maner est, lou tenāt en le taile seisie de certaine terre dont le remainder est a vn auter en le taile, ou a vn auter en fee. Si le tenant en le taile alienast en fee, ou en fee taile, et puis deuiast sans issue, ceux en le remainder ne poiēt enter, mes sont mis a lour briefe de Formedon en le remainder, &c. et pur ceo que per force de tielx feoffments et alyenations en les cases auantdits, et en semblables cases, ceux queux ont title et droit apres la mort de tiel feoffour ou alienour, ne poient pas enter, mes sont mises a lour actions Vt supra, et p̄ ceo cause tiels feoffments et alienations sont appels discontinuances.

IN the same manner is it where tenant in taile is seised of certaine land whereof the remainder is to another in taile, or to another in fee. If the tenant in taile alien in fee, or in fee taile, and after die without issue they in the remainder may not enter, but are put to their writ of *Formedon* in the remainder, &c. and for that that by force of such feoffments and alienations in the cases aforesaid, and the like cases, they that haue title and right after the death of such a feoffor or alienor may not enter, but are put to their actions, *Vt supra*, and for this cause such feoffments and alienations are called discontinuances.

¶ *Fait feoffment &c.* Here is implyed Fee simple, Fee taile, or estate for life, and in this and the next Section Littleton putteth two cases, where if the issues in taile faile, they in the reuersion and remainder are driuen to their Formedon in reuersion or remainder, and this remaineth as it was when Littleton wrote not altered by any Statute. And the reason whereof these Alienations in the seuerall cases in this and the next Section doe make a Discontinuance, and put him in the reuersion or remainder that right had to his Action, and tooke away his entrie, was for that hee was priuie in estate, and for the benefit of the Purchasor, and for the safegard of his Warrantie, so as euery mans right might bee preserued, viz. to the Demandant for his ancient right, and to the Feoffee for the benefit of his Warrantie, which was founded vpon great reason and equity, which benefit of the warranty should bee preuented and auoyded if the entrie of him that right had were lawfull, and therby also the danger that many times happeneth by taking of possessions was warily preuented by Law. But then it may bee demanded, seeing that there was no reuersion or remainder expectant vpon any estate taile at the Common Law, nor the issue in taile had any remedy by the Common Law, if the Tenant in taile had aliened, then by what Law is the alienation of Tenant in taile a Discontinuance at this day to the issue in taile?

Vid. Sect. 592. 597. 601. 937. 638.

30. E. 1. Formedon 65. 10. E. 2. Formedon, 61. 18. E. 3. 46. 12. E. 4. 3.

taile or to him in reuersion or remainder. Whereunto it is thus answered, That it is prouided by the Statute of W.2.ca.1. De donis conditionalibus, quod non habeant illi quibus tenementum sic fuerit datum potestatem alienandi, &c. Upon these words the Sages of the Law haue construed the said Act according to the rule and reason of the Common Law, and that in diuers and sundrie variable manners. For some Alienations of Tenant in taile, they haue adiudged voydably by the Issue in taile by action only: some at the election of the Issue in taile to auoyde it by Action, Entrie, or Clayme, some are meerely voyde by the death of the Tenant in Taile: which seuerall Constructions were made upon the selfe same words aforesayd.

18.E.3.12.19.E.3.Bre.468 24.E.3.28. 36.Ass.8. 22.R.2.Discon. 5.E.4.3. 4.H.7.17. 33.E.3. Formdon. & 13.H.7. Pl. Com. Smith & Staplotons case.

As for example, If Tenant in Taile make a Feoffement in fee, this driues the Issue in Taile to his Action, which is called in Law a Discontinuance, and this Construction was made, for that at the Common Law the Feoffement of an Abbot or Bishop, or of the husband seised in the right of his wife, did worke a Discontinuance, and did driue the Successor and the wife to their Action, and foreclosed them of their entrie: and as the entrie of the issue was taken away, so consequently of them in reuersion and remainder. Also if an Abbot, Bishop, or husband in the right of his wife, seised of a Rent, or of any other Inheritance that lieth in Graunt had aliened, it was in the election of the Successour or wife after the death of her husband to claime the rent, &c. or to bring an Action, for that alienation did not worke a Discontinuance, and so it is by construction in case of Tenaunt in Tayle. Lastly, If the Abbot, Bishop, or Husband, had granted a Rent newly created out of the land &c. to another in fee, this had utterly ceased by their death; and so it is also by construction in case of Tenant in Taile. So as these words, (Non habent potestatem alienandi) doe worke these effects, viz. as to Lands, That a Feoffement barreth not the Issue, &c. of his Action, but worketh a Discontinuance to barre him of his Entrie: as to Rents or any thing in esse, that lie in grant, that the sayd words doe take away his power to make any Discontinuance: as to Rents, &c. newly created, that they take away his power to make them to continue longer than during his life.

But there is a diuersitie betweene an Alienation working a discontinuance of an estate which taketh away an entrie, and an Alienation working, diuesting or displacing of Estates which taketh away no entrie. As if there be Tenant for life, the remainder to A. in Tayle, the remainder to B. in fee, if Tenant for life doth alien in Fee, this doth diuest and displace the remainders, but worketh no discontinuance. And therein it is to be obserued, That to euerie Discontinuance there is necessarie a diuesting, or displacing of the Estate, and turning the same to a right: for if it be not turned to a right, they that haue the Estate cannot be driuen to an Action. And that is the reason that such Inheritances as lie in Grant cannot by Grant bee discontinued, because such a Grant diuesteth no Estate, but passeth onely that which hee may lawfully grant, and so the estate it selfe doth discend, reuert, or remaine, as shall be sayd hereafter in this Chapter.

A. maketh a gift in Taile to B. who maketh a gift in Taile to C. C. maketh a Feoffement in Fee and dieth without Issue, B. hath Issue and dieth, the Issue of B. shall enter, for albeit the Feoffement of C. did discontinue the reuersion of the Fee simple which B. had gayned upon the Estate taile made to C. yet could it not discontinue the right of Intaile which B. had, which was discontinued before: and therefore when C. died without Issue, then did the discontinuance of the estate Taile of B. which passed by his Liuerie, cease, and consequently the entrie of the Issue of B. lawfull, which case may open the reason of many other cases.

Also note, That a Discontinuance made by the husband, did take away the entrie onely of the wife and her heires by the Common Law, and not of any other which claimed by title paramount aboue the Discontinuance. As if Lands had beene giuen to the husband and wife and to a third person, and to their heires, and the husband had made a Feoffement in Fee, this had beene a discontinuance of the one moitie, and a disseisin of the other moitie: if the husband had died, and then the wife had died, the suruiuor should haue entred into the whole, for hee claimed not under the discontinuance, but by title paramount from the first Feoffor, and seeing the right by Law doth suruiue, the Law doth giue him a remedie to take aduantage thereof by entry, for other remedie for that moitie he could not haue.

¶ *Fee, ou Fee taile.* **And so it is of an estate for life.**

Sect. 598.599.600.

¶ Item si Tenant en Taile soit disseisie, et il relessa per son

ALso if Tenant in Taile be disseised, and he release by his

son fait a le Disseisor et a ses heires tout le droit, le quel il ad en mesme les tenements, ceo nẽ pas discontinuance, pur ceo que rien de droit passa al Disseisor forsque pur terme de vie del tenant en le Taile que fist le Release, &c.

Deed to the Disseisour and to his heires all the right which he hath in the same Tenements, this is no discontinuance, for that nothing of the right passeth to the Disseisor, but for terme of the life of tenant in Taile, which made the release, &c.

Sect 599.

¶ Mes per feoffment del tenant en le Taile, fee simple passa per mesme le feoffement per force de Liuerie de seisin, &c.

BVt by the Feoffement of Tenaunt in Taile, Fee simple passeth by the same Feoffement by force of the Liuerie of Seisin, &c.

Sect. 600.

¶ Mes per force dun release rien passera forsque le droit que il poet loyalmẽt, & droituralment relesser, sans leydõ ou damage as auters persons q̃ur ent aueront droit apres son decease, &c. Issint il est graund diuersitie perenter vn Feoffement dun tenant en le taile, et vn Release fait per tenant en le taile.

BVt by force of a Release nothing shall passe but the right which he may lawfully and rightfully release, without hurt or dammage to other persons who shall haue right therin after his decease, &c. So there is great diuersitie betweene a Feoffement of Tenant in Taile, and a release made by Tenant in Taile.

¶ OUr Author hauing put examples of Estates passing by transmutation of an Estate and possession, both in this and the two Sections following put a diuersitie betweene a Feoffement and a release or confirmation of a bare right: for it is a rule in Law, That the Disseisee or any other that hath a right onely by his Release or Confirmation, cannot make any discontinuance, because nothing can passe thereby but that which may lawfully passe. But otherwise it is of a Feoffment in respect of the Liuerie of Seisin, for that it is the most solemne and common assurance in the Countrie, and to be maintained for the common quiet of the Realme: and by the Feoffement the Freehold (which is so much esteemed in Law) doth passe by open Liuerie to the Feoffee, and by the release a bare right. 9.E 4.18.12.E.4.12. 5.H.4.8.21.H.6.58.

Section 601.

¶ Mes il est dit, que si le tenant ẽ tail en cest cas relessa a son disseisor, et oblige luy et ses h̃rs

BVt it is said, That if the Tenant in Taile in this case release to his Disseisor, and bind him and his heires to Warran-

¶ The reason why the additiõ of the warrantie in this case maketh a Discontinuance, is that which hath been sayd, viz. If the Issue in Tayle should enter, the Warrantie (which is so much fauoured in Law) should be destroyed, And 3.H.4.9.22.R 2.Discont.5. 12.E.4.11.21.H.7.9. 43.E.3.8.15.E.4.sit.Discont.30. Vi.Sect. 596.602.637.658.

and therefore to the end that if Assets in Fee simple doe discend, he to whom the Release is made, may plead the same, and barre the Demandant: by which meanes all rights and advantages are saved. And that I may note it once for all, an (Il est dit) with Littleton, is as good as a Concessum in a Booke case.

a Garranty et mort, et cest garranty discendist a son Issue, ceo est discontinuance per cause de le garrantie.

tie, and dieth, and this Warrantie discend to his Issue, this is a Discontinuance, by reason of the Warrantie.

Section 602.

¶ MEs si vn home ad Issue fits per sa Feme, et sa Feme morust, et puis il prent auter Feme, et tenements sont dones a luy et a sa second Feme, et a les heires de lour deux corps engendres, et ils ont issue vn auter fits, et l' second Feme morust, et puis le Tenant en le taile est disseisie, et il relessa al Disseisor tout son droit, &c. et oblige luy & ses heires a le garrantie, &c. et deuia, ceo nest pas discontinuance al issue en le Taile per l' second feme, mes il poit bien enter, pur ceo que le garrantie discendist a son eigne frere que son pier auoit per le primer feme, &c.

BVt if a man hath issue a Sonne by his Wife, and his Wife dieth, and after hee taketh another wife, and Tenements are giuen to him and to his second wife, and to the Heires of their two bodies engendred, and they haue issue another sonne, and the second Wife dieth, and after the Tenant in taile is disseised, and hee release to the Disseisor all his right, &c. and bind him and his heires to Warrantie, &c. and die, this is no Discontinuance to the Issue in Taile by the second wife, but he may wel enter, for that the Warrantie discendeth to his elder brother which his Father had by the first wife, &c.

Sect. 603.

¶ EN mesme le manner est, lou tenements sont discendable a le fits puisne solonqs le custome de Burgh English, queux sont entailes, &c. et le tenant en le taile ad deux fits, & est disseisie, et il relessa a son Disseisor tout son droit oue garrantie, &c. et morust, le puisne fits poit enter sur le Disseisor, nient obstant le garrantie, pur ceo que le garrantie discendist al eigne fits, car touts foits le Garrantie

IN the same manner is it, where Lands are discendible to the youngest sonne after the Custome of Burrough-English, which are entayled, &c. and the Tenaunt in Taile hath two sonnes, and is disseised, and he releaseth to his Disseisour all his right with Warrantie, &c. and dieth, the younger sonne may enter vpon the Disseisor notwithstanding the Warranty, for that the Warrantie discendeth to the elder son: for always the War-

tie discendera a celuy que est heire per le common ley.

rantie shall discend to him who is heire by the Common Law.

¶ By these two examples in this and the Section next following, it appeareth that a warrantie being added to a release or Confirmation, and discending upon him that right hath to the Lands maketh a Discontinuance, otherwise it is out of the reason of the Law, and worketh no Discontinuance if the warrantie discendeth upon another.

¶ *Oue garrantie, &c.* Here is implyed that he doth bind him and his heires to warrant to the releasee and his heires.

¶ *Touts foits le garrantie discendist sur le heire al Common ley.* This is a Maxime of the Common Law, and hereof more shall be said in the Chapter of Warrantie. Sectione 718. 735 736 737. so as it is not the warrantie only that maketh a discontinuance, but the warrantie and the Discent upon him that right hath together. 13. H. 4. Garrantie 94. 19. R. 2. Garrantie 100.

Sect. 604.

¶ Item si un Abbe soit disseisie, & il relessa al disseisor ouesque garrantie, ceo nest pas discontinuance a son successor, pur ceo que rien passa per cel releas, forsque le droit que il ad durant le temps que il est Abbe, & le Garrantie est expire per son priuation, ou per sa mort.

Also if an Abbot bee disseised and hee releaseth to the disseisor with warrantie, this is no Discontinuance to his successor, because nothing passeth by this release but the right which hee hath during the time that he is Abbot, and the Warrantie is expired by his priuation, or by his death.

¶ The reason hereof yeelded by Littleton is for that the warrantie is expired by his priuation or death.

¶ *Per son priuation ou per sa mort.* Note, that priuation is here resembled to death, and so is translation also. Wherein this diuersitie is worthy of obseruation, that when a Bishop, &c. make an estate, lease, grant of a Rent charge, warrantie, or any other Act which may tend to the dimination of the reuenues of the Bishopricke, &c. which should maintaine the successor, there the priuation or translation of the Bishop, &c. is all one with his death. But where the Bishop is Patron and Ordinarie, and confirmeth a Lease made by the Parson without the Deane and Chapter, and after the Parson dieth, and the Bishop collateth another, and then is translated, yet his Confirmation remayneth good; for the Reuenues that are to maintaine the Successor are not thereby diminished. And the like diuersitie doth hold in case of resignation, notwithstanding (m) the authority to the contrary. Vide 19. E. 3. 16. (m) 19. E. 3. 16. tit. grant. 99.

Sect. 605.

¶ Item si home seisie en droit sa feme est disseisie, & il relessa, &c. ouesque garrantie, ceo nest pas discontinuance a la feme si el suruesquist son baron, mes que el poit enter &c. Causa patet.

Also if a man seised in the right of his Wife be disseised, and he releaseth, &c. with warrantie, this is no discontinuance to the wife if shee suruiueth her husband, but that she may enter, &c. *Causa patet.*

¶ This is euident, unlesse the wife be heire to the husband (as by law shee may bee) and then it is a discontinuance for the cause aforesaid.

Section 606.

¶ Item si tenant en taile de certaine terre, lessa mesme la terre a un auter pur term des ans, per force de quel le lessee ent eit possession, en quel possession le tenant en taile per son fait relessa tout le droit que il auoit en mesme le terre, a auer & tener a le lessee & a ses heires a touts iours ceo nest pas discontinuance, mes apres le decease le tenant en taile son issue poit bien enter, pur ceo que per tiel releas riens passa forsque pur terme de la vie de le tenant en le taile.

ALso if Tenant in tayle of certaine Land letteth the same Land to another for tearme of yeares, by force whereof the Lessee hath thereof possessiō, in whose possession the Tenant in tayle by his Deed releaseth all the right that he hath in the same Land. To haue and to hold to the Lessee and to his heires for euer. This is no discontinuance, but after the decease of the Tenant in tayle, his issue may well enter, because by such Release nothing passeth but for tearme of the life of the Tenant in tayle.

¶ *Car per tiel releas riens passa.* Here is one of the maximes of the Common Law rehearsed by our Author, whereof hee doth put divers examples hereafter.

Sect. 607.

¶ En mesme le manner est, si le tenant en le taile, confirma lestate le lessee pur terme des ans, a auer & tener a luy & a ses heires, ceo nest pas discontinuance, pur ceo que riens passa per tiel confirmation forsque lestate que le tenant en le taile auoit pur terme de sa vie, &c.

IN the same manner it is if the Tenant in tayle confirme the estate of the Lessee for yeares. To haue and to hold to him and to his heires, this is no discontinuance, for that nothing passeth by such Confirmation, but the estate which the Tenant in tayle hath for tearme of his life, &c.

¶ *Riens passa per tiel confirmation.* Here is another of the maximes of the Common Law rehearsed by our Author, whereof he putteth examples hereafter.

More shall be said hereof in the next Section following.

Section 608.

¶ Item si tenant en taile apres tiel leas granta le reuersion en fee per son fait a auter, & voile que

ALso if tenant in taile after such lease grant the reuersion in fee by his Deed to another, and wil-

que apres le terme fine, q̄ mesme le terre remaindroit a le grantee et a ses heires a touts iours, & le tenant a term̄ dans atturna, ceo nest pas discontinuance. Car tiels choses queux passont en tiels cases de tenant en le taile tantsolement per voy de graunt, ou per confirmation, ou per tiel release, rien poit passer pur faire estate a celuy a que tiel graunt, ou confirmatio͂ ou release est fait forsque ceo que le tenant en taile poit droiturelment faire, et ceo nest forsque p̄ terme de sa vie, &c.

leth that after the terme ended, that the same land shall remaine to the grantee and his heires for euer, and the tenant for yeares attorne, this is no discontinuance. For such things which passe in such cases of tenant in taile only by way of grant, or by confirmation or by such release, nothing can passe to make an estate to him to whom such grant, or confirmation or release is made, but that which the tenant in taile may rightfully make, and this is but for terme of his life, &c.

Sect. 609.

CAr si ieo lessa terre a vn hom̄ pur terme de sa vie, &c. et le tenant a terme de vie lesse mesm̄ la terre a vn auter pur terme des ans, &c. et puis mon tenant a terme de vie graunta le reuersio͂ a vn auter en fee, et le tenant a terme des ans atturna, en cest case le grantee nad en le franktenement forsq; estate pur terme de vie son grauntor, &c. & ieo que suis en le reuersion de fee simple, ne puisse enter per force de cel grant del reuersion fait per mon tenant a terme de vie, pur ceo que per tiel grant mon reuersion nest pas discontinue, mes tout temps demurt a moy, sicome il fuit adeuant, nient obstant tiel grant del reuersion fait al grantee a luy et a ses heires, &c. pur ceo que riens passa per force de tiel grant forsque estate que le grantor auoit, &c.

FOr if I lett land to a man for terme of his life, &c. and the tenant for life letteth the same land to another for terme of years, &c. and after my tenant for life grant the reuersion to another in fee, and the tenant for yeares attorne, in this case the grantee hath in the freehold but an estate for terme of the life of his grantor, &c. And I which am in the reuersion of the fee simple may not enter by force of this grant of the reuersion made by my tenant for life, for that by such grant my reuersion is not discontinued, but alwayes remaine vnto me as it was before notwithstanding such grant of the reuersion made to the grantee, to him and to his heires, &c. because nothing passed by force of such grant, but the estate which the grantor hath, &c.

Sect. 610.

¶ EN mesme le maner est, si le tenant a terme de vie, per son fait confirme lestate son lessee pur terme des ans, a auer et tener a luy et a ses heires, ou relessa a son lessee et a ses heires, uncore l' lessee a terme dans nad estate forsque pur terme de vie de le tenant a terme de vie, &c.

¶ IN the same manner is it, if tenant for terme of life by his Deed confirme the estate of his Lessee for yeares, To haue and to hold to him and his heires, or release to his Lessee and his heires, yet the Lessee for yeares hath an estate but for terme of the life of the tenant for life, &c.

¶ *Ar tiels choses que passont en tiels cases de tenant en le taile, &c.* Here is rehearsed another Ancient maxime of the Common Law touching Grants, and hereby it appeareth that a Feoffment in fee (albeit it be by Parol) is of a greater operation and estimation in Law, then a grant of a reuersion by Deed though it be enrolled and Attornement of the Lessee for yeares of a Release, or a Confirmation by Deed for the reasons aforesaid. And this is manifested by the Examples which our Author here in these three Sections putteth.

Sect. 611.

¶ *Forsque estate per term dans, &c.* Here it is implyed that albeit the feoffment made by Lessee for yeares be a feoffment betweene the Feoffor and feoffee, and that by this feoffment the fee simple passeth by force of the liuery, yet is it a disseisin to the Lessor. And here it is worthy to bee obserued, that our Author saith that Tenant for terme of yeares may make a feoffment, whereupon it followeth, that the Feoffor may thereunto annexe a Warrantie, whereupon the Feoffee may vouch him, but of this you shall reade more in the Chapter of Warranties, Sect. 698.

¶ Mes autrement est quant tenāt a terme de vie, fait un feoffmēt en fee, car per tiel feoffment le fee simple passa. Car tenant a term̄ dans poit faire feoffment en fee, et per son feoffment le fee simple passera, et uncore il nauoit al temps del feoffment fait forsque estate pur terme dans, &c.

BVt otherwise it is when tenant for life maketh a feoffment in fee, for by such a feoffment the fee simple passeth. For tenant for yeares may make a feoffment in fee, and by his feoffment the fee simple shall passe, and yet he had at the time of the feoffment made but an estate for terme of yeares, &c.

Sect. 612.

¶ ITem si ten̄ en le taile granta son terre a un auter pur terme de vie de mesme le tenant en taile, et liuer a luy seisin, &c. et apres per son fait il relessa a le tenant et a ses heires tout le droit

ALso if tenant in taile grant his land to another for terme of the life of the said tenant in taile and deliuer to him seisin, &c. and after by his Deed hee releaseth to the tenant and to his heires all the

droit que il auoyt en mesme la terre, en cest cas lestate del tenant de la terre nest pas enlarge per force de tiel releas, pur ceo que quant le tenant auoit lestate en le terre pur terme de vie de le tenant en le taile, donque il auoit tout le droit que le tenant en le taile puissoit droiturelment granter ou relesser, issint que per tiel releas nul droit passa, entant que son droit fuit ale adeuant.

right which hee hath in the same land, In this case the estate of the tenant of the land is not enlarged by force of such release, for that when the tenant had the estate in the land for terme of the life of the tenant in taile, hee had then all the right which tenant in taile could rightfully grant or release. So as by this release no right passeth, inasmuch as his right was gone before.

Sect. 613.

¶ Item si tenant en le taile per son fait grant a vn auter tout son estate que il auoit en les tenements a luy tailes, a auer et tener tout son estate al auter et a ses heires a touts iours, et deliuera a luy seisin accordant, en cest cas le tenant a que lalienation fuit fait, nad auter estate forsque pur terme de vie del tenant en taile, et issint il poit bien estre proue, que le tenant en taile ne poit pas graunter ne aliener, ne faire ascun droiturel estate de franktenement a auter person, forsque pur terme de sa vie demesne, &c.

ALso if tenant in taile by his Deed grant to another all his estate which hee hath in the tenements to him entailed, To haue and to hold all his estate to the other, and to his heires for euer, and deliuer to him seisin accordingly. In this case the tenant to whom the alienation was made hath no other estate but for terme of the life of tenant in taile. And so it may bee well proued, that tenant in taile cannot grant nor alien, nor make any rightfull estate of freehold to another person, but for terme of his owne life only, &c.

¶ The meaning of Littleton in both these cases in this and in the Section next preceding is, that hauing regard to the issue in taile, and to them in reuersion or remainder, Tenant in taile cannot lawfully make a greater estate then for terme of his life, and therefore this Release or Grant is no Discontinuance. But in regard of himselfe this Release or Grant leaueth no reuersion in him, but put the same in abeiance, so as after this Release or Grant made he shall not haue any action of Waste, &c. 13.H.7.16.a. Brooke Release 95.

¶ *Grant tout son estate, Vid. Sect. 650.* Action of waste, &c. there is implyed that he shall not enter for a forfeiture if after the Release or Grant the Lessee maketh a feoffment in fee.

Sect. 614.

¶ CAr si ieo done Terre a vn home en taile, sauant

FOr if I giue land to a man in taile, sauing the reuersion to my

¶ HEre Littleton proueth, that the feoffee of Tenant in Taile hath no rightfull estate hauing having respect to two persons, the one is to the Donor, whose reuersion is diuested and displaced, and the other to the Issue in Taile, who is driuen to his Action to recouer his Right.

A tort luy deforce.

(n) Brast. li. 4. fo. 238. Flet. li. 5. ca. 11.

(n) Deforciare is a word of Art, and cannot be expressed by any other word, for it signifieth, To withhold lands or tenements from the right owner, in which case either the entrie of the right owner is taken away, or the Deforceor holdeth it so fast, as the right owner is driuen to his reall Præcipe, wherein it is sayde, Vnde A. eum iniustè deforceat, or the Deforceor so disturbeth the right owner, as hee cannot enioy his owne: and therefore it is sayd, Per hoc autem quod dicitur in breui vltimæ præsentationis deforceant, videtur quibusdam quod querens innuat per hoc quod deforcians sit in seisina, sicut in breui de recto, sed reuera non est ita, sed satis deforceat qui possessorem vti seisina non permiserit omnino vel minus commode impediat præsentando, appellando, impetrando secundum quod dicitur de disseisitore, satis facit disseisinam, qui vti non permisit possessorem vel minus commode licet omnino non expellat. In this case that Litleton putteth, the Discontinuee being in by wrong, is no Disseisor, Abator, or Intrudor, but a Deforceor, and hereof commeth Deforcement, and thus did Antiquitie describe it: (o) Deforcement, come si asun enter en auter tenement tout come le veray Seignior est al Market, ou ailors, & retorne, & ne poet auer entre eins est celuy deforce & debotue. And for that at the first the withholding was with violence and force, it was called a deforcement of the Lands or Tenements, but now it generally extended to all kind of wrongfull withholding of Lands or Tenements from the right owner. There is a writ called a Quod ei deforceat, and lieth where Tenant in Taile, or Tenant for life, looseth by default, by the Statute he shall haue a Quod ei deforceat against the Recoueror, and yet he commeth in by course of Law.

Brast. & Flet. vbi supra.

(o) Mir. ca. 2. §. 13.

Westm. 2. ca. 4.

le reuersion a moy, et puis le tenant en le Taile enfeoffa vn auter en fee, le feoffee nad pas droiturell estate en les tenements pur deux causes. Un est, pur ceo que per tiel Feoffement ma Reuersion est discontinue, le quel est a tort fait, et nemy a droit fait. Un auter cause est, si le Tenant en taile morust, et son issue suist Briefe de Formedon enuers le feoffee le briefe dirra, et auxy le count &c. que le feoffee a tort luy deforce, &c. Ergo sil a tort luy deforce, &c. il nad pas droiturel estate.

selfe, and after the Tenant in tayle infeoffeth another in Fee, the Feoffee hath no rightfull estate in the Tenements for two causes: One is, For that by such Feoffement my reuersion is discontinued, the which is a wrong and not a rightfull Act. Another cause is, If the Tenant in Taile dieth, and his Issue bring a Writ of *Formedon* against the Feoffee, the Writ and also the Declaration shall say, &c. That the Feoffee by wrong him deforces, &c. *ergo* if he deforceth him by wróg, he hath no right estate.

Sect. 615.

Item si terre soit lesse a vn home pur terme de sa vie, le remainder a vn auter en le Taile, si celuy en le remainder voile graunter son remainder a vn auter en fee per son fait, et le Tenant a terme de vie attourna, ceo nest pas discontinuance de le remainder.

ALso if Land bee let to a man for terme of his life, the remainder to another in Taile, if he in the remainder will grant his remainder to another in Fee by his Deed, and the Tenaunt for life attorne, this is no discontinuance of the Remainder.

Sect. 616.

¶ ITem si home ad Rent seruice ou Rent charge en Taile, et il granta le dit Rent a vn auter en fee, et le tenaunt attorna, ceo nest pas discontinuance, &c.

ALso if a man hath a Rent seruice or Rent charge in Taile, and hee graunt the sayd Rent to another in Fee, and the Tenaunt attorne, this is no Discontinuance, &c.

Sect. 617.

¶ ITem si home soit Tenant en Taile de vn aduowson en grosse, ou de vn Common en grosse, sil per son fait voile graunt laduowson, ou le Common a vn auter en fee, ceo nest pas discontinuance. Car en tielx cases les Granteez nont estate forsque pur terme de vie de le Tenant en Taile que fist le Grant, &c.

ALso if a man bee Tenaunt in Taile of an Aduowson in Grosse, or of a Common in grosse, if he by his Deed will graunt the Aduowson or Common to another in Fee, this is no Discontinuance; for in such cases the Grauntees haue no estate but for terme of the life of Tenant in Taile that made the Grant, &c.

¶ BY the cases in these three Sections it appeareth, That if a Remainder or a Rent seruice, or a Rent charge, or an Aduowson, or a Common, or any other Inheritance that lieth in Grant, be granted by Tenant in Taile, it is no Discontinuance, as formerly hath beene sayd.

Bract. li. 2. fo. 53. & fo. 366. 378. Brit. fo. 187. Mir. ca. 2. §. 17. Flet. li. 3. ca. 15.

(p) Note, here is an Aduowson named by Littleton, as a thing that lieth in Grant, and passeth not by Liuerie of Seisin.

(p) 5. E. 3. 58. 21. B. 3. 37. 38. 43. E. 3. 1. b. 11. H. 6. 4. 5. H. 7. 37. 18. H. 8. 16. El. Dy. 303. b.

Section 618.

¶ ET nota, que de tiels choses que passont per voy de graunt per fait fait en pays, et sans liuerie, la tiel graunt ne fait pas discontinuance, come en les cases auantdits, & en auter cases semblables, &c. et coment que tiels choses sont graunts en Fee per fine leuie en le Court

ANd note that of such things as passe by way of grant, by Deed made in the Countrie, and without Liuery, there such Grant maketh no discontinuance, as in the cases aforesayd, and in other like cases, &c. And albeit such things bee graunted in Fee, by Fine leuied in the Kings Court, &c.

¶ HEre is the generall reason yeelded of the precedent cases and the like, for that it is a Maxime in Law, That a Grant (d) by Deed of such things as doe lie in Graunt, and not in Liuerie of Seisin, doe worke no discontinuance. But the particular reason is, for that of such things the Grant of Tenant in Tayle worketh no wrong, either to the Issue in Taile, or to him in reuersion or remainder, for nothing doth passe but onely during the life of Tenant in Taile, which is lawfull, and euery discontinuance worketh a wrong, as hath beene sayd.

(d) 6. E. 3. 56. 32. E. 3. Discont. 2. 33. Ass. 8. 4. H. 7. 17. 21. H. 7. 42. 15. H. 7. 19. 21. H. 6. 52. 53. 5. E. 4. 3. 21. E. 4. 5. 22. R. 2. Discon. 56. 38. H. 8. Discont. 35. Brooke. 19. E. 3. Bre. 468. Pl. Com. 435. 18. Ass. p. 2.

(q) If

le Roy, &c. uncore ceo ne fait discontinuance, &c.

yet this maketh not a Discontinuaunce, &c.

(q) 33.E.3.Formd. 47. 13.H.7.10. 36.Ass. 8. 4.H.7.17.

(q) If Tenant in Tayle of a Rent seruice, &c. or of a Reuersion, or Remainder in Taile, &c. grant the same in Fee with warrantie, and leaueth Assets in Fee simple, and dieth, this is neither barre nor discontinuance to the Issue in Taile, but he may distraine for the Rent or seruice, or enter into the land after the decease of Tenant for life. But if the Issue bringeth a Formedon in the Discender, and admit himselfe out of possession, then he shal be barred by the warrantie and Assets.

(r) 3.H.7.12. 9.E.4.22.

(r) Tenant in Taile of a Rent disseiseth the Tenant of the Land, and maketh a Feoffement in Fee with warrantie and dieth, this is no discontinuance of the Rent, but the Issue may distreyne for the same, and albeit the warrantie extend to the Rent, yet by the rule of Litleton, it lieth not in Discontinuance: and where the thing doth lie in Liuerie, as Lands and Tenements, yet if to the conueyance of the Freehold or Inheritance, no Liuerie of Seisin is requisite, it worketh no discontinuance. (s) As if Tenant in Taile exchange lands, &c. or if the King being Tenant in Taile, grant by his Letters Patents the Lands in Fee, there is no Discontinuance wrought.

(s) 38.H.8.Patен.Br.101. Pl.Com.233. Li.1.fo.26. Alton Woods case.

48.E.3.23.

¶ *Per Fine.* Of a thing that lieth in Grant, though it bee granted by Fine, yet it worketh no Discontinuance, and this is regularly true.

(t) 15.E.4.tit.Discont.30. 6.E.56.57.

(t) If Tenant in Taile make a Lease for yeares of Lands, and after leuie a Fine, this is a Discontinuance, for a Fine is a Feoffement of Record, and the Freehold passeth. But if tenant in Taile maketh a Lease for his owne life, and after leuie a Fine, this is no Discontinuance, because the Reuersion expectant upon a state of Freehold which lieth onely in Grant passeth thereby.

Sect. 619.

¶* Nota, si ieo done terre a un auter en taile, et il lessa mesme la terre a un auter pur terme dans, et puis le Lessor graunta le reuersion a un auter en fee, et le tenant a terme dans attourna al Grantee, et le terme est expire durant la vie le tenant en taile, per que le Grantee enter, et puis le tenant en taile ad issue et duie, en ceo case ceo nest discontinuance, nient obstant que le Grant soit execute en la vie le Tenaunt en Taile, pur ceo que al temps de Lease fait a terme dans nul nouel Fee simple fuit reserue en le Lessor, eins le Reuersion demurt a luy en Tail sicome il fuit deuant le Lease fait. *

Note, If I giue Land to another in Taile, and hee letteth the same land to another for terme of yeares, and after the Lessor graunteth the reuersion to another in fee, and the Tenant for yeares attorne to the Grantee, and the terme expireth during the life of the tenant in Tayle, by which the Grauntee enter, and after the Tenant in Taile hath Issue and die: in this case this is no Discontinuance, notwithstanding the Grant be executed in the life of the tenant in Taile, for that at the time of the Lease made for yeares, no new Fee simple was reserued in the Lessor, but the Reuersion remained to him in Taile, as it was before the lease made.

¶ *This is added to Littleton, and not in the Originall, and therefore I purposely omit it: Yet is the case good in Law, because neither the Lease for yeares, nor the grant of the Reuersion diuesteth any Estate.

Sect. 620.

¶ MEs si le tenant en taile fait leas a terme de vie le lessee, &c. en cest case le tenant en le tayle ad fait vn nouel reuersion de fee simple en luy, pur ceo que quant il fist leas pur terme de vie, &c. il discontinua le taile, &c. per force de mesme le leas, & auxy il discontinua ma reuersion, &c. & il couient que la reuersion de fee simple soit en ascun person en tiel cas, et il ne poit estre en moy que sue donor, entant que mon reuersion est discontinue, Ergo il couient que la reuersion de fee soit en le tenant en le taile, que discontinua ma reuersion per tiel leas, &c. En si en cest case le tenant en le taile graunta per son fait cest reuersion en fee a vn auter, et le tenant a terme de vie atturna, &c. & puis le tenant a terme de vie morust, viuant le tenant en le taile, et le grantee de le reuersion entra, &c. en la vie le tenant en le taile, donques ceo est vn discontinuance en fee, & si apres le tenant en le taile morust, son issue ne poit entrer, mes est mis a son briefe de Forme-

BVt if the Tenant in taile make a lease for tearme of the life of the Lessee, &c. In this case the Tenant in tayle hath made a new reuersion of the fee simple in him, because when hee made the Lease for life, &c. he discontinued the tayle, &c. by force of the same Lease, and also hee discontinued my reuersion, &c. And it behoueth that the reuersion of the fee simple be in some person in such case. And it cannot be in me which am the donor inasmuch as my reuersion is discontinued, *Ergo* the reuersion of the fee ought to be in the tenant in tayle who discontinued my Reuersion by Lease, &c. And if in this case the Tenant in tayle grant by his Deed this Reuersion in fee to another, and the Tenant for life attorne, &c. and after the Tenant for life dieth, liuing the Tenant in taile & the grantee of the reuersion enter, &c. in the life of the Tenant in taile, then this is a discontinuance in fee, and if after the Tenant in tayle dieth, his issue may not enter, but is put to his Writ of *Formedon.*

¶ *PVr terme de vie del lessee, &c.* Here is implyed or for tearme of another mans life.

¶ *Nouel reuersion de fee simple.* Which must bee vnderstood of a fee simple determinable vpon the life of the Lessee, which our Author here calleth a fee simple, for if the Lessee dieth, the Donee is Tenant in tayle againe as he was before, and that is the reason that if in that case hee granteth ouer the reuersion and dieth, and after the death of Tenant in taile the Lessee dieth, the entry of the issue is lawfull, because by the death of the Lessee the Discontinuance is determined; and consequently the grant made of the reuersion gained vpon that discontinuance is void also. 15.E.4. Tit Discont. 30.

If Tenant in tayle maketh a lease for three liues according to the Statute of 32.H.8. that is no discontinuance of the estate tayle or of the reuersion, because it is authorised by Act of Parliament whereunto euery man in iudgement of Law is partie. 32.H.8 cap. 28.

And yet in some cases the freehold may bee discontinued and not the reuersion. (u) As if the husband and wife make a lease for life by Deed of the wiues Land reseruing a rent, the husband dieth, this was a Discontinuance at the Common Law for life, and yet the reuersion was not discontinued but remayned in the wife. Otherwise it is if

(u) 38.E.3.32. 18. Ass. 2. 18.E.3.54. 22.H.6.24.

don. Et la cause est, pur ceo que cestuy q̃ auoit l' grant de tiel reuersion en fee Simple, auoit le seisin & execution de mesmes les terres ou tenements dauer a luy et a ses heires en son demesne come de fee, en la vie l' tenant en taile, et ceo est per force de grant de mesme le tenant en taile.

And the cause is for that he which hath the grant of such reuersion in fee simple hath the seisin and execution of the same lands or tenemẽts. To haue to him and to his heires in his Demesne as of fee in the life of the tenant in taile. And this is by force of the grant of the said Tenant in tayle.

if the husband had made the Lease alone.

21.H.6.52. 15.E.4.tit. Discont. 30.

¶ *Et puis le tenant a terme de vie morust, &c.* The like Law it is if the tenant for life surrender to the Grantee, or if the Grantee recouer in an Action of waste, or enter for the forfeiture.

32.E.3.Discont 2. 43 E.3.Entr.Cong.31. 3.H.4.9 22.R.2.discont 50 34.Ass.6. Pl.4 38. Ass 6 p. 6. 43.Ass.6.48.18.E.2.43. 21.H.6.52.15.E.4.110 Discontinuance 30.Brooke.tit.discont.3.& 14.4.H.7.17. 21.H.7.11.

¶ *Auoit seisin & execution.* And here it is to be obserued, that when the reuersion in this case is executed in the life of Tenant in tayle, it is equiualent in iudgement of Law to a feoffment in fee, for the state for life passed by liuery

(w) 21.H.6.52.53.

(w) If Tenant in tayle make a lease for life, the remaynder in fee, this is an absolute Discontinuance albeit the remaynder be not executed in the life of Tenant in tayle, because all is one estate and passeth by one liuery. And so note a diuersity betweene a grant of a reuersion, and a limitation of a remaynder. B. Tenant in tayle maketh a gift in tayle to A. and after B releaseth to A and his heires, and after A. dieth without issue, the issue of the first Donee may enter vpon the collaterall heire, because A. had not seisin and execution of the reuersion of the land in his Demesne as of fee, as Littleton here speaketh. But if Tenant in tayle make a lease for the life of the Lessee, and after releaseth to him and his heires, this is an absolute Discontinuance, because the fee simple is executed in the life of Tenant in tayle.

(y) 34.E.1.Quare Impedit 179. 22.E.3.6. 17.E.3.3. 33.E.3.Quare Imp.196. 23.Ass.8. 50.E.3.26.

(y) If Tenant in tayle of a Mannor whereunto an Aduowson is appendant maketh a feoffment in fee by deed (as it ought to be) of one Acre with the Aduowson, and the Church becommeth void, and the feoffee present, Tenant in tayle dieth, the Church becommeth voide, the issue shall not present vntill he hath recontinued the Acre. But if the feoffee had not executed the same by presentment, then the issue in tayle should haue presented. And so was it at the Common Law of the husband seised in the right of his wife, mutatis mutandis

36.Ass.8. 42.E.3.20. 22.R.2.Discont. 50.

If a fine be leuied to a Tenant in tayle, and hee granteth and rendreth the Land to him and his heires and die before execution, this is no Discontinuance. Otherwise it is, if it had beene executed in the life of Tenant in tayle.

21.H.6.52.53. Brooke tit. Discontin. 3. 21.H.7.11.Lib 1.fol.85. Lib.10.fol.96.97.

If Tenant in tayle make a Lease for life of the Lessee, and after grant the Reuersion with Warrantie, and dieth before execution, this is no Discontinuance, because the Discontinuance was (as hath beene said) but for life, and the Warrantie cannot enlarge the same.

(*) 15.E.4.Discont.30. Vide Sect.642.

¶ *Et ceo est per force del grant de mesme le tenant en tayle.* Hereupon Littleton himselfe is of the same opinion, (*) as it appeareth he was in our Bookes, that if Tenant in tayle make a Lease for life, and grant the Reuersion in fee, and the Lessee attorne, and that Grantee granteth it ouer, and the Lessee attorne, and then the Lessee for life dieth, so as the Reuersion is executed in the life of Tenant in tayle, yet this is no Discontinuance, but that after the death of Tenant in tayle the issue may enter, because as Littleton here saith, he is not in of the grant of the Tenant in tayle, but of his Grantee.

If at this day Tenant in tayle make a Lease for life, and after by Deed indented and inrolled according to the Statute he bargaineth and selleth the Reuersion to another in fee, and the Lessee dieth, so as the Reuersion is executed in the life of Tenant in tayle, albeit the bargainee is not in the per by the Tenant in tayle, yet in asmuch as hee clayneth the Reuersion immediately from him, which is executed in his life time, this is a Discontinuance. And so it is and for the same cause if Tenant in tayle had granted the Reuersion to the vse of another and his heires If Tenant in tayle maketh a Lease for life, and after disseiseth the Lessee for life and maketh a feoffment in fee, the Lessee dieth, and then Tenant in tayle dieth, albeit the fee be executed, yet for that the fee was not executed by lawfull meanes, (as in all the Cases of Littleton it appeareth it ought to be) it is no Discontinuance.

Sect. 621.

¶ En mesme le manner serra, si en le case auantdit, le tenant a terme de vie apres lattournement al grantee vst alien en fee, & le grantee vst enter pur forfeiture de son estate, & puis le tenant en taile vst deuie, cest vn discontinuance, Causa qua supra. ¶.

IN the same manner shall it be, if in the case aforesaid the Tenant for tearme of life after the Attornement to the Grantee had aliened in fee, and the Grantee had entred by forfeiture of his estate, and after the Tenant in tayle had died this is a Discontinuance, *Causa qua supra*. ¶.

¶ This is added in this place, but in the Originall it commeth in after in this Chapter. 21.H.6.52.53. 15.E.4.Discont.30.

Section 622.

¶ Mes en cest cas, si tenãt en taile que granta le reuersion, &c. morust, viuant le tenant a terme de vie, et puis le tenant a terme de vie morust, & puis celuy a que le reuersion fuit graunt enter, &c. donque ceo nest pas discontinuance, mes que lissu del tenant en taile poit bien enter sur le grauntee del Reuersion pur ceo que le Reuersion que le grauntee auoit, &c. ne fuit execute, &c. en le vie le tenant en taile, &c. Et issint il est graund diuersitie quant tenant en taile fait vn leas pur terme dans, & lou il fait leas pur terme de vie, car en lun cas il ad reuersion en taile, & en lauter cas il ad vn reuersion en fee.

BVt in this case if Tenant in taile that grants the reuersion, &c. dieth liuing the tenant for life, and after the Tenant for life dieth, and after hee to whom the reuersion was granted enter, &c. then this is no discontinuance, but that the issue of the tenant in tayle may well enter vpon the Grantee of the reuersion, because the Reuersion which the Grantee had &c. was not executed, &c. in the life of the tenant in taile, &c. And so there is a great diuersitie when Tenant in tayle maketh a Lease for yeares, and where hee maketh a Lease for life, for in the one case hee hath a reuersion in tayle, and in the other case he hath a reuersion in fee.

¶ Of this sufficient hath beene said before, and is of it selfe manifest and needeth no explication.

Like Law was at the Common Law of a husband seised of Land in right of his wife, Mutatis mutandis. 18.Ass.6. 21.H.6 53.

Sect. 623.

¶ Car ſi terre ſoit done a vn hōe et a ſes heires males de ſon corps engendres, le quel ad iſſue deux fits, et leigne fits ad iſſue file et deuy, et le ten̄ en taile fait vn leas pur terme des ans, et deuy, ore le reuerſion diſcendiſt a le fits puiſne, pur ceo que le reuerſion fuit forſque en le taile, et le fits puiſne eſt heire male, &c. Mes ſi le tenant vſt fait vn leas pur terme de vie, &c. et puis mouruſt, ore le reuerſion diſcendiſt a le file del eigne fits, pur ceo que le reuerſion eſt en fee ſimple, et la file eſt heire general, &c.

For if land bee giuen to a man and to his heires males of his body engendred, who hath iſſue two ſonnes, and the eldeſt ſonne hath iſſue a daughter and dieth, and the tenant in tayle maketh a leaſe for yeares and die, now the reuerſion diſcendeth to the younger ſonne, for that the reuerſion was but in the taile, and the youngeſt ſonne is heire male, &c. but if the tenant had made a leaſe for life, &c. and after died, now the reuerſion diſcend to the daughter of the elder brother, for that the reuerſion is in the fee ſimple, and the daughter is heire generall, &c.

This is euident alſo and needeth no explanation.

Section 624.

¶ Item ſi home ſoit ſeiſie en taile de terres deuiſables per teſtament, &c. et il ceo deuiſa a vn auter en fee, et mourust, et lauter enter, &c. ceo neſt pas diſcontinuance, pur ceo que nul diſcontinuance fuit fait en la vie del tenant en le taile, &c.

Alſo if a man be ſeiſed in taile of lands deuiſable by Teſtament, &c. and hee deuiſeth this to another in fee, and dieth and the other enter, &c. this is no diſcontinuance, for that no diſcontinuance was made in the life of the Tenant in taile, &c.

9.E.4.32. 30.H.6.14. Vet.18.E.3.8.

¶ This is manifeſt and needeth no explanation; Only this is to be obſerued, that no Diſcontinuance can be made by Tenant in taile, but ſuch as is made, and taketh effect in his life time, which is here implied in the (&c.)

Sect. 625.

(a) 9.E.4.24.b.

And of this opinion is Littleton (a) in our bookes, and ſaith that ſo it was adiudged.

¶ *Enfeoffe le donor, &c.* This muſt bee vnderſtood where the reuerſion of the Donor is immedi-

Lib.1.fo.140.in Chudleys caſe

¶ Item ſi terr̄ ſoit done en taile, ſauant le reuerſion al donor, et puis le tenāt en taile per ſon fait enfeoffa l' donor,

Alſo if land be giuen in taile, ſauing the reuerſion to the Donor, and after the Tenant in taile by his deed enfeoffe the Do-

a auer et tener a luy et a ses heirs a touts iours, et liuer a luy seisin accordant, &c. ceo nest pas discontinuance, pur ceo que nul poit discontinuer lestate en le taile, si non q̃ il discontinue le reuersion celuy que ad le reuersion, &c. ou le remainder, si ascun ad le remainder, &c. & entant que per tiel feoffment fait a le Donor (le reuersion adonq; esteant en luy) son reuersion ne fuit discontinue ne alterate, &c. cest feoffmēt nest pas discontinuance, &c.

nor, To haue and to hold to him and to his heires for euer, and deliuer to him seisin accordingly, &c. this is no discontinuance, because none can discontinue the estate taile, vnlesse he discontinueth the reuersion of him who hath the reuersion, &c. or remainder, if any hath the remainder, &c. and in asmuch as by such feoffment made to the Donor (the reuersion then being in him) his reuersion was not discontinued nor altered, &c, this feoffment is no discontinuance, &c.

ately expectant vpon the estate of the Donee (b) for if a man make a Gift in taile the remainder in taile, reseruing the reuersion to himselfe; In this case if the Donee enfeoffe the Donor, this is a discontinuance because there is a meane estate, and so doth Littleton here put his case of a reuersion immediately expectant vpon the gift in taile. Also it is to be intended of a feoffment made to the Donor soly or only, for if the Donee enfeoffe the Donor and a stranger, this is a discontinuance of the whole land.

(b) 41. Ass. 2. 41. E. 3. 2.

28. H. 8. Dier. 12.

But if Tenant for life make a Lease for his owne life to the Lessor, the remainder to the Lessor and an estranger in fee. In this case forasmuch as the limitation of the fee should worke the wrong, it enureth to the Lessor as a surrender for the one moyty, and a forfeiture as to the remainder of the stranger, for he cannot giue to the Lessor that which he had before, as our Author here saith, and as to the remainder to the stranger, it is a forfeiture for his moity, and when the Lessor entreth he shall take the benefit of it. But if two Ioyntenants be, and one of them enfeoffe his Companion and a stranger, and make Liuery to the stranger, this shall vest only in the stranger, because the Liuery cannot enure to his Companion.

¶ *Nul poet discontinuer lestate en taile, sinon que il discontinue le reuersion, &c. ou le remainder, &c.* And therefore for this cause if the reuersion or remainder be in the King, the Tenant in taile cannot discontinue the estate tayle. (c) But Tenant in taile, the reuersion in the King, might haue barred the estate taile by a Common recouery vntill the Statute of 34. H. 8 ca. 20. which restrayneth such a Tenant in taile, but that common recouery neither barred nor discontinued the Kings reuersion.

40. Ass 36. 21. Ass 36. 18. E. 3. 45. F. N. B. 142. d. Pl Com. 555.

(c) 33. H. 8. tit. Taile. Br. 41. Pl. Com. vbi supra.

Note the reuersion may be reuested, and yet the Discontinuance remaine. (d) As if a Feme Couert be Tenant for life, and the husband make a Feoffment in fee, and the Lessor enter for the forfeiture, here is the reuersion reuested, and yet the Discontinuance remained at the Common Law.

(d) 27. Ass. P. 60. 29. Ass. 43. 11. Ass. 11. 16. Ass. 11. 18. E. 3. 45.

Sect. 626.

¶ En mesme le maner est, lou terres sont dones a vn hōe en taile, le remainder a vn auter en fee, et le tenāt en taile enfeoffa celuy, que est en le remainder, a auer et tener a luy, et a ses heirs, ceo nest pas discontinuance, Causa qua supra.

IN the same manner is it where lands are giuen to a man in taile, the remainder to another in fee, and the tenant in taile enfeoffe him that is in the remainder, To haue and to hold to him & to his heires, this is no discontinuance, *Causa qua supra.*

¶ *Le remainder a vn auter.* Here it appeareth that (as hath bin said in case of a reuersion) that the remainder must be immediately expectant vpon the estate taile.

Sect. 627.

¶ ITem si vn Abbe ad vn Reuersion ou Rent seruice, ou Rent charge, et voile graunter cel reuersion, ou Rent seruice, ou Rent charge a vn auter en fee, et le tenant atturna, &c. ceo nest pas discontinuance.

ALso if an Abbot hath a Reuersion, or a Rent seruice, or a Rent charge, and he will grant this Reuersion, or Rent seruice, or Rent charge to another in Fee, and the Tenant attorne, &c. this is no discontinuance.

Of Inheritances that lie in Grant, sufficient hath beene sayd before.

Section 628.

¶ EN mesme le manner lou Abbe est seisie dun Aduowson, ou de tielx choses que passont per voy de grant sans liuerie de seisin, &c.

IN the same manner where an Abbot is seised of an Aduowson, or of such things which passe by way of Grant, without Liuerie of seisin, &c.

¶ HEre it appeareth, (as hath beene sayd) That an Aduowson doth not lie in Liuery, but in Grant.

Section 629.

¶ ITem si Tenant en Taile lessa sa terre a vn auter pur terme de vie, et puis il graunta en fee le Reuersion a vn auter, et le tenant atturna, & puis le tenant a terme de vie aliena en fee, et le Grantee de reuersion entra, &c. en le vie le Tenant en le Taile, et puis le Tenant en le Taile mourust son Issue ne poet enter, mes est mis a son Briefe de Formedon, pur ceo que le Reuersion en Fee simple que le Grauntor auoit per le grant del tenant en le Taile, fuit execute en le vie de mesme le tenaunt en le Taile, et pur ceo est vn discontinuance en fee, &c.

ALso if Tenant in Tayle letteth his Land to another for life, and after he granteth in Fee the Reuersion to another, and the Tenant attorne, and after the Tenant for life alien in Fee, and the Grauntee of the Reuersion enter, &c. in the life of the Tenant in Taile, and after the Tenant in Taile dieth, his Issue shall not enter, but is put to his Writ of *Formedon*, because the Reuersion in Fee simple which the Grauntor had by the Graunt of the Tenant in Tayle, was executed in the life of the same Tenant in Tayle, and therefore it is a discontinuance in Fee, &c.

Of this sufficient hath beene sayd before.

Section 630.

¶ ET nota que ascuns font discontinuances p̄ terme de vie. Sicome Tenaunt en le taile fait vn Lease pur terme de vie, sauant le reũsion a luy, auxy longement que le reuersion est al tenant en taile, ou a ses heires, ceo nest discontinuance, forsque durant la vie le tenant a terme de vie, &c. Et si tiel tenant en taile dona les tenements a vn auter en taile, sauant le reuersion, donques ceo est discontinuance durant le second taile, &c.

AND note that some make discontinuances for terme of life. As if Tenant in Tayle make a Lease for life, sauing the reuersion to him as long as the Reuersion is to the Tenaunt in Tayle or to his Heyres: This is no discontinuance but during the life of Tenaunt for life, &c. And if such Tenant in Taile giueth the lands to another in Tayle, sauing the Reuersion, then this is a Discontinuance during the second Tayle, &c.

¶ This is manifest, and hath beene handled before, and needeth no explanation, onely this is to be obserued, where Littleton putteth hereafter cases of Discontinuances by Feoffement, &c. he hath a double entendment: First, By Feoffement or by any other Conueyance which may make a Discontinuance. Secondly, (&c.) implieth a Discontinuance by a gift in Taile, or a lease for life, &c.

Sect. 631.

¶ MES sou le tenant en tayle fait vn lease pur terme dans, ou pur terme de vie, le remainder a vn auter en fee, et deliuer liuerie de seisin accordant, ceo est discontinuance en fee, pur ceo que le Fee simple passa per force de liuerie de seisin, &c.

BVt where the Tenant in Tayle maketh a Lease for yeares or for life, the remainder to another in Fee, and deliuereth Liuerie of Seisin accordingly, this is a Discontinuance in Fee, for that the fee simple passeth by force of the Liuerie of Seisin, &c.

This is euident also, and hereof sufficient hath beene spoken before.

Sect. 632.

¶ ET est ascauoir, q̄ ascuns tiels discontinuances sont fait sur condition, &c. et pur ceo que les conditions sont enfreints, &c. ou pur

AND it is to be vnderstood, That some such Discontinuances are made vpon Condition, &c. and for that the conditions be broken, &c. or for

¶ *Discontinuances fait sur Condition, &c.* Heere is to be vnderstood a Diuersity betweene a Condition in Deed, whereof Littleton here speaketh, and a Condition in law, whereof somewhat hath beene sayd before in this Chapter, viz. where the Feme is tenant for life, and the husband maketh a Feoffement in Fee, and the Lessor entreth for the Condition in Law.

¶ *Conditions sont enfreints, &c.* Here is implied, Or any cause giuen either by disabilitie of the feoffees, or by any condition performed on the part of the feoffor, or otherwise, whereby the state is in any sort auoyded.

¶ *Come si le Baron soit seisie de certain terre en droit sa feme, &c.* Here it appeareth, That for the Condition broken, the heire of the husband may enter, for albeit no right discend from the husband to his heire, yet the title of entry by force of the Condition which the husband created vpon the Feoffement, and reserued to him and his heires, doth discend to his heyre, and Littleton saith truly, That so it hath beene adiudged.

4.H.6.3.9.H.7.24.b. Lib.8.fo.43.44. Whittinghams case.

¶ *Sur le heire.* Nota, when the heire in this case hath entred for the Condition broken, and hath auoyded the Feoffement, the estate of the heire vanisheth away, and presently the Estate vesteth in the Feme or her heires, without any entrie or claime by her or them; for the heire entreth in respect of the Condition, vpon the reall Contract, and not of any right, as hath beene sayd, and if the husband himselfe had re-entred, the state had vested in his wife: And therefore where Littleton and our Bookes say, That the wife shall enter vpon the heyre, the meaning is, that after the re-entrie of the heire she may enter.

Whitinghams Case vbi supra.

auters causes, solonque le course de la ley, tiels estates sont defeates, donques sont les discontinuances defeates, et ne tollet ascun home per force de eux, de son entrie, &c. Come si le Baron soit seisie de certeine terre en droit sa feme, et fait Feoffement en fee sur condition, et deuie, si le heire apres enter sur le feoffee pur le Condition enfreint, lentrie la feme est congeable sur le heire, pur ceo que per lentrie del heire le discontinuance est defeat, come est adiudge.

other causes, according to the course of Law such Estates are defeated, then are the Discontinuances defeated, and shall not by force of them take any man from his entrie, &c. As if the husband be seised of certaine land in right of his wife, and maketh a Feoffement in Fee vpon Condition, and dyeth, if the Heire after enter vpon the Feoffee for the condition broken, the entrie of the wife was cogeable vpon the heire, for that by the entry of the heire the discontinuance is defeated, as is adiudged.

Sect. 633.

Whittinghams Case vbi supra.

¶ The reason here rendred by Littleton, is, for that the husband cannot enter in his own right, but in the right of his wife; and the heire of the Husband cannot enter, for no right or title discends vnto him, and the wife in this case shall take benefit of the nonage of her husband, and enter into the land.

If an Infant be Tenant for another mans life, and make a Feoffement in fee, and Cesty que vie dieth, the Enfant himselfe shall not enter, because he hath no right at all.

¶ Item si feme inheritrix q̃ ad vn Baron, quel Baron est deins age, et il esteant deins age fait vn Feoffement de les Tenements son feme en fee, et morust, il ad este question, si la feme poit entrer, ou non, &c. Et il semble a ascuns, que lentry la feme

ALso if a Woman Inheritrix hath a husband who is within age, and hee beeing within age maketh a Feoffement of the Tenements of his wife in Fee, and dieth, it hath beene a question, If the Wife may enter or not, &c. And it seemeth to some, that the

feme apres la mort sa baron, est congeable en cest cas. Car quant sa baron feasoit tiel feoffment, &c. il puissoit bien enter, nient contristeant tiel feoffment, &c. durant la couerture, & il ne puissoit enter en son droit demesne, mes en le droit la feme, *Ergo* tiel droit que il auoit dentrer en droit sa feme, &c. cest droit dentrer demurt al feme apres son decease.

entrie of the wife after the death of her Husband is congeable in this case, for when her Husband made such feoffment, &c. he might well enter notwithstanding such feoffment, &c. during the couerture, and he could not enter in his owne right but in the right of his wife, *Ergo* such right as hee had to enter in the right of his wife, &c. this right of entrie remayneth to the wife after his decease.

If the husband within age take to wife feme tenant in tayle generall, and the husband make a gift in tayle and dieth within age, in this case the wife may enter, as Littleton here holdeth, or the heire of the husband in respect of the new reuersion discended vnto him may enter. But if the heire enter presently thereupon his estate vanisheth. If tenant in tayle being within the age of one and twenty yeeres make a feoffment in fee, and after is attainted of felonie and dieth, the entry of the issue is not lawfull, for his entry is not lawfull in respect of his estate only, but of his blond also which is corrupted, and therefore in that case he is driuen to his Formedon.

If husband and wife be both within age, and they by Deed indented ioyne in a feoffment reseruing a rent, the husband dieth, the wife may enter or haue a Dum fuit infra ætatem: But if she were of full age, she shall not haue a Dum fuit infra ætatem, for the nonage of her husband, albeit they be but one person in Law. 14.E.3.Bre.282. 14.E.3. *Dum fuit infra ætatem* 6. F.N.B 192.

Sect. 634.

ET il y ad ee dit, que si deux ioyntenants esteants deins age, font vn feoffment en fee, et lun des enfants deyt, et lauter suruesquist, entant que les ambideux enfants puissont ent ioyntment en lour vies, cel droit accruist tout a luy que suruesquist, et pur ceo, celuy que suruesquist poit enter en lentiertie, &c. Et auxy lheire le baron que fist le feoffment deins age ne poit enter, &c. pur ceo que nul droit discendist a tiel heire en le cas auantdit, pur ceo que le baron nauoit vnques riens forsque en droit de sa feme, &c.

AND it hath beene said that if two Ioyntenants being within age make a feoffment in fee and one of the Infants die, and the other suruiueth in as much as both the Infants might enter ioyntly in their liues, this right accrueth all to him which suruiueth, and therefore hee that suruiueth may enter into the whole, &c. And also the heire of the husband which made the feoffment within age cannot enter, &c. because no right discendeth to such heire in the case aforesaid, for that the husband had neuer any thing but in right of his wife, &c.

P*Oet enter en lentiertie, &c.* And the reason hereof is implyed in this (&c.) for that they may ioyne in a Writ of right, and therefore the right shall suruiue, But they cannot ioyne in a Dum fuit intra ætatem, because the nonage of the 21.E.3.50.18.E.2.Bre.838 6.E.3.4. 9.H.6.6. 19.H.6.6. 39.H.6.42. 34.H.6.31. F.N.B.192.

See of this in the Chapter of Joyntenants.

one is not the nonage of the other. In this case if one Joyntenant had made a feoffment in fee and died, the right should not haue surniued, for the Joynture was seuered for a time. If two Joyntenants be, and the one is of full age, and the other within age, and both they make a feoffment in fee, and he of full age dieth, the Infant shall enter or haue a Dum fuit infra ætatem, but for the moitie.

Section 635.

¶ Et auxy quant vn enfant fait vn feoffment esteant deins age ceo ne luy greeuera ne ledra, mes que il poit enter bien, &c. car ceo serroit encounter reason, que tiel feoffment fait per celuy que ne fuit able de faire tiel feoffment, greeuera ou ledera auter, de toller eux de lour entre, &c. Et pur ceux causes il semble a ascuns, que apres la mort de tiel baron issint esteant deins age al temps de le feoffment, &c. que sa feme bien poit enter, &c.

And also when an infant make a feoffment being within age, this shall neither grieue nor hurt him, but that hee may well enter, &c. for it should be against reason that such feoffment made by him that was not able to make such a feoffment, shall grieue or hurt another to take them from their entry, &c. And for these reasons it seemeth to some, that after the death of such husband so being within age at the time of the feoffment, &c. that his wife may well enter, &c.

Bract. fol. 14. Bretton fol. 88. a. Fleta lib. 3. cap. 3.

¶ *Mes que il poet enter bien, &c.* Here is implyed that he might enter either within age, or at any time after full age, and likewise after his death his heire may enter. Meliorem enim conditionem facere potest minor deteriorem nequaquam.

Nota, A speciall heire shall take aduantage of the infancie of the Ancestor. As if Tenant in tayle of an Acre of the custome of Borow English make a feoffment in fee within age, and dieth, the yongest sonne shall auoyd it, for he is priuie in bloud, and claymeth by discent from the Infant.

And so if Tenant in tayle to him and the heires females of his bodie make a feoffment in fee and dieth within age, hauing issue a sonne and a Daughter, the Daughter shall auoyd the feoffment. And so note that a cause to enter by reason of Infancy is not like to Conditions, warranties, and Estoppels, which euer discend to the heire at the Common Law.

The residue of this Section vpon that which hath beene said is euident.

Section 636.

¶ *Surrender.* Sursum redditio properly is a yeelding vp of an estate for life or yeares to him that hath an immediate estate in reuersion or remaynder, wherein the estate for life or yeares may drowne by mutuall agreement betweene them.

¶ Item si feme enheritrix prent baron, et ont issue fits, et le baron morust, & el prent auter baron, et le second baron lessa la terre que il ad en droit sa feme a vn auter

Also if a woman inheritrix taketh husband; and they haue issue a sonne, and the husband dieth, and she takes another husband, and the second husband letteth the Land which he

ter pur terme de sa vie, et puis la feme morust, et puis le tenant a terme de vie surrendist son estate a le second baron, &c. Quære si le fits le fem poit enter en cest cas sur le second baron durant la vie le tenant a terme de vie, &c. Mes il est cleere ley, q̃ apres la mort le tenant a terme de vie, le fits la feme poit enter, pur ceo que l' discontinuance que fuit tantsolemẽt pur terme de vie, est determine, &c. per la mort de mesme le tenant a terme de vie.

hath in right of his wife to another for terme of his life, and after the wife dieth, and after the tenant for life surrendreth his estate to the second husband, &c. *Quære* if the sonne of the wife may enter in this case vpon the second husband during the life of tenant for life, &c. but it is cleere Law, that after the death of the Tenant for life the son of the wife may enter, because the discontinuance which was only for terme of life, is determined, &c. by the death of the same Tenant for life.

Note there be three kinds of Surrenders, viz. a Surrender properly taken at the Common Law, which is here before discribed, and whereof Littleton speaketh. Secondly, a Surrender by custome of lands holden by Copie, or of customary estates whereof you haue read before, Sect. 74. and a Surrender improperly taken (as appeare before, Sect. 550.) of a Deed. And so of a Surrender of a Patent, and of a Rent newly created, and of a fee simple to the King.

2. Eliz. Dier 176. 14. H. 7. 3. 27. Ass. 37. 49. E. 3. 2. 11. H. 4. 2. 12. H. 4. 21. 13. H. 4. 13.

A Surrender properly taken is of two sorts, viz. a surrender in Deed, or by expresse words, (whereof Littleton here putteth an example) and a surrender in Law wrought by consequent by operation of Law. Littleton here putteth his case of a Surrender of an estate in possession, for a Right cannot bee surrendred. And it is to be noted that a surrender in Law is in some cases of greater force, then a surrender in Deed. As if a man make a Lease for yeares to begin at Michaelmasse next, this future interest cannot bee surrendred, because there is no Reuersion wherein it may drowne, but by a Surrender in Law it may be drowned. As if the Lessee before Michaelmasse take a new Lease for yeares either to begin presently, or at Michaelmasse, this is a Surrender in Law of the former Lease, Fortior & æquior est dispositio legis quam hominis.

14 H. 8. 15. 37 H. 6. 17. 21. H. 7. 6. 40. E. 3. 24. 31. Ass. 26. 50. E. 3. 6. 44. Ass. 3. 35. H. 8. Dier 37. 8. Ass. 20. 4. Ma. Dier 141 11. Eliz. Dier 280.

6. H. 7. 9. 37. H. 6. 17. 21. H. 7. 5. 14. H. 7. 4. Lib. 6. fo. 67. Sir Moyle Finches case.

Also there is a surrender without Deede, whereof Littleton putteth here an example of an estate for life of lands, which may be surrendred without Deed, and without Liuery of seisin, because it is but a yeelding, or a restoring of the state againe to him in the immediate reuersion or remainder, which are alwayes fauoured in Law. And there is also a surrender by Deed, and that is of things that lye in grant, whereof a particular estate cannot commence without Deed, and by consequent the estate cannot be surrendred without Deed. But in the example that Littleton here putteth, the estate might commence without Deed, and therefore might be surrendred without Deed. And albeit a particular estate be made of lands by Deed, yet may it be surrendred without Deed, in respect of the nature and quality of the thing demised, because the particular estate might haue beene made without Deed, and so on the other side. If a man be Tenant by the Curtesie, or Tenant in Dower of an Aduowson, Rent or other thing that lye in grant, albeit there the estate begin without Deed, yet in respect of the nature and quality of the thing that lyes in grant, it cannot be surrendred without Deed. And so if a Lease for life be made of lands, the Remainder for life, albeit the remainder for life began without Deed, yet because remainders and reuersions though they be of lands are things that lye in grant, they cannot be surrendred without Deed. See in my Reports plentifull matter of surrenders.

19. H. 6. 33. 27. Ass. 46. 14. H. 7. 4. 1. H. 6. 1. Pl. Com. 541.

¶ *Quære si le fits la feme poet enter, &c.* Here Littleton maketh a quære. So as graue and learned men may doubt without any imputation to them, for the most learned doubteth most, and the more ignorant for the most part are the more bold and peremptorie.

It is holden of some, that after the surrender the issue in taile during the life of Tenant for life may enter, for that hauing regard to the issue the state for life is drowned, and consequently the inheritance gained by the Lease is by the acceptance of the surrender banished and

gone, as if Tenant in taile make a Lease for life, whereby he gaineth a new reversion (as hath beene said) if Tenant for life surrender to the Tenant in taile, the estate for life being drowned, the reversion gained by wrong is, banished and gone, and he is Tenant in taile againe a-
21.H.6.53. gainst the opinion Obiter of Portington, 21.H.6.53.

But herein are two diversities worthy of observation. The first is that having regard to the partyes to the surrender, the estate is absolutely drowned, as in this case betweene the Lessee and the second baron. But having regard to strangers, who were not parties or privies thereunto, least by a voluntary surrender they may receive prejudice touching any right or interest they had before the surrender, the estate surrendred hath in consideration of Law a con-
45.E.3.13. 5.H.5.9. 9.E.4.18. tinuance. As if a Reversion be granted with warrantie and Tenant for life surrender, the Grantee shall not have Execution in value against the Grantor who is a stranger during the life of Tenant for life, for this surrender shall worke no prejudice to the Grantee who is a stranger.

40.E.3.13. 9.E.4.18. 1.H.6.1. 24.E.3.77. So if Tenant for life, surrender to him in reversion being within age, he shall not have his age, for that should be a prejudice to a stranger, who is to become Demandant in a reall action.

5.H.5.8. 26.Ass.38. 7.H.6.2.b. If Tenant for life grant a Rent cherge, and after surrender, yet the rent remaineth, for to that purpose he commeth in under the charge. Causa qua supra.

If a Bishop be seised of a Rent-charge in fee, the Tenant of the land enfeoffe the Bishop and his Successors, the Lord enter for the Mortmaine, he shall hold it discharged of the rent, for the entrie for the Mortmaine affirmeth the alienation in Mortmaine, and the Lord clay-meth under his estate, but if Tenant for life grant a rent in fee, and after infeoffe the Grantee, and the Lessor enter for the forfeiture, the rent is revived, for the Lessor doth claime above the
48.E.3.16. Feoffment. But if I grant the reversion of my Tenant for life to another for terme of his life, and Tenant for life attorne, now is the waste of Tenant for life dispunishable. After-wards I release to the Grantee for life and his heires, or grant the reversion to him and his heires, now albeit the Tenant for life be a stranger to it, yet because he attorned to the Grantee for life, the estate for life which the Grantee had, shall have no continuance in the eye of the Law as to him, but he shall be punished for waste done afterward.

The second diversity is, that for the benefit of an estranger the estate for life is absolutely determined. As if he in the reversion make a Lease for yeares or grant a Rent-charge, &c. and then the Lessee for life surrender, the Lease or rent shall commence maintenant. So in the case of Littleton, first betweene the Lessee, and the second husband, the state for life is determined, and secondly for the benefit of the issue it shall be so adiudged in Law. Here note a diversity, when it is to the prejudice of a stranger, and when it is for his benefit.

If a man maketh a Lease to A. for life reserving a rent of 40. shillings to him and his heires, the remainder to B. for life, the Lessor grant the reversion in fee to B. A attorne, B. shall not have the rent, for that although the fee simple doe drowne the remainder for life betweene them, yet as to a stranger it is in esse, and therefore B shall not have the rent, but his heire shall have it.

Adiudge Mich. 16. & 17. Eliz. int. Turner Pl. & Gray def. in eiectione firme in Communi banco. Rot. 945. Sir Francis Flemings case. (a) 6.H.4.7. Pl. Com. 418. (b) 32.H.8. Br. surrender 52. A Master of an Hospitall being a sole Corporation by the consent of his brethren make a Lease for yeares of part of the possessions of the Hospitall, afterwards the Lessee for yeares is made master, the terme is drowned, for a man cannot have a terme for yeares in his owne right, and a freehold in auter droit to consist together (as if a man Lessee for yeares take a feme Lessor to wife.) (a) But a man may have a freehold in his owne right and a terme in auter droit, and therefore if a man Lessor take the feme Lessee to wife, the terme is not drowned, but he is possessed of the terme in her right during the Coverture. (b) So if the Lessee make the Lessor his Executor, the terme is not drowned. Causa qua supra.

But if it had beene a Corporation aggregate of many, the making of the Lessee Master had not extinguished the terme, no more then if the Lessee had beene made one of the brethren of the Hospitall.

Sect. 637.

Nota que un estate taile ne poit este discontinue, mes la ou cestuy que fait le discontinuance fuit un foits seisie per force de le taile, sinon

que

Note, that an estate taile cannot bee discontinued, but there where hee that makes the discontinuãce was once seised by force of the taile, vnles it be

Vid. Sect. 638. Un foits. Here it is to bee observed that it is not necessary that the Tenant in taile bee ever seised of an estate taile at the time when the Discontinuance of the whole estate is begun, as if Tenant in taile make a lease for life, whereby he gaineth,

que soit per reason de garrantie, &c. Come si soit aiel, pier, & fits, et layel soit tenant en taile, et est disseisie per le pier que est son fits, et le pier fait vn feoffment de ceo sans garranty & deuie, et puis laiel deuie, le fits bien poit enter sur le feoffee, pur ceo que ceo ne fuit pas discontinuance, entant que le pier ne fuit seisie per force de le taile al temps del feoffment &c. mes fuit seisie en fee per le disseisin fait al ayel.

by reason of a warranty, &c. As if there be grandfather, father, & son, & the grandfather is tenant in taile, & is disseised by the father who is his son, & the father maketh a feoffment of this without warranty & die, & afterwards the grandfather dies, the son may wel enter vpon the feoffee, because this was no discontinuance, inasmuch as the father was not seised by force of the entaile at the time of the feoffment, &c. but was seised in fee by the disseisin of the grandfather.

as hath beene said, a fee simple by wrong, in this case if he grant the Reuersion in fee, and the Lessee dieth, the whole estate is discontinued, and yet at the time of the grant (by which the Discontinuance continueth) he was not seised by force of the taile, and therefore Littleton materially added these words (Vn foits) that is, that he was once seised by force of the estate taile: and seeing that (as hath beene said) a Discontinuance is a priuation, the rule of Law agreeth well with the rule of Philosophie that Omnis priuatio præsupponit habitum, and therefore he cannot discontinue that estate which he neuer had. *Vid. Sect. 592. 596. 597. 601. 640. 658.*

¶ *Sinon que il soit per reason del garrantie, &c.* For in many cases a warranty added to a Conueyance is said to make a discontinuance Ab effectu, although hee that made the conueyance was neuer seised by force of the estate taile, because it taketh away the entrie of him that right hath, as a Discontinuance doth. As if Tenant in taile be disseised and dieth, and the issue in taile release to the Disseisor with warranty; in this case the issue was neuer seised by force of the taile, and yet this hath the effect of a Discontinuance by reason of the warranty, and the reason hereof appeareth before in this Chapter. *9.E.4.19. 12.E.4.12. 21.E.4.97.*

¶ *Le fits poet enter.* But if the father that made the feoffment had suruiued the Grandfather he should neuer haue entred against his owne feoffment, but albeit the Father had suruiued, yet after his decease the Sonne should haue entred for the reason here yeilded by Littleton. But if the feoffment had beene with warranty, then it had wrought the effect of a Discontinuance, and therefore Littleton saith Sauns Garranty, without warrantie. *15.E.4. Discont. 30. & entr. Cong. 21. 21.E.4.97. 9.E.4.19. 39.H.6.45. 21.H.6.52. 12.E.4.11. 1. Mar. Dier 98.*

Sect. 638.

¶ Item si Tenant en Taile fait vn lease a vn auter pur terme de vie, et le Tenant en taile ad Issue et deuie, et le reuersion discendist a son Issue, et puis lissue granta le reuersion a luy discendue a vn auter en fee, et le tenant a terme de vie attourna & deuie, et le Grantee del reuersion enter, &c. et est seisie en fee en la vie del Issue, et puis issue en le taile ad issue fits et deuie, il semble

ALso if Tenant in Taile make a Lease to another for terme of life, and the Tenaunt in Tayle hath Issue and dieth, and the Reuersion discendeth to his Issue, and after the Issue granteth the reuersion to him discended, to another in Fee, and the Tenant for life attorne and die, and the Grantee of the Reuersion enter, &c. and is seised in Fee in the life of the Issue, and after the Issue in Tayle hath

ble que ceo nest pas discontinuance a le fits, mes que le fitz poit enter,&c. pur ceo que son pier a que le reuersion de Fee simple discendist, &c. nauoit unques riens en la terre, per force de le Taile,&c.

Issue a son and dieth, it seemes that this is no discontinuance to the son,but that the son may enter,&c. for that his father, to whom the reuersion of the fee simple discẽded, had neuer any thing in the land by force of the entaile,&c.

15.E.4.Discont.30.43.Ed.3. 8. 21.H.6.52.4.H.7.17.

¶ Of this opinion is Littleton in our Bookes.

¶ *Le Grantee del reuersion enter,&c.* Here it is to be understood and obserued, That in this case of the grant of the Reuersion, Littleton doth not say, Sans garrantie, because if a warrantie had beene added, it had wrought no discontinuance, for that (as hath beene said) the Discontinuance in iudgement of Law was but for life: but when the addition of a warrantie doth worke a Discontinuance, then Littleton saith, Sans garrantie, as you may obserue often in this Chapter.

21.H.6.52.53.

Sect. 639.

¶ Car si home seisie en droyt sa feme, lessa mesme la Terre a un auter pur terme de vie, ore est le reuersion de fee simple a le Baron,&c. Et si le Baron morust, viuant sa feme et le Tenant a terme de vie, et le reuersion discendist al heire le Baron, si le heire le Baron grant le reuersion a un auter en fee, et le tenant attourna,&c. et puis le tenaunt a terme de vie morust, et le Grauntee del Reuersion en cel Case enter: En cest case ceo nest pas Discontinuance a le Feme, mes la feme bien poit enter sur le Grantee,&c. pur ceo que l'grantor nauoit riens al temps del Graunt, en le droit la Feme, quant il fist le graunt del Reuersion.

For if a man seised in the right of his Wife, letteth the same land to another for terme of life, now is the reuersion of the Fee Smple to the Husband, &c. And if the Husband dyeth, liuing his Wife, and the Tenant for life, and the Reuersion discend to the heire of the Husband, if the Heire of the Husband grant the reuersion to another in Fee, and the Tenant attorne,&c. and afterwards the Tenant for life dieth, and the Grantee of the reuersion in this case enter: In this case this is no discotinuance to the wife, but she may well enter vpon the Grantee,&c. because the grantor had nothing at the time of the Graunt, in the right of his Wife when hee made the Graunt of the Reuersion.

14.E.3.Discont.5.18.assp.2 18.E.3.54.38.E.3.32. 22.H.6.24. 21.H.6.52.53. 15.E.4.Discont.30.

¶ *Car si home seisie en droit sa feme, lessa,&c.* Here Littleton putteth his case where the Baron onely makes a Lease for life, for if he and his wife ioyne in a Lease by Deed, there the Reuersion is not discontinued. See before, Sect.620. More need not to be sayd hereof, in respect the like case of Tenant in Taile hath beene explained before.

Section 640.641.

¶ Et iſſint il ſemble, coment que homes queux ſont inheritables per force de le Taile, et ils ne fueront unques ſeiſſes per force de meſme le Taile, que tiel feoffements ou grants p eux fait ſans clauſe de Garrantie, nẽ pas diſcontinuance a lour iſſues apres lour deceaſe, mes q̃ lour Iſſues poyent bien enter, &c. coment que ceux queux fierent tielz grants en lour vies fueront forbarres dentrer per lour Fait demeſne, &c.

And ſo it ſeemeth, That men which are inheritable by force of an Entaile, and neuer were ſeiſed by force of the ſame entaile, that ſuch Feoffements or grants by them made without clauſe of warrantie, is no diſcontinuance to their Iſſues after their deceaſe, but that their Iſſues may well enter, &c. albeit they which made ſuch Graunts in their liues were forebarred to enter by their owne act, &c.

Sect. 641.

¶ Et ſi le tenant en Tail ad iſſue deux fits, et leigne diſſeiſiſt ſon pier, et ent fait feoffment en fee ſans clauſe de Garrantie, et deuia ſans Iſſue, et puis le pier deuie, le puiſñ fits poit bien enter ſur le feoffee, pur ceo que l' Feoffment ſon eigne Frere ne poit eſtre diſcontinuance, pur ceo que il ne fuit unques ſeiſie p force de meſme le Taile. Car il ſemble encounter reaſon, que per matter en fait, &c. ſans clauſe de Garrantie, home poit diſcontinuer un Fait, &c. que ne fuit unques ſeiſie per force de meſme le Taile.

And if Tenant in Taile hath Iſſue two Sonnes, and the eldeſt diſſeiſeth his Father, & thereof maketh a Feoffement in Fee, without clauſe of Warrantie, and die without iſſue, and after the father die, the yongeſt ſon may well enter vpon the Feoffee, for that the Feoffement of his elder brother cannot be a diſcontinuãce, becauſe he was neuer ſeiſed by force of the ſame Tayle. For it ſeemeth to be againſt reaſon, that by matter in fact, &c. without clauſe of Warrantie, a man ſhould diſcontinue a Deed, &c. that was neuer ſeiſed by force of the ſame Taile.

¶ Note, here alſo in theſe two Sections appeareth, That (as hath beene ſayd before) a Warrantie, though he were neuer ſeiſed, by force of the Tayle may worke the effect of a Diſcontinuance. *Vid. Sect. 592. 596. 597. 601. 658.*

¶ *Home poet diſcontinuer vn fait, &c.* This is miſtaken, & ſhould be, Home poet diſcontinuer vn taile, and ſo is the Originall.

Sect. 642.

¶ NOta si soit Sir, et tenāt, et le tenant dona les tenements a vn auter en taile, le remainder a vn auter en fee, et puis le tenant en taile fait vn leas a vn home pur terme de vie, &c. sauant le reuersion, &c. & puis granta le reuersion a vn auter en fee, et le tenant a terme de vie atturna, &c. et puis le grantee del reuersion morust sans heire, ore mesme l' reuersion deuient al seignior per voy descheate. Si en cest cas, le tenant a terme de vie deuiast, et le Seignior per force de son escheate enter en la vie le tenant en le taile, et puis le tenant en le taile morust, il semble en ceo cas que ceo nest pas discontinuance al issue en le taile ne a celuy en le remainder, mes que il poit bien enter pur ceo que le Seignior est eins per voy descheat, et nemy per le tenant en le taile, &c. Mes secus esset, si le reuersion vst este execute en le grauntee en le vie le tenant en le tayle, car adonque vst le grauntee este eins en les tenements per le tenant en le tayle, &c.

NOte if there be Lord and Tenant, and the Tenant giueth lands to another in taile, the remainder to another in fee, and after the Tenant in taile makes a lease to a man for a terme of life, &c. sauing the reuersion, &c. and after granteth the reuersion to another in fee and the tenant for life attorne, &c. and after the Grantee of the reuersion die without heire, now the same reuersion commeth to the Lord by way of escheate. If in this case the Tenant for life dieth and the Lord by force of his escheat enter in the life of Tenant in taile, and after the Tenant in taile dieth, it seemeth in this case that this is no discontinuance to the issue in taile, nor to him in the remaynder, but that he may well enter, because the Lord is in by way of escheate, and not by the Tenant in tayle, but otherwise it should bee, if the reuersion had beene executed in the Grantee, in the life of Tenant in tayle, for then had the Grantee beene in the Tenements by the Tenant in taile, &c.

Vide Sect. 620.

Lib. 1. fol. 136.
Lib. 3. fol. 62. 63.

¶ The reason of this case is here rendred (as before it was in this Chapter) that albeit the reuersion be executed in the Lord by escheate in the life of Tenant in tayle, yet because he is not in by the Tenant in tayle but by escheate, it worketh no Discontinuance. But if it had beene executed in the life of Tenant in tayle in the Grantee which was in by Tenant in tayle, then the Lord by escheate should haue taken aduantage of it, but of this sufficient hath beene said before in this Chapter.

Sect. 643. 644. & 645.

¶ PArcel de son Glebe &c. In whom the fee simple of the glebe is,

¶ ITem si vn parson dun Esglise, ou vn Vicar dun Esglise

ALso if a Parson of a Church or a Vicar of a Church alien

Esglise, alien certaine terres, ou tenements parcel de son glebe, &c. a un auter en fee, et morust, ou resigne, &c. son successor poit bien ent, nient contristeant tiel alienation, come est dit en un Nota 2. H. 4 Terme Mich, quod sic incipit.

certaine Lands or Tenements parcell of his Glebe, &c, to another in fee, and die or resigne, &c. his successor may well enter notwithstanding such alienation, as is said in a *Nota* 2. *H.* 4. *Termino Mich.* which beginneth thus.

Sect. 644.

¶ Nota quod dictum fuit pro lege en un briefe de accompt port per un master dun colledge, vers un Chapleine, que si un Parson. ou un Vicar, graunt certaine terre, quel est de droit son Esglise a un auter & devie, ou permute, le successor poit enter, &c. Et ieo croy que la cause est, pur ceo que le Parson, ou Vicar, que est seisie, &c. come en droit de son Esglise, nad pas droit de fee simple en les tenements, et le droit de fee simple de ceo demurt en ascun auter person, et pur cel cause son success. poit bien enter, nient contristeant tiel alienation, &c.

N*Ota quod dictum fuit pro lege*, in a Writ of Account brought by a Master of a Colledge against a Chaplaine, that if a Parson or Vicar grant certaine Land, which is of the right of his Church to another and die, or changeth, the Successor may enter, &c. And I take the cause to bee, for that the Parson or Vicar that is seised, &c. as in right of his Church hath no right of the fee simple in the tenements, but the right of the fee simple abideth in another person. And for this cause his Successour may well enter, notwithstanding such alienation, &c.

is a question in our Bookes: (a) some hold that it is in the Patron, but that cannot bee for two reasons, first, for that in the beginning the Land was given to the Parson and his Successors, and the Patron is no Successor. Secondly, the wordes of the Writ of Iuris vtrum bee, si sit libera Eleemosina Ecclesiæ de D. and not of the Patron. Some others doe hold that the fee simple is in the patron & Ordinary, but this cannot bee for the causes abouesaid And therefore of necessitie the fee simple is in abeyance as Littleton saith. And this was prouided by the Prouidence and Wisdome of the Law; for that the Parson & Vicar haue Curam animarum, and were bound to celebrate Diuine Seruice, and administer the Sacraments, & therefore no Act of the Predecessor should make a discontinuance to take away ye entry of the successor, and to driue him to a reall action whereby he should be destitute of maintenance in the mean time; vpon consideration of all our Bookes I obserue this diuersitie, that a Parson or Vicar for the benefit of the Church and of his Successor is in some cases esteemed in Law to haue a fee simple qualified but to doe any thing to the preiudice of his Successor in many cases, the Law adiudgeth him to haue in effect but an estate for life, Causæ Ecclesiæ publicis causis æquiparantur, and summa ratio est quæ pro religione facit. And Ecclesia fungitur vice minoris meliorem facere potest conditionem suam deteriorem nequaquam.

(a) 8. H. 6. 24. 12. H. 8. 8.

Vide Registr. 307 a. 45. E. 3. tit. Eschange. 12. H. 8. 9.

F. N. B. 49. L.

Bracton lib. 4. fol 226.

Britt. fol. 143.

As a Parson, Vicar, Archdeacon, Prebend, Chantery Priest, and the like may haue an Action of Waste, and in the Writ it shall be said ad exhæredationem Ecclesiæ, &c. ipsius B. or Præbendæ ipsius A.

F. N. B. 55. D. & 57. E. F. 10. H. 7. 5.

And the Parson, &c. that maketh a Lease for life shall haue

F. N. B. 49. l. m. a. 30. E. 3. tit. Iuris utrum. Temps E. 3. Iuris utrum 14. 1. 14. E. 3. ibid. 4. F. N. B. 50. 30. E. 3. 26. 21. E. 3. 21. tit. Entrie 10. F. N. B. 206. F. Regist. 237. 4. E. 4. 2. 8. E. 3. tit. Entrie 3. 7. E. 3. 54. 55.

haue à Consimili casu during the life of the Lessee, and a Writ of entry ad communem legem after his death, or a Writ Ad terminum qui præterijt, or a quod permittat in the debet, and none can maintaine any of these writs, but a Tenant in fee simple or fee taple.

And a Parson, &c. may receiue homage, which Tenant for life cannot doe, Temps E. 1. Incumbent 19.

(c) F. N. B. 49. l. 50. a.

(c) Likewise a Parson, &c. shall haue a Writ of mesne and a Contra formam feoffamenti.

But a Parson cannot make a discontinuance as Littleton here teacheth, for that should bee to the preiudice of his Successor, to take away his entrie, and to driue him to a reall action.

Also if a Parson, &c. make a lease for yeares reseruing a rent & dieth, the lease is determined by his death, as if Tenant for life had made a lease, no acceptance of the rent by the Successor can make it good. Also in a reall action a Parson, Vicar, Archdeacon, Prebend, &c. shall haue aide of the Patron and Ordinary as tenant for life shal haue. So as it is euident that to many purposes a Parson hath but in effect an estate for life, and to many a qualified fee simple, but the entire fee and right is not in him, and that is the reason that hee cannot discontinue the fee simple that he hath not, nor euer had, for as it hath beene said, Omnis priuatio præsupponit habitum. And for the same cause he cannot haue a writ of right right, nor a Writ of right in his nature, as a Writ of Right Sur disclaimer of customes and seruices, Ne iniuste vexes, rationabilibus diuisis, quo iure, and the like.

30. E. 3. tit. Aide 30. 25. E. 3. 34. 8. E. 3. 45. 8. H. 6. 21. 11. H. 6. 9. 6. E. 3. 45. 43. Ass. Pl. 13. F. N. B. 229.

But here it appeareth by Littleton that such bodies politique or corporate as haue a sole seisin, and may haue a Writ of right for that the fee and right is in them (albeit they cannot absolutely conuey away their Lands, &c without assent of others) may make a Discontinuance, as a Bishop, an Abbot, a Deane, a Master of an Hospitall and the like. But this is to bee vnderstood, where a Deane or a Master of an Hospitall, &c. are soly seised of distinct possessions, for if the bodie that is seised be aggregate of many, as the Deane and Chapiter, Master and Confreres, &c. then the feoffment of the Deane or Master is so farre from a Discontinuance as it is a disseisin.

44. E. 3. 11. 12. H. 4. 68. 9. E. 4. 16. 18. E. 3. 7. 6. E. 3. 11. 9. E. 2. Aide 167. 12. H. 4. 21. 32. E. 3. Aide 39. 38. E. 3. 19. 14. E. 3. Iuris utrum 4.

And these that haue the fee and right in them shall not haue aide in respect of their high and large estate, albeit any of them be presentable: but a Deane that is collatiue shall haue aide of the King.

And it is to be obserued, that the remedy is euer agreeable to the right, and therefore the Bishop, Deane, Master of an Hospitall, that hath Colledge and common Seale, or the like, shall haue a Writ of Right Right, which is the highest remedie, for that they haue the highest estate.

Sect. 645.

CAr vn Euesq̃ poit auer bře de droit de tenemẽts de droit de son Esglise, pur ceo que le droit est en son Chapiter, et le fee simple demurrant en luy et en s̃ Chapiter. Et vn Deane poit auer bře de droit, pur ceo que le droit demurt ẽ luy. Et vn Abbe poit auer briefe de droit, p̃ ceo que le droit demurt en luy, et en son couent. Et vn Master dun Hospitall poit auer briefe de droit, pur ceo que le droit demurt en luy, et en ses confreres, &c. Et sic de alijs casibus consimilibus. Mes vn parson ou vn Vicar ne poit auer briefe de droit, &c.

FOr a Bishop may haue a writ of right of the tenements of the right of his Church, for that the right is in his Chapiter, and the fee simple abideth in him and in his Chapiter. And a Deane may haue a writ of right, because the right remaynes in him. And an Abbot may haue a writ of right for that the right remaynes in him and in his Couent. And a Master of an Hospitall may haue a Writ of Right because the right remayneth in him and in his Confreres, &c. And so of other like cases. But a Parson or Vicar cannot haue a Writ of Right, &c.

Here Littleton citeth the Booke Case, Mich.2.H 4. as an authoritie whereupon he groundeth his opinion. And it is to be obserued, that the yeares of H.4. were published before Littleton did write.

But at this day, the Bishop, Deane, Master of an Hospitall, or the like that haue the fee and right in them, as hath beene said, cannot discontinue, neyther can they or any Parson, Vicar, Archdeacon, Prebend, or any other hauing any Ecclesiasticall Liuing with assent of Deane and Chapiter, Patron and Ordinary, or the consent of any others make any Lease, Gift, Grant or Conueyance, Estate, Charge or Incumberance to bind his Successor other then for tearme of one and twentie yeares, or three liues in possession, whereupon the accustomed Rent or more shall be reserued. These be excellent Lawes, and haue beene well expounded for the maintenance of Religion; and the good of Gods Church, for otherwise it is to bee feared that holy Church would lose more then it would gaine in these dayes.

*Vide Sect.*527.593.*&c.* 1.*Eliz ca.*18. 13.*Eliz.ca.*10 1.*Iacobi cap.*3.

*Lib.*2 *fol.*46. *Lib.*4.*fol.*76.*&* 20. *Lib.*5.*fol.*9.*&*.14. *Lib.*6 *fol* 37. *Lib.*7.*fol.*8. *Lib.*11.*fol.*67.

But where Littleton in this and other Sections make mention of Masters of Hospitals, the Reader must know, that since Littleton wrote, there hath beene a great alteration made by diuers Acts of Parliament concerning Hospitals.

37.*H.*8. 31 *H.*8. 32 *H.*8. 37.*H.*8. 1.*E.*6.*&c.*

¶ *Master del Hospitall.* These points concerning Hospitals were resolued (c) by the Iustices.

(c) *Pasch.*24.*Eliz. The Lord Cheneys case. Lib.*2.*fol.*48.49. *Euesque de Canterburies case.*

First, That no Hospitall was giuen to the Crowne by the Statute of 27.H.8. nor any Hospitall is within the Statute of 31.H.8. of Monasteries, but only religious and Ecclesiasticall Hospitals, and that no Lay Hospitall was within those Statutes.

Secondly, If vpon the foundation of any lay Hospital or after it was ordained, That one or diuers Priests should be mayntained within the Hospitall to celebrate Diuine Seruice to the poore, and to pray for the soule of the Founder, and all Christian soules, or the like, and that the poore of such Hospitall should make the like Orisons, yet such an Hospitall is not within the said Statutes, for the Hospitall is Lay, and not Religious, and all or the most part of ancient Lay Hospitalls were founded or ordained after the like sort, and the makers of those statutes neuer intended to ouerthrow workes of Charitie, but to take away the abuse.

Thirdly, That no Hospitall was giuen to the King by the Statute of 37.H.8. but in two cases, where the Donors, Founders or Patrons, &c. had entred and expulsed the Priests, Wardens, &c. betweene the fourth day of February, Anno 27.H.8 and the fiue and twentieth of December, Anno 37.H.8. or where King Henrie the eighth by Commission according to that Act should enter and seise the same, but that determined by the death of that King.

*Lib.*1.*fol.*24. *Porters case.*

Fourthly, That the Statute of 1.E.6. extended not to any Hospitall whatsoeuer eyther Lay or Religious, as by the same appeareth.

*Porters case vbi supra. Lib.*4.111.113.114.116. *In Lamberts case.*

And I was of Counsell with the Lord Cheney in this case, which, seeing it may doe good for mayntenance of Charitable vses, I thought good summarily to report it, to this I will adde Panis pauperum vita pauperum, qui defraudat eos vir sanguinis est.

*Ecclesiasticus ca.*34.*verse.*22.

Nota, of Hospitals some are Corporations aggregate of many, as of Master or warden, &c. and his Confreres: some where the Master or warden hath only the estate of Inheritance in him, and the Brethren or Sisters power to consent hauing Colledge and Common Seale, Some where the Master or warden hath the state in him, but hath no Colledge and common Seale, and such a Master or warden shall haue a Iuris vtrum: and of these Hospitals some be eligible, some donatiue, and some presentable.

14.*E.*3.*Iuris Vtrum.*4.

Sect. 646.

¶ MEs le pluis haut briefe q̃ ils poient auer est le brief de Iuris vtrum, le quel est graund proofe que le droit de fee nest en eux ne en nul auters, &c. Mes le droit de fee simple est en abeiance &c. ceo est adire, que il est tantsolement en le remembrance, entendement, & consideration de la ley, &c. Car moy semble que tiel chose

BVt the highest Writ that they can haue is the Writ of *Iuris vtrum*, which is a great proofe that the right of fee is not in them, nor in any others, &c. but the right of the fee simple is in abeiance, that is to say, that it is only in the remembrance, intendement and consideration of

chose et tiel droit que est dit en diuers Lieurs estre en abeyance, est a tant adire en Latyne, (s.) Talis res, vel tale rect' quæ vel qd' non est in homine adtunc superstite, sed tantummodo est, & consistit in consideratione & intelligentia Legis, & quod alij dixerunt, talem rem aut tale rectum fore in nubib⁹. Mes ieo suppose que ils intenderont per ceux parols, In nubibus, &c. come ieo aye dit adeuant.

the Law, &c. for it seemeth to me, That such a thing, and such a Right which is sayd in diuers bookes to be in abeyance, is as much to say in Latine, (s.) *Talis res, vel tale Rectum quæ vel quod non est in homine adtunc superstite, sed tantummodo est, & consistit in consideratione & intelligentia legis, & quod alij dixerunt, talem rem aut tale rectum fore in nubibus.* But I suppose, that they meane by these words, *(In nubibus, &c.)* as I haue said before.

44.E.3.63. Vi. Sect. 648. 649. 650. 651.

¶ E*N abeiance.* That is in in expectatiō, of the French word Bayer to expect. For when a Parson dyeth we say that the freehold is in Abeiance, because a Successor is in expectation to take it, and here note the necessitie of the true interpretation of words.

Vid. Sect. 1.

If Tenant Pur terme dauter vie dyeth, the freehold is said to be in Abeiance untill the occupant entreth. If a man make a Lease for life the remainder to the right heires of I.S. the fee simple is in Abeiance untill I.S. dieth. And so in the case of the Parson, the fee and right is in Abeiance, that is in expectation, in remembrance, entendment or consideration of Lawe I. In consideratione siue intelligentia legis, because it is not in any man then liuing, and the right that is in Abeiance is said to be In nubibus in the Clouds, and therein hath a qualitie of fame whereof the Poet speaketh;

Virg. 4. Æneid.

Insequiturque solo, & caput inter nubila condit.

Section 647.

¶ ITē si vn parson dun esglise deuie, ore le franktenement del glebe del personage est en nulluy durant le temps que le parsonage est voide, mes in abeiance, cest ascauoir, in consideration & en le intelligenc de le ley, tanque vn auter soit fait parson de mesme leglise, et immediat quant vn auter est fait parson, le franktenement en fait est en luy come successor.

ALso if a Parson of a Church dieth, now the freehold of the glebe of the Parsonage is in none during the time that the Parsonage is voide but in abeiance, *viz.* in consideration and in the vnderstanding of the Law vntill another be made Parson of the same Church, and immediatly when another is made Parson, the freehold in Deed is in him as Successor.

¶ S*I vn Parson dun Esglise deuie, &c.* So it is of a Bishop, Abbot, Deane, Archdeacon, Prebend, Viccar, and of euery other sole Corporation or body politique presentatiue, electiue, or donatiue, which inheritances put in abeiance are by some called Hæreditates jacentes, and some say, Que le fee est en balaunce.

Bract. li. 1. ca. 2. Brit. fo. 249.

Sect. 648.

¶ Item aſcuns peradventure voilent arguer & dire, que entant que vn parſon oue laſſent del patron & ordinarie poit granter vn rent charge hors del glebe del parſonage en fee, et iſſint charger l' glebe del parſonage perpetualment ergo ils ont fee ſimple, ou deux, ou vn de eux, avoit fee ſimple al meins. A ceo poit eſtre reſpondue, que il eſt principle en le ley, que de cheſcuns terres il y ad fee ſimple, &c. en aſcun hom̄, ou auterment le fee ſimple eſt en abeyance. Et vn auter principle eſt, Que cheſcun terre de Fee ſimple poit eſtre charge de vn Rentcharge en fee per vn voy, ou per auter. Et quant tiel rent eſt graunt per le Fait le Parſon, et l' Patron, et l'Ordinarie, &c. en Fee, nul auera preiudice ou parde p force de tiel Grant, forſque les Grantors en lour vies, et les Heires le Patron, et les ſucceſſors del Ordinary apres lour deceaſe. Et apres tiel charge, ſi le

ALſo ſome peradventure will argue and ſay, that inaſmuch as a Parſon with the aſſent of the Patron and Ordinary, may grant a rent charge out of the Glebe of the Parſonage in fee, and ſo charge the glebe of the Parſonage perpetually, *ergo* they haue a Fee ſimple, or two or one of them haue a fee ſimple at the leaſt. To this may bee anſwered, That it is a Principle in Law, That of euerie land there is a Fee ſimple, &c. in ſome bodie, or otherwiſe the fee ſimple is in abeyance. And there is another Principle, that euery Land of Fee ſimple may bee charged with a Rent charge in Fee by one way or other. And when ſuch Rent is granted by the Deede of the Parſon, and the patron, and Ordinarie, &c. in Fee, none ſhall haue preiudice or loſſe by force of ſuch Grant, but the Grantors in their liues, and the Heires of the Patron, and the ſucceſſours of the Ordinarie after their deceaſe. And after ſuch charge

¶ *IL eſt vn Principle en la Ley, &c.* Principium, quod eſt quaſi primum caput, from which many caſes haue their originall or beginning, which is ſo ſtrong, as it ſuffereth no contradiction; and therefore it is ſayd in our Bookes, that antient Principles of the law (a) ought not to be diſputed, Contra negantem principia non eſt diſputandum. That which our Author here calleth a Principle, Sect. 3. & 90. hee calleth a Maxime. (a) 11. H. 4. 9. Sect. 3. & 90.

Here Littleton in anſwer to an obiection alledgeth two Principles. Firſt,

¶ *Que de cheſcun terre il y ad Fee ſimple, &c.* This is Perſpicue verum, and needeth no explanation. Secondly,

¶ *Cheſcun terre de Fee ſimple poet eſtre charge en Fee per vn voy ou auter.* Hereby it appeareth, That albeit the right of the Fee ſimple be in abeyance, yet it may be charged by one way or another. And ſo it may bee aliened in Fee, albeit the right of the fee be in abeyance, or in conſideration of Law. And herein is a diuerſitie worthie the obſeruation to be made, That when the right of Fee ſimple is perpetually by iudgement of Law in abeyance, without any expectation to come in eſſe, there hee that hath the qualified fee concurrentibus hijs quæ in iure requiruntur, may charge or alien it, as in the caſe of Parſon, Vicar, Prebend, &c. But where the Fee ſimple is in abeyance, and by poſſibilitie may euerie houre come in eſſe, there the fee ſimple cannot bee charged vntill it commeth in eſſe. As if a Leaſe for life be made, the remainder to the right heires of I.S. the Fee ſimple cannot be charged

Parson deuie, & successour ne poit vener a le dit Esglise d'estre Parson de mesme le Esglise per la Ley, forsque per presentment del Patron, et admission et institution del Ordinarie. Et pur cel cause il couient que le Successor soy teigne content, et agree de ceo, que son Patron et Lordinary loyalment fesoyent adeuant, &c. Mes ceo nest proofe que le Fee simple, &c. est en le Patron et Lordinarie, ou en ascun de eux, &c. Mez la cause que tiel grant de Rent charge est bone, est pur ceo que ceux queux aueront interest, &c. en la dit Esglise, s. le Patron solonque la Ley temporal, et Lordinarie solonque la Ley spirituall, fueront assentus, ou parties a tiel charg, &c. Et ceo semble estre la verie cause que tiel Glebe poit estre charge en perpetuitie, &c.

if the Parson die, his successor cannot come to the sayd Church to be Parson of the same, by the Law, but by the presentment of the Patron, and admission and institution of the Ordinarie. And for this cause the Successour ought to hold himselfe content, and agree to that which his Patron and the Ordinarie haue lawfully done before, &c. But this is no proofe that the Fee simple, &c. is in the Patron and the Ordinarie, or in either of them, &c. but the cause that such graunt of rent charge is good, is for that they who haue the interest, &c. in the sayde Church, *viz.* the Patron according to the Law Temporall, and the Ordinarie, according to the law spiritual, were assenting, or parties to such charge, &c. And this seemeth to be the true cause why such Glebe may be charged in perpetuitie, &c.

charged till I.S. be dead. And so is Littleton to bee vnderstood, viz. that either it may be charged in præsenti or in futuro.

¶ *Chescun Terre de Fee simple.* And so it is of Lands entailed, for they may bee charged in Fee also, for the Estate Taile may bee cut off by Fine or Recouery. Also the Estate taile may continue, and yet Tenant in taile may lawfully charge the land and bind the Issue in Taile. As if a Disseisor make a gift in Taile, and the Donee in consideration of a Release by the Disseisee of all his right to the Donee, granteth a rent charge to the Disseisee and his heires, proportionable to the value of his right, this shall bind the Issue in Taile: Vide Sect. 1. Bridgewaters Case: which Lands by the rule of Littleton may be charged: and therefore if the owner of those thirteene acres grant a Rent charge out of those thirteene Acres generally, lying in the Meadow of eightie, without mentioning where they lie particularly, there as the state in the land remoues, the charge shall remoue also. But since our Author wrote, all Ecclesiasticall persons are disabled to charge in Fee any of their Ecclesiasticall possessions, as before hath beene spoken of at large.

Vi. Sect. 1. Bridgewaters case. & 59.

Vi. Sect. 593.

¶ *Et quant tiel rent est grant, &c.* This is an excellent interpretation and limitation of the sayd Principle, viz. That none shall haue preiudice or losse by any such Grant, but such as are partie or priuie thereunto, as the Patron and his Heyres, the Ordinarie and his Successors, and the Parson and his Successors: which Successors of the Parson are to be presented by the Patron or his heires, and admitted and instituted by the Ordinarie or his Successors. The like is to be sayd of an Archdeacon, Prebend, Vicar, Chauntrie Priest, and the like.

31. E. 1. tit. Grant 90. 8. R. 2. Annuit. 53.

¶ *Per le Fait le Parson, & Patron, & Lordinarie, &c.* Yet if the Parson die, and in time of vacation, the Patron of the assent of the Ordinarie, or the Patron and Ordinarie grant an annuitie or Rent charge out of the Glebe, this shall (as hath beene sayd) binde the succeeding Parsons for euer.

16. E. 3. tit. Annuit. 24. 40. E. 3. 30. 3. E. 3. 17. Reg. 38

If there be Parson, Patron, and Ordinarie, and the Parson by the Ordinance and assent of of the Ordinarie grant an Annuitie to another, having quid pro quo in consideration thereof, this shall bind the successor of the Parson, without the consent of the Patron.

6 E. 3. 4. 55. 7 E. 3. 40. 41. F. N. B. 152. 17. E. 3. 32. 39 E. 3. 17. b. 11. H. 4. 68. 8. H. 3. 23.

A Church Parochiall may be donatiue and exempt from all ordinarie iurisdiction, and the Incumbent may resigne to the Patron, and not to the Ordinarie, neither can the Ordinarie visit, but the Patron by Commissioners to be appoynted by him: And by Litl. rule, the Patron and Incumbent may charge the Glebe, and albeit it be donatiue by a Lay man, yet mere laicus is not capable of it, but an able Clerke infra sacros Ordines is, for albeit he come in by Lay donation, and not by admission or institution, yet his Function is spirituall, and if such a Clerke donatiue be disturbed, the Patron shall haue a Quare impedit of this Church donatiue, and the Writ shall say, Quod permittat ipsum præsentare ad Ecclesiam, &c. and declare the speciall matter in his Declaration. And so it is of a Prebend, Chanterie, Chappell donatiue, and the like, and no Laps shall incurre to the Ordinarie, except it be so specially prouided in the Foundation. But if the Patron of such a Church, Chanterie, Chappell, &c. donatiue, doth once present to the Ordinarie, and his Clerke is admitted and instituted, it is now become presentable, and neuer shall be donatiue after, and then Laps shall incurre to the Ordinary, as it shall of other Benefices presentable. But a presentation to such a Donatiue by a stranger, and admission and institution thereupon, is meerely voyd. And all this was resolued by the whole Court of Kings Bench, for the Rectorie Parochiall donatiue of Saint Burian in the Countie of Cornewall.

Vi. Sect. 133. 536. 11. E. 3. Iur. utr. 3. 8. Ass. 29. 31. 13. Ass. 2.
14 H. 3. Quar. imp. 183. 17. E. 3. 12. & 9. 14. H. 4. 11. F. N. B. 33. e. 16. E. 3. bre 660
13. E. 4. 3. 6. H. 7. 14.
Vi Sect. 530.
22. H. 6. 26. F. N. B. 35. e.
Hil. 1. Iac. coram Reg. rot. 601 inter Wil. Fairchild, Pl. & Wil. Gayer def. in Trespas.

It appeareth by our Bookes, and by diuers Acts of Parliament, That at the first all the Bishoprickes in England were of the Kings foundation, and donatiue per traditionem baculi, (id est) the Crosier, which was the Pastorall Staffe, & annuli, the Ring whereby hee was married to the Church. And King Henrie the first beeing requested by the Bishop of Rome to make them electiue, refused it: but King Iohn by his Charter bearing date quinto Iunii, anno decimo septimo, granted that the Bishopricks should be eligible. If the King doth found a Church, Hospitall, or free Chappell donatiue, he may exempt the same from ordinarie Iurisdiction, and then his Chancellor shall visit the same. Nay, if the King doe found the same without any speciall exemption, the Ordinarie is not, but the Kings Chancellor, to visit the same. Now as the King may create Donatiues exempt from the visitation of the Ordinarie, so he may by his Charter licence any subiect to found such a Church or Chappell, and to ordaine that it shall be donatiue, and not presentable, and to be visited by the Founder, and not by the Ordinarie. And thus began Donatiues in England, whereof common Persons were Patrons.

17. E. 3. 40. 6. E. 3. 10. 25. E. 3. ca. vide ce Prouisor. Math. Par. pa. 10. & 61.
F. N. B. 35 E. 42. A. B. 27 E. 3. 84 & 85. 8 Ass. 29. 8. E. 3. Ass. 150. 18. E. Scire Fac. 11. 6. H. 7. 14. 16. E. 3. Briefe 660. 21. E. 3. 60. Register 40. Dyer 10. Eliz. f. 273. 14. El. ca. 5. 2. H. 5. c. 1.

¶ *Ordinarie.* Ordinarius is he that hath ordinarie iurisdiction in causes Ecclesiasticall, immediate to the King and his Courts of Common Law, for the better execution of Iustice, as the Bishop or any other that hath exempt and immediate iurisdiction in Causes Ecclesiasticall.

¶ *Ley temporel.* which consisteth of three parts, viz. First, On the Common Law, expressed in our Bookes of Law and iudiciall Records. Secondly, On Statutes contained in Acts and Records of Parliament. And thirdly, On Customes grounded vpon reason, and vsed time out of mind, and the Construction and determination of these doe belong to the Iudges of the Realme.

¶ *Ley Spiritual, &c.* That is, the Ecclesiasticall Lawes allowed by the Lawes of this Realme, viz. which are not against the Common Law (whereof the Kings Prerogatiue is a principall part) nor against the Statutes and Customes of the Realme, and regularly according to such Ecclesiasticall Lawes, the Ordinarie and other Ecclesiasticall Iudges doe proceed in causes within their Conusance. And this Iurisdiction was so bounded by the antient Common Lawes of the Realme, and so declared by Act of Parliament.

The Statute of 25. H. 8. ca. 19. 33. H. 6. 34. 32. H. 6. 28.

¶ *Admission & Institution.* In proprietie of speech, Admission is, when the Bishop vpon examination admitteth him to be able, and saith, Admitto te habilem. (d) Institution is, when the Bishop saith, Instituo te rectorem talis Ecclesiæ cum cura animarum, & accipe Curam tuam & meam. (e) But sometime in a more large sence, admissus doth include Institutus also, Cuius præsentatus sit admissus, (i.) institutus. And it is to bee obserued, That Institution is a good plenartie against a common person, (but not against the King, vnlesse he be inducted) and that is the cause that regularly plenartie shall be tried by the Bishop, because the Church is full by Institution, which is a spirituall Act, but voyd or not voyd shall be tried by the Common Law.

(d) Lib. 4. fo. 75. & 79. Lib. 6. fo. 49. Lib. 7. fo. 46.
(e) W. 2. cap. 5. 13. E. 1.
22. H. 6. 27. 38. E. 3. 4.

At the Common Law if an estranger had presented his Clerke, and hee had beene admitted and instituted to a Church, whereof any Subiect had beene lawfull Patron, the Patron had no other remedie to recouer his Aduowson, but a writ of Right of Aduowson, wherein

Glanvill lib. 13. ca. 18. 19. 20. Mirror cap. 5. § 5. Bracton Lib. 4. fol. 238. 240. 244. & c. 291. Flet. li. 5. c. 11. 16. 17. Brit. fo. 220, 223. 224

6.E.3.28.39 52. 39.E.3.24 43.E.3.25.45 E.3. Quar. imp 139.10.E.2.Com.22. 31.E.1.Quar.imp.186.

in the Incumbent was not to be remoued: and so it was at the Common Law, if an vsurpation had beene had vpon an Enfant or Feme Couert, hauing an Aduowson by discent, or vpon Tenant for life, &c. the Infant, Feme Couert, and he in the reuersion were driuen to their Writ of Right of Aduowson; for at the Common Law, if the Church were once full, the Incumbent could not be remoued, and Plenartie generally was a good Plea in a Quare impedit, or Assise of Darreine presentment, and the reason of this was, to the intent that the Incumbent might quietly intend & applie himselfe to his spirituall Charge. And secondly, the Law intended, that the Bishop that had cure of soules within his Diocesse, would admit and institute an able man for the discharge of his dutie and his owne, and that the Bishop would doe right to euerie Patron within his Diocesse. But at the Common Law, if any had vsurped vpon the King, and his Presentee had beene admitted, instituted, and inducted, (for without induction the Church had not beene full against the King) the King might haue remoued him by Quare impedit, and beene restored to his presentation, for therein he hath a Prerogatiue, Quod nullum tempus occurrit Regi, but he could not present, for the plenartie barred him of that, neither could he remoue him any way but by Action, to the end the Church might bee the more quiet in the meane time: * Neither did the King recouer dammages in his Quare impedit at the Common Law. But the sayd Statute (a) hath altered the Common law in the cases aforesayd, as namely, Quoad hoc, quod si pars rea accipiat de plenitudine Ecclesiæ per suam propriam præsentationem, non propter illam plenitudinem remaneat loquela, dummodo breue infra tempus semestre impetretur, &c. And also hath prouided remedie in the other cases, as by the sayd Act appeareth.

F.N.B.36 k.243.a.35.E.3. ca.3.13.R.2.ca 1. 4.H.4. ca.21. 1.H.fo.19.

* Li.6 fo.51.Li.7 fo.19. 3.H.6.Dam.17.34.H.6. 28.12.E.3.Champerty9 18.E.3.2.Temps E.1.Quar. imp.181.

(a) W.2.ca 5.13.E.1.

(g) 45 E.3.35.38.E.3.4. 25.E.3.47.13.El.Dy.292. Reg.302.&ca.18.El.Dy.348. 14.E.4.2.7.H.4.32.31.E.1 Quar.imp.185. W.2.vb.sup. (h) 17.E.3.64.

(g) And if the King doe present to a Church, and his Clerke is admitted and instituted, yet before induction the King may repeale and reuoke his presentation. But regularly no man can be put out of possession of his Aduowson, but by admission and institution vpon a vsurpation by a presentation to the Church, Cum aliquis ius præsentandi non habens præsentauerit, &c. and not by collation of the Bishop: (h) And therefore if the Bishop collate without title, and his Clerke is inducted, this shall not put the rightfull Patron out of possession, for it shall be taken to be onely prouisionally made for celebration of diuine Seruice vntill the Patron do present, and therefore hee is not driuen to his Quare impedit, or Assise of Darreine presentment, in that case, but an Usurpation by collation shall take away the right of Collation that is in another.

9.H.6.32.& 56.19.H.6.68

It is to be obserued, That an vsurpation vpon a Presentation shal not only put out of possession him that hath right of presentation, but right of Collation also. Therefore at this day the Incumbent shall be remoued in a Quare impedit, or Assise of Darreine presentment, if there be not a Plenartie by sixe moneths before the Teste of the Writ, but then the Incumbent must be named in the Writ, or else he shall neuer be remoued: yet at the Common law, if the Ordinarie refused to admit and institute the Clerke of the Patron, or when any disturbed him to present, so as he could not preferre his Clerke, he might haue his Quare impedit, or Assise de Darreine presentment, and if the Church were not full, haue a Writ to the Bishop to admit his Clerke: but so odious was Symonie in the eye of the Common Law, that before the Statute of W.2. he recouered no dammages. At the Common Law, if hanging the Quare impedit against the Ordinarie for refusing of his Clerke, and before the Church were full, the Patron brought a Quare impedit against the Bishop, & hanging the Suit, the Bishop admit & institute a Clerk at the presentation of another, in this case if Judgement be giuen for the Patron against the Bishop, the Patron shall haue a Writ to the Bishop, and remoue the Incumbent that came in pendente lite by vsurpation, for pendente lite nihil innouetur, and therfore at the Common Law it was good policie to bring the Quare impedit against the Bishop as speedily as might be. And it is to be obserued, That albeit the Clerke that comes in pendente lite, by vsurpation, shall be remoued, yet if the rightfull Patron, being a stranger to the Writ, present pendente lite, and his Clerke is admitted and instituted, he shall not be remoued, for else by the bringing of such Quare impedit against the Ordinarie, the rightfull Patron might bee defeated of his Presentation: and therefore euer after the Statute of Westm 2. amongst other things it was inquired ex Officio, if the Church were full, and of whose presentation, &c. and if the Plaintife should haue a Writ to the Bishop, and his Clerke admitted (as in most cases he ought) yet may the rightfull Incumbent haue his remedie by Law.

18.E.2.Presentment 20. 50.E 3.Encumbent 10.21.H. 7.8 a & b 9.Eliz. Dyer.260 F.N.B.32.14.H.8,31. 19 E.2.Dar.Pres.21. 10.E.3.17.9.H.6.31.

30.E.3.tit.Quar.imp.Stath. 45.E.3.15.9.H.5.32.56. 19.H.6.68. L.5.E.4.115. 9.E.4.30.

And as it was good policie (as hath beene sayd) to bring a Quare impedit as speedily as might be against the Bishop, so it is good policie at this day to name the Bishop in the Quare impedit, for then he shall not present by Laps. But seing the Bishop shall not present by Laps because he is named in the Writ, what then, after that the time be deuolued to the Metropolitan, shall not he present by Laps because he is not named? To this it is answered, That he shal not in that case present by laps, for the Metropolitan shal neuer present or collate by laps after sixe moneths, but when the immediate Ordinarie might haue collated by Laps within the sixe moneths, and had surceased his time. And so it is if the time be deuolued to the King

11.H.4.80.

for

for the first step or beginning faileth, and in humane things Quod non habet principium, non habet finem. And all these points were resolved (*) in a Writ of Error brought by Richard Bishop of London, and Iohn Lancaster against Anthony Lowe upon a Iudgement given against them in a Quare impedit in the Common Place for the Church of Winwike. But now let us heare what our Authour will saye unto us. (*) Mich. 3. Iacobi.

Section 649.

¶ Item si tenant en taile ad issue & soit disseisie, et puis il relessa per son fait tout son droit al disseisor, en cest case nul droit de taile poit estre en le tenant en taile, pur ceo que il auoit releas tout son droit. Et nul droit poit estre en lissue en le taile durant le vie son pere. Et tiel droit del enheritance en le taile nest pas tout oustrement expire per force de tiel releas, &c. Ergo, il couient que tiel droit demurt en abeiance, vt supra, durant la vie le tenant en taile, que relessa, &c. & apres son decease donque est tiel droit maintenant en son issue en fait, &c.

ALso if Tenant in tayle hath issue and is disseised, and after he releaseth by his Deed all his right to the Disseisor. In this case no right of taile can be in the tenant in taile, because hee hath released all his right. And no right can bee in the issue in taile during the life of his father. And such right of the Inheritance in the taile is not altogether expired by force of such release, &c. *Ergo*, it must needs be that such right remain in abeiance, *vt supra*, during the life of Tenant in taile that releaseth, &c. And after his deceased such right presently is in his issue in deed, &c.

Sect. 650.

¶ En mesme le maner est, lou tenant en taile granta tout son estate a un auter, en cest cas le grauntee nad estate forsque pur terme de

IN the same manner it is where Tenant in taile grant all his estate to another. In this case the Grantee hath no estate but for terme of life of the Tenant

¶ Littleton hauing declared where a fee is in abeiance, & where a freehold and fee is in abeiance by Act in Law, & where a fee that is in abeiance may be charged. Here hee putteth two cases where a right of an estate taile may bee in abeiance by the act of the partie, which are so cleere and euident, as there needs no further proofe or argument, then Littleton hath iustly and artificially made, albeit some obiections of no weight haue beene made against it. If tenant in taile of Lands holden of the King bee attainted of felony, and the King after office seiseth the same, the estate taile is in abeiance, there said to be in suspence. Pl. Com fol. 552. 563. in Walsinghams case. 14. E. 3. Discent. 5. 19 H. 6. 60. 29. Ass. p. Walsinghams case vbi supra.

¶ *Grant son estate concedit statum suum.* State or estate signifieth such Inheritance, Freehold, terme for yeares, Tenancie by statute Merchant, Staple, Elegit or the like, as any many hath in Lands or tenements, &c. And by the grant of his estate, &c. as much as he can grant shall passe, as here by Littletons case appeareth Tenant for life the remaynder in taile, the remaynder to the right heires of Tenant for life, Tenant for life grant totum statum suum to a man and his heires, both estates doe passe. Vide Sect. 65. 524. 525. 526. 44. E. 3. 10. 44. Ass. 28. 43. Ass. 8. 5. H. 7. 30. 44. Ass. 28. 44. E. 3. 10.

¶ *Right.* Ius, siue rectum (which Littleton often useth) signifieth properly, and specially in Writs and pleadings, when an estate is turned to a right, as by Discontinuance, Disseisin, &c. where it shall be said, Quod ius discendit & non terra. But (right) doth also in- 20. H. 6. 9.

vie del tenant en le taile et le reuersion del taile nest pas en le tenant en taile, pur ceo que il auoit graunt tout son estate et son droit, &c. Et si le tenant a que le graunt fuit fait fist wast, le tenant en le taile ne vnques auera breife de wast, pur ceo que nul reuersion est en luy. Mes le reuersion et le enheritance de le taile, durant le vie le tenant en le taile, est en abeiance, cestascauoir, tantsolement en le remembrance, consideration, et intelligence de la ley.

in taile, and the reuersion of the taile is not in the Tenant in taile, because he hath granted all his estate and his right, &c. And if the Tenant to whom the grant was made make waste, the Tenant in taile shall not haue a Writ of waste, for that no reuersion is in him; but the reuersion and inheritance of the taile during the life of the Tenant in taile is in abeiance, that is to say, only in the remembrance, consideration, and intelligence of the Law.

Vide Sect.465. Pl.Com.484 Lib.8.fol.153. Althams case 39.H.6.38.

clude the estate in esse in conueyances; and therefore if Tenant in fee simple make a Lease for yeares, and release all his right in the land to the Lessee and his heires, the whole estate in fee simple passeth.

And so commonly in fines, the right of the Land includeth and passeth the state of the Land, as A. cognouit tenementa prædicta esse ius ipsius B. &c. And the Statute (a) saith, Ius suum defendere, (which is) statum suum. And note that there is Ius recuperandi, ius intrandi, ius habendi, ius retinendi, ius percipiendi, & ius possidendi.

(a) W.2.Cap.3. Pl.Com.484.& 487.b.

Title, properly (as some say) is when a man hath a lawfull cause of entrie into Lands whereof another is seised, for the which hee can haue no Action, as title of condition, title of Mortmaine &c. But legally this word (Title) includeth a right also, as you shall perceiue in many places in Littleton: and title is the more generall word, for euery right is a title, but euery title is not such a right for which an Action lyeth, and therefore Titulus est iusta causa possidendi quod nostrum est, and signifieth the meanes whereby a man commeth to land, as his title is by fine or by feoffment, &c. And when the Plaintife in Assise maketh himselfe a title, the Tenant may say, Veniat Assisa super titulum, which is asmuch to say, as vpon the title which the Plaintife hath made by that particular Conueyance, Et dicitur titulus à tuendo, because by it he holdeth and defendeth his Land, and as by a release of a right a title is released, so by release of a title a right is released also. See more hereof in Fitzherbert and Brookes Abridgements in the title of Title.

Vide Sect.429.659.&c.

6.H.7.8.a. Althams case vbi supra.

Pl.Com fol.374.in Seignior Zouches case et fol.487.& 448.in Nichols case.

¶ *Interest*, Interesse is vulgarly taken for a terme or chattle real, and more particularly for a future tearme, in which case it is said in pleading that hee is possessed De interesse terimni. But Ex vi termini in legall vnderstanding it extendeth to Estates, Rights and Titles, that a man hath of, in, to, or out of Lands, &c. for he is truly said to haue an interest in them: and by the grant of totum interesse suum in such Lands as well reuersions as possessions in fee simple shall passe. And all these words singularly spoken are nomina collectiua, for by the grant of totum statum suum in Lands all his Estates therein passe. Et sic de cæteris.

23.H.8.Taile Br.32. 35.H.8.Grant Br.150. Vide 16.Eliz. Dier 325.b. Titulum.

43.Ass.p.13.41.E.3.tit Waste 83. 11.H.4.67. 13.H.7.10. Pl.Com.482. Ter Dier 27.H.8.20.

¶ *Ne vnques auera briefe de waste, &c.* So it is if Tenant for life be, the remaynder in tayle, and he in the remaynder release to the Tenant for life, all his right and state in the Land. Hereby it is said in our Bookes, that the estate of the Lessee is not inlarged, but the release serueth to this purpose to put the estate taile into abeiance, so as after that he in the remaynder cannot haue an Action of waste; yet in that case (sauing reformation) the Lessee for life hath an estate for the life of Tenant in tayle expectant vpon his owne life. But if Tenant in fee release to his Tenant for life all his right, yet he shall haue an Action of waste. And if Tenant in taile make a Lease for his owne life, hee shall haue an Action of waste.

42.E.3.23.

F.N.B.60.H.41.E.3.Wast 83. 42.E.3.18.

Section 651.

¶ Item si vn Euesque alien terres que sont parcel de son Euesquery & deuy, ceo est vn discontinuance a son successor, pur ceo que il ne poit enter, mes est mis a son briefe De Ingressu sine assensu capituli.

ALso if a Bishop alien lands which are parcell of his Bishopricke and die, this is a discontinuance to his successor, because he cannot enter, but is put to his writ of *De Ingressu sine assensu capituli.*

Of this sufficient hath beene said (how the Law standeth at this day) before in this Chapter.

Sect. 652.

¶ Item si vn Dean alien terres queux il ad en droit de luy et son Chapiter, & morust, son successor poit enter. Mes si le Deane est sole seisie come en droit son Deanry donque son alienation est discontinuance a son successor come est dit adeuant.

ALso if a Deane alien lands which he hath in right of him and his Chapter and dieth, his successor may enter. But if the Deane bee sole seised as in right of his Deanry, then his alienation is a discontinuance to his successor as is said before.

¶ HEreof also that which was necessary is before said in this Chapter, and Littletons owne words are plaine and euident. 21.E.4 tit.Feoffment, & faits 29. 21.E.4.85.86.

Sect. 653.654.655 & 656.

¶ Item peraduenture ascuns voilont arguer et dire, que si vn Abbe et son Couent sont seisies en lour demesne come de fee de certaine terres a eux et a lour successors, &c. et Labbe sans assent de son Couent alien mesmes les terres a vn auter et deuie, ceo est vn discontinuance a son successor, &c.

ALso peraduenture some will argue and say, that if an Abbot and his Couent bee seised in their demesne as of fee of certaine lands to them and to their successors, &c. and the Abbot without the assent of his Couent alien the same lands to another and die, this is a discontinuance to his successor, &c.

Sect. 654.

¶ Per mesme le reason ils voilent dire, que lou vn Dean et Chapter sont seisies de certain terre a eux et a lour successors, si le Dean alien mesme la terre, &c. ceo

BY the same reason they will say, that where a Deane and Chapter are seised of certaine lands to them and their successors, if the Deane alien the same lands,

ceo serroit vn discontinuance a son successor issint que son successor ne poit enter,&c. A ceo poit estre respondue que il y ad grand diuersity penter les deux cases.

&c. this shall be a discontinuance to his successor, so as his successor cannot enter,&c. To this it may be answered, that there is a great diuersitie betweene these two cases.

Sect.655.

CAr quant vn Abbe & le Couent sont seisies, vncore sils sont disseisie, Labbe auera assise en son nosm demesne, sans nosmer le Couent,&c. Et si ascun voile suer Præcipe quod reddat, &c. de mesmes les terres quant ils fueront en le maine Labbe et Couent, il couient que tiel action real soit sue enuers Labbe solement sans nosme la Couent, pur ceo que touts sont morts persons en la ley, forsque Labbe que est le soueraigne,&c. Et ceo est per cause del soueraigntie; Car auterment il serroit forsque come vn de les auters Moignes de le Couent,&c.

FOr when an Abbot, and the Couent are seised, yet if they bee disseised, the Abbot shall haue an assise in his owne name without naming the Couent,&c. And if any will sue a *Præcipe quod reddat, &c.* of the same lands when they were in the hands of the Abbot and Couent, it behoueth that such action reall be sued against the Abbot only without naming the Couent, because they are all dead persons in Law, but the Abbot who is the soueraigne,&c. and this is by reason of the soueraignty; For otherwise he should bee but as one of the other Monkes of the Couent,&c.

Sect.656.

MEs vn Dean et le Chapter ne sont morts persons en la ley,&c. car chescun de eux poit auer action per soy en diuers cases. Et de tiels terres ou tenements que le Deane et Chapter ont en common,&c. sils soient disseisies, le Deane et Chapter aueront vn assise, et nemy le Deane sole,&c. Et si auter voile auer action real de tiels terres ou tenements enuers le Deane,&c. il couient de suer enuers le Deane et chapter, et nemy enuers le Deane sole,&c. et issint il appiert

BVt Deane and Chapter are not dead persons in Law,&c. for euery of them may haue an action by himselfe in diuers cases. And of such lands or tenements as the Deane and chapter haue in common,&c. if they bee disseised, the Deane and Chapter shall haue an assise, and not the Deane alone,&c. And if another will haue an action reall for such lands or tenements against the Deane,&c. he must sue against the Deane and Chapter, and not against the Deane alone, &c. and so there appeareth a

appiert grand diuersitie perenter les deux cases, &c.

great diuersitie betweene the two cases, &c.

These are apparant and need no explanation. Sauing in the 655. Section mention is made of the Præcipe quod reddat which in this place is intended of a reall action whereby land is demanded, and is so called of the words in every such writ.

And the reason of this, diuersity betweene the case of the Abbot and Couent, and Deane and Chapter is, for that (as hath beene said) the Monkes are regular, and ciuilly dead, and the Chapter are secular, and persons able and capable in Law. But by the pollicy of Law the Abbot himselfe (here termed the soueraigne) albeit he be a Monke and regular, yet hath he capacity and ability to sue and be sued, to enfeoffe, giue, demise and lease to others, and to purchase and take from others, for otherwise they which right haue should not haue their lawfull remedy, nor the house remedie against any other that did them wrong, neither could the house without such capacitie and ability stand. And the Couent haue no other ability or capacitie, but only to assent to estates made to the Abbot, and to estates made by him, which for necessities sake, though they be ciuilly dead, they may doe. *Vid. Sect.* 200. 8. *E.* 3. 27. 11. *H.* 4. 84. 21. *E.* 4. 86. 11. *H.* 7. 12.

Sect. 657.

Item si le Master dun Hospitall discontinue certaine terre de son Hospitall, son successor ne poit entrer, mes est mis a son briefe de ingressu sine assensu confratrum & consororum &c. Et touts tiels briefes pleinment appearōt en l'Register, &c.

ALso if the Master of an Hospitall discontinue certaine land of his Hospitall, his successor cannot enter, but is put to his writ of *De ingressu sine assensu confratrum & consororum, &c.* And all such writs fully appeare in the Register, &c.

This must also be understood where the Master of the Hospitall hath sole and distinct possessions, and not where he and his brethren are seised as a body politique aggregate of many. And here Littleton (as diuers times before) doth cite the Register.

Sect. 658.

Item si terre soit lesse a un home pur terme de sa vie, le remainder a un auter en le taile, sauant le reuersion al lessor, et puis celuy en le remainder disseisist le tenant a terme de vie, et fait un feoffment a un auter en fee, et puis morust sans issue, et le tenant a terme de vie morust, il semble en cest cas, q̄ celuy en la reuersion bien puit enter sur le feoffee, pur ceo que celuy en le remainder que fist le feoffment, ne fuit unque seisie en le taile per force de mesme le remainder, &c.

ALso if land bee lett to a man for terme of his life, the remainder to another in taile sauing the reuersion to the Lessor, and after he in the remainder disseiseth the Tenant for terme of life, and maketh a feoffment to another in fee, and after dyeth without issue, and the Tenant for life dyeth. It seemeth in this case that hee in the reuersion may well enter vpon the Feoffee, because hee in the remainder which made the feoffment was neuer seised in taile by force of the same remainder, &c.

Vid. Sect. 637. 592. 596. 597. 601. 640. 641. Vid. Sect. 637.

¶ HEre it appeareth, That albeit the Feoffor hath an Estate Taile in him expectant vpon an estate for life, yet his Feoffement worketh no Discontinuance. Wherein Littleton doth adde a limitation to that which in this Chapter he had generally said, viz. That an Estate Taile cannot be discontinued, but where he that maketh the Discontinuance was once seised by force of the Taile, which is to be vnderstood when hee is seised of the Freehold and Inheritance of the Estate in Taile, & not where he is seised of a Remainder or a Reuersion expectant vpon a Freehold: which Freehold (as often hath been sayd) is euer much respected in Law.

Chap.12. Of Remitter. Sect.659.

¶ HEere our Author hauing next before treated of a Discontinuance, very aptly beginneth this Chapter with a description of a Remitter.

¶ *Remitter est vn antient terme en la Ley*, and is deriued of the Latyne Verbe Remittere, which hath two significations, either, To restore and set vp againe, or to cease. Therefore a Remitter is an operation in Law vpon the meeting of an antient right remediable, and a latter state in one person where there is no follie in him, whereby the antient right is restored and set vp againe, and the new defeasible estate ceased and banished away. And the reason hereof is, for that the law preferreth a sure and constant right, though it bee little, before a great Estate by wrong and defeasible, and therefore the first and more antient is the most sure and more worthy title, Quod prius est, verius est, & quod prius est tempore, potius est iure: (a) Therefore manie Bookes in stead of Remitter, say, That he is En son primer estate, or en son melior droit, or En son melior Estate, or the like.

(a) 25. Ass. pl. 4. 35. Ass. pl. 11. 26. E. 3. 69. 11. H. 4. 50. a. 42. E. 3. 17. b. Et tit. Remitter 11. 6. E. 3. 17.

¶ *Lou home ad deux Titles*. Heere this word (Titles) is taken in the largest sence, including rights, for being properly taken (b) as in case of a condition, mortmaine, assent to a Rauisher,

(b) V. Sect. 429. & 659. & 34. H. 8. tit. Remitter Br. 50. 44. E. 3. Attaint. 22. 38. Ass. pl. 7.

¶ REmitter est vn antiẽt term̃ en la Ley, et est lou home ad deux titles a terres ou tenẽts, s. vn plus antient title, et vn auter title plus darrein, et sil vient a la terre per le pluis darreine title, vncore la Ley luy adiudgera eins per force del plus eigne title, pur ceo q̃ le pluis eigne titl' est le pluis sure title, et pluis digne title. Et donque quant home est adiudge eins per force d son eigne titl', ceo est a luy dit vn remitter, pur ceo que la ley luy mitter destre eins en la terre per le pluis eigne et sure title. Sicome tenãt en t' taile discontinua la taile, et puis il disseisist s̃ discontinuee, et issint morust seisie, per que les tenemẽts discendont a son issue ou cosine, inheritable per

REmitter is an antient terme in the Law, and is where a man hath two titles to Lands or Tenements, *viz.* one a more antient title, and another a more latter title, and if he come to the land by a latter Title, yet the Law will adiudge him in by force of the elder title, because the elder title is the more sure and more worthie Title. And then when a man is adiudged in by force of his elder title, this is sayd a Remitter in him, for that the Law doth admit him to be in the Land by the elder and surer Title. As if Tenaunt in Taile discontinue the Taile, and after hee disseiseth his Discontinuee and so dieth seised, whereby the Tenements discend to his Issue or cosine inheritable by

per force de le Taile, en cest case, ceo est a luy a que les Tenements discendont q̄ ad droit per force de le Taile, un remitter a le Taile, pur ceo q̄ le Ley luy mitte et adiudge deste eins p force de l' taile que est son eigne title, car sil serroit eins per force de le discent, donques le Discontinuee puissoit auer Briefe de Entre sur disseisin en le Per, enuers luy, et recoueroit les tenem̄ts et ses dammages, &c. Mes entāt que il est eins en son remitter per force de le Taile, le title et le interest le discontinuee, est tout oustermeut anient et defeat, &c.

force of the Tayle: In this case this is to him to whom the Tenements discend, who hath right by force of the Tayle, a Remitter to the Tayle, because the Law shall put and adiudge him to bee in by force of the Tayle; which is his elder Title: for if hee should bee in by force of the discent, then the Discontinuee might haue a Writ of Entrie *Sur Disseisin* in the *Per* against him, and should recouer the Tenemēts & his dammages, &c. but in as much as he is in his remitter by force of the taile, the title & interest of the Discontinuee is quite taken away and defeated, &c.

and the like, there is no remitter wrought vnto them, because these are but bare titles of Entrie, for the which no Action is giuen, but a Remitter must be to a precedent right: And Lit. in this Chapter putteth all his cases onely of Remitters, to Rights remediable.

Et vn auter Title plus darreine, &c. Here is to bee obserued; That an Estate must worke a Remitter to an antient right, for albeit two rights doe discend, there can be no Remitter, because one right cannot worke a Remitter to another: for regularly to euerie remitter there be two incidents, viz. an antient right and a defeasible estate of Freehold comming together. 19.H.6.50.48 45. tit. Entre Cong. 3.Tl Com 246.a.

Le pluis eigne title est le pluis sure Title, & pluis digne title. So as the eldest title is worthily (as hath beene sayd) preferred, because it is the more sure and more worthie.

Sicome Tenant en Taile discontinue le taile, &c. Here our Author according to his accustomed manner, to illustrate his description putteth an example of a Remitter, where the Law preferreth the antient estate by right, before a new Estate defeasible. And this Remitter is wrought by an Estate cast vpon the Issue in Taile by discent, which is an Act in Law, and the discent of the land in possession, and the right of Estate Taile discend together. 19.H.6.61.62.

Est tout ousterment anient & defeat, &c. Here be two things implied and to be vnderstood: First, That this Remitter is wrought in this case by operation of Law vpon the Freehold in Law discended without any entrie Secondly, That the Law so fauoureth a Remitter, (being a restoring to right) that if the Discontinuee be an Enfant or a Feme couert, and Tenant in Tayle after a Discontinuance disseise them and die seised, the Issue shall be remitted without any respect of the priuiledge of Enfancie or Couerture, and therefore our Author sayd, Le title & interest le Discontinuee est tout ousterment anient & defeat. 11.E.4.1.

Donques le Discontinuee, &c. Heere is a reason added in this particular Case, that fitteth not other cases of Remitter, for in this case and many other, the Law that abhorreth Suits of vexation, doth auoyd circuitie of Action, for the Rule is, Circuitus est euitandus. 11.E.3.tit.Ass.85.4.E.4.35 11.R.2.Bar.242. 30.E.3.8. 6.E.3.7. 19.H.6.63.24.E.3 70. 14.H.4.27. 10.H.7.11. F.N.B. Mesne & Wast.

Sect. 660.

ITem si le tenāt en Tayle enfeoffa son fits

ALso if Tenant in Tayle infeoffe his Sonne in Fee,

OUr Author hauing put one example where both the Rights discend together, now puts another example where the Tempt E.1.Remit.13.11.E.3 Age 5.38.E.3.24.40.E.3. 43.21.E.4.19.

the Issue in Tayle claimeth by purchase in the life of Tenant in Taile, and the antient right discendeth after to the same Issue.

Car coment que tiel Heire fuit de pleine age al temps del mort, &c. The reason is; Because no follie can bee adiudged in the Infant at the time of the acceptance of the Feoffement. Therefore the Law respecteth the time of the Feoffement, and not the time of the death: and albeit hee might haue waiued the estate which hee had by the Feoffement at his full age, yet here it appeareth, that the right of the Estate taile discending to him either within age, or of full age, shall worke a Remitter in him, for that the waiuer of the state should haue bin to his losse and preiudice.

27. H. 8. c. 10. of Vses. 35. H. 8. Dy 54. b. 6. E. 6. ib. 77. 1. & 2. P. & M. 116. 2. & 3. P. & M. 129. 191. 28. H. 8. 23. b. Pl. Com. Amy Townshends case fo. 34. H. 8. tit. Remit. Br. 49.

Since Littleton wrote, and after the Statute of 27. H. 8. cap. 10. if Tenant in Tayle make a Feoffement in Fee to the vse of his Issue being within age, and his Heyres, and dyeth, and the right of the Estate Tayle discend to the Issue being within age, yet he is not remitted, because the Statute executeth the possession in such plite manner and forme as the vse was limited: Et sic de similibus, so as there is a great change of Remitters since Littleton wrote.

Pl. Com. vb. sup.

But if the Issue in Tayle in that case waiue the Possession, and bring a Formedon in the Discender, and recouer against the Feoffees, hee shall thereby be remitted to the Estate Taile, otherwise the Lands may be so incumbred, as the Issue in Tayle should be at a great inconuenience: but if no formdon be brought, if that Issue dieth, his Issue shall bee remitted, because a state in fee simple at the Common Law discendeth vnto him.

Esteant de pleine age il charge per son fait,

en fee, ou son Cosine inheritable per force de le taile, le quel fits ou cosin al temps de feoffement est deins age, et puis le tenant en l' taile deuia, et celuy a que le feoffemẽt fuit fait est son heyre per force de le Taile, ceo est vn remitter al heire en le taile a que le feoffment fuit fait. Car coment que durant la vie le Tenãt en le taile que fist le Feoffement, tiel heire serra adiudge eins p force de le feoffment, vncore apres la mort le tenant en le tayle, lheire serra adiudge eins per force de le taile, et nemy p force de le Feoffment. Car coment que tiel heire fuit de pleine age al temps de le mort de le Tenaunt en le Taile que fist le Feoffement, ceo ne fait ascun matter, si lh̃e fuit deins age al tẽps del feoffmt fait a luy. Et si tiel heire esteant deins age al temps de tiel Feoffement, vient al pleine age viuant le Tenãt en le Taile, que fist l' Feoffement, et issint esteant de pleine age, il charge per son fait mesme la Terre oue

or his Cosine inheritable by force of the Taile, which Sonne or Cosine at the time of the Feoffment is within age, and after the Tenant in Taile dieth, and hee to whome the Feoffement was made is his heire by force of the Taile, this is a Remitter to the heire in taile to whom the Feoffement was made: for albeit that during the life of the Tenant in Tayle who made the Feoffement, such heire shall bee adiudged in by force of the Feoffement, yet after the death of Tenant in Taile, the heire shall be adiuged in by force of the Taile, & not by force of the feoffment. For although such heire were of full age at the time of the death of the Tenant in Taile who made the Feoffment, this makes no matter, if the heire were within age at the time of the feoffement made vnto him. And if such heire beeing within age at the time of such feoffmẽt, commeth to full age, liuing the tenant in tayle that made the feoffement, & so being of full age he charges by his deed

vn common de pasture, ou oue vn rent charge, & puis le tenant en le taile morust, oze il semble que le terre est discharge del common, et de le rent, pur ceo que le heire est eins de auter estate en la terre, que il fuit al temps de le charge fait, entant que il est en son remitter per force de le tayle, & issint le state, que il auoit al temps de le charge, est oustermēt defeat, &c.

the same Land with a common pasture or with a rent charge, and after the Tenant in tayle dieth, now it seemeth that the Land is discharged of the Cōmon, and of the rent for that the heire is in of another Estate in the Land then hee was at the time of the charge made, in as much as hee is in his Remitter by force of the tayle, and so the estate which hee had at the time of the charge is vtterly defeated, &c.

&c. The reason is because the Grantor had not any right of the estate in taile in him at the time of the grant but only the estate in fee simple gained by the feoffment, which (as Littleton here saith) is wholy defeated. And the state of the land out of which the rent issued, being defeated the rent is defeated also.

But if Tenant in tayle make a Lease for life whereby he gaineth a new reuersion in fee, so long as Tenant for life liueth, and he granteth a rent charge out of the Reuersion, and after Tenant for life dieth, whereby the Grantor becommeth Tenant in tayle againe, and the Reuersion in fee defeated, yet because the Grantor had a right of the entayle in him, clothed with a defeasible fee simple, ye rent charge remayneth good against him, but not against his issue, which diuersitie is worthy of obseruation, for it openeth the reason of many Cases. 11.H.7.21. Edrichers case.

If the heire of the Disseisee disseise the Disseisor, and grant a rent charge, and then the Disseisee dieth, the Grantor shall hold it discharged, for there a new right of entrie doth discend vnto him, and therefore he is remitted.

So if the father disseise the Grandfather and granteth a Rent charge, and dieth, now is the entry of the Grandfather taken away, if after the Grandfather dieth, the Sonne is remitted, and he shall auoid the charge. So as where our Author putteth his example of a fee tayle, it holdeth also in case of a fee simple.

¶ *Vn common de pasture, ou vn rent charge, &c.* Here Littleton putteth his case of things granted out of the Land. But what if the issue at full age by Deed indented, or deed poll make a Lease for yeares of the Land, and after by the death of Tenant in tayle he is remitted, whether shall he auoide the Lease or no. And it is holden he shall not, because it is made of the Land it selfe, and the Land is become by the Lease in another plight, then it is in the case of a grant of a Rent charge, which I gather out of our Authors owne words in another place. 33.H.8. Dier 51.b. Vide Sect.289.

¶ *La terre est discharge del rent, &c.* Littleton doth adde these words materially because the whole grant is not thereby auoyded, but the Land discharged of the Rent charge, for the Grantee shall haue notwithstanding a writ of Annuitie and charge the person of the Grantor. Lib.2.fol.36.b. Wards case.

Section 661.

¶ Item vn principall cause pur que tiel heire en les cases auandits & auters cases semblables serra dit en son remitter, est pur ceo que il ny ad ascū person enuers que il poit suer son briefe d

ALso a principall cause why such heire in the Cases aforesaid, & other like cases shall bee said in his Remitter, is for that there is not any person against whom he may sue his writ of *Formedon*. For against

¶ *VN principall cause pur que, &c.* And of this opinion is (d) Littleton in our Bookes. (d) 12.E.4.20. 41.E.3.18.11.H.4.50.

¶ *Il nad ascun person enuers que, &c. sicome il auoit loialment recouer mesme la terre vers vn auter, &c.* Here it is to be vnderstood that regular-

Lib.3 fol.3. the Marquesse of Winchesters case.

ly a man shall not bee remitted to a right remedilesse, for the which he can haue no Action for Littleton here saith, that there is no person against whom the issue when becommeth to the land without folly may bring his Action and sayth also, that this is the principall cause of the Remitter, for neither an Action without a right, nor a right without an Action can make a Remitter. As if tenant in tayle suffer a common recouery in which there is error, and after Tenant in taile disseiseth the recoueror and dieth, here the issue in tayle hath an Action, viz. a Writ of Error, but as long (as the recouerie remayneth in force) he hath no right, and therefore in that case there is no Remitter.

Formedon. Car enuers luy mesme, il ne poit suer, & il ne poit suer enuers nul auter, car nul auter est tenant del franktenement, et pur cel cause la ley luy adiudge eins en son remitter, s. e tiel plite, sicome il auoit loialment recouer mesme la terre enuers vn auter, &c.

himselfe he cañot sue, and hee cannot sue against any other, for none other is Tenant of the freehold; and for this cause the Law doth adiudge him in his Remitter, s. in such plite, as if hee had lawfully recouered the same Land against another, &c.

If B. purchase an Aduowson and suffereth an vsurpation and sixe moneths to passe, and after the vsurper granteth the Aduowson to B. and his heires, B. dieth, his heire is not remitted because his right to the Aduowson was remedilesse, viz. a right without an Action.

5.H.7.35. Tenant in tayle of a Mannor whereunto an Aduowson is appendant maketh a Discontinuance, the Discontinuee granteth the Aduowson to Tenant in Tayle and his heires, Tenant in Tayle dieth, the Issue is not remitted to the Aduowson, because the Issue had no Action to recouer the Aduowson before hee recouered the Mannor whereunto the Aduowson was appendant. And so it is of all other Inheritances, regardant, appendant, or appurtenant, a man shall neuer bee remitted to any of them before hee recontinueth the Mannor, &c. whereunto they are regardant, appendant, or belonging.

Britton fol. 126. Car nul ne poet claimer droit en les appurtenances ne en les accessories que nul droit ad en le principall.

(c) Bract. lib. 4. fol. 243. b. (c) Item, excipi potest, &c. quamuis ius habeat in tenemento & pertinentijs, primo se recuperare debet tenementum ad quod pertinet aduocatio, & tunc postea præsentet & non ante, & de hac materia in Rottulo de termino Sancti Michaelis, anno Regis Henrici tertio in comitatu Norff. de Thoma Bardolfe.

8.R.2. Quare Imp. 199. 2.H.4.18. 14.H.6.15.16. 8.H.6.17. 33.H.6.15. F.N.B. 35.B. & 36.F. 24.E.3 Disceit. 16. 33.H.8. Dier 48.b.

But on the otherside, if a man be remitted to the principall, he shall also be remitted to the appendant or accessory albeit it were seuered by the Discontinuee, or other wrong doer. And therefore if Tenant in tayle be of a Mannor whereunto an Aduowson is appendant, and infeoffeth A. of the Mannor with the appurtenances. A. re-infeoffeth the Tenant in tayle sauing to himselfe the Aduowson, Tenant in tayle dieth, his issue being remitted to the Mannor is consequently remitted to the Aduowson, although at that time it was seuered from the Mannor. So it is in the same case if Tenant in tayle had beene disseised, and the Desseisor suffer an vsurpation, if the Disseisee enter into the Mannor, hee is also remitted to the Aduowson.

Sect. 662.

ITem si terre soit taile a vn home & a sa feme, et a les heires de lour deux corps engendres, les queux ont issue file, et le feme deuy, et le baron prent auter feme, et ad issue vn auter file, & discontinua le tayle, & puis disseisie le discontinuee et issint morust seisie, ore le terre discendera

ALso if Land bee entailed to a man and to his wife, and to the heires of their two bodies begotten, who haue issue a daughter, and the wife dieth, and the husband taketh another wife, and hath issue another daughter, and discontinue the taile, and after he disseiseth the Discontinuee and

dera a les deux files. Et en cest case quant al eigne file, que est inheritable per force de le tayle, ceo nest vn remitter forsque de le moity. Et quant al auter moity el est mis a suer son action de Formedon envers sa soer. Car en cest cas les deux soers ne sont pas tenants en parcenary, mes sont tenants en common, pur ceo que ils sont eins per diuers titles. Car lun soer est eins en son remitter per force de le taile quāt a ceo que a luy affiert, et lauter soer est eins quant a ceo que a luy affiert en fee simple per le discent son pier, &c.

so die seised, now the Land shall discend to the two Daughters. And in this case as to the eldest daughter, who is inheritable by force of the tayle, this is no remitter but of the moitie. And as to the other moitie shee is put to sue her action of *Formedon* against her sister. For in this case the two sisters are not tenants in parcenarie, but they are Tenants in common, for that they are in by diuers titles. For the one sister is in in her remitter by force of the entaile, as to that which to her belongeth, and the other sister is in as to that to her belongeth in fee simple by the discent of her father, &c.

C*Eo nest remitter forsque pur le moitie, &c.* Here Littleton putteth a case where the issue in taile shal be remitted to a moity, because but a moitie of the Land discended vnto her, and there cannot be any remitter, but for so much as commeth to the issue by discent, or by any other meanes without his folly, and in this case by act in Law the Coparcenarie is defeated for the daughters are in by severall Titles, viz the eldest daughter is Tenant in tayle per formam doni by the remitter of the one moitie, and the youngest seised in fee simple by discent of the other moitie, against whom the other sister in tayle may haue her Formedon. 44. E. 3. 18. 19. H. 6. 59.

Sect. 663.

EN Mesme le manner est, si tenant en taile enfeoffa son heire apparant en le taile esteant lheire deins age, et vn auter iointenant en fee, et le tenant en tayle morust, ore lheire en taile est en son remitter quāt a lun moity, et quant a lauter moity il est mis a son briefe de Formedon, &c.

IN the same manner it is if tenant in taile enfeoffe his heire apparant in tayle, (the Heire beeing within age) and another ioyntenant in fee, and the Tenant in tayle dieth, now the heire entayle is in his Remitter as to the one moitie, and as to the other moitie, hee is put to his Writ of *Formedon*, &c.

L*E heire, &c. est en son remitter quant a lun moitie, &c.* Hereby it appeareth, that albeit ioyntenants bee seised pro indiuiso per my & per tout yet each of thē hath in iudgement of Law but a right to a moitie, & therefore the issue in tayle in this case is remitted but to a moity & is tenant in Cōmon but with the other Feoffee. And so it is if the Discontinuee after the death of Tenant in tayle make a Charter of feoffment to the issue in tayle being within age who hath right, and to a stranger in fee, and make liuerie to the Infant in name of both: the issue is not remitted to the whole but to the halfe, for first hee taketh the fee simple, & after the Remitter is wrought by operation of Law, and therefore can remit him but to a moitie. But of this sufficient hath beene said in the Chapter of Ioyntenants. Vide Sect. 288.

Section 664.

¶ Item si ten̄ en taile enfeoffa son heire apparant, lheire esteant de pleine age al temps de feoffment, et puis le ten̄ en taile morust, ceo nest remitter al heir, pur ceo que il fuit sa folly que il esteant de pleine age voile prender tiel feoffment, &c. Mes tiel folly ne poit estre adiudge en lheire esteāt deins age al temps del feoffment, &c.

Also if Tenant in taile enfeoffe his heire apparant, the heire being of full age at the time of the feoffment, and after Tenant in taile dieth, this is no remitter to the heire, because it was his folly, that being of full age hee would take such feoffment, &c. but such folly cannot bee adiudged in the heire being within age at the time of the feoffment, &c.

40. E. 3. 44. 18. E. 4. 25.

¶ By this Feoffment albeit the heire apparant hath some benefit in the life of his Ancestor, yet is he thereby (besides his owne) subiect during his life to all charges and incumbrances made or suffered by his Ancestor. And therefore our Author saith well, Que il fuit sun folly que il esteant de pleine age voile prender tiel feoffment, but folly shall not be iudged in one within age in respect of his tender yeares, and want of experience.

Sect. 665.

¶ Item si tenant en taile enfeoffa vn feme en fee, et morust, et son issue deins age prent mesme la feme a feme, ceo est vn remitt̄ al enfant deins age, et la feme donq; nad rien, pur ceo que le baron et sa feme sont forsque come vn person en ley. Et en cest cas le baron ne poit suer briefe de Formedon, sinon que il voiloit suer enuers luy mesm, le quel seroit enconuenient, et pur cel cause la ley adiudgera lheire en son remitter, pur ceoque nul folly poit estr̄ adiudge en luy, esteāt

Also if Tenant in taile enfeoffe a woman in fee, and dyeth, and his issue within age taketh the same woman to wife, this is a Remitter to the infant within age, and the wife then hath nothing, for that the husband and his wife are but as one person in Law. And in this case the husband cannot sue a writ of *Formedon*, vnlesse he will sue against himselfe, which should be inconuenient, and for this cause the Law adiudgeth the heire in his Remitter, for that no folly can bee adiudged in him being

¶ Here Littleton putteth a case where the husband within age by the intermarriage may bee remitted albeit hee gaineth but a freehold during the Couerture en auter droit.

Also here is to bee obserued that the estate which doth in this case worke the Remitter could not haue continuance after the decease of the wife. And soon the other side, if the husband make a Discontinuance and take backe an estate to him and his wife, during the life of the husband, this is a Remitter to the wife presently albeit the estate is not by the limitation to haue Continuance after the decease of the husband, which case is proued by the reason of the case which our Author here putteth. And here our Author obserueth the diuersity when the husband is within age, and when he is of full age, for when hee is within age no folly can be adiudged in him, as in this Chapter hath beene often said.

deins

deins age al temps despousels, &c. Et si lheire soit en son remitter per force de le taile, il ensuist per reason, q̃ la feme nad riens, &c. Car entant que le baron et sa fem̃ sont come un person, la terre ne poit estre severe per moities, et pur cel cause le baron est en son remitter de lentiertie: Mes autrement est si tiel heir fuit de plein age al temps de les espousels, car donques le heire nad riens forsque en droit sa feme, &c.

within age at the time of the Espousells, &c. And if the heire bee in his remitter by force of the entaile, it followeth by reason that the wife hath nothing, &c. for inasmuch as the husband and wife be as one person the land cannot be parted by moities, and for this cause the husband is in his remitter of the whole. But otherwise it is if such heire were of full age at the time of espowsells, for then the heire hath nothing but in right of his wife, &c.

Here is also to bee noted that presently by the marriage within age, the husband is remitted, and the freehold and inheritance of the wife vanished cleane away.

Prist mesme la feme al fem. Here it is good to be seene what things are given to the husband by marriage. First it appeareth here by Littleton, that if a man taketh to wife a woman seised in fee (f) he gaineth by the intermarriage an estate of freehold in her right, which estate is sufficient to worke a Remitter, and yet the estate which the husband gaineth dependeth upon uncertaintie, and consisteth in privity, (g) for if the wife be attainted of felony, the Lord by eschcate shall enter and put out the husband, otherwise it is if the felony be committed after issue had. Also if the husband bee attainted of felony, the King gaineth no Freehold but a pernancie of the profits during the Coverture and the Freehold remaineth in the wife. (h) Secondly, if shee were possessed of a terme for yeares, yet he is possessed in her right, but he hath power to dispose thereof by Grant or Demise, and if hee be Outlawed or attainted, they are gifts in Law.

(f) 13 H.4.6. Stanf pr 7.b. 18.E.4.5. 11.H.7.19. 10.H.6.11. 7.H.6.9 b.

Vid. Sect. 58.

(g) 4. Ass P.4. 4.E.3. Assise 166.

(h) Pl. Com fo.260.b. Dame Hales case, 50. Ass.5. 38 H.6.23. 21.E.4.35. 7.E.4.6. 7.H.7.2. 10.H.6.11.

(*) Upon an Execution against the husband for his debt, the Sherife may sell the terme during her life: but the husband can make no disposition thereof by his Last will. Also if hee make no disposition or forfeiture of it in his life, yet it is a gift in Law unto him if hee doe survive his wife, but if he make no disposition and die before his wife, shee shall have it againe. And the same Law is of estates by Statute Merchant, Statute Staple, Elegit, wardships and other chattels realls in possession.

(*) Mich. 26. & 27. Eliz. inter Amner & Lodington in Brie'e de error adiudge in both Courts, lib.8 fo.96. Mar: Manning. case.

But if the husband charge the Chattell reall of his wife, it shall not binde the wife if shee survive him.

7.H.6. fo.2.

If a Feme sole be possessed of a Chattell reall, and be thereof dispossessed, and then taketh husband, and the wife dieth, and the husband surviveth, this right is not given to the husband by the intermarriage, but the Executors or Administrators of the wife shall have it, so it is if the wife hath but a possibility.

Vid. Sect. 58.

In the same manner it is if the wife be possessed of Chattells realls in auter droit, as Executrix or Administratrix, or as Gardeine in Socage, &c. and she intermarrieth, the Law maketh no gift of them to the husband although he surviveth her. In the same manner if a woman grant a terme to her owne use, taketh husband, and dieth, the husband surviving shall not have this trust, but the Executors or Administrators of the wife, (i) for it consisteth in privity, and so hath it beene resolved by the Justices. Chattells realls consisting meerely in Action the Husband shall not have by the intermarriage, unlesse he recovereth them in the life of the wife, albeit he survive the wife, as a Writ of Right of ward, a valore maritagii, a forfeiture of marriage, and the like, whereunto the wife was intitled before the marriage.

Pl. Com. fo.294. Osbornes case and there fo.192.b. Wrotesleys case.

(i) Pasch 32. Eliz. in Cancellar. in Withams case. Hill. 38. Eliz. in Cancell. in Water houses case. Wrotesleys case, ubi supra.

But Chattells realls being of a mixt nature, viz. partly in possession, and partly in Action, which happen during the Coverture, the husband shall have by the intermarriage, if hee survive his wife, albeit he reduceth them not into possession in her life time: but if the wife surviveth him, she shall have them. As if the husband be seised of a Rent service, Charge, or Seck, in the right of his wife, the rent become due during the Coverture, the wife dieth, the husband shall have the arrerages; but if the wife survive the husband, she shall have them, and not the Executors of the husband. So it is of an Advowson, if the Church become voyd during the Coverture, (k) he may have a Quare impedit in his owne name, as some hold: but the wife shall

13.E.3. Quare Imp.57. 14.H.4.12. 38 E.3.35.b. 50.E.3.13. 10.H.6.11. F.N.B.121. 22.H.6.25. 29.E.3.40. 11.R.2. Accompt 49. 12.R.2. briefe 639. 5.E.3. Execut.99.

(k) 50.E.3.13. 28.H.6.9. 7.H.7.2.

shall haue it if she suruiue him, and the Husband, if he suruiue her, Et sic de similibus.

26.E.3 64.10.H.6.11. F.N.B.121.22.H.6.25.

But if the arrerages had become due, or the Church had fallen voyd before the marriage, there they were meerely in Action before the marriage, and therefore the husband should not haue them by the Common Law, although he suruiued her. And so it is of Reliefes, Mutatis mutandis: (l) But now by the Statute of 32.H.8.cap.37. if the husband suruiue the wife, he shall haue the arrerages as well incurred before the marriage, as after.

(l) Li.4 fo.51. in Ognels case Hil.17.El.Rot.457. in Com. Banco, Sharps case. 21.E.4.4.21.H.7.29. 11.H.7.4.26.H.8.7.43.E.3 10. 3.H.6.23.37 4.H.6.5. 14.E.2.Det.173.5.E.2.ibid. 169.30.E.3. 48.E.3.12. 12.R.3.Bre.638.639. 16.E.4 8 16.H.6.Bre 939. (m) 43.E.3.8.V.10.H.6.11 39.E.3.17.

But the marriage is an absolute gift of all Chattels personalls in possession in her owne right, whither the husband suruiue the wife or no; but if they bee in Action, as debts by Obligation, Contract, or otherwise, the husband shall not haue them vnlesse he and his wife recouer them. And of personall Goods en auter droit, as Executrix or Administratrix, &c. the marriage is no gift of them to the husband, although he suruiue his wife.

(m) If an Estray happen within the Mannor of the wife, if the husband die before seisure, the wife shall haue it, for that the propertie was not in the wife before seisure.

But as to personall Goods there is a diuersitie worthie of obseruation, betweene a propertie in personall goods, (as is aforesayd) and a bare possession, for if personall goods bee bayled to a Feme, or if she finde goods, or if goods come to her hands as Executrix to a Bailife, and taketh a husband, this bare possession is not giuen to the husband, but the Action of Detinue must be brought against the husband and wife.

But now let vs heare Littleton.

Vi.Sect.87.&c.

¶ *Le quel serra inconuenient.* This argument ab inconuenienti, our Author hath vsed in many places.

Section 666.

¶ Item si Feme seisie de certaine terre en fee prent baron, le quel aliena mesme la terre a vn auter en Fee, lalienee lessa mesme la terre al Baron et sa Feme pur terme de lour deux vies, sauant le reuersion al Lessor et a ses heires, en cest cas la Feme est eins en son Remitter, et el est seisie en Fait en son demesne come de Fee, sicome el fuit adeuant, pur ceo que le reprisel del Estate serra adiudge en Ley le Fait le Baron, et nemy le Fait la Feme, issint nul folly poit estre adiudge en la Feme, que est couert en tiel Case, et en cest case le Lessor nad rien en le Reuersion, pur ceo que la Feme est seisie en fee, &c.

Also if a woman seised of certaine Land in Fee, taketh Husband, who alieneth the same Land to another in Fee, the Alienee letteth the same Land to the husband and wife for terme of their two liues, sauing the reuersion to the Lessor and to his Heires; In this case the wife is in in her Remitter, and she is seised in Deed in her Demesne as of Fee, as she was before, because the taking back of the Estate shall be adiudged in law the fact of the Husband, and not the fact of the Wife; so no follie can be adiudged in the wife, which is Couert in such Case. And in this Case the Lessor hath nothing in the Reuersion, for that the Wife is seised in Fee, &c.

21.E.3.26. 29.E.3.43. 41.E.3.Remit.11. 19.E.3.Remit.14.35.Ass.12.38.E.3.24 39.E.3.29.30 41.E.3.17. 46.E.3.20.b. 26.E.3.69. Vi.Sect.676. 11.R.2.Remit.12.44.E.3.17.

¶ *La feme est en son Remitter.* By this it appeareth, That albeit there be no moities betweene husband and wife, yet this is a Remitter presently, and standeth not vpon the suruiuor of the wife, as some haue thought, for if the Estate gained by intermarriage be a sufficient Estate to worke a Remitter, à fortiori, an Estate made to the husband and wife shall worke a Remitter in the wife. And so it is if Tenant in Taile infeoffe his Issue being within age, and his wife in Fee, and dieth, this is a Remitter to the Issue presently, by the death of Tenant in Tayle, though some haue thought the contrarie.

Here also it appeareth, That no follie in this case can be adiudged in a Feme Couert, for the taking backe of the Estate shall be adiudged in Law the act of the Husband. The Marques of Winch. case, vb. sup.

Note in the case of the Feme Couert, she may be remitted in the life of the Discontinuor, because she hath a present right: but in the case of Tenant in Taile, the Issue cannot bee remitted in the life of the Discontinuor, because the Issue hath no right untill his decease.

Section 667.

¶ Mes en cẽ case si le Lessour voile suer Action de wast vers le Baron et sa Feme, pur ceo que le Baron auoit fait wast, le Baron ne poit barrer le Lessor pur monstre ceo que le reprisel del estat fait a luy et a son Feme, fuit vn Remitter a sa feme, pur ceo que le Baron est estoppe a dire ceo que est encounter sõ feoffment et son reprisel demesne del estate p̃ terme de vie a luy et a sa Feme. Et vncore le Lessor nad vn Reuersion, pur ceo que le Fee simple est en la feme. Et issint home poit veier vn matter en ceo case, q̃ home serra estoppe per vn matter en fait coment que nul Escripture soit fait per Fait indent ou auterment.

BVt in this Case if the Lessor wil sue an Action of Wast against the husband and his Wife, for that the husband hath committed Wast, the husband cannot barre the Lessor by shewing this, That the taking backe of the Estate to him and to his wife, was a Remitter to his wife, because the husband is stopped to say that which is against his owne Feoffement, and taking backe of the Estate for terme of life to him and to his Wife. And yet the Lessor hath no reuersion, for that the Fee simple is in the Wife. And so a man may see one thing in this case, That a man shall bee stopped by matter in Fact, though there bee no Writing by Deede indented, or otherwise.

¶ Pvr ceo que Baron est estoppe a dire, &c.

¶ Estoppe commeth of the French word Estoupe, from whence the English word Stopped: and it is called an Estoppel or Conclusion, because a mans owne Act or acceptance stoppeth or closeth up his mouth to alledge or plead the truth: And Littletons case heere prooueth this description. *I. 2. fo. 4. b. Goddards case. V. Sect. 41. & 693. 695. 679.*

Touching Estoppels, which is an excellent and curious kind of learning) it is to obserued that there be three kind of Estoppels, viz. By matter of Record, By matter in writing, and By matter in Paiis.

(a) By matter of Record, viz. By Letters Patents, Fine; Recouerie, Pleading, taking of Continuance, Confession, Imparlance, Warrant of Atturney, Admittance. *(a) 43. Ass. 29. 8. H. 4. 7. & 22. Ass. 54. 15. E. 3. Estop. 239. 4. E. 3. ib. 133.*

(b) By matter in writing, as by Deed indented, by making of an Acquittance by Deed indented, or Deed poll, (c) by Defeasance by Deed indented or Deed Poll. *(b) 4. H. 4. 8. H. 7. 6. 13. H. 7. 24. 15. E. 4. 28. 41 E. 3 Estop. 12 12. R. 2. ib. 212.* *(c) 8. R. 2. Estop. 283. 35. H. 6. 18. 3. H. 6. 16. 16. H. 7. 5 34. H. 6. 19. 14. H. 4. 29.*

By matter in Paiis, as by Liuerie, by Entry, by Acceptance of Rent, by Partition, and by Acceptance of an Estate as heire in the case that Littleton putteth, whereof Littleton maketh a special obseruation, that a man shall be estopped by matter in the Countrie, without any writing.

To make the Reader more capable of the learning of Estoppels, these few Rules, amongst others, are to be knowne.

(d) First, That euerie Estoppell ought to be reciprocall, that is to bind both parties; and this is the reason, that regularly a Stranger shall neither take aduantage, nor be bound by the Estoppell, (e) Priuies in Blood, as the Heire, Priuies in Estate, as the Feoffee, Lessee, &c. Priuies in Law, as the Lords by Escheat: Tenant by the Curtesie, Tenant in Dower, the *(d) 33. H. 6. 19. 50. 30 H. 6. 2 31. E. 3. Estop. 240. 32 ass. 18. 30. ass. 51. 14. ass. 9. 18 E. 4. 1 (e) 8. ass. 33. Br. Fines 73. 8. H. 6. 17 21. E. 3. 35. 38. E. 3. 31. 20. E. 3. Estop. 187.*

Incumbent

Incumbent of a Benefice, and others that come vnder by Act in Law, or in the Post, shall bee bound and take aduantage of Estoppels, and that a Rebutter is a kind of Estoppell.

(f) 21. E. 4. 4. 23. Ass. 14. 17. H. 6. Estop. 273. 18. E. 3. 30. 7. H. 7. 6. & 16.

(f) Secondly, That euerie Estoppell, because it concludeth a man to alledge the truth, must be certaine to euerie intent, and not to be taken by argument or inference.

(g) 46. E. 3. 33. 29. Ass. 38. Pl. Com. 398.

(h) 35. H. 6. 33. 46. E. 3. 12. 49. E. 3. 14. 8. Ass. 3. 45. Ass. 5. 3. El. Dy. 196. 21. El. ibid. 280. 9. H. 6. 60.

(g) Thirdly, Euerie Estoppell ought to be a precise affirmation of that which maketh the Estoppell, and not be spoken impersonally, as if it be sayd, Vt dicitur, quia impersonalitas non concludit, nec ligat: impersonalis dicitur, quia sine persona. (h) Neither doth a recitall conclude, because it is no direct affirmation.

(i) 5. E. 4. 7. 8. E. 4. 19. 10. E. 4. 12. 22. E. 4. 38. 32. Ass. 9. 35. H. 6. 20.

(i) Fourthly, A matter alledged that is neither trauersable nor materiall, shall not estoppe.

(k) 33. H. 6. 16. 4. E. 3. 22. 6. H. 4. 7. 31. E. 1. Gard. 155. F. N. B. 142. E.

(k) Fiftly, Regularly a man shall not bee concluded by acceptance or the like, before his Title accrued.

(l) 12. H. 7. 4. 20. H. 6. 29. 3. H. 4. 9. 41. E. 3. 4. 11. H. 4. 30.

(l) Sixtly, Estoppell against Estoppell doth put the matter at large.

(m) 2. R. 3. 14. 2. R. 2. Estoppel. 20. 40. E. 3. 21. 12. E. 4. 13. 18. E. 3. 31. 35. 44. E. 3. 45. 27. Ass. 27. 45. E. 3. 2. 21. H. 7. 24. 5. E. 4. 7. 7. E. 4. 19. 3. E. 4. 11. 4. E. 3. 54. 7. E. 6. Br. Estop. 162. 11. H. 4. 30. 30. E. 3. 21. 31. Ass. 14.

(m) Seuenthly, Matters alledged by way of supposall in Counts, shall not conclude after Non-suit: otherwise it is after iudgement giuen; and after Non-suit, albeit the supposall in the Count shall not conclude, yet the Barre, Title, Replication, or other pleading of either partie, which is precisely alledged, shall conclude after Non-suit, and hereby are the Bookes reconciled.

(n) 37. Ass. 17. 38. H. 6. 12. 5. El. Dy. 222.

(o) 7. El. Dy. 244.

Eightly, where the veritie is apparant in the same Record, there the aduerse partie shal not be estopped to take aduantage of the truth, for he cannot be estoppad to alledge the truth, when the truth appeareth of Record. (n) If a Fine be leuied without any originall, it is voydable, but not voyd, but if an Originall be brought, and a Retraxit entred, and after that, a Concord is made, or a Fine leuied, this is voyd, in respect the veritie appeareth of Record. (o) An Impropriation is made after the death of an Incumbent, to a Bishop and his Successors, the Bishop by Indenture demiseth the Parsonage for fortie yeares, to begin after the death of the Incumbent, the Deane and Chapiter confirmeth it, the Incumbent dieth, this Demise shall not conclude, for that it appeareth that he had nothing in the Impropriation till after the death of the Incumbent.

(p) Brall. fo. 420. 26. Ass. 64. 39. Ass. 10. 11. H. 4. 84. 7. H. 6. 7. 33. Ass. 5. 11. E. 3. Estop. 229. 21. E. 3. 39. 19. R. 2. Estop. 282. 3. E. 3. ib. 23. 33. E. 3. Estop. Stath. Lestat. de 9. H. 6. ca. 11. 30. H. 6. 2. Doct. & Stud. 69. 34. H. 6. 39. 18. E. 4. 1. b. 10. E. 4. 16.

(p) Ninthly, where the Record of the Estoppell doth run to the disabilitie or legitimation of the person, there all strangers shall take benefit of that Record, as Outlawrie, Excommengement, Profession, Attainder of Præmunire, of Felonie, &c. Bastardie, Muliertie, and shall conclude the partie, though they be Strangers to the Record, Vide in Littleton, cap. Villenage, Sect. 196, 197. &c. But of a Record concerning the name of the person, qualitie, or addition, no estranger shall take aduantage, because he shall not be bound by it. But note Reader, That in case of the Mulиertie prima facie, an Estranger shall take benefit of it, &c. But yet because he may be a Mulier by the Ecclesiasticall Law, and a Bastard by the Common Law, therefore against such a Certificate pleaded, the aduerse partie may alledge the speciall matter, and confesse the Certificate of the Bishop according to the Ecclesiasticall Law, and alledge further the speciall matter according to the Common Law, whereunto the aduerse party must answer, and so are the Books that treat of this matter, to be reconciled. But now let vs returne to Littleton.

Sect. 668.

<table>
<tr>
<td>¶ La Feme pria deste resceiue & soit resceiue.</td>
<td>¶ Mes si en action de Wast le baron fait default a le graund distresse, et la feme pria destre receiue et soit receiue el monstra bien tout le matter, et coment el est en son Remitter, et el barrera le Lessor de son Action, &c.</td>
<td>But if in the Action of Waste the Husband make default to the grand Distresse, and the Wife pray to be receiued, and is receiued, shee may well shew the whole matter, and how shee is in her Remitter, and shee shall barre the Lessor of his Action, &c.</td>
</tr>
</table>

10. E. 3. Defensio iuris.

(a) W. 2. ca. 3.

(b) Brall. fo. 393. Mir. li. 3. cap. Exceptions.

Receipt, Receptio commeth of the Latyne Verbe Recipere, so called because the wife vpon the default of her husband, is receiued as a Feme sole alone, without her husband, to defend her right, and it is also called Defensio iuris: and in this case the wife may bee receiued by the (a) Statute, and yet (b) antient Authors who wrote before the Statute, doe speake of a kind of Receit at the Common Law. The Ciuilians call Receit, Admissionem tertij pro suo interesse, which more properly is resembled to the receit of him in the reuersion or remainder, that is no partie to the Writ.

Sect. 669.

¶ CAr en chescun cas lou feme est receiue pur default son baron, el pledera & auera m̄ ladvantage en plee pledant, come el fuissoit feme sole, &c. Et coment que lalienee fist le leas al baron & a sa feme, per fait endent, uncore ceo est remitter a la feme. Et auxy coment que lalienee rendist mesm̄ la terre al baron & a sa feme per fine pur terme de lour vies, uncore ceo est un remitter al feme, pur ceo que feme couert que prent estate per fine, ne serra my examine per les Iustices, &c.

FOr in euery Case where the wife is receiued for default of her husband, shee shall plead and haue the same aduantage in pleading, as shee were a woman sole, &c. and albeit that the alienee made the lease to the husband and wife by deed indented, yet this is a Remitter to the wife. And also albeit the alienee rendreth the same Land to the husband and his wife by fine for tearme of their liues, yet this is a remitter to the wife, because a feme couert which takes an estate by fine shall not be examined by the Iustices, &c.

¶ COme el fuissoit feme sole, &c.

In this Section foure things are to bee understood.

First when a Feme couert is receiued that she shall plead as if she were sole. And this is regularly true, yet holdeth not in all cases, (c) for if a Feme couert bee receiued in an Assise and plead a Record and faile, therefore shee shall not bee adiudged a Disseisor as shee should bee if shee were sole, &c. So if a Feme couert only leuie a fine executorie, and a Scire facias is brought against her and her husband, if shee bee receiued upon the default of her husband, shee shall barre the Conusee, which if shee had beene sole, she could not doe, and in some other Cases. (c) 37. Ass. 1. 17. Ass. 17. 29. E. 3. 43. 5. E. 3. Voucher 178.

Secondly, that though the estate taken backe bee by deed indented, yet that shall not hinder the Remitter in case of a Feme couert, or an Infant. Thirdly, that though it be by fine sur render, yet that shall not hinder the Remitter, because a Feme couert is not to be examined upon any fine, but when shee and her husband passe some estate or interest, or release her right by a fine of the Lands or Tenements.

¶ *Ne serra my examine per les Iustices, &c.* The examination of a Feme Couert ought to be secret, and the effect is to examine her whether she be content to leuie a fine of such Lands (naming them particularly and distinctly, and the state that passeth by the fine) of her owne voluntarie free will, and not by threats, menaces, or any other compulsarie meanes.

Fourthly, if the husband leuie a fine of his wiues Lands, and the Conusee grant and render the Land to the husband and wife, although the wife bee not partie to the originall nor to the Conusans, and therefore she ought not by the Law to take any present estate but by way of Remainder only, yet here it is proued by Littleton, that the grant and render de facto to the wife in præsenti is not void, for then it could not worke a Remitter, but voidable by Writ of Error, and that avoidable estate doth worke a Remitter. Trin. 27. Eliz. Inter Owen & Morgan Rot. 276. in Banco Communi. Lib. 3. fol. 5. the Marquesse of Winchesters Case. 7. E. 3. 64. 13. E. 3. Voucher 119.

Sect. 670.

¶ ET hic nota, que quant ascun chose passera de la fem̄ que est couert de baron per force dun

ANd here note, that when any thing shall passe from the wife which is couert of a husband by

dun fine, sicome le baron et la fem̃ fesont vn conusance de droit a vn auter, &c. ou fesoyent vn grant & render a vn auter, ou relessent per fine a auter, & sic de similibus, lou le droit del fem̃ passeroit del feme p force de mesme le fine, en touts tielx cases la feme serra examine deuaunt q̃ la fine soit accept pur ceo que tiels fines concluderont tiels fem̃s couerts a touts iours, &c. Mes lou riens est moue en le fine forsque tantsolement que le baron, & la feme preignont estate per force de mesme le fine, ceo ne concluder la feme, pur ceo que en tiel cas el iammes ne serra my examine, &c.

force of a fine. As if the husband and wife make Conusance of right to another, &c. or make a grant & render to another, or release by fine vnto another, *& sic de similibus*, where the right of the wife shall passe from the wife by force of the same fine, in all such cases the wife shall bee examined before that the fine bee taken, because that such fines shall conclude such femes couerts for euer. But where nothing is moued in the fine but only that the husband and wife do take an estate by force of the said fine, this shall not conclude the wife, for that in such case shee shall not bee at all examined, &c.

(d) 15.E.4.28. 24.E.3.31. 42.E.3.6. 3.H.6.42. 20.E.3.tit. Cui in vita 10.
(*) 29.E.3.43. 46.E.3.5.

Quant ascun chose passera de la feme couert, &c: per force dun fine, &c. And of this opinion is (d) Littleton in our Bookes.

*Therefore if the husband and wife be Tenants in speciall tayle, and they leuie a fine at the Common Law, and after the husband and wife take backe an estate to them and their heires in this case the estate tayle is not barred, and yet against a fine leuied by her selfe she cannot be remitted, because thereupon she was examined: but in that case if the Land discend to her issue he shall be remitted.

Section 671.

Item si tenant en taile discontinua le taile & ad issue file, & morust, & la file esteant de pleine age prent baron, & le discontinuee fait vn releas de ceo al baron & a sa feme pur terme de lour vies, ceo est vn Remitter al feme, et la feme est eins per force de le taile, Causa qua supra.

Also if tenant in tayle discontinue the taile, and hath issue a daughter & dieth, & the daughter being of full age taketh husband and the Discontinuee make a release of this to the husband & wife for terme of their liues, this is a Remitter to the wife, and the wife is in by force of the Tayle, *Causa qua supra, &c.*

Et la feme esteant de plein age prent baron, &c. Here it appeareth that her full age when she tooke Baron is not materiall, but her couerture at the taking backe of the estate. And so note a diuersitie betweene a Remitter and a Discent. For if a woman be disseised, and being of full age taketh husband, and then the Disseisor dieth seised, this Discent shall binde the wife, albeit shee was couert when the Discent was cast, because shee was of full age when shee tooke husband, as appeareth before in the Chapter of Discents. But albeit the wife that hath an ancient right, and being of full age taketh a husband, and the Discontinuee letteth the Land to the husband and wife for their liues, this is a Remitter to the wife. For Remitters to ancient rights are fauoured in Law.

Sect. 672.

¶ Item si terre soit done a le baron et a sa feme, a auer et tener a eux et a les heirs de lour deux corps engendres, et puis le baron aliena la terre en fee, et reprent estate a luy et a sa fem̃ pur terme de lour deux vies, en cest cas il est remitter en fait a le baron et a sa feme maugre l' baron. Car il ne poit est̃ vn remitter en cest cas a la feme, sinon que soit vn remitter a le baron, pur ceo que le baron et sa feme sont tout vn mesme person en ley, coment que le baron est estoppe de claymer. Et pur ceo, ceo est vn remitter ẽ luy encounter son alienation et son reprisel demesne, come est dit adeuant.

ALso if land be giuen to the husband and to his wife, to haue & to hold to them & to the heires of their two bodies begotten, and after the husband alien the land in fee, and take backe an estate to him and to his wife for terme of their two liues, in this case this is a remitter in deed to the husband and to his wife mauger the husband. For it cannot bee a remitter in this case to the wife, vnlesse it bee a remitter to the husband, because the husband and wife are all one same person in Law, though the husband be stopped to claime it, and therefore this is a remitter against his owne alienation and reprisel, as is said before.

¶ HEre it appeareth that the husband against his owne alienation if hee had taken the estate to him alone could not haue been remitted. But when the estate is made to the husband & wife, albeit they be but one person in Law, and no moyties betweene them, yet for that the wife cannot be remitted in this case, vnlesse the husband be remitted also, and for that remitters, as hath beene often said, are fauoured in Law because thereby the more antient and better rights are restored againe, therefore in this case in iudgement of Law both husband and wife are remitted, which is worthy of great obseruation.

Sect. 673.

¶ Item si terre soit done a vn feme en taile, le remainder a vn auter en taile, le remainder a le tierce en taile, le remainder al quart en fee, et la fem̃ prent baron, et le baron discontinua la terre en fee, p cel discontinuance touts les remainders sont discontinues. Car si la fem̃ deuiast sans issue, ceux en le remainder naueront ascun remedie forsque de suer lour briefes de Formedon en le remainder quant

ALso if land bee giuen to a woman in taile, the remainder to another in taile, the remainder to the third in taile, the remainder to the fourth in fee, and the woman taketh husband, and the husband discontinue the land in fee, by this Discontinuance all the remainders are discontinued, for if the wife die without issue, they in the remainder shall not haue any remedie but to sue their writs of *Formedon* in the remainder, when

quant il auient a lour temps. Mes si apres tiel discontinuance, estate soit fait a le baron et sa feme pur terme de lour deux vies, ou pur terme dauter vie, ou auter estate, &c. pur ceo que ceo est vn remitter al feme, ceo est auxy vn remitter a touts ceux en le remainder. Car apres ceo que la feme que est en son remitter mourust sans issue, ceux en le remainder poyent enter, &c. sans ascun action suer, &c. En mesme le maner est de ceux que ount la reuersion apres tiel tailes.

it comes to their times. But if after such discontinuance, an estate be made to the husband and wife for terme of their two liues, or for terme of another mans life, or other estate, &c. for that this is a remitter to the wife, this is also a remitter to all them in the remainder. For after that that the wife which is in her remitter be dead without issue, they in the remainder may enter, &c. without any action suing, &c. In the same manner is it of those which haue the reuersion after such entailes.

¶ Littleton hauing spoken of Remitters to the issue in taile who is priuie in blood, and to the wife who is priuie in person, now he speaketh of Remitters to them in reuersion or remainder expectant vpon an estate taile who are priuie in estate. And this case proueth that the wife is remitted presently, for the equity of the Law requireth that as the discontinuance of the estate in taile is a discontinuance of the reuersion or remainder, so, that the Remitter to the estate in taile should be a Remitter to them in the reuersion or remainder.

41. E. 3. 17. 41. Ass. 1. 36. Ass p. 4.

44. Ass. p. 15. 44 E. 3. 30. Tenant for life the remainder to A in taile, the remainder to B. in fee, Tenant for life is disseised, a collaterall Ancestor of A releaseth with warrantie and dyeth, whereby the estate taile is barred, the Tenant for life re-entreth, the Disseisor hath an estate in fee simple determinable vpon the state taile, and the remainder of B is reuested in him, and so note in this case the estate for life and the remainder in fee are reuested and remitted, and an estate of inheritance left in the Disseisor. 30. E. 3. Aid. 29. If a Fine be leuied sur grant & render to one for life or in taile, the remainder in fee, if Tenant for life or in taile execute the estate for life or in taile, this is an execution of the remainder.

Vid. Pl. Com. 489. Nichols case & 10. 553. in Walsinghams case. 17. Eliz. Dier 344. 25. E. 3. 48. tit. Resceit 28. 49. E. 3. 16. (a) Seignior Staffords case, Lib. 8. fo. 76. b. (b) Cholmleys case, lib. 2. 53. 7. R. 2. Aide le Roy, 61. 22. E. 3. 7.

A gift in taile is made to B the remainder to C. in fee, B. discontinueth and taketh backe an estate in taile, the remainder in fee to the King by deed inrolled, Tenant in taile dieth, his issue is remitted, and consequently the remainder as Littleton here saith, and the diuersitie is (a) betweene an act in Law, for that may deuest an estate out of the King, and a tortious act, or entrie, or a false and a feyned recouery against Tenant for life or in taile which shall neuer deuest any estate, remainder, or reuersion out of the King. (b) But a recouery by good title against Tenant for life or in taile where the remainder is to the King by defeasible title shall deuest the remainder out of the King, and restore and remit the right owners.

Sect. 674. 675.

¶ Feint & faux action. i. Actio ficta & falsa, But hereof Littleton speaketh himselfe in this Chapter.

(c) W. 2. cap. 4. ¶ Quod ei deforceat, is a Writ that is giuen by (c) Statute to any Tenant for life or in taile vpon a Recouery by default against them in a Præcipe, and lyeth against the

¶ Item si hom lessa vn mease a vn feme pur terme de sa vie, sauant le reuersion al lessour, et puis vn suist vn feint et faux action enuers la feme et recouerast le mease enuers luy per default, issint que la

Also if a man lett a house to a woman for terme of her life, sauing the reuersion to the Lessor, and after one sue a feyned and false action against the woman, and recouereth the house against her by default, so as the

la feme puit auer enuers luy vn Quod ei deforceat, solonque le Statute de Westm̃ 2. ore le reuersion le Lessor est discontinue, issint que il ne poit auer ascun action de wast. Mes en cest case si la fem̃ prent baron, et celuy que recouerast lessa le mease al baron et a sa feme pur terme de lour deux vyes, la feme est eins en son remitter per force del primer lease.

woman may haue against him a *Quod ei deforceat*, according to the Statute of Westm. 2. now the reuersion of the Lessor is discontinued, so that he cannot haue any action of wast. But in this case if the woman take husband, and hee which recouereth lett the house to the husband & his wife for terme of their two liues the wife is in her Remitter by force of the first Lease.

Sect. 675.

¶ Et si le baron et la feme font wast, le primer lessor auera enuers eux brẽ de wast, pur ceo que entant que la feme est en son remitter, il est remise a son reuersion. Mes semble en cest cas si celuy que recouerast per l' faux action, voile porter auter briefe de wast enuers le baron & sa feme, le baron nad auter remedie enuers luy, mes de faire default a la graund distres, &c. et causer la feme destre receiue, et de pleder cel matter enuers le secõd lessor, et monstrer coment laction per que il recouerast fuit faux & feint ẽ ley, &c. issint l' fẽe poit luy barrer, &c.

AND if the husband and wife make wast, the first Lessor shall haue a writ of wast against them, for that inasmuch as the wife is in her remitter, he is remitted to his reuersion. But it seemeth in this case if hee that recouereth by the false action will bring another writ of waste against the husband & his wife, the husband hath no other remedy against him, but to make default to the grand distresse, &c. and cause the wife to be receiued, and to plead this matter against the second Lessor, and shew how the action wherby he recouered was false & fained in law, &c. so the wife may barre him.

recoueror and his heires in which case the particular Tenant was without remedy at the Common Law, because hee could not haue a writ of right. And it is called a Quod ei deforceat, for that they are part of the words of that writ, viz. Præcipe A. quod, &c. reddat B. vnum mesuagium, &c. quod clamat esse jus & maritagium suum, & quod idem A. ei iniuste deforceat. *Bracton lib.* 4. 367. *Fleta, lib.* 5. *c. p.* 22. & *lib.* 6. *cap.* 14. 7. *E.* 3. 62. *F. N. B.* 155.

¶ *Recouerast &c. per default.* There hath beene a question in our bookes vpon these words (By default) as for example, whether a recouery had by default in an action of waste against Tenant in Dower, or by the Curtesie, a Quod ei deforceat lyeth by the said Statute. *W.* 2. *ca.* 4. And diuers hold opinion, that in that case no Quod ei deforceat lyeth, for that iudgement is not giuen, for notwithstanding the default, there goeth out a writ to enquire De vasto facto, & quod vastum prædictum A. (le defendant) fecit. So as the Defendant may giue euidence, and the Jurors may finde for the Defendant, that no waste was done: As in the Assise albeit it bee awarded by Default, yet may the Tenant giue euidence, and the Recognitors of the Assise may finde for the Tenant, and therefore in those cases, the Defendant or Tenant Non amittit per defaltam, as the Statute and Littleton speaketh, and they cite F. N. B in the point. *F. N. B. fo.* 155. *E.*

Secondly, they hold that a Quod ei deforceat lyeth where the Tenant can haue no remedie by attaint, but in this case (say they) an attaint doth lye. 2. *H.* 4. 2. 21. *H.* 6. 56. 41. *E.* 3. 8. 3. *H.* 6. 29. 22. *E.* 3. 19.

Thirdly, they hold, that in an Action of waste although

though it be brought against a Tenant in Dower or Tenant by the Curtesie that haue a freehold, yet the dammages are the principall, for they were recouerable against Tenant in Dower and by the Curtesie by the Common Law, and the Statute of Glocester gaue the place wasted but for a penaltie, so as the nature of the Action (say they) remaineth still to bee personall, for that the dammages are the principall; (d) and in proofe hereof they cite diuers Authorities in Law. And if two bring an Action of wast, the release of one of them is a good bar against the other, (e) and so resolued by the whole Court; which prooueth (say they) that the dammages are the principall, for if the Land were the principall, the release of one of them should not barre the other, no more then in an Assise, a Writ of Ward, an Eiectione firmæ, &c.

(d) 34. H. 6. 7. 40. E. 3. 37. & 38. E. 3.

(e) 9. H. 5. 15.

30. H. 6. tit. Bar. 59.

Lastly, they say, That in Actions where dammages are to be recouered, and the land is the Principall, the Demandant neuer counteth to dammages, and yet shall recouer them: but in an Action of wast the Plaintife counteth to his dammage, and if the dammages be the Principall, then cleerely no Quod ei deforceat lieth.

Others doe hold the contrarie, and as to the first they say, That albeit that in the writ of wast iudgement is not onely giuen vpon the default, yet the default is the principall, and the cause of awarding of the writ to enquire of the wast as an incident thereunto: and the Law alwayes hath respect to the first and principall cause, and therefore vpon such a Recouerie (*) a writ of Deceit lieth, and that writ lieth not but where the Recouerie is by default. So in an Action of wast against the husband and wife, vpon the default of the husband the wife shal be receiued, and yet the Statute there speaketh also, per defaltam. So vpon such a recouerie in wast against the Baron and Feme by default, the wife shall haue a Cui in vita by the Statute, and it speaketh where the Recouerie is per defaltam. And albeit the Defendant may giue in euidence, if he knoweth it, yet when he makes default the Law presumeth hee knoweth not of it, and it may be that he in truth knew not of it; and therefore it is reason, that seeing the Statute, that is a beneficiall Statute, hath giuen it him, that he be admitted to his Quod ei deforceat, in which writ the truth and right shall be tried. And so it is of a recouerie by default in an Assise, albeit the Recognitors of the Assise giue a verdict, a Quod ei deforceat lieth. And all this as to this poynt was resolued by the whole Court of Common Pleas, and so the doubt in 41 E. 3. 8. well resolued. Nota, if Tenant for life make default after default, and he in the reuersion is receiued and plead to Issue, and it is found by verdict for the Demandant, the default and the verdict are causes of the Judgement, and yet the Tenant shall haue a Quod ei deforceat.

(*) 17. E. 3. 58. 29. E. 3. 42. F. N. B. 98. b. 12. H. 4. 4. 19. E. 2. Disceit 56. W. 2. ca. 3. 3. H. 4. fo. 1.

W. 2. ca. 3. 9. E. 4. 16.

41. E. 3. 8. b. 2. H. 4. 2. 21. H. 6. 56. 44. E. 3. 43. br. tit. Quod ei deforc. 4. Pasch. 33. El. Rot. 1125. inter Ed. Elmer & El. sa feme, ten. en Dower. demandants, & Wil. Thacker ten. in Quod ei deforceat.

As to the second obiection, That the Defendant may haue an Attaint, First it was vtterly denied of the other part, (f) that an Attaint did lie in this case, for though it be taken by the Oath of twelue men, yet it is but an Enquest of Office, whereupon no Attaint did lie on either partie, as vpon an enquirie of Collusion, although it be by one Jurie, nor vpon a Verdict in a Quale ius. Secondly, Admitting that an Attaint did lie in that case, yet it followeth not ex Consequenti, that a Quod ei deforceat did not lie, (g) for if an Assise be taken by default, a Quod ei deforceat doth lie, and yet the partie may haue an Attaint, for this is no Enquest of Office, but a Recognition by the Recognitors of an Assise, who were returned the first day, and not returned vpon the awarding of the Assise by default. And as to the second Obiection, of this opinion was the whole Court in Edward Elmers case aboue mentioned. As to the third Obiection, That the dammages should bee the principall, because they were at the Common Law, that is an argument (say the other side) that they are more antient, but not that they are more principall, and treble dammages were not at the Common Law, (for the Common Law neuer giueth more dammage than the losse amounteth vnto) but are giuen by the Statute of Glocester, but the place wasted is worthier being in the Realtie, than dammages that be in the personaltie, Et omne maius dignum trahit ad se minus dignum, quamuis minus dignum sit antiquius, & à digniori debet fieri denominatio. And it is confessed, That in an Action of wast against Tenant for life, or for yeares, the place wasted is the principall, because the Statute of Glocester doth giue the place wasted and treble dammages at one time; for no prohibition or Action of wast lay against them at the Common Law, and in an Action of wast, if the Defendant confesse the Action, the Plaintife may haue iudgement for the place wasted, and release the dammages, which prooueth (and so Fitzherbert collecteth) that the dammages are not the principall, for a man shall neuer release the principall, and haue iudgement of the accessorie: and an Action of wast against Tenant for life, is as reall as an Action against Tenant in Dower. And as to the case of 9. H. 5 cited on the other side, it was answered that it was an Action in the Tenuit, which is onely in the personaltie, and then the Release of the one doth bar both, neither could summons and seuerance lie in that case, (h) but in an Action of wast (in the Tenet) either against Tenant for life or for yeares, the release of the one doth not barre the other, and in both these cases summons and seuerance doth lie, and this poynt was also resolued accordingly in Edward Elmers Case. But when these three poynts were resolued by the Court for the Demandant, then the Councel of the Tenant mooued in arrest of iudgment another point,

(f) 33. E. 3. Qd. ei deforc. Pl. vlt. F. N. B. 156. V. Flet. li. 5. ca. 21. 48. E. 3. 19. 40. Ass. 23. 33. H. 6. 25. 39. H. 6. 1. F. N. B. 107.

(g) 17. E. 2. Attaint 69. 21. H. 6. 56. 34. H. 6. 12.

34. H. 6. 7. Wast. 50.

(h) 6. E. 3. 47. 48. E. 3. 19.

viz.

viz. That the iudgement was giuen vpon a Nihil dicit, which is alwayes after apparance, and not per defaltam, and thereupon iudgement was stayed.

But to returne to Littleton. Here he openeth a secret of Law, for the cause of this remitter is, for that the Tenant for life in this case might haue a Quod ei deforceat, for so Littleton sayth, Issint que il poet auer Quod ei deforceat: Now it appeareth by our Bookes, That the Tenant for life at the Common Law was remedilesse, because he could not haue (as hath beene sayd) a Writ of Right, and consequently the Feme couert in this case could not bee remitted by the taking of an Estate to her husband and her, because her right was remedilesse, and could haue no Action. But when an Act of Parliament or a Custome doth alter the reason and cause thereof, thereby the Common Law it selfe is altered, if the Act of Parliament and Custome be pursued, for Alterata causa & ratione legis, alteratur & lex, & cessante causa seu ratione legis cessat & lex: as in this case the Statute of W.2 giuing remedie to this Feme Tenant for life, in this it giueth her abilitie to bee remitted, because her right is not now remedilesse, but she hath an Action to recouer it.

Vide for the Cases upon this ground. 14 H.7.11 p Fineux 27.H 8 4.b. And 35.H.6. Gard 2.27 E 3.5. p Wilbie Custome l.1.3 fo.86. Iustice Windhams case, a. & b.

And Littleton warily putteth his case, That the recouerie was had against the Feme while she was sole, for there was a time when it was a question, whither a Recouerie beeing had by default against the husband and wife, (the wife being Tenant for life) the sayd Statute gaue a Quod ei deforceat to the husband and wife, for that the Statute gaue it against tenant in Dower and Tenant for life, &c. and here the husband is not Tenant for life, but seised in the right of his wife, and therefore out of the Statute: and of this opinion is one (g) Booke, but (apices iuris non sunt iura, & parum differunt quæ re concordant) the contrarie hath beene adiudged, and so that poynt is now in peace: and the like in case of receit for him in reuersion. But if the husband and wife lose by default, & the husband die, the wife shall not haue a Quod ei deforceat, for a Cui in vita is giuen to her in that case by a former Statute, viz. W.2. cap.3. These things are worthie of due obseruation, and poynts of excellent learning; and Littleton in our Bookes speakes of another kind of Quod ei deforceat at the Common Law, vpon a Disseisin, which you may read. But now let vs heare him in his Booke.

(g) 4.E.3.38.33.E.3.Annotr 255. 5.E.3.4.33.E.3.Annotr 255 F.N.B.155 a. 5.E.3.5.2.E.4.13. F.N.B. 156.C. 33.H.6.46.2.E.4.11. 19.E.4.2.

Le reuersion est discontinue, issint que il ne poet auer Action de Waste.

45.E.3.21.44.E.3.34.35. F.N.B.60.23.H.8.tit.Wast. Br.138.

Here it appeareth, That when the Reuersion is deuested, the Lessor cannot haue an Action of Wast, because the writ is, That the Lessee did wast ad exhæredationem of the Lessor, and that Inheritance must continue at the time of the Action brought: And it is to bee obserued, That in an Action of wast brought by the Lessor against the Lessee, the Lessee in respect of the priuitie cannot plead generally, Riens en le Reuersion, viz. (h) That the Lessor hath nothing in the Reuersion, but he must shew how and by what meanes the reuersion is deuested out of him: and this holdeth (as hath beene sayd) betweene the Lessor and the Lessee; but if the Grantee of a Reuersion bringeth an Action of wast, the Lessee may plead generally, That hee hath nothing in the reuersion. And yet in some speciall cases an Action of wast shall lie, albeit the Lessor had nothing in the Reuersion at the time of the wast done. As if Tenant for life make a Feoffement in Fee vpon condition, and wast is done, and after the Lessee re-enter for the condition broken, In this case the Lessor shall haue an Action of wast. And so if a Bishop make a Lease for life or yeres, & the Bishop die, the lessee, the Sea being voyd, doth wast, the successor shall haue an Action of wast. So if Lessee for life be disseised, and wast is done, the Lessee re-enter, an Action of wast shall be maintained against the Lessee, and so in like cases: and yet in none of these cases the Plaintife in the Action of wast had anything in the Reuersion at the time of the wast made, but these especiall cases haue their seuerall and especiall reasons, as the learned Reader will easily find out.

(h) 46.E.3.20.8.H.6.13. 30.H.6.7.

Here note, That albeit the Action be false and feigned, yet is the recouerie so much respected in Law, as it worketh a Discontinuance. (i) But if Tenant for life suffer a common Recouerie, or any other Recouerie by couine and consent betweene the Tenant for life and the Recoueror, this is a forfeiture of his estate, and he in the Reuersion may presently enter for the forfeiture. Since our Author wrote, the statute of 14.El.ca.8. hath bin made concerning this matter, which is to be considered, (k) and hath beene well construed and expounded, and needs not here to be repeated.

(i) 5.Ass pl.3. 5.E.3.Entre Cong 42.15.E.3.Ass 95. 41.E.3.18 p Finchden. 22 E.3.2.b.Li.1.fo.15.Sir Wil.Pelhams case. 14.El.ca.8. (k) Li.3.fo.60.Li.1.fo.15.

And it is to be obserued, That although the Discontinuance groweth by matter of Record, yet the Remitter may be wrought by matter in Paiis: And of the residue of these two Sections sufficient hath beene sayd before.

Sect. 676.

Item ſi l baron diſcontinua le terre de ſa feme, et puis repriſt eſtate a luy & a ſa feme, & al tierce perſon pur term̃ de lour vies, ou en fee, ceo neſt vn remitter a la feme, forſque quant a la moity, et pur lauter moity el couient apres la mort ſon baron de ſuer vn briefe de Cui in vita.

ALſo if the husband diſcontinue the land of his wife, and after taketh backe an eſtate to him and to his wife, & to a third perſon for terme of their liues, or in fee, this is no remitter to the wife, but as to the moity, and for the other moity ſhe muſt after the death of her husbād ſue a writ of *Cui in vita*

44.E.3.17. 44.Aſſ.2. 43.Aſſ.3. Vid.Sect.666.

Ceo neſt remitter forſque quant al moity, &c. Albeit there is Authority in our bookes to the contrary, yet the Law is taken, as Littleton here holdeth it, and as before it appeareth in the like caſe in this Chapter, and for the reaſon therein expreſſed.

Section 677.

Item ſi le baron diſcõtinue la terr̃ ſa feme, et ala ouſter le mere, et le diſcontinuee leſſa meſme la terre al fem̃ pur term̃ de ſa vie, & liuer a luy ſeiſin, & puis le baron reuyent, & agreea a cel liuerie de ſeiſin, ceſt vn remitter a la feme, & uncore ſi la feme fuiſſoit ſole al temps de le leas fait a luy, ceo ne ſerroit a luy vn remitter. Mes entant que el fuit couert de baron al temps de la leas, & de le liuery de ſeiſin fait a luy, coment que el priſt ſolement le liuery de ſeiſin, ceo fuit vn Remitter a luy, pur ceo que feme couert ſerra adiudge

ALſo if the husband diſcontinue the land of his wife, and goeth beyond ſea, and the Diſcontinuee let the ſame Land to the wife for tearme of her life, and deliuer to her ſeiſin, and after the husband commeth backe, and agreeth to this Liuery of ſeiſin, this is a Remitter to the Wife, and yet, if the Wife had beene ſole at the time of the leaſe made to her, this ſhould not bee to her a Remitter, but in as much as ſhe was couert baron at the time of the Leaſe, and liuery of ſeiſin made vnto her, albeit ſhee taketh only the liuery of ſeiſin, this was a Remitter

15.4.1.b. 7.H.4.17. 1.H.7.16.b. 39.E.3.30. 27.H.8.24.

ET puis le baron reuient & agrea, &c. In this caſe the eſtate is in the Feme Couert preſently by the liuery before any agreement by the husband and of this opinion is Littleton in our Bookes.

Ala ouſter le mere. If hee had beene within the Realme, it doth not alter the caſe.

Quære en ceſt caſe ſi le baron, &c. Here is a queſtion moued by Littleton whether the diſagreement of the Husband ſhall ouſte the wife of her Remitter. And it ſeemeth that the diſagreement ſhall not deueſt the Remitter: Firſt, becauſe the ſtate made to the wife which wrought the Remitter is baniſhed and wholy defeated, and therefore no diſagreement of the husband can deueſt the ſtate gained by the leaſe, which by the Remitter was deueſted before.

Secondly, for that the Law hauing once reſtored her ancient and better right will not ſuffer the diſagreement of the husband to deueſt it out of her, and to reuiue the Diſ-

ſicome enfant deins age en tiel cas, &c. Quære en ceſt cas ſi l' barō quant il reuiẽt, voil diſagree a l' leas & liuery de ſeiſin fait a ſon feme en ſon abſence, ſi ceo ouſtera ſon feme de ſon Remitter, ou nemy, &c.

to her becauſe a Feme couert ſhall bee adiudged as an Infant within age in ſuch a caſe, &c. *Quære* in this caſe if the Husband when hee comes backe will diſagree to the leaſe and liuery of ſeiſin made to his wife in his abſence, if this ſhall ouſte his wife of her Remitter, or not, &c.

continuance and reueſt the wrongfull eſtate in the Diſ-continuee.

Thirdly, for that Remitters tending to the aduancement of ancient Rights are fauoured in Law.

And ſo it is for the ſame cauſes if the wife ſuruiue her husband ſhe cannot claime in by the purchaſe made during the couerture but the Law adiudgeth her in her better right. But if both eſtates be waiueable, there albeit the wife *prima facie* is remitted, yet after the deceaſe of her husband, ſhee may elect which of the eſtates ſhee will. As if Lands bee giuen to the Husband and wife and their heires, the husband make a feoffment in fee, the feoffee giueth the Land to the husband and wife and the heires of their two bodies, the husband dieth. In this caſe the wife may elect which of the eſtates ſhe will, for both eſtates are waiueable, and her time of election and power of wayuer accrewed to her firſt after the deceaſe of her husband. If Lands bee giuen to a man and the heires females of his bodie, and hee maketh a feoffment in fee, and take backe an eſtate to him and his heires, and dieth hauing iſſue a daughter leauing his wife groſſement enſeint with a ſonne and dieth, the daughter is remitted, and albeit the Sonne be afterwards borne, hee ſhall not deueſt the Remitter.

41.E.3.18.

18.Eliz.Dier 351.

Sect. 678.

ITem ſi le baron diſcontinua les tenements ſon feme, & le diſcōtinuee eſt diſſeiſie, & puis le diſſeiſour leſſa meſmes l's tenements a l' baron & a ſon fem̃ pur term̃ de vie, ceo eſt vn remitter a la feme. Mes ſi le baron et ſon feme fueront de couin & conſent que l' diſſeiſin doit eſte fait donques il neſt Remitter a ſon fem̃ pur ceo que el eſt diſſeiſereſſe: Mes ſi l' baron fuit de couin & conſent a le diſſeiſin, et nemy la feme, donq̃

ALſo if the Husband diſcontinue the Lands of his wife, and the diſcontinuee is diſſeiſed, and after the Diſſeiſor letteth the ſame lands to the husband and Wife for tearme of life, this is a Remitter to the wife. But if the husband & his Wife were of couin and conſent that the diſſeiſin ſhould be made, then it is no remitter to his Wife becauſe ſhe is a Diſſeiſereſſe. But if the husband were of couin & conſent to the Diſſeiſin, and not the Wife

ET puis le diſſeiſor leſſa meſme les tenements, &c. Note ſo much are remitters fauoured in law, that the ſtate made by the Diſſeiſor (which commeth to the Land by wrong, and vpon whom the entry of the Diſcontinuee is lawfull) doth remit the wife, and deueſteth all out of the Diſcontinuee, albeit hee hath a Warrantie of the Land. 18.E.4.2.b.

Mes ſi le baron & feme fuer' de couin & conſent, &c. Here it appeareth that couin and conſent of the husband and wife doth hinder the remitter of the wife, for couine and conſent in many caſes to doe a wrong doth choake a meere right, and the ill manner doth make a good matter vnlawfull. 18.E.4,vbi ſupra.

Couin. Couina commeth of the French word Couine, & is a ſecret aſſent (c) Pl.Com.546. in Wimbiſhes caſe.

 Dee

determined in the hearts of two or more to the defrauding and prejudice of another.

tiel leas fait al feme est un remitter, pur ceo que nul default fuit en la feme.

then such Lease made to the wife is a Remitter, for that no default was in the wife.

44.E.3 46. 11.H.4.60. 44.Ass.29. 19.H.8.12. 18.H.8.5. 11.E.4.2. 7.H.7.11.

A woman is lawfully intitled to haue Dower, and shee is of couine and consent, that one shall disseise the Tenant of the Land against whom shee may recouer her lawfull Dower all which is done accordingly, the Tenant may lawfully enter upon her, and auoid the recouery in respect of the couine. But if a Disseisor, Intrudor, or Abator doe endow a woman that hath lawfull title of Dower, this is good, and shall bind him that right hath, if there were no such couine or consent before the Disseisin, Abatement, or Intrusion.

41.Ass 28. 25.Ass pl.1. 27.Ass 74. 15.E.4.4 a. 12. Ass.p.20.

And so it is in all cases where a man hath a rightfull and iust cause of Action, yet if he of couine and consent doe raise up a Tenant by wrong against whom he may recouer, the couine doth suffocate the right, so as the recouery though it be upon a good title shall not bind, or restore the demandant to his right.

11.E.4.2. 15 E.4 23. 14.H.8.13. 33.H.6.5. 12.E.4.21.b.

If Tenant in tayle and his issue disseise the discontinuee to the use of the Father, and the Father dieth, and the Land discendeth to the issue, he is not remitted against the Discontinuee in respect he was priuy and partie to the wrong, but in respect of all others he is remitted, and shall deraigne the first warrantie. And so note a man may be remitted against one, and not against another.

A. and B. Joyntenants be intitled to a reall Action against the heire of the Disseisor, A. cause the heire to be disseised, against whom A. and B. recouer and sue execution. B. is remitted for that he was not partie to the couine, and shall hold in common with A, but A. is not remitted for the reason that Littleton here sheweth.

F.N.B.179.g. 12.E.4.9. 35.Ass 5. 44.E.3.9.23.13.Ass.1. Temps E.1.Wast 128. 16.Ass.p.7. 21.E.4.53. 21.H.7.35. 3.H.4.17.

¶ *Pur ceo que el est disseisoresse.* Nota, It is regularly true that a Feme Couert cannot be a Disseisoress by her commandement or procurement precedent, nor by her assent or agreement subsequent, but by her actuall entry or proper act she may bee a Disseisoresse. And therefore some doe hold that Littleton must be intended that the husband and wife were present when the Disseisin was done, and others doe hold that Littleton is good Law albeit she were absent, for that if her procurement or agreement bee to doe a wrong to cause a Remitter unto her in this speciall case she shall faile of her end, and remitted she shall not bee, but in this speciall case she shall be holden as a Disseisoresse by her couine and consent quatenus to hinder the Remitter. And here it appeareth, that albeit the husband bee of couine and consent, &c yet if the wife were not of couine and consent also, she shall be remitted, because as Littleton saith, there was no default in the wife.

Sect. 679.

¶ Item si tiel discontinuee fesoit estate de franktenement al baron & a son feme per fait endent. sur condition, s. reseruant al discontinuee un certaine rent, & pur default de payment un reentry, & pur ceo que le rent est aderere, le discontinuee enter, donques de cel entrie le fem auera un Assise de Nouel disseisin, apres la mort son baron enuers le discontinuee, pur ceo que le condition fuit tout oustrement aniente, entant que la feme fuit en son remitter, uncore le baron ouesque sa feme

Also if such discontinuee make an estate of freehold to the husband and wife by Deed indented upon condition, s. reseruing to the discontinuee a certain rent and for default of payment a re-entrie, and for that the rent is behind the discontinuee enter, then for this entry the wife shall haue an Assise of *Nouel disseisin*, after the death of her Husband against the Discontinuee, because the condition was altogether taken away, inasmuch as the Wife was in her Remitter, yet the husband with his wife can-

feme ne poient auer Assise, pur ceo que le baron est estoppe, &c.

not haue an Assise because the husband is estopped, &c.

IT is hereby to be obserued, that the wife is presently remitted, and that the conditions and rents and all other things annexed to or reserued vpon the state (that is banished and defeated by the Remitter) are defeated also.

Pl. Com. in Amy Townesends Case.
12. R. 2. tit. Remitter 12.

Sect. 680. & 681.

Item si le baron discontinua les tenements sa feme, & reprist estate a luy pur terme de sa vie, le remainder apres son decease a sa feme pur terme de sa vie, en cest cas ceo nest vn remitter a la feme durant la vie le baron, pur ceo que durant la vie le baron, la feme nad riens en le franktenement. Mes si en ceo cas la feme suruesquist le baron, ceo est vn remitter a la feme, pur ceo que vn franktenement en ley est iect sur luy maugre le soen. Et entant que el ne poit auer action enuers nul auter person, & enuers luy mesme el ne poit auer action, pur ceo el est en son Remitter. Car en cest cas, coment que la feme ne entra pas en les tenements, vncore vn estrange que ad cause de auer action, poit suer son action enuers la feme de mesmes les tenements, pur ceo que el est tenant en ley, coment que el ne soit tenant en fait.

ALso if the Husband discontinue the tenements of his wife, and take back an estate to him for life, the remaynder after his decease to his wife for tearme of her life, in this case this is no Remitter to the Wife during the life of the husband, for that during the life of the Husband the Wife hath nothing in the freehold. But if in this case the wife suruiueth the Husband, this is a Remitter to the Wife because a freehold in Law is cast vpon her against her will. And in as much as shee cannot haue an action against any person, and against her selfe shee cannot haue an Action, therefore shee is in her remitter. For in this case although the Wife doth not enter into the tenements, yet a stranger which hath cause to haue an Action, may sue his Action against the Wife for the same tenements, because shee is Tenant in Law, albeit that she bee not Tenant in Deed.

Sect. 681.

Car tenant de franktenement en fait est celuy, que si il soit disseisie de franktenement, il poit auer Assise. Mes tenant de franktenement en ley deuant son entre en fait, nauera my assise. Et si home soit seisie de certeine terre, et ad issue fits quel prent feme

FOr tenant of freehold in deed is he, who, if hee bee disseised of the freehold, may haue an Assise, but tenant of freehold in Law before his entrie in deed, shall not haue an Assise. And if a man bee seised of certaine Land, and hath issue a sonne who taketh wife, and

feme, & le pier devie seisie, et puis le fitz devie devant ascun entrie fait per luy en la terre, le feme le fitz serra endowe en le terre, et uncore il navoit nul franktenement en fait, mes il avoit un fee & franktenement en ley. Et issint nota, que Præcipe quod reddat poit auxybien estre maintenus envers celuy que ad franktenement eu ley, sicome envers celuy que ad le franktenement en fait.

the father dieth seised, and after the sonne dies before any entrie made by him into the land, the wife of the sonne shall be endowed in the land, and yet he had no freehold in Deed, but he had a fee and freehold in Lawe. And so note, that a *Præcipe quod reddat* may as well bee maintained against him that hath the freehold in Law, as against him that hath the freehold in deed.

18.H.8.3.

¶ Here five things are to be observed; First, that a remainder expectant upon an estate for life worketh no Remitter, but when it fall in possession: for before his time he can have no action, and no free hold is in him. Secondly, though the woman might waive the remainder, yet because she is presently by the death of the husband Tenant to the Præcipe, it is within the rule of Remitter, and her power of waiver is not materiall. Thirdly, that a freehold in Law being cast upon the woman by act of Law without any thing done or assented to by her, doth remit her, albeit she be then sole and of full age. Fourthly, that a Præcipe lyeth against one that hath but a freehold in Law. Fiftly, that a woman shall bee endowed where the husband hath the inheritance and but a freehold in Law, as hath beene said in the Chapter of Dower.

Vid. Sect. 44.7.
Bracton lib.4. fol. 206.237.
Britton 83.b.
Fleta lib.3. cap.15.

Sect. 682.

¶ Item si tenant en taile ad issue deux fitz de pleine age, et il lessa la terre taile al eigne fitz pur terme de sa vie, le remainder al fitz puisne pur term de sa vie, et puis le tenant en taile morust, en cest cas leigne fitz nest pas en son Remitter, pur ceo que il prent estate de son pier. Mes si leigne fitz morust sauns issue de son corps, donque ceo est un remitter al puisne frere, pur ceo que il est heire en le taile, et un franktenement en le ley est escheate, et iecte sur luy per force de le remainder, et il y ad nul envers que il poit suer son action.

Also if Tenant in taile hath issue two sonnes of full age, and he letteth the land tailed to the eldest sonne for terme of his life, the remainder to the younger sonne for terme of his life, and after the Tenant in taile dieth, in this case the eldest sonne is not in his remitter, because he tooke an estate of his father, but if the eldest die without issue of his body, then this is a remitter to the younger brother, because hee is heire in taile, and a freehold in lawe is escheated & cast upon him by force of the remainder, and there is none against whō he may sue his action.

(a) 12.E.4.20.
(b) Sect. 684.685.

¶ Of this opinion is (a) Littleton in our bookes, and of this sufficient hath beene said in the next Section before. See hereafter (b) some explanation hereof.

Section 683.

EN mesme le maner est, lou home soit disseisie, & le disseisor morust seisie, et les tenits discendont a son heire, et lheire le disseisor fait vn leas a vn hõe de mesmes les tenements pur terme de vie, le remainder a le disseisee p̄ terme ď vie, ou in taile, ou en fee, le tenant a terme de vie morust, ore ceo est vn remitter al disseisee, &c. Causa qua supra, &c.

IN the same manner it is, where a man is disseised, and the disseisor dieth seised, and the tenements discend to his heire, and the heire of the disseisor make a lease to a man of the same tenements for terme of life, the remainder to the disseisee for terme of life, or in taile, or in fee, the tenant for life dieth, now this is a remitter to the disseisee, &c. *Causa qua supra, &c.*

AND this standeth upon the same reason that the cases in the two Sections precedent doe. See the next Section following.

Sect. 684.

*NOta, si tenant en taile enfeoffa son fits et vn auter per son fait de la terre taile en fee, et liuery ď seisin est fait a lauter accordant al fait, & le fits rien conusant de ceo agreea a le feoffment, & puis celuy que prist le liuery de seisin deuy, & le fits ne occupia la terre, ne prent ascun profit del terre durant la vie le pier, & puis le pier morust, ore ceo est vn remitter al fits, pur ceo que le franktenement est iect sur luy per le suruiuor: Et nul default fuit en luy, pur ceo que il ne vnque a-

NOte if Tenant in taile infeoffe his sonne and another by his deed of the land intailed, in fee, and liuery of seisin is made to the other according to the Deed, and the son not knowing of this agreeth to the feoffment, and after hee which tooke the liuery of seisin dieth, and the sonne doth not occupie the land, nor taketh any proffit of the land during the life of the father, and after the father dieth, now this is a remitter to the sonne, because the freehold is cast vpon him by the suruiuor. And no default was in

*IT should seem by this marke that this was an addition to Littleton, but it is of Littletons owne worke, and agreeth with the originall, sauing the originall begun this Section thus, Itẽ si tenãt en taile, &c.

Per son fait, &c. Here Littleton materially addeth by his Deed, for if a man intendeth to (b) make a feoffment by parol to A. and B, and he and B. come upon the land, A. being absent, and make Liuery to B. in the name both of B. & A. & to their heirs this shall enure only to B, for neither can a man absent take Liuery nor make Liuery without Deed.

(b) *Temps H.* 8. *Feoffments.* *Br.* 72. 40. *E.* 3. 41. 10. *E.* 4. 1. 4. 15. *E.* 4. 18. 18. *E.* 4. 12. 22. *H.* 6. 12.

Et liuery de seisin est fait a lauter accordant al fait, &c. Note Liuery being made to one according to the Deede, enureth to both, because the Deede whereunto the Liuery referreth is made to both, for the rule is, That Verba relata hoc maxime operantur per referentiam vt in eis inesse videntur.

greea, &c. en la vie son pier, et il ad nul enuers que il poit suer Briefe de Formedon, &c.

him, because hee did neuer agree, &c. in the life of his Father, and hee hath none against whom hee may sue a Writ of *Formdon*, &c.

¶ *Et le fits nient conusant de ceo, ne agreea a le Feoffement.* Here it appeareth, That if the son be Conusant, and agreeth to the Feoffement, &c. this is no Remitter to him. And therefore if the Feoffement were made by Deed indented, and the son with the other sealeth the Counterpart, and then the feoffor maketh liuerie to the other according to the Deed, and the other dieth, the sonne is not remitted, because he was Conusant of the Feoffement, and agreed to the same, and Littleton saith in the Case that he putteth, That there was no default in the sonne, because hee agreed not to the Feoffement in the life of the Father: And so it seemeth, That if A. be seised in Tayle, and haue Issue two sonnes, and by Deed indented betweene him of the one part, and the sonnes of the other part, maketh a Lease to the eldest for life, the remainder to the second in Fee, and dieth, and the eldest Sonne dieth without Issue, the second sonne is not remitted, because he agreed to the remainder in the life of the Father, or if the like Estate had beene made by Parol, if in the life of the father the Tenant for life had beene impleaded, and made default, and he in the remainder had beene receiued, and thereby agreed to the remainder, after the death of the father and the eldest sonne without Issue, the second sonne should not bee remitted, because he agreed to the remainder in the life of the father, all which is well warranted by the reason yeelded by our Author in this Section.

Vide Sect. 682.

Sect. 685.

¶ CAr si home soit disseisie de certaine terre, et le Disseisor fait vn Fait de Feoffment, per que il infeoffa B. C. et D. et le liuerie de seisin est fait a B. et C. mes D. ne fuit al Liuerie de seisin, ne vnques agreea a le Feoffment, ne vnque voile prender les profits, &c. et puis B. et C. deuieront, et D. eux suruesquist, et le Disseisee port son Briefe Sur disseisin en le Per, enuers D. il monstra tout le matter, coment il ne vnques agreea a le Feoffment, et issint il dischargera luy de damages, issint que le Demandant ne recouera ascuns dammages enuers luy, coment que il soit Tenant del franktenement del tre. Et vncore le statute de Gloucester cap. 1. voit, que le Disseisee recouera damages en briefe de Entre, foundue sur Disseisin vers celuy que est troue tenant. Et ceo est vn proofe en lauter case, que entant

FOr if a man bee disseised of certaine land, and the Disseisour make a Deed of Feoffement, wherby hee infeoffeth B. C. and D. and Liuerie of seisin is made to B. and C. but D. was not at the Liuerie of Seisin, nor euer agreed to the feoffment, nor euer would take the profits, &c. and after B. and C. die, and D. suruiue them, and the Disseisee bringeth his Writ vpon Disseisin in the *Per* against D. hee shall shew all the matter, how he neuer agreed to the feoffement, and hee shall discharge himselfe of Dammages, so as the Demaundant shall recouer no dammages against him, although he be Tenant of the freehold of the Land. And yet the Statute of *Gloucester cap. 1.* will, That the Disseisee shall recouer dammages in a Writ of Entrie founded vpon a Disseisin against him which is found Tenant. And this is a proofe in the other Case,

que

que lissue en le Taile auient à le franketenement, et nemy per son fait, ne per son agreement, mes apres la mort son pier, ceo est vn Remitter a luy, entant que il ne poit suer Action ď Formedon, enuers nul auter person, &c.

that for as much as the Issue in taile came to the Freehold, and not by his Act, nor by his Agreement, but after the death of his father, therefore this is a Remitter to him, in as much as he cannot sue an Action of *Formedon* against any other person, &c.

¶ This case standeth vpon the same reason that the next precedent case doth.

¶ *Mes celuy que est troue Tenant, &c.* Here it appeareth, that Acts of Parliament are to be so construed, as no man that is innocent or free from iniurie or wrong, be by a literall construction punished or indammaged: and therefore in this case albeit the letter of the Statute is generally to giue dammages against him that is found Tenant, and the Case that Littleton here putteth, D. being suruiuor is consequently found tenant of the Land; yet because he waiued the Estate, and neuer agreed to the Feoffment, nor tooke any profits, he shall not be charged with the dammages.

Section 686. 687.

ITem si vn Abbe aliena la terre de son meason a vn auter en fee, et Lalienee per son Fait charge la terre oue vn rent charğ en Fee, et puis lalienee infeoffa Labbe oue licence, a auer et teñ al Abbe et a ses successors a touts iours, et puis Labbe morust, et vn auter est eslieu, et fait Abbe: en cest case Labbe que est le successor, et son Couent, sont ẽ lour Remitter, et tiendront la terre discharge, pur ceo que mesme Labbe ne poit auer ascun Actiõ, ne Briefe Dentre sine assensu Capituli, de mesme la terre enuers nul auter person.

ALso if an Abbot alien the lãd of his house to another in Fee, and the Alienee by his Deed charge the land with a Rent-charge in Fee, and after the Alienee infeoffe the Abbot with Licence, To haue and to hold to the Abbot and to his successors for euer, and after the Abbot die, and another is chosen and made Abbot: in this case the abbot that is the successor, & his Couent, are in their remitter, & shal hold the lãd discharged, because the same Abbot cannot haue an Action, nor a writ of *Entre sine assensu Capituli*, of the same Land, against any other person.

Sect. 687.

¶ EN mesme le maner est, lou vn Euesque, ou vn Dean, ou auters tiels Persons aliena, &c. sans assent, &c. et Lalienee charge la terre, &c. et puis Leuesque reprist estate de mesme la terre per Licence, a luy et a ses suc-

IN the same manner is it, where a Bishop or a Deane, or other such persons alien, &c. without assent, &c. and the Alienee charge the land, &c. and after the Bishop takes backe an estate of the same land by Licence, to him and his Succes-

Successors, et puis Leuesque deuie, son Successor est en son Remitter, come en droit de son Esglise, et defeatera le charg, &c. Causa qua supra, &c.

sours, and after the Bishop dieth; his Successour is in his Remitter as in right of his Church, and shall defeat the Charge, &c. *Causa qua supra.*

OUr Author hauing spoken of Remitters to singular or naturall persons, as Issues in Taile, and to Feme Coverts, and to their Heires, and to them in Reversion or Remainder, and their Heires; now he speaketh of Remitters to Bodies politique and incorporate, as to Abbots, Bishops, Deanes, &c. And as Discents doe remit the heire which comes in the Per, so succession doth remit the Successor, albeit he commeth in the Post. And so in other cases where the Issue in Taile of full age shall be remitted, there in the like case shall the Successor be remitted also, and defeat all meane charges and incumbrances.

One Licence, &c. That is, of the King and the Lords immediate and mediate, to dispence with the Statutes of Mortmaine, whereof see more before, Sect. 140.

Sect. 688.

ITem si home suist faux action enuers le Tenant en Taile, sicome home voile suer enuers luy vn Briefe Dentre en le Post, supposant per son briefe que le tenant en taile nad pas entre, sinon per A. de B. que disseisist lapel le demandant, et ceo est faux, et il recouer enuers le Tenant en le Taile per default, et suist execution, et puis l'Tenant en taile morust, son Issue poit auer Briefe de Formedon enuers luy que recouera, et sil voile pleader le recouerie enuers le Tenant en taile, lissue poit dire que le dit A. de B. ne disseisist poynt lapel celuy que recouerast, en le maner come son Briefe supposa, et issint il faurera le recouerie. Aury posito, que ceo fuit voyer, que le dit A. de B. disseisist lapel le demandant que recouerast, et que apres le disseisin le demandant, ou son Pier, ou son apel per vn fait auoient relesse al tenant en Tail, tout le droit que il auoit en la Terre, &c. et ceo nient contristeant

ALso if a man sue a false Action against Tenant in Taile, as if one will sue against him a Writ of Entrie in the *Post*, supposing by his Writ, That the Tenant in Tayle had not his entrie, but by A. of B. who disseised the Graundfather of the Demaundant, and this is false, and he recouereth against the Tenant in Taile by default, and sueth Execution, and after the Tenant in Tayle dieth, his Issue may haue a Writ of *Formedon* against him which recouereth, and if hee will plead the Recouerie against the tenant in taile, the Issue may say, That the said A. of B. did not disseise the Grandfather of him which recouered in maner as his writ suppose, and so he shall falsefie his recouery. And admit this were true, That the sayd A. of B. did disseise the Graundfather of the Demaundant which recouered, and that after the Disseisin, the Demandant, or his father, or his Grandfather by a deed had released to the Tenant in Taile all the right which hee had in the

ant il ſuiſt vn Briefe Dentre en le Poſt enuers le Tenant en Taile, en le manner come eſt auauntdit, et le Tenaunt en Taile pleda a celuy, Que le dit A. de B. ne diſſeiſiſt pas ſon ayel, en le manner come ſon Briefe ſuppoſa, et ſur ceo ſont a Iſſue, et liſſue eſt troue pur le Demandant, per que il ad iudgement de recouer, et ſuiſt execution, et puis le Tenant en le Taile moruſt, ſon Iſſue poit auer vn Briefe de Formedon enuers celuy que recouera, et ſil voile plead le recouerie per laction trie enuers ſon pier, que fuit Tenant en Taile, donque il poit monſtrer et pleader le Releaſe fait al ſon pier, et iſſint laction que fuit ſue, feint en Ley.

land, &c. and notwithſtanding this hee ſueth a Writ of Entrie in the *Poſt*, againſt the Tenant in Taile, in manner as is aforeſayd, and the Tenant in Taile plead to him, That the ſayd A. of B. did not diſſeiſe his Grandfather, in ſuch manner as his Writ ſuppoſe, and vpon this they are at Iſſue, and the Iſſue is found for the demandant, wherby he hath iudgement to recouer, and ſueth execution, & after the Tenant in Taile dieth, his Iſſue may haue a Writ of *Formdon* againſt him that recouered, and if he will plead the recouery by the Action tried againſt his father who was Tenant in taile, then he may ſhew and plead the Releaſe made to his father, & ſo the Action which was ſued, feint in Law.

¶ IL *recouera enuers le tenant en taile per default.* Littleton addeth (by default) becauſe if the (c) recouery paſſed vpon an iſſue tried by verdict, hee ſhall neuer falſifie in the point tryed, becauſe an attaint might haue beene had againſt the Iurors, and albeit all the Iurors be dead, ſo as the attaint doe faile, yet the iſſue in taile ſhall not falſifie in the point tried, which, vntill it be lawfully auoyded, pro veritate accipitur. As if the Tenant in tayle be impleaded in a Formedon, and he trauerſeth the gift, and it is tryed againſt him, and thereupon the Demandant recouer In this caſe the iſſue in tayle ſhall not falſifie in the point tryed [redacted] but he may falſifie the recouery by any other matter: as that the Tenant in tayle might haue pleaded a collaterall warrantie, or a Releaſe, as Littleton here putteth the caſe, or to confeſſe & auoid the point tried. And Littletons caſe holdeth not only in a recouery by default, whereof he ſpeaketh, but alſo vpon a nihil dicit, or Confeſſion or Demurrer.

(c) 12.*E*.4.19. 13.*E*.4.3. 11.*H*.4.89. 7.*H*.4.17. 14.*H*.7.11.28.*Aſſ*.32.52. 34.*Aſſ*.7. 10.*H*.6.5. 21.*H*.6.13 *b*. *Brooke tit. Fauxifier de Recouerie* 55.

Sect. 689.

¶ ET il ſemble que feint action eſt autant adire en Engliſh, a fained action, ceſtaſcauoir, tiel action, que coment que les parolx de le briefe ſont voyers, vncore pur certaine cauſes il nad cauſe ne title per la ley de recouer pur meſme laction. Et faux action eſt, lou les parolx de briefe ſont faux. Et en les deux caſes auantdits, ſil le cas fuit tiel, que apres tiel recouery & execution ent

AND it ſeemeth that a faint action is aſmuch to ſay in Engliſh, *a fained action*, that is to ſay ſuch an Action as albeit the words of the Writ bee true, yet for certain cauſes he hath no cauſe nor title by the Law to recouer by the ſame action. And a falſe action is, where the wordes of the Writ bee falſe. And in theſe two Caſes aforeſaid, if the caſe were ſuch that after ſuch recouery, and execution

ent fait, le tenant en taile vst disseisse celuy que recouera, et ent morust seisse, per que la terre discendist a son issue, ceo est vn remitter al issue, & lissue est eins per force de le taile, & pur cel cause ieo aye mis les deux cases precedents, pur enformer toy, mon fits, que lissue en taile per force dun discent fait a luy apres vn recouery & execution fait enuers son auncester poit estre auxy bien en son remitter scome il serroit per le discent fait a luy apres vn discontinuance fait per son auncester de les terres tailes, per feoffement en pais, ou autrement, &c.

thereupon done the tenant in tayle had disseised him that recouered, and thereof died seised whereby the Land descended to his issue, this is a Remitter to the issue, and the issue is in by force of the taile, and for this cause I haue put these two cases precedent, to enforme thee (my Sonne) that the issue in tayle by force of a discent made vnto him after a recouerie and Execution made against his Ancestor, may be aswell in his remitter as he shold be by the discēt made to him after a Discontinuance made by his Ancestor of the entayled lands by feoffment in the Countrie or otherwise, &c.

¶ HEre Littleton explayneth what a faint action is, and what a false action is, which is plaine and perspicuous. And here it is to bee obserued, that a Remitter may bee had after a recouery vpon a faint action by a disseisin and a discent, aswell as by a discent after a discontinuance by a feoffment, &c.

Section 690.

¶ ITem ē les cases auantdits, si le cas fuit tiel, que apres ceo que le demandant auoit iudgment de recouer enuers l' tenant ē taile, & mesme le tenant en taile morust deuaunt ascun execution eiwe enuers luy: p que les tenements discendōt a son issue, et celuy q̄ recouera suist vn Scire facias hors de le iudgement dauer execution de le iudgement enuers lissue en taile, lissue pledera le matter

ALso in the cases aforesaid, if the case were such, that after that the Demandant haue iudgement to recouer against the Tenant in tayle, and the same Tenant in tayle dieth before any execution had against him whereby the Tenements discēd to his issue, & he who recouereth sueth a *Scire facias* out of the iudgement to haue execution of the iudgement against the issue in taile, the issue shal plead the matter as aforesaid, and so

28. Ass. 32. 34. Ass. Pl. 7. 15. E. 3. Age 95. 11. H. 4. 89. 7. H. 4. 17. 33. E. 3. Entree cong. 31. 21. H. 6. 13. 10. H. 5. 6. 12. E. 4. 20. 14. H. 7. 11. 23. Eliz. Dier 376. lib. 1. fol. Shelleys case. Pl. Com. 55.

¶ HEere it appeareth, that if a iudgemēt be giuē against a tenāt in tayle vpon a faint or false action, and Tenant in tayle die before execution, no execution can bee sued against the issue in tayle. But if in a common recouery iudgement bee had against Tenant in tayle where hee voucheth, and hath iudgement to recouer ouer in value, albeit the Tenant in Tayle dieth before execution, yet the recouerer shall execute the iudgement against the issue in tayle in respect of the intended recompence, and for that it is the common assurance of the Realme, and is well warranted (d) by our Bookes, and was not inuented by Iustice Choke who was a graue and learned Iudge in the time of E. 4. (as some hold by tradition) but it may bee

See hereafter Sect. 709. 15. E. 3. briefe 324. 42. E. 3. 53. 44. E. 3. 21. 48. E. 3. 11. 1. E. 4. 5. 5. E. 4. 2.

(d) 12. E. 4. 20. Dier 23. Eliz. 376. lib. 10. fol. 37. 38. In Mary Portingtons Case.

matter come auaunt est dit: Et issint proua que le dit recouery fuit faux, ou feint en ley, & issint luy barrera dauer execution de le iudgement.

proue that the said recouery was false or faint in Law, and so shall barre him to haue execution of the iudgment.

that it was vpon former Authorities and opinions of Judges discouered by him, assented vnto by the rest of the Judges.

If a recouery bee had against Tenant for life without consent or Couine, though it be without title, and Execution bee had, and Tenant for life dieth, the reuersion or remainder is discontinued, so as he in the reuersion or remainder cannot enter, but if such a recouery be had by agreement and Couine betweene the Demandant and the Tenant for life, then, as hath beene said, it is a forfeiture of the estate for life, and he in the reuersion or remainder may enter for the forfeiture. So it is if the Tenant for life suffer a common recouery at this day, it is a forfeiture of his estate, for a common recouery is a common conueyance or assurance, whereof the Law taketh knowledge. Since Littleton wrote there were two Statutes (e) made for preseruation of Remainders and Reuersions expectant vpon any manner of estate for life, the one in 32. H 8. the other in 14. Eliz. but 32. H. 8. extended not to recoueries when Tenant for life came in as Vouchee, &c. and therefore that act is repealed by 14. Eliz. and full remedie prouided for preseruation of the entrie of them in reuersion or remainder. But the Statute of 14. Eliz extendeth not to any recouery, vnlesse it bee by agreement or Couyne. Secondly, (f) if there be Tenant for life, Remainder in taile, the Reuersion or remainder in fee, if Tenant for life be impleaded by agreement, and he vouche Tenant in taile, and he vouch ouer the common Vouchee, this shall barre the Reuersion or Remainder in fee, although hee in the reuersion or remainder did neuer assent to the recouery, because it was not the intent of the act to extend to such a recouerie in which a Tenant in taile was vouched, for he hath power by common recouery, if he were in possession, to cut off all reuersions and remainders. And so if Tenant for life had surrendred to him in Remainder in taile, hee might haue barred the remainders and reuersions expectant vpon his estate. Thirdly, where the prouiso of that act speaketh of an assent of Record by him in reuersion or remainder, it is to bee vnderstood, that such assent must appeare vpon the same Record either vpon a Voucher, Aid prier, receite, or the like; for it cannot appeare of Record, vnlesse it be done in course of Law, and not by any extraiudiciall entrie, or by Memorandum.

5. Ass. 3. 5. E. 3. entre Cong. 42. lib 1. fo. 15. 16. Sir William Pelhams case.

(e) 32. H. 8 ca. 31. 14. Eliz. ca. 8.

(f) Lib. 3 fo. 60. 61. Lincolne Colledge case.

Section 691.

¶ Item si tenant en taile discontinua le taile, et morust, et son issue port son briefe de Formedon enuers le discontinuee (esteant tenant de franktenement del terre) et le discontinuee pleda que il nest tenant, mes oustermēt disclaima de le tenancy en la terre, en cest cas le iudgement serra, que le tenant alast sans iour, et apres tiel

ALso if Tenant in taile discontinue the taile, & dieth, and his issue bringeth his writ of *Formedon* against the discontinuee (being tenant of the freehold of the land) and the Discontinuee plead that he is not tenant, but vtterly disclaymeth from the tenancy in the land. In this case the iudgement shall bee that the Tenant goeth without day, and after such

¶ Here it appeareth that vpon the plea of non-tenure, or of a disclaimer of the tenant in a Formedon in the Discender, albeit the expresse iudgement be that the tenant shall goe without day, yet in iudgement of Law the Demandant may enter according to the title of his Writ, and bee seised in taile notwithstanding the Discontinuance. And here Littleton saith the Demandant shalbe adiudged in his Remitter, where he taketh Remitter in a large sence, for in this case the Demandant hath not two rights, but hath only one ancient right, and is restored to the same by course of Law, and so Remitter here is taken for a recontinuance of the right.

5. E. 4 1. 36. H. 6 29. 6. E. 3. 8. 4. E. 4. 38.

Non-tenure Vid. Bracton lib. fol. 331. 432. & 414. Britton cap. 84.

(f) 13.H.7.28. 36.H.6.29. 22.H.6.44 4.E.4.38. 5.E.4.1. 6.E.3 8.

(g) 8.E.3.434. 24.E.3.9. 11.H.4.16.& 7.H.6.17.

5.E.4.1.

¶ *Ou le demandant ne recouera damages.* Here is to bee obserued that in such a Præcipe where the Demandant is to recouer damages, if the Tenant pleade non-tenure or disclaime, (f) there the Demandant may auerre him to be tenant of the land, as his Writ suppose for the benefit of his damages, which otherwise hee should lose, or pray iudgement & enter. (g) But where no damages are to be recouered, as in a Formedon in the Discender, and the like, there hee cannot auerre him tenant, but pray his Iudgement and enter, for thereby hee hath the effect of his suite Et frustrà fit per plura, quod fieri potest per pauciora.

¶ *Auerrer.* To auerre or auouch, or verifie, verificare, whereof commeth verificatio an auerment, and is so said as well in English as in French. And is twofold, viz. generall and particular. A generall auerment, which is the conclusion of euery plea to the Writ, or in barre of replications and other pleadings (for Counts or Auowries in nature of Counts need not bee auerred) containing matter affirmatiue, ought to be auerred, & hoc paratus est verificare, &c. Particular auerments are, as when the life of Tenant for life, or Tenant in taile are auerred, and there, though this word (verificare) be not used, but the matter auouched and affirmed, it is upon the matter an auerment. And an auerment containeth aswell the matter as the forme thereof.

¶ *Que le tenant alast sans iour.* Quod tenens eat sine die. This is the entrie of the iudgement in that case, that the Tenant shall goe without day, that is to be discharged of further attendance, and this is some-

iudgement lissue en le taile que est demādant, poit entrer en la terre, nyent contristeant le discontinuance, et per tiel entrie il serra adiudge eins en son Remitter. Et la cause est, pur ceo que si ascun hōe suist Præcipe quod reddat, enuers ascun tenant de franktenement, en quel action l' demandant ne recouera damages, et le tenant pledast nontenure, ou autrement disclaima en le tenancy, le demandant ne poit auerrer son briefe, et dirra q̄ il est tenāt cōe le briefe suppose. Et pur cel cause le demādant apres ceo que iudgement est done q̄ le tenant alast sans iour, poit entrer ē les tenemēts demands, le quel serra auxy graund aduantage a luy en ley, sicome il auoit iudgement d̄ recouerer enuers le tenant, et per tiel entrie il est en son remitter per force del taile. Mes lou le demand recouera damages enuers le tenant, la le demandant poit auerrer, que il est tenāt come le briefe supp, & ceo pur laduantage

Del

iudgement the issue in the taile that is demandant may enter into the land notwithstanding the discontinuance, and by such entry hee shall be adiudged in his Remitter. And the reason is for that if any man sue a *Præcipe quod reddat* against any tenant of the freehold in which action the demandant shall not recouer damages, and the tenant pleads nontenure, or otherwise disclaime in the tenancie, the demandant cannot auerre his writ, and say that hee is tenant as the writ supposeth. And for this cause the demandāt after that that iudgemēt is giuen that the tenant shall goe without day, may enter into the tenements demanded, the which shall bee as great an aduantage to him in law, as if he had iudgement to recouer against the tenant, and by such entrie hee is in his remitter by force of the entaile. But where the demandant shall recouer damages against the tenāt, there the demandant may auerre that he is tenant, as the writ supposeth and that for the aduan-

del demandant pur recouer ses damages, ou autermēt il ne recoueroit ses damages, queux sont ou fueront a luy dones per la ley.

tage of the demandant to recouer his damages, or otherwise hee shall not recouer his damages, which are or were giuen to him by the law.

time finall for that action whereof Littleton here putteth an example, & sometime temporarie, whereof Littleton also hath put an example, as when excommengement is pleaded in disability of the Plaintife or demandant, there the award is, that the Tenant or Defendant shall goe without day, and yet when the Demandant or Plaintife haue purchased his Letters of absolution, vpon shewing them to the Court, he may haue a resommons or reattachement to recontinue the cause againe. But it is to be knowne, that when iudgement is giuen against the Tenant or Defendant vpon a plea in barre, or to the Writ, &c. the iudgement is all one, viz. Quod tenens or defendens eat inde sine die, and shall haue reference to the nature and matter of the plea, and so bee taken either to goe in barre, or to the Writ. So on the other side when iudgement is giuen against the Plaintife either in barre of his action or in abatement of his Writ, &c. the iudgement is all one, viz. Nihil capiat per breue, and it appeareth by the Record whether the plea did goe in barre or to the Writ. And the cause of the iudgement is neuer entred in the Record in any case, for that vpon consideration had of the Record it appeareth therein.

Vid. Sect. 101.

3.H.4.2.11.

Section 692.

¶ Item si home soit disseisie, & le disseisor deuy, son heire esteant eins per discent, ore lentrie de le disseisee est tolle, et si le disseisee porta son briefe dentrie sur disseisin en le Per, enuers lheire, et lheire disclaime en le tenancy, &c. le demandant poit auerrer son briefe que il est tenant come le briefe suppose sil voyt, pur recouerer ses damages, mes uncore sil voyt relinquisher le auerment, &c. il poit loialment entrer en la terre per cause del disclaimer, nient obstant que son entry adeuant fuit tolle, et ceo fuit adiudge deuant mon master sir R. Danby iades Chief Justice de la common banke & ses compagnions, &c.

ALso if a man be disseised, and the disseisor die his heire being in by discent, now the entrie of the disseisee is taken away, and if the disseisee bring his Writ of entrie *Sur disseisin* in the *Per* against the heire, and the heire disclaime in the tenancie, &c. the Demandant may auerre his writ that hee is tenant as the writ suppose, if he will, to recouer his damages, but yet if he will relinquish the auerment, &c. he may lawfully enter into the land because of the disclaimer, notwithstanding that his entrie before was taken away, and this was adiudged before my Master Sir *R. Danby* late chiefe Iustice of the Common place and his Companions, &c.

¶ *Item si home soit disseisie, &c.* Albeit in this case and in the case before the entrie of the Demandant is his owne act, and the Demandant hath no expresse iudgement to recouer, yet shall he be remitted, because he in iudgement of the Law shall be in according to the title of his Writ, and by his entrie defeate the Discontinuance, and consequently is remitted to his ancient estate. 36.H.6.fo.29.

¶ *Sir Robert Danbye* Knight was a Gentleman of an ancient and faire discended family, and chiefe Iustice of the Court of Common pleas, a graue, reue- 5.E.4.41. 4.E.4.38.

rend & learned judge, of whom our author speaketh here with very great reuerence, as you may perceiue. And here is to be noted how necessarie it is, after the example of our Author, to obserue the iudgements, and resolutions of the Sages of the Law.

Sect. 693.

¶ ITem lou lentry dun home est congeable, coment que il prent estate a luy quaunt il est de pleine age pur terme de vie, ou en taile, ou en fee, ceo est vn Remitter a luy, si tiel prisel de estate ne soit per fait indent, ou per matter de record, que concludera ou estoppera. Car si hõe soit disseisie, et reprẽt estate de le Disseisor sans fait, ou per fait polle, ceo est vn remit al disseisee, &c.

ALso where the entrie of a man is congeable, although that he taks an estate to him when he is of full age, for terme of life, or in Taile, or in Fee, this is a Remitter to him, if such taking of the Estate be not by Deed indented, or by matter of Record, which shal cõclude or estop him: for if a man be disseised, and takes backe an Estate from the Disseisor without Deed, or by deed pol, this is a remitter to the Disseisee, &c.

29. Ass. p. 26. 43. Ass. p. 3. 11. H. 7. 20. 3. H. 6. 19. 40. E. 3. 43.

¶ HEere appeareth a diuersitie betweene a right of entrie, and a right of Action; for if a man of full age hauing but a right of Action, taketh an Estate to him, hee is not remitted: but where hee hath a right of Entrie, and taketh an Estate, he by his entry is remitted, because his entry is lawfull. And if the Disseisor infeoffe the Disseisee and others, the Disseisee is remitted to the whole, for his entry is lawfull: otherwise it is if his entrie were taken away.

8. R. 2. Quar. im. 199. 19. H. 6. 30. 8. H. 6. 17. 21. H. 6. 2. 3. H. 4. 8. 14. H. 6. 15. 16. 37. H. 6. 18. 26. H. 8. 4. F. N. B. 36. f. & 35. b.

¶ *Lou le'ntrie est congeable.* A. is disseised of a Mannor, whereunto an Aduowson is appendant, an Estranger vsurpe to the Aduowson, if the Disseisee enter into the Mannor, the Aduowson is recontinued againe, which was seuered by the vsurpation. And so it is if Tenant in Tayle be of a Mannor, whereunto an Aduowson is appendant, the Tenant in Tayle discontinueth in Fee, the Discontinuee granteth away the Aduowson in Fee, and dieth, the Issue in Tayle recontinueth the Mannor by recouerie, he is therby remitted to the Aduowson, and in both cases he that right hath shall present when the Church becommeth voyd.

22. Ass. p. en le case de Thebald Grimule.

The Patron of a Benefice is outlawed, and the Church becommeth voyd, an Estranger vsurpeth, and sixe moneths passe, the King doth recouer in a *Quare impedit*, and remooue the Incumbent, &c. the Aduowson is recontinued to the rightfull Patron. And so note a diuersitie betweene a Recontinuance and a Remitter, for a Remitter cannot be properly vnlesse there be two titles, but a recontinuance may be where there is but one.

13. H. 4. 5. 3. H. 4. 17. 8. H. 4. 8. 12. H. 4. 19. 35. Ass. 8. 17. Ass. 3. 29. Ass. 53. 43. E. 3. 17. Parkers case. 44. E. 3. Estop. 10. 21. H. 6. 2. 8 Pasch. 8. H. 6. 17. 8 Cotismore.

¶ *Per fait indent, &c.* Here it appeareth, That if the Disseisor by Deed indented make a Lease for life, or a gift in Taile, or a Feoffement in fee, whereunto Liuerie of Seisin is requisite, yet the Deed indented shall not suffer the Liuerie made according to the forme and effect of the Indenture, to worke any remitter to the Disseisee, but shall estoppe the Disseisee to claime his former estate: and if the Disseisor vpon the Feoffment doth reserue any rent or condition, &c. the rent or condition is good: and the reason wherefore a deed indented shall conclude the taker more than the Deed polle, is, for that the Deed poll is onely the Deed of the Feoffor, Donor, and Lessor, but the Deed indented is the Deed of both Parties, and therefore as well the taker as the giuer is concluded.

¶ *Ou per Record.* As by Fine, Deed indented, and inrolled, and the like.

Sect. 694.

Item si home lessa terre pur terme de vie a un auter, le quel aliena a un auter en fee, et lalienee fait estate a le Lessour, ceo est un Remitter al Lessor, pur ceo que son entrie fuit congeable, &c.

Also if a man let land for terme of life to another, who alieneth to another in Fee, and the Alienee make an Estate to the Lessour, this is a Remitter to the Lessour, because his Entrie was congeable, &c.

This is euident enough vpon that which hath beene sayd.

Section 695.

Item si home soit disseisie, et le Disseisor lessa la terre al disseisee per fait pol, ou sans fait pur terme des ans, per que le disseisee entra, cest entre est un Remitter a le disseisee. Car en tiel case lou lentre dun home est congeable et un Lease est fait a luy, coment que il claima p parols en pais, que il ad estate per force de tiel lease, ou dit ouertment que il ne claima riens en la terre sinon per force de tiel lease, uncore ceo est un remitter a luy, car tiel disclaimer en le pais nest riens a purpose. Mes sil disclaimer en court de Record que il nad estate forsque per force de tiel lease, et nemy autrement, donques il est conclude, &c.

Also if a man be disseised, and the Disseisor let the Land to the Disseisee by deed pol, or without Deed, for terme of yeares, by which the Disseisee entreth, this entrie is a Remitter to the disseisee. For in such case where the entrie of a man is congeable, and a Lease is made to him, albeit that he claimeth by words in *Pays*, that hee hath estate by force of such Lease, or saith openly, That hee claimeth nothing in the Land but by force of such lease, yet this is a Remitter to him, for that such disclaimer in *Pays* is nothing to the purpose. But if he disclaime in court of Record, that hee hath no estate but by force of such Lease, and not otherwise, then is hee concluded, &c.

Here appeareth a Diuersitie betweene a Claime in Paiis of an Estate, and a Claime of Record, for a Claime in Paiis shall not hinder a Remitter. Otherwise it is of a claime of Record, because that doth worke a Conclusion.

Sect. 696.

Item si deux Joyntenaunts seisie de certain tenements en Fee, lun

Also if two Ioyntenants seised of certaine Tenements in Fee, the one being of

Here note a diuersitie worthy the obseruation, that where Ioyntenants or Coparceners haue one and the same remedie, if the one enter, the

esteant de pleine age, lauter deins age sont disseisies, &c. et l' disseisor morust seisie, et son issue entra, lun de les Jointenants esteant adonqz deins age, et apres que il vient al pleine age, lheire le disseisor lessa les Tenements a mesmes les Joyntenants pur terme de lour deux vies, ceo est un remitter (quant al moitie) a celuy que fuit deins age, pur ceo que il est seisie de cest moitie que affiert a luy en fee, pur ceo que son entre fuit congeable. Mes lauter Jointenaunt nad en lauter moity forsque estate pur terme de sa vie, per force de le lease, pur ceo que son entre fuit tolle, &c.

full age, the other within age, bee disseised &c. and the Disseisor die seised, and his Issue enter, the one of the Ioyntenants being then within age, and after that he commeth to full age, the heire of the Disseisor letteth the Tenements to the same Ioyntenants for terme of their two liues, this is a Remitter (as to the moitie) to him that was within age, because hee is seised of the moitie which belongeth to him in fee, for that his entry was congeable. But the other Iointenant hath in the other moity but an estate for terme of his life by force of the lease, because his entry was taken away, &c.

10 H.6.10. 19.H.6.45. 32.H.6.111. Entr.cong.

the other shall enter also: but where remedies bee seuerall, there it is otherwise. As if two Joyntenants or Coparceners joyne in a reall Action, where their entrie is not lawfull, and the one is summoned and seuered, and the other pursueth and recouereth the moitie, the other Joyntenant or Coparcener shall enter and take the profits with her, because their remedie was one and the same. But where two Coparceners bee, and they are disseised, and a Discent is cast, and they haue issue and die, if the Issue of the one recouer her moitie, the other shall not enter with her, because their remedies were seuerall, and yet when both haue recouered, they are Coparceners againe. So here in this Case that Littleton putteth, the two Joinetenants haue not equal remedie, for the Infant hath a right of entrie, and the other a right of Action, and therfore the Infant beeing remitted to a moitie, the other shall not enter and take the profits with her.

If A. and B. Jointenants in Fee, be disseised by the father of A. who dieth seised his sonne and heire entreth, he is remitted to the whole, and his Companion shall take aduantage thereof. Otherwise heere in the Case of Littleton, for that the aduantage is giuen to the Infant more in respect of his person, than of his right, whereof his Companion shal take no aduantage. But if the Grandfather had disseised the Joyntenants, and the Land had discended to the father, and from him to A. and then A. had died, the entrie of the other should be taken away by the first discent, and therefore he should not enter with the heire of A.

V. 35. Ass. Pl. Vltimo.

But here in the case of Littleton, if after the discent the other Joyntenant had died, and the Infant surviued, some say that he should haue entred into the whole, because he is now in iudgment of Law, solely in by the first Feoffement, and he claimeth not vnder the Discent.

Chap. 13. Of Warrantie. Sect. 697.

V. Sect. 288. 332.

Il *est communement dit*. Here by the opinion of Littleton, Communis opinio is of authoritie, and stands with the rule of Law, A communi obseruatia non est recedendum:

Il est communement dit, Que trois Garranties y sont, scilicet, Garrantie lineal, Garrantie

It is commonly said that there be three Warranties, *scilicet*, Warrantie Lineall, Warrantie Co-

rantie collaterall, et Garrantie que commence per disseisin. Et est ascauoir, que deuant lestatute de Glouc, touts Garranties queux discendont a eux queux sont heires a eux que fesoyent les Garranties, fueront barres a mesmes les heires a demander ascuns terres ou tenements encounter les Garranties, forprise les garranties que commencerent per disseisin, car tiel Garrantie ne fuit unque barre al heire, pur ceo que le Garrantie commence per tort, s. per disseisin.

laterall, and Warrantie that commence by disseisin. And it is to bee vnderstood, that before the Statute of Glouc'. all Warranties which discended to them which are heires to those who made the Warranties, were barres to the same heires to demand any Lands or Tenements against the warranties, except the Warranties which commence by disseisin. For such warranty was no barre to the heire, for that the Warrantie comméced by wrong, *viz.* by disseisin.

and againe, Minime mutanda sunt quæ certam habuerunt interpretationem.

Here our Author beginneth this Chapter with an exact diuision of Warranties. A warrantie is a Couenant reall annexed to Lands or Tenements whereby a man and his heires are bound to warrant the same, and eyther vpon voucher or by iudgement in a Writ of Warrantia cartæ to yeild other lands and Tenements (which in olde Bookes is called in excambio) to the value of those that shall be euicted by a former Title, or else may be vsed by way of Rebutter.

Bract. lib. 2. fol. 37. lib. 5. fol. 380. 381. &c. Glanuil. lib. 3. cap. 1. 2. 3. Lib. 7. cap. 2. 3. lib. 9. cap. 4. Britton cap. 105 fol. 249. 250. &c. & fol 88. 106. b. 196. 197. Fleta lib. 5. cap. 15. Lib. 6. cap. 23. Mirror cap. 2. §. 17.

38. E. 3. 21. 45. E. 3. 18.

¶ *Rebouter* is a French word, and is in Latine repellere, to repell or bar, that is in the vnderstanding of the Common Law, the action of the heire by the warranty of his Ancestor, and this is called to Rebutte or repell. (c) Britton saith, Garranter en vn sence signifie a defender son tenant en sa seisin, & en auter sence signifie que si il ne defende que le garrant luy soit tenue a eschanges, & de faire son gree a la vaillaunce. (d) Bracton sayth, Warrantizare nihil aliud est, quam defendere & acquietare tenentem qui Warrantum vocauit in seisina sua. (e) Fleta saith, Warrantizare nihil aliud est quam possidentem vocantem defendere & acquietare in sua seisina vel possessione erga petentem, &c. & tenens de re Warranti excambium habebit ad Valentiam.

(c) *Britton. fol. 197. b.*

(d) *Bracton lib. 5. fol. 380.*

(e) *Fleta lib. 5. cap. 15.*

It is to be obserued that there be two kind of Warranties, that is to say Warrantia expressa, & tacita, vulgarly said warrantie in deed, because they be expressed, & warranties in law, because the law doth tacitely imply them. And this diuision of Warranties that Litt. here speaketh of, he intendeth of Warranties in deed. And of Warranties in Law more shall bee said hereafter in this Chapter. As for promises or Contracts annexed to Chattels reall or personall they are not intended by our Author in his said diuision, but only Warranties concerning Freeholds and Inheritances.

Lib. 4. fol. 81. Nokes Case.

Vide Sect. 733.

¶ *Deuant le statute de Glouc.* This Statute was made at a Parliament holden at Glocester in the first yeare of the raigne of King E. 1. and therefore it is called the Statute of Glocester.

Gloc. cap. 3. *Vide Sect. 724. 725. & 727. &c.*

¶ *Sont barres a mesmes les heires a demander ascuns terres, &c.* For the Statute, as hath beene said, being made in 6. E. 1. (was before the Statute of Donis conditionalibus which was enacted 13. E. 1.) when all states of Inheritance were fee simple. But after the Statute of 13. E. 1. the heire in tayle is not barred by the warrantie of his Ancestor vnlesse there be Assets, as shall be said hereafter more largely in this Chapter.

Bracton lib. 4. fol. 321. b. Fleta lib. 5. cap. 34. 7. E. 3. Garr. 47.

By the Statute of Glocester foure things are enacted.

First, that if a Tenant by the curtesie alien with warrantie and dieth, that this shall bee no barre to the heire in a writ of Mordancester without Assets in fee simple. And if Lands or Tenements discend to the heire from the Father hee shall bee barred hauing regard to the value thereof.

Secondly, That if the heire, for want of Assets at that time discended, doth recover the lands of his Mother by force of this Act, and afterwards Assets discend to the heire from the Father, then the Tenant shall recover against the heire the Inheritance of the Mother by a writ of Judgement, which shall issue out of the Record, to resommon him that ought to warrant, as it hath beene done in other Cases, where the heire beeing vouched commeth into the Court, and pleadeth that he hath nothing by discent.

Thirdly, That the issue of the Sonne shall recover by a Writ of Cosinage, Aiel and Besaiel.

And lastly, that the heire of the wife after the death of the Father and Mother shall be barred of his Action to demand the Heritage of the Mother by writ of Entrie, which his Father aliened in the time of his Mother, whereof no fine was levied in the Kings Court.

Concerning the first, there be two points in Law to be observed.

(e) 11. E. 2. tit. Garr. 83. 4. E. 3. Garr. 63. 18. E. 3. 51. Pl. Com. 110. 7. E. 3. 53. Temps E. 1. Garr. 87.

First, Albeit the Statute in this Article name a writ of Mordancester, and after writs of Cosinage, Aiell and Besaiel (e) yet a writ of Right, a Formedon, a writ of Entry Ad Communem Legem, and all other like Actions are within the purview of this Statute, for those Actions are put but for examples.

27. E. 3. 89. 14. E. 4. Garr. 5. Dier quarto Mar. 148. a.

Secondly, where it is said in the said Act, (if the Tenant by the curtesie alien) yet his release with warranty to a Disseisor, &c. is within the purview of the Statute, for that it is in equall mischiefe, and if that evasion might take place, the Statute should have beene made in vaine.

22. Ass. 9. & 37. Temps E. 1. Garr. 86. (o) 11. H. 7. cap. 20.

If Tenant by the curtesie be of a Seigniorie, and the Tenancie escheate unto him, & after he alieneth with warrantie, this shall not bind the issue, unlesse Assets discend, for it is in equall mischiefe. But notwithstanding this Statute, if Feme Tenant in Dower had aliened in fee with warranty and died, the warranty had bound the heire untill the Statute (o) of 11. H. 7. since our Author wrote. By which Statute the heire may enter notwithstanding such warrantie.

18. E. 3. 9.

But note there is a diversitie betweene a warranty on the part of the Mother, and an estoppell. For an estoppell of the part of the Mother shall not bind the heire, when hee claimeth from the Father. As if Lands bee given to the husband and wife, and to the heires of the husband, the husband make a gift in tayle, and dieth, the wife recovereth in a Cui in vita against the Donee supposing that she had fee simple, and make a feoffment and dieth, the Donee dieth without issue, the issue of the husband and wife bring a Formedon in the Reverter against the Feoffee, and notwithstanding that he was heire to the Estoppell, and the Mother was estopped, yet for that he claymed the Land as heire to his Father, hee was not estopped. Note, that warranties are favoured in Law being part of a mans assurance, but estoppels are odious.

21. R. 2. Judgement 263.

If a feme heire of a Disseisor infeoffeth me with warrantie, and marrieth with the Disseisee, if after the Disseisee bring a Præcipe against me, I shall rebut him, in respect of the warrantie of his wife, and yet hee demandeth the Land in another right. And so if the husband and wife demand the right of the wife, a warranty of the collaterall Ancestor of the husband shall barre.

If a woman had beene Tenant for life, the remaynder or Reversion to her next heire, and the woman had aliened in fee and died, this warranty had barred her heire in Remaynder or Reversion, but this is partly holpen by the said Act of 11. H. 7. viz. where the woman hath any estate for life of the Inheritance or Purchase of her husband, or given to her by any of the Ancestors of the husband, or by any other person seised to the use of her husband or of any of his Ancestors, there her Alienation, Release, or Confirmation with warranty shall not bind the heire.

11. H. 7. cap. 20. Vide Sect. 595. See this Statute of 11. H. 7. cap. 20. well expounded. Lib. 1. fol. 176. in Sir Anth. Mildmayes Case. 3. & 4. Ph. & Mar. Dier. 146 Lib. 3. fol. 59. 60 61. 62. Lincolne Coll. Case. Pl. Com. fol. 56. 20. Eliz. Dier 362. Doct. & Student. 8. Eliz. Dier 248. 19. Eliz. Dier 354 21. Eliz. ibid. 363. lib. 3. fol. 50. 51. Sir George Brownes Case Lib. 5. f. 79. ot Smiths Case. 27. H. 8. 23. (f) Mich. 13. Iac inter Harley & West in ejectione firme in Communi Banco. Lincoln.

To the Authorities quoted in the margent which may serve as Commentaries upon the said Statute, I will only adde two cases, the one was. (f) A man seised of Lands in fee levied a fine to the use of himselfe for life, and after to the use of his wife, and of the heires males of her bodie by him begotten for her Joynture, and had Issue male, and after he and his wife levied a fine and suffered a common recovery, the Husband and Wife died, and the Issue male entred by force of the said Statute of 11. H. 7. And it was holden by the Justices of Assise (the case comming downe to be tryed by Nisi prius) that the entry of the Issue male was lawfull, and yet this case is out of the Letter of the Statute, for shee neither levied the fine, &c. being sole, or with any other after-taken Husband, but is by her selfe with her Husband that made the Joynture. Sed qui hæret in littera hæret in cortice, and this case beeing in the same mischiefe is therefore within the remedy of the Statute by the intendement of the makers of the same to avoyd the disherison of heires who were provided for by the said Joynture, and especially by the Husband himself that made the Joynture, which (as it was said) is a stronger case then the examples set downe in the Statute. The other was, (g) A man is seised of

(g) Pasch. 17. Eliz. in

Lands

Lands in the right of his wife, and they two levy a fine, and the Conusee grant and rendreth the Land to the Husband and wife in speciall tayle, the remaynder to the right heires of the wife, they haue issue, the Husband dieth, the wife taketh another Husband, and they two leuie a fine in fee, and the issue entreth, this is directly within the Letter of the Statute, and yet it is out of the meaning, because the state of the Land moued from the wife, so as it was the purchase of the Husband in letter, and not in meaning. But where the woman is Tenant for life by the gift or conueyance of any other, her alienation with warranty shall bind the heire at this day. So if a man bee Tenant for life (otherwise then as Tenant by the curtesie) and alien in fee with warranty, and dieth, this shall at this day bind the heire that hath the Reuersion or Remaynder by the Common Law not holpen by any Statute. But all this is to be understood, unlesse the heire that hath the Reuersion or Remaynder doth auoide the estate so aliened in the life of the Ancestor, for then the estate being auoyded, the warranty being annexed unto the estate is auoyded also, whereof more shall be said in this Chapter in his proper place. And therefore it is necessary for the heire in such cases to make an entry as soone as hee hath notice or probable suspition of such an alienation.

Com. Banco. Lattons Case which I my selfe heard and obserued.

Sect. 725.

As to the second clause of the Statute of Glocester. There are two points of Law to bee obserued.

First, That by the expresse purview of the Statute, if Assets doe after discend from the Father, then the Tenant shall haue recouery or restitution of the Lands of the Mother. But in a Formedon if at the time of the warranty pleaded no Assets be discended, whereby the Demandant recouereth, if after Assets discend, there the Tenant shall haue a Scire facias for the Assets, and not for the Land intayled. And the reason hereof is, that if in this case the Tenant should be restored to the Land intayled, then if the Issue in Tayle aliened the Assets, his Issue should recouer in a Formedon, and therefore the Sages of the Law to preuent future occasions of suits resolued the said diuersitie in the Cases abouesaid upon consideration and construction of the Statute of Glocester, and of the Statute De donis conditionalibus.

Pl. Com. Fulmerstons case 110. a. Lib. 8. fol. 53. Syms Case.

Secondly, It is to be obserued, that after Assets discended, the recouerie shall be by Writ of iudgement which shall issue out of the Rolle of the Justices, &c. And here two things are to be declared and explayned. First, by what Writ, &c. and that is cleere, viz. by Scire facias. But the second is more difficult, and that is upon what manner of iudgement the Scire facias is to be grounded: for explanation whereof it is to be understood, that if the Tenant will haue benefit of the Statute he must plead the warranty, and acknowledge the title of the demandant, and pray that the aduantage of the Statute may be saued unto him. And then if after Assets discend, the Tenant upon this Record shall haue a Scire facias. And if Assets discend but for part, he shall haue a Scire facias for so much. But if the Tenant plead the warranty, and plead further that Assets discended, &c. and the Demandant taketh issue that Assets discended not, &c. which issue is found for the Demandant, whereupon hee recouereth, the Tenant albeit Assets doe after discend, shall neuer haue a Scire facias upon the said Judgement, for that by his false plea he hath lost the benefit of the said Statute.

Lib. 8. fol. 53. 54. Syms Case. Ibid. 134. Mary Shipleys case.

Touching the third sufficient hath beene spoken before. For the last it is to bee obserued, That if the Husband be seised of Lands in the right of his wife, and maketh a feoffment in fee with warranty, the wife dieth and the Husband dieth, this warranty shall not binde the heire of the wife without Assets, albeit the Husband be not Tenant by the curtesie. But of this you shall reade more hereafter.

8. E. 2 tit. Garr. 81. 18. E. 3. 51.

In the meane time know this that the learning of warranties is one of the most curious and cunning Learnings of the Law, and of great use and consequence.

Vide Sect. 725.

¶ *A demander ascuns terres ou tenements.* **A warrantie may not** only be annexed to Freeholds or Inheritances corporeall which passe by Liuery, as Houses and Lands, but also to Freeholds or Inheritances incorporeall which lie in grant as Aduowsons, and to Rents, Commons, Estouers, and the like, which issue out of Lands or Tenements. And not only to Inheritances in esse, but also to Rents, Commons, Estouers, &c. newly created. As a man (some say) may grant a Rent, &c. out of Land for life, in tayle, or in fee with warranty, for although there can bee no title precedent to the Rent, yet there may be a title precedent to the Land, out of which it issueth before the grant of the Rent, which Rent may bee auoyded by the recouery of the Land, in which case the Grantee may helpe himselfe by a Warrantia cartæ upon the especiall matter. And so a warrantie in Law may extend to a Rent, &c. newly created, and therefore if a Rent newly created bee granted in Exchange for an Acre of Land, this Exchange is good, and euery Exchange implyeth a warranty in Law. And so a Rent newly created may bee granted for oweltie of partition.

2. H. 4. 13. 30. H. 8. Dier 42.

Temps E. 1. admesurement 16. 32. E. 1. Voucher 294. 30. E. 1. Exchange 16. 9. E. 4. 15. E. 4. 9. 29. Ass. 13.

Vid.Sect.741. 45.E.3.Voucher 72. 9.E.3.78. 18.E.3.55. 30.E.3.30. 21.H.7.9. 3.H.7.4.7.H.4.17. 10.E.4.9.b. 21.E.4.16. 14.H.8.6. 30.H.8.Dier 42.

A man seised of a Rent secke issuing out of the Mannor of Dale taketh a wife, the husband releaseth to the Terre tenant & warranteth Tenementa prædicta and dyeth, the wife bringeth a writ of Dower of the rent, the Terre tenant shall vouche, for that albeit the release enured by way of extinguishment, yet the warranty extended to it, and by warranting of the land all rents, &c. issuing out of the land, that are suspended or discharged at the time of the warrante created, are warranted also.

Sect. 698.

Garranty q̃ cōmence p disseisin est en tiel forme, sicome lou il est pier et fits, et le fits purchase terre, &c. et lessa mesme la terre a son pier pur terme dans, & pier per son fait ent enfeoffa un auter en fee, & oblige luy & ses heires a garranty, et le pier deuy, per que l' garranty discendist al fits, ceo garranty ne barrera my le fits, car nient obstant cel garrantie, le fits poit bien enter en la terre, ou auer un assise enuers lalienee sil voit, pur ceo que l' garranty commence per disseisin, car quant le pier que nauoit estate forsque pur terme des ans, fist un feoffment en fee, ceo fuit un disseisin al fits del franktenemēt que adonqz fuist en le fits. En mesme le maner est, si le fits lessa a le pier la terre a tener a volunt, & puis le pier fait un feoffment oue garrantie,

Warrantie that commence by disseisin is in this manner, As where there is father and son, and the sonne purchaseth land, &c. and letteth the same land to his father for terme of years, and the father by his deed thereof infeoffeth another in fee, and binde him and his heires to Warranty, and the father dies, whereby the warranty discendeth to the son, this warranty shall not barre the son, for notwithstanding this warranty the sonne may well enter into the land, or haue an Assise against the Alienee if he will, because the Warranty commenced by disseisin, for when the father which had but an estate for term of yeares made a feoffment in fee, this was a disseisin to the son of the freehold which then was in the sonne. In the same manner it is if the son letteth to the fa-

Warranty que cōmence per disseisin, &c. It is called a warranty that commenceth by Disseisin, because regularly the conueyance whereunto the warranty is annexed doth worke a Disseisin.

In this Section Littleton putteth fiue examples of a warranty commencing by Disseisin, viz. of a feoffment made with warranty by Tenant for yeares, by Tenant at will, by Tenant by Elegit, by Tenant by Statute Merchant, and by Tenant by Statute Staple: all these and the other examples that Littleton putteth of this kinde of warranties in the succeeding Sections haue foure qualities.

7.E.3.41. 43.E.17. 50 E.3.12. Vid.Sect.611.

First, that the Disseisin is done immediately to the heire that is to be bound, and yet if the father be Tenant for life, the remainder to the son in fee, the father by Couyn & consent maketh a Lease for yeares, to the end that the Lessee shall make a feoffment in fee, to whom the father shal release with warranty, and all is executed accordingly, the father dieth, this warranty shall not binde, albeit the Disseisin was not done immediately to the sonne, for the feoffment of the Lessee is a disseisin to the father, who is particeps criminis. So it is if one brother make a gift in taile to another, and the uncle disseise the Donee, and infeoffeth another with warranty, the uncle dieth and the warranty discendeth upon the Donor, and then the Donee dieth without

Lib.5.fo.79.b. Fitzherberts case.

31.E.3.tit.Garrantie 28.

garrantie, &c. Et sicome est dit de pier, issint poit estre dit de chescun auter auncester, &c. En mesme le maner est, si tenaunt per Elegit, tenant per Statute Merchant, ou tenant per Statute de le Staple fait feoffment en fee ouesque garranty, ceo ne barrera my lheire que doit auer la terre, pur ceo que tiels garranties cõmencerent per disseisin.

ther the land to hold at will, & after the father make a feoffment with warranty, &c. And as it is said of the father, so it may be said of euery other ancester &c. In the same mãner is it, if tenant by *Elegit*, tenant by Statute Merchant or tenant by Statute staple make a feoffment in fee with warranty, this shall not bar the heire which ought to haue the land, because such warranties cõmence by disseisin.

nee, albeit the disseisin was done to the Donee and not to the Donor, yet the warranty shall not binde him. The father, the sonne and a third person are joyntenants in fee, the father maketh a feoffment in fee of the whole with warranty, and dyeth, the sonne dyeth, the third person shall not only auoide the feoffment for his owne part, but also for the part of the sonne, and hee shall take aduantage that the warranty commenced by Disseisin, though the Disseisin was done to another.

The second quality appearing in Littletons examples is, that the Warranty and Disseisin are simul & semel both at one and the same time. (y) And yet if a man commit a Disseisin of intent to make a feoffment in fee with warrantie, albeit he make the feoffment many yeares after the disseisin, notwithstanding because the Warranty was done to that intent and purpose, the Law shall adiudge vpon the whole matter, and by the intent couple the Disseisin and the warranty together.

(y) 19.H.8.12. lib.5. fo 79.b. Fitzh.case.

The third quality is that the Warranty that commenceth by Disseisin by all these examples (if it should binde) should binde as a Collaterall Warranty, and therefore commencing by Disseisin shall not binde at all.

Ne barrera my le heire, &c. For by the Authority of our Author himselfe a Lessee for yeares may make a feoffment, and by his feoffment a fee simple shall passe, so as albeit as to the Lessor it worketh by disseisin, yet between the parties the Warranty annexed to such estate standeth good: vpon which the Feoffee may vouche the Feoffor or his heires as by force of a lineall Warranty. And therefore if a Lessee for yeares or Tenant by Elegit, &c. or a Disseisor incontinent make a Feoffment in fee with Warranty, if the Feoffee be impleaded, he shall vouche the Feoffor, and after him his heire also, because this is a Couenant reall, which binde him and his heires to recompence in value, if they haue assets by discent to recompence, for there is a Feoffment de facto, and a Feoffment de iure: (*) And a Feoffment de facto made by them that haue such interest or possession, as is aforesaid, is good betweene the parties, and against all men, but only against him, that hath right. And therefore if the Lord be Gardeine of the land, or if the Tenant maketh a Lease to the Lord for yeares, or if the Lord be Tenant by Statute Merchant or Staple, or by Elegit of the tenancie, and make a Feoffment in fee, he hereby doth extinguish his Seigniory, although hauing regard to the Lessor it is a Disseisin.

Vid. Sect. 611. 699. Bracton fo. 216. 223. 224. Fleta lib. 4 ca. 17. 1. 2. Britton cap. Disseisin. 50 E.3. 12 b 8. H.7. 5. 7. E.3. 11. 14. E.3. Feoffments on fait 67. 18 E.3. Issue 36. 4. E 2. briefe 790. 19. E.2. Ass. 402. 43. E.3. 9. 17. E.3. 41. 43. E.3. Diss. 5. 3. E.4. 17. 12 E.4. 12. 10. E.4. 18. F N. B. 201. Lib. 3. fo. 78. in Fermors case. (*) Temps E.1. Counterplea de Voucher 126. 50. E.3. Ibidem 124. Vid W.1. cap. 48. in the second part of the Institutes.

The fourth quality is a Disseisin, but that is put for an example, and the rather for that it is most vsuall and frequent, but a warranty that commenceth by abatement or intrusion (that is when the abatement or intrusion is made of intent to make a Feoffment in fee with Warrantie) shall not binde the right heire, no more then a Warrantie that commenceth by Disseisin, because all doe commence by wrong. And so it is if the Tenant dyeth without heire, and an Ancestor of the Lord enter before the entry of the Lord, and make a Feoffment in fee with warranty, and dyeth, this warranty shall not binde the Lord, because it commenceth by wrong, being in nature of an Abatement, Et sic de similibus.

Sect. 699.

Item si gardein en Chiualrie, ou gardein en Socage fait

ALso if Gardeine in Chiualrie or Gardeine in Socage make

fait vn feoffement en fee, ou en fee taile, ou pur terme de vie ouesque garranty, &c. tiels garranties ne sont pas barres a les heires, as quex les terres serront discendus, pur ceo que ils commence per disseisin.

a Feoffement in Fee, or in Fee taile, or for life, with Warrantie, &c. such Warranties are not barres to the Heyres to whome the Lands shall bee discended, because they commence by Disseisin.

16. E. 3. Gar. 20. 8. Ass. 2. 43. E. 3. 7. and the Books above sayd. Vi. Sect. 698.

HEre Littleton addeth the Case of Gardeine in Chiualrie; and Gardein in Socage, and Gardeine because of Nurture is also in the same case.

Sect. 700.

Item si le pier et le fits purchase certaine Terres ou tenements, a auer et tener a eux iointmēt, &c. et puis le pier alien lentier a vn auter, et oblige luy et ses heires a garrantie, &c. et puis le pier deuie. cel Garrantie ne barrera my le fits de le moitie que a luy affiert de les dits terres ou tenemēts, pur ceo que quaunt a cel moitie que affiert a le fits, le Garranty commence per Disseisin, &c.

ALso if Father and Sonne purchase certaine Lands or Tenements, To haue and to hold to them iointly, &c. and after the Father alien the whole to another, and binde him and his Heyres to Warrantie, &c. and after the Father dieth, this Warrantie shall not barre the sonne of the moitie that belōgs to him of the said Lands or Tenements, because as to that moitie which belongs to the Sonne, the warrantie commences by Disseisin, &c.

13. Ass. 8. 13 E. 3. Gar. 24. 25. 37. 22. H. 6. 51. 8. H. 7. 6.

A *Auer & tener a eux iointmēt, &c.* This is to be intended of a ioynt purchase in fee, for if the purchase were to the father and the sonne, and the heyres of the sonne, and the father maketh a Feoffement in Fee with warrantie, if the sonne entreth in the life of the Father, and the Feoffee re-enter, the father dieth, the sonne shal haue an Assise of the whole, and so is the Booke of 22 H. 6. to be understood. But if the sonne had not entred in the life of the father, then for the fathers moitie it had beene a bar to the sonne, for that therein he had an estate for life, and therefore the warrantie as to that moitie, had beene collaterall to the sonne, and by Disseisin for the sonnes moitie, and so a Warrantie defeated in part, and stand good in part. And this appeareth by the example that Littleton hath put. But if the purchase had been to the father & sonne, and to the heires of the Father, then the entrie of the sonne in the life of the father, as to the auoydance of the warrantie, had not auailed him, because his father lawfully conueyed away his moitie.

Temp. E. 1. Vouch. 207. 39. E. 3. 26. John Londons case. 14. H. 6.

If a man of full age and an Infant make a Feoffement in Fee with warrantie, this warrantie is not voyd in part, and good in part, but it is good for the whole against the man of full age, and voyd against the Infant: for albeit the Feoffement of an Infant passing by Liuerie of Seisin bee voydable, yet his warrantie which taketh effect onely by Deed, is meerly voyd.

Section 701.

¶ ITem ſi A. d B. ſoit ſeiſie dun meſe, et F. de G. que nul droit ad dentrer en meſme le meaſe, claimaunt meſme le meaſe, a tener a luy et a ſes Heires, entra en meſme le meaſe, mes le dit A. de B. adonque eſt continualmẽt demurrant en meſme le meaſe: En ceſt cas le poſſeſſion d frank-tenement ſerra tout temps adiudge en A de B. et nemy en F. de G. pur ceo que en tiel caſe lou deux sõt en vn meaſe, ou auters Tenements, et lun claima per lun title, et lauter p lauter title, la Ley adiudgera celuy en poſſeſſion que ad droit dauer le poſſeſſion de meſmes les Tenements. Mes ſi en le caſe auantdit, l dit F. de G. fait vn Feoffment a certaine Barrettors et extortioners en le pais, p̃ maintenance de eux auer, de meſme le meaſe per vn fait de Feoffement oue garrantie, per force de quel le dit A. de B.

ALſo if A. of B. bee ſeiſed of a Meſe, and F. of C. that no right hath to enter into the ſame Meſe, claiming the ſayde Meſe to hold to him and to his heires, entreth into the ſayd Meſe, but the ſame A. of B. is then continually abiding in the ſame Meaſe: In this Caſe the poſſeſſion of the Free-hold ſhall bee alwayes adiudged in A. of B. and not in F. of G. becauſe in ſuch Caſe where two bee in one Houſe or other Tenements, and the one claimeth by one Title, and the other by another Title, the Law ſhal adiudge him in poſſeſſion, that hath right to haue the poſſeſſion of the ſame tenements. But if in the Caſe aforeſayd, the ſayde F. of G. make a Feoffement to certaine Barrettors and Extortioners in the Countrie, to haue maintenance from thẽ of the ſayd houſe, by a Deed of Feoffment with Warrantie, by force whereof the ſaid

¶ L*ou deux ſont en vn meſe, &c. & lun claima per lun title, & lauter per auter title, &c.* For the rule is, Duo non poſſunt in ſolido vnam rem poſſidere. 19.H.6.fo.28.b. 3 Newton.

Theſe words of our Author be ſignificant and materiall: (h) for if a man hath iſſue two daughters Baſtard eigne and Mulier puiſne, and die ſeiſed, and they both enter generally, the ſole poſſeſſion ſhal not be adiudged onely in the Mulier, becauſe they both claime by one and the ſame title, and not one by one title, and the other by another title, as our Author here ſaith. (h) 17.E.3.59.11.Aſſ.

(i) If the Tenaunt in an aſſiſe of an houſe deſire the Plaintiſe to dine with him in the houſe, which the Plaintiſe doth accordingly, and ſo they be both in the houſe, and in truth one pretendeth one title, and the other another title, yet the Law in this caſe ſhall not adiudge the poſſeſſion in him that right hath, becauſe our Author here ſaith, he claimed not his right, and it ſhould be to his preiudice if the Law ſhould adiudge him in poſſeſſion; and a Treſpaſſer he cannot be, becauſe he was inuited by the Tenant in the Aſſiſe. (i) Pl.Com.92. the Parſon of Honylanes caſe.

¶ *Barretors.* A Barrettor is a common mouer and exciter or maintainer of ſuits, quarrells, or parts, either in Courts or elſewhere in the Countrie. In Courts, as in Courts of Record, or not of Record, as in the Countie, Hundred, or other inferiour Courts. In the Countrie in three manners, Firſt, in diſturbance of the Peace. Secondly, in taking or keeping of poſſeſſions of lands in controuerſie, not onely by force, but alſo by ſubtiltie

See the Inditement of a common Barrettor. W.1.ca 18. & 32 40.E.3.33. Lib.8.fo.36.b. Caſe de Barretry.

ne osast pas demurrer en le Mease, mes alast hors de le mease, cest garranty commence per Disseisin, pur ceo que tiel Feoffement fuit la cause que le dit A. de B. relinquist le possession de mesme le Mease.

A. of B. dare not abide in the House, but goeth out of the same, this Warrantie commenceth by Disseisin, because such Feoffement was the cause that the sayde A. of B. relinquished the possession of the same House.

tie and a deceit, and most commonly in suppression of truth and right. Thirdly, by false inventions, and sowing of calumniations, rumors, and reports, whereby discord and disquiet may grow betweene neighbours.

33 E.1.Stat.de Conspiracie. Li.8.vb.sup.

¶ *Barrettor* is derived of this word (Barret) which signifieth not onely a wrangling suit, but also such brawles and quarrels in the Countrie, as are aforesayd.

Pl.Com fo.64. Li.10 fo.101.102. Beausages Case.

¶ *Extortioners*. Extortion in his proper sence is a great misprision by wresting or unlawfully taking by any Officer by colour of his Office any money or valuable thing of or from any man, either that is not due, or more than is due, or before it be due, Quod non est debitum, vel quod est ultra debitum, vel ante tempus quod est debitum: For this it is to be knowne, that it is provided by the (l) Statute of W.1. That no Sherife nor any other Minister of the King, shall take any reward for doing of his Office, but onely that which the King alloweth him, upon paine that he shall render double to the partie, and be punished at the Kings pleasure. And this was the antient Common Law, and was punishable by fine and imprisonment, but the Statute added the aforesayd penaltie. But some latter Statutes having permitted them to take in some cases, by colour thereof the Kings Officers and Ministers, as Sherifes, Coroners, Escheators, Feodaries, Gaolers, and the like, doe offend in most cases; and seeing this Act yet standeth in force, they cannot take any thing but where, and so farre as latter Statutes have allowed unto them. But yet such reasonable Fees as have beene allowed by the Courts of Justice of antient time to inferiour Ministers and Attendants of Courts for their labour and attendance, if it bee asked and taken of the Subiect, is no extortion.

(l) W.1.c.26.&c.W.1.c.10. 41 E.3.5.27.Ass.14. Pl.Com.68.

23.H.6.ca.10.33.H.6.22. 21.H.7.17.Stanf.49. 3.E.3.Cor.372.

(n) Hil.13.Ia.Reg.

And all this was resolved (n) by the whole Court of Kings Bench, betweene Shurley Plaintife, and Packer Deputie of one of the Sherifes of London, in an Action upon the Case in the Kings Bench.

See the Statute of 21.H.8. cap. 5. setting downe the Fees of Ordinaries, Registers, and other Officers, in certaine Cases, and many other Statutes, as for example the Statute of 19.H.7.cap.8. against taking of Shewage (that is, taking of any thing for shewing of Wares and Merchandises that be truly customed to the King before) and the like.

Pl.Com.in Dive & Manninghams case. Mir.ca.5.§.1.

Of this crime it is sayd, That it is no ther othan Robberie: And another saith, That it is more odious than Robberie, for Robberie is apparant, and hath the face of a crime; but Extortion puts on the visure of Vertue, for expedition of Justice, and the like, and it is ever accompanied with that grievous sinne of periurie.

7.E.4.21.

But largely Extortion is taken for any oppression by extort power, or by colour or pretence of right, and so Littleton taketh it in this place. Extortio is derived from the Verbe Extorqueo, and it is called Crimen expilationis or concussionis: And here Barrettors and Extortioners are put but for examples, for if the Feoffement bee made to any other person or persons, the Law is all one.

¶ *Pur maintenance de eux auer.* Maintenance, Manutenentia is derived of the Verbe Manutenere, and signifieth in Law, a taking in hand, bearing up or upholding of quarrels and sides, to the disturbance or hinderance of common right; Culpa est rei se immiscere ad se non pertinenti, and so is two fold, One in the Countrie, and Another in the Court. For quarrells and sides in the Court (k) the Statutes have inflicted grievous punishments. But this kind of maintenance of quarrells and sides in the Countrie, is punishable onely at the suit of the King, (r) as it hath beene resolved. And this Maintenance is called Manutenentia, or Manutentio ruralis, for example, as to take possessions, or to keep possessions, whereof Littleton here speaketh, or the like.

(k) 1.E.3.ca.14. 20.E.3.ca.4.5.

(r) Mich.7.Ia. in the Starre-Chamber.

The other is called Curialis, because it is done pendente placito, in the Courts of Justice, and this was an Offence at the Common Law, and is threefold.

33.E.1.Stat.2.in fine. Regist.183. 6.E.3.33.22.H.6.7. 9.H.7.22.

First, To maintaine, to have part of the Land, or any thing out of the Land, or part of the Debt, or other thing in Plea or Suit, and this is called Cambipartia, Champertie.

The second is, when one maintaineth the one side, without having any part of the thing in

Plea

Plea or Suit, and this maintenance is two-fold, generall maintenance, and speciall maintenance, whereof you shall reade at large in our Bookes, which were too long here to be inserted.

The third is when (u) one laboureth the Jurie, if it bee but to appeare, or if hee instruct them, or put them in feare, or the like, he is a mayntainer, & hee is in Law called an Embraceor, and an Action of Mayntenance lyeth against him, and if hee take monie a decies tantum may be brought against him. And whither the Jury passe for his side or no, or whither the Jurie giue any verdict at all, yet shall he be punished as a Mayntainer or Embraceor eyther at the suite of the King or party.

30. Ass. 5. 19. E. 4. 3. 20. H. 6. 12. 34. H. 6. 2. 11. H. 6. 11. 8. H. 5. 8. 10. E. 4. 19. W. 1. ca. 25. 28. W. 2. cap. 49. Artic super Cart. cap. 11. F. N. B. 171. 172. Mirror cap. 1. §. 5. (u) 13. H. 4. 16. b. F. N. B. 171. 11. H. 6. 10. 37. H. 6. 3[illegible]

Here in this case that Littleton putteth the feoffment is void by the Statute (a) of 1. R. 2. for thereby it is enacted, that feoffments made for Mayntenance shall bee holden for none, and of no value, so as Littleton putteth his case at the Common Law, for hee seemeth to allow the feoffment where he saith, tiel feoffment fuit le cause, &c. but some haue said that the feoffment is not void betweene the Feoffor and Feoffee, but to him that right hath.

(a) 1. R. 2. cap. 9. Vid. 27. H. 8. fol. 23.

Now since Littleton wrote there is a notable Statute (b) made in suppression of the causes of vnlawfull mayntenance (which is the most dangerous enemie that Justice hath) the effect of which statute is.

(b) 32. H. 8. cap. 9.

First, That no person shall bargaine, buy or sell, or obtaine any pretensed Rights or Titles.

Secondly, Or take, promise, grant, or couenant to haue any Right, or Title of any person in or to any Lands, Tenements, or Hereditaments, but if such person which so shall bargaine, &c. their Ancestors, or they by whom hee or they clayme the same haue beene in possession of the same, or of the Reuersion or Remaynder thereof, or taken the Rents or Profits thereof by the space of one whole yeare, &c. vpon paine to forfeit the whole value of the Lands, &c. and the buyer or taker, &c. knowing the same, to forfeit also the value.

Thirdly, Prouided that it shall be lawfull for any person being in lawfull possession by taking of the yeerely Farme, Rents or Profits to obtaine and get the pretensed Right, or Title, &c. of any Lands whereof he or they shall be in lawfull possession.

For the better vnderstanding of which Statute, you must obserue, that title or right may be pretensed two manner of wayes.

First, when it is meerely in pretence or supposition, and nothing in veritie.

Secondly, when it is a good right or title in verity, and made pretensed by the act of the partie, and both these are within the said Statute; for example, If A bee lawfull Owner of Land and is in possession, B that hath no right thereunto granteth to or contracteth for the land with another, the Grantor and the Grantee (albeit the grant bee meerely void) are within the danger of the Statute. For B hath no right at all but only in pretence. If A bee disseised in this case A. hath a good lawfull right, yet if A being out of possession granteth to or contracteth for the Land with another, hee hath now made his good right of entrie pretensed within the Statute, and both the Grantor and Grantee within the danger thereof. A fortiori of a right in action. Quod nota.

Pl. Com fol. 80. &c. Partridges Case

It is further to bee knowne, that a right or title may bee considered three manner of wayes.

First, As it is naked and without possession. Secondly, When the absolute right commeth by Release or otherwise to a wrongfull possession, and no third person hath eyther Ius proprietatis, or Ius possessionis. The third, when he hath a good right, and a wrongfull possession. As to the first, somewhat hath beene said, and more shall bee said hereafter. As to the second, taking the former example, if A be disseised, and the Disseisee release vnto him, hee may presently sell, grant, or contract for the Land, and need not tarrie a yeare, for it is a rule vpon this Statute, that whosoeuer hath the absolute Ownership of any Land, Tenements, or Hereditaments (as in this case the Disseisor hath) there such Owner may at his pleasure bargaine, grant, or contract for the Land, for no person can thereby be prejudiced or grieued. And so if a man morgage his Land, and after redeeme the same, or if a man recouer Land vpon a former title, or be remitted to an ancient right, he may at any time bargaine, grant, or contract for the Land for the reason aforesaid. As to the third, if in the case aforesaid the Disseisor dieth seised, and A the Disseisee entreth, and disseise the heire of the Disseisor, albeit he hath an ancient right, yet seeing the possession is vnlawfull, if hee bargaine or contract for the Land before hee hath beene in possession by the space of a yeare, hee is within the danger of the Statute, because the heire of the Disseisor hath right to the possession, and he is thereby grieued, & sic de similibus, and albeit he that hath a pretensed right (and none in veritie) getteth the possession wrongfully, yet the Statute extendeth vnto him, as well as where he is out of possession.

Pl. Com. Partridges case vbi supra: 6. E. 6. Brook Tit. Maintenance. 38.

Note the words of the Statute be (any pretensed right) therefore a Lease for yeares is within the Statute, for the Statute saith not (the right) but any right) and the offendor shall forfeit the whole value of the Land. And where the Statute speaketh of rights in the plurall number, yet any one right is within the Statute. (a) But yet if a man make a lease for yeeres to another to the intent to try the title in an ejectione firmae that is out of the Statute,

23. Eliz. Dier 374. Pl. Com. Partridges case f. 8[illegible] (a) Mich. 30. & 31. Eliz. 2811. inter Finch & Cosham in Cōi Banco.

because it is in a kind of course of Law, but if it be made to a great man, or any other to sway or countenance the cause, that is within this Statute.

(b) Lib.4.fol.26. Copihold Cases.

Also the Statute speaks (of any right or title to any Land, &c.) (b) A customarie right or a pretence thereof to Lands holden by Copie is within this Statute.

6.E.6.tit.maintenance Brooke 38.

The said prouiso (which is rather added for explanation then of any necessitie) extendeth only to a pretensed right or title, and to a good and cleere right; and therefore without question, any that hath a iust and lawful estate may obtaine any pretensed right by release or otherwise; for that cannot bee to the preiudice of any, nay, as hath beene said, a Disseisor that hath a wrongfull estate may obtaine a release of the Disseisee, and that is not within the body of the Act, and consequently standeth not in need of any prouiso to protect him.

(c) 34.H.8.Dier 52.

And therefore (c) if there be Tenant for life, the Remaynder in fee by lawfull and iust title, he in the Remaynder may obtaine and get the pretensed right or title of any stranger, not only for that the particular Estate and the Remaynder are all one, but for that it is a meane to extinguish the seeds of troubles and suites, and cannot be to the preiudice of any, as hath beene said. And where the Statute saith, (being in lawful possession by taking the yearly Rent, &c.) those words are but explanatorie, and put for example, for howsoeuer hee be lawfully seised in possession, Reuersion, or Remaynder, it sufficeth though hee neuer tooke profit. But the matter obseruable vpon this Prouiso, which is worthy of obseruation, is, that if a Disseisor make a Lease for life, liues, or yeares, the Remaynder for life, in tayle, or in fee, hee in Remaynder cannot take a Promise or Couenant, that when the Disseisee hath entred vpon the Land or recouered the same, that then hee should conuey the Land to any of them in Remaynder thereby to auoid the particular estate, or the interest or estate of any other, for the words of the Prouiso be, (buy, obtaine, get or haue by any reasonable way or meane) and that is not by promise or couenant to conuey the Land after entry or recouery, for that is neyther lawfull being against the expresse purulew of the bodie of the Act, and not reasonable, because it is to the preiudice of a third person. But the reasonable way or meane intended by the Statute is by Release or Confirmation, or such Conueyances as amount to as much, and this agreeth with the letter of the Law, viz the pretensed Right or Title of any other person, and Rights and Titles are by Release or Confirmation, as by reasonable wayes and meanes lawfully transferred and extinct, and the words of Promise or Couenant, &c. which are prohibited by the body of the Act, are omitted in the Prouiso.

¶ *Relinquist le possession, &c.* This must bee vnderstood, that before liuery of seisin vpon the feoffment, A de B departed out of the house, for otherwise the liuery and seisin should be void, because A de B was in possession. And Littleton here saith, Per vn fait de feoffment, so as albeit the Deed were made before the departure it is not materiall, but the departure must be before the liuery of seisin, for that doth worke the disseisin. And yet that which Littleton saith is true, that the feoffment was the cause that he relinquished his possession, for otherwise he would not haue done it.

But admit that A de B had departed for any other cause, yet if F de G enter and enfeoffe certaine Barretors or Extortioners, or any other with warrantie, this is a warrantie that commenceth by disseisin, for that the feoffment worketh a disseisin.

Sect. 702.

See before in the Chapter of Releases.

¶ This doth explane that which hath beene said before. And albeit Littleton vseth the words (and incontinently thereof make a Feoffment) and that in this case of Littleton the Disseisin & Feoffment were made quasi vno tempore) yet if the Disseisin were made to the intent to make a feoffment with warranty, albeit the Feoffment be long after, this (as hath beene said) is a warranty

46.E.3.6.

¶ Item si hom̃ que nul droit ad denter en auters tenements, entra en mesmes les tenements, & incontinẽt ẽt fait vn feoffment as auters per son fait oue garranty, & deliuer a eux seisin, cel garranty commence per disseisin

Also if a man which hath no right to enter into other tenements enter into the same tenements, & incontinently make a feoffment therof to others by his deed with warranty & deliuer to them seisin, this warranty comence

sin, pur ceo que le disseisin et le feoffment fueront faits quasi uno tempore. Et q̃ ceo est ley, poiez veier en un plee M.11.Ed.3. en un briefe de Formedon en le reuerter.

by disseisin, because the disseisin and feoffment were made as it were at one time. And that this is lawe you may see in a plee *M.11 E.3.* in a writ of *Formedon* in the reuerter.

that commenceth by Disseisin.

¶. *Mich.* 11. *E.3.* This is mistaken and should be (d) 31.E.3. and so is the originall, which case you shall see in Master Fitzherberts Abridgement, for there is no booke at large of that yeare, whereby you may perceiue that learned men looke not only to the cases reported, but unto Records, as you may see Littleton did, for Fitzherb. put this case in print long after, as elsewhere hath beene shewed. (d) 31.E.3.tit.Garr.28.

Sect. 703.

¶ Garranty lineal est, lou home seisie de terres en fee, fait feoffment per son fait a un auter, & oblige luy et ses heires a garrantie, et ad issue et morust, et le garrantie discendist a son issue, ceo est lineal garranty. Et la cause pur ceo q̃ est d't lineal garrantie, nest pur ceo que le garranty discendist de le pier a son heire, mes la cause est pur ceo que si nul tiel fait oue garranty fuissoit fait per le pier, donque le droit d les tenemẽts discenderoit al heire, et lheire conueyeroit le discent de son pier, &c.

WArranty lineall is where a man seised of lands in fee, maketh a feoffment by his Deed to another, & bindes himselfe & his heires to warranty, and hath issue and die, and the Warranty discend to his issue, this is a lineal warranty. And the cause why this is called lineall warranty is not because the warrãty discendeth from the father to his heire, but the cause is for that if no such deed with warranty had beene made by the father, then the right of the tenements should discend to the heire, and the heire should conuey the discent frõ his father, &c.

¶ G*arranty lineal, &c.* A Warranty lineall is a Couenant reall annexed to the land by him which either was owner, or might haue inherited the land, and from whom his heire lineall or collaterall might by possibility haue claimed the land as heire from him that made the warranty, whereof Littleton himselfe putteth diuers cases, which shall bee explained in their proper places. And in this case put in this Section Littleton (once for all) sheweth, that the reason of the example here put, is because if no such alenation with Warranty (for so is Littleton to be intended) had beene made, the very lands had discended to the heire, so as the case being put of lands in fee simple, the alienation without the warranty had barred the heire. And note that it is called a lineall warranty, not because it must discend upon the lineall heire, for bee the heire lineall or collaterall, if by possibility he might claime the land from him that made the warranty, it is lineall, hauing regard to the Warrantie, and title of the land. And also it is called lineall, in respect that the warranty made by him that had no right or possibility of right to the land is called Collaterall, in regard that it is collaterall to the title of the land. And it is also to be obserued, that in all the cases that Littleton hath put or shall put the lineall or collaterall warranty doth binde the heire, and therefore the successor clayming in another right, shall not be bound by the warranty of any naturall Ancestor. For which cause (c) in a Iuris vtrum brought by a Parson of a Church, the collaterall warranty of his Ancestor is no barre, for that hee demandeth the land in the right of his Church in his politique capacitie, and the warrantie descendeth on him in his naturall capacitie. (d) But some haue holden that if a Parson bring an Assise, that a Collaterall warranty of his

35.E.3.Garr.73.

(c) 37.H.6.Garr.48.

(d) 34.E.3.Garr.72.

his Ancestor shall binde him, and their reason is, for that the Assise is brought of his possession and seisin, and he shall recouer the meane profits to his owne vse. But seeing he is seised of the freehold, whereof the Assise is brought in jure Ecclesiæ, which is in another right, then the Warranty, it seemeth that it should not be any barre in the Assise. The like Law is of a Bishop, Archdeacon, Deane, Master of an Hospitall, and the like, of their sole possessions, and of the Prebend, Vicar, and the like.

(*) 45. Ass. 6. 6. E. 3. 56. Pl. Com. 234. & 553. 554.

Et oblige luy & ses heires. * King H. 3. gaue a Mannor to Edmund Earle of Cornwall, and to the heires of his body, sauing the possibility of Reuerter, and dyed. The Earle before the Statute of W. 2. cap. 1. De donis conditionalibus by Deede gaue the said Mannor to another in fee with warranty in exchange for another Mannor, and after the said Statute in the 28. yeare of E. 1. dyeth without issue, leauing Assets in fee simple, which warranty and Assets descended vpon King E. 1. as Cosin germaine, and heire of the said Earle, viz. sonne and heire of King Henry the third, brother of Richard Earle of Cornwall, father of the said Earle Edmund. And it was adiudged, that the King as heire to the said Earle Edmund, was by the said warranty and Assets barred of the possibility of Reuerter, which he had expectant vpon the said gift, albeit the warranty and Assets descended vpon the naturall body of King E. 1. as heire to a subiect, and King E. 1. claymed the said Mannor, as in his Reuerter in jure Coronæ in the capacity of his body politique, in which right he was seised before the gift. In this case how by the death of the said Earle Edmund without issue, the Kings title by Reuerter, and the warranty, and Assets came together, and that the warranty was collaterall, yet the King shall not be barred without Assets as a subiect shall be, and many other things are to be obserued in this case which the learned reader will obserue.

Vid. 27. H. 6. Garr. 48. 34. E. 3. Garr. 71.

Vid. Sect. 711. 712.

Sect. 704. 705.

Car si soit pier & fits & le fits purchase terres en fee, et le pier de ceo disseisist son fits, et aliena a vn auter en fee per son fait; et per mesme le fait oblige luy et ses heires a garranter mesmes les tenements, &c. et le pier morust, ore est le fits barre dauer les dits tenements, car il ne poit per ascun suit, ne per auter meane de la ley, auer mesmes les terres per cause del dit garranty, et ceo est vn collateral garranty, et vncore le garranty discendist lynealment de le pier a le fits.

For if there be father and sonne, and the sonne purchase lands in fee, and the father of this disseiseth his sonne and alieneth to another in fee by his Deede, and by the same deed binde him and his heires to warrant the same tenements, &c. and the father dieth, now is the son barred to haue the said tenements, for hee cannot by any suite, nor by other meane of law haue the same lands by cause of the said warranty. And this is a collaterall Warranty, and yet the Warranty discendeth lineally from the father to the sonne.

Sect. 705.

Mes pur ceo que si nul tiel fait oue garr. vst estre fait, le fits en nul maner puissoit conueyer le title que il ad a les tenements de son pier a luy, entant que son pier nauoit ascun estate

But because if no such Deed with Warranty had beene made, the sonne in no manner could conuey the title which hee hath to the tenements from his father vnto him, inasmuch as his fa-

estate en droit en les tenements, pur ceo tiel garrantie est appel collateral garranty, entant que celuy que fist le garranty est collateral a le title de les tenemēts, et ceo est a tant adire que cestuy a que le garranty discendist, ne puissoit a luy conueier l' title que il ad de les tenements per my cestuy que fist le garrantie en cas que nul tiel garrantie fuit fait.

ther had no estate in right in the lands, wherefore such Warranty is called Collaterall warranty, inasmuch, as he that maketh the warranty is collateral to the title of the tenements, and this is as much to say, as hee to whom the warranty descendeth, could not conuey to him the title which hee hath in the tenements by him that made the warranty, in case that no such warranty were made.

¶ Here Littleton putteth an example, prouing that it is not called Lineall, because it descendeth lineally from the father to the sonne, for in this case the warranty descendeth lineally, and yet is a collaterall warranty. In this example you must intend that the Disseisin was not of intent to alien with warranty to barre the sonne, but here the Disseisin being done to the sonne, without any such intent, the alienation afterwards with warranty doth barre the sonne, because that albeit the warranty doth lineally discend, yet seeing the title is Collaterall, that is, that the sonne claymeth not the land as heire to his father, therefore in respect of the title it is a Collaterall warranty. And thus doth Littleton agree (c) with the Authority of our bookes. So as the diuersities doe stand thus. First, where the Disseisin and feoffment are vno tempore, and where at seuerall times. Secondly, where the Disseisin is with intent to alien with warranty, and where the Disseisin is made without such intent, and the alienation with warranty afterwards made.

5.E.3.14. 46.E.3.6. 19.H.8.12. 8.R.2.Gar.102. Vid.Sect.716.

(c) 46.E.3.6. 5.E.3.14. 19.H.8.12.

Sect. 706.

¶ Item si soit aiel, pier, et fits, et le aiel soit disseisie, en que possession le pier releas p son fait oue garrantie, &c. et morust, et puis laiel morust, ore le fits est barre dauer les tenements per le garranty del pier. Et ceo est appel lineal garrantie, pur ceo que si nul tiel garranty fuit, le fits ne puissoit conueyer le droit de les tenements a luy, ne monstre coment il est heire al Aiel fors-

Also if there bee grandfather father and son, and the grandfather is disseised, in whose possession the father releaseth by his Deed with warranty, &c. and dieth, and after the grandfather dieth, now the son is barred to haue the tenements by the warranty of the father. And this is called a lineal warranty, because if no such warranty were the son could not conuey the right of the tenements to him, nor

¶ Here Littleton putteth an example where the son must clayme the land as heire to his grandfather, and yet because hee cannot make himselfe heire to his grandfather but by his father, it is lineall.

And it is to bee obserued that the warranty in this case descended upon the son, before the discent of the right, which happened by the death of the grandfather in whom the right was, vide Littleton cap. de Releases, and after in this Chapter, Sect.707. & 741.

¶ *Pier release per son fait oue garranty.*

(f) It is to be knowne that upon euery conueyance of Lands, Tenements, or Hereditaments, as upon Fines, Feoffments, Gifts, &c. Releases and Confirmations made to the Tenant of the land,

1.H.4.33. 35.E.3.Gar.73.

(f) 14.E.3.voucher 108. 16.E.3.ibid.87. 18.E.3.ibid.6. 10.E.3.52. 21.E.3.27. 11.H.4.22. 44.E.3.Cont. de Vouch.22. 12.H.7.1. Vid.Sect.733.738.745.

land, a Warrantie may bee made, albeit he that makes the Release or Confirmation, hath no right to the Land, &c. but some do hold, That by release or confirmation, where there is no estate created, or transmutation of possession, a Warrantie cannot be made to the Assignee.

que per meane del pier.

shew how hee is heire to the grandfather but by means of the father.

Sect. 707.

¶ ITem si home ad issue deux fits & est disseisie, & leigne fits relessa al disseisor per son fait oue garranty, &c. & morust sans issue, & apres ceo le pier morust, ceo est vn lineall Garrantie al puisne fits, pur ceo que coment q leigne fits morust en la vie le pier, vncore pur ceo que per possibilitie, il puissoit estre q il puissoit conueier a luy le title dl terre per son eigne frere, si nul tiel Garrantie fuissoit. Car il puissoit estre que apres la mort le pier, leigne frere entroit en les tenements & morust sans issue, & donque le puisne fits conueyera a luy le title per leigne fits. Mes en tiel cas si le puisne fits relesse oue Garrantie a le disseisor, et morust sans issue ceo est vn collaterall Garrantie al eigne fits, pur ceo que de tiel terre que fuit al pier, leigne per nul possibility poit conueyer a luy le title per meane de le puisne fits.

ALso if a man hath issue two sonnes, and is disseised, and the eldest sonne release to the disseisor by his deed with Warranty, &c. and dies without issue, and afterwards the father dieth, this is a lineall warrantie to the younger sonne, because albeit the eldest sonne died in the life of the father, yet by possibility it might haue beene, that hee might conuey to him the Title of the Land by his elder brother, if no such Warranty had beene. For it might bee that after the death of the father the elder brother entred into the Tenements and died without issue, and then the yonger sonne shall conuey to him the title by the elder son. But in this case if the yonger son releaseth with warr' to the disseisor, & dieth without issue, this is a collateral war. to the elder son, because that of such lād as was the fathers, the elder by no possibility can conuey to him the title by meanes of the younger sonne.

35.E.3.Gar.73.11.H.4.33. ¶ HEre Litl. putteth an example, where the heire that is to be barred by the Warranty, is not to make his discent by him that made the Warrantie, as in the case before; and yet because by possibilitie he might haue claimed by the eldest sonne, if hee had suruiued the father, & died without issue, & so the yonger brother might by possibilitie haue been heire to him, the Warrantie is lineall.

And here it is to be noted, that the Warrantie of the eldest sonne discended before the right discended, whereof more shall be sayd hereafter Sect.741. and the opinion of Littleton in this Case is holden for Law, against the opinions in 35.E.3.Gar 73.

9.E.3.16. 38.E.3.21. 46.E.3.26.8.R.2.Gar.101. ¶ *Mes en tiel case le puisne fits release oue Garrantie, &c.* This Warrantie in this case is collaterall to the eldest sonne, and to the Issues of his bodie: but if the eldest sonne dieth without Issue of his bodie, then the Warrantie is lineall to the Issues of the bodie of the youngest: and so the Warrantie that was collaterall to some persons, may become lineall to others.

Sect. 708.

¶ Item si Tenant en le taile ad issue trois fits, et discontinue le Taile en fee, et le mulnes fits relessa per son fait al Discontinuee, et oblige luy et ses heirs a garrantie, &c. et puis le tenant en l' Tayle morust, et le mulnes fits morust sans issue, ore leigne fits est barre dauer ascun recouerie per Briefe de Formedon, pur ceo que le garrantie del mulnes frere est collaterall a luy, entant que il ne poit per nul manner conueyer a luy per force del taile ascun discent per le mulnes, et pur ceo cest vn colateral garrantie. Mes en cest Cas si leigne Fits deuie sans issue, ore l' puisne frere poit bien auer vn briefe de Formdon en le discender, et recouera mesme le tre, pur ceo que le Garrantie del mulnes est lineal al fits puisne, pur ceo que il puissoit estre que p possibilitie le mulnes puissoit estre seisie p force dl taile apres la mort son eigne frere, et

ALso if Tenaunt in Taile hath issue three sonnes, and discontinue the Tayle in fee, and the middle son release by his Deed to the Discontinuee, and bind him and his heirs to warrantie, &c. and after the tenant in taile dieth, and the middle sonne dieth without issue, now the eldest Son is barred to haue any recouerie by writ of *Formedon*, because the Warrantie of the middle brother is collaterall to him, in as much as he can by no meanes conuey to him by force of the Tayle any discent by the middle, and therefore this is a collateral warrantie. But in this case if the eldest sonne die without issue, now the yongest brother may well haue a writ of *Formdon* in the discender & shal recouer the same land, because the Warrantie of the middle is lineall to the yongest sonne, for that it might bee that by possibilitie the middle might be seised by force of the taile after the death of his eldest

¶ HEreby it also appeareth, That a warranty that is collaterall in respect of some persons, may afterwards become lineall in respect of others. whereupon it followeth,* That a Collateral warrantie doth not giue a Right, but bindeth onely a Right so long as the same continueth: but if the Collaterall warrantie be determined, remooued, or defeated, the Right is reuiued; (f) And yet in an Assise the Plaintife hath made his title by a Collateral warrantie.

8.R.2.Gar.101.

* 43.Ass.44. 24 H.8. tit. Taile Br. 7.H.5.6.tit. Ass.359. 34.E.3. Droit 29. 19.H.6.59. 21.H.7.40. 5.H.7.29. 3.H.7.9.b.

(f) 16.Ass.p.16. 27.Ass.74. 29.Ass.50. 43.Ass.8. 14.H.4.13. 19.H.6.60.

¶ *Barre* is a word common as well to the English as to the French, of which cometh the nown, a bar Barra. It signifieth legally a destruction for euer, or taking away for a time of the Action of him that right hath. And Barra is an Italian word, and signifieth Barre, as we vse it, and it is called a Plea in Barre, when such a Barre is pleaded. Here Littl. putteth an example of a barre of an estate taile by a Collaterall warrantie. It is to be obserued, That in some Cases an Estate taile may be barred by some Acts of Parliament made since Littleton wrote, and in some cases an Estate taile cannot be barred, which might when Littleton wrote haue beene barred. For example, If Tenant in Tayle leuie a Fine with Proclamations according to the statute, this is a barre to the Estate taile, but not to him in reuersion or remainder, if hee maketh his claime, or pursue his Action within fiue yeares after the state Taile spent.

4.H.7.ca.24. & 32.H.8.c.36

(b) If a gift be made to the eldest sonne, and to the heires of his bodie, the remainder to the father and to the heires of his bodie, the father dieth, the eldest sonne leuieth a Fine with proclamations, & dieth with-

(b) Dalison 2.El. & 7.El. Vi.li.3.fo.84. le case de Fines.

without issue, this shal barre the second sonne for the remainder descended to the eldest.

If tenant in taile bee disseised, or haue a right of action, and the Tenant of the land levy a fine with proclamations, and fiue yeares passe, the right of the estate taile is barred.

donque le puisne frere puissoit conueyer son title de discent per le mulnes.

brother, and then the yōgest brother might conuey his title of discent by the middle brother.

(b) 26.H.8.ca.13. 33.H.8.ca 20. 5.&6.E.6.ca.11. Stanf.Pl.Coron.18.

(b) If Tenant in taile in possession, or that hath a Right of entrie bee attainted of high treason, the estate taile is barred, and the land is forfeited to the King; and none of these were barres when Littleton wrote. A lineall Warrantie and Assets was a barre to the estate tayle when Littleton wrote, whereof more shall be said hereafter.

(c) 12.E.4.19. Taltarums case.
(d) Vid.devant Sect.690. Vid.lib.3.fo.5. Cuppledikes case, & fo.94.97.106. Lib.1.fo.62. Capells case. Lib.2 fo.16.52.74 77. Lib.6.fo.41.32.lib 10.fo.37. Mary Portingtons case.
(e) 33.H.8.taile Br.41. Pl.Com.fo.555. 29.H.8.D.er 52.
(f) 34.H.8 ca.20.

(c) A common recouery with a Voucher ouer, and a Judgement to recouer in value was a barre of the estate taile when Littleton wrote. (d) And of Common recoueries there be two sorts, viz. one with a single Voucher, and another with a double Voucher, and that is more common and more safe: there may be more Vouchers ouer.

(e) If the King had made a gift in taile, and the Donee had suffered a Common recouery, this should haue barred the estate taile in Littletons time, but not the reuersion or remainder in the King. And so if such a Donee had levied a fine with Proclamations after the Statute of 4.H.7. this had barred the estate taile, although the reuersion was in the King. (f) But since Littleton wrote a Common recouery had against Tenant in taile of the Kings gift, or such a fine levied by him, the reuersion continuing in the Crowne, is no barre to the estate taile by the Statute of 34. H, 8. And where the words of the Statute bee (whereof the reuersion or remainder at the time of such recouery had shall be in the King) these Ten things are to be obserued upon the construction of that act.

First, that the estate taile must be created by a King, and not by any subiect, albeit the King be his heire to the reuersion, for the Preamble speakes of gifts made to subiects, and none can haue subiects but the King. And also in the Preamble it is said (for seruice done to the Kings of the Realme) and the body of the act referreth to the Preamble. (g) And therefore if the Duke of Lancaster had made a gift in taile, and the reuersion descended to the King, yet was not that estate tayle restrained by that Statute, and so of the like.

(g) Trin.23.Eliz.inter Dively & Ashton resolued in the Court of Wards. Lib.2.fol.15. & 16.in Wisemans case.

Secondly, If the King grant ouer the Reuersion, then a recouery suffered will barre the state tayle, because the King had no Reuersion at the time of the recouery.

Lib 8.fol.77.78. The Lord Staffords case.

Thirdly, If the King make a gift in tayle, the remaynder in tayle, or grant the Reuersion in tayle, keeping the Reuersion in the Crowne, a recouery against Tenant in tayle in possession shall neyther barre the estate tayle in possession by the expresse purview of the Statute, nor by consequence the state in Remaynder or Reuersion, for that the Reuersion or Remaynder cannot be barred, but where the Estate tayle in possession is barred.

Lib.2.fol.15.16.Wisemans case. Lib.2.fol.52.Cholmleis Case.

Fourthly, If a subiect make a gift in tayle, the Remaynder to the King in fee, albeit the words of the Statute be, (whereof the Reuersion or Remaynder of the same, &c.) yet seeing the estate in tayle was not created by a King, as hath beene said, the estate tayle may be barred by a common recouery.

Fiftly, If Prince Henry Sonne of Henry the Seuenth, had made a gift in tayle, the Remaynder to Henry the Seuenth in fee, which Remaynder by the death of Henry the Seuenth had discended to Henry the Eighth, so as he had the Remaynder by discent, yet might Tenant in tayle, for the cause aforesaid, barre the estate tayle by a common recouery.

Lib.2.fol.16.Wisemans case

Sixtly, The word (Remaynder) in the Statute is no vaine word, for the words of the preamble be, The King hath giuen or granted or otherwise prouided to his Seruants and Subiects. The word (Reuersion) in the body of the Act hath reference to these words (giuen or granted) and (Remaynder) hath reference to these words (otherwise prouided.) As if the King in consideration of Money, or of assurance of Land, (or for other consideration by way of prouision, procure a Subiect by Deed indented and inrolled to make a gift in tayle to one of his Seruants and Subiects for recompence of seruice, or other consideration, the Remaynder to the King in fee, and all this appeare of Record, this is a good prouision within the Statute, and the Tenant in tayle cannot by a common recouery barre the estate tayle. So it is, if the Remaynder be limited to the King in tayle: but if the Remaynder be limited to the King for yeares, or for life, that is no such Remaynder, as is intended by the Statute, because it is of no Remaynder of continuance, as it ought to bee, as it appeareth by the preamble, and it ought to haue some affinitie with a Reuersion, wherewith it is ioyned.

Seuenthly, where a common recouery cannot barre the state tayle by force of the said Statute, there a fine levied in fee, in tayle, for liues, or yeares with Proclamations according to the Statutes, shall not barre the state tayle, or the issue in tayle where the Reuersion or Re-

maynder

mayner is in the King, as is aforesaid, by reason of these words in the said Act, (the said recouery or any other thing or things hereafter to be had, done, or suffered by or against any such Tenant in tayle to the contrary notwithstanding) which words include a fine leuied by such a Donee, and restrayneth the same.

So resolued Pasch. 31. Eliz. Rot. 1645. in Netleys case in Communi Banco.

Eightly, But where a common recouery shall barre the estate tayle, notwithstanding that Statute, there a fine with Proclamations shall barre the same also.

Ninthly, where the said latter words of the Statute be (had, done, or suffered by or against any such Tenant in tayle) the sence and construction is, where Tenant in tayle is partie or priuie to the Act, be it by doing or suffering that which should worke the barre, and not by meere permission he being a stranger to the Act.

As if Tenant in tayle of the gift of the King, the reuersion to the King expectant, is disseised, and the Disseisor leuie a fine, and fiue yeares passe, this shall barre the estate tayle: and so if a collaterall Ancestor of the Donee release with warrantie, and the Donee suffer the Warranty to discend without any entry made in the life of the Ancestor, this shall bind the Tenant in tayle, because hee is not partie or priuie to any Act, either done or suffered by or against him.

So holden Trin. 39. Eliz. Rot. 1914. inter Stratford & Dower in Communi Banco.

Tenthly, Albeit the preamble of the Statute extend only to gifts in tayle made by the Kings of England before the Act (viz hath giuen and granted, &c.) and the bodie of the Act referreth to the preamble (viz that no such feined recouerie hereafter to be had against such Tenant in tayle) so as this word (such) may seeme to couple the bodie and the preamble together, yet in this case (such) shall be taken for such in equall mischiefe, or in like case, and by diuers parts of the Act it appeareth, that the makers of the Act intended to extend it to future gifts, and so is the Law taken at this day without question.

A recouery in a Writ of Right against Tenant in tayle without a Voucher is no barre of any gift in tayle.

If Tenant in tayle the remaynder ouer in fee cesse, and the Lord recouer in a Cessauit, this shall not barre the estate tayle, for the issue shall recouer in a Formedon: neither were eyther of these barres when Littleton wrote. But let vs now heare Littleton.

33. E. 3. iudgement 252. 3. H. 6. 55. 10. H. 6. c. 14. E. 4. 5. b. 15. E. 4. 8. F. N. B. 134. b. Pl. Com. 237. 28. E. 3. 95. F. N. B. 28. I.

Section 709.

Item si Tenant en taile disconti- nua le taile, & ad issue & deuy, & luncle del issue relessa al discontinuee oue Garrantie, &c. & morust sans issue, ceo est collateral Garrantie al issue en tayle, pur ceo que le Garrantie discendist sur lissue, le quel ne poit soy conueyer a le tayle per meane de son vncle.

Also if tenant in tayle discontinue the taile and hath issue and dieth, and the Vncle of the issue release to the Discontinuee with Warrantie, &c. and dieth without issue, this is a collaterall Warrantie to the issue in tayle, because the Warrantie discendeth vpon the issue, that cannot conuey himselfe to the entayle by meanes of his vncle.

The reason wherefore the warrantie of the Vncle hauing no right to the Land entailed shall barre the issue in tayle is for that the Law presumeth that the Vncle would not vnnaturally disherit his lawfull heire being of his own bloud, of that right which the Vncle neuer had, but came to the heire by another mean, vnlesse hee would leaue him greater aduancement. Nemo præsumitur alienam posteritatem suæ prætulisse. And in this case the Law will admit no proof against that which the Law presumeth. And so it is of all other Collaterall warranties for no man is presumed to doe any thing against nature.

Pl. Com. fol. 307. a. in Shelingtons case.

(k) And the like holdeth in some other Cases, as if a Rent be behind for twenty yeares, and the Lord make an Acquittance for the last that is due, all the rest are presumed to bee paid, and the Law will admit no proofe against this presumption. (l) So if a man bee within the foure Seas, and his wife hath a child, the Law presumeth that it is the child of the husband, and against this presumption the Law will admit no proofe.

(k) 11. H. 4. 33. 10. Eliz. Dier 271.

(l) 7. H. 4. 9.

(m) If a man that is innocent bee accused of Felony, and for feare flieth for the same, al-

(m) 3. E. 3. Corone Staunf.

beit he iudicially acquitteth himselfe of the Felonie, yet if it be found that he fled for the Felony, he shall notwithstanding his innocencie forfeit all his Goods and Chattels, Debts and Duties, for as to the forfeiture of them the Law will admit no proofe against the presumption in Law grounded vpon his flight: and so in many other Cases. But yet the generall rule is, Quod stabitur presumptioni donec probetur in contrarium. But as you see it hath many exceptions.

Bracton lib. 1. cap. 9.

(n) It hath beene attempted in Parliament, that a Statute might bee made, that no man should be barred by a warrantie collaterall, but where Assets discend from the same Ancestor: but it neuer tooke effect, for that it should weaken common Assurances.

(n) Rot. Parliament. 50. E. 3. num. 77.

Sect. 710.

¶ Item si le tenant en taile ad issue deux files & morust, et leigne entra en le entierty & ent fait vn feoffment ē fee oue garrantie, &c. et puis leigne file morust sans issue, en cest cas le puisne file est barre quant al vn moity, et quant al auter moity el nest pas barre. Car quant a la moity que affiert a le puisne file, el est barre, pur ceo que quant a cel part el ne poit conueyer le discent per my le maine de son eigne soer et pur ceo quant a cel moity, ceo est vn collaterall Garranty. Mes quant al auter moity que affiert a son eigne soer, le Garranty nest pas barre a le puisne soer, pur ceo q̄ el poit conueyer s̄ discent, quant a cel moity que affiert a son eigne soer per mesme le eigne soer, issint quant a cest moity que affiert al eigñ soer, le Garran-

ty

ALso if the Tenant in tayle hath issue two daughters and dieth, and the elder entreth into the whole, and thereof maketh a feoffment in fee with warrantie, &c. and after the elder daughter dieth without issue. In this case the yonger daughter is barred as to the one moitie and as to the other moitie she is not barred. For as to the moitie which belōgeth to the yonger daughter, shee is barred, because as to this part shee cannot conuey the discent by means of her elder sister, and therefore as to this moitie, this is a collaterall Warrantie. But as to the other moitie, which belongeth to her elder sister, the Warrantie is no bar to the younger sister because she may conuey her discent as to that moitie which belongeth to her elder sister by the same elder sister, So as to this moitie which be-

¶ *A Dissue deux files.* If husband and wife Tenants in especiall tayle haue issue a Daughter, and the wife die, the husband by a second wife hath issue another daughter, and discontinueth in fee and dieth, a collateral Ancestor of the Daughters releaseth to the discontinuee with warrantie and dieth, the warrantie discendeth vpon both daughters, yet the issue in taile shall be barred of the whole, for in iudgement of Law the entire warrantie discendeth vpon both of them.

5. E. 2. Garr. 78. lib. 8. fol. 41. Symes Case.

¶ *Et leigne enter en lentiertie & ent fait vn feoffement, &c.* Here it is to bee vnderstood, that when one Coparcener doth generally enter into the whole, this doth not deuest the estate which discended by the Law to the other, vnlesse she that doth enter claymeth the whole, and taketh the profits of the whole, for that shall deuest the freehold in Law of the other Parcener.

See before in the Chapter of Discent, Sect. 398.

Otherwise it is after the Parceners be actually seised, the taking of the whole profits or any clayme made by the one cannot out the other out of possession without an

ty est lineall al puisne soer.

longeth to the elder sister the Warrantie is lineal to the yonger sister.

Sect. 711.

¶ E nota q̃ quant a celuy que demanda fee simple per ascun de ses auncesters, il serra barre per Garranty lineall que discendist sur luy, sinon que soit restraine per ascun estatute.

AND note, that as to him that demandeth fee simple by any of his Ancestors he shall be barred by Warrantie lineall which discendeth vpon him, vnlesse he be restrained by some Statute.

Sect. 712.

¶ Mes il que demande fee taile per briefe de Formedon en discender, ne serra my barre per lineall Garrantie, sinon que il ad assets per discent en fee simple per mesm launcester que fist le Garranty. Mes collateral Garranty est barre a celuy que demanda fee, et auxy a celuy que demaunda fee tayle sans ascun auter discent de fee simple, sinon en cases queux sont restraines per les estatutes, & auters cases pur certaine causes, come serra dit en apres.

BVt hee that demandeth Fee tayle by Writ of *Formedon in discender*, shall not bee barred by lineall Warrantie, vnlesse hee hath assets by discent in fee simple by the same Ancestor that made the Warrantie. But collaterall Warrantie is a barre to him that demandeth fee, and also to him that demandeth fee Tayle without any other discent of fee simple, except in cases which are restrained by the Statutes, and, in other cases for certaine causes, as shalbe said hereafter.

actuall putting out or disseisin. And in this case of Littleton, when one Coparcener entreth into the whole, and maketh a feoffment of the whole, this deuesteth the freehold in Law out of the other Coparcener.

Now seeing the entry in this case of Lit. deuested not the estate of the other Parcener, if no further proceeding had beene, then it is to bee demanded, that seeing the feoffment doth worke the wrong, & bee the wrong either a disseisin or in nature of an abatement, how can the Warrantie annexed to that feoffment that wrought the wrong be collaterall or bind the youngest Sister for her part? To this it is answered, that when the one sister entreth into the whole, the possession being void, and maketh a feoffment in fee, this Act subsequent doth so explaine the entrie precedent into the whole, that now by construction of Law, shee was only seised of the whole, and this feoffment can bee no disseisin, because the other sister was neuer seised, nor any abatement, because they both made but one heire to the Ancestor, and one Freehold and Inheritance discended to them. So as in iudgement of Law the Warranty doth not commence by disseisin or by abatement, and without question her entrie was no intrusion. *Pl. Com.* 543.

Tenant in tayle hath issue two daughters, and discontinueth in fee the youngest disseiseth the discontinuee to the vse of her selfe and her sister, the Discontinuee ousteth her, against whom she recouereth in an Assise, the eldest agreeth to the Disseisin, as she may against her sister, and becoms Ioyntenant with her. And thus is the Booke in the 21. Assise (n) to be intended, the case being no other in effect, but A disseiseth the one to the vse of himselfe and B, B agreeth, by this he is Ioyntenant with A. (n) 21. *Ass. p.* 19.

¶ *Et nota que quant a celuy que demanda fee simple, &c.* **In these two** Sections there are expressed foure legall conclusions:

3. E. 3. 22. 4. E. 3. 28 50. 6 E. 3 56. 7. E. 3. 54 57. 9. E. 4. 16 10. E. 3. 14. 13. E. 3 Garrant. 27. 20. E. 3 Iudg 29. 25. E. 3. 50. 37. E. 3. 8 3. 41. E 3. Garr. 16. Mich 38 E. 3 Coram Rege Abbot de Colchesters case. 45 Ass 6. Pl. Com. 554. 19. E. 4 10. Vid. Sect. 703 747.

First, That a lineall warrantie doth bind the right of a Fee simple.

Secondly, That a lineall warrantie doth not bind the right of an Estate taile, for that it is restrained by the Statute of Donis conditionalibus.

Thirdly, That a lineall warrantie and assets is a barre of the right in Taile, and is not restrained (as hath beene sayd) by the sayd Act.

Fourthly, That a Collaterall warrantie made by a Collaterall Ancestor of the Donee, doth bind the right of an estate taile, albeit there be no Assets, and the reason thereof is upon the Statute of Donis conditionalibus, for that it is not made by the Tenant in taile, &c. as the lineall warranty is.

To this may be added, that the warranty of the Donee in taile which is collaterall to the Donor, or to him in remainder, being heire to him doth binde them without any assets. For though the alienation of the Donee after issue doth not barre the Donor, which was the mischiefe provided for by the Act, yet the warranty being collateral doth barre both of them, for the Act restraineth not that warranty, but it remaineth at the Common Law as Littleton after saith: and in like manner the warranty of the Donee doth barre him in the remainder.

¶ *Assets.* (id est) quod tantundem valet, **sufficient by discent.**

Fleta lib. 2. ca. 65. Britton 185. 4 E. 3. Garr. 63. 16. E. 3 Assets 4. 42. E. 3. 9. 7. H. 6. 3. 11 H. 4 20.

Note Assets requisite to make a lineall warranty a barre must have sixe qualities. First, it must be assets (that is) of equall value, or more at the time of the Discent. Secondly, it must be of discent, and not by purchase or gift. Thirdly, as Littleton here saith, it must be assets in fee simple and not in taile, or for another mans life. Fourthly, it must descend to him as heire to the same Ancestor that made the warranty as Littleton also here saith. Fiftly, it must be of lands or tenements, or rents or services valuable, or other profits issuing out of lands or tenements and not personall inheritances as Annuities, and the like. Sixtly, it must be in state or interest, and not in use or right of actions or rights of entrie, for they are no assets untill they be brought into possession. (a) But if a rent in fee simple issuing out of the land of the heire descend unto him whereby it is extinct, yet this is assets, and to this purpose hath in iudgement of Law a continuance.

24. E. 3. 47.

(a) 22. E 3. Assets 5. 31. E. 3. Recovery in value 17. E 6. 1. fo 31 Butler & Bakers case. (b) 14. E. 3 Mesne 3. Regist. 253. (c) Fleta lib. 2. ca 65. Britton, fo. 185. Extent. manerii. 3. H. 7. 37. 32. H. 6. 21. 33 E. 3. Gar. 102

(b) A Seigniory in free Almoigne is no assets, because it is not valuable, and therefore not to be extended, and so it seemeth of a Seigniory of Homage and fealty But an Advowson is Assets whereof (c) Fleta saith; Item de Ecclesiis quæ ad donationem domini pertinent quot sunt, & quæ, & vbi, & quantum valeat quælibet Ecclesia per annum secundum veram ipsius æstimationem, & pro marca solidus extendatur, vt si Ecclesia centum marcas valeat per annum, ad centum solidos extendatur aduocatio per annum. And herewith agreeth Britton, and others have reckoned a shilling in the pound, and Britton addeth further, Mes si la aduowson duist estre vendue, adonques sert' le reasonable price solonque le value en vn an a ccl extent. Wherein it is to be observed, that Antiquity did ever reckon by markes.

Sect. 713.

¶ Item si terre soit done a un home et a les heires de son corps engendres, le quel prent feme, et ont issue fits enter eux, & le baron discontinua le taile en fee, et deuy, et puis la feme relessa al discontinuee en fee oue garrantie, &c. et morust, & le garrantie discendist a le fits, c̄ est un collateral garrantie.

ALso if land bee given to a man and to the heires of his body begotten, who taketh wife, and have issue a sonne betweene them, and the husband discontinues the taile in fee and dieth, and after the wife releaseth to the Discontinuee in fee with warranty, &c. & dyeth, and the warrantie discends to the son, this is a collaterall warranty.

¶ This case standeth upon the same reason that divers other formerly put by our Author, doe, viz. that because the heire claymeth only from the father Per formam doni, and nothing from the wife, that therefore the warrantie of the wife is collaterall, and the warrantie made by any Ancestor male or female of the wife bindeth, and here the warrantie descended after the discent of the right.

Section 714.

¶ Mes si tenements soyent dones a le baron et a sa feme, et a les heires de lour deux corps engendres, queux ont issue fits, et le baron discontinua le taile et morust, et puis la feme relessa oue garrantie et morust, cest garranty nest forsque un lineal garranty a le fits: Car le fits ne serra barre en ceo cas de suer son bre de Formedon, sinon que il ad assets per discent en fee simple per sa mere, pur ceo que lour lissue en briefe de Formedon covient conveyer a luy le droit come heire a son pere et a sa mere de lour deux corps engendres, per forme del done, et issint en tiel case, le garrantie de le pere, et le garrantie de la mere ne sont forsque lyneal garr̃ al heire, &c.

BVt if lands be giuen to the husband & wife, and to the heires of their two bodies begotten, who haue issue a son, and the husband discontinue the taile and dyeth, and after the wife release with warranty and dieth, this warranty is but a lineall warranty to the son: For the sonne shall not be barred in this case to sue his writ of *Formedon*, vnlesse that he hath Assets by discent in fee simple by his mother, because their issue in the writ of *Formd.* ought to conuey to him the right as heire to his father and mother of their two bodies begotten *Per formam doni*, and so in this case the warranty of the father and the warrantie of the mother are but lineall warranty to the heire, &c.

¶ HEre is a point worthy of obseruation, that albeit in this case the issue in taile must claime as heire of both their bodyes, yet the warranty of either of them is lineall to the issue, and yet the issue cannot claime as heire to either of them alone, but of both. 33.E.3.tit. Garr.73.

If lands be giuen to a man and to a woman vnmarried, and the heires of their two bodyes, and they entermarry, and are disseised, and the husband release with warranty, the wife dieth, the husband dieth, albeit the Donees did take by moyties, yet the warranty is lineall for the whole, because as our Author here saith, the issue must in a Formedon conuey to him the right as heire to his father and his mother of their two bodyes engendrez, and therefore it is collaterall for no part.

Sect. 715.

¶ Et nota que en chescun cas ou home demanda tenements en fee taile per briefe de Formedon, si ascun del issue en le taile que auoit possession ou que nauoit ascun possession fait un garranty, &c. si celuy que suist le briefe d Formedon puissoit per ascun possibility per matter que puissoit estre en fait, conueyer a luy per my celuy que fist le garranty

ANd note that in euery case where a man demandeth lands in fee taile by Writ of *Formedon* if any of the issue in taile that hath possession, or that hath not possession make a warranty, &c. if hee which sueth the writ of *Formedon* might by any possibility by matter which might bee in fait, conueye to him, by him that made the warranty *Per formam doni*, this is a li-

ranty per forme del done, ceo est vn lineal garr, & ney collateral.

neall warranty and not collaterall.

35. E. 3. Garr. 73.

¶ Of this sufficient hath beene said before, Sed nunquam nimis dicitur quod nunquàm satis dicitur, for it is a point of great vse and consequence.

Sect. 716, 717.

¶ Item si home ad issue trois fits, et il dona Terre al eigne fits, a auer et tener a luy et a les heires de son corps engendres, et pur default de tiel Issue, le remainder al mulnes fits a luy, et a les heires de son corps engendres, et pur default de tiel issue del mulnes, le remainder al puisne fits et les heires de son corps engendres, en cest cas si leigne discontinua le Tayle en fee, et oblige luy et ses heyres a garrantie, et morust sans Issue, ceo est vn collaterall Garrantie al mulnes fits, et serra barre a demaunder mesme la Terre per force del remainder, pur ceo que le remainder est son title, et son eigne frere est collaterall a cel title, que commence per force del remainder. En mesme le maner est, si le mulnes fits auoit mesme la terre per force del remainder, pur ceo que son eigne frere ne fist ascun discontinuance, mes morust sans issue de son corps et puis le mulnes fait vn discontinuance oue garrantie, &c. et morust sans issue, ceo est vn collaterall Garrantie a le puisne fits. Et auxy en cest case si ascun de les dits fits soit disseisie, et le pere que fist le done, &c. relessa a le Disseisor tout son droit oue Garrantie, ceo est vn collaterall garrantie a celuy fits sur que le Garranty discendist, Causa qua supra.

ALso if a man hath Issue three sonnes, and giueth land to the eldest sonne, to haue and to hold to him and to the heires of his bodie begotten, and for default of such issue, the remainder to the middle sonne, to him and to the Heires of his bodie begotten, and for default of such issue of the middle sonne, the remainder to the yongest Son and to the heires of his bodie begotten; In this case if the eldest discontinue the taile in fee, & bind him & his heires to Warrantie, and dieth without issue, this is a collaterall warrantie to the middle son, & shal be a bar to demand the same land by force of the Rem', for that the remainder is his title, and his elder brother is collaterall to this title, which commenceth by force of the remainder. In the same manner it is if the middle son hath the same land by force of the Remainder, because his eldest brother made no discontinuance, but died without Issue of his bodie, and after the middle make a discontinuance with warrantie, &c. and dieth without issue, this is a collaterall warrantie to the youngest son. And also in this case if any of the sayd sonnes be disseised, and the Father that made the gift, &c. releaseth to the disseisor all his right with war, this is a collaterall warranty to that Son vpon whom the warranty discendeth, *Causa qua supra*.

Sect. 717.

ET sic nota, Que lou home que est collateral a le Title, et ceo release oue Garrantie, &c. ceo est un Collaterall Garrantie.

ANd so note, That where a Man that is collaterall to the Title, and releaseth this with Warrantie, &c. this is a collaterall Warrantie.

HEre it appeareth, That it is not adjudged in Law a Collaterall warrantie, in respect of the blood, for the warrantie may be collaterall, albeit the blood be lineall, and the warrantie may be lineall, albeit the blood be collaterall, as hath beene said. But it is in Law deemed a Collaterall warrantie, in respect that he that maketh the warrantie is collaterall to the title of him upon whom the warrantie doth fall, as by the example which Littleton here putteth, and by that which hath beene formerly sayd, is manifest. 8.E.2.*Gar*.101.*V.Sect*.704

Sect. 718.

ITem si Pier dona Terre a son eigne fits, a auer & tenir a luy & a ses heires Males de son corps engendres, le Remainder a le second fits, &c. si leigne fits alienast en fee oue ceo Garrantie, &c. et ad issue female, et morust sans issue male, ceo nest pas collaterall Garrantie al second fits, car il ne serra barre de son action de Formedon en le remainder, pur ceo que le Garranty discendist al file del eigne fits, et nemy al second fits. Car chescun Garrantie que discendist, discendist a celuy que est heire a luy que fist le Garrantie per le Commõ Ley.

ALso if a father giueth land to his eldest sonne, to haue and to hold to him and to the Heirs males of his bodie begotten, the remainder to the second sonne, &c. if the eldest sonne alieneth in fee with warranty, &c. & hath issue female, & dieth without Issue male, this is no collaterall warrantie to the second Son, for he shall not be barred of his Action of *Formedon* in the Remainder, because the warr discended to the daughter of the elder son, & not to the secõd son: for euery warrãty which discends, discẽdeth to him that is heir to him who made the Warrantie by the Common Law.

HEre is rehearsed a Maxime of the Common law, that euery warrantie doth discend upon him that is heire to him that made the warranty, by the Common Law, as by this example it appeareth. V.Sect.3.603.735.736.737.

A celuy que est heire a luy que fist le Garrantie per le Common ley, &c. Hereupon many things worthie to bee knowne are to be understood. (a) First, That if a man infeoffeth another of an acre of ground with warrantie, and hath Issue two sonnes, and dieth seised of another acre of land, of the nature of Burrough English, the feoffee is impleaded, albeit the warrantie discendeth onely upon the eldest sonne, yet may hee vouch them both; the one as heyre to the warrantie, & the other as heire to the land: for if he should vouch the eldest sonne onely, then should hee not haue the fruit of his warrantie, viz. a recouerie in value, the yongest sonne only he cannot vouch, because hee is not heire at the Common Law, upon whom the warrantie discendeth. (a) 40.E.3.14.

(b) So it is of heyres in Gauelkind, the eldest may be vouched as heire to the warrantie, and the other sonnes in respect of the Inheritance discen- (b) 22.E.4.10.4.E.3.35. 47.E.6.1.4.[illegible].E.3.Vou.

ded

(c) 49. Aſſ. 4. 38. E. 3. 22.

(d) 32. E. 3. Vouch. 94. 35. H. 6. 33.

ded unto them. (c) And in like sort, the heire at the Common Law, and the heire of the part of the mother shall be bouched. But the heire at the Common Law may bee bouched alone in both these cases, at the election of the Tenant, & *sic de similibus*. (d) In the same manner if a man dieth seised of certaine lands in fee, hauing issue a sonne and a daughter by one Venter, and a sonne by another, the eldest sonne entreth and dieth, the land discends to the sister, In this case the Warrantie discendeth on the sonne, and he may be bouched as Heire, and the Sister as heire of the Land: In which and the other case of Burrough English, the sonne and heyre by the Common Law hauing nothing by discent, the whole losse of the recouerie in value lieth upon the heires of the land, albeit they be no heires to the Warrantie. Then put the case that there is a Warrantie paramount, who shall deraigne that Warrantie? and to whom shall the recompence in value goe? Some haue sayd, That as they are bouched together, so shall they auouch ouer, and that the recompence in value shal enure according to the losse, and that the effect must pursue the cause, as a recouerie in value by a Warrantie of the part of the mother shall goe to the heire of the part of the mother, &c.

Pl. Com. 515.

Some others hold, That it is against the Maxime of Law, that they that are not heyres to the Warrantie should ioyne in Voucher, or to take benefit of the Warrantie which discended not to them, but that the heire at the Common Law, to whom the Warrantie discended shall deraigne the Warrantie, and recouer in value, and that this doth stand with the rule of the Common Law.

(e) 17. E. 2. tit. Recouer. in value 33. 1. E. 3. 12. 33 Edw. 3. Iudgm. 222, 14. E. 3. ib. 160. 10. E. 3. 52. 18. E. 3 51. Li. 1. fo. 96. Shelleys case. (f) 32. E. 3. Vouch. 94. & Greene.

Others hold the contrarie, and that this should be both against the rule of Law, and against reason also; for by the rule of Law (e) the Vouchee shall neuer sue to haue execution in value, untill execution be sued against him. But in this case Execution can neuer be sued against the heire at the Common Law, therefore he cannot sue to haue execution ouer in value. Secondly, It should be against reason, that the heire at the Common Law should haue *totum lucrum*, and the speciall heires *totum damnum*. I find in our Bookes, (f) that this reason is yeelded, that the speciall heire should not be bouched onely; For (say they) if the speciall heires should bee bouched onely, then could not they deraigne the Warrantie ouer, which should bee mischieuous, that they should lose the benefit of the Warrantie, if they should be bouched onely. But if the heire at the Common law were bouched with them, (as by the law he ought) all might bee saued, and therefore studie well this poynt how it may be done.

(g) V. Pl. Com. fo. 514.

(g) If Tenant in generall Tayle be, and a common recouerie is had against him and his wife, where his wife hath nothing, and they bouch, and haue iudgement to recouer in value, tenant in Taile dieth, and the wife suruiueth; for that the Issue in Tayle had the whole losse, the recompence shal enure wholly to him, and the wife, albeit she was partie to the iudgement, shall haue nothing in the recompence, for that she loseth nothing.

(h) 17. E. 3. 59. 20. E. 3. Vouch. 129. 32. E. 3. Vouch. 94. 5. H. 7. 2.

(h) If the Bastard eigne enter and take the profits, he shall be bouched onely, and not the bastard & the Mulier, because the Bastard is in apparance heire, and shall not disable himselfe.

(i) 11. H. 7. 12. 11. E. 3. tit. Det. 7. Dy. 5. El. 238.

(i) If a man be seised of lands in Gauelkind, and hath issue three sonnes, and by Obligation bindeth himselfe and his heires, and dieth, an Action of Debt shall be maintainable against all the three sonnes, for the heire is not chargeable unlesse he hath lands by discent.

(k) 11. H. 7. 12.

(k) So if a man be seised of Land on the part of his mother, and bind himselfe and his heirs by Obligation, and dieth, an Action of Debt shall lie against the heire on the part of the mother, without naming of the heire at the Common Law. And so note a diuersitie betweene a personall lien of a Bond, and a reall lien of a Warrantie.

Sect. 719.

(l) 24. E. 3. 36. 27. E. 3. age 108. 38. E. 3. 26. 40. E. 3. 9. 37. H. 8. Br. Nesme. 1. & 40. & tit. Done & Rem. 61.

¶ Heere it appeareth, That (l) whensoeuer the Ancestor taketh any estate of freehold, a limitation after in the same Conueyance to any of his heires; are words of limitation, and not of purchase, albeit in words it be limitted by way of remainder: and therefore heere the remainder to the heires Females vesteth in the Tenant in Tayle himselfe. And it is good to bee

¶ Nota, si tre soit done a un home, et a les heires males de son corps engendres, et pur default de tiel Issue, le rem̃ ent a ses heyres females de son corps engendres, et puis le Donee

Note, if Land bee giuen to a man and to the heirs males of his bodie begotten, and for default of such Issue the Remainder thereof to his Heires femals of his body begotten, and after the

donee en le taile fait feoffment en fee oueſque garrantie accordant, & ad iſſue fits et file et moruſt, cel Garrantie neſt forſque lineall Garrantie a le fits a demaunder per briefe de Formedon en le diſcender, & auxy il neſt forſque lineall a l' fil', a demaunder meſme la terre per briefe de Formedon en le remaynder, ſinon frere deviaſt ſans iſſue mal', pur ceo que el claime come heire female de la corps ſon pere engendres. Mes en ceſt cas, ſi ſon frere en ſa vie releaſaſt al diſcontinuee, &c. oue garranty, &c. & puis moruſt ſauns iſſue, ceſt un collateral garrantie a le file, pur ceo q̃ el ne puit conueyer a luy le droit que el ad per force de le remaynder per aſcun meane de diſcent per ſon frere, pur ceo que le frere eſt collaterall a le title ſa ſoer, & pur ceo ſon Garrantie eſt collaterall, &c.

donee in tayle maketh a feoffment in fee, with warrantie accordingly and hath iſſue a ſonne and a daughter and dieth, this warrantie is but a lineall warrantie to the Son to demand by a Writ of *Formedon* in the diſcender, and alſo it is but lineall to the Daughter to demand the ſame Land by Writ of *Formedon*, in the remaynder, vnleſſe the brother dieth without iſſue male, becauſe ſhee claymeth as heire female of the bodie of her father ingendred. But in this caſe, if her brother in his life releaſe to the diſcontinuee, &c. with warrantie, &c. and after dieth without iſſue this is a collateral warrantie to the daughter, becauſe ſhee cannot cõuey to her the right which ſhee hath by force of the remaynder by any meanes of diſcent by her brother, for that the brother is collateral to the title of his ſiſter, and therefore his warranty is collaterall, &c.

knowne, that for Learning ſake, and to find out the reaſon of the Law, theſe limitations to the heires males of the bodie, and after to the heires females of the bodie may bee put, but it is dangerous to vſe them in Conueyances, for great inconuenienceſ may ariſe thereupon, for if ſuch a tenant in tayle hath iſſue diuers Sonnes, and they haue iſſue diuers Daughters, and likewiſe if Tenant in tayle hath iſſue diuers Daughters; and each of them hath iſſue Sonnes, none of the Daughters of the Sonnes, nor the Sonnes of the Daughters ſhall euer inherit to either of the ſaid eſtates tayle: and ſo it is of the Iſſues of the Iſſues, for that (as hath beene ſaid) the Iſſues inheritable muſt make their clayme either only by Males, or only by females, ſo as the Females of the Males, or Males of the Females are wholy excluded to bee inheritable to eyther of the ſaid Eſtates tayle: but where the firſt limitation is to the heires Males, let the limitation be, for default of ſuch iſſue to the heires of the bodie of the Donee, and then all the Iſſues, bee they Females of Males, or Males of Females are inheritable.

If a man giue Lands to a man, to haue and to hold to him and the heires Males of his bodie, and to him and to the heires Females of his bodie, the eſtate to the heires Females is in remaynder, and the Daughters ſhall not inherit any part, ſo long as there is Iſſue Male, for the eſtate to the heires Males is firſt limited, and ſhall bee firſt ſerued, and it is as much to ſay, and after to the heires females, and Males in conſtruction of Law are to bee preferred.

1. *H.* 6. 4. 11. *H.* 6. 13. 14. 28. *H.* 6. *deuiſe* 18. *Statham. Deuiſe.* Pl. *Com.* 414. 20. *H.* 6. 43. *Vide Litt. cap. taile. Sect.* 24. 37. *H.* 8. *Br, done & rem.* 61. *& tit. nosme* 1. *&* 40.

Sect. 720.

Item ieo ay oye dire que en temps le Roy Richard le second, il y fuit vn Iustice del Common Banke, demurrant en Kent, appel Richel, q̄ auoit issue diuers fits, & son entent fuit, que son eigne fits aueroit certaine terres & tenements a luy, et a les heires de son corps engendres, et pur default dissue, le remainder a le second fits, &c. & issint a l' tierce fits, &c. & pur ceo que il voile que nul de ses fits alieneroit, ou ferroit Garrantie pur barrer ou leder les auters, queux serront en le remainder, &c. il fist faire tiel Indenture, a tiel effect, cestascauoir, que les terres & tenements fueront dones a son eigne fits sur tiel condition que si leigne fits aliena en fee, ou en fee tayle, &c. ou si ascun de ses fits alienast, &c. que adonque lour estate cessera, & serroit void, et q̄ adonque mesmes les terres & tenements immediate remaindront a le second fits, et a les heires de son corps engendres, & sic vltra, le remaind as auters de ses fits, et liuery de seisin fuit fait accordant.

Also I haue heard say, that in the time of King *Richard* the second, there was a Iustice of the Common Place dwelling in *Kent*, called *Richel*, who had issue diuers sonnes, and his intent was that his eldest sonne should haue certaine Lands and Tenements to him and to the heires of his bodie begotten, and for default of issue, the remainder to the second sonne, &c. and so to the third sonne, &c. and because hee would that none of his sonnes should alien or make Warrantie to barre or hurt the others that should be in the remainder, &c. he causeth an Indenture to be made to this effect, *viz.* That the Lands & Tenements were giuen to his eldest Son vpon such condition that if the eldest sonne alien in fee or in fee tayle, &c. or if any of his sonnes alien &c. that then their estate should cease and be void, and that then the same Lands and Tenements immediately should remayne to the second sonne, and to the heires of his bodie begotten, *& sic vltra*, the remaynder to his other sonnes, and liuerie of seisin was made accordingly.

21.H.6.fol.33.lib.6.fo.42.b. *Sir Anthony Mildmayes case.*

Ieo ay oye dire, &c. Those things that one hath by credible hearesay, by the example of our Author are worthy of obseruation. This inuention deuised by Iustice Richel in the Raigne of King Richard the Second, who was an Irishman borne, and the like by Thirning Chiefe Iustice in the Raigne of H.4. were both full of imperfections for Nihil simul inuentum est & perfectum, and sæpe viatorem noua non vetus orbita fallit: And therefore new inuentions in Assurances are dangerous. And hereby it may appeare, that it is not safe for any man (be he neuer so learned) to bee of councell with himselfe in his owne case, but to take aduice of other great and learned men.

Non prosunt Dominis quæ prosunt omnibus, artes.

And the reason hereof is, in suo quisque negotio hebetior est, quam in alieno.

(m) 2.H.4.fo.11.in Action sur le case.

(m) And the same Iudge in his owne name, &c. brought an Action vpon his case against others and obtained a verdict, so as the right of the cause was tried on his side, yet for that vpon his owne shewing in his Count the Action did not lie, Ex assensu omnium Iusticiariorum præter querentem Richel iudgement was giuen against him, but let vs now leaue this Iudge for example to others, and let vs returne to our Author.

turn over one leaf

son in fee take wife, now by act in Law is the wife intitled to the third presentation, if the husband dye before: the husband grant the third presentation to another, the husband die, the heire shall present twice, the wife shall haue the third presentation, and the Grantee the fourth, for in this case it shall be taken the third presentation, which he might lawfully grant, and so note a diuersitie betweene a title by act in Law, and by act of the party, for the act in Law shall worke no preiudice to the Grantee.

¶ *Auxi si tiel remainder serroit bone, &c.* **The force of this argument** is, that seeing the estate of the Alienee (albeit the words of the Condition be, that the state should cease and be voide) being an estate of inheritance in lands or tenements cannot cease or be voide before the state be defeated by entrie, then if this remainder should bee good, then must it giue an entrie vpon the Alienee to him that had no right before, which should bee against the expresse rule of Law, *viz.* that an entrie cannot be giuen to a stranger to auoide a voydable act, as before hath beene said in the Chapter of Conditions.

¶ *Le quel serr' enconuenient.* **Here note three things. First, that** whatsoeuer is against the rule of Law is inconuenient. Secondly, that an argument Ab inconuenienti is strong to proue it is against Law, as often hath beene obserued. Thirdly, that new inuentions (though of a learned Judge in his owne profession) are full of inconuenience *Vid. Sect. 87. &c.*

Periculosum est res nouas & inusitatas inducere,

Euentus varios res noua semper habet.

Sect.723.

¶ La tierce cause est, quant la condition est tiel, que si leigne fits alienast, &c. que son estate cessera, ou serroit voide, &c. donques apres tiel alienation, &c. poit le Donor enter per force de tiel condition, come il semble, & issint le Donor ou ses heires en tiel case doient pluis tost auer la tre que le second fits, que nauoit ascun droit deuant tiel alienation, & issint il semble que tielx remainders en le cas auantdit sont voides.

The third cause is, when the condition is such, that if the elder sonne alien, &c. that his estate shall cease or be voide, &c. then after such alienation, &c. may the Donor enter by force of such condition as it seemeth, and so the Donor or his heires in such case ought sooner to haue the land then the second sonne, that had not any right before such alienation, and so it seemeth that such remainders in the case aforesaid are voide.

¶ Here it is to bee obserued that part of the condition that prohibiteth the alienation made by Tenant in taile is good in Law with such distinction as hath beene before said in the Chapter of Conditions. And the consequent of the Condition, *viz.* that the lands should remaine to another, &c. is voide in Law, and by the opinion of Littleton the Donor may re-enter for the Condition broken, for vtile per inutile non vitiatur. which being in case of a Condition for the defeating of an estate, is worthy of obseruation.

And it is to be noted, that after the death of the Donor, the Condition descendeth to the eldest sonne, and consequently his alienation doth extinguish the same for euer, wherein the weakenesse of this inuention appeareth, and therefore Littleton here saith, that it seemeth that the Donor may re-enter, and speaketh nothing of his heires. A man hath issue two sonnes, and maketh a Gift in taile to the eldest, the Remainder in fee to the puisne, vpon condition, that the eldest shall not make any Discontinuance with warranty to barre him in the remainder, and if he doth, that then the puisne sonne and his heires shall re-enter, the eldest make a Feoffment in fee with warranty, the father dyeth, the eldest sonne dyeth without issue, the puisne may enter, but if the Discontinuance had beene after the death of the father, the puisne could not haue entred. In this case foure points are to be obserued. First, as Littleton here saith, the entrie for the breach of the Condition is giuen to the father, and not to the puisne sonne. Secondly, that by the death

 of

41. E. 3. fo. of the father the condition discends to the elder son, & is but suspended, & is reuiued by the death of the eldest sonne without Issue, and discendeth to the youngest sonne. Thirdly, That the Feoffement made in the life of the father cannot giue away a Condition that is Collaterall, as it may doe a right. Fourthly, That a Warrantie cannot bind a title of entrie for a Condition broken, (as hath beene sayd) but if the discontinuance had beene made after the death of the father, it had extinct the Condition: which Case is put to open the reason of our Authors opinion.

Vi. Sect. 446.

In these last three Sections our Author hath taught vs an excellent poynt of Learning, That when any innouation or new inuention starts vp, to trie it with the Rules of the Common Law, (as our Author here hath done) for these be true Touchstones to seuer the pure gold from the drosse & sophistications of nouelties & new inuentions. And by this example you may perceiue, That the rule of the old Common Law being soundly (as our Authour hath done) applied to such nouelties, it doth vtterly crush them and bring them to nothing; and commonly a new inuention doth offend against many rules and reasons (as here it appeareth) of the Common Law; and the antient Judges and Sages of the Law haue euer (as it appeareth * in our Bookes) suppressed innouations and nouelties in the beginning, as soone as they haue offered to creepe vp, lest the quiet of the Common Law might bee disturbed: and so haue (a) Acts of Parliament done the like, whereof by the authorities quoted in the Margent, you may in stead of many others, vpon this occasion take a little taste. But our excellent Author in all his three Bookes hath sayd nothing but Ex veterum sapientium ore & more.

* 31. E. 3. Gaor deliuerance 5. 22 ass. 12. 38. E. 3. 1. 2. H. 4. 18. &c.
(a) 1. E. 3. ca. 15. Stat. 3. 18. E. 3. ca. 1. & 6. 4. H. 4. ca. 2. 11. H. 6. ca. 23. 12. E. 4. ca. 8, &c.

Section 724. 725.

¶ ITem a le Common ley deuant lestatute de Gloucester, si tenant p le Curtesie vst alien en fee ouesque Garrantie, apres son decease ceo fuit vn barre al heire, sicome appiert per les parols de mesme lestatut, mes il est remedy p mesme lestatute, que le Garrantie de le Tenant per l' Curtesie, ne sẽ my bar al hẽe, sinon que il y ad assets per discent per le tenant per le curtesie, car deuant le dit estatute, ceo fuit vn collaterall Garrantie al hẽe, pur ceo que il ne puissoit conueyer ascun title de discent a les tenements per le tenant p l' Curtesie, mes tantsolement per sa mere, ou auters de ses ancestors, et ceo est le cause pur que il fuit collaterall Garrantie.

ALso at the Common Law before the Statute of Gloucester, if Tenant by the Curtesie had aliened in fee with Warrantie, after his decease this was a barre to the heire, as it appeareth by the words of the same Statute: but it is remedied by the same Statute, That the Warrantie of Tenant by the Curtesie shall bee no barre to the heire, vnlesse that hee hath Assets by discent by the Tenaunt by the Curtesie, for before the sayd Statute this was a Collaterall warrantie to the heire, for that hee could not conuey any title of Discent to the tenements by the tenant by the Curtesie, but onely by his mother, or other of his Ancestors, and this is the cause why it was a collaterall Warrantie.

Sect. 725.

¶ MEs si home enherit prist feme, les queux ont fits enter eux, et le pier deuie, et le fits

BVt if a man Inheritor taketh wife, who haue issue a sonne betweene them, and the father di-

Sect. 721.

¶ MEs il semble p reason, que touts tielx remainders en la forme auantdit sont voides et de nul value, et ceo pur trois causes. Un cause est, pur ceo que chescun remainder q̄ cōmence per un fait, il couient que le remainder soit en luy a que le remainder est taile per force de mesme le fait auant liuerie de seisin est fait a luy que auera le franktenemēt, car en tiel case le nessance et le estre de le remainder est per le liuery de seisin a celuy que auera le franktenement, et tiel remainder ne fuit al second fits, al temps de liuery de seisin en le cas auantdit, &c.

BVt it seemeth by reason, that all such remainders in the forme aforesaid are voide and of no value, and that for three causes. One cause is, for that euery remainder which beginneth by a Deed, it behooueth that the remainder be in him to whom the remainder is entailed by force of the same deed before the liuery of seisin is made to him which shall haue the freehold, for in such case the growing and the being of the remainder is by the liuery of seisin to him that shall haue the freehold, and such remainder was not to the second sonne at the time of the liuerie of seisin in the case aforesaid, &c.

¶ HEre our Author is of opinion, that these remainders in the forme aforesaid, are void and of no value for three causes.

¶ *Vn cause est, &c.* Here he setteth downe a rule concerning remainders, viz, Euery remainder which commenceth by a Deed ought to vest in him to whom it is limitted, when Liuery of seisin is made to him that hath the particular estate.

First Littleton saith by Deed, (n) because if lands bee granted and rendred by Fine for life, the remainder in taile, the remainder in fee, none of these remainders are in them in the remainder untill the particular estate be executed.

(n) 7.R.2.*Scire fa.*

Secondly, that the remainder be in him, &c. at the time of the Liuery. This is regularly true, but yet it hath diuers exceptions. First, unlesse the person that is to take the remainder be not in rerum natura, (o) as if a Lease for life be made the remainder to the right heires of I.S. I.S. being then aliue, it sufficeth that the inheritance passeth presently out of the Lessor, but cannot vest in the heire of I.S. for that liuing his father he is not in rerum natura, for non est hæres viuentis, so as the remainder is good upon this Contingent, viz. if I.S. dye during the life of the Lessee.

(o) 32.*H.6.tit. Feoffments & faits*,99. 27.*E.*3.87. 11.*R.*2.*Detinue*,46. 2.*H*7.13. 12.*H*.7.27. 12.*E*.4.2. 21.*H*.7.11. 7.*H*.4.23. 11.*H*.4.74. 18.*H*.8.3. 27 *H*.8.42. 38.*E*.3.26. 30.*Ass*.47. 6.*R*.2.*qu.Iur.dum*.20.

(p) And so it is if a man make a Lease for life to A.B and C. and if B. suruiue C. then the remainder to B. and his heires. Here is another exception out of the said rule, for albeit the person be certaine, yet inasmuch as it depends upon the dying of B before C. the remainder cannot vest in C. presently. And the reason of both these cases in effect is, because the remainder is to commence upon limitation of time, viz upon the possibility of the death of one man before another, which is a common possibility.

(p) *Pl.Com.in Colthirsts case*, *fo*.25.29.

A man letteth lands for life upon condition to haue fee, and warranteth the land in forma prædicta, afterward the Lessee performeth the Condition, whereby the Lessee hath fee, the warranty shall extend and inccease according to the state. And so it is in that case if the Lessor had dyed before the performance of the Condition, the warranty shall rise and increase according to the estate, and yet the Lessor himselfe was neuer bound to the warranty, but it hath relation from the first Liuery. And by this it appeareth that a warranty being a Couenant reall executorie may extend to an estate in futuro, hauing an estate, whereupon it may worke in the beginning. But if a man grant a Seigniory for yeares upon Condition to haue fee with a warranty in *forma prædicta*, and after the Condition is performed, this ſhall not extend to the fee, becauſe the firſt eſtate was but for yeares which was not capable of a warranty. And ſo it is, if a man make a Leaſe for yeares the remainder in fee, and warrant the land *in forma prædicta*, he in the remainder cannot take benefit of the warranty, becauſe he is not partie to the Deed, and immediately he cannot take, if he were partie to the Deed, becauſe he is named after the *Habendum*, and the eſtate for yeares is not capable of a warranty. And ſo it is if Land be giuen to A and B. ſo long as they ioyntly together liue, the remainder to the right heires of him that dyeth firſt, and warrant the land *in forma prædicta*. A. dyeth his heire ſhall haue the warranty, and yet the remainder veſted not during the life of A, for the death of A. muſt precede the remainder, and yet ſhall the heire of A. haue the land by diſcent.

Section 722.

¶ Le ſecond cauſe eſt, ſi le primer fits alienaſt les tenements en fee, adonques eſt le fráktenement, et le fee ſimple en lalienee, et en nul auter, et ſi le Donour auoit aſcun reuerſion, per tiel alienation l' reuerſion eſt diſcontinue, donques coment per aſcun reaſon poit ceo eſtre, q̃ tiel remainder commencera ſon eſtre, & ſon neſſance immediat apres tiel alienation fait a vn eſtrange, que ad per meſme lalienation franktenement, & fee ſimple, &c. Et auxy ſi tiel remainder ſeroit bone, adonques purroit il enter ſur lalienee, lou il nauoit aſcun maner d' droit auant lalienation, que ſerra inconuenient.

THe ſecond cauſe is, if the firſt ſon alien the tenements in fee, then is the freehold and the fee ſimple in the Alienee, and in none other, and if the Donor had any reuerſion, by ſuch alienation the reuerſion is diſcontinued, then how by any reaſon may it be, that ſuch remainder ſhall commence his being and his growing immediatly after ſuch alienation made to a ſtranger, that hath by the ſame alienation a freehold and fee ſimple, &c. And alſo if ſuch remainder ſhould bee good, then might hee enter vpon the Alienee, where hee had no manner of right before the alienation, which ſhould bee inconuenient.

¶ *Si le primer fits alienaſt, &c.* By the alienation of the Donee two things are wrought.

Firſt, the Franktenement and fee is in the Alienee.

Secondly, the Reuerſion is deueſted out of the Donor.

(q) 21.H 7.11. 27.H.8.24 (q) And therefore by the alienation that transferreth the freehold & fee ſimple to the Alienee there can no remainder be raiſed and veſted in the ſecond ſonne. *(r) 6.R.2.quid iuris clam.20.* (r) As if a man make a Leaſe for life vpon condition that if the Leſſor grant ouer the reuerſion, that then the Leſſee ſhall haue fee, if the Leſſor grant the reuerſion by Fine, the Leſſee ſhall not haue fee, for when the Fine transferreth the fee to the conuſee, it ſhould be abſurd, and repugnant to reaſon, that the ſame Fine ſhould worke an eſtate in the Leſſee, for one alienation cannot veſt an eſtate of one and the ſame land to two ſeuerall perſons at one time. *Argumentum ex abſurdo.*

In a mans owne grant, which is euer taken moſt forcibly againſt himſelfe, the reaſon of *Littleton* doth hold, for it hath beene reſolued by the Iuſtices (ſ) that if a man ſeiſed of an Aduowſon in fee by his Deed granteth the next preſentation to A and before the Church becommeth voide by another Deede grant the next preſentation of the ſame Church to B. the ſecond grant is voide, for A. had the ſame granted to him before, and the Grantee ſhall not haue the ſecond auoydance by conſtruction, to haue the next auoydance, which the Grantor might lawfully grant, for the grant of the next auoydance doe not import the ſecond preſentation, (t) But if a man ſeiſed of an Aduowſon

(ſ) 20.H.8.Preſentment al Eglise Br.52. 33.H.8 ibid.55. 29.H 8. Dier 35. 11.Eliz.282.283.

(t) 15.H.7.7. 19.E.3.quar.Imp.154.

fits entra en la terre, et endowa sa mere, et puis le mere alien ceo que el ad en sa Dower, a un auter en fee oue Garrantie accordant, et puis morust, et le Garrantie discendist a le fits, ore le fits serra barre a demaunder mesme la terre per cause de la dit Garrantie, pur ceo que tiel collaterall Garrantie de Tenaunt en Dower nest pas remedie per ascun Estatute. Mesme la Ley est lou Tenaunt a terme de vie fait un Alienation ouesque Garrantie, &c. et morust, et le Garrantie discendist a celuy que auoit le reuersion ou le remainder, ils serront barres per tiel Garrantie.

eth, and the sonne entreth into the land, and endow his mother, and after the mother alieneth that which shee hath in Dower to another in Fee with Warrantie accordant, and after dieth, and the Warrantie discendeth to the sonne, now the son shall be barred to demand the same Land by cause of the sayd Warrantie, because that such Collaterall Warrantie of Tenaunt in Dower is not remedied by any Statute. The same Law is it where Tenant for life maketh an Alienation with Warrantie, &c. and dieth, and the warranty discendeth to him which hath the reuersion or the rem̃, they shall be barred by such Warrantie.

¶ Of this and the subsequent Section sufficient hath beene sayd before in this Chapter Sect. 697.

¶ *Nest pas remedie per ascun Statute.* But by a Statute made since, this Case is remedied, as you see before Sect. 697.

Section 726.

¶ Item en le dit Case, si issint fuit que quant le tenant en Dower alienast, &c. son heire fuit deins age, et auxy al temps que le garrantie discendist sur luy, il fuit deins age, en cest cas lheire poit apres enter sur lalienee, nient contristeant le garranty discẽdist, &c. p̃ c q̃ nul lachesse serra adiudg̃ en lheire deins age que il nentra pas sur lalienee en la vie le tenãt en Dower. Mez

ALso in the Case aforesaid, if it were so that when the Tenant in Dower aliened, &c. his heire was within age, and also at the time that the warrantie discended vpon him hee was within age, In this Case the heire may after enter vpon the Alienee, notwithstanding the warrantie discended, &c. because no Lachesse shal be adiudged in the heire within age, that he did not enter vpon the Alienee in the life

¶ Here note this diuersitie, if the heire bee within age at the time of the discent of the warrantie, he may enter and auoyd the Estate either within age, or at any time after his full age: And Littleton saith well, That the Enfant in this Case may enter vpon the Alienee, for if he bring his Action against him, he shalbe barred by this warrantie, so long as the state whereunto the warrantie is annexed continue, and bee not defeated by entrie of the heire: but if he be within age at the time of the Alienation with warrantie, and become of full age before the discent of the warrantie, the warranty shal barre him for euer. Our Author putteth his cases where the entrie of the Infant is lawfull, (a) for where the entrie of the Infant is not lawfull

(u) 18.E.4.13. 35.H.6.63. 28.Ass.28. 32.Eq.Garr.30.

35.H.6.63.

(a) 3.H.7.9. 35.H.6.63. Br.tit.War.54. 33.H.8.Tit. War.Br.84.Li.1.fo.67.a. in Archers case, & 140.Chudleys case.

si l'heire fuit deins age al temps del alienation, &c. et puis il devient al pleine age en la vie de le tenant en Dower, et issint esteant de pleine age, il nentra pas sur lalienee en la vie de le tenant en Dower, et puis le Tenaunt en Dower morust, &c. la peraduenture l'heire serra barre per tiel Garrantie, pur ceo que il serra recte sa follie, que il esteant de plein age, ne entra pas en la vie de le Tenaunt en Dower, &c.

of Tenant in Dower. But if the Heire were within age at the time of the alienation, &c. and after he commeth to full age in the life of Tenant in Dower, and so being of ful age he doth not enter vpon the Alienee in the life of Tenant in Dower, and after the tenant in Dower dieth, &c. there peraduenture the heir shal be barred by such Warranty, because it shall bee accounted his folly, that hee beeing of full age did not enter in the life of tenāt in dower, &c.

full when the Warrantie discendeth, the Warrantie doth bind the Enfant, as well as a man of full age, and the reason thereof is, because the state whereunto the Warrantie was annexed, continueth and cannot be auoyded but by Action, in which Action the Warrantie is a barre: and for the same reason likewise it is of a Feme Couert, if her entrie be not lawful, a warrantie discending on her during the Couerture, doth bind her.

(w) 18.E.3.3.

(w) And albeit the husband be within age at the discent of the Warrantie, yet if the entry of the wife be takē away, the Warrantie shal bind the wife.

(q) 30.E.3. Audit. quer. 27. F.N.B. 104. k. 6.E.3.39. 17.E.3.76. 17. Ass. 53.17. 31.E.24.13.E.3. Aud. quer. 30.18.E.3. Infant 61.16.H.7 5.15.E 4.5.8.H.6.30. 1.H.7.15.

(q) And herein a diuersitie is to bee obserued betweene matters of Record done or suffered by an enfant, and matters in Fait, for matters in Fait he shal auoid either within age, or at full age, as hath beene sayd: but matters of Record, as Statutes merchants, & of the staple, Recognisances knowledged by him, or a Fine leuied by him, recouerie against him by default in a reall Action (sauing in Dower) must bee auoyded by him, viz. Statutes, &c. by Audita quærela, and the fine and recouerie by writ of Error during his minoritie, and the like. And the reason thereof is, because they are iudiciall Acts, and taken by a Court or a Judge, therefore the nonage of the partie to auoyd the same shall be tried by inspection of Judges, and not by the Countrie. And for that his nonage must be tried by inspection, this cannot be done after his full age: and so is the Law clearely holden at this day, though there be some differenc in our Bookes. But if the age be inspected by the Judges, and recorded that he is within age, albeit hee come of full age before the reuersall, yet may it be reuersed after his full age, * And so was it resolued by the whole Court of Kings Bench in the case of Kekewiche.

6.H.8. Sauer de default Br.50 3.H.6.10. 1. Mar. Dy. 104.

* Pasch. 13. Ia. R. in the Kings Bench.

If, lands had beene giuen to the husband and wife and their heires, and the husband had made a Feoffement to another, to whom a Collaterall Ancestor of the wife had released and died, and the husband died, (and this had beene before the Statute of 32.H.8.) this warrantie had so bound her waiueable right, as shee could not waiue her estate, and claime Dower. Otherwise it is of an Estate determined: for if a Disseisor make a Lease to the husband and wife during the life of the husband, and the husband dieth, she may disagree to this Estate determined, to saue her selfe from dammages. And so note a diuersitie betweene an estate determined, and and an estate bound by Warrantie.

Nul laches serra adiudge en le heire deins age. Laches or Lasches is an old French word for slackenesse, or negligence, or not doing. And the Rule (That no negligence shall be adiudged in an Enfant) is true, where he is thereby to be barred of his entry in respect of a former right, as by a discent, or of his former right, (as Littleton doth heere put an example) by a Warrantie where his entrie is congeable. But otherwise it is of Conditions, charges and penalties going out of, or depending vpon the originall Conueyance, for the Laches or negligence shall be adiudged in those cases as wel in the Infant as in any other. (y) Vide Pl. Com. Stowels Case per totum. And see further there, where an Infant being tenant for life or yeares, shall be punished for doing or suffering of wast; and where he claimeth by purchase, a Cessauit shall lie against him, if he pay not his Rent by two yeares. And some haue sayd, If he haue the Tenancie by discent, and he himselfe cesse, a Cessauit doth lie, and he shal not haue his age because it is of his owne Cesser, 31.E.3. Age 54. But other Bookes (as some conceiue them) be against that: Vide 9.Edw.3.50. 28.E.3.99. 14.E.3. Age 88. 2.E.2. Age 132.

(y) Pl. Com. Stowels case. 355, &c.

and

and others, which Bookes doe not prove that the Cessavit doth not lie in that case, but the contrarie, that he shall have his age to the end, he may at his full age certainly know what to plead, or what arrerages to tender, for the Land was originally charged with the Seigniorie and Services,

Sect. 727.

¶ MEs ore per lestatute fait 11.H.7.cap.10. il est ordeine, si ascun feme discontinue, alien, release, ou confirme ove Garrantie ascun terres ou tenements que el tient en dower pur terme de vie, ou en tayle del done sa primer baron, ou de ses Ancesters, ou del done dascun auter seisie al use le primer baron, ou de ses Ancesters, que touts tiels garranties, &c. serront voides, & q̄ bien lirroit a cestuy q̄ avoit ceux terres ou tenements apres la mort de m̄ la feme dentrer.

BVt now by the Statute made 11.*H*,*cap*.10. it is ordained if any woman discontinue, alien, release or confirme with warrantie any Lands or Tenements which shee holdeth in Dower for tearme of life, or in tayle of the gift of her first husband, or of his Ancestors, or of the gift of any other seised to the use of the first Husband or of his Ancestors, that all such warranties, &c. shall bee void, and that it shall be lawfull for him which hath these Lands or Tenements after the death of the same woman to enter.

¶ THis is an addition to Litleton, and therefore to bee passed over. And hereof sufficient hath beene said before Sect.637.

Sect. 728.

¶ ITem il est parle en le fine de l'dit estatute de Gloucest. que parle del alienation ouesque garrantie fait per le tenant per le curtesie en cest forme. Ensement, en mesme le manner ne soit lheire la feme apres la mort le pere & le mere barre daction, sil demanda lheritage ou l'mariage, sa mere per briefe Dentre, que son pere aliena en temps sa mere, dont nul fine est levy en la Court le

ALso it is spoken in the end of the said Statute of *Glocest.* which speaketh of the alienation with Warrantie made by the tenant by the curtesie in this forme. Also, in the same manner, the heire of the woman after the death of the father and mother shall not bee barred of action, if hee demandeth the heritage or the marriage of his Mother by Writ of Entry, that his father aliened in his mothers time,

Ddddd

¶ *Dont nul fine est levie en le Court le Roy, &c.* Here are three things worthy of observation concerning the construction of Statutes, First, that (a) it is the most naturall and genuine exposition of a Statute to construe one part of the Statute by another part of the same Statute, for that best expresseth the meaning of the makers. As here the question upon the generall words of the Statute is, whether a fine levied only by a husband seised in the right of his wife with warrantie shall barre the heire without Assets. And it is well expounded by the former part of the Act, whereby it is enacted, that alienation made by Tenant by the courtesie with warrantie shall not bar the heire, unlesse Assets discend,

(a) *Pl.Com.fol.*73. 7.*E*.3.89.

*Vide Bracton lib.*4.*fol.*321. *Fleta lib.*5.*cap.*34.

Roy: & issint p force de m̄ lestatute, si l' baron del feme aliena lheritage, ou mariag̃ sa feme en fee oue garranty, &c. per son fait en pais, ceo est clere ley, que cest garranty ne barrera my lheir, si non que il nad assets per discent.

whereof no fine is leuied in the kings court And so by force of the same Statute, if the Husband of the wife alien the heritage or mariage of his wife in fee with warrantie, &c. by his Deed in the Countrey, it is cleere Law, that this warrantie shall not barre the heire, vnlesse hee hath assets by Discent.

cend. And therefore it should be inconuenient to intend the Statute in such manner, as that he that hath nothing but in the right of his wife should by his fine leuied with Warrantie barre the heire without Assets. And this exposition is ex visceribus actus.

Secondly, The wordes of an Act of Parliament must bee taken in a lawfull and rightfull sence, as here the words being (whereof no fine is leuied in the Kings Court) are to be vnderstood, whereof no fine is lawfully or rightfully leuied in the Kings Court, And therefore (b) a fine leuied by the Husband alone is not within the meaning of the Statute, for that fine should worke a wrong to the wife, but a fine leuied by the husband and wife is intended by the Statute, for that fine is lawfull and worketh no wrong. (c) So the Statute of W.2.cap.5. sayth (Ita quod Episcopus Ecclesiam conferat) is construed Ita quod Episcopus Ecclesiam legitime conferat, and the like in a number of other Cases in our Bookes. And generally the rule is Quod non præstat impedimentum quod de iure non sortitur effectum.

(b) *Pl.Com.246.b. Seignior Barkleyes Case. lib.9. fol.26. in case del Abbot de Strata mercella.*
(c) 11.H.4.80.9.E.4.12. 21.H.6.28.4.E.4.31. 12.H.4. Formedon 15.

Thirdly, That construction must be made of a Statute in suppression of the mischiefe, and in aduancement of the remedie, as by this Case it appeareth. For a fine leuied by the Husband only is within the letter of the Law, but the mischiefe was, the heire was barred of the Inheritance of his Mother by the warrantie of his Father without Assets, and this Act intended to apply a remedie, viz. that it should not barre vnlesse there were Assets, and therefore the mischiefe is to be suppressed, and the remedie aduanced. Et qui hæret in littera, hæret in cortice, as often before hath beene said.

Sect. 729. 730. & 731.

¶ Mes le doubt est, si le baron alienast lheritage sa feme, per fine leuy en la Court l' Roy ouesque Garrantie, &c. si ceo barrera lheire sans ascun discent en value. Et quant a ceo, jeo voile icy dire certaine reasons que jeo ay oye dit en cest matter. Jeo ay oye mon Master Sir Richard Newton iades chief Justice de Common Banke dire vn foits en mesme le Banke, que tiel Garrantie que le baron fait per fine leuie en le Court le Roy, barrera lheire, coment que il ad riens per discent, pur ceo que lestatute dit (dont nul fin̄ est leuy en le Court le Roy) et issint per son opinion

BVt the doubt is, if the husbād alien the heritage of his wife by fine leuied in the Kings Court with warrantie, &c. if this shall barre the heire without any discent in value. And as to this I will here tell certaine reasons, which I haue heard said in this matter. I haue heard my Master Sir *Richard Newton* late Chiefe Iustice of the Common Pleas once say in the same Court, that such Warrantie as the husband maketh by fine leuied in the Kings Court shall barre the heire, albeit hee hath nothing by discent, because the Statute saith (whereof no fine is leuied in the Kings Court) and so by his opinion cel garrantie per fine demurt vncore vn collaterall Garrantie, come il fuit a le common ley, nient remedy per le dit eſtatute, pur ceo que l' dit eſtatute except alienations per fine oue garrantie.

opinion this Warrantie by fine remayneth yet a collaterall warrantie as it was at the Common Law not remedied by the ſaid Statute, becauſe the ſaid Statute excepteth alienations by fine with warranty.

Sect. 730.

¶ ET aſcuns auters ont dit, et vncore diont le contrarie, et ceo eſt lour proofe, que come per meſme le chapiter de dit eſtatute il eſt ordeine, que le garrantie le tenant per le curteſie ne ſerra my barre al heire, ſinon que il ad aſſets per diſcent, &c. coment que le tenant per le curteſie leuy vn fine de meſmes le tenements oueſque garranty, &c. auxy fortment come il poit faire, vncore cel Garranty ne barra my lheire ſinon que il ad aſſets per diſcent, &c. & ieo croy que ceo eſt ley, & pur ceo ils diont, que ſerroit inconuenient dentender leſtatute en tiel forme, que vn home que nad riens forſque en droit ſa feme purroit per fine leuie per luy de meſmes les tenements queux il ad forſque en droit ſa feme oue Garrantie, &c. barre lheire de meſmes le tenements ſans aſcun diſcent de fee [ſi]mple, &c. lou le tenant per le [cur]teſie ceo ne puit faire.

AND ſome others haue ſaid, and yet doe ſay the contrarie, and this is their proofe, that as by the ſame Chapter of the ſaid Statute it is ordained that the warrantie of the tenant by the curteſie ſhall bee no bar to the heire, vnleſſe that he hath aſſets by diſcēt, &c. although that the tenant by the curteſie leuy a fine of the ſame tenements with warrantie, &c. as ſtrongly as hee can, yet this warrantie ſhall not bar the heir, vnleſſe that he hath aſſets by diſcent, &c. And I beleeue that this is Law, and therefore they ſay, that it ſhould be inconuenient to intend the Statute in ſuch manner, as a man that hath nothing but in right of his wife might by fine leuied by him of the ſame Tenements which hee hath but in right of his wife with warranty, &c. barre the heire of the ſame tenements without any diſcent of fee ſimple, &c. where the Tenant by the curteſie cannot doe this.

Sect. 731.

¶ M[e]s ils ont dit, que le [ſta]tute ſerra entend ſolonque cel forme, ſ. lou le Statute dit, dont nul fine [eſt] leuie en Court le Roy, ceo eſt a[di]re, dont nul loial fine

BVt they haue ſaid that the ſtatute ſhal be intended after this manner, s. where the Statute ſaith, whereof no fine is leuied in the Kings Court, that is to ſay,

fine est droiturelment leuy en la Court le Roy, ceo est adire, dont nul loial fin̄ est droiturelm̄t leuy en la court le Roy: Et c̄ est dont nul fine de l' baron et sa feme soit leuie en le Court le Roy, car al temps de le fesans del dit estatute, chescun estate de terres ou tenements que ascun home ou feme auoit, que discenderoit a son heire, fuit fee simple sans condition, ou sur certaine conditions en fait, ou en ley. Et pur ceo que adonques tiel fine poit droiturelment estre leuie per le baron et sa feme, et les heires le baron garronteront, &c. tiel garranty barrera lheire, et issint ils diont que cest lentendement de lestatute, car si le baron et sa fem̄ fieront vn feoffment en fee per fait en pais, son heire apres le decease le baron et sa feme auera briefe Dentre sur Cui in vita, &c. nient obstant le garrantie de le baron, donque si nul tiel exception fuit fait en lestatute de le fine leuie, &c. donque lheire aueroit le briefe Dentre, &c. nient obstant le fine leuie per le baron & sa fem̄, pur ceo q̄ les parolx de lestatute deuant lexception de fine leuie, &c. sont generals, &c. cestascauoir que lheire la feme apres le mort le pere et la mere ne soit barr̄ daction, sil demaund lheritage, ou le mariage sa mere, per briefe Dentre, que son pere aliena en temps sa mere, & issint coment que le baron et la feme alienent per fine, uncore ceo est voier, que le baron aliena ē temps la mere, et issint il serroit en case de lestatute, si non que tielx parolx fueront

whereof no lawful fine is rightfully leuied in the Kings Court, and that is, whereof no fine of the husband and his wife is leuied in the Kings Court, for at the time of the making of the said Statute, euery estate of lands or tenements that any man or woman had which should descēd to his heire, was fee simple without condition, or vpon certaine conditions in Deed or in law. And because that then such fine might rightfully bee leuied by the husband and his wife, & the heires of the husband should warrant, &c such warranty shall barre the heire, & so they say that this is the meaning of the statute, for if the husbād & his wife should make a feoffment in fee by Deede in the countrie, his heire after the decease of the husband and wife shall haue a Writ of entrie *sur Cui in vita, &c.* notwithstanding the warranty of the husband, then if no such exception were made in the statute of the fine leuied, &c. then the heire should haue the Writ of entrie, &c. notwithstanding the fine leuied by the husband and his wife, because the words of the statute before the exception of the fine leuied, &c. are generall, viz. that the heire of the wife after the death of the father and moth[er] is not barred of action, if he demand the heritage or the [ma]rriage of his mother by writ [o]f entrie, that his father aliene in the time of his mother, an[d] so albeit the husband and wi[fe a]liened by fine, yet this is true [th]at the husband aliened in t[h]e time of the mother, and so [s]hould be in that

rent, s. dont nul fine est leuie en la Court le Roy, & issint ils diont que ceo est a entender, dont nul fine per le baron et sa feme est leuy en la Court le Roy, le quel est loialment leuie en tiel case, car si les Justices ont conusans, que home que nad riens forsque en droit sa feme voile leuier vn fine en son nosme solement, ils ne voylont, ne vnque deuoient prender tiel fine destre leuie per le baron solement sans sa feme, &c. Ideo Quære de cest matter, &c.

case of the statute, vnlesse that such words were, *viz.* whereof no fine is leuied in the Kings Court, and so they say that this is to be vnderstood, whereof no fine by the husband and his wife is leuied in the Kings Court, the which is lawfully leuied in such case, for if the Iustices haue knowledge that a man that hath nothing but in the right of his wife will leuie a fine in his name only, they will not, neither ought they to take such fine to bee leuied by the husband alone without his wife, &c. *Ideo quære* of this matter, &c.

¶ I*Eo ay oye mon maister Sir* R. Newton, *&c.* Who was a Gentleman of an ancient family; in Latyn de noua villa, in French de neufe ville, and a reuerend learned Judge, and worthily aduanced to be chiefe Justice of the Court of Common pleas, whom our Author remembers with great reuerence, as by his words you may perceiue, calling him his master, and citeth his opinion deliuered once in the Court of Common pleas which our Author heard and obserued (whose example therein, it is necessary for our student to follow) but the latter opinion (as hath beene before obserued) being Littletons owne, is against the opinion of the Lord Newton (d) and the Law is holden cleerely with our Author at this day, and our Author (as in all other cases) hath good Authority in Law to warrant his opinion, Nullius hominis authoritas tantum apud nos valere debet, vt meliora non sequeremur si quis attulerit.

(d) Bracton 321. Fleta, lib. 5 cap. 34. 8. E. 2. Garr. 81. 18. E. 3. 51. 7. E. 3. 84. Pl. Com. 57.

¶ *Car si les Iustices ount conusance, &c.* Hereby it appeareth (e) that the Judge, if he knoweth it, ought not to take knowledge of a Fine that worketh a wrong to a third person.

Sect. 731. (e) 33. H. 6. 52. 5. E. 3. 56. 2 Eliz. Dyer. 178. 1. H. 7. 9. 1. Mar. 89 4. E. 3. 41. 7. Eliz. Dier 246. Vid. Sect. 87 &c.

¶ *Que serroit inconuenient.* Argumentum ab inconuenienti is very forcible in Law, as often hath beene obserued.

Of the rest of these three Sections sufficient hath beene said before.

Sect. 732.

¶ ITem est ascauoir, que en ceux parolx, ou lheire demande lheritage, ou le mariage sa mere, cest parol (ou) est vn disiunctiue, et est autant adire, si lheire demande le heritage sa mere, s. les tenements que sa mere auoit en fee simple per discent, ou per purchase, ou si lheire demaund le mariage sa mere, cest ascauoir, les tenemets que

ALso it is to bee vnderstood, that in these words where the heire demands the heritage, or the marriage of his mother, this word (or) is a disiunctiue, and is asmuch to say, if the heire demand the heritage of his mother, *viz.* the tenements that his mother had in fee simple by discent or by purchase, or if the heire demand the mariage of his mother, that is

que fueront dones a sa mere en frankmariage.

to say, the tenements that were giuen to his mother in frankmariage.

Some doe expound heritage of the mother to be the lands which the mother hath by discent. And that construction is true, but the Statute by the Authority of Littleton extendeth also where the mother hath it by purchase in fee simple, for so saith Littleton himselfe, that this word (Inheritance) is not only intended where a man hath lands by discent, but where a man hath a fee simple by purchase, because his heires may inherite him. And albeit it be true, that the Statute extendeth to an estate in Frankmariage acquired by purchase, yet doth it extend also to all estates in tayle, as well by discent as by purchase, for that Frankmariage is put but for an example.

V. Sect. 9.

Sect. 733.

Item come est moue en diuers faits, ceux parols en Latyne, Ego & Hæredes mei, warrantizabimus, & imperpetuum defendemus, il est a veier quel effect ad cel parol, Defendemus, en tiels faits, et il semble que il nad pas leffect de Garrantie, ne emprent en luy la cause de Garrantie, car sil issint serroit, que il prent effect ou cause de Garrantie, donque il serroit mitte en ascuns fines levies en la Court le Roy: Et home ne veiet ceo unque, que cest parol Defendemus, fuit en ascun fine, mes tansolement cest parol Warrantizabimus, per que semble que cest parol et Verbe Warrantizo, fait la Garrantie, & est la cause de Gar-

Also where it is contained in diuers Deedes these wordes in Latyne, *Ego & Hæredes mei warrantizabimus & imperpetuum defendemus*; it is to be seene what effect this word (*Defendemus*) hath in such Deedes: And it seemeth that it hath not the effect of Warrantie, nor comprehendeth in it the cause of warrantie, for if it should be so that it tooke the effect or cause of warrantie, then it should bee put into some Fines leuied in the Kings court, and a man neuer saw, that this word (*Defendemus*) was in any Fine, but onely this word (*Warrantizabimus.*) By which it seemeth, That this word and Verbe (*Warrantizo*) maketh the warrantie, and is the

Ego & hæredes mei warrantizabim° & imperpetuũ defendemus. Wherein three things are to be obserued: First, That Hæredes mei are words of necessitie, for otherwise the heyres are not bound. (a) Secondly, Though in the clause of the warrantie it be not mentioned to whome, &c. yet shall it bee intended to the Feoffee. (b) Thirdly, That the Feoffor may by expresse words warrant the land for the life of the Feoffee, or of the Feoffor, &c. but the recouerie in value shall bee in Fee. (c) Of this Bracton writeth in this manner, Et ego & hæred̃ mei warrãtizabim° tali et heredibus suis tantum vel tali & hæredibus & assignatis, & hæredibus assignatorum, vel assignatis assignatorum, & eorum hæredibus, & acquietabimus & defendemus eos totam terram illam cum pertinentijs, contra omnes gentes, &c. per hoc autem quod dicit (ego & hæredes mei) obligat se & hæredes ad warrantiam propinquos, & remotos, præsentes & futuros, & succedentes in infinitum. Per hoc autem quod dicit (Warrantizabimus) suscipit in se obligationem ad defendendum suum tenementum in possessione rei datæ & assignatos suos & eorum hæredes & omnes alios, &c. Per hoc autem quod dicit (acquietabimus) obligat se & hæredes suos ad acquietandum si quis plus petie-

(a) 6. E. 2. Vouch. 258. 12. E. 2 ib. 262. 14. H. 4. 15.

(b) 38. E. 3. 14.

(c) Bract. fo. 37. 238. & li. 5. 380, 381. Brit. fo. 106. b. Flet. li. 5. ca. 15. & li. 6. ca. 23. 35. H. 8. B. Gar. 90. F. N. B. 134. b

Brit. vb. sup. Flet. vb. sup. 21. H. 6. 48. 6. E. 2. Gar. 262.

Gar-

Garrantie, et nul auter Verbe en nostre Ley.	cause of warrantie, and no other word in our Law.	ris seruitij vel aliud seruitium quam in carta donationis continetur. Per hoc autem quod dicit (Defendemus) obligat se & hæredes suos ad defendendum si quis velit seruitutem po-

nere rei datæ contra formam suæ donationis. (d) Hereby it appeareth, That neither Defendere nor Acquietare doth create a Warranty, but Warrantizare onely. And as Ego & hæredes mei warrantizabimus, &c. in Latyne doe create a Warrantie; so, I and my heires shall Warrant, &c. in English, doth create a Warrantie also.

(d) 46. E. 3. 28. 11. H. 4. 41. 6. E. 2. Vouch. 262. 2. E. 4. 15. 6

(e) If a man be bound to A. in an Obligation, to defend such lands to A. whereof the Obligor had infeoffed him for 12. yeares, &c. in this case if he be ousted by a stranger without being impleaded, the Obligation is forfeit: but if hee bee bound to warrant the Land, &c the Bond is not forfeited, unlesse the Obligee be impleaded, and then the Obligor must bee readie to warrant, &c.

(e) 2. E. 4. 15. nu. Det. 71.

Donques il serra mit en ascuns fines, &c. Heere Littleton draweth an Argument from the forme & words of a Fine, & his reason is this, That seeing that a Fine is the highest and surest kind of assurance in Law, if Defendemus had the force of a warranty it would haue beene contained in Fines: and on the other side seeing this word Warrantizo is contained in Fines to create a Warrantie, that therefore that word doth implie a Warrantie, and not the other.

Et nul auter Verbe en nostre Ley. Heere it appeareth, That no other Verbe in our Law doth make a Warrantie, but Warrantizo onely, which is onely appropriated to create a Warrantie.

46. E. 3. 28. Vi. Sect. 1.

But, Qui bene distinguit, bene docet, and here, of necessitie you must distinguish, * First, betweene a Warrantie annexed to a Freehold or Inheritance, (whereof Littleton here speaketh) and a Warrantie annexed to a ward, which is a Chattell reall, for there, Grant, Demise, and the like, doe make a Warrantie. And of Warranties annexed to Freeholds and Inheritances, some be Warranties in Deed, and some be Warranties in Law. A Warrantie in Deed, or an expresse Warrantie, (whereof Littleton here speaketh) is created onely by this word Warrantizo, but Warranties in Law are created by many other words; they be therefore called Warranties in Law, because in iudgement of Law they amount to a Warrantie without this verb Warrantizo. (f) As Dedi is a Warrantie in Law to the Feoffee and his heires during the life of the Feoffor, but Concessi in a Feoffement or Fine implieth no Warrantie. But before the Statute of Quia emptores terrarum, if a man had giuen lands by this word Dedi, to haue and to hold to him and his heires, of the Donor and his heires, by certaine seruices, then not onely the Donor but his heires also had beene bound to Warrantie. But if before that statute a man had giuen lands by this word Dedi, to a man and to his heires for euer, to hold of the chiefe Lord, there the Feoffor had not beene bound to Warrantie, but during his life, as at this day he is.

Sect. 697.
* 31 E. 3. Vouch. 24. 12. Rich. 2. tit. Cont. de Vouch 35. 29. E. 3. 48. 10. Edw. 3. 6. & Symtin: Symons case 8. E. 3. 61. 12. Ed. 3. Vouch. 27. Temps E. 1. Vouch. 302. 3. H. 6. 17.

(f) Le stat. de Bigamis cap. 6. 2. H. 7. 7. 6. H. 7. 2. 48. E. 3. 2. 32. E. 1. tit. Vouch 390. Fitz. N. B. 134. 6. E. 2. Vouc. 258

And albeit the words of the Statute of Bigamis be, In cartis autem vbi continentur (Dedi & concessi, &c.) yet if Dedi be contained alone, it doth import a Warrantie, for the Statute doth conclude, Ipse tamen feoffator in vita sua ratione proprij doni sui tenetur warrantizare. So as Dedi is the word that implieth Warrantie, and not Concessi. Also where the words of the Statute be further, sine clausula quæ continet Warrantiam, the meaning of the Statute is, That Dedi doth import a Warrantie in Law, albeit there bee an expresse Warrantie in the Deede.

For if a man make a Feoffment by Dedi, and in the Deed doth warrant the land against I. S. and his heires, yet Dedi is a generall Warrantie during the life of the Feoffor, and so was the Statute expounded in both poynts, (g) Hil. 14. El. in the Court of Common Pleas, which I my selfe heard and obserued. (h) And if a man make a Lease for life reseruing a rent, and adde an expresse Warrantie, here the expresse Warrantie doth not take away the Warrantie in Law, for he hath election to vouch by force of either of them. And in Nokes Case note a diuersity betweene a Warrantie that is a Couenant reall, and a Warrantie concerning a Chattell. (i) Also this word Excambium doth implie a Warrantie.

Also a Partition implieth a Warrantie in Law, as in the Chapter of Parceners appeareth. And Homage auncestrell doth draw to it selfe Warrantie, as hath beene sayd in the Chapter of Homage Auncestrell.

And it is to be obserued, That the Warrantie wrought by this word Dedi is a speciall Warrantie, and extendeth to the heires of the Feoffee during the life of the Donor onely. But vpon the exchange and homage auncestrell the Warrantie extendeth reciprocally to the heires, and against the heires of both parties: and in none of the Cases the Assignee shall vouch by force

(g) Hil. 14. El. in Com. Banc.
(h) Li. 4 fo. 80. in Nokes case. 8. E. 3. 69. 9. E. 3. 15. 10. Ed. 3. 11. 20. E. 3. Count. de Gar. 7. 31. E. 3. Vouch. 280. 32. Ed. 3. ib. 102. 43. E. 3. 3. 7. E. 2. Tit. Cui in vita 17. 3. E. 3. Formedon 44.
(i) 4. E. 2. Vouch 245. 22. E. 3. 2. 14. H. 6. 2. 20. H. 6. 14. Li. 4 fo. 122. in Bastards Case. 15. E. 3. Bar. 265. 43. Ed. 3. 30. Li. 1 fo. 96 Li. 5 fol. 17 Spencers case. Li. 8. fo. 95. Sr. Staffords case.

of any of these warranties, but in the case of the exchange and Dedi the Assignee shall rebutt, but not in the case of Homage ancestrell.

(k) 28. Ass. 33. 14. Hen. 4. 5. 18 E. 3. 18 3. E. 2 auowr. 201 & 202. 19 E. 3. Auowr. 201, 202. 11. E. 3. Auowr. 100. 30. H. 6. 7. 33. H. 8. Dyer 51. 10. H. 7. 11. b. F. N. B. 163. a.

(k) And so no man shall haue a writ of Contra formam collationis, but onely the Feoffee and his heires which be priuie to the Deed, but an Assignee may rebutt by force of the Deede.

(l) 6. E. 2. Cont. de Vouch 105. 3. E. 3. 67. 4. E 2. ibid. 102. 6. E. 3. 11. 50. 7. E. 3. 6. 18. E. 3. 8. 22. Ed 3. 3. 3. H. 7. 13. 6. H. 7. 2. 14. E. 3. gar 32. F. N. B. 134. g. 5 E. 3. 87. 20. E. 3. tit. Counterplea de Gar. 7.

(l) If a man make a gift in Tayle or a Lease for life of land, by Deed or without Deed, reseruing a Rent, or of a Rent seruice by Deed, this is a warrantie in Law, and the Donee or Lessee being impleaded shall vouch and recouer in value. And this warrantie in Law extendeth not onely against the Donor or Lessor, and his heyres, but also against his Assignees of the reuersion, and so likewise the Assignee of Lessee for life shall take benefit of this warrantie in Law.

(m) 4. E. 3. 36. 33 Ed. 3. tit. Cont. de Vouch. 122. 43. ass. 32 50. E. 3. 7. F. N. B. 149 m.

(m) When Dower is assigned there is a warrantie in Law included, that the Tenant in Dower being impleaded, shall vouch and recouer in value a third part of the two parts whereof she is dowable.

(n) 14. H. 6. 2. 15. E. 3. Bar. 255.

And it is to be vnderstood, That a warrantie in Law and Assets is in some cases a good bar. (n) In a Formedon in the discender the Tenant may plead, That the Auncestor of the Demandant exchanged the Land with the Tenant for other Lands taken in exchange, which discended to the Demandant, whereunto he hath entred and agreed: or if he hath not entred and agreed vnto the Lands taken in exchange, then the Tenant may plead the warrantie in Law, and other Assets discended.

(o) 38 E. 3. 22. 23. 24. 13. E. 3. Garr. 35.

(o) If Tenant in Taile of Lands make a gift in Taile or a Lease for life, rendring a Rent, and dieth, and the Issue bringeth a Formedon in the discender, the Reuersion and Rent shall not barre the Demandant, because by his Formedon he is to defeat the Reuersion and Rent, Et non potest adduci exceptio eiusdem rei, cuius petitur dissolutio.

(p) 16. E. 3. Age 45. 18. E. 3. 8. 31. E. 3. Garr. 29.

(p) But if other assets in Fee simple doe discend, then this warrantie in Law and assets is a good barre in the Formedon.

Here foure things are to be obserued: First, That no warrantie in Law doth barre any Collaterall title, but is in nature of a Lineall warrantie: wherein the equitie of the Law is to be obserued.

Secondly, That an expresse warrantie shall neuer binde the heires of him that maketh the warrantie, vnlesse (as hath been sayd) they be named: as for example Littleton here sayth (Ego & hæredes mei) but in case of warranties in Law, in many cases the heyres shall be bound to warrantie, albeit they be not named.

Vide lib. 4. fol. 121. Bustards Case.

Thirdly, That in some cases warranties in Law doe extend to execution in value, of speciall Lands, and not generally of Lands discended in Fee simple, as you may see at large in my Reports.

(q) 45. E. 3. 20. b.

(q) Fourthly, That warranties in Law may be in some cases created without Deed, as vpon gifts in taile, Leases for life, Exchanges, and the like.

And seeing somewhat hath beene sayd out of Bracton and other antient Authors, concerning Assignees, it is necessarie to shew who shal take aduantage of a warrantie as Assignee by way of Voucher to haue recompence in value.

(r) 14. E. 3. Garr. 33. 13. E. 1. Garr. 93.

Lib. 5. fol. 17. b in Spencers case. 38. E. 3. 21.

(r) If a man infeoffe A. and B. to haue and to hold to them and their heires, with a Clause of warrantie, Prædictis A. & B. & eorum hæredibus & assignatis: In this case if A. dieth, and B. suruiueth and dieth, and the heire of B. infeoffeth C hee shall vouch as Assignee, and yet he is but the Assignee of the heyre of one of them, for in iudgement of Law the Assignee of the heyre is the Assignee of the Auncestor, and so the Assignee of the Assignee shall vouch in infinitum, within these words. (His Assignes.)

(s) 12. E. 2. Vouch. 263. 19. E. 2 gar. 85. 13. E. 1. ib. 93 Li. 5. fo. 17 Spencers case. 7. E. 3. 34. 10. E. 3. 9. 14. E. 3 Gar. 33. Bract. vb. sup. 9. Ed. 2 Gar de Chart. 30. 36. Edw. 3. Gar. 1. 4. H. 8. Dy. 1. F. N. B. 135.

(s) If a man infeoffeth A. To haue and to hold to him, his heyres and Assignes; A. infeoffeth B and his heyres, B dieth, the heyre of B shall vouch as Assignee to A. So as heyres of Assignees, and Assignees of Assignes, and Assignees of Heyres are within this word (Assignes) which seemed to be a question in Bractons time. And the Assignee shall not onely vouch, but also haue a Warantia Cartæ.

(t) 43. E. 3. 23. 26. Ed. 3 68. 40. E. 3. 14. 24. E. 3. 36. 11 H. 4. 94. 30. E. 3. 17. 5. E. 3. Age 19. Pl. Com. 418

If a man doth warrant Land to another without this word (Heyres,) his heyres shal not vouch: and regularly if he warrant Land to a man and his heyres; without naming Assignes, his Assignee shal not vouch. (t) But if the father bee infeoffed with warrantie to him and his heyres, the father infeoffeth his eldest son with warrantie and dieth, the Law giueth to the sonne aduantage of the warrantie made to his father, because by act in Law the warrantie betweene the father and the sonne is extinct.

But note there is a diuersitie betweene a warrantie that is a Couenant reall, which bindeth the partie to yeeld lands or Tenements in recompence, and a Couenant annexed to the Land, which is to yeeld but dammages, for that a Couenant is in many Cases extended futher than the warrantie. As for example:

(u) 42 E. 3 b. 3 Finchden.

(u) It hath beene adiudged, That where two Coparceners made partition of Land, and the one made a Couenant with the other, to acquite her and her heires of a Suit that issued out of the land, the couenantee aliened. In that case the assignee shall haue an action of couenant, and yet he was a stranger to the couenant, because the acquitall did runne with the land.

(w) A seised of the Mannor of D whereof a Chappell was parcell, a Prior with the assent of his Couent couenanteth by deed indented with A. and his heires to celebrate Diuine Seruice in his said Chappell weekly for the Lord of the said Mannor, and his Seruants, &c. In this case the assignees shall haue an action of Couenant, albeit they were not named, for that the remedie by couenant doth runne with the land to giue dammages to the partie grieued, and was in a manner appurtenant to the Mannor. (y) But if the couenant had beene with a stranger to celebrate Diuine Seruice in the Chappell of A. and his heires, there the assignee shall not haue an action of couenant, for the couenant cannot bee annexed to the Mannor because the couenantee was not seised of the Mannor. See in Spencers Case before remembred diuers other diuersities betweene Warranties, and Couenants, which yeild but dammages

(w) 42.E.3.3.a. Laur. Takehams case. 2.H.4.6. 6.H.4.1. & 2. Rasse Brabsons Case. Lib. 5. fol. 17.18. Spencers Case.

(y) 2.H.4.6. Henry Hornes Case. 6.H.4.1. Lib. 5. fol. 17.18. Spencers Case.

And here it is to be obserued, that an assignee of part of the land shall vouche as assignee. (*) As if a man make a feoffment in fee of two Acres to one with warrantie to him his heires and assignes, if he make a feoffment of one Acre, that feoffee shall vouch as Assignee, for there is a diuersitie betweene the whole estate in part, and part of the estate in the whole, or of any part. As if a man hath a warrantie to him his heires and assignes, and he make a lease for life, or a gift in tayle, the Lessee or Donee shall not vouch as assignee because he hath not the estate in fee simple whereunto the warrantie was annexed, but the Lessee for life may pray in ayde, or the Lessee or Donee may vouche the Lessor or Donor, and by this meanes hee shall take aduantage of the warranty. But if a lease for life, or a gift in tayle be made, the Remaynder ouer in fee, such a Lessee or Donee shall vouche as assignee, because the whole estate is out of the Lessor, and the particular estate, and the Remaynder doe in iudgement of Law to this purpose make but one estate.

(*) 18.E.3.52. 10.E.3.58. 5.E.3.49. 12.E.3. Counterplea de Vouch. 42. 14.E.3. Voucher 108. 5.E.3. ibid. 178. 13.E.3. ibid. 119. 40.E.3.22. 41.E.3. Vouch. 69. & 100. 32.E.3. ibi. 96. And this diuersitie was agreed Hill. 14. Eliz. in Communi Banco, which I heard and obserued.

(a) If a man infeoffe three with warrantie to them and their heires, and one of them release to the other two, they shall vouche, but if he had released to one of the other, the warrantie had beene extinct for that part, for he is an assignee.

(a) 40.E.3.14. 40. Ass. 5. 33.H.6.4. 37.H.8. alienation sans licence 31. 8.H.4.8.

(b) If a man doth warrant Land to two men and their heires, and the one make a feoffment in fee, yet the other shall vouch for his moitie. If a man at this day bee infeoffed with warrantie to him, his heires, and assignes, and he make a gift in tayle, the Remaynder in fee, the Donee make a feoffment in fee, that feoffee shall not vouche as assignee, because no man shall vouche as assignee, but hee that commeth in in priuitie of estate, but hee must vouche his feoffor, and he to vouche as assignee, but such an assignee may rebutte. If the warrantie be made to a man and his heires without this word (assignes) yet the assignee, or any tenant of the Land may rebutte. And albeit no man shall, vouche or haue a Warrantia cartæ either as partie, heire, or assignee, but in priuity of estate, yet any that is in of another estate, bee it by disseisin, abatement, intrusion, vsurpation or otherwise, shall rebutte by force of the warrantie as a thing annexed to the Land which sometime was doubted (c) in our Bookes. But herein is a diuersitie to be obserued when in the Cases aforesaid, hee that rebutteth claymeth vnder the warranty. And when hee that would rebutte claymeth aboue the warranty, for there hee shall not rebutte. And therefore if Lands bee giuen to two Brethren in fee simple with a warranty to the eldest and his heires, the eldest dieth without issue, the Suruiuor albeit he bee heire to him, yet shall he neyther vouche nor rebutt, nor haue a Warrantia cartæ, because his title to the Land is by relation aboue the fall of the Warrantie, and hee commeth not vnder the estate of him, to whom the warranty is made, as the Disseisor, &c. doth.

(b) 11.R.2. Detinue 46. 7.E.3.35. 46.E.3.4.

(c) 38.E.3.21. 26.E.3.56. Lib. 10. fo. 96.b. Seymors case. 7.E.3.34.35. 8.E.3.10. 46.E.3.4. 10.E.3.42. 45.E.3.18. 10. Ass. 5.35. Ass. 9.22. Ass. 30. 88. 31. Ass. 13.

(d) If a man make a gift in tayle at this day, and warrant the Land to him his heires and assignes, and after the Donee make a feoffment and dieth without issue, the warrantie is expired as to any Voucher or Rebutter, for that the estate in tayle whereunto it was knit is spent: otherwise it is, if the gift and feoffment had beene made before the Statute of Donis conditionalibus, for then both the Donee and Feoffee had a fee simple, and so are our Bookes to be intended in this and the like Cases.

(d) Lib. 3. fol. 62.63. Lincolne Colledge Case.

(e) If A. be seised of Lands in fee, and B releaseth vnto him or confirmeth his estate in fee with warrantie to him his heires and assignes; all men agree this warrantie to be good: but some haue holden, that no warranty can be raysed vpon a bare Release or Confirmation without passing some estate or transmutation of possession. (f) But the Law as it appeareth by Littleton himselfe is to the contrarie, and that both the partie, and (as some do hold) his assignee shall vouche, but he that is vouched in that case must be present in Court, and ready to enter into the warrantie and to answere, and the Tenant must shew forth the Deed of Release or Confirmation with warrantie, to the intent the Demaundant may haue an answere thereunto and eyther denie the deed or auoid it, for that at the time of the Confirmation made, he to whom it was made, had nothing in the Land, &c. for otherwise the Demaundant may counterplead the

(e) 14.E.3. Garr. 108. 12.H.7.1.

(f) 11.H.4.22. 10.E.3.52. 21.E.3.27. Vide Sect. 706. 738. & 745.

W. 1. cap. 40.

Vide 20. E. 1. Statute de vocat. ad warant.

(g) 22. H. 6. 15. 19. H. 6. 73. 20. H. 6. 73. 2. H. 4. 12. 41. E. 3. Garr. 15. 43. E. 3. 17. 43. Ass. 42. 12. Ass. 17. 12. E. 3. tayle 3. 22. E. 4. 16. b. 44. E. 3. 10. 44. Ass. Bassingbeons Ass. Lib. 10. fol. 97. Seymors Case.

(h) Lib. 3. fol. 63. Lincolne Colledge Case.

(i) 29. E. 3. 70. 17. E. 2. Ioinder in action. 1. 11. R. 4. 8.

(k) 14. H. 4. 3.

Voucher by the Statute of W. 1. viz. that neither Vouchee nor any of his Ancestors had any seisin whereof he might make a feoffment. And this is grounded upon the said Statute of W. 1. the words whereof be, Sil neit son garrantie en præsent, que lun voile garranter de son gree, & maintenant enter en respons. Otherwise the Tenant must be driven to his Warrantia cartæ.

(g) But a warrantie of it selfe cannot enlarge an estate, as if the Lessor by Deed release to his Lessee for life, and warrant the Land to the Lessee and his heires, yet doth not this enlarge his estate.

(h) If a man make a feoffment in fee with warrantie to him his heires and Assignes by Deed (as it must bee) and the Feoffee enfeoffeth another by paroll, the second Feoffee shall vouche, or have a Warrantia cartæ (as hath beene said) as assignee, albeit hee hath no deed of the assignement, because the deed comprehending the warrantie doth extend to the Assignees of the Land, and he is a sufficient assignee albeit he hath no Deed.

(i) If a man infeoffe two, their heires and assignes, and one of them make a feoffment in fee, that Feoffee shall not vouch as Assignee.

If a man make a feoffment in fee to A. his heires and assignes. A. infeoffeth B. in fee, who re-enfeoffeth. A. He or his assignes shall never vouche, for A. cannot be his owne Assignee. But if B. had infeoffed the heire of A. he may vouche as assignee, for the heire of A. may be assignee to A, in as much as he claymeth not as heire.

(k) If a man make a feoffment by deed of Lands to A. To have and to hold to him and his heires, and bind him and his heires to warrant the Land in forma prædicta, this warrantie shall extend to the feoffee and his heires. But if he had warranted the Land to the feoffee, the warranty had not extended to his heires, except the words had beene to him and his heires.

If a man letteth Lands for life the Remaynder in tayle, the Remaynder eadem forma, this is a good estate tayle, quia idem semper refertur proximo præcedenti.

Section 734.

Item si tenant en taile soit seisie des terres deuisables per testament solonque le custome, &c. et le tenant en tayle alien mesmes les tenements a son frere en fee, et ad issue, et deuie, & puis son frere deuisa per son testament mesmes les tenements a un auter en fee, et oblig̃ luy et ses heires a garranty, &c. et morust sans issue, il semble que cest Garrantie ne barrera my lissue en tayle, sil voit sues son briefe de Formedon, pur ceo que cest Garrantie ne discend my al issue en le tayle, entant q̄ le uncle del issue ne fuit my oblige a le Garrantie en sa vie: ne que il ne puissoit Garranter les tenemēts en sa vie, entant que le deuise ne puissoit prender ascun execution ou effect, forsque apres son decease. Et entant que le uncle en son vie ne fuit tenus de Garranter, tiel Garrantie ne poit discender

Also, if tenant in taile be seised of Lands deuisable by Testament after the custome &c. and the tenant in the taile alieneth the same tenements to his brother in fee, and hath issue and dieth, and after his brother deuiseth by his Testament the same tenements to another in fee, and bindeth him and his heires to warrantie, &c. and dieth without issue, it seemeth that this Warrantie shall not barre the issue in the taile, if he will sue his Writ of *Formedon*, because that this Warrantie shall not descend to the issue in taile, insomuch as the Vncle of the issue was not bound to the same warrantie in his life time: neither could hee warrant the tenements in his life, insomuch as the Deuise could not take any execution or effect vntill after his decease. And insomuch as the Vncle in his life was not

der de luy al issue en le tayle, &c. car nul chose poit discender del aunceester a son heire, sinon que mesme ceo fuit en launcester.

held to warrantie, such warrantie may not discend from him to the issue in the taile, &c. for nothing can discend from the Ancestor to his heire, vnlesse the same were in the Ancestor.

¶ Here our Author declareth one of the Maximes of the Common Law, that the heire shall neuer be bound to any expresse Warranty, but where the Ancestor was bound by the same warranty, for if the Ancestor were not bound, it cannot descend vpon the heire, which is the reason here yelded by Littleton. (l) If a man make a Feoffment in fee, and binde his heires to Warranty, this is voyde by the warrant of this Maxime, as to the heire, because the Ancestor himselfe was not bound. Also if a man binde his heires to pay a summe of money, this is voide. And of the other side if a man binde himselfe to Warranty, and binde not his heires, they be not bound, for he must say, as it appeareth before, Ego & hæredes mei warrantizabimus, &c. (m) And Fleta saith, Nota quod hæres non tenetur in Anglia ad debita antecessoris reddenda, nisi per antecessorem ad hoc fuerit obligatus, præterquam debita regis tantum: A fortiori in case of Warranty, which is in the realty.

(l) 31.E.1.Grant 85.

Bracton, lib.2.fo.37.238. Britton, fo.106.b. (m) Fleta, lib.2.ca.55. Britton, fo 65.b. 21.H.6.48.

But a Warranty in Law may binde the heire, although it neuer bound the Ancestor, and may be created by a Last Will and testament. (n) As if a man deuise lands to a man for life or in taile reseruing a rent, the Deuisee for life or in taile shall take aduantage of this Warrantie in Law, albeit the Ancestor was not bounden, and shall binde his heires also to Warrantie although they be not named. Also an expresse warrantie cannot bee created without Deede, and a will in writing is no Deede, and therefore an expresse warrantie cannot bee created by will.

(n) 18.E.3.4.

Sect. 735.736.

¶ Auxy vn garrantie ne poit aler solonque la nature des tenements per le custome, &c. mes tantsolement solonque le forme del Common ley. Car si le tenant en taile soit seisie des tenements en Burgh English, lou le custome est, que touts les tenemēts deins mesm le Borough, deuoyent discender a le fits puisne, et il discontinua le tayle oue garrantie, &c. et ad issue deux fits, et mourust seisie des auters terres ou tenements en mesme le burgh en fee simple a le value, ou pluis de les tenements tailes, &c. uncore le puisn fits auera vn Formedon de les terres tailes, et ne serra my barrē per le garranty son pere, coment que assets a luy discendist en fee simple de mesme le pere, solonqs le

Also a Warranty cannot goe according to the nature of the tenements by the custome, &c. but only according to the forme of the Common Law. For if the tenant in taile bee seised of tenements in Borough English, where the custome is, that all the tenements within the same Borough ought to discend to the youngest sonne, and hee discontinueth the taile with warranty, &c. and hath issue two sonnes, and dyeth seised of other lands or tenements in the same Borough in fee simple to the value or more of the lands entailed, &c. yet the youngest sonne shall haue a *Formedon* of the lands tailed, and shall not bee barred by the warranty of his father, albeit assets discended to him in fee simple from his said father

le custome, &c. pur ceo que le garrantie discendist a son eigne frere que est en pleine vie, et nemy sur le puisne. Et en mesme le maner est de collaterall garrantie fait de tiels tenements, lou le garrantie discendist sur leigne fits, &c. ceo ne barrera my le puisne fits, &c.

according to the custome, &c. because the warranty discendeth vpon his elder brother who is in full life, and not vpon the youngest. And in the same manner is it of collaterall warrantie made of such tenements where the warranty discendeth vpon the eldest son, &c. this shal not barre the younger son, &c.

Sect. 736.

En mesme le maner est de tenements en le Countie de Kent, queux sont appelles Gauelkind, les queux tenements sont departibles enter les freres, &c. solonque la custome, si ascun tiel garrantie soit fait per son auncester, tiel garrantie discendera tantsolement al heire que est heire al common ley, cestascauoir al eigne frere, solonque la conusans del common ley, et nemy a touts les heirs queux sont heires de tiels tenements solonque le custome.

IN the same manner is it of lands in the County of Kent, that are called Gauelkinde, which lands are deuidable betweene the brothers, &c. according to the custome, if any such warranty bee made by his Ancestor, such warranty shall descend only to the heire which is heire at the Common law, that is to say, to the elder brother, according to the conusance of the Common Law, and not to all the heires that are heires of such tenements according to the custome.

Vid Sect. 603. 718. & 737.

HEreupon a diuersitie is to be obserued betweene the Lien reall, and the Lien personall. For the Lien reall, as the Warranty, doth euer discend to the heire at the Common Law, (n) but the Lien personall doth binde the speciall heires, as all the heires in Gauelkinde, and the heire on the part of the mother, as hath beene said.

(o) If two men make a Feoffment in fee with a warranty, and the one die, the Feoffee cannot vouche the suruiuor only, but the heire of him that is dead also, but otherwise if two ioyntly binde themselues in an Obligation, and the one die, the suruiuor only shall be charged.

(n) 11. E. 3. Det. 7. 11. H. 7. 12.
(o) 17. E. 3. Ioint. 41. 16. H. 7. 13. 29. E. 3. 46. 12. H. 7. 3. 22. E. 3. 1. 17. E. 3. 8. 30. E. 3. 40. 19. H. 6. 55. lib. 3. fo. 14. Mathew Herberts case.

Sect. 737.

ITem, si tenant en le taile ad issue deux files per diuers venters, et morust, & les files entront, et vn estrange eux disseisist de mesmes les tenements, et lun de eux relessa per son fait a le disseisor tout son droit, et oblige luy et ses heires a garranty, et morust sans issue, en cest case la soer

ALso if Tenant in taile hath issue two daughters by diuers venters and dieth, & the daughters enter, & a stranger disseiseth them of the same tenements, and one of them releaseth by her Deed to the disseisor all her right, and binde her and her heires to warranty, and die without issue. In this case the

soer que surviesquist poit bien enter et ouster le disseisor de touts les tenements, pur ceo que tiel garranty nest pas discontinuance, ne collateral garrantie a la soer que surviesquist, pur ceo que ils sont de demy sanke, et lun ne poit estre heire a lauter, solonque le cours del Common ley. Mes autrement est, lou y sont files del tenant en taile per un mesme venter.

sister which surviueth may well enter, and oust the disseisor of all the tenements, because such warrantie is no discontinuance nor collaterall warrantie to the sister that suruiueth, for that they are of halfe blood, and the one cannot bee heire to the other according to the course of the Common Lawe. But otherwise it is where there bee daughters of tenant in taile by one venter.

¶ The reason of this is in respect of the halfe blood, whereof sufficient hath beene said in the first booke in the Chapter of fee simple.

Two brothers bee by demy venters, the eldest releaseth with warranty to the Disseisor of the Uncle, and dyeth without issue, the Uncle dyeth, the warranty is removed, and the younger brother may enter into the land.

Section 738.

¶ Item si tenant en taile lessa les tenements a un home pur terme de vie, le remainder a un auter en fee, et un collaterall auncester confirma le state del tenant a term de vie, & oblige luy & ses heires a garranty pur terme de vie del tenant a terme de vie & morust, & le tenant en taile ad issue, & devie, ore lissue est barre a demander les tenements per briefe de Formedon, durant le vie le tenant a terme de vie, per cause del collateral garrantie discendu sur le issue en le taile. Mes apres le decease de le

Also if tenant in taile letteth the Lands to a man for terme of life, the remainder to another in fee, and a collaterall Ancestor confirmeth the state of the tenant for life, and bindeth him, and his heires to warranty for terme of the life of the tenant for life, and dyeth, and the tenant in taile hath issue & dies, now the issue is barred to demand the tenements by writ of *Formedon* during the life of tenant for life, because of the collaterall warranty discended vpon the issue in taile. But after the decease of the tenant for life,

¶ Here it appeareth that a Warrantie may be raysed by a Confirmation which transferreth neither estate nor right, whereof sufficient hath beene said before. Vid. Sect. 733. & 7[illegible]

¶ *A garranty pur terme de vie, &c.* (p) This proveth that a Warranty may bee limitted, and that a man may warrant Lands aswell for terme of life, or in taile, as in fee. (p) 38. E. 3. 14. 16. E. 3. Vouch. 85.

If Tenant in fee simple that hath a Warrantie for life either by an expresse Warranty, or by Dedi, be impleaded and vouche, hee shall recover a fee simple in value albeit his warranty were but for terme of life, because the Warranty extended in that case to the whole estate of the Feffee in fee simple, but in the case that Littleton here putteth, the Tenant for life shall recover in value but an estate for life, because the Warranty doth extend to that estate only.

¶ *Vn briefe de Formedon, &c.* Here is implyed that a Collaterall Warrantie

Warrantie giueth no right, but shall barre onely for life, and after the partie is restored to his Action.

tenant a terme de vie, lissue auera vn briefe de Formedon, &c.

the issue shall haue a Writ of *Formedon*, &c.

It is also to bee obserued, That a warrantie may discend to the heyres of him that made it during the life of another.

Section 739.

¶ ET sur ceo ieo aye oye vn reason, que cel case prouera vn auter case, s. si vn home lessa ses terres a vn auter, A auer et tener a luy et a ses heires pur terme dauter vie, et le Lessee morust viuant celuy a que vie, &c. et vn Estrange enter en la Terre que le heire le Lessee luy poit ouster, &c. pur ceo que en le case procheine auantdit, entant que home poit obliger luy et ses heyres a Garranty al Tenant a terme de vie tantsolement durant la vie le Tenant a terme de vie, & cel Garrantie discendist al heyre celuy, que fist le Garrantie, le quel Garrantie nest pas Garrantie denheritance, mes tantsolement pur terme dauter vie, per mesme le reason lou Tenements sont lesses a vn Home, A auer et tener a luy et a ses heyres pur terme dauter vie, si le Lessee morust, viuant celuy a que vie, son heire auera les Tenements, viuant celuy a que vie, &c. car ont dit, Que si home grãt vn annuitie a vn auter, A auer et perceiuer a luy et a ses heyres pur terme dauter vie, si le Grantee morust, &c. que apres son mort son Heyre auera lannuitie durant la vie celuy a que vie, &c. Quære de ista materia.

AND vpon this I haue heard a reason, That this Case will prooue another Case, *viz*. If a man letteth his Lands to another, To haue and to hold to him and to his heires for terme of anothers life, and the Lessee dieth, liuing *Celuy a que vie*, &c. and a stranger entreth into the land, That the Heyre of the Lessee may put him out, &c. because in the case next aforesayd, in as much as a man may bind him and his heires to warrantie to Tenant for life onely, during the life of the Tenant for life, and this warrantie discendeth to the Heire of him which made the warranty, the which Warrantie is no Warrantie of Inheritance, but only for terme of anothers life. By the same reason where Lands are let to a man, To haue and to hold to him and his Heires for terme of anothers life, if the Lessee die, liuing *Celuy a que vie*, his Heyres shall haue the Lands, liuing *Celuy a que vie*, &c. For they haue sayd, That if a man grant an Annuitie to another, To haue and to take to him and his Heyres for terme of anothers life, if the Grantee die, &c. That after his death his heyre shall haue the Annuitie during the life of *Celuy a que vie*, &c. *Quare de ista materia.*

Tei

[Eo ay oye vn reason. Here our Student is taught after the example of our Author, to observe every thing that is worth the noting.

Si vn home lessa terres a vn auter, &c. This case is without question, (q) That the heyre of the Lessee shall have the land to prevent an Occupant. And so it is (as Littleton here sayth) in case of an Annuitie, or of any other thing that lieth in Grant, whereof there can be no Occupant. And of this somewhat hath beene sayd in the Chapter of Discents.

(q) 17. E. 3. 48. 18. Ed. 3. 12. 11. H. 4. 42. 7. H. 4. 46. 8. H. 4. 15. Dy. 8. El. 253. 18. H. 8. 3. 27. H. 8. 21. H. 8. tit Estates Br. 50. 19. Ed. 3. tit. Account 56. 33. Ass. p. 17. 22. H. 6. 33. 39. E. 3. 37. Vid. Sect. 387.

Sect. 740.

Mes lou tiel Lease ou Grant est fait a vn home et a ses heires pur terme dans, en cest Case lheire le Lessee ou le Grantee nauera vnques aps la mort le Lessee, ou le Grantee ceo que est issint lesse ou grant, pur ceo que est chattel real, et chateux realx per l' common Ley viendra al Executors del grantee, ou del Lessee, et nemy al heyre.

BVt where such Lease or Grant is made to a man and to his heyrs for terme of yeares; In this case the heire of the Lessee or the Grauntee shall not after the death of the Lessee or the grantee have that which is so let or granted, because it is a Chattel reall, and Chattels realls by the Common Law shall come to the Executors of the grantee, or of the Lessee, and not to the Heire.

Here is a generall rule, That Chattels realls as wel as Chattels personalls shall goe to the Executors or Administrators of the Lessee, and not to his heyres. For as Estates of Inheritance or Freehold discendible shall goe to the heyre, so Chattells, as well reall as personall, shall goe to the Executors or Administrators.

11. E. 3. tit. Ass. 88. 11. Ass. 21. 10. El. Dy. 276.

(r) But if the Kings Tenant by Knights service in Capite be seised of a Mannor, whereunto an Advowson is appendant, and the church become voyd, the Tenant dieth, his heyre within age, the king shall present to the Church, and not the Executor or Administrator: but if the land be holden of a Common Person, in that Case the Executor shall present, and not the Gardein.

(r) 24. E. 3. 26. F. N. B. 33. b. F. N. B. 34. a.

(f) If a Bishop hath a ward faine and dieth, the King shall not have the Ward nor the Successor, but the Executor, and the ward shall be Assets in his hands. So it is of Heriot, Reliefe, and the like. (t) But if a Church become voyd in the life of a Bishop, and so remain untill after his decease, the King shall present thereunto, and not the Executor or Administrator, for nothing can be taken for a presentment, and therefore it is no assets.

(f) 40 Ed. 3. 14.

(t) 9. H. 6. 58. 11. H. 4. 7.

Sect. 741.

ITem en ascuns cases il poit estre, que coment que vn collaterall Garrantie soit fait en fee, &c. vncore tiel Garrantie poit estre defeat, et anient. Sicome te-

ALso in some cases it may be, That albeit a collateral warrantie be made in Fee, &c. yet such a Warranty may be defeated and taken away: As if Tenant in Tayle discontinue the Tayle

ET morust sans Issue, &c. Here (as before in this Chapter hath beene noted) the Collaterall Warrantie doth discend upon the Issue in Tayle, before any right doth discend unto him, wherein this Diversitie is to bee observed: Where the right is in esse in any of the Ancestors of the heyre, at the time of the discent

V. Sect. 707.

nant en taile disconti- nue le taile en fee, et le Discontinuee est disseisie, et le frere del tenant en le taile relessa per son fait a le disseisor tout son droit, &c. oue garrantie en fee, & morust sans issue, & le tenant en l' taile ad issue et devie, ore lissue est barre de son action per force de collateral garrantie discendue sur luy, mes si apres ceo le Discontinuee enter sur le disseisor, donque poit lheire en le taile aver bien son action de Formedon, &c. pur ceo que l' garrantie est aniente et defeat, car quant garranty est fait a un home sur estate que adonques il avoit, si lestate soit defeate le Garrantie est defeate.

in fee, and the Discontinuee is disseised, and the brother of the tenant in taile releaseth by his Deed to the Disseisor all his right, &c. with warranty in fee, and dyeth without issue, and the tenant in taile hath issue and die, now the issue is barred of his action by force of the collaterall warrantie descended vpon him. But if afterwards the Discontinuee entreth vpon the Disseisor, then may the heire in taile haue well his action of *Formedon, &c.* because the warranty is taken away and defeated, for when a warrantie is made to a man vpon an estate which hee then had, if the estate be defeated the Warranty is defeated.

cent of the Collaterall Warrantie, there albeit the Warranty discend first, & after the right doth discend, the Collateral Warrantie shall binde, as here in this case of our Author expresly appeareth. But where the right is not in esse in the heire, or any of his Ancestors, at the time of the fall of the warrantie, there it shall not binde.

(u) 7.E.3.48. 30.H.8.42.

(u) Asif Lord and Tenant be; and the Tenant make a Feoffment in fee with Warrantie, and after the Feoffee purchase the Seigniory, and after the Tenant cesse, the Lord shall have a Cessavit; for a Warrantie doth extend to Rights precedent, and never to any right that commenceth after the warranty, whereof more shall be said in this Section. Also a Warranty shall never barre any estate that is in possession, reversion or remainder, that is not devested, displaced, or turned to a right before, or at the time of the fall of the warrantie.

(w) Lib. 1. fo. 67. Archers case.

(w) If a Lease for life be made to the Father, the remainder to his next heire, the Father is disseised and releaseth with Warranty and dyeth, this shall barre the heire, although the warranty doth fall, and the remainder commeth in esse at one time.

(y) Temps E. 1. Voucher 296. 31. Ass. 13. 22. Ass. 36. 41. Ass. 6. 33. E. 3. tit. Gar. 74. lib. 10. fo. 97. E. Seymors case.

(y) If there be Father and Sonne, and the Sonne hath a Rent service, suite to a Mill, Rent charge, Rent Secke, Common of pasture, or other profit apprender out of the land of the Father, and the Father maketh a Feoffment in fee with warranty, and dyeth, this shall not barre the Sonne of the Rent, common, or other profit apprender, quamuis clausula specialis warrantie vel acquietancie in cartis tenentium, inseratur quia in tali casu transit terra cum onere: and he that is in seisin or possession need not to make any Entrie or Claime: and albeit the Sonne after the Feoffment with warranty, and before the death of the Father had beene disseised, and so being out of possession the warrantie discended upon him, yet the warranty should not binde him, because at the time of the warrantie made, the Sonne was in possession. (*) So if my Collaterall Ancestor release to my Tenant for life, this shall not binde my Reversion or Remainder, because that the Reversion or Remainder continued in me. But if he that hath a Rent Common, or any profit out of the Land in taile, disseise the Tenant of the land, and maketh a Feoffment of the land, and warrant the land to the Feoffee and his heires, (a) regularly the warranty doth extend to all things issuing out of the land, that is to say, to warrant the land in such plight and manner, as it was at in the hand of the Feoffor, at the time of the Feoffment with warranty, and the Feoffee shall vouche, as of lands discharged of the rent, &c. at the time of the Feoffment made.

(*) 45.E.3.31. 21.H.7.11.

Vid. Sect. 698.

(a) 21.E.4.26. 21.H.7.9. 3.H.7.4. 7.H.4.17. 30.H.8. Dier 42. 30.E.3.30. 9.E.3.78. 45.E.3. Voucher 72. F.N.B.125. 14.H.8.6.

A woman that hath a Rent charge in fee entermarieth with the Tenant of the Land, an estranger releaseth to the Tenant of the Land with warrantie, he shall not take advantage of this warrantie eyther by Voucher or Warrantia cartæ, for the wife, if her husband die, or the heire of the wife living the husband, cannot have an action for the Rent upon a Title before

the

the warrantie made, for if the heire of the wife bring an Assise of Mordancester, this action is grounded after the warrantie, whereunto as hath beene said, the warrantie shall not extend.

So it is if the Grantee of the Rent grant it to the Tenant of the Land upon condition, which maketh a feoffment of the Land with warrantie, this warrantie cannot extend to the Rent, albeit the feoffment was made of the Land discharged of the Rent, for if the condition be broken, and the Grantor be intituled to an Action, this must of necessitie bee grounded after the warrantie made.

But in the Case aforesaid, when the woman Grantee of the Rent marrieth with the Tenant, and the Tenant maketh a feoffment in fee with warrantie, and dieth, in a Cui in vita brought by the wife (as by Law she may) (b) the feoffee shall vouche as of Lands discharged at the time of the warranty made for that her title is Paramont, so if tenant in tayle of a Rent charge purchase the Land, and make a feoffment with warrantie, if the issue bring a Formedon of the Rent, the Tenant shall vouche Causa qua supra.

(b) 7.H.4.17.

(*) But some doe hold, that a man shall not vouche, &c. as of Land discharged of a Rent Service.

(*) 10.E.4.9.b. 18.E.3.55 44.E.3.19.

(c) Also no warrantie doth extend unto meere and naked Titles, as by force of a condition with clause of re-entrie, Exchange, Mortmaine, consent to the ravisher and the like, because that for these no action doth lie, and if no action can bee brought, there can bee neither Voucher, Writ of Warrantia cartæ, nor Rebutter, and they continue in such plight and essence as they were by their originall creation, and by no Act can be displaced or devested out of their originall essence, and therefore cannot be bound by any warrantie.

(c) Lib.10.fo.97. E.Seymores case. 22.Ass.pl.38. 31.Ass.p.13. 41.Ass.p.6. 33.E.3.garr.74.

(d) And albeit a woman may have a Writ of Dower to recover her Dower, yet because her title of Dower cannot be devested out of the originall essence, a collaterall warrantie of the Ancestor of the woman shall not barre her. So it is of a feoffment Causa matrimonij prælocuti.

(d) 34.E.3.tit.droit 72. 21.E.4.82.

(e) A warranty doth not extend to any Lease though it be for many thousand yeares, or to estates of Tenant by Statute Staple, or Merchant, or Elegit, or any other Chattle, but only to Freehold or Inheritances, as it appeareth in all Littletons Cases which hee putteth in this Chapter. And this is the reason, that in all Actions which Lessee for yeares may have, a warranty cannot be pleaded in barre, as in an Action of Trespasse, or upon the Statute of 5.R.2. and the like. But in those Actions when the Freehold or Inheritances doe come in question, there the warranty may be pleaded. But in such Actions which none but a Tenant of the Freehold can have, as upon the Statute of 8.H.6. Assise, or the like, there a warrantie may be pleaded in barre.

(e) 21.E.4.18.82. 1.H.7.12.22. 11.H.7.15.16 20.H.7.2.b. 14.H.7.22. 43.E.3.25.per Finch.in quar.Imp.15.H.7.9. Lib.10.fo.97.

¶ *Quant Garrantie est fait a un home sur estate, que adonques il auoit, si lestate soit defeat, le Garrantie est defeat.* **Here it appeareth, that although** a collaterall warrantie be discended, (f) yet if the state whereunto the warranty was annexed be defeated, albeit it be by a meere stranger, (as in this case that Littleton here put by the discontinuee) the warranty is defeated, and although the Discontinuance remaine and no remitter wrought to the heire, yet the warrantie is defeated, and barre removed, so as the issue in tayle may have his Formedon and recover the Land. Sublato Principali tollitur adiuncturn.

(f) 3.H.7.9.b. 16.E.3. tit. Continuall Claime 10. 9.H.4.8. Pl.Com.158.

Sect. 742.

¶ En mesme le manner est, si le discontinuee fait feofement en fee, reseruant a luy un certaine rent, & pur default de payment un re-entry, &c. & un collaterall Garranty de ancester est fait a celuy feoffee q̃ ad estate sur condition, &c. & morust sans issue, coment que cel Garrantie discendet sur lissue ẽ taile, uncore si apres le rent soit aderer et le dis-

IN the same manner it is if the discontinuee make a feoffmẽt in fee reserving to him a certain rent, and for default of payment a re-entrie, &c. and a collateral warrantie of the Ancestor is made to the feoffee that hath the estate upon condition, &c. and dieth without issue, albeit that this warranty shall discend upon the issue in tayle, yet if after the rent be behind, and the

discontinuee entra en la terre, adonque auera lissue en tayle son recouery per briefe de Formedon, pur ceo que le collaterall garrantie est defeat. Et issint si ascun tiel collateral garranty soit pled̄ enuers lissue en le tayle, en son action de Formedon, il poit mr̄er le matter come est auantdit, coment le garrantie est defeat, &c. & issint il poit bien maintener son action, &c.

discontinuee enter into the Land, then shall the issue in taile haue his recouery by Writ of *Formedon*, because the collaterall warranty is defeated. And so if any such collateral warranty be pleaded against the issue in tayle in his action of *Formedon* he may shew the matter as is aforesaid, how the warrantie is defeated, &c. and so he may wel mayntaine his action, &c.

¶ Here Littleton putteth another case vpon the same ground and reason, viz. where the state whereunto the warranty is annexed, is defeated, there the warranty it selfe is defeated also, which is one of the maximes of the Common Law.

Sect. 743.

¶ Item si ten̄ en taile fait vn feoffment a son vncle, & puis luncle fait vn feoffment en fee ouesq; garranty, &c. a vn auter, et puis le feoffee del vncle enfeoffa areremaine luncle en fee, & puis luncle enfeoffa vn estrange ē fee sans garranty & morust sauns issue, & le tenant en tayle morust, si issue en le tayle voyle port son bre de Formedon, enuers lestrange q̄ fuit le darrein feoffee, & ceo per luncle, lissue ne serra vnque barre per le garranty que fuit fait per le vncle al dit primer feoffee de son vncle, pur ceo que le dit garrantie fuit defeat & anient, p̄ ceo que luncle a luy reprist cy grand estate de son primer feoffee a que le garranty fuit fait, sicome m̄ le feoffee auoit de luy. Et la cause p̄ que le garranty est anient en ceo cas, est ceo, s. que si le garranty estoieroit en sa force, donq; luncl̄ garrantel̄ a luy mesm̄, q̄ ne poit estre.

ALso if Tenant in tayle make a feoffment to his vncle, and after the vncle make a feoffment in fee with warrantie, &c. to another, and after the feoffee of the Vncle doth re-enfeoffe againe the Vncle in fee, and after the Vncle enfeoffeth a stranger in fee without warrantie, and dieth without issue, and the Tenant in tayle dieth, if the issue in tayle will bring his Writ of *Formedon* against the stranger that was the last feoffee, and that by the Vncle, the issue shall not be barred by the warranty that was made by the Vncle to the first feoffee of his Vncle, for that the said warrantie was defeated and taken away because the Vncle tooke backe to him as great an estate from his first feoffee to whom the Warranty was made, as the same feoffee had from him. And the cause why the warrantie is defeated, is this, *viz.* that if the Warrantie should stand in his force, then the Vncle should warrant to himselfe which cannot bee.

Here

¶ HEre Littleton putteth another case, where a warranty may be defeated, as when the Uncle taketh backe as large an estate, as he had made, the warrantie is defeated because he cannot warrant land to himselfe. (g) And so it is if the Uncle had made the warrantie to the feoffee his heires and assignes, and taken backe an estate in fee, and after infeoffed another, yet the warrantie is defeated for that he cannot be assignee to himselfe, and a man shall not regulary vouche himselfe as assignee of a fee simple, and the Law will not suffer things inutile and unprofitable. (h) And yet if the father be infeoffed with warrantie to him and his heires, the father infeoffeth his heire apparant in fee and dieth, he (as it hath been said) shall vouch himselfe, and the heire in borow English by reason the act in Law determined the warrantie betweene the Father and the Sonne.

(i) But if a man maketh a feoffment in fee with warranty to the feoffee his heires and assignes, and the feoffee re-enfeoffeth the feoffor and his wife, or the feoffor and any other stranger, the warrantie remayneth still, or if two doe make a feoffment with warrantie to one and his heires and assignes, and the feoffee re-enfeoffe one of the feoffors, the warrantie doth also remayne.

(g) Temps E.1. Voucher 268. 40.E.3.14. 44.E.3.38. 25.E.3.43.b. 26.E.3.68. 14.E.3.Vouch.106. 16.E.3. Voucher 87. 19.E.3.Vouchee 122. 17.E.3.73.74. 20.H.6.29.
(h) 40.E.3.14.a. 41.E.3.25.a.
(i) 11.H.4.20.42. 17.E.3.47.59. 18.E.3.56. 27.E.3.46. 39.E.3.9.

Section 744.

¶ MEs si le feoffee fesoit estate al uncle pur terme de vie, ou en taile, sauant le reuersion, &c. ou que il fait done en taile al uncle, ou un leas pur term de vie, le remainder ouster, &c. en cest cas le garrantie nest pas tout oustermẽt aniẽt, mest est mis en suspence durant lestate que luncle ad. Car apres ceo que luncle est mort sans issue, &c. donques celuy en le reuersion, ou celuy en le remainder barreroit lissue en taile en son briefe de Formedon per le collateral garranty en tiel cas, &c. Mes autrement est lou luncle auoit auxy graund estate en la terre de le feoffee, a que le gar-

BUt if the feoffee had made an estate to his vncle for terme of life, or in taile, sauing the reuersion, &c. or a gift in Tayle to the vncle, or a lease for terme of life, the remainder ouer, &c. In this case the warranty is not altogether taken away, but is put in suspence during the estate that the vncle hath. For after that, that the vncle is dead without issue, &c. then he in the Reuersion, or he in the Remainder shall barre the issue in taile in his writ of *Formedon* by the collaterall warrantie in such case, &c. But otherwise it is where the vncle hath as great estate in the land of the Feoffee to whom the Warrantie was made, as the Feoffee

¶ P*Vr terme de vie, ou en taile.* Here it appeareth (k) that by taking a (l) Lease for life, or a gift in taile, the warranty is suspended.

A man enfeoffeth a woman with Warranty; they intermarry and are impleaded, upon the default of the husband the wife is receiued, shee shall vouche her husband &c. notwithstanding the warranty was put in suspence. (m) And so on the other side, if a woman infeoffe a man with warranty, and they intermarry and are impleaded, the husband shall vouch himselfe and his wife by force of the said Warranty.

(n) An infant en ventre sa mere may bee vouched if God giue him a birth, and if not, such a one heire to the warranty, but he cannot be vouched alone without the heire at the Common Law, for Proces shall be presently awarded against him.

¶ *Mes est mise en suspence.* (o) Tenant in taile maketh a feoffment in fee with warranty, and disseiseth the Discontinuee, and dyeth seised, leauing assets to his issue. Some hold that in respect of this suspended warranty and assets, the issue

(k) 16.E.3. Vouch.87. 44.E.3.38. 26.E.3.56. 17.E.3.47. 10.E.3.30. 12.E.3.Counterple de vouch 42. 14.E.3.Ibid.12.
(l) 6.E.2.vouch.257. 3.E.3. Ibid.201. 5.E.3.ibid.178. 18.E.3.52. 14.E.3.vouch.109. 31.E.3.ibid.25. 43.E.3.7. 44.E.3.38. 32.E.3.Voucher 102.
(m) 4.E.2.Voucher 243.446
(n) Temps E.1.Gard.153. 31.E.1.briefe 873. 8.E.2.vouch.237. 11.E.3.ibid.13. 11.E.3.quar.imp.158. 38.E.3.7.& 29. 41.E.3.in dower. 9.H.6.24. Pl.Com. Stowells case per Saunders & Browne
(o) 31.E.3.36.a.& b. 38.E.3.21. 44.E.3.254. 45.E.3.title 32. 44.E.3.ibid.31. 33.E.3.ibid.4.

ranty fuit fait, come le feoffee auoit de luy, Causa patet.

hath himselfe. *Causa patet.*

issue in taile shall not bee remitted, but that the Discontinuee shall recouer against the issue in taile, and he take aduantage of his warranty, if any he hath, and after in a Formedon brought by the issue, the Discontinuee shall barre him in respect of the warranty and Assets, and so euery mans right saued.

Sect. 745.

ITem si luncle apres tiel feoffment fait oue garrantie, ou release fait per luy oue garranty soit attaint de felony, ou utlage de felony, tiel collateral garrantie ne barreſt my, ne greeuera lissue en le taile, pur ceo que per le attainder de felonie, le sanke est corrupt enter eux, &c.

ALso if the vncle after such feoffment made with warrantie, or a release made by him with warrantie, be attaint of felony, or outlawed of felony, such collaterall warranty shall not barre nor grieue the issue in the taile, for this that by the attainder of felony, the blood is corrupted betweene them, &c.

Sect. 733. 746. ¶ *Or release fait per luy oue garranty.* Note a Warranty grounded vpon a Release, whereof you shall reade before in this chapter.

8. E. 2. Voucher 237. ¶ *Soit attaint de felony, ou vtlage, &c.* Note according to Littleton here, there be two manner of Attainders, the one is after apparance, and that in three manners, by Confession, by Battell, or by Verdict, the other vpon Proces to bee Outlawed, which is an Attainder in Law. But (as hath beene said) there is a great diuersitie, as to the forfeiture of Land, betweene an Attainder of felony by Outlawry vpon an Appeale, and vpon an Inditement: for in the case of an Appeale, the Defendant shall forfeit no lands, but such as he had at the time of the Outlawry pronounced, but in case of Inditement, such as he had at the time of the felony committed, and the reason of this diuersity is euident, for that in the case of Appeale there is no time alledged in the Writ when the felony was done, and therefore of necessitie it must relate in that case only to the iudgement of the Outlawry: but in the case of Inditement, there is a certaine time alledged, and therefore in that case it shall relate to the time alledged in the Inditement when the felony was committed. But in the case of the Inditement there is also a diuersitie to be obserued, (o) for as hath beene said, it shall relate to the time alledged in the Inditement for auoyding of estates, charges, and incumbrances, made by the Felon after the felony committed, but for the meane profits of the land it shall relate only to the iudgement, aswell in this case of Outlawry as in other cases. And where Littleton saith, (Attaint de felony) if a man be conuicted of felony by verdict, and deliuered to the Ordinary to make Purgation (p) he cannot be vouched, for that the time of his purgation (if any should be) is vncertaine, and the Demandant cannot be delayed vpon such an vncertaintie, but the Tenant is not without remedy, for he may haue his Warrantia cartæ.

(o) 39. E. 3. Forfeiture 30. 38. E. 3. 31. 3. E. 4. 25. 19. E. 4. 2. Pl. Com. 488. b.

(p) 8. E. 2. Voucher 237. Vid. 38. E. 3. 29 b Simile.

¶ *Attaint.* **Of this word hath beene spoken in the second booke** in the chapter of Villenage.

Vpon seuerall Attainders of Felonyes, there lye three seuerall writs of Escheate, viz. (*) First, when he hath iudgement to be hanged. Secondly, when hee is outlawed. Thirdly, when he abiureth the Realme.

(q) The Defendant in an appeale of death did wage battaile, and was slaine in the field, yet Iudgement was giuen that he should be hanged, and the Iustices said, that it is altogether necessary, that such a Iudgement be giuen, for otherwise the Lord could not haue a Writ of Escheate. (r) And in Eire it hath beene seene, that a man hath beene attainted after his death by presentment, &c. The difference betweene a man Attainted and Conuicted is, that a man is said Conuict before hee hath iudgement, as if a man bee conuict by Confession, Verdict, or Recreancy. And when he hath his iudgement vpon the Verdict, Confession, or Recreancy,

(*) Dame Hales case in Pl. Com. fo. 262.

(q) 8. E. 3. Iudgement 225.

(r) 15. E. 3. Petition 2.

Recreancy; or upon the Outlawry, or Abjuration, then is he said to be Attaint. And thus is the Law taken at this day, notwithstanding (s) some diversitie of opinions in our bookes.

(s) 40.E.3.12. 3.E.3. Corone 365. 8.E.2.ibid.293. 21.H.7.

If a Felon be convicted by Verdict, Confession, or Recreancy, he doth forfeit his goods and chattells, &c. presently. (t) For where a reason hath beene yeelded in our bookes, that the praying of his Clergie, was a refusall of the judgement of the Lawe, and a flight in Law, and for that cause he forfeited his goods and chattells, that doth not hold, for if a man bee Convict of pettie treason, or murder, or any other crime for which he cannot have his Clergie, yet by the very Conviction he forfeiteth his goods and chattells before Attainder. And (u) Stanford (speaking of a Felon convict by Verdict) saith, that he shall forfeit his goods, which he had at the time of the Verdict given, which is the conviction in that case, and by the Statute of 1.R.3. cap.3. no Sherife, Baylife, &c. shall seise the goods of a Felon before he bee convicted of the felony, whereby it appeareth, that the goods may be seised as forfeit after conviction. And the (x) old Statute is worthy of noting, Provisum est in curia nostra coram Iusticiarijs nostris quod de cetero nullus homo captus pro morte hominis vel alia felonia pro qua debet imprisonari, disseisietur de terris & tenementis vel catallis suis quousque convictus fuerit. So as by a conviction of a Felon, his goods and chattells are forfeited, but by Attainder, that is by judgement given, his Lands and Tenements are forfeited, and his blood corrupted and not before.

(t) Dame Hales case, Vbi supra. 8.H.4.2.

(u) Stanf. Pl. cor. fo. 192. Lib. 5. fo. 110. Foxleis case. Vid. 7.H.4.41. 1.R.3.ca.3.

(x) Statute de catallis felonum vet. Magna Carta, fo.66. 2.part.

(y) If the partie upon his Arraignement refuse to answer according to Law, or say nothing, he shall not be adjudged to be hanged, but for his contempt, to paine fort & dure, which worke no Attainder for the felony, nor forfeiture of his lands or corruption of blood. But in case of high treason if the party refuse to answer according to Law, or say nothing, hee shall have such judgement by attainder, as if he had beene convicted by verdict or confession.

(y) Stanf. Pl. Cor. 139.185.

¶ *Felony*. (*) Ex vi termini significat quodlibet capitale crimen felleo animo perpetratum, in which sence murder is said to be done per feloniam, and is so appropriated by Law, as felonice cannot be expressed by any other word. (a) And in ancient times this word (felonice) was of so large an extent as it included high treason; and therefore in our ancient bookes, by the pardon of all felonies, high treason, or counterfeiting of the great Seale, and of the Kings coine, &c. was pardoned. (b) But afterwards it was resolved, that in the Kings Pardon or Charter, this word (felony) should only extend to common felonyes, and that high treason should not be comprehended under the same, and therefore ought to be specially named. And yet that a pardon of all felonyes should extend to petite treason, wherefore by the Law at this day under the word (Felony) in commissions, &c. is included Petite treason, Murder, Homicide, burning of houses, Burglary, Robbery, Rape, &c. Chance-medly, se defendendo, and petite Larceny. (c) For such of these crimes for the which any shall have this judgement to be hanged by the necke till he be dead, hee shall forfeit all his lands in fee simple, and his goods and chattells: for Felony by chance-meddly or se defendendo, or petite Larceny, he shall forfeit his goods and chattells, and no lands of any estate of freehold or inheritance. And all felonyes punishable according to the course of the Common Law, are either by the Common Law, or by Statute. There is also a Felony punishable by the Civill Law, because it is done upon the high Sea, as Pyracie, Robbery, or Murder, whereof the Common Law did take no notice, because it could not be tried by twelve men. If this Pyracy be tryed before the Lord Admirall in the Court of the Admiraltie according to the Civill Law, and the Delinquents there attainted, yet shall it worke no corruption of blood, nor forfeiture of his lands, otherwise it is if he be attainted before Commissioners by force of the Statute of (d) 28 H.8. By the expresse purview of that Statute about the end of the raigne of Queene Elizabeth certaine English Pyrats that had robbed on the Sea, Merchants of Venice in amity with the Queene being not knowne, obtained a Coronation pardon, whereby amongst other things the King pardoned them all felonies. It was (e) resolved by all the Judges of England upon conference and advisement that this did not pardon the Pyracy, for seeing it was no felony whereof the Common Law tooke Conusance, and the Statute of 28.H.8. did not alter the offence, but ordaine a tryall and inflict punishment, therefore it ought to be pardoned specially, or by words which tant amount, and not by the generall name of Felony, and according to this resolution the delinquents were attainted and executed.

(*) Glanvill, lib. 14 ca. 15. Merlbr. ca 25. W.1. ca 15.

(a) 3.E.4.14. 18.E.4.10. 22. Ass. 49. 1.E.3.13. Stanf. Pl. Cor 102.E. Stanf. Pl. Cor. 102.B. 8 H.4.2.

(b) 22. Ass. 49.

(c) Stanf. prar. 45.b. 16.E.3. Coron 116. & 3.E.3 Coron. 302.

(d) 28.H.8.cap.15.

(e) Hill. 2. Ia. Regis.

Vid. Mich. 7. & 8. Eliz. Dier 241. 14. Eliz. Dier 308.

Pirata commeth of the word πειρατὴς which signifieth a Rover at sea. Attainder of heresie, or Præmunire worketh no corruption of blood; nor heresie, forfeiture of lands, but in case of Præmunire forfeiture of lands in fee simple, but not of lands in taile as formerly hath beene said. (f) By some Statutes it is said, Sur forfeiture de corps & de avoire, or Sub forisfactura omnium quæ in potestate sua obtinet, or to be at the Kings will, body, lands and goods, and the like, these are not extended to the losse of life or member, but to imprisonment, lands and goods. (g) But if an Act of Parliament saith, Soit judgement de vie & member, or subeat judicium vitæ vel membrorum, in that case judgement of death shall be given as in case of felony, viz. that he be

(f) Statute de Magna moneta tempore E.1. 35.E.1. de Carlisle 20.E.3 ca.4.

(g) W.2. Ca 34. Rot. Parliam. 25.E.1. 1.E.2. de frang. prisonam. 14.E.3. cap.10. Stanf. Pl. Coron 30 31. 3.E.3. Coron. 153. Brooke tit. Coron. 203. 9.E.4.26.

(h) Bract. li. 4. fo. 348. 48. E. 3. 3. 13. R. 2. ca. 2. Rot. Parl. 21. Ric. 2. nu. 19. 1. H. 4. c. 14. 13. H. 4. 4. & 5. 37. H. 6. 21. Rotul. Parl. 8. R. 2. nu. 31. Fortesc. ca. 32. Rot. Par. 2. H. 4. 74. 11. H. 4. 24. 30. Hen. 6. 6. Stanf. Pl. Cor. 65. Stat. de Assignat. 4. E. 3. Br. Cor. 196. Rot. Par. 2. H. 6. nu. 9. Rot. Par. 5. H. 4. nu. 39. Rot. Vast. 9. H. 4. nu. 14. 8. H. 6. nu. 38. 21. E. 4. 17. b. Catesby. 10. H. 7. Vauasor. 18. E. 2. Quar. imp. 175. 6. E. 3. 41. Pasc. 14. E. 3. in Scac. le Count. de Kents case. p. 39. Ed. 3. cor. Reg. Rot. 49. le Count. de Lanc. case. Rot. Parl. 28. E. 3. nu. 8. Mortimers case. Rot. Parl. 28. E. 3. nu. 13. Le Countee de Arundels case.

* Stanf. li. 3. Pl. Cor. 195. b. 27. E. 3. 77. 13. H. 4. 8.

V. Lit. li. 1. in the Chap. of Dower.

hanged by the necke till he be dead, and consequently his bloud is corrupted, (as our Authour here saith) and shall forfeit as in case of Felonie.

(h) There is also a Court of the Constable and Marshall, who have Conusance of Contracts, of Deedes of Armes, and of warre out of the Realme, and also of things touching warre within the Realme, which may not be determined or discussed by the Common Law, and also all Appeales of offences done out of the Realme, and they proceed according to the Civile Law: but these things more properly pertaine to another kind of Treatise, and therefore I shall speake no more thereof in this place, but onely for the satisfaction of the studious reader, to quote some Authorities of Law touching the iurisdiction of that Court, that he may have some tast thereof.

In the same manner it is if a man be attainted of High Treason, the Warrantie is also defeated.

Le sanke est corrupt enter eux, &c. *Aptly is a man sayd to be attainted, attinctus, for that by his attainder of Treason or Felonie his bloud is so stained and corrupted, as first, His Children cannot be heyres to him nor to any other Auncestor, and therefore the warrantie cannot bind, for thereby heyres onely are to be bound.

Secondly, If he were noble or gentle before, he and all his children and posteritie are by this Attainder made base and ignoble, in respect of any Nobilitie or Gentrie which they had by their birth.

Thirdly, This corruption of bloud is so high, that regularly it cannot bee absolutely salved but by authoritie of Parliament: All which is implied in the same (&c.)

Sect. 746. 747.

Le issue in Tayle poet enter. And the reason is, For that by the attainder of the father, it is now in iudgment of Law but a release without warrantie, for albeit the warranty at the time of the Release was effectuall, yet it worketh no discontinuance unlesse it discendeth upon the Issue in Tayle, so as if it be defeated, extinct, or determined in the life of the tenant in Tayle, then no discontinuance is wrought: and so it is if Tenant in Tayle hath Issue, and releaseth to the Disseisor with warrantie, and after is attainted of felonie, and after obtaineth his pardon and dieth, the Issue in Taile may enter; *for the Pardon doth not restore the Bloud, as to the warranty nor maketh the Issue in that case inheritable to the warrantie. But if the Issue in Taile in that case had been attainted of Felonie in the life of his father, and obtained his Charter of pardon, and then his father had died, the issue cannot enter into the

* 37. E. 3. 77. 1. E. 3. 4. 6. E. 3. 55. 9. H. 5. 9. 31. E. 1. Discont. 17. 46. E. 3. Petit. 20. 26. ass. 2. 49. Ass. 4. 29. ass. 11. 13. H. 4. 8. 13. H. 7. 17. Pl. Com. in Walsinghams case. 3. E. 2. Discont. Br. 64. Stanf. Pl. Cor. 195. 196. See in the Chapter of Tenant by the Curtesie, touching this matter.

Item si Tenāt en Taile soyt disseisie, et puis fait release al Disseisor oue Garrantie en fee, et puis le Tenāt en taile est attaint, ou utlage de felonie, et ad issue et morust, en cest case lissue en taile poet enter sur le Disseisor. Et la cause est, pur ceo que rien fait discontinuance ē cest case forsque le Garrantie, et Garrantie ne poit discender al Issue en tayle, pur ceo que le sanke est corrupt perenter celuy que fist le Garrantie et Issue en Taile.

Also if Tenant in Tayle bee disseised, and after make a Release to the Disseisor with Warranty in Fee, and after the Tenant in Taile is attaint or outlawed of felony, and hath issue & dieth; In this case the Issue in Taile may enter upon the Disseisor: and the cause is, for this, That nothing maketh Discontinuance in this case but the warranty, and warranty may not discend to the Issue in Taile, for this, that the bloud is corrupt betweene him that made the Warrantie, and the Issue in Tayle.

Sect. 747.

¶ CAr l'Garrāty touts foits demurt a l'Common Ley, et la Common Ley est, Que quant home est attaint ou utlage de Felonie, quel utlagarie est un attainder en Ley, que le sanke perenter luy et son fits, et touts auters queux serra dits ses heires est corrupt, issint que riens per discent poit discender a ascun q̄ poit estre dit son hēre per le Common Ley. Et la Feme de tiel home que issint est attaint de felonie, ne serra iammes endow de les Tenements sa Baron issint attaint. Et la cause est pur ceo que homes pluis eschuerent de faiē ascuns felonies. Mes l'issue en Taile quant a les Tenements tayles nest pas en tiel cas bar, pur ceo que est enherit per force de le Statute, et nemy p le course de Common Ley, et pur ceo tiel attainder de son pier ou de son ancestor en le Tayle, ne luy ouster de son droit p force de le taile, &c.

FOr the Warrantie alwayes abideth at the Common Law, and the Common law is such, That when a man is attaint or outlaw'd of felony, which Outlawrie is an Attainder in Law, that the bloud betweene him and his sonne, and all others which shall be sayd his heyres, is corrupt, so that nothing by discent may discēd to any that may bee said his heyre by the Common Law: And the wife of such a man that is so attaint shal neuer be indowed of the Tenements of her husband so attainted. And the cause is, For that men should more eschew to commit Felonies. But the Issue in Taile as to the Tenements tayled is not in such Case barred, because he is inheritable by force of the Statute, and not by the course of the Common law: And therefore such attainder of his Father or of his Auncestor in the Taile, shall not put him out of his Right by force of the Taile, &c.

Land in respect of the corruption of bloud upon the Attainder of himselfe. (h) And it is a generall rule, That hauing respect to all those whose bloud was corrupted at the time of the attainder, the Pardon doth not remoue the corruption of Bloud neither upward nor downward. As if there bee Grandfather, father, & son, & the Grandfather and father haue diuers other sonnes, if the father bee attainted of Felonie and pardoned, yet doth the bloud remaine corrupted not onely aboue him and about him, but also to all his children borne at the time of his attainder. But in the case of Litleton, if Tenant in Taile at the time of his attainder had no Issue, & after the obtaining of his pardon had issue, that Issue should haue bin bound by the Warrantie, for by the pardon he was as a new creature, Tanquam filius terræ, whose bloud upwards remaine corrupted, but for the Issue had after the Pardon, he is inheritable to his Father, and if his father had Issue before the Pardon, and had issue also after and dieth, nothing can discend to the youngest, for that the eldest is liuing and disabled. But if the eldest sonne had died in the life of the father without Issue, then the yongest should inherit.

(h) *Bract. li.* 3 *fo.* 132 133. 276 & *li.* 5. 374. *Brit. f.* 215. *b. Flet. li.* 1, *ca.* 28.

¶ *Le Garrantie demurt al Common Ley.* The Collaterall warrantie is not restrained by the Statute of Donis Conditionalibus, but a lineall warrantie is restrained by the Statute, unlesse there be Assets, as formerly at large hath beene sayd.

Vi. Sect. 711. 712.

¶ *Et la Feme de tiel home que issint est attaint, &c. ne serra iammes endow, &c.* It is to be obserued, That the iudgment against a man for felonie, is, That hee bee hanged by the necke untill he be dead, but implicatiuè, (as hath bin sayd)

sayd) he is punished first in his wife, That she shall lose her Dower. Secondly, In his children, That they shall become base and ignoble, as hath beene sayd. Thirdly, That hee shall lose his posteritie, for his bloud is stained and corrupted, that they cannot inherit unto him or any other Auncestor. Fourthly, That he shall forfeit all his lands and tenements which hee hath in Fee, and which he hath in Tayle, for terme of his life. And fiftly, All his Goods and Chattels. And thus severe it was at the Common Law, and the reason hereof was, That men should feare to commit felonie, Vt pœna ad paucos, metus ad omnes perueniat. And it is truly sayd, Etsi meliores sunt quos ducit amor, tamen plures sunt quos corrigit timor. And so it is à fortiori in case of High Treason. But some Acts of Parliament haue altered the Common Law in some of these poynts: First, By the Statute of Donis conditionalibus, Lands intailed were not forfeited neither for Felonie nor for Treason, but for the life of Tenant in
(i) 5.E.3.14.9.E.3.22 (k) 7.H.4.32.19.H.6.71. See Lit.li.1.ca.Dow.Sect.55 Tayle: This Act was made by King Edw the first, who (as our Bookes (i) speake) was the most sage King that euer was: (k) and the cause wherefore this Stat. was made, was to preserue the Inheritance in the bloud of them to whom the gift was made, notwithstanding any attainder of Felonie or Treason. And this Act in Historie is called Gentilitium municipale, For that by this Act the families of many Noblemen & Gentlemen were continued & preserued to their posterities. And this Law continued in force from the thirteenth yere of King Edward
(l) 26.H.8.ca.13.33.H.8.ca.20.5.E.6.ca.11. the first, untill the (l) twentie sixth yeare of King Henrie the eighth, when by Act of Parliament Estates in Taile are forfeited by attainder of high Treason. But as to Felonies (whereof our Author here speaketh) the Statute of Donis Conditionalibus doth yet remaine in force, so as for attainder of Felonie Lands or Tenements entailed are not forfeited, but only (as hath beene sayd) during the life of Tenant in Tayle, but the Inheritance is preserued for the Issues.

(m) Staunf. Pl Cor. 195. (m) The wife of a man attainted of high Treason or petit Treason, shall not bee receiued to demand Dower, unlesse it be in certaine cases specially prouided for. But the wife of a person attainted of Misprision of Treason, Murther, or Felonie, is dowable since our Author
(n) 1.E.6.ca.13.5.E.6.c.11 5.El.ca.1.& 11.18.El.ca.1. 12 H.4.3.V.Sect.55. wrote, (n) by the Statute in that case made and prouided, which is more fauourable to the woman than the Common Law was.

(o) 6.H.4.1.45.E.3.Vouch.72.Pl.Com.292.16.Edw.3.Age 46.18.H.3.Vouch.281.23.E.3 Garr.77. (o) If a Seigniorie be granted with warrantie, and the Tenancie escheate, the Seigniorie whereunto the warrantie was annexed is extinct, and consequently the warranty defeated, and it shall not extend to the Land, & sic in similibus.

See in the Chapter of Villenag Sect.202. If a Collaterall Auncestor release with warrantie, and enter into Religion, now the warranty doth bind; but if after he be deraigned, now it is defeated.

Sect. 748.

¶ Item si Tenant en le Taile enfeoffa son Uncle, l' quel enfeoffa un auter en fee oue garr̃ &c. si aps̃ l' feoffee p̃s fait relessa a s̃ Uncle touts manners des garranties, ou touts manners de Couenants real, ou touts manners de dões, p̃ tiel Release le Garrantie est extinct. Et si le Garrantie en cel case soit pleade enuers le heire en taile, que porta son Briefe de

ALso if Tenant in Taile infeoffe his Vncle, which infeofs another in fee with warr̃, if after the feoffee by his Deed releas to his Vncle all manner of Warranties, or all manner of Couenants realls, or all manner of Demaunds, by such Release the Warrantie is extinct. And if the Warranty in this case bee pleaded against the heire in Tayle that bringeth his writ of *Forme-*

¶ Littleton hauing spoken in what Cases Warranties may be defeated and extinguished by matter in Law, now he sheweth how a Warrantie may bee discharged or defeated by matter in Deed: and hereupon he putteth an example of a Release in 3 seuerall manners:

Vid Lib.8.fo.153.154. Althams Case. 46.E.3.2. 45.E.3.22. Vid. before in the Chapter of Releases. Sect.508

First, By a release of all Warranties.

Secondly, By a Release of all Couenants reall.

And thirdly, By a Release of all demands.

(q) 14.Ass pl.2. 3.Eliz.Dyer.188.9.E.4.52.b

(q) If a man make a gift in Taile with warranty, this warrantie is also implyed, and therefore a Release made by Tenant in Tayle of the warrantie, shal not bar the issue, no more than his Release shal bar the issue to bring an attaint upon a false verdict, or a writ of error upõ an eronious

de Formedō p̄ barrer le heire de ſon action, ſi lheire auoit le dit releas & ceo pledaſt, il defetera le plee en barre, &c. Et mults auters caſes et matters y ſont, p q̃ux hōe poit defeater garrantie, &c.

don, to barre the heire of his action; if the heire haue and plead the ſaid releaſe, &c. he ſhall defeat the plee in barre, &c. and many other caſes and matters there be whereby a man may defeate a warrantie, &c.

iudgement giuen againſt the Father, nor his gift can barre the iſſue of the Deede that create the eſtate taile, nor of any other Deede neceſſary for defence of the title.

¶ *Apres le feoffee releſſa.* Littleton here putteth his caſe where one is bound to warrant: put the caſe (r) then that two make a Feoffment in fee, and warrant the land to the Feoffee and his heires, and the Feoffee releaſe to one of the Feoffors the warranty, yet hee ſhall vouche the other for the moytie. And ſo it is if one infeoffe two with warranty, and the one releaſe the warranty, yet the other ſhall vouch for his moytie. (r) 45.E.3.23.

¶ *Si le heire auoit le dit releaſe, &c.* Here it appeareth that the releaſe being made to the vncle being his Anceſtor, the Deed doth after the deceaſe of the vncle belong to him, and therefore he cannot plead it, vnleſſe he ſheweth it forth.

¶ *Et mults auters caſes & matters y ſont per queux home poet defeater garranty, &c.* As namely by a Defeaſance, as other things executory may. Alſo a warranty may loſe his force by taking benefit of the ſame. In a Præcipe the Tenant voucheth, and at the Sequatur ſub ſuo periculo, the Tenant and the Vouchee make default, whereupon the Demandant hath iudgement againſt the Tenant. And afterwards the Demandant brings a Scire facias againſt the Tenant to haue Execution, in this caſe the Tenant may haue a Warrantia Cartæ And if in that caſe a ſtranger had brought a Præcipe againſt the Tenant, he might haue vouched againe, for by the iudgement giuen againſt the Tenant the warranty loſt not his force, but if the Tenant had Iudgement to recouer in value againſt the Vouchee, he ſhould neuer vouche againe by reaſon of that warranty, becauſe hee had taken aduantage of the warranty. And it is to be obſerued that vpon the proces of Sommoneas ad warrantizandum, if the Sherife returne the Vouchee ſummoned and he make Default, the Tenant ſhall haue a Capias ad valentiam, but if he returne that the Vouchee had nothing, then after the ſicut alias & plures a ſequatur ſub ſuo periculo ſhall iſſue, and there if the Vouchee make default, the Tenant ſhall not haue Iudgement to recouer in value, for hee was neuer ſummoned, and it appeareth of Record that he hath nothing, but in the Capias ad valentiam it appeareth that he had Aſſets, and he had beene ſummoned before, But in ſome ſpeciall caſes there ſhall be two recoueries in value vpon one warrantie. As if a Diſſeiſor giue lands to the husband and wife, and to the heires of the husband, the husband alieneth in fee with warranty and dieth, the wife bringeth a Cui in vita, the Tenant vouche and recouereth in value if after the death of the wife, the Diſſeiſee bring a Præcipe againſt the Alienee, hee ſhall vouch and recouer in value againe. 43.E.3.17. Pl.Com.in Brownings caſe.

(ſ) So it is where the wife bringeth a writ of Dower againſt the Alienee hee ſhall recouer in value, and after her death he ſhall recouer in value againe, vpon the ſame warrantie. (ſ) 45.E.3.Voucher 72.

In the ſame manner it is if a man be ſeiſed of a rent by a defeaſible title, and releaſeth to the Tenant of the land all his right in the land, and warranteth the land to him and his heires, if he be impleaded for the rent, he ſhall vouch & recouer in value for the rent, and if after he be impleaded for the land, he ſhall vouche and recouer in value againe for the land: but in theſe and the like caſes, the reaſon is in reſpect of the ſeuerall eſtates recouered, but for one and the ſame eſtate he ſhall neuer recouer but once in value, and though the land recouered in value be euicted, yet ſhall he neuer take benefit of that warranty after. And as warranties may bee defeated in the whole, ſo they may be defeated as to part of the benefit that may be taken of the ſame. (t) As hee that hath a warranty may make a Defeaſance not to take any benefit by way of Voucher: In the like manner that he ſhall take no aduantage by way of Warrantia Cartæ or by way of Rebutter. (t) 7.H.6.43. 13.Aſſ.8. 13.E.3. Gar.24.25.37. 22.H.6.51. 8.H.7.6.

Sect. 749.

¶ Et est ascauoir, que en mesme le maner come garranty collateral poit estre defeate pur matter en fait, ou en ley, en mesme le maner poit lineal garranty estre defeat, &c. Car si lheire en taile porta briefe de Formedon, & vn lineal garranty, de son ancester enheritable per force de le taile, soit plede enuers luy, oue ceo que assets a luy discendist de fee simple, que il ad per mesme launcester que fist le garranty, si lheire que est demandant poit adnuller, & defeater le garrãty, ceo suffist a luy. Car le discent des auters tenements de fee simple ne fait riens ꝑ barrer lheire sans le garranty, &c.

AND it is to be vnderstood, that in the same manner as the collaterall Warranty may bee defeated, by matter in Deed, or in Law; In the same manner may a Lineall warranty be defeated, &c. For if the heire in taile bringeth a writ of *Formedon*, and a lineall warranty of his Ancestor inheritable by force of the Tayle, be pleaded against him, with this that Assets discended to him of fee simple, which he hath by the same Ancestor that made the warrantie, if the heire that is demandant may adnull and defeate the warranty, that sufficeth him; For the discent of other tenements of fee simple maketh nothing to barre the heire without the warranty, &c.

¶ HEre Littletõ sheweth that in the same manner that a collaterall warrantie may be defeated by matter in Deede, or by matter in Law, so may to all intents and purposes a lineall warrantie, whereof hee putteth an example of a lineall warranty and assets.

¶ *Et vn lineal garranty, &c. ouesque ceo que assets a luy discendist, &c.* Here it appeareth by Littleton, that a lineall warranty and assets is a good plea in a Formedon in the Discender; wherein it is to be knowne that if Tenant in taile alieneth with warranty, and leaue assets to discend, if the issue in taile doth alien the assets, and die, the issue of that issue shall recouer the land, because the lineall warranty discendeth only to him without assets, for neither the pleading of the warranty without the assets, nor the assets without the warranty is any barre in the Formedon in the Discender. But if the issue to whom the warranty and Assets discended had brought a Formedon, and by Judgement had beene barred by reason of the warranty and Assets. In that case albeit he alieneth the Assets, yet the estate Tayle is barred for euer: for a barre in a Formedon in the Discender, which is a writ of the highest nature that an issue in tayle can haue, is a good barre in any other Formedon in the Discender, brought afterwards vpon the same gift.

Temps E.1.Garr.89. 34.E.1. ibid.88. 11.E.2.ibid.83. 4.E.3.24. 5.E.3.14. 40.E.3.9. 14.H.4.39. 24.H.8.taile Br.33. 4.Mar. Dier 139. Lib.10 fo.37.38. in Mary Portingtons case.

¶ ORe ieo ay fait a toy mon fitz trois liures.

NOw I haue made to thee my sonne three bookes.

¶ *A Toy mon fitz, &c.* Here our Author calleth (as many times in these bookes hee hath done) not only his sonne Richard, but euery student of the Law to be accounted his sonne, and worthily, for that seeing our Author had the honour to be in his time the Father of the Law, and all good students in the Law iustly account themselues the sonnes of the Law, (for otherwise they are not worthy of the profession) our author, as a carefull and prouident Father, as it hath manifestly appeared, gaue excellent instructions in these his bookes both to his owne son, and to his adopted sons, to make them from age to age the more apt and able to vnderstand the arguments and reasons of the Law.

¶ Le primer Liure est de Estates que homes ount en terres ou tenements: cestascauoire,

The first Booke is of Estates which men haue in Lands and Tenements: That is to say,

Le second Liure.

¶ Et ceux deux petits lieurs ieo ay fait a toy pur le melior entender de certaine Chapters de les antiēt Liures de Tenures.

And these two little Bookes I haue made to thee for the better vnderstanding of certain Chapters of the antient Booke of Tenures.

¶ *Meliour entender, &c.* And these Institutes haue I collected and published to the end that these three Bookes of our Author may be the better understood of the studious Reader.

¶ *Antient Liure des Tenures.* This Booke may well be accounted antient, for it was composed in the raigne of King Edward the third, (as Justice Fitzherbert saith) by a graue and discreet man. *Fitz. in his Preface to his N. B.*

Le tierce Liure.

Epilogus.

CE Tsaches mon fits, Que ieo ne voil que tu croies, que tout ceo q̃ ieo ay dit en les dits liures soit Ley, car ieo ne ceo voile enprender ne presumer sur moy. Mes de tiels choses que ne sont pas Ley enquires, et apprendres de mes sages Masters appris en la Ley. Nient meins coment que certaines choses, queux sont motes et specifies en les dits Liures, ne sont pas ley, uncore tielx choses ferra toy plus apt et able de entender et apprender les arguments, et les reasons d̃l ley, &c. Car p̃ les arguments et les reasõs en la Ley home pluſ tost auiendra a le cer-

And know my son, That I would not haue thee beleeue, that all which I haue sayd in these Bookes is Law, for I will not presume to take this vpon me, but of those things that are not Law, enquire & learne of my wise masters learned in the law; notwithstanding albeit that certaine things which are mooued & specified in the sayde Bookes, are not altogether Law, yet such things shall make thee more apt, and able to vnderstand and apprehend the Arguments and the reasons of the Law, &c. For by the Arguments and Reasons in the Law, a man more sooner shall come to the certain-

Ieo ne voile enprender ne presumer, &c. Here obserue the great modestie and mildenesse of our Author, which is worthie of imitation, for nulla virtus, nulla scientia locum suum & dignitatem conseruare potest sine modestia. And herein our Author followed the example of Moses, who was a Judge, and the first writer of Law, for he was Mitissimus omnium hominum qui fuit in terris, as the holy Historie testifieth of him.

¶ *Les arguments & les reasons del Ley, &c.* Ratio est anima Legis, for then are we sayd to know the Law, when we apprehend the reason of the Law, that is, when we bring the reason of the Law so to our owne reason, that we perfectly vnderstand it as our own, and then and neuer befor, we haue such an excellent and inseperable propertie and ownership therein, as we can neither lose it, nor any man take it from vs, and will direct vs (the learning of the Law is so chayned together) in many other Cases. But if by your studie and industrie you make not the reason of the Law your owne, it is not possible for you

certaintie & a la conusans de la ley.	tie and knowledge of the Law.	long to retaine it in your memorie. And well doth our Author couple arguments and reasons together, Quia argumenta ignota & obscura ad lucem rationis proferunt & reddunt splendida:

Lex plus laudatur quando ratione probatur.

and therefore argumentari & ratiocinari are many times taken for one. And that our Author may not speake any thing without Authority (which in these Institutes we haue as we take it manifested) his opinion herein also agreeth with that of the learned and reuerend chiefe Justice of the Court of Common pleas Sir Richard Hankford, (y) Home ne scauera de quel mettal vn campane est, si ne soit bien bate, ne le ley bien conus sans disputation. And another saith, (*) Ieo aye dispute cest matter pur la apprender la ley. So as our Author hath made a most excellent Epilogue or Conclusion with a graue aduice and councell, together with the reason thereof, which all good students are to know and follow, and with tenere and sequi I will conclude our Authors Epilogue.

(y) 11.H.4.37.

(*) 41.E.3.22. Kirton. Vid. Sect.377.

¶ *Lex plus laudatur quando ratione probatur.*

This is the fourth time that our Author hath cited verses.

Vid. Sect.384.443.550.

When I had finished this worke of the first part of the Institutes, and looked backe and considered the multitude of the conclusions in Law, the manifold diuersities betweene cases and points of learning, the variety almost infinite of Authorities, Ancient, Constant and Modern, and with all their amiable, and admirable consent in so many successions of ages, the many changes and alterations of the Common Law & additions to the same, euen since our Author wrote, by many Acts of Parliament, and that the like worke of Institutes had not bin attempted by any of our profession whom I might imitate, I thought it safe for me to follow the graue and prudent example of our worthy Author, not to take upon me, or presume that the reader should think, that all that I haue said herein to be Law: yet this I may safely affirm, that there is nothing herein, but may either open some windowes of the Law, to let in more light to the student by diligent search to see the secrets of the Law, or to moue him to doubt, & withall to inable him to inquire, & learne of the Sages, what the Law together with the true reason thereof in these cases is: Or lastly upon consideration had of our old Bookes, Lawes, and Records, (which are full of venerable Dignity and Antiquitie) to finde out where any alteration hath beene, upon what ground the Law hath beene since changed, knowing for certaine, that the Law is unknowne to him that knoweth not the reason thereof, and that the knowne certaintie of the Law is the safety of all. I had once intended for the ease of our Studient to haue made a Table to these Institutes, but when I considered that Tables and Abridgements are most profitable to them that make them, I haue left that worke to euery studious Reader. And for a farewell to our Jurisprudent I wish unto him the gladsome light of Jurisprudence, the louelinesse of Temperance, the stability of Fortitude, and the soliditie of Justice.

FINIS.

Errata.

FOlio 2.a. Linea 41. For *Gratiuta*, read *Gratuita.* fo.3.b. lin.2. *for* no heire, *read* no heire but of his body. l.18.*omit*, Bastards. l.41. *after* cosens, *adde*, Mes. l.58. for *brugam*, r. *brigam.* l.62. cauiat, *r.* caueat. f.4.a.l.41. *after* Lammas *adde* to her. *and to the notes in the marg, there*, add *Vt.li.1.f.87.per Walmsl.* f.4.b.l.8 *quarum*, r. *quare.* l.49. *for* of higher, *read* or higher. f.5.b.l.35. *metebant*, r. *metebant.* l.41. *Birquabia*, r. *Berquarium.* l.44. after *Domesday*, adde, It signifieth also, & more legally, a Sheep-coat, of the French word *Bergerie.* l.50. *Arpeu*, r. *Arpen.* l.61. Iug. *r.* Ing. f.6.a. l.29. *for* where, *r.* whereof. f.7.b.l.6. *Audigauiæ*, r. *Andiganiæ.* f.9. b.l.38. in writ, *r.* in the writ. f.10.a.l. 1. oweetie, *r.* oweltie. fol.13.a.l.34. stall, *r.* shall. l.19. in marg. 19.*Et.* r. 19.*E.1.* f.13.b.l.10. seuersl, *r.* seuerall. l.23. with, *r.* which. f.15.a.l.5. as, *r.* or. f.15.b.l.16. in marg. 23.*E.3.* r. 25.*E.3.* f.16.b. l.44. *for* the degree, *r.* vnder the degree. f.17.a. l.43. *seitus*, r. *seisitus.* fo.18.a.l.41. two simples, *r.* two fee simples. f.20 a l.11. *in the text*, their, *r.* her. fo.21.a.l.6. *after* for euer, *adde* It hath been holden that. l.10. *after* expectant, *adde* but *Vid. lib.7.fo 154.b.* otherwise resolued, *vt patet ibi.* f.21.b.l.23. *for* not the, *r.* not of the. fo.22.b.l.6. *in the text*, Donors, *r.* Donees. f.23.b. l.18. *in the text, for* Issue, *r.* Issues. l.34. ib. 21.*E.3.* r. 31.*E.3.* fo.24.a. l.49 and to exclude, *r.* and not to exclude. f.26.b.l.40. *Matilda*, r. *matildæ.* l.41. *procreata*, r. *procreatæ* f.30.a.l.44. But, *r.* By. l.13. in marg. to 29.*E.3.* adde *f.27.* f.31.a.l.31. *tallegys*, r. *tallagys.* f.31.b.l.30. Northampt. *r.* Northumb. l.48. generall, *r.* special. f.32.a.l.55. *omit*, during the couerture. lin.22. in marg. *Hillingstons*, r. *Lillingstons.* f 33.a.l.26. *iun'*, r. *iunior.* *promer'*, r. *promerere.* *victum sustin'* r. *virum sustinere.* l.37 *viz.* r. *viri.* l.7. in marg. 13.*E.1.* *Dower*. r. 3.*E.1.* *Dower*, 172. f.34.b.l.26. habitatirn, *r.* habitation. l.29 riuen, *r.* driuen. fol.35.a l.1. this companions, *r.* his companions. f.38.a.l.18. to ends, *r.* to no end. f 39.a.l.59. he, *r.* she. f 42.a.l.6. of, *r.* or. l.8. foreiture, *r.* forfeiture. f.44.a.l.4. in marg. 3.*Ia* r. 1.*Ia.* f 44 b.l.31. owne, *r.* one. l.36. tenant *r.* tenants. f.46.a l.3. for, *r.* of. l 25. *Thraing*, r. *Thirning.* f.46.b.l.60. case, *r.* lease. f.47.a.l.11. chattell, *r.* cattell f.47 b.l.17. if they distreyned, *r.* if they be distreyned. f.48 a.l.30. deuise, *r.* demise f 48, b l.45.46 *for* make writing of lease, *r.* make a writing of a lease f.49.a. l.15. *omit*, in. l.55. liuery the, *r* liuery to the. f 49 b. l.4. remainder, *r* remainders. l.50. *omit*, as. f.50.b.l.9. *pariphrasis*, r. *periphrasis* f 53.b l.20. fell, *r.* sell. f.54.a. l 45. and term, *r.* and the terme. f.58.b. l.13. disseisors, *r.* disseisees. f.59.b.l.33. concuslusion, *r* conclusion. fo.61.b. l.vlt. in marg. to *cap.67.* adde & 69. f 62.a l.3. *appruatore plegiatu*, r. *appruatore cognitus plegiatus.* l.4. for *electus*, r. *Clericus.* *moribus & legibus*, r. *communioribus legibus.* l.7. *puer*, r. *piger.* fol.63.a.lin.33. *lebris*, r. *libri.* f.65.a.l.26. saith, *r.* faith. f.66.a.l.23. rcords, *r.* records. f.67.a l.vlt *for* they within, *r.* they be within. 67.b. *the latter part of the Text of the 91. Sect. is to be added.* l.2. *fædum*, r. *feodum.* f.68. l.37. *sine*, r. *fine.* f.69.a.l.59. these, *r.* this. f.71.a. l.20. *diuinet*, r. *dimicet.* l 41. *omit* that. fo.71.b. l 47. but, *r.* and. f.73.b.l.2. *in the text*, were by, *r.* were giuen by. f.74 b l.18.19. *fædum*, r. *feodum.* f.75.b. l.29.34. 56. *fædi*, r. *feodi.* f 77.b. l.24. said office, *r.* sayd offices. f.78. b.l.6. in marg. to 27 *H.8.* add *fo.10* f.80.a.lin.28. in the text, *matrimonium*, r. *matrimonio.* f.81.a.l.11. in marg. *ca.3.* r. *ca.1.* f.83.b.l 6. *fædū*, r. *feodum.* l.39. by, *r.* of. f.84.a.l.31. of, *r.* to. f.85.b.l.11. Sxe, *r* Six. lin.27. Sheep-men, *r* Sheepe men. f 88.b.l.10. *fecus*, r. *tecus.* l.43. *for* a, *r* of. f 90.a.lin. vlt. in marg to *Sect.* adde 740. f.91.b. l.3. as presently as conueniently may, *r.* as presently and as conueniently as he may. fo.93.b.l.vlt voluntaries, *r.* votaries. f.94.a l.29. Diocesse, *r.* diocesses. and l vlt. for *fædum*, r. *feodum.* fol.95.a. l.28. take succession, *r.* take in succession. *sic*, r. *sid.* f.97.a. l.2. in marg to 33.*H.6.* adde, *fo.6.l.30.* put out the * before *Stephen*, and place it, l.28. *before* And of them. f.100.a. l.4. for *medio*, r. *medy.* f.100. b.l.9. to the disherison, *r.* or the disherison. f.107. a.l.44. *Seriantie*, r. *Seriantiam.* f.110.a.l.39. *comities*, r. Counties. f.111.a.l 52. of deuisor, *r.* of the deuisor. f 114.b.l.30 cessor, *r.* cesser. l.44 suspensation, *r.* suspension. f.115.a.l 9. to be a formdon, *r.* to a formdon. fo.116.a.l.43.47. bound, *r.* bond. 119.b. l.15. *for* may claime, *r.* may not claime. f.120.b. l.38. *coppe*, r. *cep.* f.121.a.l.55. tenure, *r.* tenancy. f.122.b.l 41.46. *vtlegat*, r. *vtlagat'.* f.123 a.l.29. *dominus*, r. *dominum.* f.128 b.l.29 vntill and a good, *r.* vntill a good. f 129. a l.58. indelibilitie, *r.* indebilitie. l.59. Priors, *r.* Prioresse. f.130.b.l 2 *for* garnish, *r.* garnishee. f.131 b.l 41 3. to 13.*R.2.* adde, *ca.16.* f 133.a l.11. *asseri, tidem*, r. *asserit idem.* f.133.b.l.40. *quandaque* r. *quandoque.* fol.135.a l.17. discouenables, *r.* couenables. l.48. *aut*, r. &. f.138.b.l.44. be, *r.* is. f 141.b.l.27. *vt*, r. &. f.142.a.l.12. *liberas*, r. *libras.* l.13. *Cometi* r. *Comiti.* 146.a.l.7. in mar. in *H.8.* *r.* in 11.*H.8.* f.146.b.l.35. *for* grantee, *r.* grantor. f.148.b.l.50. is wholly apportioned, *r.* is to be apportioned. fol.150.a.l.47. *omit*, and so it is. f.150.b.l.13. of the grantee, *r.* of the grantor. f.155.a. l.50. bound, *r.* bond. fo.155.b. l.27.28. and this, *r.* and how this. fol. 157.a. l.53. it nor, *r.* it is not. f.157.b. l.21. change, *r.* charge. l.38. pincipal, *r.* principal. l.39. one, *r.* owne. f.158 a.l.vlt. tie, *r.* trie. fol.159.a.l.44. Cambr. *r.* Cambridge. f.159.b.l.19. *Claredon*, r. *Claredon.* l.15. in the text, *auoit*, r. *nauoit.* fol. 160. b.l.13. as the poynt, *r.* as to the poynt. f.164 a.l.5. of full age, *r.* within age. f.164.b.l.13. in mar. to 2.*H.6.* add *fo.11.* f.165.b.l.9. *in the text*, Aunt, *r.* Aunts. fol.172.a.l.36. shal be allowed, *r.* shal not be allowed. f.176.b.l.3. remant, *r.* remmant.

Errata.

nant. Folio 178.a lin. *vlt*, *for*, is, *reade* it. fol. 179 b.l.30 for his, *r.* her. f.180.a.l.24. *for*, if 1 *r.* if it. f.180.b.l.5. Saile, *r.* Sale. l.47.48. *Cætitrabitio*, r. *ratihabitio*. f.181.b.l.39. tenants, *r.* ioyntenants. f.186.a.l.40. *in the text*, for her, *r.* him. fol.187. b.lin.59. Feoffee or Deuisee, *r.* Feoffor, or Deuisor. line 11, in marg. 11.*H*.7. r. 10.*H*.7.20. f.188.a.l.25. for deuiseth *r.* demiseth. f.189.a. l.2. inheritance, *r.* estate f.192.a.l.26. a lease, *r.* a lease for life. f.194.b.l 23. after Feoffees, *adde* is for that the Feoffees. f 199 a.l 2. in mar. *tit.* 8 r. *Vit.* aide. f.200.a.l.36 37. right lands, *r* right of lãds. f.201.a.l 3. omit (so it is) & after parsonals adde *virtute cuius fuit inde possessionatus*. lin.21. 22. for an equalitie, *r.* a quality. fo.202.a.l.42. possibility, *r.* impossibilitie. f.202 b.6. after escheate, omit (be) f.206.a.l.2 for morgagor, *r.* morgageor. f.206.b.l.13. whereof, *r.* wherfore. f.207 a.l.1.2 for morgage, *r* morgagee. and lin. 2. morgagee, *r.* morgageor. f.213.b.l.28. before *Littleton*, place (*d*) f.214.b l.40. the lease, *r.* the gift or lease. f.220.b.l.42 *omit*, so. f.221.b. in marg. to *Iulius Winningtons case*, adde, *Lib.* 2. *fo.* 59.60. f.223.b.l.9. for *directo*, *r. ex directo*. fol. f.226.a.l.30, morgagee, *r.* morgageor. f.230.a. l.38. r. *inuentum est, & perfectum*. fol.230 b.l. 36. euery, *r.* any. f.232.b.l.32. is, *r. est*. f.234 a. l.31. then, *r.* the. l.38. *officio*, r. *officia*. l.46. for example, *r.* certainely. f.238, b.l.2. in marg. for 15.*H*.4. r. 13.*H*.4. fol.241.a.l.11. Coment, *r.* Commentarie. f.247.a.l.26. shall take, *r.* shall not take. f.250.b.l.26. doe, *r.* enter. f.252.a. l.1. and 2. actually, *r.* actiuely. f.253.a.l.38. tenures, *r.* view. f.258.a.l.38. limitation, *r.* limitations. f.261.b.l.29. 33.*H*.8. r. 35.*H*.8 *& sic in marg.* f.264.b.l.49. debt, *r.* action. f.268.b.l.16 lands, *r.* hands. fo.272.a.l.33. or, *r.* and. f.275. a.14. if the Disseisor, *r.* if the Disseisee. f.275. b.l.21. the actions, r. all actions. f.276.a.l.9. *for* Lessee, *r.* Donee. lin.44. after *Companion*, adde out. fo.285.b.20. in marg. 13.*E*.4. r. 13.*H* 4. f.290.a.l.33. to 23.*H*.8. adde, *cap.* 6. and *lin.* 1. in marg. to 44.*E*.3. adde, *fo.* 10. f.292.a.l.38. for *deriuantur*, r. *deriuatur*. fol.293.a.l.2. in marg. to *ca.* adde, 2. f.295.a l.11. *for*, without, *r.* with. lin.36. for debt rent, *r.* debt for a rent. and for Indowment, *r.* Indenture. fol.297.a.l.25. *for*, forty, *r.* forty acres. lin.47. to fee, *r.* to the fee. f.297.b.l.36. shall haue, *r.* shall not haue. fol. 298.a. against the 10.11. lines place in the marg. *reported by Sir Iohn Popham chiefe Iustice*. f.298 b. to the note in the margent, adde, *Pl.* 15. f.299 b.l.14. in marg. to *Caryes* case, adde. *lib.* 5. *fo.* 76.*b.* f.300.b.l.58. *for*, Prior Couent, *r.* Prior and Couent. f.307.a.l. *vlt.* in marg. 3.*E*.12. *Ass.* 7. r. 3.*E*.3.12. & 3. *Ass.* 7. f.307.b, in the margent to 34.*H*.6. adde, *fo.* 41. f.309.b.l.47. after, attorne, *r.* to the Grantee by Deede. and lin.51. *omit*, in a barre. f.310.a l.13. after, Grantee, *adde*, the Lessee attorne to the husband. And in the margent against the same line, adde to the note there, *Lib.* 4. *fo.* 61. *Hemlings* case. f.310.b.l.2. in marg. adde, *Hemlings case vbi supra*. f.312.b.17. for rent charge, *r.* rent charge in fee. f.343.b.l.16. adde in marg. 44 E.3.21.22. f.349.a. l.30. heire, *r.* heire apparant. f.352.a.45. heire, *r.* here f.355.a l 31. after giuen, *adde*, by default. f.361.a.l 3. in the margent, for, 14.*H* 7.11, r 14.*H* 7.10.11. lin.5. *ibid.* for, 21.*H*.6.13. r. 19.*H*.6 39. and adde to the notes there, 22.*H*.6.21. 36 *H*.6.32. 36.*H*.6. *fauxer de recouery* 27. fol.361.b.l.5. in marg. *for*, 10.*H*.5. *r.* 10.*H*.6. lin.7. to *fol.* adde 106. f.362. a.l.11. in marg. nonteape, *r.* non-tenure l.12. *ib.* to *lib.* adde 5. and for 331. *r.* 431. fol.363.a.l.14. *for*, against, *r.* for. line 17. *omit*, on the other side. f.363.b.10. in marg. to 22. *Ass. p.* adde 33. f.364.b.l.2. in marg. to *Entr. Cong.* adde 54. fol. 365.b.l.21. in marg. to student, adde. 55. fol. 368.a.l.2. in marg. to *Ass.* adde, *p.* 23. fol.368.b. 39. *for*, nether othan, *r.* no other than. lin. 51. *for*, so, *reade*, it.

CPSIA information can be obtained
at www.ICGtesting.com
Printed in the USA
BVHW09*1103160818
524721BV00009B/157/P

9 780266 925750